The Insider's Guide to the Colleges

2005

The Insider's Guide to the Colleges

2005

Compiled and Edited
by the Staff of the
Yale Daily News

St. Martin's Griffin
New York

Readers with comments or questions should address them to Editors, *The Insider's Guide to the Colleges*, c/o *The Yale Daily News*, 202 York Street, New Haven, CT 06511-4804.

Visit *The Insider's Guide to the Colleges* Web site at www.yaledailynews.com/books.

The editors have sought to ensure that the information in this book is accurate as of press time. Because policies, costs, and statistics do change from time to time, readers should verify important information with the colleges.

www.stmartins.com

ISBN 0-312-32384-0
EAN 978-0312-32384-4

First Edition: July 2004

10 9 8 7 6 5 4 3 2 1

Contents

Preface 1

Acknowledgments 3

How to Use This Book 5

Getting In 7

The College Spectrum 27

Introduction for International Students 39

Students with Disabilities 42

Terms You Should Know 44

The College Finder 49

A Word About Statistics 63

The Colleges Listed by State 67

Index 1001

The Insider's Guide to the Colleges

2005

Preface

Congratulations! No matter how excited, scared or nervous you are about the college process, you are beginning your search on the right foot simply by picking up this book. Choosing a college is a huge decision—in fact, it is so big that no one source will give you all the answers you need. However, this 31st edition of *The Insider's Guide to the Colleges* will provide you with the tools necessary to give you an advantage in the hectic college-choosing process.

We have one central objective: to paint the *real* picture of what it is like to be a college student. Rankings and statistics are not the best or only measure of a school. In each college write-up, we avoid boring glossy brochure-talk and instead rely on countless hours of personal interviews with actual college students so that you can get a true sense of the color of a school and the day-to-day life of its students. After all, we have been through the process ourselves, and we owe it to you to tell you the truth. We tell you what we would have wanted to know when we were in your shoes.

College is the experience of meeting hundreds of students in your first few weeks, of dining halls where the lines are long and the food is bad, and of making friends who skip class to help you out when you're in trouble. It's about pulling all-nighters on papers due the next morning or engaging in late-night talks until the sun comes up. It's about trying things you never thought you would, and probably will never have the chance to do again. It's about driving halfway across the country to see your football team win, walking onto a sports team knowing you'll probably get cut, or volunteering at the local elementary school when you still have 300 pages of reading to do. During your college search, keep in mind that it is these experiences and friendships that you will look back on when you are old and gray, not your SAT score (we hope).

All of this is well and good, but you're probably thinking that it doesn't help you much. After all, you have to get there first. Among the thousands of colleges that span the continent, you can apply to no more than a handful. Maybe you have a vague idea of what you are looking for, but how do you begin to narrow your choices?

This is where *The Insider's Guide* comes in. In this 31st edition, we've taken special care to review our entire book to ensure that it provides an accurate portrayal of life at each of 315 colleges and universities in United States and Canada. We give you the inside scoop on these places, directly from the students who attend these institutions. We research each school in *The Insider's Guide* by interviewing friends, friends of friends, and a random selection of students at each school. This gives *The Insider's Guide* a unique perspective from students whose opinions we trust. It also means that we are only as accurate as our sources. Though we have worked hard to make each article factually correct and current, the college experience is unique for every individual—after all, one student's closet-sized dorm room is another student's palace.

In addition to articles on each college, *The Insider's Guide* includes a number of special features to help you in your search. "The College Finder" gives you a rundown on various schools according to selected attributes. "Getting In" takes you step-by-step through the intricacies of the admissions process. In "The College Spectrum," we discuss some of the most important factors to consider when choosing between schools, as well as give you a look at current trends in college life. "Introduction for International Students" provides some tips on applying to American schools if you live outside of the United States, while "Disabled Student Services" introduces students with learning or physical disabilities to issues they should be aware of when applying to college. Finally, we have included "Terms You Should Know," a glossary to help you decode confusing college slang.

We know how stressful the college process is. After all the hard work of preparing and applying, acceptance letters or rejections often appear to have been decided at random. It may sound difficult, but try not to worry. The majority of students love their college. In part, this is because they chose a school that was right for them. But remember, every single college will provide you with new people to meet, new freedoms to explore, and new experiences to enjoy and learn from. So whatever college you end up going to, take it from us: four years goes fast, so make the most of it! —*Amanda Stauffer*

Acknowledgments

A special thanks to Tom Mercer, our editor at St. Martin's Press, who has been instrumental in getting this book out as early as possible and in excellent shape. We would also like to thank all the interviewees who were kind enough to let us get a personal peek into their lives and their colleges: without you, this book would not have been possible. Finally, a special thanks to those Yalies who 31 years ago decided to devote their time and energy toward creating a helpful guide for high-schoolers about to go to college. We hope you enjoy.

Carolyn Abram
David Adams
Carmen Allen
Ken Alvord
John Anderson
Donald Andres
Christine Beaudry
Katie Berglund
Audrey Bishop
Jenny Bloom
Sarah Bolos
Ted Bonanno
Sara Bouchard
Jessica Brandenburg
Katherine Britt
Amy Cadros
Michelle Carrera
Chris Carrico
Kate Carter
Nicholas Casey
Vanessa Casino
Godhuli Chaudhuri
Tyler Chen
Thomas Chew
Joanna Collier
Meredith Coogan
Jeremy Cowie
Lauren Davey
Jennifer Davis
Latrisha Dean
Kristen Deane
Cindy DeVries
Jackie DeCicco
Claire Diamond
Patricia Diez
Amber Dreher
Emily Eddren
Christopher England
Kara Evans
Kevin Faddis
Eric Feeny
Sara Fisher
Michael Forte
Emily Fourmy
Allison Fuller
Justine Haemmerli
Abigail Hartnett
Molly Heintz
Ruth Henkes
Allison Hiden
Sana Hong
Edmond Johnson
Delight Jones
Lacey Jones
John Joseph
Alex Kehlenbeck

Young-Ghee Kim
Dennis Kisyk
Matthew Klaus
Gregory Larsen
Stephanie Levner
Sea Ah Lim
Arthur Liu
Deidre Loftus
Amanda Malayer
Lauren May
Maryl Mazepa
Janet McKay
Stephanie McOean
Ted Meriam
Jenn Mestl
Ian Mohler
Judith Ann Montiel
Eunice Na
Joanna Naamo
Sean Nealon
Scott Novich
Leslie O'Loughlin
Terren O'Reilly
Nicholas Pagoria
Lydia Petell
Shelby Peterson
Cresa Pugh
Allison Raino
Matthew Rosenberg
Elisha Rudolph
Lori Saeki
Jessica Sapaugh
Ruth Schauble
Jessica Selby
Sharmin Shahjahan
Liz Shiland
Lily Siegal-Gardner
Mollie Simms
Jacquelyn Simoneau
Tania Simyar
John Rex Smith III
Carolyn Snell
Brian Solomon
Deanna St. Onge
Zoe Stern
Eve Stevenson
Jeff Torrance
Cole Trautmann
Molly Tuttle
Ben Volta
Tim Walter
Jeremiah Wander
Corey Watson
Ashley Webster
Debra Weinstein
Elle Weislitz
Barry White
David White
Abbye Wingram
Kevin Wissner
Andrea Wolf
Liza Wolfe
Jack Wu
David Zhu

How to Use This Book

How We Select the Colleges

One of the most difficult problems we wrestle with here at *The Insider's Guide* is which schools to include in each year's edition. From more than 2,000 four-year institutions nationwide, we cover only 320 schools. Our first priority in selecting a college is the quality of academics the institution offers. After academic quality is assessed, we then must look at a number of factors to determine which colleges we select. One key factor that we carefully consider is the need to offer a diversity of options in the book. Thus, we have included institutions from all 50 states as well as the top institutions in Canada. Many of the largest institutions are state-affiliated and we have made a point to include those because such a large majority of students apply and matriculate to their state schools. Each year, we review our list of schools and try to include new schools that we have not had space to write about before.

We have also made every effort to include a broad cross-section of the smaller colleges because they offer a very different kind of education. The smaller the school, the more we tend to look at the quality of the student body. Many of these small schools are top liberal arts schools generally clustered in the Northeast that offer a broad but personalized education. The range of extracurricular options was also factored into our decision as to which schools to include.

To add to the diversity of schools reviewed by *The Insider's Guide*, we included selections from the most prominent technical schools and creative and performing arts schools. These schools provide a more specialized education that combines general knowledge with a specialty in a specific field. The sampling of schools in this category is by no means entirely conclusive and we encourage students looking into specialized schools to explore more deeply into these options.

In sum, this book includes the colleges we believe to be among the most noteworthy in both the United States and Canada. This does not imply in any way that you cannot get a good education at a school not listed in the *Guide*. We strongly encourage students to use strategies discussed within this book to explore the wide variety of schools that we did not have space to explore here, including community colleges, state schools, international schools, and professional schools. Nor does this mean that you are guaranteed a happy and prosperous four years if you attend one of these schools. Rather, we believe that every school in the *Guide* offers students the raw materials for constructing an excellent education.

It's All Up to You

We have found that everyone can use *The Insider's Guide* in their own unique way. A few dedicated readers digest the book from start to finish, determined to gain the most complete understanding of the college process. Others pick up the *Guide* for only a few minutes to read funny quotes taken from nearby colleges. Another good strategy is to use the College Finder and statistics that begin each article to learn more about colleges that students may not have heard of before because they are in a distant region of the country. We encourage all of these approaches. Above all, we hope that the *Guide* is both fun to read and educational, and it makes the college process as stress-free as possible. The opening features of the book are designed to help you zero in on what is unique and important about the schools you might be considering.

You will notice that we have avoided the temptation to pigeon-hole the colleges with some kind of catch-all rating system, or worse, to numerically rank these schools. Our reason is that the "best" college for one person may come near the bottom of the list for another. Each student has his or her own particular set of wants and needs, so it would be pointless for us to try to objectively rank the schools. Whereas most rankings focus on academic factors, the college experience is a balance of academics, social life, extracurriculars, and living.

Even so, many continue to ask, "Can't you rate the colleges just on the basis of academic quality?" We think not. There are too many variables—from the many factors that contribute to the quality of a department and school as a whole to the articulateness and accessibility of the professor who happens to be your academic advisor. Furthermore, it is useless to try to compare a college of 2,000 students with a university of 10,000 (or a university of 10,000 with a state school of 40,000 for that matter) on any basis other than individual preference. Despite all of these reasons not to, reportedly reliable sources such as national magazines often insist on publishing numerical rankings of colleges. We warn you from taking these rankings too seriously. Often times the determining factor in the rankings is a statistic such as "percent of alumni who donate money," a factor that does not mean much to most high school students.

For 31 years, *The Insider's Guide* has always been dedicated to the notion that the best rankers of schools are students themselves, not magazine writers. Our goal, therefore, is to help you train your eye so that you can pick the college that is best for you. Remember, we may describe, explain, interpret, and report—but in the end, the choice is always yours.

Getting In

The task of applying to college can seem as intimidating as the thickness of this book. In the spring of your sophomore year of high school your Aunt Doris, whom you have not seen in seven years, pinches your cheek and asks you where you are going to college. *How the heck should I know?* you think to yourself. That fall, your mom tells you that the girl down the street with the 4.0 grade point average is taking the SAT prep course for the fifth time to see if she can get a perfect score and win thousands in scholarship money. You reply that you are late for school. You keep ducking the subject, but the hints come with increasing regularity. Not only has dinnertime become your family's "let's talk about Joe's college options" hour, but friends at school are already beginning to leaf through college catalogs. Soon you find the guidance counselor's office crowded with your wide-eyed peers, and it seems clear that they aren't all asking for love advice. Finally, you decide to make an appointment with the counselor yourself.

When you first talk to your counselor, preferably in the early part of your junior year, you may have only just begun to feel comfortable in high school, let alone prepared to think about college. The entire prospect seems far away, but picking and getting into the best school for you takes a good amount of thought and organization—and a visit to your counselor is a good start. You may even be wondering if college is the way you want to go after high school. If you aren't sure that you want to delve into more books immediately after graduating, keep in mind that a good number of people choose to take a year or two off to work or travel.

One important asset in making a decision about any post-graduation plans is your counselor. College counselors have many resources to pull from, and can help you lay out a plan in the direction you wish to take. If you decide that college is your next step, you will have a lot options. Many schools are surveyed in this book—but we have not included technical schools, professional schools, or community colleges, all of which also offer numerous opportunities. With research of your own and the aid of your counselor, you should be able to find a place that will give you just what you want.

To make sure that you find your best college, however, it is wise to do a little exploring of your own before sitting down with your counselor. Counselors can be invaluable advisors and confidants through the college admissions process, but only if their goals line up with yours. Some counselors limit your search by only recommending noncompetitive schools, or, conversely, by assuring you that you'll get into whichever school you want. A few may even try to dissuade you from colleges that you are seriously considering. In these cases—which aren't common, but do happen—it is best if you already have an idea of what your looking for, so that you can express it to your advisor. In the end, you should always follow your gut instincts.

So read up, and ask yourself questions. What factors about a school make a difference to you? What do you want in a college? A strong science department? A Californian landscape? A small student body? A great social life? Although each college is a mix of characteristics, your best advice (in case your parents have not told you yet) is to place your academic needs first. However, since most college students change their majors repeatedly before finally settling down, look for schools that have good programs in all the areas you would consider majoring in.

Of course, it isn't possible to think of all the angles from which you should approach your college search. You can't be sure what your interests will be three or four years from now, or what things will prove most important to you at the college you attend. After all, those realizations are a big part of what the college experience is all about! But by taking a hard look at yourself now, and proceeding thoughtfully as you begin looking at colleges, you can be pretty confident that you are investigating the right colleges for the right reasons.

In the early winter of your junior year

you'll receive your PSAT scores. Unless you request otherwise, your mailbox will soon become inundated with letters from colleges around the country. The College Search Service of the College Board provides these schools with the names and addresses of students who scored in various percentiles, and the schools crank out thousands of form letters to those who show promise. These colleges often send letters to students who they feel are underrepresented in their student population.

While sorting through these masses of glossy brochures, you'll probably notice that most of them contain lofty quotes and pictures of a diverse, frolicking student body. The only way to find out if these ideals are also truths is to visit the college. But before that, you can verify some of what you read by comparing it to nationally published articles and statistics. Of course, that level of investigation need only be pursued if you like what you see in the brochures sent to you. However, you will probably find your most compatible colleges through your own research, and the majority of these wait for you to contact them before they send information. In that case, create a form letter that briefly expresses your interest in the college and requests materials. You'll get your name on their mailing list and they'll smile on the fact that you took the initiative.

While you're opening up the field, make sure to listen to the people who often have good things to say—namely, your parents. Some students find their parents a great help through the entire college search, whether as chauffeurs on college trips or supporters when opening acceptance letters. Besides having some ideas of schools you might enjoy attending, your parents also have great insight into how your education can and will be financed. If you come to an early understanding with your family about prospective colleges and financial concerns, things will move much more smoothly down the road. Be warned, though, the college search is also one of the most trying times in any parent-child relationship. More often than not, parents "stick their noses in the process" more than most students want. The best advice that we can give is to always remember that calm, patient, discussions are a better tactic than yelling matches.

When consulting other people's opinions, it is helpful to keep a few things in mind. Every piece of advice you get will be a reflection of a particular person's own life experiences, and is likely to be highly subjective. Most adults will suggest schools located in regions that they know or that they have visited or attended. Also, opinions are often based on stereotypes that can be false, outdated, or just misleading. Still, the more people you talk to, the better perspective you gain on the colleges you are considering. Once you have a few outside ideas, this book can give you some inside information. If you like what you have heard about a particular school, follow up with some research and find out if it's still a place that calls to you.

As you approach the time when your final college list must be made, you will probably have visited college fairs and attended various college nights. Real-life representatives from the schools are always good to meet. Talking to current college students is an even more important step, as is visiting the schools that make it to your last list. During these encounters, ask the questions that are on your mind. Be critical and observant. When it's time for the final leg of the college selection process, you'll be calm and satisfied if you know you've really looked hard into yourself and all your options.

The Visit

Ideally, much of your visiting will have been completed by the fall of your senior year. You will have some kind of list made up of 10–15 schools that you are interested in attending. Campus visits are a good way to narrow down and prioritize the schools on your list. There is no better way to get an idea of where you will most want to spend the next four years of your life.

When you visit a campus, you should keep in mind why you are there. You have probably already seen the college viewbook with glossy pictures of green lawns and diverse groups of students holding test tubes. Now is the time to find out what the campus is really like. Is the student population actually that diverse? Do people actually gather and play Frisbee on plush green lawns? What do the dorms actually look like? And most importantly, do you feel comfortable there?

If you are visiting a campus for an interview, make sure that you schedule one early. Sometimes space books up, and you will not even get to speak to an admissions officer. Making the decision not to interview on campus may be a good one; while some schools require an on-campus interview, some insiders recommend that you request an alumni interview instead. Alumni interviews tend to be more significant in your application and less grueling than on-campus interviews. In any case, make sure you check a school's policy regarding interviews before you visit, and schedule your visit accordingly.

Some people find that summer vacation is a good time to visit—others prefer spring break or weekends during their junior year. Keep in mind that if you choose to visit during the summer, very few students will be on campus. The feeling of the student culture and vibrancy (or lack thereof) will be difficult to read. During the college's academic year, your questions about the campus are much more likely to be answered. You'll get a feeling for the type of people at the school, and you'll get an idea of what it's like to be a student living on campus. You want to be able to get a good feeling of what daily life will be like.

Before you visit any school, you should come up with some kind of system to evaluate all of the schools that you will visit. You should make a list of characteristics that are important to you, so that you are better able to compare each school to the next. Things like how academic (or nonacademic) a school is, what freshman dorms are like, and how big the campus is might be some areas to keep in mind. Make sure you write down some notes about the schools during and after your trips. Although the schools you visit may seem easy to differentiate at the time, it certainly will not be so easy to remember each school once you are back home with ten identical-looking applications in front of you.

You should probably try to stay overnight with undergraduates. Most admissions offices have students on call who are happy to have you stay a night, take you to some classes and parties, and show you around campus. If you have friends there, they are a good resource as well. Either way, staying with students will help you get the most inside look at what a school is really like. One student said, "I found that it didn't matter much if I stayed over or not, as long as I got to talk to students. But if you do stay over, Thursday or Friday night is the best time." Sometimes it is hard to connect with students during a single day when everybody is rushing around to classes. Try to spend a night late in the week when students will have more time for you. It is possible that you will end up with socially withdrawn hosts. Don't let bad hosts completely dictate your feeling about a school however—do everything you can to get out into the student body and explore what the school has to offer.

Keep in mind that college life doesn't consist entirely of classes. Sample the food, which is, after all, a necessity of life. Check out the dorms. Take the campus tour. Though you are sure to be inundated with obscure facts about the college that don't interest you, it can be useful to see the buildings themselves and the campus as a whole. If you have any questions, do not hesitate to ask. Tour guides are often students, and are a great resource for any information you want about the school.

Should you bring your parents along? Maybe. If you feel comfortable going alone and can actually convince them to stay, your best bet is probably to leave them at home. Although they mean no harm, parents can sometimes get in the way. Your discomfort at having them around you when you're trying to get along with new students may cloud your opinion of a school. When you enter college they will not be there with you, so to get the best idea of what that will be like, they shouldn't be with you during the visits, either. However, don't completely discount any advice they may have. They are a useful resource to bounce ideas off of, particularly regarding the pros and cons of the various schools you have seen.

Most importantly, keep in mind your sense of the campus atmosphere. How does it feel to walk across the main quad? Does the mood seem intellectual or laid-back? Do T-shirts read "Earth Day Every Day" or "Co-ed Naked Beer Games"? Look for postings of events; some campuses are alive and vibrant while others will seem pretty dead. Check your comfort level. Imagine yourself on the campus for the next four years and see how that makes you feel. Focus on these characteristics while you are on campus; you can read about the distribution requirements when you get back home. Most of all, enjoy yourself! The campus visit is an exciting chance to get a taste of exciting things to come.

The Interview

Just about every college applicant dreads the interview. It can be the most nerve-wracking part of the college application process. But relax—despite the horror stories you might have heard, the interview will rarely make or break your application. If you are a strong candidate, don't be too cocky (many have fallen this way); if your application makes you look like a hermit, be lively and personable. Usually the interview can only help you, and at some schools it is nothing more than an informational session. "I was constantly surprised at how many questions they let me ask," one applicant reported.

It is best to look at the interview as your chance to highlight the best parts of your application and possibly to explain the weakest parts without being whiny or making excuses. Are your SAT scores on the low side? Did your extracurricular section seem a little thin? An interview gives you the opportunity to call attention to your successes in classes despite your scores, or explain that of the three clubs you listed, you founded two and were president of the third.

There are a few keys to a successful interview. The first and most important is to stand out from the crowd. Keep in mind that the interviewer probably sees half a dozen or more people every day, month after month. If you can make your interviewer laugh, interest him or her in something unusual you have done, or somehow spice up the same old questions and answers, you have had a great interview. Don't just say that you were the president of something; you *must* be able to back up your titles with interesting and genuine stories. Second, do not try to be something you are not. Tell the truth. By doing so, you will be more relaxed and confident. Even if you feel that the "real you" isn't that interesting or amazing, think hard about your years of high school; you'll surprise yourself with the stories that will surface in your mind.

A few days before the actual interview, think about some of the questions you might be asked. Some admissions officers begin every interview by asking, "Why do you want to go to this school, and why should we let you?" You should not have memorized speeches for every answer, but try not to get caught off guard. Make sure you really know why you want to attend this college. Even if you are not sure, think of a few plausible reasons and be prepared to give them. Students often make the mistake of giving a canned answer, which is okay since most answers are similar, but admissions officers look to admit students who want to take advantage of all that is available at their school. Your answer must include the three essential elements of a good reply: your interests, whether academic or extracurricular; what you believe the school will provide; and how and why you are excited about the opportunity to take advantage of them. Other common questions include those about your most important activities, what you did with your summers, and what vision you may have for your future.

A note of caution: If your interview takes place after you have submitted your application, the interviewer might ask you questions about some of the things you included. One student wrote on his application that he read *Newsweek* religiously. During his interview, the admissions officer asked the student about a story in a recent issue of the magazine. The student had no idea what the interviewer was talking about. He was not accepted. Back up your claims or don't talk the talk.

It is always an excellent idea to indicate that you have a special interest in something, but make sure the interest is genuine—you may wind up in an hour-long conversation on the topic. Do not start talking about how you love learning about philosophy if you have only dabbled in it once. Do not try to use big words simply to sound impressive during what should be just a friendly chat. An open, thoughtful manner can do as much as anything else to impress your interviewer.

Being spontaneous in a contrived situation usually amounts to having a successful interview. If you are nervous, that's okay. Said one applicant, "I felt sick and I didn't eat for a day before the interview." The most common misconception is that admissions officers are looking for totally confident individuals who know everything and have their entire future planned out. Almost the opposite is true. An admissions officer at a selective private college said, "We do not expect imitation adults to walk through the door. We expect to see people in their last year or two of high school with the customary apprehensions, habits, and characteristics of that time of life." Admissions officers know that students get nervous. They understand.

If everything in your life is not perfect, do not be afraid to say so when appropriate. For example, if the conversation comes around to your high school, there is no need to cover up if problems do exist. It is okay to say you did not think your chemistry lab was well equipped. An honest, realistic critique of your school or just about anything else will make a better impression than false praise ever could. Even more, someone with initiative who overcomes adversity is often more appealing than a person who goes to the "right" high school and coasts along.

If something you say does not come out quite right, try to react as if you would with a friend. If the interviewer asks about your career plans, it is all right to say that you are undecided. As a high school student, no one expects you to have all the answers—that is why you are going to college. Above all, remember that the admissions officer is a person interested in getting to know you as an individual. As one interviewer explained, "I'm not there to judge the applicants as scholars. I'm just there to get a sense of them as people."

Do not get so worried about saying all the right things that you forget to listen carefully to the interviewer. The purpose of the interview is not to grill you, but to match you with the school in the best interest of both. Sometimes the interviewer will tell you, either during the interview or in a follow-up letter, that you have little chance of getting in. If she says so or implies it, know that such remarks are not made lightly. On the other hand, if she is sincerely encouraging, listen to that, too. If an interviewer suggests other schools for you to look into, remember that she is a professional and take note. Besides, many interviewers appreciate a student's ability to listen as well as to talk.

Your interviewer might ask you whether you have a first choice, particularly if her college is often seen as a backup. If the school is really not your first choice, fudge a little. Mention several colleges, including the one you are visiting, and say you have not made up your mind yet. Your first choice is your business, not theirs. If the school really is your first choice, though, feel free to say so, and to give a good reason why. A genuine interest can be a real plug on your behalf.

Also know that you can direct the conversation. Do not worry about occasional lapses as some interviewers wait to see how you will react to a potentially awkward situation. Calmly ask a question, or mention something that really interests you. It is your job to present the parts of you and your background that you want noted.

Selective colleges need reasons to accept you. Being qualified on paper is not always enough. Think of the interviewer's position: "Why should we accept you instead of thousands of other qualified applicants?" The answer to that question should be evident in every response you give. Use the interview to play up and accentuate your most memorable qualities. Show flashes of the playful sense of humor that your English teacher cites in his or her recommendation; impress the interviewer with the astute eye of politics about which your math teacher raves.

Too many applicants are afraid to talk confidently about their accomplishments. If the interviewer is impressed by something, do not insist that it was not much, or he might believe you. If he is not impressed by something you think is important, tactfully let him know that he should be. But do not, under any circumstances, be "too cool" for the college. One well-qualified applicant to a leading college was turned down when the interviewer wrote, "It obviously isn't going to be the end of his world if he doesn't get in. And it won't be the end of our world, either. " If there is any quality you want to convey, it is a sincere interest in the school.

Almost all interviewers will eventually ask, "Do you have any questions about our school?" Come to the interview armed with a good question or two and not one whose answer is easily found in the college's view-book. Do not ask if they have an economics department, for example—ask the average class size in introductory economics courses. If you are excited to learn more about the school and have already done some homework, it goes a long way in the eyes of the interviewer.

You will probably wonder what to wear. This is no life or death decision, but remember that your appearance is one of the first things the interviewer will notice about you. Wear something you will be comfortable in—a jacket and a tie or a nice dress are fine. Do not, however, be too casual. Faded jeans and a T-shirt will give the impression that you are taking the interview too lightly.

One crucial point: Keep your parents a thousand feet and preferably a thousand miles away from the interview session. When parents sit in, interviews tend to be short, boring, and useless. If the interviewer feels you cannot handle and hour without your parents, she might be concerned about your ability to survive the pressures of college life. Take the risk of hurting your parents' feelings and ask them to wait outside.

Once the interview is over, it is perfectly all right for your parents to ask any questions they may have if the interviewer walks with you back to the waiting room. Even if this makes you uncomfortable, do not let it show. Admissions officers can learn as much about you by the way you treat your parents as they do in the interview. The interviewer is not judging your parents. As long as you conduct yourself calmly and maturely, you have got nothing to worry about.

All of this advice applies for interviews given by alumni as well as those conducted by admissions staff. Alumni interviewers sometimes carry slightly less weight with the admissions office, but they are valuable contacts with the schools and should not be taken lightly. Expect on-campus interviews to be a bit more formal than alumni interviews.

What if you do not have an interview at all? Perhaps you live too far away, and you cannot get to the school itself. Or, perhaps you feel that your lack of poise is serious enough that it would work against you in any interview you had. Talk it over with your guidance counselor. In general, geographic isolation is a valid excuse for not having an interview, and most colleges will not hold it against you. Ask if they will allow a phone interview instead. Yet, if the college is fairly close and makes it clear that applicants should have an on-campus interview if at all possible, make the effort to go. Otherwise, the college will assume that for some reason you were afraid to interview, or worse, that you simply did not care enough to have one. If the prospect is genuinely terrifying, schedule your first interview for a safety school, or ask your guidance counselor to grant you a practice interview. You might discover that the process is not as horrible as you originally thought.

The Tests

Whether you are an Olympic hopeful, a musical prodigy, or a third-generation legacy, you cannot avoid taking standardized tests if you want to go to college. Approximately 90 percent of all four-year institutions now require some type of admissions test. Certainly tests do not tell the whole story; grades, recommendations, extracurricular activities, the application essays, and personal interviews round out the picture. However, standardized test scores are often the only uniform criteria available to admissions committees. They are meant to indicate the level of education you have had in the past, as well as your potential to succeed in the future.

Virtually all of the nation's colleges require applicants to submit SAT I or ACT scores. In addition, some colleges will ask their applicants for SAT II subject test scores. If you are an international student with a native language other than English (or recently moved from an education system using a foreign language), you may be required to take the TOEFL as well. If you take AP tests or are in an IB program, your scores could help you earn college credit if they agree with the score requirements of the college you are applying to. Does all this seem overwhelming to you? Read this section and hopefully we can help you understand each test a little better.

The Scholastic Assessment Test (SAT) is the most widely chosen admissions test by college applicants. Administered by the Educational Testing Service (ETS) and created by the College Board, the SAT I: Reasoning Test currently has a math and a verbal section. A three-hour test, there are a total of seven sections; three are math, three are verbal, and the last is variable and could be either. All that you will need to know for the math section of the SAT I is material through Algebra I and, to your benefit, you are allowed to use calculators. It has 5-choice multiple-choice questions, questions where you produce the answer yourself, and quantitative comparison questions. In the verbal section, you will find sentence completions, analogies, and passages with reading comprehension questions.

The SAT I scores the math and verbal sections separately on a 200 to 800 scale. Therefore, your combined score can be a minimum of 400 and a maximum of 1600. One disadvantage with the SAT I is that you are penalized for wrong answers, so avoid guessing haphazardly. The average score is a 1000 based on the recentered scale that the ETS implemented starting in 1995. When the SAT was originally calibrated, it was done so that the average score for the math and verbal sections would each be 500. Over several decades, the average dropped—some say as a result of the declining American education system. However, others argue that the perceived "decrease" is not surprising considering that today's over two million SAT-takers are much more representative of American education as a whole than the 10,000 primarily affluent prep-school students who took the test when it was implemented in 1941. As a result, the scoring was recentered in 1995 (recentered scores have an 'R' next to them) in order to redistribute scores more evenly along the 200 to 800 scale. All colleges and scholarship institutions are aware of this new scoring calibration, so even though it may be easier to get that rare 1600, your percentile *rank* among other students who took the exam will not change.

In March 2005, ETS will begin to administer a new SAT I. As a result of continued study regarding fair assessment of high school students' education and the skills needed to succeed in college, a writing section will be added to the exam. Students will be asked to write an essay as well as answer multiple-choice questions testing their ability to use standard written English. The current verbal section will be renamed Critical Reading and will include shorter reading passages along with the existing longer reading passages. Analogies will be eliminated from this section, but the sentence completion questions will remain. For the math section, the material covered will expand to include Algebra II and the quantitative comparison questions will be removed. The length of the exam will increase slightly. Those graduating from high school in 2006 will be the first to be affected by this change since many students tend to take the SAT I in March of their junior year. For those of you who take the SAT I before March 2005, don't worry. Most colleges have indicated that they will accept scores from the old or new SAT I for the class of 2006. However, you should check with the college of your choice since each college sets its own rules regarding the admissions process.

There are five ways to register for the SAT. The two most common methods are to complete an online registration at *www.collegeboard.com* or mail in a registration form, which you can get from your high school counselor's office. If you've registered for an SAT Program test before, you can complete the registration over the phone. For those students living outside of the U.S., U.S. territories, and Puerto Rico, there is an option to fax in your registration. International students have the option of registering through a representative found in the International Edition of the SAT Registration Bulletin.

Before you take the test, be sure to take advantage of two services offered by the College Board upon registration. The first is called the Student Search Service and allows universities, colleges, and scholarship programs to get general information about you, as well as what range your score falls into. You will receive a flood of information about different universities, colleges, and scholarship programs in the mail in addition to information regarding financial aid opportunities. This is a good way to obtain a list of colleges to which you intend to apply.

The second service will mail your test scores to a maximum of four specified schools or scholarship programs for free. You can send additional score reports for a fee. Be aware that if you have taken the SAT I more than once, all of your previous scores will be sent when reporting to schools and scholarship programs. If you have second thoughts and want to cancel your scores, you must do so by the Wednesday following your exam by email, fax, or mail.

The American College Test (ACT) was required mostly by colleges in the southern and western regions of the country, but is now accepted by most colleges all over the nation. The exam covers English, Reading, Mathematics, and Science Reasoning in the format of 215 multiple-choice questions. One distinguishing factor of the ACT is that it tests what you have already learned in the high school curriculum rather than your aptitude.

The ACT, unlike the SAT I, does not deduct any points for incorrect answers. You will receive a score on a scale of 1 to 36 for each of the four subject areas; your Composite score is just an average of the four scores rounded to the nearest whole number. Based on the over 1.1 million students who choose to take the test, the average Composite score is around 21. Registration is much like the SAT I, with a mail-in option, online registration at www.act.org, or telephone preregistration. There is a stand-by registration option for those who forget to register. As far as score reporting goes, you can choose up to six schools or scholarship programs on your registration to have the scores sent to for free. The great thing about the ACT is that you can choose to just send one testing date's scores instead of having your whole history of scores sent, as is done with the SAT I.

Many of the more selective colleges also require up to three SAT II exams, formerly called Achievement Tests. Available subjects include English, a variety of foreign languages, math, history, and several of the sciences. One thing about the SAT II is that you don't have to choose which tests you want to take until you're at the test center on the test date. The scores are reported on a 200 to 800 scale, but no longer with the Score Choice option. Score Choice had allowed students to put their subject tests on hold until they had decided which scores to send to universities, colleges, and scholarship agencies. It posed problems in giving those who could pay for more tests an unfair advantage and also in that students would often forget to send their scores later on. After the June 2002 testing date, the College Board abandoned this option; now all SAT II scores are reported, but only your highest in each subject will be taken into consideration.

The Test of English as a Foreign Language (TOEFL) is an English proficiency test provided for international students who want to study in the U.S., Canada, or other English-speaking countries. It is administered on the computer or by paper-and-pencil depending on the location you choose. The scale for your total score is from 0 to 300 along with a score of 0 to 6 for the essay, which is scored separately. The TOEFL will test your listening, structured writing, and reading skills—giving a better picture of your English to the schools you apply to.

Advanced Placement (AP) exams are another animal altogether since their purpose is not to get you into college, but instead to earn you credits once you get there. Administered in May, each test covers a specific subject area and scores you from 1 to 5. Different schools require different scores for granting college credit. Some will offer credit but still require you to take classes in a subject that you aced on the AP exams. Since the tests require in-depth knowledge of specific subjects, do not put off studying for them. It is generally a good idea to take the exam in a particular subject the May right after you have finished (or are in the midst of finishing) a course in that area. Not only can you get college credit with a high score, but you can also help your college applications with AP exams taken before your senior year.

If you attend an International Baccalaureate (IB) school, you might be able to receive college credit for your coursework depending on your score. A score of 4 or 5 are the required minimum by a college for credit and/or placement, but many institutions require a higher score of 6 or 7. Although not as popularly embraced by colleges and universities across the nation for giving college credit, they will definitely recognize you for the rigorous work you have completed in the program.

You may have already taken the PSAT/NMSQT, which is usually administered to sophomores or juniors through their high school. This is a great practice exam for the SAT I because it has a lot of the same type of questions. Be sure to take part in this because it is a good way to qualify for merit scholarships if you get a high score. The PSAT will change its format in the fall of 2004 to complement the new SAT I in 2005.

The most reliable way to keep up-to-date on test dates, sites, and registration deadlines is through your high school guidance office. After the PSAT, you will be on your own about when and where you take the tests. Find out way ahead of time which ones are required by the colleges you are interested in; deadlines have a way of sneaking up on you. It is a good idea to begin taking the tests by the spring of your junior year. If you take the SAT I in March or May of your junior year and do not do as well as you think you should, you will have a couple of other opportunities to improve your score. The required SAT II's should be taken by June of your junior year so that if you decide to apply to an early-action or early-decision program, you will have completed the required testing.

Avoid postponing required testing until November, December, or January of your senior year. One new college student, who put off his exams until the last minute, recalled his college freshman faculty advisor saying to him, "I just don't understand it . . . you went to one of the best high schools in Chicago and did very well. How could your SAT scores have been so low?" He told her how lucky he felt just getting into college; he had contracted a nasty flu and thrown up before, during, and after the test! On the other hand, do not repeat tests over and over. The ETS reports that students can gain an average of 25 points on both the math and verbal sections of the SAT I if they take the test a second time. Two or three shots at the SATs are sufficient.

If you've got the time and money, you may want to consider taking a prep course given by a professional test-preparation service. National test-prep companies like Kaplan and the Princeton Review, as well as dozens of local companies, attempt to give helpful tips on how to take tests for those willing to shell out hundreds of dollars. If you do decide to take a prep course, take it seriously. You may have six or seven high school classes to worry about, but you cannot hope to get your money's worth if you do not attend all of the sessions and complete the homework in these prep courses.

Many people choose not to take practice courses. A good student who is confident about taking tests can probably do just as well studying on his or her own. You can find practice exams online or in commercially marketed practice books. Get acquainted with the tests you plan to take beforehand; you should not have to waste time during your exam re-reading instructions and trying to figure out what to do. It's a good idea to even simulate an actual test by timing yourself with no interruptions on a real test that was previously administered.

The College Board puts out a book called *10 Real SATs* that proves to be one of the most effective ways to prepare for the SAT I. True to its title, the book has official SATs from the past, along with hints, test-taking strategies, and exercises to help you improve your test score. The ACT has a similar book called *Getting Into the ACT* with two complete exams plus ACT's own analyses and explanations designed to help you with the test. Getting the chance to practice exams in a real test-like situation (no pets, family, or friends to distract you) will help you to get a keener sense of the overall structure of the test and help you work faster during the actual exam. It might also help you relax!

Do not cram the night before the exam. Get plenty of sleep and relax. "My teacher encouraged us to go out and have a good time the day before," recalled one first-year college student. "So I went to the movies as a distraction. I think it worked!" On the day of the test, eat a full breakfast that isn't too heavy, dress comfortably, and do not forget to bring two pieces of ID, a calculator, a couple of number two pencils, and a pencil sharpener. Make sure you are up early and know where you will be taking the test as well as how to get there. The test center may be overcrowded, there may be no air-conditioning or heat, and a hundred construction workers may be drilling outside the nearest window—be prepared for anything!

The key to success on any of these exams is to keep calm. During the exam, keep track of how many problems there are and allot time accordingly. Read and attempt to answer every question since you do not get more credit for the hard ones than the easy ones. If you are stuck on a question, try to eliminate as many answers as possible and select from the remaining choices. Only if you really have no clue about the question should you leave it blank on the SAT. Just remember to also leave a blank on your answer sheet!

A word of warning: Do not even think about cheating. It is not worth it, and your chances of getting caught and blackballed from college are high. To weed out cheaters, the ETS uses the mysterious K-index, a statistical tool that measures the chance of two students selecting the same answers. If your K-index is suspect, a form letter goes out to the colleges you are interested in, delaying your score until you retake the exam or prove your innocence. Know that looking at another person's test is not the only activity that the ETS considers cheating. Going back to finish work on a previous section is also against the rules. Do not tempt fate—a low score is better than no score at all.

At the beginning of this section, we stressed that standardized tests are important. How important? It varies depending on the school you are applying to. At many state schools, admission depends almost entirely on test scores and grades; if you score above the cutoffs, you are in. With the more selective schools, scores are usually only one of many important factors in the admissions process. According to the dean of admissions at Harvard University, "If scores are in the high 500 to low 700 range, they probably have a fairly small impact on our decisions." Each of the schools in this book lists a mean score range for the SAT I. Remember that there are students who score below this range and above this range that were accepted to that college. Unless you score far below or far above the mean of your desired college, most likely your SAT I score will not make or break your chances of getting in. If you attended an inner-city school or a school in an area of the country where education standards are below the norm, your apparent deficit might, in fact, indicate a strength—as long as you are above the minimum levels.

Many students mistakenly believe that the SAT is the only test that "really matters" in competitive college admissions. In fact, SAT II scores taken as a whole are usually of equal importance. Colleges will often view these scores as a more accurate predictor of future performance than the SAT I. Aside from tests, it's important to remember that your high school record is weighed heavily. If you bomb your admissions tests, but have a decent grade, there's a chance that your high school performance can outweigh the bad test scores. However, a poor GPA is hard to overlook, even if your scores are high. Remember that your admissions test scores are just a portion of the whole picture you present to the colleges. So try your best to make it advantageous for you, but don't worry if you don't get a perfect score!

The Application

It's the fall of your senior year of high school. You've done your research, and found a few schools that you're interested in. You've taken the standardized tests, you've visited the campuses, and you may even have had some on-campus interviews. You still have one major hurdle ahead of you, however: The Application. Though the piles of paperwork may seem daunting, with some advance planning you can make the application process as painless as possible.

First, you have to decide where you want to apply. You should have this done no later than the first few weeks of your senior year. After talking to students and visiting campuses, you should be able to narrow down your original list of colleges to somewhere between five and 15. Applying to any more schools than this is probably overkill. Not only is it a waste of time to apply to more schools than necessary, it's also a waste of money to apply to any school you won't be happy attending—application processing fees can run as high as $65 per school. However, you want to apply to enough schools that you'll be sure to get accepted somewhere.

It's also important to think about the selectivity of the schools you apply to. Don't be scared to apply to your dream school even if your SAT score or GPA is a bit low. On the other hand, make sure to apply to at least one or two "safety schools," where you'll both be happy and where you stand an excellent chance of getting accepted. A good rule of thumb is to apply to at least one "reach" school, a school where it may be a long-shot for you to get in but where you'd love to go, at least one "safety school," and a few schools in between.

After you've listed the schools where you'll apply, get the applications and figure out when each of them are due. Many schools allow you to download their applications from their Web sites. Others send them to you in the mail; if this is the case, make sure you request the application in plenty of time to fill it out carefully and send it in. Whatever you do, make sure you get your applications in on time. Many schools won't even look at applications that they receive late, so make deadlines a priority.

Different schools accept applications in a variety of ways. A brief description of the **major types of applications** follows:

- *Rolling Admissions:* Most large public schools and many less-selective colleges accept "rolling applications," which means that they process applications continuously, in the order that they receive them. You hear back from the school a few weeks after you send in your application. Though these schools often accept applications into the spring, it is important to send in your application early because admittance often becomes more challenging as these schools accept more and more students. Try to send in applications to schools with rolling deadlines as early as you can.

- *Regular Decision:* Colleges that don't offer rolling admissions typically require all your application materials to be sent by a specific date, usually in December or sometimes in January. The applications are processed and evaluated all at the same time, so while it is still an excellent idea to send in your application materials as early as possible, there is no automatic advantage to applying as soon as you can, as there is with rolling admissions. Whereas with rolling admissions, you'll hear back from the college within a few weeks, with regular decision all applicants hear back from the school at the same time. Many schools have separate parts of the application with different deadlines, so be prepared to organize your calendar so as not to miss any deadlines. Acceptances and rejections get mailed in early April.

- *Early Decision:* Many schools offer an "early decision" option as part of their regular decision program. However, a recent push by presidents of several top universities (including Harvard, Stanford, Yale and others) is working to erode this option since it hurts economically disadvantaged students who would need to compare financial aid packages in making their decision. Typically available at more selective colleges, the early decision program allows you to apply to one school by mid-October or November, and will respond to you by mid-December either with an acceptance, a rejection, or a deferral. An acceptance to a school under an early decision program is binding. This means that when you apply early decision, you sign a contract stating that you absolutely commit to attending that school if you are accepted. Rejections are final. A deferral means that the admissions committee will wait to make a decision about your application until they see what the regular pool of applicants is like. If you are deferred from an early decision acceptance but are accepted with the regular pool, the contract is no longer binding, and you may choose to attend a different school. Failure to comply with the agreement can lead to unpleasant consequences like being blackballed from other schools.

Early decision does have some advantages. By expressing a clear interest in one school, you may gain some advantage in admissions, and if accepted you'll already know where you're going to school in December. However, by no means feel that you need to apply to a school under an early decision commitment. You should not apply to a school early decision unless you are totally, completely, positively sure that the school is your first choice, and you should not apply early decision if you feel like your credentials will improve significantly during your first semester of your senior year. Since rejections under early decision are final, and if you think your application will be stronger after another semester, you should wait to be able to provide the best application possible.

- *Early Action:* Early action has been increasingly common among extremely selective schools such as M.I.T., Georgetown, Stanford, University of Chicago, Harvard, Yale, etc. Like early decision, early action offers applicants a chance to find out in December if they've been admitted. However, the acceptance is not binding; if you get accepted to another school in April that you would prefer to attend, you're welcome to do so. This provides a convenient alternative for students who want to hear back from a school as soon as possible, but aren't ready to commit to attending a particular school right away.

Once you know when your applications will be due, it's time to start filling out the paperwork. There are a few general guidelines to follow. First, read the entire application carefully before you begin. Plan what you are going to say in each section before you write anything. It is a great idea to make a photocopy of the application to "practice" on before you fill out the official form. Always fill out or type the application yourself. If you're going to hand-write the application, try to use the same pen for the entire thing, to remain consistent in ink color and thickness. If you're going to use a printer, use a standard font like Times New Roman or Arial, and use the best printer you can find. Presentation and neatness count. If the application specifically suggests that you hand-write anything, be sure to do so, but draft exactly what you're going to write on scrap paper so that you don't have to make any corrections on the actual application.

More and more colleges nationwide are coming to accept the Common Application in lieu of applications specifically tailored for their schools. With a standard format and several general essays, you can fill out this application—online or on paper—once and submit to any of the 60 participating schools. It makes the application process somewhat less burdensome and time-consuming, although you may still want to consider tweaking essays to better fit the demands of each individual college.

Applications are usually divided up into several sections. All of them are important, and you should use all of them to your advantage. The following explanations of the **application sections** include some things you should remember when filling out your application:

- *Personal Information:* This section is fairly straightforward. It asks for general information about you, your school, and your family. Since all applications will ask for pretty much the same information, it's a good idea to keep it all on an index card so that you can easily reference it whenever you need to. This section often includes a question about race. Though this question is optional, you can go ahead and answer it; it won't hurt you, and the answer could help you. If you do answer, don't try to "stretch the truth;" answer it the way you would on a census form. Legal debates about affirmative action have gotten a lot of attention lately, but you still should not worry about answering this question.

- *Standardized Tests:* This is another relatively easy section to fill out. Most applications require you to fill in your tests scores here, but also require you to have copies of your scores sent from the testing companies to the admissions offices. Make sure you do this in enough time for the test scores to arrive at the admissions office well before applications are due. Also, be sure you pay attention to which tests are required by your school. Some schools don't require test scores at all, others require either SAT and SAT II or ACT scores, still others specify which they want. Be sure your school receives all of the scores that it needs.

- *Extracurricular Activities:* This is the first section where your personality and accomplishments can shine through; be sure to make the most of it. Your extracurriculars allow the admissions office to see what you do when you're not studying. Sports, clubs, publications, student government, jobs, and volunteer positions are examples of some of the activities that fall into this category. Make sure to follow directions carefully when filling out this section. Some schools want you to write your activities directly on the form; others allow you to attach a typed list to the application instead. If you have the option to type a list it's a good idea to do so, even if the rest of your application is handwritten. It looks neater, you'll have more space for all your activities, and you can just print out a copy of the list for each school that requests it. Just make sure to adapt the list to the particular requirements of the school. If the application instructs you to list your activities in chronological order, do so. Otherwise it is best to list activities in order of their importance to you.

  A last word about extracurriculars—quality is more important than quantity. It's infinitely better to have long-term involvement and leadership positions in a few activities than it is to join a thousand groups to which you devoted an hour a month. Admissions officers can tell when you're just trying to pad your résumé with activities. They look more highly on passion and commitment to a few activities that reflect who you are and what interests you.

- *Transcript:* Your transcript is a window into your academic history. Admissions officers look at your grades and class rank, and they also look at the types of classes you've taken. A high GPA is important, but so is the number of AP or Honors courses you've had. Colleges look for students who challenge themselves. At this point you can't go back and fix that C you got in freshman biology, but you can do a few things to make your transcript look as good as possible. First, make sure everything is accurate. Check that your grades are correct, and that every honors class you've taken is listed as such. Second, remember that colleges *will* see your grades from senior year. Don't pad your schedule with blow-off courses; make sure to continue to take challenging classes. Try not to let yourself develop a serious case of "senioritis," because admissions committees will think that you don't take academics seriously. Lastly, request transcripts from your school as soon as you can. They can take a while to print, and you don't want your application to be late because you did not get your transcript in time.

- *Recommendations:* Many schools request letters of recommendation from teachers, coaches, or other adults who know you well. These letters let the admissions officers see how others view you and your potential. Most people will be happy to write a good recommendation for you. If a teacher doesn't feel comfortable recommending you, he or she will most likely not agree to write a letter for you, so don't worry about a teacher trashing you behind your back; it won't happen.

  Do think carefully about whom you choose to write these letters, though. You want to choose teachers who know you personally and with whom you have a good relationship. It's a good idea to choose teachers in your strong subjects, but it's also important to demonstrate some diversity of interest. For example, it's better to have your English teacher and your physics teacher write recommendations than it is to have two math teachers write them. Whomever you choose, make sure to provide them with plenty of time to write and revise a strong recommendation. Many colleges want your teachers to send recommendations in separate from the rest of your application. If so, don't forget to give teachers a stamped and addressed envelope in which to send it. Be assertive; there's nothing wrong with reminding your teachers about the recommendation, and asking before the deadline if they'd gotten it done. Most teachers are careful about these deadlines, but it does not hurt to make sure.

  Additionally, most recommendation forms have a line asking you to waive your right to see the recommendation.

You should probably sign it. Most teachers will show you a copy of what they write anyway, and signing the waiver shows confidence that your teachers respect you. Finally, though most schools only require two recommendations from teachers, some allow you to send additional recommendations from others who know you well. Though by no means required or necessary, this is a good opportunity for students with significant activities outside of school-affiliated activities to get people like coaches, art tutors, or employers to say something helpful. Don't go overboard on these though; one extra recommendation is more than enough. Content is more important than the person who writes it. It's not impressive to get your state senator to write a recommendation for you if he's never met you before.

- *The Essay:* The college essay strikes fear in the hearts of high school seniors every fall, but you should not think about it as something scary. Instead, consider it an opportunity to show your wonderful, special, unique personality while telling the admissions officers a bit about yourself. If you give yourself plenty of time and have some fun with it, it can actually be the most enjoyable part of your application.

  Think about your topic carefully, but do not kill yourself trying to come up with a topic that you think an admissions officer will like. It's a good idea to brainstorm several topics, and choose the one that feels the most exciting. Being yourself is the most important thing. If you feel strongly about something it will show through in your writing, and that will catch an admissions officer's attention. Too many students write about a class project or winning the state championship—try to describe any experiences that are less common. You want your personality to shine through, and the best way to do that is to write about something that is important to you. Though it might seem obvious, it's worth restating that you should be sure to answer whatever question the application asks. Sometimes you can reuse an essay for more than one school, but don't try to make an essay fit a topic just so you don't have to write another essay. Be prepared to write several different essays if you're applying to a lot of schools.

  Once your topic is chosen, give yourself enough time to write a good rough draft. It's sometimes intimidating to begin writing, but just put your pen to paper and start. It doesn't matter what your draft looks like at first; you'll have plenty of time to correct and edit it later. Since the essay is the part of the application where you can be yourself, write in a way that feels natural to you, whether that's humorous or serious or something completely different. You should never submit a first draft to a college. Revise your essay a few times, both for style and for content. If the application gives you a word limit, stick to it.

  Once you feel confident about the essay, it's a good idea to have a teacher, parent, older sibling, or counselor look over it for you. They can both help you find technical mistakes in spelling and grammar, and can point out places where you could be more clear in your content. By all means have others help you out with your essay in these ways, but under no circumstances should you ever, ever let anyone else write your essay for you. Not only is this dishonest, admissions officers read thousands of essays every year, and so have a good eye for essays that do not seem to be written by a particular student. Once your essay has been drafted, revised, edited, and perfected, you can either hand-write it on the application form, or, if the school allows, you can attach a typed version to the form.

Once your application is complete, put a stamp on the envelope, and pat yourself on the back. Your application was honest, well thought-out, neat, and will show the admissions committee who you are. Though you might want to call the admissions office in a week or so to make sure that they've received all your materials, there is not much left to stress out about. Once the application is in the mail it's out of your hands, so kick back, relax, and enjoy the end of your senior year. You deserve it.

The Wait

There is probably nothing anybody can say to you at this point to make you feel secure and confident regarding your applications. Your worries of the last few months about application deadlines and teacher recommendations are now petty concerns, replaced with the general unease that comes with the uncertain ground of your fate resting in somebody else's hands. Your applications are in the mail (and by now they have arrived at various admissions offices across the state and country). You hope they did, anyway. You are finished with the applications, but have only just begun the long road of anxiety.

Well, all is not lost. While it is nearly impossible to distract you from the near-constant pressure of the uncertainty regarding your future, we can at least let you know a little more about what is going on in the office.

Your application will arrive and most likely be put into an anonymous-looking, plain envelope. It will then be given to the admission officer who is in charge of your district or school. In some larger schools, you will not get much individual attention: There are often grade and SAT/ACT score cutoffs that they use to determine who gets admitted.

In smaller, private schools that can afford it, your application will be considered much more closely. Generally, your application will be read by up to three or four officers. Some schools use a numbering system to rate your academic record, your standardized test scores, and your extracurricular activities. There are some "bonus points" that you may end up with for uncontrollable variables such as your economic or racial background, or your relationship to an alumnus of the school.

Mostly, your application will speak for itself. While some schools weigh academics over extracurriculars, others might want to see high levels of community involvement or strong standardized test scores. This is where things are entirely out of your control. Each school is looking for a diverse group of students. The schools keep their academic standards relatively high, while looking for people from every possible background with every possible interest. If there happen to be 20 other students just like you from Houston, Texas, with 1350 SATs, a 3.5 GPA, roles in several school plays, and playing time on the varsity basketball team, all 20 will probably not be accepted. Likewise, if you happen to be the only student applying with an 1100 SAT, 2.8 GPA and work founding a non-profit organization to help teach English to needy children in Africa, you would probably look more unique and attractive to the admissions officer.

It is fantastically frustrating, but in the end much of this process is out of your control. You are not only competing to be good enough for a school, but you are competing against everybody else who is applying to the school. When the decision has been made, the myth is generally true: Big, thick envelopes often have big admit letters inside. The thin ones often bring bad news. Watch out, though, each year you will hear horror stories of mistaken acceptance or rejection letters. You will probably be receiving a mix of these, so don't let a poor first response get you down. Each year, more schools are experimenting with letting students find out their acceptance status online as well.

The good news is that thin envelopes sometimes bring news of a place on the wait list. The last thing you want to do in this situation is anger the admissions office. Surely, a place on the wait list is disappointing. There are only two things that can help you get off, however. First and foremost, the best you can hope for is a lot of luck. Your eventual admission depends a lot on how many people reject their offers of admission. The second factor is how you act: Admissions offices do like to see people eager to attend their school. A simple letter stating your excitement about the school and your eagerness to attend may help nudge things in your direction. Anything pestering or negative directed at the admissions office will ensure you a rejection letter.

Admissions officers are quick to admit that they turn away an incredible number of qualified applicants every year; enough, in fact, to more than fill two separate classes of equal strength. The decision process, therefore, often seems arbitrary. You may end up on the wait list of one of your safety schools, and find yourself accepted at the strongest school you applied to. You simply cannot know what is going to happen until you receive the letters. In the end, you should choose the school where you feel most comfortable.

If you can afford to, visit the schools you are considering. Otherwise, try to call students there and get a better feel for the campus. Even if one school has a better name than another, you may not be as happy there. There is no absolute way to measure your potential happiness at a school, and although it may not seem this way now, you will probably be happy anywhere you end up. The best advice we can offer you is to follow your instincts. If you get some kind of feeling about a school, go with it! There is no better reason out there to make a decision.

For now, sit back and relax. It's your senior year, your very last semester in high school. While you can't start failing your classes now, there is plenty of room left for you to chill out. Do what you can to forget about your applications (and stress about work) and instead think about how you can make the most out of your last couple months of high school. Be proud that your applications are finished and go out and have some fun!

The Money

Best case scenario: you get into the college of your dreams. Worst case scenario: you get into the college of your dreams and you realize you cannot pay for it. Once you get into college, you've only won half the battle; now you have to figure out how to pay for it. With many of the nation's most expensive colleges quickly passing the $25,000 annual tuition mark, adding up to $100,000+ for a four-year education, it is no wonder that many students are talking as much about finances as they are about SAT scores. Although few families can afford this expensive price tag, especially if there is more than one member of the family attending college, there are many resources to aid families in paying for college. You should never hesitate to apply to a college simply because of its "sticker price." Many colleges meet most, if not all, of a family's financial need with a combination of scholarships, grants, loans, and work-study programs.

The most important step you can take as a student is to openly discuss your family's financial situation at the outset of your college search. Talk about how much your family is able to pay for college, how much your parents are willing to take out in loans, and other financial topics. By initiating this discussion with your family, you are showing them that you are both responsible and sensitive to your family's financial situation.

Your biggest advantage in the financial aid game is to be organized. As you will find out, there are many forms that you must fill out in order to even begin applying for financial aid. Getting organized helps you to see exactly where you stand in the financial aid process. The money is not going to come to you, so you have to be proactive in looking for it. There are plenty of resources available to you, but you have to know where to look for it.

A good place to start is with your college guidance counselor. Counselors have the knowledge and experience in helping students like yourself get into college and in paying for college. Oftentimes, they receive information from colleges regarding scholarships and will post them around the school. Take note of these announcements and fill out the applications as soon as possible. The applications can be time consuming, but if you are well-organized, there should be no problem. The following Web sites also provide useful information for students seeking financial aid: www.finaid.org and www.fastweb.com. The more persistent and diligent you are in your search, the better your chances will be for finding the resources you need.

The best sources for financial aid are the colleges themselves. Colleges oftentimes earmark large sums of money specifically for financial aid. Many colleges also receive money from federal and private sources for financial aid purposes. Scholarships come in a variety of forms, including need-based, and merit and/or achievement awards. You will need to look at what types of financial aid the colleges that you are considering offer. Please be aware which colleges offer only need-based financial aid packages and which colleges offer merit and/or achievement scholarships. The policies and practices at each school may vary differently, so it is important that you have the information you need.

Carefully read the bulletins provided by the colleges you are considering. If you have any questions, e-mail or call the admissions office or financial aid office right away. As the saying goes, the only stupid question is the one not asked. Find out what the colleges' admissions policies are regarding financial aid applicants. Some of the nation's wealthier schools have need-blind admissions, which means that you are considered for admission without taking into account your family's ability to pay. However, at some schools, financial need may play a part in the final admission decision, especially in borderline cases where preference may be given to those with the ability to pay. Even if you do not think you can afford it, apply to the school and for the financial aid. Then, just wait and see. You might be pleasantly surprised. Sometimes it is cheaper to attend a more expensive college because they often provide superior aid packages. Of course this is not always the case, but it does prove that you should never decide against a school because of money until you have a financial aid offer (or rejection) in your hand.

As a financial aid applicant, you will soon notice all that paperwork involved. Most schools require you to file a standardized need analysis form to determine an expected family contribution (EFC). Depending on the school, the form will either be the College Board's Profile form or the U.S. Department of Education's Free Application for Federal Student Aid (FAFSA), or in some cases, both. The school will also have its own financial form for you to fill you, which you have to send along with the family's income tax forms for verification. The school will determine a reasonable family contribution for one year. (The student is also usually expected to contribute around $1,000 from summer earnings.) To come up with an estimate, a formula established by Congress is used. The formula takes into account family income, expenses, assets, liabilities, savings accounts, and other data. The cost of attendance minus this expected family contribution yields an approximate financial need. The school then designs a financial aid package that may consist of a low-interest, federally guaranteed loan, a work-study job, and a combination of different types of grants. This would lead one to believe that all packages would be similar, yet this is not always the case. Even though all schools receive the same input data, they do not all use the same formula. The family contribution will thus vary slightly, but there should not be a big difference. The difference in aid packages comes mainly from the way the school issues money. Some schools may require you to get more loans, or they might give you more money.

Some schools will always make better offers than others. Wealthier schools guarantee to meet the full "demonstrated" need of every applicant that they accept. At other colleges, however, the financial aid package may leave an "unmet" need that you will have to cover on your own. In unfortunate cases like these, students can bear the extra financial burden or choose a college that gives them a better offer.

There are a few things that you can do to improve your chances of receiving an adequate financial aid package from a school. First of all, be efficient in getting all of the forms in as early as possible. Some schools have a limited supply of funds available for financial aid, and the earlier they look at your application, the better your chance of receiving a larger share. Getting your forms in early shows a good-faith effort on your part, and schools are more likely to be cooperative with you if they feel you are being cooperative with them. Another thing you can do is write a letter to the financial aid office explaining any special family circumstances that are not reflected on the financial aid forms. If you do not let the school know about such situations, there is no way they can take them into account.

If a school offers you a financial aid package that you consider inadequate despite your best efforts to let them know about your family situation, all is still not lost. After you have been accepted at the school, make a polite call to the school's financial aid office. If you noted any special circumstances either on the financial aid form or in a separate letter, ask if they took them into account when determining the award. Sometimes letters or comments get overlooked in the haste to get the aid awards out on time. If they say they took the circumstances into account, or if you did not mention any, tell them, that you would really like to attend the school but do not think you can without more aid. If another school has offered you more aid, mention that, especially if the school is a competitor of the one you're talking to. Calling may not help, but they are not going to withdraw your acceptance once you are in.

If you are eligible for money on the basis of need, then the school may list some federal government assistance. The first of the types of federal government assistance are grants. Grants do not have to be paid back, unlike loans, but they are also harder to obtain. The federal government offers two grants: the Federal Pell Grant and the Federal Supplemental Education Opportunity Grants. You have to demonstrate "exceptional" financial need for either, but the latter is harder to obtain since the government does not guarantee as much. A Pell Grant is as high as $2,340, and the FSEOG is as high as $4,000 annually.

The federal government also offers lower-interest loans. If you demonstrate "exceptional" financial need, you may be eligible for a Perkins Loan, which can be loaned at 5 percent interest up to a maximum of $3,000. There are two types of Stafford Loans, one subsidized and the other unsubsidized. The subsidized Stafford Loan is only for people who demonstrate financial need, and it has a cap of 8.25 percent interest. The government pays for the interest while you are in school and during the grace period after you graduate. The unsubsidized loan is for those who do not demonstrate financial need, and they have to pay interest the whole time. There is also a new loan called the Federal Direct Student Loan which is just like the Stafford except that the lender is the federal government and not a bank.

There is also a federal government sponsored loan for parents called the PLUS loan. It is particularly valuable for those who qualify for little or no financial aid. Each year, parents are allowed to borrow the full amount of tuition less any financial aid the student receives. The loan requires good credit, repayment while the child is still in school, and interest rates that are not far from market rates. Still, it can help to ease the burden on middle-class families.

You will also probably be required to take a job through the federal work-study program. Many applicants worry that working part-time will detract from studying or, equally important, playtime. Yet, if you work on campus, you certainly will not be the only one: Most colleges report that about half of their students hold term-time jobs. It is possible to take a full load of courses, participate in extracurricular activities, and work ten or 15 hours per week, all while maintaining a good grade point average. Although freshmen tend to get the least exciting jobs on campus, in later years you may well find yourself working on interesting research, in a lab, or in a library job.

Many private colleges also provide scholarships based on academic, athletic, or artistic ability. As competition among colleges for the best students intensifies, more and more colleges are offering lucrative merit awards to well-qualified students. There are many excellent schools, including many state universities, that offer merit scholarships in ever-increasing numbers. The best sources for information are your high school counselor and state Department of Education.

Be sure not to overlook the millions of dollars of aid available from private sources. Organizations ranging from General Motors to the Knights of Columbus offer money for college, often as prizes to assist students from your community. Sometimes large companies offer scholarships to children of their employees, so have your parents find out if their employers have such programs. There are also several scholarships out there related to specific majors, religions, or even ethnic heritage. Or if you scored very high on the PSAT, you could be in the running for a National Merit Scholarship. There is often a catch to merit-based awards, however: If you qualify for awards from private sources, your school will often deduct some or all of the amount from any need-based aid you receive.

The only other significant source of federal aid available that is not based on need is the ROTC (Reserve Officers Training Corps) scholarship program. Thousands of dollars are available annually for students willing to put in several years in a branch of the armed forces. Sometimes they will even repay a portion of the federal government loans.

More and more, federal aid is being reserved exclusively for the very needy. Many families with incomes over $35,000 who qualify for PLUS loans must now pass a needs test to get Stafford Loans. Yet, if you play your cards right, your family should not have to undergo severe financial hardship to put you through school.

Advice for Transfers

If you are already in college and are thinking about transferring to another school, the preceding advice is mostly old news to you. Theoretically you know what to do now, but there are actually a number of new considerations that all potential transfers should keep in mind.

Most importantly, you need to seriously consider your decision to transfer. If you are unhappy, it is easy to blame your school first. However, the cause of your troubles may not be your school in particular, but issues with the college experience itself, such as roommate troubles, work overload, or homesickness. Don't assume that you'll necessarily be happy at another university. One student left Stanford in search of "greener pastures." Instead, she found New England "cold, gray, and without pastures at all." According to another student, "It's a big risk. You have to really want to leave where you are or really want to go where you will be." There are no guarantees that you will be better off at another school, and the process itself may make things even less satisfactory for you. Ultimately, you need to reassess your reasons for transferring. Do other schools have what you need to make your life any better? You should seriously consider taking a semester or two off to reevaluate your situation, or giving a more honest effort at making your current situation work. Transferring is a difficult and often disappointing process.

Most schools accept transfer students who have up to two years of credit at another university. It is safer, however, to transfer after your first year, because your old university will be more likely to take you back if you change your mind. One student advised that it is better to take a leave of absence from your original school than to withdraw completely.

The application process is also slightly different for transfer students. Be aware that colleges tend to consider a transfer student in a different light from a high school senior. Few students tend to leave top private universities, so the acceptance rate for transfers at top schools is much, much lower than that for first-time applicants. The situation can be different at larger state schools.

Each school looks for different students, but grades, recommendations, and the essay that explains why you want to transfer are usually the three most important parts of the application. Make sure that you find classes with professors who will be able to write you good recommendations, or it is almost not worth applying to transfer. Standardized test scores and extracurriculars are less important. One exception to this may be if you decide to take time off and do something exceptional during your time away from school. Keep in mind that your college transcript is incredibly important. As much as you might want to leave your school, do not ease up on your academics.

Because colleges will expect you to prove that you have developed during your first year or two of college and to show why you absolutely cannot stay at your old school, your essay (and interview if you can arrange one) is critical. Be definite and clear about your reasons for transferring and what you expect to find in a new environment. Academic reasons are best; personal ones are only as convincing as you can make them. It also helps if the department in which you want to major is under-subscribed at the new school.

Make sure you know a lot about the school you are applying to. Not only will this show through in your application, but you will also be much more prepared for the experience ahead. If what you need is an active, social campus in which to get involved, then make sure that you will be guaranteed on-campus housing. If you are going to need financial aid, check and see that it will be available for transfer students. Also, be sure you look into how your credits will transfer at the new school. Will you get credit towards a major, or only towards graduation? If you don't have a major already picked out, it can be difficult, if not impossible, to graduate in four years.

Making the decision to transfer is not a walk in the park. Make sure that you are confident in your decision, and be ready for anything. Most importantly, have a backup plan for the upcoming year. If it doesn't work out and you don't get accepted, make sure you have options. Be prepared to make another run at getting the most out of your school, or have a plan of what you might do with a year off. If everything does work out for you, make sure you have covered all of the bases before you make the final decision to commit to a new school.

The College Spectrum

Current Trends and Comparing Colleges

At first glance, the sheer number of colleges included in this book might seem a bit overwhelming—clearly you would never consider applying to over 300 schools. Since colleges and their student bodies vary in so many ways, it can be difficult to identify schools at which you would feel comfortable. One piece of advice is to be aware of the general social, political, and academic trends that schools are experiencing in the early years of the new millennium (hey, we had to throw the word "millennium" in at least once in a book this long). When *The Insider's Guide* was first written 31 years ago, these changing trends included coeducation, breaking racial barriers, and providing access for the disabled. These issues are still present, but the current hot issues include affirmative action, the fairness of standardized testing, expanding financial aid, and how to treat "legacies" (students whose parents or relatives attended a college).

Another way to get some perspective on different colleges is to identify where they stand in terms of various criteria—to figure out where they fall on a continuum we call the College Spectrum. Most importantly, it is not our place to judge which types of schools are best, but instead to present a variety of perspectives and observations that can help you with the decision-making process. Here are some of the many areas in which you can compare different schools.

Size

The total enrollments of the schools in this book range from 26 at California's Deep Springs to nearly 50,000 at the University of Texas at Austin. Considering the size of the campus you want to attend is helpful in the initial narrowing-down process; the feel of a school can be very dependent on how many students are around. There are two main parts of your experience that will be affected by the size of the school you choose: academics and social life.

Academically, two important areas of comparison between large and small schools are class size and the accessibility of senior faculty. In this case, smaller colleges decidedly have the advantage simply because a smaller population usually translates into smaller classes. Students at small schools have great opportunities for one-on-one student-faculty interaction. At large schools, students are more likely to complain of impersonal instruction and "being treated as a Social Security number."

To make up for this apparent disadvantage, many larger schools offer special programs intended to create the sense of community among professors and students that small colleges enjoy. Different universities have different approaches. Some offer honors programs for a limited number of students and some schools house all the students who are in special programs together. Generally, students in such programs all take the same or similar courses, most of which are small, discussion-oriented classes. Bear in mind that many honors and special programs are highly selective; do your best to make a realistic assessment of your chances to be accepted. Additionally, don't be snowed by the glossy pictures in admissions booklets: If you are considering a large university, take a close look at the quality of its special programs. Very often, there is a gap between the description of the program in the brochures and the reality.

Another important factor to remember is that no matter how large a school is, not all of the classes it offers will be huge and overcrowded, and some of the huge classes will break into smaller discussion groups. Thus, although most schools do have some very large classes, you can almost always find small ones of interest. In this case however, it is important to remember that in bigger schools, it is often difficult to get into small classes as an underclassman.

Also, pay attention to who teaches the classes. At most liberal arts colleges, only professors do. Many large universities pad their student-faculty ratios by including graduate students, or they advertise discussion classes that turn out to be taught by people who are still working toward a Ph.D. By reading guides such as this one and by talking to students, you can find out roughly how many graduate students teach and whether or not senior professors teach undergraduates at all. Having younger, less experienced professors teach is not always a bad thing. Many times, courses taught by graduate students allow for a rapport between teachers and students that does not develop with some of the stodgier old professors. However, if graduate students appear to dominate the teaching, even if only for the freshman year, you should definitely consider this as you make your decision. These facts also give a good idea of how much the administration cares about the typical undergraduate student.

For highly specialized fields that require extensive facilities, the resources at small schools are generally limited. For facilities not associated with academics, such as the gym or the library, size and showiness are not nearly as important as accessibility. You will not care how many racquetball courts the gym has as long as one is available when you want to play and it's not a three-mile walk away. Instead of asking how many volumes there are in the library, find out whether everyone has full access to all its resources, and if the library holds long hours. While the facilities at smaller schools may be less impressive than those at big universities, they are often more accessible to undergraduates.

Social life, too, is affected by the size of the school. Consider carefully what kind of social life you plan to have and which type of school would be more conducive to your interests. The people you associate with will likely to be determined by your extracurricular interests—a sports team, a student newspaper, or student government. This is especially true for universities that do not provide more than one year of campus housing.

The key is finding your own comfortable niche within any school. While there are usually more niches to be discovered in large colleges, finding yours may require some initiative. The larger the school, the more subgroups there are likely to be within the student body. Frats and sororities tend to be more abundant and popular on bigger campuses. An advantage to being a member of a very large community is that the supply of new faces never runs out. If you get tired of one circle of friends, you can always find another. But it is also important to keep in mind that when you are on your own in the midst of all those unfamiliar people, it is also possible to feel very lonely. On the other hand, small environments can be more welcoming and friendly. Small schools often have a greater sense of community and people can find that making friends is easier. Some students find that small schools can be a little too small, because "everybody knows everybody else's business."

One common misconception about smaller schools is that they are inevitably more homogenous and have less school pride or spirit. On the contrary, many of them, especially the more selective ones, have just as many different types of people as do most large universities, only in smaller numbers. Although larger schools, especially those with a big emphasis on athletics, may have tremendous school spirit, smaller ones foster their own brand of pride, usually stemming from rich tradition and a strong sense of community.

Schools come in all different sizes. No matter how big or small a school is, make sure it prioritizes what is important to you. Be sure to keep in mind both academic and social consequences of the size of your school: Both have the potential to drastically change your college experience.

Location

At some point, if not right away, you will find yourself thinking about the town in which one of your college choices is located. Can you see yourself living there for a few years? What sounds better to you—a college where all the buildings are completely surrounded by trees, or a college with easy access to shops and malls? Before you answer these questions, be sure you really understand the difference between urban and rural settings, and more importantly, what this difference would mean for your life at school. Often, what some students perceive to be "life in the city" or "life on a farm" are not the reality of what living at the college would be like. There are many factors that need to be considered in order to get an accurate idea of how location would affect your whole college experience.

Whether you've found your way through corn fields for eighteen years, or you've wandered around Times Square by yourself since you were ten, going away to college, while invigorating and rewarding, can also be an intimidating experience. Many people arrive at school the very first day completely oblivious to the opportunities and the challenges of being out of their town, their state, or their region. If you are from a rural area and are considering the big move to the city, expect adjustment (to noise, traffic, people, crime, the hectic pace), but try not to make or accept any assumptions about "the horrors" of city life. If you are from an urban area and are considering the peace and quiet of a smaller school tucked in the woods somewhere, also expect adjustment (to relatively silent nights, no movie theater or department store, the slower pace), but also try not to make or accept any assumptions about 'life with the cows." Your thoughts about the location of the school should be balanced by the fact that every school will inherently have some sort of community; is this community, along with the city the school is located in, right for you?

College is a great time to try new things, including a new location—a new city, a new state, maybe a whole new region of the United States or even Canada. In general, you do need to be aware of certain broad characteristics of each type of campus. At a campus in a big city, for example, there is a greater chance of no on-campus nightlife, as everyone will head towards the major clubs and bars to relax. At the same time, however, after a week of academic work, extracurricular activities, dorm parties, visiting speakers, football games, and the multitude of other school-sponsored events, being in an urban environment means that there is still the option of seeing a Broadway show or going to a world-renowned museum. As for a campus in a smaller town, the exact opposite may be true. Without anything to do around town, students will have all of their activities and create all of their own nightlife on campus. While you may sometimes wish you did have the major clubs and bars, the tight-knit community that forms among students at the school may very well more than make up for any of those longings. Whichever setting you do end up choosing should depend on your own realizations of how you would feel in those surroundings.

Another point to consider is how comfortable you would be living so close to or so far away from home. Does leaving the Pacific Ocean for the Atlantic Ocean sound like a real adventure, or does being even two hours away from your family make your hands start to tremble? Are you at the point in your life where you still need to be with all of your friends going to the same school near or in your hometown, or can you not wait for all of your new friends and your "whole new life" out of state? Distance is definitely another one of those factors that requires thinking about everything in context.

Your life will change in college, whether you pack your bags to travel far away or keep your room at home. Anywhere you end up, even if you do stay close to home, your old relationships will change at least a little bit. When it comes down to it, make sure you are honest with yourself about your reasons for choosing a particular school. It may be helpful to talk to current students at the school to get a sense of where they came from and what they think about the location. It may also be helpful to fold a piece of paper in half and come up with a list of positives about the location of the school on one side, and negatives on the other. Include everything that will affect your life: the weather, the people, the travel expenses, and the homesickness, without forgetting to take into account the school's own community. Life at college will require at least some adjustment, but it may be that exact adjustment which completes your college experience.

Private vs. Public

The question of whether to attend a public or private school is best answered through a cost-benefit approach. Don't worry, we know you haven't had Econ 101, so consider this a free lesson. Let's first divide the universities in the U.S. into three categories: large private, public, and small private.

The greatest distinction between a private and a public university is, of course, the cost. However, in recent years this divide has dramatically diminished as private schools have allocated increasingly more funds to financial aid packages. These packages are almost always a combination of loans and grants, meaning that they do not always diminish the cost of college, but simply postpone it to a future date.

Most top-tier private institutions have adopted *need blind admissions* policies which mean that they admit irregardless of your ability to pay and then work with you to create a financial aid package which will allow you to attend. Princeton led the pack in this respect by announcing in 2001 that it would replace loans with outright grants; soon many other colleges followed suit.

Smaller private schools, however, do not have the high-powered endowments necessary to fund such *need blind* policies. In this area, public universities definitely have an advantage. Subsidized by state taxpayers, they offer an outstanding education at a fraction of its actual cost—this means everyone is basically a financial aid recipient.

If you do decide to break the bank and attend a private school, you will often be rewarded with smaller class size and greater student-teacher interaction. There is, however, a not-so-obvious advantage to the small private colleges. At larger private or state universities much of the teaching duty has been increasingly placed on the shoulders of ill-equipped, barely comprehensible, and many times foreign teaching-assistants (graduate students). Additionally, at large private universities, professors must devote a significant amount of time to research in order to stay ahead in their field. Small private colleges offer teaching environments in which the professors are not burdened with this dictum of *publish or perish;* they can devote all their time to teaching the material instead of contributing to it.

Although their numbers at private schools are staggering, not all students attended New England prep schools such as Exeter or Deerfield. Indeed, it might be said that private universities offer the best socio-economic racial mix because state schools reserve the majority of their spaces for state residents. Also, highly selective private colleges have an intellectual atmosphere rarely matched at state universities. This is an important consideration because at any good college, public or private, much of the valuable learning takes place through interaction with students of backgrounds different from yours.

Different types of students undoubtedly create different social scenes. While many state schools have the reputation as centers for Greek life, private schools tend to develop an equivalent, but alternatively labeled approach. You will find that many private and public schools have banned frat houses on campus, but never fear, almost all schools develop clubs or societies that ultimately fill the same role.

Lastly, when deciding which type of school to attend, make sure that you look beyond its label as either public or private. While some applicants consider attending a state university second-best when compared to an elite private school, others make a public institution their first choice. It is important to consider department-specific academic strengths along with the overall reputation of the university as whole. Public schools such as UC Berkeley, UCLA, and University of Michigan rank among some of the top academic institutions, public or private, in the country. So after all of this, in the end, you should never be swayed too much by a school's private or public designation. Instead, try to choose the school that's best suited to you.

Coed or Single-Sex?

Since co-education became the norm at American universities in the 1960s, the number of single-sex schools in the nation has dropped significantly. There are only four men's colleges remaining in this book: Deep Springs College, Hampden-Sydney College, Morehouse College, and Wabash College. The students here chose to attend mainly because of their belief that the absence of the opposite sex allows greater dedication to academics and a friendlier, more fraternal atmosphere. Tradition and conservatism prevail at these all-male institutions, and men that work best in these atmospheres find themselves very content.

Women's colleges have similar reasons for existence as all-male colleges, but with a few twists. There are many more women's colleges, as the whole movement for women's education came later and is still firmly rooted in feminine beliefs. Most women who attend single-sex colleges cite the supportive, nurturing environment as their college's asset. In an arguably male-dominated culture, women's schools provide a learning environment where there is support for developing one's female identity, no academic competition with men, and numerous leadership opportunities. Women's colleges are usually very liberal, with focus on current events and debates on different points of view.

There is no debate, however, about the fact that life at a single-sex institution is very different from life at a co-ed one. Because single-sex schools tend to be smaller, there are often fewer academic programs and resources than at larger co-ed colleges. Also, the atmosphere is somewhat contrived, since one of the sexes is missing. There are always outlets through which students can find the opposite sex, such as "brother universities," but the social life and vivacity of the campus is usually at a much "calmer" level than co-ed schools. For students who want the best of both worlds, there are a few colleges that are part of co-ed consortia. Women at Mount Holyoke and Smith can take classes at the neighboring Amherst and Hampshire Colleges and the University of Massachusetts, and the women at Barnard are paired with the co-ed Columbia University.

Single-sex atmospheres can be ideal for some people, but not everyone finds benefits from such an experience. Most college-bound seniors end up enrolling in co-educational schools—but in these colleges the issues of co-ed bathrooms and dormitories come to the fore. There are, however, many different housing options, and administrators work to make you comfortable. So after choosing whether a single-sex or co-ed college is right for you, your institution will send you information on handling all the details.

The most famous all-female schools are the Seven Sisters, a group of seven Northeastern colleges that self-organized in 1927 to promote single-sex education. The seven sisters—Barnard, Bryn Mawr, Mount Holyoke, Radcliffe (now joined with Harvard), Smith, Vassar (now co-ed), and Wellesley—hoped to compete with the image of the Ivy League schools. Interestingly, it was not until 1978 that all seven schools had female presidents.

Besides the actual experience, one final thing to keep in mind is a certain stigma attached to many single-sex schools. Since the majority of these schools are extremely liberal, they are generally known for strong activism in women's and gay rights. This reputation exists despite the more conservative nature of some of the top academic single-sex schools. Whether accurate or not, this is another factor to consider in your choice.

Advising and Tutoring

The first few weeks of college can be confusing. There are placement tests to take, forms to fill out, questions about AP credits to ask, and parents to kiss goodbye. Many freshmen are often unaccustomed to the breadth of courses from which to choose. Also, it's hard to plan your academic year when you're in the midst of meeting new friends, moving into your dorm room, trying to go to as many parties as possible, and asking out that cute German down the hall. However, do not be daunted.

Almost all colleges provide students with faculty advisors for at least the first year. Their function is twofold: they can both rubber stamp your schedule and be used as reference for everything from course selection to general questions about the college. Though most of the students agree that faculty advisors are usually only good for placing their John Hancocks on your schedule, there were a few who are adamant that faculty advisors do have some value. If you are not one of those who knows what you want to major in from day one, don't worry, your advisor can help you plan your schedule and think things through.

If you still have unanswered questions, ask upperclassmen (often the best source for good, quick information). For more detailed, department-specific questions about graduation/major requirements, ask a faculty member in that department.

Once you have chosen your classes, remember that this is only half the battle! Fortunately, most colleges and universities offer tutoring resources free of charge to help you succeed. If you find yourself in a large class with a professor who rushes through the most important points in the last five minutes of lecture or have a foreign TA who can barely speak English, you should consider getting a tutor. Professors' office hours are usually insufficient for detailed explanations. Even the brightest students can benefit from going over the subject matter once per week.

Many times tutors are graduate students or particularly advanced undergraduates proficient in that specific academic discipline. However, ask upperclassmen for old study guides for more general insight into acing specific courses when exam time roles around.

A Minority Perspective

As a minority student or a person of color, there might well be some additional factors to consider in your decision. You may, for example, be searching for a school with a high population of minority students or for a school that is predominantly African-American. A school with a high minority population may prove to be more supportive and even more comfortable. Regardless of size, though, a strong minority community can be helpful during the next four years and can even help reduce the racism and ignorance on some campuses.

Another factor to consider is the general attitude of both the administration and the student body. Unfortunately, racism still exists at many colleges, but do not assume a defensive attitude while visiting schools. Instead, be aware of possible situations and attitudes that may make you feel excluded and uncomfortable. What might have seemed like a diverse college in the brochures may not seem so open-minded after all. Take note of how integrated the minority community is, and what the school does to recognize and support other cultures. Some schools may foster a pressure to conform; if the school has a large population of a certain race, there may be a distinct sense of separatism. For some this may provide a stronger sense of belonging, while for others it will only increase the stress of college life.

To determine the true attitude of the administration, look at how it attempts to support the minority communities. Some schools assign ethnic counselors to help minority students adjust to college life. Some students appreciate this; others resent it. One student reported that her school was doing so much to accommodate her minority status she felt separated rather than integrated. Many students, however, get used to the idea of special resources and ultimately find them supportive.

Another thing to look at is the extracurricular life. What kinds of organizations are there for specific minority groups or minority students in general? The school may have cultural centers and politically oriented associations that focus on the traditional arts and dances of their culture. With any luck, the school's primary form of minority student recognition will not be an ethnic theme dinner once a semester.

For African-American students, an important decision may be whether to attend a predominantly black college over another school. Despite the improving financial situations of most private black colleges, you are likely to find better facilities and larger academic departments at majority white schools. Unfortunately, the continuing decline of federal funding is likely to exacerbate this situation, since black colleges rely heavily on such resources. Nevertheless, many students choose to attend a predominantly black college for many of the same reasons other students choose to attend a single-sex school. Some black students find them a more congenial and accepting community that is more conducive to personal growth. Likewise, students often have a better chance to attain key leadership positions at a college where they do not have minority status. At a predominantly black school, the African-American experience is one of the central issues on campus. What does it mean to be a black person in America at the turn of the 21st century? Of what importance is African-American heritage? At predominantly black schools, these questions are addressed in a manner and with a fervor unrivaled by other institutions.

In this book, we include reports on five of the best-known predominantly black schools in the United States: Howard University in Washington, D.C.; Spelman and Morehouse Colleges in Georgia; Florida A&M University; and Tuskegee University in Alabama. For a more complete listing, we suggest you consult *The Black Student's Guide to Colleges*, written by Barry Beckham and published by Beckham House. Another school with an ethnic majority is the University of Hawaii, which is predominantly made up of Asian students.

Ultimately, you have to decide where you will feel most comfortable. Whatever your choice, it is important to remember that your ethnicity is an integral part of yourself and is not something you should have to compromise in choosing a school.

Sexual Minorities

The first question that a gay, lesbian, bisexual, or transgender student should ask when considering choosing a college is the same one that straight students ask: where will I be the most comfortable and happiest for four years? Students planning on being openly gay at college will want to choose a campus where they can come out to their roommates, friends, and even professors without worrying about the consequences. But how can you tell on one or two trips to a college whether or not you'll get a positive reception?

The good news is that, as one transfer student put it, "there are sensitive people everywhere—at large schools and small ones." Another student said she sought out a campus with diversity, guessing that a diverse population "would create more understanding." Beyond these general statements, however, there are other aspects of campus life to observe. Check out a school's listing of organizations, for instance. A school with several gay alliances and clubs, for example, probably has a more accepting environment, even if you don't think you'll end up being active in any of them. One student pointed out that the surrounding community can be just as important. "Knowing that there were gay bars and events in the town made me more comfortable in my choice." The more town-gown interaction there is, the more important it is that a perspective student feels comfortable being gay in that city. A lesbian student who chose a Quaker school commented that she "guessed the school's principles would attract a more accepting student body." In other words, there are countless characteristics that imply a college's atmosphere welcomes gay students.

In looking for a school, all students search for a place with unlimited options. As a gay, lesbian, or even questioning student, the best college is going to be one where your opportunities are not constrained by your sexual orientation. As one gay member of a fraternity pointed out, "I wanted to join a frat in college, so it was important that I found a place where my sexuality wouldn't be as big a deal. At a school where the Greek scene isn't predominant, it's been easier to be openly gay." In other words, there are countless schools where gay and lesbian students participate in every aspect of campus life—and fortunately it isn't too hard to track them down. This is not to say life for gay students is always perfect; gay students do risk running up against prejudices, but it is reassuring to know that gay and lesbian students at large and small schools, public and private, have managed to find their niche, be active members of the undergraduate community, and simply have a good time.

Politics

How politically active a campus is may affect how comfortable you are there. You will find that many schools have clubs of all alignments, and political journals of all bents as well, from the left-wing liberals to the Green Party to the ultra-conservatives. Generally these partisan organizations are most active in presidential election years. If this is what you're interested in, you will have no trouble finding your political niche.

When our parents were in school, political activism was as common as bell bottoms and tie-dye. Today though, the number of students strongly involved in politics on campus is generally a minority. One student remarked that a majority of her fellow students stay away from politics for social reasons: many people at her university look down on those with strong convictions because they assume them to be closed-minded. Instead of joining political organizations, many students channel their activism into volunteer programs that confront specific problems such as urban blight or environmental destruction.

Usually it is the small liberal arts schools that are the most politicized. "At my school, you don't just put your name on name tags, you put your cause, your oppressor, your god, and your sexual orientation," said one student. Before selecting a school, you may want to see if it has a political forum that brings in outside speakers and organizes discussions and lectures.

Although only a few years ago campus activism was moving towards being institutionalized and domesticated, recent events, such as the September 11 attacks and the war in Iraq, have provoked an increasing amount of activity on behalf of students. Student protests, petitions, and marches have garnered much support as well as media recognition.

Additionally certain incidents and issues, particularly those involving racism and sexuality, receive community-wide attention. On Columbus Day at one school, for example, indignant students covered sidewalks with brightly colored chalked polemics against racism and genocide. The gay- and lesbian-rights activists at a different school sponsor a kiss-in where same-sex couples cluster around the campus' central promenade and neck. Gay rights, AIDS awareness, and race-related issues are commonly on the collegiate slate of activist causes. Today, to be politically correct (PC)—manifested by a tolerance for others' ideas and political affiliations and an attempt to be inoffensive to any and all groups in speech as well as in print—is something of a secondary issue. Although PC was a hot topic on campus in the nineties, the debates on the spelling of "woman" and whether your roommate is disabled or "differently abled" seem to have faded.

The PC contingent has won some battles, though. Many schools now require students to take courses that focus on non-Western cultures, or courses aimed at raising sensitivity to minority issues and concerns. Additionally more and more schools have started classifying "Women and Gender Studies" as a major, as well as "Latin-American Studies," and "African-American Studies."

As a general rule of thumb, the more liberal the campus, the more concerned students are about political issues. If you enjoy informal political debates or thrive on dinner conversations about the Middle East or Title IX athletics, you might want to consider a more liberal school, even if you are a radical Republican.

By visiting a college you can quickly pick up on how important politics are to the student body. Read posters and skim student newspapers to gauge whether or not the political climate on that campus is right for you. The best schools may be those that can absorb all viewpoints, so that no matter what you think, there will be others who will embrace your thoughts, challenge them, or respect your decision not to vocalize them.

Preprofessionalism vs. Liberal Arts

Preprofessionalism is a term you will see repeated throughout this book. Not all curriculums are the same, and depending on what track or major you choose, you will receive either a preprofessional or a liberal arts education.

Majors that do not lead directly to a specific career fall into the liberal arts category. Even if a student plans to be an accountant, for example, he or she might get a liberal arts degree in philosophy or English, and then go on to study accounting at the appropriate professional school. The goal of a liberal arts education is to teach students how to think creatively and analytically, thus preparing them to pursue any career.

There are pros and cons to both tracks.

Some argue that a liberal arts education is the key to a solid education and to becoming a well-rounded individual. Others believe that a liberal arts degree can be a waste of four years and thousands of dollars for those who already have their career plans mapped out. Many preprofessional programs require students to take general education courses in liberal arts departments. In fact, almost all colleges insist that you take some courses outside your chosen field.

If you don't yet know your interests well enough to decide now which option is for you, you may be pleased to learn that the largest colleges and universities have both liberal arts and preprofessional students. The University of Michigan, for example, has a strong undergraduate school of business; many students in Michigan's liberal arts school also plan to go into business eventually but are pursuing a B.A. in a more general field first. The case is similar with Cornell.

If you do know what you want from a school in terms of career preparation, then you may prefer to attend a preprofessional institution. But keep in mind that getting a liberal arts education and getting a good job are not mutually exclusive. Moreover many report that the learning environment at a preprofessional university is more competitive, and would therefore not be as enjoyable to a student who enjoys the intellectual exchange more common to liberal arts campuses.

In the past two decades there has also been a revival of interest in ROTC (Reserve Officers Training Corps) programs. These scholarships from the four branches of the armed forces help pay for tuition, books, and room and board during college. When you graduate, you are committed to anywhere between four and eight years of reserve or active duty, depending on the program. As the supply of financial aid declines and the cost of college education continues to climb, more and more students are coming to see ROTC scholarships as worthwhile. However, be very thorough when investigating ROTC programs at different schools. Some colleges tend to be very anti-military, and you may find yourself part of a controversial program. Even so, the benefits of the program can be substantial for a student who joins after careful consideration and research.

Greek Life and Other Social Options

When choosing a college, you are choosing a place in which to live and learn. In this way the social life at colleges becomes a large factor in choosing your school and many people claim that when they visited colleges, the people they met made them love or hate the campus more than any other aspect. You will find that in some places you just click with the students at particular schools. Although most schools are large enough that you will find your social niche anywhere, it is also important to consider how that overall social atmosphere will affect you while you are there.

Collegiate life in the United States often conjures images of a social scene dominated by exclusive fraternities and sororities. While this is true of some schools, there are many schools where Greek life is either non-existent or less central to college life than some would believe. Thus, Greek life can run the gamut from a dominating institution to a relatively unknown and tame element of college life. It is also true that while many fraternities and sororities have high levels of membership, some of the numbers are dropping across the country. This is due mostly to increasingly strict policies on campuses to curb hazing as well as alcohol abuse that has made Greek life so infamous in today's media.

Although the most widely publicized side of Greek organizations has to do with their partying habits, belonging to a Greek organization is not necessarily just for those who like to party. In fact, many organizations have reformed their policies to reduce or eliminate such practices as pledge hazing and many require that Greeks be dry at official functions (although that does not mean they cannot party together outside of meetings).

Beyond being a social group, Greek organizations offer many advantages to students including a nationwide network of alumni, community service opportunities and housing (which is often very difficult to find for upperclassmen). The emphasis on community service is particularly important to most Greek organizations and most chapters have an office dedicated specifically to organizing the chapter to participate in local charitable activities. On some campuses, the fraternities and sororities are the most active social-service organizations.

In terms of housing considerations, most organizations are on campus and thus are financially supported by the school, national chapter, and students. Because of this, Greek houses are some of the nicest housing available, often as free standing buildings with manicured lawns and beautifully decorated interiors. However, an increasing trend among colleges is to kick Greek organizations off campus. This trend is especially marked among fraternities that gain the reputation of being unkempt and raucous. Without campus funding, many of the organizations lose a large amounts of their financial support and thus cannot run as well as those that are on campus.

Whether Greek life appeals to you or not, when choosing a college it is essential to know just how influential the Greek organizations are each school. At some campuses, not rushing could seriously limit your social options. On the other hand, there are many schools where fraternities and sororities are most certainly not part of campus life and are regarded as conformist. There are also schools, especially among the Ivy League, where although Greek life is present, there is a strong residence system that fills many of the social functions that Greek organizations occupy elsewhere. As a rule of thumb, Greek life is more dominant at the largest schools where practical concerns keep the organizations strong and smallest at the most specialized schools where campus life is intimate enough that smaller social organizations may prove stifling.

However, even at the most Greek-dominated campuses, there are always other social outlets. Your interests will largely determine who your friends are. Therefore, you should choose a school that has groups that represent your interests. Greek organizations, athletics, cultural organizations, or theater groups will all be part of your college experience and the people you meet in any of these organizations will generally become some of your closest friends.

Ultimately, the best way to tell if a school's social scene is right for you is to visit the campus or talk to friends who go there. Most college applicants worry that they will not find people like themselves when they get to college, but when they get there realize that making friends was much easier than expected. Find what you think will be the right combination of organizations, Greek or otherwise, and you will meet the right people.

Security

Security as an issue on college campuses is not simply a response to a few well-publicized campus murders. Although the tragedies at some colleges are by no means insignificant, crime in general is increasing on campuses across the country. In response to this trend, federal legislation has made it mandatory for all colleges receiving federal aid (which is almost every one) to publish crime statistics in several categories. At your request, the appropriate office (usually the public relations or admissions offices) at any college or university should release to you the crime count for the last calendar year.

Many colleges have also taken measures to beef up security. If you visit a campus and notice very stringent security measures (at the University of Pennsylvania, for example, you have to show your ID just to get into the quadrangle), remember that this means two things: there is a need for security measures, and the administration is responding to this need.

There are a number of features that any safety-conscious campus should have. Doors to individual dorm rooms and to the building entrances should be equipped with locks. All walkways should have bright lights, not only so that you can see, but so friends and classmates would be able to see you from a distance in case of danger. Another important security measure is a safety phone system with one-touch access to an emergency line. Each safety phone should have a distinct light to make it easily recognizable at night. Ideally, there should be enough units so that you are never more than a half a block from a phone. For getting around campus late at night, colleges should provide bus service or student safety escorts, free of charge. At least one of these services should be available 24 hours a day and should travel to every possible destination on campus. Every school should employ some type of security guard, whether unarmed monitors in or near the dorms or full-time police officers responsive solely to students and the affairs of the college.

Security problems are not limited to urban campuses. Some rural schools have crime rates as high as the urban ones. The sad truth is that most non-violent crimes are committed by other students, not outsiders. Why is campus crime such an issue now? College students are ideal targets—they keep expensive stereo and computer equipment in badly guarded areas, and they often walk alone across dark, seemingly safe campuses.

Therefore, it is important to understand that you cannot judge the safety of a campus simply by eyeing it from the safe confines of a brochure. Yet, by using a little common sense and preventive measures, the security problems of a given school should not prevent you from attending that school. By making yourself aware of potential problems and following the school's security guidelines, you can improve your chances of enjoying a safe four years. Security may be a fundamental problem with college life, but you can certainly do something about it.

Computers

As Internet and e-mail usage continue to expand, computers and networking are becoming more and more essential in all aspects of college life. Whether you are an art major, a computer science major, or an expert procrastinator, computers will be an important part of your college experience. Looking up information for that research paper due in 12 hours, searching for your classmate's phone number in the online directory, and downloading the next problem set from the class Web site are just a few examples of the countless ways that computers will be part of your everyday life. With that in mind, here are a few things to look for when evaluating a college's computing facilities:

24-Hour Computer Clusters: Make sure that there are at least a few accessible computer clusters to rely on when your computer or printer stops cooperating once you finally sit down to start your homework. Many people also like to work on their papers in computer clusters to get away from the distractions of their own room. Easily accessible clusters with numerous, fast computers are always a plus.

Macs vs. PCs: The networks at some schools may be preferentially built for Macs or PCs. If you are looking into buying a new computer, make sure your school provides adequate support for your machine. If you are required to purchase a new computer through your school, you can be certain that they will provide support, and the price may be factored into financial aid as well.

Support Staff: Another important thing to consider is the availability of computer assistants. Many schools will hire students or other staff to troubleshoot the problems you may encounter with networking, hardware, or software licensed by the school. This can be especially helpful at the beginning of each semester when you have to register your computers with the school network and install the necessary software.

Internet and e-mail Access: Most schools provide Ethernet access from dorm rooms and e-mail accounts that you can use during both the semester and your breaks. Another feature to look for is the availability of wireless Ethernet at your school. In addition to getting rid of an extra wire on your desk, it also allows you to check your e-mail or chat with your roommate from anywhere on campus.

School-Provided Software: Colleges will purchase licenses of software that can be used by student and faculty while on campus. Examples of commonly offered programs are antivirus software and networking software.

Academic Usage of the Internet: More and more professors are beginning to use the Internet as an important resource for their classes. Being able to find class notes, handouts, or homework assignments posted on a Web site can be an aspect to consider when choosing a class or a school.

Although not every school excels in all of these categories, finding a school that is adequate in each of them will help make your life slightly easier over the next four years.

One recent hot topic surrounding computers is the widespread use of illegally downloaded mp3s on college campus. Many universities have sought to fight back by restricting access to certain popular Web sites or by sending warning messages to students who use excessive bandwidth on the network. Although many students continue to download songs for free unabated, be aware of what the university's policy is towards Internet usage.

A Final Note About Quality of Life

If you started at the first page and you've read up to here, you are probably thinking *there are just way too many things to think about in choosing a college*! Certainly, you already have many reasons why, right off the bat, you would add a college to, or eliminate a college from, your list. Perhaps the school has the best zoology program in the nation. Or maybe you have always wanted to be in the stands cheering as your school's basketball team wins the championship game. Either way, a final but crucial criterion for your decision is the overall quality of life you can expect to have at college.

Everyone goes to college to learn more, right? Yes, of course. Continuing your academic education will provide you with even more ways of thinking as well as more opportunities after graduation. You have to remember, though, college is someplace you will be for three or more years of your life. Academics are the most important reason to go to college, but when it comes down to everyday life, the college you choose will basically be your new world. Everything from extracurricular activities to housing, social life, and even weather will affect the way you eat, dress, study, and relax. Don't go to Michigan State if there is no way you would even go outside when it is cold; for the same reason, don't go to the University of Miami if you cannot stand the sun! Have you always thought about joining a fraternity or a sorority, and there just aren't any on campus? Or perhaps your favorite weekend activity is to curl up on a chair in a coffee shop; is the college in such a small town that there is no coffee shop? What about the housing situation? Could you see yourself coming "home" every day to that closet-sized room you are sharing with five other students? Speaking of the other students, would you be comfortable being around them—or any of the people walking down the street? All of these factors can and will make a difference in how you feel about a school. The best way to really get an idea of what it would be like to be a student at the college is to visit the school, maybe stay over for a night or two, talk to the students around you, and browse through the student newspaper. Do you like what you see and how it feels to be there?

As you figure out what you like about a college, you may also want to check that those aspects of the school will still be there when you enroll. When the economy is doing poorly, an increasing number of schools, both public and private, will face a shortage of funds; administrations at the schools have no choice but to make budget cuts. Without adequate funding, programs or even entire departments may be eliminated, the number of tenured professors may be reduced, campus renovations and additions may be delayed, extracurricular activities and sports teams may be cut, or worse yet, a combination of all of these possibilities may take place. If you are the star of your high school's varsity swimming team and want to continue swimming in college, check with the coach or the current swimmers to make sure the team is not rumored to be next on the list of programs to be cancelled. If you know that you want to major in biomedical engineering, make sure the department is big enough so that it is not one of the smaller and less popular departments that would be first to go. As recent newspaper headlines will tell you, even the best-endowed schools are tightening their purse strings.

We hope that we have given you a stronger sense as to what to think about and what to focus on as you continue to make the decisions necessary for finding the college of your choice. Just remember, in the end you are the one who will be attending the college, so you should be the one who is happy. Best of luck!

Introduction for International Students

International students who decide to apply to colleges in the U.S. might find a daunting and unfamiliar path before them. Unlike in many other countries, admission to U.S. colleges depends not only on grades and scores, but on the whole package: what you have done outside of schoolwork, what your teachers have to say about you, and what you have to say about yourself. The international student's task is to put together the most attractive application, while dealing with linguistic and cultural differences, scarcity of information, and communication delays. An "international student" formally refers to anyone who is applying to American universities from a non-U.S. address. Thus, if you are a U.S. citizen or a permanent resident applying from abroad, you are still placed in the international category. Many schools review this applicant pool differently from the domestic applicants—admissions committees might place less emphasis on SAT test scores, for example. Many schools also look for geographical and cultural diversity, which could work in your favor if only few students are applying from your country, or against you if there are many other applicants.

With these advantages and disadvantages in mind, here are some tips about the application process that might be especially helpful to international students. You should also read the **Getting In** section of this book for more general information. The best advice is: *get started early.* Deadlines for American universities can be as early as November for fall admissions. As one student said, "make sure you take care of everything well ahead of time—last minute surprises are harder to deal with abroad."

Pre-Application Preparations

If you decide that you want to go to an American university, start getting involved. While in many countries extracurricular activities are not taken seriously, American universities place emphasis on what you achieve outside of the classroom. These activities might highlight your leadership, talent, or determination. If your school does not offer many extracurricular activities, look for opportunities to get involved in the community or take the initiative to organize something yourself. When application time rolls around, be sure to list everything to which you have devoted your time. Extracurricular activities can include a variety of activities such as taking piano lessons, participating in organizations, doing volunteer work, or working part-time.

Academically, international students might want to think about taking Advanced Placement (AP) tests and courses related to them. Although not required for college admission, the results will demonstrate the level of your knowledge in the subject as compared to American high school students. As an added bonus, high scores might let you bypass some classes in college or accelerate and graduate early. Arranging to take an AP test internationally might be difficult; try to see if an American school in your area will arrange it. If you can take it and you have recently completed a course corresponding to one of the tests, it would be risk-free way to increase your chances at admission—students can choose whether to report individual AP scores. Students studying under the International Baccalaureate (IB) system, and even students that do not take either of these tests, might be able to negotiate for acceleration in their first year of college. Acceleration policies, however, vary greatly from college to college.

Deciding that you want to go to college in the U.S. and figuring out where to apply might be the rocky starting point for many international students because of the relative lack of information. Research, however, is an essential part of the college application process and what many internationals said they wished they had spent more time doing. The United States is a huge country, and it will make a difference whether you are in California or Massachusetts, whether you are in a city or a rural area. The U.S. also has a large number of schools with excellent programs, beyond the names that people outside of the U.S. would recognize.

If you have a college guidance counselor in your school who is knowledgeable about admissions to U.S. schools, take advantage of the resource. If no such help is available, seek out a counselor outside of school, possibly at the American school in your area. You might also want to seek out someone who has recently gone through a similar decision-making process, or talk to an American expatriate. Libraries and the Internet are also prime sources of information. If possible, try to visit the colleges. It will make a difference in your opinion about each school.

Testing

Most American colleges require international students to take the SAT (Scholastic Assessment Test), a selection of SAT II tests, and the TOEFL. The Educational Testing Service (ETS) has many international test sites, although the tests might still be hard to come by in certain countries. Students from such diverse countries as Israel, Japan, and Guatemala all attested that signing up was easy, particularly with online registration. However, some people might have to travel hours out of the way to get to the testing center. To avoid any unnecessary travel, register for these tests early before popular testing centers fill their seats. To find out where the nearest testing center is located, write to ETS or visit their Web site.

Many colleges require the TOEFL (Test of English as a Foreign Language) if English is not your first language or the language of instruction in your high school. While taking another test might seem like a hassle, TOEFL is easier than the SAT and could work to your advantage since many schools will substitute a TOEFL score for the SAT Verbal score. If you are satisfied with your SAT Verbal scores, you should probably not bother taking TOEFL—although a near perfect score could never hurt.

Application Package

In getting teachers to write recommendations for you, be sure to approach those who not only know your work, but know you and will be willing to write enthusiastically about you. Many international teachers tend to be more reluctant to award superlatives or write a personalized recommendation than their American counterparts. If you went to a school taught in a non-English language, you can ask the teachers to write you recommendations in English, have them translated, or send them to the colleges to have them translated. You could also offer your services in helping the teacher translate the letter into English. It is often a good idea to have the recommendations translated in your own country to make them easier for the admissions officers to read.

The essay is the personal reflection of yourself and an opportunity to have the different parts of your application come together. Think of what will be interesting to the admissions officers reading the essay, and allow for more creativity than might be acceptable in college applications in your own country. Many internationals choose to write about living in different countries or experiencing cultural differences, which might be more interesting than the fact that you won a national academic award—the latter point can be listed elsewhere in the application.

Financial Aid and Visas

While some large and wealthy colleges can afford to be need-blind in its admission of international students, the consensus is that there is very little financial aid available for non-U.S. citizens and residents. If you will definitely need aid, you should research the financial aid policy of each college before applying. Depending on which country you are from, you might be able to look to sources in your home country for financial support. If, on the other hand, you are an American citizen applying from abroad, the financial aid process is the same as for any other American student.

Once all the applications are in and the big, fat envelopes arrive in your mailbox, most of the hard work is over. Although visa regulations differ from country to country and you will still have to go through the paperwork, you should not have any problems. The student visa will allow you to work inside the university, but be forewarned that it will be difficult for you to find a job outside.

There are certainly obstacles that challenge the international student applying to American universities, but they are surmountable with some research and planning. One international student, now a sophomore in college, summed it up, "Although it is an endless process, it is worth it!" *—Mariko Hirose and Staff*

Students with Disabilities

Many students at the college level will have one or more disabilities. These may include health disorders, physical disabilities, learning disabilities, emotional or behavior disorders, autism, attention deficit hyperactivity disorder, hearing loss or visual impairments. Students with disabilities that limit their functioning are entitled to reasonable accommodations, but services vary widely from school to school. It is important to know your particular strengths and needs and to visit schools with a critical eye. Talk with campus community members (other students, staff and faculty) in order to learn more. Below are some specific suggestions when visiting college campuses.

If You Use a Wheelchair: The most important criteria for wheelchair users is to check to see if there are adequate ramps around campus. Schools that are truly committed to making their campuses accessible for wheelchair users will not only have many ramps available, but those ramps will be attractive and blend in naturally with the immediate environment. Make sure the ramps aren't too steep and that they have safe borders running along each edge. Also, at the bottom of each ramp there should be adequate "turn around" room. Furthermore, make sure that doorways are wide enough to get through comfortably, that classrooms have appropriate and adequate spaces for wheelchairs, and that restrooms are wheelchair accessible. Be warned, many older universities have buildings that are still not wheelchair accessible, so try to determine how much of a problem this will be. If you see someone on your visit using a wheelchair, you may consider asking her/his opinion concerning the accessibility of the campus.

If You Have a Learning Disability: The best bet for finding out a school's policy for students with a learning disability is a quick visit to the Office for Students with Disabilities. Although this office provides services for students with a wide variety of disabilities, the most common are learning disabilities. Ask about the specific services and resources that are offered. Such services and resources may include extended time on tests, note-takers, books-on-tape, and assessments to further understand your particular learning differences. Ask about the procedures that you would need to undertake in order to use such services and resources. What is the atmosphere of the office? Welcoming? Situated in a convenient location? Does the office offer peer support groups for study skills? Social challenges? Is technological equipment available for use by students? Are there courses offered in the course catalog on learning disabilities? These are usually found in the education or psychology departments and could be a useful avenue for you to pursue. Most importantly, do not be afraid to be honest about your learning needs; most school officials and fellow students will only be more than happy to help.

If You Suffer From Depression: Although services may also be offered through the Office of Students with Disabilities, the Office of Psychological Services would most likely be your primary source of help. Depression is now recognized as relatively common in college-age individuals, so schools are becoming increasingly better at providing services and resources in this area. Find out what kind of counseling the school's health services provide as well. What is the typical wait to visit a counselor? Does the office provide peer support groups? Crisis hot lines? You may want to ask for samples of the brochures they offer. Don't be shy about asking questions in this area. Many schools now even include information on depression in their orientation materials for new students and their training for resident hall leaders.

Students suffering from depression often have a harder time socially. Many students do not want to share their feelings with anyone but their closest friends. Others are unsure whether they have a serious problem or are just overloaded with work and stress. There is no easy way to handle depression, but never be afraid to speak to a professional if you are concerned.

For students suffering from other disabilities, many schools have an ADA (Americans with Disability Act) and Section 504 compliance officer. This person could give you information concerning the procedures for filing grievances, as well as other services that are available. Also, investigate whether each school has a disability issues department or a faculty member who specializes in special education or disability law. If so, these would be additional great resources for you. Whether or not you want to disclose that you have a disability is totally up to you. By law, schools may not demand such information. However, either way—whether or not you disclose that you have a disability—with a little detective work, you should be able to find the school that best fits your strengths and needs. *—Rae Lynne and Adam Rein*

Terms You Should Know

Advanced Placement (AP)—College credit earned by students while still in high school. Many high schools offer specially designed AP courses that prepare students for the College Board's AP Exams. Administered in May, they can qualify students who score well for advanced standing when they enroll in college.

American College Test (ACT)—Test administered to high school juniors and seniors by the American College Testing Program. Traditionally it has been used as an admissions criterion primarily by Midwestern schools. Some Southern and Western schools use it as well.

American College Testing Program (ACTP)—The organization that produces the American College Test (ACT) and the Family Financial Statement (FFS). Many Midwestern universities use the ACT and the FFS in admissions instead of the SAT and the Financial-Aid Form (FAF). (See also "Family Financial Statement" and "Financial-Aid Form.")

arts and sciences (also called liberal arts)—A broad term that encompasses most traditional courses of study, including the humanities, social sciences, natural sciences, mathematics, and foreign languages. A liberal arts college is also a college of arts and sciences. (See also "humanities" and "social sciences.")

bagging—You're in bed. It's 9:30 A.M. You've got a class at 9:30. You are about to "bag" this class.

beer goggles—People start to look interesting when you've had too much to drink. If you hook up as a result of this phenomenon, you've been looking through "beer goggles."

candidate's reply date—The May 1 deadline, observed by most selective colleges, by which the applicant must respond to an offer of admission, usually with a nonrefundable deposit of several hundred dollars. Colleges that require students to respond by May 1 in almost all cases notify them of their acceptance on or before April 15.

College Board—The organization that sponsors the SAT, the SAT IIs, the Advanced Placement tests, and the Financial-Aid Form (FAF). College Board admissions tests are developed and administered by the Educational Testing Service (ETS). (See also "Advanced Placement" and "Financial-Aid Form.")

Common Application—A form produced by a consortium of about 100 colleges (mainly selective liberal arts schools) that may be filled out and sent to member colleges in lieu of each school's individual application.

comprehensive exams (comps)—Also known as "generals," these tests, administered by some colleges (usually during the senior year) are designed to measure knowledge gained over a student's entire college career. Schools that give comps usually require students to pass the test in their major field in order to graduate.

computing assistant (CA)—A university employee, often an undergraduate, who helps students with all varieties of computing problems, from how to use a word processor to how to download games from the network.

consortium—A group of colleges affiliated in some way. The extent of the association can vary widely. Some consortiums—usually among colleges in close proximity—offer a range of joint programs that may include cross-registration, interlibrary loans, residential exchanges, and coordinated social, cultural, and athletic events.

co-op job—A paid internship, arranged for a student by his or her college, that provides on-the-job training, usually in an occupation closely related to the student's major.

core curriculum—A group of courses all students in a college must take in order to graduate. Core curricula are becoming widespread.

couch duty—There are two people in your bedroom that you share with your roommate, and you are not one of them. Guess where you get to sleep? Also known as "sexile."

cramming—The process by which students attempt to learn a semester's worth of course material in a short period, often 24 to 48 hours. Cola, coffee, and/or caffeine pills are the staples of most all-night cramming sessions.

crew (rowing)—A sport, more familiar to those who live on or near either coast than to those from the South and Midwest, in which teams of two, four, or eight oarsmen or oarswomen race in long, narrow boats, usually on inland waterways. Crew is very "Ivy," very popular at many schools, and usually requires no high school experience.

deferral—A college's postponement of the decision to accept or reject an early-action applicant. The applicant's file is entered in with those of regular-action candidates and is reviewed once again, this time for a final decision.

distribution requirements—Requirements stipulating that students take courses in a variety of broad subject areas in order to graduate. The number and definition of subject areas and the number of courses required in each varies from school to school. Typical categories include the humanities, social sciences, fine arts, natural sciences, foreign languages, and mathematics. Unlike a core curriculum, distribution requirements do not usually mandate specific courses that students must take. (See also "humanities," "social sciences," and "core curriculum.")

dry—as in "dry campus." A school that does not allow alcohol for any students in its dorms or other campus facilities.

early action—A program that gives students early notification of a college's admissions decision. Unlike early decision, it does not require a prior commitment to enroll if accepted. Early action is far less common than early decision and is only offered by a handful of schools: Harvard, University of Chicago, and in a recent policy change, Stanford and Yale. Deadlines for early-action applications are usually in late fall, with notification in December, January, or February. An applicant accepted under early action usually has until May 1, the candidate's reply date, to respond to the offer of admission. (See also "early decision" and "candidate's reply date.")

early decision—A program under which a student receives early notification of a college's admissions decision if the student agrees in advance to enroll if accepted. Students may apply early decision to only one college; it should be a clear first choice. Application deadlines for early decision are usually in November, with decision letters mailed by mid-December.

Ethernet—A direct, high-speed means of access to the World Wide Web and the Internet, as well as a way to keep in touch with friends via e-mail. Most campuses are either "wired" with Ethernet, or will be in the near future.

family contribution—The amount of money that a family can "reasonably" be expected to pay toward a student's education, as determined by one of the two standardized needs-analysis forms. (See also "Financial-Aid Form" and "Family Financial Statement.")

Family Financial Statement (FFS)—The financial-needs analysis form submitted to the American College Testing Program (ACTP), which, like the FAF, determines the expected family contribution. Colleges that use the American College Test (ACT) for admissions purposes usually require a copy of the FFS report from students applying for financial aid. (See also "American College Testing Program," "family contribution," and "Financial-Aid Form.")

fee waiver—Permission, often granted upon request, for needy students to apply for college admission without having to pay the application fee.

Financial-Aid Form (FAF)—The financial-needs analysis form submitted to the College Board by students applying for financial aid. Like the Family Financial Statement (FFS), it yields the expected family contribution. Colleges that require the Scholastic Assessment Test (SAT) for admission typically use the FAF as the basis for financial-aid awards. (See also "Family Financial Statement," "family contribution," and "College Board.")

financial-aid package—The combination of loans, grants, and a work-study job that a school puts together for a student receiving financial aid.

five-year plan—The practice of stretching a four-year degree program over a five-year period.

four-one-four—An academic calendar consisting of two regular four-month semesters with a short "winter" or "January" term in between. Variations include four-four-one and three-three-two. In most cases, these numbers refer to the number of courses a student is expected to complete in each segment of the year, although at some schools they refer to the number of months in each segment.

freshman 15—A reference to the number of pounds students often gain during the freshman year. Usually caused by a combination of too little exercise, unlimited helpings in the dining hall, too many late-night runs for pizza, and overconsumption of alcoholic beverages.

government aid—Money that federal or state governments make available to students, most of which is administered through the colleges on the basis of need. Government aid can come in the form of grants, loans, and work-study jobs. Stafford Loans (formerly Guaranteed Student Loans) and PLUS parent loans of up to $2,625 and $4,000 per year, respectively, are made available through commercial lending institutions. For further information on government aid programs, contact the state and federal departments of education.

grade inflation—A situation in which average work is consistently awarded a higher letter grade than it would normally earn. At most schools, the grade for average work is about B-/C+. But in classes or entire colleges with grade inflation, it can be as high as B or even B+.

Greek system—The fraternities and sororities on a particular campus. They are called "Greek" because most take their names from combinations of letters in the Greek alphabet.

gut—A course widely known to be very easy, often with enrollments well into the hundreds. Guts are traditionally favorites among second-semester seniors.

hook up—To enjoy a person's nonplatonic company, often used in reference to a one-night event. A very vague term that can range from an innocent kiss to sex, depending on usage.

humanities—Subjects in which the primary focus is on human culture. Examples include philosophy, language, and literature. (See also "social sciences.")

independent study—A course, usually in a student's major field, in which he or she studies independently and meets one-on-one with a professor on a topic of the student's choosing. Some colleges require an independent study essay or research paper for graduation.

interdisciplinary major—A major that combines two complementary subjects from different fields, such as biology and psychology. Students completing these majors take courses in each area as well as courses that explicitly join the two.

International Baccalaureate (IB)—A high school program found across the world which, like AP courses, can earn a student advanced standing upon college enrollment.

intramurals—Athletic leagues informally organized within a college. Students are free from the burden of tryouts and play with and against fellow classmates.

language requirement—A rule at many colleges that requires students to study a foreign language before graduation. Two years on the college level are usually required, although credit from Advanced Placement or SAT IIs often allows students to bypass the requirement.

legacy—An applicant whose mother or father is a graduate of a particular school. Students with legacy status are often given preferential treatment in admissions.

merit scholarship—A financial grant for some part of college costs, usually awarded for academic achievement or special skill in an extracurricular activity and not based on need. Private corporations and many colleges offer merit scholarships.

need-based aid—Money awarded solely on the basis of need, usually administered through the colleges. Some schools agree to pay the difference between their total fees and the expected family contribution; others pay only part of it, leaving some "unmet" need. Most financial-aid packages consist of some combination of three components: grants, loans, and work-study jobs. Some of the money comes from the college's own resources, although part is financed by federal and state governments. (See also "government aid.")

need-blind admissions—A policy in which the applicant's ability to pay does not affect the college's consideration of his or her application. Some schools with need-blind admissions also guarantee to meet the full demonstrated financial need of all accepted applicants as determined by one of the two standardized needs-analysis forms; others do not. (See also "family contribution," "Financial-Aid Form," and "Family Financial Statement.")

office hours—A period during which a professor agrees to be available in his or her office for the purpose of talking with students about their coursework. Professors are not always required by their colleges to have office hours, but most do anyway.

open admissions—A policy under which any applicant with a high school diploma is accepted. State universities that have this policy usually limit open admission to state residents.

parietals—Regulations that govern the times when students of one sex may visit dorms or floors housing the opposite sex. Usually found only at the most conservative schools nowadays.

pass/fail or CR/F or CR/D/F—An option offered by some schools in certain classes. A student may enroll in a class and simply receive credit or failure (or a D in "CR/D/F") for it on his or her transcript instead of a specific grade; God's gift to college students everywhere.

PLUS parent loans—A component of the Stafford Loan, for parents. (See also "government aid.")

problem set—An annoying weekly assignment you're inevitably faced with in any given science or quantitative class. This thankless task will keep you up 'til 2 A.M. Sunday nights but can count for 1/50 of your grade or one-half. Previously known as homework.

quad—An abbreviation for "quadrangle"; many dorm complexes are built in squares (quadrangles) with a courtyard in the middle. Quad can also refer to a suite of dormitory rooms in which four students live together.

quarter system—An academic calendar under which the school year is divided into four quarters, three of which constitute a full academic year. Less common than the semester system, it is most often used by large universities with extensive programs in agricultural and technical fields.

resident advisor/assistant (RA)—A student, usually an upperclassman, who lives in a dorm and helps to maintain regulations and enforce school policy, as well as offering advice and support to dorm residents. RAs receive compensation from the school for their services, usually in the form of free room and board.

rolling admissions—A policy under which a college considers applications almost immediately after receiving them. Decision letters are mailed within a month after the application is filed. Colleges with rolling admissions continue to accept applications only until the class is filled, so it is best to apply early.

Scholastic Assessment Test (SAT)—Test administered to high school juniors and seniors by the College Board of the Educational Testing Service, with math, verbal, and written-language sections. Used as an admissions criterion at most colleges nationwide.

senior project—Many majors at many colleges require seniors to complete a special project during their senior year. This could involve a thesis (anywhere from 15 to 100 pages), a research project, some sort of internship, or all of the above. Some colleges offer seniors a choice between taking comps or doing a project. (See also "comps.")

social sciences—Subjects that deal systematically with the institutions of human society, most notably economics and political science. The behavioral sciences, which include psychology, sociology, and anthropology, are often included in this group as well.

study break—An institutionalized form of procrastination involving food and talk. Often informally arranged—"I'm sick of calculus, let's take a study break at——" (insert name of local hangout)—but can be sponsored by RAs, cultural groups, or even school administrators. Some nights, study breaks can take more of your time than the actual studying.

teaching assistant (TA)—A graduate student who assists a professor in the presentation of a course. Usually the professor gives two to four lectures a week for all the students in the class; the TAs hold smaller weekly discussion sections.

three-two program (3–2)—A program in which students can study three years at one school, followed by two at another, more specialized school. Upon completion, many of these programs award both the bachelor's and the master's degrees.

town-gown relations—The contact between a college (students, employees, buildings) and its host town (citizens, businesses, local government) and the set of issues around which this contact revolves. Such issues include taxes, traffic, local employment practices, and government services like road maintenance, sewage, and trash collection.

townie—A resident of a college town or city who is not enrolled in the college, but who might sit beside you at the local pub. Often involves a them-versus-us mentality.

trimesters—An academic calendar that divides the school year into three terms of approximately equal length. Schools on the trimester system generally have one term before the winter break and two after.

tutorial major (also self-designed or special major)—A program offered by many schools in which a student can plan his or her own major, combining the offerings of two or more traditional majors, usually in consultation with a faculty member. An example is Medieval studies, in which the student might study the history, literature, philosophy, and art of the period, taking courses from a number of departments. (See also "interdisciplinary major.")

waiting list—A list of students who are not initially accepted to a certain school, but who may be admitted later, depending on the number of accepted students who enroll. Most colleges ultimately accept only a fraction of the students on the waiting list, who are notified during the summer.

work-study—Campus jobs, for financial-aid recipients, that are subsidized by the federal government. Work-study jobs are a component of most need-based financial-aid packages. Students typically work 10 to 20 hours a week to help finance their education.

The College Finder

With so many colleges from which to choose, how can you zero in on one that is right for you? The lists that follow are designed to help you match your interests with a selected group of colleges. Our hope is that the Finder will introduce you to a number of colleges you might not otherwise have considered.

Regions

New England: Connecticut, Maine, Massachusetts, New Hampshire, Rhode Island, Vermont. Also includes Eastern Canada.

Mid-Atlantic: Delaware, District of Columbia, Maryland, New Jersey, New York, Pennsylvania, West Virginia

Midwest: Illinois, Indiana, Iowa, Kansas, Kentucky, Michigan, Minnesota, Missouri, Nebraska, North Dakota, Ohio, South Dakota, Wisconsin

Southeast: Alabama, Arkansas, Florida, Georgia, Louisiana, Mississippi, North Carolina, South Carolina, Tennessee, Virginia

West: Alaska, Arizona, California, Colorado, Hawaii, Idaho, Montana, New Mexico, Nevada, Oklahoma, Oregon, Texas, Utah, Washington, Wyoming. Also includes Western Canada.

Schools with 1,500 Undergraduates or Fewer

New England

Bennington College
College of the Atlantic
Hampshire College
Marlboro College
Simmons College
United States Coast Guard Academy

Mid-Atlantic

Bard College
Bryn Mawr College
Cooper Union for the Advancement of Science and Art
Eastman School of Music
Goucher College
Haverford College
Juilliard School, The
Sarah Lawrence College
Swarthmore College
Trinity College
Wells College

Midwest

Alma College
Antioch College
Beloit College
Centre College
Cornell College
Earlham College
Grinnell College
Kalamazoo College
Knox College
Lake Forest College
Lawrence University
Wabash College

Southeast

Agnes Scott College
Birmingham-Southern College
Hampden-Sydney College
Hendrix College
Hollins College
Millsaps College
New College of the University of South Florida
North Carolina School of the Arts
Randolph-Macon Woman's College
Sweet Briar College
University of the South (Sewanee)
Wofford College

West

California Institute of Technology
California Institute of the Arts
Claremont McKenna College
Deep Springs College
Harvey Mudd College
Mills College
Pitzer College
Reed College
Scripps College
St. John's College (NM)

University of Dallas
Whitman College

Schools with 1,501 to 3,000 Undergraduates

New England
Amherst College
Babson College
Bates College
Bowdoin College
Clark University
Colby College
Connecticut College
Holy Cross, College of the
Middlebury College
Mount Holyoke College
Rhode Island School of Design
Smith College
Trinity College
Wellesley College
Wesleyan University
Wheaton College
Williams College
Worcester Polytechnic Institute

Mid-Atlantic
Alfred University
Allegheny College
Barnard College
Catholic University of America
Clarkson University
Colgate University
Dickinson College
Drew University
Franklin & Marshall College
Gettysburg College
Hamilton College
Hobart and William Smith College
Lafayette College
Manhattanville College
Muhlenberg College
Parsons School of Design
Skidmore College
St. Lawrence University
St. Bonaventure University
St. John's College
Stevens Institute of Technology
Susquehanna University
Union College
Vassar College
Yeshiva University

Midwest
Albion College
Carleton College
Denison University
DePauw University
Gustavus Adolphus College
Kenyon College
Macalester College
Oberlin College
Ohio Wesleyan University
Rose-Hulman Institute of Technology
St. Olaf College
Valparaiso University
Wheaton College (IL)
Wittenburg University
Wooster, The College of

Southeast
Davidson College
Florida Institute of Technology
Florida Southern College
Furman University
Morehouse College
Rhodes College
Rollins College
Spelman College
Stetson University
Tuskegee University
Washington and Lee University

West
Colorado College
Colorado School of Mines
Lewis and Clark College
Occidental College
Pomona College
Rice University
St. Mary's College of California
Trinity University
University of Puget Sound
University of Tulsa
Willamette University

Schools with Over 20,000 Undergraduates

New England
McGill University
University of Toronto

Mid-Atlantic
Pennsylvania State University

Rutgers, The State University of New Jersey
Temple University
University of Maryland/College Park

Midwest
Indiana University
Iowa State University
Michigan State University
Ohio State University
Purdue University
University of Illinois/Urbana-Champaign
University of Iowa
University of Kansas
University of Michigan
University of Minnesota
University of Wisconsin

Southeast
Florida State University
Louisiana State University
North Carolina State University
University of Florida
University of Georgia
Virginia Polytechnic Institute and State University

West
Arizona State University
Brigham Young University
Colorado State University
Texas A&M University/College Station
Texas Tech University
University of Arizona
University of British Columbia
University of California/Davis
University of California/Los Angeles
University of Colorado/Boulder
University of Houston
University of Oklahoma
University of Texas/Austin
University of Utah
University of Washington

Some Schools Over 200 Years Old

Bowdoin College
Brown University
Columbia University
Dartmouth College
Dickinson College
Franklin & Marshall College
Georgetown University
Hampden-Sydney College
Harvard University
Middlebury College
Princeton University
Rutgers, The State University of New Jersey
St. John's College
Union College
University of Delaware
University of Georgia
University of North Carolina/Chapel Hill
University of Pennsylvania
University of Pittsburgh
University of Tennessee/Knoxville
University of Vermont
Washington and Lee University
William and Mary, College of
Williams College
Yale University

Some Schools Less Than 50 Years Old

California Institute of the Arts
College of the Atlantic
Eugene Lang College of the New School for Social Research
Evergreen State College
Florida Institute of Technology
George Mason University
Hampshire College
Harvey Mudd College
New College of the University of South Florida
North Carolina School of the Arts
Oral Roberts University
Pitzer College
SUNY/Stony Brook
United States Air Force Academy
University of California/Irvine
University of California/Riverside
University of California/Santa Cruz
University of Dallas
University of Waterloo

Single-Sex Schools

Women
Agnes Scott College

Barnard College
Bryn Mawr College
Hollins College
Mills College
Mount Holyoke College
Randolph-Macon Woman's College
Scripps College
Simmons College
Smith College
Spelman College
St. Mary's College (IN)
Sweet Briar College
Trinity College (D.C.)
Wellesley College
Wells College

Men
Deep Springs College
Hampden-Sydney College
Morehouse College
Wabash College

Predominantly Male Schools (More Than Two-Thirds Male)

California Institute of Technology
Clarkson University
Colorado School of Mines
Cooper Union for the Advancement of Science and Art
Florida Institute of Technology
Georgia Institute of Technology
Harvey Mudd College
Rensselaer Polytechnic Institute
Rochester Institute of Technology
Rose-Hulman Institute of Technology
Stevens Institute of Technology
United States Air Force Academy
United States Coast Guard Academy
United States Military Academy
United States Naval Academy
Worcester Polytechnic Institute

Predominantly Female Schools (More Than Two-Thirds Female)

Adelphi University
Bennington College
CUNY/Hunter College
Eugene Lang College of the New School for Social Research
Goucher College
Howard University
Loyola University
Manhattanville College
Parsons School of Design
Sarah Lawrence College

Some Schools with High Minority Enrollment (More Than 30%)

New England
Harvard University
Massachusetts Institute of Technology
Wellesley College
Wesleyan University
Yale University

Mid-Atlantic
Barnard College
Columbia University
Cooper Union for the Advancement of Science and Art
CUNY/City College of New York
CUNY/Hunter College
CUNY/Queens College
Drexel University
Howard University
Johns Hopkins University
Juilliard School, The
New York University
Rutgers, The State University of New Jersey
Stevens Institute of Technology
SUNY/Stony Brook
Swarthmore College
Temple University
Trinity College (DC)
University of Pennsylvania

Midwest
DePaul University

Southeast
Florida A&M University
Morehouse College
Old Dominion University
Spelman College
Tuskegee University
University of Miami

West

California Institute of Technology
California Polytechnic State University/ San Luis Obispo
California State University/Fresno
Claremont McKenna College
New Mexico State University
Occidental College
Oral Roberts University
Pitzer College
Pomona College
Scripps College
Stanford University
University of Alaska/Fairbanks
University of California/Berkeley
University of California/Davis
University of California/Irvine
University of California/Los Angeles
University of California/Riverside
University of California/San Diego
University of California/Santa Barbara
University of California/Santa Cruz
University of Hawaii/Manoa
University of Houston
University of New Mexico
University of Southern California

Schools Accepting 25% or Less of Their Applicant Pool

Amherst College
Bowdoin College
Brown University
California Institute of Technology
Columbia University
Cooper Union for the Advancement of Science and Art
Dartmouth College
Deep Springs College
Duke University
Georgetown University
Harvard University
Juilliard School, The
Massachusetts Institute of Technology
Pomona College
Princeton University
Rice University
Stanford University
Swarthmore College
United States Air Force Academy
United States Coast Guard Academy
United States Military Academy
United States Naval Academy
University of California/Berkeley
University of California/Los Angeles
University of Pennsylvania
Washington University
Williams College
Yale University

Schools Accepting 26% to 40% of Their Applicant Pool

Babson College
Bard College
Barnard College
Bates College
Boston College
Bucknell University
California Institute of the Arts
Carleton College
Carnegie Mellon University
Claremont McKenna College
Colby College
Colgate University
Connecticut College
Cornell University
CUNY/City College
CUNY/Hunter College
Davidson College
Eastman School of Music
George Washington University
Hamilton College
Harvey Mudd College
Haverford College
Johns Hopkins University
Lafayette College
Middlebury College
Muhlenberg College
New York University
Northwestern University
Oberlin College
Pepperdine University
Rhode Island School of Design
Sarah Lawrence College
Trinity College
Tufts University
University of North Carolina/ Chapel Hill
University of Notre Dame
University of Richmond
University of Southern California
University of Virginia

Vassar College
Wake Forest University
Washington and Lee University
Wesleyan University
William and Mary, College of

Schools Accepting 41% to 50% of Their Applicant Pool

Babson College
Bard College
Brandeis University
California Polytechnic State University/San Luis Obispo
CUNY/Queens College
Emerson College
Holy Cross, College of the
Lehigh University
Macalester College
McGill University
New Jersey, The College of
Occidental College
Parsons School of Design
Skidmore College
Spelman College
SUNY/Binghamton
Union College
University of California/San Diego
University of Chicago
University of Delaware
University of Maryland/College Park
University of Miami
University of Michigan
Vanderbilt University
Villanova University
Wellesley College
Wheaton College (MA)
Whitman College

Private Schools

New England
Amherst College
Babson College
Bates College
Bennington College
Boston College
Boston University
Bowdoin College
Brandeis University
Brown University
Clark University
Colby College
Connecticut College
Dartmouth College
Emerson College
Fairfield University
Hampshire College
Harvard University
Holy Cross, College of the
Marlboro College
Massachusetts Institute of Technology
McGill University
Middlebury College
Mount Holyoke College
Northeastern University
Quinnipiac University
Rhode Island School of Design
Simmons College
Smith College
Trinity College
Tufts University
Wellesley College
Wesleyan University
Wheaton College
Williams College
Worcester Polytechnic Institute
Yale University

Mid-Atlantic
Adelphi University
Alfred University
Allegheny College
American University
Bard College
Barnard College
Bryn Mawr College
Bucknell University
Carnegie Mellon University
Catholic University of America
Clarkson University
Colgate University
Columbia University
Cooper Union for the Advancement of Science and Art
Cornell University
Dickinson College
Drew University
Drexel University
Eastman School of Music
Eugene Lang College of the New School for Social Research
Fordham University

Franklin & Marshall College
Georgetown University
George Washington University
Gettysburg College
Goucher College
Hamilton College
Haverford College
Hobart and William Smith College
Hofstra University
Howard University
Johns Hopkins University
Juilliard School, The
Lafayette College
Lehigh University
Manhattanville College
Muhlenberg College
New York University
Parsons School of Design
Princeton University
Rensselaer Polytechnic Institute
Rochester Institute of Technology
St. Bonaventure University
St. John's College
St. Lawrence University
Sarah Lawrence College
Skidmore College
Stevens Institute of Technology
Susquehanna University
Swarthmore College
Syracuse University
Trinity College
University of Pennsylvania
University of Rochester
Union College
Vassar College
Villanova University
Wells College
Yeshiva University

Midwest
Albion College
Alma College
Antioch College
Beloit College
Carleton College
Case Western Reserve University
Centre College
Cornell College
Creighton University
Denison University
DePaul University
DePauw University
Earlham College
Grinnell College
Gustavus Adolphus College
Hope College
Kalamazoo College
Kenyon College
Knox College
Lake Forest College
Lawrence University
Loyola University of Chicago
Macalester College
Marquette University
Northwestern University
Oberlin College
Ohio Wesleyan University
Rose-Hulman Institute of Technology
St. John's University/College of St. Benedict
St. Olaf College
University of Chicago
University of Notre Dame
Valparaiso University
Wabash College
Washington University
Wittenburg University
Wooster, The College of

Southeast
Agnes Scott College
Birmingham-Southern College
Davidson College
Duke University
Emory University
Florida Institute of Technology
Furman University
Hampden-Sydney College
Hendrix College
Hollins College
Millsaps College
Morehouse College
Randolph-Macon Woman's College
Rhodes College
Spelman College
Stetson University
Sweet Briar College
Tulane University
Tuskegee University
University of Richmond
University of the South (Sewanee)
University of Miami
Vanderbilt University
Wake Forest University
Washington and Lee University
Wofford College

West
Baylor University
Brigham Young University
California Institute of Technology

California Institute of the Arts
Claremont McKenna College
Colorado College
Colorado School of Mines
Deep Springs College
Harvey Mudd College
Lewis and Clark College
Mills College
Occidental College
Oral Roberts University
Pepperdine University
Pitzer College
Pomona College
Reed College
Rice University
Scripps College
Southern Methodist University
St. John's College (NM)
Stanford University
Texas Christian University
Trinity University
University of Dallas
University of Denver
University of Puget Sound
University of Redlands
University of Southern California
University of Tulsa
Whitman College
Willamette University

Some Schools with Religious Affiliation

Agnes Scott College
Albion College
Allegheny College
Alma College
American University
Baylor University
Birmingham-Southern College
Brigham Young University
Catholic University of America
Centre College
Creighton University
Davidson College
DePauw University
Duke University
Earlham College
Emory University
Fairfield University
Georgetown University
Gustavus Adolphus College
Hampden-Sydney College
Holy Cross, College of the
Hope College
Kenyon College
Lafayette College
Lake Forest College
Loyola University of Chicago
Macalester College
Marquette University
Millsaps College
Muhlenberg College
Notre Dame
Ohio Wesleyan University
Pepperdine University
Randolph-Macon Woman's College
Rhodes College
St. Bonaventure University
St. John's University/College of St. Benedict
St. Olaf College
Southern Methodist University
Susquehanna University
Texas Christian University
Trinity College (DC)
Trinity University
University of Notre Dame
University of Denver
University of Dallas
University of the South (Sewanee)
University of Tulsa
Valparaiso University
Villanova University
Willamette University
Wittenburg University
Wofford College
Wooster, The College of

Small Liberal Arts Colleges (Under 3,000 Undergraduates)

New England
Amherst College
Babson College
Bates College
Bennington College
Bowdoin College
Brandeis University
Clark University
Colby College
College of the Atlantic
Connecticut College
Emerson College

Fairfield University
Hampshire College
Holy Cross, College of the
Marlboro College
Middlebury College
Mount Holyoke College
Simmons College
Smith College
Trinity College
Wellesley College
Wesleyan University
Wheaton College
Williams College

Mid-Atlantic
Allegheny College
Bard College
Barnard College
Bryn Mawr College
Clarkson University
Colgate University
Dickinson College
Drew University
Franklin and Marshall College
Gettysburg College
Goucher College
Hamilton College
Haverford College
Hobart and William Smith Colleges
Manhattanville College
Muhlenberg College
St. John's College (MD)
St. Lawrence University
Swarthmore College
Sarah Lawrence College
Skidmore College
Trinity College (DC)
Union College
Vassar College
Wells College

Midwest
Albion College
Alma College
Antioch College
Beloit College
Carleton College
Centre College
Cornell College
Denison University
DePauw University
Earlham College
Grinnell College
Gustavus Adolphus College
Kalamazoo College
Kenyon College
Knox College
Lake Forest College
Lawrence University
Macalester College
Oberlin College
Ohio Wesleyan University
St. Olaf College
Wabash College
Wheaton College (IL)
Wittenburg University
Wooster, The College of

Southeast
Agnes Scott College
Birmingham-Southern College
Davidson College
Florida Southern College
Furman University
Hampden-Sydney College
Hendrix College
Hollins College
Millsaps College
Morehouse College
New College of the University of South Florida
Randolph-Macon Woman's College
Rhodes College
Spelman College
Stetson University
Sweet Briar College
University of Richmond
University of the South (Sewanee)
Washington and Lee University
Wofford College

West
Claremont McKenna College
Colorado College
Deep Springs College
Lewis and Clark College
Mills College
Occidental College
Oral Roberts University
Pitzer College
Pomona College
Reed College
Rice University
Scripps College
St. John's College (NM)
Trinity University
University of Dallas
University of Puget Sound
University of Redlands
University of Tulsa

Whitman College
Willamette University

Large Fraternity/Sorority Systems (More than 30%)

Large Fraternity/Sorority Systems (More Than 30%)
Albion College
Allegheny College
Birmingham-Southern College
Bucknell University
Centre College
Colgate University
Cornell College
Creighton University
Denison University
DePauw University
Dickinson College
Duke University
Emory University
Franklin & Marshall College
Furman University
Gettysburg College
Johns Hopkins University
Kansas State University
Lafayette College
Lehigh University
Massachusetts Institute of Technology
Miami University
Millsaps College
Muhlenberg College
Northwestern University
Ohio Wesleyan University
Rensselaer Polytechnic Institute
Rhodes College
Rose-Hulman Institute of Technology
Stetson University
Stevens Institute of Technology
Syracuse University
Susquehanna University
Texas Christian University
Trinity University
University of Mississippi
University of Pennsylvania
University of Puget Sound
University of Richmond
University of the South (Sewanee)
Union College
Valparaiso University
Vanderbilt University
Villanova University
Wabash College
Wake Forest University
Washington and Lee University
Whitman College
Willamette University
William and Mary, College of
Wofford College
Worcester Polytechnic Institute

Schools with No Fraternities or Sororities

Agnes Scott College
Antioch College
Bard College
Barnard College
Bates College
Bennington College
Boston College
Brandeis University
Brigham Young University
Bryn Mawr College
California Institute of the Arts
California Institute of Technology
Carleton College
Carleton University
Claremont McKenna College
Clark University
Colby College
CUNY/City College of New York
CUNY/Hunter College
CUNY/Queens College
Deep Springs College
Drew University
Earlham College
Eugene Lang College of the New School for Social Research
Evergreen State College
Fairfield University
Fordham University
Georgetown University
Goucher College
Grinnell College
Hampshire College
Harvey Mudd College
Haverford College
Hendrix College
Hollins College
Holy Cross, College of the
Juilliard School, The
Kalamazoo College
Lewis and Clark College
Macalester College
Manhattanville College

Marlboro College
McGill University
McMaster University
Middlebury College
Mills College
Mount Holyoke College
New College of the University of South Florida
North Carolina School of the Arts
Oberlin College
Oral Roberts University
Parsons School of Design
Pitzer College
Queen's University
Randolph-Macon Woman's College
Reed College
Rhode Island School of Design
Rice University
St. Bonaventure University
St. John's College (MD and NM)
St. John's University/College of St. Benedict
St. Olaf College
Sarah Lawrence College
Scripps College
Simmons College
Skidmore College
Smith College
Sweet Briar College
Trinity College (D.C.)
United States Air Force Academy
United States Coast Guard Academy
United States Military Academy
United States Naval Academy
Vassar College
University of California/Santa Cruz
University of Dallas
University of Notre Dame
University of Toronto
University of Washington
University of Waterloo
University of Western Ontario
Wellesley College
Wells College
Wheaton College
Williams College
Yeshiva University

Some Schools with Very High Graduation Rates

Amherst College
Bates College
Brown University
Bryn Mawr College
Bucknell College
California Institute of Technology
Carleton College
Claremont McKenna College
Colby College
Colgate University
Columbia University
Connecticut College
Cornell University
Dartmouth College
Davidson College
Dickinson College
Duke University
Emory University
Florida A&M University
Georgetown University
Hamilton College
Harvard University
Haverford College
Holy Cross, College of the
Johns Hopkins University
Kenyon College
Middlebury College
Mount Holyoke College
Northwestern University
Rhode Island School of Design
University of Notre Dame
University of Richmond
University of the South (Sewanee)
Swarthmore College
Trinity College (CT)
Union College
United States Air Force Academy
Villanova University
Washington and Lee University
William and Mary, The College of
Yale University

Tuition, Room and Board

When a school is followed by (I), that figure refers to in-state tuition only; out-of-state tuition is higher.

Under $6,000

NEW ENGLAND
United States Coast Guard Academy

MID-ATLANTIC
CUNY/City College of New York (I)
CUNY/Hunter College (I)
CUNY/Queens College
United States Military Academy
United States Naval Academy

MIDWEST
Kansas State University (I)
University of Nebraska/Lincoln (I)
University of North Dakota (I)
University of South Dakota (I)
University of Wisconsin (I)

SOUTHEAST
Florida A&M University (I)
North Carolina School of the Arts (I)
North Carolina State University (I)
University of Mississippi (I)

WEST
Brigham Young University
Deep Springs College
New Mexico State University (I)
University of Idaho (I)
University of Texas/Austin (I)
United States Air Force Academy

$6,000 to $11,999

NEW ENGLAND
Carleton University (I)
McGill University
McMaster University (I)
Queen's University (I)
University of Connecticut (I)
University of Maine/Orono (I)
University of Massachusetts/Amherst (I)
University of New Hampshire (I)
University of Rhode Island (I)
University of Toronto (I)
University of Waterloo (I)
University of Western Ontario (I)

MID-ATLANTIC
CUNY/City College of New York
CUNY/Hunter College
New Jersey, The College of (I)
Pennsylvania State University (I)
Rutgers, The State University of New Jersey (I)
SUNY/Albany
SUNY/Binghamton (I)
SUNY/Buffalo (I)
SUNY/Stony Brook (I)
Temple University (I)
University of Delaware (I)
University of Maryland/College Park (I)
University of Pittsburgh (I)
West Virginia University (I)

MIDWEST
Bowling Green State University (I)
Illinois State University (I)
Indiana University (I)
Iowa State University
Kansas State University (I)
Kent State University (I)
Miami University (I)
Michigan State University (I)
Ohio State University (I)
Ohio University (I)
Purdue University (I)
Southern Illinois University/Carbondale (I)
University of Cincinnati (I)
University of Illinois/Urbana-Champaign (I)
University of Iowa (I)
University of Kansas
University of Kentucky
University of Michigan (I)
University of Minnesota (I)
University of Missouri/Columbia (I)
University of Nebraska/Lincoln
University of North Dakota
University of South Dakota
University of Wisconsin

SOUTHEAST
Auburn University
College of William and Mary (I)
Clemson University
Florida A&M University
Florida State University (I)
George Mason University (I)
Georgia Institute of Technology (I)
James Madison University (I)
Louisiana State University
Mississippi State University
New College of the University of South Florida
North Carolina State University
Old Dominion University (I)
University of Alabama
University of Arkansas
University of Florida (I)
University of Georgia

University of Mississippi
University of North Carolina/Chapel Hill
University of South Carolina
University of Tennessee/Knoxville
University of Virginia (I)
Virginia Polytechnic Institute and State University (I)

WEST

Arizona State University
California Polytechnic State University/San Luis Obispo
California State University/Chico
California State University/Fresno
Colorado School of Mines (I)
Colorado State University (I)
Evergreen State College
New Mexico State University
Oklahoma State University
Oregon State University
Texas A&M University/College Station (I)
Texas Tech University
University of Alaska/Fairbanks
University of Arizona
University of British Columbia (I)
University of California/Berkeley (I)
University of California/Davis (I)
University of California/Irvine (I)
University of California/Los Angeles (I)
University of California/Riverside (I)
University of California/Santa Barbara (I)
University of California/Santa Cruz (I)
University of Colorado/Boulder (I)
University of Hawaii/Manoa (I)
University of Houston
University of Idaho
University of Montana
University of Nevada/Reno
University of New Mexico
University of Oklahoma
University of Oregon (I)
University of Texas/Austin
University of Utah
University of Washington (I)
University of Wyoming
Washington State University (I)

$12,000 to $17,999

NEW ENGLAND

Carleton University
Queen's University
University of Maine/Orono
University of Massachusetts/Amherst
University of Rhode Island
University of Toronto
University of Vermont (I)
University of Waterloo
University of Western Ontario

MID-ATLANTIC

Adelphi University
Cooper Union for the Advancement of Science and Art
Howard University
New Jersey, The College of
Pennsylvania State University
Rutgers, The State University of New Jersey
SUNY/Binghamton
SUNY/Buffalo
SUNY/Stony Brook
Temple University
University of Delaware
University of Maryland/College Park
West Virginia University
Yeshiva University

MIDWEST

Bowling Green State University
Creighton University
DePaul University
Illinois State University
Indiana University
Kansas State University
Kent State University
Miami University
Michigan State University
Ohio State University
Ohio University
Purdue University
Southern Illinois University/Carbondale
University of Cincinnati
University of Illinois/Urbana-Champaign
University of Iowa
University of Minnesota
University of Missouri/Columbia

SOUTHEAST

Florida State University
George Mason University
Georgia Institute of Technology
Hendrix College
James Madison University
Morehouse College
North Carolina School of the Arts
Old Dominion University
Spelman College

Tuskegee University
University of Florida
Virginia Polytechnic Institute and State University
Wake Forest University

WEST
Baylor University
Colorado State University
Oral Roberts University
Rice University
Texas A&M University/College Station
Texas Christian University
University of British Columbia
University of California/Davis
University of California/Irvine
University of California/Santa Barbara
University of Colorado/Boulder
University of Dallas
University of Hawaii/Manoa
University of Oregon
University of Tulsa
University of Washington
Washington State University

$18,000 to $23,999

NEW ENGLAND
McMaster University
University of Connecticut
University of New Hampshire

MID-ATLANTIC
Catholic University of America
Drew University
Drexel University
Fordham University
Hofstra University
Juilliard School, The
Muhlenberg College
Rochester Institute of Technology
St. Bonaventure University
Trinity College (D.C.)
University of Pittsburgh
Wells College

MIDWEST
Alma College
Case Western Reserve University
Centre College
DePauw University
Earlham College
Grinnell College
Gustavus Adolphus College
Knox College
Loyola University of Chicago
Marquette University
St. John's University/College of St. Benedict
St. Olaf College
University of Michigan
Valparaiso University
Wabash College
Wittenburg University

SOUTHEAST
Agnes Scott College
Birmingham-Southern College
Florida Institute of Technology
Furman University
Hampden-Sydney College
Hollins College
Millsaps College
Randolph-Macon Woman's College
Rhodes College
Stetson University
Sweet Briar College
University of Richmond
University of the South (Sewanee)
University of Virginia
Washington and Lee University
William and Mary, College of
Wofford College

WEST
California Institute of Technology
California Institute of the Arts
Colorado School of Mines
Mills College
Southern Methodist University
Trinity University
University of California/Berkeley
University of California/Los Angeles
University of California/Riverside
University of California/San Diego
University of California/Santa Cruz
University of Denver
University of Puget Sound
University of Redlands

A Word About Statistics

You want to narrow your search, size up a school quickly, or check out your chances of getting admitted? Statistics are a useful place to start when you are browsing colleges, and they are also helpful in creating that perfect list of reach, mid-range, and safety schools to which you will apply. A statistical profile precedes every college in the *Insider's Guide*. The colleges themselves provide the data. The letters "NA" (not available) either represents data that the school did not report, or figures under one percent. For the most up-to-date information, as well as for all data not included in the *Insider's Guide*, you should contact the colleges directly.

As a rule, the statistics provided are from the most recent year for which the college has information. In most cases, this means either the 2002–2003 or 2003–2004 academic year. In general, percentages have been rounded to the nearest whole-number percent. Statistically speaking, there is no significant difference between an acceptance rate of 30 percent and 30.4 percent; in fact, even a difference of 3 to 5 percent would hardly be noticeable.

Below the name of each school the **World Wide Web (WWW) site** is listed, as well as the admissions office e-mail address for the school.

The **address** and undergraduate **admissions phone number** are the ones that a school's admissions office prefers applicants to use when corresponding.

Location describes the setting of the college, which is either rural, suburban, small city, or urban. This description gives only a general idea of the surroundings.

The designation **private** or **public** refers to private schools versus publicly-funded state schools.

Founded is the year that the school first accepted students.

Religious affiliation indicates whether a school is affiliated in any way with a particular religious establishment. This affiliation may vary from traditional school history to strong religious and cultural sentiments in the student population and administration.

Undergraduate enrollment is the number of full-time undergraduate students for the most recent year available at the time of publication, whereas **Total enrollment** gives the total number of students, including part-time and full-time undergraduates, graduate students, and professional students. Often the ratio of undergraduate to graduate students gives an indication of the relative emphasis an institution places on each.

Percent male/female (M/F) gives the percentage of undergraduates of each sex.

Percent minority is the percentage of enrolled students who indicated on their applications that they consider themselves members of a minority group. This figure is followed by percentages of students in four broad minority groups—African-American, Asian-American, Hispanic, and Native American—to give a measure of the ethnic diversity of the school. Many students of different ethnicities, such as international students and biracial students, are not included in this section. You may want to contact the college directly for more specific information.

Percent in-state/out-of-state is the percentage of enrolled undergraduates who are residents of the state in which the school is located. For Canadian schools, the percentage is that of students from within Canada. This figure gives an approximation of the regional diversity of the school. Obviously, the in-state numbers will usually be much higher for public schools than for private schools, although in most cases, states provide incentives for private schools to take in-state students. **Percent Pub HS** is, of course, the percentage of students whose secondary education took place in a public school.

Number of applicants is the number of completed first-year undergraduate applications received by the university.

The **percent accepted** figure is the number of applicants accepted for the most recent entering freshman class (in this case, usually the class of 2008) divided by the total number of applicants.

This is an imperfect measure of a college's selectivity, and does not necessarily reflect academic quality, since many factors can influence acceptance rates. One example of this is that some schools with reputations for being easy after admission tend to attract larger numbers of applicants. For another example, public schools offer lower tuition to in-state residents, which is an attractive incentive for those applicants. Even winning sports teams can increase application numbers. There are many other factors that can influence the quality and size of the applicant pool even from year to year.

Despite these caveats, the percent accepted figure is a revealing statistic. Colleges that accept relatively small numbers of applicants are usually in the best position to maintain high academic standards. When the acceptance rate is less than one-third, you can be assured that the school is one of the best around.

Percent accepted who enroll is the number of students who enroll divided by the number of students accepted. This figure, commonly called the "yield" by the admissions offices, is another way to assess how well a school attracts qualified applicants. Since many applicants have to decide between several schools, the yield is a good indicator of which schools are first-choice and which are "safety" schools. The latter usually have yields below 40 percent.

The main use of yields is to compare colleges that have similar applicant pools. State universities tend to have high yields because some applicants are in-state students who do not apply elsewhere.

Size of entering class tells the number of first-years and transfers on campus at the beginning of the year.

Number of transfers reports the number of students who were accepted for transfer to that institution each year. The transfers accepted is a better indication of an applicant's chances of gaining admission than the actual number of transfers matriculated, since often the number of transfers accepted is large compared to the number of matriculating transfer students. Keep in mind that "NA" here does not mean that there were no transfers, only that the schools did not report a number. Of course, not every school accepts transfer students, but those that do may restrict the number or have as many students leaving as transferring. Many big state schools are known for accepting lots of transfers from local community colleges. For these reasons, the number of transfers is not a good measure of a school's popularity.

The **application deadline** is the final deadline for completed applications (except for second-term grade reports and late admissions tests) for freshman students. Early decision and early action programs have different deadlines, and rolling admissions may have priority deadlines after which an application is at a disadvantage. Transfer student applications usually are due one or two months after freshman applications. Nevertheless, submitting your application early gives the admissions committee more time to become familiar with your application and increases your chance of getting in.

Many colleges no longer report **mean SAT scores** (SAT I), as they do not wish to discourage potential applicants. Instead, they either report a range of SAT scores or none at all. The important thing to remember about mean scores is that there are approximately as many students with scores higher than the mean as those with scores lower than the mean.

The College Board prefers schools to use the **middle 50% SAT range** when discussing scores. The range represents where half of a particular school's new freshman students' scores fell. A mathematics range of 550 to 650 would mean that half the incoming freshmen had SAT mathematics scores between 550 and 650. The middle 50 percent range are the numbers between the twenty-fifth and seventy-fifth percentile boundaries; someone whose SAT score falls on the seventy-fifth percentile scored higher than 75 percent of the people who took that particular test. The same applies for someone whose score falls on the twenty-fifth percentile; the median is a score at the fiftieth percentile. Therefore, if your SAT score falls within the middle 50 percent range, you are on par with the SAT scores of last year's successful applicants. This does not mean that you have a 50–50 chance of getting in. Instead, view this figure as an indication of your own competitiveness against the overall applicant pool that the school evaluates.

Schools in the South and Midwest often prefer the American College Test (ACT). We report the **middle 50% ACT range** as well as the SAT for this reason. The scale for this test is 1 to 36, and the middle 50 percent range for this test means the same as it does for the SAT.

Most popular majors lists the top three majors among the seniors in the most recent graduating class for which the college has data. Remember, though, that popularity is not necessarily a measure of quality. Also, the exact number of students majoring in any given field can vary widely from year to year. Certain schools, however, are well-known for specific programs (e.g., criminology, biomedical engineering, government, journalism).

The **retention rate** is the percentage of first-year students who remain enrolled at a given institution for their second (sophomore) year. This statistic is an indicator of the quality of life, resources, and general satisfaction of the students at a particular college. Like the statistics on percent accepted who enroll, these numbers are most useful in comparisons between schools of the similar academic caliber, size, and student body.

The **graduation rate** represents the percentage of students who graduate successfully over a certain time period: for example, "70 percent in five years." Different institutions will report this statistic over four-, five-, or six-year periods. Many students take five years to obtain their bachelor's degree. Contact a school directly to find out how long the average student takes to complete the requirements for his or her degree. Generally students are more likely to take over four years to graduate in public schools than private schools.

On-campus housing, first year gives the percentage of students living in school-controlled housing for their first year. Be prepared to seek off-campus housing arrangements early if a school's housing percentage is less than 90 percent, or if no figure is listed.

The figures for membership in **sororities** and **fraternities** represent the approximate percentage of male students joining fraternities and female students joining sororities, as reported by the administration. Fraternity and sorority enrollment over 30 percent usually indicates a strong Greek system. Note that fraternity and sorority figures do not include non-Greek exclusive clubs or secret societies.

Library figures list the physical number of volumes possessed by the college library system. This includes book, audio and video recordings, but not microreproductions or volumes available through cooperation with other libraries.

Tuition and fees and **room and board** figures are given for the most recent year available. In cases where costs differ for in-state and out-of-state students, both figures are listed. Also, many public schools charge tuition that varies with the course load taken. Remember that these figures are meant as an estimate of the cost for a year at a given institution, and do not include travel, book, and personal expenses. These figures tend to increase every year. Use these figures as a relative index of how expensive one college is compared to another. For Canadian schools, these figures are reported in Canadian dollars.

For **financial aid, first-year figures,** schools are asked to report the percentage of the entering class receiving need-based financial assistance from the institution out of those applying for aid. In some cases, though, schools responded with the total percentage of students on financial aid. This does not include students receiving only merit-based scholarships, federal loans not given out by the institution, and students who did not apply for aid. These figures are most relevant for comparing similar institutions. Questions about schools' particular financial aid programs should be addressed directly to their financial aid offices.

Another statistic recently added to the *Insider's Guide* is **varsity or club athletes,** a number that represents the percentage of students who play a varsity or club sports at the college. Like the fraternity and sorority figures, this statistic helps to give an impression of the general composition of the student body and campus life.

Early decision or early action acceptance rate is a recent addition to the *Insider's Guide.* There has been a growing population of students applying early to college to demonstrate commitment or to increase chances of admission. A school's policy for early admission may include "early action" (EA) or "early decision" (ED). Both programs have application due dates far in advance of regular admission, so check with the school to make sure your application will arrive on time. Remember that while early action is advance acceptance with the option of applying and matriculating elsewhere, early decision requires a commitment to matriculate and to rescind all outstanding applications to other schools. The fact that these programs exist should not exert any pressure on an applicant to commit to an institution early, and many institutions in fact prefer to use regular or rolling admissions.

A Note About Some Statistics We Do Not Include

We do not list student-faculty ratios in our statistics because we believe that such ratios form an inappropriate basis for judging student-faculty interaction. Large universities often pad their ratios by counting as faculty graduate students who teach undergraduate courses. Other schools distort their figures by including part-time professors, or full-time research and emeritus faculty who do not teach at all.

Previous editions of the *Insider's Guide* included a percentage of international students. Since the international student percentage was generally under nine percent, the figure was dropped in favor of others that would better serve the audience. International students should not feel slighted by this.

Other statistics an applicant might wish to research independently are: the percentage of students involved in community service, the average loan debt of a typical graduate, the number of transfers from a community college at your state university, or the percentage of graduates who continue their education within five years of graduation.

Alabama

Auburn University

Address: 202 Martin Hall; Auburn University, AL 36849-5145
Phone: 334-844-4080
E-mail address: admissions@auburn.edu
Web site URL: www.auburn.edu
Founded: 1856
Private or Public: public
Religious affiliation: none
Location: suburban
Undergraduate enrollment: 19,603
Total enrollment: NA
Percent Male/Female: 52%/48%
Percent Minority: 9%
Percent African-American: 7%
Percent Asian: 1%
Percent Hispanic: 1%
Percent Native-American: 0%
Percent in-state/out of state: 69%/31%
Percent Pub HS: NA
Number of Applicants: 13,264
Percent Accepted: 83%
Percent Accepted who enroll: 38%
Entering: 4,184
Transfers: 1,297
Application Deadline: 1 Aug
Mean SAT: NA
Mean ACT: NA
Middle 50% SAT range: V 490-600, M 510-610
Middle 50% ACT range: 21-26
3 Most popular majors: business, engineering, education
Retention: 82%
Graduation rate: 68%
On-campus housing: 16%
Fraternities: 22%
Sororities: 37%
Library: 2,591,255 volumes
Tuition and Fees: $3,784 in, $11,084 out
Room and Board: $5,586
Financial aid, first-year: 28%
Varsity or Club Athletes: NA
Early Decision or Early Action Acceptance Rate: NA

"Why do they have two mascots?" As you turn off the interstate on the way to Auburn University you'll drive over large tiger-paw prints showing you the way to the campus. Upon your arrival you'll meet Aubie the Tiger, who was 1997 NCAA mascot national champion. But at football games, you'll sing the War Eagle fight song and witness the Eagle in his cage outside Jordan-Hare Stadium. What does it all mean? At Auburn University, a school that prides itself on both its football and its friendliness, one emblem just isn't enough.

Two Heads Are Better Than One

Auburn University is divided into 12 different colleges. Students graduate with a major from one of these colleges, which include: Agriculture; Architecture, Design, and Construction; Business; Education; Engineering; Forestry; Nursing; Human Sciences; Liberal Arts; Pharmacy; Science and Mathematics; and Veterinary Medicine. Once students declare their major at the end of their sophomore year, students are not ultimately bound to it and a change of major even between different colleges is easily accomplished. With some noted exceptions, Auburn students are pleased overall with their academic experiences. Grading is seen as fair, and homework is not too much of a burden, although as one student put it "your time here is all what you make of it. You can walk out without ever picking up a book, but you can also study your head off." While there are certainly exceptions, education is largely known as a "slack" major, while engineering and veterinary medicine are both considered "tough" and "prestigious." In addition to its tough subject matter, the math and science departments at Auburn also draw student criticism related to the attentiveness of some faculty members. One student stated, "my teacher seemed to fall asleep during his own lecture, so I went in for a little personal help during office hours, and he fell asleep there too!" Other complaints stem from the fact that getting a professor or TA who speaks fluent English is often a rarity, although another student noted that the university has made efforts to address this problem.

To Dorm or Not to Dorm

Freshmen aren't required to live on campus so many choose among other options available to them. For those who do decide to reside in university housing, there are two main areas of the campus to live in: the Quad and the Hill. Dorms in both of these areas are divided by sex but have regular visiting hours for students of the opposite sex. Dorms are also segregated according to student interests. For example, there is Sewell, the dorm for athletes, and Broun and Harper, which house many honors-program students. Another point of interest surrounding dorm life is that the majority of the dorms are strictly female. For unknown reasons, many more Auburn women decide to spend their freshman year in the dorms than their male counterparts.

For the majority of students who live off campus, housing options are plentiful. Many students decide to rent apartments or houses. Residential complexes often have reputations associated with them, like the College Park Apartments, which is known as "party central." Other options include the Commons, an interesting blend of apartment and dorm that is not run by the university but still supplies younger students with an RA system in order to help them with any problems they may have adjusting to college life.

Students rate the food at Auburn's two main dining halls, War Eagle Court and Terrell, "just average," but they consider their overall food choices plentiful. There are several fast-food chains around campus for students on the go, as well as other university-run options like the Dow Deli, where students can make their own pizza and sandwiches. There is no common meal plan at Auburn, but students can and often do make use of their "Tiger Club" card to send the bill for any food purchases home to Mom and Dad. For more upscale dining, the town of Auburn offers an array of popular restaurants like Applebee's and Ruby Tuesday's, along with local favorites like Gutherie's, where students joke that one can choose from "chicken fingers, chicken fingers, or chicken fingers."

Y'all Come Back Now, Ya Hear?

Socially, Auburn considers itself one of the preeminent universities nationwide. Students pride themselves on their southern hospitality and amiability, although the university is somewhat homogeneous. "There is definitely a student stereotype here," said one upperclassman, "and those who don't fit in might feel a little out of it."

"There is definitely a student stereotype here, and those who don't fit in might feel a little out of it."

On weekends, Auburn students know how to have fun. "Friday night party, Saturday night party, and Sunday recuperate" is how one student described her weekend schedule. Most of these parties occur either in private apartments or at the many fraternities and sororities around campus. The Greek scene of Auburn is somewhat different from that at other large Southern universities. While the Greek presence is large, the frats and sororities don't have their own houses and students reside in the dorms. Thus, the first three floors of most dorms are populated with members of one particular fraternity or sorority.

This doesn't keep the Greeks from having a good time, however. Their large band parties and dressy formals keep members entertained and active. The band parties are attractive to Greek and non-Greek alike, and while police are required to be present at these get-togethers, students claim limitations on underage drinking are virtually never enforced. The cops do, however, enforce one popular safety rule known as "Sober Drivers" at major parties. Volunteers give their services to get partiers home safely at the end of the night, and are required to be on call at all times. Students say that non-Greeks don't feel particularly pinched by a lack of activity at Auburn.

Sports also play a large role in campus activities for all levels of commitment. Auburn football is followed with incredible zeal, especially when such noted rivals as the University of Georgia, Florida, and of course, Alabama come knocking. While no other varsity sport garners the attention given to football, Auburn plays host to a large group of well-supported intercollegiate teams. For those who take their sports a little less seriously, there are also many intramural and pickup games occurring on the campus at all times, as well as a bevy of local lakes and parks to which students frequently retreat.

Many students also engage in social and community service organizations present on campus. Popular groups include the University Program Council, commonly known as the UPC, which strives to bring famous entertainers and musicians to campus, and Campus Crusade for Christ, which regularly boasts over 800 members. Service groups include Habitat for Humanity, which builds housing for the underprivileged in the area, Impact and Uplift, two groups that work with local families and children, and the Circle K, which works in conjunction with the local Kiwanas Club in community efforts.

A Walk in the Park

When asked to describe the campus, virtually every Auburn student replies "beautiful," "pretty," and "green." The campus is large enough that students don't feel cramped, yet not so big that getting from place to place is a problem. Grass and trees abound, and comparable redbrick buildings complete the campus.

When asked which of these buildings is the most noteworthy, most students reply with authority "the Haley Center." This behemoth of college life contains the university bookstore, cafeteria, and most of the large lecture halls on the campus. It is shaped into four quadrants that point (as rumor has it) towards four symbols of Auburn life: from Jordan-Hare Football Stadium to Draughton Library to Foy Student Union and finally to a four-way intersection. Perhaps the importance of the intersection rests in Auburn's large automobile population. Cars have caused a slight dilemma on the campus due to a limited number of parking spaces. Most Auburn students do bring a vehicle to school, because as one student puts it, "a car is not a necessity for getting to classes, but socially it's a big plus." In fact, Auburn students seem to regard their entire collegiate experience as a big plus and with two mascots, how could you go wrong? —*Robbie Berschinski*

FYI

If you come to Auburn, you'd better bring "an Auburn sweatshirt."

What is the typical weekend schedule? "Hang out in the park during the day, and hit the bars at night."

If I could change one thing about Auburn, I'd "add more parking spaces."

Three things every Auburn student should do before graduating are "go to a "Beat 'Bama" pep rally, relax during Splash into Spring week, and run in the 2.7 mile Cake Race across campus."

Birmingham-Southern College

Address: 900 Arkadelphia Road; Birmingham, AL 35254
Phone: 205-226-4696
E-mail address: admission@bsc.edu
Web site URL: www.bsc.edu
Founded: 1856
Private or Public: private
Religious affiliation: Methodist
Location: urban
Undergraduate enrollment: 1,316
Total enrollment: NA
Percent Male/Female: 42%/58%
Percent Minority: 9%
Percent African-American: 6%
Percent Asian: 2%
Percent Hispanic: 1%
Percent Native-American: 0%
Percent in-state/out of state: 74%/26%
Percent Pub HS: NA
Number of Applicants: 1,040
Percent Accepted: 90%
Percent Accepted who enroll: 36%
Entering: 341
Transfers: 46
Application Deadline: rolling
Mean SAT: NA
Mean ACT: NA
Middle 5NA SAT range: V 540-650, M 540-640
Middle 5NA ACT range: 23-29
3 Most popular majors: business, multi/-interdisciplinary studies, social sciences
Retention: 83%
Graduation rate: 74%
On-campus housing: 88%
Fraternities: 53%
Sororities: 74%
Library: 232,330 volumes
Tuition and Fees: $17,185
Room and Board: $5,980
Financial aid, first-year: 48%
Varsity or Club Athletes: NA
Early Decision or Early Action Acceptance Rate: NA

While solid academics can be found at many an institution, and certainly are present at Birmingham-Southern, according to students, small class sizes and highly accessible faculty are what make Birmingham-Southern special to them.

Polymaths!! So Many Polymaths!!

First and foremost, BSC is a liberal arts university, and it requires of its students a working knowledge of numerous subjects. Students must accrue one unit credit in each of the following subjects: art, history, lab science, language, literature, math, philosophy and religion, social science, and writing. Following these initial core courses, students must take two additional arts and humanities courses, and then an additional math or science followed by two units outside of one's major or minor. Undaunted by the requirements, many students immerse themselves in pre-medical and pre-law tracks, which are both grueling career-oriented majors. Slacker majors, according to one student, are non-existent: "Everything is hard here, because it's a hard school."

But finding interesting and enjoyable classes is not difficult, so fulfilling the general education requirements is rarely looked upon as a burden. For 50 of the best and the brightest, BSC offers an honors college which has accelerated courses and even smaller class sizes largely taught in seminar format. Other options include the Leadership Studies Program and the Service Learning Program. Students are assigned an advisor, often within the student's major, who assists with course selection, provides general guidance, and calms the student during the trying academic times that they will likely encounter while enrolled at BSC. Good time management skills are necessary to survive here.

One aspect of their education that students universally praise is the "interim" session held every January. BSC has the two-semester system, during which students generally take four classes, but the January interim session allows them to either take one class or travel abroad. Traveling abroad to such exotic destinations as Greece, England, and France is always a popular option for the Alabama-weary student.

The administration is reportedly very responsive to student complaints and concerns. The president routinely e-mails the student body, informing them of the latest high-level decisions and he takes substantive complaints lodged against faculty very seriously.

Healthy, Wealthy, and Wise

Affluence is the hallmark of BSC students. Students report that most of their peers are upper-middle-class, white, and from some sort of prep or boarding school. While the environment may, from this brief description, sound relatively homogenous, the school has a minority enrollment of almost 20 percent and a substantial body of foreign students. But despite the apparent ethnic diversity, geographic diversity is lacking. Almost 80 percent of BSC students come from in state, as BSC is a popular college option within the Alabama private school community.

"This school is hard."

Social life on campus centers around the Greek system at the school, with "Naty Light" being the preferred beer. Frat Row is a frequent destination for weekend partiers and the majority of students on campus are involved with either a sorority or fraternity. Sigma Nu and SAE are known to throw particularly big parties. Parties, save formal events, are generally open to all students regardless of Greek membership. Some, however, decry what they say is an over-reliance among students on the Greek system. Thus, travel into the south side of Birmingham is also a popular pastime. There one can find myriad clubs and bars, generally for ages 18 and up. The drinking age is 21, of course, but no worries for the campus minors, as BSC is a "very wet" campus according to students.

Major campus-wide events include the Entertainment Festivals in the fall and spring. The college also sponsors free movie nights at the local cinema for interested students. The dating scene on campus is small, and the result is that most students search off campus for potential mates. Therefore maintaining a relationship with a significant high school sweetheart or off-campus beau is usually not a problem. With most students coming from Alabama and the campus being a mere five-minute drive from downtown Birmingham, getting to campus is also no problem at all. Of course, not everyone is involved in serious commitments—casual dating is common.

Living Large

Living conditions are regarded as adequate. The campus architecture runs the gamut from modern to neoclassical with everything well contained and within easy walking distance. The dorms themselves are all single-sex with the most liberal option being 24-hour visitation. Hansen and Bruno are the most spacious and well outfitted of all the dorms. Living options range from singles to large suites with common rooms and bathroom. Other suites have community bathrooms and kitchens. Each floor of the dorms has a residential advisor (RA) who, depending upon temperament, may or may not strictly enforce all university policies. Students report that RAs are readily available to lend help or a comforting ear to the concerned freshman.

The rest of the campus contains some fairly modern buildings including the Norton Campus Center, which holds the food court, movies, computers, and games. The Cellar, a coffee shop on campus, is a popular hang out for students and hosts an open mike night on Thursdays and always provides a convenient place to study and chat with friends. The Learning Center is the place for hardcore studiers. The "caf," BSC vernacular for the cafeteria, has numerous dining options designed to please the palate, including Pizza Hut, homestyle cooking, a grill, deli, and salad bar.

As BSC recently moved into Division I play, baseball and basketball are fairly big on campus. Besides sporting options, students wholly devote themselves to community service activities. BSC is, after all, a Methodist school with a tradition of lending a helping hand to the less fortunate. In addition, the student newspaper, the *Hilltop News*, attracts student writers while the Student Government reigns in the budding politicians on campus. BSC provides budding scholars with the opportunity to live, learn, and grow while at the same time offering up a healthy dose of southern comfort, hospitality, and charm. *—Sean McBride*

FYI

If you come to BSC, you'd better bring "a car, because the campus is pretty darn hilly."

What is the typical weekend schedule? "Thursday, party all night in Birmingham; Friday and Saturday, go to campus parties, and Sunday get some homework done."

If I could change one thing about BSC, I'd "make it more independent of the Greek system."

Three things every student should do before graduating are "go to Frat Row, pull an all-nighter with friends, and get fined by your RA."

Tuskegee University

Address: PO Box 1239; Tuskegee, AL 36088
Phone: 334-727-8500
E-mail address: admissions@tuskegee.edu
Web site URL: www.tuskegee.edu
Founded: 1881
Private or Public: private
Religious affiliation: none
Location: rural
Undergraduate enrollment: 2,608
Total enrollment: NA
Percent Male/Female: 43%/57%
Percent Minority: 81%
Percent African-American: 81%
Percent Asian: 0%
Percent Hispanic: 0%
Percent Native-American: 0%
Percent in-state/out of state: 41%/59%
Percent Pub HS: NA
Number of Applicants: 1,902
Percent Accepted: 81%
Percent Accepted who enroll: 49%
Entering: 747
Transfers: 91
Application Deadline: 15 Mar
Mean SAT: NA
Mean ACT: NA
Middle 50% SAT range: V 340-540, M 370-550
Middle 50% ACT range: 17-20
3 Most popular majors: electrical engineering, biological sciences, animal sciences
Retention: 72%
Graduation rate: 51%
On-campus housing: 55%
Fraternities: 6%
Sororities: 5%
Library: 500,000 volumes
Tuition and Fees: $11,360
Room and Board: $5,940
Financial aid, first-year: 75%
Varsity or Club Athletes: NA
Early Decision or Early Action Acceptance Rate: NA

Founded in 1881 by Booker T. Washington, Tuskegee University (formerly Tuskegee Institute) has drawn generations of African-American men and women searching for a strong, higher education and cultural enrichment. Tuskegee's close-knit student community lives and studies in one of America's most important African-American universities.

Changing Tradition

Tuskegee was founded upon the concept that African-Americans ought to train in specific, technical fields in order to gain a competitive stance in the job market. This approach has changed over the years, however, and today the school provides its undergraduates with a liberal arts education. Even with the change in curriculum, all freshmen are required to take an orientation course, which consists of history of the university—including the mandatory reading of Booker T. Washington's Up from Slavery—and advice for adapting to college life. Other requirements include two semesters each of English and math.

Most Tuskegee students are engineering or science majors. Prevet, premed, and nursing programs receive high student praise. Many introductory classes enroll between 40 and 50 students, but the average class size ranges from 20 to 30 students. The small class sizes and the fact that very few courses use TAs allow for interaction between students and faculty.

Overall, students give Tuskegee's academics a high rating, calling the school "demanding."

Tuskegee's history is clearly visible around its campus. Some of the brick buildings were built by students when the school was founded. Many of these buildings' interiors have been recently renovated. Although administrators claim that these renovations have produced air-conditioning, increased ethernet access, and an overall increase in comfort, students complain that the renovations were "incomplete because of funding problems." Despite such recent work, however, students argue that the library still "needs work." It is small and limited in resources, and as a result students doing research projects often have to travel to nearby Auburn University to find information. In an effort to improve their library system, Tuskegee joined an interlibrary loan system and began a renovation project, to be completed shortly.

In Loco Parentis, or Just Loco

Dorms are the other main source of student complaints. Students must remain on campus for their freshman and sophomore years. One student called the dorms "ancient." A typical room is sparsely furnished. "You had better bring things that make you feel at home," said one undergrad, because "there's no real cozy feeling." Also, because the school's traditional atmosphere lends itself to conservative social rules, all dorms are single-sex, and members of the opposite sex are never permitted to visit each other's rooms. To help enforce these rules, male and female dorms are separated by a 10-minute walk. In addition, the university staff keeps a close eye on dorms; students are not allowed to be on the "wrong" side of campus after 11 P.M. and, if caught, may face punishment.

As a result of the strict rules and old facilities, many upperclassmen choose to move off campus. One student said of the co-ed policies, "I love my campus, but I had to leave it because of the rules." In an attempt to persuade more students to stay, however, the administration has announced plans for the construction of new on-campus apartments, but little has been said about the relaxation of rules.

Students tend to meet in the student union, which contains a movie theater, a grill, a game room, and offices for student organizations. The new cafeteria is another popular meeting place. Students report that the food quality is "ten times better" than it was several years ago.

Tuskegee's many clubs and organizations also help to bring students together. Some of the biggest clubs are the state clubs, which unite students hailing from the same states to plan activities relating to their home turf. African-American groups such as the National Society of Black Engineers are also popular. Students are active in community service, and many students volunteer at the local hospital.

"The town of Tuskegee offers nothing except seclusion from the modern world, but you learn a lot trapped in the wilderness."

Football and basketball games generate great excitement at Tuskegee. Students are sure to use their tickets for games against Morehouse College and Alabama State University. Homecoming is one of the biggest social events of the year. Aside from football, however, varsity sports tend not to be so popular.

Student Solidarity

Social life at Tuskegee changes with the season. In the fall, football brings the student body together. In the spring, Greek Weeks and Springfest attract large crowds. While the Greek system is a strong presence on campus, students report that they do not feel an urge to rush. There is little animosity between the fraternities, but they reportedly have a "friendly rivalry." Officially, alcohol is prohibited on campus and students who are caught with it face fines or other penalties. As a result, on-campus drinking is not a big activity; those wishing to drink can just search for off-campus parties.

Many students consider the town of

Tuskegee "slow," but students agree that it contains the basics for college life. And, as one student put it, "Tuskegee has a lot of potential to grow," adding, "but you come for the school—not the town."

Tuskegee students say their campus is safe and claim that it is "getting better." Additional lights have been installed around campus in the past few years, and security patrols keep increasing. Security is "much, much better about patrolling both night and day," said one student. It has "really increased from years past," she added.

Tuskegee has a history of enriching young minds both culturally and academically. To this day, students take pride in the beliefs upon which their school was founded. The administration is more conservative and tradition-bound than the student body, but students are willing to accept this conservatism in return for the Tuskegee experience. As one student said, "There are a lot of good people here and you can meet a lot of great minds—not to mention we're friends for life. People might complain about things here, but in the end, you don't want to leave." *—Melissa Chan and Staff*

FYI

If you come to Tuskegee, you'd better bring a "car. The nearest mall is like 20 minutes away."

What is the typical weekend schedule? "Go to a football game if we're playing at home, and then party at a fraternity at night."

If I could change one thing about Tuskegee, I'd "make the town more fun!!!"

Three things every student at Tuskegee should do before graduating are "try the food at the Chicken Coop, go to Homecoming, and visit the George Washington Carver Museum on campus."

University of Alabama

Address: 1530 Third Avenue S; Birmingham, AL 35294
Phone: 205-348-5666
E-mail address: uaadmit@enroll.ua.edu
Web site URL: www.ua.edu
Founded: 1831
Private or Public: public
Religious affiliation: none
Location: suburban
Undergraduate enrollment: 10,501
Total enrollment: NA
Percent Male/Female: 40%/60%
Percent Minority: 35%
Percent African-American: 31%
Percent Asian: 3%
Percent Hispanic: 1%
Percent Native-American: 0%
Percent in-state/out of state: 95%/5%
Percent Pub HS: NA
Number of Applicants: 3,532
Percent Accepted: 91%
Percent Accepted who enroll: 46%
Entering: 1,471
Transfers: 965
Application Deadline: 1 July
Mean SAT: NA
Mean ACT: NA
Middle 50% SAT range: NA
Middle 50% ACT range: 19-25
3 Most popular majors: business, health sciences, education
Retention: 73%
Graduation rate: 38%
On-campus housing: 13%
Fraternities: 6%
Sororities: 6%
Library: 1,224,842 volumes
Tuition and Fees: $3,880 in; $7,810 out
Room and Board: NA
Financial aid, first-year: 50%
Varsity or Club Athletes: NA
Early Decision or Early Action Acceptance Rate: NA

University of Alabama students have an enormous amount of pride in their school. It's not just the beautiful architecture ("This place must have more Greek columns than Athens!") that gets raves from undergrads. Rather, in the words of one senior, "The spirit I saw here is what attracted me in the first place. I've lived in college towns and have never seen anything like this place on a game day." In all likelihood, if you attend the University of Alabama a significant portion of your free time is going to be spent supporting tremendously successful athletic teams. In addition, Alabama students manage to fit academics and many extracurricular activities into their busy lives on the warm, southern campus.

The Necessities

Ferguson Center, the student union, houses the supply store, post office, dining hall, small movie theater, and food court with fast-food chain restaurants such as Burger King, Blimpie, Manchu Wok, and Chick-Fil-A. Taco Casa, students claim, "puts Taco Bell to shame!" On the meal plan, students buy five, 10, or 15 meals a week plus $200 of credit per semester to use at the Ferguson Center and restaurants near campus. Students agree the food is acceptable for cafeteria cuisine. "It's nothing to write home about," one student said, and another added he "wouldn't call it home cooking." What does get raves, however, is the City Café's homemade biscuits with molasses on top.

For students who don't reside in Greek houses, dorm life is typical of campus living, getting "pretty loud" at times. "The dorms are not an ideal living situation, but you don't spend much time in them anyway." Freshmen are not required to live on campus, but for those who want to, suites with bathrooms and kitchens are available, as are coed and single-sex dorms. Friedman Hall is popular for its newer stoves and refrigerators. A junior advised that the smaller dorms tend to have bigger rooms.

Academics at Alabama

While some students study in their rooms, many study in Gorgas Library, which is the main library. Other options include the Science and Engineering Library, the Business Library (where many go to socialize while studying), Mclure Library and the Arts and Sciences Library.

The options of what to study are diverse as well. In addition to the College of Arts and Sciences, Alabama houses a business school and colleges of engineering, nursing, and communication. Other schools include the College of Education, the College of Human Environmental Sciences and the College of Social Work. At the College of Arts and Sciences (which contains undergraduate liberal arts majors as well as many pre-professional programs) distributional requirements ensure that graduates of UA are well-rounded. These requirements include writing-intensive courses, computer or foreign-language literacy, humanities, literature, fine arts, history, social and behavioral sciences, natural sciences, and mathematics.

"The homecoming pep rally is an unforgettable event involving fireworks, the Million Dollar Band, old alumni, a four-story bonfire, and 20,000 of your closest friends."

'Bama undergrads may take advantage of the prestigious honors program incoming freshmen with high test scores and grades. This program allows for more student-faculty interaction, since participants work and research with professors. Also prestigious is the Computer-Based Honors Program. Along with the program's prestige comes a lot of hard work: one student recalled an assignment in which he was given a week to learn JAVA and write a complex program for presentation. The Women's Honors Program also allows students to capitalize on the intellectual resources of the University.

One of the biggest concerns for UA students is the lack of recognition given to its solid academics. Despite the school's vibrant and respected business and law schools, its noted communications program, and the successful accounting department, for the most part, UA's academics go unrecognized. Some students lament the lack of recognition; others consider UA "our treasured little secret."

Crimson and White

As the team with the most national championships of any college football team, the Crimson Tide garners the passion and spirit of many loyal Alabama fans. It would not be an overstatement to say that football is life for much of the student body.

Much of the excitement centers around an intense rivalry with Auburn University. Not to be outdone, the women's gymnastics team, the men's baseball team, and the girls' softball team sporting events are also very well attended. Intramural sports are also popular: students devote time to flag football, Ultimate Frisbee, soccer, and basketball. One popular place where students can be found playing casual sports is the Quad. One student remarked, "With its oaks and gentle breeze, this 10-acre park in the middle of campus makes the school's character."

The Machine

Besides athletics, Greek life is one of the main binding factors among University of Alabama students. *Esquire* magazine once ran an article on the country's most powerful fraternity located at Alabama titled "The Machine." The article reported that this UA organization, a secret fraternity of fraternities, allegedly controlled student government.

According to students, the majority of voters in SGA elections still are Greek, and although Alabama students held a constitutional convention on the electoral system, a staff member of the *Crimson White*, the campus daily newspaper, said he believes the changes were purely cosmetic. "In a race in which a Greek was running a Greek won," he said of a recent SGA election. Despite the strong presence and influence of fraternities and sororities, students say there is no great pressure to rush and that it is possible to have a social life, if not political power, outside the Greek system. Students note that other popular activities are the Campus Crusade for Christ, the *Crimson White* newspaper, the national championship-winning debate team, the honorary organizations, and the community services groups. Active theatre, dance, and music programs also contribute to the diversity of cultural entertainment that UA has to offer.

The University of Alabama is known as a party school by outsiders and students don't go out of their way to discourage this view. Homecoming in late October is the biggest social event of the year. The homecoming pep rally is an unforgettable event involving "fireworks, the Million Dollar Band, old alumni, a four-story bonfire, and 20,000 of your closest friends." During homecoming, students can see the bond between the school and the community as "frat boys rally next to families."

In the spring, a big-name band performs on campus. Past performers have included Jimmy Buffett, Tom Petty, and James Taylor. On the weekends, students frequent the Strip, a street lined with restaurants, bars, and clubs. Many students have cars to get around in Tuscaloosa, which many call a typical college town. About five minutes away is the community of Northport while Birmingham is less than an hour's drive. Something that every student should do, one senior claims, is to "drive somewhere insane on the weekend before exams and drive straight back that night." Popular roadtripping destinations have included Atlanta and the beach. On weekends without big basketball or football games, many students head home or to nearby Auburn.

The UA Student

"Most people think of UA as a typical white, southern, Greek school with a lot of alcohol. Few people actually fit the stereotype. There are students from many backgrounds here, though most are from Alabama and, reflecting the region, the majority are white." Students say they believe that all races and religions are welcome at UA, though they acknowledge that their school is relatively conservative. Efforts by the Student Government Association are aimed at improving diversity awareness and relations, to ensure a comfortable environment for all students on UA's campus. —*Marti Page*

FYI

If you come to the University of Alabama, you'd better bring "a car, to get around campus, town, and beyond. They're good for road trips, too!"

What is the typical weekend schedule? "Greek parties dominate on Friday nights. The rest of the weekend may be more devoted to other activities, like sleep and homework."

If I could change one thing about the University of Alabama, I would "try to do something about the division between Greeks and non-Greeks."

The three things that every student should do before graduating from the University of Alabama are "eat breakfast at City Café at 5 in the morning after an all-nighter, attend the homecoming pep rally, and road trip to random locations."

University of South Alabama

Address: 307 University Boulevard; Mobile, AL 36688-0002
Phone: 334-460-6141
E-mail address: admiss@jaguan1.usouthal.edu
Web site URL: www.usouthal.edu
Founded: 1963
Private or Public: public
Religious affiliation: none
Location: urban
Undergraduate enrollment: 9,723
Total enrollment: NA
Percent Male/Female: 41%/59%
Percent Minority: 23%
Percent African-American: 18%
Percent Asian: 3%
Percent Hispanic: 1%
Percent Native-American: 1%
Percent in-state/out of state: 78%/22%
Percent Pub HS: NA
Number of Applicants: 2,512
Percent Accepted: 93%
Percent Accepted who enroll: 60%
Entering: 1,389
Transfers: 1,060
Application Deadline: 2 Aug
Mean SAT: NA
Mean ACT: NA
Middle 50% SAT range: NA
Middle 50% ACT range: 20-25
3 Most popular majors: nursing, elementary education, communications
Retention: 70%
Graduation rate: 34%
On-campus housing: 21%
Fraternities: NA
Sororities: NA
Library: 517,293 volumes
Tuition and Fees: $2,916 in; $5,672 out
Room and Board: $5,312
Financial aid, first-year: 82%
Varsity or Club Athletes: NA
Early Decision or Early Action Acceptance Rate: NA

The University of South Alabama, "South" or "USA" to students, offers a bit of everything. It provides both a traditional Greek scene for the typical college-age student, and unique dorm accommodations for non-traditional older students. The campus itself reflects a mixture of environments—the main campus sprawls across several grassy acres in the western outskirts of the city of Mobile, but many classes, particularly in health-related fields, are located in the much more urban downtown area. Although relatively young, South is growing into a more traditional university as it ages.

Academic Options

South offers a variety of academic options to its students, including traditional degrees, an honors program, and several degrees geared towards older students returning to school. The university is divided into nine colleges: Arts and Sciences, Computer and Information, Business, Education, Medicine, Nursing, Engineering, Allied Health, and Continuing Education. The core requirements differ from college to college; however, all students must take two classes with a writing emphasis, though they do not necessarily have to be English classes. Workloads vary according to majors as well. Health-related majors, such as nursing and physical therapy are considered strong departments, and students must have GPAs in the 3.8 range to be considered for admission to the BS/MS programs in these majors in their junior year. The Continuing Education program offers many night classes for students that work during the day and many students pursue this option. "Going to school here certainly is convenient for those of us who work all day," noted one night student.

Students generally praise their professors as "very helpful, not intimidating at all." Most classes are small enough to allow professor-student interaction, with average class size between 20 and 40 students. Professors teach nearly all the classes, which are primarily in lecture format. Students complain that due to poor English speaking skills, math professors are close to impossible to understand, but reading the textbook usually gave adequate instruction. Professors are happy to meet with students during office hours. "Go visit your professors," one student advised. "It's the best advice that I got freshman year—professors are helpful and inspiring as well as being nice people." The Honors Program offers opportunities for extended involvement with faculty. It pairs students with a faculty mentor with whom they do research and community service projects.

One student described her fellow classmates as "not extreme—you don't see a bunch of people with spikes or piercings running around here."

Registration for new students is conducted on campus during orientation. Everyone else registers over the phone, and priority is dictated by GPA. There are caps to classes, but students say they can often get around these by talking to professors and administrators. South recently changed its academic calendar from the quarter to the semester system. One student wonders if professors have completely adapted to the longer terms, commenting that the number of tests in some classes have not changed despite the lengthier time period.

Commuter Campus?

In years past, South has been primarily a commuter school, with many of its students living in Mobile or surrounding areas and driving to class every day. This is still true for many students, and, as a result, their interactions in the campus social life are limited. Clubs meet in the afternoon, for instance, which is an inconvenient time for students who work full-time. Many attribute the lack of school spirit to the fact that so many students do not live on campus or participate in campus events. "You have to jump into campus life here; nothing is going to pull you in like the school spirit that other schools have," admitted one frustrated student.

There are signs that this stereotype is beginning to fade, however, as more efforts are made to involve commuters. A newsletter, for example, tells commuter students about campus events. The recent completion of on-campus housing for Greek organizations is in part aimed at increasing student residence on campus. Another sign of growth is the Mitchell Center, the home to the basketball team and site of concerts (such as the Indigo Girls and Better Than Ezra) as well as other campus-wide events. However, the administration's attempt to field a football team, which many believe would bolster school spirit, fell through do to a lack of community support. In a region so dominated by football, this continues to set South apart with other state universities that have strong football programs, namely Alabama and Auburn.

Few live on campus all four years, but for those who do, dorm life is a great opportunity to meet other students. Epsilon dorms are newer, and their interior hallways are more conducive to getting to know others in the dorm. Other dorms include Beta and Gamma, which are set up like apartments, and Delta, which resembles hotel rooms. All freshmen who live on campus must have the university meal plan. But limited cafeteria hours on weekends reportedly create problems for meal plan holders. Resident assistants in each dorm occasionally sponsors activities to build community spirit. "Living in dorms is a terrific way to meet people—most of the people I hang out with now I met freshman year in dorms," raved one junior. South recently implemented the Essence Program designed to ease the transition to college life and encourage greater student involvement. It has several components, including living on campus, eating together with other students in the program, and an emphasis on mentoring and advising.

BYOB

The Greek system is responsible for most of the on-campus social scene. The membership is not huge, but they have a strong presence on campus since most of the students who join sororities or fraternities are also active in other activities at South. Non-Greeks are welcome at all social functions except date parties. The campus is officially dry, so frat parties do not usually supply alcohol (they can obtain licenses for special occasions). Party-goers are encouraged to bring their own drinks. Written warnings are given for alcohol violations and for storing alcohol in dorm rooms. Nevertheless, students emphasize that South is a dry campus "in name only."

A myriad of other activities cater to a range of interests. Outdoor movies, clubs relating to a particular major or to specific interests—such as backpacking and rock climbing—and student government are a few of the more popular extracurricular activities. Religious alternatives are numerous, and include student fellowships, Bible studies, and mission trips. Students can also found a club if they so desire. Organizations often develop theme weeks to focus attention on a particular issue, like rape awareness, and speakers regularly visit campus in conjunction with these events. Sports are another option for students—the basketball team made an appearance in the NCAA Tournament as recently as 1998 and the baseball team regularly plays in the postseason. Intramurals cater to less serious athletes, and the on-campus gym is more than adequate for students looking for a good workout.

While the university's administration has made several changes to enrich the life of the school, characteristics of the student body remain the same. Nearly all students are from Alabama or surrounding states. Many are older students returning for a degree as they change careers or parents going back to school—as many as half the students are over twenty-one. Regardless of their age, students seem pretty uniform. One undergrad described her fellow classmates as "not extreme—you don't see a bunch of people with spikes or piercings running around here."

With the advent of new programs and buildings however, South is going through growing pains as well. Poor investing, by the committee that controls the school's endowment, has led to the loss of a substantial amount of money. The administration is facing questions after its failure to institute a football team and as students protest the school's status as a dry campus. Nevertheless, the concerted effort to improve the quality of students' experiences has resulted in many changes that are fostering a great sense of community in this deep South school. *—Alexa Frankenberg*

FYI

The three best things about attending South are "helpful, knowledgeable professors, strong programs in health-related fields, and a wide variety of activities."

The three worst things about attending South are "no school spirit, parking, and no football team."

Three things that every student should do before graduating from South are "play oozeball (volleyball in a knee-deep mud pit), go to an event in the Mitchell Center, and take advantage of the fine arts offerings."

One thing I'd like to have known before coming here is "that it's much different from other colleges in that it lacks school spirit."

Alaska

University of Alaska / Fairbanks

Address: PO Box 757480; Fairbanks, AK 99775-7480
Phone: 800-478-1823
E-mail address: fyapply@uaf.edu
Web site URL: www.uaf.edu
Founded: 1917
Private or Public: public
Religious affiliation: none
Location: urban
Undergraduate enrollment: 6,727
Total enrollment: NA
Percent Male/Female: 42%/58%
Percent Minority: 26%
Percent African-American: 4%
Percent Asian: 3%
Percent Hispanic: 3%
Percent Native-American: 16%
Percent in-state/out of state: 85%/15%
Percent Pub HS: NA
Number of Applicants: 1,721
Percent Accepted: 85%
Percent Accepted who enroll: 64%
Entering: 942
Transfers: 451
Application Deadline: 1 Aug
Mean SAT: NA
Mean ACT: NA
Middle 50% SAT range: V 460-590, M 450-580
Middle 50% ACT range: 18-24
3 Most popular majors: engineering, security and protective services, business
Retention: 61%
Graduation rate: 25%
On-campus housing: 30%
Fraternities: NA
Sororities: NA
Library: 608,575 volumes
Tuition and Fees: $3,850 in; $9,580 out
Room and Board: $4,950
Financial aid, first-year: NA
Varsity or Club Athletes: NA
Early Decision or Early Action Acceptance Rate: NA

There are very few universities in the United States where one can list "reindeer tending" as an activity, but at the University of Alaska at Fairbanks taking care of the local wildlife is just another part of the college experience. At Alaska's largest university, anyone who can brave the long, cold winter is offered a unique opportunity to study in America's beautiful wilderness.

Science, Indoors and Out

A student's first two years spent at University of Alaska at Fairbanks (UAF) are centered on completing core requirements. The demands of the core program are relatively strict, though students report no trouble in completing their required classes. Included are courses in the humanities, English, math above the calculus level, and art appreciation. Students enjoy the broad nature of instruction in their core classes, but are disappointed to find that not many professors teach these courses.

Though UAF offers undergraduate degrees in countless academic, pre-professional, and vocational programs, students say that the greatest strength of their university is the natural science program. UAF is home to one of the nation's most respected and unique biology departments. Though students view the biology major as one of the university's more difficult offerings, the opportunity to interact with the environment of Alaska draws many students. The cold climate and mountainous terrain of Alaska are characterized by a wonderful array of plants and animals not found elsewhere in the

United States. Ecology and biology students routinely make use of their environment to expand their academic horizons.

Students also cite the business school as a very popular choice for academic pursuit. This pre-professional school is nationally accredited and attracts many top students. Many business school students go on to graduate business programs. In addition, attending medical school is popular among students, especially those graduating with a major in biology. Other popular science majors include physics, computer science, and mathematics. The electrical engineering program at UAF is also very strong, and the new Natural Sciences Building has attracted many students to the sciences over the past several years.

Students are not as quick to praise the non-science programs at UAF. One senior remarked that the liberal arts "aren't so hot." Regardless, students take courses in all disciplines and gain much from their liberal education. After the core courses are completed, professors teach all courses, which are generally small. "My favorite part about UAF is the low student-to-faculty ratio," said one sophomore. Professors at UAF are very accessible and charismatic, making classes exciting and interactive.

Cold Parties

The social scene at UAF revolves around the on-campus student apartments. Students of all classes trek to the apartments, mostly occupied by upperclassmen, on Friday and Saturday nights for campus parties. Students maintain that the university has a relatively lax policy about alcohol consumption. Alcohol is permitted in the apartments, but not in freshman dormitories. Many students drink on weekends, but non-drinkers never feel excluded. UAF offers an incredible amount of university-sponsored campus activities. Intramurals are a very popular activity, and student-organized teams compete in soccer, basketball, and volleyball, as well as other sports. The annual broomball tournament pits teams of students against each other, wielding nothing but brooms and their athletic prowess on ice.

In addition to parties, much socializing at UAF revolves around the housing arrangements. Each dormitory has a Residential Association that is very active in campus life. These committees plan dances and social activities for the students in each dorm, and students report that the activities foster feelings of friendship and community.

"If you enjoy nature and can deal with the dark winters, this place is great!"

The student government at UAF is also very active. Officers and delegates to the student government are responsible for planning annual campus-wide events that excite the student body. Every year there is an ice sculpture contest between the different dorms. Students compete to form the best sculpture out of the natural snow and ice around their buildings. "Spring Melt Down" is another favorite student activity. Every spring when the ground begins to thaw and the snow starts to melt, students participate in activities ranging from mud volleyball to class-oriented olympics. Students also call Melt Down "Case Day," as each student is supposed to try to finish one case of beer.

We Love the Outdoors

One student described the average UAF student as a "20-year-old guy who lives in a cabin." Because of Alaska's distinct environment and climate, a very particular student attends UAF. Many students are characterized as "outdoorsy" and environmentally aware. Fewer than 20 percent of UAF students are Alaskan natives, but all students attending the school must be able to stand the cold weather. The winter at UAF is extremely long and cold, and there are only three hours of sunlight per day in the dead of winter.

Students at UAF are generally concerned with the well-being of the environment, and enjoy spending time in the wilderness. One group of hardy students lives in off-campus cabins with no plumbing or electricity. These adventurers enjoy the serenity of nature, and utilize their time in Alaska to appreciate the pristine environment. Students not living in cabins or apartments live in the on-campus dorms. Though the dorms are considered small, there is a great feeling of community among the students living on campus. There are eight dorms, which are split into Lower and Upper Campus. A rivalry exists between the two campuses, and students engage in healthy competitions like "Starvation Gulch," which pits the Upper against the Lower in a contest of bonfire-making. Residential Assistants live in the dorms, but these upperclassmen are not particularly strict according to some students, and they usually let students live their lives uninterrupted.

Did You See That Moose?

UAF is situated outside of Fairbanks, one of Alaska's largest cities. Citizens of Fairbanks refer to the college as situated on "The Hill." Though the Alaskan wilderness is quite stunning, students maintain that UAF is "not a pretty campus." One senior reported that, "all of the buildings look really bleak, and none of them seem to match." The campus does, however, offer a number of wonderful facilities. The Wood Center is the campus's social center, which contains It's a Pizza, a popular student eating place, student activity offices, and a ballroom. The Student Recreation Center houses a pool, an indoor track, and an ice-skating rink. Many students use this center throughout the winter, citing exercise as the only way to forget how difficult it can be to go outside. Students also routinely head to The Pub, which serves only students who are of legal drinking age.

If UAF's campus isn't your style, the city of Fairbanks is only a five-minute drive from the university. Many students have cars, but those who don't take advantage of the excellent shuttle system. A student position on the Fairbanks Chamber of Commerce encourages a strong relationship between the city and the college. The movie theater in Fairbanks is a popular hangout, as are the clubs. Students frequent The Underground, Club Detour, and The Blue Loon. These clubs require an ID for entry, so students make sure to be appropriately "armed."

So Much Winter Fun

There are countless activities in which to get involved at UAF. The Student Government Association is very active, and has delegates from all of the dorms and housing areas on campus. In addition, there is "a club for everything" according to one sophomore. UAF offers everything from a fencing team to an Asian dance team.

Sports are also very popular at UAF. The Division I hockey team is the most well-known team on campus. Friday nights find all students heading to the hockey rink to cheer on their men on skates. Though not as popular, the rifle team is always among the top in the nation. Even non-varsity athletics attract students. Intramural sports pit students against one another in all different types of sports. Most notable, however, are the winter sporting opportunities at UAF. Many students choose to attend UAF for its incredible winter terrain. The cross-country skiing team has miles of on-campus trails that they utilize for training. For snowboarders and downhill skiers, mountains are nearby. Students fly down Birch Hill, Moose Mountain, and the Ester Dome, all of which are a short ride from campus. "There is great snow for a solid seven months of winter . . . The skiing is great!" exclaimed one excited junior.

Students at UAF find themselves in what most characterize as a very unique academic experience. "If you enjoy nature and can deal with the dark winters, this place is great," remarked one senior. The UAF student body embraces their college and environment, making it an exciting place to live and study.—*Justin Cohen*

FYI

If you come to UAF, you'd better bring "a heavy coat."

What is the typical weekend schedule? "Hockey game on Friday night, party at apartments or the frat on Saturday, work and student government meetings on Sunday."

If I could change one thing about UAF, "I would get rid of the darkness that persists throughout November, December, and January."

Three things that every student at UAF should do before graduating are "go to Chena Hot Springs, participate in Meltdown or Case Day, and learn to cross country ski."

Arizona

Arizona State

Address: Tempe, AZ 85287-0112
Phone: 480-965-7788
E-mail address: information@asu.edu
Web site URL: www.asu.edu
Founded: 1885
Private or Public: public
Religious affiliation: none
Location: suburban
Undergraduate enrollment: 36,802
Total enrollment: NA
Percent Male/Female: 48%/52%
Percent Minority: 21%
Percent African-American: 3%
Percent Asian: 5%
Percent Hispanic: 11%
Percent Native-American: 2%
Percent in-state/out of state: 77%/23%
Percent Pub HS: NA
Number of Applicants: 18,155
Percent Accepted: 85%
Percent Accepted who enroll: 41%
Entering: 6,348
Transfers: 4,029
Application Deadline: rolling
Mean SAT: NA
Mean ACT: NA
Middle 50% SAT range: V 480-590, M 490-610
Middle 50% ACT range: 20-26
3 Most popular majors: business, multi/-interdisciplinary studies, journalism
Retention: 76%
Graduation rate: 52%
On-campus housing: 17%
Fraternities: 6%
Sororities: 7%
Library: 2,380,457 volumes
Tuition and Fees: $3,595 in; $12,115 out
Room and Board: $5,866
Financial aid, first-year: NA
Varsity or Club Athletes: NA
Early Decision or Early Action Acceptance Rate: NA

In a climate where you can wear shorts ten months out of the year, it is no wonder that most students at Arizona State care more about their tan lines than their grade-point average. Situated in Tempe, in the heart of what the locals call the Valley of the Sun, Arizona State is often a victim of its location. The sun provides the students with what is, in one undergrad's opinion, "a nine-month vacation." And as much as the university has tried, with numerous new programs over the past few years, ASU has not yet shed its reputation as one of the nation's top party schools.

Serious Sun Devils

The Sun Devils of Arizona State are a curious lot. Amid all of the distractions and beautiful weather, there *are* those who are serious about their studies. Arizona State's best programs are primarily pre-professional, and students rate the business, engineering, architecture, and broadcasting colleges as the university's best. The music program is also highly regarded. The main student complaint is the overall size of Arizona State, which includes more than 32,000 undergrads and 47,000 students overall. "Seemingly simple things like registration for classes in my major can sometimes become a real hassle because of a required signature of a professor who has, on short notice, decided to take a vacation," one student noted. To help ease this problem, Arizona State has implemented a phone registration process that has enabled students to check their grades, class schedules, and even their financial charges.

Introductory classes tend to be huge: classes such as Introduction to Sociology and Human Sexuality often enroll as many as 500 students. Undergrads report, however, that as they progress in their major, the class size radically decreases. Another student complaint centers on the English skills of some TAs. According to one undergrad, "Chemistry is hard enough as it is. It is almost impossible when the lab assistants can't speak English."

Students can sidestep some of these problems in ASU's nationally regarded Honors College. Housed in McClintock Hall at the center of the university, the program accepts top high school applicants as well as older undergraduates who have performed well. The program includes such benefits as priority registration and extended library checkout, as well as the opportunity to enroll in honors seminars taught by the university's best professors.

Living Off

With rare exceptions, only freshmen live in the campus dorms. The rest of the students can choose to live in nearby apartments, condominiums, or Greek houses. On campus, students have the choice of single-sex, coed, or theme dorms. Off-campus, students say having a car is a virtual necessity. Public transportation is poor in Tempe, and vast distances between many of the city's attractions cause even the most ambitious student to acquire a car. Arizona State does, however, provide ample parking on campus for a small fee. Many students also purchase a bike to travel around the vast campus.

"You really have to be dedicated to be a good student here."

Between classes, students have a wide variety of activities to pass the time. Many choose just to lounge around the many lawns and quads, while others opt to study in the university library or hit the Memorial Union, the student center. Students generally rate the library system as "good" and "easy to use." Hayden, the main university library, is centrally located and provides students with ample study space and high-tech research equipment. Inside the enormous Memorial Union are various restaurants, a movie theater, a video arcade, lounges, and the popular basement bowling alley.

The Best Bodies on Campus

ASU's intercollegiate athletic program is perennially regarded as one of the best in the nation—the baseball and golf teams are among the nation's best annually. Every Saturday night in the fall, almost religiously, thousands of students head over to Sun Devil Stadium to watch the football team compete before they go, just as ritualistically, to the fraternity parties. The varsity athletes, however, are not the only ones working up a sweat. The enormous and well-equipped Student Recreation Complex is home to thousands of students who hope to add muscle to their already tanned and toned bodies. As one students said, "The lack of competition in the classroom is more than made up for by the extreme competitiveness for the best bodies on campus."

Many students also take advantage of Phoenix's professional sports scene. Football, basketball, baseball, and hockey games all take place during the academic year. For just a 20-minute drive west of campus, students can enjoy Arizona Diamondbacks and Phoenix Suns games in the Bank One Ballpark and American West Arena, respectively, in downtown Phoenix.

Party Central

No one can completely forget the world-class social life at ASU that attracts so much media attention and annual rankings by college and national publications alike. The social life is heavily divided between those who are 21 (or, students say, those who have a fake ID) and those who are not. For the under-21 crowd, students say that dorm, apartment, and fraternity parties are the primary sites to socialize. Greek life at ASU is influential, with 36 chapters and over 3,000 pledges. Many students report feeling some pressure to rush, as "there is really no better way to meet other people."

For the over-21 crowd, Tempe offers students a large choice of bars, dance clubs, and pool halls that attract almost every eligible student. In fact, Mill Avenue, the city's most famous street for bars and entertainment, has become so crowded by partying university students that police have enacted measures to stop the frequent cruising by voyeuristic drivers. The more experienced barhoppers venture away from the trendy Mill Avenue and praise such places as Maloney's, Famous Door, Cajun House, Martini Ranch, and Club Rio as the top bars. For the truly adventurous and less thrifty types, North Phoenix and Scottsdale offer the Valley's most upscale clubs and bars.

Those who are tired of the bar scene or just want to experience something different from the bustle of Phoenix can, in a few hours by car, travel to Tucson, Flagstaff, or the Grand Canyon. For spring break or long weekends, many ASU students pile into cars and head down south to Rocky Point, Mexico, for more temperate weather, a little beach time, and unlimited alcohol. As much as it tries, Arizona State University cannot escape its party-school reputation. As one student said, "You really have to be dedicated to be a good student here."

Over the last few years this young university has made strong strides in developing programs to provide its students with a solid, well-rounded education. But for now, ASU's beautiful winter weather, attractive people, and world-class social life promise a social experience that is hard to beat.—*Alison Pulaski and Staff*

FYI

If you come to ASU, you'd better bring "a lot of money—tuition and dorms are really expensive."

What is a typical weekend schedule? "Go to sporting events, party hearty, sleep, and work."

If I could change one thing about ASU, I'd "eliminate the bureaucracy of the university."

The three things every student at ASU should do before graduating are "go bar-hopping, go to the football games, and attempt to study."

University of Arizona

Address: PO Box 210066; Tuscon, AZ 85721-0066
Phone: 520-621-3237
E-mail address: appinfo@arizona.edu
Web site URL: www.arizona.edu
Founded: 1885
Private or Public: public
Religious affiliation: none
Location: urban
Undergraduate enrollment: 28,278
Total enrollment: NA
Percent Male/Female: 47%/53%
Percent Minority: 26%
Percent African-American: 3%
Percent Asian: 6%
Percent Hispanic: 15%
Percent Native-American: 2%
Percent in-state/out of state: 70%/30%
Percent Pub HS: NA
Number of Applicants: 19,832
Percent Accepted: 86%
Percent Accepted who enroll: 34%
Entering: 5,808
Transfers: 1,959
Application Deadline: 1 Apr
Mean SAT: NA
Mean ACT: NA
Middle 50% SAT range: V 490-600, M 500-620
Middle 50% ACT range: 21-26
3 Most popular majors: psychology, communications, elementary education
Retention: 77%
Graduation rate: 55%
On-campus housing: 18%
Fraternities: 11%
Sororities: 13%
Library: 4,359,195 volumes
Tuition and Fees: $3,603 in; $12,373 out
Room and Board: $6,810
Financial aid, first-year: NA
Varsity or Club Athletes: NA
Early Decision or Early Action Acceptance Rate: NA

Sunbathing and studying go hand in hand at the University of Arizona, located in a region that receives more sun than Florida. Among the palm trees that dot this 350-acre desert oasis, students enjoy first-class research facilities, and top-notch preprofessional programs. The combination of quality academics and the unbelievable weather make it easy to understand why students display "incredible school spirit." Of course, Arizona's top-ranked basketball team also offers a likely explanation why "half the campus wears school colors on a daily basis."

Every Field Under the Sun

With over 150 academic majors in subjects ranging from hydrology to criminal justice administration, every student can find an academic niche at Arizona. Students report that the architecture and business programs are highly competitive and challenging, and engineering is considered a "hard" major. Science departments like astronomy and physics are well regarded, as is information systems management, a major within the business school. Slackers choose communications, education, and "any major in the family and consumer sciences department." Yet as one junior noted, " Majors are only as easy or hard as you make them." Effort equals results at Arizona because grade inflation, according to one sophomore, is "non-existent."

Before students can take classes within their major, they must satisfy mandatory general education requirements which include English and math classes, a foreign language requirement, and a course in gender, race, class, ethnicity or non-western area studies. These courses tend to be "very large" with 150 to 300 students in each, and academically "leave something to be desired." Although the material is often "interesting" and "well-taught," "it is difficult to keep up with the tedious and asinine busy work assigned in most of the general education." A drawback of the university's large size is that these courses and other introductory level classes can be difficult to get into to. Priority is given to upperclassmen during online registration. Popular classes fill very quickly, and "unfortunate freshmen... are stuck taking whatever the rest of the university leaves behind." Still, one freshman claimed she was thoroughly enjoying her required courses, and felt they would prepare her well for upper-level coursework. First-year colloquial courses are also available and are generally capped at 30 students, offering some students a more intimate classroom experience.

Most students found academic advising to be adequate at all levels. Once students declare their major, they are assigned to advisors within their departments. Those still undecided about a major are encouraged to schedule an appointment with a general advisor. The Freshman Year Center offers a full range of counseling services to first-year students. Tutoring services and a writing center also provide academic assistance. For those with learning disabilities, the Strategic Alternative Learning Techniques (SALT) program is reportedly one of the best of its kind in the nation, and requires separate admission. Students describe professors as "accessible;" even if class size sometimes restricts personal interactions, all professors hold weekly office hours. Some undergrads feel that TAs teach too many courses, especially introductory English offerings, and are assigned too many students for discussion sections.

> **"You never sleep because there is so much going on."**

For students seeking a more intense academic experience, the university offers a well-regarded honors program that "strives to provide liberal arts education in a large research-oriented university." Undergrads can be offered a spot in the program upon admission to the university, or can be recommended later by a professor. Honors students enroll in specially designated sections and are assigned additional work. For their efforts, the program offers perks such as early registration privileges and extended borrowing time from the library. While students benefit from the program's intensity, "we are worked to the bone," reported one junior.

A+ Partying

Academics are not the only thing Arizona students take seriously, giving new meaning to the old college mantra "work hard, play hard." The Greek scene is alive and well at Arizona, with 15 percent of students involved in one of the 44 campus fraternities. Despite some recent problems, including the university's formal revocation of Pi Kappa Alpha's recognition in May 2003, one fraternity brother said that Greek parties remain well-attended and rushing is a popular option for first- and second-year students. Beyond Frat Row, many upperclassmen choose to drink at private parties or in Tucson's many bars and clubs. For freshman, drinking can be more difficult since "being underage is a huge problem . . . the [campus police] are leading a witchlike hunt to curb underage drinking." While some try fake IDs, most first-year students stick to hanging out on campus on the weekends where, as one student put it, they "go to parties, drink, and get wasted." Some make the 45-minute road trip to Nogales, Mexico, to take advantage of that country's lower drinking age. Despite the emphasis on alcohol at some campus parties, non-drinkers say they "definitely do not feel out of place" and that "everyone has their place/niche within the whole campus community."

Endless opportunities for procrastination exist at the brand new Student Union Memorial Center, one of the largest student centers in the nation. Complete with dozens of restaurants, an art gallery, post office, TV and game lounges, a comedy club, and even a movie theater, the center provides students with a whopping ten acres of entertainment possibilities. With about 22,000 students visiting the union daily, it truly serves as the center of campus. The university also attracts an impressive list of speakers and performers to campus, including Sugar Ray, Buena Vista Social Club, and AIDA. Clubs, extracurricular activities, and on-campus jobs occupy most students' remaining free time. As one sophomore exclaimed, "You never sleep because there is so much going on." Literally hundreds of student organizations exist on campus, with groups related to academic majors and ethnic organizations drawing the largest memberships. The university generously funds many student-run endeavors and encourages students to create their own clubs.

The "very fit and athletic student body" always "packs" the enormous Student Recreation Center, which offers, among other things, a weight room, an indoor track, and continuous pick-up games on its many basketball courts. Students agree that looks are important to many on campus, and that while the Arizona population is "very attractive," they work hard for it. "The frat brothers are always lifting and the sorority girls are always on the treadmills," said one senior. Some see this as representative of the university's lack of diversity. The campus is "very white," and while the admissions office actively recruits minorities, the numbers tell the tale. As one junior put it, "I was born here and I want the population of the university to reflect the diverse population of the state of Arizona." However, minorities do report a "quite pleasant" experience and praise the ethnic organizations "that help to cushion students." An international student also described her time at Arizona as from "far from traumatic" thanks to the help of the "fabulous international students office."

Look Mom, My Own Apartment!

On-campus housing is limited and dorm space is not even guaranteed for freshman. The majority of upperclassmen choose to reside off campus. Since there are plenty of "extremely reasonably priced" and "luxurious" apartments close to campus, and because many students live in their Greek "mansions," the small amount of dorm housing poses little problem. That being said, upperclassmen and freshman alike encourage first-year students to apply to live on campus, stressing that it is the best way to "form the friendships that last the next four years." Undergrads generally found the residence halls to be quite comfortable, even "posh," with Pima, La Paz, and Coronado being the most popular options. Single-sex dorms, theme floors, and honors housing are all available.

Dining options at Arizona skip the traditional cafeteria in favor of on-campus restaurants. Over 35 different eateries are sprinkled around campus, allowing students to eat wherever and whenever they chose. Students applaud this flexibility and praise the wide variety of cuisines available, ranging from "fantastic" Mexican food at Café Sonora to the Oy Vey Café's high quality vegetarian and kosher options. Students can munch on burgers and fries at McDonald's, or scarf platefuls of food at Reddington Restaurant's all-you-can-eat buffet. The food plan works on a debit system that allows students to add money to their CatCards (student IDs) at any time. Many off-campus students said they often venture into town for dinner, but do sometimes prepare their own meals. Residence halls are equipped with kitchen access, and most rooms have small fridges included. Students living on and off campus alike agree that eating at school was "just more convenient" and a great way to socialize with friends.

Hoop Dreams

No matter where they live or eat, what Arizona students have in common in their "unsurpassed" sense of school pride. Cheering students pack the stands at sporting events, decked out in a wardrobe of Arizona red and blue. When it comes to Wildcats basketball, Arizona students are all business. Tickets are in extremely high demand, and sales even sparked riots in 2003 when the team won the PAC 10 conference championship. One sophomore advised that students "attend every basketball game possible" before graduation.

University of Arizona students love their school, and it shows. When lying under a palm tree, encircled by Old Main, the campus's first building, and other "beautiful" Spanish-influenced brick buildings framed by the surrounding mountains, "what's not to like?" asked one senior. —*Amelia Page*

FYI

If you come to the U of A, you better bring "sunscreen."

What is the typical weekend schedule? "Friday and Saturday nights are for partying, and then all of Sunday (including wee hours of Monday morning) is homework and study time."

If I could change one thing about U of A, I would "stop all the endless construction on campus."

Three things every student at U of A should do before graduating are "attend a Wildcat B-ball game, swim in the fountain in front of Old Main at 3 A.M., and go to Dirtbags (a seniors-only bar)."

Arkansas

Hendrix College

Address: 1600 Washington Avenue; Conway, AR 72032
Phone: 800-277-9017
E-mail address: adm@hendrix.edu
Web site URL: www.hendrix.edu
Founded: 1876
Private or Public: private
Religious affiliation: Methodist
Location: suburban
Undergraduate enrollment: 1,082
Total enrollment: NA
Percent Male/Female: 45%/55%
Percent Minority: 10%
Percent African-American: 4%
Percent Asian: 3%
Percent Hispanic: 2%
Percent Native-American: 1%
Percent in-state/out of state: 66%/34%
Percent Pub HS: NA
Number of Applicants: 1,071
Percent Accepted: 83%
Percent Accepted who enroll: 36%
Entering: 317
Transfers: 18
Application Deadline: rolling
Mean SAT: NA
Mean ACT: NA
Middle 50% SAT range: V 570-690, M 550-670
Middle 50% ACT range: 25-31
3 Most popular majors: social sciences, biology, psychology
Retention: 85%
Graduation rate: 68%
On-campus housing: 80%
Fraternities: NA
Sororities: NA
Library: 211,374 volumes
Tuition and Fees: $15,630
Room and Board: $5,340
Financial aid, first-year: 52%
Varsity or Club Athletes: NA
Early Decision or Early Action Acceptance Rate: NA

A small, Methodist, liberal arts college in the middle of Arkansas may seem less than thrilling at first. The fact that there are no fraternities or sororities could also give you the impression that this school is a pretty boring place, the kind of place you would want to leave on the weekends. Don't be fooled though—thanks to the diverse student body at Hendrix College, your first impression might be proven completely wrong.

Reputation for Diversity

Because of its extremely diverse student body, Hendrix has gained a reputation in the south as being a very liberal school. Students say that there are a lot of outside stereotypes about the liberal nature of the school, but as one student corrected, "When I got here, all the stereotypes were disproved."

Even though over two-thirds of Hendrix students are from Arkansas and there is minimal racial variation, students use the word "diverse" repeatedly in their descriptions of their school, with some even claiming that they hadn't expected such diversity. Students credit this feeling to the fact that, although most Hendrix students come from similar geographic locations, there is a multitude of different ideas, opinions, and values that all come together at the school. As one student put it, "There is definitely not a single kind of 'Hendrix student.'"

Many students stress the fact that Hendrix is neither the typical frat-oriented Southern school nor the liberal school full of "rich, drug-taking intellectuals" that people might expect. Certainly, no one is characterized by what he or she does: one senior described Hendrix as a "pseudo-bohemian bubble." As one freshman explained, "So many people do so many things that knowing someone from one activity is only knowing a little bit about him or her." Hendrix students pride themselves on being active and accepting of all people.

The Hendrix Experience

For students at Hendrix, the college experience starts before they even arrive on campus freshman year. All incoming freshmen are required to go on one of the school's famous week-long orientation trips before the start of the school year. There are a wide variety of trips, ranging from white water rafting or rock climbing, to shopping in and exploring downtown Nashville, Tennessee. In other words, there are trips to suit many interests.

Not only do incoming freshmen get to meet and greet one another, but, since the groups are all led by Hendrix upperclassmen, they also get to meet more than one experienced Hendrix student. All students mentioned that they felt the orientation trips were extremely valuable experiences. One freshman said, "I had 12 people I could hang out with as soon as I got to school." Freshmen appreciate the opportunity to bond with other freshmen as well as to ask questions of their group leaders, who are already wise in the ways of Hendrix.

Just because the orientation trips come to an end doesn't mean these freshmen stop socializing or slow down. While most students say their workload can vary considerably from class to class, they admit that it is usually "just average." Luckily for Hendrix students, this manageable workload gives them a chance to relax and take advantage of their school's vast array of activities. Students report that not only does Hendrix provide a variety of nonparty weekend choices, but the college also brings in lecturers, shows, and film festivals during the week: "Campus-wide activities occur almost daily. There is something for everyone at Hendrix."

Although Hendrix students have every opportunity to immerse themselves in an endless stream of cultured activities, on occasion they do like to party. Unlike many colleges, which start their weekends on Thursday nights, the Hendrix weekend is Friday and Saturday, plus Tuesday. Because almost nothing but science classes meet on Wednesday, "Tuesdayfest" is a regular event for those who have no classes the next day, and even for some who do. Students report the administration is rather lenient regarding alcohol, and allows dorm and other on-campus parties.

Survival Basics

Living at Hendrix is apparently as easygoing as the social life. Of the six dorms on campus, only one is considered to be in the undesirable range, and that judgment is based primarily on its outward appearance. The majority of the rooms on campus are doubles and triples, although RAs usually live in singles. Hendrix has a system of allowing all students to choose where they would prefer to live each year. This means that there are no "freshman dorms," and people from every class live together.

Eating at Hendrix is ranked high in comparison with other schools. Most students feel that the food is definitely edible and the only real complaint is about the frequent repetition of meals. Students do enjoy the express bar in the cafeteria, which serves burgers, hot dogs and other alternatives to the daily homestyle meal. The rave, however, is all about the Burrow, the new student center which serves food when the cafeteria is closed. Despite the fact that there is a limit on the amount of food and number of meals that can be transferred to the Burrow for each student per week, students rate the food as excellent and regard the Burrow as a popular hangout.

"There is definitely not a single kind of 'Hendrix student.'"

Not only is the Burrow an alternative source of food, it is also the newly remodeled student center. Aside from a place to eat, it houses the student post office and a pool table. The Burrow is just one of the popular spots on campus to mill around, especially for freshmen. The other notable social areas on campus include the pecan courts, a central area of campus filled with cracked pecan shells, as opposed to the average wood chips.

Aside from on-campus areas, there are a few key places in Conway, Arkansas, that are student favorites. Across the train tracks from the Hendrix campus is Prince Street, which, though considered "the other side of the tracks," is popular due to the fact that it houses an abundance of fast food restaurants. While Prince Street is definitely within walking distance, many students take the occasional drive around Conway to visit local restaurants, the most famous of which is Los Amigos. The occasional trip to Little Rock, especially during Razorback season, is also a student favorite.

Out With the Old

Hendrix recently changed its academic calendar from the trimester schedule to the semester schedule. The trimester system was hard on both professors and students because it conflicted with outside internship and summer-school programs. Along with the schedule change, many Hendrix classes were also revised. The most drastic of these changes was the elimination of WIT, the freshman program that served as an introduction to liberal arts, and the addition of Journeys, a course on cultures and diversity.

Hendrix is a school that relishes its diversity and acceptance. This could be the reason why there is a surprising amount of school spirit coming from a school with no football team. Students feel most strongly about the sense of community they feel at Hendrix, and they strive to contribute to that community. Hendrix is a school whose students feel comfortable in an environment in which they can bond with each other from the very beginning.
—Lauren Rodriguez

FYI

If you come to Hendrix, you'd better bring "an open mind."

What is the typical weekend schedule? "Friday, party; Saturday, a bit less partying; Sunday, some homework and laundry."

If I could change one thing about Hendrix, I'd "move it closer to a major metropolitan area."

Three things every student at Hendrix should do before graduating are "get thrown in the fountain for their birthday, become involved in the college in some capacity, and go skinny dipping in the pool."

University of Arkansas

Address: 200 Silas Hunt Hall; Fayetteville, AR 72701
Phone: 501-569-3127
E-mail address: adminfo@uair.edu
Web site URL: www.uark.edu
Founded: 1871
Private or Public: public
Religious affiliation: none
Location: urban
Undergraduate enrollment: 12,889
Total enrollment: NA
Percent Male/Female: 51%/49%
Percent Minority: 13%
Percent African-American: 6%
Percent Asian: 3%
Percent Hispanic: 2%
Percent Native-American: 2%
Percent in-state/out of state: 88%/12%
Percent Pub HS: NA
Number of Applicants: 5,025
Percent Accepted: 86%
Percent Accepted who enroll: 52%
Entering: 2,251
Transfers: 915
Application Deadline: 15 Aug
Mean SAT: NA
Mean ACT: NA
Middle 50% SAT range: V 510-640, M 520-650
Middle 50% ACT range: 22-28
3 Most popular majors: marketing, adult and continuing education, data processing
Retention: 81%
Graduation rate: 46%
On-campus housing: 41%
Fraternities: 14%
Sororities: 18%
Library: 851,714 volumes
Tuition and Fees: $4,768 in; $11,518 out
Room and Board: $5,087
Financial aid, first-year: 43%
Varsity or Club Athletes: NA
Early Decision or Early Action Acceptance Rate: EA 93%

Imagine this thrilling experience: You are attending a sold-out football game and the roar of the crowd surrounds you. There are thousands of people dressed in red and white cheering for the home team at the top of their lungs. School spirit fills the stadium and you can feel the excitement in your body as you root for the Razorbacks. If this situation appeals to you, then you would probably love attending the University of Arkansas.

Pick a College

Similar to the policy at many other universities, undergrads at the University of Arkansas are required to take a core curriculum consisting of 44 hours of core courses. Students can take examinations to place out of certain core classes they feel they are already proficient in. There is also a second-language requirement for the core, which can be satisfied by successfully completing a competency exam or taking foreign language classes at the school. Although some students may feel that the core limits them from taking all the classes they are most interested in, there seems to be a general feeling that completing the core "prepares students well for more advanced courses and introduces them to new and different ways of thinking."

Undergraduates at Arkansas can enroll in one of several colleges: the College of Education and Health Professions; the College of Engineering; Dale Bumpers College of Agricultural, Food and Life Sciences; J. William Fulbright College of Arts and Sciences; Sam M. Walton College of Business Administration; and the School of Architecture. Each of these colleges has slightly different graduation requirements and programs, but students are not left alone in the dark. The university provides an Office of Academic Advising to keep students on the right track and make sure they take the courses they need.

One aspect of academics that Arkansas students commented positively about was the accessibility of the faculty. Professors hold regular office hours and even go to meals with students. Some students, however, regret that not all classes are taught by professors. Teaching assistants supervise labs, and they occasionally teach introductory freshman classes. "Many TAs know the material well and are helpful, but they just don't have the same teaching experience yet as regular professors," commented one student. Due to the large student population at Arkansas, intro and core courses can top 400 students, and even some of the upper-level courses can be large.

Students generally consider accounting and engineering to be among the more difficult majors at the University of Arkansas. However, interested students should not be worried or frightened away by this. One student wisely commented, "if you are interested in the subjects, then the workload isn't too bad." Although some students may be a little busier depending on what they choose to study, their schedules are "challenging, but definitely manageable." In addition to getting help by studying with fellow students, "the professors and TAs are always there to help you if you have trouble understanding the material."

Life in Fayetteville

According to students, Fayetteville is "definitely a great college town." With its moderate size, the school is located in a place with "the benefits of a city but the intimacy of a small town." Students enjoy a feeling of safety when at school and enjoy making use of what the city has to offer. Favorite spots include many different restaurants and several popular bars, such as George's and River City. Dickson Street, which runs through the middle of the campus, "a fun and convenient place to find something cool to do," commented one sophomore.

Aside from going out, there are plenty of activities that students can occupy themselves with while staying on campus. The Arkansas Union, which contains a movie theater, a post office, a travel agency, a large ballroom, as well as other resources, always attracts a large number of students. The school also holds larger special occasions, such as the annual non-alcoholic Red-Eye party featuring bands, dancing, and other entertainment. For a slightly more personal evening, many students also choose to spend time talking or watching a video in their dorms with friends.

Although there is definitely a Greek

presence on campus, students are not pressured in any way to get involved if they are not interested. Only a small fraction of the student body actually pledges to the fraternities and sororities but anyone looking for a weekend party can usually find one at the houses, which are located near the middle of campus. The administration at Arkansas is attempting to be a little stricter on their alcohol policies, but as one student commented, "you won't get into trouble unless you are drinking in the street or doing something that makes it obvious you are drunk."

When they are not studying or out partying, Arkansas students also enjoy just relaxing in their dorms. People have mixed opinions of the housing, depending on whether they were fortunate enough to get one of the better dorms. The Gregson and Gibson houses, which are in a convenient location on campus and recently renovated, are among the preferred dorms. In the words of one junior who lived in Gibson, "I feel sorry for the people who are stuck in Pomfret and Humphreys . . . those are definitely the worst."

"I can feel the adrenaline pumping through my body every time I go to a game."

Another popular living option for students is off-campus housing. Residences, such as College Park Apartments, offer an inexpensive and convenient place to live for Arkansas students. Students living off-campus can either drive to school or take a bus provided by the university's shuttle service. "The shuttles are useful because it's hard to find parking and the police are not afraid to give out tickets if you leave your car anywhere convenient," explained one senior.

Let's Go Hogs!

Anyone who follows college athletics will be familiar with the teams from the University of Arkansas. The Razorbacks have been nationally recognized as a perennial powerhouse in a wide range of sports. The most popular squads are the basketball team and the football team, which are consistently ranked among the top in the nation. The school's track team has also enjoyed much success over the years, at one point having captured 17 consecutive indoor national titles. In addition to their tremendous talent and success, the school's teams draw even larger crowds due to the lack of a professional sports team in the state. The high attendance at games is due to a combination of tremendous school pride on the part of the students and the support from members of the community. As one enthusiastic student explained, "The Hogs represent all that we stand for! I can feel the adrenaline pumping through my body every time I go to a game." Yet another student declared that "every student should experience a basketball game! The Bud Walton Arena can get so loud and fun." The rivalries between Tennesse, Ole Miss, Alabama, and LSU are pretty intense. With all the motivation from watching the Razorbacks, many students take the opportunity of participating in intramural sports and working out at the House of Physical Education and Recreation (HPER). The "Hyper" building provides tracks, pools, racquetball courts, weight rooms, dance floors, basketball courts, and multi-purpose rooms for students to use.

Getting Involved

In addition to the intramurals and academics, students can participate in various on-campus organizations and activities. Most students agreed that the extracurricular activities they chose play a big role in their college experience. Students can immerse themselves into KUAF radio or UATV, the campus television station. Students who are interested in campus publications can contribute to the *Arkansas Traveler*, the campus newspaper that is released three times each week, *The Harbinger* magazine, or the yearbook. "You can find people interested in almost anything here. You just have to be willing to go out and look for them," stated one junior.

For sports fans or anyone else looking for an enjoyable college experience, the University of Arkansas should not be overlooked. Students describe themselves as "friendly and bursting with pride." One tradition at the university is the Senior Walk, which began in 1905 and has the names of over 100,000 graduates

etched into it. The path, which already stretches over five miles, will surely continue to grow as future students experience the thrill of being a Razorback.
—Robert Wong

FYI

If you come to Arkansas, you'd better bring "your car or enough money to buy one."

What is the typical weekend schedule? "Fridays find a house party, Saturdays check out a ballgame and then party, and Sundays sleep and forget about your hangover."

If I could change one thing about Arkansas, I'd "advertise for more campus events so people hear about them before they're already over."

The three things that every student should do before graduating from Arkansas are "watch a football game, get involved in extracurriculars, and go to a frat party."

California

California Institute of Technology

Address: 1200 East California Boulevard; Pasadena, CA 91125
Phone: 626-395-6341
E-mail address: ugadmissions@caltech.edu
Web site URL: www.caltech.edu
Founded: 1891
Private or Public: private
Religious affiliation: none
Location: suburban
Undergraduate enrollment: 939
Total enrollment: NA
Percent Male/Female: 67%/33%
Percent Minority: 35%
Percent African-American: 1%
Percent Asian: 27%
Percent Hispanic: 6%
Percent Native-American: 1%
Percent in-state/out of state: 42%/58%
Percent Pub HS: NA
Number of Applicants: 2,615
Percent Accepted: 21%
Percent Accepted who enroll: 46%
Entering: 252
Transfers: 10
Application Deadline: 1 Jan
Mean SAT: NA
Mean ACT: NA
Middle 50% SAT range: V 710-780, M 760-800
Middle 50% ACT range: NA
3 Most popular majors: engineering, physical sciences
Retention: 96%
Graduation rate: 85%
On-campus housing: 90%
Fraternities: NA
Sororities: NA
Library: 1,107,226 volumes
Tuition and Fees: $24,117
Room and Board: $7,560
Financial aid, first-year: 54%
Varsity or Club Athletes: NA
Early Decision or Early Action Acceptance Rate: EA 35%

"Anyone with the slightest chance of maybe sort of thinking a little bit about not majoring in science/math should stay very far away from this campus. Do not pass Go, do not waste your money on the application fee." This is how one student at the California Institute of Technology, better known as Caltech, described the atmopshere of this science-heavy university. However, for those willing to make a commitment to science and engineering and looking for topnotch programs, Caltech is the place to be.

Like Drinking from a Fire Hose . . . A Caltech Education

The academic year of Caltech students, or "Techers," is split into three terms. Dividing the required 486 credit units over four years yields an average of 40.5 units per term. Each unit is designed to equal one hour students are expected to spend on work in or out of class, however, because of required classes, students usually take between 45 and 48 units, and course loads of over 50 units are not unheard of. Although some admit that the actual hours spent on the work are often less than the number of units, students are quick to point out the notorious difficulty of the problem sets that make up a significant part of their grades. Students generally spend anywhere from 2 to 10 hours on problem sets, and some report spending more than 15 hours on particularly difficult ones. According to one student, "it's possible that some work just as much, but I cannot believe that people at other schools work more than we do".

Freshman year and most of sophomore

year, the source of these problem sets is Caltech's demanding core program, which includes five terms of math and physics, two of chemistry, one of biology, and two lab courses. Although they aren't Caltech's focus, students must also take 12 terms of humanities and social sciences. Students add that many of the humanities faculty are better teachers than the rest of the professors—they just don't get as much respect.

Caltech professors include some of the most highly respected researchers in their respective fields, but students overwhelmingly remark that amazing researchers do not necessarily make for great teachers. "Professors here are almost always available, and are, as a rule, willing to give you a second chance, but they're not generally good lecturers," remarked one student. "But if you want to do research, this is a great place. If you like to attend classes, this might not be the best place."

TAs at Caltech receive high ratings from students, although English-speaking ability is sometimes a problem. TAs are ready and willing to help with course work, and because it's easy to change sections, leaving a TA with poor English skills doesn't seem to be a major issue.

Although it's clear that there's no easy way through Caltech, students report quite a variation in the difficulty of the major programs. Others claim that Literature and Economics are relatively easy, but it's important to note that students rarely get these degrees solo; usually students majoring in a humanities subject will combine it with one of the easier science programs. On the other hand, Physics is notorious for being the hardest major, while Electrical Engineering is rumored to be the most time consuming.

Caltech students constantly speak about the sheer amount of knowledge they are expected to acquire in their four years. A popular school slogan is that "Getting an education at Caltech is like drinking from a fire hose." In fact, prefrosh orientation T-shirts depict the school mascot, a beaver, trying to drink from a hose of rushing water.

Due to the huge workload, Techers are more often seen working than anything else. Even though the first two terms of their core classes are graded pass/fail, freshmen usually have to adjust to the overwhelming amount of work. Typical students work and attend class for about 10 to 14 hours a day, leaving little time for other activities. Not surprisingly, sleep is usually the first thing to go. "It's not unusual to see students up until 4 A.M., even frosh taking pass/fails—sleep is a very precious commodity," said one student.

Although most freshman work is pass/fail, grading for other classes seems to be quite fair overall. One student remarked, "Professors are not afraid to give you an honest grade. If you did C work, you get a C. And they're not afraid to fail you, either. If you get good grades here, you're either very smart, or you have no social life, or both." Because of the academic pressures, group work is encouraged and students find that working together not only makes the work go a lot easier, but that commiserating builds friendships. Another example of freedom within this workload is the Honor Code, which students really seem to like and respect. The Honor Code System is based on the idea that "no member of the Caltech community shall take unfair advantage of any other member of the community." Because of the Code, students have access to most campus facilities at all times of day and night, and are often given take-home tests and exams. One student explained: "The Honor Code is so respected that we get take-home exams; the professors trust us not to cheat, and the students, with few exceptions, honor that trust. That's why the students have so much freedom to explore the campus, underground and indoors, after-hours, whatever. The Honor Code is one of the things that makes Caltech bearable."

Rotate, Please

At the beginning of freshman year, all students spend a week called Rotation touring the seven undergraduate houses, which can best be characterized as pseudo-frats. Each house has its own character and traditions, and since everyone is a member of one of them, no one is left out and social skills are honed. As one upperclassman recalled, "Rotation lasts through the first week of classes, and is designed to help frosh choose Houses and Houses choose frosh. Frosh have dinner at each House, one per night, and then there's a whole lot of secret meetings where the Houses talk about the frosh, and then the House Presidents get together for a grueling 12 or 14 hours and hash it all out." After being assigned to a house, frosh may choose their roommates and suite mates, and are given a considerable amount of freedom in the house. After being placed in the houses, students select their own resident advisors (RAs) who act as their counselors and sometimes supervisors. RAs are usually graduate students or younger Caltech employees, and overall students find them to be cool and laid-back, more like mentors or older siblings than disciplinarians.

Diversity?

One thing that strikes almost all students is a perceived lack of ethnic diversity. There is a decent amount of economic diversity, and most students come from public schools; however, students lament the overwhelming number of white and Asian males. Females comprise roughly one-third of the student body, about the same as Asian students, but African-American and Latino students make up only a combined seven percent of students. Time and time again, students report sensing a lack of African-American students.

As for dating, many Techers describe strange phenomena that occur on campus such as the "instant couple," whereby two individuals suddenly decide to go out, with little warning or dating. Such relationships often end as quickly as they begin, only to be repeated with different people. Like everything else at Caltech, dating is intense. Because of the disproportionately large male population, many men on campus complain about the lack of quality females. According to some, make-up is rarely seen, and many students pay little attention to appearance beyond basic grooming. Others praised this natural look, feeling it minimizes sexual tensions. Homosexual couples on campus seem to be completely accepted, and students report a very tolerant and accepting atmosphere on campus toward sexual diversity.

Everybody Likes a Prankster

Despite their heavy course load, most Techers have pretty active social lives. Although there are occasionally parties in off-campus housing, Caltech social life centers around the Houses. Each weekend a party can usually be found at one of the houses, but students are quick to note that Caltech house parties differ considerably from parties at other schools. At the beginning of every academic year the Caltech administration advises the students on the university drinking policy, but in reality it doesn't seem to be strictly enforced. One student recalls, "The administration has some sort of policy about underage drinking. I'm pretty sure they're opposed to it, at least in principle. They send out an annual flyer stating that drinking under the age of 21 is illegal in the state of California, and there's something about student bartenders and a spreadsheet full of things like '30% of undergraduates are of legal drinking age, so for a party of 200 people, you should buy one bottle of rum.'" Apparently, the students don't take the administration's policy very seriously, but they add that drinking and partying are done with restraint, due to the small and largely respectful student body. Basically, as long as the police don't get involved, students are given plenty of liberty. Drug use on campus isn't a major issue, and most students note that it involves only a tiny proportion of the student body.

Caltech students'affinity for pranks carries over to parties too, and Techers boast of pulling off an amazing array of stunts. One upperclassman recalls "the time we flooded our courtyard to eighteen inches and built boats to take us across it, all for a one-night party." Another popular prank is "the annual Pumpkin Drop, when Darbs freeze 30 pumpkins in liquid nitrogen and drop them off of Milikan Library, the tallest building on campus, in an amazing display of gravitation. It is rumored that there was once a 'blue flash' seen when a pumpkin struck the concrete. People have been looking out for the blue flash ever since..." Like most activities at Caltech, pranks generally involve math and science, such as reprogramming the scoreboard at a football game to show that Caltech was beating MIT.

> **"Getting an education at Caltech is like drinking from a fire hose."**

Stemming from the prank tradition is the Senior Ditch Day, in which seniors leave their rooms unoccupied for the day and the underclassman must break through or solve a series of "stacks" in order to gain entrance to the rooms and "redecorate." The stacks may be simple physical challenges or they may involve more sophisticated puzzles and challenges. Once the underclassmen gain entrance to the rooms, they usually find a food "bribe" left by the seniors in order to persuade the underclassmen from rearranging the rooms too ridiculously.

Another way to relieve the stress caused by the work is by participation in athletics, either varsity or intra-house. Intra-house athletics are more popular, and are as much a social event as an athletic endevor. These games add to the spirit of friendly competition between the houses, and foster bonding within the houses.

Varsity athletics follow the same principle, as membership is based on desire and commitment more than ability. Anyone can participate on any team, and indeed some Techers take up entirely new sports in college. Winning is hardly a concern, and laughing about how bad many of the teams are is a great bonding experience. Everyone who comes to practices and makes an effort gets to play, even women on some of the men's teams, due to the small number of females. Since Caltech doesn't recruit athletes, everyone is given a fair shot at athletic glory. Because of the no-recruitment policy, it's understood that all athletes have an obligation first to academics, and coaches are extremely understanding about missing games or practices due to such commitments.

Pasadena and Beyond

According to some students, the campus is beautiful and scenic, but rather uninspiring for the average underclassman. They admire its architectural dichotemy—the early 20th century buildings contrast nicely with the newer labs and buildings. The campus is fairly safe, and there is an excellent escort service for students walking home late or who need a ride home.

Any student venturing off campus will find a wealth of activities in nearby Pasadena, which is only a short drive away. There students will find movie theaters, clubs, and dozens of great restaurants. Caltech students' meal plan covers five dinners and five lunches each week—the dining hall is open all day to purchase snacks or breakfast, but once the food grows boring, nearby restaurants see more business. Even though it's quite close, students still need a car to get into town or will need to find friends with one. During the day, hiking, skiing and swimming are feasible in the nearby mountain range.

Indeed, enjoying the fresh air may be a great way to take a break from what students describe as "the hardest school I could ever imagine." The workload is said to be ridiculous at some times, and overwhelming the rest of the time, but students at Caltech are willing to work through it. Even if Techers could never imagine doing any more work than they already do, they somehow fight off procrastination and get it done, emerging from four years of attempting to drink from a fire hose with an unparalleled education. —*Brendan Muha*

FYI

If you come to CalTech, you'd better bring "at least a TI-83, but preferably the TI-92 to crunch the numbers."

What is the typical weekend schedule? "Study, study, and study some more."

If I could change one thing about Caltech, I'd "reduce the ludicrous amount of assigned work and enlarge the student body."

The three things that every student should do before graduating from Caltech are "pull an all-nighter or four (or 10 . . . or 30 . . .), drive a Daihatsu (the electric carts on campus), and see the steam tunnels."

California Institute of the Arts

Address: 24700 McBean Parkway; Valencia, CA 91355
Phone: 661-255-1050
E-mail address: admiss@calarts.edu
Web site URL: www.calarts.edu
Founded: 1961
Private or Public: private
Religious affiliation: none
Location: suburban
Undergraduate enrollment: 787
Total enrollment: NA
Percent Male/Female: 59%/41%
Percent Minority: 29%
Percent African-American: 7%
Percent Asian: 11%
Percent Hispanic: 9%
Percent Native-American: 2%
Percent in-state/out of state: NA
Percent Pub HS: NA
Number of Applicants: 2,608
Percent Accepted: 33%
Percent Accepted who enroll: 13%
Entering: 116
Transfers: 138
Application Deadline: rolling
Mean SAT: NA
Mean ACT: NA
Middle 50% SAT range: NA
Middle 50% ACT range: NA
3 Most popular majors: Visual and performing arts
Retention: 75%
Graduation rate: 53%
On-campus housing: 40%
Fraternities: NA
Sororities: NA
Library: 95,316 volumes
Tuition and Fees: $24,695
Room and Board: $7,120
Financial aid, first-year: 66%
Varsity or Club Athletes: NA
Early Decision or Early Action Acceptance Rate: NA

There's rarely a dull moment at the California Institute of the Arts. On its small campus in Valencia, California, students are constantly creating new ways to portray life, whether it be through devising a new interpretation of Hamlet, preparing for an exhibit opening, making a song completely out of Chewbacca sounds, or celebrating at the "My Bloody Valentine" party. Although the students are from an array of different backgrounds, they are tied together by their love of and total immersion in the arts. The result is a true cornucopia of passionate artists and an extremely focused yet admittedly eccentric student body.

Arts Aplenty

There is never a lack of daily activities at CalArts. Between academic responsibilities and alluring extracurricular activities, some students are at school for as much as 14 hours each day—and loving every minute of it. One sophomore's biggest complaint was that "classes are too short." CalArts is divided up into five different schools: music, art, dance, film/video, and theater. Within each school, there is a rough progression of classes that everyone must take, though this schedule is more defined in the music, theater, and dance schools. While academic requirements are different in each school, a senior found that "school politics make it hard to get into classes that aren't required. You really have to work at getting in the good classes, and it doesn't always pan out." However, students are required to take some classes outside of their school, and introductory courses in other schools are relatively easy to get into.

The assignments at CalArts are not traditional essay papers. One art student recounted, "I had to make art out of garbage and then sell it to someone. Then, I had to use the money to buy candy and bring it to class!" Students are also encouraged to join forces in their extracurricular activities; for many productions, theater students will make movies with the help of film students while music students write the score and art students create the sets.

Students are required to take 48 credits in the Critical Studies department in order to gain a strong liberal arts foundation.

Some students feel restricted by these "annoying" requirements, but many find the Critical Studies department a wonderful opportunity to explore unusual fields. One theater student was taking Narcissism, Holography, and a Theater Management class to fulfill his requirement, and found Critical Studies to be "a little tedious, but you can find some gems in there." For the most part, students consider Critical Studies little more than an interesting obstacle in their pursuit of the arts.

Cutting-Edge Arts

CalArts professors receive rave reviews from all students. "The student-teacher ratio is seven to one, and they can really focus on me. That's why I'm here," remarked one student. The professors are not just instructors, but usually also active participants in their field. "The training here is absolutely phenomenal. My theater professor took time off from Broadway to teach at CalArts, and she went back to be in a production with Uma Thurman. We're being trained by the professionals for the professionals," reported a junior. Professors are very accessible and friendly, and the school also manages to attract an impressive crop of guest speakers. Noted alum Ed Harris frequently makes appearances, while jazz virtuosos Charlie Hayden and Tim Allen have each held workshops in previous years. "There is always someone cutting edge here."

Although the CalArts campus is minuscule by most standards, students can lay claim to some of the best art resources on the West Coast. There are studios and practice spaces galore, not to mention the acclaimed Walt Disney Modular Theater, constructed entirely out of 3' × 3' blocks. Hydraulic pistons make it possible to raise and lower segments of the wall, floor, and ceiling, paving the way for some bizarre sets. It is rumored that scenes from The Empire Strikes Back were filmed there, and one junior recalled a terrific modernized version of Edward II reorganized under the auspices of "the Mod." The animation department has just received expanded studios, and CalArts also boasts one of the biggest photo enlargers in the country. However, some students claim that getting access to facilities, even in your own school, can be trying.

Everyday Life with Not Your Everyday People

Students can live off campus all four years, but those who remain on campus don't complain about much. "The rooms are huge, and I have my own sink in the bathroom." However, not all experiences are positive. One student complained that "Ants really ruined my freshman year." The halls are also well-decorated by the students. "There is some really fantastic artwork; they make all these illusions. One hallway looks like it goes on forever. It's amazing!" Resident Advisors preside over the dorms, but like most CalArts students, they are fairly laid-back. "They might come in to tell us to stop smoking weed if they can smell it, but usually they're pretty cool." Half the students are blessed with a view directly over the courtyard and site of the CalArts heated swimming pool, which has inspired some unusual behavior. "I never expected so much skinny-dipping when I decided to come here!" exclaimed a junior.

Many cook at home or eat out, but CalArts does have a pretty good cafeteria. "Even though it's got a pretty wide range of choices, after a while it gets monotonous. But overall, it's pretty decent." Meals can be cooked to order and the food is considered fresh by most, although some students have gripes with the "rip-off" meal plan. If the meal plan gets old, there is always the student-run Mom's Cafe or the Tatum Coffee Lounge on campus. For those up for a journey, the Claimjumper in Valencia was lauded, but students also have the entire city of Los Angeles to peruse for an incredible array of dining options.

Tiny Town, Tall Talent

Valencia itself is considered one of the main drawbacks to CalArts. Although it boasts plenty of movie theaters, bowling alleys, and restaurants, students complain that "Valencia is really a cookie-cutter, soccer mom kind of place. You can always pick out the students." There is a Six Flags Magic Mountain in town, but to many "there's only so many times you can twist around the looping loops or swish down a hundred feet without getting bored." Fortunately, Valencia is only 20 minutes from L.A. and a half hour from the country, so students have a smorgasbord of options. Many have cars, and for those not swamped with rehearsals, jaunts into L.A. transpire several times a week. Students swing at the Derby, go clubbing around Hollywood, or just go out for a bite to eat.

"Someone made up a T-shirt last year that said 'CalArts Varsity Football,' but that's as close as we get to having a sports team."

Those who opt to stay on campus are not living in a ghost town. The Rendezvous is a popular drinking hole, and there are always performances or art openings sponsored by the school. "Most Saturday nights there are raving parties on campus, too; I usually don't go anywhere," remarked a junior. CalArts is renowned for its wild Mardi Gras party and especially the annual Halloween party, which necessitates the LAPD for security. "The costumes are awesome. Last year there was some guy dressed up as Jesus, and he actually nailed a cross through the thin skin in his hands!" Creativity even pervades the graduation ceremonies. There are no cap and gowns; instead each year, commencement is based on a theme. One year the theme was the circus, so "the dean dressed up as a magician, people wore outfits, they served peanuts and hot dogs, and there was hay everywhere. It was wild!"

Yet, very little at CalArts is as wild as the students who go there. "People here are very eccentric and different. They are all really into their work and have green hair and a lot of piercings," remarked a junior. Another student admitted, "there are a lot of freaks. But, they're nice freaks." CalArts students find ways to express themselves in all aspects of life, from their work to their appearance.

This sense of individuality is heightened by CalArts' lack of organized sports teams. "Someone made up a T-shirt one year that said 'CalArts Varsity Football,' but that's as close as we get to having a sports team." While arts are the main focus, many students miss sports—there isn't even a school gym! "There's no school spirit. I kind of wish we all had something to rally around like a football team." Fortunately, for the casual athlete, Nerf football and Ultimate Frisbee games have been know to pop up in students' spare time.

If you like doodling in the margins during boring classes, the California Institute of the Arts is probably not for you. These students are extremely dedicated to their artwork and goals, and the overflowing creativity pervades everything from their personal appearance to their environment and even to their parties. But don't be scared off if you're not a pro just yet. For the truly motivated, CalArts provides an unparalleled opportunity to develop and refine your understanding of art as well as your ability to create it. *—Matt Stewart and Staff*

FYI

If you come to CalArts, you'd better bring "an artsy outlook on life."

What is the typical weekend schedule? "Thursday night: go to a school-sponsored art opening party. The rest of the weekend: party, rehearse, and head to L.A. for a break."

If I could change one thing about CalArts, I'd "get some school spirit going."

Three things that every student should do before graduating from CalArts are "take a good dose of non-art classes, attend as many student shows and presentations, and hit the L.A. club district."

California State University System

The California State University system has continually grown since the enactment of the Donahoe Higher Education Act of 1960, which brought together a collection of individual colleges to form the California State University. The expansive system now contains 22 colleges, including the first public university in California, San Jose State University, and the more recently established CSU Monterey Bay. A 23rd campus opened in Ventura County in the fall of 2002 and is known as CSU Channel Islands. From the metropolitan Los Angeles campus to rural CSU Sonoma to the coastal San Diego State, the individual campuses that make up the system are distinctive and vary greatly. San Diego State University, known for its party atmosphere and close proximity to fine beaches, is the largest campus, with about 31,000 full-time students. Maritime Academy and CSU Monterey Bay are the smallest, with total enrollments of 450 and 1,960 respectively.

CSU or UC?

Although often overshadowed by the better-known University of California system, the CSU system offers many features that the UC system does not. With campuses located throughout the state, the CSU system allows many Californians the option of commuting to a college close to home. For students concerned with the high costs of financing higher education, the tuition of the California State Universities are half that of UC schools, while still providing larger and better resources than two-year junior colleges. Even for an out-of-state student seeking California weather, the CSU system is still an attractive deal.

Differences and Similarities

All CSU schools offer financial aid and over 60 percent of the students are currently receiving aid. The larger campuses offer Division I varsity sports, while the smaller schools are in Division II. All campuses have organized club and intramural sports. Each campus differs greatly and prospective students should research the academic focus, size, location, and student makeup of each campus before deciding. To help high school students decide which of the 23 campuses is right for them, Cal State has implemented a specialized Web site named CSUMentor System (www.csumentor.edu). This site is very helpful and anyone interested in CSU should check it out.

Unlike the research-oriented UC system, CSU schools concentrate most of their resources on undergraduate teaching.

Education, Not Just Research

The most popular undergraduate majors in the system are business and management, social science, and interdisciplinary studies. At the graduate level, education, business, and management majors top the list. The CSU system gives out more degrees in business, computer science, and engineering than all other California schools combined, reflecting the career-oriented focus of the programs.

Unlike the research-oriented UC system, CSU schools concentrate most of their resources on undergraduate teaching. Although the professors are less prestigious, it is for this reason that they can spend less of their efforts maintaining their reputation and more time focused on teaching. As tuition skyrockets at private colleges, the CSU system's offer of a good education at a reasonable price looks better and better. —*Seung Lee and Staff*

California Polytechnic State University / San Luis Obispo

Address: 1 Grand Avenue; San Luis Obispo, CA 93407
Phone: 805-756-2311
E-mail address: admprosp@calpoly.edu
Web site URL: www.calpoly.edu
Founded: 1901
Private or Public: public
Religious affiliation: none
Location: suburban
Undergraduate enrollment: 17,401
Total enrollment: NA
Percent Male/Female: 56%/44%
Percent Minority: 23%
Percent African-American: 1%
Percent Asian: 11%
Percent Hispanic: 10%
Percent Native-American: 1%
Percent in-state/out of state: 94%/6%
Percent Pub HS: NA
Number of Applicants: 19,739
Percent Accepted: 39%
Percent Accepted who enroll: 34%
Entering: 2,601
Transfers: 727
Application Deadline: 30 Nov
Mean SAT: NA
Mean ACT: NA
Middle 50% SAT range: V 530-570, M 570-670
Middle 50% ACT range: 23-28
3 Most popular majors: engineering, business, agriculture
Retention: 89%
Graduation rate: 65%
On-campus housing: 16%
Fraternities: 10%
Sororities: 9%
Library: 763,651 volumes
Tuition and Fees: $3,381 in; $10,149 out
Room and Board: $7,479
Financial aid, first-year: 29%
Varsity or Club Athletes: NA
Early Decision or Early Action Acceptance Rate: ED 22%

For those students who know they want (and can handle) a highly regarded technical education in a small-town atmosphere, Cal Poly at San Luis Obispo may be the ideal school. With a practical approach to learning and numerous opportunities for lab work, students do not just learn from a textbook. As an added benefit, California's sunny beaches and beautiful mountains surround the campus, providing educational adventures that go far beyond the classroom.

Hands-On Learning

Cal Poly's "learn-by-doing" philosophy distinguishes it from most other schools. The General Education (GE) requirements demonstrate this modern approach to learning: 15 credits each are required in science and technology distributions (labs included), as well as in Social, Political, and Economic Institutions and Life Understanding (psychology). Humanities classes add to the school's offerings, but as one student said, "liberal studies" are slacker majors at a college where laboratory work is highly valued. Most students will find their schedule dominated by technical courses.

Another aspect of the "learn-by-doing" philosophy is the commitment to small classes. One senior said that he had "only had a handful" of classes that had more than 35 students in his four years at Cal Poly. Another student said that classes usually have fewer than 60 people for lectures and less than 16 for labs. Small classes allow for close contact with professors, who are "very willing to help" and "really try to get to know the students." One student said that a professor's office hours "help tremendously in getting to know the teacher, which will hopefully help your grade as a result."

Although situated in sunny California right by the beach, Cal Poly students know how to get down to work. As one student said, "the grade scale really depends on which department the class you're in is from. An A in a philosophy department class doesn't mean the same as an A in a physics class." Not surprising for a tech school, the majority of students major in engineering, technology, or science-related fields. Students claim that the toughest majors include Materials, Electrical and Aeronautical Engineering, and Architecture. On the other side of the coin, "slacker majors" include Business, Liberal Arts, Child Development, and IT-industrial technology, commonly known as "I Tried."

California Dreamin'

The town of San Luis Obispo, or "SLO" in campus slang, is a small, comfortable town on the California coastline, halfway between Los Angeles and San Francisco. Students at Cal Poly love spending time outdoors in the West Coast warmth. The hills and beaches around the town provide plenty of opportunities to take a well-needed break from studying. The diversity of natural attractions gives students different options for exercise; biking, hiking, and swimming are all popular depending on the season. One student professed, "the weather is perfect: not too hot and not too cold. The sky is bright blue, the trees are luscious green, and the sun is shining." Perhaps due to the cheery weather, SLO is also home to a "great social element." The sun naturally draws people from their studies to mix and mingle around campus. One student explained, "You always see people you know around, but it's not too congested, and there are always new people to meet."

This social charm carries forward into the weekends, which typically include a mix of entertainment. Outdoor activities, shopping, partying, and studying complete a student's weekend routine. Although the college administration claims Cal Poly is a dry campus, students say that drinking is popular yet does not pose much of a problem. One student even claimed, "everyone drinks in lab all the time." Another student who said that she wasn't personally a part of the drinking scene did comment that the students who do drink "aren't big drinkers. They are not the type to get drunk every weekend." Students say that Greek life on campus is also not very important for those who are not involved, but plays a big role for those who choose to spend their time with other fraternity and sorority members. Similarly, students do not boast much school spirit for their sports teams. However, there is an opportunity for more athletic-minded students to participate in a variety of intramural sports.

Other options for entertainment around town include the U-U Hour. Every Thursday afternoon the school hosts the University Union Hour, where no classes are scheduled and different bands play outside in the university's main quad. When in the mood to study, students often frequent coffee shops, including "some of the best," such as Linnea's, Uptown, Rudolph's, and the "infamous Starbucks." Another student said that "Juliens is the best coffee shop ever. Woodstock's is always a fun hangout, as are the bars downtown."

"An A in a philosophy department class doesn't mean the same as an A in a physics class."

After boasting about the school's surrounding landscapes, students complain most vigorously about Cal Poly's buildings, housing, and parking. "The campus is older," said one student. "We have mostly Spanish-style buildings. The newer ones are concrete from the 1950s that look like war bunkers." Construction is in constant motion as Cal Poly renovates older buildings from the mid-1900s and builds new ones, including a new building for the College of Architecture and Environmental Design and a new Center for Science and Mathematics. One undergrad assessed the situation by spouting, "The construction is ridiculous around town. It never ends, and it's very frustrating. It's not so bad on campus, though, but parking is a huge problem still." Parking tends to be a pain for all students except for freshmen, who are guaranteed on-campus housing and don't have to worry about a vehicle. Upperclassmen (who mostly live off campus) have to struggle to get to school, but cars aren't a necessity and usually "a bike will do."

A Typical Student?

According to Cal Poly students, a typical undergraduate "wears sandals year-round and a light sweater for most of the year" due to the town's beautiful weather. Some undergrads claim that Cal Poly students belong to the "preppy" stereotype, and wear clothing from the Gap, Abercrombie & Fitch, and J. Crew. One student mused, "More students at Cal Poly could be mistaken for high school kids than at other universities. That wears off a little after their freshman year, though."

In general, the student body at Cal Poly is dominated by white, upper-middle-class Californians. Students say that the student body is "not really" diverse, although a good number of Hispanic and Asian students do attend the school. One undergrad estimated that the student body is about 75 percent white, but did not mention any segregation among the different ethnicities.

Cal Poly students know that they are fortunate to obtain a valuable technical education with a hands-on learning approach, while having California's beautiful mountains and beaches as their playground. Students like to think that very few other universities could offer such a wonderful combination. As one student said, Cal Poly is "perfect for me. It wouldn't fit everyone, though. What differentiates it is that it is a highly regarded school in a very small town. You don't get that very often." For prospective students looking for a great technical education combined with even greater weather, Cal Poly might just be the place for you, too. —*Lisa Siciliano*

FYI

If you come to Cal Poly, you'd better bring "a bike."

What is the typical weekend schedule? "Sleeping, any kind of outdoor activity, shopping, partying, and then studying on Sunday."

If I could change one thing about Cal Poly, I'd improve "the quality of the architecture labs and campus landscaping."

Three things that every student at Cal Poly should do before graduating are "attend U-U hour, take a bowling class, and do a study abroad program through the school."

California State University / Chico

Address: 400 West First Street; Chico, CA 95929-0722
Phone: 800-542-4426
E-mail address: info@csuchico.edu
Web site URL: www.csuchico.edu
Founded: 1887
Private or Public: public
Religious affiliation: none
Location: rural
Undergraduate enrollment: 14,356
Total enrollment: NA
Percent Male/Female: 47%/53%
Percent Minority: 18%
Percent African-American: 2%
Percent Asian: 5%
Percent Hispanic: 10%
Percent Native-American: 1%
Percent in-state/out of state: 98%/2%
Percent Pub HS: NA
Number of Applicants: 8,502
Percent Accepted: 78%
Percent Accepted who enroll: 31%
Entering: 2,037
Transfers: 1,234
Application Deadline: 30 Nov
Mean SAT: NA
Mean ACT: NA
Middle 50% SAT range: V 460-560 M 470-580
Middle 50% ACT range: 18-24
3 Most popular majors: business, liberal arts, social sciences
Retention: 80%
Graduation rate: 46%
On-campus housing: 12%
Fraternities: 6%
Sororities: 7%
Library: 942,322 volumes
Tuition and Fees: $2,275 in; $10,735 out
Room and Board: $7,245
Financial aid, first-year: NA
Varsity or Club Athletes: NA
Early Decision or Early Action Acceptance Rate: NA

California State University at Chico is set among the foothills of the Sierra Nevada Mountains. The campus is replete with matching brick buildings, "tons of trees and flowers," and the Big Chico Creek running through its center. Strolling around Chico, one often finds students and locals wandering through the twice-weekly farmers market that fills the streets of the small town; its homey feel welcomes students warmly.

A Varied Environment

Though some students feel isolated, others rave about the beauty of their surroundings: "Ten minutes from here there is snow, and five minutes the other direction is fishing, hiking, and the best mountain biking in the country." Students are quick to take advantage of their beautiful location. The salmon fishing is reported to be fantastic, and Chico also boasts Feather Falls, the sixth-largest waterfall in the country. A university-sponsored program, "Adventure Outings," takes groups of students on outdoor expeditions. They also offer day-long classes on subjects such as wilderness survival. The group has sponsored whitewater rafting, long hiking trips, and even ventured outside of the country. Students looking for a less formal hike or mountain-biking trip walk downtown to Bidwell Park, a huge area with watering holes, places to relax, and a massive trail system.

Hitting the Books

Students don't flock to Chico for the environment alone; many believe that the small class size and the accessible professors are the school's best assets. The undergraduate program consists of six academic colleges as well as a School of Nursing and a College of Business. While core requirements are strenuous, students have few complaints. The average class size is 35 students. Students study diligently during the week, but admit that their books gather dust when the weekend hits.

TRAC, a telephone registration process, makes selecting classes easy, allowing students to plan their schedules up to two years ahead of time. Students report having very little trouble getting into the classes they want. An honors program is available to incoming freshmen with a high school GPA of 3.5 or higher. This program offers more one-on-one attention from professors, smaller classes with an average of 12 students, and an off-campus Honors House. Even if not enrolled in the honors program, students get to know their professors very well. "You see your professors out and about with the students." TAs are very rare, but when present, they get rave reviews as being very in touch with students' needs. Students claim that the friendly atmosphere and size of school leads to more networking with professors and other students, and therefore better jobs after graduation.

Dorm Living

Freshmen live in the dorms, which are coed by hall, and consist of small double rooms with "jail beds." The Resident Assistants program in the dorms is quite strict, as the campus is ". . . supposed to be . . . uhh, is, a dry campus." Any student caught with alcohol on campus must endure harsh penalties including community service and attendance at alcohol-related classes. Shafta is a dorm specifically for transfer students, while Whitney Hall is the largest dorm and the only one containing a dining hall. Sophomores traditionally move into Creekside Apartments and the upperclassmen to other off-campus complexes. The dorms tend to be noisy, and have recently become overcrowded.

Students linger over meals in the dining hall to chat about the weekend, but upperclassmen tend to avoid eating there altogether. Rather they choose to use their meal cards at the student union, the BMU, sometimes referred to as "the Moo." Here students gather at The Rainbow Cafe, a snack area where they can pay or use their meal cards. Students also frequent other area restaurants.

Wildcat Spirit

Cheering for the school colors—maroon and white—is also a popular activity. The football team was recently cut completely in order to fund golf and swimming teams, though few students seem upset by the loss. The gym itself is unpopular, with students choosing instead to join independent local gyms. The basketball and baseball teams are particularly popular.

The Greeks

The Greek system at Chico is a prominent part of campus life. Approximately 40 percent of students join either a sorority or fraternity. The Greeks also sponsor intramural games for less serious athletes, and this often attracts students to the Greek system. Though a division exists between those within the system and those outside of it, students claim that the division is neither extreme nor hostile. The Greek organizations on campus host parties, which are well attended. Students do not date traditionally, but rather travel in large groups. The largest Greek-sponsored activity is Greek Week, a week filled with activities, including relay races to benefit various charities.

"The students are laid-back party animals."

Halloween is the biggest social event of the year; people park all along the streets and get out their folding chairs to watch the costume parade-a town tradition. During this party, which lasts the whole week, the population of Chico nearly doubles. Parties abound, and students wander the streets attending haunted houses and admiring each others' costumes.

Local bands often frequent the Chico campus, and distinguished visitors are also common. The Cherry Poppin' Daddies and Red Hot Chili Peppers are bands who have played in front of the Rose Garden, a large grassy area backed by a large garden of roses. Prominent speakers such as the President of the Honda Corporation have also made appearances. A Free Speech area allows campus groups to voice their opinions and gain support for their causes.

Chico is home to the Sierra Nevada Brewery, and many students are proud to drink their locally brewed ales. Going to bars is a favorite weekend activity, with the Bear, a restaurant and bar, and the Crazy Horse, which has a mechanical bull, rating among the top hot spots off-campus. The beverage of choice remains beer, though martinis are a close second. Texas Tea, a stronger version of a Long Island Iced Tea, is thought to have developed in Chico. Students also say that marijuana is prevalent on campus.

Students laud the friendliness of Chico, and say that it is not unusual to smile and wave as they stroll across campus. The student body in general is quite liberal. In fact, the town of Chico holds the largest per capita lesbian population in California. Largely consisting of preppy, middle-class students, diversity at Chico is small, but improving. Described as "laid-back party animals," students are very happy with their experiences at Chico. "It is the typical college experience that you see in the movies," explained one student. Renowned for their partying, Chico students describe themselves as social: "We're like an island, secluded, but we still know how to have a good time." —*Cynthia Matthews*

FYI

If you come to Chico, you'd better bring "a spirit for the outdoors and the equipment to match."

What is the typical weekend schedule? "Friday: bars; Saturday: party, hiking or mountain biking; Sunday: relax."

If I could change one thing about Chico, I'd "make the drinking rules more lenient."

Three things every student at Chico should do before graduating are "see Feather Falls, participate in Adventure Outing, and share a glass of Sierra Nevada's best with a friend."

California State University / Fresno

Address: 5150 North Maple; Fresno, CA 93740-8026
Phone: 559-278-2261
E-mail address: vivian_franco@csufresno.edu
Web site URL: www.csufresno.edu
Founded: 1911
Private or Public: public
Religious affiliation: none
Location: urban
Undergraduate enrollment: 17,338
Total enrollment: NA
Percent Male/Female: 43%/57%
Percent Minority: 44%
Percent African-American: 4%
Percent Asian: 12%
Percent Hispanic: 27%
Percent Native-American: 1%
Percent in-state/out of state: 99%/1%
Percent Pub HS: NA
Number of Applicants: 9,013
Percent Accepted: 66%
Percent Accepted who enroll: 34%
Entering: 2,005
Transfers: 1,974
Application Deadline: 28 July
Mean SAT: NA
Mean ACT: NA
Middle 50% SAT range: V 400-530, M 420-550
Middle 50% ACT range: 16-22
3 Most popular majors: humanities, business administration, social sciences
Retention: 78%
Graduation rate: 41%
On-campus housing: 6%
Fraternities: 3%
Sororities: 3%
Library: 977,198 volumes
Tuition and Fees: $2,275 in; $10,735 out
Room and Board: $7,245
Financial aid, first-year: NA
Varsity or Club Athletes: NA
Early Decision or Early Action Acceptance Rate: NA

Looking for an urban agriculture school? Interested in education, engineering, or health sciences? In the center of the state of California, between San Francisco and Los Angeles, lie Fresno and California State University, Fresno (a.k.a. Fresno State University). In the past decade, the city has developed into a metropolis, home to many software and Internet companies, and the university has matured into a diverse and well-respected state school.

Diversity is one of Fresno's strongest points. As one student put it, "There is awesome racial and ethnic diversity at this school, which I have not seen in many places, it truly makes it fantastic." In the heart of the San Joaquin Valley, Fresno has the resources and enthusiasm that make for an incredible agricultural department. However, it doesn't stop there. Students all have particular interests and ideas, preventing Fresno State from becoming an exclusively agriculture school. According to students, Fresno has highly respected education, engineering, health sciences, and criminology departments. "It can be hard to get into the more popular majors, but it's totally worth it," one student commented.

The Brain Part

Freshman and sophomore years at Fresno are mostly spent fulfilling General Education requirements, commonly known as the "breadth." These classes strive to "expose students to a variety of disciplines within a structured framework." A relatively new format has been adopted, expanding the program and dividing it into four basic categories. Now students will be required to take their 21 class GE requirements from each of the four groups: "Foundation, Breadth, Integration, and Multicultural / International Studies."

Along with this change in format, Fresno State has adopted an ambitious program to improve the school, both academically and socially. The staff and faculty's "Vision for the 21st Century" included the development of an honors program, an intensification of research projects, and an increase in the overall diversity of the campus. The president of the university and his staff are "extremely committed to this school and its improvement," said one student.

The "breadth" allows students to explore many different areas before selecting a major, and is rarely an obstacle when it comes to taking classes in which one is interested. A second-year student confessed, "There are usually a few classes in the divisions that are required by your major anyway." Some of the required courses include a speech course and an English class. While many frosh are daunted by the prospect of giving speeches, this, according to one third-year, is the point, "Every student should take a good speech class their freshman year; it helps bring out some of those shy ones."

Getting into the classes you want is rarely a problem. Even students in popular majors, such as animal science, still found that they were almost never barred from a class and that most of the introductory courses remained relatively small. However, in some instances, when the phone registration system failed to cap the numbers registered, popular courses could end up with up to 300 people. On average, introductory science courses reportedly tend to enroll between 80 and 100 students, but most English and speech courses for freshmen are capped at 30. While few students have had problems with TAs teaching courses, as one junior stated, she has "had a few problems with teachers not being able to speak English too well."

There aren't any notorious "slacker majors," or awful classes that everyone avoids. As one student pointed out, "Everyone has their own hopes and aspirations, which of course gives way for diversity"—one of Fresno's greatest qualities.

To escape the distractions of dorm or apartment life, many students choose to study in the Henry Madden Library, which is large enough and modern enough to accommodate a number of different study areas. Moreover, the digital "card catalog" is accessible from any computer.

The Life Part

Student life at Fresno centers around the University Student Union (USU). This building contains many student resources, including a food court, bank, post office, Tower Records, information center, lounge, balcony (for enjoying the beautiful California weather), administrative offices, graphic design center, and meeting rooms for student organizations. In the recreation center one can find billiards, bowling, chess, cards, pinball, video games, and even dominoes. "One could never leave the college and still have an awesome four years," noted one student.

However, most students do choose to leave campus occasionally. While Fresno is not a "commuter school," a fair number of students do live at home, and most after freshman year choose to live off campus. Generally people have cars and if they don't live in one of the "tons of apartments located very close to campus and at reasonable costs," then there are houses within a five- to 10-minute drive.

"If I had to go back and pick a school again, I would pick Fresno . . . the campus is beautiful and the diversity amongst students and faculty is incredible."

Dorms are without question a "great way for frosh to meet people," and most of them are organized "like mini-apartments." The bathrooms are single-sex and "the facilities are actually very nice." However, there are Resident Advisors (RAs) and certain "strictly enforced" regulations. Only eight people are allowed in a room at a time, and quiet hours are enforced from 11 P.M. to 7 A.M. on weekdays, and from 1 A.M. to 7 A.M. on weekends. In addition, there are no kegs allowed on campus.

When not in their rooms, students participate in a variety of activities, from varsity athletics to jobs to community service. On weekends, one sophomore found that "Fresno does not have that much to offer if you are under 21." However, there are movie theaters, restaurants, and clubs located near campus. People do date regularly, and it is not uncommon to see couples walking around the school. Great date spots are Romano's Macaroni Grill, the Bulldog Café, and later in the evening, Williker's or Baja's. Fresno is located almost exactly between San Francisco and Los Angeles, making both a four-hour drive away, a distant, but not impossible, weekend excursion. Closer by are Shaver Lake and Yosemite, two "beautiful escapes from urban life."

The Outside World

Fresno State's 327-acre main campus and its 1,083-acre University Farm are located at the northeast edge of Fresno, California, at the foot of the Sierra Nevada mountain range. The San Joaquin Valley, one of the richest agricultural areas in the world, surrounds the city. Fresno is the sixth-largest metropolitan area in California and has all the amenities of a major urban area.

The campus itself is spread out enough to seem full of lawn and trees, yet not so large that one can't walk to classes. Sitting in the middle of campus one would find "a large fountain with a row of roses up the center of campus . . . with trees and a grassy area." Directly across are the Student Union and the bookstore.

While crime is a problem off campus, within Fresno State there are special designated paths that are very well lit at night, and there are emergency phones scattered throughout campus. In regards to on-campus crime, one student warned, "just like anywhere else, be wary; it's a cool place to meet people, but always keep your eyes open." A third-year added, "I feel safe on campus for the most part, but having a late class is not always a good thing." While for many students living in such an urban environment is quite a shock, the sizable number of students from surrounding areas creates an excellent town-gown relationship. Fresno State has grown up with the city, for the benefit of both, and that connection is not easily forgotten. Every year the Associated Student Body puts on Vintage Days, a celebration where people from all over the Central Valley come together for wine tastings, antique auto shows, sales, and other entertainment. Non-students also find interest in the University due to its dynamic sports teams, where the Red Wave (Fresno fans, wearing their color, "cardinal") have managed to break multiple records in numbers of spectators attending competitions.

The Cheering Part

Varsity sports are a huge part of Fresno State life, ranging from football to the equestrian team. The Bulldog Stadium was expanded to add 11,000 seats to accommodate the increasing number of fans. The fans, called the Red Wave, financially support the entire Fresno athletic program. The athletic boosters club, Bulldog Foundation, has also had the number-one fund drive since 1986. While football reigns as the most popular sport on campus, the men's basketball team is "a close second" and the men's basketball team's new coach Ray Lopes has been making a splash and leading the team to numerous victories. Enthusiasm for athletics infects everyone at Fresno; as one student put it, "the sports here at Fresno are awesome. I really don't know too much about their programs, but the facilities and the games are always good."

And those facilities have gotten even better. The Save Mart Center opened in the fall of 2001 and is an arena for Bulldog basketball, volleyball, and wrestling. Sponsored primarily by Save Mart and Pepsi, this facility serves not only for sporting events, but also concerts and cultural gatherings. It includes classrooms, banquet facilities, shops, and a gym. The enthusiasm of the student body and the surrounding population for sports is responsible for its creation. The Red Wave is "deafening" at games, and literally looks like a "sea of red" in their Fresno school color.

Fresno State is a school with "an endless amount of opportunities, and a highly involved staff." It enjoys an urban setting in a rural area, meaning students have the best of both worlds. The school is diverse both in students and in faculty, allowing learning to span far beyond the classroom. —*Kyla Dahlin*

FYI

If you come to Fresno State, you'd better bring "some sunscreen—it's easy to sit down on the grass or under a tree and end up with a sunburn."

What is the typical weekend schedule? "Go out on Friday and Saturday nights—mostly at dance clubs or frat parties."

If I could change one thing about Fresno State, I'd "increase the number of students accepted into certain academic programs like Nursing or Physical Therapy."

Three things everyone should do before graduation are "go to Shaver Lake, go to Vintage days, and participate in as many activities as possible."

The Claremont Colleges

The Claremont Colleges are a cluster of five small liberal arts colleges and two graduate schools, nestled in a suburban valley about 35 miles east of Los Angeles. The member colleges are Claremont McKenna, Harvey Mudd, Pitzer, Pomona, and Scripps, as well as Claremont Graduate University and Keck Graduate Institute, both of which are separate from the undergraduate colleges. Each college is independent, with its own faculty, campus, and academic focus. However, the schools' being adjacent to one another gives their respective students the best of both worlds: the feel of a small college with the resources of a large university.

Academic Integration

Cross-registration of classes between the colleges is easy and commonplace. The five campuses make up about 12 blocks total, so commuting is not a problem. Since each college has a particular academic focus and expertise, students can take advantage of specialized instructions in almost every subject. Claremont McKenna offers 26 majors with strengths in economics, government, and international relations. Harvey Mudd specializes in science and engineering with the option of a five-year master's program. Pitzer offers liberal arts majors with an emphasis on social and behavioral sciences. Pomona offers a variety of majors in arts, humanities, and social and natural sciences with a para-professional bent. Scripps is a liberal arts college for women. All the libraries are integrated as is the campus bookstore.

Campuswide Activities

The Claremont Colleges are also linked through athletic, social, and extracurricular activities. Pitzer and Pomona together comprise a NCAA Division III team, while Claremont McKenna, Harvey Mudd, and Scripps make up another. However, most athletic competition is usually among one another. Parties thrown in one college draw people from the other colleges. And there are several all-college parties thrown throughout the year. Many student organizations are comprised of undergrads from all the colleges, including the Claremont Collage, the student daily newspaper; the Claremont Colleges Model U.N.; and the Claremont Shades, an a cappella group. The Claremont Center is the hub for social groups, organizations, and administrations on each campus, and orchestrates the activities of all five schools.

As integrated as the five colleges are, they still retain distinct characteristics, and prospective students should look to find the right fit. As one student summed it up, "It's really a matter of your academic interests as well as your personality. There is something for everyone at each of the colleges, but one college will definitely be the best fit." —*Seung Lee*

Claremont McKenna College

Address: 890 Columbia Avenue; Claremont, CA 91711-6425
Phone: 909-621-8088
E-mail address: admission@claremontmckenna.edu
Web site URL: www.claremontmckenna.edu
Founded: 1946
Private or Public: private
Religious affiliation: none
Location: suburban
Undergraduate enrollment: 1,027
Total enrollment: NA
Percent Male/Female: 53%/47%
Percent Minority: 29%
Percent African-American: 4%
Percent Asian: 15%
Percent Hispanic: 9%
Percent Native-American: 1%
Percent in-state/out of state: 49%/51%
Percent Pub HS: NA
Number of Applicants: 2,918
Percent Accepted: 28%
Percent Accepted who enroll: 31%
Entering: 250
Transfers: 36
Application Deadline: 2 Jan
Mean SAT: NA
Mean ACT: NA
Middle 50% SAT range: V 650-740, M 660-740
Middle 50% ACT range: 28-32
3 Most popular majors: economics, political science
Retention: 94%
Graduation rate: 84%
On-campus housing: 96%
Fraternities: NA
Sororities: NA
Library: 998,823
Tuition and Fees: $27,770
Room and Board: $9,180
Financial aid, first-year: 57%
Varsity or Club Athletes: NA
Early Decision or Early Action Acceptance Rate: ED 31%

Claremont McKenna College fits the portrait of a small, cozy liberal arts college almost perfectly. Nestled in Claremont, California, this tiny Southern California school offers its students an intimate environment to bond with peers and professors. At the same time, four other colleges in the Claremont system provide a larger community feeling and an outlet from the limiting factor of a smaller school, making Claremont McKenna a school that can be whatever size a student wants it to be. With a solid academic program, plenty of college-wide activities, and a number of clubs, CMC offers a personalized and community-oriented experience.

Classes No Joke

Claremont's academic reputation and standards are very high. Students must complete twelve General Education (GE) requirements in addition to the nine or ten specific to their major, with an overall graduation requirement of 32 courses. The GE classes are spread among several different disciplines, but everyone has to take the "primary four," which is a specific set of economics, history and government classes. Other requirements include one class of choice in the humanities, foreign literature, philosophy, religious studies, and two in literature. Most students actually enjoy the benefits of GE requirements because they get a solid liberal arts education. "The system [also] encourages you to figure out what you *want* to major in as you go along." Students are also free to cross-register in the four surrounding colleges if a class is not offered on campus.

Although about fifty percent of classes may be taught lecture style, these "lectures" are hardly the normal college lecture—an intimate feel in the classroom is evident, for about ninety percent of classes are twenty students or fewer. "Our professors actually know us," one student remarked. And class dinners are a common occurance. The smaller classroom atmosphere provides opportunity for discussion and unique projects. One student reminisced about a final project for an organizational psychology course that involved establishing an imaginary corporation, inventing a product, marketing it on campus, and taking student surveys to see how it would sell.

CMCs government and economics departments are their strongest, and approximately seventy five percent of undergrads major in one or the other. Some of the earlier economics courses in particular are more difficult to discourage the fainter of heart from the major. The lack of science and engineering majors is reflective of the school's humanities emphasis, but those who do survive the pre-med path are rewarded upon graduation: a very high ninety percent of them get into medical school.

Despite the small feel of the school, administrative issues can sometimes be a hassle. CMC still does registration manually, which often makes for a long, drawn-out process for getting classes. Although "persistence usually pays, getting into popular classes can be tough" and students comment that the bureaucratic aspect of signing up each semester "really needs to be moved online." This is something administration says is in the works for next year.

School-Centric Social Life

An important connection between academics and social life at CMC is the Athenaeum, a place designated for speakers and classes to convene outside the classroom environment. It consists of a large auditorium where speakers or performers can be found four nights a week. Its two connected rooms are reserved as a professors' space for class with a guest speaker. "We get the really awesome chance to talk to the speakers in an informal environment," explained one student. All students in CMC and those members from the other four Claremont colleges on a meal plan are invited to the performances, which include dinner. Recent speakers in the Athenaeum have included Newt Gingrich and Aaron McGrudder, the animator of the comic strip "Boondocks." As one student put it, "sometimes there are people who aren't famous outside their fields, but it is still incredible to hear them talk."

Claremont McKenna is very much a residential college, and students say that "you work here, you sleep here, you go out here . . . you live here." Consequently, social life generally revolves around parties and events on campus. The five Claremont colleges sponsor many events collectively and students from all five schools often attend these large parties. "Most of the parties during weekends are either pre- or post-parties for some larger campus event," said one student. There is no Greek life, but the college council is creative in planning a wide variety of events: the Monte Carlo, the Claremont Formal held during Homecoming, Sumo Wrestling Night, and interesting theme parties like foam or nakedness (held primarily at Pomona) are all well attended.

"You work here, you sleep here, you go out here . . . you live here."

Campus administration recognizes the prevalence of alcohol in colleges, and the school buys kegs for campus-wide events. Underage drinking is discouraged, however, and all events with alcohol must have security and a definitive carding policy. Most drink, but others say "alcohol doesn't have to rule your life." There is music and drama to appreciate and comedy to laugh at every weekend on campus, and since most students have cars, it is possible to escape the confines of CMC to procure adventure elsewhere.

Around Campus

CMC itself sponsors fifty clubs and there are an additional hundred and fifty that are spread amongst all five colleges. Most students are active in at least one extracurricular activity, and the majority participates in at least one sport, varsity or intramural. The school, whose teams are Division III and do not recruit, is still able to get riled up about many of its athletic events. Proud students run around the goals with a giant flag after each goal is scored in soccer games and the big football game against Redlands University every year draws a sizable crowd.

Living conditions at Claremont McKenna are generally praised. With mild weather year-round and an idyllic campus, students spend a lot of time outside, which fosters the family spirit. Dorms themselves are monitored by RAs who are encouraged to enforce the rules, but "really are college students that understand what it is to be in college." Students are required to live on campus only their freshman year, but ninety-six percent of students elect to continue living on campus after. There are a variety of housing options: North Quad offers suite living, MidQuad offers standard double hallway-style living, and on-campus apartments. Although the apartments are located "very far away," they do include kitchens and living rooms which "makes living there worth it." The food "isn't bad" and students are given a number of dining options. Meals can be used anywhere among the five colleges, and each campus offers a dining hall where full meals can be eaten and an eating alternative that takes cash or "flex dollars." For example, Pitzer offers the "Grove House," which sells smoothies and sandwiches. Claremont McKenna's alternative is the "Hub," a grill that caters to college students' need for snacks and fried food.

The city of Claremont itself is more or a less a "bedroom community," with little commercial activity. However, the beaches in the surrounding area are frequented by all and spice up the suburban feel. The spread out nature of Southern California makes having a car a definite bonus, but in all, students seem to be satisfied with their lives on campus. CMC is what students make of it, whether they branch out to the other four colleges, or whether they focus their attentions on their own tightly knit campus community. Either way, Claremont offers an enriching academic experience in a tranquil setting. *—Stephanie Teng*

FYI

If you come to Claremont McKenna, you'd better bring "shorts, sunscreen, and a refrigerator to hold all the free beer."

The typical weekend schedule includes: "Friday: hit up a BBQ or the pool, find a good off-campus event; Saturday: go to the 5C (5 College) party; Sunday: brunch and catch up on work."

If I could change one thing about Claremont McKenna, I'd "make the student body less Californian."

Three things everyone should do before graduating are: "complete the CMC 'triathalon,' including going to the beach, skiing, and hitting Las Vegas all in one day, take a class from Marc Massoud, and get 'ponded' on your birthday."

Harvey Mudd College

Address: 301 East 12th Street; Claremont, CA 91711-5990
Phone: 909-621-8011
E-mail address: admission@hmc.edu
Web site URL: www.hmc.edu
Founded: 1955
Private or Public: private
Religious affiliation: none
Location: suburban
Undergraduate enrollment: 703
Total enrollment: NA
Percent Male/Female: 67%/33%
Percent Minority: 24%
Percent African-American: 0%
Percent Asian: 18%
Percent Hispanic: 5%
Percent Native-American: 1%
Percent in-state/out of state: 41%/59%
Percent Pub HS: 80%
Number of Applicants: 1,669
Percent Accepted: 37%
Percent Accepted who enroll: 30%
Entering: 187
Transfers: 9
Application Deadline: 15 Jan
Mean SAT: NA
Mean ACT: NA
Middle 50% SAT range: V 650-750,M 720-790
Middle 50% ACT range: NA
3 Most popular majors: engineering, computer science, physics
Retention: 95%
Graduation rate: 79%
On-campus housing: 96%
Fraternities: NA
Sororities: NA
Library: 2,380,457 volumes
Tuition and Fees: $29,794
Room and Board: $7,796
Financial aid, first-year: 34%
Varsity or Club Athletes: 5%
Early Decision or Early Action Acceptance Rate: EA 55%

Strolling past its basic concrete buildings—covered in "warts" (random, purposeless square protrusions), one might never recognize the intense learning that occurs within the walls of Harvey Mudd. Harvey Mudd's no-frills exterior projects its hard working interior. It is no secret: Harvey Mudd is no walk in the park. Though listed as a liberal arts school, Mudd's curriculum is geared towards the scientifically inclined. The school offers only seven majors: physics, math, computer science, engineering, chemistry, biology, and math / CS. These heavily technical majors are earned through an intense four years of work. When asked about gut courses, one Mudd student responded, "To tell you the truth, I've never even heard that phrase before. I think that's just a foreign concept here. You come here with the assumption that all your classes will be hard."

No Guts, But Such Glory

Students agree that classes are hard but believe that Mudd's programs make it worthwhile. At such a science-concentrated school, students are able to obtain research opportunities not present at other schools. Another part of the Harvey Mudd experience is the clinic program. Designed to give students hands-on experience in their future professions, the clinic program introduces many out of classroom skills vital to work survival. Corporations such as Kodak or Techtronics contact the school with particular problems, and groups of five or so students join together to solve them. Their creations are working prototypes that often eventually become products employed by the companies. The clinic program is far from an elite activity for only the brightest at Mudd. In fact, all students majoring in a related area are required to participate in a clinic.

Another trademark of the Harvey Mudd experience is intense academic study. A typical day for a student would include three or four classes, which for most unfortunate freshmen, start at eight or nine A.M. Nights are often consumed by the eight or ten hours of homework that professors assign. At Mudd, the majority of exams are given as take home tests, which often take hours to complete. Mudders don't hide the fact that for them, college does mean a lot of work.

All Work and All Play

With such an intense academic program, it is not surprising that Mudders are also strong believers in the idea of "play as hard as you work." They may be passionate students, but when the weekend arrives the social scene comes alive on campus. With a budget of $38,000 per semester devoted entirely to entertainment, weekends are filled with original and creative parties. Everything from tequila nights and roses for all the girls to Nevada night and parties with batting cages, Mudders really know how to brighten the twilight hours.

> **"It's going to be hard, you should come here knowing that you're going to work hard, but just know that everything you put into it, you'll get out of it. No matter what, you'll find your place here."**

But if partying isn't your scene, there is still a place for you at Harvey Mudd. Students are split into dorms based on detailed questionnaires that determine a student's studying style and social habits. Each dorm carries its own personality and a separate social circle. Do you love sports? You'll find yourself at home in the North Dorm, the stereotypically "jock dorm". Of a quieter mind? Down in South Dorm a more serene atmosphere exists for those who prefer the peace. Living amongst the more socially tame are unique and quirky groups such as the unicyclers. Mudd's slightly bizarre claim to fame is the high percentage of unicyclers that circle the campus. For an unbeknownst reason, travel by one wheel is of abnormal popularity—just another example of Mudd's diverse personality. One student ventured to admit, "There are definitely some strange people here. During one of the speeches given at orientation it was said that, 'All of us have some nerd tendencies, but just to varying degrees.'"

Spacious Living

Housing for this eclectic collection of science lovers isn't too shabby at all. The spacious rooms come in various styles, from suites to singles and doubles, and are furnished with the basics for student life. With an average of only four students to each bathroom, the inevitable fight for the shower each morning may only be a small standoff, rather than a full-on battle. Freshman enjoy the benefit of being integrated within upperclassmen in dorms, providing them with interaction with those who may help them assimilate to campus life.

Amongst these upperclassmen is the ever-present authority figure, a college residential advisor. Known as proctors at Mudd, RA's play a slightly less fearful role, their presence more as a parental figure than policeman. "They're job is not to make sure people don't drink, but to make sure people don't hurt themselves. The school lets the students take care of each other and take care of themselves," one freshman stated.

The community lifestyle is instilled in students as soon as they reach campus. Each freshman is assigned an upperclassman sponsor who takes them through orientation, on shopping trips, and generally helps them through the first couple of days of college. Beyond that, throughout the year students find themselves taking care of one another. As on student put it, "You're all writing the same paper at four in the morning, so you look out for each other."

There is, however, some faculty support as well. When first arriving at Mudd, each student is given a freshman advisor who help students choose classes and sign off on schedules through the third semester. Afterward, students are given a choice as to which faculty member they want as an academic advisor. In addition to the academic advisor, students also have a humanities advisor, who guides them through the task of fulfilling Mudd's high humanities requirements.

The Fab Five

Harvey Mudd, though a very science oriented school, is listed as a liberal arts college, and has the graduation requirements back that claim. A third of the average student's classes will be more humanities oriented classes. In fact, ten courses of humanities beyond the freshman classes are required for any degree, four or five of which must be in the same concentration. Five of the classes must also be on campus.

Which brings up the question, five on campus? Where else would they be from? At Mudd class selection is not limited to the science heavy course manual. Harvey Mudd also has the unique quality of being a part of the Claremont College System, or 5C system. As one of five schools in this southern Californian town, its students can cross register for courses at any of the other four colleges. Can't find a course that goes in depth into Russian literature at Mudd? Simply go across the street to Scripps or to nearby Pomona to find the classes the Mudd may be lacking.

Classes aren't the only things students in the 5C system share. Everything from gym facilities to dining halls are communal. When Mudd students sometimes find the menu repetitive (it's cycled every four weeks) or slightly greasy, they simply can head to one of the other four dining halls. Sports teams are also a group effort. Harvey Mudd's NCAA athletic teams are formed in collaboration with Claremont McKenna and Scripps, while Pitzer and Pomona make up another team. Most club sports, and other extracurricular activities for that matter, are shared between the five schools.

The 5C system also provides a broader social scene, allowing students to go beyond the tiny Harvey Mudd campus. With a ratio of females to males that one student jokingly pointed out was, "nothing significant to a ton", Mudd men may find relationships a little hard to come by were it not for Scripps, an all female college, just across the street. Coupling within Mudd students is also difficult because of the schools small town feel. With such a small class, gossip travels fast. To avoid the chatter of curious classmates, most students look to one of the other four colleges to find romance.

Despite the work, Mudd students are proud of where they are. What makes it all worth it? One student answered, "The fun and knowing everyone here will be doing something cool." Students looking at Harvey Mudd should recognize that, "its going to be hard, you should come here knowing that you're going to work hard, but just know that everything you put into it, you'll get out of it. No matter what, you'll find your place here." —*Vivian Hsu*

FYI

If you come to Harvey Mudd, you better bring "an air conditioner. It's hot!"

What is the typical weekend schedule? "Friday: classes, a relaxed afternoon with some work, the dorm BBQ for dinner, and parties through the night starting at nine. Saturday: a late brunch, homework or sports or clubs to fill the day, dinner at another college cuz it isn't too good on Saturday then off to parties. Sunday: a late rise and homework . . . all day."

If I could change one thing about Harvey Mudd, I'd "want there to be more attractive women."

Three things every student at Harvey Mudd should do before graduating are "pull off a big prank, get whirled or showered, and go to Long Tall Glasses (a formal where the drinks are served from, you guessed it, long tall glasses!)."

Pitzer College

Address: 1050 North Mills Avenue; Claremont, CA 91711
Phone: 909-621-8129
E-mail address: admission@pitzer.edu
Web site URL: www.pitzer.edu
Founded: 1963
Private or Public: private
Religious affiliation: none
Location: suburban
Undergraduate enrollment: 954
Total enrollment: 921
Percent Male/Female: 38%/62%
Percent Minority: 32%
Percent African-American: 6%
Percent Asian: 10%
Percent Hispanic: 15%
Percent Native-American: 1%
Percent in-state/out of state: 50%/50%
Percent Pub HS: NA
Number of Applicants: 2,323
Percent Accepted: 56%
Percent Accepted who enroll: 18%
Entering: 235
Transfers: 21
Application Deadline: 15 Jan
Mean SAT: 1218
Mean ACT: 25
Middle 50% SAT range: V 570-670, M 550-670
Middle 50% ACT range: 25-27
3 Most popular majors: social sciences, visual and performing arts, psychology
Retention: 85%
Graduation rate: 66%
On-campus housing: 69%
Fraternities: NA
Sororities: NA
Library: 2,232,086 volumes
Tuition and Fees: $27,150
Room and Board: $9,890
Financial aid, first-year: 52%
Varsity or Club Athletes: 30%
Early Decision or Early Action Acceptance Rate: ED 33%

Known as the most laid back of the Claremont Colleges, Pitzer has developed a reputation that students truly appreciate. With a wide range of course offerings, activities, and opportunities on-campus as well as off, Pitzer has attracted a diverse student population. Students defy the stereotype of "stoner radical left-wing hippie" by getting involved in their community and expressing themselves through various venues at Pitzer.

Best of Both Worlds

Located 35 miles outside of Los Angeles, Pitzer provides students access to both the big city as well as the smaller town of Claremont. This is very important to students because they can easily get off campus with the town nearby, but also make use of everything in LA. The town of Claremont is considered very safe and the campus itself is very manageable because it "is a ten minute walk from the two farthest separate points." Also, because the campuses of the other Claremont Colleges surround it, students have a great number of resources available to them.

Academics: Smaller Is Better

One of the most important things about academics at Pitzer is the small size of the school, because this allows students to form relationships with their professors and delve into the more specific areas of their majors. As one student said, "Because Pitzer is so small, we have the opportunity to take classes with the same professor more than once, which I think is really great." Another way students can become familiar with their teachers is through a program that allows them to bring a faculty member to the dining hall. The idea behind this is to encourage contact between students and professors outside of the classroom.

Another significant aspect of academics is the availability of classes taught at the other colleges in the consortium of the five Clarement Colleges. As one student noted, "One semester I only had one Pitzer class out of my five," attesting to the wide variety of academic options available to students in the Claremont Colleges. Some students do complain about the lack of required courses, but others feel that this gives them more opportunity to take the classes they are interested in and probe more deeply into their majors.

At Pitzer, there are three types of courses: core, breadth, and depth. The first category is for general classes within the major, while depth courses are for focusing within the major. Finally, breadth classes are defined as entirely outside of the major and are required in order to give students a more well-rounded education. One student said these areas provide "an excellent way to graduate broadly knowledgeable students—since you're not allowed to only focus on your strength or major, you learn more, and can apply your knowledge in a cross-disciplinary manner."

Psychology, economics, and sociology are considered the best of the school's departments and are also among the most competitive. Since classes are kept quite small (class size is generally kept somewhere between seven and 20), it can be difficult for students to enroll in the more popular classes. However, with the Joint Classes at the other colleges, there is always something to fulfill a student's academic needs.

Three Dorms . . . Where to Live?

Freshmen are required to live on campus, and most are placed in Sanborn. Starting sophomore year, students have the option to move off campus, but more choose to stay in the dorms. The other two on-campus options are Holden, which is the mirror image of Sanborn and primarily for freshman and sophomores, and Mead. Some sophomores are eligible to live in Mead, though predominantly juniors and seniors live there. As one student said, "Mead tends to be looser about rules," but otherwise the dorms are generally the same. One way students can make their living experience more unusual is to live on a theme hall. Examples of these are the "Involvement Tower" in Mead, where students support each other through similar academic and non-academic interests, and "Wellness Quarter" in Sanborn, where students commit not to smoke or drink. It can be difficult to get a single until senior year, but students generally tend to be happy with living options on campus.

Many seniors and a growing number of juniors opt to live off campus because, as one students pointed out, "Rent is decent and sometimes people prefer to move off campus so that they can live with friends from the other colleges." This means that available housing tends to be equidistant from all the Claremont schools.

Students who live on campus are required to buy a meal plan, which means much more than eating at the one dining hall on campus, McConnell. Pitzer students have the option of eating at any of the seven dining halls shared by the Claremont Colleges. There are also "flex dollars" that can be used for food at any of the six on-campus restaurants at the different colleges. The student-run Gold Mine is the most recently built eatery on the Pitzer campus.

Groove at the Grove

"The Grove House is my favorite building on the Pitzer campus," said one student about an on-campus hangout where students gather. They often come to Grove to get a freshly baked cookie or latte at the coffeehouse. On Thursday nights, the house's women's center sponsors "Groove at the Grove," where students hang out and listen to DJs and live bands. Students also occupy themselves at the Gold Center, Pitzer's student union, which has an arcade room, a TV lounge, and a swimming pool, as well as meeting rooms for student organizations.

> **"Pitzer College has a 100 percent community service participation rate among undergraduates."**

Since Pitzer is such a small campus, it shares a number of its facilities with the nearby colleges. For example, students usually go to Honnold Library at Pomona because there is no library at Pitzer. Varsity sports teams are also shared by the colleges, so there is a strong rivalry between the Pitzer-Pomona Sage Hens and the team formed by Claremont McKenna, Harvey Mudd, and Scripps. Moreover, the competition between Pitzer-Pomona and Occidental is the third-oldest college sports rivalry in the country. Although a fair number of students attend sporting events, there is a general feeling of apathy about athletics. As one student commented, "Pitzer students don't really care about sports" beyond frisbee on the Mounds, a grassy area in the middle of campus.

Community Involvement Is Key

While there are a number of different extracurricular activities available to Pitzer students, community service tends to be the most popular. "Pitzer College has a 100 percent community service participation rate among undergraduates. We all do it," said one student. "Some like it more than others, but all do it." There is not a vast number of clubs at Pitzer, but students get involved in student government, the newspaper (*The College* is available to all the colleges), or the radio station operated by the Claremont Consortium.

Weekend activities tend to be oriented around parties at the upperclass dorms and Pomona, Claremont McKenna, and Harvey Mudd, which are attended by upper and underclassmen alike. As one student said, "It's a pretty integrated group of partiers here." Drugs and alcohol are part of the party scene at Pitzer, but for the most part "it's no easier to get or use here than anywhere else." Students really enjoy the opportunity to party with all five colleges in the Consortium because everybody, no matter what their interest, wants to participate.

Pitzer throws some parties that are particular to the college, such as "The SuperFly" (which features hip-hop and house music) and "Screw Your Homey" (which is for setting up roommates on blind dates). Yet, the biggest party at Pitzer is Kahoutek, a music festival on campus that lasts for two days in April. There are different bands, craft booths, and various other activities to celebrate the coming of spring.

Pitzer College is clearly a unique place with much to offer on its own as well as through the connection to the other Claremont Colleges. It is a school that both serves and employs the community so as to give students a greater experience, while preserving an intimate setting. Students who desire the feeling of a smaller community with the benefits of a large school can offer should look no further than Pitzer College.—*Rebecca Ives*

FYI

If you come to Pitzer you'd better bring "a bathing suit, blanket, and your guitar for some lazy afternoons on the grassy mounds."

What is the typical weekend schedule? "Thursday nights at Grove House are followed by Fridays on the beach. Friday and Saturday nights spent at Five-College parties, whether at Pitzer or one of the other campuses. Sundays are dedicated to studying, but there are always kids on the Mounds or at the pool."

If I could change one thing about Pitzer, I would "try to improve the overall lack of motivation of students."

Three things every student at Pitzer should do before graduating are "go to the Grove House, dance 'til dawn at a desert party, and travel abroad."

Pomona College

Address: 550 North College Avenue; Claremont, CA 91711
Phone: 909-621-8134
E-mail address: admissions@pomona.edu
Web site URL: www.pomona.edu
Founded: 1887
Private or Public: private
Religious affiliation: none
Location: suburban
Undergraduate enrollment: 1,562
Total enrollment: 1,574
Percent Male/Female: 50%/50%
Percent Minority: 26%
Percent African-American: 5%
Percent Asian: 12%
Percent Hispanic: 8%
Percent Native-American: 1%
Percent in-state/out of state: 34%/66%
Percent Pub HS: 64%
Number of Applicants: 4,230
Percent Accepted: 23%
Percent Accepted who enroll: 38%
Entering: 374
Transfers: 5
Application Deadline: 2 Jan
Mean SAT: NA
Mean ACT: NA
Middle 50% SAT range: V 690-760, M 680-750
Middle 50% ACT range: 30-33
3 Most popular majors: economics, biology/biological sciences, political science
Retention: 99%
Graduation rate: 89%
On-campus housing: 97%
Fraternities: 5%
Sororities: NA
Library: 998,823 volumes
Tuition and Fees: $27,100
Room and Board: $8,600
Financial aid, first-year: 49%
Varsity or Club Athletes: 40%
Early Decision or Early Action Acceptance Rate: ED 78%

Thirty-five miles east of Los Angeles, California are five prestigious undergraduate schools collectively called the Claremont Colleges. Among them is Pomona College, a leading liberal arts college that boasts a unique blend of tradition and academics. With their school consistently ranked as one of the top national liberal arts colleges, Pomona students generally love every aspect of their small environment—from the outstanding student-faculty ratio to the chirping freshmen during orientation week: "Even if I had the chance, I wouldn't exchange my experience at Pomona for anything else."

Choose What You Learn

The Pomona faculty ensures that their students complete a well-rounded curriculum during their four years at the school. Students are allowed to enroll in classes offered at any of the 5-C (five Claremont Colleges), giving them a wide breadth from which to choose. The general education requirements include 10 courses in Perception, Analysis, and Communication (PAC) that allow students to explore 10 different categories of academics in order to develop a well-rounded base. Also required of freshmen is the Critical Inquiry Seminar, a writing-intensive course that teaches students critical thinking skills. Younger students feel that the requirements are "annoying and too demanding," but upperclassmen "understand the reasons behind them and eventually come to appreciate their purpose."

Easy classes are hard to find at a challenging school like Pomona. However, as one biology major reports, "Science courses require a lot more work than the business courses." Popular majors for sage hens (as students at Pomona call themselves) include economics, biology, history, chemistry, and psychology.

"The great thing about Pomona is that we get so much individual attention from our professors," said one junior. Professors are easily accessible outside of the classroom setting for meals and tutoring sessions. Overall, sage hens are "very pleased" with the efforts Pomona professors make to build relationships with them. One freshman said that on the last day of his neuroscience class, the professor brought the students pizza and played croquet with them.

Chill in Sun

According to those on campus Claremont, California is somewhat of a "dead town." Students say that the town is mostly residential with a few tiny stores interspersed. Most students with cars go to Los Angeles for more adventure. Another nearby town that is frequented by sage hens is Roland Heights: "Go to RH to eat! They have the best Asian cuisine," raved one student. If you can't afford to bring your own car to school, don't despair. Students say there are enough who do own cars at school that odds are you'll have at least one friend with a car.

One can find parties on campus, but most people migrate to Claremont McKenna (one of the other 5-C's) for the nightlife. Just like at any other college, alcohol plays a major role in the social scene at Pomona. The administration's stance on alcohol is lenient compared to many other colleges. Some students say that non-drinkers "feel very out of place" at Pomona and attribute it to the lack of things to do on campus. Other students think that there are plenty of social alternatives, such as dances and impromptu performances, and theme parties, which have included nights entitled "Harwood Halloween" and "Smiley 80s."

Although sports don't play a major role in the life of Pomona students, the gym facilities are "decent." The Claremont Colleges are divided into two teams, the Pomona-Pitzer joint team and the Harvey Mudd-Scripts-Claremont McKenna joint team. The two teams end up being each other's rivals in Division III. But as one student put it, sage hens "don't really concentrate on sports."

The student body at Pomona is composed of individuals from nearly all 50 states and many foreign countries. Though geographically diverse, some minority students wish there were higher percentages of African-American and Hispanic students. Nevertheless, Pomona still offers an array of cultural clubs and activities in which one can participate. In their free time, students also play intramural sports and do community service.

"The atmosphere at Pomona is really laid back," said one senior. It isn't uncommon to see sage hens go to class in their pajamas. Although most people dress casually, there are always those who "dress to impress."

The Improving Campus

Described as "cute" by some and "aesthetically pleasing" by others, Pomona's campus is small and full of ivy-covered modern and 19th-century architecture. The newest addition to the campus is the Smith Campus Center, built in 1999. Called the "Coup" by sage hens, the facility houses two restaurants, a student store, mail service, and other modern amenities, making it a prime hangout spot.

> **"Even if I had the chance, I wouldn't exchange my experience at Pomona for anything else."**

Dining at Pomona is "not bad considering it's dining hall food." Students can purchase a plan with a certain number of meals per week and some amount of "flex" dollars that can be used during the semester. Meals can be used at any of the 5-C's, and flex dollars can be used to purchase drinks and snacks at the student store. "Being able to transfer your meals to the other colleges is really convenient, especially if you're taking classes there or visiting friends." But some still prefer dining out at local restaurants like Viva Madrid's Spanish cuisine and Aruffo's Italian restaurant.

Living in the dorms of Pomona, however, is simply "terrible," said one student. "We boast to have the oldest dorm on this side of the Mississippi." But not to worry! Renovations are currently underway to install air-conditioning and better insulation into all of the dorms. The most recently renovated dorm is Mudd-Blaisdell. With a shortage of housing, some students are temporarily required to live in portables which are said to be "very spacious" but have "the worst location and sound insulation."

Generally, North Campus dorms are for the upperclassmen while South Campus dorms house the freshmen. Each of the five South Campus dorms has slightly different personalities. For the most part, students can choose whether they want to be housed co-ed or single-sex. Most floors are co-ed and some bathrooms are also co-ed, but Pomona also sets aside some housing to be single-sex.

Those Quirky Sage Hens

What makes Pomona so great? Some students say the professors. Others say the California weather. And still others mention that Pomona's unique traditions make this Claremont school unbeatable. During freshman orientation, "the freshmen run through Pomona's gates yelling 'Chirp! Chirp! Chirp!' while upperclassmen throw blue and white carnations (the school colors) at them." Another interesting thing sage hens do is throw their friends into the Fountain on their birthdays.

One thing many students at Pomona rave about is the number 47. The tradition reportedly started when Pomona math students wanted to prove that the number 47 appeared in nature more than any other number. For starters, the Pomona motto "Pomona College: Our Tribute to Christian Civilization" has 47 characters. To get to Pomona, one must take exit 47 from the freeway. There were 47 students enrolled at the school in the first graduating class of 1894 and 47 valedictorians entering the freshman class in the year 2000. Whether the occurrences are by chance or not, students and alums make a big deal about the phenomenon. For example, Joseph Menosky '79, co-producer and writer of Star Trek, incorporated the number 47 into almost every episode of the famous television series.

Because Pomona has a total of fewer than 2000 students, it is an environment conducive to "knowing everyone." Students love that it is a small school "where getting to know the professors is an option and where people can really make a difference on campus." Pomona offers all of the opportunities of a larger university through its joint systems with the other Claremont Colleges, and yet preserves the intimacy of a small college. One student captured his experience at Pomona best by saying, "The sun here makes me smile. The professors here challenge me to be the best I can be. My friends here know how to have fun. What more could I ask for?" —*Jane Pak*

FYI

If you come to Pomona, you'd better bring a "trusty alarm clock. There's so much work that sooner or later your sleeping schedule will get messed up."

What is the typical weekend schedule? "People party or hang out with friends on Friday and Saturday nights. Occasionally students will venture out of Claremont to neighboring cities where they can find more to do. Sundays are all about studying and catching up on work."

If I could change one thing about Pomona, I'd "change the grading system. The 12-point scale makes getting a good GPA a lot tougher than with a 4.0 scale."

Three things every student should do before graduating are "get thrown into the Fountain on their birthday, go to the other 5-C parties, and explore the diversity available in the vicinity of Claremont and Los Angeles."

Scripps College

Address: 1030 Columbia Avenue; Claremont, CA 91711
Phone: 800-770-1333
E-mail address: admission@scrippscollege.edu
Web site URL: www.scrippscol.edu
Founded: 1926
Private or Public: private
Religious affiliation: none
Location: suburban
Undergraduate enrollment: 830
Total enrollment: NA
Percent Male/Female: 0%/100%
Percent Minority: 24%
Percent African-American: 3%
Percent Asian: 15%
Percent Hispanic: 6%
Percent Native-American: 0%
Percent in-state/out of state: 45%/55%
Percent Pub HS: 64%
Number of Applicants: 1,371
Percent Accepted: 58%
Percent Accepted who enroll: 28%
Entering: 224
Transfers: 19
Application Deadline: 1 Feb
Mean SAT: NA
Mean ACT: NA
Middle 50% SAT range: V 620-720, M 600-690
Middle 50% ACT range: 26-30
3 Most popular majors: English language and literature, psychology, fine/studio arts
Retention: 86%
Graduation rate: 68%
On-campus housing: 98%
Fraternities: NA
Sororities: NA
Library: NA
Tuition and Fees: $25,700
Room and Board: $8,300
Financial aid, first-year: NA
Varsity or Club Athletes: 10%
Early Decision or Early Action Acceptance Rate: NA

If life among independent, motivated women strolling between Spanish Mediterranean architecture, sprawling lawns, and rose gardens sounds appealing, check out Scripps College. This small, all-female institution boasts the intimacy and community of a single-sex school, and the resources and entertainment of the surrounding four colleges and nearby Los Angeles.

Students are quick to point out that they are not members of a stereotypical women's college. "It's not about feminism and activism, but about equality and community spirit." The advantages of a single-sex environment range from the supportive environment and relaxed atmosphere, to the attention given to women's educational issues. Most students did not choose Scripps because of its all-female status, but rather fell in love with the school itself.

All in the Family

Scripps is part of a consortium with Claremont McKenna, Pomona, Pitzer, and Harvey Mudd. Students cross-register frequently, and claim that doing so is easy, and often rewarding. "Going to one of the other schools is just like walking to another part of campus." Claremont McKenna, Pitzer, and Scripps have a Joint Science Center, where resources, and often classes, are shared between the schools. This state-of-the-art facility allows Scripps to benefit from resources that it would not be able to afford alone.

Students rate academics highly, praising their professors, as well as their small classes. The campus is evenly divided between humanities and science majors. With an average of 10 to 15 students in a Scripps class, and up to 150 in a joint science lecture, personal attention is one of Scripps' greatest attributes. There are no teaching assistants, and the professors are helpful and always willing to talk.

A core curriculum is required of all Scripps students. Students must also fulfill general requirements, which include three semesters of foreign language, one of laboratory science, two of social sciences, and one inter-cultural class. Students note that these requirements are not difficult to meet.

Scripps registers students by randomly choosing a letter, and proceeding alphabetically from that point, circling back around to cover the letters passed initially. This provides a fair way to register students, though some students are occasionally denied their first-choice classes.

"Going to one of the other schools is just like walking to another part of campus."

The Scripps campus is located in the rather upscale town of Claremont, dubbed "the village" by students, and student interaction with the townspeople is very congenial. The campus is built in a loose square, with lawns and walled gardens filling the middle. A set of steps forming a semi-circle in the middle of campus is laughingly called "the Miss America Steps." Add Spanish Mediterranean architecture and rose gardens to these lawns, and it is easy to understand why the Scripps campus is a National Historic Landmark. Students feel extremely safe on the Scripps campus. It is a quiet and closed community in which students "never feel endangered." The dorms have an escort policy stating that a Scripps student must always accompany visitors to the dorms.

Home Sweet Home

Dorms at Scripps vary widely but all have resident assistants. Scripps has a few newer dorms, which are largely suite-style, with air-conditioning, and several older dorms, which students often prefer. "The older dorms have more character, with larger rooms, vaulted ceilings, and just more charm," one student explained. Designed to foster a close community, the older dorms each have a living room with a piano, and a fireplace, as well as a "browsing room" in which students may make use of uninterrupted quiet, reference books, and couches. One particularly unique dormitory, Toll Hall has a star-shaped fountain in its courtyard with balconies running around it. Students call residing in this part "living on star court."

Students live in double rooms their first year, and singles thereafter. Further campus additions include a Commons, to make dining at Scripps more accessible to students at other Claremont schools. Commons also houses administrative offices, student organizations, and mailboxes.

A new food service was introduced recently, and students were not happy with the results. Students unhappy with the menu can use their meal plans at grills and pizza places off-campus, as well as at the Motley Coffee House, which shows movies every Friday night, and hosts bands every Sunday night.

Athletics, Activities, and Dateless Dances?

Sports are played in conjunction with the other four colleges, with Pitzer and Pomona forming one league, and Claremont McKenna, Scripps, and Harvey Mudd forming another. There is intense rivalry between the two leagues. Within the Scripps league students can participate in intramural sports. Though many Scripps students are involved in sports, the Scripps campus houses few athletic facilities. However, the gym facilities at the other colleges are easily accesable.

Other extracurricular activities abound, from student government to NOW, the National Organization for Women, or the literary magazine. One sorority recently opened a local chapter on campus, though it received a lot of student resistance. This chapter associates largely with the three fraternities at Pomona, and is not a large part of campus life.

Weekend activities often involve cultural events such as concerts, guest speakers, or art openings. Some of Scipps' most memorable speakers include Supreme Court Justice Sandra Day O'Connor, and author Jane Smiley. Students also travel to the other colleges for Five College parties. Until this year, a Five College Organization worked to organize a large party at one campus each weekend. This organization has broken up for administrative reasons, and is currently being reconstructed. The Dean of Students organizes several Saturday afternoon trips into Los Angeles. Students might also spend several weekends a semester visiting LA, or going to Disneyland.

Scripps students attend several formal occasions a year, one where Scripps women get dressed up and go to a dance on their campus without dates. A more conventional Spring Formal is also held on the Scripps campus.

Other Scripps traditions include students signing their names in a book of Scripps students as freshmen, and as seniors having a special champagne brunch, after which some streak the campus. The Dean of Students serves students cookies and tea during the traditional Scripps Tea.

Students at Scripps form a tight community based on mutual support. "Scripps is a small college with personal attention, yet you don't know every person that you see, every day." For many, Scripps presents the best of both worlds, one where diverse students can bond and "not be on guard all the time," experience small class sizes, and yet reap the benefits of an active college town. —*Cynthia Matthews*

FYI

If you come to Scripps, you'd better bring a "a strong sense of community spirit."

What is the typical weekend schedule? "Friday: lay in the sun, party; Saturday: homework then leave campus; Sunday: homework."

If I could change one thing about Scripps, I'd "get rid of the smog."

Three things that every student should do before graduating Scripps are, "go to one of Professor Hao Huang's concerts, take a professor to the Motely for coffee and talk about anything but class work, and find an excuse to spend time in the Rare Books room in Denison Library."

Deep Springs College

Address: Application Committee, Box 45001, Dyer, CA 89010
Phone: 760-872-2000
E-mail address: appcom@deepsprings.edu
Web site URL: www.deepsprings.edu
Founded: 1917
Private or Public: private
Religious affiliation: none
Location: rural
Undergraduate enrollment: 26
Total enrollment: 26
Percent Male/Female: 100%/0%
Percent Minority: NA
Percent African-American: NA
Percent Asian: NA
Percent Hispanic: NA
Percent Native-American: NA
Percent in-state/out of state: NA
Percent Pub HS: NA
Number of Applicants: 145
Percent Accepted: 9%
Percent Accepted who enroll: NA
Entering: 13
Transfers: NA
Application Deadline: 15 Nov
Mean SAT: NA
Mean ACT: NA
Middle 50% SAT range: NA
Middle 50% ACT range: NA
3 Most popular majors: liberal arts
Retention: NA
Graduation rate: NA
On-campus housing: 100%
Fraternities: NA
Sororities: NA
Library: 28,000 volumes
Tuition and Fees: tuition free
Room and Board: NA
Financial aid, first-year: NA
Varsity or Club Athletes: NA
Early Decision or Early Action Acceptance Rate: NA

At Deep Springs College, located in a large desert valley set deep in the mountains, isolation is the name of the game. Even *The New York Times* arrives a couple of days late. "The joke is it's the best place to be if the world ends because we'll have a couple of days," smirked one student. Of course, that is the least of what this unique and very special school has to offer.

Just the 26 of Us

Probably the most glaring feature that sets Deep Springs apart from other colleges is its tiny student body. At Deep Springs, it is composed of only 26 students, all male. Each year, out of around 200 applicants, a committee composed of mainly students in addition to a few faculty members chooses between 10 and 13 new students for admission to the two-year associate degree program. Ethnically and racially, there is not much diversity, though a committee devoted to diversity has been formed to address the issue. In other regards though, "there is a good variety of people," said one student. "We have some international students, a fair spread in economic background, and we have a wide range of views on different issues. We didn't *all* vote for Nader." An admissions committee member agrees that Deep Springs looks for no one type of student. "Some are just straight amazingly intelligent people who were incredible in high school," he explained, "while others just seem like they're really interested in service and have a lot of potential even if they didn't necessarily live up to it in their high school years."

Serving Time

The idea of service is central to Deep Spring's philosophy. The education students receive is tuition-free, but by taking it, students are agreeing to devote their lives to serving others, even if they're not doing it directly but are just remaining conscious of it. "A dedication to service and desire to serve mankind—that's something we look for in our applicants," said another admissions committee member. "I don't think there's a particular type we accept. Some people would say weirdos, but I would like to contest that."

It's certainly true that Deep Springs is not for everyone. After all, living in seclusion in the California desert with only 25 guys is not exactly everyone's cup of tea. A good thing about it, though, is that the guys form incredibly tight relationships, compared by many to a brotherhood. "They are really incredible people to be around, and very, very smart," said a second-year student. "They can also be gigantic assholes. I mean, living with the same 25 people, we get on each other's nerves sometimes."

The lack of girls also takes some getting used to. "It's really hard on some people," said one student. "We don't meet or interact with any girls, and it's a death trap for long-distance relationships." Still, the student added, "I like to think it's worth it." Another student said the upside is that "you can concentrate better, and honestly, I do find that I can concentrate better here than anywhere else." Other students agree that the situation precludes distractions from studies and labor.

"We didn't *all* vote for Nader."

By labor, they mean *farm* labor, because Deep Springs is an almost entirely self-sufficient farm. Students work on the farm about 20 to 30 hours per week, rotating duties ranging from harvesting and planting to shoveling horse dung to milking cows. The fresh milk at every meal is a definite bonus, but for every glass some poor student has to get up at six in the morning to milk ol' Bessie (even on Saturdays!).

I Want to Be a Fireman When I Grow Up

In addition to staying up to task on farm duties, the guys also have to stay on top of a large workload for classes in a curriculum chosen by a student committee. Each of the three long-term and two short-term faculty members has a list of classes they can teach, voted on by the committee each semester. Past offerings have included classes on the civil rights movement, the history of higher education, German philosopher Heideger, painting, and the literature of love. There are no majors, and only two requirements—"Composition" and "Public Speaking." Students can do independent studies, too. Not surprisingly, the say that students have over what's offered has caused some tension between students and faculty. "We granted leave to one student so he could take an emergency medical technician course because he wants to become a firefighter," said a member of the curriculum committee, "and it really ticked off a bunch of the faculty members."

Students are mostly very satisfied with their professors. One student said the only class he hasn't liked was one on conservation biology, and not because of the subject matter. Actually, "I was the only student in the class, so there wasn't much in the way of class discussion, which would have been interesting." Classes usually have about six or seven students, providing an intensely personalized educational experience. After getting their two-year associate degree at Deep Springs, most students transfer to prestigious colleges throughout the nation to earn their Bachelor's degree. Students who chose to transfer have gone to Yale, the University of Chicago, Swarthmore, and Harvard.

Got Milk? Got Beef? Get Bessie

Though Deep Springs is almost entirely student-governed, it has strict rules. There are two big ones. First is the isolation policy: visitors usually don't come into the valley, and students are not permitted to leave the valley. The second forbids the students from using drugs and alcohol. Still, the guys don't feel totally imprisoned. For one thing, the quality of life at Deep Springs, labor aside, is pretty excellent. The buildings in the beautiful valley were remodeled, and double and triple dorm rooms are "absolutely gigantic, it's almost ludicrous," said one student.

The farm-fresh food that sustains the hard workers is described as "amazing. We have a chef who used to work at a really good restaurant in the Bay area," said a second-year Deep Springster. "Tonight we had herb-roasted chickens for each table, risotto and vegetables, homemade ice cream and cake, and salad from the green houses. We always have our own fresh milk and beef, too. We are definitely spoiled."

Nothin' Like Sliding Your Bare Butt Down a Giant Sand Dune

In their rare free time, the guys enjoy outdoors activities like rock-climbing, hiking, camping, and horseback riding. When it's hot, they also like to go swimming to cool off. Guys also look forward to silly traditions like the yearly "naked lunch" followed by a game of naked frisbee, and sand-dune sliding: "In the summer, when it's warm at night and there's a full moon, we go out to the really big sand dunes and slide down them. It's a lot of fun." Students also get together at some of the staff's satellite-equipped houses to watch the Super Bowl. Sometimes they get bands together and periodically put on performances. "One kid is really into techno music, so he's put on a few dance parties," said a student. Also, almost all of the guys leave Deep Springs with an affinity for country music, "since the only radio station we get is a country music station. It's hard not to get a thing for it."

It's not hard to see why attending Deep Springs is a life-changing experience. "It's hard to say how it's changed you," said one second-year student. "We struggle with that all the time. I mean, I've learned so many things I never thought I would—how to horseback ride, how to plant alfalfa. But it's changed me in so many more important ways that I can't even describe." Another second-year agrees that his time at the school has been an incredible journey. "I would come back to Deep Springs in a second. I really love it here, and I don't think I could have been as happy anywhere else. Now I'm really looking forward to going out in the world and doing something worthwhile." There couldn't be a better preparation for it than attending an inspiring institution like Deep Springs. —*Patricia Stringel*

FYI

If you come to Deep Springs, you'd better bring a "a deep love, or at least tolerance, for isolation."

What is the typical weekend schedule? "Videos, brunch, Frisbee, meetings, and, oh yeah, work."

If I could change one thing about Deep Springs, I'd "probably have to say admit more girls, but I think that would change this place too much."

Three things every student at Deep Springs should do before graduating are "hike to The Druid (a rock formation in the mountains), milk a cow, and slide naked down the sand dunes in the light of the full moon."

Mills College

Address: 5000 MacArthur Boulevard; Oakland, CA 94613
Phone: 510-430-2135
E-mail address: admission@mills.edu
Web site URL: www.mills.edu
Founded: 1852
Private or Public: private
Religious affiliation: none
Location: urban
Undergraduate enrollment: 763
Total enrollment: 1,162
Percent Male/Female: 0%/100%
Percent Minority: 29%
Percent African-American: 10%
Percent Asian: 8%
Percent Hispanic: 10%
Percent Native-American: 1%
Percent in-state/out of state: 72%/28%
Percent Pub HS: 78%
Number of Applicants: 484
Percent Accepted: 85%
Percent Accepted who enroll: 33%
Entering: 137
Transfers: 100
Application Deadline: 1 Feb
Mean SAT: 1133
Mean ACT: 24
Middle 50% SAT range: V 500-640, M 480-620
Middle 50% ACT range: 23-28
3 Most popular majors: English language and literature, psychology, fine/studio arts
Retention: 80%
Graduation rate: 60%
On-campus housing: 57%
Fraternities: NA
Sororities: NA
Library: 233,835 volumes
Tuition and Fees: $24,441
Room and Board: $8,930
Financial aid, first-year: 76%
Varsity or Club Athletes: 13%
Early Decision or Early Action Acceptance Rate: EA 71%

Having initially opened as a women's seminary to educated gold miners' daughters, Mills evolved under the influence of the Bay Area's liberal spirit into a modern liberal arts women's college. Mills College's focus on the woman came into the spotlight in the 1990s when the Board of Trustees decided to open Mills to male undergraduates. The entire undergraduate student body went on strike right before final exams, refusing to attend classes. When the students won and the Board reversed its decision, Mills' commitment to women's education was permanently reinforced.

Focus on the Individual Woman

Students describe a Mills education as intimate and personal, citing typical class sizes of eight to 12 students in which the professor knows each student personally and a campus environment in which strangers smile at each other on the way to study. Classes "are really small," explained one sophomore, "so you have a wonderful relationship with the professor." Mills women consistently praised the accessibility of their professors, and students unanimously cited small class size as their favorite aspect of Mills academics. Students also report that getting into classes is generally really easy, even as a "freshwoman," and is definitely not a problem as an "upperclasswoman."

A Variety of Opportunities

As a liberal-arts college, Mills does not have an engineering major, but it does offer science majors like chemistry and biology and also has a premedical program that students describe as excellent. A Mills workload is what you make of it, one sophomore explained. Depending on what classes you take, "you can have a total slacker semester, or you can also pile on the work."

All Mills women, however, do have to take at least two classes from each of the four major distributions: humanities, fine arts, social sciences, and natural sciences, in addition to one semester of English, one of the many writing-intensive courses offered in different fields, and one course on another culture: either a foreign one or an American minority culture.

The main drawback of Mills' small size however, is the somewhat limited variety of course offerings within each field. Standard, practical courses are always available, but "we don't have the random, more specific classes" found at some other schools, one student reported. Because of the school's small size, moreover, some upper-level classes can only be offered every other year, so students interested in these courses have to plan their schedules carefully and with foresight. However, students are allowed to cross-register for classes at UC Berkeley and at other colleges in the Oakland area—a measure of flexibility that widens Mills women's options and is praised by students despite a number of somewhat "bothersome" restrictions that Mills places on cross-registration.

Some students also occasionally experience problems with TAs. Because Mills TAs are usually undergrads, they do not always know the material as well as grad-student TAs would. However, students also reported excellent experiences with some undergrad TAs, and the small class size ensures that the professor plays a central role in the course anyway, with TAs only assisting as needed. Students reported no courses taught entirely by TAs.

Students are generally satisfied with Mills' library offerings, although deep, specialized research sometimes requires a trip to UC Berkeley's library, which is not open to the public but is open to students from Mills and some other schools. Regular shuttle service between Mills and Berkeley makes such trips convenient. By and large students were very happy with the academic opportunities they find at Mills.

Beyond the Books

Mills throws a few large dances and parties each year, including the popular "Fetish Ball," which encourages minimal amounts of clothing. In general, however, partygoers head to UC Berkeley or Stanford on the weekends. The shuttle carries students to and from Berkeley makes a final pickup at Berkeley as late as 12 A.M. to minimize strandings. "If you're looking for a party school," one student said simply, "don't come here." Another student commented that parties are easily accessible by making a short trip to nearby schools but agreed that students looking for big parties without going off-campus would be inconvenienced at Mills: small, friendly parties are common on campus, but big, wild ones are not.

Because Mills' immediate vicinity is predominantly residential, shops and restaurants of interest to college students are in short supply, but regular shuttles bring students to downtown Oakland as well as to San Francisco, making such excursions both popular and convenient. Freshwomen often go shopping with friends on the weekend, hang out downtown, or watch movies. Upperclasswomen sometimes go skiing or camping together at nearby sites.

Being underage can be a slight problem for students looking to drink, as liquor vendors in the area definitely card. However students report that they can usually get an upperclasswoman to buy alcohol on their behalf. Moreover, while large parties are rare at Mills, students seeking alcohol can generally find keg parties at UC Berkeley and Stanford. A sophomore reports, however, that non-drinkers are common at Mills and do not feel excluded from the social scene, even if they attend events at which other students are drinking.

"Mills is a place for women who are into thinking and want to make a difference in the world."

For students seeking weekend getaways, the athletics staff also hosts "rec trips," which are exciting outdoor excursions. Previous rec trips have included ski trips, rafting trips, horseback riding on the beach, and visits to the mudbaths at Calistoga.

What About Guys?

If you're at Mills, one sophomore said, you're probably not looking for a guy. It is true that many Mills women bring their boyfriends from home, and Mills policy allows male guests to stay overnight in the dorms for up to seven nights each month. Mills women looking for men also often meet them at Berkeley and Stanford. Mills' grad school is co-ed, as is a year-round ESL program on campus that draws international students from around the world and is called "the English School" or "ES" by Mills women. If you are looking for guys, suffice it to say, there are places to find them. Also, female-female couples at Mills are both common and accepted. All students interviewed explained that Mills is more open than other environments and that its liberal spirit makes it totally gay and lesbian friendly. Interracial couples are also welcomed. A sophomore reports however, that romance is definitely not what brings Mills women to college and that the predominant sentiment on campus is one of "I'm a woman, but I don't really need a man." To put it simply, Mills women are independent.

The Women of Mills

"Mills women: proud women, strong women," is the student image, according to one sophomore, who describes the characterization as very true. Another student described Mills women as "individualistic" and "outspoken" but said that beyond those traits, the Mills student body fit no stereotypes. Mills is diverse—"not homogenous at all," said one woman.

The student body at Mills is diverse not only ethnically, culturally, and ideologically but also geographically, as Mills draws students from around the U.S. and from many foreign countries. The many international students in the English School further add to geographic diversity. Students also report that Mills women represent a full, diverse cross-section of family backgrounds and income levels. The women of Mills, however, are characterized by one particular form of diversity found at few other colleges: diversity of age.

Mills has many resumers; "resumers" is the Mills term for women older than the traditional college ages of roughly 18 through 26, though these numbers are general ideas and not hard borders. Resumers are usually women who have taken time off of education in order to pursue careers or raise families and have now decided to go back to the books. Many resumers are aged 40 or over; while the resumers have their own dorm wing and a warm community, there is no social divide between resumers and "traditional-age" students. Students report that Mills women of all ages mix easily and entirely, bonding across age differences to build a strong, shared society.

An Urban Oasis

Students describe the Mills campus as "absolutely gorgeous" and "like a park" with grassy meadows and eucalyptus trees. The part of Oakland surrounding Mills is relatively uninteresting and somewhat "impoverished," but students call Mills an oasis—"something you would not expect to find in Oakland." Students report that the campus, which is enclosed and has only one entrance, is beautiful, and you can't see Oakland unless you're on top of a hill.

On the note of hills, Mills is somewhat hilly. The main dining hall, Founders Commons, rests atop one of two main hills, and two dorms sit atop the other. Women living in the "hill dorms" try to plan their daily routes carefully to minimize trips up and down the hill. The other dorm buildings are on flat ground, and four of the five dorms even have their own dining halls, making trips to Founders unnecessary—unless students crave hot breakfasts, which are served only at Founders while the other dining halls offer continental breakfast. The only dorm that does not have its own dining hall, Reinhardt, is close to Founders.

Students are happy with the food at Mills, and agree that it is very good and better than the food at most colleges. Options for vegetarians and other special dietary needs are available, although special arrangements are sometimes required. Students can use their meal plans at several dining halls and have the option of transferring one meal per day to one of two on-campus cafés. One reservation students have, though, is that such transfers are worth only $3.40 although students pay more than $3.40 per meal for their meal plans.

Students are also very happy with on-campus housing. Freshwomen live in singles or doubles, and Mills generally honors requests for single rooms. For sophomore year and beyond, all Mills women living on campus receive singles unless they specifically arrange with other students to live in doubles or one of several larger suites. Students are generally really happy with their large, comfortable rooms, even in first-year housing.

One common student concern is the lack of an ATM on campus. Many bank branches are accessible by Mills shuttle, but the nearest ATM within walking distance is in a 7-11 facility, three or four blocks off-campus. The area around Mills was described by one woman as "not a college town." Students reported feeling safe off-campus during the day but were less comfortable walking alone at night and usually bring a friend when leaving campus after dark. There are a few small businesses in the area, but most students head into nearby cities for serious shopping and entertainment. Many students have cars, but Mills operates shuttles and also has a bus stop right outside its front gate, making getting around easy even for non-drivers.

Fun and Games

As a Division III school, Mills does not award athletic scholarships, but it does actively recruit students. At American colleges and universities, the sports team traditionally generating the most hype is the football team. As an all-women's school, Mills does not have a football team, but it does have six intercollegiate sports teams. "We support our athletes," said one student. "We go to the games," she explained, although athletic spirit at Mills is "definitely not as big as you would get at one of the larger schools." Mills athletes do, however, win certain regional and national tournaments and awards regularly despite coming from a small, all-female school.

One student praised the fact that at Mills, interested beginners have a chance to join varsity teams even if they never played varsity sports in high school. For students not seeking varsity play at Mills, there are still a variety of club and intramural sports, as well as P.E. classes in a wide range of sports—from rugby to tai chi. These classes are universal enough in appeal that both casual players and varsity athletes sign up for them.

Outside of athletics, Mills also has a host of clubs and organizations, and students are encouraged to start new ones. "There's something out there for everybody," said one student. "If people aren't doing anything, it's not because they couldn't be." Particularly interesting organizations include the Cheese Lovers United Club and Mouthing Off, "an LGBT group that sponsors quite a few events on campus and puts up amusing signs to advertise them."

Empowering the Woman

Mills has a number of traditions, ranging from the assignment of a class color to each year, to Paint Night, on which the senior class storms the campus, painting steps, walls, and other objects the senior class color, to the Ghost Walk, a Halloween event in which seniors wake up the freshmen at two or three in the morning, bring them to a dining hall, and tell them ghost stories as other seniors banged pots and pans spookily in the kitchen. The greatest and foremost Mills tradition, however, has always been the empowering of the woman.

Said one sophomore, "Mills is a place for women who are into thinking and want to make a difference in the world." Through means ranging from small, intimate classes to single dorm rooms to the emphatically all-female undergraduate program, Mills focuses on the individual woman and underscores her independence. One sophomore said, "I'm definitely supported here in everything I do," while another lauded the abundance of "smart women and strong women" at this academic institution, which she and other students described as "really empowering." It's no wonder then that when interviewed students were asked whether they would choose Mills again, every student emphatically said yes. As one woman explained, "Mills is a place where almost anything can happen if you're willing to put in the work to do it." —*Jacob Jou*

FYI

If you come to Mills, you'd better bring "an open mind."

The typical weekend schedule at Mills includes "daytrips to San Francisco or downtown Oakland, shopping, perhaps a movie or a visit to a year-round farmer's market, and maybe a party at night. Oh, and a lot of homework on Sunday."

If I could change one thing about Mills, "I'd move it out of Oakland."

Three things every student at Mills should do before graduating are "go on a rec trip, have lunch with a professor, and attend the Fetish Ball."

Occidental College

Address: 1600 Campus Road; Los Angeles, CA 90041-3314
Phone: 323-259-2700
E-mail address: admisssion@oxy.edu
Web site URL: www.oxy.edu
Founded: 1887
Private or Public: private
Religious affiliation: none
Location: urban
Undergraduate enrollment: 1,808
Total enrollment: NA
Percent Male/Female: 42%/58%
Percent Minority: 36%
Percent African-American: 7%
Percent Asian: 14%
Percent Hispanic: 14%
Percent Native-American: 1%
Percent in-state/out of state: 53%/47%
Percent Pub HS: 67%
Number of Applicants: 4,172
Percent Accepted: 43%
Percent Accepted who enroll: 25%
Entering: 447
Transfers: 58
Application Deadline: 15 Jan
Mean SAT: NA
Mean ACT: NA
Middle 50% SAT range: V 580-670, M 590-680
Middle 50% ACT range: NA
3 Most popular majors: economics, psychology, English language and literature
Retention: 90%
Graduation rate: 76%
On-campus housing: 76%
Fraternities: NA
Sororities: NA
Library: 493,216 volumes
Tuition and Fees: $28,298
Room and Board: $7,830
Financial aid, first-year: 61%
Varsity or Club Athletes: 30%
Early Decision or Early Action Acceptance Rate: NA

Nestled in the green suburbs of northeast LA, Occidental College is a gem of a liberal arts college dedicated to recruiting students of diverse backgrounds. An "Urban Oasis," Oxy is one of the oldest colleges on the West Coast, and strives to provide motivated students with opportunities to work together and with the resources of LA to forge educational paths all their own.

Academics at the Core

Occidental's core curriculum encourages students to explore a wide variety of subjects; the core "creates more open-minded, pluralistic individuals," said one senior. It "enables students to take different classes, sometimes outside of their major, to understand and partake in different disciplines so that they can further develop their knowledge." One-third of a student's education is devoted to this core. Requirements include classes in foreign languages, the sciences (including a lab science), the arts, and "a social studies-type requirement where you have to take three to four classes from different geographical areas," a student described. One particular core class is a year-long freshman writing requirement; "the core [writing] class is really nice because we are in a dorm with the other people in the core, so we form a close bond," said a freshman. Popular majors at Oxy include economics for business management, which is highly competitive as "Oxy students want to make a lot of money after they leave," commented a senior, and biology, for whose majors the college offers many research opportunities.

Class size generally ranges from small to medium, and even in the few larger classes, there is ample communication between students and professors. Getting into the class you want is relatively easy, especially for upperclassmen, because professors are often willing to add extra students. There are places reserved for freshmen in all entry-level courses, and the system for priority is fair: freshmen are placed in numerical order in terms of priority for getting into a class, and this order switches around at the start of the second semester.

In general, students find that the workload at Occidental is pretty heavy, and though it can depend on the classes you are taking, it is manageable if you budget your time well. If you need help, there are many resources within the college and the peer community. Professors are required to hold office hours, and the Center for Teaching and Learning, run by the college library, has advisors available in nearly every subject, every night.

Always Getting Involved

Oxy students may work hard, but the academic atmosphere is relaxed enough that it does not impede students' involvement in extracurriculars. Quite the contrary: Occidental is home to an incredibly active and involved student community. "Everyone that I meet is part of a larger organization on campus; people want to get involved," said a freshman. There are over 100 organizations—quite a lot for a student population of only about 1,700! These groups cover all possible areas of student interest on the diverse campus. From the Asian-Pacific Islander Alliance to the Pre-Dental Club, Oxy students create their own opportunities to explore LA, tutor younger students, engage in student government, political activism, and venture into the outdoors.

There are club sports teams, and despite their popularity among Oxy athletes, one freshman said that, "right now, club sports are having trouble getting field space. From what I gather, the school needs money, so they are leasing the fields," and it is the club sports that suffer. There is, however, "a lot of talking going on," she said, so the problem has not gone unaddressed.

Chill Out, With Choices

Wherever your interests lie, there are many social activities offered to Oxy students in their free time, and not just on weekends: cultural, social and educational events are offered daily by clubs or the college. There is a movie every Wednesday night, and the ICC (Inter-Cultural Community) hosts weekly events open to the public.

A typical Oxy weekend "can be bland," one senior admits, but if you make the effort, there are a lot of things to do. Drinking can be prominent at parties, and many students feel that marijuana is common on campus. While the Greek system isn't big, frat parties do occur in off-campus houses. The school has taken measures to limit on-campus pre-parties, notorious for hard alcohol, but binge drinking can still be found. "The pressure is not too bad, but freshmen are usually targets for peer pressure," a student remarked. One freshman agreed: "Sometimes it does feel like all anyone wants to do is sit in a room and drink." In the end, it is a student's decision whether or not to drink. If students choose not to, "you can find people who don't want to drink and want to do something else besides go to a party," this freshman remarked. Recently, the college has been successful in preparing "wonderful themed parties" free of charge, which spices up the usual routine of mingling with your friends in one another's houses and dorm rooms.

LA Livin'

When it comes to social life, if all else fails, there is always LA. "One wonderful thing about Oxy is that it is so close to LA that students can enjoy off-campus life when the parties aren't so happening," said a student. Oxy's array of student activities meshes well with Los Angeles' great weather, and the resources really add to campus life as both a bridge and an escape to the real world. Students leave campus to attend parties off campus, eat (especially on the weekends), and go to the beach. The weather is a huge draw for many Oxy kids—when East Coasters are beginning to bundle up for fall and winter, Oxy students are still sunning themselves while studying and hanging out! The campus is relatively close to Pasadena; students can take the college's Bengal Bus to Old Town Pasadena or the Glendale Gallery, but having a car is a definite plus. "Bumming rides off of people is fine," remarked a student, "until you miss dinner on Friday and no one wants to get food." Some students complain that Old Town Pasadena can be expensive, but if you know where to go, you won't break the bank.

A Beautiful and Diverse Campus

It's hard not to see Occidental's appeal when you visit the campus glistening and green in the LA sun. One student described the Beaux-Arts architecture as "very Grecian, yet modern," and it retains a definite California flavor in the terra cotta rooftops. Everything is within walking distance and the view is amazing from the hilltop on which Oxy is perched. Campus and the surrounding area are well patrolled, and students consistently report feeling very safe. The freshman dorms get mixed reviews, described as both "decent" and not "overwhelmingly too small." Upperclassmen "can live anywhere on campus, depending on their room draw number," said a senior, and while only some halls have air conditioning, all will eventually get it as Oxy updates the facilities. While the majority of students live on campus, there are many options for off-campus living, and the school provides a wealth of information about available apartments.

Occidental students praise not only their physically beautiful campus, but also the very diverse, active, and friendly student community. A lot of students come from multiracial backgrounds, but race is not the only type of diversity here at Oxy. "Diversity ranges from ethnicity to socio-economic background to hobbies to types of music," remarked one student. With such varied interests, Oxy students enrich their community by being involved in the many, varied activities offered. In addition, "the things that Oxy lacks—art studio space, field space, etc.—are made up in the friendliness of the people who go here," gushed a freshman.

"Everyone that I meet is part of a larger organization on campus; people want to get involved."

At Oxy, students experience diversity on all fronts: in academics, in the people they meet, in the activities they do, and in the events offered by the relationship between the college and the city. With all these things to offer, Oxy is an invigorating and inviting place to spend four years.—*Samantha Wilson*

FYI

If you come to Occidental, you'd better bring "shower sandals and a lot of room decorations."

What is the typical weekend schedule? "Friday, Farmer's Market for dinner, a movie or party of the week either on or off campus; Saturday, go to brunch at 12 P.M., do some homework, go shopping, or trek to the beach to "study," and finally head out to LA for a club."

If I could change one thing about Occidental, I'd "make the campus bigger with more facilities for students that are open 24 hours."

Three things every student at Occidental should do before graduating are "go tunneling, hike Mt. Fiji, and attend the 'Sex on the Beach' party."

Pepperdine University

Address: 24255 Pacific Coast Highway; Malibu, CA 90263-4392
Phone: 310-506-4392
E-mail address: admission-seaver@pepperdine.edu
Web site URL: www.pepperdine.edu
Founded: 1937
Private or Public: private
Religious affiliation: Church of Christ
Location: suburban
Undergraduate enrollment: 3,153
Total enrollment: NA
Percent Male/Female: 44%/56%
Percent Minority: 28%
Percent African-American: 7%
Percent Asian: 9%
Percent Hispanic: 11%
Percent Native-American: 1%
Percent in-state/out of state: 52%/48%
Percent Pub HS: NA
Number of Applicants: 5,503
Percent Accepted: 37%
Percent Accepted who enroll: 39%
Entering: 802
Transfers: 60
Application Deadline: 15 Jan
Mean SAT: NA
Mean ACT: NA
Middle 50% SAT range: V 540-640, M 550-660
Middle 50% ACT range: 23-28
3 Most popular majors: business, communications, liberal arts
Retention: 88%
Graduation rate: 75%
On-campus housing: 49%
Fraternities: 24%
Sororities: 29%
Library: 315,078 volumes
Tuition and Fees: $27,520
Room and Board: $8,270
Financial aid, first-year: 58%
Varsity or Club Athletes: 8%
Early Decision or Early Action Acceptance Rate: EA 31%

Perched atop its own hill overlooking Malibu and the Pacific Coast stands Pepperdine University, a liberal arts college rich in tradition and beauty. In the words of one student, "this place is absolutely gorgeous. I don't think I'll have this view again until years after graduation." Students rave about the varied and intimate undergraduate academic program coupled with the resources of a well-endowed school. "Pepp," as it is affectionately known on campus, is a private, Christian and somewhat conservative institution that offers small classes and a chance to meet and live with fellow students from all over the nation.

California Dream School

Pepperdine is one of several liberal arts-centered universities in California with a national reputation. George Pepperdine, who wanted to create a college with high academic standards that was based on the spiritual and ethical ideals of Christian faith, founded the University in 1937. For much of its history, the college was a small undergraduate-only program located in south central Los Angeles. In 1971, the schools of law, business, and education were added and the growing university moved to its current 830-acre Malibu campus in 1972.

Consistently ranked in the top 50 by U.S. News over the past three decades, Pepperdine has risen from its humble beginnings to hold its own with the more established institutions on the East coast. As one student put it, "students here had a lot of choices; they came here because they loved it." Many such students take advantage of the school's non-binding early action admissions program. Students applying to Pepperdine can submit an application in November and have a response by December 15, but do not have to commit to attending until May 1 after considering their other options.

When asked why they came to Pepperdine, many students singled out the small classes and intimate relationships Pepp students build with their professors and fellow students. Pepperdine is known for its small classes. This attention and devotion to undergrads makes Pepperdine somewhat unique among the giant public UC schools that dominate the Californian education system. "The profs and administration are great," said one freshman. In addition to regular office hours, the "accessible" and "friendly" professors often invite students to dinner and go out of their way to be helpful and understanding. "I was considering going to [UC] Riverside, but the huge classes turned me off—all my classes here have less than 20 students," one student said.

The Pepperdine curriculum includes a general education (GE) core that all students in the college must fulfill before they move on to take courses in their major. The GE requirements—including classes in English, math, religion, physical education and the Western Tradition—are very interesting according to students. Almost all provide the same intimate faculty contact as more specialized classes. "Of my GEs I only have one lecture class, and even there the professor knows everyone's names," said one freshman. The only requirement that seems to irk some students is the one on religion. "The religion one gets kind of old because you have to take four years of it," complained one Pepperdine student.

Students seem to be satisfied with the amount of ethnic and geographical diversity that the school offers. Although the single largest group of students is made up of California residents, who constitute over one-third of the student body, there are a fair number of students from all over the country. In addition, the administration has made a concerted effort over the last few years to increase minority enrollment. One student sums up that "it's not incredibly diverse, but somewhat," and most others agree with that statement. The school also has its fair share of international students. Despite their differences, "everyone seems to get along," commented a freshman, noting that "the freshman housing system is designed to put people from different backgrounds together."

Problematic Party Policies

The beautiful campus that Pepperdine students enjoy has just one big problem according to students: its strictness when it comes to parties. Because of the extremely strict on-campus party and alcohol policies, many students spend their weekends in nearby Los Angeles at schools such as USC and UCLA instead of staying at Pepp. "We're not allowed to party much on campus, and the parties here aren't great because it is dry; people go off campus a lot," commented one student. The upside to this is that students visiting area colleges can often find groups of other students from Pepperdine partying along with them. However, the penalties for being caught with prohibited substances—including alcohol—on campus are extremely harsh. If you are cited for possession by your RA, you can be asked to appear before the judicial committee and multiple offenses can lead to suspension or dismissal. According to one freshman, even a single offense can reduce your chances of being able to study abroad.

Because most students choose, in any case, to spend their weekends off campus—whether partying it up in Los Angeles, heading home, or simply taking advantage of the natural beauty surrounding the school—the actual campus is generally pretty quiet from Friday to Sunday. "People go off campus a lot and lots of people take mini-trips. Almost no one is here on the weekends," said one student. He added, however, that since "you'll be off too, it doesn't really make much of a difference." Since home is not far for many students, many also decide to head there for the weekends. "A lot of people are from LA metro area and go home every other week," said a student.

"This place is absolutely gorgeous, I don't think I'll have this view again until years after graduation."

On-campus social events—for the students who are around to enjoy them—are often hosted by the various Greek organizations. Fraternities and sororities are some of the most popular activities at Pepperdine and are growing more so each year. A majority of male students end up joining a fraternity, and nearly half the females pledge sororities. Since a change in policy in 1995, Pepperdine organizations are now allowed to join national chapters, whereas before they were limited to being local only.

Many students say one of the best things about the Greek system is its inclusivity. According to one freshman girl, "if you want to join a sorority you can—there will always be one for any girl who wants to join." The trend towards Greek life was spurred by the undergraduate organization Campus Life, which is designed to provide students with a better and more varied social scene. From working with the Greek system to putting on annual cultural and social events, the organization is responsible for much of Pepp's on-campus fun.

It's Good to Be King Neptune

A big part of the academic program for some—and a dull requirement for others—is Pepperdine's required convocation. These weekly sessions usually feature a lecture by a guest speaker or some other form of community building activity. "With the big cross out in front of the school, I was actually expecting a lot more religion," said one student. Another added, "I thought it was going to be like a cult," but both were pleasantly surprised by the actual programs on campus. Although church services and bible study are available on campus, neither is required. Indeed, most students say they are able to fit their beliefs into the Pepperdine structure. Even "convo" is often not religiously based—it can feature celebrity guests and musicians and really helps build school spirit.

Pepperdine "has great school spirit" according to students. The university mascot, King Neptune or "the wave," appears at most games, and students rally behind their teams. "A lot of people go to soccer and water polo games, but basketball is the really intense sport," explained one student. One Pepp tradition related to this basketball frenzy is Midnight Madness: at midnight on the day that the basketball season starts, the whole student body heads down to the gym to celebrate. The event is often well attended by celebrities. Adam Sandler recently made an appearance at it according to students.

Sweet Suites

Freshmen at Pepperdine live in suites with either a mountain or a beach view. Upperclassmen can live in the main buildings or in a new apartment tower. One thing students find disappointing about the living system is the curfew. Members of the opposite sex must be out of the dorms by 1 A.M. Other than that, however, students express overall satisfaction with the living conditions. Food, too, is "pretty good—for the most part," said one student. There is one main dining hall on campus, which serves a wide variety of food choices. For late-night snacking and hanging out there's the Sand Bar, a cyber café on campus that's open all night.

Between the "great" classes, "friendly" people, and "absolutely gorgeous" location, Pepperdine students are a happy bunch. Despite complaints over rules and administrative regulations, Pepperdine students delight in the fact they are getting an excellent education coupled with all the fun provided by having one of America's most active cities in the backyard. —*Chaitanya Mehra*

FYI

If you come to Pepperdine, you'd better bring "a car."

What is the typical weekend schedule? "Party in the city on Friday and Saturday nights, or go home. Saturday and Sunday are mostly used for studying, sports, or other extracurriculars."

If I could change one thing about Pepperdine, it would be "the religious aspects of the school."

Three things every student at Pepperdine should do before graduating are: Paint the rock, take in a day at the beach, and take advantage of the school's proximity to Los Angeles.

St. Mary's College of California

Address: PO Box 4800; Moraga, CA 94575
Phone: 925-631-4224
E-mail address: smcadmit@stmarys-ca.edu
Web site URL: www.stmarys-ca.edu
Founded: 1863
Private or Public: private
Religious affiliation: Catholic
Location: suburban
Undergraduate enrollment: 3,061
Total enrollment: 4,127
Percent Male/Female: 40%/60%
Percent Minority: 28%
Percent African-American: 6%
Percent Asian: 9%
Percent Hispanic: 16%
Percent Native-American: 1%
Percent in-state/out of state: 89%/11%
Percent Pub HS: 60%
Number of Applicants: 3,230
Percent Accepted: 77%
Percent Accepted who enroll: 23%
Entering: 580
Transfers: 162
Application Deadline: 1 Feb
Mean SAT: NA
Mean ACT: NA
Middle 50% SAT range: V 500-590, M 500-590
Middle 50% ACT range: NA
3 Most popular majors: business, communications, political science
Retention: 79%
Graduation rate: 60%
On-campus housing: 62%
Fraternities: NA
Sororities: NA
Library: 203,000 volumes
Tuition and Fees: $20,885
Room and Board: $8,550
Financial aid, first-year: 91%
Varsity or Club Athletes: 20%
Early Decision or Early Action Acceptance Rate: EA 32%

Although St. Mary's is located close to the bustling urban centers of San Francisco and Berkeley, the school manages to provide the feeling of an intimate, quiet community. This Catholic private school's lush, green campus of roughly 2,500 undergraduates has plenty of resources to provide what students say is a nurturing and stimulating experience; "Gaels" can boast of strong academic as well as athletic programs.

Not Just a Number

Applicants to St. Mary's apply under one of four schools: the School of Liberal Arts, the School of Science, the School of Economics and Business Administration, or the Intercollegiate Nursing Program. Each of these programs (except for the Intercollegiate Nursing Program) has its own collection of majors. Among the most popular majors are Business, Psychology, and Communications, but there are a wide variety of others to choose from. St. Mary's also allows its students to create their own major. Students say that St. Mary's is known for its undergraduate teacher's preparation program. In it, students complete a unique teaching degree program in five years, after which they earn their teaching credentials.

While there are requirements for the fulfillment of every major, there are also general education requirements for all students. Included among these are four "seminars," or intensive discussion-based classes. They range from Greek Thought to The Renaissance and allow student exposure to four specific genres of books. These requirements need only be completed by the time of graduation.

When St. Mary's advertises its average class size at 21 students, it really means it. All classes are capped at 30 students, and the school creates more classes rather than overfilling existing ones. Unlike many other colleges, there are no large freshman lectures, so there is no need for graduate student teaching assistants. Students are taught only by professors, and are happy to say that they "actually know our names."

Direct interaction with teachers is encouraged to give freshmen an extra opportunity to interact more with the faculty, each freshman seminar professor also doubles as a "Freshman Advisor." These faculty members serve as an academic as well as a personal resource to their students. The seminar groups also function as a social group: "We went to a Mexican restaurant and then to the Exploratorium," remarked one freshman. Another student's Greek Thought seminar got to go to "a full-out Greek dinner."

A particularly unique aspect of St. Mary's is its academic calendar. There are two regular semesters; the first from September to December and the second from February through May. Then there is "Janterm," short for the January Term. This takes place after the December holiday break but before second semester begins. Janterm classes meet four days a week for only three weeks, during which students only take one or two classes. The purpose is to "focus on one thing" so that you can explore new interests. Students can concentrate on developing one subject they are really interested in or, if they need to, can work towards major requirements. One student taking theater for Janterm said, "We get to put on Hansel and Gretel for inner-city children, and it's a time where I get to do one thing I like without having to worry about homework or other classes."

Living and Dining

St. Mary's guarantees housing for all freshmen and sophomores who submit their paperwork on time. While not all upperclassmen are guaranteed housing, there is some available. Freshman dorm buildings are clustered together on campus. Every dorm building is separated into single-sex floors, and each floor consists of a hallway of rooms with two bathrooms. Unlike many other schools' dorms, St. Mary's dorms do not share a lounge; students have to make an extra effort to get together in each other's rooms.

The students live with "RAs," Residence Advisors, and "RDs," Residence Directors. The RAs are generally juniors or seniors, and are responsible for regulating other students' activity. According to students, "they're mostly just your friends unless you really mess up." The RDs however, nicknamed "the Wardens," are "your parents' age and kind of strict." Watch the rules—no being on the other sex's floor after 2 A.M. or drinking in the dorms, or you can be written up.

The freshman dorm rooms are generally pretty small, as many are doubles that have been converted into triples. If you can afford it, paying more money can keep you out of a triple and even a double room if you don't want them. Rooms do get better as you get older. Most sophomores live in suites and the lucky upperclassmen who get on-campus housing are provided with "comparatively luxurious" townhouses. Off-campus housing varies in distance and quality—often found in the neighboring high-end suburbs of Lafayette and Walnut Creek—and while it is generally quite nice, it can be pricey. Student housing discounts help make this problem "not so bad."

St. Mary's is known for its undergraduate teacher's preparation program.

While there are some on-campus dining options, there aren't many. Students who live on campus are required to purchase a meal plan, which varies in meals per week as well as in the number of supplementary "flex dollars." The meals are redeemable throughout the week in the one cafeteria that serves the entire campus, which has "pretty good hours." "Sometimes the [hot] food is [unrecognizable]," said one student, but there is always a salad bar, a sandwich bar, and about ten types of cereal. In addition to the normal breakfast, lunch, and dinner that most dining facilities offer, St. Mary's cafeteria has a "late-night" meal period from 9 to 11 P.M. where junk food and snacks are available. The flex dollars are redeemable at the on-campus café, Taco Bell, and a grill known as the "Brickpile."

Religion Doesn't Wreck Your Life

Socially, it's possible to find almost anything at St. Mary's. "Some people like to think this is the biggest party school in the country, and drink every weekend," said one student. Another student noted that "chilling in the room and watching movies is just fine." There are a number of school-sponsored social activities throughout the year. Concerts, lectures, and shows take place in a central building known as Soda Hall, and all students are invited via e-mail to attend.

While there is no Greek life at St. Mary's, there are plenty of other options. Regular weekend parties are "usually going on in the upperclassman townhouses" and there are school-organized dance parties in Soda Hall as well as parties at other locations around the Bay Area. The Catholic nature of the school dictates some rules on campus—like no sex or alcohol—but students find plenty else to do around campus.

Many students attending St. Mary's are from California, so it isn't uncommon for them to go home for the weekend. Trips to nearby Berkeley and San Francisco are also popular weekend excursions. While it isn't necessary to have a car, it is very useful to have one or know someone who does. Parking is not a problem—there are a good number of commuter students—and it isn't difficult to find someone who can drive you where you need to go. Supermarkets, restaurants, and movie theaters are all within five or ten minutes from campus but are not very "realistic walks." Public transportation is available by way of buses and BART, the local rapid transit system, but somewhat inconvenient.

Not Lacking in Sports

There is a good deal of school spirit at St. Mary's, and all students are urged to attend events. Sporting events tend to bring large student crowds, and the teams are well funded and fielded. St. Mary's recruits top athletes and the school offers a number of sports scholarships each year, keeping St. Mary's teams strong. Each game has a particular area of the stands reserved for the "Gael force," or the pep group on campus. All students are welcome to sit in the section, and the entire St. Mary's crowd enjoys ringing St. Mary's large historic bell and making a lot of general commotion.

Despite the religious affiliation of the school and the fact that the majority of the student body is Christian, students say that the atmosphere is not one that makes people feel "dominated or pressured to convert in any way." There are Christian organizations on campus, but there a number of other clubs in which to participate as well: These range from Performing Arts and Accounting to the Gay and Lesbian Association, or Circle K, the community service club. "There's pretty much something for anyone," said one student. Despite some students' complaints that the school is just a "bunch of yuppies," and "a Ken-and-Barbie school," many students do hold jobs on and off campus.

All in all, students enjoy the small school, great location, and strong academics at St. Mary's: Undergraduates certainly boast an enjoyable college experience. *—Stephanie Teng*

FYI

If you come to St. Mary's, you'd better bring "a good attitude—you'll need it to juggle the work with extracurriculars and hang out time."

The typical weekend schedule at school includes: "going to San Francisco or Berkeley, eating at off-campus restaurants, taking it easy."

If I could change one thing about St. Mary's, "I would take away the Christian affiliation."

Three things every student should do before graduating are: "paint the 'SMU,' figure out the mystery of the catacomb, and attend a sporting event."

Stanford University

Address: Old Student Union;Stanford, CA 94305
Phone: 650-723-2091
E-mail address: admission@stanford.edu
Web site URL: www.stanford.edu
Founded: 1885
Private or Public: private
Religious affiliation: none
Location: suburban
Undergraduate enrollment: 7,360
Total enrollment: 14,173
Percent Male/Female: 49%/51%
Percent Minority: 51%
Percent African-American: 10%
Percent Asian: 25%
Percent Hispanic: 11%
Percent Native-American: 2%
Percent in-state/out of state: 50%/50%
Percent Pub HS: 70%
Number of Applicants: 18,599
Percent Accepted: 13%
Percent Accepted who enroll: 68%
Entering: 1,639
Transfers: 85
Application Deadline: 15 Dec
Mean SAT: NA
Mean ACT: NA
Middle 50% SAT range: V 660-760, M 690-780
Middle 50% ACT range: 28-33
3 Most popular majors: economics, interdisciplinary studies, computer science
Retention: 98%
Graduation rate: 93%
On-campus housing: 94%
Fraternities: 17%
Sororities: 12%
Library: 7,000,000 volumes
Tuition and Fees: $28,563
Room and Board: $9,073
Financial aid, first-year: 49%
Varsity or Club Athletes: 10%
Early Decision or Early Action Acceptance Rate: ED 23%

Located right outside San Francisco, Stanford is one place where students can gather on the grass year-round, enjoying the academia, sports, and arts all fostered by their red-roofed university. With a community of brilliant scholars—and a reverence for a more laid-back way of life—Stanford University gives its students unlimited opportunities to work hard while still taking the time to enjoy moments in the sun.

Fuzzies and Techies

Stanford's unique school year calendar begins in late September and consists of three 10- to 11-week quarters and one summer session. Since 180 units of credit are required to graduate and most courses are worth four to five units, students generally take four or five classes per quarter. Before graduating, students must fulfill writing, language, general education, and major requirements. The general education requirements include four areas of concentration from which students pick courses: introduction to humanities (I-Hum); science, technology, and mathematics; humanities and social sciences; and world culture, American culture, and gender studies.

Eventually, every Stanford student must decide whether he is a "techic" or a "fuzzy" (majoring in math/sciences or the humanities). While there is a clear distinction between the two macro-disciplines, students report that the quality of teaching in both areas is consistent. Generally, there can be less structure and emphasis in the fuzzy courses, but, as one sophomore notes, "that comes with the territory." Students are quick to say that they feel confident in most departments at Stanford, and came largely because "Stanford does everything well."

The departments where Stanford stacks up particularly well, and enrolls the most students, include computer science, economics, and human biology. Psychology and sociology are also cited as very popular majors, while studio art and managerial science are not as well respected by the students. Recently, there has been consolidation of the language departments (French and Italian are now grouped together, as are Spanish and Portuguese). However, while this restructuring is taking place, an intensified emphasis is being placed on "special languages" (languages hailing from non-Western countries).

Stanford boasts incredible professors in virtually all areas. Philip Zimbardo, the psychologist who headed the Stanford Prison Experiment in the 1970s, teaches the Psychology I course, while David Kennedy lectures on U.S. history and Tobias Wolff teaches short story writing. One junior notes that while these professors could be "cloistered with graduate students," they end up teaching mainly freshmen and "try to pull the freshman on their side." Because of all these great opportunities, it can be hard to choose a major. TAs are considered to be quite good at Stanford, and contact with the actual professors seems to be easy to make. When students go to their professors' office hours, they find their professors "genuinely happy to have [them] there." An anthropology major observed that Stanford promises to take good care of its undergraduates with its programs and professors, and "if students take them up on it, they come through."

Special academic programs that students often enjoy at Stanford include the various study abroad opportunities and three-week overseas seminars. Students also point out that while all Stanford's academic opportunities are full of work, it is "really hard to do poorly," and fairly easy to get a B. Getting an A, however, takes much more energy.

Stanford Duck Syndrome

One student said, "the typical Stanford student goes abroad, learns a language or two, and does too many activities for his health." The student population here is involved in a huge number of things, but somehow remains "laid-back, friendly, open, and relaxed," thus maintaining the "low-stress" environment that Stanford is so proud of. But Stanford students reveal that they, like most other top university students, are "trying to manage something really unmanageable." There is much fun by day, but when few are looking, there's hard work by night. One sophomore cited this as "Stanford Duck Syndrome"; the duck (Stanford student) appears to be sitting still against the rush of the stream, but is actually paddling like mad to stay in place. As one junior mathematics major commented, "We work hard, but there's just not very much complaining about it."

Stanford students come from all over—from public schools, private day schools, and boarding schools. Fifty percent of the undergraduate population is classified as belonging to a minority group, and students often feel like they have "the whole world in one place." It is also noted, however, that while there is complete representation, it is not equal; there are more people with upper-class backgrounds, and much of the campus ("like the U.S.," one student remarked) is white.

Amidst the diversity at Stanford is a definite hippie population, as well as a homosexual-friendly scene. Some of this seems to stem from the nearby San Francisco's progressive politics. Although Stanford is on the whole a very liberal campus, even Stanford students point to their rival, UC-Berkeley, as being the most liberal place around.

Under the Red-Tiled Roofs

Stanford University stretches across 8,000 acres, meaning it takes "20 minutes of hard biking to get off Stanford land in any direction." The middle of this huge campus is filled with the non-engineering buildings, all of which are low and roofed with Stanford's trademark red tile. Throughout the rest of the campus, there are "palm trees and fountains all over the place." Students gather year-round on the sprawling lawns, and also congregate in CoHo (the on-campus coffee house), the Student Union, the dining halls, and the dorms.

Many students say they meet most of their friends through their co-ed dormitories, which are assigned to students based on a random draw in which seniority doesn't count. While there is some frustration with this system, it has never been abolished. As one sophomore commented, "it's been around for a long time and I don't think anyone likes it." Nevertheless, most people live on campus and eat in their dormitory's dining hall.

Of the many dormitories on campus, some are only for freshmen while others are "four-class." Some also have reputations, such as the dilapidated Roble, rowdy Branner, and lovely Bob. There is a lot of variation in room sizes and conditions, though the university is executing a plan to renovate all the dormitories. Despite the renovations, there is currently a housing crunch, as more freshmen than expected are matriculating. Doubles have turned into triples, and what singles are left "seem to be gobbled up by the seniors." Living off campus isn't an option for most, as rents in surrounding Palo Alto are sky high.

"We work hard, but there's just not very much complaining about it."

Each major dorm has its own dining hall (one student described the food as "college mediocre"), where students can choose either an a la carte or all-you-can-eat meal plan. The dining situation is different for the other housing options at Stanford. Instead of living in a normal dormitory, students have the option (according to where they fall in the random draw) of living in one of the seven co-ops, The Row, or theme dorms. The co-ops, where students do their own cooking and cleaning, are mainly peopled by "bare-footed, tree-hugging hippies," while houses on The Row are the most elite living arrangements on campus. Theme dorms attract students who want to share a language, lifestyle, or ethnicity. Ethnic dormitories are fairly controversial at Stanford, as some students feel that it fosters the formation of cultural cliques. In theory, these dorms attempt to avoid such effects by allowing only 45 percent of the dorm to be people of the specified race, and having the other 55 percent be people who want to live with the said race. As students weigh over the pros and cons, debate continues.

Into Palo Alto, Out to San Francisco

The relationship between Palo Alto and Stanford is, as one junior described, "strange." Palo Alto is populated by "middle-aged dot-comers" and is decidedly not a college town, but it does have class. Though most places close before nine, students do stop by the shop Tea Time and the Stanford Theater, which shows movies from the 1930s–50s. By general consensus, "you don't go to Palo Alto unless you're going to dinner or the movies."

Though Palo Alto isn't a popular hangout, the industries and corporations surrounding it lend energy and excitement to the Stanford campus. A mathematics major described the "sense of creation" students feel being radiated from such nearby businesses as Google, Netscape, and Apple. The excitement only intensifies as one gets closer to San Francisco, where not only technology but theater, restaurants, and natural sights abound. Though it takes a bit of planning to carve out time, many Stanford students make day trips into the city. At only $10 roundtrip by train, students have a great opportunity to get to know a great city.

While on Stanford's turf, the social and party scenes are dominated by fraternities, most of which are on The Row. Students also go to movies, veg in the dorms, or throw dormitory parties. The hard (non-pot) drug scene is considered "virtually non-existent," and the drinking scene is described as "laid-back, like most things here." Still, the new head of the Stanford police recently implemented an anti-alcohol plan to "turn things around." Alcohol is no longer allowed in freshman dorms, and when it is found, it creates obvious friction between RAs and their charges.

Outside of partying, Stanford students keep busy with all kinds of extracurriculars, including the Stanford Daily, dozens of a cappella groups, and, of course, athletics. Students report a high level of palpable energy on campus—one-sixth of the student body is on varsity teams, and most of the others keep very active. As a member of the crew team observed, "there's lots of basketball, Frisbees, and running all the time." The surrounding area has "great outdoor places—the possibilities are endless," and the weather is always "perfect here—no one can deny it except the people from Hawaii."

The state-of-the-art fitness centers are open to all when the varsity teams aren't practicing, and the club and intramural sports have large followings. Often the level and intensity of these non-varsity sports are higher than they are at other colleges, mainly because some people who would make varsity teams at other schools don't make them here.

While the football game against UC-Berkeley and the NCAA tournament bring out the most fan spirit, all the varsity sports have fan support. The soccer team has a group of fans who call themselves the "Back of the Net Club"; they stand bhind the opposing team's goal and make a formidable ruckus. Opposing teams dread having to play at Stanford—both because of Stanford's amazing level of play and the incredible enthusiasm of their fans.

Students are quick to note that while the most palpable on-campus culture is the sports scene, the arts are also very well represented through Stanford's excellent music programs, visiting artists (YoYo Ma, Joshua Bell), and an active dance culture. All dance classes at the university are consistently booked solid, and formals are a distinctive part of the undergraduate experience. The student dance culture has established itself best through the traditional and elaborate Viennese Ball, held every February. Other Stanford traditions take a different turn, such as Full Moon on the Quad, where freshman and seniors meet up at midnight during the first full moon of the year and kiss. Some say this practice "has degraded into a swapping of saliva and an influx of mono," but like many traditions at Stanford, it is based on a real love of fun.

While balancing all these traditions, absorbing the energy and wisdom of world-renowned scholars, and experiencing the area of San Francisco, Stanford students cash in on an incredible education—one that always makes time for those relaxed moments in the sun. *—Elizabeth Dohrmann*

FYI

If you come to Stanford, you'd better bring a "bike."

What's the typical weekend schedule? "Begin the weekend on Thursday night; sleep as late as humanly possible on Friday and Saturday; go to the city or a sports game during the day, a club or concert at night; and work all day on Sunday."

If I could change one thing about Stanford, I would "have school year be in sync with the rest of the world, not start late in September and go so late into June."

Three things every student at Stanford should do before graduating are: "attend a sport you've never seen before, go to the Viennese Ball, and get to know San Francisco."

University of California System

The schools comprising the University of California System are renowned as some of the top research and academic institutions in the world. Since the founding of the first school in Berkeley in 1868, the UC schools have produced over 20 Nobel Prize winners. Currently, the system spans the entire state with universities in Berkeley, Davis, Irvine, Los Angeles, Riverside, San Diego, Santa Barbara, and Santa Cruz and one medical school in San Francisco. A tenth university, UC Merced, is currently under construction and is set to open in the fall of 2004. UC Merced is located on over 5,000 acres in the San Joaquin Valley and will have a high focus on environmental sensitivity and technology. Each of the eight undergraduate institutions receives a large number of applications from all over the nation and competition to enroll is high.

Distinctive Campuses

The foremost determining factor for many applicants is the location and climate of the schools. UCLA and Berkeley are in urban settings, and offer the exciting bustle and sophistication of cities. San Diego, Irvine, Santa Barbara, and Santa Cruz are near beaches, settings that tend to lull their respective students to take a day off to surf or sunbathe. Davis and Riverside are in more secluded rural areas, surrounded by the tranquil outdoors. Perhaps because their urban atmospheres appeal to more people, LA and Berkeley tend to have the most applicants and most competitive admissions process. Academically, all eight schools are top-notch and were recently recognized by *U.S. News & World Report* as some of the best schools in both the national public universities category as well as the national universities category.

Fall of Affirmative Action

With the fall of affirmative action in California, a casualty of Proposition 209, the demographic shift in the student body of the UC schools was dramatic. At UCLA and Berkeley, the Asian-American population has skyrocketed to the mid-40 percent range, while African-American and Hispanic acceptance rates have suffered. In addition to the lower acceptance rates, many African-Americans and Hispanics who were accepted have declined admission in favor of more "minority-friendly" campuses with higher African-American and Hispanic enrollment. Many students have noticed that with this change has come greater self-enforced segregation among the student body. The future ramifications of this decision are still hard to foresee, but as of now, California has become the testing ground for a non-affirmative action educational policy.

Why Attend a UC School?

Despite the recent admissions changes and financial hardships, the hard fact is that the UC System provides a great education at a comparably cheap price. The tuition for an in-state resident is six times less than tuition at an Ivy League college, and out-of-state students still pay half what they would at a similar private college. With the warm and temperate California weather, it is no wonder that students from all over the U.S. and the world choose one of the UC System universities to spend four blissful years. *—Seung Lee*

University of California / Berkeley

Address: 110 Sproul Hall; Berkeley, CA 94720
Phone: 510-642-3175
E-mail address: ouars@uclink4.berkeley.edu
Web site URL: www.berkeley.edu
Founded: 1868
Private or Public: public
Religious affiliation: none
Location: urban
Undergraduate enrollment: 23,835
Total enrollment: NA
Percent Male/Female: 46%/54%
Percent Minority: 57%
Percent African-American: 4%
Percent Asian: 42%
Percent Hispanic: 10%
Percent Native-American: 1%
Percent in-state/out of state: 89%/11%
Percent Pub HS: 85%
Number of Applicants: 36,466
Percent Accepted: 24%
Percent Accepted who enroll: 42%
Entering: 3,653
Transfers: NA
Application Deadline: 30 Nov
Mean SAT: NA
Mean ACT: NA
Middle 50% SAT range: V 570-700, M 610-740
Middle 50% ACT range: NA
3 Most popular majors: engineering, English, political science
Retention: 95%
Graduation rate: 84%
On-campus housing: 65%
Fraternities: 11%
Sororities: 10%
Library: 13,915,488 volumes
Tuition and Fees: $4,895 in; $18,375 out
Room and Board: $11,212
Financial aid, first-year: 48%
Varsity or Club Athletes: 9%
Early Decision or Early Action Acceptance Rate: NA

Hailed as the best public university in the country, the University of California at Berkeley attracts the state's best students. An elite faculty provides close instruction that rivals an Ivy League education, and as one of the states oldest universities, UC Berkeley has a rich tradition with loyal alumni.

"Bazerkeley" and its Radical Roots

Right on the bay, a subway ride away from San Francisco, the campus lies just under the beautiful eucalyptus hills of the Northern California. Besides being beautiful, the city of Berkeley also has a reputation for its radicalism. The campus is full of left leaning political energy that gives it a lively idealistic spirit. The revolutionary attitude of the 1960s has been best preserved on Telegraph Avenue, which includes a mixture burnt out hippies and young alternative activists. Demonstrators might be seen in Sprawl Plaza with picket signs side by side with naked men bearing signs saying, "Legalize Pot!" One junior girl said the best thing about Berkeley was the constant activity and entertainment in the center of campus. She commented, "Any afternoon I would walk out of my way through Sprawl Plaza just to see musicians, dancers, student a cappella groups, or political speeches." Just down the street are two solid blocks where vendors selling hemp bracelets and tie-dye pants litter the sidewalk.

In the same vein as the widespread liberalism, the student body shares a collective appreciation for cultural dynamism and diversity. Large cultural and ethnic clubs are very active and popular on campus. The surrounding area provides some of the best ethnic food in the U.S. Berkeley is a place where indy movie theatres and falafel restaurants can truly thrive.

Is It Too Big?

Well it's pretty big. With an undergraduate population around 40,000 many say it is difficult to find a niche at first. But freshmen are organized into colleges based on academic interests, so on the first day students are already provided with an easy social outlet. One freshman said she had been frustrated at the beginning of the year because she did not like the students in her dorm. She added that once she asserted herself socially she found many ways of meeting new and interesting people. Another junior corroborated, "Obviously you can't be friends with everyone, but if you make an effort, it is easy to find your niche." Many turn to the Greek life to expand their social horizons, and subsequently the Greek scene thrives and dominates the campus social scene. There are many fraternities and sororities, several of which are ethnically or culturally defined. But that does not mean that CAL is preppy, white, frat-boy-free. The Greek system allows for a very social and coed environment. Most of the major sororities and fraternities have an invitational or a date party in which they rent out clubs in San Francisco. Each brother or sister invites either a date or a few friends. One senior sorority member said "The most fun I've had at school is at invitationals in the City."

But don't let the traditional Greek scene scare you off; the many uppercrust students raised in California's affluent suburbs are balanced out by the diversity of the out-of-staters. There is a fraternity or sorority fit for almost everyone, but if that does not appeal to you, there are clubs, intramural sports, club sports, political groups, and the amazingly spirited "Booster Club."

Cal Spirit

Every weekend in November you can hear the chants around campus; "Stanford Sucks!" "Stanford Sucks!" It's true. The CAL-Stanford rivalry competes only with the ferocity of the USC-UCLA competition for California's biggest football rivalry. During a recent CAL football game against Oregon, Cal scored a touchdown just before the half for the lead. The crowd stood and cheered and sat back down. Soon after, they announced the score of Stanford game. When everyone realized Stanford was losing, the stadium went nuts and the band started playing the school fight song. In the middle of one of CAL's biggest games of the season the only thing audible in the stands were choruses of "Stanford Sucks!" Students were so thrilled to beat Stanford last year that they stormed the field by the thousands, took out the goal post, and marched it several blocks down campus.

The school is not just about football though. Basketball, volleyball, swimming and water polo are very competitive division I teams that receive a lot of support from the school. Just two years ago the school was furnished with a new Olympic size swimming pool and fitness center.

Academic Rigors

One film professor claimed CAL was as good as any Ivy League school if you know how to pick your major. If you pick one of the smaller departments for a major, some say you can get as much expert teaching and personal attention as at the best private universities. Berkeley's many graduate schools are generally ranked among the top five in each field. Fortunately this reputation carries over to the undergraduate level as well. Many classes are very large, however, holding up to five hundred students for general lecture classes. But also one can find as few as 20 peers in a given English or Literature class. Classes are said to be difficult and competitive. One sophomore applying to Haas business school for his junior year said, "Everyone is trying to beat each other out since most of the grades are curved. It is ultra-competitive."

"Obviously you can't be friends with everyone, but if you make an effort, it is easy to find your niche."

Each major offers a subset of various concentrations. The Biology and Chemistry departments are favorites of many, but considered rather tough, especially because they attract a large number of students hoping to apply to medical school. Computer science is also popular, but similarly considered to entail a lot of work. To liven up the rigors of traditional classes, every semester CAL offers fun classes such as "The History of Tupac" or "Black Jack."

Housing—Tough Luck!

Freshmen are provided with modest freshmen dorm rooms, while sophomores are left to face the "rat race" of Berkeley housing. Fraternities and sororities are cited as a great way to avoid this hassle. But if you have to brave the off-campus market, be forewarned that it is expensive. There are several apartment buildings scattered around campus, but you need to plan well in advance before they fill up. There are quite a few old beautiful houses owned by not only the fraternities, but also by the cultural houses or other large groups; some even rent rooms or floors from families from Berkeley residence. So while housing is tough to find and relatively pricey, you do find yourself in one of the best locations in California. If you are lucky you might even get a view of the Golden Gate from your window.

Where's the Beer

There are two choices when it comes to finding beer on the weekend: you can peruse frat row or hit up the bars. There are many popular bars within walking distance of campus, but sadly only good fake i.d.'s will buy you a drink. Fraternity or sorority parties are the most popular on-campus option. On a typical Saturday night the streets are hopping with eager partygoers looking for the frat house with the most kegs.

Overall, CAL, according to one enthusiastic freshman, is the "most diverse place I've ever been in my entire life. There's definitely something happening in here . . . and it's definitely groovy. —*Quinn Fitzgerald*

FYI

If you come to Berkeley, you'd better bring "an unfettered liberal spirit."

What is the typical weekend schedule? "Homework on Friday afternoon until it's party-time, repeat on Saturday, and don't forget the occasional protest!"

If I could change one thing about Berkeley, "I'd end the controversy over affirmative action."

The three things you have to do before graduating are "eat at a Thai restaurant, tear down the goal posts after winning the Cal-Stanford football game, and give change to a bum who claims it will go to his pot fund."

University of California / Davis

Address: One Shields Avenue; Davis, CA 95616
Phone: 530-752-2971
E-mail address: undergradadmissions@ucdavis.edu
Web site URL: www.ucdavis.edu
Founded: 1905
Private or Public: public
Religious affiliation: none
Location: suburban
Undergraduate enrollment: 22,786
Total enrollment: NA
Percent Male/Female: 44%/56%
Percent Minority: 50%
Percent African-American: 3%
Percent Asian: 36%
Percent Hispanic: 10%
Percent Native-American: 1%
Percent in-state/out of state: 97%/3%
Percent Pub HS: 86%
Number of Applicants: 28,794
Percent Accepted: 63%
Percent Accepted who enroll: 26%
Entering: 4,672
Transfers: 1,941
Application Deadline: 30 Nov
Mean SAT: NA
Mean ACT: NA
Middle 50% SAT range: V 510-630, M 560-670
Middle 50% ACT range: 21-27
3 Most popular majors: agricultural business and management, psychology, English language and literature
Retention: 91%
Graduation rate: 78%
On-campus housing: 19%
Fraternities: 8%
Sororities: 9%
Library: NA
Tuition and Fees: $5,498 in; $18,478 out
Room and Board: $9,410
Financial aid, first-year: 42%
Varsity or Club Athletes: 5%
Early Decision or Early Action Acceptance Rate: NA

Located in the heart of the Central Valley, University of California at Davis is the largest of the nine UC campuses with 5,200 plush acres. Although Davis started out as the "University Farm," you'd be terribly wrong in calling it that today! Its academics are among the best offered in the nation, and is one of the top public universities. Its sports put numerous other schools to shame with many NCAA titles. And the students that walk its campus are friendly and diverse in their interests. Davis students still get a hint of the farm that the campus once was with the cows and large open spaces, but "this school is just like any other college. Parties, dating, you name it. We've got it."

Do U.C. Intensity Here?

Although Davis was once an institution for those only interested in agriculture, today it offers its students an opportunity to learn from a broad range of disciplines. The school has a GE (General Education) requirement, which has three components: Topical Breadth, Social-Cultural Diversity, and Writing Experience. To fulfill this requirement, six courses must be taken from the two topical breadth subjects that don't include your major, one course must be taken from the social-cultural diversity component, and three courses are required from the writing experience component. One student comments that "the GE system really helps us get a better background in subjects outside of our concentration. I like it a lot." UC-Davis also has University Requirements and separate requirements for whichever college the student decides to enter (College of Agricultural and Environmental Sciences, College of Engineering, and College of Letters and Science). Although it seems as though the school has way too many requirements, one student says "it's not too rigid and strict nor loose and easy. I just take what I want to."

But it's not always easy to get the courses you want at Davis. "A lot of people don't get into the classes they want because the school is so big," said one student about the courses at Davis. With such a large student body, people complain that the courses have too many enrollees, making interaction with professors almost impossible. Another complaint students have is that some of the professors and "way too many TAs are foreign," making it hard for them to understand lectures and the weekly discussion sessions. Some students say that they are "happy with a lot of the professors and TA's. They're usually willing to help you out if you ask." On the other hand, one sophomore says, "I think our professors aren't qualified to tell you the truth, and the TAs are pretty weak all around so far."

Davis offers a couple of different honors programs including the Davis Honors Challenge Program and the Integrated Studies Program. Davis Honors Challenge involves an application process while Integrated Studies is an invitational, first-year, residential honors program limited to the top 3 percent of the entering class. Both programs require members to be highly motivated and grant students the opportunity to enhance their educational experience at Davis. When asked about the Davis Honors Challenge, one student in the program commented that "the seminars we're required to take are a joke!"

Students claim that Biological Sciences, Psychology, and Computer Science are among the more popular majors at Davis. "Computer Science is hard as heck and so competitive!" Some students comment that Managerial Economics and Design are probably the easiest majors at their school. As far as classes go, "Everyone seems to want to do design and nutrition . . . probably since they are so easy." The overall workload at Davis is "easier than high school" for some students and quite the opposite for others. "The work they give here is by no means unbearable," says one student. "As long as you keep up with the reading and seek help when you need it, you'll be on top of things." Indeed, students must keep up with their studies because it's fast-paced at Davis. Their 10-week quarter system requires students to "take in a lot of information in a very short time period." Some students complain that they don't get as much out of their classes because of this, while others think that it's a great system that allows them to take more classes. One thing that Davis students *do* agree on is the necessity of the weekends to recuperate and relax.

Where Do You Want To Go Today? Off Campus!

The social life at Davis is pretty limited. Some students party at the frat houses, some catch movies that the campus organizes, and others just chill with their friends. If they have access to a car, Davis students will probably leave campus for their fun. With Sacramento to the east and the San Francisco Bay Area to the west, students can find a plethora of places at which to eat, shop, and go clubbing. The campus tries to engage its students with many speakers, performances, and dances. "Turbulence" is a dance that freshmen go to every year to meet new people. "I think it's easy to meet new people here. It's just a matter of whether or not you're willing to go out and actually meet them," says one junior.

Even though there is a Greek system at Davis, it only consists of about 20 percent of the student body. So non-Greeks definitely don't feel left out. Alcohol is pretty big among the frats and smoking is prevalent all over campus, but if you don't do either, you won't feel out of place. The student body is ethnically pretty diverse, although predominantly Caucasian and Asian. Most of the students are California residents from a wide range of economic backgrounds. The typical look varies widely as well with some students looking "like they just rolled out of bed" and others dressing up in nice clothes. But on the average, students at Davis are very fit and athletic. "Everyone wants that Cali bod," laughed one student.

You can't beat a place that has smiling faces and Cali's sunny weather to complement it!

As far as extracurriculars go, with such a large student body and over 300 different organizations, there's sure to be something that interests each individual. "Everybody tries to do something to get involved on campus." Intramural sports are pretty big as are the religious groups at UC-Davis. Students say that "it's a good way to make friends and find out more about yourself."

Davis Got Game

Even though Davis doesn't offer athletic scholarships, its sports teams consistently rank among the top in Division II of the NCAA. In addition, Davis has won the Sears Directors' Cup for overall excellence in both men's and women's athletic programs for NCAA Division II schools and was recently named the top Division II school for female athletes by *Sports Illustrated.* The annual Causeway Classic football game against Sacramento State University usually attracts a lot of Davis students cheering for their school. With the "Aggie Pack," Davis's cheer organization (acclaimed as the largest in the nation), students get pretty hyped for their teams as shirts, food, and other items are thrown into the crowd. "The Aggie Pack really gets us going! It's amazing how the school spirit just rises to a different plane when they come out!" The facilities for non-athletes at Davis are "wonderful, but there could always be more of everything since there are always so many guys working out and playing basketball all the time." The campus offers a swimming pool, tennis courts, and even a roller hockey rink!

Green Acres Is the Place to Be

The open areas of green and abundant trees on campus make it a "peaceful and enjoyable place to be, whether you are by yourself or with other people." Most of Davis is flat, spread out, and very nature-oriented. "I don't think I could survive without my bike here. The campus is way too big to walk." Some students complain about the odor from the cows near Tercero dorm, but most say that it's bearable after a while. "The arboretum is a great place to go. It's so relaxing to be surrounded by the ducks and the serenity there," said one student when asked about his favorite hiding place on campus. The surrounding town of Davis is "small, quiet, and suburban-like . . . it's nothing different from any small college town."

Students say they feel safe on campus despite some small crime incidents here and there. Recent disturbances on campus include some racially motivated hate crimes. Violent confrontations between an Asian American frat and a Caucasian frat have resulted in an increased awareness of racial tensions within the student body. Still, Davis students say that for the most part they still feel safe, just more wary of their surroundings.

Most freshmen live on campus in the dorms with Residential Advisors, but the bulk of upperclassmen live in apartments. The dorms usually have air-conditioning with co-ed floors and single-sex bathrooms. Some dorms have different programs and all dorms vary in size. "I met most of my closest friends in my dorm. Everyone should live in a dorm their freshman year because you get to meet and live with so many interesting people!" After freshman year, most people are booted off-campus to apartments. The rent is "good compared to other schools nearby like Stanford and Berkeley" but the degree of expense really varies depending on whether you get a shack or a model home. One accommodation Davis makes for its students living off-campus is the UNITRANS bus system that connects to the main campus.

The meal plan is pretty flexible. Students choose how many meals they want and pay accordingly. One student complained "It's a rip-off for the quality of food we get," while another said that "it's fine." With plenty of restaurants surrounding the campus, however, students don't starve to death. There are the usual fast food restaurants like Jack in the Box, McDonald's, KFC, and Wendy's. Some of the more favorite restaurants are Woodstock's Pizza, Pluto's, and Fuji's all you can eat sushi bar. And one can't forget about the late-night Chinese food deliveries!

Nothing's Better Than Some California Sunshine

The small-town, country atmosphere of UC-Davis is what attracts most students to the school. Although the fast-paced schoolwork and abundant extracurriculars provide challenging opportunities, it doesn't keep the students from maintaining a laid-back attitude and friendly ambiance. "The one thing that separates us from other schools is our friendly and open student body. You can't beat a place that has smiling faces and Cali's sunny weather to complement it!" —*Jane Pak*

FYI

If you come to Davis, you'd better bring "a bike for campus and a car by sophomore year—campus is so spread out that I feel tempted to drive to class."

What is the typical weekend schedule? "Hanging out with friends and maybe going to room parties or the Frats."

If I could change one thing about Davis, I'd "change the way you feel like you're a number rather than a person."

The three things every student should do before graduating from Davis are "make a trip to Sacramento, get lost in the boonies at night with some friends, and live in the dorms."

University of California / Irvine

Address: 204 Administration Building; Irvine, CA 92697-1075
Phone: 949-824-6703
E-mail address: oars@uci.edu
Web site URL: www.uci.edu
Founded: 1965
Private or Public: public
Religious affiliation: none
Location: suburban
Undergraduate enrollment: 19,179
Total enrollment: NA
Percent Male/Female: 48%/52%
Percent Minority: 64%
Percent African-American: 2%
Percent Asian: 51%
Percent Hispanic: 11%
Percent Native-American: 0%
Percent in-state/out of state: 98%/2%
Percent Pub HS: 82%
Number of Applicants: 30,598
Percent Accepted: 56%
Percent Accepted who enroll: 24%
Entering: 4,027
Transfers: 1,447
Application Deadline: 30 Nov
Mean SAT: NA
Mean ACT: NA
Middle 50% SAT range: V 510-620, M 560-670
Middle 50% ACT range: NA
3 Most popular majors: biology, economics, computer sciences
Retention: 93%
Graduation rate: 76%
On-campus housing: 29%
Fraternities: 8%
Sororities: 8%
Library: 2,560,259 volumes
Tuition and Fees: $5,804 in; $18,784 out
Room and Board: $7,520
Financial aid, first-year: 47%
Varsity or Club Athletes: 7%
Early Decision or Early Action Acceptance Rate: NA

One of the first things that students at UC Irvine comment on when asked about their school is how much they love their campus. The 1,500-acre modern, beautiful campus is located in Orange County, only minutes from the Pacific Ocean. In addition to being close to the water, UCI is also close to home for much of the student body. And although it is one of the younger campuses in the UC system, UCI is "one of the fastest growing in stature and size" and is the first public university to have faculty members awarded two Nobel prizes in two separate fields the same year.

A Wide Variety of Classes

To accommodate its large student population, UCI boasts a renowned faculty and a broad range of course offerings. Academics are considered intense, and students are happy with the diverse course offerings at UC Irvine. UCI offers majors in seven schools: Engineering, Social Ecology, Art, Humanities, Physical Sciences, Biological Sciences, and Social Sciences. The biology department is particularly strong and boasts the most majors. UC Irvine is on the 10-week quarter system, and the first thing students mention when asked about their courses is the heavy workload. General education requirements (or "breadth requirements" as students call them) are extensive and varied, and include competence in a foreign language, three natural science courses, and three writing courses. While some complained about the hassle of the requirements, they were quick to mention "cool and interesting" classes such as Greek Literature and the History of Jazz.

Students need 180 credits to graduate, which means most undergrads take three to four classes a quarter. Some mentioned difficulties enrolling in classes at times, and anticipated taking five years to graduate. UCI is a large public university with an undergraduate enrollment of over 12,000 students, and class size can often reach "intimidating proportions." Introductory courses often enroll about 400 students, though discussion sections with only about 15 to 20 students provide a more interactive atmosphere.

A Growing Campus

When UCI was founded in the 1960s, the campus consisted of 1,500-acres of treeless terrain. Less than forty years later, it has been filled with facilities that make life easier for the thousands of students at UCI. Among the newest buildings on campus is the Anteater Recreation Center (known among students as the ARC), where students participate in sports and other planned activities, such as dance lessons, karate classes and rock climbing. The Bren Center, UCI's student activity center, hosts banquets, exhibitions, concerts, and other events. Some of the center's more popular recent events have been the World Championship Wrestling tournaments and MTV's Campus Invasion Tour. The center can also be rented out to the general public for activities, such as dance competitions and sporting events. As one student says, "Residents from all over Orange County and other areas of California often visit the Bren Center for its most popular events."

The Irvine Barclay Theatre hosts orchestras, cabaret, concerts, and other performances several times a week. The theater sponsors an arts education program called ArtsReach that is designed to provide students with knowledge and appreciation of the performing arts. Crawford Hall is where men's and women's volleyball games are held. Students who are fond of water sports should be sure to visit the Aquatic Complex, where they can watch the Anteaters compete against other colleges. The Anteater Pool, which holds nearly one million gallons of water, is one of the largest competitive pools in the United States.

Go Anteaters!

Although UCI does not have a football team, sports still play a major role in the lives of students. As one student commented, "All we are missing is a football team." Despite this shortcoming, students at UCI still have plenty of enthusiasm for their school's athletics. Perhaps the most popular team on campus is the men's basketball team, which consistently does well and was recently seeded third in the Western Division of the Big West Tournament. A lot of students enjoy participating in intramural sports, where different organizations and fraternities engage in friendly competition for an invigorating break from their studies.

Life On and Off Campus

While the percentage of students involved in the Greek system is relatively small, fraternity and sorority mixers are cited as the places to go for parties. Thursday and Friday nights are party nights, and fraternities and sororities provide the alcohol. But there is very little pressure to participate in the Greek system, and ethnic fraternities and sororities are also options. Fraternities and sororities are prevalent at UCI, where "students can often be found hanging out with their brothers or sisters at the food court." Every Thursday night, people at UCI look forward to attending frat parties, since Irvine can reportedly be boring at times. The surrounding cities also offer much to do for students. As one student noted, "Ring Road is like the promenade of UCI. There is always something going on, whether it be a fair, clubs offering food, games to attract people, or speakers." Popular options include Newport Beach, Costa Mesa and Los Angeles, as well as clubbing and going to raves, where students "dress to impress."

Flashy cars are known in the parking lots, and many of them are "fixed up and lowered to the ground with great sound systems." However, many students don't feel a pressure to conform to this "fashion show," because they can easily blend into the large student body. A portion of the student body at UCI takes fashion very seriously. As one student, "many people are indifferent about what they wear, while for others their clothing is a top priority."

Freshmen are guaranteed housing, and in their subsequent years usually seek off-campus housing in apartments and homes in town, which are plentiful. Two housing complexes named Mesa Court and Middle Earth are freshman residences, each accommodating about 1,200 students. A fairly large portion of the student body commutes, and as a result "parking can be a hassle at times."

In addition to the regular weekly options for hanging out, there are numerous special events held at UCI each year. "Celebrate UCI" is the annual open house held each April. This event gives the community, alumni, prospective students and their families the opportunity to tour the campus and observe performances throughout the day. The semi-annual formal dance also allows students a chance to get dressed up and have fun with their classmates and meet some new people. As one student put it, "as long as you make an effort, it is not hard to meet a lot of great people here."

"When you are tired of school, just chill at the beach."

Students who live on or off campus enjoy the all-you-can-eat dining facilities on campus, which also provide the option of packing a bag lunch for those with classes during regular meal times. There are two main dining halls, which students feel are not bad at all, although one cautioned, "Keep away from the pasta sauces."

Although academics at UCI are a top priority for students, it is often difficult to take for granted many of the various opportunities. Whether it be intramural sports, research, studying abroad, clubs, or organizations, students have an array of opportunities to take advantage of at the University of California at Irvine. —*Robert Wong*

FYI

If you come to UCI, you'd better bring "tennis shoes—while Irvine is flat, the campus is remarkably hilly."

What is the typical weekend schedule? "Our big party night is Thursday because most students go home for the rest of the weekend."

If I could change one thing about UCI, I'd "get rid of the de facto segregation that has become institutionalized through the social options available to students."

The three things that every student should do before graduating from UCI are "to go to a concert at the Bren Center, hang out at the beach, and get to know people."

University of California / Los Angeles

Address: 405 Hilgard Avenue; Los Angeles, CA 90095-1436
Phone: 310-825-3101
E-mail address: ugadm@saonet.ucla.edu
Web site URL: www.ucla.edu
Founded: 1919
Private or Public: public
Religious affiliation: none
Location: urban
Undergraduate enrollment: 24,899
Total enrollment: NA
Percent Male/Female: 46%/54%
Percent Minority: 57%
Percent African-American: 4%
Percent Asian: 38%
Percent Hispanic: 15%
Percent Native-American: 0%
Percent in-state/out of state: 93%/7%
Percent Pub HS: 80%
Number of Applicants: 43,443
Percent Accepted: 24%
Percent Accepted who enroll: 41%
Entering: 4,257
Transfers: 2,271
Application Deadline: 30 Nov
Mean SAT: NA
Mean ACT: NA
Middle 50% SAT range: V 550-670, M 590-720
Middle 50% ACT range: 22-29
3 Most popular majors: economics, psychology, English language and literature
Retention: 97%
Graduation rate: 85%
On-campus housing: 30%
Fraternities: 12%
Sororities: 9%
Library: 7,616,016 volumes
Tuition and Fees: $4,878 in; $17,257 out
Room and Board: $10,452
Financial aid, first-year: 52%
Varsity or Club Athletes: 10%
Early Decision or Early Action Acceptance Rate: NA

Surrounded by Bel Air, Beverly Hills, and the Santa Monica Mountains, a picturesque Southern California campus is home to one of the UC's most premier academic institutions. With a huge undergraduate population of 35,000, UCLA offers a panoply of academic, athletic, and extracurricular opportunities for every type of student. UCLA distinguishes itself from universities of similar size and reputation through its expressed commitment to undergraduate education.

First-Rate Academics

In spite of their university's size, UCLA students do not report feeling neglected. While students claim that classes fill up quickly, very few are unable to take their top choices. "It is also great if you are an athlete or an honors student, because you get to pick your classes before everyone else," explained one junior. In addition, most describe accessible professors and small class sizes in upper-level courses. These qualities make UCLA academically competitive with the top universities in the country, and give its students a sense of community in such a large institution.

A unique aspect of academics at UCLA is the modified quarter system which consists of three ten-week periods. Students take three sets of classes each academic year compared with the normal two at universities on the semester system. Although students like to complain about the general education (GE) requirements, which include courses in departments they do not necessarily major in, they often grudgingly admit that it opens their eyes to subjects they never thought they would be interested in. At the completion of the GE requirements, students take prerequisite courses for the major they plan on applying to. Engineering and business-economics are two majors with a competitive application process, while more popular majors are economics, chemistry, and particularly biology.

The courseload around finals week often takes its toll on students' sanity, but don't be frightened during finals week when loud, desperate yelps are heard from the street late at night. The traditional Midnight Yells take place every night during finals to offer therapy for those who need to release their test-taking anxiety. The event has become a social, stress-relieving fanfare, and in years past it has gotten out of control with students burning furniture in the street. Now every finals night LAPD patrols the streets in riot gear just to keep students in check.

Party LA-Style

The social scene at UCLA during the weekends is dominated by the fraternities and sororities. At such a large school these are popular social niches that make the social scene less intimidating. "It isn't necessary to be in a frat or sorority; it just makes the school a little smaller for you," explained one sophomore. In-demand underclass girls need not join a sorority to be involved in the weekend Greek scene. This is less true for underclass boys, who have a harder time gaining entrance to Greek parties if they are not in a fraternity themselves.

Alternatives to Greek life include apartment parties and local bars within walking distance. However, being underage can be a problem even with fake identification. "Tons of people use fake IDs all the time, but I got arrested and you have to deal with the LAPD if you get caught," said one embarrassed freshman.

UCLA students often venture off campus for social events, as many of them are from the area and have cars. Some students choose to go home for the weekend, treating UCLA more like a commuter school. On the other hand, there are nights on the LA strip when there is no dearth of lively hot spots teeming with attractive college students. Even trips to Mexico are not unheard of, with the border only a couple of hours away.

Eat, Sleep, and Be Merry

The residential plan for UCLA students is quite varied. Freshman live in one of four high-rise dormitories. These buildings are described as madhouses due to the number of excited, bewildered, and reportedly drunk freshman. Upperclassmen look back on these dorms with nostalgia from the tamer confines of university-owned apartment buildings. Such accommodations are more like hotels, many with picnic and volleyball areas. For those not living in a fraternity or sorority house, another option is finding an apartment in one of the local neighborhoods such as Santa Monica, Culver City, or Westwood. Private apartments are often luxurious compared to the freshman dorms and Greek houses, but may be further from campus.

"I love UCLA but it was not what I expected. I was a little shocked. I guess I didn't prepare myself for the LA mentality,"

Unlike most college food, the UCLA meal plan gets rave reviews. Students enjoy hanging out in the Ackerman Union for hours, studying, socializing and taking advantage of the fast-food dining options such as Taco Bell. Others enjoy the meal plan because they can use allotted funds at many other eateries on campus.

Being a Bruin

What does it mean to be a UCLA Bruin? Well, whatever you want it to mean. If you're an athlete, you find yourself at a highly competitive Division I school with plenty of campus recognition. *Sports Illustrated* named UCLA the number one "jock school" in the country two years ago. The university has won over 80 NCAA championships in basketball, football, volleyball, and water polo. Home football games are always an occasion for an enthusiastic display of school spirit, especially when the Bruins play UCLA's rival, USC.

There are plenty of community service opportunities and a countless number of clubs, societies, and club sports on and off campus. Moreover, at such a large and diverse school, students have access to interesting jobs on campus. "What makes this place different from other schools is the opportunity we have to work on research projects and get involved with faculty that are well-known in their fields," boasts one female junior.

Another aspect students consistently mention is the LA mindset. "I love UCLA but it was not what I expected. I was a li tle shocked. I guess I didn't prepare myself for the LA mentality," said one sophomore boy. The "LA mentality" is a Hollywood-infused, fast-paced, image-oriented social stance that is both loved and hated. Whether students embrace it or reject it, this attitude has found its way into the UCLA campus dynamic. While many are disgusted by the superficiality, with its make up, hair bleach, and who-you-know name dropping, they find relief in the kicked-back mentality pervasive in the sun-soaked Southern California Coast. —*Quinn Fitzgerald*

FYI

If you come to UCLA you'd better bring "a parking pass."

What is the typical weekend schedule? "An overnight getaway with a fraternity or sorority, nights out at the local bars, or a quiet weekend of hanging out and studying."

If I could change on thing about UCLA, I would "make it more personable."

Three things every student at UCLA should do before graduation are "attend a USC vs. UCLA football game, eat at Diddy Reese's famous cookie shop, and cruise the Sunset strip."

University of California / Riverside

Address: 900 University Avenue; Riverside, CA 92521
Phone: 909-787-3411
E-mail address: discover@pop.ucr.edu
Web site URL: www.ucr.edu
Founded: 1954
Private or Public: public
Religious affiliation: none
Location: urban
Undergraduate enrollment: 14,124
Total enrollment: NA
Percent Male/Female: 46%/54%
Percent Minority: 70%
Percent African-American: 6%
Percent Asian: 41%
Percent Hispanic: 23%
Percent Native-American: 0%
Percent in-state/out of state: 99%/1%
Percent Pub HS: 87%
Number of Applicants: 18,162
Percent Accepted: 82%
Percent Accepted who enroll: 24%
Entering: 3,563
Transfers: 859
Application Deadline: 30 Nov
Mean SAT: NA
Mean ACT: NA
Middle 50% SAT range: V 450-570, M 490-620
Middle 50% ACT range: 18-23
3 Most popular majors: business, social sciences, biology
Retention: 85%
Graduation rate: 66%
On-campus housing: 28%
Fraternities: 3%
Sororities: 3%
Library: 2,081,146 volumes
Tuition and Fees: $5,078 in; $18,558 out
Room and Board: $9,350
Financial aid, first-year: 56%
Varsity or Club Athletes: 4%
Early Decision or Early Action Acceptance Rate: NA

Although UC Riverside is often overshadowed by more prominent universities within the University of California system, UCR holds true to the UC tradition of public school excellence as a major research center. Nestled within the quiet suburban town of Riverside, less than an hour away from metropolitan Los Angeles, UCR affords its students a tranquil academic atmosphere, as well as the resources of a major city. Its relative newness and smaller size offers students a certain charm that differentiates it from other UC schools.

With Room to Grow

To date, UCR remains one of the smallest UCs in terms of student body size, but the largest of the UCs in terms of acreage. Its undergraduate student body of roughly 13,000 is considered "just right for the size of the school." Ten minutes is all it takes to walk from one edge of campus to the other, and much of the outlying land is used for research or is slated for development. The architectural design of the campus is characterized by a lack of uniformity; according to several students, there seems to be no underlying theme that connects the modern buildings. UCR is under constant construction and renovation as it works for continual campus improvement. A recent addition to the campus is the Fine Arts Building—a distinctive, angular, "smoky plum" structure. New dorms are being built to keep up with the demand for housing, and ongoing refurbishments of existing residential halls make living at UCR "pretty comfortable, with heating, air conditioning, and plenty of space." Most dorms are doubles, with a few singles and triples. Pentland, one of the three residential halls, consists of all suites. The majority of freshmen live in the dorms, and on-campus housing is guaranteed for two years. However, living on-campus is not a requirement, even for freshmen, and many students choose to live in apartments on or off campus, or in one of the many fraternity houses.

A Stone's Throw

Riverside, located east of downtown Los Angeles, is a quiet town somewhat isolated from the bustle of the neighboring city sprawl. One freshman states, "Riverside is just a stone's throw away from L.A., but it's nothing like L.A." (However, even with picturesque grass and mountains in the background, the town inherits the smoggy air characteristic of L.A. without the urbanity.) Students have easy access to all the cultural resources that Los Angeles has to offer, while living in a tranquil working environment that facilitates education.

A Quiet Place to Study

With reportedly few attractions within the immediate area, "Riverside is a place where you can concentrate on studying because, well, there isn't much else to do." One of UCR's most heralded aspects is its Biomed Program, a joint association with UCLA Medical School. Twenty-five spots are made available in UCLA Med each year for graduates of the program, and competition for these spots is fierce. Riverside students often gripe about the class curve being set by "those overachievers in the Biomed Program." The most popular majors at UCR are business, engineering, and the life sciences. As one senior noted, "I haven't met that many people in the humanities, but I am sure there are some out there."

Students report an environment supportive of homosexuals and interracial couples, and, as one student said, "UCR has an abundance of attractive people."

Because many classes are held in large lecture halls, one common complaint among students is the size of most introductory courses for common majors. Even when these classes are broken down into discussion sections run by TAs, they often have 15 to 40 people, resulting in "less individual attention and less interaction with the professor." Among underclassmen, the biggest frustration is capping enrollment. Stated one freshman, "we're the last to choose classes, so it's incredibly hard to get the classes you want, and even if you can, it's impossible to get them in the right time slots." Said another, "course selection is done either over the phone, by appointment, or on the web, and it really sucks to be late."

Commuters, Greeks, and the UCR Night Life

Many Riverside students live in the surrounding area, and weekends are less lively than those of other universities, as a large number of students commute from home. For those who choose to stay, Downtown Riverside is five to 10 minutes away, yet few undergrads have cars, leaving many students with the common sentiment that "besides fast food and a movie theater, there's nothing to do here." However, the Greek scene is prominent on campus, and frat parties are fairly inclusive. In addition, there are many dances open to the entire student body, a few clubs, and a popular UCR Movie Night once a week. While both random hook-ups and long-term relationships exist to some extent, the dating scene is also quite lively.

Students report an environment supportive of homosexuals and interracial couples, and as one student said, "UCR has an abundance of attractive people."

Although the social scene lags somewhat on campus, some students argue: "Come on. It's L.A. There's always something to do; you just have to look around and deal."

Sagging Spirit

There is not much school spirit for athletics at UCR, a Division I school. On the whole, students seem apathetic about their teams and many feel that they are "at the bottom of the Division I totem pole." However, as one student stated, "I think that over time, now that we're part of Division I and playing better teams, school spirit will increase when it comes to athletics."

One source of pride that many students mention is the "C." All UC schools have a "C" located somewhere near campus. Riverside's "C" is carved into a mountain, reportedly "the biggest 'C' of all the UCs." Getting to the "C" is a fair hike, but a must-do for spirited or adventurous UCR students.

While students do not appear to rally behind their teams, involvement in sports certainly exists. Intramural sports are particularly popular, and according to one student, "with nice weather year-round, getting involved in intramurals is easy and a welcome break from studying."

Although it is somewhat isolated from the heart of Los Angeles, many students appreciate Riverside for its "quiet environment that invites hardcore studying." Students often forget that UCR was not their first choice college because of all that it has to offer. According to one student, "Despite its unpolished reputation, UCR is more like the underdog of the UC system." If a good education is more important to you than bragging rights, UCR is not a bad choice at all. *—Theresa Nguyen*

FYI

If you come to UCR, you'd better bring "sunblock."

What is the typical weekend schedule? "Drive home on Friday and come back on Sunday."

If I could change one thing about UCR, I'd "liven up the city, because it gets pretty boring here."

Three things every student should do before graduating from UCR are "go to a frat party, climb to the 'C,' and explore Los Angeles."

University of California / San Diego

Address: 9500 Gilman Drive; La Jolla, CA 92093-0337
Phone: 858-534-4831
E-mail address: admissionsinfo@ucsd.edu
Web site URL: www.ucsd.edu
Founded: 1960
Private or Public: public
Religious affiliation: none
Location: urban
Undergraduate enrollment: 19,088
Total enrollment: NA
Percent Male/Female: 48%/52%
Percent Minority: 47%
Percent African-American: 1%
Percent Asian: 36%
Percent Hispanic: 10%
Percent Native-American: 0%
Percent in-state/out of state: 95%/5%
Percent Pub HS: NA
Number of Applicants: 41,354
Percent Accepted: 41%
Percent Accepted who enroll: 25%
Entering: 4,243
Transfers: 1,498
Application Deadline: 30 Nov
Mean SAT: NA
Mean ACT: NA
Middle 50% SAT range: V 540-650, M 600-700
Middle 50% ACT range: 26-29
3 Most popular majors: psychology, communication and media studies, biochemistry
Retention: 94%
Graduation rate: 81%
On-campus housing: 35%
Fraternities: 10%
Sororities: 10%
Library: 3,086,871 volumes
Tuition and Fees: $5,150 in; $18,630 out
Room and Board: $8,672
Financial aid, first-year: 50%
Varsity or Club Athletes: 10%
Early Decision or Early Action Acceptance Rate: NA

Soaked in sun and minutes from beautiful California beaches, the University of California at San Diego offers its students a world of opportunities in the idyllic setting of the San Diego suburb of La Jolla. How, you may ask, does anyone ever work with great waves and warm beaches closer to your dorms than your classes are? However, in spite of the weather, UCSD students do find time to get their academics in and live up to the school's reputation as one of the top academic institutions in the country.

Beach Reading

Like many California schools, UCSD is on the quarter system. Most students attend three quarters a year and do not take classes during the fourth quarter, which is during the summer. Because of the quarter system, each student gets to take a wide variety of classes. However, many students complain that because of the short duration of quarters, they are not able to study material in depth. One student observed, "the quarter schedule is pretty hectic—you're either in the middle of midterms or getting ready for finals!"

Apart from the quarter system, students are generally pleased with their academic experience. One of UCSD's most unique aspects of academics is the college system. There are five colleges, each with different core requirements and mission statements. Marshall College emphasizes diversity and public policy. Muir College emphasizes the humanities, Warren College emphasizes a liberal arts education, Roosevelt College is focused on international policy, and Revelle College is directed towards math and the hard sciences. Because of UCSD's core requirements, introductory classes are often large in size with as many as 300 to 400 students.

The complaint at many universities is that TAs do not speak English. However at UCSD, the problem is not the TAs (often undergraduates themselves), but the professors. In fact, students report a recent decrease in English proficiency among the faculty. At the upper level, class size decreases dramatically and professors are generally better. However, as one student reported, "Classes are becoming hard to get because of overcrowding." How do students get into classes? Throughout the UC system students register by phone or on the Internet. Priority is given to more advanced students—freshmen with AP credits are able to register before those without. However, students who are not able to get into a class that they are adamant about taking are often able to get into the class by talking with the professor once the semester starts.

Students must work for their grades once they have gotten into their classes. The biggest complaint about UCSD is that students are constantly studying. Because students must apply to be in some of the majors, there is reportedly a high level of competition among students. As one student reported, "it is not totally uncommon for pre-meds and engineering students to be victims of sabotage or commit academic dishonesty in the form of cheating." However, there were no reports of such competition among students in less quantitative subjects. And if you want to take it easy with academics, the majors to think about are communications or economics.

Creative Campus

With all this studying, one might wonder where students go to do work and research papers. The center of academia on the UCSD campus is Geisel Library. Besides housing the bulk of texts on the UCSD campus, the Geisel Library is one of the most architecturally unique structures on campus: a massive building that widens until the sixth floor after which it tapers up to the top. And if the library is not unique enough, the way that you get to the library is—by the "snake path." "Everyone likes to walk on the snake path on their way to the library, it's a path with colorful tiles in the shape of a snake."

California Casa

Besides the library, the UCSD campus is sprawling and many students need cars to get from where they live to their classes. For freshmen however, this is not the case. Housing is guaranteed for freshmen and sophomores and most students live in doubles along hallways. Dorm life is far and away the most complained about part of life as a UCSD student. According to one student, "dorms and dorm living is difficult for most people because the residents and RAs (residential advisors) tend to be uptight about everything. Also, dorms are usually about a 15-minute walk from most classes." According to another student, "from the first week of school freshman year, I quickly discovered that partying was a big no-no."

"Nine out of 10 girls in San Diego are pretty and the tenth one goes to UCSD."

The best part of dorm living is the food. Each of the five colleges (Marshall, Warren, Revelle, Roosevelt, and Muir) has its own "restaurant" which means you can always find people you know at dinner. Also, the food is apparently well liked by most students.

Because of such a limiting dorm life, students tend to move off campus as soon as they are able to find housing. However, this is easier said than done. Not only is La Jolla the most expensive area of San Diego, but all housing is a good drive away from campus "and if you're a freshmen, don't bother bringing a car" because parking is absolutely unavailable. And even if you are able to park, it is still a good walk to class. However, the upside to this ritzy area of California is that the town of La Jolla is generally safe for students. Also, there is a campus escort service for students who find themselves alone at night.

What Football Team?

Because studying takes so much time, "people at UCSD aren't really into organized extracurriculars." Many students can be found studying or relaxing at the heart of campus at the "Price Center." Price Center has a bunch of restaurants, a theater, a travel agency, a smoothie joint, a coffee shop, and the bookstore, as well as a pool hall. Most people hang out there between classes. In spite of the apparent apathy of many students towards extracurriculars, UCSD does offer a wide range of student organizations that allow for everyone to get involved if they so desire. One example is the *UCSD Guardian*, a student newspaper listing all the campus happenings.

For athletes, UCSD is a Division III school with sports available on the varsity level. However, one apparent gap is the lack of a football team, a factor to which many students attribute the lack of school spirit. However, the absence of a football team does not discourage all athletics. UCSD has a good water polo team and by rallying behind water polo, "School spirit has increased in the past few years."

"Take Genesee to Governor . . ."

As for evening activities, student opinions vary widely. It depends on who your friends are and what kinds of things you like to do. The on-campus party scene is fairly subdued and most parties are broken up by 10 P.M. due to the strict policies of the campus police and RAs. Off-campus parties tend to be the most talked about. According to one student, "I think everyone who has ever gone to UCSD knows the intersection of Genesee and Governor. About 75 percent of the off-campus parties start with the directions 'Take Genesee to Governor . . .'" Also, the fraternity scene is not as omnipresent as it is on many state school campuses due to the fact that the frats do not have their own on-campus houses. Thus, frat parties are held at one of the member's apartments or houses and it can sometimes be a drive to get there. Furthermore, recent laws passed in La Jolla to limit the noise level can result in eviction if offences are committed multiple times.

With strict laws on parties, most under-21 undergraduates find themselves hanging out with friends or going to the movies. For those over 21, there are a few local bars that students frequent. Also, brand new last year was the first on-campus club in the UC system; "Club Ritmo's" hopes to cater to the students' desire to party and features DJs from UCSD's DJ club, "The Vinylphiles."

Besides the weekly party scene, the most anticipated event of the year is the campus-wide "Sun God Festival." Not only is it near the end of the academic year, but it is one of the only times in the year that the whole campus comes out to celebrate and take some time off. Huge obstacle courses are set up on the athletic field and top name bands such as Cypress Hill, Reel Big Fish, and others play for students under the rays of San Diego sun.

As for the students themselves, the running joke is that "nine out of 10 girls in San Diego are pretty and the tenth one goes to UCSD." Whether this is true or not, is a matter of opinion. With the sun always shining, the campus is conducive to athletic participation and many people play intramural sports and jog on a regular basis. There is also a state-of-the-art gym facility on campus known to students as RIMAC (Recreation and Intramural Athletic Complex). Also, there is always the possibility of going to the beach nearby if you want a real tan.

The warm climate and beautiful beaches, along with top-ranked academics make UCSD one of the most highly sought-after schools in California. After all, who could turn down a school that has a campus-wide festival dedicated to a celebration of "The Sun God"? *—Sophie Jones*

FYI

If you come to UCSD, you'd better bring "a beach towel."

What is the typical weekend schedule? "Friday night: go out. Saturday: goof off and go out at night. Sunday: wake up late and study frantically all day."

If I could change one thing about UCSD, I'd "have more things to do on the weekends."

The three things that every student should do before graduating from UCSD are "go to Black's Beach (a local nude beach) for a night bonfire, go to BJ's pizza, and go to Ralph's in La Jolla."

University of California / Santa Barbara

Address: 1210 Cheadle Hall; Santa Barbara, CA 93106
Phone: 805-893-2485
E-mail address: appinfo@sa.ucsb.edu
Web site URL: www.ucsb.edu
Founded: 1909
Private or Public: public
Religious affiliation: none
Location: suburban
Undergraduate enrollment: 17,714
Total enrollment: NA
Percent Male/Female: 46%/54%
Percent Minority: 35%
Percent African-American: 3%
Percent Asian: 15%
Percent Hispanic: 16%
Percent Native-American: 1%
Percent in-state/out of state: 95%/5%
Percent Pub HS: 82%
Number of Applicants: 34,703
Percent Accepted: 51%
Percent Accepted who enroll: 22%
Entering: 3,842
Transfers: 1,342
Application Deadline: 30 Nov
Mean SAT: NA
Mean ACT: NA
Middle 50% SAT range: V 510-620, M 550-660
Middle 50% ACT range: 22-27
3 Most popular majors: business, sociology, communications
Retention: 91%
Graduation rate: 73%
On-campus housing: 21%
Fraternities: 8%
Sororities: 10%
Library: 2,700,000 volumes
Tuition and Fees: $5,259 in; $18,739 out
Room and Board: $9,236
Financial aid, first-year: 44%
Varsity or Club Athletes: 3%
Early Decision or Early Action Acceptance Rate: NA

You are taking a peaceful stroll at sunrise on a typical Sunday morning. Life is great at your new beachside home in Santa Barbara. As you look down at the sand caught in your Reef sandals you notice the beer stain on your khakis. You realize that you are not on a morning stroll, but on your way home from the biggest Saturday night of the year. With every ache of your pounding head you are knocked back into reality as you remember the sociology paper due Monday morning. While deciding how to spend the next 24 hours before the paper is due, you realize that you do not remember the last time you saw your bed. After several aspirin and a quick nap, you wake up just in time to catch a late dinner before setting out to write your paper. Six cups of coffee, and two burritos later you snatch the paper from the printer and race to your sociology class. As you vigorously take notes, the intellectual stimulation reminds you why you chose UCSB. But with ten minutes left in lecture even the most interesting topic fades into the background and you find yourself daydreaming about the afternoon you are going to spend on the beach.

The Perfect Vacation Spot

The University of California, Santa Barbara is located ten minutes outside the elegant beach town of its namesake in the city of Galeta. The campus is wedged between the soaring Santa Barbara Mountains and some of California's most pristine beaches. Scattered with palm trees and beachside bike trails the campus feels more like a resort than a school. The campus is small but most people ride bikes to class anyway. Besides classrooms, the school has a brand new recreational center complete with two Olympic-sized swimming pools, an extensive weight room, and several indoor and outdoor basketball courts. This is ideal for the exercise conscious Santa Barbara students who can be seen waiting in line for the treadmill, running along the beach, or playing beach volleyball.

The Ocean As Your Classroom

Besides frequenting the beaches, SB students spend much of the rest of their day in the classroom. SB is known for having a large number of required classes that are meant to ensure a broad liberal arts education for all students. These requirements are "not difficult to fulfill since most classes cover more than one area requirement," noted one SB sophomore. Beyond required classes, all students must pick a major. Santa Barbara is best known for the quality of its sciences departments. However, there are an equal number of students in the humanities, with some of the most popular majors being communications and sociology. In these majors, there is often competition for spots. But, as one sophomore boasted, "if you are assertive and persistent, you can always get in the classes you want." Introductory classes, on the other hand, tend to be fairly large—ranging in numbers from 200 to 1,200. In these classes, it is mostly teaching assistants (TAs) who do the grading and handle most student questions. However, the professors are known to be very friendly and accessible as well. Some of the unique classes offered at UCSB are due to its beach location. For a touch of diversity in your schedule, classes like sailing and hands-on oceanography are offered.

The Triple Kegger

Outside of the classroom, students take plenty of time to party off the stress of the day. If you were to go out on virtually any night of the week you might tell someone you were going to a triple kegger at 347 DP. This would indicate that you would be drinking out of one of the three kegs at a given address on the biggest party street on campus, Del Playa. Every Thursday, Friday, and Saturday night herds of blond girls in skimpy attire, and eager well-dressed boys funnel down DP looking for the best parties. Almost every house has people spilling out the door and over the balcony while beer flows and music blasts. The houses on DP compete with each other to gain the coveted title of Best Party House. Many lure guests by throwing theme parties devoted to decades (70s and 80s) or by only admitting those with very small amounts of clothing. It is not until two or three each morning that the parties start to die down. And even at that hour, many rowdy groups can be seen heading to Free Birds for a late-night burrito.

Your Own Beach Front Home

After a night of partying, the thing most college students desire most is their own bed. Most of the dorms are privately owned and have names like Fountain Blue and Tropicana. Only two stories high and built surrounding a courtyard and swimming pool, these dorms look more like hotels than classic college housing. Every dorm has RAs who are supposed to control drinking and help students settle into college life. However, students agree that there is a "don't ask don't tell attitude in regards to alcohol. And RAs are pretty cool to have around." The only stipulation is that no kegs are allowed. After freshman year this is not an issue because almost all students move off campus. The most social students move into one of the nice houses along the beachfront streets so that they can host parties. Renting tends to be pricey but most everyone agrees it is the only way to go. More affordable apartment complexes are scattered throughout the city and many upperclassmen who choose this option commute to school.

> **"Our varsity drinking team is undefeated."**

Who Goes Here Anyway?

Are you white? Does any member of your family drive an SUV? Do you live in California? Do you like to drink beer? If you answered yes to all of these questions, you will fit in well at UCSB. Compared with other UC campuses, SB is the least ethnically diverse. It is a predominately white upper-middle-class student body whose roots can be traced to the high schools in California's suburbs. About half of the students are from northern California while the other half are from the various regions of southern California.

What? No Football Team!

The regional divide between NorCal and SoCal according to one student is more predominant on campus than rivalries with other schools. When asked to comment about the lack of a football team at UCSB one junior responded, "who cares? Our varsity drinking team is undefeated." Most people seem not to mind the fact that there is no game to go to on Saturdays and it is not uncommon for students to replace what would be an afternoon football tailgate with what is known as a "day keg." However, some do miss the feeling of a fall football game that is stereotypical of most college experiences. One sophomore lamented, "football games were always something I associated with the college experience. I feel cheated at SB without them," and two freshmen said they noticed a lack of school spirit on campus. "I attribute that to the lack of spectator sports," said one of them. UCSB is known for its lacrosse, swimming, and volleyball, but none of these sports draw the kind of crowds a football game would.

Image Renovation

Even without a football team, UCSB has the nationwide reputation as a classic party school. However, UCSB administration has been working hard to increase its prestige in the last several years. Successfully recruiting high-level professors to do research, the school can boast three Nobel laureates just last year and is noted as an "up-and-coming school." To the dismay of many students, part of renovating the school's image is an attempt by the administration to disband its notorious reputation as a party school. Several students have noted an increase in the police intervention during the weekend. One angry sophomore said, "ever since this new crackdown, the cops hassle us at night and the frats can't throw parties anymore." If one thing can be said about UCSB, "it's a school where everyone wants to have a good time—in and out of class." —*Quinn Fitzgerald*

FYI

If you come to UCSB you'd better bring "a surfboard."

What is the typical weekend schedule? "Nights: beer. Days: beach."

If I could change one thing about UCSB "I would make it smaller."

Three things that every student should do before graduating from UCSB are "go surfing, go to the bars downtown, take an oceanography class."

University of California / Santa Cruz

Address: 1156 High Street; Santa Cruz, CA 95064
Phone: 831-459-4008
E-mail address: admissions@cats.ucsc.edu
Web site URL: admissions.ucsc.edu
Founded: 1965
Private or Public: public
Religious affiliation: none
Location: suburban
Undergraduate enrollment: 12,881
Total enrollment: 13,170
Percent Male/Female: 44%/56%
Percent Minority: 32.3%
Percent African-American: 2.3%
Percent Asian: 17%
Percent Hispanic: 14%
Percent Native-American: 1%
Percent in-state/out of state: 94%/6%
Percent Pub HS: 76%
Number of Applicants: 23,931
Percent Accepted: 80%
Percent Accepted who enroll: 19%
Entering: 3,159
Transfers: 912
Application Deadline: 30 Nov
Mean SAT: 1149
Mean ACT: NA
Middle 50% SAT range: V 500-620, M 520-630
Middle 50% ACT range: 21-26
3 Most popular majors: psychology, English literature, economics
Retention: 86%
Graduation rate: 67%
On-campus housing: 45%
Fraternities: 1%
Sororities: 1%
Library: NA
Tuition and Fees: $5,283 in; $18,763 out
Room and Board: $10,314
Financial aid, first-year: 41%
Varsity or Club Athletes: 4%
Early Decision or Early Action Acceptance Rate: NA

You might think attending a school where you suddenly become referred to as a banana slug sounds like an unattractive prospect. Actually, UC Santa Cruz, in its beautiful beach setting amidst a forest of trees, offers much to compensate for its slimy mascot. The California coast, spread-out campus, and freedom of programs provide a relaxed atmosphere for both academic studies and socializing.

Academics Smorgasbord

UC Santa Cruz offers competitive academics in almost every field. The marine biology program is "very good" and the psychology department is said to be "phenomenal." Professors in every subject are generally described as "interesting" and important in providing UCSC students with a unique learning experience. As for class selectivity, students say that if they sign up by phone or online in a timely manner, they almost always get into their top-choice classes. Most lower-division classes are taught lecture-style with discussion sections—an actual professor gives the lectures, but students are at the mercy of their teaching assistants, usually graduate students, for grades. The grading system has recently made a change for the better. Up until only a couple of years ago, UCSC students could opt to take as many classes as they wished towards their major pass/fail with nothing differentiating an A from a C- except brief evaluations. The system was criticized for making it difficult for students to get into graduate schools, and it is now far less common to find people taking courses without letter grades.

The very minimal graduation course requirements at UCSC earn student praise for allowing for a lot of flexibility in course choice. They require that students take courses in each of four different academic areas: introduction to humanities and arts, social sciences, natural sciences, and a "topical requirement," which consists of a social issue analysis class.

According to students, the workload at USCS can vary from heavy to "not so bad." Classes vary widely in both size and difficulty. Many courses are large lectures, as is the case with most of the colleges in the large California public university system; however, there are also writing seminars and upper-division classes that give USCS a smaller student-to-teacher ratio. A variety of interesting classes are offered as well. "One class I am taking this semester is called, 'Muppet Magic,'" said a student. "It's a class on the history of the Muppets and Jim Henson." Another student described a great assignment for a social documentation class—creating a five- to six-minute documentary on 9/11. At UCSC, students concur that academic opportunities, if you seek them out, abound.

> **"One class I am taking this semester is called, 'Muppet Magic.'"**

A Mixed Social Scene

The atmosphere at UC Santa Cruz is laid back and spread out, giving the social scene on the whole a "very relaxed feeling." Despite the student body's reputation as being full of potheads and stoners, the drug scene does not dominate the school. "You could probably find drugs if you went looking for them," said one student, "but they're not in your face or anything like that." Mostly, the student body consists of a lot of California residents with some "random out-of-staters" thrown in, and is described as diverse in race, culture, and interests.

Most on-campus socializing is confined to hanging out in the floor lounges or at tables outside the building or the dining halls. Students are divided into ten residential colleges with different themes—Merrill, for example, is the college with "cultural emphasis." The only formal distinction between the colleges is the core class associated with them, which is a class all students in the college take (Merrill's is a cultural class); however, students have made other distinctions between them. Oaks, for example, is reputed to be "more of a party college." When applying for housing, freshmen list the colleges of their choice based on a sheet they get sent describing the different themes and things they've heard from other students. Each college hosts a "College Night" once a quarter, which brings its students together for good food and some socializing. The college nights are the extent of college-sponsored social events.

A definite party atmosphere can be found, however, in upperclassman apartments off campus. "Most juniors and seniors don't get housing, and it's sometimes difficult even for sophomores to get housing," explained one student, so the dorms aren't very mixed. Housing in Santa Cruz "can be quite expensive, but there are always advertisements looking for roommates or tenants," and "the school does try to facilitate housing in the community," say students. Cars are not a big part of on-campus living. No freshmen get parking permits, and the school "makes it very difficult for students to get them in general," said one student. However, he added, "the buses run frequently and often." The spread-out nature of the campus creates some isolation, however, and it can be "something of a hike" to get from one end to the other.

Greek life at UCSC is almost nonexistent. The sororities and fraternities do not have houses. This makes it difficult for them to have the parties that can make Greek groups so notorious on other campuses. "They were present at the beginning of the year," remarked one freshman, "but it was kind of inconvenient to rush and you had to go out of your way." Several students agree that they wouldn't be surprised if some students didn't even know that there were frats or sororities on campus.

Escaping Paradise

Varsity sports are barely an aspect of the campus lifestyle. For one, there is no football team; there is a limited range of sports for men and women. Despite this fact, however, most students are in pretty good shape. Lots of people consider hiking around the huge campus a workout in itself, but if this isn't enough, "the gym is brand new and hella nice," said one student.

Intramural sports are the other athletic alternative. Santa Cruz fields an activity fair each year that makes it easy to sign up for a pre-existing team or get a new club started. "It isn't difficult to get involved in extracurriculars," a student said. There is a breadth of activities to go with the equally wide variety of students, such as tutoring, environmental work, and cultural clubs.

Just outside campus lies the beach, a favorite spot of students. There is also the nearby boardwalk, which is a collection of rides and arcade games, although closed during the winter. Other attractions are the local town, which contains "a lot of restaurants—everyone has their local places," and "a nice movie theatre." San Francisco and the Berkeley region are only a bus ride away, though "if you walk out, you're pretty much in the forest." —*Stephanie Teng*

FYI

If you come to UC Santa Cruz, you'd better bring "bug spray."

The typical weekend schedule includes: "sleeping in, eating brunch, partying, studying, and seeing a movie."

If I could change one thing about UC Santa Cruz, "I'd improve the food."

Three things every student at UC Santa Cruz should do before graduating are: "go to the gym, hit the beach and the boardwalk, and play an intramural sport."

University of Redlands

Address: PO Box 3080; Redlands, CA 92373-0999
Phone: 800-455-5064
E-mail address: admissions@redlands.edu
Web site URL: www.redlands.edu
Founded: 1907
Private or Public: private
Religious affiliation: none
Location: suburban
Undergraduate enrollment: 3,071
Total enrollment: NA
Percent Male/Female: 41%/59%
Percent Minority: 27%
Percent African-American: 5%
Percent Asian: 6%
Percent Hispanic: 15%
Percent Native-American: 1%
Percent in-state/out of state: 74%/26%
Percent Pub HS: 77%
Number of Applicants: 2,499
Percent Accepted: 76%
Percent Accepted who enroll: 32%
Entering: 602
Transfers: 105
Application Deadline: 1 July
Mean SAT: NA
Mean ACT: NA
Middle 50% SAT range: V 520-610, M 520-630
Middle 50% ACT range: 21-26
3 Most popular majors: business, liberal arts, social sciences
Retention: 81%
Graduation rate: 59%
On-campus housing: 76%
Fraternities: 22%
Sororities: 51%
Library: 251,053 volumes
Tuition and Fees: $24,096
Room and Board: $8,478
Financial aid, first-year: 68%
Varsity or Club Athletes: 32%
Early Decision or Early Action Acceptance Rate: NA

Majestic mountains rise out of the Californian desert landscape. Nestled at the foot of the mountains among a patch of greens is University of Redlands, a small liberal arts college of about 2,000 undergraduate students. One week during Christmas season, students trail on the greens to attend the Festival of Lights, a three-hour performance by the orchestra and the choir in their chapel. "It's beautiful, and it's a big deal at the school," said one student. The Festival of Lights displays the essence of University of Redlands—its quaint and serene existence among the mountains.

Academics Without Distractions

While the remoteness of Redlands can keep students from getting distracted, its small size can also be a blow for the students. On the positive side, with the class size of about seven people, it means professors pay a lot of attention to each student. "All my professors know me by name and greet me when I see them outside class," said one student fondly. But having a small school also means that course selection may be limited. The problem is especially true for the Liberal Arts Foundation, LAF, in which certain core requirements must be taken before graduating. "There are lots of requirements for students not in a specialized program," said one student. To avoid these requirements, students can use Advanced Placement exam credits. Every student must, however, complete the community service requirement for the school before graduating.

Redlands excels in the humanities, in particular the music, art, and creative writing departments. But some other facilities may fall short of student expectations. "It's inconvenient that the computer cluster is only open until midnight," noted one student. Such inconveniences are one of the problems of being in a small school.

There are many options for getting away, however, such as the winter term and study abroad programs. Winter term refers to one month of intensive study in January, usually undertaken abroad. The school has an impressive gamut of study abroad programs, in countries from Japan to Africa, which any student can pursue for her winter term or for a junior term/year abroad. The biggest study abroad available is in Germany, especially popular among music students.

Overall, students seem satisfied with the academics at their school. "Redlands is not really easy, but it's not really difficult either," commented one student. "If you want to work, you can, but here you are not as stressed out as you might be in some other schools."

Activities—from Sports to Music Theater

Being such a humanities-oriented school, students admit readily that the athletics are not the strongest part of their school. "I've never gone to a sports game, or heard of anyone going to one," said one student, trying to remember who Redlands' rival school is. Another student explained that there is some school spirit: "The sports teams are not that good, so we get excited when we win."

Outside organized sports, however, there are plenty of opportunities for the athletically minded. The location of Redlands makes it an ideal campus for those who love skiing or swimming. Hiking in the nearby mountains is another popular activity. One student described one of her favorite activity as "hiking into the mountains and looking at the stars."

Redlands also boasts a variety of clubs and organizations, including choir, mock trial team, and Christian organizations, and the school hosts lecture series and other academic events. Students note the visibility of Christian organizations and events on campus, although their popularity does not compare to that of musical theater, which involves an excellent orchestra and a trained choir. Traditionally, an opera is staged one semester, and a musical the other semester. The theaters, as well as the Festival of Lights, are school-wide celebrations showcasing students' musical talents.

Town of Redlands and Beyond

Redlands is a small Southern Californian town that students describe as relatively safe. The tradeoff, however, is that it does not offer much by way of fun. "The only thing we can do is watch movies, and that's what we do for dates," said one student, referring to the nearby Krikorian Theater. About 30 minutes away from campus in downtown, there are cute restaurants with Italian and Mediterranean foods, as well as coffee shops. "We don't hang out in the town though," claimed one student. "You would get bored of it if you stayed here for four years."

"The small community feel is nice because you get to know people really well, but you probably want to go out sometimes."

That is why Redlands students recommend having a car. Having a car allows them to shop at outlet malls, take a trip to Walmart, and to get some food after the student eatery closes at midnight. Equipped with a car, students can also venture into LA, which is only about one hour away. Also within driving distance are San Diego, Las Vegas, a 4.5-hour trip, and San Francisco, about nine hours away.

Social Life on Campus and the Myths of Johnson

"Parties at Redlands suck," exclaimed one student. The party scene at Redlands revolves around the Greek system, which reportedly provides students an ample supply of alcohol and pot for those who want it. Less prevalent are hook-ups, which people feel happen less frequently than dating because of the size of the school. All in all, students feel that the administration knows of the party activities, but that it generally adheres to a "hear no evil, see no evil" approach to maintaining order.

Students would say the Johnson Center is the exception. The Johnson Center is a competitive program that lets students design their own majors. The students in the program live in one dorm, and are seen by outsiders as being "really smart, but really weird." Johnson Center adds spice to campus life; its parties are notoriously crazy, lewd, and fun. Theme parties such as kissing parties are open to all students, but rumor has it that plenty of mysterious activities go on behind closed doors.

Food and Living

The living situation for Redlands students depends on the dorm that they are placed in. Single-sex dormitories have the largest rooms, while Cortner is popular because of its central location, and Melrose for its hotel-like quality. All dorms have a kitchen and washing machines, albeit some students would complain there are not enough. While the university does not separate freshmen housing, first-years typically end up in the worst dorms. Students must live on campus the first year, and can decide to live off campus after first year if they so desire.

Students feel that the food at Redlands is not bad compared to other colleges. They do complain, however, about the inflexibility of the meal schedules and plans. Students who live on campus must select from one of the complicated meal plans, which do not reimburse students for missed meals. The Plaza, the student center, is only open until 12, and the menu hasn't changed in the past few years. The Plaza cafe is the only eatery open on campus late at night, and if you miss those hours, there is nowhere within walking distance to buy food.

"The small community feel is nice because you get to know people really well, but you probably want to go out sometimes," said a student, summarizing the majority of opinions expressed about her school. Redlands seems to be about unexpected surprises however, whether in the form of its large international population, the Johnson Center, or the Festival of Lights. It is through uncovering these hidden treasures that the students of the University of Redlands survive their four years out in the oasis of the Californian desert. *—Mariko Hirose*

FYI

If you come to Redlands, you'd better bring "a car! The town is so small you get bored easily here!"

What is the typical weekend schedule? "going to the movies or hanging out with friends. Greek parties are usually big on Saturday."

If I could change one thing about Redlands, I'd "increase the limited class choices, and the lack of economic diversity among the students."

The three things every student should do before graduating from Redlands are "hike in the mountains, visit market night in town, and attend the Festival of Lights."

University of Southern California

Address: University Park; Los Angeles, CA 90089
Phone: 213-740-1111
E-mail address: admitusc@usc.du
Web site URL: www.usc.edu
Founded: 1880
Private or Public: private
Religious affiliation: none
Location: urban
Undergraduate enrollment: 16,145
Total enrollment: NA
Percent Male/Female: 50%/50%
Percent Minority: 42%
Percent African-American: 7%
Percent Asian: 21%
Percent Hispanic: 13%
Percent Native-American: 1%
Percent in-state/out of state: 67%/33%
Percent Pub HS: 58%
Number of Applicants: 28,362
Percent Accepted: 30%
Percent Accepted who enroll: 33%
Entering: 2,766
Transfers: 1,108
Application Deadline: 10 Jan
Mean SAT: NA
Mean ACT: NA
Middle 50% SAT range: V 600-700, M640-720
Middle 50% ACT range: 27-31
3 Most popular majors: business, visual and performing arts, social sciences
Retention: 94%
Graduation rate: 76%
On-campus housing: 37%
Fraternities: 15%
Sororities: 18%
Library: 3,526,134 volumes
Tuition and Fees: $28,692
Room and Board: $8,632
Financial aid, first-year: 46%
Varsity or Club Athletes: 4%
Early Decision or Early Action Acceptance Rate: NA

Upon her admission to the University of Southern California, one girl remembers being told: "When you come to USC, you will become a part of the Trojan family." As cheesy as that may sound, it may not be too far from the truth. Upon arriving in sunny South Central Los Angeles, students find themselves steeped in the Trojan spirit whether it is in classrooms, at football games, or at Greek parties. The ties founded during the undergraduate years continue after graduation, assuring USC students that "there will be a Trojan always, wherever you go."

Studying in the City of Angels

One sentence sums up the academic strengths of USC: this is LA. The popular undergraduate programs reflect the city's status as the world headquarters of cinema and communications. "The music program, communications, and the film programs are really wonderful," raved one student majoring in cinema and minoring in music industry, "these popular programs have a lot of funding and top-line equipment." Also popular is the business school, which students agree is not too intense. The five-year architecture program, on the other hand, is nicknamed "archi-torture;" no explanation necessary there. For most of the programs, however, "your workload depends on how well you want to do." One student in the Arts and Sciences explained, "if you want an A in the class, you have to put in an A effort."

USC programs tend to emphasize preprofessional focus. A slew of internships available in the areas of communications, film, music, and business support such a focus. "We're in LA, so we get a lot of cool internships," boasted one student. Being situated in Los Angeles is also an advantage when looking for speakers to educate the students outside the classrooms. USC invites an impressive list of speakers each year; in the recent past, they have had Jason Alexander from *Seinfeld*, Reverend Jesse Jackson, and former President George Bush Sr.

Sometimes, the big names that stand at the podium at USC are not guests, but professors. One cinema undergrad, for example, was excited to take a class with a cool, Oscar-winning professor. World-renowned or not, however, students agree that their professors are "well-educated and experienced" in their fields, and easy to approach. "Every year I have at least one class where the professor is excellent," commented a student in the arts and sciences.

Despite all the focus on preprofessional programs, USC has not abandoned its liberal arts education. Students in all programs are encouraged to take classes outside of their schools to fulfill the general education requirements and to pursue a minor in another field of study. General education (GE) requires credits from various categories of study, plus a writing requirement. "It is not that bad, and I understand why they have it," said one student, "but it's not very interesting either." For students in the small programs like architecture or cinema, the big GE classes are social occasions where they can easily meet people outside their major. If students ever get tired of LA, studying abroad is a popular option for junior year. The school itself has a selection of programs, and students can also petition to go on a separate program.

The Other Face of LA

For all the glitz and glamour associated with LA, prospective students might be disappointed if they expect Hollywood and Beverly Hills to be at the footsteps of USC. "South Central LA (where USC is located) is a pretty bad area," warned one student, "there is not much around it." The campus of USC is like a little island, beautiful and traditional Ivy League style brick buildings surrounded by an area undergoing development. Students hanging around campus restrict themselves to visiting friends off campus, grocery shopping at University Village, or UV, or visiting one of the "hole-in-the-wall" bars. New clubs targeted towards USC students such as Club Envy have also emerged in the recent past.

Despite the relatively wealthy population that attends USC, students agree that Trojans still interact with the community. "College kids go out and tutor inner city kids and do other community service activities," said one student. Outside the USC neighborhood, LA is the Trojan's playground; there are clubs along the Sunset Strip, beaches for the warm days, and lots of shopping. Many students leave the campus on weekends to frolic in the glamorous parts of the city. However, one student warned, "Having a car is the only way to get around. Absolutely."

Partying with Beautiful People

Staying on campus can't be that bad, though, when yours is one of the ten most beautiful schools in the United States. "Everyone at this school is like a model," said one sophomore girl. If you are looking for a long-term prince-in-shining-armor, however, you may not find him here. One sophomore testified, "I don't think many people long term date here." "I hear a lot more about random hook-ups than about people going out for a long time," confirmed one guy: "People are busy doing a lot of other things, and they just want to have fun."

> **"Staying on campus can't be that bad . . . when yours is one of the ten most beautiful schools in the United States."**

After all, having fun is what USC is about. Students think that it is fairly easy to meet people, and just as easy to find alcohol, even if you are underage. The Greek system is big, and the Row (frat row) is open to non-Greeks on Thursdays for parties. One student commented that the center of social life is focused on the Greek system, although less now that the University is cracking down a little bit. Overall, however, the consensus remains that the school is a paradise for party-lovers.

Fighting, the Trojan Way

There is no better way to cultivate the Trojan fraternity (outside of the Greek system) than at football games. The King of all games is the one against USC's major rival: UCLA. "The rivalry is so intense that they tape up the mascot on our campus a couple of weeks before the game to protect it," said one student. Tradition on the day of the big game dictates that the whole school walks together to the Coliseum, kicking the flagpole on the way to bring luck to the Trojans.

Besides football, basketball and swimming are also popular, as well as Cal Week and games against Stanford or UC Berkley. Because of the focus on athletics, the school has good fitness facilities, which one student called "intimidating, but nice." On the negative side, one student complained, "the school is too athletic and obsessed with the sports people."

Typical Living and Dining

Students at USC have no complaints about any of the facilities on campus, including their living situations. Most students agree that the dorm is where people meet each other freshman year. "I think it's virtually impossible to live in a dorm freshman year and not to make friends," said one sophomore. The rooms in the dormitories are allegedly big, although it depends on the dorm. Upperclassmen may live in apartments or off campus.

Trojans generally like the food at their school. Students agree that the cafeteria does a good job, considering the number of students in the school. "The quality of the food depends," clarified one student, "but there is always diversity." The ice cream, Betty Crocker, and sushi that embellish their main dining hall confirm such diversity. Such good food lures students to hang out in Commons, the central area with the food court and a bookstore.

Big on Diversity

Diversity seems to be the theme of this urban campus. "I'm very surprised at the diversity, especially racially," said one student from the East Coast who had grown up in less diverse areas. "Contrary to the stereotype that USC is a rich people's school, there is a large financial aid pool," said one Trojan proudly.

Activities offered on campus, however, reflect the diverse interests of the student body. According to students, intramural sports, the Student Senate, and Christian campus organizations are popular. Special interest clubs, like the sky-diving club, also exist for the adventurous and the risk-loving. Whatever a student chooses to do, there is a place for him in the Trojan family. It is obvious that there is no stereotypical USC student.

Diversity reaches beyond race and activities at USC. Diversity for the loyal Trojans is about maintaining a mixture of a myriad of experiences and activities. "I feel like there is enough academics and academic reputation at this school, so I am getting a good education without frying out," said one student. USC nurtures strong and healthy Trojans by allowing them to enjoy a balance of sports, academics, the arts, real-life preparation, and most of all, fun. —*Mariko Hirose*

FYI

It you come to USC, you'd better bring "a car."

What is the typical weekend schedule? "Hitting the frats on Thursday or Friday and heading into LA to a club on Saturdays. During the fall, the football games are also a huge part of everyone's Saturday."

If I could change one thing about USC, I'd "make the bad neighborhood a little better."

Three things every student at USC should do before graduating are "go to a frat party, go to a football game, and go to the beach."

Colorado

Colorado College

Address: 14 East Cache La Poudre Street; Colorado Springs, CO 80903-3298
Phone: 719-389-6344
E-mail address: admission@coloradocollege.edu
Web site URL: www.coloradocollege.edu
Founded: 1874
Private or Public: private
Religious affiliation: none
Location: urban
Undergraduate enrollment: 1,902
Total enrollment: NA
Percent Male/Female: 44%/56%
Percent Minority: 14%
Percent African-American: 2%
Percent Asian: 4%
Percent Hispanic: 7%
Percent Native-American: 1%
Percent in-state/out of state: 33%/67%
Percent Pub HS: 70%
Number of Applicants: 3,411
Percent Accepted: 53%
Percent Accepted who enroll: 27%
Entering: 497
Transfers: 41
Application Deadline: 15 Jan
Mean SAT: NA
Mean ACT: NA
Middle 50% SAT range: V 590-670, M 590-670
Middle 50% ACT range: 26-30
3 Most popular majors: biology, English language and literature, economics
Retention: 93%
Graduation rate: 83%
On-campus housing: 76%
Fraternities: 13%
Sororities: 13%
Library: 535,657 volumes
Tuition and Fees: $27,635
Room and Board: $6,840
Financial aid, first-year: 41%
Varsity or Club Athletes: 21%
Early Decision or Early Action Acceptance Rate: EA 65%

Snug beneath the Rocky Mountains and Pike's Peak, Colorado College is a small liberal arts school with a rustic, yet modern feel to it. Students appreciating the scenery from their dorms will see beautiful natural surroundings and a high-tech campus waiting to be explored. Yet it is the closely knit community of open-minded and liberal students who truly characterize the CC academic and social scene.

The Plan—One at a Time

The Colorado College Plan, commonly known as the block system, is the college's truly unique scheduling system, in which students take an intense course in one subject for three-and-a-half weeks. Students usually take eight courses a year and are completely immersed in this subject for three hours a day in the classroom. Small classes, usually ranging from 15 to 25 students with one or two professors, are key for in-depth interactive discussions that focus on one subject. The block system requires full devotion to one topic, but it also spares the stress of having to juggle four or five different subjects at once. As one student said, "the block plan is excellent for students who are easily distracted and overwhelmed." Both students and teachers can concentrate on doing one thing and doing it well. Having only one three-hour class leaves students with the rest of the day free to pursue other interests, but mostly to look for jobs or internships related to the subject they are studying.

Moreover, teachers are free all day for post-class discussions or fieldwork. One student claimed, "teachers are friendly and always approachable." The small classes and close contact often builds strong student-teacher bonds.

The block system is intense, but perhaps only as demanding as students make it. One senior summed up what he had noticed throughout his four years: "there is a heavy, challenging workload, but nothing insane." The curriculum tends to focus on reading—teachers may assign 150 pages per night—and critical analysis. Certainly the block system will not suit all tastes. Those with one-track minds often do well, as do those who know more or less what they want to study. Academic success "depends on motivation and interest. If you don't like the subject, it can be painful."

Going Once, Going Twice . . .

Sold. The unconventional seems to be the convention at CC, with class registration just as extraordinary as the block system. Like in an auction, students are given 80 "points" at the beginning of the semester and are required to "bid" for their classes. Each class is given a certain number of points depending on its desirability; most students get their first or second choice out of five. Introductory classes are the most popular, as are anthropology courses, and the famous Human Sexual Behavior course.

Requirements at CC are not considered courses that are taken just to get them out of the way. They can usually be included in any major and are not seen as obligations. By their sophomore year, students are expected to complete four blocks of "Alternative Perspectives," which include two courses in Western culture and two in non-Western culture. In addition, students have the full four years to complete two blocks of both lab and natural sciences. Requirements help to keep students well-rounded and open-minded, and they require critical thinking skills no matter the subject.

> **"Colorado College is for the adventurous."**

The more popular majors include biology, psychology, economics, and English, while the hardest majors tend to be physics and mathematical economics. As one student noted, "there is no engineering program, but the sciences are very strong." Many students pursue double majors, interdisciplinary programs, and prelaw. Overall, CC attracts individual and independent students who are usually high-spirited. These strong personalities make for passionate discussions, creativity, and a diverse student body. Also, an astonishing 90 percent of students engage in the arts programs at CC before graduating. Colorado College's commitment to the arts is evident in their brand new Cornerstone Arts Center, which offers state-of-the-art performance centers, studios, galleries, and rehearsal areas.

Decompression Time

After working long and hard for nearly a month, students at CC need to stop and catch their breath. Block breaks are the four-day weekends between each block in which students have no class: this is a time for relaxing, socializing, and traveling. "A typical student here is highly enthusiastic about learning, but block breaks are always welcome."

Although many students go off campus on breaks, especially to Denver, partying and exploring the picturesque natural surroundings on campus is also quite popular. "We like outdoor activities such as rafting, climbing, and skiing and the more urban people can always take advantage of the many museums and theatres in Colorado Springs." The Garden of the Gods National Park is also a scenic favorite for picnics and hiking.

The downtown area is only a five-minute walk away, so nightlife is replete with movies, performances, assorted cafes and restaurants, and party hopping at off-campus housing. Frats do not play a big part in the social life, nor does drinking. Some traditional parties are the Harley-Davidson party, the "Denver University Sucks" party, and beach parties. As for campus rules: kegs are not allowed and substance-free dorms are actually meant to be substance-free. At parties, "you basically drink your own alcohol." The dating scene is somewhat limited. Not many couples are seen, and dating is casual and "laid back," according to one student. Another student said the "hook-up scene is normal. There's no pressure, but since it's a small school, everybody knows everybody. Stuff gets around in 16 hours max." CC can certainly be deemed a "close-knit community."

Nestled Away

Although near the Colorado Springs downtown area, more than one student would describe CC as an island-like place. "The CC campus is like a world of its own," according to one student. The students are very liberal and diverse, creating a "good, healthy, balance" on campus, where "whatever," as one student said, is acceptable. However, they don't necessarily blend with the townspeople, who tend to be conservative and upper-class. The rivalry with the Air Force Academy is also fairly visible on campus.

If this isolationist sentiment seems contrary to the laid-back atmosphere of the school, CC is making a huge integration effort through its community service programs. First and foremost, an outreach program called "Streetwise" aims to connect with the locals in many different ways.

On and Off the Field

Besides community service, intramurals are very popular on campus. About 75 percent of students play intramural or club sports, while many choose to play Division III varsity. Ice Hockey and Soccer are the only Division I sports on campus.

CC also offers a lifestyle replete with opportunities beyond sports. Many participate in drama groups, go ice-skating, go on outdoor excursions, write for student-run publications, or join ethnic or cultural organizations. The Worner Campus Center—at the center of campus life—is where students can be found advertising for upcoming events or just hanging out.

CC's dorms are fairly new and modern. Students are also generally happy with the food and meal plans. The main freshman dorm is Loomis, while others include Slocum and Messians (a.k.a. the "old" dorm). Most dorms are co-ed, but there are all-girl dorms as well. By and large, students are comfortable in their residences, and none can complain about the beautiful view out their windows. CC's green-fielded campus, often blanketed with snow, provides for an academically challenging environment amidst stunning scenery. Its liberal students, always up for experimenting with new endeavors, enjoy great freedom at this small institution, and many would agree that "Colorado College is for the adventurous." —*Carolina Galvao*

FYI

If you come to Colorado College, you'd better bring a "pair of ice skates, a ski jacket, and an open mind."

What is the typical weekend schedule? "Work, procrastinate, read, eat, hot chocolate, snuggle. . . . Party? . . . Sleep, its freezing out!"

If I could change one thing about Colorado College, I'd "make the breaks longer and the winters shorter."

Three things every student at Colorado College should do before graduating are "take a retreat to the Baca campus, go skiing, and watch an ice hockey game."

Colorado School of Mines

Address: 1600 Maple Street; Golden, CO 80401-1842
Phone: 303-273-3220
E-mail address: admit@mines.edu
Web site URL: www.mines.edu
Founded: 1874
Private or Public: public
Religious affiliation: none
Location: suburban
Undergraduate enrollment: 2,504
Total enrollment: 3,350
Percent Male/Female: 76%/24%
Percent Minority: 14%
Percent African-American: 1%
Percent Asian: 5%
Percent Hispanic: 7%
Percent Native-American: 1%
Percent in-state/out of state: 79%/21%
Percent Pub HS: 90%
Number of Applicants: 2,720
Percent Accepted: 67%
Percent Accepted who enroll: 32%
Entering: 583
Transfers: 87
Application Deadline: 1 May
Mean SAT: 1230
Mean ACT: 27
Middle 50% SAT range: V 540-640, M 610-700
Middle 50% ACT range: 25-29
3 Most popular majors: engineering, math and statistics, physics
Retention: 86%
Graduation rate: 62%
On-campus housing: 30%
Fraternities: 20%
Sororities: 20%
Library: 150,000 volumes
Tuition and Fees: $6,380 in; $19,570 out
Room and Board: $6,100
Financial aid, first-year: 60%
Varsity or Club Athletes: 27%
Early Decision or Early Action Acceptance Rate: NA

Looking at the landscapes of the Rocky Mountains, the glorious foliage and the breathtakingly mountainous terrain, it is very easy to overlook Golden, Colorado, an uneventful town harboring about 15,000 people. However, to 3,000 Colorado School of Mines students, this is home. Offering 15 degree programs of which ten contain the word "engineering," Mines is strongly slanted towards the technical disciplines. Even for the most optimistic and open-minded college student, the School of Mines is "lame at first," as one senior described, but the expansive scenery and unique student body eventually become a welcoming home.

Golden Academics in Golden

According to most students, Mines does not have enough parties to really call the party scene a scene, but the parties are not what guides most students to apply to the school. Academics are clearly the main attraction at the School of Mines. The extremely rigorous curriculum challenges students with a "basically prescribed" schedule of classes for the first three years, including extensive mathematics, from calculus through differential equations, as well as physics, economics, and computer programming. A typical freshman schedule includes classes (and class-related meetings) from eight to five, three times a week, and a marginally lighter load on the off-days; 19 credit hours is standard for most freshmen. Professors are generally very knowledgeable, but also have a reputation as being harsh and unforgiving. In fact, the professors in the extremely demanding physics department—one of the most demanding in the nation—were placed on probation a few years ago for failing too many students. Nonetheless, on the whole, the teaching staff is considered unmatched and many students cite the "opportunities for interactions with professors" as one of Mines's key advantages.

Another program mandated by the school is its EPICS program, an acronym for Engineering Practices Introductory Course Sequence. With EPICS, students are given real-world engineering problems and are asked to find innovative solutions to those problems. Additionally, in the summer following their freshman year, students participate in a Field Session program where they are introduced to skills unique to their particular area of specialization.

According to one student, the university strives to teach "the stuff you really need to be an engineer." Other students complain, however, that labs engulf three to four hours a week but earn no credit. Also, students point to a lack of well-taught liberal arts classes as being the school's weakest point. With engineering as the unequivocal focus of the university, few resources are dedicated to other disciplines. One last complaint by students is that some of the classes are superfluous and are designed to "weed out" many of the students. These "weeder" classes are seen as the main contributor to Mine's unusually high dropout rate—16 percent. Of these 16 percent most transfer to Colorado State University and other state colleges around the country. For those who remain, most are satisfied with the rigor and quality of their education. As one student put it, "it is gratifying to see how much work you actually get done by the end of each term."

Beyond the Classroom?

According to one junior, the party scene at Mines is "best thought of as a desert country . . . a quiet, lonely realm with sporadic oases of people and alcohol." Another student complained that there is "no social atmosphere and the frats are lame." There is also "no cool football, no good sports, and no school spirit." Perhaps some of the trouble with social life at Colorado School of Mines lies in the fact that dorms are only for freshmen. After their first year the established Miners must find housing elsewhere. On a good note, housing is not a problem in Golden. Most students find reasonably priced apartments or housing for rent within five or ten minutes of the campus. With most people in apartments, parties are usually small groups of friends hanging out at various locations off campus, as opposed to large, campus-wide parties. One senior said that the best change for Mines would be to "open [the party scene] more to freshmen and let them get involved." Although the social scene at Mines may not be as raucous as at other schools, one student stated that, "I have class with the same people, I study with the same people, I eat dinner with the same people. CSM helps to build a real sense of community and friendship that I couldn't find anywhere else."

What about the Coors Brewery?

Given the lack of gathering places on campus, the Coors Brewery, which also calls Golden, Colorado, home, serves to fill this void (literally). The brewery packs with Miners "Monday, Tuesday, Wednesday . . . every night." One student described the brewery phenomenon as the "cultural and social center of CSM." While the brewery traditionally serves free beer at the conclusion of a half-hour-long tour, with a Mines identification card, students can take "the short tour" on their way to three free servings of Colorado's best beer. Drinkers and non-drinkers should not stray from the Coor's experience, advised one Mines junior. "It is the brewery that captures the best of CSM's social life."

> **"I would definitely come back. Great education, great people, great friends!"**

For students wishing to evade the enduring call of barley and hops, the university offers a number of highly patronized alternatives. The Fellowship of Christian Athletes (or FCA) attracts many students, and athletic participation is not a prerequisite. While the FCA is a religious organization, its activities are mostly social events and community service projects. One student said that while religion (specifically Christianity) is a "big deal on campus," those who do not observe are not isolated from other students. Additionally, a large number of students associate through club sports. Although "homework is still the varsity sport of the weekends," rugby and soccer are the perennial favorites among the Miners.

Let's Party—Mines-Style

Noting the dominance of engineering in Colorado School of Mines academics, it is not surprising that the grandest production of the university is also engineering-related. In the first week of April, the school hosts "E-Days," short for—of course—Engineering Days. During this well-respected and highly anticipated event, the university presents a carnival-type fair demonstrating the newest engineering technologies. Besides a healthy dose of engineering, E-Days also boasts a spectacular pyrotechnics show. In fact, Mines is famous for their spectacular fireworks, bringing local and national bands, alumni, and students from neighboring colleges to their E-Days festival.

Beyond the Mines

When not celebrating their E-Days, Colorado School of Mines, due to its geographical location, provides numerous escapes for its students. Major cities are within a short driving distance. Denver and Boulder are within 15 minutes, while Colorado Springs is about 30 minutes away. Activities such as skiing and kayaking are frequent forms of amusement for Mines students. A senior said, "There is always something available to do, just not always time."

Clearly, Colorado School of Mines is a departure from the traditional state school education. By centering engineering as the locus of the Mines experience, the university may have segregated its enrollment and narrowed its curriculum, but it has produced a praiseworthy and noteworthy academic experience. Even with the complaints about social life, Mines students are satisfied with their college experiences. As one senior put it, "Colorado is a great place, and I like CSM." Another stated, "I would definitely come back for a second time. Great education, great people, great friends!" Those who are looking to call themselves Mines students should nevertheless heed the warning of a CSM veteran: "I would like to have known how hard it would be once I got here. The school is great but very hard."—*Anatoly Brekhman*

FYI

If you come to CSM, you'd better bring "a calculator and get ready to study hard!"

A typical weekend schedule at CSM includes "homework, going to the Coors Brewery and doing more work."

If I could change one thing about CSM, "I'd get the freshmen more into parties."

Three things every student at CSM should do before graduating are "go to E-Days for the fireworks, get to know a professor well, and take a non-engineering class."

Colorado State University

Address: 200 West Lake Street; Fort Collins, CO 80523-0015
Phone: 970-491-6909
E-mail address: admissions@colostate.edu
Web site URL: www.colostate.edu
Founded: 1870
Private or Public: public
Religious affiliation: none
Location: urban
Undergraduate enrollment: 21,884
Total enrollment: NA
Percent Male/Female: 48%/52%
Percent Minority: 14%
Percent African-American: 2%
Percent Asian: 3%
Percent Hispanic: 6%
Percent Native-American: 1%
Percent in-state/out of state: 80%/20%
Percent Pub HS: NA
Number of Applicants: 12,249
Percent Accepted: 77%
Percent Accepted who enroll: 41%
Entering: 3,829
Transfers: 1,791
Application Deadline: 1 July
Mean SAT: NA
Mean ACT: NA
Middle 50% SAT range: V 500-600, M 500-610
Middle 50% ACT range: 22-26
3 Most popular majors: business, journalism, biology
Retention: 82%
Graduation rate: 63%
On-campus housing: 24%
Fraternities: 9%
Sororities: 11%
Library: 1,909,882 volumes
Tuition and Fees: $3,744 in; $14,216 out
Room and Board: $6,045
Financial aid, first-year: NA
Varsity or Club Athletes: 5%
Early Decision or Early Action Acceptance Rate: NA

It's been called by *Your Future* one of the four "Best Places to be Young." *Money Magazine* ranked it among the 20 safest cities in the U.S. *Reader's Digest* noted that it was the third best city in the country to live based on the absence of crime, low rate of drug and alcohol abuse, clean environment, and affordable cost of living. Find where the Great Plains meet the Rocky Mountains, and you'll see the vibrant city of Fort Collins; and nestled within the heart of Fort Collins are 642 green acres, home to Colorado State University.

Students come from Colorado and beyond to enjoy the beauty of Fort Collins, experience the "exceptional academics" without exceptional cost, and join in the multitude of activities that CSU has to offer. Students report that they love CSU and its "exciting and relaxed" environment.

Hidden Resources

Students claim that the solid academics at CSU are consistently underrated. The university boasts eight academic colleges with concentrations in agricultural science, applied human science, business, engineering, literary arts, forestry and natural resources, veterinary medicine, and biomedical sciences. Students who haven't decided on a major can postpone enrollment in a specific college and register with the more generic "open option." Although liberal arts are offered at the school, its strengths lie in the natural sciences. The well-respected veterinary school is ranked among the top in the nation, the business school is "top notch," and the forestry and natural resource management school is well respected. The engineering program is earning increased attention and respect, due in part to extensive facility renovations, an easily accessible internship program in Fort Collins, and great research opportunities.

With this respect, however, comes a "kind of challenging" workload. CSU requires its students to take classes from each of five general categories, including Communications and Reasoning, Natural Sciences, Arts and Humanities, Behavioral and Social Sciences, and Physical Education and Wellness. Although most students claim these requirements are relatively simple to fulfill, some students have complained that these requirements ensure that "there will always be that one semester when you cannot avoid an 8 A.M.

class." Students also get frustrated with class sizes in some of the introductory courses, some of which enroll 200 to 300 students. Whether the class has 10 or 300 students, however, students claim that "professors genuinely care for their students on an individual level and make themselves accessible."

The workload varies by class. Many perceive studio art to be easy but time consuming, and some students report that psychology is relatively easy. Science courses, particularly engineering, tend to be more challenging. One student joked that "if you're a genius, even the sciences will be easy, and if you're not, you'll have to work fairly hard."

So where do people do this hard work? Some students study in their rooms, but usually that's a luxury of people who have singles. Popular places to study include the Sunken Lounge at Lory Student Center, the renovated Morgan Library, or outside on the grass. Despite the work load that CSU students can expect, students guarantee that "there's always time to have fun!"

Fort Fun

The new Lory Student Center provides not only the Sunken Lounge for study, but also a popular place to take a break from the books. After the old facility flooded, the school decided to renovate its main gathering place. After the student center underwent complete renovation, the *New York Times* ranked Lory as one of the country's ten best student centers. Given Lory's video arcades, pool tables, a ballroom, a theater, a computer store, a bookstore, restaurants, bowling alleys, comfortable places to sit and sleep, TVs, and more, this ranking was no shock to CSU students.

Despite the workload that CSU students can expect, students guarantee that "there's always time to have fun!"

Some of the noteworthy buildings on campus include the engineering building, the environmental sciences building, and the student recreation center/gym. Students report that the engineering building is "very attractive," but the real enthusiasm is for the environmental sciences building, with its copper fountain cascading from three stories. Students consider the new gym to be a "great facility," but professors are not allowed.

Students are required to live on campus for their freshman year. Those who live on campus prefer Corbett, the party dorm, and Braiden, the closest dorm to central campus. Dorm rooms tend to be small, but students enjoy the "great big windows" from which you can enjoy Colorado's 300 days of sunshine. After freshman year, many students move off campus. Fort Collins offers many apartment complexes like Rams Village for its college students.

Many students opt to live off campus because the on-campus alcohol policy strictly enforces that no alcohol be consumed in the dorms. Fraternities and sororities, while they do constitute about ten percent of the student body, aren't a huge presence. Students have a wide selection of bars and clubs in Fort Collins from which they can choose. Some of the more popular clubs include Ramskellar (on campus, actually), Linden's and Felipe's (in Old Town Fort Collins), Suite 152, the Matrix, the Martini Bar, and Washington's. Students who want to get a bite to eat off campus enjoy Coopersmith's, a brewery with reportedly good food, El Burrito and Rio Grande, Bisetti's, Canino's, the Charcoal Broiler, CB & Potts, Young's Vietnamese Cuisine, and the Red Dragon. Students have a similarly broad selection in coffee places: Starry Night, Starbucks, Déjà vu Coffeehouse, and the Coffee Connection to name a few.

300 Days of Sunshine

Colorado boasts of nice weather, but Fort Collins has the added benefit of avoiding "those huge storms that Denver gets." Students capitalize on this weather by hanging outside, hiking, biking, roller-blading, running, skiing (two hours away), snowshoeing, and rock-climbing. River rafting is popular, as are the water sports on nearby Horsetooth Reservoir. With the exception of surfing, Fort Collins offers almost everything for the outdoors enthusiast.

This enthusiasm for outdoor activity extends into sports: CSU students enjoy participating in and watching the many sports that CSU has to offer. The women's basketball team has had strong performances in the past, making bids for the NCAA tournament. Both the community and students come out to support the games.

Intramurals are a popular activity on campus. Team lists, sometimes arranged by dorm floor or apartment complex, fill up quickly. Students are especially eager to play softball, basketball, inner-tube water polo, soccer, flag football, volleyball, tennis, racquetball, and inline hockey (a new offering). Part of the popularity of intramurals stems from the fact that students recognize them as a fun way to get to know people and to get some exercise.

Student enthusiasm isn't limited to sports and outdoor activity; students have a wide selection of extracurricular activities from which to choose. Those interested in writing can work for the *Rocky Mountain Collegian*, and those interested in television can participate in Campus Television, which one student claimed "has won more Emmy's than the cast of Seinfeld." His claim might be slightly exaggerated, but students agree that the television and the radio station, KCSU, are great. The arts are also popular at CSU. The dance school hosts recitals, there are open auditions for plays and musicals, and there are frequent poetry and fiction readings. Community service is also a popular activity. CSU students can volunteer to tutor in the Fort Collins community, give time to the Northern Colorado AIDS Project, run and bike in marathons to help raise support for various causes, and conduct food drives for the homeless and needy.

Students at CSU, therefore, benefit not only from a strong academic program, but also from gorgeous surroundings and countless opportunities to get involved in social and community life. —*Marti Page*

FYI

If you come to Colorado State, you'd better bring "a bicycle. Things are pretty spread out around here."

What is the typical weekend schedule? "Get up at 8 A.M., go skiing or biking, and then have dinner with friends."

If I could change one thing about Colorado State, I'd "change the architecture—it's ugly."

Three things that every student should do before graduating from CSU are "go to a lady Rams basketball game, hike to the Aggies sign above Fort Collins, and go into Old Town on Friday night."

United States Air Force Academy

Address: HQ USAFA/RRS, 2304 Cadet Drive; Suite 200; USAF Academy, CO 80840-5025
Phone: 719-333-2520
E-mail address: rr_webmail@usafa.af.mil
Web site URL: www.usafa.af.mil
Founded: 1954
Private or Public: public
Religious affiliation: none
Location: suburban
Undergraduate enrollment: 4,219
Total enrollment: NA
Percent Male/Female: 84%/16%
Percent Minority: 11%
Percent African-American: 6%
Percent Asian: 5%
Percent Hispanic: 6%
Percent Native-American: 1%
Percent in-state/out of state: 5%/95%
Percent Pub HS: NA
Number of Applicants: 9,041
Percent Accepted: 17%
Percent Accepted who enroll: 79%
Entering: 1,207
Transfers: NA
Application Deadline: 31 Jan
Mean SAT: NA
Mean ACT: NA
Middle 50% SAT range: V 590-680, M 617-700
Middle 50% ACT range: E 26-31, M 28-32
3 Most popular majors: engineering, business, management, marketing, and related support services
Retention: 88%
Graduation rate: 77%
On-campus housing: 100%
Fraternities: NA
Sororities: NA
Library: 500,000 volumes
Tuition and Fees: NA
Room and Board: NA
Financial aid, first-year: NA
Varsity or Club Athletes: 26%
Early Decision or Early Action Acceptance Rate: NA

Day to day life at the United States Air Force Academy has seen many schedule changes in the past year. Entering freshmen, or fourth degrees, will find themselves initiated into all the traditions of the Academy, but 6:20 A.M. inspection and flag raising have been replaced by optional buffet breakfast before the start of first-period class at 7:30. Still, changes such as these do not compromise the traditionally "hardcore" way of life that makes Air Force as rigorous as the other service academies. Freshman cadets will find that life at the Academy is demanding, particularly in the first year, and that most of their time is occupied with challenging course load, extracurricular activities, required seminars, and intramural sports.

Not So Basic Training

Freshman cadets, known as "doolies," spend the first five weeks at Air Force making the transition from civilian to military life through the Basic Cadet Training Program, or BCT, which more than lives up to any outsider's idea of boot camp. In BCT, cadets learn basic military skills, practice teamwork, and undergo a thorough physical evaluation. The end of BCT is marked by the Acceptance Parade, the first of many parades in which freshmen will participate as cadets, wherein they formally join the rest of the student body and begin their fourth-class academic year. While freshman year is referred to across the board as "rough" due to restrictive rules, many of these regulations are balanced by the addition of privileges in the spring. Some of the rules to which freshmen must acclimate themselves include squaring corners, walking straight lines along the sides of hallways, and greeting all upperclassmen on campus pathways.

Cadets are assigned to one of 36 squadrons, each of which contains 110 to 120 students. Squadrons draw from all four of the class years, and are combined into two larger groups. Together, the 4,000 cadets form the Cadet Wing. All cadets are housed by squadron in two large dormitories, Vanderberg and Sijan Halls, where most of the rooms are doubles, with the occasional freshman triple mixed in. One senior remarked that by the end of four years, "you'll know all 120 cadets in your squadron pretty well." Women make up about 20 percent of the student body and are mixed into the dorms evenly across squadrons. Students feel that life for female cadets, while different from that for males, is still both demanding and rewarding.

After buffet breakfast, cadets attend four morning classes, from 7:30 A.M. to 11:30 A.M., and then the entire Cadet Wing meets up in formation and marches together to "Noon Meal," where "waiters serve all 4,000 people in a period of five to ten minutes." Fifteen minutes later, lunch is over and cadets head to their last three class periods of the day. After 3 P.M., cadets splinter off, some to intercollegiate athletics, which run generally from 3 to 6 P.M. in the evening, while the rest head to required intramural and club sports practices, which take up time from around 4 to 5:30 P.M. Some students would "rather be using their time to work out on their own," but for the most part Air Force cadets enjoy the time spent at athletic pursuits.

Under the new schedule, 3:30 P.M. to 7:00 P.M. is now referred to as "Excellence Time," and is "an effort to give more time back to the cadets and also set aside specific times where everyone can be together for military training." Like breakfast, dinner is also optional and buffet-style, served in the main Air Force cafeteria, Mitchell Hall. After dinner is Military Call to Quarters, MCQ, when squadrons meet and have talks on various military topics of note. Clubs meet during Excellence Time, and one student guessed, "anywhere from one-half to three-quarters of people are involved in different clubs."

Like any college or university of its size, Air Force is host to an array of clubs, "everything from Ultimate Frisbee and chess club to debate team." Many cadets are involved in the Soaring or Jump Programs: one teaches gliding, the other parachuting. These two clubs are popular uses of time in the spring of freshman year, and if a third-year student desires, he or she can spend time in that year being trained by seniors ("firsties, or "first years") to become an instructor in one of the two programs. The Jump and Soaring programs are both "pretty much cadet run," and upperclassmen comment on the awe they feel in "the responsibility of teaching someone to fly." At 8 P.M. all underclassmen have Academic Call to Quarters until 10 P.M., and most students study in their rooms, although some take advantage of the library. The Academy issues each cadet a personal computer, and this year the freshman class was equipped with laptops, which they can bring to class, or to work in a library. Freshmen have a bedtime of 11 P.M., but the lights out rule, as one senior described it, is "not really enforced. We all know it's kind of unreasonable to expect even freshman to get homework done by eleven." Also at 11 is DI, or Dormitory Inspection, run by one senior who goes around the squadron to check that everyone is accounted for and at work.

Work Hard, Play Hard

The course load at the Air Force Academy is challenging no matter which major track you select. Students agree that the engineering programs are the standouts, whether astronomical or mechanical. At the same time, so called "fuzzy" majors, such as Political Science, are gaining ground against the ever-strong "techie" majors. In the past few years, Management has become one of the school's most popular majors. The Cadet Wing is reported to be fairly evenly split between fuzzies and techies. The core curriculum for freshmen is quite rigorous, requiring courses in humanities, foreign language, engineering, and both social and hard sciences. Many cadets report having about 20 to 21 credit hours of work weekly per semester. Air Force offers some remarkable opportunities that might not otherwise be afforded to undergraduates at larger research universities. NASA ventures are available, as well as interesting projects such as building an Indy 500 car. The faculty is made up of both civilian and military personnel, and the student-professor connections are described as "simply amazing." Many of the professors are graduates of the academy, and "care deeply about cadets' learning and overall health, since they've done it themselves." Of the civilian members of the faculty, students have said that they provide "a good mix," and that "it's good to see people in normal clothing!"

In addition to standard academic classes, each year cadets take several physical education classes that meet for three hours several times a semester and, like many things at Air Force, are described as "pretty tough." Freshmen take basic swimming, sophomores take water survival (a rough course also known as "water haze"), juniors are enrolled in unarmed combat classes ranging from judo to karate, and seniors can pick from a variety of options.

Many of the professors are graduates of the academy, and "care deeply about cadets' learning and overall health, since they've done it themselves."

On top of grade point average, cadets have a military performance average, or MPA, and are tested several times annually on two tests. The first test is the Physical Fitness test, which consists of pushups, sit-ups, a long jump, and a 600-yard run. The other test is the Aerobic Fitness test and is simply a mile and a half timed run.

Weekends at Air Force are designated as "blue" or "silver." Blue weekends are the more open of the two, when seniors come and go almost as they please, while sophomores and juniors balance their set number of weekend passes. Freshmen are permitted to leave only infrequently. On blue weekends cadets will generally drive to Colorado Springs, where there is a lot to do, from "grabbing pizza to seeing your significant other—which many cadets, male and female, actually have." Seniors are not required back on weeknights until the 11 P.M. Dormitory Inspection, and so a lot of them do some community service work, such as coaching junior league soccer. Silver weekends are entirely different, starting with Friday afternoon uniform and room inspections. On Saturday there is a parade and then attendance is required at the football game where about half the Cadet Wing will do formations before the kickoff.

Life at Air Force is by no means easy, and many students note that by senior year some become cynical about the bureaucracy of the Academy. "Cadets are encouraged to feel like we're running things, then when officers put their hands in the mix, a lot of people get bent out of shape about not being trusted," noted one senior. Still, for those who have always wanted to fly, and who value responsibility and order, Air Force can be an amazing four years. Upon graduation, cadets are committed to five years of active duty, a prospect most find an exciting portal to the future. It is imperative to look carefully at Air Force, more so perhaps than with other colleges, and to be sure that you are prepared to test yourself both mentally and physically in order to better yourself and your country. *—Charlotte Taft*

FYI

If you come to the United Stated Air Force Academy, you'd better bring a "toothbrush, since you're issued just about everything else."

What is the typical weekend schedule? "Uniform and room inspection Friday, parade and football game Saturday morning, go into Colorado Springs in the evening, work on Sunday."

If I could change one thing about Air Force, "I'd add more free personal time."

The three things that every student should do before graduating from the USAFA are "go skiing, climb Eagle Peak, where the Rockies begin, and jump out of an airplane."

University of Colorado / Boulder

Address: Regent Administration Center, Room 125, 552 UCB; Boulder, CO 80309-0552
Phone: 303-492-6301
E-mail address: apply@colorado.edu
Web site URL: www.colorado.edu
Founded: 1876
Private or Public: public
Religious affiliation: none
Location: urban
Undergraduate enrollment: 22,697
Total enrollment: NA
Percent Male/Female: 59%/41%
Percent Minority: 15%
Percent African-American: 2%
Percent Asian: 6%
Percent Hispanic: 6%
Percent Native-American: 1%
Percent in-state/out of state: 67%/33%
Percent Pub HS: 80%
Number of Applicants: 19,152
Percent Accepted: 80%
Percent Accepted who enroll: 35%
Entering: 5,428
Transfers: 1,380
Application Deadline: 15 Jan
Mean SAT: NA
Mean ACT: NA
Middle 50% SAT range: V 520-620, M 540-640
Middle 50% ACT range: 22-27
3 Most popular majors: psychology, communications, English
Retention: 83%
Graduation rate: 67%
On-campus housing: 24%
Fraternities: 8%
Sororities: 12%
Library: 2,255,315 volumes
Tuition and Fees: $3,884 in; $20,336 out
Room and Board: $6,648
Financial aid, first-year: 26%
Varsity or Club Athletes: 3%
Early Decision or Early Action Acceptance Rate: NA

Students at the University of Colorado, Boulder, or "CU" as it is known to most Coloradoans, are free spirits. At CU, life is pretty laid back—not surprising since it is located in one of the "chillest" towns in the United States. Students say they tend to live in the "Boulder Bubble," where "nothing gets out, and the outside world is not a factor." CU provides academics that range from rigorous to easy, depending on the student and the major. CU is all about opportunity, fittingly providing a mellow environment for college students to develop and explore themselves academically.

Many Possible Paths

When applying to CU, prospective students have a choice of possible paths. Out of 26,000 undergraduates, 15,000 follow the general Arts and Sciences track, but CU's School of Business has 3,000 students, and the School of Engineering and Applied Science 2,600. Undergraduate degrees in Architecture and Planning, Journalism and Mass Communication, Music, and Education are also available. Each school has an assortment of required core classes, which must be completed within the first two years. These courses, many of which students have completed before they enter CU, include foreign language proficiency, writing, and basic math. Students comment that the graduation requirements "[do not] take too long to complete," and that they are excited that "pretty good teachers" teach them. Some range from 300 to 400 people and "can be pretty crowded, which sucks." After freshman year, though, classes are much smaller: 48 percent of courses have fewer than 20 people, and as many as 84 percent have fewer than 50. In terms of libraries and facilities, "the resources are just amazing," said one student, and "they've got everything you'd ever need." The "sciences are really big," and the school has definitely marked its dedication to them with the construction of the "Discovery Center," which houses an array of resources. As an additional credit to the University's strong science core, two CU professors were awarded the Nobel Prize in Physics in 2001. Despite some big names, students call most professors "accessible," but say that for the bigger lectures, students need to go to office hours to get a more personal connection. CU's 14 to 1 student-to-faculty ratio is best felt in the smaller seminars, where professors trade ideas in open forums with 10 to 30 students.

The specialized majors, especially Engineering, are considered more difficult than the open option School of Arts and Sciences. Classes generally considered easy, such as Psychology 1 and "Deviance in US Society" "end up being harder" because they have begun to require more reading. One Business major went so far to say, "I haven't been in a class that's been really easy," and that it would be hard to find a full four years of easy classes. The Arts and Sciences program allows students to take a variety of classes towards graduation credit and postpone declaring a major until the end of sophomore year. Anthropology, Political Science, and Psychology are historically very popular departments. "Profiles in American Enterprise" is one example of the interactive course offerings at CU. The class brings in a CEO of a major corporation weekly to lecture, and then lets the group break down into small discussion sections, or "recitations," to talk about the issues raised. Recitations are common across the University, and are taught by Teaching Assistants, or TAs. Student feedback on TAs ranges from complaints about foreign language barriers and those who "had no idea how to keep people interested," to praise for TAs who "have been very high quality," and "made us get really into the topic."

Nightlife: Greek and Beyond

"Drinking is pretty big," admitted one student. While drinking is not allowed in the dorms, house parties and an active fraternity scene provide ample opportunity for those out for a good time. With about 15 percent of students in fraternities and sororities, "the Greek scene is not really big, but it gets a lot of attention." Recently, the university has heavily monitored the Greek system. Still, frats tend to throw parties, more often than do sororities. The frats with the biggest campus presence are Sigma Alpha Epsilon, Alpha Tau Omega, and Pi Kappa Phi. The sororities provide more formal social opportunities for female students, which is especially desirable as most do not live on campus after freshman year. Halloween is reported to be pretty crazy around CU, as is any night on which CU is in a championship game.

Apart from Greek life, social activities center around houses and the relaxed atmosphere of downtown Boulder. The bar scene attracts many to digs such as the Walnut Brewery or the Sink. Student groups, including frats, often rent out clubs and host dance parties. As far as romantic social encounters go, students describe the process as "random hookup first, then dating," often involving someone met through parties. Though students acknowledge a gay and lesbian presence on campus, few feel that there is much public homosexual dating, especially compared with other schools.

Relaxed Homogeneity

CU students enjoy their reputation as relaxed and laid back. They laughingly admit to a presence of drugs, particularly marijuana, on campus, but say that use is confined to a relatively small portion of the student body. On the 20th of April at 4:20 A.M., many of those students meet up to smoke marijuana together. One student notes that over four years, it would be difficult not to come into at least some contact with marijuana. This is a factor of environment, to some degree. CU is located in downtown Boulder, a "very liberal, laid-back place, known for a lot of hippies." Students also feel that the town is "wealthy and not diverse at all," but enjoy the mountain-grown feel to it, concluding that it is all in all a "really, really unique town."

Nonetheless, CU students are not impressed by the school's diversity statistics. With approximately 15 percent minority enrollment, "homogenous" was the first adjective to come to many students. Students joke about a "Boulder uniform," composed of "a North Face jacket, jeans, and Reef sandals." Students are definitely aware of the fairly Caucasian feel to campus, distinguishing between "outdoorsy," and "hippies," as distinct subgroups of the CU student type. However, CU students are by no means homogenous when it comes to their interests. "There is always something going on," said one student, describing the active extracurricular scene. From women's football to the arts, CU's 300 clubs offer ample ways to fill up students' time. CU's student government controls one of the largest budgets in the nation, nearly 25 million dollars, devoted to campus programs and improving student life. "Whatever you're into, you can definitely find something to do."

Off-Campus Migration

Dorm life is not central to CU. One student mentioned, "it feels like about 90 percent [of students] live off campus." While freshmen are required to live in the dorms, by senior year, the number of students still living in the Halls is small. The freshman year experience, however, is a happy one. Most students express pleasure at the efforts made by CU to integrate first-year students and make them feel more at home. RAs and "academic advisors" live on every floor of freshman dorms. RAs make nightly rounds to check on their advisees, and organize fun events "to promote people getting to know each other." Academic advisors serve as resource bases in case of late-night academic difficulties. The CU dorms are intended as study spaces, so "quiet hours" are fairly strictly enforced, following a lot of criticism for rowdiness. Halls are co-ed, though they differ sometimes by floor, room, or entryway.

Students are neither impressed nor discouraged by dining hall food, "depending on what's being served." The dorms with dining halls in them are "preferred," despite mixed feelings about food quality. Once students move off campus, they "basically never" eat in the dorms again. Students admit to eating out regularly, "once or twice a week," in Boulder, if only for a slice of pizza or a burrito.

Rocky Mountain High

CU's campus is very attractive, nestled in some of Colorado's best scenery. "All the buildings are done up the same way," described a student, "so it seems all packed in, since it's the same architectural style." Some students complain that the interiors do not always reflect the pristine exteriors, but that the university has begun to improve the building facilities in the past years. From Folsom Stadium, home to the CU football team, spectators look directly out onto the Rockies. Students agree that Norlin Library is one of the better-known landmarks on campus, in addition to providing outstanding research opportunities. Campus is thoroughly suburban and for the most part, students feel very safe walking alone.

Students cite "outdoorsy" and "hippy" as distinct subgroups of the CU student type.

CU loves its sports teams. CU fields a Division IA football team, which is consistently among the best in the nation. Ralphie, the much-loved mascot, represents the Buffaloes, or the "Buffs," at games. The CU-Nebraska football game is not to be missed, and homecoming weekend is celebrated with a parade, masses of alums back on campus, and a slew of rowdy parties. CU students who are not varsity athletes are by no means inactive. Skiing and snowboarding are hugely popular with CU's convenient proximity to stellar resorts, as are other outdoorsy pastimes such as rock climbing and mountain biking.

Expectations and Opportunity

"CU exceeded my expectations," commented one student, mentioning the opportunities he might never have had at a smaller school. At CU, students have a real chance to define their own educations, just as they do their lifestyles, and as a result students are involved, interested, and relaxed, but they also know when to party. If someone is looking for a chance to explore and excel in a variety of subjects without the pressure to fit a high-stress ultra-academic personality mold, CU could be a perfect fit. —*Charlotte Taft*

FYI

If you come to CU, you'd better bring a "pair of skis or a snowboard."

What is the typical weekend schedule? "Go out Thursday, go out Friday with the people who didn't go out Thursday, watch football and chill out on Saturday, do homework Sunday night."

If I could change one thing about CU, "I'd make it smaller."

The three things that every student should do before graduating from CU are "have sex in Norlin library, eat at Illegal Pete's, and go see a CU-Nebraska football game."

University of Denver

Address: Office of Admissions, University Hall, Room 110; Denver, CO 80208
Phone: 303-871-2036
E-mail address: admission@du.edu
Web site URL: www.du.edu
Founded: 1864
Private or Public: private
Religious affiliation: none
Location: urban
Undergraduate enrollment: 3,898
Total enrollment: NA
Percent Male/Female: 48%/52%
Percent Minority: 15%
Percent African-American: 3%
Percent Asian: 5%
Percent Hispanic: 6%
Percent Native-American: 1%
Percent in-state/out of state: 50%/50%
Percent Pub HS: NA
Number of Applicants: 4,305
Percent Accepted: 77%
Percent Accepted who enroll: 30%
Entering: 1,004
Transfers: 209
Application Deadline: 1 Feb
Mean SAT: NA
Mean ACT: NA
Middle 50% SAT range: V 500-610, M 510-620
Middle 50% ACT range: 22-27
3 Most popular majors: business management, social sciences, communication
Retention: 85%
Graduation rate: 69%
On-campus housing: 43%
Fraternities: 23%
Sororities: 22%
Library: 1,212,392 volumes
Tuition and Fees: $24,873
Room and Board: $7,275
Financial aid, first-year: 40%
Varsity or Club Athletes: 15%
Early Decision or Early Action Acceptance Rate: EA 90%

The "oldest independent university in the Rockies" is getting a face-lift. Students agree that the focus of the school has shifted noticeably in the past several years. The existing emphasis on community leadership and involvement is being matched by a set of construction projects aimed at centralizing and modernizing the campus. The administration has also cracked down on the wild Greek scene. The result? A mellow, focused, and more academically oriented feel pervades the school that was known for its tradition of good times, great skiing, and rousing school events.

Personalized Academics

To start off their time at DU, freshmen are required to take a medley of courses, including a foreign language, oral communication, math, computer science, and English. Most students are in agreement that the core curriculum let them explore the school's strengths before choosing a major. "My favorite class to date was definitely my freshman year Spanish class, no question," comments one sophomore. The student-to-faculty ratio is an impressive 14 to 1, and many commented on the personal attention received from teachers. The result is that students enjoy very small class sizes and foster "interactive" relationships with professors. TAs are a concept pretty foreign to DU students, except in a few science courses. DU also boasts a freshman-mentoring program, which assigns all entering freshmen a faculty mentor to see them through the major decisions of the first year. After freshman year, students split their range of studies in various directions, from Arts and Literature to Creative Expression.

Popular majors include business, reflecting DU's impressive Business School, psychology, and biology. Science majors are generally considered more difficult, and include killer courses in organic chemistry and cellular biology.

For all majors, DU makes an effort to foster a merit-based academic feel on campus from the very start. Freshmen can apply to be in the Pioneer Leadership Program the summer before they arrive. This highly selective program fits into their curriculum as a minor, applicable to any primary major later on. Equally selective is the Honors Program, which offers students with a 3.4 GPA or higher access to special lectures and seminars. The Pioneer Leadership and Honors Programs students live on special, separate floors in freshman housing.

Another popular offering is the Interterm Program, which provides students with intensive programs between the formal academic quarters, both based at DU and abroad. Past Interterm opportunities, which are available in the fall, winter, and spring recesses, have included An Economic History of the Caribbean taught on St. Kitts and Nevis in the West Indies, a course on the European Union on location in London, and a course on gaming and gambling taught from the casinos of Las Vegas.

Students at DU generally like the academic term system, which divides the school year into quarters. Some complain that it is a bit fast paced at times, leaving "no room for screwing up." The daily workload is manageable, and more than two or three classes per day are rare.

DU students are motivated and engaged, but not over-the-top intense. One student describes academics as "strong, but nothing I can't handle. I'm challenged, but not killing myself over work on a daily basis." The University has tried to unify and raise the quality of the academic experience by, for the last four years, requiring all students to have a laptop computer. Classes make use of online discussion groups, note taking, and in-class Internet access.

Central and Modern

"Copper is big here," commented one DU student when describing the campus. A nice blend of fresh, modern architecture and older structures makes for a very pleasant campus feel. The red brick tower of University Hall meets the low lines of Pembrose Library, while pathways snake through manicured lawns and green open spaces. The wide Colorado sky and view of the Rockies add to the picturesque feel of the campus. The university prides itself on its accomplishments in enhancing the beautiful surroundings as well, with additions such as the beautiful Humanities Gardens near the center of campus. Students call the campus "very central and modern," and praise the large capital project devoted to the recently completed residence hall and science center. Recent construction projects are part of the University's efforts to move much of DU's satellite campus, Park Hill, closer to the action on the central grounds. The Ritchie Center for Sports and Wellness is another highly visible landmark, as well as a state-of-the-art athletic facility for varsity athletes and gym-rats alike.

"Those who don't ski can feel a little excluded."

The campus is manageably sized, so that "it never takes more than ten or so minutes to get to class, at the extreme," one student explained. Freshmen and sophomores are required to live on campus. Freshmen are housed in two dormitories, Johnson-McFarlane, or J-Mac, and Centennial Halls. Both buildings are air-conditioned, and comprised of suites with kitchenettes. Centennial Halls is the home of Special Interest floors, which group students by interests such as substance free, business, math/science, all male or all female, and the Honors Program. Members of the Pioneer Leadership Program and others live in J-Mac, generally regarded as the "dorkier" of the two freshman residences. The dorms are described as "decent," and "kinda gross." Freshmen live with RAs on each floor, who keep tabs on alcohol, which is forbidden, and noise violations.

Students eat in cafeterias located in both of the freshman dorms, and the upperclassman dorm. After freshmen year, many sophomores choose to eat in their fraternity or sorority, and there are few upperclassmen in the cafeterias at all. DU offers a "point system" allowing students extra meal points with which they can eat in local restaurants and "get a Starbucks fix."

Greek Festivities

The area around campus is "residential and cute," made up of mostly student houses. There is a small, "adequate" commercial area a few blocks from campus, and downtown Denver is only a ten-minute drive from campus. A majority of students have cars on campus, and they are permitted for freshmen. The social life at DU has many ties to the Greek system, and 23% of students are members of the eight fraternities and five sororities. Those inside the Greek system say that "it does not entirely dominate the social scene, but it is strong," and say that there are "tons of alternative, non-Greek weekend options," though some are more adamant that the Greek system "*is* the social scene." Students lament the increased frequency with which house parties are broken up, and say that the party scene has begun to shift towards "bar parties," where a group will rent a bar, and allow anyone over 18 (those under 21 get a wristband) to enter and enjoy dancing and drinking. Traditional fraternity events at the ever popular SAE, Lambda Chi Alpha, and Sigma Chi fraternities include annual theme parties, such as Western, Pajama, and Principals and Schoolgirls. All formal events are Greek based. One of the major non-Greek events is the yearly Winter Carnival, a hugely popular campus-wide event in January.

Involved and Evolving

Like all universities of its size, DU has a long list of interesting extracurricular possibilities, from public service organizations to professional honors societies and dance troupes. The student newspaper, *The Clarion*, is a popular involvement, and the Alpine Club is known for organizing frequent outdoor excursions.

The student body at DU is "not extremely diverse," and one student commented that with regards to breaking the stereotype that it's a school of rich kids, "they try but it's pretty white, fairly preppy, not a lot of punks." The 15 percent of the student of body of minority background does not fail to make an impression on campus. However, forming a strong community within a community through ethnic clubs and organizations.

One student remarked that arts opportunities are not at the forefront at DU, but that with the completion of the new music building on central campus, which will include a larger theater space, there is hope that students will no longer "need to be in the know to hear about the arts."

Winter Sports Rule

Skiing is a huge campus pastime and "those who don't ski can feel a little excluded," as many students hit the slopes every weekend throughout the winter. Aside from skiing, DU offers many athletic choices to the sports-minded. Club sports are popular. They do not make any cuts and are "a lot of fun" for all involved. DU also fosters strong Varsity sports teams, the most popular of which is its successful hockey team, followed by the lacrosse, soccer, and swim teams. There is generally "good turnout" to games, though hockey is unquestionably king. Division I hockey games take the place of football games, as DU has no football team, and the annual game against rival Colorado College is "not to be missed."

Traditions such as the enthusiasm for the hockey team unify DU as it continues to establish itself as a rising academic institution. Students are as relaxed and ready to take advantage of its opportunities to hit the slopes and fraternity row as they are to hit the books. —*Charlotte Taft*

FYI

If you come to the University of Denver, you'd better bring "a fake ID."

What is the typical weekend schedule? "Rest up, go out, squeeze in the homework."

If I could change one thing about DU, "I'd change the rules about social activities—make them less anal about breaking up house parties."

The three things that every student should do before graduating from the University of Denver are "travel around the area because Colorado is beautiful, realize what downtown has to offer, and go to the Colorado College-DU hockey game."

Connecticut

Connecticut College

Address: 270 Mohegan Avenue; New London, CT 06320
Phone: 860-439-2200
E-mail address: admission@conncoll.edu
Web site URL: www.connecticutcollege.edu
Founded: 1911
Private or Public: private
Religious affiliation: none
Location: suburban
Undergraduate enrollment: 1,890
Total enrollment: 1,897
Percent Male/Female: 40%/60%
Percent Minority: 10%
Percent African-American: 3%
Percent Asian: 3%
Percent Hispanic: 4%
Percent Native-American: 0%
Percent in-state/out of state: 19%/81%
Percent Pub HS: 50%
Number of Applicants: 3,915
Percent Accepted: 35%
Percent Accepted who enroll: 36%
Entering: 500
Transfers: 21
Application Deadline: 1 Jan
Mean SAT: 1310
Mean ACT: 27
Middle 50% SAT range: V 612-687, M 602-682
Middle 50% ACT range: NA
3 Most popular majors: economics, English language and literature, political science and government
Retention: 91%
Graduation rate: 83%
On-campus housing: 96%
Fraternities: NA
Sororities: NA
Library: 955,749 volumes
Tuition and Fees: NA
Room and Board: NA
Financial aid, first-year: 42%
Varsity or Club Athletes: 30%
Early Decision or Early Action Acceptance Rate: ED 65%

Set in the quiet town of New London, Connecticut College provides a safe environment for its close-knit student community while stressing the importance of its honor code, strong academic program, and lively social life.

Education at Conn and Beyond

As a "general education" requirement, each student at Connecticut College is required to take one course in each of seven offered areas, in addition to a foreign language and two writing intensive or writing enhanced courses. A wide range of classes gives students the opportunity to design their own majors, double majors, minors, and areas of concentration. However, students find "Conn has too many requirements for graduation and the faculty is looking to change the number of non-major classes that need to be taken." Professors are easily accessible as there are no teaching assistants, and students report this feature as the most rewarding aspect of their academic experience. Students find Biology, History, and Pre-med to be among the most demanding majors, while Human Development is mentioned as the easiest. Small class sizes and the accessibility of professors ease the difficulty of courses. Students also benefit from a wide range of library sources in their research. As a part of a consortium with Trinity and Wesleyan, students can freely exchange library materials between the three schools free of charge.

In addition to the true spirit of liberal arts, Conn also offers academic centers with different certificate programs. The Center for International Studies and Liberal Arts (CISLA), the Public Policy Certificate Program in Community Action (PICA), and the Career Enhancing Lif

Skills program (CELS) help students discover their strengths and find internships and jobs. PICA provides students with community service internships while CISLA is oriented around internships abroad as a way of enriching Conn's liberal arts education. Students are encouraged to spend one semester or summer abroad with CISLA internships, as well as making use of Study Away Teach Away (SATA) and Traveling Research and Immersion (TRIP) programs. SATA, a small program of 10 to 20 students, offers applicants the opportunity to study with their professors in socially, politically, and economically different environments for one semester. Past programs have taken place in Prague, Tanzania, India, South Africa, Greece, Egypt, Rome, Mexico and Vietnam. TRIP, funding research projects abroad, is also a part of Conn's Comprehensive Strategic Plan, aiming to provide students with multicultural experiences.

Active Social Life . . .

Despite student complaints of a lack of social life in the New London area, students report a vibrant drinking and dating scene. Said one junior: "Drinking is the number-one social activity at Conn, followed by sex in a very close second." "Casual hook-ups are always happening," another noted. As there is no Greek scene on campus, drinking takes place in dorm rooms, while parties usually continue on to the Campus Bar. Though students observe that the administration is implementing a tougher alcohol policy as of late, one senior warned "Don't be a nondrinker at Conn! You feel left out!"

Students and Dorm Life

Students find their student body to be mostly upper- or middle-class white students from Massachusetts or New York. One student described the typical Conn student as "Educated at a private school, wears J-Crew or Abercrombie, drives a Volvo or Saab. Loves Dave Matthews, but listens to Jay- Z at a party." The student body feels its percentage of minority students is fairly small, but is contrasted by a larger body of international students.

After freshman year, almost all students are provided with on-campus singles. The number of students electing off-campus housing is therefore relatively low. Recent dormitory renovations now offer rooms with air-conditioning systems. The size of the campus allows easy access to dorms, classrooms, and other facilities. Students mention that their campus is not well-connected with the greater New London community, though Conn's "Camel Van" provides transportation to students wishing to volunteer in schools and community organizations around the city. The campus is praised as "beautiful, especially when you can overlook Long Island Sound and the Thames."

The friendly and entertaining "Camelympics" are named for the school mascot and pit dorms against each other in events like "glow-in-the-dark kickball."

For dining options, students choose between one of the following: Harris, the main dining hall, which offers a "hot line," vegetarian line, deli, bakery, and sweets; Harkness, which specializes in the deli foods; and Freeman, the "stir-fry" dining hall. The Crozier-Williams Student Center also has food service and a bar for students to grab a quick pizza or beer. Eating out is also popular among students. Mystic and Recovery Room for pizza, Fortune Cookie for Chinese, and Margaritas for Mexican are casual dine-outs, while Bravo Bravo and Anthony J's are spots for dates.

An Involved Student Body

Despite the small class size, students find Conn's facility centers to be satisfying. The athletic center, situated on the Thames River, is a great place for Conn's rowing and sailing teams, as well as offering a motivating environment for track runners. Basketball, sailing, hockey, and lacrosse are among the school's most popular sports. In the past, Conn's women's sailing team has ranked second in Sailing World Magazine, while co-ed stood at 16th place. On the club-sports level, equestrian and Ultimate Frisbee are popular. The friendly and entertaining "Camelympics" are named for the school mascot and pit dorms against each other in events like "glow-in-the-dark kickball, jigsaw puzzle races, and arm wrestling."

Due to early practice hours, sports teams usually eat together and form close-knit groups. Students find it easy to meet people during their freshman year, but note that most social groups form during this time. As one student warned transfers: "Watch out if you are a transfer—it might not be the best thing to do if you enjoy the company of others and need to make friends easily."

Volunteer work also takes an important place in the social life of many Camels, though many student-run organizations complain that they "struggle to reach the campus as a whole." Students feel that the Unity House, Conn's multicultural center, does not reach out to a majority of the student body, even though it's open for everyone. The Cro, Conn's student center, holds "Take over Cro" weekends throughout the year where there are many theme parties and where student organizations exhibit their current projects. Students also play an active role in their academic departments' advisory boards, as well as in the control of the judiciary board for honor code violations.

Connecticut College is a place where students can learn in an academically supportive atmosphere with small classes and accessible professors. Conn students learn the value of responsibility and integrity through the honor code. They are proud of their school, of their mascot, and of Conn's emphasis on acquiring multicultural experiences. As one student said, "Conn is a fun and interesting place to go to school. I am excited about what my future here will bring." —*Yakut Seyhanli*

FYI

If you come to Connecticut College, you'd better bring "a Nalgene bottle and a car."

What is the typical weekend schedule? "Party on Thursday and Saturday nights, hang out on Friday, go to a sports game on Saturday and work on Sundays."

If I could change one thing about Connecticut College, "I would move it out of New London."

Three things that every student at Connecticut College should do before graduating are "take a walk at the arboretum, go to Harkness beach, and study abroad."

Fairfield University

Address: 1073 North Benson Road; Fairfield, CT 06824-5195
Phone: 203-254-4100
E-mail address: admis@mail.fairfield.edu
Web site URL: www.fairfield.edu
Founded: 1942
Private or Public: private
Religious affiliation: Jesuit
Location: suburban
Undergraduate enrollment: 4,073
Total enrollment: NA
Percent Male/Female: 44%/56%
Percent Minority: 10%
Percent African-American: 2%
Percent Asian: 3%
Percent Hispanic: 4%
Percent Native-American: 0%
Percent in-state/out of state: 24%/76%
Percent Pub HS: 62%
Number of Applicants: 6,974
Percent Accepted: 50%
Percent Accepted who enroll: 23%
Entering: 814
Transfers: 65
Application Deadline: 15 Jan
Mean SAT: NA
Mean ACT: NA
Middle 50% SAT range: V 540-630, M 570-650
Middle 50% ACT range: 25-27
3 Most popular majors: marketing, English, communications and media
Retention: 89%
Graduation rate: 79%
On-campus housing: 80%
Fraternities: NA
Sororities: NA
Library: 219,893 volumes
Tuition and Fees: $26,135
Room and Board: $8,920
Financial aid, first-year: 52%
Varsity or Club Athletes: 25%
Early Decision or Early Action Acceptance Rate: ED 67%

Evidence of its recent transformation is gradually receding from the campus of Fairfield University. The school recently finished its three-year project of revamping each of its eight student dorms, as well as renovating the campus center, library, and science buildings. The result is likely to go well beyond aesthetics and significantly improve the quality of life at Fairfield.

A Unique Academic Experience

Fairfield's Jesuit tradition is still extremely visible in the academic arena. Rising sophomores are offered the opportunity to apply to the college's Honors Program, based on first-year GPA, which exempts its students from some of the distributional requirements in favor of an interdisciplinary program that is writing intensive. Students say that the foreign languages are the weaker programs academically and the arts program is small. The college is divided into four schools: the School of Arts and Sciences, the Business School, the School of Nursing, and the Graduate School. The nursing and business programs are especially well-regarded and popular. The core curriculum, consisting of three semesters of English, and two semesters each of math, science, language, history, social science, and fine arts. Besides these, "Stags" are required to take two semesters of religious studies and philosophy, with one additional semester in either religion, philosophy, or ethics. Such a complicated core is not ideal for those who dislike the liberal arts. But even for those who do, Fairfield's program is intellectually rewarding and, most importantly, improves writing skills. Besides the core curriculum, another respected Fairfield institution is its pre-med program. About academics in general, students say that "with a little time and effort you will be fine" because professors "are more than willing to help you out."

Fairfield's small size makes individual attention available and classes small enough to foster stimulating discussions with the professors. Introductory lecture classes rarely enroll more than 40 people and seminars often have around 12 or less. Because of the class sizes and the helpful attitude of most professors, Fairfield students have plenty of time to develop extracurricular interests.

What's a Naked Mormon?

Extracurriculars at Fairfield are as diverse as those of any other school of its size and quality. Prospective freshmen can look forward to participating in activities ranging from the community service oriented Campus Ministry, to campus radio, to Glee Club, which is a large group, and FUSA, the extremely enthusiastic Fairfield student government. One extracurricular that Fairfield does not offer is fraternities and sororities. The activity that most excites the average student at Fairfield is drinking alcohol. Students here love their "Beach," a four-square-mile strip of houses rented out to students, most of which are "right along the Long Island Sound."

In recent years, there has been more tension between the town of Fairfield and the University, because of the party scene at the Beach. As a result, fewer students are living off campus and more weekend activities seem to be shifting back to the campus area. However, these houses are still where the best partying is, and often they have fun, wacky names like the "Naked Mormon," the "Dugout," and the "Red Barn." Right near the Beach is the Sea Grape, or just the Grape, which is the most popular student bar.

When students are not at the Beach or the Grape, they sometimes head to Norwalk for its nightclubs. The most popular for Fairfield students is the Van Dome, but a new club called Risk just opened with college Thursdays. One student said that the social life at Fairfield revolves "totally and utterly" around alcohol. When asked about the presence of drugs on campus, one student said that while marijuana has always been around, recently 'shrooms and ecstasy have become more visible.

Incoming Frosh Without ID—Fear Not!

The college itself has begun to devote more attention to enhancing the weekend activities available to its undergrads. Free bowling, discounted movie tickets, and trips to see Broadway shows are all being sponsored with greater frequency. Sometimes bands play at the Levee, the campus bar. There are two major semi-formals during basketball season: the Harvest and the Dogwood-Midnight Madness, but the best-loved college-sponsored event at Fairfield is its Spring Weekend. In the words of one student, "there are bands, games, contests, and lots of activities, and of course tons of drinking."

"[Most students look like] they just stepped out of a J. Crew or Abercrombie catalog."

When it comes to sports, Fairfield holds its own in men's and women's soccer, and women's volleyball. All three have made it to the NCAA tournament in the past few years. Men's basketball games at the Arena at Harbor Yard in Bridgeport get the greatest turnout when it comes to fans. Students consistently rate school spirit very poorly, and in general, the student body is just not as sports-oriented as most Division I schools. Intramurals at Fairfield are a good way to combat stress, with floor hockey, flag football, soccer, and basketball being most popular.

Chemistry at Fairfield: Not Just a Science

The student body is a homogenous group, and students complain about a lack of diversity. When asked what the typical Fairfield student is like, students responded that most look like "they just stepped out of a J. Crew or Abercrombie catalog." The majority are Christian, hail from New England, and are middle- to upper-class. Students warn that some of their fellow classmates are very snobby. The advantage of having an attractive student body is obvious: "there is a lot of chemistry between students here," and "meeting people is not a problem." However, as at many colleges, the dating scene is nearly non-existent. With some exceptions, one-night hook-ups are predominant.

Fairfield, Connecticut

The college is located in southwestern Connecticut, and the most central and visible building on campus is the Egan Chapel of St. Ignatius Loyola, a reminder that Fairfield is a school founded upon the Jesuit ideals of education and community service. The town of Fairfield, Connecticut, is the typical New England college town, but it is on the quiet side. In this part of Connecticut, town stoplights turn off after 11:30 P.M. The closest mall is in Trumbull, and for undergrads with transportation, Fairfield is about a half hour from New Haven, seven minutes from Bridgeport, and an hour from New York City on MetroNorth. New York is a popular trip, especially for upperclassmen, but Fairfield is by no means a "suitcase school." There are many little shops in Fairfield, but few restaurants. Students generally enjoy going to Joe's, which is close to campus and has good food.

Dining and Housing Options: For Better or Worse

The dining experience at Fairfield University, according to the upperclassmen, is no different from those of other colleges. There are many choices, but for those nights when nothing looks appetizing there are the old standbys: peanut butter and jelly, cereal, and grilled cheese. The campus has two dining halls, one for freshmen and one for upperclassmen, but the school has been experimenting to see which dining hall is best for the freshmen. Campus residents are on either a 19- or 14-meal-a-week plan, and off-campus residents have the option of a seven-, 10-, or 12-meal plan. There are Stagbucks which can be purchased in order to obtain snacks during the day. Those tired of cafeteria food can go to Joe's, Spazzi's, or Sidetracks.

There's good news for freshmen in the housing department: the renovated frosh dorms are in the central Quad, making it easier for new students to feel like a part of the college immediately. Another bonus at Fairfield is that housing is guaranteed for all four years. Upperclassmen enter a lottery to get into beach houses or condominium-like townhouses on campus, and the newly constructed apartment "villages" also on campus. Many students who are granted off-campus living status enter into agreements with landlords of houses at the Beach—Beach housing is not affiliated with nor arranged by the University.

The Fairfield Experience

Student body diversity is one issue Fairfield has taken steps to improve. The creation of the Multicultural Task Force is an important addition, as it emphasizes awareness and tolerance by sponsoring guest lecturers to give talks and by sponsoring ethnic and cultural awareness days. Also, the administration added a class in diversity to its distributional requirements, and though their course loads are already heavy, the students were very pleased by this step. It requires students to take at least one course in another culture, religion, or ethnic group during their four years.

Between extensive renovations projects, the creation of a football team, and the recent addition of a diversity requirement and the Multicultural Task Force, Fairfield University is a school both steeped in the tradition of reputable academics and an enthusiasm for continued improvement of both the structural body of the school and students themselves.—*Christina Merola*

FYI

If you come to Fairfield, you'd better bring "a car, so you can get around our campus."

What is the typical weekend schedule? "Friday night, drinking until you pass out. Saturday, repeat Friday. Sunday, sleep."

If I could change one thing about Fairfield, I'd "bring 'Clam Jam' back. A while ago the school got hit with a lawsuit and now won't allow the party."

Three things every student should do before graduating from Fairfield are "go to New York City for the night, attend Spring Weekend, and spend a night at the Beach."

Quinnipiac University

Address: 275 Mt. Carmel Ave; Hamden, CT 06518
Phone: 800-462-1944
E-mail address: admissions@quinnipiac.edu
Web site URL: www.quinnipiac.edu
Founded: 1929
Private or Public: private
Religious affiliation: none
Location: suburban
Undergraduate enrollment: 5,317
Total enrollment: NA
Percent Male/Female: 39%/61%
Percent Minority: 8%
Percent African-American: 2%
Percent Asian: 2%
Percent Hispanic: 4%
Percent Native-American: 0%
Percent in-state/out of state: 22%/78%
Percent Pub HS: NA
Number of Applicants: 8,881
Percent Accepted: 61%
Percent Accepted who enroll: 24%
Entering: 1,318
Transfers: 200
Application Deadline: rolling
Mean SAT: 1070
Mean ACT: 24
Middle 50% SAT range: V 510-580, M 520-610
Middle 50% ACT range: NA
3 Most popular majors: health sciences, liberal arts, business
Retention: 84%
Graduation rate: 78%
On-campus housing: 95%
Fraternities: NA
Sororities: NA
Library: 165,000 volumes
Tuition and Fees: $21,120
Room and Board: $9,450
Financial aid, first-year: 70%
Varsity or Club Athletes: NA
Early Decision or Early Action Acceptance Rate: NA

This small college provides great vocational opportunities in a quaint New England setting. The campus' rural feel creates a pretty environment with a family-like faculty. While Sleeping Giant State Park looms over the campus and provides a popular hiking spot, students can still enjoy the urban nightlife of neighboring New Haven. "The combination of nature and urban convenience is major bonus for Quinnipiac." Most of the students come from Connecticut and surrounding New England states.

Campus Commuters

If you're looking for a school that compliments the New England fall, this is the place. Directly across the street sits a large state park which, according to one sophomore, "looks like a patchwork quilt in the fall." An elegant pine-grove path meanders through campus providing a scenic walk to class, the library, or the new gym. When asked to describe the campus, one sophomore girl said, "It looks like a little village. Everything is pretty close together and within walking distance. It's very picturesque too!" Although the campus may feel like a small village, many of the buildings are architecturally modern or even futuristic. Renovated three years ago, the gym now contains a suspended indoor track hanging over new tennis courts. The library also has a modern feel with a whole wall made of glass that makes it easy to enjoy the winter scenery while studying cozily in the warm library. The dorms may not be quite as elegant as the gym and library, but nonetheless students had few complaints. Freshmen dorms are the smallest, but still not cramped. They are co-ed and accessible to all the essential campus buildings. Freshman bathrooms are communal but in upperclass suites they are in each room. Suites after freshmen year vary in size from three to ten students depending on who you want to live with. Some students move off campus as juniors, but all seniors live off campus. Almost everyone at Quinnipiac either has a car or wishes they did. Unfortunately freshmen are not allowed to have cars; one freshman complained, "I hate waiting for shuttles and taxis when I want to get off campus; I can't wait until next year."

Partying

Yes, indeed, they like to party at Quinnipiac. According to most students it is only a minor setback that kegs are not allowed on campus. "It's not a big deal. We usually just drink in our rooms until we want to go to the bars anyway." There is not much of a Greek scene at Quinnipiac, so weekend festivities revolve around the various bars surrounding campus.

One favorite hot spot, especially for girls, is Toad's Place in New Haven located next to the Yale University campus. Just ten minutes away from Quinnipiac, Toad's has dance parties every Wednesday and Saturday and often good bands on other nights. One freshman girl said, "Toad's is my favorite place on Saturday nights because I get to meet hot Yale boys." While upperclassmen tend to get off campus more, this is due mostly to the accessibility of cars rather than the limitations of being underage. Consensus among underclassmen is that fake IDs are common and rarely scrutinized. But even if students don't make it off campus on the weekend there are usually options for partying on campus.

> **"The combination of nature and urban convenience is major bonus for Quinnipiac."**

Every student at Quinnipiac loves to talk about the tradition of May weekend. Every year in May the school spends large amounts of money for fun events like concerts. One senior girl said "the entire campus turns in to a drunken carnival. People run around and go crazy. It's my favorite weekend of the year."

Other social events include the school's basketball and hockey games. Both teams are quite good and the school gets excited for home games. Many students resent the lack of a football team and stadium. Other varsity sports are not as popular, but many students participate in intramural sports. "It's a great way to meet people and actually get some decent exercise," said one sophomore girl.

Preparing for a Job

Quinnipiac does not offer a liberal arts education. The academic curriculum, however, provides students with training in various career paths. Among these options, Quinnipiac has gained a solid reputation in the health sciences; unfortunately, students claim majors in the health sciences are also the most difficult. A junior physical therapy major said "Even though I know I'm working harder on the weekends while my friends are out partying, it's worth it knowing I can get a good job right out of college."

Mass communications and business stand on the other end of the workload spectrum, according to several students. But students in all majors note very accessible faculty members. "Teachers can be really good and even if they aren't they are usually always accessible." Classes tend to be quite small, but most students have found it relatively easy to get in to the classes they want. Teachers are often flexible about letting students in even when the classes are full. Several people recommended a popular art class in which students hike outdoors and make natural sculptures inspired by existing works of art. The outdoor sculptures are displayed along campus' central pathway for all the students to admire.

By providing a rigorous preprofessional education within a small close-knit and spirited community, Quinnipiac is, in the words of one student, "a perfect fit for so many of us. I would never choose to go anywhere else."—*Quinn Fitzgerald*

FYI

If you come to Quinnipiac you'd better bring "a car and a fake ID."

What is the typical weekend schedule? "Sleeping in, homework, campus events, bars."

If I could change one thing about Quinnipiac, "it would be the lack of student enthusiasm for on-campus events."

Three things every student at Quinnipiac should do before graduating are "hike through Sleeping Giant State Park; become a leader of a team, club, or organization; and go crazy on May weekend with the rest of campus."

Trinity College

Address: 300 Summit Street; Hartford, CT 06106
Phone: 860-297-2180
E-mail address: admissions.office@trincoll.edu
Web site URL: www.trincoll.edu
Founded: 1823
Private or Public: private
Religious affiliation: none
Location: urban
Undergraduate enrollment: 2,098
Total enrollment: NA
Percent Male/Female: 48%/52%
Percent Minority: 18%
Percent African-American: 6%
Percent Asian: 6%
Percent Hispanic: 5%
Percent Native-American: 0%
Percent in-state/out of state: 22%/78%
Percent Pub HS: 45%
Number of Applicants: 5,417
Percent Accepted: 36%
Percent Accepted who enroll: 28%
Entering: 550
Transfers: 8
Application Deadline: 15 Jan
Mean SAT: NA
Mean ACT: NA
Middle 50% SAT range: V 590-690, M 600-690
Middle 50% ACT range: 24-29
3 Most popular majors: economics, political science, history
Retention: 91%
Graduation rate: 83%
On-campus housing: 95%
Fraternities: 27%
Sororities: 22%
Library: 988,536 volumes
Tuition and Fees: $28,602
Room and Board: $7,380
Financial aid, first-year: 44%
Varsity or Club Athletes: 42%
Early Decision or Early Action Acceptance Rate: ED 50%

Set atop a hill overlooking downtown Hartford, Trinity is a small liberal arts college with a reputation for being academically rigorous. Students here work and play hard. With a football team that has been steadily improving over the past few years and the number one squash team in the nation, the Bantams are full of school spirit. Students rave about Trinity's picturesque scenery and architecture, the most recent addition to which is a brand new library, which one student called "the nicest in the NESCAC."

Innovative Academic Programs

Trinity is home to a number of unique academic programs not found at any other colleges or universities in the country. From freshman to senior year students have the opportunity to study in a variety of environments that integrate residential and academic life. Through the First-Year Program all freshmen are assigned to a seminar with 12 to 15 classmates. The professor of the seminar advises the students on academic matters, including declaration of a major, while an upperclassman who lives in the freshman dorm serves as a mentor for the seminar members.

As sophomores, students may opt to continue the residential-learning tradition through participation in Tutorial College. A multi-disciplinary "college within the college" tutorial brings together 60 sophomores and five professors from five different departments. Students live together in a new residence hall, which also houses the classrooms used for the program's lectures, seminars, and conversations. Tutorial students take two courses outside of the college each semester. Upperclassmen from all majors are encouraged to study away from campus, either internationally or domestically, and the college has programs and campuses all over the country and the world.

Other curricular opportunities include the country's first undergraduate human rights program, CityTerm, through which upperclassmen work in Hartford; guided studies, a two-year intensive program in Western history, literature and philosophy; and numerous programs in the arts.

Like these special program courses Trinity's other Liberal Arts course offerings are typically small in size, which encourages high levels of teacher-student interaction. Students generally enjoy their classes, even though the workload tends to be on the heavy side. One junior warned prospective students to "be prepared to read a ton and write many papers." Economics and the sciences are known as the hardest majors at Trinity, the latter because the college does not give credit for lab time. Sociology was cited as an example of a relatively easy major.

Living It Up on Campus

With its wide array of residential setups, Trinity tends to keep its students living on campus. Each year students are presented with more housing options, and upperclassmen usually have access to kitchens and their own bathrooms. Freshmen described their rooms as "small, but cozy and very friendly:" so friendly that the majority of people meet their closest buddies in their first-year dorms. Most freshmen live in doubles, but some live in quads. Although floors are co-ed, the communal bathrooms are single-sex. Alcohol is not allowed in the freshman dorms. Upperclassmen usually have their own rooms, either within suites or on their own. There are a few dorms that house mostly seniors, and Vernon is only for students who are at least 21 years-old. Students can also choose to live in a community service dorm, a quiet dorm, an alcohol-free dorm, or in various other theme rooms. RAs, who oversee dormitory discipline, and mentors, who deal with academic and mental health issues, receive free room and board, along with a stipend. Very few students live off campus, but there are two streets right next to campus where some students rent apartments and houses. Within walking distance of all of the academic buildings, off-campus housing ranges in price from $350 to $500 per room per month.

> **"We have this beautiful campus in the middle of one of the poorest neighborhoods in the country."**

The Trinity dining experience is generally favorable, and most students described the food as "great but repetitive." In addition to the normal dining halls, students can use dining points in The Cave, an on-campus burger joint, and The Bistro, a gourmet sandwich and soup shop.

Capitol City

Although they agree that their campus is gorgeous, Trinity students are divided in their opinions of Hartford. "There is a lot of tension," explained one senior, "because we have this beautiful campus in the middle of one of the poorest neighborhoods in the country." For some this means more opportunities to volunteer in the community, while for others it means spending the vast majority of their time on campus.

Hartford, once known as the "insurance capitol of the country," is bustling with activity during the day, but more or less empty at night, since most of the city's employees leave after 5 P.M. This does not stop students from taking advantage of the cultural and educational opportunities Hartford has to offer. Those who spend time in the city see past its tough reputation and come to appreciate what one sophomore called its "amazing diversity," which stands in contrast to the more or less homogeneous student body (although students say that campus diversity is improving every year).

Trinity is centrally located in the city, with a plethora of restaurants and two malls within a five-minute drive. While having a car is not a necessity, it does facilitate exploration of the city. In order to encourage those without access to wheels to venture out, Trinity offers students a free bus pass as well as extensive shuttle service.

Between Class Time and Frat Time

Most people at Trinity are members of numerous clubs and organizations. Athletics of all levels are extremely popular on campus. Whether cheering the varsity teams to victory, playing with friends on an intramural team, or working out at the gym, students devote a good deal of time to sports. Students said that although the gym facilities are functional they "could use some improvement." The athletic fields and courts, on the other hand, are "outstanding."

A cappella groups, the debate team, and the student newspaper also draw large numbers of participants. Because it is "pushed pretty hard at Trinity," community service clubs abound at Trinity, and most students find time to volunteer each semester. The administration organizes an annual Do-It Day, on which students go into the city to clean up and help out. Working, on campus or in Hartford, is not hard, and many students have jobs to generate spending money. Students on financial aid are given work-study positions.

Camp Trin-Trin

In the words of one junior, "At Trinity if you pick your classes correctly, your weekends can start Thursday night and end Tuesday morning." Being underage at Trinity is not a problem, as fraternity parties, dorm room get-togethers, and school-sponsored parties at the social center provide fun times for students of all legal statuses. The administration also brings popular music acts to campus for the Fall Concert and Spring Weekend.

With only five fraternities and three sororities Trinity's Greek scene is relatively small, but its parties are very well attended. Formals are the only exclusive events; non-Greeks are welcome at all other parties. One senior feels that "sometimes frat parties are the only things to do on campus. However, 'late night' at frats and sororities is usually more popular than spending the whole night there." Rush usually lasts an entire semester.

The Greeks host many theme parties, including Tropical, one of the most popular annual events. It has been included on *Playboy*'s list of best parties in the nation.

Those who are 21 frequent the Tap, the on-campus bar, and some take advantage of the Hartford nightlife.

During the winter months the student-run Coffeehouse and the Cinestudio are popular destinations. When the weather warms up, students gather on the main quad to toss a Frisbee, listen to music, and hang out with friends. Just be careful not to step on the plaque on Upper Long Walk: according to Trinity legend doing so means that you will not graduate in four years.—*Alexis Ortiz*

FYI

If you come to Trinity you'd better bring "a pastel polo shirt with, preferably with the collar up for guys, and your best pearl earrings for girls."

What is the typical weekend schedule? "The weekend begins on Thursday night. Most people attend sports games in the early evenings and then go to parties in dorm rooms. Late-night at the fraternities is a popular way to end the night."

If I could change one thing about Trinity I'd "better integrate the college with the city of Hartford."

Three things every student at Trinity should do before graduating are "get drunk at the Tap (the on-campus bar), explore the underground tunnels, and get to know the amazing professors on campus."

United States Coast Guard Academy

Address: 31 Mohegan Avenue; New London, CT 06320-4195
Phone: 860-444-8500
E-mail address: admissions@cga.uscg.mil
Web site URL: www.cga.edu
Founded: 1931
Private or Public: public
Religious affiliation: none
Location: suburban
Undergraduate enrollment: 940
Total enrollment: NA
Percent Male/Female: 72%/28%
Percent Minority: 19%
Percent African-American: 5%
Percent Asian: 4%
Percent Hispanic: 7%
Percent Native-American: 1%
Percent in-state/out of state: 6%/94%
Percent Pub HS: 82%
Number of Applicants: 4,911
Percent Accepted: 8%
Percent Accepted who enroll: 74%
Entering: 291
Transfers: NA
Application Deadline: 15 Dec
Mean SAT: NA
Mean ACT: NA
Middle 50% SAT range: V 580-670, M 610-680
Middle 50% ACT range: 25-30
3 Most popular majors: engineering, business, social sciences
Retention: 75%
Graduation rate: 65%
On-campus housing: 100%
Fraternities: NA
Sororities: NA
Library: 153,046 volumes
Tuition and Fees: none
Room and Board: none
Financial aid, first-year: NA
Varsity or Club Athletes: 80%
Early Decision or Early Action Acceptance Rate: EA 29%

Have you been looking for a college that can turn you into the ideal image of yourself conjured up while daydreaming in high school English class? The United States Coast Guard Academy provides its students with the discipline and skills useful for all tracks of life, turning its cadets into the leaders of the future. With military employment following graduation and several opportunities for development while in the Academy, cadets receive much more than a four-year education. The USCGA holds firm to its rigorous academic curriculum, strong athletics program and varied extracurricular offering. Each graduate leaves the Academy with a sense of accomplishment, one that leads to future success post-graduation.

Core Values

The United States Coast Guard Academy boasts much more than a commanding name and intimidating reputation. Started as the School of Instruction for the Revenue Marine in 1876, the USCGA harbors an impressive combination of tradition, rigor, and discipline that continually shapes future leaders of America. In fact, the leadership skills developed during the four-years at USCGA are what many cadets attribute as the best aspect of the Academy. The USCGA's set of core values is threefold—first, honor; second, respect; and finally, devotion to duty—and transcends all programs in the Academy. With such a hefty reputation, the Academy often intimidates students from applying to enter its undergraduate pool. However, prospective candidates should "consider the broad range of opportunities that the Academy has to offer and acknowledge the diverse student body that enjoys the benefits of the USCGA."

The USCGA draws a student body that is about 70 percent male and 30 percent female. All cadets receive equal treatment with respect to academics, housing and athletic training. The promise of equal opportunities at the Academy is one of the most treasured aspects of the institution, as reported by many cadets. The USCGA provides an equal playing field whether a cadet is male or female, first-class or fourth-class. You might ask: what is the difference between a first class and a fourth class cadet? How can delineating classes exist within a system of fair play?

All freshmen at the Academy are called fourth-class cadets, and each year students climb on rung on the ladder. Each class has special roles and duties at the Academy; this reflects the hierarchical structure of military life and prepares cadets for post-graduation military employment. Fourth-class cadets are like understudies, learning the ropes of military life and following closely in the paths of their elders. Third-class cadets advise one or two fourth-class cadets in a mentoring role, while second-class cadets assume the responsibility of Assistant Division Officers, leading the younger cadets during training. Finally, first-class cadets, who have already gone through the stages of development at the Academy, have the opportunity to become Regimental Staff Officers, Company Commanders, Department Heads and Division Officers. This specific regimentation at the Academy prepares cadets for the structured system of military duty and creates a progressive path toward more responsibility, learning, and opportunity. At the end of four years, first-class cadets have had the experience of being followers, mentors, assistant leaders, and commanders. Each of these roles provides potential for growth and enrichment unique to the mission and mores of the Academy.

Cadets Uniform: The Typical Day

With such a close parallel to military structure and core values, discipline plays a tremendous role in the lives of USCGA cadets. Although cadets' names and roles change from year to year, the typical weekday schedule "falls equally upon all cadets alike." The wake-up alarm sounds at "0600" and breakfast quickly follows. Academic instruction begins promptly at 0800 and ends at 1200 for lunch. Classes then resume after lunch and end for the day at 1600. The Academy's curriculum offers a Bachelor of Science degree for all of its students. Classes are often competitive, though many cadets enjoy the academic challenges laid before them. The classroom setting encourages cadets to think quickly, observe objectively and analyze deeply. Most classes do not exceed 40 students, and this fosters close relationships between students and professors as well as interactive learning. The Academy has set core requirements, which students often complete during their first two years there.

"The friends you meet here will be the ones you keep for the rest of your life."

The USCGA ensures the well-roundedness of its cadets whether in the classroom or beyond. Sports period runs from 1600 to 1800, and the school encourages all of its cadets to pursue athletics. The majority of students play for a varsity team, though some cadets take sports less seriously and wish there was less emphasis on it at the Academy. They insist that many of their fellow classmates "have never picked up a baseball or shot a basketball in their life." This sentiment, though not universal, shows the diversity of interests among cadets. In addition to intramural and varsity sports, a cadet may choose from 18 other clubs and activities. These range "from glee club to aviation club to ski club to pep band." Cadets may develop a wide variety of talents and delve into many of their special interests.

Sports period doesn't end the day for cadets. Buffet dinner follows from 1700 to 1900. Then, 1900 marks the beginning of military period, and from 2000 until 2200 is study hour. Sleep becomes an option only at 2200, and all cadets must be in bed by 2400. Cadets must stay on the base during the week, and the Academy requires its students to live on the base all four years. Cadets say that living "on base" gives them a strong sense of unity with the whole student body, an Academy quality that cadets value highly. Cadets report that homesickness does not often occur because of the strong bonds that cadets form while living, training, and learning together. One sophomore cadet reports that "the best thing about the Academy is the people you are surrounded by. The friends you meet here will be the ones you keep for the rest of your life."

Life Beyond the Coast

Cadets need not apply for jobs after graduation since the Academy leads them into a career with the United States Coast Guard. Immediately following graduation, cadets receive positions as Deck Watch Officers or Engineers in Training for their first two-year tour. This embarks them on a military journey that further develops their minds, bodies and spirits. The work ethic taught at the USCGA prepares cadets for a successful life within the military or in civilian surroundings.

Alumni of the Academy make their mark in the outside world, often receiving honors in fields such as medicine, business and law. They attribute much of their success to the training at the USCGA and often come back to the Academy for lectures and conferences. A strong alumni network really kindles the spirit at the Academy and shows the way the Academy's core values never die in the minds of its cadets.

The job security that the USCGA offers is one of the most attractive features of the Academy. After the first tour, cadets can apply for advanced degree programs that the U.S. Coast Guard finances. Flight school also stands as an appealing option for many graduates. Pay and benefits, including full medical and dental plans, continue during any tenure of employment by the Coast Guard. Cadets admit that many of them choose the USCGA because it ensures them job security when they finally embark into the world. Graduating the USCGA is not the end for cadets but rather the beginning of a fruitful career of military life and much more. The USCGA asks a lot of its students but gives back just as much, if not more. *—Aleksandra Kopec*

FYI

If you come to the U.S. Coast Guard Academy, you'd better bring "a sense of humor for the many disciplining challenges you will encounter."

What is the typical weekend schedule? "Live large while freedom reins. Leisure time increases as cadets get closer to graduation, but getting off the base is something most cadets try to do during the weekend. Maybe a little bit of studying on Sunday would ease the workload for the rest of the week, but it is important to get outside the gates and enjoy yourself."

If I could change one thing about the U.S. Coast Guard Academy, I'd "give cadets the option to get into bed before 10 P.M."

Three things every student at U.S. Coast Guard Academy should do before graduating are "go to the Caribbean for five weeks on a 300-foot sailboat, experience swab summer—a rigorous orientation program prior to the beginning of freshman year—and become part of an athletic team."

University of Connecticut

Address: 2131 Hillside Road, Unit 3088; Storrs, CT 06269-3088
Phone: 860-486-3137
E-mail address: beahusky@uconn.edu
Web site URL: www.uconn.edu
Founded: 1881
Private or Public: public
Religious affiliation: none
Location: rural
Undergraduate enrollment: 14,716
Total enrollment: NA
Percent Male/Female: 48%/52%
Percent Minority: 17%
Percent African-American: 5%
Percent Asian: 6%
Percent Hispanic: 4%
Percent Native-American: 0%
Percent in-state/out of state: 77%/23%
Percent Pub HS: NA
Number of Applicants: 13,760
Percent Accepted: 62%
Percent Accepted who enroll: 37%
Entering: 3,185
Transfers: 645
Application Deadline: 1 Mar
Mean SAT: NA
Mean ACT: NA
Middle 50% SAT range: V 520-610, M 530-630
Middle 50% ACT range: NA
3 Most popular majors: business, social sciences, health professions
Retention: 88%
Graduation rate: 69%
On-campus housing: 72%
Fraternities: 7%
Sororities: 7%
Library: 2,987,772 volumes
Tuition and Fees: $6,800 in; $17,584 out
Room and Board: $6,888
Financial aid, first-year: 48%
Varsity or Club Athletes: NA
Early Decision or Early Action Acceptance Rate: EA 78%

Could you cheer "GO HUSKIES!" for one of the nation's finest basketball teams? Perhaps you are also interested in a solid liberal arts education at an affordable price? If so, the growing athletic and educational programs at the University of Connecticut might have just what you are looking for.

A Broad Education

Undergraduates at the University of Connecticut are offered a comprehensive education, and the freedom to choose classes that best suit their interests. All students must fulfill requirements for the core curriculum by taking credits in a variety of disciplines including art, science, philosophy, and computer science. Most students meet these requirements by sophomore year, and feel that the core classes help rather than hinder the education process: "It's great being able to take classes in so many interesting subject areas that we want to learn about and have them count towards graduation." The level of technological advancement at UConn is also highly beneficial to its students. Most classrooms are equipped with Internet access, and many classes are run primarily through the Internet; students are even able to observe on-screen research occurring in a separate facility on campus.

By their junior year, students must apply to one of nine schools of specialized study. Undergraduates finish their years at UConn with the majority of their remaining classes taken within the focus of their school. The schools of pharmacy, engineering, and physical therapy are three of the most popular of the specialized schools. The business school is not only very popular as well, but also very widely recognized on campus because "the econ department at UConn is really awesome". When it comes to class size, there are a fair number of large introductory lectures, but the average class size ranges from 18 to 25 students. For those students seeking smaller classes and more difficult work, a challenging honors program is available. Overall, as one sophomore put it: "I feel the university has some very good teachers here, but at such a big school, it's always up to the student to make the most of it all."

Where to Live, What to Eat?

Dormitories are both single-sex and coed, consisting of high-rises as well as smaller buildings. The majority of the rooms are doubles, with some singles and triples. Upper- and lower-classmen are mixed in the dorms, allowing for integration and bonding among the classes. Floor regulations are relatively lax. As long as alcoholic beverages are not carried in their original containers, RAs usually do not bother students. Many students do complain, however, that dorms are barely in satisfactory condition due to a lack of upkeep and renovation. "Our living conditions aren't the best; you're lucky if you can get to live in the recently built dorms on South Campus," commented one undergrad. Buckley, and Shippe (an all-female dorm) are considered two of the better dorms available. As freshmen, many students choose to live and party together in "the jungle"—a dorm on North Campus rumored to throw wild parties. A good number of upperclassmen live in apartments and houses off-campus. The apartments are not very close to class buildings and can be expensive. Off-campus houses include Blue, White, Yellow, Brick, Stone, and Fire Houses.

"I thought there'd be much less of a social life here because of the location, but there is lots of fun to be had."

In regard to food, "the meal plan itself is fine, it's the food that sucks." Another student stated just as plainly, "The dining halls serve food that you really just shouldn't eat." Although the food may be horrible, students enjoy the luxury of having an on-campus creamery that offers delicious fresh-made ice cream and milk. Located in rural Storrs, UConn is a virtually self-sufficient campus: on-campus stores and facilities meet most students' needs. "We're in the middle of cow country, but that's not really a problem," remarked one undergrad.

Partying, For Sure—But That's Not All

Well-known as a party school, UConn does not disappoint. Fraternities, sororities, and the Rugby House are all notorious for their huge parties. Students also head to Carriage House, and Celeron apartments to let loose. Popular hangouts on campus are Ted's—a restaurant, Civic Pub—a pool hall/bar, and Huskies—a bar/dance club. Although alcohol is the central focus of the party scene, non-drinkers do not feel left out, as UConn's social activities include much more than just alcohol and parties. The campus is a popular stop on the tours of many famous entertainers such as Jewel, Reel Big Fish, Harry Belafonte, and David Spade. The Student Union sponsors weekly dances and movie nights while the Student Union Board of Governors (SUBG) plans such large events as homecoming weekend, a winter party, and spring fling weekend. "I thought there'd be much less of a social life here because of the location, but that's not the case at all," insisted one sophomore.

Extracurricular activities and service-oriented clubs also play a major part in the non-academic pursuits of undergraduates at the University of Connecticut. Varied opportunities exist to accommodate the full-range of interests. Students can play in bands and sing in groups, join political unions, or write for the *Daily Campus* newspaper. Many undergrads join the Student Union Board of Governors to voice their opinion in the student government, while other students choose to pledge fraternities and sororities in order to be part of a more tight-knit community. The Public Interest Research Group (PIRG) is a protest group focused on improving government environmental issues. Other outlets of service allow students to volunteer with children, the elderly, and the state government in nearby Hartford, Connecticut's capital.

Not Just Basketball

Ranking among the top teams in the nation, UConn's men's and women's basketball teams have recently been major contenders for both the NCAA Division I Big East Conference and national championships. The two teams command the spirit of the students who fill the stands of Gampel Pavilion to cheer for UConn's primary sports teams. In recent years, men's and women's soccer have also become increasingly popular, as has football. In its effort to upgrade the football team to Division I-A status, UConn has recently constructed a new state-of-the-art football facility, with help from the state of Connecticut. For those students not involved in a varsity sport, intramurals are a great way to be involved in sports.

The University of Connecticut is an excellent example of a school that offers top-notch athletic and educational programs as well as a great social atmosphere—all at a very affordable price. —*Victoria Yen*

FYI

If you come to UConn, you'd better bring "your voice to cheer for all the UConn teams."

What is the typical weekend schedule? "Friday: party at the Rugby House; Saturday: go out to dinner and play pool with friends; Sunday: catch up on sleep and homework."

If I could change one thing about UConn, "I'd build a shopping mall closer to campus."

The three things that every student should do before graduating from UConn are "go to a basketball game—of course, go to the big party at X-lot on spring weekend, and pee on the electric fence."

Wesleyan University

Address: 237 High Street; Middletown, CT 06459-0265
Phone: 860-685-3000
E-mail address: admissions@wesleyan.edu
Web site URL: www.wesleyan.edu
Founded: 1831
Private or Public: private
Religious affiliation: none
Location: urban
Undergraduate enrollment: 2,733
Total enrollment: NA
Percent Male/Female: 48%/52%
Percent Minority: 26%
Percent African-American: 8%
Percent Asian: 8%
Percent Hispanic: 6%
Percent Native-American: 0%
Percent in-state/out of state: 10%/90%
Percent Pub HS: 57%
Number of Applicants: 6,474
Percent Accepted: 28%
Percent Accepted who enroll: 40%
Entering: 720
Transfers: 59
Application Deadline: 1 Jan
Mean SAT: NA
Mean ACT: NA
Middle 50% SAT range: V 640-740, M 650-730
Middle 50% ACT range: 29-32
3 Most popular majors: English language and literature, political science, psychology
Retention: 95%
Graduation rate: 89%
On-campus housing: 94%
Fraternities: 5%
Sororities: 1%
Library: 1,224,750,volumes
Tuition and Fees: $29,998
Room and Board: $8,226
Financial aid, first-year: 45%
Varsity or Club Athletes: 50%
Early Decision or Early Action Acceptance Rate: ED 46%

You are curled up in front of a rented video: *PCU*, the movie. The camera pans over a beautiful college campus of dignified ivy-covered buildings and a chapel. You wonder, is there really a college campus that looks like that? Indeed there is. Go to Wesleyan University and you will recognize that the scene was a scroll across Wesleyan's college row. The ivy-covered buildings include the Psychology Department building, the 92 Theatre, and the administration buildings (North and South College).

A Comfortable Learning Environment

Freshman year begins with a special orientation program where students have the option of community service or a two-day camping adventure. A great way to meet other students, the program is also intended to give students the feeling that they can accomplish anything. "It definitely put me in the right frame of mind going into first semester freshman year," noted one student. Meeting the general educational requirements is probably less challenging. In order to graduate, undergraduates at Wesleyan must take two classes in natural sciences, two in behavioral and social sciences, and two in arts and humanities. For students, these requirements are considered "very few, almost non existent." As one sophomore describes it: "The dearth of requirements really allows the student to pursue any academic venture unimpeded . . . one of the beauties of attending this small, liberal college."

For the student who wants to be challenged, there are two interdisciplinary programs to which students may apply during their sophomore year. The College of Letters combines work in English, writing and languages while the College of Social Studies, which has earned the nickname "College of Suicidal Sophomores," focuses on history, philosophy, political science, and sociology. There is also the Science and Society program, which enables participants to double major in one natural and one social science simultaneously, or to concentrate solely on science and medicine and their implications in society. Even though students feel their workload can be overwhelming at times, Wesleyan does not have a very competitive environment. Students feel that they are there to genuinely help each other, and that they "have the privilege of going to school with extremely intelligent people, but are not hampered by the competitiveness that is often detrimental to students at other schools." Getting into classes is not really a problem: "if you want a class badly enough, odds are you will be able to get in." The "drop and add period" also helps students take the classes from which they may originally have been denied. For freshmen, the First-Year Initiative Program affords the opportunity to take small seminar classes in several departments, enabling them to get to know professors early on in their college years. The school also has Student Forums—classes on any topic that are organized and governed by students, who are sponsored by a faculty advisor. These programs are just examples of how intimate the academic environment is at Wesleyan: "Undergrads really do get a lot of individualized attention here; it's a common reason why many students choose Wesleyan over Ivy League schools."

A Good Time for All

Weekends offer almost every type of student the opportunity to get out, meet people, and have a good time. And since the surrounding area of Middletown has little to offer students and is not considered by many to be the safest of places, most students stick around on weekends, making campus life busy and exciting.

The partying and drinking scenes are based on the fraternity and residential houses. Each weekend, several fraternities and residential houses throw parties that are open to all students. Fraternities are "ridiculously easy" to rush because not many people really want to rush. "I rushed for a few days and instead of being hazed, it seemed more of a courtship; they need you to keep the frat going," quipped one student. "We only use them for the dancing, drinking and grinding," said another. According to students, being underage is "HAHA, not a problem at all". "Freshmen are welcome anywhere," said one such freshman, "whether it be a frat house or a house party—or it that is not your cup of tea, you can take in a show, go to a concert." The general rule of the administration about alcohol seems to be "if they don't see it, they don't care." Besides the weekly parties, big events such as the Fall Hall, Spring Fling, Homecoming, Halloween dance, the Valentine's Day Party, Screw-Your-Roommate dances, and the '80s theme dance also draw big crowds throughout the year.

"If there weren't decent vegetarian options here, the student body would mobilize and protest; that is what we do at Wesleyan."

All kinds of couples find acceptance at Wesleyan. There are many homosexual and interracial couples and, according to students, they are accepted on campus. When it comes to dating, however, well . . . there is none. One student woefully reported, "I am an ex-Homecoming King, and I haven't been on a date in a year." Meaningful relationships tend to become marriage-like while "random hook-ups are what make the party world go round."

Great Housing, Not-So-Bad Meal Plans

Freshmen dorms are scattered throughout the campus, but most freshmen reside in Clark and Butterfield halls. They can also live in student-governed Wesco, where the residents do not have to wear clothes (some call it "the naked dorm"), or on "well-being" floors, which specifically forbid any use of drugs and alcohol. The rooms range from nice-sized singles to quads, and some rooms even have balconies. One RA lives on each floor of each dorm. For the most part, students report that the RAs allow you to do whatever you want: "They aim to be a friend and usually end up to be. They are really no different than any of the other residents." Floors and bathrooms are coed, but students can vote for the latter not to be.

After freshman year, students enter a lottery for housing, either with the group of people they want to live with, or alone if they want a single. In this lottery, drawn in order of seniority, each student or group gets to list housing preferences. Upperclassmen also have the option of living in residential houses, some of which cater to particular interests. For example, students can live in the Malcolm X House, La Casa, the Gay and Lesbian House, or one of a few literary societies.

Most students feel that "the food's not too too bad, especially since there are many options." As freshmen, students have the option of choosing a plan consisting of either 19 meals per week or 13 meals per week and flex points. The meals can be eaten in a few places, the most popular of which is "Mocon," the McConaughy cafeteria, which always offers a salad bar, a deli-car, and a buffet of hot foods. Flex points can be used at various on-campus eateries and mini-grocery stores. The points can also be used at the supermarket for students who want to make the food themselves. As upperclassmen, students have even more meal plan opportunities, including a completely point-based plan. Diners nearby are also very popular amongst students at Wesleyan. Athenian is one such diner that is open late and "perfect for an omelet when you are not all there . . . if you know what I mean." There is also the renowned Oroukes Diner, which makes "a mean breakfast."

A Passion and Energy—Outside of Class

When not in class, Wesleyan students put their passion and energy to work. "People tend to do things that make them stand out and show that they aren't just another smart kid." Wesleyan boasts more than 180 undergraduate organizations, many of which perform community service in Middletown. A cappella groups, theater troupes, and the student newspaper, *Argus*, are among the most popular student activities. "Activities here are awesome because they give you something to do and people to know without forcing you to identify yourself as one type of person," remarked one student. In short, nearly anyone could find his or her niche in the extracurricular world of Wesleyan.

Though recruited, athletes at Wesleyan, are fairly low-key. Wesleyan sports fans, however, take their sports very seriously, and several teams have recently met with great success. Football, crew, and Ultimate Frisbee are particularly hard-core, competitive teams. The teams also foster different traditions as well as close friendships. One soccer player recounts the night before the first soccer game of the year: "We soccer folk, the night before the first game, strip down to our nakedness, run laps and take penalty kicks. It is a real bonding experience." Those interested in participating in athletics on a less competitive level can choose from a large and active array of noncompetitive club and intramural sports at the Freeman Athletic Center, which houses "an amazing pool and field house".

The Wesleyan campus is very diverse and open to virtually any sort of personality or activity: "Kids are really laidback; no one cares what you look like. It's a comfortable, accepting, awesome environment." Many students even claim that the idea of being politically correct began here. As one student asserted, "If there weren't decent vegetarian options here, the student body would mobilize and protest; that is what we do at Wesleyan."—*Victoria Yen*

FYI

If you come to Wesleyan, you'd better bring "your credit card and a sense of humor."

What is the typical weekend schedule? "Friday: work and then go catch a movie; Saturday: watch TV, eat out and party; Sunday: sleep late, work out, then study."

If I could change one thing about Wesleyan, "I'd integrate the local eateries into the meal plan."

The three things that every student should do before graduating from Wesleyan are "study abroad, take advantage of all the programs, both academic or extracurricular, and spend time on Foss Hill in the spring (it's easy to get wrapped up in school work, but one afternoon on Foss Hill will remind you what college is really about)."

Yale University

Address: PO Box 208234; New Haven, CT 06520-8234
Phone: 203-432-9316
E-mail address: undergraduate.admissions@yale.edu
Web site URL: www.yale.edu/admit
Founded: 1701
Private or Public: private
Religious affiliation: none
Location: urban
Undergraduate enrollment: 5,339
Total enrollment: NA
Percent Male/Female: 50%/50%
Percent Minority: 34%
Percent African-American: 8%
Percent Asian: 13%
Percent Hispanic: 6%
Percent Native-American: 0%
Percent in-state/out of state: 8%/92%
Percent Pub HS: 54%
Number of Applicants: 15,466
Percent Accepted: 13%
Percent Accepted who enroll: 65%
Entering: 1,300
Transfers: 25
Application Deadline: 31 Dec
Mean SAT: NA
Mean ACT: NA
Middle 50% SAT range: V 680-780, M 690-780
Middle 50% ACT range: 28-33
3 Most popular majors: history, political science, biology
Retention: 98%
Graduation rate: 95%
On-campus housing: 87%
Fraternities: 10%
Sororities: 6%
Library: 10,900,000 volumes
Tuition and Fees: $28,400
Room and Board: $8,600
Financial aid, first-year: 43%
Varsity or Club Athletes: 20%
Early Decision or Early Action Acceptance Rate: ED 26%

At Yale University, students wear their hearts (and spirit) on their sleeves. And on their sweatpants. And on their faces. At the annual "Exotic Erotic" party where the slogan is "the less you wear, the less you pay," while some girls are clad in fishnets and skimpy leopard-print skirts, every year more than a handful wear nothing but their school pride—in the form of a Yale banner wrapped around their body. "I've never met anyone who doesn't love this place!" one sophomore remarked. "Every where you look kids are donning their Yale hooded sweatshirts or baseball caps." At Harvard-Yale, the much-anticipated yearly football game against Yale's archrival, there are "dozens of Yalies with their faces or chests painted blue and white. Some guys even shave 'Y's' into their hair!"

This elite academic institution boasts some of the top professors in the nation, a diverse, enthusiastic and involved student body, and "old blue"—Yale's devotion to its three-century-long history and its ongoing sense of tradition. Located smack in the middle of New Haven, a vibrant community that has been revamped in the last decade to become "about 100 times cleaner, safer and more fun than everyone thinks," Yale University is cited by many as "the best damn college in the country."

Steeped in Academia

Yale bases its academic curriculum on the idea that every student should receive a liberal education but still have the freedom to design an individual program of study. Students must fulfill several requirements before graduation, but no specific courses are required. Every class falls into one of four distributional groups. Group I contains all languages, both English and foreign; Group II deals with art, film, history, music and philosophy; Group III covers the social sciences; and Group IV encompasses the natural sciences and mathematics. In order to graduate, Yalies must take at least three classes in each of the four distributional groups as well demonstrate proficiency in one foreign language.

By and large, students like the group system of distributional requirements because it is less intensive than the "core" curriculums of several rival universities but it still forces students to expand their academic horizons. Finding three classes in Group IV is considered "a pain in the neck" by most humanities-centered Yalies, while filling the humanities classes is equally annoying for pre-meds. But never fear: popular "gut" courses (bearing colorful nicknames, of course) help make fulfilling these requirements a bit easier. There's "rocks for jocks" (Intro Geology) and "physics for poets" (Intro Physics), "clapping for credit" (Intro to Music Theory), "Science Fiction, Science Fact," and "History of the Olypics," to name a few.

On cold winter days, "group IV's"—those who major in the sciences—can often be spotted trekking up "Science Hill," where most of the university's science-related buildings and labs are located. However, many non-science majors can earn their Yale diploma without ever venturing up the Hill. One junior noted, "Science Hill is kind of a mystery to the humanities-oriented folks like myself. I don't even know what's actually up there." Thanks to a new $500 million project to provide new science facilities, update existing labs, and hire more faculty and researchers, the administration is currently in the process of improving Yale's science departments.

History, political science and economics are the most popular majors, with English trailing at a close fourth. The history and English departments are lauded for having the best professors and the most prestigious faculty overall. Said one junior English major, "I couldn't believe I got to take a class with Harold Bloom . . . He practically wrote my high school research papers as editor of all the critical editions of popular American novels. And of course, he's also today's Shakespeare scholar extraordinaire." Professor John Gaddis's Cold War class is another perennial favorite among students of all disciplines. Gaddis teaches his class using clips from the television documentary he helped produce for TBS, and the course is known for being particularly difficult to gain entry to, even though the lecture holds 400 spots. In the spring of 2004, Dr. Ruth, famed sex therapist, even taught a seminar on intimacy and the American family.

No matter their major, virtually all Yalies will tell you that they work hard. Yale requires 36 course credits to graduate, in comparison with the standard 32 at most of the other Ivies. Workloads are "intense," noted one senior, "but contrary to popular belief, we party just as hard as we work, so it all evens out."

An Architect's Paradise

The residential college system is one of Yale's defining characteristics and one its most appealing aspects to prospective students. Based on the housing at Oxford and Cambridge Universities in England, Yale developed its system in the 1930s to organize students into small communities within the larger university. Upon admission to the university, every student is randomly assigned to one of the 12 residential colleges. One senior praised the system because "it is great to be thrown into such a close network of people right away," but lamented that "it makes it difficult to get to know people in other colleges." More than just a dorm, each college has its own dining hall, fitness center, library, common room, intramural teams, and any number of other unique characteristics. Silliman College, for example, has its own movie theater, "Silliflicks," where the college holds screenings every Saturday night, while Berkeley College has its own studio for woodworking and furniture design. Freshmen in 10 of the 12 colleges do not live within their college for their first year—instead most freshmen are housed together on Old Campus, which, as the name implies, contains many of the campus's oldest buildings.

Although Yale's dominant architectural style is Gothic, many of its colleges and academic buildings display various other styles: Pierson and Davenport are Georgian, Connecticut Hall and McClellan are colonial, while Morse and Ezra Stiles are modern masterpieces designed by renowned architect Eero Saarinen. Another famed architect, Louis Kahn, built the Art and Architecture building as well as the Yale Art Gallery, which houses well-known works by Monet, Van Gogh, Pollock and Hopper. One junior architecture-major noted, "The campus is really the most beautiful of any American university. The buildings are historic landmarks as well as architectural ones." He continued, "It's neat to be flipping through my architecture books and to say to myself, 'Oh, that's Harkness Tower. I walked by there ten minutes ago.'"

Currently the university is engaged in a major renovation project for its residential colleges that will span 12 years and cost over $1 billion. A new college is renovated each year, and its displaced students reside in "Swing Space," a newly constructed dorm that "is nice because each room has air conditioning and a kitchenette"—features the regular dorms lack—"but is hideously ugly and has a hospital-like sanitary feel."

"I have a teacher who leaves school mid-week to advise the President on foreign policy, a teammate who's a Marshall Scholar, and a sorority sister who won a Westinghouse—and they all seem so *normal*."

Although the food is considered "subpar" by many, the dining system has variety working in its favor—in addition to the 12 college halls, students can eat in the dining rooms of any of Yale's various professional and graduate schools, as well as in Commons, a massive dining hall replete with a columned façade, a marble rotunda, and portraits of American presidents and famous alumni watching over you as you eat. Noted one student, "It's a perfect example of how cool it is to go to Yale."

Berkeley College even has an organic food menu created by chef Alice Waters of the famed restaurant Chez Panisse in California, although entrance to this dining hall is limited to Berkeley students. While other dining options abound, the food itself hardly elicits praise. One senior noted, "Like dining hall food around the world, Yale's dining halls are far from gourmet and the options get quite redundant after two weeks when they recycle menus." One student recounted, "Last week they served macaroni and someone had taken a plate and turned their dinner into a sculpture of a cat. While it was cool to see how creative Yalies can be, food isn't supposed to be so sticky and moldable!"

Social Heaven in New Haven

Although not known as a party school, "Yalies can throw one heck of a party!" Noted one senior, "I've rarely heard anyone complain about a lack of social options. There's always plenty going on and you're never going to get bored in your four years here." While freshmen tend to party mostly with other freshmen on Old Campus, underclassmen in general find themselves at frat parties or in a variety of the party suites ("Book World," "The Jungle," "The God Quad") sprinkled throughout the residential colleges. While not involving a large percentage of the campus, fraternities and sororities throw open parties nearly every weekend. Additionally, Yale hosts a variety of college-sponsored theme parties throughout both semesters, open to all students regardless of residential college affiliation. These parties include: Morse & Stiles' Casino Night, which was written up in *Rolling Stone* as one of the top ten best college parties in the country; Pierson Inferno, a Halloween masquerade dance; Exotic Erotic; the Winter Ball, a school-wide formal dance; and "Screw Your Roommate" dances sponsored by each residential college throughout the fall during which students are set up on blind dates for the night by their roommates.

Older Yalies take full advantage of New Haven, which has undergone a drastic redevelopment in recent years. As the city tries to diversify and improve its options, a plethora of bars and classy restaurants have sprouted up. Popular bars include Rudy's, Olde Blue, Anna Liffey's (known for their Guinness Stew), and BAR. Also popular are local dance clubs like Image and Bottega, which tend to fill up with both Yalies and "townies" on most weekend nights. On Saturday nights after the parties have died down, "all roads lead to Toad's," as the saying goes, and Yalies flock to this famous club (which has hosted such popular bands as U2, the Rolling Stones and more recently, Shaggy and the Black Eyed Peas) for late night DJ-ed dance parties.

For God, For Country, and For Yale!

"At a school like this, the spectrum of activities is out of control," noted one senior. "They run the gamut from the mainstream Habitat for Humanity and tutoring groups to the Freestyle Dueling Association, the Anti-Gravity (juggling) Society to the Fried Chicken 'n Porn Club." Students can write for the *Yale Daily News*, the country's oldest college daily paper, or any number of journals with prestigious sounding names like *The Politic* and *The Yale Journal of Ethics*. Fifteen a cappella groups call Yale home, including the oldest group in the country, the Whiffenpoofs, who have recently appeared on *The West Wing*, *Jeopardy*, and *The Today Show*. For those with a political bent, the Yale Political Union hosts numerous debates and lectures, while the Yale College Council acts as a student government body.

In addition, every week the University brings in guest lecturers for broad audiences while residential college masters bring in speakers for more intimate "Master's Teas" at which politicians, artists, actors and scholars meet with students to discuss their work or contemporary issues over tea and cookies. Students are given the opportunity afterwards to meet with and ask questions of these great minds. In the past two years, students have had the opportunity to hear George W. Bush, Bill Clinton, Tom Wolfe, Ed Norton, and Oliver Stone among others share their thoughts and insight. On occasion masters will invite students to accompany the guest speaker to Mory's, an establishment at Yale more than a century old at which customers "do cups"—that is, drink alcoholic concoctions of strange colors (velvet, gold, purple, red) out of huge silver chalices. "Mory's is such an institution here. It sort of typifies the wackiness of Yalies," one junior explained. "It's sort of elitist as a coat-and-tie, member's only type of place, but then it's totally quirky. There are all these rules, like when passing cups, you have to turn them 180 degrees and they can't touch the table." Then when you near the last dregs, "everyone has to sing 'the Mory's song,' as the drinker spins the cup on his head!"

Sports are also highly regarded at Yale. Fall Saturdays are spent tailgating outside the Yale Bowl and then heading inside to the football games, although the mammoth Yale Bowl (seating capacity 64,269) usually dwarfs the small but loyal crowds. However, the annual Yale/Harvard football game ("The Game"), is a different story—legions of fans and alumni from both schools pack the stadium every two years to cheer on a rivalry dating back to 1875. Yale has 32 other varsity sports; the hockey, squash, and crew teams perennially vie for league or national championships. For those without the time for varsity-level commitment, club sports, like rugby, wrestling and Ultimate Frisbee, offer athletic outlets. Intramurals that pit residential college teams against one another in a year-long quest for the cherished "Tyng Cup," are also quite popular. IM sports range from soccer and basketball to ping pong and inner-tube water polo.

Bright College Years

"Everyone comes here because of the students," one sophomore noted, "I think this is the most diverse campus in the country." Although Yale students are stereotyped to be "preppy and privileged," "no two people here are the same, even though everyone was their high school president . . . and most are decidedly liberal." A senior pointed out that the greatest aspect of Yale is that "everyone has a genuine interest in learning about and from each other." Whether its "politics, drama, or even biology, [everyone] really cares about whatever it is they're involved in and they want to share their passions with their peers." Because of this, they create "an atmosphere where conversations are never dull and you're continuously learning, mostly outside of the classroom." One sophomore bragged, "I have a teacher who leaves school midweek to advise the President on foreign policy, a teammate who's a Marshall Scholar, and a sorority sister who won a Westinghouse—and they all seem so *normal.*" On a campus where "everyone's interest*ed* and interest*ing*," a sophomore insisted you "will undoubtedly find your niche—whether you're a surfer from California or a nerd from New Hampshire!" —*Amanda Stauffer*

FYI

If you come to Yale, you'd better bring "a hooded Yale sweatshirt, a dictionary, and a taste for pizza since New Haven is the pizza capital of America."

What is the typical weekend schedule? "Thursday, after classes and dinner hit up the bars or a frat party; Friday, work by day and attend a play, dance performance, a cappella show, or sporting event by night; Saturday, spend the day tailgating or at the art gallery or working on Old Campus and then hop between campus parties, house parties, and Toad's; Sunday, catch up on sleep, go to brunch in your pajamas, and then get comfy in a library with your books."

If I could change one thing about Yale, "I'd eliminate the inequalities between the residential colleges—we all pay the same tuition, and it's not fair that some kids get gourmet organic food every day and free sweatshirts and nalgenes, while others have to pay for their T-shirts and eat fried cheese day after day."

The three things that every student should do before graduating from Yale are "tailgate and cheer on the Bulldogs at 'The Game,' go to a Master's Tea, and pass cups at Mory's."

Delaware

University of Delaware

Address: Newark, DE 19716-6210
Phone: 302-831-8123
E-mail address: admissions@udel.edu
Web site URL: www.udel.edu
Founded: 1743
Private or Public: public
Religious affiliation: none
Location: suburban
Undergraduate enrollment: 17,486
Total enrollment: NA
Percent Male/Female: 42%/58%
Percent Minority: 12%
Percent African-American: 5%
Percent Asian: 3%
Percent Hispanic: 3%
Percent Native-American: 0%
Percent in-state/out of state: 41%/59%
Percent Pub HS: 80%
Number of Applicants: 20,365
Percent Accepted: 48%
Percent Accepted who enroll: 35%
Entering: 3,420
Transfers: 645
Application Deadline: 15 Feb
Mean SAT: NA
Mean ACT: NA
Middle 50% SAT range: V 530-620, M 550-650
Middle 50% ACT range: 22-27
3 Most popular majors: social sciences, business, education
Retention: 88%
Graduation rate: 72%
On-campus housing: 48%
Fraternities: 15%
Sororities: 15%
Library: 2,540,162 volumes
Tuition and Fees: $6,498 in; $16,028 out
Room and Board: $6,118
Financial aid, first-year: 43%
Varsity or Club Athletes: 5%
Early Decision or Early Action Acceptance Rate: ED 49%

The University of Delaware is a large state college nestled in the rolling hills of picturesque Newark, Delaware. It is a place where intellectuals and frat boys co-exist in eternal bliss. As one Delaware freshman stated, "we talk about everything from Heideggar to Heineken."

Rollin' with the Scholars—Academics

The University of Delaware offers the full range of the usual college majors. Particularly intense majors, according to some students, are Engineering, Visual Communication, Chemistry, and Physics. Chemical Engineering is of special interest to many students since the DuPont Company endowed the university with millions of dollars resulting in a Chemical Engineering program that rivals the best technical schools in the United States. On the other end of the spectrum, for those not interested in masochism, the Psychology major is apparently a popular option for the slacker student population. But one student emphatically asserted that Delaware has "no joke majors."

In order to attract top-notch students the university has also implemented numerous programs. In particular, the Honors Program provides students with challenging classes in small settings. Honors students praise the close contact between students and professors that they enjoy.

The Jefferson Scholars program offers would-be doctors guidance and aide in applying to medical school and gives them a slight competitive edge. For minority students interested in engineering there is the RISE (Resources to Insure Successful Engineers) program, which offers them tutelage and career counseling. In addition to these programs Delaware also offers the Dean's Scholar Program whereby students can devise their own major.

When it comes to academic distributions Delaware students are fairly lucky. They are required only to fulfill basic core courses that include such courses as E110—otherwise known as Freshman English. Full-time students are required to take 12 credits per semester but most studious Blue Hens opt for 15.

Although there are some large introductory courses, many students enjoy schedules where none of their classes have more than 30 or 35 students. Despite the perks of small classes and "incredible professors," one student complained that she has a mere 3.5 hours of sleep a night and has absolutely a "TON" of work.

To help students diminish the intensity of the workload the university offers a much taken "winter term" during which students remain in school to take classes during their incredibly long winter break. The university, however, does not require anyone to partake in this pseudo-semester.

Many would-be college students are greatly concerned about having TAs as teachers. At Delaware, many large lecture courses are actually taught by the professors but have TAs leading sections. But take heart pre-frosh—there are some excellent professors at the University of Delaware including big names such as Robert Straight and Katherine Varnes who one student called "absolutely incredible!"

Students love to relax at some of the university's most popular study locations. Morris Library is called "indispensable" by one student and the Chemistry, Physics, and Honors Centers are notoriously quiet locales ideal for the angst-ridden student. Overall, "the University of Delaware has a strong academic program. What you get out if depends on how you treat the courses."

For those looking to kick back, there are also some nice off-campus hangouts that include the famous Klondike Kates and the ever hip Iron Hill Brewery. According to several sources the Hartsoe House, located in Nonantum Hills, is *the* location for popular parties and cool sounding music. Local musical talent includes Phil Lamplugh and his band *The Grieder's*. All three locations offer food and some places accept UD flex dollars whereby students "pay" for off-campus food with specially distributed UD cards. Many students complain about the meal plan and the varying quality of the food, as one student did by calling Delaware's meal plan an absolute "rip-off." Unfortunately, many students list dining hall food as one of the worst aspects of university life.

The Social Scene

Social life at UD centers heavily on the drinking scene. According to some upperclassmen, freshmen have been spotted in huge groups desperately trying to locate parties they hear about through the grapevine. The upperclassmen, on the other hand, are the ones who throw these much sought-after parties. On a more serious note, drug use exists on campus but it is not widespread and mainly consists of marijuana usage.

There is a definite frat scene on campus and as much as 15 percent of UD students belong to either a frat or a sorority. For those interested in rushing frats or sororities, the process of joining one isn't difficult. According to students, the most popular frats and sororities are Sigma Chi and Alpha Zeta Delta. Though Greek life is a presence on campus, it is not an integral part of the social scene at UD.

> **"We talk about everything from Heidegger to Heineken."**

Dating is rare but according to one student, there is "a load of random hookups." Sex is apparently commonplace on campus and "attractive individuals," according to one sophomore girl, "abound." For students lucky enough to find a date, Klondike Kate's followed by a movie is always a popular option for burgeoning couples.

Students wary of the drinking scene have available to them a large number of on-campus non-alcoholic activities. There are frequent movies screened, as well as "art under the stars."

It is very easy to meet new people on campus and most people form friendships with individuals from classes and activities. When asked about stereotypes of UD students, some boldly state that none exist while others characterize their fellow classmates as "upper-middle-class white kid beer guzzlers." Many students feel there is a definite categorization of the student body along the lines of athletes, Greeks, nerds, etc. A common complaint from the students center on the lack of diversity at the school. Many students come from Delaware and the surrounding Mid-Atlantic States, so geographical diversity is not commonplace. As for racial diversity there is very little interracial mixing on campus but race relations are still described as "good."

Leaving Campus—Extracurriculars

Extracurricular life at Delaware is booming. When asked about the workload at Delaware one student replied that he was "swamped" with mainly extracurricular activities. Like any major state school Delaware has the ROTC, theater groups, and some singing groups. There is a very active Black Student Union, as well. The inter-varsity Christian Fellowship and the Greek groups are active in community service in and around Newark. Many students at Delaware enjoy actual paying jobs on and off the campus. Popular places of employment are clothing stores, restaurants, and on-campus jobs.

Of all extracurricular activities, the largest and most popular one at Delaware is athletics. Delaware has a superb men's basketball team that has reached the NCAA Tournament and helps drum up school support for the Fighting Blue Hens. The football team is also a popular source of school spirit. The opening game versus archrival West Chester University is always a fun-filled and exciting event for all involved.

Living at UD

Housing problems, with the recent increase in the number of students, is one of the greatest problems on campus today. Two years ago, some students were forced to live in common rooms until suitable accommodations could be found. Freshmen describe the dorms as comfortable but certainly not "palaces." One dorm to particularly avoid is the Dickinson dormitory. The RAs at Delaware are notoriously strict and hand out offenses for underage drinking and other frowned-upon dormitory activities. One RA claimed that Delaware RA s are as "strict as they have to be" in order to enforce the alcohol policy on campus despite the fact that many students maintain that alcohol still flows freely at Delaware.

Most upperclassmen move off campus and housing is apparently readily available to students in the Newark area. Some others choose, however, to live in the house of their respective fraternity or sorority. Theme houses, such as the French house, also exist on campus.

Ultimately, most students are content with their decision to attend the University of Delaware. With wonderful professors and interesting visiting speakers (from Chris Rock to Maya Angelou), the experiences students enjoy while at the University are extraordinary and "eye opening." Overall Delaware students are healthy, somewhat sober, and very, very wise.—*Sean McBride*

FYI

If you come to the University of Delaware, you'd better bring "a Nintendo."

What is the typical weekend schedule? "Hit the frat parties, sleep all day, and maybe make a trip to Philly."

If I could change one thing about the University of Delaware, I'd "make the food better."

Three things every student should do before graduating from the University of Delaware are "learn how to take an ice block shot, walk around campus at night and appreciate the architecture and lighting, and to visit Nonantum Mills."

District of Columbia

American University

Address: 4400 Massachusetts Avenue NW; Washington, DC 20016-8001
Phone: 202-885-6000
E-mail address: afa@american.edu
Web site URL: www.american.edu
Founded: 1893
Private or Public: private
Religious affiliation: United Methodist
Location: urban
Undergraduate enrollment: 5,872
Total enrollment: NA
Percent Male/Female: 39%/61%
Percent Minority: 29%
Percent African-American: 6%
Percent Asian: 4%
Percent Hispanic: 5%
Percent Native-American: 0%
Percent in-state/out of state: 24%/76%
Percent Pub HS: 60%
Number of Applicants: 9,879
Percent Accepted: 63%
Percent Accepted who enroll: 21%
Entering: 1,312
Transfers: 386
Application Deadline: 1 Feb
Mean SAT: NA
Mean ACT: NA
Middle 50% SAT range: V 560-670, M 550-650
Middle 50% ACT range: 24-29
3 Most popular majors: business/commerce, international relations, political science
Retention: 86%
Graduation rate: 66%
On-campus housing: 64%
Fraternities: 17%
Sororities: 18%
Library: 763,000 volumes
Tuition and Fees: $24,839
Room and Board: $9,916
Financial aid, first-year: 49%
Varsity or Club Athletes: 10%
Early Decision or Early Action Acceptance Rate: ED 66%

Located on an 84-acre campus just miles from Capitol Hill, American University is a diverse school consisting of more than 5,000 undergraduate students from over 140 different countries. Understanding that a college education should consist of more than just hours spent in classrooms, AU actively encourages its students to take advantage of the plentiful internship and international opportunities available both in D.C. and abroad.

Small Classes, Thoughtful Professors

The undergraduate population at American University, or "AU" as its students call it, is divided into five schools: the College of Arts and Sciences, the School of Business, the School of Communication, the School of International Service, and the School of Public Affairs. Each school is affiliated with several different majors—some of the most popular are international relations, in the School of International Service; government, in the College of Arts and Sciences; and public communication, in the School of Communication.

When asked what the best parts of academics at AU are, students invariably responded with how approachable their professors are or the small size of their classes. With only two lecture halls on campus, almost all of AU's classes are taught in a seminar setting that averages only 19 students per class. Coupled with AU's policy of not allowing TAs to teach classes, the result is an academic environment that allows a large amount of interaction between students and professors. Furthermore, the professors at AU are noted to be very flexible and often make accommodations to deadlines or help students catch up on missed classes whenever possible.

AU has a strong academic program centered on its General Education core curriculum. The "GenEd" program is required of all undergraduates, regardless of their major or school, and consists of 30 semester-hours of course work that draws from five diverse areas ranging from the creative arts to the natural sciences. As one student said, "[GenEd] really helps students get a better feel for the world around [them] and often sparks interests in areas [that they] thought they had no interest in." Although most students are happy with the GenEd program, some do complain that its requirements are too strict since it comprises one-quarter of the courses required to graduate. Students note that having AP credits from high school will pay off, as APs often can be used to satisfy GenEd requirements.

AU has an honors program that consists of smaller seminars, more individual attention, and unique access to special resources in D.C. Entrance to the program is usually offered on the basis on SAT scores and high school GPA, but it's possible to move into the honors program based on first semester grades. However, due to its rigorousness, it's not uncommon for students to drop out of honors after their freshman year.

D.C. Interns

Since AU places such a strong emphasis on the importance of internships, class schedules at AU have been centered around it with most classes meeting on Mondays and Thursdays, or on Tuesdays and Fridays. This gives most students Wednesday off to take on internship opportunities with some of the most popular being those on Capitol Hill, at the Kennedy Center, or at NBC. In addition, many of these internships either are paid or can be taken for credit. Although most of these opportunities are targeted towards juniors and seniors, freshmen or sophomores who are passionate about finding an internship can usually get one. In addition to internships, AU also emphasizes the importance of having a global perspective on the world. As such, it encourages its students to study abroad by taking advantage of its AU Abroad Program, which allows students to study in one of more than twenty cities around the globe. The success of this program is demonstrated by the fact that more than 50 percent of students at AU participate in some sort of study abroad, usually during their junior year.

Living and Dining

Dorms at AU consist of six residence halls on campus made up of mostly doubles with no difference between freshmen and upperclassmen rooms. All dorms are co-ed, but all-girls floors, along with themed floors such as the "community service floor" or the "honors floor," are available in most residence halls. Each room comes with air-conditioning, cable TV, telephone, and high-speed internet.

AU does have an RA system with each floor in a residence hall having one or two RAs. For the most part, RAs "don't get in your way or try to find you out. You just have to be careful when you do something bad." One such bad thing might be getting caught with alcohol on campus, which can result in fines or community service, since AU maintains a strict dry campus policy.

The campus itself consists of mostly modern-looking buildings dispersed throughout a relatively green campus. Many students praise the landscaping, especially about the abundance of flowers that decorate every part of campus. In fact, students often joke about an "endowment" that funds the replanting of flowers on AU every six weeks.

The meal plan at AU has two components: the block plan and 'EagleBuck$.' Buffet-style meals are offered at the Terrace Dining Room (TDR), the main cafeteria on campus, with each meal being a swipe off the 200-block plan that freshmen are automatically enrolled in. Many students had mixed feelings about dining hall food, especially the lack of variety over time and difficulty in maintaining a healthy diet. One freshman complained, "Food [at AU] is apparently ranked sixth in the country. I don't really see how that's possible because it's not all that great. Everything is starting to taste the same." Fortunately, alternatives to TDR exist on campus including a Subway, Chick-fil-A, McDonald's, Häagen-Dazs, and Salsa, which is a popular Tex-Mex restaurant. All of these places, along with some off-campus restaurants, transact in EagleBuck$ by debiting from a student's meal plan.

Louis Vuitton, Gucci, and Burberry—Oh My!

AU is a very diverse campus in terms of the number of different cultures and religions—it is by no means a homogeneous mixture. One of the largest groups on campus is the Jewish population, which comprises approximately one-quarter of the AU student body. In addition, several Christian groups, such as the United Methodists, along with Muslim groups have strong presences on campus. While everyone at AU is generally very open towards everyone else in terms of religion, one freshman did complain that religion played a larger part than she thought it should at AU. Also, a sophomore mentioned that international students had a tendency to segregate amongst themselves. Many AU students come from wealthy families and this is certainly flaunted around on campus, from clothing (think Gucci, Burberry, and Louis Vuitton) to spending habits to cars. As such, status is a very important part of the school, much to the disappointment of some. Finally, at a nearly 3:1 girl-to-guy ratio (coupled with a large homosexual male population) it is not surprising that girls lament the lack of male targets on campus.

Fun and Games

The fact that AU is a dry campus, does not completely restrict a student's access to alcohol nor does it prevent students from having fun. The club scene in D.C. plays a large part in many students' lives, especially since promoters for clubs often hire students to advertise on campus. The only drawback to clubbing seems to be the fact that "you have to take a cab everywhere if you're drinking and this gets somewhat expensive." Apart from clubbing, a strong Greek scene on campus offers plenty of excitement on weekends ranging from small mixers to large parties on Halloween and Mardi Gras. Since many students have Wednesday off, Tuesday tends to be a big party night for students both on and off campus. As such, most clubs fill with AU students only on Tuesdays, which many students like since it removes the sometimes unwanted presence of local D.C. residents.

If you are not into drinking or the Greek scene, students assure that there are plenty of alternatives to clubs and frats. The student government organizes many social events throughout the year including concerts, speakers, and other special events. These have included a "beach day" one year when two tons of sand was dumped on to the central quad and a "snow day" another year when fake snow was piled onto the ground. AU is known for its ability to attract great speakers to its campus with recent notables including Gorbachev, the Dalai Lama, and Spike Lee. The student government has also attracted some great bands to campus including the Barenaked Ladies, Weezer, and Nickelback.

> **"The food is apparently ranked sixth in the country. I don't really see how that's possible . . ."**

In terms of extracurricular activities, AU has a tremendous number of clubs and organizations ranging from community service organizations to political clubs to musical and performing groups. Basically, "AU has a club for almost every interest and if there isn't one, you can petition to start one." It should be noted that sports at AU take on a much less importance than at other schools, due partly to the lack of a football team. Although other varsity sports teams such as basketball and soccer exist and do reasonably well, students note a general lack of enthusiasm for sports. One girl mentioned that "sports are not a big deal to students that go [to AU]" and that she was "a little disappointed by the lack of school spirit," both of which are feelings echoed by many other AU students.

Undoubtedly, one of the best things about being at AU is its location near the heart of Washington, D.C. With shuttles running from campus to the local Metro (subway) station every 10 to 15 minutes, traveling into the city is extremely easy. Once you are there, there is simply no lack of things to do with possibilities ranging from shopping at Dupont Circle, to eating in Georgetown, to catching a show at the Kennedy Center. It seems that if there is one thing AU students can all agree on, it is that life in D.C. is "FUN, FUN, FUN." —*Anthony Xu*

FYI

If you come to American University, you'd better bring "a cell phone" and a "political perspective."

What is the typical weekend schedule? "Friday afternoon, relax and hangout; Friday night, go clubbing or watch a movie; Saturday afternoon, shopping in Georgetown; Saturday night, go clubbing; Sunday, do homework."

If I could change one thing about American University, "I'd change how much it costs."

The three things every student at American should do before graduating are "tour every square-inch of D.C., watch the Fourth of July fireworks, and get an internship."

The Catholic University of America

Address: Cardinal Station; Washington, D.C. 20064
Phone: 800-673-2772
E-mail address: cua-admissions@cua.edu
Web site URL: www.cua.edu
Founded: 1887
Private or Public: private
Religious affiliation: Roman Catholic
Location: urban
Undergraduate enrollment: 2,668
Total enrollment: NA
Percent Male/Female: 45%/55%
Percent Minority: 19%
Percent African-American: 6%
Percent Asian: 3%
Percent Hispanic: 3%
Percent Native-American: 0%
Percent in-state/out of state: 4%/96%
Percent Pub HS: 40%
Number of Applicants: 2,708
Percent Accepted: 82%
Percent Accepted who enroll: 32%
Entering: 712
Transfers: 125
Application Deadline: 15 Feb
Mean SAT: NA
Mean ACT: NA
Middle 50% SAT range: V 530-640, M 520-640
Middle 50% ACT range: 21-28
3 Most popular majors: engineering, architecture, political science
Retention: 84%
Graduation rate: 65%
On-campus housing: 75%
Fraternities: 1%
Sororities: 1%
Library: 1,026,238 volumes
Tuition and Fees: $23,600
Room and Board: $9,002
Financial aid, first-year: 78%
Varsity or Club Athletes: 18%
Early Decision or Early Action Acceptance Rate: NA

For some reason the idea of a "religious" school always seems to strike fear into the hearts of prospective students. Fear not, my friends! Despite its ominous name, CUA is not Vatican City. In fact, it might be more aptly characterized as the prototypical American institution of higher learning.

Although Roman Catholics are the majority at CUA, all faiths are not only tolerated but also openly studied. The administration encourages students to study and explore the numerous faiths of the world. According to one student, "There isn't the least bit of pressure to convert to anything!" Although Intro to Religion is a thorn in the students' sides of most freshmen, non-Catholic freshmen report feeling very little discomfort attending class.

God Loves Smart People

CUA does have numerous core requirements for many of its majors. Some students enjoy the regimentation while others find it particularly annoying. According to one student, "sometimes the core courses don't make sense in light of your major." Despite having an exceptional architecture program, students who intend to major in this field must fulfill requirements in such oddly incongruous courses such as Religion and Philosophy. Many students regard the large introductory classes in math and English as rudimentary to the point of ridiculousness.

The core requirements, for most majors, include courses in English, the humanities, philosophy, social science, foreign language, science, and math. One of the more popular majors, and considered by some to be a slacker major, is political science. CUA is, after all, centered in Washington, DC, the heart of what we fondly call the "political process." As a consequence, many of the incoming freshmen at Catholic are interested in political science, political philosophy, and history. There are myriad internships available for these future practitioners of democracy. Special programs in Europe are available for the particularly scholar of history, as well. Professors are readily available to help out the student-in-need. As one student creatively put it, "My English professor is the best thing since Shakespeare and mangos!"

In terms of the actual facilities on campus, students give them mixed reviews. The main library, Mullin, is good, in part because of the quiet rooms for studying. However, the actual card catalog is somewhat confusing and on occasion the book the student so desperately needs cannot be found. Membership in the DC College Consortium, consisting of CUA, Howard, George Washington, and American, help many hapless students find much-needed research material. The Library of Congress, the largest library in the United States, is also a few metro stops away.

Perhaps the best features of academics are CUA is the superb graduate schools. The Nursing School is consistently ranked in the Top 10 and offers motivated future RNs an absolutely superb education. The Law School also carries a positive reputation. Perhaps one of the more popular graduate schools is the School of Drama, which has graduated such blockbuster stars as Jon Voight of *Deliverance* and the versatile Susan Sarandon. The strong graduate schools attract top-notch professors and great graduate students so that the TAs are "excellent and very helpful," according to one student.

And on the Fifth Day He Created Dorms . . .

Are you tired of the same old cookie cutter dorm room with your hand-held fan being the only source of relief from the sometimes-stifling humidity of the Mid-Atlantic? Do you like *The Sopranos* as much as the next college freshman? Go no further! CUA has two of the greatest luxuries afforded to the college freshman—air-conditioning and cable. And for you "playas" out there, CUA offers coed floors and wings, with the only all-female dorm being Conaty. The prize of these palatial housing options is Centennial Village. CUA has an odd policy regarding dorm visitation. All visitors must be signed in by 8 P.M. and must leave the dorm by 2 A.M. As a result, many students complain of a "booty gap" that exists at Catholic. Centennial Village is popular for several reasons, foremost of which are its lackadaisical guards who, according to one senior, are "easily bypassed." Those who cannot find housing in Centennial usually move off campus, a once popular option that has fallen by the wayside in recent years. The two apartment complexes near campus, Heights and the Cloisters, provide many upperclassmen with adequate housing. But why, you ask, has this option declined in popularity? According to one student, there is a growing racial tension in the neighborhood in and around Catholic. "The neighborhood seems to be getting worse, not better." Fewer and fewer upperclassmen opt to live off campus because of the safety issue that now exists. The administration encourages students to avoid walking alone anywhere in the area. "The campus itself is incredibly safe with the guards and all . . . but just watch out when you step outside the gates. Use common sense and you'll be fine." The university provides escorts to concerned students.

But, living on campus is not all bad. The campus itself is "gorgeous" and overflowing with green things (a.k.a trees and shrubs). Students have nicknamed the campus "The Mall II" after a more famous mall in Washington, DC. On sunny days, students can be seen reading and doing other collegiate activities on the Mall. Students have also been able to enjoy a relatively new athletic center. Also nearby is the third largest Catholic Church—The National Shrine—in the whole world.

"You just step outside and you're in the nation's capital. It's kind of awe-inspiring."

Finding food on campus is a different story. Catholic is notorious for "shitty" meals. A popular option among students is to eat in DC, which has "some really fine restaurants." However, there are some decent meals on campus and the campus Taco Bell is a popular destination. The neighborhood around Catholic is also replete with fast food joints and surly counter people.

God Hates Keggers

Don't go to CUA expecting to find kegs all over campus—the administration forbids underage drinking on campus. But for all you hedonists out there, there are a plethora of off-campus bars and pubs that'll liquor you up to your heart's content. But be forewarned that late night drinking in DC also means a late night walk through the hospitable streets of DC. By hospitable, I mean there are a lot of muggings. Thankfully for the inebriated CUA student, blue phones are in abundance on campus. Blue phones allow students to contact the police in the event of an emergency.

Although there is no Greek System, fun does exist on campus. The Program Board dominates campus social activities. The board brings in cool bands and popular guests to talk to students. They also sponsor such infamous dances as the "Screw Your Roommate Dance," where you have to have sex with your roommate. Just kidding. "The Screw" involves roommates setting each other up on blind dates. Other popular on campus events are the Mistletoe Formal, and Movies on the Mall nights.

Although Catholic is a Division III school, sports are still popular on campus. The football team and basketball teams are perennial favorites. The team mascot is the Cardinal. Although most teams at Catholic are Division III, the rugby team is at the Division I level and routinely performs well. Games against cross-town Jesuit rival Georgetown are heavily attended.

CUA, on the whole, is a place where students can allow their own individual talents to flourish. The social life in a major city, especially one chock full of college students, cannot be beat. "You just step outside and you're in the nation's capital. It's kind of awe-inspiring." Although the school has its Catholic traditions, which many students praise, DMX can also be routinely heard in the hallways. And as DMX would say, "Stop, Drop . . . and come to The Catholic University of America."—*Sean McBride*

FYI

If you come to Catholic University, you'd better bring "a love for politics to enjoy D.C. even more."

What is the typical weekend schedule? "Friday: go clubbing in D.C.; Saturday: spend time with friends and party at night; Sunday: go to church and study at 'The Mall II.'"

If I could change one thing about Catholic University, "I'd improve the quality of the food."

Three things that every student at Catholic University should do before graduating from are "go clubbing in D.C., visit the Shrine, and kick Georgetown's ass."

George Washington University

Address: 2121 I Street NW; Washington, D.C. 20052
Phone: 202-994-6040
E-mail address: gwadm@gwu.edu
Web site URL: www.gwu.edu
Founded: 1821
Private or Public: private
Religious affiliation: none
Location: urban
Undergraduate enrollment: 10,328
Total enrollment: NA
Percent Male/Female: 44%/56%
Percent Minority: 27%
Percent African-American: 6%
Percent Asian: 10%
Percent Hispanic: 5%
Percent Native-American: NA
Percent in-state/out of state: 3%/97%
Percent Pub HS: NA
Number of Applicants: 16,910
Percent Accepted: 40%
Percent Accepted who enroll: 34%
Entering: 2,292
Transfers: 357
Application Deadline: 15 Jan
Mean SAT: NA
Mean ACT: NA
Middle 50% SAT range: V 580-680, M 590-680
Middle 50% ACT range: 25-29
3 Most popular majors: social sciences, business, management, marketing, psychology
Retention: 92%
Graduation rate: 73%
On-campus housing: 63%
Fraternities: 14%
Sororities: 16%
Library: 1,984,094 volumes
Tuition and Fees: $29,070
Room and Board: $10,040
Financial aid, first-year: 40%
Varsity or Club Athletes: 5%
Early Decision or Early Action Acceptance Rate: ED 61%

It's a lazy Thursday afternoon in autumn, and you're a George Washington University student looking for something exciting and fascinating to do. Your options are almost endless. How about exploring the National Archives and reading the original Declaration of Independence or watching your favorite member of Congress passionately deliver a policy proposal on Capitol Hill? You could also go for a run in front of the White House and continue past Embassy Row to the Vice-President's house. There is always the option of visiting one of the Smithsonian Museums or just taking a leisurely walk around the monuments. The possibilities in our nation's capital are limitless, and George Washington University sits in the heart of it all. Located three short blocks from the White House, GW attracts most of its students with an opportunity to be educated not only academically but also politically and socially in one of the world's most awe-inspiring cities.

A Mix of Politics and Academia

George Washington University is comprised of seven individualized schools with their own requirements. Freshmen apply directly to one of the seven: The Colombian College of Arts and Science, The School of Media and Public Affairs, The School of Business and Public Management, The School of Medicine and Health Sciences, The School of Public Health and Health Services, The Elliot School of International Affairs, and The School of Engineering and Applied Science. Despite the narrow focus of these individual schools, each student must fulfill general liberal arts requirements, and students are permitted to take classes outside of their specific school. GW also offers a number of specialized programs including an eight-year Integrated Engineering/M.D. program, a seven-year B.A./M.D. program, and an Integrated Engineering and Law Program. The University Honors Program is a smaller, selective college within the university that allows students a four-year, multidisciplinary, interschool undergraduate experience. Acceptance to the Honors Center also carries a significant merit-based scholarship to help defray tuition.

The GW faculty and classes receive

solid overall reviews. Most students are "happy with the accessibility of the faculty and the quality of teaching." The work load is described as "intense at times, but manageable." Double majoring is fairly common, and not overly difficult. Academic advisors are readily available for guidance and support. Class sizes vary with introductory lectures maxing out at 200. Other classes are "better, between 20 to 50," reported one student. Another student reported that "TA grad students are helpful and the small discussion groups are my favorite part of the academics."

Academics at GW also means taking advantage of all that Washington has to offer. Many students are able to take part in internships and work during the school year, and the faculty is quick to bring expert speakers to class and campus. Students also enjoy taking field trips to museums and other attractions as part of class.

Learn to Schmooze and Booze, but Off Campus

"Clubbing!" one freshman said enthusiastically when asked what students do on weekends. Other students report that the novelty of dance clubs (and more precisely the cover charges) wears off soon, and students look to other alternatives. Parties on campus and in rooms are prevalent, but there is officially no alcohol allowed in campus housing, and the policy of "three strikes and you're out" concerning alcohol on campus is strictly enforced, making things "harder than most students would like." Community facilitators (CFs) are good resources for information in dorms, but are also quick to write up students with alcohol. Any student caught with illegal substances is immediately required to leave campus housing. Drinking is still prevalent, however, and is a major part of social life. "A fake I.D. is almost a necessity to survive here," said one student. "Don't ever order a Shirley Temple in a bar. It's rather embarrassing." Upperclassmen are more likely to hit the bars, especially in the Adams Morgan neighborhood on the weekends. Students also take advantage of the multitude of restaurants all over the city, but "M street in the Georgetown neighborhood is a favorite destination," according to one student. Fraternities and Sororities are also an option for some students, but many feel that joining the Greek system inhibits taking advantage of all that the city has to offer. The University in recent years has looked to provide more on-campus entertainment for students. In keeping with Washingtonian custom, formal balls on campus have increased in popularity and are well-attended. One freshman was "excited to gown shop for the Turkish-American Ball."

"Academics at GW also means taking advantage of all that Washington has to offer. Many students are able to take part in internships and work during the school year, and the faculty is quick to bring in expert speakers to class and campus."

Students at GW characterize themselves as fit, and most take part in intramurals. However, GW does not officially recognize contact sports. Non-contact athletic teams are competitive in the Atlantic 10 Conference as well as NCAA Division I tournament play, and students show their school spirit by attending basketball games. The loss of popular coach Mike Jarvis decreased attendance in recent years, but "basketball is still the most popular and dominant sport on campus." Extracurricular activities are also a big part of student life, and most students get involved with at least one organization. Political activism is popular, and many students use the city's resources to get involved in a cause. In terms of other organizations, "everything is well-respected" said one student. Students are generally not categorized by their activities or groups.

Can You Say "Location, Location, Location"?

The location of George Washington is its greatest draw to students. The main Foggy Bottom campus (there is a smaller campus in Mount Vernon, VA) is composed of four-by-four square city blocks. "Most of the buildings blend into the city, and are almost indistinguishable from the federal government buildings that surround them," said one student. "It is definitely an urban, city campus." Students also complain about a lack of grass and open space. Many report feeling generally safe around campus, and security was increased after the tragic terrorist attacks on the World Trade Center and Pentagon on September 11.

Freshman and sophomore students are required to live on campus, and freshmen are usually split between Thurston (or "the tenements") and Hobo Hall. Thurston is the largest dorm on campus, and offers suites with up to four students. Juniors and seniors are not guaranteed on-campus housing and take their chances in a lottery that awards seniors first pick for apartment-style rooms. Mitchell Hall is most sought after, offering the most attractive living conditions complete with a veranda and subway shop. Many upperclassmen also opt for apartments in the city and some live in the suburbs of Maryland or Virginia.

The center of campus life is the student union, known as the Marvin Center. Besides housing the headquarters and offices of student organizations, the center has many fast-food and chain restaurants. Meals can be eaten in the Marvin Center or in the standard dining halls, where food is described as "good but unhealthy." The center also has a travel agency, grocery store, and lounges used to study or relax. As one student summed up, the Marvin Center "has pretty much anything that you would ever need."

Statistics show a geographically and racially balanced student population at GW, however students complain that many of them are extremely wealthy, and that people are not afraid to show their money. "People dress very well here. A lot of chic, urban Black is the norm," said one student. Another described the student stereotype as "extremely rich, white, Jewish, and from the Northeast."

Located in the hub of the political world, George Washington University provides an education in academics, politics, and real-life living. With the White House, Kennedy Center, and Vietnam War Memorial all within walking distance of campus, "no one is ever bored, and there is never a dull moment. And that is what we love about GW." —*Nirupam Sinha*

FYI

If you come to George Washington University, you'd better bring "a fake I.D."

What is the typical weekend schedule? "Typical weekend days consist of sleeping until 3, doing laundry and a little bit of work, going grocery shopping, starting to drink in the dorm at 10, going to a club from 12 to 1, stumbling back to the room at 3, babbling until 5, and falling into bed."

If I could change one thing about George Washington University, I'd "add more healthy food to the dining plan."

Three things every student at George Washington University should do before graduating are "go on a 'Drunken Monument' tour, take part in an internship, and utilize D.C. and its resources."

Georgetown University

Address: 37th and O Streets NW; Washington, DC 20057
Phone: 202-687-3600
E-mail address: guadmiss@georgetown.edu
Web site URL: www.georgetown.edu
Founded: 1789
Private or Public: private
Religious affiliation: Roman Catholic
Location: urban
Undergraduate enrollment: 6,332
Total enrollment: NA
Percent Male/Female: 47%/53%
Percent Minority: 27%
Percent African-American: 7%
Percent Asian: 10%
Percent Hispanic: 5%
Percent Native-American: 0%
Percent in-state/out of state: 2%/98%
Percent Pub HS: 42%
Number of Applicants: 15,536
Percent Accepted: 21%
Percent Accepted who enroll: 46%
Entering: 1,497
Transfers: 225
Application Deadline: 10 Jan
Mean SAT: NA
Mean ACT: NA
Middle 50% SAT range: V 640-730, M 640-730
Middle 50% ACT range: 27-32
3 Most popular majors: business/commerce, international relations, English language and literature
Retention: 97%
Graduation rate: 94%
On-campus housing: 69%
Fraternities: NA
Sororities: NA
Library: 2,234,338 volumes
Tuition and Fees: $28,384
Room and Board: $10,056
Financial aid, first-year: 41%
Varsity or Club Athletes: 10%
Early Decision or Early Action Acceptance Rate: ED 51%

At Georgetown, liberal arts and pre-professional students mingle, weaving into campus and out to the nation's capital, looking for everything from a good education to a prestigious internship to the next party. Georgetown students have at their disposal one of the nation's finest universities and a magnificent city.

The Capital of Learning

Prospective students applying to Georgetown send their applications to one of four schools: the College of Arts and Sciences, School of Foreign Service (SFS), School of Business, or the School of Nursing. Each college has slightly different academic guidelines.

The College of Arts and Sciences requires two courses each in Philosophy, English, Theology, and Natural Sciences or Math. Students must declare their major by sophomore year. Humanities and history are given high marks. English is also popular majors, and although Computer Science is considered one of the hardest, some find Georgetown's science department relatively weak. Sociology is often considered a slacker major.

The Business school requires students to take two classes in History or Government, Philosophy, Theology, and English, as well as a semester each of Psychology and Sociology.

The distributional requirements for SFS (School of Foreign Service) are somewhat stricter. Freshmen in the school must take Economics, Political Theory, English, History, and a foreign language (proficiency is required for graduation). The school boasts the most rigorous programs of study and is considered Georgetown's strongest undergraduate program.

One of Georgetown freshmen's biggest complaints is the large class size, especially in SFS and the philosophy department. All classes are taught by professors, but many lectures break down into weekly sections led by TAs. Students are generally happy with the professors and academics. "They know what they're talking about" and often try to make the material interesting, according to one undergraduate. One student cited "impromptu guitar/

piano singalongs," as one of the coolest things a professor has done in class. The typical student will have a five-course load, with three to eight hours per week of work per course.

Students are required to study theology, a result of Georgetown's Jesuit origins. One will also find nuns on the faculty, crucifixes in the classrooms, and representations of saints decorating the walls. "Sometimes you can really tell Georgetown is a Catholic school, and other times it's not very pervasive," explained one student.

Search for Alcohol and Happenings

The freshman dorms are all dry, and those caught with alcohol in the dorms are assigned community service and fined $25 for the first offense, with increased punishments for subsequent offenses. Thus, freshmen often go to on-campus parties, or to those thrown by off-campus students. One student claimed that the ratio of good to bad parties is 1 to 7. Formal events include a number of balls throughout the year, including the Dip(lomatic) Ball in April.

The dating scene does exist, though it may not easily appear so. Many people hook up, but only "two to three times per year" says one student. The best way to get to know people, recommended a student, is to join a club. No one will find the classic frat house here as fraternities are officially banned, but they exist in some form, some throwing big house parties or posing as community service clubs.

Students can easily access all the happenings off campus by taking the subway system, avoiding the hassle of parking. They take advantage of the dining options, such as Middle Eastern, Egyptian, Vietnamese, and Indian cuisine, as well as the bars nearby. In the last few years, enforcement of underage drinking and checking of fake IDs has dramatically increased, but many can manage to drink when they'd like.

"There's a great mix of studying and real-life experiences."

Students also enjoy the off campus theater, as well as on-campus appearances by notable guests such as former President Clinton, Justices Scalia and O'Connor, along with Dave Chapelle and Billy Joel. Students sometimes feel frustrated that they do not take more advantage of their surroundings, especially since the city is loaded with sights, from the Capitol Building, White House and Washington Monument to the Kennedy Center for the Performing Arts.

Campus on a Hill

The campus consists of many small 17th-century brick buildings, some with a Gothic influence, and the occasional modern building. One complaint is that everything on campus is uphill—the entrance to one building will be on the first floor, but when you walk into the building next door, you're already on the fourth floor. Luckily, the distances between buildings are short.

Freshmen live in one of four dorms on campus: Harbin and New South are older dorms built in typical dormitory style while Village C East and Village C West are newer dorms with smaller rooms and private bathrooms (a definite plus for the residents). Halls are co-ed with common areas and kitchens on each floor, and students enjoy air-conditioning in their rooms. Students from all the schools live together, which "eliminates any feeling of segregation between the colleges." An upperclassmen is assigned to each freshman hall, and these RAs range "from sweet to evil," explained a student who had been through the experience. RAs patrol the halls at night to ensure that noise is kept down and to check that the rooms remain free from alcohol.

After freshman year, some students live off campus. In the past, students have had to move off involuntarily due to a housing crunch, but the situation should improve after a new dorm is completed. Students generally feel safe in the halls, as security guards are on duty on the ground floor.

Freshmen often find friends in their hallway, and one will often see large groups heading off together to one of Georgetown's two dining halls. Students find the quality of the food to be adequate, though most do not consider the choices to be satisfactory. Students can opt to live off campus and drop the meal plan, as many do.

Capitalizing on Opportunities

Living in D.C. allows students to take advantage of the city's political life and community service opportunities. D.C. Reads, an elementary school tutoring program, and Increase the Peace, workshop seminars with troubled teens, are some examples of volunteer opportunities. Many students, instead or in addition, get hooked up with internships such as working with members of Congress or working in the Smithsonian. The student government, on the other hand, is looked down upon because "student government has no power."

Georgetown also has the International Relations Club and various special-interest groups on campus, and the arts scene is given high ratings. "It's big, it's good," claimed a student with regards to theater and studio art. Many students are also involved with sports. "Athletics is a big part of campus life for those who participate in it, but our on-campus facilities are pretty weak," said one student. Sports are not too popular for spectators, although spirit is often high during basketball season.

Georgetown combines the challenges of rigorous academics with one of the world's most impressive cities. Students often say that their years at Georgetown have given them more than an academic education. As one undergraduate said, "There's a great mix of studying and real-life experiences."—*Andrew Hamilton*

FYI

If you come to Georgetown, you better bring "a polo shirt for the guys or black pants for the girls."

What is the typical weekend schedule: "Friday: class, go to a movie; Saturday: sleep in, basketball with friends, watch a performance, or go partying; Sunday: homework."

If I could change one thing about Georgetown, "I'd put less emphasis on fashion."

Three things that every student should do before graduating from Georgetown are: "spend some time in southeast D.C., eat a Chicken Madness at Weismiller's, see the sunrise from a rooftop.

Howard University

Address: 2400 Sixth Street NW; Washington, D.C. 20059
Phone: 202-806-2763
E-mail address: admission@howard.edu
Web site URL: www.howard.edu
Founded: 1867
Private or Public: private
Religious affiliation: none
Location: urban
Undergraduate enrollment: 6,892
Total enrollment: NA
Percent Male/Female: 34%/66%
Percent Minority: 1%
Percent African-American: 69%
Percent Asian: 1%
Percent Hispanic: 0%
Percent Native-American: 0%
Percent in-state/out of state: 12%/88%
Percent Pub HS: 80%
Number of Applicants: 7,488
Percent Accepted: 56%
Percent Accepted who enroll: 33%
Entering: 1,368
Transfers: 407
Application Deadline: 15 Feb
Mean SAT: NA
Mean ACT: NA
Middle 50% SAT range: V 440-680, M 430-680
Middle 50% ACT range: 20-29
3 Most popular majors: biology, radio and television, journalism
Retention: 85%
Graduation rate: 53%
On-campus housing: 58%
Fraternities: 2%
Sororities: 3%
Library: 2,465,152 volumes
Tuition and Fees: $10,935
Room and Board: $5,570
Financial aid, first-year: 72%
Varsity or Club Athletes: 1%
Early Decision or Early Action Acceptance Rate: NA

Through its dedication to academics and community outreach, Howard University has created a reputation of excellence. Its prestige is further enhanced by the fact that Howard has turned out more African-American students with advanced degrees than any other university in the nation, including such alumnae as Nobel Prize–winning author Toni Morrison and acclaimed singer Roberta Flack.

Academics: "You Get What You Put In"

Howard is made up of several different colleges, within which students can focus on specific areas of study. Most subjects fall under the College of Arts and Sciences, where students must take 127 credits to graduate. There are specific academic requirements for the college including four semesters of a language, two English composition courses, and two classes in math, algebra and statistics. Howard's emphasis on practical education manifests itself with even a swimming requirement, which students appreciate despite its unusual nature. One student said, "I wish it was mandatory at every school to take swimming." Other areas considered strong are communication, business, and engineering, which students attribute to the strong connection between professors and students. One student commented, "They feel that we have the power to strengthen the African-American community."

Students at Howard find that the workload reflects the amount of effort each individual student invests. A famous saying about classes at Howard is "you get what you put in," which acknowledges that classes greatly range in difficulty. Slacking off, however, is not a widely accepted way of life. One student said, "If you try and breeze through your classes, it will show later." One way students can make their academic curriculum a little more challenging is by joining the honors program after their freshman year. This translates into a heavier course load than the typical five courses per semester.

Something for Everyone

With more than 200 student organizations open to them, Howard students with passions can find like-minded peers, get together, and do great things. One student commented, "Everybody does something. Whatever your idea, want, desire, need . . . there is a club for it." Community service, student government, and sports tend to be the most popular extracurriculars. Howard students have long-standing involvement in the local neighborhood and can get involved in the D.C. metro area through various community service organizations. Students note that tutoring organizations that go into neighboring elementary and high schools abound. Students also get experience in the media through the newspaper, *The Hilltop*, or the campus radio station, WHUR. Also popular, the student-produced TV program *Spotlight* has been nominated for an Emmy award and aired on a national black-owned and operated television station.

While the immediate area surrounding Howard does not provide much in the way of entertainment, students find creative ways to amuse themselves. One student described, "The social scene is amazing to the point of potential distraction. There are always activities for the entire student body." Campus events including a luau kick off the year, followed by movie screenings at Crampton Auditorium and occasional celebrity appearances. School spirit comes out in full force during Homecoming, when the Howard Bisons play their rival, Morehouse. Howard students generally cite a spirited and enthusiastic student body as one of the main appeals of the college. Football and basketball tend to be the most popular sports, and even though Howard's teams don't perform exceptionally well, students continue to come out and support their teams. One junior said, "I'm extremely proud of the sports because of the family environment and innate pride that comes with being a Howard Bison."

"That's the key to HU, everyone here is family. Once you become a Bison, you're a Bison for life."

Washington, D.C., itself provides a number of options for students both in terms of education and nightlife. This does not really present any problems for students; as one commented, "Almost no one complains about the social alternatives at HU." There are a number of 18-and-over clubs, such as VIP and Platinum, and students can also attend special events called "college nights." The campus itself is alcohol-free with very strict rules pertaining to drinking and using drugs.

Segregating the Sexes

The majority of freshmen live in single-sex dorms that have fairly strict visitation policies for the opposite sex. The amenities (from laundry rooms to air conditioning) vary from dorm to dorm. Drew Hall (the men's freshman dorm) is described as "a sort of initiation for Howard men" because it has no air conditioning and is far from the cafeteria. However, Howard has recently built a new dorm to replace Drew Hall, which will soon be closing.

After freshman year, students enter a lottery to live in Howard Plaza Towers, the most desirable upperclass housing. Other options are Meridian, Slowe, and Carver, all of which are off-campus dorms. Students can also opt to live off campus in rented housing or apartments.

There are a number of dining options for students both and on campus and off. The three different dining halls are the Café (the closest thing to a traditional cafeteria), the Restaurant (intended for faculty), and the Punch-Out (a "social hub of campus"). There is a special option for vegetarians at the School of Business and there is always vegetarian fare available at The Café. Students also partake of the restaurants on U Street in Adams-Morgan among other off-campus possibilities presented by the dynamic city.

Howard's main student gathering site, the Blackburn Center, is located in the center of campus along with Frederick Douglass Hall, the political science building, and Founder's Library. Another important area is the yard, where many students can be found on Friday afternoons. The president of the university often comes out "to hang out with the students," a testament to his close relationship with them, many of whom he knows personally.

A Greek Tradition

The Greek presence is unanimously cited as an important element of Howard life. A number of national black fraternities actually found their start at the university. All of these groups strive to be more than social organizations, emphasizing community service and African-American unity. "Stepping," or step dancing, is a special element of Greek life, which distinguishes it from many other schools. Students at Howard and other black universities compete in contests of these complex dance routines that are based on rhythmic stomping and chanting to a beat. Students report that they can be identified by their Greek organization and that sometimes those who do not participate feel outside of the wider social scene. For the most part the fraternities and sororities contribute a great deal to Howard, both for those who participate and those who do not.

One stereotype of Howard is that students are "stuck-up and rich," but nothing could be further from the truth. While fashion is an important element of daily life at Howard (some students have been described as "walking billboards for whatever hot designer"), students are more interested and involved in their community than in the latest trends.

Howard students cherish the bond they feel with each other based on their strong sense of school pride and unity, one that gives them the confidence to excel and lead. Through close friendships, students feel connected to Howard for the rest of their lives and wish to foster this spirit in others. As one student described it, "That's the key to HU, everyone here is family. Once you become a Bison, you're a Bison for life." —*Rebecca Ives*

FYI

If you come to Howard, you'd better bring "a pocket full of patience to deal with student services."

What is the typical weekend schedule? "Friday night, go to Dream for clubbing; Saturday, hang out at City Place or Pentagon City or go to VIP, if you aren't burnt out from Dream; Sunday, go to chapel at Howard and finish studying!"

If I could change one thing about Howard, I'd change "the perception that HU is a fashion show."

Three things every student at Howard should do before graduating are "attend a Homecoming game, take Dr. Carr's Afro-American studies class, and join a Greek organization."

Trinity College

Address: 125 Michigan Avenue NE; Washington, DC 20017
Phone: 800-492-6882
E-mail address: admissions@trinitydc.edu
Web site URL: www.trinitydc.edu
Founded: 1897
Private or Public: private
Religious affiliation: Roman Catholic
Location: urban
Undergraduate enrollment: 1,050
Total enrollment: NA
Percent Male/Female: 0%/100%
Percent Minority: 76%
Percent African-American: 68%
Percent Asian: 2%
Percent Hispanic: 9%
Percent Native-American: 0%
Percent in-state/out of state: 51%/49%
Percent Pub HS: 79%
Number of Applicants: 373
Percent Accepted: 74%
Percent Accepted who enroll: 47%
Entering: 174
Transfers: 31
Application Deadline: rolling
Mean SAT: NA
Mean ACT: NA
Middle 50% SAT range: V 420-520, M 410-480
Middle 50% ACT range: 16-22
3 Most popular majors: psychology, business, communications
Retention: 68%
Graduation rate: 50%
On-campus housing: 21%
Fraternities: NA
Sororities: NA
Library: 207,000 volumes
Tuition and Fees: $16,380
Room and Board: $7,170
Financial aid, first-year: 86%
Varsity or Club Athletes: 30%
Early Decision or Early Action Acceptance Rate: NA

In the heart of the nation's capital is a place where women's issues always receive a fair hearing—Trinity College. This small college has been educating women in the liberal arts, while maintaining its Catholic roots, for a century. According to students, Trinity is a melting pot of political activity, tradition, new ideas, and learning.

New Ideas in Academics

Upon acceptance, undergraduate students enter the School of Arts and Sciences. Political science is said to be the most popular major, a fact likely influenced by the school's proximity to Washington, DC. In order to graduate from Trinity, students must complete the Foundation for Leadership curriculum, which includes courses from six areas. Communication Skills enables students to develop critical reasoning and to speak or write a second language. Cultural Diversity explores the traditions and civilizations of different groups worldwide, and Knowledge and Beliefs involves the study of religious and intellectual perspectives. Traditions and Legacies looks at Western civilization, Scientific and Mathematical Inquiries requires study in those two areas, and Individual and Society investigates how individual and group behaviors affect societal institutions.

Within these areas, classes are designated as either Group One or Group Two, and students must take some of each group. For Group One, they must take a set number of hours. Then, students choose at least three out of the six areas available and take a Group Two course out of each of these. Most undergrads find these core requirements a bit on the extensive side, although they can usually complete them by the end of their sophomore year. One recent grad said, "You definitely have to keep it in mind, but it's really not a headache to fulfill." Recently, students have been given more choice within the core requirements. Instead of a list of specific courses, students now have more course options in the required areas of study, which makes the requirements less of a hassle.

> **"The neighborhood isn't very good. When you walk onto campus, it's like stepping into a different world."**

Small classes are the norm at Trinity. Classes range in size from 4 or 5 students to 20 at the most, and the majority have between 10 and 15 students. Students value the approachability of their professors. "The professors are involved in and become a part of your life," one sophomore stated. Unproctored tests are also routine for Trinity women, who are serious about upholding their honor code. The code also includes restrictions on underage drinking and men in the dorms after hours, but rumor has it that reports of these social violations are less common. Trinity also offers a highly popular Weekend College Program for working women through which adult students may take classes on the weekends to earn their undergraduate degrees.

Social Life and Migration Patterns

The social scene at Trinity always involves both its own campus and the lively areas surrounding it. Transportation on the Metro, DC's subway system, provides easy access to the movies, shopping (at Union Station, Pentagon City, and Dupont Circle), dance clubs, and bars. Other college hangouts in the neighborhood also enhance the social scene; undergrads frequently migrate to nearby Georgetown, Howard, and Catholic Universities for mixers or just to hang out in a coed environment. While the surrounding area has its attractions, the campus has its fair share of hangouts as well. Most popular is the Pub, which offers fast food, video games, billiards, occasional dances, and karaoke nights.

Certain campus social events and traditions are an integral part of the Trinity experience. Twice a year, each class convenes on one of the four floors of the Main dorm to sing canons. The college sponsors a Christmas party called the Holly Hop, and a Beaux-Arts weekend during the spring semester. Towards the end of the year, rising juniors don their graduation caps and gowns for the first time at a special mass. Class dinners and class color days take place as well, but according to one student, these are "nothing special."

Politicking and Other Activities

Because Trinity is in Washington, DC, political involvement is naturally the most popular extracurricular activity for the Trinity undergrad. A good number of students work on Capitol Hill and are active on campus in various leadership roles. The student government plays an important role at Trinity and has a strong rapport with the administration. Interning is common for students, who sometimes to receive course credit and in other cases for enjoyment and experience. Some travel to other states in order to work on political campaigns. In general, students interested in politics find that at Trinity their extracurricular activities and academic endeavors complement, if not overlap, each other.

It's Like Stepping into a Different World

Although many Trinity students find politics near or at the top of their priority list, other activities also have their place. The monthly paper, the Trinity Times, and the literary magazine, the Record, attract aspiring writers. The school has a strong a cappella group, the Bells, the Pan American Symphony Orchestra is in residence at Trinity, and some students play for the orchestra. Some students also take piano or voice lessons for credit. Trinity has six varsity sports teams—lacrosse, soccer, tennis, field hockey, crew, and track and field—all of which are quite popular. Because of the small student body, the teams will accept anyone who wants to play. Trinity entered the NCAA Division III a decade ago in 1995, and as a result both the number of participants and spectators have surged. In addition, February 2003 marked the opening of the Trinity Center, a $20 million dollar project that is now the largest athletic center in the country dedicated to women and girls.

Living Standards

Overall, Trinity students are satisfied with the quality of the housing on campus. Although single rooms are not available to first-year students, the doubles are reportedly roomy. Some undergrads prefer Main for its convenient location, and Cuvilly Hall remains a favorite because of its spaciousness and easy staggering distance from the Pub. Seniors and some fortunate juniors live in Alumni Hall, which is popular for its two-bedroom suites with private bathrooms, an underground tunnel leading to Main, and its proximity to the cafeteria. Students are required to purchase a 19-meal plan the first semester of their first year, but after that they may choose either 19, 14, or 10 meals a week. Some students are also pushing for a pay-as-you-eat plan, citing the inflexibility and inefficiency of the set meal plans. Approximately 25 percent of all students, including commuters, live off campus.

Relations between the school and the largely residential area that surrounds it are reportedly good, although the area surrounding the campus is not flourishing quite as well as the university. According to one senior, "The neighborhood isn't very good. When you walk onto campus, it's like stepping into a different world." Security, however, is not a problem. Campus buses leave for the Metro stations every twenty minutes, and escort services are always available.

Trinity students say that over the years they have earned a reputation for being "white, Catholic, feminist snobs," but many report that this stereotype is outdated and incorrect. Trinity's Catholic population is down to approximately 50 percent, minority enrollment is increasing, and need-based student financial aid is prevalent. According to one first-year student, "There are some snobs—but the stereotype is really misleading."

At Trinity, women find a small, friendly environment, enlivened by the excitement of being in a major city. In the political center of the nation's capital, Trinity students thrive and learn, receiving hands-on experience to complement their work in the classroom.—*Lisa E. Smith and Staff*

FYI

If you come to Trinity, you'd better bring "a camera to capture all those moments."

What is the typical weekend schedule? "Friday, explore the D.C. nightlife; Saturday, explore the D.C. nightlife; Sunday, study and recover from exploring the D.C. nightlife."

If I could change one thing about Trinity, "I'd make the surrounding neighborhood nicer."

Three things that every student at Trinity should do before graduating are "get a great internship, use this opportunity to network, and do something spectacular—there are a lot of opportunities here."

Florida

Florida A & M University

Address: Tallahassee, FL 32307
Phone: 850-599-3796
E-mail address: admissions@famu.edu
Web site URL: www.famu.edu
Founded: 1887
Private or Public: public
Religious affiliation: none
Location: urban
Undergraduate enrollment: 10,853
Total enrollment: 44%/56%
Percent Male/Female: NA
Percent Minority: 97%
Percent African-American: 96%
Percent Asian: 0%
Percent Hispanic: 1%
Percent Native-American: 0%
Percent in-state/out of state: 78%/22%
Percent Pub HS: 85%
Number of Applicants: NA
Percent Accepted: 71%
Percent Accepted who enroll: NA
Entering: NA
Transfers: NA
Application Deadline: 10 May
Mean SAT: NA
Mean ACT: NA
Middle 50% SAT range: NA
Middle 50% ACT range: NA
3 Most popular majors: NA
Retention: NA
Graduation rate: 43%
On-campus housing: NA
Fraternities: NA
Sororities: NA
Library: NA
Tuition and Fees: $2,789 in; $11,071 out
Room and Board: $4,752
Financial aid, first-year: NA
Varsity or Club Athletes: 3%
Early Decision or Early Action Acceptance Rate: NA

While most of the country braves the winter cold, Florida A&M students, with sunblock and books in hand, settle back on well-manicured, flower-filled lawns. Located in quiet and scenic Tallahassee, Florida A&M University (also known as FAMU) provides solid educational opportunities in a variety of disciplines.

Preprofessionals

Academics at FAMU are centered on specific preprofessional programs. Students report that the business, architecture, engineering, and pharmacy departments are among the strongest. While one senior particularly praised the administration for "teaching us practical information with tons of realistic applications instead of abstract ideas and principles that we will forget an hour after the final," another freshman complained that "my academic program is way too narrowly defined and there is little room for personal exploration." All classes at FAMU, including some recitation sections, are taught by professors. Graduate TAs only help with labs and occasionally substitute for faculty. While each department has its own specific requirements for graduation, all students must complete at least one course each in history, English, math, humanities, and a physical or biological science. The academic program on the whole is considered both "very manageable" and "reasonable, with enough work to make you feel like you are learning without being ridiculously overwhelmed."

Most of the facilities at FAMU are reportedly satisfactory. Although Coleman Library "needs a bigger collection," according to one student, it is a great space to "spread out your stuff, get focused, and accomplish a lot." Empty classrooms are also popular places to get to work when classes are done for the day. Several students said that the sports facilities are "small and mediocre at best" due to a lack of modern gym equipment. Yet, students are also quick to compliment the administration for investing in building improvements and point to the newer music building and ongoing commitment to general classroom building.

An Off-Campus Student Body

Most undergraduates at FAMU live off campus in either rented houses or apartments. The situation draws mixed reviews. While an off-campus student body can be "great because you are really living on your own without dealing with the bullshit regulations that often accompany on-campus housing arrangements at other schools," others are not as convinced. One undergrad said "off-campus living is limiting socially because you are confined to your own group of friends and lose the close proximity that on-campus dorms offer." Residents consider campus housing "fine—nothing great, nothing awful." All students who live on-campus must be on a meal plan. The food ranges from "nasty" to "fair." Several students reported that the quality and variety of the meal plan has improved under a new policy that allows them to take their meals in delis and pizza places as well as in the school cafeterias. Off-campus, students enjoy eating at Jake's, "a greasy BBQ dive," and Shingle's, "a decent seafood restaurant."

> **"I love this community, but I also think there is much to be desired in terms of creating a more diverse student body."**

FAMU's campus is relatively self-contained and somewhat separated from the town of Tallahassee. Students say town-gown relations are "great." Undergrads enjoy shopping, hanging out at several local clubs, or just wandering around the city's two malls. As one junior reported, "Everything you need is right here." Tallahassee is also only an hour and 15 minutes away from the beach. Fraternity parties are another social venue for those who have exhausted the Tallahassee club scene. Students agree that FAMU's top on-campus hangout is the "Set," a common area near the Student Union Building, which has a post office, TV room, bookstore, and market. As one sophomore said, "It is great to have the Set so that off-campus people like myself can still stay connected with the rest of the student body." One senior added, "It is awesome to be able to come to campus for something more than just going to class."

Getting Involved

Many undergrads are quick to praise the active student government at FAMU for helping to get students involved in campus life. One person noted that student government leaders "have a really tough task trying to keep an off-campus student body involved with the school, but they do a terrific job." The student government is responsible for planning many social events throughout the year including their biggest event of the year, "Be-out day," which occurs in the spring and features food, games, and contests on the athletic field. It also organizes the extensive homecoming festivities, activities that "we all look forward to each year," one student said.

Most undergraduates join extracurricular activities connected to their future professions, such as the pre-medical society. Some students also participate in FAMU's theater group, which stages four performances every semester. The gospel choir, several bands, and the *Faumuan*, FAMU's weekly paper, are also popular among students. Community service activities are largely sponsored by fraternities and sororities. Varsity sports also draw student support, and intramural competition is reportedly "fierce and fun." Students rally behind the school mascot, the Rattler, and FAMU students show their school spirit during game weeks when the "whole school is covered" with orange and green, FAMU's colors.

Diversity at FAMU?

The students at FAMU are predominantly African-Americans from in-state. Some students have questioned the lack of diversity at FAMU. As one senior reported, "I love this community, but I also think there is much to be desired in terms of creating a more diverse student body—I look outside and everyone is so much like me." While not ethnically diverse, FAMU students say that they have very different interests and backgrounds. The small number of openly lesbian and gay students, however, are not organized, and according to one sophomore, not very welcome on campus. "Students are not very open-minded when it comes to that," said one student. FAMU undergrads also consider themselves more environmentally than politically aware.

FAMU offers an opportunity to take advantage of a strong pre-professional academic program in a warm, relaxed environment. In the words of one senior, "I am going out into the real world with not only solid academic training, but a host of life experiences that I won't soon forget."—*Jeff Kaplow and Staff*

FYI

If you come to FAMU, you'd better bring "some sunglasses, not for the sun, but for all the gold teeth that will hurt your eyes."

What is the typical weekend schedule? "Friday, catch up on sleep; Saturday, go out and party; Sunday, do all the work from the previous week."

If I could change one thing about FAMU, "I'd improve the landscape. There are too many bushes around here."

The three things that every student at FAMU should do before graduating are "chill at the Set, volunteer in Tallahassee, and attend Homecoming."

Florida Institute of Technology

Address: 150 West University Boulevard; Melbourne, FL 32901-6975
Phone: 800-888-4348
E-mail address: admissions@fit.edu
Web site URL: www.fit.edu
Founded: 1958
Private or Public: private
Religious affiliation: none
Location: urban
Undergraduate enrollment: 2,168
Total enrollment: NA
Percent Male/Female: 70%/30%
Percent Minority: 39%
Percent African-American: 4%
Percent Asian: 3%
Percent Hispanic: 5%
Percent Native-American: 0%
Percent in-state/out of state: 56%/44%
Percent Pub HS: 81%
Number of Applicants: 1,982
Percent Accepted: 84%
Percent Accepted who enroll: 31%
Entering: 519
Transfers: 172
Application Deadline: rolling
Mean SAT: NA
Mean ACT: NA
Middle 50% SAT range: V 500-610, M 550-650
Middle 50% ACT range: 22-27
3 Most popular majors: aviation, engineering, business administration
Retention: 76%
Graduation rate: 53%
On-campus housing: 48%
Fraternities: 15%
Sororities: 11%
Library: 262,222 volumes
Tuition and Fees: $22,600
Room and Board: $6,140
Financial aid, first-year: 71%
Varsity or Club Athletes: 10%
Early Decision or Early Action Acceptance Rate: NA

After a day of classes at the Florida Institute of Technology, some students head for nearby beaches along Florida's Space Coast while others study under the tall palm trees on campus. The motivated pre-professional student who chooses FIT is rewarded not only with its picturesque, tropical setting but also with its intense, challenging curriculum.

Sun and Studies

Despite the temptations of the sun and beach, students at FIT take academics seriously. The core curriculum includes heavy doses of science and math (something most FIT students are happy about), along with courses in English composition and rhetoric. Many FIT students have a strong sense of what they want to do later in life and focus on their major early in their college career at one of the five undergraduate schools: the College of Engineering, the College of Science and Liberal Arts, the School of Aeronautics, the School of Business, or the School of Psychology.

Each major requires an intensive curriculum in addition to the core requirements, so freshmen and sophomores have little flexibility in their schedules. According to one student, FIT "gives you a schematic for your major—there aren't too many electives." One sophomore described the first-year program as "rather difficult. They test you to see whether or not you can handle it." The rigorous course load, however, does not translate into cutthroat competition: students report that they "don't go after each other." On the contrary, study groups are popular, and some professors encourage team problem solving. Easy courses are hard to come by in the science departments, but many students use their elective opportunities to take stress-free courses such as scuba diving or sailing.

The College of Engineering is especially popular at FIT. The School of Aeronautics and the departments of oceanography and marine science are also well respected. According to one oceanography major, FIT is one of the few places where students receive "in-the-field" training from almost the first day of class. FIT maintains an extensive co-op program with many of the major companies on the Space Coast, which enables undergrads to alternate semesters in the classroom with semesters on the job. Students can become involved as early as sophomore year, and one participant said of his job experience, "You're not a gopher. You are asked to do the work and get it done. It is a real job." Students work (earning course credits and money) at places such as NASA, Rockwell International, Martin Marietta, McDonnell Douglas, Harris, and Lockheed.

Living Arrangements

Dorm life at FIT is quiet, but as one RA confirmed, "there are parties." The six campus dorms surround a large quad. Evans and Brownly are considered upperclass dorms, although some upperclassmen live on halls with freshmen in the other four dorms, two of which are single-sex. Most rooms are designed for three people, although freshmen generally live in doubles. Residents consider the rooms "quite large." Brownly Hall is especially popular: although the rooms are smaller on average, each has its own bathroom. All rooms at FIT are air-conditioned, and many also have ceiling fans. While freshmen must live on-campus, many upperclassmen move to the university-owned Southgate Apartments or to other off-campus housing. Southgate units typically have two or three bedrooms, a large living room, and a kitchen.

> **"Who else takes their calculators to the beach?"**

Students say they feel safe hanging out on campus. University security officers, most of whom are ex–law enforcement or ex-military officers, are on duty 24 hours a day. Call boxes are located around campus, and an escort service walks students from place to place at night.

Students call the food in FIT's Evans cafeteria "decent—it could be better, it could be worse." Freshmen are required to be on the meal plan. Students looking for tastier food head for the popular campus hangout called the Rat (short for Rathskeller), whose specialties include burgers, grilled chicken, and sub sandwiches. Pool tables, a large-screen TV, and small bar make the Rat a favorite place for eating, talking, and hanging out. Seven fraternities and two sororities dominate campus social life by hosting parties and events. According to one student, "The most fun you have in Melbourne is at the fraternities and sororities. You're not going to die if you're not involved in one, but they're pretty big." Drinking is a popular pastime despite the administration's efforts to curb it, but students say that those who don't want to drink are under no pressure to do so.

The surrounding city of Melbourne, home to a large retirement community, has little to offer students (who have nicknamed it "Melboring"). Many students drive or find rides to the bars, malls, and other entertainment venues outside the Melbourne area. Orlando is an hour away, and the beach is a mere ten minutes from campus. Hangouts just off campus include a pizza place called the Mighty Mushroom (locally known as "the 'Shroom"), the local bowling alley, and a miniature golf course. There is also a 7-Eleven store for late-night snack runs.

FIT's lopsided male-female ratio affects campus social life. Many male students lament that it is difficult to meet women, and one female student reported that the situation sometimes causes "a little tension" between the sexes. Another student pointed out that as more women enroll at FIT, the ratio and the tension are slowly improving.

The FIT student body hails from all parts of the globe, with especially large contingents from the Northeast, Florida, and the Caribbean. A burgeoning international community on campus has led to the formation of a number of ethnic clubs, including the Caribbean Students Association. FIT supports many extracurricular organizations, ranging from student government to the school newspaper, the Crimson, and from a biology fraternity to a theater group called the College Players.

The FIT Panthers compete in the NCAA Division II Sunshine State Athletic Conference. Popular varsity teams include women's volleyball, men's and women's basketball, crew, cross-country, softball, and baseball. The administration's efforts to start a football program have been unsuccessful so far; homecoming revolves around basketball instead. Many students are active in intramural flag football, inner-tube water polo, and cycling. For the size of the school, students consider the athletic facilities "pretty good."

In general, FIT students take a lot of pride in and are happy with their school. ("Who else takes their calculators to the beach?" one tanned undergrad questioned). As one student emphasized, "if you work hard, you will receive a good education here." And the weather and waves aren't bad, either.—*Ellen Lee Moskowitz and Staff*

FYI

If you come to FIT, you'd better bring "some cold drinks to get through the heat."

What is the typical weekend schedule? "Friday, go over a friend's place and relax; Saturday, go to the beach and surf; Sunday, go to the beach and study."

If I could change one thing about FIT, "I'd bring more girls to campus."

Three things that every student at FIT should do before graduating are "learn how to dive, go see Cape Canaveral, and attend the Daytona 500 at least once."

Florida Southern College

Address: 111 Lake Hollingsworth Dr.; Lakeland, FL 33801
Phone: 863-680-4131
E-mail address: fscadm@flsouthern.edu
Web site URL: www.flsouthern.edu
Founded: 1885
Private or Public: private
Religious affiliation: Methodist
Location: urban
Undergraduate enrollment: 1,881
Total enrollment: NA
Percent Male/Female: 44%/56%
Percent Minority: 12%
Percent African-American: 6%
Percent Asian: 1%
Percent Hispanic: 5%
Percent Native-American: 0%
Percent in-state/out of state: 77%/23%
Percent Pub HS: NA
Number of Applicants: 1,668
Percent Accepted: 78%
Percent Accepted who enroll: 38%
Entering: 304
Transfers: 130
Application Deadline: rolling
Mean SAT: NA
Mean ACT: NA
Middle 50% SAT range: V 470-570, M 460-560
Middle 50% ACT range: 20-25
3 Most popular majors: business, communications, psychology
Retention: 71%
Graduation rate: 54%
On-campus housing: 65%
Fraternities: 15%
Sororities: 16%
Library: 173,000 volumes
Tuition and Fees: $17,042
Room and Board: $6,050
Financial aid, first-year: 78%
Varsity or Club Athletes: NA
Early Decision or Early Action Acceptance Rate: NA

Shake, rattle and roll for the water moccasins of Florida Southern—they'll be sure to show you a good time with hospitality in keeping with Southern tradition and parties to rival the Greeks. Though Florida Southern itself is small, and nestled into the not-so-large city of Lakeland, students warn that "it's not the country," and one even said "Parts of it look like New York, in the Old District." What you'll find at Florida Southern, though, is a little warmer and maybe a little more hospitable. One freshman said, "I only wanted to come to this school because it was close to home, but when I came here, I found out people were so nice and so genuine and so helpful that I decided to stay."

ACE is Wild

Some students complain, "There's really not to much to do around here," but ACE is around to fix that. The Association for Campus Entertainment schedules events every month for students on campus. From concerts to community service activities, ACE keeps commuting students and those who live on campus in touch by bringing them together for some good wholesome fun. Comedians, hypnotists, and other entertainers host audiences in the school auditorium or in classrooms, usually at no cost to students. ACE also hosts bands, but don't look for too many weekend events. "They don't put a lot of stuff on the weekends," students said, "because no one will come. A lot of the students go away on the weekends." Because "there aren't too many parties" at Florida Southern, many students opt to go to Tampa or Orlando for party weekends, and many commuters spend the weekends at home.

Intramurals keep Florida Southern students busy, as do trips to local rock-climbing and ice-skating facilities. There are even horseback riding trips on offer, and all such trips are free for students. If there isn't enough entertainment to suit your fancy, join ACE! Like any club, ACE is open to non-elected members of the student body, and your fun streak might be just what your peers have been looking for.

Water Moccasins on a Dry Campus

When Florida Southern does get down and party, students look to their fraternities and sororities to host the shindigs. This is due in part to their enthusiastic party publicity. "They're always putting banners up that say everyone's invited," one student said. "They're very welcoming, even if you don't belong to the sorority." Frats and sororities are also the main party source because their houses are not on school property and alcohol is forbidden on campus. This means that even those of legal drinking age are not allowed to bring alcohol into the dorms. "People are known to go out, and a lot of people drink, because normally dry campuses are like that," one student said. But the school safeguards against excessive drinking when students are away from their campus homes. "If you go out to club and you're drunk," a program called Safe Ride ensures that "the school pays for you to come back to campus," students report.

Livin' La Vida Florida

Freshmen at Florida Southern start out in freshman dorms, which are manned by RAs like all the other on-campus dorms. A large percentage of Florida Southern students are commuters, often because they are in-state residents and it makes more sense for them to live at home. Students who choose to live on campus get their own dose of parental supervision from their RAs. "My RA is one of my best friends," one student said, "but you can be stuck with a pretty strict one." Other rules include a curfew that prohibits visitors past a certain hour as well as sleepovers with the opposite sex. On the other hand, RA-supervised dorm life means the school sponsors pizza parties and movie outings with your hallmates.

"I only wanted to come to this school because it was close to home, but when I came here I found out people were so nice and so genuine and so helpful that I decided to stay."

Freshmen at Florida Southern are required to take a freshman introduction course, worth an hour of credit, for the first half of their first semester. This is the only class at Florida Southern where you can get credit for going on a tour of the college! Other features of the freshmen orientation include introductions to faculty members and to the tutoring resources available for students looking for extra help. The CORE then guides undergraduates through their course of study, requiring that all students take classes in areas like fitness and wellness, psychology, theater, English, religion, and sociology. Students are in favor of the requirements for different reasons. "I think everyone should take a religion class even if you're not that into going to church—it's just something you learn," one student said. Another added "They want to introduce you into everything the college offers in case you want to change your major."

Students say their "classes are really small, so it's more hands on," and they "get more one-on-one time" because of the intimate learning environment, where "the teachers are very helpful." Still, one student said, "It's nothing like high school."

Moccasins Shed Their Skin

Sometimes commuters have a hard time being hooked into on-campus life, so the school administration does a number of things to unite the student body. Off-campus residents are invited to regular lunches in the dining hall to join their campus-dwelling classmates. Convocation is another tradition at Florida Southern. Once a month the entire student body congregates in the auditorium to hear speakers—a professor, a reverend—talk about a given topic. January, for example, focused on the Martin Luther King Jr. holiday and its value as a human rights holiday, not an African-American holiday.

Students take great pride in the diverse and welcoming environment their school fosters. "You'll find all different kinds of people here," one student said. "We have people that are rich, people that are poor, blacks, whites, Hispanics. It's really nice to see all these people. It's really cool to have a college where everyone's welcome." Mr. Moc is a great example of Florida Southern's welcoming arms and warm spirit. Mr. Moc is the unofficial mascot of the school, and students say "he's gotta be like 85." A Florida Southern alumnus himself, Mr. Moc heads up traditional cheers at basketball games and joins the most spirited fraternities in dressing up in Florida Southern's colors. "I think he even goes on the road with the basketball team!" one student said. "I think he's pretty representative of the school. You don't have to be a certain race or a certain age. There's people here that I think are professors that are actually students—everyone from 17 to 70."

The diversity extends to religious leanings, too. "It's a Methodist school, but we have students that are Jewish, students that are Muslim." Above all, students comment on the warmth of their classmates. "I love that everyone's so nice here," one freshman said. "Everyone's very friendly to you. That's one of the reasons I'm going here."—*Stephanie Hagan*

FYI

If you come to Florida Southern, you'd better bring "extra money."

What is the typical weekend schedule? "Go to Cows Thursday night; Friday night, go on a date; Saturday mornings, Habitat for Humanity; and spend the whole day Sunday doing work."

If I could change one thing about Florida Southern, "I'd make it snow."

Three things every student at Florida Southern should do before graduating are "go to Cows, go to a Convocation, and join a fraternity or a sorority."

Florida State University

Address: Tallahassee, FL 32306
Phone: 850-644-6200
E-mail address: admissions@admin.fsu.edu
Web site URL: www.fsu.edu
Founded: 1851
Private or Public: public
Religious affiliation: none
Location: suburban
Undergraduate enrollment: 29,195
Total enrollment: NA
Percent Male/Female: 44%/56%
Percent Minority: 24%
Percent African-American: 12%
Percent Asian: 3%
Percent Hispanic: 9%
Percent Native-American: 0%
Percent in-state/out of state: 85%/15%
Percent Pub HS: 88%
Number of Applicants: 21,046
Percent Accepted: 70%
Percent Accepted who enroll: 43%
Entering: 6,386
Transfers: 1,963
Application Deadline: 1 Mar
Mean SAT: NA
Mean ACT: NA
Middle 50% SAT range: V 520-620, M 520-620
Middle 50% ACT range: 22-27
3 Most popular majors: communications, criminal justice, finance
Retention: 86%
Graduation rate: 63%
On-campus housing: 16%
Fraternities: 14%
Sororities: 13%
Library: 2,488,398 volumes
Tuition and Fees: $2,713 in; $13,741 out
Room and Board: $6,772
Financial aid, first-year: 38%
Varsity or Club Athletes: 2%
Early Decision or Early Action Acceptance Rate: NA

Almost every weekend during football season, the streets around Florida State University (FSU) are blocked off, and an organized chaos engulfs the campus. Such is the atmosphere during football season, when thousands of students and alumni pack in to watch their Seminoles destroy the competition. Waves of painted faces enthusiastically cheer their team to victory but also revel in their school's social atmosphere and dedication to academics.

Studying Seminole Style

Although their university is consistently ranked among the top party schools in the nation, FSU students are quick to point out that there is much more to the school than its reputation implies. "Despite what a lot of people think, we actually dc to work and have to study to do well in classes," said one sophomore. Most students enter the School of Arts and Sciences, but the university has a number of specialty schools. Some of the stronger ones include the School of Music, the College of Engineering, the College of Business, and the nationally renowned School of Motion Picture, Television, and Recording Arts. The degree requirements vary from school to school, but in general all students must receive course credit in English, mathematics, history, social sciences, humanities, and natural science. They were described as "nothing you can't finish easily, and they usually overlap with a major's requirements as well." In addition, all students must satisfy the statewide Gordon Rule, which requires students to write 24,000 words by graduation. FSU students must also take two "x-and-y" multicultural classes before graduation. "Some of the requirements are really annoying. They can be very large courses and in some of them I never really learned anything," said one sophomore.

Most people generally agree that one of the easiest and most popular majors is psychology. Communications was cited as an easier concentration, which was explained as "something you do when you don't know what else to do." Several introductory courses were described as easy, or in some cases, "easy As." Introductory sociology, religion, and theater were among the most popular. "The hardcore science classes are definitely the hardest, and they usually weed out a large portion of students who thought they were going to be premed," said one junior.

Many classes at FSU tend to be very large, especially introductory courses. "Some of the lectures are so large, I feel like an anonymous number," said one freshman. While some classes can enroll upwards of several hundred students, FSU tries to keep most classes twenty students or under. "The more individualized attention in my music class is spectacular," exclaimed one sophomore. For those looking for more personalized attention, the Honors program is ideal. Applicants who graduate from high school with 3.8 GPA and 1300 SAT score are invited into the program, which includes special classes and colloquiums.

One student described FSU's registration system as "absolutely horrible. It can be extremely hard to get into classes." Students can register either by phone or through the Internet. Undergrads commonly complain that classes fill up quickly and jammed phone lines prevent registration. In addition, three summer courses are required for graduation. AP credit earned in high school is often used to get out of these requirements, but one student warned, "They'll charge extra if you take too many classes." One happy undergrad said of his FSU education, "I feel that my major has really prepared to send me out into the world."

Sunning Like a 'Nole

In the capital of Florida, a wide variety of social options await Seminoles. On campus, the fraternities reportedly, "dominate a large portion of your social life," and alcohol can be a big part of that scene. Some students claim that it can be easy to feel left out if you don't drink. "Sometimes there can be a real limit on your social life if you don't drink. It seems that a lot of people plan their weekend schedules around getting drunk," claimed one freshman. Marijuana use is present on campus, but not something that is overwhelming. Recently, the university has been cracking down on underage drinking on campus. "You can get arrested if you're not careful," said one freshman.

"Going to FSU football games is one of the most incredible experiences. Looking out and seeing thousands of people do 'the chop' just fills you with such a sense of school pride."

Although it may appear as if the Greek system dominates social at FSU, there are a number of alternatives that await students. Among one of the more popular options is to go to a movie at Moore Auditorium. The screenings are sponsored by the Student Government Association and are shown every few days. "They actually play really good movies and they're free," exclaimed one freshman of the movie screenings. The Oglesby Union also has many different things for students to do, such as a bowling alley and art studio. The Leach Center, FSU's incredible gym and recreational building, offers a myriad of activities to keep students entertained. The Fitness Center offers state-of-the-art cardiovascular and strength training machines. Multipurpose courts can be used to play anything from basketball to badminton, and an indoor running track and pool are available. Racquetball courts are also housed here, and students make good use of this popular fitness center. Intramurals ranging from basketball to tennis run year-round for students who are interested in becoming involved in organized sports, but don't have the time to make a serious commitment. Students with other extracurricular interests can participate in a wide variety of clubs and activities, such as Habitat for Humanity or the Student Government Association.

Off campus, many students frequent clubs and bars in the city of Tallahassee. One student claimed that "clubbing" is one of the biggest social alternatives. Floyd's is a particularly popular destination. Students gave the city of Tallahassee varying reviews. "The city seems kind of dirty, and there are some parts I really wouldn't want to walk into," said one sophomore. The city has two shopping malls for the most essential shopping, and an IMAX theatre under construction should add even more options for off-campus relaxation. Bike trails and a nearby lake invite swimmers and canoeists year round, thanks to Florida's temperate climate.

Picturesque and Poor Parking

Dotted with old red brick architecture, and set amid a rolling countryside, FSU's campus has been described as "very pretty. There are lots of nice brick buildings and it's usually very well maintained." "I was kind of surprised when I got here. I thought all of Florida was supposed to be really flat, but around FSU it's really hilly," said one freshman. The campus is spread out over a large area, so many students take advantage of the campus-wide bus system. A large percentage of students, including freshmen, bring cars, and insufficient parking is, by far, the most widespread complaint of students. "The parking sucks here. It's hard as hell to even find a spot. I've gotten hit twice because of the way the lot is laid out, and I've only been up here a few months!" said one freshman.

Many students choose to bring a car because off-campus housing is a very popular alternative for upperclassmen. The surrounding area of Tallahassee has a wide array of affordable housing. Many freshmen choose to live on campus, but dorm quality varies. "If you're not in a renovated dorm—watch out!" warned one sophomore. Reynolds, Bryan, Gilchrist, and Broward dormitories have all been redone and are considered to be very clean. Sally and Kellum are known as the party dorms, but they have not been renovated anytime close to recently, and according to students, do not provide the most pleasant living accommodations. Dorms are coed by floor, except for the all-female Dorman and Jennie Murphree Halls. Rooms are assigned on a first-come, first-serve basis and also by class seniority. Thus, the older students leave freshmen to fend for themselves, as the nicer dorms fill up quickly. RAs (residential advisors) are available on each floor for counsel and friendly advice. Off-campus private dormitories are ideal for those who want a college atmosphere without actually living on campus.

A surprising number of students do not use FSU's meal plan. Most go to the Food Court, which has a Burger King and Pizza Hut, among others. "I wasn't terribly impressed with the school's food. I think that's why a lot of people just cook for themselves," said one junior. The dining halls "don't seem to be very social places. Sometimes if you're not in a clique it can be hard to find people to sit with," said one sophomore. FSU is a school filled with southern charm and friendly students, but many find that tight social groups tend to form, making it difficult to meet new people.

Football at Its Finest

Not surprisingly, the most popular activity on campus is attending football games. FSU's football team consistently ranks among the best in the nation, and the entire student body supports them. Painted faces and bodies clad with Seminole merchandise, fill the stadium during the season. "Going to FSU football games is one of the most incredible experiences. Looking out and seeing thousands of people do 'the chop' just fills you with such a sense of school pride," said one freshman. When students make the tomahawk motion and sing the sacred tune, they are carrying on a tradition that characterizes Florida State as much as football itself. Although football is the most popular and well known FSU sport, others, like baseball and crew are gaining prominence.

FSU students exhibit an enormous amount of school spirit. They are proud of their school's success in the field and in the classroom. Being one of the top party schools in the nation has not permitted academics to fall through the cracks. The school may be extremely large, but southern hospitality allows most students to feel welcome. Says one student, "FSU is the best of both worlds. The party scene is incredible, but you can really come out after four years with a great education if you take advantage of the resources made available to you."—*Aaron Droller*

FYI

If you come to FSU, you'd better bring "a car so you don't have to bum rides off friends."

What is the typical weekend schedule? "Friday: go clubbing in Tallahassee; Saturday: go to a football game and do 'the chop'; Sunday: work out and homework."

If I could change one thing about FSU, "I'd make the classes smaller."

Three things that every student should do before graduating from FSU are "live in a dorm as a freshman, get thrown in the fountain on your birthday, and go to class."

New College of the University of South Florida

Address: 700 North Tamiami Trail; Sarasota, FL 34243-2197
Phone: 941-359-4269
E-mail address: ncadmissions@sar.usf.edu
Web site URL: newcollege.usf.edu
Founded: 1960
Private or Public: public
Religious affiliation: none
Location: suburban
Undergraduate enrollment: 649
Total enrollment: NA
Percent Male/Female: 37%/63%
Percent Minority: 15%
Percent African-American: 3%
Percent Asian: 3%
Percent Hispanic: 6%
Percent Native-American: 0%
Percent in-state/out of state: 73%/27%
Percent Pub HS: NA
Number of Applicants: 405
Percent Accepted: 70%
Percent Accepted who enroll: 57%
Entering: 163
Transfers: NA
Application Deadline: 1 May
Mean SAT: NA
Mean ACT: NA
Middle 50% SAT range: V 630-720, M 580-670
Middle 50% ACT range: 26-29
3 Most popular majors: liberal arts
Retention: 88%
Graduation rate: 66%
On-campus housing: 99%
Fraternities: NA
Sororities: NA
Library: 255,000 volumes
Tuition and Fees: $2,616 in; $11,422 out
Room and Board: $4,879
Financial aid, first-year: NA
Varsity or Club Athletes: NA
Early Decision or Early Action Acceptance Rate: NA

With a name like "New College" there's no mistaking the small Sarasota, Florida, school for a traditional undergraduate institution. With only 600 students and no grades or core curriculum, New College attendees report that their four years of striving for success takes place "in an experimental milieu."

Independent Intellectuals

New College students make much of the fact that self-motivation is key for success at their school. There is no core curriculum. Rather, students design their course plan with the help of a faculty advisor. Students can easily design their own majors, though many choose from the variety of already-established ones. Traditional liberal arts majors like anthropology, literature, and biology are common. Students caution, though, that the "literature theory classes will completely exhaust your brain and overload your reading time." In addition, "Psychology is very popular . . . but the department walks you through the thesis, which is the most difficult aspect of New College." Some even get degrees in "general studies," which is "sort of a catch-all." As for those who plan to continue their education, faculty members can suggest programs of study appropriate for future graduate students.

"You'll definitely have professors who know you well—some'll probably cook your whole class dinner."

Another hallmark of the New College education is the lack of grades. Said one sophomore, "There can't really be competition—there's nothing to compete about." Nevertheless, one student did note that "it can be a hard adjustment from high school. You have to train yourself to study for the right reasons." Students don't point to any particularly strong area of faculty expertise, but note, rather, that they are all "high-caliber." Like the college as a whole, class sizes are almost universally small. As a result, professor-student interaction is lauded at New College. "You'll definitely have professors who know you well—some'll probably cook your whole class dinner." There are TA's, but they only assist professors and students and do not teach classes.

Students say that at least partly as a result of the atmosphere of "intellectualism," most students spend more time on academics than any other aspect of college. The Jane B. Cook Bancroft Library, the main library, is complimented for having "the best librarian I've ever met." Because New College is a state school, it is part of an inter-library book exchange program with other Florida colleges. Upperclassmen are also pleased that they get their own study carrels. Other places to study, which tend to be more social than Bancroft, are the student center and individual dorm rooms.

Time Flies When You're Saving the World

While studying occupies the biggest chunk of a New Collegian's life, many students are involved in extra-curricular activities. The *Catalyst* is the weekly paper written by students. Other popular activities include student government (through the New College Student Alliance) and Amnesty International. Politically, "the overwhelming majority is liberal." A senior cautioned, though, that "more than being of one view or another we are open-minded." Nevertheless, students noted that the campus isn't as good at activism as it is at "theorizing about activism." New College does not have a varsity sports program, but its athletic facilities include a gym, racquetball, tennis, and basketball courts, a soccer field, and a pool.

On the weekends, New College students party like their peers at other institutions—sort of. There are no fraternities or sororities, and students say that the social scene is "fairly laid-back." The majority of socializing takes place on campus. "Walls" are parties randomly thrown together whenever the urge hits. Cross-dressing is reportedly popular at these parties. A more organized dance is the Palm Court Party (PCP), where a laid-back atmosphere of tie-dyeing, listening to music, and dancing pervades. Students say that both drinking and drugs are prevalent at the school, though the latter is mostly confined to marijuana. "Cops look the other way most of the time," said one student. Outside of campus Sarasota does not offer much for night-time activity, though its tourist-friendly beaches are appreciated by New College students. Said one student, "Sarasota is a small, artsy town with not a lot to do, but it's beautiful and has more cultural opportunities than any other city in Florida. Which I guess makes me a bit sad for the rest of Florida . . ." Tampa is less than an hour way and students in need of a break from the quiet suburban life occasionally make the trip.

Sleeping and Snacking in Sarasota

Most freshman and sophomores live on campus while upperclassmen generally move off campus. All B and Viking rooms are singles, while Pei residents share doubles. Viking is actually a converted motel, which some students say, has "charm." The newer Dort and Goldstein dorms are said to be much better than their counterparts. Dort features large suites with single bedrooms, complete with appliances. In all the dorms, though, residents often keep their doors open, which contributes to a more suite-like atmosphere. Security concerns are minimal among students; locking doors is the only precaution most students take. There are two RA's for each dorm. Students enjoy the "very Florida" campus, calling the architecture "'70s Spanish" style. The school is located on a bay, which, "during good weather, is awesome." In general, students appreciate going to school in sunny Florida. "I don't know why my friends put up with snow up north!" said one.

Campus residents eat in one central cafeteria and are required to be on the meal plan. The food is prepared by the Marriott food service, and students can use their meal cards at the local convenience stores as well. Many undergrads complain about the quality of the food. As one student explained, "There's a reason we were ranked as the worst college food in the South." Students also enjoy eating at the Granary, a health-food restaurant, and at Taco Bell.

Lack of Cultural Diversity

While students have diverse interests, they generally come from similar backgrounds: white, upper-middle-class, and suburban. Said one student, "I wouldn't say New College is particularly diverse, unless you consider a school nearly 85 percent full of white, suburban, overly intelligent kids diverse. Of course, everyone welcomes diversity, but it's part of the 'program' here." The homosexual community is said to be "well-accepted." In general, said one student, "due to self-selection, we're a pretty alternative, easy-going bunch. Students are proud to be a part of their "thoughtful—in both senses of the word" community and don't mind missing the "traditional" college experience. "I belong here. I can't imagine most of us truly belonging anywhere else." —*Ellen Moskowitz*

FYI

If you come to NCF, you'd better bring "your stamina and social skills."

What is the typical weekend schedule? "Friday, relax and get ready for the party in Palm Court; Saturday, relax and play some sports; Sunday, nothing else but studying."

If I could change one thing about NCF, "I'd make the student population more diverse."

Three things that every student at NCF should do before graduating are "dance naked in Palm Court, listen to one of John More's storytimes, and win a game of one-on-one with John Newman."

Rollins College

Address: 1000 Holt Avenue; Winter Park, FL 32789-4499
Phone: 407-646-2161
E-mail address: admission@rollins.edu
Web site URL: www.rollins.edu
Founded: 1885
Private or Public: private
Religious affiliation: none
Location: suburban
Undergraduate enrollment: 1,723
Total enrollment: NA
Percent Male/Female: 40%/60%
Percent Minority: 18%
Percent African-American: 4%
Percent Asian: 3%
Percent Hispanic: 7%
Percent Native-American: 1%
Percent in-state/out of state: 52%/48%
Percent Pub HS: 57%
Number of Applicants: 2,307
Percent Accepted: 63%
Percent Accepted who enroll: 32%
Entering: 467
Transfers: 65
Application Deadline: 15 Feb
Mean SAT: NA
Mean ACT: NA
Middle 50% SAT range: V 540-620, M 530-630
Middle 50% ACT range: 22-26
3 Most popular majors: international business, English, economics
Retention: 84%
Graduation rate: 62%
On-campus housing: 63%
Fraternities: 38%
Sororities: 40%
Library: 237,333 volumes
Tuition and Fees: $26,250
Room and Board: $8,050
Financial aid, first-year: 39%
Varsity or Club Athletes: 19%
Early Decision or Early Action Acceptance Rate: ED 69%

Students at Rollins have a lot on their minds—a tasteful, elegant Spanish-Mediterranean-style campus, perpetually sunny Florida weather, and Disneyworld, which is just a short drive away. At least if it all gets to be too much for them, they can pull on a bathing suit and hop into the pool, or lay out by the lake around the back of the campus. In reality, although the campus (which the students call "amazing" and "truly beautiful") is well situated and designed, life isn't all laying out in the sun at "Rolly." Students also take full advantage of the academic and extracurricular offerings on their campus, and manage to have a significant amount of fun while they do it.

Well-Rounded Academics

The academic program at Rollins has a wide range of offerings. Students must complete both general education requirements and a major program in order to graduate with a Bachelor of Arts degree. The "gen ed" courses fall under areas such as writing, foreign languages, quantitative reasoning, literature, and laboratory science. Students must complete a total of 140 credit hours, which averages out to around 18 per semester to graduate in four years. 60 of these make up the general education requirement, and the major programs generally comprise about 30. While most students agree that it gives them a well-rounded education in a lot of areas, a few could do without such rigorous rules, because as one said, "a few of them seem like a waste of time"—most specifically the gym requirement.

Popular majors include English, psychology, and economics. Students seem to agree that "schoolwork can be as hard as you want to make it for yourself." More difficult majors include politics, math, natural sciences, and anthropology, while economics is generally regarded as somewhat easier. The arts programs are also cited as being strong as well as competitive. Rollins offers an honors program and a program with the Crummer Graduate School of Business, both of which are seen as being more difficult than the average course load.

One of the defining characteristics of Rollins classes is their small size—there are no lecturers with more than 30 students, and most classes have between eight and 25. The limited class size leads to an intimate atmosphere and good discussions with professors. For example, one English major reports that "in the English department, each classroom has a gigantic oval-shaped wood table, and only 16 students can sit around it." However, this small size can make it difficult to get into some courses, especially some of the general education courses. Just to add to the intimacy, "most classes have attendance policies, and if you miss more than two classes your grade drops by a letter for each additional class missed." The low number of students means that professors are often available to help outside of class when desired.

There is a week-long optional intersession offered in January, when students can take classes from more diverse, hands-on offerings before returning for the second semester. They can also participate in internship programs in nearby Orlando, a rapidly growing business community.

Playing Hard

Several students are rather blunt about the composition of the student body: "The stereotype is that all Rollins students are rich, white, and barely getting through school. To an extent, that's true." While not everyone fits this label, most students agree that Rollins' population is rather homogenous, and puts a heavy emphasis on looking put-together. One lamented the large number of "skinny blonde girls who spend $300 per pair of jeans," and another said that "the last person I saw in workout clothes in class was probably a long time ago. Even people who wear jeans and T-shirts always look polished."

Students at Rollins also like to party. The Greek system is huge, with nearly 60 person of the campus pledging, and although they can dominate the social scene, as one student says, "the frats have to go through a big thing to throw a party [and] campus safety always breaks it up early." Another commented that "those who aren't involved [with the Greek system either] don't hang out much, are in the arts departments, live in one of the non-Greek fraternities, or live off campus." Most students agree that the party environment leads to "a lot of hooking up," but is not as conducive to longer relationships. Winter Park offers alternatives as well, which students take increasing advantage of as they get older. The nearby University of Central Florida has a less scrutinized party scene, and there are many clubs and bars in the town.

Rollins has a reputation for heavy drinking and drug use, and students find that to be true to some degree. One student says "non-drinkers find their place, but if I didn't drink I would feel uncomfortable at a lot of the parties." There are other social options, though, some organized weekly by the "All Campus Events (ACE)" organization, through which different student groups sponsor events with different themes. "Most of them actually get a pretty big turnout," reported a senior. "We have a 'Day of Peace' where we have yoga and healthy choice sorts of things on the main lawn. There are also jousting competitions, powder puff football, drum circles, pool parties, barbecues, and more."

"Even people who wear jeans and T-shirts always look polished."

Although the campus is well stocked with options for students, many agree those with cars are at a big advantage. The proximity of Disneyworld and the other Orlando theme parks, as well as the nearby social options, lead most students to bring cars, although that also means that "there is always someone with a car willing to take you where you need to go." Off-campus students can have difficulty parking.

Sun-Drenched

In general, most students don't often actually see a need to leave the campus—in fact, they consistently cite their beautiful physical environment as one of the aspects that sets Rollins apart from other schools. A senior commented, "The buildings are stucco and tile and the grounds are very well manicured. I love it when it rains." The campus also boasts a rose garden and a brand-new entrance archway made from Italian marble, and the student center is widely used and well-stocked with food.

Most freshmen live in dorms, which have "nice, comfortable rooms with working A/C." Many upperclassmen live off campus, although it can be difficult to find other local options and the rent is high at whatever apartments may be available.

There are also several theme houses for students with a variety of different interests. The main complaint of most students living on campus is the dining hall food, which one undergrad cites as "the major incentive for most of the people who move off campus."

Extracurricular activities encompass a huge scope of options, ranging from the familiar to the more eclectic. One student said, "The Star Trek club is both well respected and funny. They're really crazy and really smart people. There is a pumpkin-carving organization, and SEA (Society of Enlightened Academics) and WPRK (radio) are well respected." Students interested in music and the fine arts have many outlets for their creativity, and there is a fair amount of community service that includes food and clothing drives and Habitat for Humanity, "as well as beach clean-ups, holiday fairs for the community, and volunteering in area schools."

Athletics are also strong, especially in golf, tennis, and crew. The Division II women's golf team won the 2003 NCAA championship, and the basketball teams also consistently perform well. The waterskiing team is also highly regarded. Although several students wish the gym were bigger, they agree that it is easy to get exercise by playing on an intramural team.

Overall, Rollins students seem to know how to have fun and how to take advantage of their beautiful setting to the fullest extent possible; they also know when to get their work done. Although some students believe that it can be necessary to withdraw from the social scene in order to put in time for academics, most believe that the collegiate environment is conducive to studying for those who can manage their time. They also extol the small environment, which leads to "professors who care about their students and who can and will take the time to get to know [their students] and make their experience here the best it can be." And if that's not enough, there's always Disney World just around the corner. —*David Carpman*

FYI

If you come to Rollins, you'd better bring a "bathing suit and a really expensive car."

What is the typical weekend schedule? "Friday night, off-campus party; Saturday, lay out by the pool and then hit up the bar; Sunday, recover and do homework if you have any."

If I could change one thing about Rollins, I would "make every student spend at least one summer flipping burgers. Most seniors have never held a job."

Three things every student at Rollins should do before graduating are "go through Greek recruitment to meet people, go abroad, and go to the amusement parks."

Stetson University

Address: 421 North Woodland Boulevard; Deland, FL 32723
Phone: 800-688-0101
E-mail address: admissions@stetson.edu
Web site URL: www.stetson.edu
Founded: 1883
Private or Public: private
Religious affiliation: none
Location: suburban
Undergraduate enrollment: 2,142
Total enrollment: NA
Percent Male/Female: 42%/58%
Percent Minority: 16%
Percent African-American: 3%
Percent Asian: 2%
Percent Hispanic: 5%
Percent Native-American: 1%
Percent in-state/out of state: 77%/23%
Percent Pub HS: 75%
Number of Applicants: 1,919
Percent Accepted: 80%
Percent Accepted who enroll: 36%
Entering: 551
Transfers: 112
Application Deadline: rolling
Mean SAT: NA
Mean ACT: NA
Middle 50% SAT range: V 510-620, M 500-610
Middle 50% ACT range: 21-27
3 Most popular majors: marketing, business, education
Retention: 79%
Graduation rate: 61%
On-campus housing: 69%
Fraternities: 33%
Sororities: 29%
Library: 377,319 volumes
Tuition and Fees: $21,505
Room and Board: $6,855
Financial aid, first-year: 59%
Varsity or Club Athletes: 21%
Early Decision or Early Action Acceptance Rate: ED 88%

In the 1860s, the Stetson hat was called the "Boss of the Plains." Indeed, the students that call themselves Hatters at Stetson University take charge of any obstacle that gets in their way. Through one-one-one academics and a fervent school spirit, students that choose to call Deland their home can be assured of obtaining a good education amidst the intimate setting of a small school.

Hats Off to Academics

Educational opportunities abound at Stetson. The university is divided into the College of Arts and Sciences, School of Business, School of Music, and the Law School, which is located in nearby St. Petersburg. The degree requirements to graduate are both broad and extensive. Students are required to take courses in English, communications, math, social and natural sciences, religion, and demonstrate proficiency in a foreign language. Many requirements can be waived by presenting satisfactory AP scores. Also required is attendance at cultural events such as music recitals and lecture series. "All the requirements can be irritating, but at the same time they help broaden your horizons. If you're an English major, at least you have the experience of having taken some science," commented one junior. Some students choose to take advantage of the Honors Program, which mandates that students take a Junior Honors Seminar. Students in the program have the luxury of being able to design their own major, but should have graduated high school in the top ten percent of their class with at least a 1270 SAT score to enter the program.

Due to Stetson's small size, students are given many opportunities to learn one-on-one with professors. Classes are kept very small and even introductory lectures will only have about 25 to 30 students. "People get to know their professors so well here. Some even invite students from their class over for dinner. I know all of my professors by first name," exclaimed one freshman. Registration is done through an advisor, and most students do not have a problem getting into desired courses. Students said that chemistry and biology are among the harder majors, but also pointed out that the music major is extremely competitive. "Watch out for the Music Theory class, it has the highest failure rate on campus!" warned one student. Easier majors were said to be Education and Communications.

Hatter Living

Although upperclassmen can request to live in suites, all freshmen live in doubles that are "definitely a little cramped" and share a hall bathroom. There are Residential Advisors (RAs) on every floor to help offer friendly advice. The two honors dorms, Carson and Hollis, are single-sex, dry, and have enforced quiet hours for study. All of the other dorms except one are coed and separated by floor. Nemick is reportedly the worst dorm because it is the oldest. Emily has a reputation for having a party atmosphere with more drinking than other dorms. Students said they felt very safe on campus. It is necessary to pass through two key locks for room access and Public Safety, Stetson's security force, is constantly walking around campus. In addition, there are phones around campus to call for escorts for those who do not want to walk home alone at night. In addition, although off-campus housing is always an option, most people choose to live on-campus all four years because finding apartments in the small town of DeLand can be costly.

"Having Daytona so close really gives you something great to do on weekends."

Many students have positive opinions of the culinary options at Stetson. The dining hall, Commons, is catered by Marriott, so "the food seems to be a level above what you would find at other colleges." There is a well-stocked salad bar and a vegetarian entrée for those who are inclined, and there are also omelets on Sunday. The meal-plan ranges between five and 17 meals per week. Those who don't use all of their meals can convert them to points that can be used at "The Hatrack," a fast food restaurant that is open until late at night. In addition, points can be used to order-in Domino's Pizza for those who don't feel like leaving the dorm. The dining hall is a social place where "you can just pick up a conversation with anyone really." In addition, minutes away by car are several restaurants, including the popular Boston Coffee Shop.

Brimming with Spirit

Stetson students say that there is a "club for almost everyone here." Many people are involved in some type of extracurricular activity. Religious organizations seem to be popular on campus such as the Wesley house, a Methodist student union, and the Baptist student union. Community service is also represented at Stetson, with such organizations as Circle K. The Council for Student Activities organizes campus-wide events like concerts, and has recently brought bands like Sister Hazel to campus. "Stetson is a very musical campus. Lots of people are in choirs or play an instrument, and the School of Music brings performers to campus throughout the year to campus," said one freshman.

Athletics plays a large role on campus. Many students choose to get involved with intramurals where offerings range from basketball to flag football. A complaint among some students is the lack of a football team, but the basketball and soccer teams are well supported at games. "Humiliating yourself by doing the Stetson cheer in front of everyone is a time-honored tradition that everyone should do," said one junior. The Hollis Center, the recently renovated gymnasium, has many facilities to keep the athletically inclined student entertained. Its offerings include basketball courts, an Olympic-sized pool, a game room, an aerobics studio, and a fitness center offering state-of-the-art workout machines.

Night on the Town

The town of DeLand, although small, is located conveniently about an hour away from Orlando and just a short ride from Daytona. In Orlando, students can go to theme parks such as Walt Disney World or Universal Studios on weekends. In Daytona, students find some of the best beaches in all of Florida and also one of the hottest Spring Break destinations for students around the country. "Having Daytona so close really gives you something great to do on weekends," exclaimed one freshman. Accordingly, many students at Stetson choose to bring cars, although some claimed that it can sometimes be difficult to find a parking spots on campus.

The town of DeLand itself, although not incredibly large, has a certain Southern type of appeal for students. It is filled with lots of "mom and pop shops" that give it the small-town America type feel. "Since Orlando is close by, I never feel smothered by how small DeLand is," said one sophomore. One student said she liked the fact that the residents of DeLand seem to get involved with what goes on around campus, such as attending sporting events to throw their support for the home team.

The weekend starts for Stetson students on Thursday night. Greek influence on campus is very noticeable at this time: fraternities throw large parties that are inclusive to everyone, and are not prone to charge admission. Drinking is noticeable, but definitely not overwhelming. Drug use is said to exist, but is not visible. "People who don't drink really do not feel pressure to do so," said one freshman. More than thirty percent of students are involved in Greek life. Those that are not in frats said there is not a terrible amount of pressure to join. Many of Stetson's students are from Florida. As a result there is often a "mass exodus of students" that choose to drive home on Friday, and the campus is not as active for the rest of the weekend.

Students at Stetson recognize both the advantages and disadvantages of attending such a small school. The intimate setting of the school allows students to truly get to know their professors and receive real individualized attention. The small town of DeLand adds to the personal atmosphere, but with Daytona and Orlando so close by, students have no problem. The small school feel ultimately adds to a feeling of togetherness that makes the time spent at Stetson a worthwhile experience.—*Aaron Droller*

FYI

If you come to Stetson, you'd better bring "your driver's license to get out of DeLand once in a while."

What is the typical weekend schedule? "Friday: drive to Daytona; Saturday: spend the afternoon in Daytona and hang out with friends; Sunday: relax in DeLand."

If I could change one thing about Stetson, "I'd make the school less claustrophobic feeling."

The three things that every student should do before graduating from Stetson are "get thrown into the fountain, the Stetson cheer, and ring the bell at the Hollis Center."

University of Florida

Address: 201 Criser Hall; Gainesville, FL 32611
Phone: 352-392-1365
E-mail address: freshman@ufl.edu
Web site URL: www.ufl.edu
Founded: 1853
Private or Public: public
Religious affiliation: none
Location: suburban
Undergraduate enrollment: 34,031
Total enrollment: NA
Percent Male/Female: 47%/53%
Percent Minority: 27%
Percent African-American: 8%
Percent Asian: 7%
Percent Hispanic: 11%
Percent Native-American: 1%
Percent in-state/out of state: 95%/5%
Percent Pub HS: NA
Number of Applicants: 20,119
Percent Accepted: 58%
Percent Accepted who enroll: 56%
Entering: 6,536
Transfers: 2,031
Application Deadline: 13 Jan
Mean SAT: NA
Mean ACT: NA
Middle 50% SAT range: V 550-660, M 580-680
Middle 50% ACT range: 24-29
3 Most popular majors: business management, marketing, engineering, social sciences
Retention: 92%
Graduation rate: 77%
On-campus housing: 21%
Fraternities: 15%
Sororities: 15%
Library: 5,024,637 volumes
Tuition and Fees: $2,581 in; $11,595 out
Room and Board: $5,640
Financial aid, first-year: 40%
Varsity or Club Athletes: NA
Early Decision or Early Action Acceptance Rate: ED 60%; EA 64%

While UF students are proud that their school has been noted as one of the top universities in the country according to *U.S. News and World Report*, they'd toss that accolade aside for a #1 ranking where outside opinion really matters: football. The school has a winning tradition in the sport, and the game against Florida State makes for the biggest weekend of the year, as well as one of the biggest pep rallies in the country. GatorGrowl, as the pep rally is known, typifies both American college life and the UF experience—quality football, parties, and fun.

Pride's for More than Saturday

Students are proud of their fun-loving reputation but emphasize that their education is both high-quality and strenuous. As admission standards of recent years have risen markedly, the school's prestige has increased accordingly. The general education core curriculum requires students to complete classes in math, English, the biological sciences, the humanities, and social and behavioral sciences. Nearly all Gators note the reputation of UF's teachers and programs as having been a decisive factor in their college choice. In particular, architecture, journalism, and engineering are quality programs. Business-related majors are popular as well. Choosing a major is a decision that should be made early at UF. Said one student, "If you are going to change your major, change it early. If not, expect to stay an extra year." An honors program is available, acceptance to which is based on SAT scores and high school GPA. In addition, study abroad programs are gaining popularity. Gripes about the academic experience at UF include lecture classes of as many as 700 students and the preponderance of graduate students in teaching positions. One junior noted, however, the "personal attention" from TAs is a valuable asset.

Prowling Grounds

The main library, used for both studying and research, is the Smathers Library, which houses 2.5 million volumes in two main libraries and nine branches. Students report that they often study in other quiet places, such as the computer labs or the Plaza of Americas Park, due to the limited hours of the libraries. Social studying is based in the dorm lobbies. Other facilities available for student use on campus include the Florida Museum of Natural History, the Center for the Performing Arts, Harn Museum of Art, and the University Art Gallery. Further contributing to the breadth of Gators' opportunities are the world's largest citrus research center, a world-renowned institute for the study of the brain, a public television and radio station, and one of the largest health centers in the Southeast, Shands Hospital. Students bask in the Florida sunshine on a gorgeous campus characterized by a variety of brick and Gothic-style buildings. One section of campus is on the National Register of Historic Places.

Quarters and Cuisine

Dorm living does not get as much praise as the dorms themselves. While one upperclassmen said, "It's good to experience it," she acknowledged that, "people are always happy to move off campus after the first year." Living on campus is optional, and most take advantage of the option freshman year in order to get acquainted with their classmates. Only upperclass students have the opportunity of getting into an ARF (apartment residence facility) and even these are rare. The rest of the dorms are generally small but comfortable doubles. There are RAs on every floor, and floor residents vote on visiting hours for members of the opposite sex. The only particularly undesirable dorms are Murphree and Buckman, which have no air-conditioning.

Students say that their dining options have improved recently and that they appreciate not being forced into a meal plan. Many take advantage of the offer, though, with food ranging from cafeteria-style and fast food at the Hub, to vegetarian at the Gator Dining Corner.

Living the Florida Life

The campus is mainly self-contained and Gators can easily keep themselves occupied on its grounds. Besides the opportunities to be a spectator at premier college sporting events, UF students can participate in popular intramural sports including football, soccer and tennis. Students can't seem to point to the most popular extracurricular activities because "there's seemingly as many groups as there are students." The *Alligator*, a student-run daily newspaper and Florida Blue Key, a campus activity involvement organization, are two of the most well-known. Popular community service activities include Habitat for Humanity and volunteering for the Shands Hospital.

"We all bleed orange and blue down here! FSU fans are the only thing we're not open-minded about."

Greek life is influential at UF. The fraternities and sororities dominate social life but non-Greeks don't feel left out. "We can still go to the parties and there's plenty other ways to meet people. You probably have to make more of an effort, though, and that's why there's some pressure to rush." All year long, Gators have plenty of opportunities for socializing and drinking. Drugs are "without question available, but completely avoidable."

Students do report that Gainesville caters to the university and that movies, malls and restaurants are easily accessible by car. Local clubs such as Torches and Maui's are popular too. Tampa, Tallahassee, Jacksonville and Orlando are all located within a two-hour drive, and students often make weekend trips to other colleges. Fans of the outdoors can take advantage of great year-round weather in Gainesville—and at the hour-away beaches located on the Gulf of Mexico or the Atlantic Ocean.

A Gator?

A junior laughed in response to the question, "Is there a student stereotype?" "With 42,000-plus students we've got 'em all," he said. Florida students come from all over the country and remarkably diverse cultural backgrounds. Cultural organizations like the Black Student Union are popular. The lesbian and gay communities are large and in general students point to a "live and let live" feeling on campus. "We all bleed orange and blue down here! FSU fans are the only thing we're not open-minded about."

The spirit UF students exhibit for more

than football reflects confidence in their school. Said one junior, "If you are looking for a good academic school and you want to experience all that college has to offer, then UF is your place." At first overwhelmed by the great size and many opportunities at the University of Florida, students ultimately find niches at UF and unite to scream "If You're Not a GATOR, You're GATORBAIT!"—*Ellen Moskowitz*

FYI

If you come to UF, you'd better bring "your football spirit."

What is the typical weekend schedule? "Friday, Greek scene; Saturday, clubbing at Torches or Maui's; Sunday, study all day in Smathers and Plaza of Americas."

If I could change one thing about UF, "I'd build a private parking lot just for myself."

Three things that every student at UF should do before graduating are "watch the bats leave the bat house at dusk, attend a UF football game, and hang out on Payne's Prairie and watch the stars on a clear night."

University of Miami

Address: PO Box 248025; Coral Gable, FL 33124
Phone: 305-284-4323
E-mail address: admission@miami.edu
Web site URL: www.miami.edu
Founded: 1925
Private or Public: private
Religious affiliation: none
Location: suburban
Undergraduate enrollment: 9,794
Total enrollment: 14,436
Percent Male/Female: 43%/57%
Percent Minority: 40%
Percent African-American: 10%
Percent Asian: 5%
Percent Hispanic: 25%
Percent Native-American: 0%
Percent in-state/out of state: 56%/44%
Percent Pub HS: 55%
Number of Applicants: 15,909
Percent Accepted: 44%
Percent Accepted who enroll: 29%
Entering: 2,059
Transfers: 555
Application Deadline: 1 Feb
Mean SAT: NA
Mean ACT: NA
Middle 50% SAT range: V 550-650, M 570-670
Middle 50% ACT range: 25-30
3 Most popular majors: business management, marketing, visual and performing arts, biological sciences
Retention: 84%
Graduation rate: 64%
On-campus housing: 41%
Fraternities: 13%
Sororities: 13%
Library: 141,578 volumes
Tuition and Fees: $26,280
Room and Board: $8,328
Financial aid, first-year: 57%
Varsity or Club Athletes: 20%
Early Decision or Early Action Acceptance Rate: ED 37%

Thousands of students nervously watch as the football sails up in the air in the closing seconds of the annual University of Miami–Florida State University matchup. The ball arches and it's . . . wide right. With a collective sigh of relief and excitement, a wave of orange and green clad students rush the Orange Bowl to celebrate a hard-earned victory and show the pride they feel by being a Hurricane. The passion students' exhibit at the University of Miami isn't just for athletics, but also for the strong academic departments that shape their education in tropical South Florida.

No Sun Tanning 101

The University of Miami is comprised of 14 schools, which include Arts and Sciences, Architecture, Business Administration, Communication, Education, Engineering, International Studies, Law, Medicine, Music, Marine and Atmospheric Science, Continuing Studies, Nursing, and Graduate. Until a major is declared, usually during sophomore year, students enroll in the

College of Arts and Sciences. Course requirements vary depending on the school, but all students must take English, social science, and natural science core courses. Many students get out of these requirements via AP credits, but most "don't mind the core at all because major requirements often overlap with required courses.

Typically there are about 15 students in each course. Large introductory lectures, such as biology and chemistry, can enroll upwards of 200 students. Students find that getting into a class does not pose a problem, though, even for freshmen. Reportedly, the science courses are "the toughest around," and weed out many pre-med students. Exclusively open to Florida residents is the extremely elite six-year medical school program, which grants automatic entrance into UM's medical school after two years. Competition to get into the program is tough, as only 25 students are granted admission per year. In addition to science, the architecture and music programs are also considered very rigorous, as is the internationally renowned School of Marine Science. Business, Education, and Communication are reportedly easier majors.

Most students enjoy their classes thanks to the excellent faculty. Professors try to be accessible to students, even in the largest of lecture courses. "I know my professors on a first name basis," said one junior. Classes are mostly taught by professors, even at the introductory level. TAs are also available to help students and often help review for exams. Freshmen are assigned to faculty advisors to help devise a course of study that is both broad but focused on specific interests. After declaring a major, students are assigned to an advisor in their respective department. Students generally agree that, "Advisors are great and supportive. They're there to help with all kinds of academic problems."

Applicants that score at least a 1360 on the SAT and rank in the top ten percent of their class are invited to join the honors program. Students enrolled in the program must maintain a minimum GPA of 3.3 and take at least one honors class per semester. In addition to the six-year medical school program, Dual Admission Honors programs are available, which offer both a bachelors and masters degree in Biomedical Engineering, Marine Geology, or Physical Therapy. The university also offers an extensive study abroad program for those who are interested in a wide variety of majors, such as International Studies and Marine Science.

Fratting It Up

The weekend begins on Thursday at UM with a wide array of social options awaiting students, both on and off campus. Advanced movie screenings at the university's theatre or outdoor screen are popular options for on-campus relaxation. Toga and patio-themed parties also provide entertainment for students. A significant portion of on-campus social events revolves around the Greek scene. Many frats advertise parties all around campus and tend not to charge admission. Some, however, are by invitation only. Although drinking is prevalent on campus, one student said "non-drinkers don't feel left out." "If you do, do, if you don't, don't," seems to be the general attitude toward drinking on campus. Alcohol is not allowed in any dorm whose residents are under 21, but it is still present in many on campus apartments. For a campus with "lots of attractive people," random hookups do happen, but not with oppressive frequency. As one junior put it, "UM is not a sex melting pot."

The University Center, with comfortable couches, TV's, an arcade, and ping-pong tables, offers a relaxing and social environment. The Rathskellar, referred to as the Rat, frequently hosts bands and comedians, and is another place where students go for a bite or a game of pool.

Salivating in South Beach

The university's close proximity to south Florida hangouts offers students a number of off-campus activities. Parking is a major problem, and many students opt not to bring cars to campus. While some find not having a car to be very constricting, they have no trouble getting around thanks to the aboveground railway, the Metrorail, which is close to campus. Just a short ride away on the Metrorail are Coconut Grove and South Beach, where students shop, go clubbing, or hangout on the beach. At South Beach, students "get an eyeful every day," compliments of the beautiful people who come from all around to sunbathe in the unique Miami atmosphere. A law was recently passed increasing the minimum age for admittance to clubs to 21 for women, who were previously let in at 18. This has made clubbing a less viable social option, although "a lot of people try to get fake I.D.'s." Students also frequent Sunset Place to catch a movie and Bayside, where they can browse the boutiques that line the streets. Although there is a lot in Miami to tempt them away from schoolwork, students claim, "You can't slack off, or the work will catch up with you." The work-hard-play-hard attitude prevails across campus.

The Comfort of Campus

Students rave about the beauty of the university's campus. Lake Osceola sits at its center, and is surrounded by palm trees and other tropical foliage. "It feels almost like a resort," said one junior. Many students enjoy the very "relaxed and laid back atmosphere." The campus is kept clean and students claim that one can rarely find graffiti. The warm tropical climate lends itself to t-shirts and shorts all year round. Students also praise the diversity of the campus. "No matter what ethnicity you come from, there is always someone [like you] here," said one freshman. Some, however, noticed that certain groups form cliques, which can make it difficult to meet people. Despite the wealthy Coral Gables neighborhood that surrounds campus, there are areas of Miami nearby that students try to stay away from.

At South Beach, students "get an eyeful every day," compliments of the beautiful people who come from all around to sunbathe in the unique Miami atmosphere.

The coed dorms include Eaton, Stanford, Walsh, Pentland, McDonalds, Pearson, Mahoney and Hecht. All dorms are air conditioned, but many students lament the fact that the windows cannot be opened. All freshmen who do not commute to school are required to live on campus in the same dorms as upperclassmen. Generally, freshmen will live in a unit consisting of two doubles and one shared bathroom. Pierson and Mahoney are regarded as the best colleges, although Eaton also received high remarks. Security is "very tight." Students are required to swipe their "Cane Card" for dorm access and have to check in with Residential Advisors who live on the same floors as freshman, late at night and early in the morning. Students who need quiet study time will head to study rooms in their dorms or to Richter Library, which is opened 24 hours a day and has copy machines and computer labs.

Dining is viewed as "adequate, but it gets tiresome." A popular food court, called The Hurricane, offers food from chains such as Panda Express and Sbarros. The general complaint about the two main dining halls, Hecht-Stamford and Pierson-Mahoney, is that their hours aren't flexible for most students' schedules. On campus students must purchase a meal plan that ranges from eight to 21 meals per week. "The Caf" is a popular place not only to eat but also to socialize. Salad bars and meal options such as quiches provide vegetarians with adequate culinary alternatives.

Hurricane Force Wins

Athletics play a huge role at the University of Miami, and the school has a long winning tradition in a multitude of sports. The biggest event of the year is the annual football game against Florida State University at the historic Orange Bowl. "If you don't go to the game, you have no school spirit," claimed one sophomore. Football isn't the only sport that the Hurricanes excel at. Recently, the University of Miami basketball team made it to the Sweet Sixteen for the first time in team history, and the baseball team won the College World Championship in 1999. Tickets to sporting events are provided to all students free of charge, and as a result, games are widely attended and enthusiastically supported.

The Wellness Center received rave reviews from almost all students. The facility contains modern weight training equipment, racquetball and basketball courts, Olympic sized swimming pools, an elevated jogging track, and even a health juice bar. At the Wellness Center, many students participate in a variety of intramurals, ranging from touch football to floor hockey. For those not looking for a huge commitment, students will head over to the Wellness Center for a quick pick-up game.

Students praise the university's strength and dedication to a wide variety of disciplines. For those who don't need cold New England winters to force them to study, UM offers a tropical climate all year round with a unique South Florida atmosphere. Students demonstrate a strong sense of pride in their school's academic and athletic accomplishments. "The focus isn't just on academics and it isn't just on partying. There's no better place to spend four years than sunny South Florida." *—Aaron Droller*

FYI

If you come to University of Miami, you'd better bring "your bathing suit and suntan lotion."

What is the typical weekend schedule? "Friday: hang out at the University Center or clubbing; Saturday: take the Metrorail to South Beach; Sunday: study in Milner."

If I could change one thing about University of Miami, "I'd renovate all the dorms."

Three things every student at University of Miami should do before graduating are "go to South Beach, visit the Everglades, and learn to speak Spanish!"

Georgia

Agnes Scott College

Address: 141 East College Avenue; Decatur, GA 30030
Phone: 800-868-8602
E-mail address: admission@agnesscott.edu
Web site URL: www.agnesscott.edu
Founded: 1889
Private or Public: private
Religious affiliation: Presbyterian
Location: urban
Undergraduate enrollment: 869
Total enrollment: NA
Percent Male/Female: 0%/100%
Percent Minority: 33%
Percent African-American: 21%
Percent Asian: 6%
Percent Hispanic: 3%
Percent Native-American: 0%
Percent in-state/out of state: 55%/45%
Percent Pub HS: 75%
Number of Applicants: 743
Percent Accepted: 73%
Percent Accepted who enroll: 43%
Entering: 234
Transfers: 9
Application Deadline: 1 Mar
Mean SAT: NA
Mean ACT: NA
Middle 50% SAT range: V 570-680, M 540-650
Middle 50% ACT range: 23-30
3 Most popular majors: social sciences, psychology, biological and biomedical sciences
Retention: 79%
Graduation rate: 72%
On-campus housing: 90%
Fraternities: NA
Sororities: NA
Library: 171,891 volumes
Tuition and Fees: $20,470
Room and Board: $7,760
Financial aid, first-year: 73%
Varsity or Club Athletes: 20%
Early Decision or Early Action Acceptance Rate: ED 73%

Hollywood, watch out! When it comes to picture-perfect campuses, not even Tinseltown can beat Agnes Scott's storybook setting. The campus, famously featured in the horror flick *Scream 2*, hosted crews for two different movies this past year alone. This all-female school, tucked away in Decatur, Georgia, attracts studious women as well as movie studios. Agnes Scott offers a strong liberal arts curriculum and a lengthy list of traditions that together form a unique "Agnes Scott experience."

A Peach of a Campus

"Agnes Scott's campus is absolutely beautiful!" exclaimed one junior. Students universally share this sentiment, and maintain that the "gorgeous surroundings" are among the school's best features. The campus, tucked away in a "quiet, mostly residential" neighborhood, overflows with Gothic and Victorian buildings. Several of the administrative buildings are so architecturally noteworthy that they are featured in the National Register of Historic Places and the American Institute of Architects Guide to Atlanta. The campus is built around a grassy expanse known as the Quadrangle, or "Quad." Big brick and stone dorms frame this "green oasis," and provide scenery for those studying and sunbathing on the "always green" lawn. As one sophomore said, "It doesn't take more than five minutes to get anywhere from anywhere else" on this small, centralized campus. Students seem to appreciate the intimacy of their secluded environment, praising the "quiet and solitude" it offers. As one amazed student commented, "You can barely even hear the cars passing by." When seeking even more peace and quiet, students frequent the "Secret Garden," a courtyard within the library. But as one senior said, "Daydreaming is possible anywhere on this campus. There are so many trees and flowers that it feels like an English country home." Another noted that "the school really prides itself on maintaining this suburban forest—the landscaping budget is through the roof!"

Recent construction and renovations have ensured that Agnes Scott has modern facilities despite its historical status. Students praised the expansion of the McCain Library and the recent opening of new Alston Campus Center, "the most popular place on campus" complete with a bookstore, e-café and post office. The Science Center is the jewel of Agnes Scott's $120 million building program. This state-of-the-art facility opened in the spring of 2003 and "is a symbol of Agnes Scott College's commitment to putting women in the field of science."

The college lies on the edge of downtown Decatur. While Decatur is full of "cute, eclectic shops and great coffee houses, the nearest supermarket is a good 20-minute walk away," moaned one freshman. For this reason, students stress the importance of having access to a car on campus. "While not a necessity, it will make your life a lot more pleasant," recommended one junior. For those without their own vehicles, borrowing cars is standard practice. Students report that because of Agnes Scott's small-town setting, "safety is simply not an issue on campus." The school police are "everywhere all the time" and "in fact there are more problems with public safety accosting boyfriends and guests than there are of public safety not being present."

Within this self-contained environment, traditions flourish. "There is the sense that you are connected to generations of Agnes Scott women," said one senior. Annual events such as senior investiture, when each senior is capped with an academic mortar board, and the ring ceremony, an evening when every sophomore receives her class ring in the school chapel, create a "strong sense of belonging." Seniors traditionally ring the bell in the tower of Agnes Scott Hall when they are offered a job or get accepted to grad school, and when Agnes Scott women get engaged they are thrown into the pond in the Alumnae Garden. The biggest annual event is Black Cat week, described by one junior as "homecoming minus the football team." Black Cat falls at the beginning of the year and "the entire week is just crazy with competitions between classes." Each class is assigned a color and a mascot and plays elaborate practical jokes on the others. The freshmen traditionally try to keep their mascot, a secret while the sophomores try to guess what it is. The week includes a bonfire where each class sings "sister songs," and the Junior Production, an hour-long series of skits satirizing administrators, professors, and the college in general. A formal followed by an awards ceremony marks the end of the festivities.

Scotties' Honor

Another long-held Agnes Scott tradition is the honor system. As one student put it, "The honor system is our defining characteristic." The code applies to all aspects of life at Agnes Scott and creates a level of trust among faculty and students rarely found at other schools. Students take unproctored, self-scheduled exams, "which are probably the best thing that we have here," said one junior. Students are expected to turn themselves in for code violations and cases go before the student-run Honor Court.

Agnes Scott students take pride in their academic integrity and many students describe classes as "extremely demanding." Professors generally have extremely high expectations, but students enjoy rising to the challenge. "I'm thrilled about being pushed to my limits and exceeding them," said one sophomore. Students also report that professors are "very accessible" and caring. "Agnes Scott professors are awesome. They will do whatever they need to do to help you succeed," raved one freshman. Except for a few foreign language sections, classes are taught exclusively by professors. Class sizes are small, and the average class "never has more than 40 girls. There are usually more like 15 or 20, although English classes can have as few as four or five." While students appreciate the individual attention such small classes allow, "sometimes it would be nice to be anonymous on those days when you didn't finish the reading."

Scotties major in a wide variety of areas, although the science and English departments are "standouts." Students stress that women should major in something that interests them: "a good major would be something that you love to do, because you going to have to work hard, no matter what you decide." Slackers beware because "to be perfectly honest, there is no such thing as an easy major because the professors here are so demanding." Grade inflation is "a dream"; in reality, "deflation is more likely; the English department is rumored to have a cap on the number of As given per class."

"There is the sense that you are connected to generations of Agnes Scott women."

All students must fulfill distributional requirements and take certain required courses in order to graduate. Requirements include an intermediate-level foreign language class, two physical education semester hours, two semesters of science (one with lab), and one semester each of fine arts, literature, history or political science, philosophy, and math. First-year students must also take a first-year seminar and English 101, a composition and literature course. Some wish the requirements were less extensive, but most acknowledged that the expectations went along with their goal of a well-rounded education. As one sophomore said, 'I think that the requirements represent a good variety of knowledge that all people need to function in the world; it's a part of the liberal arts education experience." Students also have few complaints about registration, although "freshman sometimes get stuck with the leftovers," as upperclassmen have priority in class selection. International study is a popular option, and over half the student body goes abroad sometime during their four years. For those looking for new experiences a little closer to campus, Agnes Scott has cross-registration privileges with all Atlanta universities. Students interested in engineering particularly appreciate the opportunity to enroll in a duel degree program with the Georgia Institute of Technology.

Atlanta: Bright Lights, Big City

Agnes Scott students appreciate nearby Atlanta for more than its academic opportunities. With downtown only six miles from campus and easily accessible through MARTA, Atlanta's rapid transit system, Scotties "don't run into that small-town problem of being bored all the time." Agnes Scott has no sororities and there are few parties on campus ("Agnes Scott should be #1 on the Stone Cold Sober College list," remarked one senior), so those who choose to party often explore the "awesome" Atlanta club scene. Attending frat parties at Georgia Tech and Emory is another popular option, especially for those under 21. Those of legal drinking age frequent Atlanta's bars and nightclubs and "some of the better Tech and Emory parties." The administration is "extremely strict" about underage drinking, and all agree that drinking on campus is "all but impossible." Although many leave campus to seeking alcohol, as one junior said, "non-drinkers are very welcome on campus. This is not a party school." Upperclassmen stress the importance of getting off campus and note "how easy it is to be consumed by academics." Yet many appreciate the studious atmosphere. As one freshman said, "I came here to get an education and Agnes Scott lets me focus on that goal."

Students do stick around campus to participate in the many clubs and extracurriculars. "It is strongly encouraged for Agnes Scott women to be involved in extracurricular activities and the majority do so," explained one sophomore. The student senate and sports are both reportedly popular, as are more unusual clubs like the handicrafts and origami clubs. Agnes Scott is a Division III school and some athletes lament the minor role of sports: "Is there any team spirit? No. We're lucky if we get 10 people to show up to our soccer games unless the dining hall decides to serve dinner at the field." Many however praise the "thriving cultural scene." "Whether it is the African–West Indian Society, the Asian Women Society, the Hispanic Association, the German House, or the Muslim Student Association, there are outlets for all groups to feel comfortable and to share their culture with the campus," said one junior.

Agnes Scott students hail from all over the United States as well as from 31 countries, creating a student body that is "ethnically, geographically, and culturally diverse, especially for a small, Southern women's college." One junior did note that despite the mix of ethnicities, "most everyone it seems is Southern and the Southern mindset can be quite a jolt for us Northerners." Still, "the student body is diverse enough to defy the Agnes Scott stereotypes that we're all either lesbians or stuck-up snobs," said one freshman.

A/C and Walk-in Closets: Living the Good Life

No matter where they call home, Agnes Scott students agree that the "palatial" dorms are "downright luxurious." That's a good thing, since all students must live on campus unless married or living at home. Freshmen live together in spacious doubles in either Winship or Walters Hall. The rooms are "bigger then any freshman dorms I have seen at other schools and have walk-in closets, a major perk," said one freshman. Visiting hours for boys, known as parietals, are stricter for first-years than for upperclassmen. Even when parietal restrictions are loosened, bringing boys home can be an awkward experience. Before a boy enters a hall, the Agnes Scott host must shout "man on the hall," at which point "every head in the hall turns and you feel ridiculous for trying to have a guest," lamented one senior. After their first year, students have the choice to either live in one of the traditional dormitories for upperclass students or move to Avery Glen, a college apartment complex near central campus. Three theme houses offer another option. Themes change annually and are chosen based on student petitions, so "they very much reflect the student body."

Students are reserved in their praise for the dining hall food. They describe Evans, the one central dining hall, as a "fried chicken and collard greens kind of place." Meal variety, or lack there of, is a common complaint, as are the limited hours. However, Mollie's Grill and the Black Cat Café, both located in the student center, offer later hours and "a welcome break from Evans." Vegetarian options are always available. All students are required to have a meal plan of some sort, ranging from five meals to all 21 meals a week. Eating out in Decatur or Atlanta is popular, but "the dining hall is great for just hanging out with friends or meeting new people." "While there are definitely cliques, they don't mind when you sit with them. Everyone is so nice here," said one sophomore.

Set in the beautiful, verdant town of Decatur just a few minutes away from Atlanta, Agnes Scott offers an excellent education to a motivated and diverse group of women who love their school. While a small, Southern, women's college is not right for everyone, those who choose Agnes Scott join a long and special tradition. As one student put it, "being at a small all-girls college isn't what you'd think. This has really been the best experience of my life and I wouldn't trade it for anything." —*Amelia Page*

FYI

If you come to Agnes Scott, you better bring "a fan, an open mind, and an umbrella, because our president rains tears during EVERY speech she gives!"

What is the typical weekend schedule? "Friday, homework and a movie on campus; Saturday, sleep in, study, party at Georgia Tech; Sunday, study, study, break for meals, study some more.

If I could change one thing about Agnes Scott, "I'd leave out the drama. With 900 girls there's a lot of drama."

Three things every student at Agnes Scott should do before graduating are "go to a Tech football game, act in Junior Production, and take advantage of the study abroad programs."

Emory University

Address: 1380 South Oxford Road, NE; Atlanta, GA 30322
Phone: 800-727-6036
E-mail address: admiss@learnlink.emory.edu
Web site URL: www.emory.edu
Founded: 1836
Private or Public: private
Religious affiliation: Methodist
Location: urban
Undergraduate enrollment: 6,285
Total enrollment: NA
Percent Male/Female: 44%/56%
Percent Minority: 30%
Percent African-American: 9%
Percent Asian: 15%
Percent Hispanic: 3%
Percent Native-American: 0%
Percent in-state/out of state: 28%/72%
Percent Pub HS: 65%
Number of Applicants: 9,789
Percent Accepted: 42%
Percent Accepted who enroll: 33%
Entering: 1,337
Transfers: 82
Application Deadline: 15 Jan
Mean SAT: NA
Mean ACT: NA
Middle 50% SAT range: V 640-720, M 660-740
Middle 50% ACT range: 29-33
3 Most popular majors: business administration, psychology, economics
Retention: 93%
Graduation rate: 87%
On-campus housing: 64%
Fraternities: 30%
Sororities: 30%
Library: 2,705,123 volumes
Tuition and Fees: $27,952
Room and Board: $8,920
Financial aid, first-year: 35%
Varsity or Club Athletes: NA
Early Decision or Early Action Acceptance Rate: ED 61%

Every fall, former President Jimmy Carter holds an open forum with students at Emory. The Georgia native answers any question a student throws at him, formal or informal, from whether he wears boxers or briefs to his thoughts on the Clinton-Lewinsky scandal. Unique opportunities like this define the undergraduate experience at Emory, a university that manages a fusion of Southern style with challenging academics.

Academics in Atlanta

With 50 majors and 42 minors, Emory offers diverse academic opportunities for its students. The large number of premed students makes science majors the most difficult and competitive. Though the programs are rigorous, one senior who plans to go to dental school said, "if you are premed here you will be very well-prepared. Emory students go to some of the best med schools in the country." The emphasis on science at Emory does not mean that other areas are overlooked; the humanities and liberal arts fields are also intense and receive high marks from students. According to one junior, "science majors spend more time in labs, but humanities students spend more time reading and writing papers. The workload evens out in the end, so it just comes down to what you want to spend your time doing." Emory also offers a few special programs for undergraduates through its business and nursing schools. Students can apply to The Gozuieta Business School, or "B school" as it is known on campus, at the end of their sophomore year to receive a BA in business administration. However, students warn that these classes can be the most rigorous on campus. There is also a program for students to receive a BS in nursing through Emory's Nursing School.

The average class size at Emory is 20-50 students, though upper-level seminar classes can be as small as five to ten. Large introductory classes usually have TAs who grade student work, however all teaching is done by professors who draw rave reviews from their students. Students consistently describe professors as "very accessible" and "accommodating." One sophomore appreciated the flexibility of his professors when he had to miss exam period to have surgery. Another senior remembered how one of her professors "stayed up with us until 3 AM at a review session the night before the midterm." Professors often have students over for dinner at their homes, and are always willing to schedule extra office hours to meet with undergraduates. One student summed up the teaching philosophy at Emory like this: "professors truly want to know students who truly want to learn from them. If you show that you want to learn, they'll give you everything they have to offer."

Frat Parties and Dooley's Ball

Emory's on-campus social scene centers on "Fraternity Row," the aptly named street that houses the school's 15 fraternities. Two or three of these frat houses (or "frat mansions," as one student called them) host parties each weekend. None of Emory's nine sororities have houses on campus, but the president and officers of each sorority often live together in an apartment or house, and the chapters frequently rent downtown bars or nightclubs for parties on the weekends. Statistically, about 40 percent of the student body is Greek, but some say that it can feel more like 80 percent, especially at parties. Still, many non-Greeks maintain they rarely feel left out of the social scene, and that many Greeks are friends with non-Greeks, as well. Rush takes place during second semester to allow freshman to make friends before joining Greek organizations, and most feel that the rush process is fairly laid-back.

Frat parties usually revolve around drinking. In theory, the frats only serve alcohol to students 21 and older, but these rules are rarely enforced. Police are strict about open container laws, dissuading students from roaming campus with open alcoholic beverages. Because Emory is located in a residential area, party-throwers must be careful to observe local noise ordinances. One junior commented that the frat scene has "broken down over last few years because of new regulations against alcohol, noise, and the number of people at parties." Still, frat parties continue to be popular social events on campus.

The Student Programming Council, composed of members of Emory's student body, sponsors other on-campus events throughout the year. The freshman semiformal dance is always well-attended. The homecoming dance is far less popular, probably because Emory has no football team. The Council also organizes band parties that bring well-known groups like Ludacris, The Dave Matthews Band, and The Ataris to campus each semester. Attendance at these events usually depends on the band, but according to one student, "most people usually leave once the free food runs out." Without a doubt, the most popular school-sponsored event of the year is Dooley's Ball, a dance held in honor of Emory's mysterious unofficial mascot. Originally, Dooley was a skeleton in an 1899 biology lab that wrote anonymous articles in the school's newspaper, the Emory Phoenix. Nowadays, Dooley takes human form and shows up at special occasions, always accompanied by a group of bodyguards dressed in black. Dooley's identity is carefully guarded, though it's common knowledge on campus that a secret society of students maintains the tradition. Dooley's Ball is the culmination of Dooley's Week, a celebration featuring theme days, special activities, and, of course, parties. The week also includes special visits by Dooley himself, who has the authority to dismiss any class on campus with a mere squirt of his water gun. The Ball, held outdoors on the intramural fields, also features a dramatic entrance by Dooley and his entourage. One student commented that the Dooley phenomenon is "strange and a little scary, but its one of the things that makes Emory really unique. Its also one of the only times that you'll see any school spirit on campus."

Welcome to Atlanta

Most students cite Emory's location just outside of downtown Atlanta as one of the best attributes of the school. Emory Village, the area just outside of campus, offers an assortment of restaurants and convenience stores to serve student needs, but many also make the 15-minute trip to downtown Atlanta to take advantage of the great shopping, eating, attractions such as Olympic Park, and the city's numerous bars and nightclubs. Off-campus nightlife forms a huge part of the social scene at Emory, and more than one student cautioned, "having a fake ID is key to enjoying Atlanta." If you can get past the bouncers at the doors, there are bars and clubs to suit every partygoer's taste. From the upscale bars in Midtown, to the dance clubs in Buckhead, to the hippy bars in Little Five Points, Atlanta offers students a variety of alternatives to the on-campus social scene. Some clubs also sponsor well-attended Emory nights on the weekends. Being in Atlanta has more serious advantages as well. Aside from its thriving nightlife, the city is a great place for students to find jobs and internships for the summer after graduation.

"There are too many designer purses here for my tastes, but they aren't necessarily a requirement."

With so much to do off campus, many students feel that having a car is necessary at Emory. While freshmen aren't allowed to have cars on campus, one junior suggested, "there are ways of sneaking them in." Despite the availability of public transportation and a school-sponsored shuttle service to the supermarket and a nearby mall, most students feel it is easier to drive. Cars are also status symbols on campus. "Something like 1 in 5 students here drives a BMW," noted one sophomore.

Preppy, Fit, and Motivated

When asked to describe their peers, many Emory students agree that the majority of the student body is wealthy, upper-class, attractive, and fit. Some feel that this contributes to a snobby and cliquish atmosphere, while others say that they had no problems getting to know people. One sophomore said, "lots of people here look snobby, but once you get to know them they can be very down to earth." Many students appreciated getting to know people when they first arrived at Emory through FAME, Emory's mandatory freshman advisory program, which matches groups of frosh with staff, faculty, and upperclassman. Still, they felt that the social scene gave way too quickly to separate cliques. Students are satisfied with the level of racial diversity, but feel that there is too much self-segregation among students, making it hard to get to know people from different backgrounds. Many also comment that a disproportionate number of their fellow students hail from Long Island and elsewhere in the Northeast.

Students at Emory are highly motivated and intelligent. One freshman commented, "the majority of kids here are overachievers." Some feel that this creates a competitive atmosphere, particularly among the premed science majors. But it also means that Emory students are actively involved and strongly opinionated about their causes. "From Free Tibet to a group that advocates better wages for university workers, to experimental theater, everyone here is involved in something," says one sophomore. Community service activities, coordinated by the Volunteer Emory program, also draw student involvement.

Looking good is a priority for many Emory students, producing an attractive and image-conscious student body. One senior related that "there are too many designer purses here for my tastes, but they aren't necessarily a requirement." Students take full advantage of Emory's spacious gym facilities and participate in many intramural and club sports. Though students are "terribly apathetic toward sports," some of Emory's Division III teams in sports like swimming, soccer, and volleyball are competitive. Many students feel that one of Emory's flaws is the lack of a football team. "It makes it difficult for students to really rally some school spirit," said one junior.

Country Club Campus

Students at Emory love their campus, which they describe as "gorgeous" and "very ritzy" with "beautiful Spanish-style architecture." Georgia's mild weather makes for beautiful landscaping, and students spend time outside year-round on Emory's spacious quads. The campus has renovated almost all of its campus buildings in the last 15 years. Students rave about the updates, which include the installation of computers in the gym and a gorgeous new reading room in the school's main library. Between the brand-new buildings and the well-manicured lawns, students gush that Emory's campus looks "just like a country club."

One senior commented, "Emory has the cleanest, nicest, newest dorms of any school I've ever visited." Ten dorms house first-year students, each with its own perks and disadvantages. Dobbs has the smallest rooms but the most central location, while Turman offers "enormous rooms" but is further from campus. Freshmen are usually assigned to double rooms, though some singles are available. All dorms are air-conditioned and most have sinks in the rooms. There are also special theme wings or floors for students who want to live with others who share similar interests. Sophomores have similar choices for on-campus living, but many choose to move off campus and into one of the many apartments or houses available in the surrounding residential area. The most coveted dorms are on the Clairmont Campus, a short shuttle ride from Emory's central campus. Available only to upperclassmen, these apartment-style dorms are "drop-dead gorgeous." One resident bemoaned, "I don't want to graduate and move out of here!" Each four-person apartment includes four bedrooms, two full bathrooms, a kitchen, washer and dryer, living room, and dining room. The facilities include four outdoor swimming pools (two of which are Olympic-size) as well as basketball courts, tennis courts, volleyball courts, an indoor gym, and a student center called the "SAC" with lots of study rooms and a grill-style cafeteria. These luxury dorms do come at a higher price than other campus housing, but almost everyone agrees that it is well worth it.

Great Weather and a Great Degree

Students at Emory seem satisfied with their experiences. Though some bemoan the "snobby attitude" and "competitiveness" of their fellow students, almost all feel that they are getting a great education and that being in Atlanta is a huge asset. As one student observed of Emory's unique atmosphere, "where else can you get Ivy League academics south of the Mason-Dixon Line? We have better weather and you still get a great degree." —*Jessica Lenox*

FYI

If you come to Emory, you'd better bring a "car and a Prada handbag."

What is the typical weekend schedule? "Thursday night, dancing in Buckhead; Friday night, fraternity party or a bar in Midtown; Saturday night, off-campus party followed by late night at Maggie's; Sunday, brunch and work, work, work!"

If I could change one thing about Emory, I'd "give it a football team!"

Three things every student at Emory should do before graduating are "take a long weekend to Mardi Gras, have lunch with the dean, and lay out at the Clairmont pool instead of studying."

Georgia Institute of Technology

Address: 225 North Avenue, NW; Atlanta, GA 30332
Phone: 404-894-4154
E-mail address: admission@gatech.edu
Web site URL: www.admission.gatech.edu
Founded: 1885
Private or Public: public
Religious affiliation: none
Location: urban
Undergraduate enrollment: 11,456
Total enrollment: NA
Percent Male/Female: 72%/28%
Percent Minority: 29%
Percent African-American: 7%
Percent Asian: 15%
Percent Hispanic: 3%
Percent Native-American: 0%
Percent in-state/out of state: 68%/32%
Percent Pub HS: NA
Number of Applicants: 8,953
Percent Accepted: 59%
Percent Accepted who enroll: 43%
Entering: 2,281
Transfers: 402
Application Deadline: 15 Jan
Mean SAT: NA
Mean ACT: NA
Middle 50% SAT range: V 600-690, M 650-740
Middle 50% ACT range: 26-31
3 Most popular majors: engineering, business, computer sciences
Retention: 89%
Graduation rate: 68%
On-campus housing: 60%
Fraternities: 23%
Sororities: 25%
Library: 2,258,892 volumes
Tuition and Fees: $3,726 in; $14,506 out
Room and Board: $6,150
Financial aid, first-year: 31%
Varsity or Club Athletes: 11%
Early Decision or Early Action Acceptance Rate: NA

When Vice President Richard Nixon met Soviet Premier Nikita Khrushchev in Moscow in 1959, the two leaders partook in a little tussle known today as the Kitchen Debate. Yet between their political bickering, they joined together in a rousing (and tension-relieving) rendition of the one song that they both knew: "The Ramblin' Wreck from Georgia Tech." While the highly-publicized event certainly boosted the preeminence of the song, the first line—"I'm a ramblin' wreck from Georgia Tech and a helluva engineer"—provides a testament to Georgia Tech's status as one of the top engineering schools in the country. Students who spend their college years at this mecca for research and learning leave with a degree that speaks for itself, attesting to the demanding and specialized undergraduate education that they have completed.

Engineering . . . or a Life?

Across the board, students report academics at Georgia Tech to be "challenging" and "time-consuming." All students, regardless of their major, must satisfy the requirements of the core curriculum, which includes two semesters of English, two lab science courses, Calculus I or II (depending upon the major), and a selection of courses from the humanities, fine arts, and social sciences. While most Tech students readily favor differentials over diction, the core curriculum appears to have its fans. "A lot of people like the core curriculum," admitted one student, "because it prepares you well for the more advanced courses that you'll take in your major." Students cite many of the engineering majors—specifically aerospace engineering, biomedical engineering, nuclear and radiological engineering, and polymer and fiber engineering—as the most difficult to complete, but likewise regard them as the cream of the crop. In fact, according to *U.S. News and World Report* in 2003, nine undergraduate engineering programs at Tech ranked among the top ten programs nationwide in their respective categories. By contrast, the management major has the distinction of being the easiest major at Tech; as one student put it, "management majors start out as engineers..." but eventually switch majors due to the intensity and rigor of the engineering programs. Still other students choose to pursue a course of study separate from either engineering or management, majoring in disciplines like international studies, psychology, or one of the biological or physical sciences.

Chemistry I, Physics I, and Calculus II are widely regarded as "weeder" courses and traditionally have lower pass rates than the analogous intro classes in other departments. Performing well in these courses, according to one student, depends heavily upon "your high school background and the professor." In general, students describe their professors as "available" and "accessible" but acknowledge that professors may be hit or miss. "People come here from all over the world to research," one student commented, "and many of the professors are foreign and have thick accents, which can make them difficult to understand." In addition, a handful of professors have been placed on academic probation in recent years for not passing enough students. Overall, however, students agree that professors "want you to pass" and "always try to make themselves available." Remarked one freshman, "My Calc professor is 'genius' but very approachable." The difficulty of a particular class can also depend upon the quality of the TAs, who lead recitation sections and generally receive positive marks from the students.

In addition to its course offerings, Georgia Tech provides a number of unique academic programs and opportunities to its students that help define the academic experience of a Tech undergrad. The Co-op program, short for the Georgia Tech Cooperative Education Program and one of the largest of its kind in the nation, is a five-year program in which students gain actual on-the-job experience in their majors by alternating between a semester of school and a semester of full-time work. Over 700 companies, including big wigs like Coca-Cola, BellSouth, and General Electric, participate in the program. Students are also privy to a vast array of research opportunities, most of which take place in Tech's cutting-edge laboratories.

Pocket Protectors, Women, and Buzz

Georgia Tech prides itself in its diverse student body. Although Georgians constitute 65 percent of the undergraduate population, the remaining 35 percent hails from across the country and the rest of the globe, including a large number of students native to China, India, and South Korea. Most students enter as prospective engineers, but, as one student puts it, not everyone fits the "nerdy guy with high-waters and glasses" stereotype. In truth, however, some students "do love calculus and do talk about it in their free time," and many students eagerly admit to studying in excess of twenty hours during the week. "Intelligent" is the adjective most frequently used to by Tech students to describe themselves, with "focused" running a close second.

Perhaps the defining feature of the Tech student body, or rather the most conspicuous feature, is summed up by "The Ratio," which refers to the disproportionate number of male to female students at Tech. "The Ratio" has remained stable at 3:1 for a number of years. The disparate composition of the student body can make dating—and social interaction in general—either "really easy or really difficult," depending upon the student's orientation. However, Tech's close proximity to other colleges and universities in Atlanta, including Emory University, Georgia State University, Spelman College, and Morehouse College, helps bring balance to the unique complexities spawned by "The Ratio."

Although many on-campus clubs and organizations throw parties on the weekends, the epicenter of the Tech social scene is the Greek system. "If you're Greek, you're social and you do things on weekends," commented one student. "If not, you tend to stay in your room." Approximately 25 percent of Tech students go Greek, usually at the beginning of their freshman year, and become members of one of the 42 chapters on campus. Fraternities tend to sponsor most of the major parties, often hosting popular local bands and other forms of entertainment; one frat recently sponsored Southern favorite Sister Hazel. However, very few parties are closed to non-Greeks, so students, especially females, who want to experience the social perks of Greek life without being affiliated with a chapter are generally free to do so.

"Not everyone fits the nerdy guy with high-waters and glasses stereotype."

For those students not interested in Greek life, Georgia Tech's location in the heart of Atlanta provides a plethora of other outlets. The Varsity, the world's largest drive-in restaurant, serves up "naked dogs with a side of strings" (i.e. plain hot dogs and french fries) from its North Avenue location. Numerous other eateries, restaurants, and pizza parlors—including Fellini's and Mellow Mushroom—are within walking distance to the campus and offer inexpensive meals. A prolific local music scene fills the many Midtown clubs in Atlanta every weekend, and the Buckhead bar scene, accessible by car or MARTA (Metro Atlanta Rapid Transit Authority), provides yet another alternative to on-campus Greek life.

Aside from nightlife and weekend parties, the campus scene revolves heavily around clubs, organizations, and varsity and intramural sports. Tech boasts one of the largest intramural sports programs in the country, with three different divisions that cater to participants at all levels. In the fall, Yellow Jacket football dominates the weekend scene, as tens of thousands of students and alumni—donned in bright yellow and black—pack into Bobby Dodd Stadium for home games. SWARM, a student organization devoted to promoting school spirit, is notorious for its conspicuous support of the school's varsity athletics, especially the football team and the perennially strong basketball and baseball teams.

East vs. West

Many Tech students are pleasantly surprised to find that the campus, despite its location in downtown Atlanta, has the appearance and atmosphere of a typical college. Commented one freshman, "The campus is designed so well, I forget that I'm in a city." Green space dots the campus, and students appear generally satisfied with the quantity of undeveloped land, although some students still lament the overriding urban character of the school.

The campus is roughly divided into two halves—east and west—each with distinct personalities. East campus is older and, according to one student, tends to "be more social because the buildings are closer together and the football stadium and the Greek houses are only a short walk away." West campus, facing in the opposite direction of the city, contains many of the newer buildings on campus, which tend to be less concentrated and thus less conducive to social interaction. East and west campus each has its own dining hall, although freshmen and some sophomores tend to be the major patrons of both. According to one student, however, most of the classes "are usually in between east and west campus, so it doesn't really matter which side you live on—it's just a matter of preference."

Students joke about "east coast" and "west coast" rivalries but agree that the campus layout is rather conducive to maintaining a collegiate atmosphere that keeps students on campus rather than dispersed throughout Atlanta. Tech has a cohesive and spirited student body, in spite of its seemingly odd combination of "ramblin' wrecks" and nerdy engineers, and boasts an academic prize lucrative enough to draw some of the world's most promising undergrads. To Tech's many aspiring engineers, it is a value unparalleled in the country.—*Kent Garber*

FYI

If you come to Georgia Tech, you'd better bring "a ruler, your TI-89, and all the other help you can get."

What is the typical weekend schedule? "Friday and Saturday, forget about work and party at the frats; Sunday, face reality and study 'til Monday."

If I could change one thing about Georgia Tech, I'd "equalize The Ratio."

Three things every student at Georgia Tech should do before graduating are "go to the UGA-Georgia Tech football game at Bobby Dodd Stadium, try waffle fries at Chick-fil-A, and spend a night in Buckhead or Midtown."

Morehouse College

Address: 830 Westview Drive, SW; Atlanta, GA 30314
Phone: 800-851-1254
E-mail address: admissions@morehouse.edu
Web site URL: www.morehouse.edu
Founded: 1867
Private or Public: private
Religious affiliation: none
Location: urban
Undergraduate enrollment: 2,738
Total enrollment: NA
Percent Male/Female: 100%/0%
Percent Minority: 99%
Percent African-American: 96%
Percent Asian: NA
Percent Hispanic: NA
Percent Native-American: NA
Percent in-state/out of state: 34%/66%
Percent Pub HS: 76%
Number of Applicants: 2,394
Percent Accepted: 64%
Percent Accepted who enroll: 57%
Entering: 879
Transfers: 80
Application Deadline: 15 Feb
Mean SAT: NA
Mean ACT: NA
Middle 50% SAT range: V 480-590, M 480-600
Middle 50% ACT range: 20-24
3 Most popular majors: business/commerce, biology, psychology
Retention: 84%
Graduation rate: 58%
On-campus housing: 48%
Fraternities: 5%
Sororities: NA
Library: NA
Tuition and Fees: $13,760
Room and Board: $8,172
Financial aid, first-year: 97%
Varsity or Club Athletes: 5%
Early Decision or Early Action Acceptance Rate: NA

Undergrads may learn engineering or biology in their time at Morehouse, but most importantly, students say they learn the true meaning and value of the word brotherhood. For many of Morehouse's illustrious alumni, such as Dr. Martin Luther King, Jr., brotherhood has been much more than just a buzzword. Morehouse, known affectionately by its graduates as the "House," changed their lives and, in turn, allowed them to change the world.

Men Only!

The only historically African-American all-male college in the United States, Morehouse prides itself on its traditions of brotherhood, which date back to the college's beginnings in 1867. Incoming students are taught the meaning of brotherhood early in their time at Morehouse with the tradition of Spirit Night. In this traditional ceremony, underclassmen link their arms and form a circle that upperclassmen try to break. Through this struggle, Morehouse men say they learn to hold on to their brotherhood above all else. As one freshman said, "Spirit Night made me realize how much I could trust my new friends. I'd only known them for a little while, but we all held on, supporting one another like we'd been together forever."

The tradition of brotherhood is supported by Morehouse's strong academic reputation, reflected today in the extensive General Studies requirements, which comprise 68 of the 124 credits needed to graduate. Each student must complete one-year courses in composition, literature, history of civilizations (which has a special focus on ancient African civilizations), social science, and physical education. Also required is one semester each of art, music, speech, religion, philosophy, physical science, and biological science, as well as two years of a foreign language. The completion of this rigorous academic program lends truth to the school's unofficial motto: "You can always tell a Morehouse man, but you can never tell him much." Academics are further supplemented with cultural instruction. Students are required to attend the Crown Forum, a weekly address by prominent African-American leaders that many students see as a vital part of the House's social mission. "The speakers at the Crown Forum are one of the most important part of a Morehouse education. Knowledge is just knowledge without the ability to make a difference in the real world. The speakers teach us that," one student said.

One major benefit of Morehouse's urban Atlanta location is its membership in the Atlanta University Center (AUC), a consortium of five schools including Clark Atlanta, Morris Brown, the Interdenominational Theological Center, and Morehouse's sister school, the all-female Spelman College. Morehouse students can cross-register at any of the other four AUC schools, provided that the chair of the department at each school grants permission and that the course is not offered at Morehouse if it is within the student's major.

Pre-professionals Rule

The most popular majors at Morehouse, Biology, Business, and Engineering, hint at the student body's strong preference toward pre-professional subjects. For students who desire further challenge and achievement, the college offers "3-2" programs in engineering and architecture. After three years at Morehouse, students can earn an advanced degree (in two years) at such schools as Georgia Tech or the University of Michigan. Morehouse also has an honors program, beginning in the freshman year, that offers dedicated students more advanced classes and a special diploma. Students report that a definite "easy A" is Intro to Visual Art, whose toughest requirement reportedly involves "just visiting a few museums in the area."

Morehouse is also notable for its professors. Spike Lee, an alumnus, returns fairly often to lecture. Students describe their relationships with professors as "extremely close." Many students say that it is common for undergrads and teachers to have lunch together, or go to museums or parks outside of class. One student claimed that he got invited to dinner at professors' homes on a regular basis.

Although some students said that the academics at Morehouse can be very competitive, many declared that the tradition of brotherhood on campus extends into the classroom. "At Morehouse all of your fellow students want you to do well. If you are having trouble, all you have to do is ask the person sitting next to you. People are always tutoring one another," said one student.

Where'd Everybody Go?

One statistic that attests to Morehouse's challenging academic regimen is its low student retention rate. One student declared "it's definitely a tough school to be successful in—people drop out of here like flies," while another added that his junior class of 600 began as a freshman class of 900. Other academic problems related by undergrads include difficulty of getting into required classes. Occasionally, seniors are forced to postpone their graduation because they were shut out of one or two classes, students said. Students cited financial aid problems as a common reason for leaving Morehouse.

Undergrads report that they spend much of their time studying at one of several libraries in the close vicinity of Morehouse. Woodruff Library, the central library for the five-member institutions of the Atlanta University Center, gets mixed reviews. While some students reported that it is especially good for "social" studying, others declared that the number and variety of students who share the library make resources hard to come by. Students who desire quietier studying travel to the libraries at either Georgia State University or Emory. Hardcore studying takes place in the Frederick Douglass Commons, a student center at Morehouse where students have access to study rooms and materials. "What you learn here, they don't teach anywhere else."

"These programs enable us to teach our code of brotherhood to younger students in Atlanta who are particularly in need of love and respect," one student said.

Undergrads live in seven dorms on campus. Graves Hall, the oldest building on campus, is reportedly the best, as it has air-conditioning. Hubert is said to be the least appealing, with no air-conditioning and small rooms. Students can unwind at Kilgore, a dorm that houses pool and Ping-Pong tables, big screen TVs, and a snack shop that stays open until midnight. Dorms have friendly rivalries and are unofficially identified by Greek letters and hand signals. Dorm restrictions include no alcohol and specific visiting hours for women. Some residents call restricted visitation "an initiation for freshmen," but admit that the rules are obeyed without much active enforcement. Undergrads seeking relaxed rules of conduct say the best bet is to move off-campus. Most students say they prefer private apartments on Fair Street to those in the West End, where there is college-owned housing removed from the main dorm area. However, residents say that facilities in this area are "run-down."

Students who live on campus are required to be on a full meal plan that they describe as "below average," but "improving." Those desperate for improved fare eat out at places like Spegal's, a popular pub and restaurant, or fast-food restaurants at West End, a mall close to campus.

Athletics play an important role at Morehouse. The most popular teams, football and basketball, draw dedicated fan support, particularly when Morehouse plays its perennial rivals Howard and Tuskegee. Students say the tennis team is also extremely popular and successful. Archer Hall, the gym, underwent several renovations for the 1996 Summer Olympics.

Reaching Out

Students say they are particularly proud of the extracurricular activities at Morehouse, citing a strong devotion to community service programs, particularly several mentoring programs in which students act as big brothers or academic tutors to inner-city youth. "These programs enable us to teach our code of brotherhood to younger students in Atlanta who are particularly in need of love and respect," one student said. Students are also quick to point out that the popular Glee Club performed at President Clinton's first inauguration. Other organizations, such as the Pre-Law Society, the Health Care Society, and the Business Association, reflect the high aspirations of Morehouse students.

Although some students report that they were skeptical about attending an all-male college at first, many say that Morehouse provides them with the best of both worlds. They feel the all-male environment on campus allows them to cultivate a strong feeling of brotherhood. In fact, undergrads say, the high female-to-male ratio of the AUC provides students with more than adequate opportunities to meet and party with women.

Students say that the Morehouse social scene is "perfect for the challenging academic atmosphere." The campus is reportedly calm during the week, to allow for plenty of studying. Over the weekend, however, students can choose from innumerable parties, AUC unity rallies, picnics, concerts, or excursions to a local nightclub called Club Garage. Many students say that homecoming is one of the prime social events of the year and is traditionally a time for graduates and their families to return to the House to reminisce. The largest social event of the year, Freaknic, is one that is alternately loved or despised by the student body. While many students report the annual event, which consumes most of Atlanta, is the best party in the entire country, others complain that the large number of visiting students, reportedly 20,000 in recent years, absolutely prevents the students from being able to drive anywhere in downtown Atlanta.

Students consistently say that the one aspect that makes Morehouse unique is its deeply ingrained sense of tradition and brotherhood. As one student said, "What you learn here, they don't teach anywhere else. And I don't mean pre-law. I mean the overwhelming sense that you are truly a part of something great and that you can accomplish anything you want, simply because you are a Morehouse man. Even today, when students say they are only attending their college for a diploma and a few connections, being a Morehouse man still means something."—*Dylan Howard and Staff*

FYI

If you come to Morehouse, you'd better bring "brotherhood and friendship."

What is the typical weekend schedule? "Friday: study in the afternoon and chill with friends at night; Saturday: hang out in Atlanta; Sunday: work out and get back to studying."

If I could change one thing about Morehouse, "I'd make the weekdays more social."

Three things that every student at Morehouse must do before graduating are "Go to Freaknic, tutor inner-city youth, and go to Spegal's."

Spelman College

Address: 350 Spelman Lane, SW; Atlanta, GA 30314-4399
Phone: 800-982-2411
E-mail address: admiss@spelman.edu
Web site URL: www.spelman.edu
Founded: 1881
Private or Public: private
Religious affiliation: none
Location: urban
Undergraduate enrollment: 2,139
Total enrollment: NA
Percent Male/Female: 0%/100%
Percent Minority: 99%
Percent African-American: 92%
Percent Asian: 0%
Percent Hispanic: 0%
Percent Native-American: 0%
Percent in-state/out of state: 30%/70%
Percent Pub HS: NA
Number of Applicants: 3,751
Percent Accepted: 44%
Percent Accepted who enroll: 30%
Entering: 496
Transfers: 14
Application Deadline: 1 Feb
Mean SAT: NA
Mean ACT: NA
Middle 50% SAT range: V 500-590, M 480-570
Middle 50% ACT range: 20-24
3 Most popular majors: psychology, economics, political science and government
Retention: 90%
Graduation rate: 76%
On-campus housing: 59%
Fraternities: NA
Sororities: 4%
Library: 727,767 volumes
Tuition and Fees: $14,125
Room and Board: $7,625
Financial aid, first-year: 71%
Varsity or Club Athletes: 5%
Early Decision or Early Action Acceptance Rate: EA 33%

Founded in 1881, Spelman College is the oldest, and arguably most prestigious, historically black college for women in the United States. The college's unique mission—to instill in its students a profound sense of cultural identity and to prepare them for roles as life-long leaders—has guided the college since its inception and serves to this day as a bulwark for its preeminent reputation. Spelman's storied legacy over the past century, coupled with its ability to grow and evolve in the face of significant obstacles, is an enduring testament to the value of a Spelman education.

Learning with a Purpose

Spelman's core curriculum reflects an emphasis on academic exploration and cultural understanding. All students are required to fulfill broad divisional requirements by taking classes from the humanities, fine arts, social sciences and natural sciences, and must also complete specific courses—"African Diaspora and the World" and a course in international or women's studies—to lay the groundwork for the dynamic study of black history that underlies their Spelman experience. Additionally, the college places strong emphasis on written communication and requires that all students show proficiency in writing, which is normally satisfied by completing the obligatory first-year composition class, English 103. According to one senior, "Most students don't complain about the requirements, because they don't prevent you from taking the classes you really want to take."

Generally speaking, Spelman students take 16 credit hours, or four courses, per semester, and need a minimum of 120 credit hours to graduate. Of that number, approximately 40–48 hours fall within the student's major. Most students declare their major at the end of their sophomore year, although students intending to pursue majors in computer science, mathematics, and the natural sciences are strongly encouraged to take the appropriate introductory course during their first year. The workload is "rigorous"; as one student put it, "There is definitely a lot of outside research and studying that goes on here." Professors generally receive positive marks and are said to be "very knowledgeable in their field of study."

In addition to 23 regular majors, Spelman offers three special degree programs: the Dual Degree Engineering Program (DDEP), a human services major, and an "independent" major. DDEP candidates pursue a liberal arts degree from Spelman, usually completed in three years, and an engineering degree from a cooperating engineering institution—including the likes of Georgia Institute of Technology, California Institute of Technology, and Columbia University—for an additional two years. The human services major, another academic program unique to Spelman, offers an interdisciplinary track that prepares students for careers in civil service. Students can also elect the "independent" major option, in which they design their own course of study under the direction of a faculty member.

Small Campus, Big City

The Spelman campus, while feeding off the many amenities of Atlanta, offers an active, independent campus life for its 2,000-plus students. Ten different residential houses—each with its own special flavor—accommodate over 1,200 students on campus. Most first-year students live in Abby, Howard-Harreld, and Manley Halls, although some first-year honor students, including Presidential and WISE Scholars, live in the Stewart Living and Learning Center with upper-class students. Other second-, third-, and fourth-year students live in MacVicar, McAlpin, Morehouse-James, Laura Spelman, and Bessie Strong Halls. MacVicar, though conveniently situated above the campus infirmary, and Laura Spelman, a relic from Spelman's early years, generally receive poor marks. Many upper-class students, rather than risk their housing fate on the yearly "selection process," choose to rent apartments off campus, which, according to one senior, "are generally inexpensive and fairly popular among upperclass students due to small size of the school."

Manley College Center houses the two major dining facilities on campus, with Alma Upshaw Dining Hall, located on the top floor of Manley, functioning as the main dining hall. Students give the dining hall lukewarm remarks; according to one student, the food is just "what you would expect at a college dining hall." Recently, the dining hall has added several restaurant-esque stations—including "Grill Works," "Itza Pizza," and "Salad Garden"—in an effort to improve to the quality and variety of its offerings. The food court occupies the lower level of Manley, offering snacks and meals from recognizable vendors like Freshens, Mrs. Fields, and Ben & Jerry's.

"Most students don't complain about the requirements, because they don't prevent you from taking the classes you really want to take."

Welcome to Atlanta

Apart from its alternative housing options, the city of Atlanta offers a plethora of social and cultural resources to Spelman students. You can amble through the Sweet Auburn district, an area central to the civil rights movement of the 1950's and 1960's that houses the birthplace of Martin Luther King, Jr., as well as several memorials to the Reverend. Lenox Mall and Underground Atlanta offer abundant shopping opportunities, while nightlife thumps in downtown Atlanta clubs like Club Envy and The Library. For dinner in the city, students can choose from a smorgasbord of dining options, ranging from a quick bite at the Three Dollar Café to a traditional southern meal at local favorite John Winan's Chicken and Waffle.

Sisterhood

Another major benefit of Spelman's location in Atlanta is its proximity to other colleges and universities. Morehouse College, Spelman's "brother" institution, is within walking distance from campus. Additionally, Georgia State University, Georgia Institute of Technology, and Clark Atlanta University are all located in downtown Atlanta. Because Spelman places a heavy emphasis on student decorum, the campus is alcohol-free, and much of the social life gravitates towards parties at Morehouse and other neighboring institutions.

Despite the hum-drum party life, the general campus scene is buzzing with activity. Sororities, which for many epitomize the Spelman ideal of "sisterhood," play a conspicuous role on campus and in the lives of many students. While none of the chapters have actual houses, the sororities at Spelman make their presence felt through on-campus activities and community service projects. Competition for admission into the sorority of one's choice is intense: students must have a 3.0 GPA to take part in the "intake process," Spelman's term for rush, and sorority membership is typically capped at 30 sisters per chapter. Sororities, however, do not dominate the campus scene; one non-Greek remarked that "while there are sororities here, I honestly couldn't tell you how many people are in them . . . it's just not that big of a deal."

Active Leaders and Athletic Women

Spelman women also tend to be active leaders in school-sponsored clubs and organizations, and such activities are highly encouraged by the administration and considered part of the school's overriding mission. Subject-specific clubs (the Chemistry Club, the Economics Club, etc.), honor societies, and the Spelman Student Government Association (SSGA) are among the organizations that attract widespread membership. For the more musically-inclined, the Spelman College Jazz Ensemble, Glee Club, and the Spelman-Morehouse Players give Spelman students the opportunity to hone their musical and performance skills. Religious clubs, ranging from the Campus Crusade for Christ to the New Life Inspirational Gospel Choir, predominate on campus as well, providing myriad spiritual outlets.

Intercollegiate athletics at Spelman have traditionally taken a back seat to more academic and socially-progressive pursuits, although interest in varsity sports teams appears to be growing. The college is currently a provisional NCAA Division III school and a new member of the Great South Conference. Moreover, the Spelman administration has recently begun backing varsity athletics in an effort to visibly promote school spirit, taking the necessary steps to gain admission as a full-fledged member of the NCAA. To date, Spelman students compete against other Division III schools in basketball, cross country, golf, soccer, volleyball, and tennis. For those students keen on staying healthy at a lower level competition, IMs are always a popular option.

The Spelman Mission

Perhaps what truly distinguishes Spelman College is its underlying philosophy. In an effort to empower its students with skills for future success, Spelman requires that all students take a course in public speaking, fulfill a community service requirement, and complete a diverse and culturally-probing curriculum. Some schools may espouse high-sounding ideals, but leave them as empty rhetoric; at Spelman, however, the guiding mission and its underlying tenets—sisterhood and leadership—underscore not only the workings of the college but the demeanor and attitudes of its students. *—Kent Garber*

FYI

If you come to Spelman, you'd better bring "both an open mind and a sense of identity."

What is the typical weekend schedule? "Friday, Morehouse parties; Saturday, hit up the city; Sunday, church and work."

If I could change one thing about Spelman, I'd "get rid of the core curriculum."

Three things every student at Spelman should do before graduating are "volunteer in the city, get to know a member of the faculty, and use the resources here to expand your awareness as an individual."

University of Georgia

Address: 212 Terrell Hall; Athens, GA 30602
Phone: 706-542-8776
E-mail address: undergrad@admissions.uga.edu
Web site URL: www.uga.edu
Founded: 1785
Private or Public: public
Religious affiliation: none
Location: urban
Undergraduate enrollment: 24,983
Total enrollment: NA
Percent Male/Female: 44%/56%
Percent Minority: 12%
Percent African-American: 5%
Percent Asian: 4%
Percent Hispanic: 2%
Percent Native-American: 0%
Percent in-state/out of state: 91%/9%
Percent Pub HS: 80%
Number of Applicants: 12,786
Percent Accepted: 65%
Percent Accepted who enroll: 51%
Entering: 4,228
Transfers: 2,056
Application Deadline: 1 Feb
Mean SAT: NA
Mean ACT: NA
Middle 50% SAT range: V 550-650, M 560-650
Middle 50% ACT range: 24-29
3 Most popular majors: finance, marketing/marketing management, psychology
Retention: 91%
Graduation rate: 70%
On-campus housing: 17%
Fraternities: 16%
Sororities: 19%
Library: 3,789,228 volumes
Tuition and Fees: $4,078 in; $14,854 out
Room and Board: $5,756
Financial aid, first-year: 27%
Varsity or Club Athletes: 5%
Early Decision or Early Action Acceptance Rate: NA

To attend the University of Georgia every student must become familiar with one word and one place. "Dawg" is the word. It's short for "Bulldawg," and it's used to denote both the sports teams and each and every student on the UGA campus. "Between the Hedges" is the place, known to outsiders as the field at Sanford Football Stadium, but understood by students to be the epicenter of this football-proud school.

And in the words of one Dawg: "What a school it is!" UGA plays host to a total enrollment of approximately 30,000 students. The size of the school, located in the "classic city" of Athens, allows for an immense range of activities, sports, clubs, and social groups. This coupled with the university's comprehensive list of degrees and programs has made UGA one of the south's premier state universities.

Keeping the Hope Alive

At UGA, academics are spelled HOPE. This is because a large percentage of student tuition is paid by Georgia's HOPE grant—a fund created through state lottery proceeds that grants any student who maintains a "B" average free tuition and $100 towards books each semester at any public school. The relatively cheap cost of attending UGA has made it very popular among Georgia's top students, and is also reflected in the school's admissions numbers. Students must now have noticeably higher GPA and average SAT scores than their predecessors in order to be eligible to walk around the famous Georgia "arch." (But don't walk through it! It's campus lore that those who prematurely pass under the arch are doomed never to graduate).

Once inside the hallowed halls, students have a large scope of classes from which to choose, ranging from pre-law and Greek lyrical poetry to calculus and chemistry. While opinions differ among students on whether the university caters more to the humanities- or science-focused student, both are thought to be very well-represented on campus.

For those who take a long time to commit to a path, the university gives students until the end of their sophomore year to declare a major, prompting one student to notice that "slackers major in undecided." Those students who wish to really flex their mental might may choose to engage the University's honors program. While time-consuming, (honors students must take at least nine honors classes throughout their career in order to graduate from the program), the honors program was cited in *U.S. News and World Report* as one of the nation's best. Other perks for honors students include smaller class sizes and closer contact with their professors.

In general, students at UGA are happy with their professors. Most class sizes are admittedly large, but are cut down to sections of only 20 or so. Teaching assistants are known to be good and grading to be fair, although some students have had occasional problems with the English-speaking abilities of their teachers.

Did Someone Say "Party"?

The social scene at UGA is considered by students to be as much of an institution as the school itself. Dawgs love their football team, and throughout the fall much of campus life revolves around the weekly games between the hedges. Tailgates and post-game parties are a rite of passage in Athens, and season tickets sell out months before the first kick-off. Students and adult alumni also support their Dawgs on the road, and for the weekend of the all-important yearly contest with the University of Florida, no classes are held on the Thursday and Friday prior, allowing most of the classic city to head south for the rumble in Jacksonville with the Gators.

"Parties can be found at UGA seven days a week, prompting many students to consider themselves at the center of the party universe."

Parties can be found at UGA seven days a week, prompting many students to consider themselves at the center of the party universe. The Greek system at UGA is very popular among students and annually holds the country's second-largest rush period. The approximately 40 fraternities and sororities at Georgia are known to party hard, but non-Greeks are invited to many of the events and do not find themselves without social alternatives. One student sums up the atmosphere by stating that "Frats have a great time, but if you're not in one then you hardly know they exist." Greek or not, the one thing that unites nearly all parties at UGA is the large quantity of alcohol, leading one student to exclaim, "a Dawg's favorite food is usually beer."

And the Winner is . . .

Make no doubt about it, *the* sport on the Georgia campus is football. With each home football game, Athens turns itself from a moderately busy college town into a sea of Dawg-crazed fans as students, past and present, swamp Sanford Stadium to see the boys in red.

While football is certainly the king of the sports scene at UGA, it is not the only game played. UGA fields many perennial powerhouses in a wide variety of intercollegiate athletics, including women's gymnastics and swimming. For those who take their sports a little less seriously, UGA also offers a wide variety of club and intramural teams to fit any level of participation. Students who just want to keep in shape can use the university's state-of-the-art Ramsey Student Physical Activity Center. The Ramsey Center, as it's known, is a sprawling gym that contains, among other things, an indoor track, two pools complete with diving equipment, a rock-climbing wall, basketball and volleyball courts, and a large weight room.

Owning to the immensity of the student body at UGA, the options for extracurricular activities and social organizations are broad. Students with a journalistic bent can work for one of the many publications including the *Pandora Yearbook* or the student newspaper, the *Red and Black*. There are also several active religious groups on campus, including the Baptist Student Union and Campus Crusade for Christ. Habitat for Humanity was started in Georgia under President Jimmy Carter, and is a very popular organization on the UGA campus. Participants help build houses for financially challenged families in the community. A broad spectrum of organizations, including the fraternities and sororities, actively engage in community service as well.

A Dawg's Pad

It is not mandatory that students live in dorms at UGA for any period, although most freshmen take advantage of this option. Two of the more popular dorms are Russell, which is known for its party atmosphere, and Oglethorpe. Many other students choose to live in Myers, but this non air-conditioned dorm tends to elicit complaints until late fall rolls around. Female students who wish to live in a single sex dorm can choose to live in Brumby, known on campus as "the virgin vault." Rules on dorm visitation vary from dorm to dorm and even floor to floor. The severity of the restriction ranges from no admittance at any time to 24-hour-a day visitation—but students are allowed to place themselves according to their preferences. UGA has a comprehensive Resident Assistant program and at least one RA lives on every floor in each dorm. Students remark that RAs do not act as police, and are not overly strict. Students at Georgia are relatively happy with their dorm experiences, but few remain in the university-provided housing for more than a year. Apartments abound on and around the campus, and the majority of students choose to move off campus after their freshman year. Students who live off campus find that having a car is a must, and even the majority of those living on campus bring a car from home. One student summed up the situation at Georgia by saying, "The traffic problem is getting rather large, but I can't imagine what I'd do here without a car."

One aspect of dorm-life consistently given high marks is the food. Students on the meal plan can eat their meals at any of the three dining halls: Bolton, Oglethorpe, (commonly known as "O-House"), and Snelling. Just as living in dorms, the meal plan at UGA is totally optional, although most freshmen tend to take advantage of the university-supplied food. Some students who do not live in the dorms also purchase full or limited meal plans for weekday stops in the cafeterias. Food off campus is rated as very good as well, although it can sometimes get expensive to eat all meals out. Many students avoid this situation by buying groceries and cooking for themselves in the apartments.

A large state university in a picturesque college town, UGA has something to offer each and every one of its students. Whether a challenging courseload or a never-ending series of parties, there is rarely a lack of things to keep someone busy at UGA. One simply has to find his or her own home among the "Dawgs." —*Robert Berschinski*

FYI

If you come to UGA, you'd better bring "a Bulldawg jersey."

What is the typical weekend schedule? "Friday: go to a frat party; Saturday: drink and watch the Dawgs win again; Sunday: homework and celebrate the Dawgs' victory."

If I could change one thing about UGA, "I'd build more parking lots."

Three things that every student at UGA should do before graduating are "Go watch the Gym Dogs, catch a concert at the Georgia Theatre or 40 Watt Club, and tailgate with the old alumni at a football game."

Hawaii

University of Hawaii

Address: 244 Dole Street; Honolulu, HI 96822
Phone: 808-956-8975
E-mail address: ar-info@hawaii.edu
Web site URL: www.hawaii.edu
Founded: 1907
Private or Public: public
Religious affiliation: none
Location: urban
Undergraduate enrollment: 12,820
Total enrollment: NA
Percent Male/Female: 44%/56%
Percent Minority: 82%
Percent African-American: 1%
Percent Asian: 70%
Percent Hispanic: 2%
Percent Native-American: 0%
Percent in-state/out of state: 88%/12%
Percent Pub HS: 67%
Number of Applicants: 4,915
Percent Accepted: 73%
Percent Accepted who enroll: 52%
Entering: 1,877
Transfers: 1,562
Application Deadline: 1 June
Mean SAT: NA
Mean ACT: NA
Middle 50% SAT range: V 470-570; M 510-610
Middle 50% ACT range: 20-25
3 Most popular majors: marketing, multi/-interdisciplinary studies, psychology
Retention: 78%
Graduation rate: 53%
On-campus housing: 22%
Fraternities: NA
Sororities: NA
Library: 3,234,881 volumes
Tuition and Fees: $3,465 in; $9,945 out
Room and Board: $5,675
Financial aid, first-year: 31%
Varsity or Club Athletes: 2%
Early Decision or Early Action Acceptance Rate: NA

While the sun, sand, and sea might first come to mind when thinking of the exotic location, the University of Hawaii has a whole lot more to offer. Its proximity to the Asia-Pacific region, a unique mix of American, Asian, and Pacific cultures, academic strengths, and a friendly environment make this major research institution a promising place to spend four years.

East Meets West

When asked about the quality of academics, students mostly agreed that academics were generally "okay," but reported that several departments were "excellent," such as marine biology, astronomy, geology, and Pacific volcanology. Ethnic studies and Pacific Asian studies were also praised for their high quality. As one student put it, "Pretty much everything is all right, but anything that specifically relates to Asia is really good." One student praised the "eminent minds" brought in by the East-West Center, a national center which sponsors scholars from all over the world to examine economic and social issues. Others liked the presence of "renowned professors" and reported that the quality of instruction was generally good, describing professors as "supportive" and the classroom environment as "progressive."

Regarding the core requirements, however, students offered differing opinions. While most liked the "breadth" offered, one student regretted that the focus was primarily on Asia. Mostly, though, students found the core requirements as satisfactory and did not have many complaints.

Fun in the Sun

Students rave about the range of social options at the University of Hawaii, noting that "you can pretty much do whatever you want." Most students go clubbing or to parties on Friday and Saturday nights and recuperate by hanging out at the beach on weekends and enjoying the fabulous weather. While the University of Hawaii has a Greek system, fraternities and sororities do not dominate social life. Students described the Greek scene as "not major," and students experience little pressure to join the Greek scene. Some students experience pressure to conform to what everyone else is doing but maintain that they are not overwhelmed by it, and students who dislike partying choose from a range of other options including going to the theater, surfing, hiking, or attending recreational classes such as scuba diving.

Get "Lei-ed"

Occasions to dress up formally are few and far between, and guys almost never get to don their tuxedos. The dating scene is alive and well, and it is common for people to go out on dates or have significant others. Random hook-ups "do happen" every once in a while, but, as one student put it, "I've been to some schools that are really promiscuous and this is not one of those." The University of Hawaii also has its fair share of attractive people, with one student raving about the "pretty girls" and their "sexy outfits." Students agreed that interracial dating is very common, but differed on the subject of interracial couples. While some described the attitude toward homosexual couples as "open and non-discriminatory," others insisted that homosexual couples generally tend to "stay low-key" because "this is not a very open climate for them."

"The campus is fantastic and really inspiring because it's surrounded by beautiful mountains and . . . on certain parts of campus . . . you can look down and see the ocean."

Athletic opportunities abound at University of Hawaii, with the most popular sports being football, volleyball, and surfing. Students are proud of their school's athletics and there is a general "sporty atmosphere." Even students not affiliated with any of the sports clubs or teams enjoy getting outside and kicking a ball around in their spare time. It is common to see groups of students getting together to play casual sports for recreation around campus, even on weekdays.

Homogenous and Happy

One student described the student stereotype as "people of Asian descent who were brought up in Hawaii." While there were some complaints about the student body being homogeneous, one student emphatically described the student body as "multicultural, diverse, with little segregation." Most were happy with the atmosphere, which they described as "supportive," "friendly," "relaxed," and "not very aggressive." Students dress very casually, with the typical student day-to-day wardrobe consisting of "jeans, shorts, T-shirt." It is easy to make friends, with students describing everyone as being "really friendly." Most students make friends in classes, activities, and intramurals. Extracurriculars are not a very major part of the lives of students, because of the fact that "we are a commuter school" and also because it is common for students to take on part-time jobs.

Paradise Found

Students described the campus as "spread-out" and liked the fact that it is "a campus unto itself." The size of the grounds was described as "just nice." A tropical oasis, the campus consists of a lot of greenery with large lawns and lots of trees. One student enthusiastically described, "The campus is fantastic and really inspiring because it's surrounded by beautiful mountains and if you are on certain parts of campus that are on higher ground, you can look down and see the ocean." The good weather and abundant sunshine also made a good impression with students. While the natural surroundings are great, the buildings seem to be the worst part of campus, with students commenting that the buildings "could be prettier," "could use more funding," and "need to be renovated."

Island Fare

While most students deem the dining hall food "acceptable" (the magical word for college dining halls everywhere), one student said that "the quality is horrible."

Cliques do exist and there "is some pressure to always be eating with a group of friends," but students report that it is not uncommon for people to walk into a dining hall and eat by themselves. There are also complaints about the lack of great eating establishments near campus, however a student said that "if you go a little further off campus, you can find some really good places, places that I wouldn't mind going to on a date."

On the whole, most students agree that the beautiful surroundings and friendly people make the University of Hawaii a great place to be. Students insist that they wouldn't trade their experiences here for anything. There is never a lack of things to do or friends to hang out with, and if classes are too stressful—as any University of Hawaii student will tell you—there's always the beach. —*Wenshan Yeo*

FYI

If you come to the University of Hawaii, you'd better bring "a swimsuit for the beach."

What is the typical weekend schedule? " Friday, go partying; Saturday, go to the beach, more partying; Sunday, watch TV, do homework."

If I could change one thing about the University of Hawaii, I would "renovate the buildings and make them look prettier."

Three things every student at the University of Hawaii should do before graduating are "learn to surf, explore the rest of Hawaii, and learn about the culture and history of Hawaii."

Idaho

University of Idaho

Address: 875 Perimeter Drive, P.O. Box 442282; Moscow, ID 83844-2282
Phone: 888-884-3246
E-mail address: admappl@uidaho.edu
Web site URL: www.uidaho.edu
Founded: 1889
Private or Public: public
Religious affiliation: none
Location: rural
Undergraduate enrollment: 9,368
Total enrollment: NA
Percent Male/Female: 54%/46%
Percent Minority: 8%
Percent African-American: 1%
Percent Asian: 2%
Percent Hispanic: 3%
Percent Native-American: 1%
Percent in-state/out of state: 81%/19%
Percent Pub HS: 95%
Number of Applicants: 3,936
Percent Accepted: 82%
Percent Accepted who enroll: 53%
Entering: 1,704
Transfers: 787
Application Deadline: 1 Aug
Mean SAT: NA
Mean ACT: NA
Middle 50% SAT range: V 480-610, M 490-610
Middle 50% ACT range: 20-26
3 Most popular majors: education, business, management, marketing, natural resources and conservation
Retention: 80%
Graduation rate: 49%
On-campus housing: NA
Fraternities: NA
Sororities: NA
Library: 1,355,911 volumes
Tuition and Fees: $3,348 in; $10,740 out
Room and Board: $4,868
Financial aid, first-year: 53%
Varsity or Club Athletes: 5%
Early Decision or Early Action Acceptance Rate: NA

One junior captured the essence of his years at the University of Idaho as "cheap, fun, and a great education." Tucked between the potato fields and rolling hills of Moscow, Idaho, the University of Idaho is wrapped up in its own world—a world immersed in frat parties, intramurals, and academics.

Engineering Future Engineers

Engineering is widely recognized as the toughest major on campus. Even so, undergrads flock to the department. The University of Idaho engineering programs are regarded as some of the best in the country. The university attracts candidates early on through an engineering camp for juniors in high school. Future engineering majors earn credit at the university during the intense two-week program. All undergrads, in regardless of major, are required to fulfill basic core requirements. These include math, science, social science, and communications. The easiest classes are found in the PE department (one can get credit for playing football or bowling) and in general studies, but most students feel that "for the most part there are not too many easy classes."

Students were split in their feelings on class size and TAs. Some undergrads thought their TAs were generally very good while others thought they "suck royally." Feelings about class sizes ran along similar lines. Opinions on class size varied from "perfect" to "fine as long as the room is big enough" to "too big." Many introductory classes fall into the "too big" category, but are broken down into sections and labs taught by TAs.

Undergrads also have the option of enrolling in classes offered by Washington

State University, located eight miles away in Pullman, Washington. Students are able to take classes at WSU that the U of I does not offer, though course selections are very limited.

It's All Greek to Me

With 18 fraternities and 8 sororities for the approximately 8,000 member campus, Greek life dominates every aspect of non-academic life at the U of I. About 27 percent of men and 19 percent of women go Greek. There is an unspoken but pronounced division between Greeks and independents. As one undergraduate put it, "There are two separate worlds. You're proud to be where you are."

Freshmen are free to choose their living arrangements. Their options include living in a fraternity or sorority house, living in a residence hall, or living off-campus. Just as each Greek house has its own personality, each dorm has its own character. Residents may choose their dorm, but dorms have unofficial designations such as "athletic" housing. Despite the variety of options, the administration has had to deal with a housing crunch in recent years, and dorms and Greek houses were renovated to provide extra space. There are also apartments available on campus. Many students opt for off-campus housing but find that a good location at a decent price is difficult to come by if they don't look early.

> **"I have only been on one date and I went to the rodeo!"**

Greeks also dominate social and extracurricular life. There are fraternity and sorority parties nearly every weekend. There is no cover charge for the parties, but they are open only to those on the guest list (usually the membership list of other Greek houses). There have been no publicized problems with Greek life recently, though one fraternity chapter lost its charter a few years ago. However, underage drinking is "the epitome of the U of I. There are constant minor-in-possession citations." Greek life revolves around dances, cruises, socials, and philanthropic events. Strong friendships are a part of the package. A sorority member claims, "The friends that I have made through the Greek system will be my friends for life."

Those not involved in Greek life take quite a different view, "[The Greek system] has TOTAL control of this place. We have the second-largest Greek system in the Northwest here (next to U. of Washington). It sucks because the Greeks here think they are God's gift to life and everything else." However, social life outside of the Greek scene is abundant. Many undergrads take advantage of the nearby mountains and rivers to camp and hike. Others head for neighboring Pullman, Washington, or for Spokane, Washington, which is about an hour's drive away.

Where's the Kremlin?

Moscow, Idaho, itself has very limited opportunities. Described as a "typical college town," this tiny town of about 18,000 boasts fast food restaurants, movie theaters, a small mall, and an abundance of bars. Students complained that there is nothing social to do off campus. Many students own cars and escape from Moscow over the weekends. The U of I campus is fairly compact. It takes about 15 minutes to get from one end to the other. With both a small campus and a small town, students said they generally feel safe on campus and in town, although like anywhere there are "certain places [where] you don't walk after dark."

Dating at the U of I is very low-key. A typical date involves attending a Greek event or going to the movies. Those who are not in serious relationships generally just try to meet people at parties. With such limited options, dating often gets creative. "I have only been on one date and I went to the rodeo! Whoa, pardner, easy!"

Vandal-izing Fun

School spirit runs high among the University of Idaho Vandals, and sporting events are heavily attended. U of I athletes, both men and women, compete in NCAA Division I as members of the Big West Athletic Conference. The men and women Vandals represent the university in 14 varsity sports, including the recently added women's soccer program. The rivalry with the Boise State University Broncos is especially intense. Outstanding recreational facilities, available to the campus and the community, include an excellent 18-hole golf course, swimming pool, indoor and outdoor tracks, indoor and outdoor tennis courts, and racquetball courts.

Extracurricular activities are unfortunately quite limited at the U of I. The engineering department offers several organizations and teams, but these usually appeal only to students in the major. Outside of academic organizations, there is a large Christian group on campus that has some presence. The campus also hosts various concerts, including the widely known Lionel Hampton Jazz Festival held every spring. The most popular activity, by far, is intramural sports, although they are often "Greek dominated."

Despite its isolated location and the deep division between Greek and non-Greek undergrads, students love the U of I. Whether they are looking for an awesome social life or a decent education at a decent price, U of I meets its students' needs, and creates many fond memories for them along the way. Students feel that they are getting the "college experience." As one enthusiastic Vandal put it, "I thought that high school was the best time of my life, until I got to college. This is where my best memories are!"—*Jennifer Rogien and Staff*

FYI

If you come to UI, you'd better bring "your sleeping bag for those camping trips."

What is the typical weekend schedule? "Friday, go to a frat party; Saturday, go camping or hiking at a nearby mountain; Sunday, sleep, exercise, do homework."

If I could change one thing about UI, "I'd move it closer to a big city."

Three things that every student at the University of Idaho should do before graduating are "make a road trip to one of the cities, attend a game against the Broncos, and participate in intramurals."

Illinois

DePaul University

Address: 1 East Jackson Boulevard; Chicago, IL 60604-2287
Phone: 312-362-8300
E-mail address: admitdpu@depaul.edu
Web site URL: www.depaul.edu
Founded: 1898
Private or Public: private
Religious affiliation: Roman Catholic
Location: urban
Undergraduate enrollment: 14,343
Total enrollment: NA
Percent Male/Female: 42%/58%
Percent Minority: 36%
Percent African-American: 12%
Percent Asian: 10%
Percent Hispanic: 13%
Percent Native-American: 0%
Percent in-state/out of state: 89%/11%
Percent Pub HS: 65%
Number of Applicants: 8,932
Percent Accepted: 78%
Percent Accepted who enroll: 32%
Entering: 2,256
Transfers: 0
Application Deadline: rolling
Mean SAT: NA
Mean ACT: NA
Middle 50% SAT range: V 510-620; M 490-610
Middle 50% ACT range: 21-27
3 Most popular majors: business management, marketing, liberal arts, computer and information sciences
Retention: 83%
Graduation rate: 63%
On-campus housing: NA
Fraternities: NA
Sororities: NA
Library: 863,848 volumes
Tuition and Fees: $16,950
Room and Board: $7,455
Financial aid, first-year: 67%
Varsity or Club Athletes: 3%
Early Decision or Early Action Acceptance Rate: NA

Within the last five years, DePaul was selected by both *Time* magazine and the *Princeton Review* as having the happiest student body of any college in the country. DePaul manages to maintain a small-school, student-oriented atmosphere where everyone is happy and nobody feels trapped or isolated. It probably helps that classes are small and almost all taught by professors, and that the main campus is in one of the best parts of Chicago, Lincoln Park. One political science major referred to the neighborhood's inhabitants as "rich, young yuppies."

Safety is rarely an issue, whether in Lincoln Park or on the downtown campus, which is located near the Art Institute of Chicago. No wonder the students of DePaul are so pleased: they can go to the nation's third-largest city for fun, get a great education, and still find time for top-notch extracurricular activities and sports.

Educational Priorities

"The school is very passionate about making education the first priority," said a pleased senior. While DePaul offers more than 100 academic programs and more than 1,000 different courses, every single class is taught by a professor as opposed to a teaching assistant, like at other large schools. More than 88 percent of the faculty have Ph.D.s, and average class sizes max out at 25 students and can be as small as 5 students. Notable professors include Wayne Steger, who teaches political science; Deena Weinstein, the authority on rock concerts and audiences (one student said that "she knows everybody in the music industry"); and Lorilee Sadler of computer science, telecommunications, and information systems. Professors and students maintain a comfortable atmosphere both in and out of class—the professors give out their home phone numbers on syllabi and are flexible with grading. As one freshman described, "You can call them up and be like, 'Hey, what happened with this grade?' A lot of times, they'll change it and be reasonable." Students are encouraged to participate in class, and one senior raved that the professors "encouraged individuality and helped guide me."

DePaul is known for being a humanities and business-oriented school, but one student pointed out that the "computer science program is gaining national attention" and that "the School of Computer Science is one of the largest in the country." Slackers can be found in any major, but, in particular, the exotic cat management major seems to attract a large share of the loafers for some reason.

DePaul is on a quarter system, and students must take at least three courses a quarter and maintain a 2.1 GPA. Those in the liberal arts program must take a core curriculum. First-year students have a special curriculum that they must follow, but they have "a lot of room for other classes," according to one freshman. Honors programs can be found in each college, and classes are even smaller in those; one honors student raved, "You end up taking the majority of your classes with the same group of people, and you get to know each other, which is nice when a school is large." However, a sophomore mentioned that while "my honors and political science classes are the most challenging, the rest seem like a joke at times." On the other hand, a freshman said that he felt like he had a ton of work, although he did say that it was manageable.

The professors are available to help those who need it. One invited students over to his house to help them with projects that he had assigned. Other positive aspects of classes at DePaul include, said a senior, "their locations. You can be in the Chicago Loop downtown in the center of business, then take a ten-minute train ride into Lincoln Park and be at a standard college campus that's surrounded with history and all kinds of things to do."

An Extracurricular Experience

Extracurricular activities are also a big part of student life. There are about 120 different student organizations: ethnic clubs, political groups, honor societies, a radio station, and many more. Students are often identified by the activity they are involved in. As one student put it, "Everyone knows who works on the *DePaulia* [the student paper], partly because our lives revolve around it. It's like that for anyone, if they are really into one thing, they will be associated with it." Many students are involved with community service, and student government is also well respected. Perhaps gaining the most attention are the sports teams, which compete in NCAA Division I. In particular, the men and women's basketball teams, which recruit heavily, are popular and bring in a lot of fans.

"I think there are some fine-looking men here!"

While DePaul is a commuter school, students did not mention that as having an adverse effect on their social lives. The most obvious reason for this is that the "city is our campus. Even if you don't drink, there's still a lot of stuff to do." Similarly, another student said that "DePaul utilizes Chicago to the extreme; it's awesome." Students can go to concerts, bars, clubs, and plays, although one upperclassman remarked that freshmen just "find the nearest party and travel there in large packs." Students agreed that it was easy to meet people, that "people are very friendly." Good parties include swing dances, Halloween parties, '70s parties, and toga parties hosted by the fraternities. There is a lot of drinking, and one sorority member pointed out that "the Greek life is really starting to grow."

Punks vs. Preppies

Because, as one senior put it, "DePaul is a very liberal school," students mentioned that there is a large gay population. "We live near one of the largest gay communities in the country, North Halstead," explained a freshman. Many students tend to be trendy, and a common stereotype is "a bunch of rich, Chicago, suburban kids." This stereotype might stem from the fact that, as one disgruntled junior pointed out, DePaul, as a rule, does not give scholarships to international students. Student dress tends to differ between the campuses. The Lincoln Park campus is really laid-back, while students at the downtown campus tend to be more dressed up. The student population is "pretty diverse," with a large number of Hispanic and African-American students, although there are not many Asian students. One thrilled female student also mentioned that "I think there are some fine-looking men here!" Music-wise, the punk scene is reputedly quite big.

Also big, although in a different sense, are the dorm (called "residence hall") rooms, for the few who opt to stay in them (students complain about the high prices of housing). All student rooms have private bathrooms, air-conditioning, and cable with movie channels; upperclassmen get to stay in "town houses and beautiful apartments with a killer view of the skyline." Freshmen must stay on-campus, but even their dorms are complete with "tall ceilings," an attribute not found at too many other universities. Cafeteria food is good, but "gets boring," (DePaul has just one cafeteria) so students often go off-campus to eat. Popular restaurants include Potbelly's, My Pie, Demon Dogs, and "Taco Burrito Place is where every DePaul student goes after hitting the bars." Campus buildings are indistinguishable from the rest of the city, and anywhere on the undergraduate campuses students can be awed by the sight of the magnificent Chicago skyscrapers.

Winner? Chicago

So there are great academics, extracurricular activities, and parties. But what epitomizes DePaul University? Students seem to love, above all, their school's deep bond with the city of Chicago. As one senior reflected, "I got to do things here that I could never do at a huge university, and I'm in the center of a huge city." Just like Chicago, the DePaul community is connected through close-knit classes and a dedication to community service. Even the sororities and fraternities are friendly with each other, said one member. What creates this great atmosphere? As one freshman put it, "The city. It's all about the city."—*Jennifer Wang and Staff*

FYI

If you come to DePaul, you'd better bring "some money to go out and eat some quality fast food."

What is the typical weekend schedule? "Friday, go to a bar in Chicago; Saturday, check out a Greek party; Sunday, problem sets and reading."

If I could change one thing about DePaul, "I'd lower housing costs."

Three things that every student at DePaul should do before graduating are "go to the Midnight Madness pep assembly in the fall, take a class on a campus other than Lincoln Park, and see different areas of Chicago other the immediate Lincoln Park area."

Illinois State University

Address: Campus Box 2200; Normal, IL 61790-2200
Phone: 309-438-2181
E-mail address: ugradadm@ilstu.edu
Web site URL: www.ilstu.edu
Founded: 1857
Private or Public: public
Religious affiliation: none
Location: urban
Undergraduate enrollment: 18,353
Total enrollment: 21,240
Percent Male/Female: 42%/58%
Percent Minority: 10%
Percent African-American: 6%
Percent Asian: 1%
Percent Hispanic: 3%
Percent Native-American: 0%
Percent in-state/out of state: 98%/2%
Percent Pub HS: 90%
Number of Applicants: 9,070
Percent Accepted: 81%
Percent Accepted who enroll: 42%
Entering: 3,108
Transfers: 1,856
Application Deadline: 1 Mar
Mean SAT: NA
Mean ACT: 22.8
Middle 50% SAT range: NA
Middle 50% ACT range: 21-25
3 Most popular majors: education, business, social services
Retention: 80%
Graduation rate: 57%
On-campus housing: 37%
Fraternities: 9%
Sororities: 15%
Library: 1,451,195 volumes
Tuition and Fees: $5,520 in; $11,880 out
Room and Board: $5,315
Financial aid, first-year: 39%
Varsity or Club Athletes: 3%
Early Decision or Early Action Acceptance Rate: NA

With over 18,000 undergraduate students, Illinois State fits the profile of a large, state school. But students at this Midwestern university are treated as individuals, not just as numbers. Students consistently praise the personal attention they receive from Illinois State's faculty and the quality education they provide. With its diverse curriculum, vibrant student body, and highly accessible faculty, students at ISU will find a challenging and diverse environment in which to pursue their goal of higher education, nestled among the Illinois cornfields.

Looking for a Good Time

Though the majority of students at ISU hail from within the state, the student body is far from homogenous. In fact, as students from the rural parts of the state and those from Chicago and its suburbs come together, they create an interesting and diverse mix. Whatever their origin, students find common ground in their commitment to having a good time. Though alcohol is outlawed in the dorms (except for a few areas, which allow students of age to have alcohol in their rooms), students looking for a party can often find one at a nearby off-campus apartment or fraternity house. "Going out" is a huge part of student social life and a chance for students to strut their stuff. As one senior commented, "people are more relaxed during the day, but at night it's like a competition to see who's hotter!" Parties usually revolve around alcohol, but one student commented that, while hard drugs aren't commonly used, "there are a lot of people here who smoke marijuana." The school does sponsor some alternative social events, and student organizations have recently brought bands 311 and Alien Ant Farm to campus. Students can also kick back at the BBC—the on-campus billiards and bowling center that offers more relaxed, alcohol-free entertainment. Most large events, like dances and parties, are sponsored by the school's many Greek organizations.

Due to recent crackdowns on underage drinking by school administration, the social scene is beginning to change. Stringent ID policies and a sign-in, sign-out procedure have cut down on the number and size of parties that fraternities can have. A division of the local police—affectionately dubbed the "Party Police" by students—has been known to break up out-of-control parties, though arrests are rarely made. Upperclassmen prefer to frequent the bars in nearby Bloomington, about a 10-minute drive from campus. Social life is not limited to the weekends, as Wednesday and Thursday are popular nights at the bars which often feature drink specials to attract students. These events are strictly for the over-21 crowd, and students caution against trying to sneak into a bar if you're not of legal age. According to one junior, "Bars can be pretty strict about checking ID's, and the police can come in and shut a place down if they're letting in underage kids."

The Land of Opportunity . . . and Requirements

ISU offers students the opportunity for a great education, with over 150 fields of study to pursue. The business and nursing programs are very popular, and also known to be the most intense, while the communications major offers a lighter workload. The largest and most renowned program at ISU is its College of Education. The administration estimates that one in seven teachers in Illinois public schools was educated at Illinois State. This ensures that ISU has its own very talented faculty who is committed to teaching undergraduate students. One senior said that she could not "imagine an institution where the professors are more approachable or accessible to students than at ISU." Professors receive high marks for their commitment both in and out of the classroom and are always available to help students, whether during office hours or at a late-night study session. One student even commented, "I've seen a few of them out at the bars once in awhile."

Though ISU students generally love their professors, the school's general education requirements are less highly praised. Opinions seem to be divided on the topic, as some students think that they are acceptable while others feel that they prevent them from taking more classes within their majors. Students are required to take one class in each of the 15 specified areas ranging from the natural sciences to United States traditions to the fine arts. Every freshman is required to take the Foundations of Inquiry (FOI) course, a seminar that helps students make the transition from high school to college and prepares them for college-level work. Many students have positive opinions of their experiences in FOI, but others feel that it was an unnecessarily hard course. Classes that fulfill general education requirements tend to be large lectures that feature separate discussion sections led by graduate students. Once students declare a major, however, class size decreases dramatically to between 20 and 30 students. Overall, students feel that they are getting a great education at ISU.

"People are more relaxed during the day, but at night it's like a competition to see who's hotter!"

Outside of the classroom, some students get involved in some of the over 200 registered organizations (RSO's) on campus. Ranging from the American Marketing Association to the Albino Squirrel Preservation Society, there is a group to suit every student's taste. However involvement tends to be limited. As one junior said, "Last I heard, only about 10 percent of students are in RSO's." Those that are involved tend to be very focused and devoted to their cause. This lack of involvement can also be seen at the school's sporting events. Though ISU has plenty of talented recruited athletes, students usually only show up "when we're playing the University of Illinois or our big rival, Bradley," according to one junior.

World-Class Accommodations

Students at ISU rave that their campus is centralized and accessible. With most classroom buildings situated around a large grassy quad, the campus is easy to navigate and avoids the sprawl of most large state schools. A walkway built over College Road, the main artery of campus, links the quad with the school's library and student center. ISU is in the process of building a number of new campus buildings, including a brand new school of business and several new athletic facilities. One senior commented, "the school looks great. They are really trying to make it new and modern."

With 13 residential buildings on campus, students at ISU have plenty of choice in their housing options. Freshman and sophomores are required to live on campus, and are usually assigned to double rooms, though some triples and singles are available. Most of the buildings have the same set-up, with rooms along a long hallway and large communal bathrooms. Some buildings feature theme areas, which group students with common interests or lifestyles. There are also both single-sex and co-ed floors available. By far the most notable residential buildings at ISU are the massive Watterson towers, a 28-floor housing complex that can be seeing rising out of the cornfields from miles away. One of the tallest dorms in the world, Watterson's two towers are divided into five "houses" of five floors each, to offer students a greater sense of community within such a large building. While Watterson is definitely the most social dorm, and features the largest rooms, some students prefer the quieter atmosphere of the other, smaller residential buildings. One junior observed,"It's all a matter of preference. I like the smaller buildings, but most of them don't have air conditioning!"

Each cluster of dorms contains it own dining facilities, but with so many students housed in one place, it is no surprise that Watterson's large dining area features the most variety on campus. One senior raved that the "dining facilities here are amazing!" In addition to the home-cooked fare and salad bars, there are a number of chain restaurants including Sbarro's, Pepe's, Chick-fil-A, and even a Ben and Jerry's in the complex. Each dining facility also has its own Subway franchise that stays open until 2 A.M. and offers student discounts. Students will soon be able to use their meal cards at nearby restaurants in downtown Normal, adding to the already large variety of meal options available to students.

The Normal Life

Most upperclassmen live in off-campus apartments, though one senior says, "They're so close, they might as well be called 'on-campus.'" Many students feel satisfied with their off-campus living situations, and appreciate the freedom that comes with escaping the dorms. But finding a suitable apartment can sometimes be difficult; as another senior cautioned, "The landlords are as shady as they come." Many of the sports teams have houses together, and along with the fraternity houses, the sports houses are the usual locations for weekend parties.

Students living off campus can have meal plans, but many chose to explore the bars and restaurants in the Bloomington-Normal area. A popular spot near campus is Avanti's, an affordable Italian restaurant known for its great breads and pastas. A typical assortment of chain restaurants is just a few minutes' drive from campus. While many students do have cars, especially those living off campus, students do not feel that they are a necessity. In fact, the lack of parking on campus can make having a car more trouble than it is worth. Many students take advantage of the free shuttle service that runs from campus to various locations around town.

From the Cornfields to Prime Time

Despite its location among the cornfields of central Illinois, Illinois State University offers an exciting environment with a great academic experience. Most students are overwhelmingly satisfied with their decision to come to ISU. A look at some of ISU's alumni proves that students there are destined for big things; among the notable alumni are actor Sean Haynes, who plays Jack on "Will and Grace," and NBA star Doug Collins. The school's location, solid academic programs, and engaged faculty are just some of the reasons it makes for a great college environment. As one senior remarked, "I can honestly say that ISU offers as fine of an education as any public university in the state, or elsewhere for that matter."—*Jessica Lenox*

FYI

If you come to ISU, you'd better bring a "jacket that is warm and waterproof, because the weather can be harsh at times!"

What is the typical weekend schedule? "Hanging out with friends, going to a party or out to a bar, homework, and eating pizza."

If I could change one thing about ISU, I'd "have there be more school spirit."

Three things every student at ISU should do before graduating are "join a club, go cosmic bowling at the BBC, and attend a concert at the new performing arts center."

Knox College

Address: 2 E. South Street; Galesburg, IL 61401
Phone: 800-678-5669
E-mail address: admission@knox.edu
Web site URL: www.knox.edu
Founded: 1837
Private or Public: private
Religious affiliation: none
Location: urban
Undergraduate enrollment: 1,121
Total enrollment: NA
Percent Male/Female: 47%/53%
Percent Minority: 23%
Percent African-American: 5%
Percent Asian: 5%
Percent Hispanic: 3%
Percent Native-American: 1%
Percent in-state/out of state: 56%/44%
Percent Pub HS: NA
Number of Applicants: 1,542
Percent Accepted: 72%
Percent Accepted who enroll: 27%
Entering: 300
Transfers: 30
Application Deadline: 1 Feb
Mean SAT: NA
Mean ACT: NA
Middle 50% SAT range: V 550-680; M 550-650
Middle 50% ACT range: 23-29
3 Most popular majors: economics, education, psychology
Retention: 87%
Graduation rate: 72%
On-campus housing: 96%
Fraternities: 30%
Sororities: 10%
Library: 185,923 volumes
Tuition and Fees: $24,369
Room and Board: $5,925
Financial aid, first-year: 71%
Varsity or Club Athletes: 30%
Early Decision or Early Action Acceptance Rate: EA 79%

The very first day of college can be a little scary for anyone. "How am I going to meet all these new people," you wonder, as Mom and Dad drive off in the now-empty station wagon. If your first day of school is at Knox, meeting people may be less of a worry. Every year at Knox College starts off with all students, faculty, and administrators getting together for "Pump Handle." Everyone lines up and shakes hands until no hand is left unshaken. This personable, "homey feeling" is exactly what Knox is all about. As one sophomore described it, "I came to Knox because I wanted to get lots of attention, and this place has really surpassed my expectations."

Professors Are Really Interested . . . in You!

Though the environment at Knox is homey, the work is serious and wide-ranging, with the professors contributing much to the students' passion for learning. Knox professors are diverse and friendly, but above all, truly interested in their students. They are described by students as, "the best quality of the school," "very open," and "inviting."

Beginning with the Freshman Preceptorial, a discussion class designed to stimulate intellectual conversation on various controversial subjects, Knox students follow the principles of a liberal education during their trimesters and take a wide variety of classes: required are two each in the social sciences, humanities, fine arts, and math and science. Independent undergraduate research is fairly common (involving about one out of five seniors) and is made possible by the nationally recognized Knox Honors Program. Students are encouraged to study overseas or in a major US city; some majors even require it. Programs in places as diverse as Zimbabwe and Florence are popular, but according to one upperclassman, the South American programs are the most "life changing."

Premed students from all over the country are attracted to Knox by the Rush Medical School early admission program. This program gives qualified freshmen a guarantee of admission into Chicago's Rush Medical School, as long as they maintain B averages over the next four years. This permits students to pursue a wide variety of interests without being constrained by the lengthy and stressful process of applying to medical schools later. The program is unique in that it allows students to shop around and apply to other schools without losing their acceptance into Rush.

An exciting new special program for all those who love the outdoors is the Green Oaks Term. In this program, students spend an entire term roughing it while studying field biology, environmental studies, and a related humanities course at Green Oaks, Knox's 760-acre wilderness preserve. Or, for those who would rather be involved in a more artsy program, the Art Department offers a semester-long program in Chicago doing internships; another program called "Knox in New York" allows students to spend several weeks studying at the New York Studio School while living in Greenwich Village.

Confines of the Campus

The gothic architecture of Seymour Library stands out from the very center of the Knox campus, although the most historic of the central buildings is Old Main, the only still-standing site of a Lincoln-Douglas debate. The bell tower mounted on top of Old Main is the model for the Knox logo. To the west is the SMAC (science and mathematics) building, alone in a lot, surrounded by a thin veil of pine trees. Students report that the SMAC facilities are excellent. Among other things they have electron and scanning microscopes, a greenhouse, and more computers than you can shake a stick at. The CFA (center for fine arts) building is home to, not surprisingly, the art department, the music department, and the theater department. There are two main halls, Kresge and Harbach, for music and theater respectively.

Knox is located in a fairly small Midwestern town, so the social scene is pretty much kept within the confines of the campus. There are, however, some nice shops in the downtown area, such as Cornucopia, a fine quality bakery and natural foods store.

A good part of the social scene revolves around the big frat parties that can be found "pretty much every weekend." A number of students, however, prefer other fun activities on campus. Many students spend a lot of weekend time doing social things with their extracurricular groups. Another popular alternative is road tripping, which seems to have developed into an unofficial Knox tradition. Students will go see concerts in cities like Chicago or St. Louis, and then spend the weekend there. As far as the dating scene goes, Knox students report a "normal atmosphere with everything from random hook-ups to serious relationships," although one girl admitted, "It's a small school so you can get a reputation pretty easily after a while."

Good at Meeting Students' Needs

Knox has a history of being a very diverse school—it was involved in the early 1800s with the civil rights and women's rights movements. The college makes a strong effort to keep that tradition of social activism and awareness alive. Both American minorities and international students are well represented at 12 percent and 11 percent of the student body, respectively. Knox encourages and celebrates this ethnic diversity; an Office of Intercultural Affairs works to enhance diversity, ethnic clubs are numerous, and a yearly International Fair brings together all the students of the school to learn about and sample the foods of countries from around the world.

> **"I came to Knox because I wanted to get lots of attention, and this place has really surpassed my expectations."**

The diverse student body at Knox enjoys a praiseworthy housing system. "Really good about meeting people's needs" is how one freshman girl described Knox housing. The rooms are generally large and well maintained, with dorms being distinctly different from each other. For example, Seymour houses first-year men, and offers markedly inferior accommodations as compared to the all-women dorm, Post. Then there is the Quad, which seems to be the center of dorm social life. There are, actually, two Quads, the old quad and the new quad, side by side forming an E-shape when looked at from above. These dorms are co-ed and house students from every class.

The food at Knox can be described as, well, "typical college food." There are essentially three dining halls, all located in one building at the center of campus: the Hard Knox Café (besides the obvious reference to Hard Rock, the School of Hard Knox is an old nickname for the college), the Oak room, and the Lincoln/Skylight rooms. Vegetarian, vegan, and Kosher-style meals are always available, according to one Jewish student. Overall, although the food is not that bad, "having some granola bars in your room is a must." For snacks at odd hours of the day or night, Knox's Gizmo is the place to go. Despite trying for a coffeehouse atmosphere, Gizmo essentially serves mozzarella sticks, burgers, and fries.

Lots of Extracurriculars

At Knox, extracurriculars are abundant. As one junior put it, "Pretty much everyone is in two or three things." Besides several ethnic and cinema clubs, there is a string ensemble directed by Bruce Polay, a Knox music professor and director of the Knox-Galesburg Symphony (which has repeatedly been named Illinois' best community orchestra). The Knox publications, *Catch*, and *Knox Student*, are both prizewinners. While *Catch* focuses mostly on the fine arts at Knox, the *Knox Student* has a wider range in its topics of interest.

Knox's "Prairie Fire" Varsity and JV athletics are secondary to academics. The varsity athlete is given time for his sport and for his work. Support for the Knox teams is greatest among the community of athletes themselves, yet big football games continue to turn out large crowds. The athletic facilities at Knox are very new, and almost always being expanded or improved in some way or another; currently, a natatorium is being built. For those interested in non-varsity athletics, club sports are big at Knox. The Ultimate Frisbee team is very popular, and a new water polo team is growing in popularity. As far as intramural sports go, indoor soccer gets a lot of players every winter, and softball is the spring's biggest event.

A School of Traditions

Flunk Day is, according to almost all Knox students, the best Knox tradition. One spring morning, without warning, a group of seniors manages to wake up all of campus at around 5 A.M. Whether they do it by banging pots and pans, or by blasting heavy metal out of the windows of their frat seems to vary from year to year, and from witness to witness. In any case, Flunk Day is a whole lot of fun. No one goes to classes, carnival rides are brought onto campus, and the day is spent outside picnicking and relaxing. It is not just the students who love Flunk Day, professors like the time off too—they can be spotted "takin' it easy on the lawns with their students and families." And that is Knox College: the interweaving of a vigorous academic life with a fun social life. *—Pete Ortner*

FYI

If you come to Knox, you'd better bring "an open mind and an industrial-size bucket of sidewalk chalk."

What is the typical weekend schedule? "A good ol' fashioned frat party, some movies with friends, and a fair amount of studying (hey, they don't call it Hard Knox for nothing)."

If I could change one thing about Knox, I'd "build tunnels between all the buildings, so you wouldn't have to deal with the weather in the winter."

Three things every student at Knox should do before graduating are "study abroad, go sledding in the Knox Bowl with cafeteria trays, and have a really good time at Flunk Day."

Lake Forest College

Address: 555 North Sheridan Road; Lake Forest, IL 60045
Phone: 847-735-5000
E-mail address: admissions@lakeforest.edu
Web site URL: www.lakeforest.edu
Founded: 1857
Private or Public: private
Religious affiliation: Presbyterian
Location: suburban
Undergraduate enrollment: 1,319
Total enrollment: NA
Percent Male/Female: 41%/59%
Percent Minority: 21%
Percent African-American: 6%
Percent Asian: 4%
Percent Hispanic: 3%
Percent Native-American: 0%
Percent in-state/out of state: 48%/52%
Percent Pub HS: 63%
Number of Applicants: 1,666
Percent Accepted: 66%
Percent Accepted who enroll: 33%
Entering: 359
Transfers: 53
Application Deadline: 1 Mar
Mean SAT: NA
Mean ACT: NA
Middle 50% SAT range: V 520-620, M 510-620
Middle 50% ACT range: 23-28
3 Most popular majors: business/commerce, communication and media studies, English Language and literature
Retention: 77%
Graduation rate: 70%
On-campus housing: 81%
Fraternities: 19%
Sororities: 27%
Library: 231,845 volumes
Tuition and Fees: $24,406
Room and Board: $5,764
Financial aid, first-year: 70%
Varsity or Club Athletes: 32%
Early Decision or Early Action Acceptance Rate: ED 63%; EA 87%

Set in the wealthy suburb of Lake Forest, a five-minute walk from the beach of Lake Michigan, a fifty minute drive from Chicago, and filled with close, extremely social, and hardworking professors and students, Lake Forest College sounds a bit too good to be true. Sure, it has the makings of a great vacation getaway, but a real, four-year college? Get out of here. There must be a catch.

It's a Ton of Fun

One junior, when asked when the weekend started at Lake Forest College, was confused by the question. "The weekend doesn't quit," he said. Then he added, "But people have got their priorities, and not a lot of people say their priority is to party." However, one student double majoring in computer science and business said that parties are great: "They're so much fun. You go there, and it's 1,300 of your closest friends. If you bring a freshman to a party, it's like a dream for them. If an upperclassman brings a frosh, he'll introduce you to everyone, and everyone wants to know where you live, what do you do. It's so cool."

Lake Forest administration allows legal-age students to consume alcohol, as long as they're in their rooms behind closed doors. "They give us a little leeway; if we [mess] up there's consequences," explained one student. After being caught outside with alcohol three times, students are "kicked off housing."

When asked what differentiated Lake Forest from other schools, one student gushed, "The socialness. I can't even express it in words. It's unbelievable. When you go to class you say hi to everybody, if you go to a party, you know everybody. If you don't know somebody, it's like a long-lost brother. You're like, 'Where have you been? Why don't I know you?' Everyone hangs out; everyone knows everyone. It's literally like an oversized family at our school."

And when students are not at the parties, which usually take place on Fridays, they can easily hop on a train (the station is about a mile away; students drive and park their cars there) downtown for $1.75, or get a $5 unlimited weekend pass. As one English major put it, "We like to mix some culture in our social/party schedule." And of course, the city of Chicago speaks for itself.

Students who want to stay on campus and sober (some undergrads estimate that between 30 to 40 percent do not drink) have plenty of options too. Lots of movies, sporting events, community service, and dry social activities run by the Student Council can be found, although one sophomore mentioned that the turnout at the events is pretty small, since "it's a small school, and people are too busy getting trashed." But even so, it seems hard to knock a social scene where, as one athlete put it, "Everyone is welcome everywhere."

And the Academics Are Good

If the weekends "don't quit," then the classes could not be too challenging, right? No. Students all agreed that classes are difficult, entail a lot of work, and ultimately, are very rewarding. A junior said that after finishing a test one time, his professor gave him a high five, saying, "You studied so hard for this." Professors invite students to their houses for dinner, attend sporting events, and "want you to succeed and come back to visit and say 'Thanks for kicking my [butt] all through college—look where I am now,'" said a student. Students are close to their professors, who tend to be relatively young. Freshmen introductory courses are sometimes a source of complaint because they average 30 to 40 students, but upper-class courses max out at 25 and average between 6 and 10 students per class. Another junior said that "the professors are very competent and willing to let students exercise intellectual freedom and reward them accordingly."

In fact, some illustrious profs can be found at Lake Forest: the inventor of holography is in the physics department. There is also a world-renowned art historian, a nationally recognized postmodern theorist, and the leading authority on the philosophy of erotics. The "all-around, most competent, rewarding prof?" asks one student. "Bob Greenfield in the English department. Ph.D. Columbia, amazing." Students also mentioned Dawn Meyer in the music department, Jason Cody in chemistry, and Ben Goluboff in English. Professor Matheson in business/economics starts off every class with a joke to "loosen everybody up." Professor Guglielmi in the psychology department is "awesome, gets so pumped up in class. He'll throw chalk and erasers at you." There are no TAs, class participation is encouraged and necessary, and as one chemistry major quipped, "I'm taking organic chemistry, which is taught by two professors. Both meet with me on a regular basis. The Dean of the College helps me out. My advisor calls me in my room, to see if I need something. Professors really care. If there's anything that stands out about this school, it's that they really care, won't let you fail. They really encourage interaction and challenge you. Students rise to the occasion and really get a decent education."

The Sports Teams Are Good, Too!

The Lake Forest handball team is the best in the nation, literally, since there is only one division and Lake Forest is on top of it. Other sports are also top-notch. The men's swimming team has won three Midwest Conference titles recently, and the women's team has a tradition of first-place finishes. Men's tennis has also won titles the last couple of years. The men's soccer team is reputedly good, but the most popular varsity teams are men's hockey and women's basketball.

> **"The music is just as diverse as the people who go here. People listen to anything from swing to alternative to jazz to metal to rap to R&B."**

Juniors referred to a poll of students taken every year that revealed "astronomical statistics. Sixty-five percent of the freshmen class has played varsity athletics. Forty percent were captains of their teams. Thirty percent had a varsity letter in three or more sports." As one student put it, "Our school goes out and gets people that are leaders, that can express their feelings, who are able to perform well in the academic world. A 36 ACT is not what they're looking for. They want students that are well-rounded."

Student organizations mentioned included the campus radio station, Student Council, an environmental organization that is helping out with the reforestation of Lake Forest, and GLASS, the gay, lesbian, and straight society, one of whose events was to watch the Grammys together and cheer for Madonna. The student in charge of the radio station, when asked what type of music the undergrads listened to, answered, "The music is just as diverse as the people who go here. People listen to anything from swing to alternative to jazz to metal to rap to R&B."

"Our school thrives on diversity," emphasized a junior. She went on to explain how students were from all over the place, both from all over the States and other countries. There are also "all sorts of minority groups, an intercultural relations center, and all sorts of scholarships." However, students tend to be quite wealthy. A junior, when asked what students typically wore to class, said, "Polo, Prada, and Banana Republic." Somewhat antithetically, he went on to say, "There is certainly a spectrum of other people [not predominantly wealthy] here." There are also quite a few homosexual and interracial couples. And what brings the diversity of students together? As one student put it, "Everyone drinks. All races, they all get drunk and plastered together."

The Dorms Finally Get Renovated

Students report Lake Forest dorms were once in a "sad condition," but recent renovations have significantly raised the caliber of on-campus living. Even without the renovations, students all agreed that the dorms are "livable," a good thing, since not many can live off-campus because of the costly surrounding neighborhood. Lake Forest is home to multimillion-dollar houses, and "one of the most expensive places to live in the entire nation." (The town is not exactly a college town, although students did mention the popularity of the Lantern, which has Wednesday-night drink specials and Rainbows for Thursdays.)

The campus itself is "very, very beautiful. It's slightly hilly, but crisscrossed with ravines and an oak forest. It's just a mile or so from the lakefront." Buildings are red brick, and one building, Holt Chapel, is the center of an unusual tradition. Every year, "these super-religious people come out and all sit around it. They meditate and try to levitate the chapel. Just the concept of trying to levitate the 120-year-old building . . . it's pretty solid." There are three campuses: North, Middle, and South. Middle is where the classroom buildings are, and "it is a lug" from South Campus, where most of the students live (and where the parties are). Five dorms are on South Campus, and "all the jocks live down there because the sports center is down there. It's usually the crazy area," explained a Middle Campus resident. Along with the class buildings, there are two dorms on Middle Campus, including the Blackstone, which students need to apply to, to live in, since it is the "academic dorm." North Campus includes Cleveland Young, a residence hall for international students and those who have lived abroad. It was "just renovated. It's really, really nice," gushed one student.

Even the food is good, because Lake Forest switched to Aramark food service a few years ago, which does "a good job," say students. There's full salad and pasta bars daily, and "compared to other colleges, it's really good," said a junior. There are a couple of exceptions, however. "Some of the meats are bad, but it's tough to get good-quality meat," said one junior, while another mentioned, "They don't have enough seating, but it's getting fixed."

Ferris Bueller, Macaulay Culkin, and Harrison Ford Are Right

So, it seems the catches are small and getting fixed, and the great parts of Lake Forest College are going to last. Reputedly, Lake Forest has produced the most CEOs of any small college. And even Hollywood likes Lake Forest. Movies like *Ferris Bueller's Day Off*, *Home Alone*, and *The Fugitive* have all been shot here. Students cannot stop gushing, and as one said, "all sorts of races and ages come together, it's a super-friendly campus." It seems there is not much to lose and a whole lot of fun, learning, and friends to gain when it comes to Lake Forest College.—*Jennifer Wang and Staff*

FYI

If you come to Lake Forest, you'd better bring "your sneakers because so many people are athletic."

What is the typical weekend schedule? "Friday, party; Saturday, take the train downtown; Sunday, sleep late, relax, and catch up on work."

If I could change one thing about Lake Forest, "I'd make the weekends longer."

Three things that every student at Lake Forest should do before graduating are "go to the Lantern and Rainbows, go to a Winter Ball, and spend the day touring Chicago."

Loyola University

Address: 820 North Michigan Avenue; Chicago, IL 60611-9810
Phone: 312-915-6500
E-mail address: admission@luc.edu
Web site URL: www.luc.edu
Founded: 1870
Private or Public: private
Religious affiliation: Roman Catholic
Location: urban
Undergraduate enrollment: 7,533
Total enrollment: NA
Percent Male/Female: 34%/66%
Percent Minority: 32%
Percent African-American: 9%
Percent Asian: 11%
Percent Hispanic: 10%
Percent Native-American: 0%
Percent in-state/out of state: 68%/32%
Percent Pub HS: 57%
Number of Applicants: 8,759
Percent Accepted: 84%
Percent Accepted who enroll: 22%
Entering: 1,623
Transfers: 483
Application Deadline: rolling
Mean SAT: NA
Mean ACT: NA
Middle 50% SAT range: V 520-630, M 520-640
Middle 50% ACT range: 22-27
3 Most popular majors: business management, marketing, social sciences, biological and biomedical sciences
Retention: 83%
Graduation rate: 70%
On-campus housing: 29%
Fraternities: 7%
Sororities: 5%
Library: 1,108,157 volumes
Tuition and Fees: $21,198
Room and Board: $7,900
Financial aid, first-year: 71%
Varsity or Club Athletes: 25%
Early Decision or Early Action Acceptance Rate: NA

Set in the heart of Chicago, Loyola University is just as bustling as its surroundings. With five campuses and a diverse student body, Loyola is an exciting place with opportunities for all.

Course of Study: Intense or Well Rounded?

Take your pick. At Loyola, possibilities are plenty, and students vary greatly in their interests. Loyola is very strong in the sciences, its nursing program being the strongest and most intense major available. Students may choose to do a 16-month intensive nursing program, while others can follow a fiercely competitive pre-med curriculum or biochemistry major. Science majors are abundant and thrive in the state-of-the-art labs and through ongoing research with professors. One student said, "although the Math department can't speak English, Loyola is definitely a school for science majors."

Other students choose to focus less in the sciences and prefer a more well-rounded education, taking advantage of Loyola's strong foundations in the liberal arts. The college offers 38 majors, the most popular being biology, psychology, and business, and can be especially noted for its many interdisciplinary programs. Some of the more unique ones include Peace Studies, Urban Research and Learning, and Ethics. The International Center also encourages students to study abroad; the program at Loyola's Rome campus is the most popular.

Loyola does have a few requirements, including a core curriculum in communicative and expressive arts, history, literature, philosophy, social or natural science, math, and theology, due to the university's Jesuit affiliation. These requirements may appear overwhelming, but Loyola students seem to deal with them well, claiming that "the curriculum is flexible and requirements generally don't get in the way." One student said that "theology classes are considered easy, and communications is the way to go for slackers." Some students elect to participate in Loyola's Honors Program, while others live in learning communities, which are floors in residence halls reserved for people enrolled in the same groups of courses, enabling them to study and work together. Students at Loyola enjoy a liberal learning environment in which teachers work closely with students and class size is small (20–30 on average), permitting active discussions and debates. With its accommodating core curriculum, intense science programs, and diverse liberal arts courses, there is a niche for everyone at Loyola.

While On Campus . . .

Loyola's main campus, Lake Shore, and its four satellite campuses are located in the heart of Chicago. Thus, many students are commuters or live off campus. Bouncing about from campus to campus for different classes or simply leaving after class does not provide for strong community life, but it does encourage bonding among the students who do remain on campus. The student body itself is very ethnically diverse, although most characterize themselves as Christians coming from upper-middle-class backgrounds. One student noted that "segregation is based on interest, not race, and students here do tend to follow trends." A large percentage of undergrads participate in athletics—most of Loyola's varsity teams participate at the Division I level, and intramural sports are always popular. Loyola's lack of a football team has often led many to cheer for Chicago's professional sports teams more than their own, but has also increased enthusiasm for soccer, volleyball, and basketball, whose teams often host popular pseudo-tailgates.

In general, students speak well of the campus, with its abundant library and computing resources, and its excellent location. For those on campus, many of the dorms have been recently renovated. As one student stated simply and firmly, "I love my dorm room." This is no joke: suites are large, some with common rooms and only five or six students to one bathroom, which is cleaned routinely for them. Simpson Hall is the newest and most coveted, with air conditioning, a computer cluster, and its own dining hall, whose food is considered, "uhhh, good, I guess."

"The entertainment and vast resources provided solely by the city of Chicago enrich the college experience immeasurably."

Interacting with the Real World

The bustling city of Chicago provides a wonderful setting for Loyola and is by far one of its main assets. Those who like an urban environment will do well at Loyola, which is a five-minute bus ride to downtown Chicago. The college prides itself on its strong ties with the community, and students take advantage of the city by enjoying its eclectic restaurants. Wolf & Kettle coffeehouse is a popular hangout for students, while musical and theatrical performances in the Chicago area always draw crowds of Loyola students. "The entertainment and vast resources provided solely by the city of Chicago enrich the college experience immeasurably," declared one student. Internships, research, and field work at major institutions cannot go without mentioning. Many students adopt projects in the community, performing various social services addressing problems such as illiteracy, poverty, and hunger. Students feel that living in Chicago has given them "a heightened sense of independence" and kept them in contact with the real world. This environment, many believe, will better prepare them for the future than if they'd gone to any other institution.

"Ad Majorem Dei Gloriam"

For the greater glory of God—Loyola's motto. The Jesuit affiliation at Loyola has shaped the college in many specific ways. First, its concern for justice and ethics in society has fueled community service programs and active political organizations throughout campus. Although there are more than 140 activities to choose from, students find that many are not as dynamic as the political groups, which often debate controversial issues such as gay rights and peace issues.

In accordance with its Catholic philosophy, students have strict dorm constraints. Members of the opposite sex are not allowed in dorm rooms after midnight on weekdays and 2 A.M. on weekends. The social life is molded by this somewhat conservative mindset, so students often search for entertainment off campus. Being underage is not seen as much of a problem, for bars and clubs have lax carding policies, and according to most students, finding alcohol is easy. One freshman said, "I don't know any non-drinkers, but I don't think non-drinkers would ever feel pressured to drink like many were in high school." Hamilton Bar is well-known for its nightly specials—including theme nights—that attract many freshmen, among whom the trend seems to be random hook-ups, and not much serious dating.

Greek life does not dominate the social scene, but frats do throw an annual ice-skating party downtown and hold the Greek Olympics, a major sporting event. Other options for entertainment include the movies and concerts that are held on campus at least every other week. Nonetheless, Chicago's luster attracts most students on weekends, and students living both on and off campus pour into downtown for Friday and Saturday nights. Students at Loyola certainly know how to party and are independent in seeking out a social life. At this cosmopolitan college, classes, nightlife, and the benefits of urban living all combine in a college experience unlike most others.—*Carolina Galvao*

FYI

If you could come to Loyola, you'd better bring a "coat. Being next to the lake brings absolutely bone-chilling winds."

What is the typical weekend schedule? "Watch games, go into the city for shopping and dinner, and always party!"

If I could change one thing about Loyola, "I'd try to change the way it is so open to the city. The amount of suspicious people walking around is kind of creepy."

Three things every student at Loyola should do before graduating are "go to a Loyola sports event, have a midnight picnic on Halas field, and sleep all day after a huge party."

Northwestern University

Address: 633 Clark Street; Evanston, IL 60204-3854
Phone: 847-491-7271
E-mail address: ug-admission@northwestern.edu
Web site URL: www.northwestern.edu
Founded: 1851
Private or Public: private
Religious affiliation: none
Location: suburban
Undergraduate enrollment: 7,946
Total enrollment: NA
Percent Male/Female: 47%/53%
Percent Minority: 31%
Percent African-American: 6%
Percent Asian: 13%
Percent Hispanic: 5%
Percent Native-American: 0%
Percent in-state/out of state: 26%/74%
Percent Pub HS: 77%
Number of Applicants: 14,283
Percent Accepted: 33%
Percent Accepted who enroll: 43%
Entering: 2,005
Transfers: 59
Application Deadline: 1 Jan
Mean SAT: NA
Mean ACT: NA
Middle 50% SAT range: V 640-730, M 660-750
Middle 50% ACT range: 28-33
3 Most popular majors: engineering, economics, journalism
Retention: 96%
Graduation rate: 93%
On-campus housing: 65%
Fraternities: 30%
Sororities: 40%
Library: 4,217,321 volumes
Tuition and Fees: $28,524
Room and Board: $8,967
Financial aid, first-year: 45%
Varsity or Club Athletes: 15%
Early Decision or Early Action Acceptance Rate: ED 53%

Known as the Ivy of the Midwest, Northwestern combines serious academics with a huge variety of extracurricular events, made apparent by the various announcements painted on "The Rock." Donated by the class of 1912, this unofficial bulletin board of the decades is covered with layer upon layer of paint and displays everything from fraternity pride to campus events like AIDS Awareness Week. To go along with this symbol of campus pride, Northwestern has highly acclaimed programs in communications, speech and journalism—the Medill School of Journalism and the School of Speech are some of the best in the country. The Rock is a monument to how diverse ideas can come together at Northwestern to create a community with strength and spirit.

Who Will I Hang Out With?

The average Northwesterner is multitalented, upper-middle class, and intelligent. Students are incredibly hard working and very goal-oriented—one senior complained about having to force her friends to "pull their noses out from their books and loosen up a little." Campus concerns are mainly political or centered on school affairs, but only when they don't interfere with studying. Although each student has his or her own style, the typical Northwesterner wears jeans, a T-shirt, and a Northface jacket. "There are members of the Abercrombie aristocracy, as well as those with dirty T-shirts and multiple piercings," observed one student.

Northwestern's student population is very diverse, with at least 50 different nationalities and almost every state in the U.S. represented. Certain ethnic groups do self-segregate, though and students note that individuals make whichever choice is most comfortable. Within this mix of students, dating is not big at Northwestern and long-term relationships are rare. Students describe each other as fairly attractive despite being a "bit nerdy." There is a sense that students are often so focused on academics and clubs that they don't really make room for a relationship. One sophomore commented, "This is definitely more of a hook-up school than a boyfriend school."

What Are the Classes Like?

Classes at Northwestern fill the spectrum from frustratingly difficult to surprisingly easy. Any hard science course at the Technological Institute is likely to be challenging. People lured by the mysticism of stars often suffer in heavily physics-based astronomy classes, while most students appear baffled by rigorous computer science courses. On the other hand, Introduction to Sociology, Introduction to Psychology, and Introduction to Music are known to allow students a mental break from intense studying. However, not all introductory classes are easy. Economics is unpopular due to its difficulty, and students say that the professors aim at weeding out freshmen. Analysis in Performance of Literature is a popular course as is "Rocks for Jocks," a notoriously easy geology class.

Introduction to Sociology is taught by Charles Moskos, a living legend at the school and once an aide to president Clinton. Other famous professors include Lane Fenrich (history), Mark Witte (economics), and Linda Gates—famed voice coach for John Cusack. Professors are described as "extremely knowledgeable" and "easily approachable." In general they are well-liked. One student fondly recalled her Russian history professor singing Russian folk songs in class and proclaiming his passion for the Slavic culture, despite being from Ohio. Teaching assistants don't usually teach classes but do lead discussion sections for some classes.

Work Hard . . .

Students must enroll in one of seven undergraduate schools: the Wineberg College of Arts and Sciences (CAS), the McCormick School of Engineering, the Medill School of Journalism, the School of Speech, the School of Music, the School of Education and Social Policy, or the School of Theology. Students recommend that freshmen come to school with a major in mind, as it is more difficult to transfer into another college after applying to CAS undecided. The university is very pre-professional, so "everyone is shooting for a place in law school or med school."

There are six distribution requirements in CAS: Natural Science, Formal Studies (math), Social and Behavioral Sciences, Historical Studies, Fine Arts and Literature, and Values (with courses in law and Buddhism). There is also a language requirement. Most students don't find these requirements a struggle, though the quarter-term system means there is an immense workload. Classes are squashed into 10-week segments, but many students love the fact that they can take so many different classes. Others praise the fact that they can count off the number of weeks left until vacation on their fingers.

Play Hard

"During your first year, you party on campus with your friends on your floor, or otherwise venture in droves of 20-plus people to an off-campus kegger," one student explained. There is a North-South divide on campus. Most of the parties are on the preppy, frat-saturated North side, whereas the artsy South side is quieter.

About 40 percent of students are involved in frats or sororities and the underclassmen scene revolves around these Greek parties. Some sororities are very highbrow—the higher the fees the higher the prestige. The sororities have gorgeous housing that make up for this while, typical to most universities, the frat houses aren't as well kept. There's a freeze on Greek activity in the fall quarter, so freshmen rush in winter quarter. Crowds of students attend frat parties that typically revolve around a keg of cheap beer, but many claim that dorm parties are often more fun. There is also a very active theater scene, with parties that charge entrance fees to raise money for productions. Non-drinkers do go to parties to hang out and generally don't feel excluded or pressured to drink.

> **"Northwestern may take a while to warm up to, but it becomes your home like no other."**

Alcohol is not allowed on campus unless you are at least 21 and are drinking with other legal students with your door closed. However, the administration, as described by one student, "pretends to take a hard line on drugs and alcohol, yet things slip through the cracks fairly easily." Drugs are not a common feature as they aren't readily available or cheap in Evanston.

There are plenty of occasions to get

dressed up at Northwestern, with formal dances often held in hotels and ballrooms. There is an annual drinking party dedicated to Frances Willard, who founded the alcohol prohibition movement. These theme parties are often used for fundraising: at the Red Party everyone dresses in red, while at other parties students go dressed Hawaiian or not dressed at all. Aside from parties, there are organized campus-wide events such as Armadillo Day ("Dillo Day") in May, a huge outdoor concert celebrating summer. One student found the array of activities "mind boggling." There are many acclaimed community service groups, many students opting for Alternative Spring Breaks where they do service or plant trees for a week. Other noteworthy activities are the 30-hour Dance Marathon, The Dolphin Show, and The Daily Northwestern.

Where Will I Live?

Freshmen and upperclassmen live together in residential colleges or dorms. The residential colleges usually have a theme, and students have to write a mini-essay to explain their choice of dorm (which is not necessarily related to any major). Some students prefer this arrangement, as the smaller residential colleges allow them to meet and befriend more people. The best dorms, Alison and Hinman, have air conditioning, elevators, lots of windows, and plenty of space. Others, such as Bobb-McCulloch, are known mostly as party dorms and are permanently messy. Many upperclassmen escape student housing entirely and move off campus after their freshman year. In general, the south side is inhabited by artsy theater-majors, while the north side houses athletes, frat guys, and sorority girls.

The Northwestern campus is picturesque; it is forested, right next to Lake Michigan and has an amazing view of downtown Chicago. Everyone goes to the rocks near Lake Michigan, and the "Lakefill" (a peninsula the university built to extend into the lake) is especially popular for cheap, romantic dates. The campus is over a mile long, but students say it is easy to walk everywhere. There are old Victorian-style buildings covered with ivy, as well as more modern buildings, such as the huge concrete library built in the 1970s. Recently there has been a lot of campus construction. The Ford Motor Company has donated $10 million to create the Ford Motor Company Engineering Design Center, slated for completion in fall 2004, while nano-technology buildings, an addition to the gym, and some new dorms are all currently being built.

Is It Edible?

"Most food at college dining halls leaves a lot to be desired, and Northwestern is no different." In fact, the food got a unanimous groan of dissatisfaction. The hours for breakfast and lunch are fine, but students complain about the early dinner times—the dining halls close at 7 P.M. Many students grab a late-night meal at Foster-Walker between 10:30 and 11:30, the only dining hall to offer this service. The Flex Plan offers students the option of bonus bucks that can be spent at the Norris Center, which serves a variety of food at different kiosks. Off-campus dining is superb; Evanston is known as the "dining capital of the North Shore." Only 15 minutes away, Northwesterners feast at Middle-Eastern, Indian, Chinese, or other ethnic restaurants. Clark's Diner and Flat Top Grill, a Mongolian BBQ, come highly recommended.

Go Wildcats!

Northwestern placed second in Big 10 football last year, and annually competes against rivals Michigan and Michigan State, as well as the other nine schools in the Big 10. Though the University has not done as well in other sports recently, sports are well-represented in general, and the fencing team is reported to look especially promising in years to come.

Facilities for non-athletes are state-of-the-art. The Sports Pavilion and Aquatic Center (SPAC) has everything—weights rooms, squash and tennis courts, a track, and a swimming pool. Club sports and intramurals are pretty popular, too.

At Northwestern, the level of intelligence and competitiveness is incredible, and students accustomed to being at the top of their class say it takes a little while to get used to their new life. Students are intensely involved in whatever they do, whether singing in an a capella group or playing intramural sports. The common complaint is that people are too busy doing their own thing to have fun, but judging from the party scene, Northwesterners can have a good time when they want to. As one upperclassman pointed out, "Northwestern may take a while to warm up to, but it becomes your home like no other."—*Niyati Gupta*

FYI

If you come to Northwestern, you'd better bring a "winter hat, as it's freezing here."

A typical weekend schedule would be to "take in a play on Broadway in the Windy City or watch a football game on Saturday, go to a frat party in the evening, and then spend Sunday recovering and cramming for Monday's lecture."

If I could change one thing about Northwestern it would be "the social scene, which is too dominated by the Greek system."

Three things every student at Northwestern should do before graduating are "watch a sunrise on Lake Michigan, paint The Rock, and take part in 'Primal Scream' on the Sunday before reading week—when everybody screams out of their windows in unison as a form of stress relief."

Southern Illinois University

Address: Mail Code 4512; Carbondale, IL 62901
Phone: 618-453-4381
E-mail address: admrec@siu.edu
Web site URL: www.siuc.edu
Founded: 1869
Private or Public: public
Religious affiliation: none
Location: rural
Undergraduate enrollment: 16,863
Total enrollment: NA
Percent Male/Female: 56%/44%
Percent Minority: 22%
Percent African-American: 13%
Percent Asian: 1%
Percent Hispanic: 3%
Percent Native-American: 0%
Percent in-state/out of state: 85%/15%
Percent Pub HS: 80%
Number of Applicants: 8,073
Percent Accepted: 78%
Percent Accepted who enroll: 40%
Entering: 2,532
Transfers: 2,121
Application Deadline: rolling
Mean SAT: NA
Mean ACT: NA
Middle 50% SAT range: V 440-560, M 450-595
Middle 50% ACT range: 18-23
3 Most popular majors: education, business management, marketing, engineering, health professions
Retention: 70%
Graduation rate: 39%
On-campus housing: 29%
Fraternities: 6%
Sororities: 5%
Library: 4,165,239 volumes
Tuition and Fees: $5,521 in; $9,766 out
Room and Board: $4,886
Financial aid, first-year: 53%
Varsity or Club Athletes: 8%
Early Decision or Early Action Acceptance Rate: NA

Southern Illinois University has long been known to be one of the biggest party schools in the Midwest. The administration has tried to correct the school's "no work, all play" image and to some extent, they have succeeded. Many upperclassmen claim that they can see a change in the school's party atmosphere, but make no mistake, partying and particularly drinking are still central features of life at Southern. The combination of an attractive and outgoing student body, a town full of bars, and plenty of "Southern Hospitality" makes SIU a great place for those looking to have a good time in college—Oh yeah, and to get a great education too.

Academics: A World of Opportunity

Southern Illinois boasts over 200 majors, specializations, and minors for undergrads, and has one of the most diverse program selections offered in the Midwest. Because it is a state school with almost 25,000 students (15,000 undergrads), SIU offers a world of academic opportunities to suit every interest and need. Students can major in anything from Retailing or Russian, to Foods or Finance. However, just because it is a relatively large school doesn't mean that students remain nameless faces in giant lecture halls. SIU's size and range of class offerings allow for plenty of small classes, discussion groups, and labs—even for introductory or required core classes.

Southern's core course requirement must be completed by graduation and consists of classes in basic areas like speech, math, composition, science, human health, arts, and humanities. Although these classes tend to be the biggest on campus (large lectures can have anywhere from 200 to 400 students), there are also opportunities for smaller, more intimate classes. Yet even in the large lecture classes, professors are always accessible. One freshman said, "Professors really encourage you to ask questions in class or to come to their office hours. They're always willing to talk to students." Although there are variations between the departments, students seem to be satisfied with their professors. One senior said, "Southern offers a melting pot of a lot of great professors. I just wish that people would realize it and take advantage of the resources they offer."

Because Southern offers so many different majors, there is a great deal of variation in workload, requirements, and quality from department to department. Southern's Aviation Program, complete with runways and its own fleet of 727s, is renowned among Midwestern schools. The university also boasts its own barns and farms for its Agricultural Studies and Pre-veterinarian majors, and a state-of-the-art broadcasting center for Radio and Television majors. Some majors are harder than others, with sciences generally being the toughest, but most students say that the workload is manageable. According to one student, "It kind of depends on how much work you want to put into your education. You can make it as easy or as hard as you want it to be."

Students are asked to declare a major when they are admitted, and they are then to assigned an advisor in that department. However, a large number of students arrive each fall unsure of what they want to do in college. These students enter the "pre-major" program and are assigned a pre-major advisor. These students work with their advisor to select a range of courses that allows the student to sample a variety of areas before choosing a major, which is usually by the end of sophomore year.

Most students are happy with their academic experiences at Southern. As one senior remarked looking back, "It has been better than my first impression of the school." Many also cite the cost-effectiveness of a Southern education as a major advantage.

Southern Hospitality

Southern students are rated by their peers as "friendly," "laid back," and "outgoing." One student attributed this friendly attitude to the "country mentality" of Southern students. There is a lot of diversity on campus, both racially and economically, and there are also many international students: "You get all kinds of people here at Southern." Because of Southern's size, once students find others like themselves, they tend to hang out in groups, making cliques fairly common—especially among Greeks and athletes. However, according to one student, "Although there are groups, everyone is still friendly and willing to hang out with anyone. You can get into any group if you want to." This social atmosphere and campus diversity makes for a vibrant student body, as well as a multitude of opportunities outside of the classroom.

There are over 150 Registered Student Organizations, or RSOs, at Southern. Ranging from international and ethnic student groups to political organizations and entertainment groups, the variety of extracurricular activities on campus is as diverse as its student body, and any student is bound to find a group of interest. Student Programming Council is a popular organization that plans events on campus like themed dances, movies, and concerts. They usually plan two or three big concerts a year, bringing artists like 311 and Pink to play on campus. About seven percent of the student body is involved in the Greek system, a surprisingly low number for such a socially focused campus. One student blamed low Greek involvement on the "very strict rules about parties in fraternity and sorority houses," which shifts the focus of the social scene to other off-campus houses or to Carbondale's bars. Although small, Southern's Greek system leaves a big mark on campus by being very involved in community service, and many chapters have been nationally recognized for their achievements.

Although there are more than enough groups to meet any student's interests, some students claim that there could be more student involvement. "Some people don't know about what is out there, or they just don't care about getting involved," said one junior. However, many report that those students who do choose to become involved in campus organizations are dedicated to what they do and are happy with their choices.

Saluki Athletics

Students are supportive of their athletic teams, but attendance is usually related to how well the team is doing and is often limited to the men's basketball and football games. SIU's unique mascot, an Egyptian hunting dog, is a source of pride for students. According to one junior, "Students show up to games in lots of Saluki apparel." With the men's basketball team making it to the Sweet 16 in 2002, SIU's teams are competitive for a small, Division I school. Intramural and club sports are very popular among students, facilitated by SIU's gigantic student rec center, which boasts basketball courts, racquetball courts, and an Olympic-sized pool. The rec center also rents out athletic equipment, including tents and camping supplies, to students. One student gushed, "If I could show prospective students one thing at Southern, the rec center would be it."

OK, So on to the Party Already!

When asked to describe the social scene at SIU, one student responded, "Have you ever seen that poster with John Belushi wearing the COLLEGE shirt from *Animal House*? That pretty much says it all." Most students at Southern definitely like to let loose and have a good time. Alcohol is not allowed on campus, except in the designated over-21 dorm, so students flock to Carbondale's bars or to off-campus houses for parties. Students who are 19 can get into bars in Carbondale, and once inside they don't have a hard time getting drinks. However, one student cautioned, "You have to be careful, because the cops do random raids in the bars and people do get fined or arrested." The same goes for parties in off-campus houses, but usually only when they are "big, out-of-control parties." Alcohol is by far the most popular drug on campus, with pot being a close second, but students say that if you are really looking, you can get almost anything and that "a lot of drugs come through Carbondale."

"Have you ever seen that poster with John Belushi wearing the COLLEGE shirt from *Animal House*? That pretty much says it all."

Students at Southern perceive their school's party scene as "just like any other big school's," and agree that it has definitely mellowed out in recent years despite the school's reputation. Some students do not drink, and others prefer to drink in a laid-back atmosphere with a few friends. Students also report that the party scene subsides dramatically after the first few weeks of school, when there are big parties every night. Southern is definitely a very social campus, but students are quick to point out that not everyone goes out to bars every night, and that there isn't necessarily a lot of pressure to do so. According to one student, "What you choose to do on the weekends depends on the type of person you are and the type of people you choose to have around you."

Where You Wake Up the Morning After

Students have traditionally been required to live on campus for their first two years at Southern, but beginning with the Class of 2007, sophomores will be able to live off campus in approved housing. Students describe on-campus housing as "typical dorms" and don't have too many complaints. There are three main residential areas—University Park, Brush Towers, and Thompson Point—each of which has its own dining hall. Freshmen usually live in University Park or Brush Towers, which are both located on the West side of campus. University Park is said to have the smallest rooms, but is located in a rustic wooded area of campus. The rooms in Brush Towers have private bathrooms shared between suites and small kitchenettes, but one student reports that it can be a chaotic place to live because there are "three buildings each with 17 floors, and that means a lot of people living in one place!" The third area, Thompson Point, is located right on Southern's Thompson Lake, and is definitely the most picturesque place to live on campus and often the most desirable. The rooms can be small, but the buildings are smaller, more personal, and located closer to the heart of campus. All three residential areas have healthy lifestyle floors, quiet floors, and special theme areas where students can live with others in their major. Most upperclassmen elect to live off campus, whereas one student reported, "the appeal comes from being able to have more independence, namely the freedom to have parties." Off campus houses vary in quality and price, but most are fairly close to campus.

Students call SIU's campus "picturesque," "woodsy," and "serene." Although the campus is large and spread out, most find that their classes tend to be in the same area, especially after they have declared their major. Many were pleasantly surprised to find rolling green hills, not vast expanses of cornfields, in this part of Illinois, and students interested in the outdoors have plenty of areas to hike and camp around campus. St. Louis is about 90 minutes away, and is a popular destination for students who want to get away for the weekend. Carbondale is described as "a typical college town," which, in addition to its bars, offers the usual assortment of chain restaurants and superstores. Some students feel that relations between the town's residents and the university are strained, but that the town benefits by having the university there. "Without SIU," said one student, "Carbondale would be just another rural Illinois town."

Southern Satisfaction

Most students say that they are satisfied with their experiences at SIU and the quality of their education. The biggest complaints are usually about the level of drinking and the relative lack of student involvement in campus organizations. However, most say that they have seen positive changes in campus life since they arrived at Southern, and that they expect more in the future. SIU is a place large enough to offer students a range of opportunities and experiences, and most feel that they have the chance to make their experiences there whatever they want them to be. —*Jessica Lenox*

FYI

If you come to SIU, you'd better bring "your older brother or sister's ID."
A typical weekend at Southern consists of "liquor, liquor, and more liquor."
If I could change one thing about SIU it would be "to get more people involved on campus."
Three things every Southern student should do before graduating are "Go to a men's basketball game, see a band off campus, and build a cardboard boat for Thompson Lake."

University of Chicago

Address: 5801 East Ellis Avenue; Chicago, IL 60637
Phone: 773-702-8650
E-mail address: college-admissions@uchicago.edu
Web site URL: www.uchicago.edu
Founded: 1892
Private or Public: private
Religious affiliation: none
Location: urban
Undergraduate enrollment: 4,236
Total enrollment: NA
Percent Male/Female: 50%/50%
Percent Minority: 36%
Percent African-American: 4%
Percent Asian: 15%
Percent Hispanic: 7%
Percent Native-American: 0%
Percent in-state/out of state: 22%/78%
Percent Pub HS: 61%
Number of Applicants: 8,139
Percent Accepted: 42%
Percent Accepted who enroll: 33%
Entering: 1,114
Transfers: 74
Application Deadline: 1 Jan
Mean SAT: NA
Mean ACT: NA
Middle 50% SAT range: V 660-750, M 650-750
Middle 50% ACT range: 28-32
3 Most popular majors: social sciences, biology, English
Retention: 95%
Graduation rate: 90%
On-campus housing: 66%
Fraternities: 12%
Sororities: 5%
Library: 6,832,833 volumes
Tuition and Fees: $29,238
Room and Board: $9,315
Financial aid, first-year: 47%
Varsity or Club Athletes: 40%
Early Decision or Early Action Acceptance Rate: EA 46%

Every year for three and a half days at the beginning of May, students at the University of Chicago get caught up in the frenzy of Scavenger Hunt, an event that can only be described as a classic example of life in Hyde Park. To win, teams try to rack up as many points a possible by finding items from the master list. Last year, members road-tripped through the Midwest to pick up objects from Big Ten universities, chugged cans of creamed corn in the Scav Hunt Olympics, and seized control of university buildings. "One year, a homemade nuclear reactor was on the list and, as it's the U of C, two students actually made one in their dorm room. I'm less frightened that someone made a nuclear reactor than by the number of students I know who know how to make them," said one senior. An interesting blend of the quirky, the creative, and the intellectual, Scav Hunt exemplifies the "sheer madness" that is an undeniable part of one of the most highly regarded schools in the nation.

Work Hard . . .

As one independent studies major put it, "U of C students are masochistic in a way. We hate it, but we love it." The University of Chicago is known for its particularly demanding academics, and most students there agreed that the work is intense. The sometimes overwhelming atmosphere of Chicago is due at least in part to the university's adherence to the quarter system. Classes run on a ten-week schedule so that students take finals three times during the year; midterms can begin as early as four weeks into the term. Using the premed requirements as an example, one student said, "It takes a year and half at most schools to finish organic chemistry and biochemistry . . . Here, you do it in one." As most would expect, these time constraints can translate into heavy assignments that are simply a fact of life. One senior student characterized the workload as "both excessive and necessary. I haven't had a class where I felt as if the problem sets or the reading assignments were not necessary. At the same time, I'm always behind in my work." Still, some people at U of C described their work as "not too bad," emphasizing that the level of difficulty often depended on an individual's course load and study habits.

In addition to the trimester-system, students must also deal with the requirements of the Common Core, a program meant to assure that graduates from the U of C receive a "true liberal arts" education. Although less stringent than in previous years, the Core requires that students take six classes in the humanities, six in mathematics and natural sciences (with at least two courses in the physical sciences and one in mathematics), and three courses in social sciences, in addition to fulfilling a language and physical education requirement. The Core takes up roughly a third of the credits required to graduate, with the remaining two-thirds split evenly between electives and classes necessary for a "concentration" (the U of C term for a major). Although they admitted that the core requirements were a source of controversy, most students praised the Core as "a way to get a taste of every subject" before committing to a particular concentration. Students can use high AP and IB tests scores to minimize the number of classes needed to fulfill the Core, but one senior felt that most people at Chicago would create a similar sampling without the graduation criteria. "Part of what makes U of C students different is our desire to know anything and everything inside out. The core plays a big part in facilitating that sort of outlook."

Such an extensive list of requirements means that relatively few classes are freshman-only, as most people are still trying to fulfill the core during their third or fourth year. The exceptions are Hum (the U of C name for the humanities requirement, pronounced "Hume") and calculus classes; most freshman take the former to improve their writing (trained by members of the Little Red Schoolhouse, Chicago's nationally renowned program for the teaching of writing) and the latter to complete the math requirement while it is still fresh from high school. Classes are split between lecture and discussion formats, with lecture classes that range from 50 to 75 students and discussion sections that generally max out at 30. Students pointed out that class size is not as important as the skill of the professor: "I was in a discussion class of about 40 that the professor made a great class because he really made discussion possible. I've also been in classes of 12 that were not handled nearly as well." Teaching assistants are particularly prevalent in large classes, but in the opinion of one freshman, "Professors, unless it's a large science intro class, don't depend too heavily on the TAs for anything other than grading." In general, students consider their professors to be accessible and open for questions. Still, the grading practices, considered "WAY too harsh" by some and "fair, but honest" by others, are universally acknowledged to be tough.

Nerd Pride

Some of Chicago's academic environment results not just from the classes but also from the students themselves. One senior fondly said, "Smart to the point of geeky is what I heard and what I expected and what I see. There *are* some stereotypically cool people on campus, however, I eventually see their nerdy sides, and then I know why they're here." This "school spirit in terms of our nerd pride" is one of the things that unites the students and makes all the studying that is necessary possible. While the vast majority of students on campus are white or Asian, students called the campus "very culturally diverse," pointing to the large number of ethnic student organizations. One freshman was particularly impressed by the visibility of these groups, "always organizing big events that the whole student body can take part in, like cultural shows, festivals, and formals." Although they are admittedly "dedicated to studying," U of C students are all quick to point out that a commitment to various extracurricular activities is the norm. Several students cited MUNUC (Model United Nations of the University of Chicago) as one of the biggest groups on campus, an organization that conducts a conference on international relations every year for roughly 2,000 high school students.

Students are unashamed of their complete lack of interest in varsity sports. A fourth-year scoffed, "I've never been to a game, and most people don't even go to playoff games if they know about them in advance." This indifference about U of C teams is consistent with the attitude about sports in general. Club sports "have been having a hard time recently" although intramural sports are more popular. Many students were underwhelmed by the quality of the athletic facilities on campus, but a new gym is under construction. One freshman summed up the concern for fitness on campus saying, "It's just not what dominates conversations."

Play Moderately

In keeping with the academic atmosphere of the University of Chicago, one freshman noted that "we aren't known for the wild parties and social extravaganzas of other universities." With six fraternities and three sororities, Greek life does not control the social scene with much force. An International Studies major noted, "Rushing is not hard. They are almost always under quota so they're always trying to recruit." Campus-wide participation is more likely to occur in events like the various lectures, theater productions, and concerts (mainly classical) typical of most colleges. One party that *is* well attended by most of the student body is Summer Breeze, scheduled just before the last round of midterms begin. The student group COUP "turns the quads into a carnival complete with hypnotists, giant sumo wrestler suits, orbitrons . . . just generally fun stuff," said one senior. MAB, an organization in charge of recruiting big-name talent to play on campus, throws its biggest show of the year, featuring performers such as Moby, Sonic Youth, Busta Rhymes, and G-Love and Special Sauce. Orientation (also known as "O-week"), "like summer camp in late September," offers similar events before school truly begins.

"Smart to the point of geeky is what I heard and what I expected and what I see."

In general, the same principle that governs life at the U of C applies to free time. As summarized by one freshman, "Here a person's experience really depends on what he or she makes it out to be." After-hours activities during freshman year seem to be focused more on campus, but upperclassmen typically venture outside of Hyde Park into the rest of Chicago. While most clubs are 21+, many are not very strict about enforcing this rule. As one upperclassman was quick to point out, "You can do so much without having to be 21. There are so many large and small theaters, plenty of film festivals, cool restaurants, ethnic neighborhoods, protests and rallies. . . ." When asked about the dating scene, one freshman replied "One thing you should know about Chicago is that it is NOT known for social aptitude . . . we're nerds, most of us at least, and we're definitely not known for an attractive population." Relationships, if they do occur, are generally more serious, lacking "the random hook-ups of other schools."

Where the Living Is Easy

"The social scene also depends greatly on where you live, as each dorm has its own social characteristics," one undergraduate observed. Currently, students are dispersed among the 11 dorms regardless of year, although buildings with dining halls that are closer to campus (Woodward, Pierce, and Burston Johnson) generally have higher concentrations of freshman. The style and layout of the rooms vary from dorm to dorm. One senior recommended, "If you want a single and want to be near the lake, you should live in Broadview. If you want a social dorm with older students and apartment-style rooms try Shoreland. Every dorm has its benefits and drawbacks." Residents are fairly devoted to the place they live because of U of C's housing system. With the exception of the small dorms, each residence hall is divided into "houses." Each house has a residential advisor who is a junior or senior (houses with over 70 students have two) and a residential head (RH) who is a member of the junior faculty or a grad student. Buildings that consist of more than one house also have a resident master drawn from the senior faculty. Masters plan large events involving the entire dorm (such as Shoreland's "infamous Karaoke Night"), while RAs and RHs organize various outing for their house each quarter, such as movie nights or trips to inexpensive plays. Only about half of the upperclassmen at Chicago live on campus. While Hyde Park has the reputation of being unsafe, students said that basic "street smarts" are all the protection that is really necessary. Even the defenders of the area will admit, "The neighborhoods surrounding Hyde Park aren't very nice," but add that these pockets are "rapidly being gentrified, which is another issue in and of itself." All students living on campus must be on the meal plan, but only freshman are required to have the full meal plan (17 per week). With vegan and vegetarian options, students generally praised the offerings in the dining hall, going so far as to call the fare "great," the single critique being the early hours for dinner.

According to one freshman, students at the University of Chicago are critical of their school by nature. "We make fun of ourselves, put ourselves and put the school down, make numerous derogatory comments, but that is the way we are, and we know it, and love it." Although this is not school spirit in a traditional sense, Chicago is not the "traditional" university of beer, frats, and footfall. With the amenities of Chicago, a star-studded faculty, and an intensely intellectual environment, the University of Chicago offers its students the resources to make their college experience their own. —*Lauren Johns*

FYI

If you come to U of C, you'd better bring "your backpack and books."

What is the typical weekend schedule? "Friday: catch a movie; Saturday: watch TV and do some reading; Sunday: relax and prepare for classes."

If I could change one thing about UChicago, "I'd give it a more social reputation."

The three things that every student at UChicago should do before graduating are "go to the Checkerboard, be on a Scav Hunt team, and step on the seal in front of Reynolds."

University of Illinois at Chicago

Address: 601 South Morgan M/C 102; Chicago, IL 60607
Phone: 312-996-4350
E-mail address: uicadmit@uic.edu
Web site URL: www.uic.edu
Founded: 1965
Private or Public: public
Religious affiliation: none
Location: urban
Undergraduate enrollment: 16,543
Total enrollment: NA
Percent Male/Female: 45%/55%
Percent Minority: 52%
Percent African-American: 9%
Percent Asian: 24%
Percent Hispanic: 16%
Percent Native-American: 0%
Percent in-state/out of state: 97%/3%
Percent Pub HS: 52%
Number of Applicants: 11,727
Percent Accepted: 63%
Percent Accepted who enroll: 41%
Entering: 3,015
Transfers: 1,973
Application Deadline: 1 Apr
Mean SAT: NA
Mean ACT: NA
Middle 50% SAT range: NA
Middle 50% ACT range: 20-25
3 Most popular majors: business management, marketing, engineering, health professions
Retention: 78%
Graduation rate: 44%
On-campus housing: 12%
Fraternities: 3%
Sororities: 2%
Library: 3,066,700 volumes
Tuition and Fees: $6,900 in; $14,600 out
Room and Board: $7,500
Financial aid, first-year: 56%
Varsity or Club Athletes: 1%
Early Decision or Early Action Acceptance Rate: NA

Nestled in the heart of downtown Chicago, the University of Illinois at Chicago offers a "real-world" academic experience and a student body as diverse as the city which surrounds it. Although it is known to be a "commuter school," with many students living and working at home or off campus, students still praise the quality of their experiences, academic and extracurricular, at UIC. One student explained, "UIC students are *real-life.* Many are working their way through college, and some are even supporting families. This keeps everyone grounded."

The diversity of its students and its location in central Chicago make UIC a vibrant campus with a myriad of opportunities for undergraduate students.

Real World (and Renowned) Academics

Most students agree that though it offers strong humanities programs through its College of Liberal Arts and Sciences, UIC is oriented more toward math and sciences because of the impressive resources offered by UIC's medical school, the second largest medical school campus in the nation. However, not all UIC students are future doctors; the schools of engineering, nursing, and business are also very popular and highly praised by students.

The presence of the Guaranteed Professional Program Admissions (or GPPA), through which selected incoming freshman are automatically admitted into specific UIC graduate programs, strengthens the math and science programs at UIC. Especially well-known is the medical program: students are guaranteed a spot at the medical school for three to five years without having to take the MCAT. One student in the program calls it "a dream for anyone who plans to go to medical school. It's great to know that I'll never have to agonize about med school admissions." GPPA students must still fulfill pre-med requirements as specified by the medical school, and all must participate in UIC's honors program, which requires students to take a special honors core course freshman year and then to complete an "honor activity" in subsequent years. The activity can take the form of other honors courses, research, or field work like study abroad, volunteering, or internships.

The advantages of the honors program are not just for GPPA students; any incoming student with an ACT of at least 25 or combined SAT score of 1240 who was ranked in the top 15 percent of his or her graduating class is also invited to join. In addition to special courses and activities, each student in the honors college is assigned a fellow, who is a faculty member in the student's major field, to serve as the student's advisor. Students in the honors program praise this highly personalized advising program, and feel that it is "much better than in the College of Liberal Arts and Sciences, where the advisors don't always know what they are talking about."

"Greek, non-Greek, religious groups, cultural groups, everyone interacts together, and there is always some way to be involved on campus. That's what makes UIC so unique."

Classes at UIC range in size depending on the subject. One English and Political Science major claims that "one of the great advantages to not being a math or science major here is having smaller classes and more personalized attention." Math and science lectures tend to be the largest classes on campus, with anywhere from 150 to 350 students. The plethora of TAs can sometimes be a source of confusion for students, especially in math and science classes, where TAs are known to have less-than-perfect English skills. Classes in the humanities, particularly English, are usually much smaller—around 30 students—and offer students the opportunity to interact more closely with professors. However, even in larger classes students claim that professors are always approachable "if you make the effort to get to know them." The workload at UIC is again subject-specific, but most agree that it is manageable. Students are also quick to note that coming to UIC with lots of AP credits can be a huge advantage, and often allows students to graduate in three years.

Learning and Commuting

The biggest complaint that students have about UIC is its "commuter-school" status. One student estimates that only about 30 percent of the students actually live on campus. Besides affecting the school's social scene, this also makes planning extracurricular activities and events very difficult. One junior student said, "It's impossible to plan meetings for organizations because everyone goes home by 3 P.M.!" However, students claim that because there are fewer students living on campus, UIC seems like a much smaller place than it actually is, fostering strong bonds among the students who live together on campus.

Students are quick to point out that UIC is an incredibly diverse campus. One student says, "UIC is the most diverse place I have ever been to. There is a little bit of every nationality and every economic level represented on campus." Although it lacks geographic diversity (almost all of the students at UIC hail from the Chicago area or elsewhere in Illinois), UIC definitely attracts a unique mix of students, including its fair share of first-generation college attendees. Students appreciate this diversity, and say that it adds a lot to campus. Some feel that ethnic students tend to self-segregate and form cliques on campus, but others perceive that their fellow students are generally approachable and willing to interact with one another. Students cite extracurricular involvement as a good way to meet people on campus.

On-Campus Living

Those students who do reside on UIC's campus have a number of possibilities for living arrangements and meal plans, and most are satisfied with their living conditions. There are three not-so-creatively-named main dorm areas, one on the East Campus (where most of the undergraduate classes are held), one on the West Campus (home to the medical school), and one on the South Campus. The East Campus offers Commons West, Commons North, Commons South, and Courtyard, which are all connected so students don't have to brave the elements of a Chicago winter in order to see their friends, get to a study lounge, or grab a bite to eat. Commons West is composed of double rooms opening onto a common hallway with bathrooms on each floor, and has an "intensive study" floor as well as an Honors College wing. Commons South has an identical set-up, but features single-sex floors. Courtyard, a triangular building, has cluster-style rooms, where doubles, singles, and triples of two to nine students are "clustered" around a common bathroom. Commons North is reserved for undergraduate students 20 years of age and older and has all single rooms in groups of three to six also clustered around a bathroom. Dorms on the West Campus are mainly for graduate and professional students, but some undergrads do reside there, either in cluster-style rooms or traditional doubles. One major disadvantage to living on the West campus is its distance from the more centralized classroom buildings and offices on the East campus; students who live there often have to take a bus to get to class. The most coveted rooms on campus, however, are in the new apartment-style dorm on the South Campus, where rooms feature individual bedrooms, full kitchens, and private bathrooms. All of the dorms on campus are relatively new, but these, which primarily house upperclassmen, are by far the nicest on campus.

For the most part, students are happy with their living conditions and with the choice between the quieter and more intimate cluster-style rooms and the more social doubles. All dorms have RAs, whom most students see as being "pretty cool" and "not too strict." Students caution that the worst part of the housing system can be just getting a room. One second-year transfer student who was forced to get an apartment off campus warned, "Get your housing in early! Dorms fill up *so fast!*" The housing situation has been somewhat remedied by the addition of the new apartment-style dorms, but UIC still does not have enough dorms to house its on-campus living demand.

UIC's dining system receives average marks from students, with some claiming that it is "way too expensive" and others praising it for its "variety and options," including Wendy's, Sbarro's, Subway, Taco Bell, and KFC in addition to your average cafeteria fare. When asked about food, most students say that they would rather be eating at the famed pizzeria Giordono's, which is only a five-minute walk from campus, or in nearby Greektown, whose restaurants are open 24/7. The surrounding area definitely offers some appetizing alternatives to traditional cafeteria meals.

Living It Up in the Windy City

Ask any student what the best part about going to UIC is, and each one will tell you the same thing: Being in Chicago! Students endlessly praise the abundance of opportunities provided by living in such a vibrant and diverse city. Not only are UIC students within walking distance of Greektown, Little Italy, and Chinatown, but each student is provided with a "Upass" (the price is included in tuition) which gives them free access to the city's public transportation. With their Upass, students are free to explore the entire city of Chicago to pursue their interests. As one might expect, the social scene at UIC tends to revolve around the many bars and clubs near campus, or parties at off-campus apartments. Being underage can pose a problem for some who want to explore the city's bar scene, but one student suggests that "there are always places that don't card, and as long as you know someone that's 21 you'll be fine." Popular student hangouts include Hawkeyes, the closest campus sports bar, and the clubs Rush and Division.

There is a Greek scene at UIC, which is, according to students, small and selective. The Greeks do not have houses, but often host parties at off-campus apartments. Students involved in the Greek system are highly enthusiastic about their experiences, but they agree that you don't have to be involved in the Greek scene to have fun on campus. One sorority member pointed out, "UIC is diverse in so many ways. Greek, non-Greek, religious groups, cultural groups, everyone interacts together, and there is always some way to be involved on campus. That's what makes UIC so unique."

Sports and Other Perks

The men's basketball team is by far the school's most popular team; students say, however, that interest in athletics is only high when the teams are doing well. One gymnast said that athletics are "a big deal within the department, but no one else seems to pay much attention to them. The commuter students have a lack of interest." Despite a lack of outside attention, UIC treats its athletes, most of whom are recruited, quite well and has given them their own multi-million dollar training facility, which regular students are not allowed to use. Non-athletes still do have ample opportunities to get involved in intramural or club sports (soccer being the most popular), and have access to workout facilities on campus.

For many students, UIC is a cost-effective way to get a great education. Students can live at home, work, and still get a great education at a great price. For more traditional students, UIC offers a diverse community and ample opportunities for extracurricular involvement. In any case, there is no denying that being in Chicago shapes the UIC experience. More than one student commented that seeing the Chicago skyline everyday as they walked to class could never get old. Although it is downtown, UIC's campus manages to carve out its own niche in the city, and students say that there is definitely a feeling of being "on campus." With its unique GPPA program, top notch facilities, affordability, and proximity to the attractions of downtown Chicago, it is easy to see why UIC comes so highly recommended by its students. —*Jessica Lenox*

FYI

If you come to UIC, you'd better bring "an open mind because this is one of the most diverse campuses in the nation."

A typical weekend at UIC consists of "getting out to the heart of the city, which is just minutes away, going out to clubs or attending house parties at night, studying and getting ready for the next week."

If I could change one thing about UIC it would be "have fewer commuter students."

Three things every student at UIC should do before graduating are "go to Greektown after a late night party, find your way around BSB (the behavioral sciences building), go shopping downtown between classes."

University of Illinois / Urbana-Champaign

Address: 601 East John Street; Champaign, IL 61801
Phone: 217-333-0302
E-mail address: undergraduate@admissions.uiuc.edu
Web site URL: www.uiuc.edu
Founded: 1867
Private or Public: public
Religious affiliation: none
Location: urban
Undergraduate enrollment: 28,947
Total enrollment: 39,291
Percent Male/Female: 52%/48%
Percent Minority: 28%
Percent African-American: 7%
Percent Asian: 13%
Percent Hispanic: 6%
Percent Native-American: 0%
Percent in-state/out of state: 89%/11%
Percent Pub HS: NA
Number of Applicants: 21,484
Percent Accepted: 60%
Percent Accepted who enroll: 49%
Entering: 6,366
Transfers: 1,077
Application Deadline: 1 Jan
Mean SAT: 1273
Mean ACT: 27.2
Middle 50% SAT range: V 550-670, M 600-720
Middle 50% ACT range: 26-30
3 Most popular majors: finance, biological sciences, psychology
Retention: 92%
Graduation rate: 80%
On-campus housing: 38%
Fraternities: 23%
Sororities: 25%
Library: 9,861,988 volumes
Tuition and Fees: $8,452 in; $18,046 out
Room and Board: $6,618
Financial aid, first-year: 42%
Varsity or Club Athletes: 2%
Early Decision or Early Action Acceptance Rate: NA

Host to the nation's first Homecoming football game, first supercomputer, oldest marching band, and the largest Greek system, the University of Illinois at Urbana-Champaign has grown from its youth in the 1860s as the chartered "land-grant" public college for the state of Illinois into one of the nation's foremost public research universities. U of I today includes eight undergraduate colleges and more than 26,000 undergrads, offering a plethora of academic, extracurricular, and social options.

Academic Powerhouse

The university's nine undergraduate divisions include the Colleges of Agriculture, Applied Life Studies, Business, Communications, Education, Engineering, Fine and Applied Arts, Liberal Arts and Sciences, and the Institution of Aviation. The university's reputation, especially in engineering, computer science, and business, is excellent, and the programs in these fields consistently rank among the best in the nation. Admission to most undergraduate schools is selective, with more than half of the student body coming from the top ten percent of their high school class. The variety of academic options makes U of I a popular destination for undecided majors; one undergrad remarked, "If a person is unsure about what major he or she wants to pursue, UIUC is a great place to come." However, transferring into a different undergraduate college—particularly into the competitive College of Engineering—can be a difficult task for students who change their minds. "It's discouraging how much red tape one needs to go through in order to switch," stated an LAS-to-engineering transfer. "But it weeds out people who don't really know what they're doing."

Graduation requirements are generally considered demanding, and some students find it difficult to fulfill both the distributional requirements and their major curriculum in four years. "Many of my friends in engineering came here knowing they'd be likely to take four-and-a-half years or more," said one freshman. Grading is also generally considered tough. "There's not a lot of grade inflation," states a junior. "It's not like high school. You work very, very hard for your courses, and sometimes an A is just not worth the extra effort." One freshman characterized her schedule as "an endless stream of work . . . there's never enough time!" However, there are known ways of circumventing the academic rigors; the Kinesiology and Leisure Studies departments in the College of Applied Life Studies, along with popular intro courses like Geology 100 ("Rocks for Jocks"), are notorious for serving as quick and easy ways to a degree.

"Like a Huge Farm"

The University of Illinois' campus is described by various students as "gigantic," "majestic," and "unbelievably flat." More than one student drew an analogy between the setting of the campus and a large farm. "There's lots of open space, the campus is entirely flat, and there's even some experimental crops growing next door to the library!" In the heart of the campus, the Quad, the architecture is primarily Georgian revival, with large brick buildings and tall white pillars. The Illini Union, sitting at the north end of the Quad and serving as the center of much of campus life, houses small shops, banks, bowling alleys, cafeterias, hotel rooms, meeting rooms for student organizations, and a branch of the University's library system, which contains more total volumes than any other public university in the country. The Undergraduate Library, situated at the south end of the Quad behind the prominent 1,750-seat Foellinger Auditorium, is a popular place to study and is almost entirely underground. It was built so as not to block the sun from shining on neighboring Morrow Plots, the country's oldest agricultural experiment fields still in use and a National Historic Landmark since 1968.

"Cliques are definitely a problem, and many of them are drawn along racial or ethnic lines."

Although the campus sprawls over nearly 1,500 acres, most buildings are grouped according to academic departments. North Campus primarily houses the sciences and the School of Engineering, while the South is home to the business and agriculture schools and the athletic complex. "I really don't have a problem with the size of the campus," said one student. "Once you're in your major and can choose where to live, it hardly feels big at all."

Beyond the large expanse of University-owned land are the cities of Urbana and Champaign, which form a combined metro area of nearly 100,000 people. Students affectionately refer to the area as "Chambana," although as several students confess, "outside of Campustown, there's really not all that much to do." Students with cars (and most U of I students have access to them) often take trips to grocery stores, movie theaters, or the mall in Champaign. Many students enjoy visiting Allerton Park, a university-owned recreation area and conference center forty minutes away in the town of Monticello. Originally a privately owned estate, the grounds were donated to the university in 1946 by the Allerton family, and the park now includes formal gardens, sculptures, hiking trails, and lots of well-maintained green space. "It's a perfect place to study, relax, or have a picnic, if you're willing to make the drive," commented one sophomore.

Social Illini

The University of Illinois' student population is one of the largest in the Midwest. Although the student body is represented by all fifty states and one hundred foreign countries, students overwhelmingly come from in-state, especially from the Chicago area. "It seems like everyone I've met is from the suburbs," noted a freshman. And while large African-American, Latino, and Asian-American populations on campus exist, most students are dismayed by how much self-segregation exists among different ethnicities. "Cliques are definitely a problem, and many of them are drawn solely along racial or ethnic lines," remarked one student. Each minority group primarily "eats, lives, and socializes" with members of their own group.

When the weekend rolls around, U of I students are no strangers to an active social life. "Campustown," a large, nearby business area with a multitude of bars, stores, and restaurants, is a popular destination. Once inside a bar, "it's very easy to score drinks, and many people go overboard with it," commented one sophomore. Because the bar entrance age is 19 in Champaign, many freshmen are initially excluded from the scene. However, fake IDs are said to be relatively easy to obtain, and many students are able to get in by knowing friends who work in the various drinking establishments.

The Greek scene maintains a huge influence on campus social life and provides the primary social outlet for a large portion of undergraduates. GDIs (the campus' "goddamned independents") had mixed responses to the question of whether they felt left out socially, though many agreed "there is plenty to do on a Friday night besides get wasted." Still, the pressure to drink, especially for those interested in becoming members of frats or sororities, can be very heavy. "Practically everyone" seems to get drunk at least one night over the weekend, lamented one critic of the "hyperactive" drinking scene.

Outside of partying, there is a wide array of events and activities to keep students entertained. Recent speakers to campus include Rubin "the Hurricane" Carter, Roger Ebert (an alum), Dr. Drew Pinsky, and Jesse Jackson. U of I is known for drawing famous musical acts to campus as well; within the past few years, the Dixie Chicks, Foo Fighters, Matchbox 20, Red Hot Chili Peppers, Smashing Pumpkins, and Cher have all come to campus to perform. The Krannert Center for the Performing Arts also brings in notable artists in other musical genres, including renowned symphonies, opera companies, and jazz ensembles. Many students throw themselves wholeheartedly into the extracurricular scene, participating in noteworthy groups like Volunteer Illini, the student newspaper (the award-winning *Daily Illini*), and a vast array of political organizations, activist groups, performing arts ensembles, and social clubs. "U of I is a very active campus. You name it and we probably have it," commented a student. Quad Day, an event that takes place at the beginning of the year, draws hundreds of student organizations to set up booths on the Quad and recruit new members. "Quad Day is huge!" exclaimed one sophomore. "You can walk around for hours and still not find all the groups that interest you."

As a member of the Big Ten athletic conference and a perennial powerhouse in many sports, the University of Illinois is also a very athletically oriented campus. Teams like men's football and men's basketball consistently sell out their venues. "Sports are very, very important here," notes a student. "Even non-athletes follow the teams, and the fitness and intramural facilities are wonderful . . . and free for students!" While one junior lamented a "slight increase in student apathy" for athletic teams over recent years, U of I is still home to some of the nation's most rabid fans.

Living in a Cage

Despite ongoing attempts by the administration to improve campus living spaces, housing still ranks among one of the largest grievances of the student population. "My freshman year dorm room was very small . . . it felt like I was in a cage," complained one upperclassman. Dorm food also gets very low marks. "The food here is awful, even by dining hall standards," commented a dorm resident. Still, many are satisfied with their arrangements; air-conditioning is available in a number of residences, and students "do a good job" of making their rooms feel like home. Most students eventually move off campus into nearby apartments or houses, some of which are maintained by the University. Fraternity and sorority houses also are popular places to live, as is the residential hall area nicknamed the "six-pack" as much for its fervent party scene as for the six towers that constitute it.

"Jewel in the Cornfields"

While the size of the university deters many would-be Illini, most students easily acclimate themselves to their surroundings and quickly fall in love with their school. In fact, many respondents cite the size of the University of Illinois as the best thing about it. "The huge size just means that there's a wealth of opportunities available here that you can't find . . . anywhere else. It's everything I'd want or need in a school," commented one enthusiastic student. Said another, "Everything about this place is engaging and exciting . . . it's truly a jewel in the cornfields."—*Jeff Sandberg*

FYI

If you come to UIUC, you'd better bring "some money to avoid the dining halls when you can."

What is the typical weekend schedule? "Friday: go to a Greek party; Saturday: hang out in Campustown; Sunday: study and go out for dinner."

If I could change one thing about UIUC, "I'd make more gut classes like 'Rocks for Jocks.'"

Three things every student at UIUC should do before graduating are "visit the echo spot in front of Foellinger Auditorium, sleep outside on the quad with Habitat for Humanity's "Shantytown," and go to lots of football and basketball games!"

Wheaton College

Address: 501 College Avenue; Wheaton, IL 60187
Phone: 630-752-5005
E-mail address: admissions@wheaton.edu
Web site URL: www.wheaton.edu
Founded: 1860
Private or Public: private
Religious affiliation: Christian, nondenominational
Location: suburban
Undergraduate enrollment: 2,395
Total enrollment: 2,844
Percent Male/Female: 49%/51%
Percent Minority: NA
Percent African-American: 2%
Percent Asian: 6%
Percent Hispanic: 3%
Percent Native-American: 0%
Percent in-state/out of state: 23%/77%
Percent Pub HS: 65%
Number of Applicants: 1,968
Percent Accepted: 54%
Percent Accepted who enroll: 54%
Entering: 569
Transfers: 83
Application Deadline: 15 Jan
Mean SAT: 1310
Mean ACT: 28.6
Middle 50% SAT range: V 620-710, M 610-700
Middle 50% ACT range: 26-31
3 Most popular majors: social sciences, English, philosophy and religious studies
Retention: 94%
Graduation rate: 86%
On-campus housing: 86%
Fraternities: NA
Sororities: NA
Library: 429,892 volumes
Tuition and Fees: $18,500
Room and Board: $6,100
Financial aid, first-year: 47%
Varsity or Club Athletes: 15%
Early Decision or Early Action Acceptance Rate: NA

When the Blanchard Hall bells ring, Wheaton students cannot help but smile. It is a school tradition that when a Wheaton couple becomes engaged, the two must climb the bell tower and ring the bell 21 times, in three sets of seven. Then they are to leave behind some sort of memorabilia or token in memory of their trip there. One of the school's most famous alumni, Christian evangelist Billy Graham, is reported to have visited the site himself more than 50 years ago with his then-fiancée Ruth. Every week, three or four couples follow his same path up the bell tower stairs.

Founded in 1860, Wheaton College is known today as one of America's premier Christian colleges. As one student joked, "People call us the Harvard of Christian colleges." And indeed it is true that many Wheaton students reject offers from top secular universities to attend Wheaton. For them, it is often a matter of where they think they will grow the most, stemming from a desire to learn in a Christian-friendly environment absent at secular institutions. Christian faith is a requisite for entrance to Wheaton, which asks its applicants to submit a personal testimony as well as a recommendation from a church pastor. At Wheaton, biblical Christian values underlie every aspect of life as the school strives to realize its motto, "Christo Et Regno Ejus"—"For Christ and His Kingdom."

In the Christian Classroom

When asked to name her favorite place on campus, one student jokingly replied, "My bed because I don't get to see it very often." Students at Wheaton work hard. All majors must fulfill a general education requirement, which includes two social science courses, Philosophy 101, two science courses, and two Bible classes concentrating on the Old and New Testaments. "We're definitely a liberal arts school," said one student. "I don't think most people realize that before coming here."

As a Christian college, Wheaton offers a number of specifically Christianity-related majors in addition to more traditional ones. Among those distinctive to Wheaton are Biblical Studies, Christian Education, and various ministry-related Music majors. Students say Communications and Christian Education are the easiest fields of study, while Chemistry and the sciences can be "absolutely killer." In the words of one science student, though, "Wheaton is really good if you're gonna major in Bible, but not-so-great if you're doing science. It is a liberal arts school, after all." Music students were said to work especially hard. "You never even see music majors because they're always in the conservatory practicing," one student noted.

Like students, all professors at Wheaton are Christian. Many will open their lectures by reciting a short prayer or bible verse. Students agree that having Christian professors can be both good and bad. As one student said, "It's good because we have the opportunity to learn in an academic atmosphere that is not hostile to the Christian faith." But because professors and students share a core of Christian beliefs, the classroom can sometimes "lack challenge and diversity of opinion." According to one student, "The environment here is conducive to close-mindedness because everyone thinks the same way. One person will say something and everyone else will just nod in agreement. Where's the challenge in that?" Another student added, "Sometimes it's like you're cheating yourself out of figuring out things for yourself by having it spoon-fed to you."

The Wheaton Pledge

Every semester, Wheaton students sign an official statement of responsibility, promising to uphold certain Christian values. In taking this Wheaton pledge, they agree to refrain from smoking, drinking alcohol, social dancing, and premarital sex. Most students do adhere to these guidelines, but there are exceptions. One student remarked, "I kinda had the impression that everyone here is a perfect Christian and never breaks any of the rules. But I've realized that's not true. It's kinda disappointing. Then again, Christians are human too—we all make mistakes."

In addition, students must attend a morning chapel service three times a week—Monday, Wednesday, and Friday. They are allowed up to 9 skips a semester; those students who miss more than nine may be placed on "chapel probation." Students on probation cannot participate in school activities and lose seniority in housing privileges. "It's not too big a deal, though," said one student.

"Bro-Sis" Housing

Almost all Wheaton students live in dorms or university-owned apartments. First-year students are required to live in dorms. Fischer was named the most social freshman dorm, while Saint and Elliot were cited as the worst places to live because of their distance from main campus. Frosh do have a curfew—midnight on weeknights and 2 A.M. on weekends—but according to one upperclassman, "it's not enforced too strictly. Coming in late is OK as long as you don't do it too much."

Males are generally not allowed in female dorm rooms and vice versa except during special hours called "open floors," which take place twice a week for about three hours. One stipulation is that dorm room doors must be kept open throughout visits, so that floor RAs (Residential Advisors) can oversee everything that goes on.

Dorms operate on a "Bro-Sis" system, in which each male floor has a corresponding "sister floor." "Brother" and "sister" floors will regularly do stuff together, including meet for weekly dinners at Saga, the campus dining hall, and have "raids," party-like get-togethers that happen a couple of times a semester. Wheaton has one dining hall to accommodate its 2300 undergrads. Officially known as Centennial Cafeteria, students informally refer to it as "Saga" after the food service Wheaton employed during the 80s. Food is cited as "pretty good—much better than what you'll find at some other schools." After hours, students can find munchies at the school eatery, called "The Stupe." Most students will only go there during certain times, though. "It's OK at night, but during the day, it's like a junior high handout, so we all kinda avoid it then," said one sophomore.

Grind-Free Zone

Primarily residential, the town of Wheaton has been nationally recognized as one of America's safest cities. "I feel really comfortable walking around even at night," said one student. But most students will agree, local life can get really boring. The handful of coffee shops and food places near campus "all close at like 8!" lamented one student.

Wheaton is a dry, Greek-free campus. But even in the absence of traditional frat party life, students find lots to do. A couple of times a month, Wheaton will host popular Christian bands, with students attending in hordes. Classical music is also a big draw. The school conducts an Artist Concert Series of six or seven concerts every year. Recent guests have included Dawn Upshaw and the Vienna Boys' Choir. Another popular event is a weekly Praise Night hosted by the campus World Christian Fellowship group every Sunday night. For a few hours, students will gather and sing Christian praise and worship songs. The school talent show and February formal are two other well-attended Wheaton events.

Wheaton does not permit its students to engage in social dancing. Square dancing performed to traditional American hoe-down music is the only kind of dancing allowed, and it is only permissible at school-sponsored events. Square dances happen a few times a semester and remain popular despite the dance's "hickish" reputation. Most students will go as singles, but it is not uncommon for people to go with dates.

Going for an M.R.S. Degree

According to one student, dating at Wheaton tends to get "very complicated." "Everyone's pretty much looking for marriage, so dating here involves a lot of pressure," noted one sophomore. Another male student explained dating at Wheaton, "The way it works, if you're seen walking around campus with a girl, people will jump to conclusions and automatically assume you're engaged. Needless to say, casual dating is lacking."

> **"I'm convinced that 99 percent of the people on this campus play the guitar."**

On the female side, a common joke circulating among Wheaton women is that "you've come to get your M.R.S. degree." One female student went so far as to call Wheaton a "meat-market." Every week the school newspaper runs a section called "Up the Tower," listing newly engaged couples; a minimum of two or three pairs of names appear each week with numbers soaring near the end of each semester.

Off Campus

Many students own cars, a luxury which makes finding fun off campus considerably easier. A big nearby movie-plex is a popular weekend destination. After shows, students often get coffee and talk at the local Borders or Barnes & Noble bookstore. The Front Street Cocina was cited as a fun place to satisfy cravings for salsa and other Mexican treats. Despite their popularity, cars are not a necessity. Said one student, "You can get by without a car, but it's nice to have one." With on-campus parking becoming scarcer many students are choosing to leave their cars at home.

Chicago is just 25 miles from Wheaton's campus. Many Wheaton students take trains there to enjoy the bustle of metropolitan life. Train fare is inexpensive—$5 for a weekend pass—and the trip takes less than an hour, making for a mass student exodus to the city on weekends.

Extracurriculars

Most Wheaton students are involved in at least one extracurricular campus activity. In particular, Christian campus ministry groups abound at Wheaton, ranging from local community service to international evangelism groups. Some well-known student organizations include the College Union, the school's social planners, which are in charge of bringing groups and speakers to campus, and Student Government, comprising Wheaton's student body representatives.

Many Wheaton students are musical, so participation in campus singing and music performance groups is naturally very high. One student joked, "I'm convinced that 99 percent of the people on this campus play the guitar. Moving in, almost everyone is carrying one."

Wheaton tends to lack ethnic diversity, but for the less than ten percent minority student population, the Office of Minority Affairs organizes a number of ethnic organizations, such as Koinonia, the Asian-American group, and Unidad Cristiana, the Hispanic and Latino-American group.

Sports at both the intercollegiate and intramural levels are very popular among Wheaton students, with soccer being especially big. Wheaton students attend school games en masse, and the crowds tend to become "very enthusiastic," said one frequent attendee.

Always Changing

In 1980, world Christian evangelist Billy Graham led a crusade at Wheaton College, celebrating the completion of the Billy Graham Center, dedicated to advancing world evangelism. Today, the Center houses its own museum, which chronicles world evangelism history using art. As the Center adapts to changing world needs and conditions, it serves as a paradigm of advancement and useful adaptation.

Wheaton, too, is a dynamic being. But the school never loses its foundation rooted in faith. Amidst a changing world, the school strives to remain a Christian bastion of higher learning. But, as the new millennium begins, recognizing the school's need to adapt and grow, the Wheaton administration announced a school-wide "New Century Challenge," which includes plans to foster greater ethnic diversity as well as more practical plans for building construction and renovation. Construction for Anderson Commons and a Sports and Recreation Center has already been completed, and the administration plans to renovate the Todd M. Beamer Student Center as well.

In a further effort to keep up with the times, Wheaton changed its mascot. Historically, the school mascot has been the Crusaders, a modern take on the medieval Christian soldiers who fought for their faith. But, some people feel the "Crusaders" image inaccurately depicts Christians and may unnecessarily offend. The new mascot name is the Wheaton Thunder.

A Personal Decision

Amidst a changing world, Wheaton can be a great place for some to grow in their Christian faith. But, as one student warned, Wheaton life can quickly become a "super-saturation of the Christian experience." As always, the final decision is a personal one. But Christian students considering Wheaton are encouraged to consider the school. As it has been for hundreds of Christian greats, it may be that the stretch in the straight and narrow leads them to places they never dreamed they would go.—*Jane H. Hong*

FYI

If you come to Wheaton, you'd better bring "an open attitude, warm clothes, and crazy dress-up outfits."

What is the typical weekend schedule? "Friday: rest and then go out to a game; Saturday: sleep late, work out, then go out with friends at night; Sunday: study all day and then rest up for the week."

If I could change one thing about Wheaton, "I'd decrease the tuition."

Three things every student should do before graduating from Wheaton are "to go up the bell tower of Blanchard Hall—or in other words, get engaged; visit Chicago; live in an apartment."

Indiana

DePauw University

Address: 313 S. Locust Street; Greencastle, IN 46135
Phone: 765-658-4006
E-mail address: admission@depauw.edu
Web site URL: www.depauw.edu
Founded: 1837
Private or Public: private
Religious affiliation: United Methodist
Location: rural
Undergraduate enrollment: 2,338
Total enrollment: NA
Percent Male/Female: 44%/56%
Percent Minority: NA
Percent African-American: 3%
Percent Asian: 2%
Percent Hispanic: 2%
Percent Native-American: 0%
Percent in-state/out of state: 57%/43%
Percent Pub HS: 67%
Number of Applicants: 3,682
Percent Accepted: 61%
Percent Accepted who enroll: 30%
Entering: 685
Transfers: 8
Application Deadline: 1 Feb
Mean SAT: NA
Mean ACT: NA
Middle 50% SAT range: V 560-650, M 570-670
Middle 50% ACT range: 25-29
3 Most popular majors: English language and literature, communication, economics
Retention: 89%
Graduation rate: 73%
On-campus housing: 92%
Fraternities: 77%
Sororities: 69%
Library: 283,735 volumes
Tuition and Fees: $24,450
Room and Board: $7,050
Financial aid, first-year: 53%
Varsity or Club Athletes: 29%
Early Decision or Early Action Acceptance Rate: ED 77%; EA 76%

In the months before the brutal cold of a Midwestern winter hits Greencastle, Indiana, students at DePauw University often spend their time playing campus golf, "the biggest thing ever." This "uniquely DePauw" sport uses golf clubs and tennis balls on student-created courses that roam all over campus—and occasionally even through buildings! Though probably not what the Methodist Church had in mind when it founded DePauw in 1837, campus golf is characteristic of the fun-loving and friendly student body that DePauw attracts.

An Academic Adventure

Life at DePauw is not all fun, games, and campus golf; rigorous academics are par for the course. Students are required to take a total of 31 course credits drawn from six categories: social and behavioral sciences; natural science and mathematics; foreign language; historical and philosophical understanding; literature and the arts; and self-expression. Students speak highly of the freedom provided by the broad requirements. "I've never been forced to take a math class!" raved one senior. A sophomore agreed, "I'm paying the university and I should be able to decide for myself which classes I want to take." The loose course groupings help "keep students open to new options." Another facet of DePauw's flexible, adventurous approach to learning is Winter Term, held during January. Winter Term is an opportunity for students to take one class intensively for a month with a diminished focus on grades. Students also use this time to take advantage of off-campus internship opportunities.

DePauw is well-regarded for its competitive honors programs; management fellows focus on prebusiness study, media fellows work in print and broadcast media, and science research fellows undertake independent lab research. These programs foster specific interests of particularly talented and ambitious students and frequently provide unusual opportunities for their participants. One media fellow said that her class spoke with an embedded journalist during the 2003 war in Iraq: "We could hear the tanks in the background. It was amazing."

Classes are widely acknowledged as "challenging but not impossible." Many DePauw students "could have gone to Ivy League schools, but for whatever reason, chose not to" and the slightly less intense academic atmosphere means that most are "notoriously over-committed" and "involved in a little bit of everything." This can have the tendency to "hamper [our] ability to do one or a couple of things really well" but students love being able to pursue their many interests.

You Can Run but You Can't Hide

Almost every class at DePauw is small and personal. "I've never been in a class with more than 32 people!" exclaimed a sophomore. Students say that professors are known for developing relationships with students that extend beyond the classroom. "My professors have me over to their houses for dessert, ask me to babysit their kids, and would do anything for me," said a senior. Students admit that the small setting does have some downsides: "you will never be able to remain anonymous, take a nap, or skip class without it being noticed." Another student's biggest complaint was about the comfort of the classrooms: "Some of the desks are really uncomfortable. They kill my back."

Several students commented on the "interesting dynamic" that exists between the "very liberal" professors and politically "moderate to conservative" student body but agree that there "is a lot of mutual respect" that extends beyond political leanings. Overall, students agree that they "love most of the professors" and that "they are good teachers." Some students complain that their professors have become increasingly reliant on technology for homework assignments and grading. Professors "overuse" the online homework system and "take a lot of liberties with the e-mail system and expect us to check our computers every ten minutes." However, most students believe that professors will tailor their use to student feedback in the future.

Greencastle Goes Greek

At DePauw, "the party scene *is* the Greek scene." Students speak highly of the Greek system, and over 70 percent of the student body belong to one of the 12 fraternities and nine sororities. Most agree that Greek life at DePauw is different from the Greek scene at other colleges simply because "it's not a cut-throat thing." Since almost everyone rushes, "it's really laid back. If you want to be in the Greek system, you can be in the Greek system." Most students look at it as "a tradition and a place to live." One sorority girl raved, "I love it. I live with 60 great girls in a beautiful house." Though most Greeks drink on the weekends, students say that non-drinkers are "never pressured" to participate in that aspect of Greek life.

> **"The party scene *is* the Greek scene."**

For "independents," students who choose not to join a Greek house, life at DePauw is markedly different. Being a "God-Damned Independent (GDI) does carry a stigma, and you can become ostracized as an arrogant elitist pretty easily. You have to try harder not to become antisocial," said a junior. Still, the average DePauw student, Greek and non-Greek alike, is friendly and outgoing, so that "once you go out and make connections, people come to accept that you're not just that weirdo who prefers dancing to AC/DC in front of his mirror" over hanging out in a frat house. Many students agree that another problem with the Greek system is that it "encourages and perpetuates an attitude of casual intimacy and stamps out the possibility of serious, and even not so serious, dating" said a student. Students say that, when they do occur, relationships tend to be long-term and with students outside of DePauw.

Some students stress that it is possible to have fun at DePauw even outside the Greek scene. As one sophomore put it, "I would argue with the nay-sayers who insist that there is nothing to do. Any time you have a group of students, you can think of something fun to do. Having a good time in Greencastle just requires a little creativity." Besides, "all you really need for fun is Wal-Mart, anyway, and we have one of those," according to another. There are also a plethora of activities like movie nights, get-togethers, and music jams hosted by various organizations for the student body.

The university adds some spice to the otherwise "pretty dull" rural town vibe in Greencastle. Still, a few popular restaurants bring students into town. Students frequent Marvin's, a "greasy spoon" famous for the garlic cheeseburger students have nicknamed the "GCB," "cute" coffee shops like Gathering Grounds, and bars like the Fluttering Duck, Toppers, and Third Degree. Many students are fond of taking short road trips to nearby Indianapolis, or "Indy." Because most of DePauw's students are from in-state, upper-middle-class families, cars are never difficult to come by and freshmen are allowed to have them on campus. Several students mentioned that this allows DePauw students "a sense of independence" which makes Greencastle a little less claustrophobic.

Life Is Beautiful at DePauw

What DePauw lacks in urban excitement, it makes up for in the rural charm of "small town America": namely, safety, physical beauty, and comfort. Students report that the campus is a place "where you never have to lock your doors." "I leave my stuff all over school and I never worry that it will be taken," claimed a freshman. Greencastle itself is mostly farmland and the campus "is always green and gorgeous." When the weather is nice, students gather in around the pond at Bowman Park for "concerts, movies, and hanging out." The "picturesque" buildings receive high praise from students, particularly East College, one of DePauw's oldest structures. The university prohibits off-campus living, so students either live in the dorms or with their fraternity or sorority. Freshman are required to live in the dorms, which are "very nice, though a little small." Most dorm floors are co-ed and the bathrooms are communal. Apartment-style dorm housing is open to upperclassmen. Many students choose to live in their Greek house after sophomore year because "it's basically like living in a mansion." The food at DePauw is decent but unexciting. One junior advised, "cereal is always a good backup." Most Greeks take meals in their house, which students agree is generally more exciting and less costly than eating in the dining halls.

Athletics and "The Game"

The DePauw student body is athletic and fit, even though the school's teams compete in Division III and do not offer athletic scholarships. Many students compete in Intramurals (IMs), which provide them a more relaxed forum to "continue the sports they played in high school." None of the varsity teams are particularly successful, and few students go to watch their games. Students insist that this is not from a lack of DePauw pride but rather an unfortunate consequence of the hectic schedules most students create for themselves.

There is one notable exception to the lack of athletic spirit at DePauw. The Monon Bell Game, often simply known as "the Game," is as clear an indication as any of the fierce love and pride DePauw students have for their school. The Game, against nearby rival Wasbash College, is "the oldest football rivalry west of the Appalachian Mountains." Despite the fact that "we're both these tiny schools," the Game is "a really big deal. Alumni pay a huge amount of money for tickets." Each year, the victorious school keeps the Monon Bell, which is "bolted into a glass case" when it is at DePauw. This tight security was imposed after a group of Wabash students tried to steal the bell from DePauw a few years ago. The near disaster amplified the rivalry to an unprecedented and enjoyable intensity.

Homogeny and Acceptance

Students say that DePauw's reputation does not seem to extend far beyond the Midwest and that the student body reflects this homogeny. However, administrators are working to recruit minority students and students from areas beyond the Midwestern states. With such a friendly, outgoing, accepting student body, students say it is only a matter of time before DePauw's population better reflects the makeup of the country. Students "always say hi to each other" and "you can meet people as you walk to class." There are social "pockets that are a bit more eclectic or extreme" than the rest of the population and there is a visible, widely accepted gay, lesbian, bisexual, and transgender organization. "A casual atmosphere" is DePauw's most pervasive characteristic, and it's not uncommon to see a things like a "woman in sweatpants, a baseball hat and a T-shirt sitting next to her friend who is wearing high heals, a skirt, and a sweater." "Everyone has their own style and everyone can find a niche," and for the most part, people "will accept you for who you are."—*Claire Gagne*

FYI

If you come to DePauw, you'd better bring a "a car, or a friend with a car" and "a cell phone, but make sure it gets reception in Greencastle."

What is a typical weekend schedule? "Friday and Saturday, take a nap, study, scrounge for food, hang out with friends, go to a Greek party; Sunday, study, work, hang out, work."

If I could change one thing about DePauw, I would "make it more diverse. We need more unusual, artistic, ethnic, and diverse people."

Three things every student at DePauw should do before graduating are "Eat a GCB or Veggie GCB, do a boulder run (even if you're in your undies), and make lasting friendships with the people here."

Earlham College

Address: 801 National Road West; Richmond, IN 47374
Phone: 765-983-1600
E-mail address: admission@earlham.edu
Web site URL: www.earlham.edu
Founded: 1847
Private or Public: private
Religious affiliation: Quaker
Location: urban
Undergraduate enrollment: 1,080
Total enrollment: NA
Percent Male/Female: 44%/56%
Percent Minority: NA
Percent African-American: 8%
Percent Asian: 3%
Percent Hispanic: 2%
Percent Native-American: 0%
Percent in-state/out of state: 32%/68%
Percent Pub HS: NA
Number of Applicants: 1,269
Percent Accepted: 78%
Percent Accepted who enroll: 29%
Entering: 283
Transfers: 27
Application Deadline: 15 Feb
Mean SAT: NA
Mean ACT: NA
Middle 50% SAT range: V 550-690, M 530-650
Middle 50% ACT range: 23-29
3 Most popular majors: biological/biomedical science, English, psychology
Retention: 84%
Graduation rate: 62%
On-campus housing: 87%
Fraternities: NA
Sororities: NA
Library: 392,100 volumes
Tuition and Fees: $24,560
Room and Board: $5,416
Financial aid, first-year: 66%
Varsity or Club Athletes: 32%
Early Decision or Early Action Acceptance Rate: ED 93%; EA 85%

Earlham College is a small liberal arts school nestled in Middle America. Despite its size, this Quaker school of just over a thousand students is anything but small-minded. Earlham confounds all the stereotypes of small town America, while embracing its community values. The result is a unique and thoroughly eclectic place centered wholeheartedly on individual growth, as well as on the process of learning how to contribute to society.

Classroom Spotlight on . . . YOU

Earlham's academic mission is manifold. All classes are small. The 11:1 student to faculty ratio allows for almost all classes to be under 30 people. "Its not at all unusual to have just seven other people in your seminar," reports one student, and "sometimes its too small—don't oversleep!" The intimate environment is integral to Earlham's endeavor to develop students in all intellectual directions. The core curriculum is also at the center of this plan, emphasizing "both traditional and emerging disciplinary and interdisciplinary fields." Freshmen, or "first years," are initiated into the "community of scholars" right off the bat in the required Freshmen Humanities Program. The Program is rigorous, but helps first year students adjust to the system of working effectively with others, as they will do non-stop in the following three years. Also required are credits in science (including time in the lab), fine arts, social sciences, philosophy or religion, language, and a multicultural/intercultural credit. Some students complain that the breadth of these prerequisites is too large, but some overlap between them is allowed. The final obligation for graduation is the time spent in "AWPE" courses, or Athletics, Wellness, and Physical Education, which is made more bearable by the exquisite fitness center. Talking with Earlham students about the requirements elicits a lot of enthusiasm about the goals of the General Education Plan. As one student says, "I graduated with a totally different sense of my place in the world, not just my community . . . Earlham forces you too see the horizon, then question what's beyond it."

Professors teach all the classes at Earlham, ensuring a level of classroom engagement higher than schools where teaching assistants are responsible for instruction. Students and faculty are on a first name basis, as is Quaker tradition, and this informality reflects the relaxed tone of academic life at Earlham. That is not to say the work is not rigorous, rather, students are able to "steer [their] own courses," and move in any and all directions they please. The accessibility of professors is part of what makes the experience at Earlham so special, and students comment on how "they are always there when you need to ask anything—inside or outside of office hours."

Earlham presents its students with many academic opportunities that most students embrace. Because of the small size of both the faculty and student body, interaction outside the classroom is frequent. Students recount everything from dinners at professors' homes to group field trips and movies as some of their favorite memories of Earlham. In recent years, the most popular majors have been psychology, biology, and history, but interdisciplinary majors allow students to combine their interests into a cumulative learning experience of their own design. All students are assigned academic advisors, who help facilitate the course selection process, and "generally just give good insights on life." Despite its size, Earlham prides itself on providing a menu of academic choices that stimulate creative and analytical processes that require students to "confront cultural paradigms," and "question the easy answers to big issues facing the world." The Peace and Global Studies program is one of the oldest in the nation, and houses the nationwide consortium on the subject.

The Heartland

Midwestern winters can be long and dark, so by the time spring rolls around, Earlham students are ready to get back outside. As the weather improves, central campus, a grassy circle called "the Heart," lives up to its name, serving as a general congregating site for those looking to relax, play Frisbee, or study outdoors. The Heart is crisscrossed by walkways, out of which contemporary redbrick dormitories and classroom buildings radiate. There have been several significant improvements made to the facilities in the last five years, much to the delight of students and professors alike. The Landrum Bolling Center for Interdisciplinary Studies and Social Sciences is a thirteen million dollar affair, which quite literally put into stone Earlham's dedication to self-initiated learning. Renovations to the science buildings helped to bring back biology as a popular major. The Health and Wellness Center offers every conceivable amenity from an indoor pool to a rock-climbing studio. The two campus libraries, Lilly Library and the Science Library, offer a variety of study spaces and computer labs. While home to several classrooms, the Runyan Center serves mainly as a place where students can "chill out, have a coffee, and hang with friends," at its coffee shop, bookstore, and small theater.

"The conservatives, if there are any, keep a pretty low profile."

While campus is "delightfully insular," the town of Richmond, Indiana, "is sort of disappointing." Beyond the usual fare of small town activities, such as bowling, the commercial options are limited to "Wal-Mart, and small stuff that closes after five o'clock." In search of entertainment, students go on jaunts to Miami University of Ohio (in Oxford, OH), Indianapolis, and Dayton. In order to do this, a car is necessary, and one student joked that those with wheels "acquire a lot of friends fast." Many students do chose to stay involved with the town, and Earlham offers Bonner Scholarships, which pay for tuition in return for volunteer work in the Richmond community.

Home Away From Home

Housing at Earlham relies on luck of the draw. Most students live on campus, but the quality of dorm facilities and personalities range greatly. Dorms like Barrett retain reputations for holding parties and raucous events, and the first floor of Olvey-Andis, "OA", is referred to as "the nunnery." If you get really lucky, you might end up in Warren or Wilson Halls, which are air-conditioned and generally "cushier." Dormitories are monitored by RAs, who are available to students of all ages and are reported to be "really helpful, especially in the first year." There are also twenty-seven college owned houses available for students to live in. A number of these are "theme houses," with themes, which vary from La Casa Hispana to the Peace House. Earlham students are fairly satisfied with the dining halls, especially since the menu has been expanded to include items that "most people like, like pizza and grilled chicken breasts." The vegetarian and vegan options are apparently "surprisingly good," but "don't limit the menu for meat-eaters like at some schools." When students don't feel like eating in the dining hall or are seized by the desire to bake, kitchens in every dorm serve as great resources.

And to the Left . . .

The number of graduation requirements pales when compared to the amount of extracurricular activities. Earlham boasts an abundance of campus clubs and activist groups. Every student can find (or, if it doesn't exist already, found) an organization that matches his or her interests. Indeed, campus activities are sometimes so charged with political fervor that one student remarked, "the conservatives, if there are any, keep a pretty low profile." The leftward lean is to some degree the work of self-selection within the admissions pool, and in recent years there has been a movement to increase political discourse. Of the more prominent groups, the Rainbow Tribe, is very active in supporting gay/lesbian/bisexual students on campus as well as gay rights on the national level. Also popular are singing groups, Habitat for Humanity, and the Film Society.

Earlham fields a number of varsity sports teams, including the consistently well-ranked Division III men's soccer team. The student body on the whole chooses to be involved in athletics rather than to watch. School spirit in regard to sports is low, but Earlham students make up for pep with intensity in intramural sports, in which about half of them participate. The Health and Wellness Center also attracts many students to work out on new machines in a friendly atmosphere.

High Times, Dry Times

Earlham has a no alcohol policy, even for students over the age of twenty-one. As a result, the party scene is "very different" from that of other schools. While there isn't a real focus on alcohol, students say that "drinking definitely goes on, no question." One tradition, "the Hash," consists of students chasing a trail (a "hash trail") of flour through the woods to find a keg at its end, thereby allowing them to drink off campus. Friday Afternoon Keg Club is also an occurrence. Student opinion on drinking diverges, while some participate in Hash, others complain of the hypocrisy of such behavior on a dry campus, and call, in Earlham trained style, for "the student body to reconsider what makes a community." This dissent aside, the social atmosphere is very laid back. Like in the classroom, Earlham students make their own way, and the variety of extracurricular offerings provides many weekend activities, such as dance performances, movie screenings, and concerts.

A Society of Friends

While not as racially and ethnically diverse as some larger universities, Earlham's eighteen percent minority students and seventy-two percent out-of-state students make it different from most schools in its region. In a small town, this small school succeeds in creating an atmosphere of buzzing intellectual activity paired with relaxed self-determination and development. Earlham's small size and strong moral dedication to creating questioning and aspiring individuals teaches its students about a great cause, the national endeavor to be a united community of engaging individuals. —*Charlotte Taft*

FYI

If you come to Earlham College, you'd better bring "an open mind."

What is the typical weekend schedule? "Finish reading, get pizza, and hang out with friends."

If I could change one thing about Earlham College, I would "increase funding for everything!"

Three things that every student at Earlham College should do before graduating are "run the Hash, go to a concert in Indy, play Ultimate Frisbee on the Heart."

Indiana University / Bloomington

Address: 300 North Jordan Avenue; Bloomington, IN 47405
Phone: 812-855-0661
E-mail address: iuadmit@indiana.edu
Web site URL: www.iu.edu
Founded: 1820
Private or Public: public
Religious affiliation: none
Location: urban
Undergraduate enrollment: 30,752
Total enrollment: NA
Percent Male/Female: 47%/53%
Percent Minority: NA
Percent African-American: 4%
Percent Asian: 3%
Percent Hispanic: 2%
Percent Native-American: 0%
Percent in-state/out of state: 72%/28%
Percent Pub HS: NA
Number of Applicants: 21,264
Percent Accepted: 81%
Percent Accepted who enroll: 41%
Entering: 7,080
Transfers: 733
Application Deadline: rolling
Mean SAT: NA
Mean ACT: NA
Middle 50% SAT range: V 490-600, M 500-610
Middle 50% ACT range: 22-27
3 Most popular majors: business, education, communication
Retention: 88%
Graduation rate: 46%
On-campus housing: 43%
Fraternities: 16%
Sororities: 18%
Library: 6,512,090 volumes
Tuition and Fees: $6,517 in; $17,552 out
Room and Board: $5,872
Financial aid, first-year: 42%
Varsity or Club Athletes: 3%
Early Decision or Early Action Acceptance Rate: NA

Ask 10 different students at Indiana University at Bloomington for the definition of a Hoosier, and expect to get 10 different answers. Located in the small city of Bloomington, IU can boast about its excellent academic reputation in addition to its nationally recognized basketball team. In fact, the only thing you may not learn at IU is the definition of a "Hoosier."

Tough Stuff

Academics at IU are reported to be tough, but not overwhelming. As one student noted, "It's only as bad as you make it." Music, journalism, and business are extremely popular majors at IU, and the business school is known to be especially demanding. While most students say that slackers are "weeded out" pretty quickly during the first year, others say the School of Public and Environmental Affairs has gained a reputation as "the school for business dropouts." Also, one student said that "the English department has a real attitude. It's impossible to get an A." The biggest academic complaints are about the strict language requirements (four semesters).

"The only thing you may not learn at IU is the definition of a Hoosier."

For those willing to work hard, the university offers several honors programs for both underclassmen and upperclassmen. On the other hand, when looking for those easy classes, students give warning about elective courses offered for credit through the HPER (Health, Physical Education, and Recreation) Departments, like archery and tae kwon do. "The teachers all know that you're probably taking them for an easy A, so they make it tough on you."

Overall, students are happy with the classes and professors at IU, but some complain about large intro classes freshman year. Freshmen are last to register, and one student said that you "sign up early and get a 30-person class, later and get a 300." However, even the smallest classes usually break up into smaller sections taught by TAs. In a sea of over 25,000 undergrads, students say that sometimes they feel like "just a number." "However," as one student countered, "something about big universities that people don't take into consideration is that once you're accepted into your chosen school . . . it feels like a family."

The Resources at IU

One of the advantages of a large university is vast number of resources it can offer. Indiana is home to the nation's largest student center, a building that includes restaurants, eateries, a bookstore, a movie theater, a bowling alley, pool tables, and a four-star hotel. There is also the new Recreational Sports Building, which students love to brag about.

Though Hoosiers complain about the food in the dining halls, there are plenty of other places to eat around campus, and most dorms now include fast-food chains like McDonald's and Sbarro's Pizza.

Most freshmen and sophomores live in the dorms, but a large number of upperclassmen live in fraternity and sorority houses or apartments off-campus. As one student described it, "people flock off-campus after freshman year." Students who do live in the dorms say they are not too bad. Most housing is coed by floor with several RAs. Students claim each dorm has a definite personality and some say that "you can usually tell what someone is like by which dorm they live in." For example, Ashton is known for its academics, Eigenmann for its international student population, and Collins Living-Learning Center is the place for "free spirits" on campus.

Though a majority of students are from in state, undergrads agree that there is no stereotypical Hoosier. Some people come in with a set group of friends from high school, but it is "very easy to meet people here." Many students mention the very liberal attitudes of students and their open-mindedness. Bloomington has a large gay and lesbian population, and the IU campus is "well known for its gay rights activism."

Greek Glory

A typical Hoosier is known as a big party fiend, and it is no coincidence that the fraternity and sorority presence on the IU campus is huge. One student reported that sometimes tension exists between Greeks and independents. While some said nondrinkers do not feel out of place (campus is "technically" dry), other students disagree, saying that "a large portion of the social life does revolve around alcohol." Drugs, mostly marijuana, are on campus, but they are "only around if you are into it." A typical weekend for underclassmen includes frat parties every night. Many of these parties are exclusive and tickets are checked at the door. However, many upperclassmen, even those who are frat members, tend to prefer the local bar scene. Other than bars, students talk about the lack of off-campus activities, saying "everything closes early here." Frequent road trips to Chicago, St. Louis, Indianapolis, or a weekend at home are also common.

One of the most anticipated events at IU is the annual "Little 500" bike race (the subject of the film *Breaking Away*, which was filmed in Bloomington). Students from all different organizations on campus participate, the days beforehand are filled with parties, and it is said to be "one of the wildest weeks ever."

100 Percent Basketball

"Basketball, basketball, basketball. That's what IU is!" Firebrand coach Bobby Knight's former program is legendary around the country, and IU school spirit reaches its peak during March Madness, the month of NCAA playoffs, known here as "Hoosier Hysteria." Students can easily get tickets, but school officials, anticipating a rush, often do not announce or downplay the opening of ticket sales.

Most IU students played a sport in high school, and many continue on in college at the intramural or varsity levels. The campus has two main athletic facilities: "HPER is a big warehouse . . . that's where all the no-nonsense people work out. The SRSC is where all the sorority and frat people go to work out . . . so they look really good in their matching workout outfits."

Extracurriculars are also important to students. *The Indiana Students* is a full-size student-run paper that most students read. Also, community service organizations abound. The IU Student Organization is recognized by the administration as the most important on-campus organization, "But no one knows exactly what they have their hands into."

Whether they come for the noteworthy academics, the Big Ten experience, or the closeness to home, the Hoosiers are happy with their school. Freshmen should be warned that the sheer size of IU can be overwhelming, however, and the transition from high school to college can often be difficult. Everyone finds their niche though, and once settled in, students can expect four years of work, fun, and basketball galore. —*Sarah DeBergalis and Staff*

FYI

If you come to Indiana University, you'd better bring "a bike, to get around campus and to compete in the 'Little 500' bike race."

What is the typical weekend schedule? "The usual rounds to parties on Friday and Saturday nights. Play catch-up with accumulated homework on Sundays."

If I could change one thing about Indiana University, I would "make the small town of Bloomington into a metropolis."

Three things that every student at Indiana University should do before graduating are "bike in the 'Little 500,' figure out what a Hoosier is, and take an HPER class for credit."

Purdue University

Address: 610 Purdue Mall; West Lafayette, IN 47907
Phone: 765-494-1776
E-mail address: admissions@purdue.edu
Web site URL: www.purdue.edu
Founded: 1869
Private or Public: public
Religious affiliation: none
Location: urban
Undergraduate enrollment: 30,908
Total enrollment: NA
Percent Male/Female: 58%/42%
Percent Minority: NA
Percent African-American: 3%
Percent Asian: 4%
Percent Hispanic: 2%
Percent Native-American: 0%
Percent in-state/out of state: 76%/24%
Percent Pub HS: NA
Number of Applicants: 22,872
Percent Accepted: 76%
Percent Accepted who enroll: 36%
Entering: 6,265
Transfers: 691
Application Deadline: rolling
Mean SAT: 1134
Mean ACT: 25
Middle 50% SAT range: V 500-610, M 530-660
Middle 50% ACT range: 23-28
3 Most popular majors: engineering, liberal arts/sciences, business
Retention: 88%
Graduation rate: 58%
On-campus housing: 51%
Fraternities: 11%
Sororities: 7%
Library: 1,200,797 volumes
Tuition and Fees: $5,860 in; $17,640 out
Room and Board: $6,700
Financial aid, first-year: 43%
Varsity or Club Athletes: 1%
Early Decision or Early Action Acceptance Rate: NA

Purdue is more than just a great engineering school. While its reputation for academic excellence in engineering draws some of the most promising prospects from all over the world, Purdue also boasts a campus teeming with school spirit, a friendly, down-to-earth student body, and a vibrant social scene.

Speaking of Engineering . . .

Known as one of the top engineering schools in the nation, Purdue gives students a run for their money not only in engineering but also in physics and computer science, all considered the hardest and most competitive majors. Anything liberal arts, interior design, and elementary education are considered somewhat easier. Even though they complain about the difficulty of many of their classes (Physics 152, one of "the toughest physics course nationwide," as one student claimed), students realize the value of their labor when recruiters start their bidding for engineers at $50,000.

Six hundred or even more are enrolled in many introductory classes, but the size of the classes decreases as students advance. Students say they don't feel that having a class of 600 affects the quality of the class since many of the lecture halls have big screens and other equipment that allow everyone to follow the lecture. However, problems may arise when the class meets in smaller groups with TAs, many of whom do not speak English as a first language.

Greeks Get to You

The lively social life on campus surpasses many students' expectations. "Call-outs, especially those of dance clubs and sports, and of many other events are handed to you all the time," said one student, who reported feeling overwhelmed by the active social life. Greek organizations play a major role in the social scene, and lots of students attend their parties. Fraternity rushes have nightmare stories compared to tamer sorority rushes, students say. And although the school has a strict policy on drinking, the Greeks continue to party on. Police visits, however, have ended in court. Purdue's alcohol policy is more strongly felt in the dorms where RAs are strict about the possession and consumption of alcohol and uphold the no-guests-after-2 A.M. rule.

For those who find the Greek scene a turn-off, Purdue boasts plenty of alternatives: Pete's Bar is popular on Wednesday nights, Neon Cactus dance bar packs them in on Thursdays, and Fridays find students at Harry's Chocolate Shop (a former chocolate shop, now a popular bar), and Where Else and Boiler Room dance bar. Theme parties such as "$5 prom," "White Trash," "Dress Your Buddy," and "Food Fight," also add color to the social life, as well as the funny organizations like the Vanilla Ice club and the Unicycle club. A great number of nearby restaurants, discount stores, malls, and many theatres are other alternatives to weekend partying and barhopping. Three campus movie theaters, each with nine screens, show first-run films.

Cheers for the Boilermakers

The huge sports complex, CO-REC, offers students everything from volleyball to swimming and weightlifting, and there are a number of golf courses close to campus. Sports is a part of almost everyone's life at Purdue; intramurals bring many to the playing field, and football holds special meaning for each student at Purdue. Tailgating, before and during the games, means great barbecue on the weekends, and the marching band entertains and enlivens the devoted supporters of the Boilermakers. The world's largest drum also adds to the excitement of games at the Ross-Ade Stadium. Most students attend the annual battle against Indiana University, where the winner keeps the Oaken Bucket, a traveling trophy that signifies the schools' strong rivalry. The basketball team also benefits from the support of the entire student body. Tickets for games at Mackey Arena quickly sell out, since fans are eager to watch the Boilermakers compete against their Big Ten rivals, and in NCAA.

Life of a Boilermaker

Purdue's campus stretches over a wide, flat terrain, and some dormitories are far away from central campus. However, if you live on campus, a car is not a necessity, or more correctly, as one student explained, "it doesn't feel like a necessity until you have to walk from your room to classes for 15 minutes during winter." Many upperclassmen and international students prefer to move off campus, while first-years and sophomores prefer living in frat houses or in the dorms. Parking is a big problem on campus: freshmen aren't given parking permits in the areas that are around central campus and the police are strict about enforcing the time limits. Therefore bringing cars freshman year is not recommended.

"As a freshman, you are the center of attention—[campus groups] come and check you out. If they like you, you join the group, if not, you've got to find new people."

Student groups are often formed along ethnic and national lines, with a great deal of interaction between all, and students say socioeconomic backgrounds don't matter at all. And new students are especially welcomed by campus groups. Said one upperclassman: "As a freshman, you are the center of attention—they come and check you out: If they like you, you join the group, if not, you've got to find new people."

All Relaxed and Spread Out

Purdue continues to grow as the administration develops its "Strategic Plan," which aims to decrease the student faculty ratio, increase interdisciplinary research opportunities, expand the diversity on campus, and make a stand for new innovations in technology, facilities, and economic development. School spirit, the lively social scene, and the satisfaction that comes from participating in such strong academic programs make for an excellent experience for Boilermakers. —*Yakut Seyhanli*

FYI

If you come to Purdue, you'd better bring "a computer—most people have desktops."

What is the typical weekend schedule? "Having fun with friends on Friday and Saturday nights, mostly at parties. Sunday, do all your last-minute homework."

If I could change one thing about Purdue, I'd "introduce more interaction with professors, and less with TAs."

Three things that every student at Purdue should do before graduating are "ride the Boilermaker train, run through all of the water fountains, and eat at the Triple X at 3 in the morning."

Rose-Hulman Institute of Technology

Address: 5500 Wabash Avenue; Terre Haute, IN 47803
Phone: 812-877-8213
E-mail address: admis.ofc@rose-hulman.edu
Web site URL: www.rose-hulman.edu
Founded: 1874
Private or Public: private
Religious affiliation: none
Location: suburban
Undergraduate enrollment: 1,642
Total enrollment: NA
Percent Male/Female: 82%/18%
Percent Minority: NA
Percent African-American: 2%
Percent Asian: 3%
Percent Hispanic: 1%
Percent Native-American: 0%
Percent in-state/out of state: 49%/51%
Percent Pub HS: 70%
Number of Applicants: 3,207
Percent Accepted: 65%
Percent Accepted who enroll: 22%
Entering: 451
Transfers: 13
Application Deadline: 1 Mar
Mean SAT: 1310
Mean ACT: 30
Middle 50% SAT range: V 570-670, M 640-720
Middle 50% ACT range: 27-31
3 Most popular majors: mechanical engineering, chemical engineering, computer science
Retention: 93%
Graduation rate: 65%
On-campus housing: 54%
Fraternities: 47%
Sororities: 46%
Library: 77,348 volumes
Tuition and Fees: $24,524
Room and Board: $6,720
Financial aid, first-year: 75%
Varsity or Club Athletes: 35%
Early Decision or Early Action Acceptance Rate: NA

For intelligent students who care more about getting a quality education than attending a name-brand university, Rose-Hulman Institute of Technology is a jewel. The small, technology specialty school lacks the name recognition of rivals MIT and Caltech but offers a relaxed environment where students are genuinely friendly and cutthroat competition is unheard of.

Scenic, Up-To-Date, and Safe

Located amidst trees and rolling hills on the outskirts of Terre Haute, Indiana, Rose-Hulman Institute of Technology is beautiful and improving every day. The campus sports two lakes, although one is "an unnatural turquoise color." While the grounds are attractive, huge amounts of money aren't shelled out for perfectly manicured lawns. "Our tuition goes to what it should—academics," one student said.

Rose has a small campus. Everything is within walking distance. Students can wake up 10 minutes before class and still get there in time, as long as they're not picky about how they look. Students brag that the quaint setting fosters a close-knit environment. "There's a very personal atmosphere here," one student said.

One of Rose's biggest assets is its state-of-the-art facilities. The multimillion-dollar Sports and Recreation Center and the observatory, technology center, and residence hall are several buildings Rose prides itself on. A new chapel and fine arts building are other up to date and comfortable buildings.

Rose is far enough away from the city of Terre Haute that safety isn't much of an issue. A car is broken into from time to time, but that's pretty much the extent of campus crime. One student claimed that she left her car doors unlocked all through freshman year and never had a problem. Dorm room doors are also left wide open even when people are gone. The only threat is friends playing a prank. "I would let my girlfriend walk across campus at 3 A.M. on a Friday night without worrying . . . it's that safe," one junior remarked. To further deter crime, emergency phones are located all over campus.

Good Things Don't Come Easy

Most Rose-Hulman students got As in high school with little difficulty. Things change. It's extremely hard to earn an A at Rose. One student said, "Getting a 4.0 is damn near impossible." However, B's are feasible if a student is willing to work hard. It's rumored that no student who's attended every class has ever failed a course.

"Getting a 4.0 is damn near impossible."

The first two years at Rose are especially difficult. The sophomore curriculum in particular is known to be a killer. It consists of a set of classes that essentially teach students the basics of all disciplines. For the first time students cannot get by with only knowing how things work. They also need to know why things work. This is the year when Rose starts teaching students to teach themselves.

To accommodate this difficult year most sophomores live in the newest dorm built largely to help with studying. There are peer tutors on every floor and study rooms at the end of each hallway. Professors are also extremely helpful. They give out home phone numbers and are available for questions at any time. All classes at Rose are taught by professors, but TAs are also available to help students with questions.

There are no easy majors at Rose, but Civil Engineering is rumored to be more painless than the rest. "The real slackers major in Economics," one student commented. Chemical Engineering is without a doubt the most difficult curriculum, but the hard work is worth the trouble. "The professors are the best in the world, and even though you will work hard and be challenged, you will be well-respected for the rest of your life," one student said. Students praise Rose's 100% job placement rate.

Living in Luxury

Most freshmen live in the impressive Deming residence hall. Others live in BSB, which is also nice. The triplets (Mees, Blumber, and Scharpenburg) are "kind of scary." For the most part, students are happy with their dorms. One senior has lived on campus all four years and said he wouldn't change much of anything. The rooms are big, most are air-conditioned, they come with nice oak furniture, and students can customize them as they wish (painting, building lofts, etc). Frosh floors are segregated by sex, but the halls are not. Upperclassmen live in co-ed floors. All dorms have RAs, and frosh dorms also have two sophomore advisors (SA). "I was an SA and would have given any of my guys the shirt off my back if they needed it," one upperclassmen said. The SAs are there to help with anything and everything freshmen could possibly need.

After their first year, students are allowed to live off campus, but many remain in the residence halls. Those who don't stay on campus typically move into fraternity or sorority houses. Some also live in off-campus housing. Nearby Village Quarter reportedly has cheap rent.

Something Edible

With a salad bar, deli, wok, main course, grill, cereals, and veggie bar in the cafeteria and "The Worx" in the basement, Rose students can "usually find something digestible." They complain, however, about having the same choices over and over. They are also unhappy with the mandatory meal plan—18 meals per week. Since the cafeteria is closed for dinner on weekends and breakfast

Making Their Own Fun

Known for Indiana State University Sycamore Larry Baird and a funny stench from a nearby paper mill, Terre Haute is not exactly an entertainment mecca. "There's really nothing to do in town besides going to Super Wal-Mart and making fun of the local 'Hautians,'" one student said. Due to this lack of options, Rose students make their own fun. With eight fraternities and two sororities on campus, Greek life dominates the social scene.

Graffiti parties are a popular event. Everyone wears a white shirt and draws on others with markers. The annual Camp Out party finds a frat house transformed into the wilderness, completely filled with leaves and a 25-foot tall tree. The popular Mafia party has hit men and fake money that can be used to give people "hits." While there's beer at all parties, students aren't pressured to drink. However, one student said "it's pretty boring at Rose without drinking."

Life Beyond Engineering

With more than 60 clubs and student organizations, Rose-Hulman students have a plethora of activities to be involved in. And if students can't find clubs that interests them, Rose encourages them to create it! One of the most popular organizations is the Solar Phantom team. The team competes in a biannual cross-country solar car race called Sunrayce. Most students are involved in several activities, but academics are their first priority. "Devotion only lasts until we have to do homework," one student said.

Intramurals are very popular, as are varsity sports. Rose is a Division III school, which means they aren't allowed to offer athletic scholarships. Consequently, school comes before sports. So is Rose-Hulman bringing home any athletic glory? "Our teams are the fighting *ENGINEERS* . . . we obviously aren't very good," one student joked. But football and basketball games still manage to draw pretty big crowds. Every year during homecoming the freshmen class constructs "an absolutely enormous, blazing hot, butt-kicking bonfire." It's built solely by manual labor. Upperclassmen try to knock it down, but the freshmen protect it.

A Less Than Satisfactory Student Body

If you're looking for a school with culture and diversity, Rose-Hulman might not be the place for you. A typical Rose-Hulman student is a white, upper-middle class male from the Midwest. "We're talking about a whole school who hasn't heard of Costco," said one East coast student. Another complained that she was the only non-white student on her freshman floor. But while there's not much diversity, there's certainly no discrimination.

With a seven-to-one male to female ratio, there is not much dating at Rose. The school has only been coed since 1995. A girl can generally get a guy if she wants to, although she might have to settle a bit. One female joked that there are too many "Steve Erkels" running around campus. Guys are not happy with the selection of females either. One male commented, "There aren't enough females, there are few girls, and absolutely no women." Many guys look for girls at nearby Indiana State University and St. Mary-of-the-Woods College.—*Alexis Wolff*

FYI

If you come to Rose-Hulman, you'd better bring "an eagerness to learn in an educational yet relaxed environment."

What is the typical weekend schedule? "A trip to Indiana State University or St. Mary-of-the-Woods college if you're a guy (not enough women at Rose-Hulman Institute of Technology), suck it up if you're a girl."

If I could change one thing about Rose-Hulman, I would "change the lack of diversity on campus."

Three things that every student at Rose-Hulman should do before graduating are "see a movie in historic Indiana Theatre, check out the locals at Super Wal-Mart at 4 A.M., have one of those conversations that keeps you up until the wee hours of the morning."

St. Mary's College

Address: LeMans Hall; Notre Dame, IN 46556
Phone: 574-284-4587
E-mail address: admission@saintmarys.edu
Web site URL: www.saintmarys.edu
Founded: 1844
Private or Public: private
Religious affiliation: Roman Catholic
Location: suburban
Undergraduate enrollment: 1,492
Total enrollment: NA
Percent Male/Female: 0%/100%
Percent Minority: 10%
Percent African-American: 1%
Percent Asian: 2%
Percent Hispanic: 5%
Percent Native-American: 0%
Percent in-state/out of state: 26%/74%
Percent Pub HS: 54%
Number of Applicants: 997
Percent Accepted: 82%
Percent Accepted who enroll: 46%
Entering: 376
Transfers: 44
Application Deadline: rolling
Mean SAT: NA
Mean ACT: NA
Middle 50% SAT range: V 530-630, M 520-610
Middle 50% ACT range: 22-27
3 Most popular majors: business administration, education, communication
Retention: 83%
Graduation rate: 73%
On-campus housing: 84%
Fraternities: NA
Sororities: NA
Library: 210,812 volumes
Tuition and Fees: $21,974
Room and Board: $7,289
Financial aid, first-year: 62%
Varsity or Club Athletes: NA
Early Decision or Early Action Acceptance Rate: ED 85%

A student at this small Catholic women's college can be assured that she will not get lost in the crowd. At St. Mary's College in Notre Dame, Indiana, one can have the best of both worlds: the intimacy of a small single-sex campus with the facilities of the large University of Notre Dame just across the street.

Liberal Arts Curriculum

Academically, St. Mary's "belles," as they're known, pursue one of five degrees: bachelor of arts, bachelor of business administration, bachelor of fine arts, bachelor of music, or bachelor of science. All students are required to declare a major at the beginning of their sophomore year. Through the core curriculum at St. Mary's, students are encouraged to pursue a broad-based liberal arts education. Most students fulfill all of the core requirements, along with the foreign-language requirement, by the end of their sophomore year, after which they take more specialized classes suited to their major. One first-year student who had not yet decided on her major said that "the core requirements are a relief. They give me some direction."

Students at St. Mary's can take classes at Notre Dame, and many do. Notre Dame students take St. Mary's courses as well. St. Mary's courses have a great advantage because of their small size: one frosh said each of her five classes had fewer than 20 students. The largest classes on campus are the introductory science classes, which are still remarkably small—around 50 students. In addition, at St. Mary's there are no teaching assistants, so students say a professor "with the highest degree in the field" will be teaching your courses. The student-teacher interactions are also excellent. In addition to having her professors' home phone numbers, one student even attended a Halloween party given by her philosophy professor.

Registration takes place over the summer. First-year students are sent a guidebook of courses, from which they select ten. A schedule is then sent home, usually including the student's top five classes. Upperclasswomen generally do not have difficulty enrolling in their first-choice courses.

Academics at St. Mary's are rigorous, but manageable. "The classes are small enough so all my questions are answered and I understand the material, which makes the classes seem easier," one student said. Undergrads claim that there are no true "gut" courses, although Beginning Acting is an easy class according to some.

An Integrated Campus

St. Mary's has its own library, named Cushwa-Leighton, which is separate from the Notre Dame facilities. To study quietly, many students go to Cushwa, which reportedly is so conducive to studying that Notre Dame students like it too. For social studying, and for simply socializing, most St. Mary's students go to the larger library at Notre Dame.

The majority of St. Mary's students live on campus in four residential halls. McCandless, the most modern of the four, provides each student with a small study carrel space across the hall from her bedroom. According to one student, "Each dorm has its own personal character." Each small study room is equipped with air-conditioning, which helps beat the hot Indiana weather at the beginning and end of the year. Students also live in one of the following: Le Mans Hall, which is relatively old, but beautiful; Holy Cross Hall, which has larger rooms and big suites; and Regina Hall, which has only singles. All of the dorms (with the exception of McCandless) as well as the computer clusters and various other facilities across campus are connected via underground tunnels.

"The classes are small enough so all my questions are answered, and I understand the material, which makes the classes seem easier."

There are stringent rules, called parietals, dictating when members of the opposite sex are allowed in the dorms. Males have to be out of the dorms by midnight during the week, and by 2 A.M. on weekends. The same rules apply at Notre Dame.

There is one main cafeteria on campus, and the food there is reasonably tasty. Students can frequent the dining hall as many times a day as they like (it's open from 7 A.M. to 7 P.M.). Vegetarian options are always available, as are a salad bar and a grill. Most students eat on campus because there are few options in the local town of South Bend. When the women of St. Mary's do leave campus for a meal, their choices "tend to be limited to fast food."

Midwestern Belles

Because South Bend has little to offer a college crowd socially and culturally, much of what happens at St. Mary's centers on life at Notre Dame. Since neither has a Greek system, the schools are interrelated through clubs and extracurriculars. One student claimed that "going back and forth to Notre Dame *is* an extracurricular activity." However, "some people have a love-hate relationship with Notre Dame," another student added. St. Mary's undergrads participate in a wide range of activities from student government to intramural sports to writing for the *Observer*, the daily paper. The main connection between the two schools is athletics. St. Mary's has its own Angela Fitness Center and Belles play competitively in basketball, volleyball, and tennis, yet their true allegiance is to Notre Dame. One frosh said, "People try to rile up some school spirit, but it's just not there. Mainly, it's for Notre Dame."

In addition to Notre Dame sports, St. Mary's students take part in Notre Dame social events. St. Mary's itself is a dry campus, but that does not stop undergrads from bussing over to Notre Dame to drink (a shuttle runs between the two schools almost 24 hours a day). Popular events on campus also include "screw your roommate" dances. At these events, roommates fix each other up on blind dates, using the "Dog Book," a book with photos of all the freshmen. Although St. Mary's does offer some social venues, the majority of St. Mary's students spend their free time socializing at Notre Dame.

Students at St. Mary's date, but random hook-ups also occur, despite the strong Catholic overtones at the school. General, informed discussions on safe sex are rare, and the administration has something of a "don't ask, don't tell" policy, according to students. The campus is politically conservative, and while the college is not as diverse as larger institutions, it makes a concerted effort to attract women from different backgrounds and geographic areas. Currently, the majority of the students at St. Mary's are from the Midwest.

St. Mary's is a small Catholic college with all the resources of a large university (as a result of its proximity to Notre Dame)—and St. Mary's students rely on their neighboring university for social, athletic, and academic enrichment. —*Heather Topel*

FYI

If you come to Saint Mary's, you'd better bring "a computer and a good fake ID."

What is the typical weekend schedule? "Go out until around 3 A.M. on Friday, sleep in on Saturday, and lay around doing homework on Sunday."

If I could change one thing about St. Mary's, I'd "change it to co-ed."

Three things that every student at St. Mary's should do before graduating are "setting up your roommate for the Screw Your Roommate dance, go to a sporting event, and take a class that you had never considered taking before."

University of Notre Dame

Address: 220 Main Building; Notre Dame, IN 46556
Phone: 574-631-7505
E-mail address: admissio.1@nd.edu
Web site URL: www.nd.edu
Founded: 1842
Private or Public: private
Religious affiliation: Roman Catholic
Location: urban
Undergraduate enrollment: 8,261
Total enrollment: NA
Percent Male/Female: 53%/47%
Percent Minority: 19%
Percent African-American: 3%
Percent Asian: 4%
Percent Hispanic: 7%
Percent Native-American: 1%
Percent in-state/out of state: 12%/88%
Percent Pub HS: 50%
Number of Applicants: 9,744
Percent Accepted: 34%
Percent Accepted who enroll: 58%
Entering: 1,946
Transfers: 129
Application Deadline: 9 Jan
Mean SAT: NA
Mean ACT: NA
Middle 50% SAT range: V 620-720, M 650-730
Middle 50% ACT range: 30-33
3 Most popular majors: business/commerce, engineering, political science
Retention: 98%
Graduation rate: 94%
On-campus housing: 75%
Fraternities: NA
Sororities: NA
Library: 2,673,446 volumes
Tuition and Fees: $27,612
Room and Board: $6,930
Financial aid, first-year: 46%
Varsity or Club Athletes: 9%
Early Decision or Early Action Acceptance Rate: EA 57%

Notre Dame: the name speaks righteously of tradition. In light of this school's academic distinction, strong faith, and excellent football team, tradition can only begin to describe its deeply ingrained values.

Academic Enlightenment

Notre Dame's rigorous curriculum baffles students with its wide variety of choices and prepares them well for the future. When freshman arrive, they enter in the First Year of Studies school, where they adjust to college life and choose what college they will further pursue out of four choices: Arts and Letters, by far the most popular, Engineering, Business, or Science. A diverse array of over 50 majors is available, and students rarely get bogged down by requirements. One student explained that "most requirements are generally fulfilled freshman year," which leaves options open for very demanding majors such as engineering or more popular majors like biology and political science.

Notre Dame students also enjoy small classes. With the exception of the large intro classes, most have fewer than 40 students, averaging about 20 per class. The university prides itself on the attention paid towards undergraduates, which students enjoy and commend, especially when it comes to attention from professors. Professors may hold dinners at their houses or even do crazy things to incite student interest. One student said his finance professor would dump a "glass of water on his head during lectures because he felt people needed to pay attention a little more." In spite of fun professors and crazy antics, academics are tough. According to most students, there is "about five to six hours of homework each night." But most who are willing to embrace the challenge of Notre Dame come expecting the level of difficulty; they generally agree that their schooling has "provided [them] with opportunities [they] never would have imagined" had they not come.

What's in a Name?

One of the most obvious traditional aspects of this respected university is that it is a Catholic institution. What does that boil down to in terms of everyday life? Many students feel that religion is not overbearing on campus, but it definitely holds a considerable place in their lifestyle. Approximately 85% of students on campus are Catholic, although not all of them practice. Notably, theology is one of the requirements for all students, although it does not necessarily have to be Catholic theology.

> **"Football games remind me of Disney World! Before the game, there is a parade through campus and huge crowds mill about."**

Each dorm has a chapel in which mass is held every day except Saturday. While many students attend, those who do not say they feel comfortable with their choice. Some students comment that they feel faith is a major unifying factor in the undergraduate population, furthering community values and a sense of family.

Crucifixes in classrooms and residence halls serve as a reminder of Notre Dame's Catholic association. Other reminders of religious beliefs include single-sex dorms, curfews, and rather stringent rules about when the opposite sex can enter a residence hall. Some students complain that "the rules get a little annoying" but in the end they say it was all worth it.

One thing that students adamantly complain about is the lack of diversity of the student body. The minority situation was described by one to be "perhaps the most disheartening aspect of this campus . . . non-white and non-Catholic is a definite minority." This lack of diversity leads a less than liberal environment, in the political, sexual, and social spheres. Notre Dame students recognize that they are "somewhat liberal, but mostly conservative."

Faith in Football

At Notre Dame, students respect their faith, but they also know how to party. Depending on their schedules, many start their weekends on Thursdays, when they go to local bars and clubs such as Corby's, Boatclub, and Heartland. Fridays are similar, and students get psyched for the next day's football game. Parties can be found on campus, but one student recommends off-campus parties "if you want a party that will last to the wee hours." Turtle Creek housing complex parties are particularly rowdy. On campus, the drinking policy is "beer only," as hard liquor was recently banned.

That beer flows well into Saturday as tailgaters gather for the football game, an amazing show of solidarity and school spirit. One Fighting Irish fan, when asked to describe a football game at Notre Dame, claims that words could not do it justice. But another says, "Football games remind me of Disney World! Before the game, there is a parade through campus and huge crowds mill about." Students, faculty, and tailgaters alike pack into the Notre Dame stadium to cheer; everyone stands throughout the entire game. Enthusiasts are usually tired after a full day on Saturdays, which tends to be a more relaxed night for parties.

Although many social events tend to be centered around sports and often drinking, other options do exist. As a student explained, "there is other stuff to do—hang out with friends, go to a show, go to a movie. There is an organization called

Flip Side that puts on a lot of non-drinking, fun activities on weekends." Every dorm has its own formal as well, which is often themed.

Life Off the Field

Other than football, students are very proud of all their athletic teams, notably basketball. Some would call Notre Dame a "workout campus," as many students double as athletes who enjoy excellent training facilities.

Apart from sports, students keep pretty busy with other activities and community service. There are myriad clubs and organizations on campus, all student-run, and for all tastes and interests. The arts and theatre scene puts on a student film festival every year, along with numerous plays. There is a Battle of the Bands, not to mention the appearance of such groups as U2 and Better Than Ezra at school sponsored concerts. Guest speakers are not uncommon to Notre Dame either, including President George W. Bush, who has come to speak at graduation.

Living in South Bend, Indiana may not be the most exciting part of the undergraduate experience at Notre Dame, but the campus has a lot to offer. It is closed off from traffic, so the landscaping is beautiful in all seasons. It really comes to life in the spring, when students lounge on the lawn and play Frisbee.

Once students are situated in a dorm, they are expected to live there for the next four years, unless they move off-campus their senior year (about 20% currently do, but the number is increasing). The dorms are well equipped, although they lack air conditioning and cable. However, students don't complain—dorms tend to foster close friendships, and take the place of the non-existent Greek life. Food options on campus received little complaint as well; students enjoy Burger King, Subway, Starbucks, and Recker's, a local sandwich shop, right on campus. Those with cars sometimes drive into town to dine out.

In general though, students are content staying on campus, where they live in a peaceful atmosphere in touch with God, with nature, and with their serious academic track. Notre Dame provides its students with rich traditions: on the surface, academics, football, and religion are major players on this campus, but deeper than that are strong feelings of community, togetherness, and progress towards a common goal. —*Carolina Galvao*

FYI

If you come to Notre Dame, you better bring "anything North Face."

What is the typical weekend schedule? "Thursday go out; Friday pep rallies and parties; Saturday tailgate and football game; Sunday recover and study."

If I could change one thing about Notre Dame, I'd "eliminate single-sex dorms."

Three things every student at Notre Dame should do before graduating are "rush the football field, attend a party to celebrate the Irish heritage on St. Patrick's day, go to the Grotto."

Valparaiso University

Address: Kretzmann Hall; Valparaiso, IN 46383
Phone: 888-468-2576
E-mail address: undergrad.admissions@valpo.edu
Web site URL: www.valpo.edu
Founded: 1859
Private or Public: private
Religious affiliation: Lutheran
Location: urban
Undergraduate enrollment: 2,910
Total enrollment: NA
Percent Male/Female: 47%/53%
Percent Minority: 10%
Percent African-American: 3%
Percent Asian: 2%
Percent Hispanic: 3%
Percent Native-American: 0%
Percent in-state/out of state: 34%/66%
Percent Pub HS: 80%
Number of Applicants: 3,117
Percent Accepted: 84%
Percent Accepted who enroll: 27%
Entering: 717
Transfers: 102
Application Deadline: 15 Aug
Mean SAT: NA
Mean ACT: NA
Middle 50% SAT range: V 530-650, M 530-650
Middle 50% ACT range: 23-29
3 Most popular majors: marketing, nursing, psychology
Retention: 86%
Graduation rate: 72%
On-campus housing: 65%
Fraternities: 24%
Sororities: 20%
Library: 521,907 volumes
Tuition and Fees: $20,638
Room and Board: $5,380
Financial aid, first-year: 69%
Varsity or Club Athletes: 16%
Early Decision or Early Action Acceptance Rate: EA 89%

Not far from the Windy City of Chicago lies Valparaiso University, a small private Lutheran school in northwest Indiana, where students enjoy nationally recognized academic programs, an active social scene, a variety of popular extracurricular activities, and, of course, a great basketball team.

"The Human Experience"

When freshmen arrive at Valparaiso (affectionately nicknamed Valpo), they are automatically enrolled in the "Valpo Core." Also known as "The Human Experience," the core covers themes such as creation, citizenship, coming of age, vocation, and love, through a year-long course that not only includes lectures and readings, but for-credit basketball game attendances and pasta gatherings in professors' homes. Most Valpo students value their core experiences. As one psychology major said, "At first I thought I would hate taking the required core. I thought it would be really boring since every freshman has to take it. Now that I've taken the courses, though, I really feel like core gave me a great background that I've built my entire Valpo education on top of."

Students who choose to enter "Christ College," the honors college at Valpo, substitute "Texts and Contexts: Traditions of Human Thought" for core credit; the class focuses on critical reading, writing, and discussion of great works of literature. This two-semester course includes a fall play written and performed by the students, and a spring debate before the campus community.

"Now that I've taken the courses, though, I really feel like core gave me a great background that I've built my entire Valpo education on top of."

Aside from core, students can take classes in four other colleges at VU: Arts and Sciences, Nursing, Engineering, or Business Administration. The meteorology program in the College of Arts and Sciences is a popular yet demanding major. Classes outside of the Core and other general education requirements are usually small, and Valpo prides itself on the absence of TAs. Most students find their workloads manageable. As one student says, "It just depends on what you do. Like at any other college, you can make Valpo what you want it to be. If you try to do everything at once, the workload's going to seem a lot bigger."

Always Something to Do . . .

Despite the fact that Valpo is a dry campus with a zero-tolerance policy on underage drinking, students at VU find many different options when it comes to the social scene. Some students have dorm parties, while others visit the fraternity houses around campus or head up to the bars and nightclubs of Chicago. While the majority of Valpo students do drink, non-drinkers rarely feel left out. The Union Board at Valpo is extremely active, constantly arranging movies, lectures, concerts, and diversity events for the entire campus.

The Greek scene at Valpo is thriving, with close to half of the students involved in fraternities or sororities. While fraternities may have houses off campus, sorority members find themselves in on-campus dorms, separated into their respective sororities by wing. The reason? As one engineering students explains, "If you have six or more girls living together in one house in Indiana, it's considered a brothel. Not that I would complain, but I think Valpo would rather avoid having all their sororities labeled as brothels. Plus, the girls probably wouldn't like it either."

Most Valpo students find it easy to meet people and make friends, especially within the student dorms, where your floor is often the source of your closest friends. Students are rarely labeled by their activities or interests, so cliques are rare at VU. Almost every student at Valpo would agree with one theology major, however, that "There is NO diversity! Everyone you meet here is white, Christian, and upper-middle-class. Practically everyone is from the Midwest, too."

From Christian Crusades to Basketball

Most students at VU are actively involved in some kind of extracurricular activity. As one student says, "Everybody has at least one thing that they do that is really theirs. Some people may do a lot of different stuff too, but everyone has got their own activity that they are really committed to." Intramural sports are very popular at Valpo, and most students are involved in some kind of community service project; and the Campus Crusade for Christ and the Voodoo Comedy Club are always fun organizations.

While many Valpo students show their school spirit and make their way out to football games in the fall, the real source of school pride is the Valparaiso basketball team. One of the most well-attended school events of the year is Midnight Madness, when the entire school turns up to watch the first basketball practice session of the year. The players are introduced to the student body one by one and a huge pep rally led by the VU Crew is held until the players begin their first practice at midnight.

Living at Valpo

Most students at Valpo live on campus, in dorms that are single-sex by floor. Students enjoy comforts such as pullout futon beds, big windows, and sinks within their bedrooms. However, the university-regulated curfew is extremely unpopular. Members of the opposite sex must be off one another's floors after 1:00 A.M. on weekdays and after 2:00 A.M. on weekends. Drinking and smoking are prohibited in the dorms as well. RAs can be found in all dorms, but they are generally friendly and welcoming, and are seen more as companions than authority figures.

There are four main cafeterias on campus. The largest is located in the student center, where, as one student says, "You come, you eat, you leave." There are three other, smaller cafeterias, which are located in three of the dorms; their residential nature means students can often be found studying or relaxing. In addition to eating on campus, Jimmy John's and various off-campus pizza restaurants are popular dining options for students.

The campus at Valparaiso is home to the second-largest university chapel in the country; its size makes it the focus of the green, gently hilly campus. Situated about an hour from Chicago and in the town of Valparaiso, Valpo creates a home for its students unlike any other. As one sociology student says, "I just love the fact that this is where I wake up every morning."

Students at VU are quickly able to find their own niches in the Valpo community and make the small Lutheran school their new home. As one Valpo student proudly boasts, "Whatever you want in a college, Valpo's got it. If you want to be in a small town community, that's Valpo. If you need the excitement of the city, Chicago's less than an hour away. If you want a lot of extracurricular activities, Valpo's got everything. If you're more concerned with the academic aspects of a college, Valpo's classes and professors are amazing. And last of all, who wouldn't want to root for our basketball team?" —*Sarah Newman*

FYI

If you come to Valparaiso, you'd better bring "a jacket, gloves, and a fan."

What's the typical weekend schedule? "Party hard on Friday night; sleep in late Saturday morning; go to the basketball game Saturday night and party with friends; go to church Sunday morning; and then study, study, study all day on Sunday."

If I could change one thing about Valparaiso, I would "make our student body more diverse."

Three things every student at Valparaiso should do before graduating are "go to El Amigos, ring the Victory Bell, and do crowd push-ups at a volleyball game."

Wabash College

Address: PO Box 352; Crawfordsville, IN 47933
Phone: 800-345-5385
E-mail address: admissions@wabash.edu
Web site URL: www.wabash.edu
Founded: 1832
Private or Public: private
Religious affiliation: none
Location: urban
Undergraduate enrollment: 912
Total enrollment: NA
Percent Male/Female: 100%/0%
Percent Minority: 18%
Percent African-American: 7%
Percent Asian: 2%
Percent Hispanic: 6%
Percent Native-American: 0%
Percent in-state/out of state: 74%/26%
Percent Pub HS: 90%
Number of Applicants: 1,287
Percent Accepted: 50%
Percent Accepted who enroll: 42%
Entering: 271
Transfers: 8
Application Deadline: rolling
Mean SAT: NA
Mean ACT: NA
Middle 50% SAT range: V 530-620, M 560-655
Middle 50% ACT range: 23-28
3 Most popular majors: history, psychology, English
Retention: 84%
Graduation rate: 67%
On-campus housing: 99%
Fraternities: 65%
Sororities: NA
Library: 420,906 volumes
Tuition and Fees: $21,215
Room and Board: $6,717
Financial aid, first-year: 77%
Varsity or Club Athletes: NA
Early Decision or Early Action Acceptance Rate: ED 81%: EA 65%

Wabash College is rich in history, tradition, and financial endowments. As one of the few remaining all-male colleges in the United States, Wabash thrives on spirited students and exceptionally loyal alumni. "People who come here support it until they die," claimed one Wabash student.

Hard-Core Curriculum

Based on a strong core curriculum, academics are rigorous at Wabash. "There are not many classes that you can blow off," one student reported. Undergraduates must take courses in the natural sciences, math, a foreign language, English composition, literature, and fine arts, regardless of their major. Sophomores must take Cultures and Traditions, a course that studies the philosophies and political ideas of various cultures in the same period in history. "It's quite politically correct, but you learn a lot," one student said. To graduate, all Wabash seniors must pass "comps," a daylong series of oral and written exams administered by professors in the student's major.

Students report that the religion and economics departments are particularly strong. The philosophy department benefits from a prestigious faculty that includes well-known philosopher William Placher. English majors say their department has a particularly cohesive faculty that works well together as a team. Art and music, however, do not fare as well in students' opinions. Many Wabash students are on a pre-professional track and hope to enroll in law or medical school after graduation; as a result, the college is reportedly strong in the pre-med sciences such as biology and chemistry.

In addition to strong academics in the classroom, Wabash offers its students the chance to study abroad or obtain various internship positions through a wide range of off-campus study opportunities and an extensive alumni network.

Super-Small Classes

Wabash's size allows not only for small classes (the largest class, a popular classics lecture, enrolls about 110), but also for maximum student-faculty interaction. Most Wabash professors live within walking distance of the campus and often eat lunch or talk informally with their students. Professors routinely give out their home phone numbers to their classes, and students say they are comfortable calling them at home for help. Students cite this open communication and sense of friendship with faculty as one of the best aspects of Wabash. The sense of community often endures long after graduation.

> **"People who come here support it until they die."**

Wabash students also benefit from the fine arts center on campus, which includes a large art gallery, auditorium, classrooms equipped with modern audiovisual equipment, and practice rooms with pianos. Salter Hall, located in the arts center, is reportedly one of the most acoustically sound halls in the state of Indiana. The Detchon Center houses the classics and foreign-language departments, a computer center, and several new classrooms. According to students, Detchon is "a good place to study." For serious study, students go to the Lilly Library, where "it is always quiet, no matter what," according to one sophomore.

No Woman, No Cry?— The Social Scene

Although Wabash is an all-male school, most students say they find no shortage of female company. Many attend social events at Purdue and Indiana University, both less than 90 minutes away. One student, however, pointed out that the lack of women, combined with the un-happening surroundings of Crawfordsville (a town of 15,000 in which "Wal-mart serves as the social epicenter"), can make the Wabash experience socially isolating in relation to the outside world. In his assessment of the social situation at Wabash, he continued, "We are encapsulated in this tiny microcosm filled with testosterone, and the result is a return to the primordial instincts of aggression and survival." But the capsule also serves as a social safe haven, a tightly knit community where "all students feel somewhat connected to one another." In this sense, Wabash can resemble a "huge male-bonding fest."

Nowhere is this more apparent than in Wabash's fraternities, which dominate the campus social scene. Rush starts during spring visitation for high school seniors and resumes as soon as freshmen arrive on campus. Beer drinking is a central activity on Greek Row and throughout Wabash, despite the college's "Gentleman Rule" that says each Wabash undergrad must "behave like a gentleman on- and off-campus at all times." One student warned that this is a "very wet campus, one of the wettest I've seen."

The largest campus-wide event happens each fall when the Wabash Little Giants and their archrival DePauw University compete for the Monon Bell in the oldest football rivalry west of the Allegheny Mountains. In 1993, the 100th anniversary game was nationally televised and covered in Sports Illustrated. Homecoming week features special events such as the Chapel Sing, in which pledge brothers assemble in front of the chapel to sing the school song. Whichever group yells and sings the loudest wins the competition, as judged by the Sphinx Club, an exclusive club whose members perform community service, promote school spirit, and symbolize "the essence of a Wabash man." The competition is more tiring than it sounds, for Wabash has the longest school song in the nation; pledges must exercise their vocal cords for over 45 minutes!

Other sports events take place in a somewhat more subdued manner, although student participation in sports remains high. "It's really hard to be cut [from a team] here, so lots of people can participate no matter what their skill or experience level," explained one junior. The swim team and the football team usually draw the most student support, as does the well-ranked cross-country team. Other teams, however, have less impressive records, and in the words of one student, "This is definitely not a jock school." Wabash students also participate in intramural sports ranging from touch football to bowling. The athletic facilities are "in need of an upgrade," according to one student, although another allows that the facilities are "not bad for Division III."

Students also participate in extracurriculars from the *Bachelor*, a widely read weekly newspaper, to the student-run radio station WNDY—the Giant. There is also a strong theater program that produces many plays throughout the year.

Food Fights

Despite the administration's reported efforts to "diversify the food scene," Wabash students report that the food, while edible, is certainly not what you would eat if you had a choice. Although each of the many fraternity houses has its own in-house cook, food in the houses is reportedly not much better than in the cafeterias. The required plan of 19 meals per week has been a recent point of contention between students and the administration, and many students want a more flexible (and less expensive) plan. Nonetheless, off-campus restaurants and bars offer a break from dining hall food. The Silver Dollar Bar currently reigns as students' favorite local bar. Little Mexico and Joe's, a bar and grill, also draw many away from dining halls.

Living Arrangements

The large majority of Wabash students live in fraternity houses during their four years at the college. But among the campus dorms, students cite the more updated Martindale and the quiet Wolcott Hall as most desirable, while dorms such as Grant are less coveted. One floor in Morris Hall was recently designated as dry in an effort to reduce peer pressure and provide a quiet haven for nondrinkers. Space reportedly abounds in all Wabash dorms except those with single rooms.

The campus is self-contained, with a mix of architectural styles. Despite the mix, however, one student said, "The buildings here are very square; they really all look the same." With generous funding from graduates, Wabash is able to maintain first-rate facilities and provide financial aid to a large percentage of students, a major draw for out-of-staters in need of financial assistance.

Although about three-fourths of the student body hails from Indiana, many different nationalities and races comprise the student population. Many students feel, however, that the campus is not diverse enough. The administration has reportedly stepped up its minority and international recruitment efforts. One student described the campus as filled with "lots of liberals in search of a well-rounded education." Others, however, say the prevailing conservative political climate can, at times, lead to closed-mindedness and stereotyping, especially in relation to such issues as feminism and homosexuality.

In spite of these complaints about the lack of diversity at Wabash, many are proud of the solid education, strong heritage, and fierce loyalty that come with being a Wabash man. "It's hard to explain, but after coming here, I wouldn't go back to a co-ed university," one Wabash transfer student said. —*Susanna Chu and Staff*

FYI

If you come to Wabash, you'd better bring "a car for all the weekend travel."

What is the typical weekend schedule? "Hang out with friends at frats and dorms at night, and work out or do laundry during the day."

If I could change one thing about Wabash, I'd "change the town—it's boring here."

The three things that every student should do before graduating from Wabash are "hang out at the Silver Dollar Bar, attend the Wabash/DePauw game, branch out and go to a social event of some sort at another nearby school."

Iowa

Cornell College

Address: 600 First Street West; Mount Vernon, IA 52314
Phone: 800-747-1112
E-mail address: admissions@cornellcollege.edu
Web site URL: www.cornellcollege.edu
Founded: 1853
Private or Public: private
Religious affiliation: Methodist
Location: rural
Undergraduate enrollment: 1,001
Total enrollment: NA
Percent Male/Female: 40%/60%
Percent Minority: 7%
Percent African-American: 3%
Percent Asian: 1%
Percent Hispanic: 2%
Percent Native-American: 1%
Percent in-state/out of state: 32%/68%
Percent Pub HS: 90%
Number of Applicants: 1,625
Percent Accepted: 62%
Percent Accepted who enroll: 31%
Entering: 314
Transfers: 29
Application Deadline: rolling
Mean SAT: NA
Mean ACT: NA
Middle 50% SAT range: V 540-660, M 540-640
Middle 50% ACT range: 23-28
3 Most popular majors: education, economics, psychology
Retention: 79%
Graduation rate: 55%
On-campus housing: 92%
Fraternities: 30%
Sororities: 32%
Library: 197,780 volumes
Tuition and Fees: $21,790
Room and Board: $6,035
Financial aid, first-year: 83%
Varsity or Club Athletes: 29%
Early Decision or Early Action Acceptance Rate: NA

Imagine starting and ending a class in just one month. It sounds impossible, but for Cornell College students, month-long classes are a reality. The small Mount Vernon, Iowa, college operates on a block system whereby students enroll in just one class at a time. While many other colleges and universities divide their academic years into fall and spring semesters, Cornell's system is comprised of nine blocks, each for three-and-a-half weeks. Many students describe the short class periods as "intense," but insist that they are "manageable."

Block Scheduling

The nine blocks are spread from late August until early May. Students typically enroll in a class for eight of the nine blocks, with the leftover block becoming three-and-a-half weeks of vacation time. However, particularly ambitious students can enroll in courses throughout all nine blocks. In such cases, the ninth block course can be taken for free. Because the winter recess is currently just one week and students do not have a spring vacation, there has been a call on campus to change the system to eight blocks, adding a spring break and lengthening the winter vacation.

All students must take four blocks of a foreign language (although testing out is possible), one of fine arts, one of math, two of physical science, and three of humanities. There are also requirements in writing and physical education. Students who choose to double-major try to fulfill the requirements in the first two years through introductory-level courses, leaving their final two years for more intense and upper-level study in their chosen fields. Although many students bubble with delight over the block system, some undergrads admit that it is difficult to fit a year's worth of a language into less than a month, and that a more "conventional" approach for teaching foreign languages would be more effective.

Not having to plan a semester full of classes in advance allows students much more time to decide on a major. In the past, many students chose triple or quadruple majors. However, two years ago Cornell limited students to two majors, with the hope of fostering a basic liberal arts education while requiring its graduates to have a sharper focus.

All of the block courses are taught for five days a week, some meeting twice a day. Classes begin on the first Monday of each month and continue until the final Wednesday of that month. According to one sophomore, "The block system lets you focus on one thing. Some nights you have a lot of stuff to do, but other nights you won't have a damn thing, which is nice." Another student described the average amount of homework per night as "around one hour."

Besides the unique block system, many students choose Cornell because of its impressive student-faculty interaction. Enrollment in most classes is capped at 25, the average class size is just 15, and all courses are taught by professors. Many students express a high level of comfort with all of their professors; home visits with profs are not uncommon.

Special Programs

Students name the sciences, especially biology, as the best departments. Cornell's special 3–2 engineering program allows students to complete three years of selected courses at Cornell and then transfer to Washington University in St. Louis to earn a joint B.A.-M.S. degree from the two schools. Cornell also has an early-acceptance predental program associated with the nearby University of Iowa. After completing their sophomore year and taking the Dental Achievement Test, students who are accepted into the program are assured a place in the U of I School of Dentistry after graduation. Another popular area of study is religion. Many students cited such religion courses as Epistles of Paul, The Idea of God, and The Question of Faith as some of the more stimulating courses at the college.

"The block system lets you focus on one thing. Some nights you have a lot of stuff to do, but other nights you won't have a damn thing, which is nice."

Many students choose to study abroad during their time at Cornell. One of the most popular Cornell-sponsored programs occurs during the fifth block, which begins after New Year's. The program consists of a trip to England for the entire length of the block to study and travel. Many students praise the creative nature of the program, calling it a "very good trip." Students may also study abroad for a year or a semester through programs of the Associated Colleges of the Midwest or by joining an approved program from another university.

Social Associations

Although the college has no Greek system, it has local groups called associations. One such association is Phi Beta Kappa, the nation's oldest scholastic honorary society. The groups are referred to by their shortened names, often Greek letters, such as the "Gammas." The associations sponsor most of the on-campus parties, including the Axetoberfest put on by the "Axes" at a farm just outside Mount Vernon in the middle of October. Pledging for the associations (six men's and six women's) occurs in the spring for freshmen and in the fall for sophomores, climaxing during the four-day break between the first and second (fall) or seventh and eighth (spring) blocks.

Besides participating in the social associations, many students choose to visit one of the two local bars or go to the University of Iowa campus in Iowa City. One student described both of the bars as "cool," but "very different from each other; Joe's is more for the athletic types and the more social-life conscious, while Randall's crowd is more mixed." Both of the bars allow anyone 19 years of age and older to enter, but you must be 21 to drink.

Although Cornell is situated in the small town of Mount Vernon, few students seem to mind the quiet setting. One student from Chicago said, "coming to Mount Vernon was a big change in that it was more rural, but once you get yourself a group of friends, you're pretty much set." Another student complained that "it takes more effort to find stuff to do on the weekends," but overall students are happy with the friendly town. According to one student, "The campus makes up the town. We keep a lot of the businesses running and they really suffer during the summer."

Moreover, Cornell is within 20 miles of both Cedar Rapids and Iowa City. The University of Iowa provides added resources, such as library materials. One junior explained that although there "is not much microfilm or microfiche at the Cornell library, students can go to Iowa City for a lot of their research."

Cornell continues to make its mark among the numerous small Midwestern colleges because of the block system. This system allows undergrads to study subjects with a degree of attention unmatched at other schools, yet still be exposed to many different people and their ideas due to the constant changeover of classes. According to students, the this system of change at Cornell provides for a stimulating and exciting four years. —*William Chen and Staff*

FYI

If you come to Cornell, you'd better bring "a couch."

What is the typical weekend schedule? "Go out and about to parties and bars on Friday and Saturday nights, then do all your homework on Sunday."

If I could change one thing about Cornell, I'd "make it be not so liberal."

Three things every student at Cornell should do before graduating are "go biking in Mount Vernon, pledge an association, and study abroad."

Grinnell College

Address: PO Box 805; Grinnell, IA 50112
Phone: 800-247-0113
E-mail address: askgrin@grinnell.edu
Web site URL: www.grinnell.edu
Founded: 1846
Private or Public: private
Religious affiliation: none
Location: rural
Undergraduate enrollment: 1,485
Total enrollment: NA
Percent Male/Female: 45%/55%
Percent Minority: 23%
Percent African-American: 4%
Percent Asian: 5%
Percent Hispanic: 4%
Percent Native-American: 1%
Percent in-state/out of state: 15%/85%
Percent Pub HS: 85%
Number of Applicants: 2,067
Percent Accepted: 65%
Percent Accepted who enroll: 28%
Entering: 369
Transfers: 29
Application Deadline: 20 Jan
Mean SAT: 1337
Mean ACT: 29
Middle 50% SAT range: V 630-730, M 620-710
Middle 50% ACT range: 28-31
3 Most popular majors: biology, history, English
Retention: 92%
Graduation rate: 83%
On-campus housing: 85%
Fraternities: NA
Sororities: NA
Library: 1,020,921 volumes
Tuition and Fees: $24,490
Room and Board: $6,570
Financial aid, first-year: 58%
Varsity or Club Athletes: 35%
Early Decision or Early Action Acceptance Rate: ED 83%

Nestled between the bridges of Madison County and baseball's field of dreams lies Grinnell, Iowa, a rural, "not exactly Manhattan" town that boasts rows of corn and a gas station that, although once called Always Open, has been renamed Almost Always Open. Don't let the town's obscure location and small size fool you, however; it's in this town that you can find Grinnell College, a liberal arts college that 1,300 Birkenstock-clad students call home. Despite its remote geography, these laid-back but dedicated Grinnellians flock to Grinnell because it offers challenging academics, eccentric opportunities, hard-core partying, and yeah . . . the six-week winter vacation.

A Recipe for Sleep Deprivation

This six-week vacation serves as a respite from the intense academic load that Grinnell's students endure. Students claim that Grinnell has "the second highest workload in the country." The 100 pages of reading that some classes demand per night has convinced one Grinnellian that "the workload is like the third level of hell." Despite the massive amount of work, students enjoy their academic experiences.

One defining mark of this academic experience is the freshman tutorial. All freshmen enroll in a tutorial where they can hone their writing skills. Past tutorials have surveyed topics like "Inside Star Trek" and "Music & Nature." With class sizes limited to 12 students, the tutorials provide freshmen with advice on how to improve their writing and analytical skills.

The class sizes don't increase after the freshman tutorial, however. While some classes like Intro to Psychology have 60-100 students, students report that most of their classes range between two and 25 students. They also promise that as topics narrow and levels advance, class sizes decrease.

In addition to small classes, students enjoy close contact with great faculty. One student proclaimed that her professor was a "goddess," yet the professors are approachable and considerate. "I had to drop one of my classes because I was having health problems. The professor was incredibly kind to me and said he hoped I'd be able to re-take the class next year." There are no TAs, but there are "mentors" who have taken the class before that help grade and tutor.

Students insist that no slacker major exists at Grinnell. All majors require dedicated work, but Bio/Chem and other science majors are especially challenging. The organic chemistry class is known for being extremely intense. Students claim that education concentrators and theatre majors put in some serious hours as well. Students can choose to take Exco classes, non-credit courses in which members of the Grinnell community or Grinnell students teach on random subjects. One student was delighted to have taken Yoing for Pleasure, a class that uncovered the secrets of yo-yos.

Where Have All the Grinnellians Gone?

Although one student announced, "We are the *royalty* of procrastination," students eventually have to hit the books and find a place to study. If you live in a single, the quiet of your room may be ideal. Burling Library offers a "really cozy" place to study. An added incentive to Burling is the opportunity to take a study break and contribute graffiti to the basement's bathroom walls. Students say that "not only does the administration not care about the graffiti, they actually encourage it."

For those who prefer background noise and a social atmosphere, the Forum Grill is a good place to whip out the books. The Forum Grill is located in one of the campus' two student centers: the Forum and the Harris Center. Students can go to the Forum to buy food ("you can get Ben and Jerry's nearly any time of day"), peruse the art gallery, play the grand piano, have a small meeting in the reserved rooms, or visit the Student Government offices. Harris provides students with a concert hall for parties and musicians, a TV lounge with couches, and a game room with pool and foosball tables.

Other notable areas on campus are the Robert Noyce Science Center, where students take science courses and have access to modern scientific equipment, and the Bucksbaum Center for the Arts, which offers excellent facilities for all types of artists. Students love the fact that "no two buildings really match." The Fine Arts building, for example, is shaped in a circular pattern "reminiscent of a nautilus shell" while the Goodnow building looks more like "a stone castle from the European Middle Ages." The architectural diversity is welcome since otherwise "you feel trapped in the middle of cornfields."

While off-campus housing is cheaper, most students opt to live on campus.

There's "no exposed plumbing, no dripping asbestos," but the suites are "not exactly hotel quality." Students can choose from Cleveland, "the smoking dorm;" Read, "the non-smokers' dorm;" Loose, the dorm with the coziest main lounge; Younker, "the party place;" and Norris, the air-conditioned building. The campus is divided into two areas: "jocks live on North campus" and "alternatives live on South campus." Between the two areas are the ever-popular Bob's Underground Café, an enclosed loggia, and a dining hall.

Students can join SCA (Society for Creative Anachronism), Free the Planet (an environmental group), Dagorhir (a blue-foam-sword fighting group), the Campus Monarchists (the group that proposed building a moat around North Campus . . . their project was denied funding), and the Vegan Coop.

The dining hall is "nothing to write home about," but students say that the food is getting better ever since Hungarian Noodlebake has been removed from the menu. Students also recommend avoiding the mozzarella sticks. Bob's Underground, the Pub, Pizza Hut, Pag's (an Italian eatery), Saint Rest's (a coffee house), and Café Phoeniz (the ritzy restaurant) are more popular places to dine.

When They're *Not* Studying

Despite the inordinate amount of reading and work required of the average Grinnell student, extracurriculars are popular and eccentric. Students can join SCA (Society for Creative Anachronism), Free the Planet (an environmental group), Dagorhir (a blue-foam-sword fighting group), the Campus Monarchists (the group that proposed building a moat around North Campus . . . their project was denied funding), and the Vegan Coop. Traditional extracurricular activities are available too: community service, the literary magazine, a comic magazine, a weekly paper, and the symphonic band, to name a few. The Grinnell Singers, an audition-only group, is also popular. All these groups tend to take the place of a Greek system, and students appreciate the absence of fraternities and sororities.

Grinnell students are generally stereotyped as "liberal, gay, pot-smoking activists." The liberal attitude, students say, is a stark contrast to the conservative mid-west town that surrounds the campus. Passionate liberalism makes for a charged political environment, and therefore the Campus Democrats is a popular club. Students attest to the fact that there are "no (out of the closet) Republicans."

Sports don't draw huge crowds. While the intramural football, Ultimate Frisbee, and rugby teams are relatively popular on campus, the varsity football team went undefeated last year and few people knew or celebrated it. Spectators at varsity events tend to be friends of the athletes.

After grueling weeks of activities and schoolwork, students relieve stress by partying hard on the weekends. Due to a lax alcohol and drug policy and the free beer at Harris parties, drinking is quite pervasive. It's not uncommon to spot a "Has anyone seen my bong" sign drifting around campus. Other activities are also available, thanks to the yearly activity fee required of each student. This fee funds free performances of groups like the Russian National Ballet and Second City. Other campus activities include house parties that are off-campus, Waltz (the semester formal), Disco (the yearly disco dance), the Drunken Titular Head Festival (an independent movie festival), Mary B. James (the annual cross-dressing party), Alice in Wonderland (a music festival with live bands), and the 10/10 progressive drinking party.

"Intense!" best describes this liberal college in Iowa. Whether it's the grueling academic life, the offbeat clubs, the creative organizations, the political aura that drapes over campus, or the big-time partying, Grinnell offers an educational experience of the utmost caliber. *—Marti Page*

FYI

If you come to Grinnell College, you'd better bring "an assortment of clothes for the numerous theme parties around campus throughout the year."

What is the typical weekend schedule? "Partying, beer-guzzling, and sleeping dominate the weekend."

If I could change one thing about Grinnell College, I would "put measures in place to reduce stress, pseudo-mindedness, and improve dining hall food."

Three things that every student should do before graduating from Grinnell are "contribute to the graffiti in Burling Library, explore the steam tunnels, and go to a Mary B. James cross-dressing dance."

Iowa State University

Address: 100 Alumni Hall; Ames, IA 50011
Phone: 800-262-3810
E-mail address: admissions@iastate.edu
Web site URL: www.iastate.edu
Founded: 1858
Private or Public: public
Religious affiliation: none
Location: urban
Undergraduate enrollment: 22,999
Total enrollment: NA
Percent Male/Female: 56%/44%
Percent Minority: 12%
Percent African-American: 3%
Percent Asian: 3%
Percent Hispanic: 2%
Percent Native-American: 0%
Percent in-state/out of state: 81%/19%
Percent Pub HS: 92%
Number of Applicants: 10,370
Percent Accepted: 89%
Percent Accepted who enroll: 56%
Entering: 4,219
Transfers: 1,537
Application Deadline: 1 Aug
Mean SAT: NA
Mean ACT: NA
Middle 50% SAT range: V 510-650, M 550-670
Middle 50% ACT range: 22-27
3 Most popular majors: business, engineering, agriculture
Retention: 84%
Graduation rate: 59%
On-campus housing: 35%
Fraternities: 13%
Sororities: 12%
Library: 2,348,646 volumes
Tuition and Fees: $5,028 in; $14,370 out
Room and Board: $5,740
Financial aid, first-year: 52%
Varsity or Club Athletes: 2%
Early Decision or Early Action Acceptance Rate: NA

Lancelot and Guinevere swim on placid Lake Laverne next to the Memorial Union. The royal swan pair are the pet darlings of Iowa State, second only to their official mascot, the Cyclone. Add the sculpture of Dutch artist Christian Petersen, Iowa State alum, to this idyllic scene and you've got Iowa State University's campus.

Upperclassmen say they can tell freshmen from returning students as they cross the campus because they're dressed up and raring to go. Upperclassmen who've been at Iowa State for a little while are all "running behind, still wearing their pajamas, and haven't combed their hair." This picture of Iowa State was pegged as "not extremely diverse." Another student put it more severely: "Since we're in the middle of Iowa, it tends to be mostly white people . . . that's what's in Iowa." Minority attendance is encouraged by a growing number of scholarships and cultural information sessions and parties, but students say the school has a difficult time retaining minority students because they're so outnumbered in the university's vast student population.

No Place Like Home

Students often start to find their niche at Iowa State by living in the dorms, and find they get a warm reception from their peers: "The doors are almost always open to everyone's rooms, and people just stop by and say hi." Resident advisors "go out of their way to make you feel part of the community." Another student added, "Up here it's pretty easy to make a small circle of friends. It's kind of hard to get lost in a crowd." The downside of the dorms is that they're none too new, though many dorm facilities are being renovated, and others are going up to replace the old buildings.

After living on campus for a year or two, most students move out of the university's old dorms. New university-owned apartments are hailed as "really really nice." There are also plenty of apartments available in surrounding Ames. While it may mean a longer walk to classes in the Iowa winter, most students choose some form of off-campus housing.

What's Doin' In Iowa

While some students complain that there's nothing to do in the corn state, they say "it's not *that* bad," even though you "have to be creative." The area surrounding Iowa State University is growing to meet college students' demand for fun. Welch Avenue, the street that separates one dorm from main campus, is lined with bars. When you're out not painting the town red, consider paintballing (a new paintballing facility is in the works), go-carting, or hanging out on the university's frisbee-golf course nearby.

Most students have cars so they can go anywhere in the city, though you won't need one on Iowa's centralized campus. The city's bus system offers another option for getting around. Wherever you are on the weekends, you can call the Moonlight Express (or, as some students have named it, "the drunk bus") to ensure a safe journey.

If you want to stay on campus for a low-key weekend, the Memorial Union has a hotel on its top floor, big halls for dances and performances, eating areas with a number of vendors, a bar, a library, and a university bookstore. On the lower level you can shoot pool or even go bowling. There's no shortage of possibilities, because "there are so many people" at Iowa State who "do so many different things." Beware of Memorial Union after dark, though. An entranceway in the building that commemorates World War II and Vietnam veterans is said to be haunted by some of the wars' nurses.

Beneath the Campanile

Iowa State's oldest and most-loved tradition is campaniling. On the Friday of homecoming, students gather under the big clock tower on campus, called the campanile. "When it strikes midnight you're supposed to kiss your significant other. That's called campaniling." Homecoming also means the height of Greek life, including a construction contest. Fraternity or sorority lawns sport such original creations as the set for PeeWee's playhouse or recreations of Cy, Iowa State's yellow-headed avion mascot.

"The joke here is [Iowa State]'s kind of the place engineers go to die."

The other big event of the year is VEISHA, an annual celebration during basketball season put together by a board of student volunteers. Events of the festival include a parade and Olympic-style competitions between teams of students. It's also a chance to reach out to the community. "They shut down a couple of the streets and they set up booths and stuff for kids and families to come," one VEISHA fan said.

VEISHA's initials represent the six original colleges at Iowa State, including veterinary medicine, engineering, industrial science, home economics, and agriculture. The original six have multiplied to include offerings such as business, education, design, and liberal arts and science. Students enter Iowa State in one of these colleges, sorted according to their major. Students who enter college undecided are automatically placed in the College of Liberal Arts and Sciences (LAS), and then they "take a bunch of classes that are designed to help you try and find what you like to do best." One student cited the difficulty of the engineering college as "really grueling, I think the 1st or 2nd in the nation" but offered business as a kinder, gentler alternative. "The joke here is it's kind of the place engineers go to die," he said. "If they fail out of engineering they go to business."

Some students complained about large class sizes that made individual attention hard to get. Class size varies depending on your college, but be reassured: students say they've gotten individual help from professors "just by going into their office and talking to them or asking questions." Really large classes have TA sections that break them down into more manageable groups. Students complain that both TAs "usually don't know what they're doing," or "know their area, but can't teach their area." The only classes you'll find you have to tolerate, TA or not, is English. Two English credits are required for students in all colleges to graduate.

Ice, Ice, Baby

For a school whose football and basketball teams "aren't too good this year," Iowa State offers a number of exciting intramural sports, which are recommended by students as "just too much fun" to pass up. Students pick their own teams and compete in sports such as broomball, an Iowa State tradition. "You take a ball to the ice rink where the hockey team plays," one senior explained, "and you just get a broom and you hit it to your goals." While billed as a low-contact sport, broomball can get pretty risky for those who don't slide around too well in tennis shoes. For those who are less athletically or icily inclined, Intramurals also offers competitions like chess and quiz bowl. Students can also compete against their professors once a year when their colleges are celebrated for a week. Business Week, for example, honors the business college, and students and teachers go up against each other in games and contests "just to get to know each other better" and have a good time.—*Stephanie Hagan*

FYI

If you come to Iowa State, you'd better bring "a beer bong."

What is the typical weekend schedule? "Friday night everybody gets dressed up, makes themselves look nice, then goes out and parties pretty much all night. Get up around noon on Saturday, sit around and watch football or study for the rest of the afternoon, and party all night. Get up at noon again on Sunday, and spend the day studying."

If I could change one thing about Iowa State, I'd "have the size of classes be smaller."

Three things every student at Iowa State should do before graduating are "go campaniling, go to VEISHA, and party—that's just gotta happen."

University of Iowa

Address: 107 Calvin Hall; Iowa City, IA 52242-1396
Phone: 800-553-4692
E-mail address: admissions@uiowa.edu
Web site URL: www.uiowa.edu
Founded: 1847
Private or Public: public
Religious affiliation: none
Location: urban
Undergraduate enrollment: 20,487
Total enrollment: NA
Percent Male/Female: 45%/55%
Percent Minority: 10%
Percent African-American: 2%
Percent Asian: 3%
Percent Hispanic: 2%
Percent Native-American: 0%
Percent in-state/out of state: 67%/33%
Percent Pub HS: 88%
Number of Applicants: 13,079
Percent Accepted: 84%
Percent Accepted who enroll: 38%
Entering: 4,184
Transfers: 1,236
Application Deadline: 1 Apr
Mean SAT: NA
Mean ACT: NA
Middle 50% SAT range: V 520-650, M 540-660
Middle 50% ACT range: 22-27
3 Most popular majors: business, social sciences, communications
Retention: 84%
Graduation rate: 61%
On-campus housing: 28%
Fraternities: 10%
Sororities: 13%
Library: 4,027,546 volumes
Tuition and Fees: $4,993 in; $15,285 out
Room and Board: $5,930
Financial aid, first-year: 46%
Varsity or Club Athletes: NA
Early Decision or Early Action Acceptance Rate: NA

Only one university in the Midwest can claim to have the nation's finest creative writing program. Besides this distinction, however, the University of Iowa also offers its students a picturesque campus, a thriving social scene, and the excitement of its Big Ten athletic teams. Through this atmosphere of academic stimulation and routine partying, most U of I students find themselves very satisfied with their college experience.

Hawkeye Academia

To many, the most distinctive features of the University of Iowa, both academically and culturally, are its world-renowned writing programs. The U of I was the first university in the United States to offer a graduate program in creative writing, and today the program continues to lead the field. Tennessee Williams and John Irving are just two of the well-known authors and graduates of the program, and notables such as Marvin Bell, Frank Conroy, Adam Haslett, and Marilynne Robinson are among the list of current teachers. The most prominent of the graduate programs are "The Writer's Workshop," "The International Writing Program," and "The Center for the Book," each sponsoring similar programs designed for undergraduates. In fact, quite a few undergraduates choose the U of I because of these opportunities to become a part of "the hub of the literary world."

The academic rigor at the University of Iowa is considered by most to be challenging but manageable. The general education requirements for graduation are described as "reasonable," and include a rhetoric or speaking/writing course (depending on AP placement), one semester's competency in a foreign language, and classes from the disciplines of interpretive literature, historic perspectives, humanities, the natural sciences, the social sciences, and quantitative or formal reasoning. Most undergraduates come in undeclared—called "open majors"—and there is no deadline by which one must choose a major. Students have 100 different areas of study to choose from, with the workload varying from major to major. Business is considered by some to be "the biggest blow off major ever," while premed and prenursing require much more focus. Not surprisingly, the English, creative writing, and music composition departments are considered excellent.

Classes at U of I are usually smaller than 50 students, and those in large lectures are put into 20-person discussion sessions with TAs. Sometimes, however, undergraduates find a lack of personal attention, as one student noticed when she was handed back an original composition that was graded but had no comments. On the whole, though, students at the U of I find that if they do their research on classes, they can find and pick ones that are pleasing to them in both rigor and instruction.

Not Just Bars

Moving beyond its writing programs, a lesser known jewel of the University of Iowa is its art museum, which houses a famous Jackson Pollock entitled *Mural*, as well as works by artists such as Léger, Matisse, Picasso, and Franz Marc. Noticing the museum's dirty carpets and handwritten captions, however, one student expressed the general conception that the art scene at U of I "has great potential, but hasn't yet found full support and funding."

> **"'Iowa's known for the wrestling and the writing.'"**

Support definitely does exist for U of I sports, though. As one freshman noted, "Iowa's known for the wrestling and the writing." Socially, football and men's basketball games provide many opportunities for one of the favorite activities of U of I students: tailgating. During football season tailgating "becomes a really big thing—people start drinking at eight in the morning and by three they're slammed." Drinking, parties, random hookups, and sports typically dominate the social scene, and Iowa City's many bars (such as The Union Bar, Gabe's Oasis, and The Green Room) are big party spots that advertise "You Call it $1.00's." The administration is aware of the heavy drinking scene and has tried to curb it, demanding strict action by the university police officers. In spite of this, to some students it seems like "security attempts to follow the rules of the administration, but it's really one big joke."

Most U of I students agree that there is a good number of socializing options for those who are non-drinkers. People often frequent coffeehouses (there are almost as many coffeehouses as bars), go to movies, and attend musical concerts. On a regular basis the university hosts speakers, and in the "Saturday Scholars" speaker series students can hear lectures on a wide variety of disciplines and issues. In addition, traditional events such the Homecoming Parade and the Dance Gala always draw a big crowd.

A Hill Amidst the Corn

There are actually no corn fields on the U of I campus, but according to one student, "to get anywhere you need to go up and down a hill." The center of campus is the Pentacrest, where the old Iowa State Capital is located. The campus itself is separated into east and west, the west being newer and closer to the medical school and hospital (which is the third largest teaching hospital in the nation). A variety of architectural styles are represented in the U of I buildings, and in between them all, right through the heart of campus, runs a river. Downtown Iowa City is very much an extension of the campus, as the bars, coffee shops, restaurants, and other businesses there all cater to the students. Outside of those venues, however, some students say that there is "not a lot going on."

Got to Eat and Sleep

There are two dining halls at U of I: one on the west side of campus in the Hillcrest dorm, and the other on the east side in a dorm called Burge. The widespread opinion is that Hillcrest has a much better cafeteria, but it's a 15-minute walk for those who live on the east side of campus. The food is generally described as "O.K.," but on weekdays a service called "Grab 'N' Go," which allows students to make to-go lunches, is very popular.

Students often eat with the people they live with, and through the university's housing system, people with similar interests can live together. There are several "learning communities" (Honors, International Crossroads, Performing Arts, and Women and Engineering) in which students can opt to be placed. Those who don't choose learning communities select a specific dormitory, each of which has its own character. Hillcrest is considered the jock dorm, while Burge, the "party dorm," is rumored jokingly to have "the highest STD rate of any dorm in the country."

Though most juniors and a fair percentage of the student body choose to live in off-campus apartments, the dorms are very clean and nicely sized. The RAs pay attention to what's going on, but are more "like friends." The dorm is, according to one composition major, a place where "a lot of crazy things go on, and I think it's all very interesting."

From Illinois to Greeks

Interestingly enough, the University of Iowa draws people mainly from two places: "Everyone you ask is either from a small town in Iowa or suburban Chicago—it really is like 'The University of Illinois at Iowa.'" Though racial diversity is lacking, there is a supportive atmosphere that accepts interracial dating and various sexual orientations. In the end, though, most students—no matter what their socioeconomic levels, interests, or orientations—merge into a unified student body that often wears jeans and University of Iowa sweatshirts.

The varying interests of U of I students is exemplified in their many extracurricular activities. There are over 360 student-run organizations, including ones that focus on equal justice, fine arts, engineering, community service, and even free bikes (the "Free Ride Bike Association" began in 2002). Over 20 of the extracurricular organizations are fraternities and sororities; about 13 percent of the campus is involved in Greek life. The rush season is described as intense, with the first day being "hell" and the last "the most awesome night." Fraternities and sororities engage in many social activities amongst themselves, but the university's social scene is not seen as being dominated by them.

A scene that does draw all U of I students is the Big Ten sports scene. Whether tailgating, playing intramurals, or watching the wrestling team bring home another title, students share their enthusiasm for a school that is the happy home to many. *—Elizabeth Dohrmann*

FYI

If you come to the University of Iowa, you'd better bring a "fleece pullover."

What is the typical weekend schedule? "Go to a bar, get drunk, take someone back to your room, get laid, sleep late, eat, get dressed, go to a bar, get drunk, take someone back to your room . . ."

What one thing would you change about the U of I? "Make the food on our [east] side of the river better."

Three things every student at the U of I should do before graduating are "Go to a poetry reading, lose your virginity, and go to the Dance Gala."

Kansas

Kansas State University

Address: Anderson Hall; Manhattan, KS 66506
Phone: 785-532-6250
E-mail address: kstate@ksu.edu
Web site URL: www.ksu.edu
Founded: 1863
Private or Public: public
Religious affiliation: none
Location: suburban
Undergraduate enrollment: 19,048
Total enrollment: NA
Percent Male/Female: 52%/48%
Percent Minority: 8%
Percent African-American: 3%
Percent Asian: 1%
Percent Hispanic: 2%
Percent Native-American: 1%
Percent in-state/out of state: 90%/10%
Percent Pub HS: 90%
Number of Applicants: 8,212
Percent Accepted: 58%
Percent Accepted who enroll: 74%
Entering: 3,537
Transfers: 1,585
Application Deadline: rolling
Mean SAT: NA
Mean ACT: NA
Middle 50% SAT range: NA
Middle 50% ACT range: 19-25
3 Most popular majors: business, agriculture, engineering
Retention: 78%
Graduation rate: 49%
On-campus housing: 30%
Fraternities: 20%
Sororities: 20%
Library: 1,573,645 volumes
Tuition and Fees: $3,444 in; $10,704 out
Room and Board: $4,500
Financial aid, first-year: 60%
Varsity or Club Athletes: 3%
Early Decision or Early Action Acceptance Rate: NA

Known to its fans as the "Happy Purple Place," K-State overflows with school spirit. Proud of their diverse student body and their beautiful campus, K-State students are often found sporting their purple gear not just to football games, but also on a daily basis. In spite of the relatively large student body of approximately 20,000, Kansas State students generally agree that their school is "warm, welcoming and truly its own community." K-Staters report that their classmates generally have a "happy-go-lucky" attitude and a "polite and social" demeanor. "People who I've never met before open doors for me," recounted one student. Others echo this belief by saying that school spirit and friendliness are the two attributes that most clearly define Kansas State University.

Grounds of Grandeur

K-State's centralized campus, set amidst the Flint Hills of northeastern Kansas, exemplifies the typical all-American college. The extensive horticultural program—which provides for a large variety of gardens and shrubbery spread over the campus—combined with limestone buildings covered with ivy, creates a visually striking and welcoming campus. The town, Manhattan, Kansas, is small and welcoming and thrives on the vitality and business students bring. When students leave for summer vacation, many of the pizza places and other college-oriented businesses shut down. The town actively supports the school and residents proudly display K-State's colors and symbols. In fact, the town firetrucks are emblazoned with three-foot-tall Powercats in honor of the school mascot, Willy the Wildcat. The school also interacts with the community through the philanthropy of the fraternities and sororities, which put in as many as 2,500 hours of community service per semester. Nevertheless, due to the town's small size, many students feel compelled to get away and drive the two hours to Kansas City or 45 minutes to Lawrence.

Dorm Life

While a large portion of K-State upperclassmen prefer to live in apartments off campus (only a couple hundred live "on" for their junior and senior years), few students complain about the dorms. The dorm area is divided into three smaller campuses, each made up of single-sex and co-ed dorms. Dorm rooms are of average size, "bordering on small," with lots of natural light. Each room has at least one wall made up of windows lined from wall to wall, giving dorm rooms an open and pleasant feel.

Although pleased with their living accommodations, students were less enthusiastic about campus food. Students can choose between plans for 10, 15 or 20 meals per week. To get away from the dining hall routine, many frequent the eateries located in the student union, which include fast-food options among several coffee shops. Students cite Pat's Blue Ribbon Café and Habachi Head as the most popular off-campus restaurants.

Kats in Class

K-State professors receive rave reviews for being "open, friendly and approachable." One student claimed, "It's funny because you run into your professors when you're out bar hopping and they talk to you like you're their friend." Students note the general high caliber of professors, but are quick to point out that math and science professors are not as good, specifically because many of them are foreign and "the language barrier in itself makes it difficult to learn from and understand them." Teaching assistants (TAs), while common in the sciences, serve primarily as lab facilitators. Class sizes vary by college, but the average lecture consists of anywhere from 150 to 500 students, while discussion classes enroll from 20 to 40. Classes known for easy grading are Natural Disasters, Introduction to Applied Architecture, and, surprisingly, Nuclear Engineering.

Running on a semester system, K-State has a set of standard academic requirements that includes classes in English composition, psychology and sociology, college algebra, history, economics, and human development. Kansas State freshmen therefore arrive to find their first semester schedule largely predetermined by these mandatory core classes. Moreover, because the registration process is based on seniority, upperclassmen report few problems getting into the classes they want, while sophomores and freshmen have a much harder time doing so. When seeking advice about scheduling, many find the advising system to be cumbersome and unhelpful, believing that the advisors are uninformative and inflexible. Some even choose to circumvent the advising system, noting that "it's easier to guide yourself."

The Miller, the Baker, the Architect Major

Academic programs are divided into nine colleges to which you apply during the second semester of sophomore year. However, the decision is flexible. One senior noted that "60 percent of KSU students switch their major three times. I'm the only one I know who kept one for all five years." K-State was originally an agricultural college, and while some students complain that the school retains an unfair image as being filled with "farmers, hicks, and country music," others are proud of the distinction that the agricultural programs have brought to the university. While the College of Agriculture is just one of the nine, it provides some of the most distinctive majors that K-State offers. Among these are Baking (K-State is the only university in the nation to offer this major) and Milling (officially known as Grain Science and Industry). Leadership Studies, another unique and popular program, deals with the theory and practical application of leadership abilities and skills. A large proportion of students attend KSU for four-and-a-half to five years in order to complete all of their requirements.

Students cite Tuttle Creek, the large lake used by the crew team, as a favorite spot to hit the books or spend a lazy Sunday afternoon. The campus libraries close at eleven, so late-night studiers crowd coffee shops in Manhattan, as well as the Village Inn, the only 24-hour restaurant in Manhattan known for its comfy booths for the sleep-deprived. Recently the student union added the "Cat's Paw" lounge, complete with large comfy sofas, reading lamps, and tables, as another "homey atmosphere ideal for a relaxed working environment."

"Gimme a K!"

K-Staters can choose from a wide range of extracurriculars in athletics, academics, and social activities. *The Collegian*, the school newspaper, and the marching band are cited as among the most popular activities. Societies based on interests and majors also abound, especially with the milling and baking majors—who use the club time for practice as well as education. K-State also offers a diverse club sports program complete with a rock climbing team, a power lifting team, a trap shooting team, and even a ski team, though Kansas rarely sees snow.

> **"You can't help but note the friendliness of the students and their southern hospitality."**

Among athletes and non-athletes alike, sports at all levels contribute heavily to the KSU community. "Everyone attends football games," said one fan. "In fact, for a game that kicks off at 11:30, many are out there in their purple gear tailgating starting at 6 A.M." At games, Willy the Wildcat spells KSU with his body while fans scream out the school letters. Non-varsity members have many opportunities to play sports as well. Students praise the well-equipped gym and a large number take part in intramural sports. Students can choose from a wide variety of sports, the most popular being flag football in the fall, volleyball in winter, and basketball in spring. Teams are made up either of dorm groups, fraternity brothers, or sorority sisters.

After Hours

Kansas State University is officially a dry campus, but most students agree that alcohol is prevalent and easy to come by. The social life for most students revolves around Aggieville, an off-campus strip that houses nearly 40 bars in a two-block radius. Aggieville is famed for having the highest concentration of bars per square meter of any area in the world. Students can choose to go to pubs, dance clubs, or themed bars such as Gilligan's or western line-dancing clubs. Underclassmen tend to congregate at the dance bars, which are deemed easier to get into without a real ID (or any ID at all).

Outside of Aggieville, nightlife revolves around the off-campus fraternities. On campus, however, events and parties are few and far between. Most students could not name any campus-wide events or parties other than homecoming that were not Greek-sponsored. One sophomore commented, "if you stay on campus for the night, there might be some people hanging out in small groups, but nothing bigger than 20 people." However students do not mind the lack of nightlife on the campus itself, because as one senior quoted, "there are always frat parties and there will always be Aggieville."

It's All Greek to Me

The Greek system is very strong at K-State (20 to 25 percent of the student body are Greek members), but students agree that participation is far from essential. Interestingly, however, Greeks tend to dominate many areas of campus life. Eighty percent of the student council is made up of Greek members, and similar figures exist for other campus-wide political, social, and service-related groups. While undergrads tend to move in either Greek or non-Greek circles, there exists almost no hostility between the groups. Said one sophomore fraternity member, "a lot of stereotypes fly between the groups, but there is no anger, just no mixing." First-year sorority members live in dorms, while males can live in their fraternity houses all four years. The sorority houses, of which there are 11, are all dry and monitored by a "housemom" to make sure that consumption of alcohol and fraternizing with males does not occur on the house grounds. The administration is beginning to crack down on parties sponsored by the 24 fraternity houses, which has resulted in an increase in dry houses.

Annual Greek theme parties include: the Rumble Stumble, a weeklong party cosponsored by two fraternities which ends with a final football game and drink off; Patty Murphy (named after a fraternity member who allegedly drank himself to death during prohibition), which features tombstones and hot tubs as decorations; and the Mud Bowl, a beach volleyball tournament to raise money for Alzheimer's research. The largest event of the year, however, is Homecoming. Planning begins in the spring for the following year's game. Fraternities and sororities are randomly paired up to compete in float building, body pyramid building, and chanting contests.

Defining the Wildcats

At a school where 75 to 80 percent of the students are from the same state, diversity may be hard to come by. Ethnic diversity on campus has improved over recent years, but it still lags behind most other universities. In general, however, students seem unconcerned, saying that the school is remarkably diverse for its location. One senior explained, "many of the kids here haven't ever experienced life or even scenery out of Kansas, but they continue to remain open-minded to new ideas and change of perspective."

There is no typical KSU student, just "a lot of athletes, a lot of Greeks, a lot of engineers, and a lot of farmer-types." One sophomore said, "If I had to describe this place in three words, they'd be 'open', 'accepting,' and 'accommodating.' You can't help but note the friendliness of the students and their southern hospitality." Although the undergraduate population is very large, students agree that the student body is close knit. One student remarked that when walking to class on an average day, he sees at least 50 students he knows. This is just another indication of what makes students proud to be at KSU. —*Amanda Stauffer*

FYI

When coming to KSU, be sure to bring "all-weather gear since it changes every five minutes and cowboy boots."

A typical weekend consists of "tailgating all day Saturday, watching the game, and hanging out in Aggieville."

If I could change one thing about KSU, "it would be that so many frats are going dry. Soon there won't be any place to party outside of Aggieville."

Three things that every student should do before graduating from K-State are "spend a day at Tuttle Creek, tailgate all morning, and do the pub crawl through Aggieville."

University of Kansas

Address: 1502 Iowa Street; Lawrence, KS 66045-7576
Phone: 785-864-3911
E-mail address: adm@ku.edu
Web site URL: www.ku.edu
Founded: 1866
Private or Public: public
Religious affiliation: none
Location: suburban
Undergraduate enrollment: 20,605
Total enrollment: NA
Percent Male/Female: 48%/52%
Percent Minority: 14%
Percent African-American: 3%
Percent Asian: 4%
Percent Hispanic: 3%
Percent Native-American: 1%
Percent in-state/out of state: 76%/24%
Percent Pub HS: NA
Number of Applicants: 9,573
Percent Accepted: 67%
Percent Accepted who enroll: 63%
Entering: 4,074
Transfers: 1,462
Application Deadline: 1 Apr
Mean SAT: NA
Mean ACT: NA
Middle 50% SAT range: NA
Middle 50% ACT range: 21-27
3 Most popular majors: business, journalism, engineering
Retention: 79%
Graduation rate: 52%
On-campus housing: 22%
Fraternities: 14%
Sororities: 20%
Library: 4,623,079 volumes
Tuition and Fees: $4,101 in; $11,577 out
Room and Board: $4,822
Financial aid, first-year: 35%
Varsity or Club Athletes: 3%
Early Decision or Early Action Acceptance Rate: NA

Located atop Mount Oread in Lawrence, Kansas, "KU" boasts gorgeous hillside scenery and a warm, friendly student body. There is something for everyone here with the large student body and the sheer range of activities it fosters.

Plenty of Choices

Everyone enrolled in the School of Liberal Arts at the University of Kansas is required to meet a core group of requirements, which includes classes in the history of Western and modern civilizations. The Western civilization classes include the study of classical thinkers like Plato and Aristotle, and the modern civilization classes focus on more recent developments and current events. While students were generally enthusiastic and deemed the course content as interesting, one student complained about the "immense amount of reading that was really demanding" and argued that "it should be pared down." Within the different programs of study, the core requirements vary greatly, and, while most students found them "helpful," one junior commented that "it would be better if the core requirements were more major-specific."

The Honors College offers a select group of students small seminar classes known for their better student-to-faculty ratio and excellent instruction. Students not in the honors program, however, found nothing to complain about, even if they are unable to get into the smaller classes. One sophomore raved that even the largest classes at KU were "still awesome" because of the first-rate teaching staff. Students were especially enthusiastic about the broad scope of classes and agreed that, while getting into classes was not a problem, "unless you're in the honors program, it can be hard for freshmen and sophomores to get into certain science classes." The same student noted "the professors are great and really know their stuff," and that one of his favorite classes at KU was, in fact, a large lecture class. Most students found the workload sufficiently demanding without being overwhelming, though one student noted that the architectural engineering program was particularly rigorous. In particular, Dennis Dailey's class on human sexuality was described as "notoriously controversial" and always attracts large numbers of curious students.

Mt. Oread or Mt. Olympus?

The Greek scene is large and active at University of Kansas, and parties are never in short supply. Most of the Greek parties are open to the entire student body, though there certain formal events hosted and attended only by Greeks. One student commented that "While the Greek system is fairly popular, it's not 'the thing,' so there's not much pressure to join." With the generally friendly atmosphere, students report that "it is pretty easy to make friends," saying that "you can just talk to people in classes and they will warm up to you." Students also maintain that most of their friends come from their dorms or halls. Furthermore, "there are not very many cliques" and no particular groups dominate student life. In terms of dating, students say that people tend to couple up, with one student noting that the majority of people have significant others. One single (and hopeful) student commented, "Even though there are lots of couples around, if you're single you can still find somebody to hook up with." And chances are the hook up will be a good one, according to one student who praised the "good selection" and "fair number of attractive people" at the university. Students described the number of homosexual couples and interracial couples as few, but did acknowledge their presence on campus.

> **"The professors are great and really know their stuff."**

Cute and Preppy

Most students agreed that there was no dominant student stereotype at KU. In the words of one student, "There are 27,000 kids, and it makes me happy that there's every type of student here." However, one student noted the lack of geographic and socio-economic diversity, stating that "there are a lot of affluent kids who come from Johnson County and drive SUVs." Another student said that the campus is "mainly Caucasian and there's a lack of diversity that way, but [it] has improved recently." Students report a good mix of preppy and casual clothing on campus, and were happy to note that fashion at KU is "pretty much up to you—you don't have to dress up for class if you don't want to." One student observed that the dressing style often develops as the day progresses, noting that "at 7 A.M. most people look like they've just rolled out of bed and are wearing jeans and pullovers, but by noon people start looking cute and preppy."

On or Off?

Students generally were satisfied and found dorms at KU ranging from "comfortable-sized" to "very nice." One student raved about the "great" facilities in the three newly renovated dorms, but described the older dorms as "basically just a 12' by 12' cubicle which two people share, unless you request a single, in which case you get the 12' by 12' cubicle to yourself." There are single-sex dorms on campus, though most of the housing is co-ed. However, it is important to note that at KU mainly freshmen and sophomores stay in the dorms, with most juniors and seniors opting to live off campus in apartments or houses for lease. Options for off-campus housing are plentiful with cheap rents and close proximity to campus, making it an attractive prospect for upperclassmen looking to escape the cubicles and save some money. Dining-hall food is generally praised by students for its good quality; they report that there is a decent range of options, including salad bars, dessert bars, and grill food. One student said that the food was relatively reliable because "the pizzas and hamburgers are pretty decent" and agreed that "you can always find something to eat." Another student, however, complained that while food quality was satisfactory, "it can be repetitive when they keep hashing the same thing." Students were happy to report that menus are posted on the Internet, making it easy to check the day's selections before setting foot in a dining hall. Most upperclassmen eat off campus, and for those students and hungry underclassmen as well, Kansas City is a popular destination "if you want to get really good food."

Picture Perfect

Students raved about the "gorgeous" campus, with its picturesque landscaping full of "trees, flowers and hilly contours." The presence of "big red roofs, beautiful stone architecture, old buildings, and bustling people" completes the idyllic scene and one student happily noted "it feels like you're in a huge park." The scenery comes at a price, though, and one student felt that the hilly landscape was a problem because it makes you develop "huge calves from walking up the hill." Due to the somewhat exhausting terrain, students generally take the bus to campus and are very happy with the efficiency of the transportation system. A female student mentioned that although "security on campus has improved recently with better lighting," she still does not feel comfortable walking alone at night and argued that improvements still were needed.

Jayhawk Rock

KU students are extremely active, as seen through the popularity of varsity sports and the prevalence of extracurricular activities. Students take great pride in their athletics. The school's basketball team is particularly strong, and basketball games are described as "always very packed—sometimes so packed that you can't get in." But while old-time favorites such as basketball and football pack the bleachers, intramural sports, community service, the law society, and the medical society were also noted as being popular. Students are happy to note that the intramurals are now free, whereas in the past a small fee was charged in order to participate. At KU, new groups and activities are formed every day; as one student commented, "This semester there are at least four or five new clubs that I've personally seen start up."

Given the strong school spirit, the active social life, and vibrant extracurriculars, the University of Kansas is definitely an exciting place to be. Add to that the gorgeous campus, strong academics and warm and friendly people, and this school is guaranteed to provide an enjoyable college experience. —*Wenshan Yeo*

FYI

If you come to the University of Kansas, you'd better bring "an open mind, because you'll meet all kinds of people here."

What is the typical weekend schedule? "Party on Friday and Saturday nights; procrastinate and do homework on Sunday."

If I could change one thing about the University of Kansas, I would "make it less hilly."

Three things every student at the University of Kansas should do before graduating are "go to a basketball game, walk through the Campanile when graduating, and enjoy a leisurely walk around the gorgeous campus."

Kentucky

Centre College

Address: 600 West Walnut Street; Danville, KY 40422
Phone: 859-238-5350
E-mail address: admission@centre.edu
Web site URL: www.centre.edu
Founded: 1819
Private or Public: private
Religious affiliation: Presbyterian
Location: rural
Undergraduate enrollment: 1,055
Total enrollment: NA
Percent Male/Female: 46%/54%
Percent Minority: 5%
Percent African-American: 2%
Percent Asian: 2%
Percent Hispanic: 0%
Percent Native-American: 0%
Percent in-state/out of state: 71%/29%
Percent Pub HS: 79%
Number of Applicants: 1,345
Percent Accepted: 78%
Percent Accepted who enroll: 28%
Entering: 298
Transfers: 8
Application Deadline: 1 Feb
Mean SAT: NA
Mean ACT: NA
Middle 50% SAT range: V 550-650, M 560-650
Middle 50% ACT range: 25-30
3 Most popular majors: English, economics, biology
Retention: 87%
Graduation rate: 76%
On-campus housing: 94%
Fraternities: 55%
Sororities: 59%
Library: 166,288 volumes
Tuition and Fees: $20,400
Room and Board: $6,900
Financial aid, first-year: 71%
Varsity or Club Athletes: 29%
Early Decision or Early Action Acceptance Rate: ED 84%: EA 90%

Rock concerts for credit. Study in England or France. No class on Wednesdays. Centre is not just your typical small-town school.

Campus Tour

Welcome to Centre College, a small yet academically challenging school located in Danville, Kentucky. As you enter the Centre campus, you will find on your left Greek Park, the biggest collection of Centre's many fraternities and sororities. Greek life is central to the Centre social scene. On your right you can find the Norton Center for the Arts, which houses a great performing arts program. Up ahead there is a collection of freshman dorms. Almost everyone lives on campus at Centre, but freshmen live in single-sex dorms with men and women on opposite sides of the campus. There are no visitation hours until after the winter homecoming freshman year, after which guests are restricted until midnight on weekdays and 2 A.M. on the weekends. Don't worry though; students agree that these visitation rules are "easy to break" and "never enforced."

According to student accounts this campus "is beautiful and small," with most everything within easy walking distance. Students here agree that they spend most of their time on campus. One of students' biggest complaints is the city of Danville. Danville is notorious for its lack of bars and good restaurants—with only fast food to feed a hungry student. There are not many friendships between Centre students and Danville "townies," and one student went so far to complain that she was "tired of being leered at by rednecks in pick-up trucks and workers who hang around Wal-mart."

Saturday Night Fever

Danville may not be loved, but students still get off campus, especially when the weekend arrives. Many students go out to dinner or go shopping with friends in the nearby city of Lexington, which helps make up for the dullness of Danville. Since Boyle County is dry, students have to drive at least a half an hour away to pick up alcohol for the weekend. However, most students find that this does not bother them and gives them a welcome chance to get off campus. In fact, one student loved that in Danville, "there aren't any bars, so on-campus parties are bigger."

Once you are ready to party, you will almost definitely want to head to the fraternity houses. One student said, "I can't imagine a school more dominated by Greek organizations." Most students welcome the Greek system, which sponsors most campus events, as an easy way to meet people and make friends. With about two-thirds of students in a fraternity or sorority, many students attend chapter meetings on Sundays and happily participate in the wide array of Greek rivalries and traditions. Centre has a "liberal drinking policy," which provides for a variety of theme parties each week (such as Dekes of Hazard and the Catholic School Girl party) that spice up the social scene.

To add to the social scene, Centre has a few crazy and popular traditions. The most famous adventure is to "Run the Flame." Tradition holds that "before you graduate, you must strip down to your birthday suit and run around "The Flame" (a flame-shaped statue in the middle of campus) and back to your clothes before getting caught with a $100 fine." Most fraternities and sororities have their own traditions and rivalries. One fraternity brings the portrait of "Dead Fred" (Frederick Vinson, a Supreme Court Chief Justice and Centre graduate) to every sporting event. Nearing its 200th birthday, Centre has accumulated its share of tradition.

First Day of Classes

There is a strong consensus that Centre is academically very challenging. Students rated the classes from "very hard" to "tough and demanding" to "harder than what everyone said." The hard work that students put in doesn't come without its rewards. Centre's size allows for small classes—none with more than 30 to 35 students. The "accessible" and "really amazing" professors at Centre have a high proportion of Ph.D.s, but are also known for the personal attention that they give to students. There is a general sentiment that the classes at Centre are hard, but the "many new outlooks on life" that students receive makes the schoolwork worthwhile.

In order to help students stay committed to this liberal arts education, Center has a unique Convocation program. From a wide variety of options, students are required to attend 12 art performances (ranging from renowned lecturers to Broadway shows). Students feel that this was a welcome opportunity to broaden their horizons, and one pondered, "I sometimes wonder where else you can get credits for going to see Art Garfunkel." Centre also has a fairly dense General Ed requirement, for which students must complete 115 course hours in areas outside their major. These include a variety of subjects—from philosophy to economics—and one student warned against the challenge of the religion courses.

Small School: Cozy or Nosey?

With an undergraduate population of a little over a thousand students, Centre encapsulates most of the typical benefits and grievances of a small school. Students agree that the biggest benefit of a small school is "the great friendships you make." The large number of on-campus activities amounts to a strong student community at Centre. The small class sizes, short walking distances, and low levels of peer pressure lead students to love Centre's cozy feel. However, this compact feeling also leads to one of students' biggest complaints—the lack of privacy. One student said that it seemed like "everyone knows everything about you and what you have done" and that "the gossip spreads to easily."

"Before you graduate, you must strip down to your birthday suit and run around 'The Flame' and back to your clothes before getting caught with a $100 fine."

Another dynamic familiar to many college campuses is the dating scene. Relationships are divided between the "typical random hook-up or long-term-boyfriend dating scene." One student claimed that there is a "constant complaint" that "casual dating is virtually unheard of." Students learn to adapt their lives around these small-school hazards and enjoy the wide variety of activities that Centre offers.

Getting Involved

To make up for the problems of being a small school, Centre offers both the opportunity for close friendships and afterschool activities that are open to students. Most students are involved in sports, whether through varsity sports or the popular intramural program. Although some sports draw low fan levels, the Centre Colonel fans get "rowdy" at the football and basketball games. Centre's soccer team is also known for being both talented and having "cute guys."

Many students agreed that Centre does not have a particularly active political atmosphere, although it does have the largest chapters of both Democrats and Republicans in the state. Most students are considered mildly conservative, and political activism seems to take the form of private debate or assisting larger campaigns in nearby Lexington.

Bye-Bye Danville, Hello World

One of Centre's strongest and mostly widely praised attributes is its study abroad program. Almost 60 percent of students study abroad. Every fall and spring trimester, Centre sends 20 students to Regent's College in London and 20 others to study in Strasbourg, France. Many biology majors go to South America during the winter term to see plant and animal life firsthand. Students unanimously praise this program and recommend that all students who attend Centre take advantage of this opportunity. Centre bends over backwards to help students explore the world. One student loved the lack of a financial burden to study abroad—"Centre foots the bill, we pay the plane ticket."

While providing all of the advantages and disadvantages of a small school, Centre's unique study abroad program and strong liberal arts education make it stand out. But what students learn most during their time at Centre is how to develop strong friendships and grow as an individual within a warm community. —*Adam Rein*

FYI

If you come to Centre College, you'd better bring "a car!"

What is the typical weekend schedule? "Usually we go out to dinner or go shopping with friends in Lexington. Also key to the weekend is the purchasing of alcohol (a 30-minute drive outside the county lines). As for the evenings, all roads lead to Greek Park for the frats."

If I could change one thing about Centre College, I'd "lessen the presence of cliques within the student body."

Three things every student at Centre should do before graduating are "run the Flame" (a tradition that entails running around campus naked starting at a flame-shaped statue), swim in the Norton fountain, and dance on the DKE pool table."

University of Kentucky

Address: 106 Gillis Building; Lexington, KY 40506-0033
Phone: 859-257-2000
E-mail address: admissio@uky.edu
Web site URL: www.uky.edu
Founded: 1865
Private or Public: public
Religious affiliation: none
Location: urban
Undergraduate enrollment: 17,830
Total enrollment: NA
Percent Male/Female: 48%/52%
Percent Minority: 9%
Percent African-American: 5%
Percent Asian: 2%
Percent Hispanic: 1%
Percent Native-American: 0%
Percent in-state/out of state: 86%/14%
Percent Pub HS: NA
Number of Applicants: 8,879
Percent Accepted: 82%
Percent Accepted who enroll: 51%
Entering: 3,718
Transfers: 1,339
Application Deadline: 15 Feb
Mean SAT: NA
Mean ACT: NA
Middle 50% SAT range: V 500-620, M 510-630
Middle 50% ACT range: 21-26
3 Most popular majors: marketing, finance, accounting
Retention: 79%
Graduation rate: 50%
On-campus housing: 25%
Fraternities: 18%
Sororities: 22%
Library: 2,989,443 volumes
Tuition and Fees: $4,547 in; $11,227 out
Room and Board: $4,285
Financial aid, first-year: 38%
Varsity or Club Athletes: 3%
Early Decision or Early Action Acceptance Rate: NA

If Wildcat basketball comes to mind when you think of the University of Kentucky, you're on the right track. The thousands of students that call this campus home all come together in support of their famed team. But the excitement doesn't end there; many students at UK find themselves satisfied with the academics, busy with all the opportunities, and ecstatic with school spirit.

Kentucky Academia

When students apply to UK, they apply to one of the university's 16 colleges, which include Agriculture, Engineering, Architecture, Arts and Sciences, Business and Economics, Communications, and five Medical colleges. No matter which college students attend, however, all must complete a core curriculum, called the "General Studies Program." Before graduation, students take courses in speaking, cross-cultural studies, humanities, and the social sciences. Additional math, English, and science class requirements depend on the individual college.

On the whole, students find that they "aren't that inspired" by core classes, as the classes are easy to let slide. But once students latch onto the department of their major, the academics are described as "pretty good." The science-oriented classes are cited as the most difficult, along with classes in the College of Architecture, where students can be working on projects "from 2 A.M. to 2 P.M., four days a week." Pharmacy and nursing are very popular areas of study, and the campus is "surrounded by hospitals, which makes for a lot of opportunities."

People choose to study many different things at UK, but most agree that "though lots come to party, those who do work find UK equally good in the humanities and the sciences." Many students receive scholarships or financial aid from the university. A good number of students also apply for the Honors Program. Once accepted into the program, students take one Honors course each semester, with the course usually focused on the humanities. All undergrads at UK have an advisor from their college and an advisor in their major, and Honors students have an additional advisor from the program.

For all students, registering for classes can be an ordeal. Though Honors students get to register first, almost everyone finds that it can be hard to get into classes. Introductory classes are often very large; one freshman commented that UK "accepts every AP credit (with a score 3 or above) to get people out of 100-level classes . . . you're lucky if you get a chair." Labs and sections for these huge classes are taught by TAs—many of whom don't speak English well. One biology major related a story of her first day in a calculus class. While students were filing into the classroom, one girl announced that the class wasn't on calculus, but a foreign language. A few minutes later, the teacher, who had a heavy Chinese accent, came out to tell the students that it really was their calculus class after all.

Despite some language barriers, many students say that they are very happy with the teachers they have had. Most adopt the ritual of asking around to find out who the best professors for each class are, and are usually not disappointed. One freshman claimed, "I've been really pleased with the faculty. They have a strong background and are interested in getting the students to do their best." Many professors encourage students to come to their office hours, and this personal attention—especially noticed in the smaller-sized Agricultural College—makes UK students feel "less like a number."

Bring Out the Bourbon

Outside of academics, most Wildcats lead a very active social life. The most dominating social force is the Greek system, which provides the central scene for partying at UK. More drinking seems to go on at UK than hard drugs; after all, "Kentucky grows tobacco and makes Bourbon." Students frequent drive-thru liquor stores, and upperclassmen often go to clubs or bars.

Students say that "there're definitely the sorority girl and fraternity boy stereotypes" at UK. Most of the undergrads are white and middle-class, and many of the girls frequent tanning beds. A freshman noted that "there's not as much diversity as I expected," especially in reference to blacks and homosexuals.

However, though "it can feel a little cliquey," those who aren't into the Greek scene find other ways to enjoy themselves. Sometimes "a lot of people who don't drink go home on the weekends," but often friends watch movies and go to coffeehouses, such as Starbuck's, Common Grounds, and Coffee Time. In addition, the university often puts on-campus events such as concerts, street parties, and pep rallies. The popular pep rallies are also sponsored by the student government, which puts on a Halloween party every year, as well.

> **"Though lots come to party, those who do work find UK equally good in the humanities and the sciences."**

On the dating front, people tend to lean towards hook-ups, but dating and steady relationships also exist. There are not many interracial or gay couples; one student said that she "doesn't see much of it" and "doesn't hear much about it."

How the Wildcats Live

The University of Kentucky is located in Lexington, where its red-brick buildings stand in green lawns full of trees. The campus is divided into three sections: North Campus, home to six dorms; Central Campus, with classroom buildings, the new library, and two dormitories; and South Campus, which has low-rise dormitory towers. Students select which dorms they want to live in on a first-come, first-serve basis. Patterson and Boyd Halls (the Honors dorms) are located on North Campus, as is Jewell Hall (the international dorm), and Blazer and Holmes Halls (all female, all male dorms, respectively). Also on North Campus is the Wildcat Lodge, the unofficial dorm for the basketball players, who are "treated like royalty."

On Central Campus is the "gorgeous and fairly easy to navigate" William T. Young Library. Nearby are the all-male Haggin Hall and the all-female Donovan Hall (said to be the hardest dorm to get into, because of the nice rooms). South Campus has Kirwan and Blanding Towers, along with several low-rises. The new, five-million-dollar athletic complex, called the Johnson Center, is also located on South Campus. While this facility is greatly enjoyed by most, some students wish the five million had been spent on "getting more teachers and more parking."

When not sleeping, partying, working out, or studying, there's a good chance that students are eating. There are three dining halls around campus, one in each campus section. Blazer Hall is on North Campus, the Student Center serves meals on Central Campus, and The Commons caters to South Campus. The library also has a highly praised café called Ovid's. Though vegetarians complain about not having many options, students can charge their meal account at on-campus eateries, such as Starbuck's. Also popular are fast-food restaurants like McDonald's and Kentucky Fried Chicken; but for a change, there's Joe Bologna's (a small Italian restaurant) and nearby restaurants like the Macaroni Grill. Tolley-Ho's, however, is the most popular off-campus restaurant. UK students have been eating and hanging out there for years, making it a real campus tradition.

We Come Together

But the biggest tradition at the University of Kentucky revolves around extracurriculars. Besides the fraternities and sororities—some of which do community outreach—students get involved in campus ministries, student boards, intramurals, the *Kentucky Colonel* (the daily newspaper), and organizations like the Green Thumb Club. As one student said, "Anything that you want to be involved in they have, or they encourage you to start yourself."

But nothing can compare to something that began a long while ago—the UK Wildcats basketball team. The men's team plays in the Rupp Arena, which now has a student section appropriately called "The Eruption Zone." Erupting is exactly what students do when they get together for a game: the "crowd is crazy" and enthusiasm skyrockets. Fireworks are set off before every home game, and afterwards the cheerleaders and band always play "My Old Kentucky Home."

No matter which UK college students are in, or what their different interests are, almost everyone comes out to support their team. Students cite this common spirit that "brings so many students and groups together" as the force that really makes their university unique. With everyone cheering their Wildcats on, it makes UK, a large research university full of opportunities, "seems so much smaller." —*Elizabeth Dohrmann*

FYI

If you come to the University of Kentucky, you'd better bring "shower shoes."

What is the typical weekend schedule? "If you don't go home for the weekend, you watch movies or go to coffeehouses with friends on Fridays, party on Saturdays, and start homework on Sundays."

If I could change one thing about UK, I'd "fix the parking problem."

Three things every UK student should do before graduating are "go to a basketball game, eat at Tolley-Ho's, and go to the library."

Louisiana

Louisiana State University

Address: 156 Thomas Boyd Hall; Baton Rouge, LA 70803
Phone: 225-578-1175
E-mail address: admissions@lsu.edu
Web site URL: www.lsu.edu
Founded: 1860
Private or Public: public
Religious affiliation: none
Location: urban
Undergraduate enrollment: 26,660
Total enrollment: NA
Percent Male/Female: 47%/53%
Percent Minority: 18%
Percent African-American: 9%
Percent Asian: 3%
Percent Hispanic: 2%
Percent Native-American: 0%
Percent in-state/out of state: 92%/8%
Percent Pub HS: NA
Number of Applicants: 10,376
Percent Accepted: 77%
Percent Accepted who enroll: 66%
Entering: 5,262
Transfers: 879
Application Deadline: 15 Apr
Mean SAT: NA
Mean ACT: NA
Middle 50% SAT range: NA
Middle 50% ACT range: 22-26
3 Most popular majors: business, engineering, education
Retention: 83%
Graduation rate: 50%
On-campus housing: 22%
Fraternities: 10%
Sororities: 16%
Library: 1,369,607 volumes
Tuition and Fees: $3,670 in; $8,970 out
Room and Board: $5,216
Financial aid, first-year: 47%
Varsity or Club Athletes: NA
Early Decision or Early Action Acceptance Rate: NA

It's a sunny Saturday afternoon, and the crowd at Louisiana State's Tiger Stadium is going wild in a sea of purple and gold. During football season, Baton Rouge, Louisiana turns into Football Town, USA. As one senior raved, "It gets pretty rambunctious at the games, but that's life. You plan your week around who we play in the game. Saturday at Tiger Stadium, it's not a date . . . it's an event!"

It Never Rains in Death Valley

The fans bleed purple and gold in Baton Rouge. The school's unofficial color seems to be orange, though—the color of Mike the Tiger, LSU's beloved mascot. Fans often try to get the tiger to roar before games for good luck; one such student admitted, "The other day I was walking by his cage and I heard a huge roar. I thought to myself 'it's going to be a good day!'"

Tigers go crazy for the pigskin at LSU. "Students come from out of state, specifically Texas, to attend the LSU football games. Football's a *huge* deal," said one sophomore. Everyone parks cars and trucks around campus the Friday night before the Saturday game. The fun begins with catered tailgates where students and visitors alike consume vast quantities of alcohol around the barbeque. Out-of-state fans often arrive in their purple-and-gold painted RVs on Thursday night, completely filling the two huge commuter parking lots by the stadium. These tailgates are elaborate affairs; one year, someone even towed along a swimming pool to the parking lot to splash around in before the game. Tiger Stadium has been nicknamed "Death Valley," where the mantra is that it never rains. Mere drizzles, however, could never keep these fans from the stands. Students sit in a section called the N-Zone. The demand for tickets in the Zone is so high that students often squish in, standing room only. As one girl said, "If you don't live on campus, you'd better get there by seven in the morning on Saturday if you want any chance of getting in." To say the least, "school spirit is definitely a big deal here."

Fans also come to cheer the marching band, called Golden Band from Tiger Land, as well as the popular Golden Girls dancers who lead cheers from the sidelines. The fans have many traditions; for instance, students claim they cheer "Geaux Tigers!" instead of "Go Tigers," as a nod to the area's Cajun-French culture. One junior explained, "it's a Southern thing!" Football games are more than just fun sporting events at LSU, they also serve as a bonding experience for the students. Cheering Tigers often wear T-shirts that read "Saturday night in Tiger Stadium is the best time spent with 92,600 of your closest friends." Many students boast that "we're like a family. It's so big here so you can't say you know everyone, but we're a football school. So that's our common ground."

Life Beyond the Stadium

Of course, not all students at LSU consider football games the highlight of their college experience. As one sophomore said with a laugh, "LSU wastes all its money on sports." Luckily for others like her, there's a wide variety of activities both on campus and in the Baton Rouge area. Greek life is a huge social force at LSU. According to one senior, over 900 girls rushed sororities this year alone. She said that "Greek life is a big deal here. There are always exchanges, socials, intermixing of fraternities and sororities, as well as different bar nights and themed parties where you can bring a date."

For those who don't want to join the Greek scene, there is still a lot to do. Many musical artists, such as Pat Green, give concerts on campus, and the Pete Maravich Assembly Center hosts a variety of theatrical performances and lectures. Students are also regulars at nearby movie theatres and the over 625 restaurants in Baton Rouge. The bar scene is another popular social option at LSU. There are at least 30 bars and clubs, though freshmen seem particularly fond of Tigerland, a strip of six bars where you only have to be 18 to enter, though you still must be 21 to drink. A "Drunk Bus" shuttles back and forth between Tigerland and campus every 15 minutes to pick up inebriated students and drop them off at their dorms. Other services like the campus transit also help to lower the rate of drunk driving, which until a few years ago was a big problem since mostly everyone on campus owns a car.

"LSU has a tremendous amount of gorgeous girls and a lot of guys lacking style."

Alcohol is not hard to find on campus, either. Students report that the administration is generally relaxed about enforcing alcohol policies. On-campus parties where alcohol will be served do have to be approved, though. If the watchful eye of campus security catches alcohol at a party that hasn't been pre-approved, the party hosts can get into a lot of trouble. Though alcohol is prevalent at LSU, many sober students "like to go out even though [they] don't drink and have no problems going to parties where alcohol is being served." Other students, however, go "wild because there's so much freedom. I wouldn't call it peer pressure, more like trying out a new lifestyle, doing things you've never done before. At home you were sheltered, but here you are responsible for yourself."

A Breeding Ground for Scholars? Maybe.

While some hard-working students maintain that LSU is not as much a party school as it is reputed to be, others say that academics are not their first priority. Most undergraduates enter LSU with a major already declared. Those who aren't sure what they want to focus on stay in a general studies program for a year or two until they do. Switching majors can be a pain, as most credits don't transfer between programs. Dealing with registration can also be a draining and frustrating experience. One sophomore suggested that "it helps if you know your major, since getting into classes becomes a lot easier." Students agree that the science classes, particularly biology, are among LSU's toughest courses. As one freshman put it, "The biology courses weed out a lot of people." Library science is well-known as the easiest class LSU offers, and it is considered a "one-hour easy A." Class size varies greatly depending on subject. Many English classes have only 15 to 30 students, while some popular biology and music lectures have to be held in the gym to accommodate the over 1,000 students that enroll in them. The average class size hovers around 150 students, though.

Generally the professors and TAs are responsive to student needs. They are good about returning student e-mails and setting up appointments. One senior was impressed that when he ran into one of his professors at the grocery store, she not only greeted him by name, but even had a conversation with him. LSU also offers a variety of free tutoring services. A center for freshmen is also available for academic counseling and for setting students up with the appropriate upperclass tutors. One student was particularly fond of the writing center, where students can get all their papers proofread. A common academic complaint, however, is that many of the foreign professors are extremely difficult to understand—so difficult, in fact, that many students drop classes because they simply cannot understand the professors. Generally the workload is decent, though the most diligent students report studying 20-30 hours weekly. Undergraduates who want to graduate within four years have to take at least 15 credit hours per semester. Often students will take lighter schedules than this, and stick around for summer school to make up the extra credits.

Beautiful Creatures in Their Natural Habitat

When one sophomore girl was asked if she thought that LSU students were on the whole an attractive bunch, she exclaimed "my freshman year I didn't see any cute people at all, but this year I see all kinds of hot people!" A similar response came from an upperclassman, who said, "The girls are *way* hotter here . . . there's a tremendous amount of gorgeous girls and a lot of guys lacking style." Needless to say, random hookups are not rare phenomena. However, the administration "strongly frowns upon shackin' up," so guys are required to sign in and out of the girls' dorms.

The students are beautiful, and "the campus is gorgeous," as well. The school invests a lot of resources to remodel buildings and to maintain the grounds. All the dorm rooms are air-conditioned, though the freshman rooms are "like closets with beds" and dorm life often involves sharing a bathroom with an entire floor of people. Many people move into off-campus apartments by sophomore year, though most agree that LSU students should try dorm life for at least one year. About 700 people live in each dorm, Herget being one of the most sought-after coed freshman dorms and Kirby Smith being one of the least desirable.

While classes are never more than a mile apart, most students opt to drive to class. The abundance of cars on campus can present a problem where parking is involved. As one frustrated sophomore confided, "There are never any parking spaces! Then the ticket people get ticket-happy and we get random parking tickets." LSU offers a great bus system that transports students from their dorms and off-campus apartments right to lecture halls, though few students actually use this service.

Despite the annoyance of parking problems, LSU students love Baton Rouge and their school. They particularly enjoy the fun atmosphere and the warm and friendly people. Most students agree that "everyone's really nice" and that "LSU is not a superficial campus." However, there seems to be conflicting views regarding diversity on campus. While one senior mentioned that "LSU is not a very diverse campus right now, the majority of students being Caucasian, and the faculty being also mostly white," several others maintained that LSU is a very diverse place where there are many international students and an impressive mix of black and white students.

LSU seems to offer a bit of something for everyone. So regardless of whether you're looking for a place to party hardy, to attend the finest football games on this side of the bayou, or to enjoy the benefits of a large university with friendly professors, LSU is definitely worth checking out. By the time you leave, you too will be bleeding purple and gold. —*Jenny Zhang*

FYI

If you come to LSU, you'd better bring "a party cup" and "a pair of walking shoes."

What is the typical weekend schedule? "Go out until the wee hours, go to the football game, and recuperate on Sunday from the strenuous weekend."

If I could change one thing about LSU, I would "have smaller classes."

Three things every student at LSU should do before graduating are "attend a football game, roll down Indian Mound, and go to a foam party."

Tulane University

Address: 6823 St. Charles Avenue; New Orleans, LA 70118
Phone: 504-865-5731
E-mail address: undergrad.admission@tulane.edu
Web site URL: www.tulane.edu
Founded: 1834
Private or Public: private
Religious affiliation: none
Location: urban
Undergraduate enrollment: 7,701
Total enrollment: 12,381
Percent Male/Female: 47%/53%
Percent Minority: 20%
Percent African-American: 9%
Percent Asian: 5%
Percent Hispanic: 3%
Percent Native-American: 0%
Percent in-state/out of state: 34%/66%
Percent Pub HS: 55%
Number of Applicants: 12,985
Percent Accepted: 56%
Percent Accepted who enroll: 21%
Entering: 1,540
Transfers: 142
Application Deadline: 15 Jan
Mean SAT: 1303
Mean ACT: 29
Middle 50% SAT range: V 630-710, M 610-700
Middle 50% ACT range: 28-32
3 Most popular majors: business, social sciences, engineering
Retention: 85%
Graduation rate: 72%
On-campus housing: 55%
Fraternities: 12%
Sororities: 15%
Library: 2,285,029 volumes
Tuition and Fees: $29,810
Room and Board: $7,641
Financial aid, first-year: 44%
Varsity or Club Athletes: 5%
Early Decision or Early Action Acceptance Rate: ED 58%: EA 65%

At Tulane, you don't have to give up good parties in order to receive a good education. What other school has a tradition that commands students to sleep on the sidewalk during its one-week recess at Mardi Gras? Just a streetcar ride away from the French Quarter, the heart of New Orleans, and the world-renown home of blues music, Tulane *is* New Orleans—fun, liberal, and crazy, with a touch of history and tradition.

The University is composed of 11 schools and colleges, and rests in the quiet Uptown section of New Orleans. Undergraduates attend two distinct colleges: Newcomb College for women and Tulane College for men, though all buildings and classes are co-educational.

The Academics: Driving at Your Own Pace

According to students, the academics at Tulane are what you make of them. The most popular major is business, while political science and English are known to be the easiest. For those who want a challenge, sciences and architecture are known to be tough. "You can either be a total slacker, or you can make it hard," said a sophomore in the Newcomb College. Most students agree that the school's general requirements are not difficult to fulfill, and that their workload is never overwhelming.

Students praise the small size of their classes—usually around 30 students—and the quality of their professors. As one student destined for law school gushed, "in my poli-sci class I got to learn stuff I would learn as a law student, and even though the professor works in the law school he gave me personal attention." Small class sizes at Tulane do not necessarily translate into a personal relationship with the professor, however. One junior complained, "My adviser barely knows who I am. You can just fool around and nobody would have any idea what you are doing." For some, the loose academic advising system is frustrating, while for others it gives them the flexibility and freedom they crave. "There's no one who is going to be pushing you at Tulane," said one student, "but if you have the motivation, it's a lot of fun and a great school."

The Social Scene: Speeding in the Front Seat

Forget band camp. "This one time, I was so wasted—," is the way most conversations at Tulane start, according to one student. "Tulane centers around drinking, and if not, then drugs," confirmed another. Students cite the frequent occurrence of freshmen drinking in their dorms in front of their RAs as proof that regulations are much less restrictive than at other universities.

> **"If you want to have a lot of fun while you're young, Tulane is the place to be."**

Parties at Tulane fire up on Tuesday, and stay hopping throughout the week. Most students make no advance plans for their nocturnal revels, but end up barhopping in Upper New Orleans or stopping by a frat party. Because Tulane does not have many on-campus parties, frat parties stand out in the campus social scene. One student cited "Pre-historic" as his favorite party—where his frat decorates its house as a cave and gives pledges a "one-inch by one-inch" cloth to wear. Despite the prevalence of frat events, older students maintain that fraternities are not necessarily the end-all of enjoying Tulane; they are only a way to secure free alcohol before the real parties begin. "You start Greek when you are young, then you burst out into New Orleans," explained one senior brother. So while the same senior admitted that it was easier for him, being in a fraternity, to find his crowd, he now prefers to frequent the bars scattered around campus or hop on the streetcar down to "the Quarter."

After a typical night out on the town, Tulane students swing by The Boot, a popular club near campus. It's there that you'll find people on the prowl. "If you want to fool around it's not very hard," shrugged one student. Dating and relationships, on the other hand, are less common according to most. All in all, students agree that Tulane is a party school and that it is easy to meet people because all one has to do is go out. "If you want to have a lot of fun while you're young, Tulane is the place to be," said one student proudly.

The Forgotten Campus and Its Delicious Surroundings

Students acknowledge that the Tulane campus has great lawns, beautiful architecture, and good facilities. A favorite building with the students is The Reily Student Recreation Center, a gym equipped with an indoor track, weight room, and swimming pools.

The Tulane campus, however, is not the hub of student activity; students are frequently seduced outside of the school's borders and into New Orleans. "No one really goes to campus, unless it's for class," said one off-campus student.

While students are required to live in dormitories for their freshman year, many people move off-campus or to on-campus apartments in the years following. Apartments are reportedly decent in size; however, on-campus housing is allegedly expensive, and many students prefer the freedom of living off campus.

A similar preference for the outside holds true for dining. "The food is livable," commented a student regarding the on-campus dining options, but "we all prefer to eat out at the mouth-watering diners next to campus." The Camellia Grill is a close local favorite, while New Orleans provides any number of culinary delights, from seafood to burgers to Cajun. At 2 A.M., however, a run to Popeye's Fried Chicken is the best place to go after a long night of partying.

Green Wave Spirit Crashes

One complaint that students have about Tulane is the lack of school spirit. It seems that with all the excitement just a few blocks out of campus, it is difficult to hold attention on campus activities. "Rarely do they have things on campus because nobody goes," said one student, despite recent crowd-drawing guests such as Kevin Spacey, frequent movie showings, and according to one student, an annual "3-D porn" showing.

Even the Green Wave football games played in the Superdome only attract a small portion of students. Most claim that they would be excited if their team did well, and point their fingers at the team's poor performance for the lack of interest. One student grumbled, "People are more interested in the Saints," referring to the New Orleans football team. Others think the excitement of the city is at fault for the lack of sports enthusiasm. "You're not going to spend your Saturday night watching basketball," said one student. "You wouldn't come to Tulane for that."

On the student-organization end of the spectrum, a fair number of students participate in government, the community service program CACTUS, school publications, and club sports. Ethnic and minority organizations are also active on campus, although students are well aware of the lack of minorities at Tulane. "For a city that has a 75-percent minority population, the situation on campus is pretty pitiful," said one student. "It's a pretty expensive school that seems to cater to the well-off," said another. "There are different kinds of people here, but you have to look for them more than at other schools."

Despite their criticisms and the lack of school spirit, Tulane students respond enthusiastically about their school, recalling fun anecdotes and having a hard time coming up with what they would want to change about their university. Would they choose this school if they were a high school senior again? The overwhelming answer: Absolutely. —*Mariko Hirose*

FYI

If you come to Tulane, you'd better bring "headphones and a tube top."

What is the typical weekend schedule? "Bar-hopping, frat parties, going to the Quarter."

If I could change one thing about Tulane, I'd "really like to see more school spirit. A lot of people are just apathetic."

Three things every student at Tulane should do before graduating are "go to a frat party, go to the Mardi Gras parade, and see a sold-out concert in the House of Blues."

Maine

Bates College

Address: 23 Campus Avenue; Lewiston, ME 04240
Phone: 207-786-6000
E-mail address: admissions@bates.edu
Web site URL: www.bates.edu
Founded: 1855
Private or Public: private
Religious affiliation: none
Location: small city
Undergraduate enrollment: 1,738
Total enrollment: NA
Percent Male/Female: 49%/51%
Percent Minority: 14%
Percent African-American: 2%
Percent Asian: 3%
Percent Hispanic: 2%
Percent Native-American: 0%
Percent in-state/out of state: 11%/89%
Percent Pub HS: 57%
Number of Applicants: 4,012
Percent Accepted: 28%
Percent Accepted who enroll: 37%
Entering: 415
Transfers: 5
Application Deadline: 15 Jan
Mean SAT: NA
Mean ACT: NA
Middle 50% SAT range: V 630-710, M 650-720
Middle 50% ACT range: NA
3 Most popular majors: social sciences, biological/biomedical sciences, psychology
Retention: 94%
Graduation rate: 86%
On-campus housing: 90%
Fraternities: NA
Sororities: NA
Library: 661,732 volumes
Tuition and Fees: NA
Room and Board: NA
Financial aid, first-year: 48%
Varsity or Club Athletes: 35%
Early Decision or Early Action Acceptance Rate: ED 40%

Founded in 1855 by abolitionists who wanted a co-ed college institution with no imposed racial boundaries, Bates College has remained one of the top liberal arts colleges in the country. Still holding fast to its founders' ideals of unity (there are no fraternities or sororities), Bates has a certain atmosphere that differentiates it from its rivals Bowdoin and Colby. From its ancient Outing Club to its intimate academic opportunities, it is not hard to see why a common senior reflection is, "I can't imagine myself not being part of the immediate Bates community."

Studying like a Batesie

The pursuit of academics at Bates is motivated by originality—no standardized test scores are required to apply (though most applicants provide them anyway), a senior thesis is required for most majors, and at least two out of four spring semesters include "Short Term" courses. As one senior noted, "Professors know that academic life can get boring so they try to mix things up, and we love it."

Characteristic of many liberal arts schools, Short Term is a five-week period at the beginning of the spring semester where students enroll in one intensive course. The actual intensity of the courses can vary, but some of the notorious ones at Bates include "History Hell," "Math Camp," and "Cell Hell."

During the rest of their career at Bates, students use online registration to choose their classes and meet their college's requirements. Bates requires three hard science courses; three classes in the social sciences (economics, anthropology, education, political science, psychology, sociology); one in quantitative techniques; and five in the humanities. There appear to be few hard feelings about these requirements, although science majors tend to be less than enthused about their humanities classes and humanities majors less than inspired by their science courses. Bates has an excellent biology program, despite the fact that the college's curriculum is centered on the liberal arts. One sophomore commented, "I assumed the school would be stronger in the humanities . . . but science is really strong here, and the humanities seem to be hit-or-miss."

The sciences/humanities division may, however, be more due to the fact that science majors have 8 A.M. classes and little time for lunch (hence forming a science "posse" that earns its high profile) than a real divergence in course quality. The most popular courses and majors at Bates, however, are mostly in the social sciences. Economics, biology, and religion (the latter with the admired professors Kaspi and Strong) are cited as some of the most popular majors, while underdeveloped programs appear to include classics, women's studies, art, and theater. Classes in these and other areas are sometimes cut because of a paucity of interest. While virtually all classes at Bates tend to be small (around 25 people), some intro courses have enrollments of over 100.

The intimacy of the Bates academic community fosters the formation of close relationships and "really amazing friendships" between students and faculty members. There are countless examples—many students work in professors' research labs, get academic advice from favorite profs, and often faculty are influential in helping students devise a study abroad plan—60 percent of Batesies study abroad before graduating. A sophomore remarked that there are certainly both "great and not-so-great" professors at Bates, but students can count on finding a supportive faculty member in their concentration, especially since many of Bates' programs are interdisciplinary.

One such interdisciplinary program that is becoming more popular is the environmental studies major. With one foot in the sciences and one in the humanities, ES doesn't fall into either grouping and thus tends to be poked fun at, even though it has the most course requirements of any major. Many students in such majors can design their own programs or projects, a freedom that highlights the variety of academic interest and dedication Batesies exhibit. While one ES major is studying rock climbing, another is designing a catalyst to break down pesticides, proving a liberal education here is "what you make of it!" This juxtaposition also elucidates a key Batesian attitude that its students are proud of: Bates students study "more for themselves than to prove anything . . . it's a really nice thing." This ethic combined with the school's resources led one biology graduate to say retrospectively, "The quality of my education is really wonderful."

The Peeps, the Booze, the Town

Lewiston, Maine—along with neighboring Auburn across the river—is described by students as "the least attractive part of the Bates community . . . the relationship between the "townies" and the Bates kids is pretty bad." Batesies mainly use the working-class, old mill town for its "restaurants, Wal-Mart, and Shaw's." But even concerning restaurants, many students venture instead to the college towns of Portland or Brunswick (both less than an hour away) to have their meals out.

Because of their interesting student community, however, Batesies don't find themselves too hindered by their location. A senior from Tennessee commented that as a student of color she values Bates' "progressive attitude towards race relations . . . it was a pleasant surprise." Still, all students point out that fair generalizations about the student body exist, such as "the conservative/athletic people and the liberal/whatever people." Fifty percent of students are from New England, many of those "just-outside-Boston kids," and it is widely noted that there's "a lot of wealth, though many people are on financial aid or have campus jobs." As one sophomore summarized, "It's Maine; it's really white and really Christian . . . Bates does a good job of being diverse and open, but as a school and city we still have a long way to go."

The general consensus on campus is that most social events revolve around the keg: "there's a lot of drinking here." Many venture into Lewiston to do it—the Den, the Goose, and the Cage are all popular drinking and hangout spots. Those who aren't hands-down into alcohol, however, don't seem to have trouble finding other social options, especially since there are no fraternities or sororities. A campus group called "The Diascordians" makes an effort to sponsor non-alcoholic student activities such as bowling or movies, but the events are rarely attended. More popular organizations are the Village Club Series, which sponsors a band every Thursday night, and the Chase Hall Committee, which brings in one headliner a year. Past performers include Ben Harper and Guster.

"I can't imagine myself not being part of the immediate Bates community."

Other traditional campus-wide events include the Winter Carnival in January; the community Harvest Dinner, which is "complete chaos—the school spends a ridiculous amount of money"; Lick It, the LGBT dance; and the President's Gala, "the one time on campus where everyone gets dressed up . . . it's like prom but amplified to a ridiculous degree." With all these events (and the ever-present booze) to look forward to year-round, the social energy at Bates remains at a constant high.

Life Bates-Style

Bates uses a random housing draw—described by some as "raggedy and frustrating"—to place students in on-campus housing. There are eight dorms, all or which are co-ed and some of which are chem-free (no alcohol or drugs). One senior commented that chem-free "is definitely the way to go when you want to be able to come back [from partying] and have a good night's sleep." RAs live among the students to "take care of the dorms," while Junior Advisors live among their 15 assigned freshmen.

Dorms with specific reputations include Hedge, a freshman dorm co-ed by floor; Smith, which houses freshman in kipper-tin-tight quads; and The Village and JB, the upperclassmen dorms with nice suites that are "drinking-intensive" and inhabited mostly by "jocks."

In addition to dorms, there is also the opportunity to live in Victorian-style houses, which hold anywhere from eight to 30 people. Moulton and Herrick are single-sex houses; other notables include the theme houses. While groups may petition each year to have a house dedicated to their theme, some themes remain constant, such as the environmental house, the cooking house, and the community service house. Since only seniors are allowed to live off campus, many sophomores and juniors choose to find a theme house to join.

Though there are numerous living arrangements at Bates, there is only one dining hall which everyone shares. Commons functions on a four-week menu rotation that includes some well-liked emphases, such as local food and two "fantastic" salad bars. Besides the overall excellence of the food, many students also applaud the intimacy that a single dining hall provides. As an anthropology major noted, "You get to know everyone's face pretty quickly . . . sometimes it can get a little claustrophobic, but for the most part it's pretty cool."

Puddle Jumping and the Rest

Many Bates students remember their first impression of Bates' campus: "when I went to Bates I just really loved it." The focal point of the campus is the block-size Quad, which is reportedly "really beautiful in the fall." The atmosphere is described as "homey, not supershowy," but with a red-brick "Harvard look." Well-known buildings include the Carnegie Science Center and the Olin Arts Center, the latter of which is faced by an amphitheater used for spring and summer concerts. Pettengill Hall, the five-story social sciences building, features lounges, an atrium, and waterfalls. Students also frequent Ronj, the on-campus coffee house. There have been plans for a new student center, but because of the recent economic slowdown the idea is currently on hold.

Safety is an issue that has permeated campus life at Bates. After the rape of a student on campus in 2002 and the murder of the lacrosse captain during a street brawl in that same year, students seem to be "overall okay" and adjusting. Safe rides and escort services increased directly after these incidents, but as of yet the promise for key-card security hasn't come through—it is expected to become a reality by fall 2005, at the latest.

One thing virtually no Bates students have qualms about is the importance of athletic activity—two-thirds of the campus participates in varsity or club sports. The others often work out individually, though the dearth of cardiovascular equipment in Bates' facilities makes that more difficult when the weather is frightful. Usually this is not such a huge problem, though, since Bates has "a ton of skiers" who flock to the mountains when the snow and cold kick in.

Each athletic team at Bates has "their own group of people" who provide fan support, and team spirit runs high when playing such rivals as Colby or Bowdoin. Of the 50 or so clubs at Bates, a good number are athletic in nature, such as the break-dance and juggling clubs. Other popular groups include the Strange Bedfellows (a comedy group), the Fishing Club, and the Environmental Coalition. Activist groups such as LGBT will sometimes stir up the campus by "chalking the Quad," an act that gets varying responses from the student body.

The "biggest and oldest" club at Bates, however, is the Outing Club, which plugs into Batesies' favorite pastime of exploring the nearby wilderness. Incredible natural beauties surround Lewiston—Bates-Morse Mountain is less than an hour away and boasts not only 574 acres, but also "one of the few sandy beaches in Maine." Another sandy Maine beach is Popham Beach State Park, where every fall and spring the club sponsors a clambake.

When the weather is too cold for a clambake and the whole campus isn't on the slopes, students have fun with their glaciered campus by doing the Puddle Jump. It happens when Lake Andrew ("the Puddle") is frozen over in the early part of the year: a hole is cut out where naked Batesies can prove their chutzpah by jumping in. If there is still ice when St. Patrick's Day arrives, the ritual is repeated. After all, students here are always ready to give new things a try, and the many "rewarding experiences of Bates" far outweigh the freezing cold. *—Elizabeth Dohrmann*

FYI

If you come to Bates, you'd better bring "a North Face jacket."

What is the typical weekend schedule? "Drink after Friday classes; sleep, ski, or hike on Saturday; do work Sunday."

If I could change one thing about Bates, "I'd change the location."

Three things every student at Bates should do before graduating are: "streak the Quad, do the Puddle Jump, and eat a lobster on the beach at a clambake."

Bowdoin College

Address: 5700 College Station; Brunswick, ME 04011-8448
Phone: 207-725-3100
E-mail address: admissions@bowdoin.edu
Web site URL: www.bowdoin.edu
Founded: 1794
Private or Public: private
Religious affiliation: none
Location: suburban
Undergraduate enrollment: 1,657
Total enrollment: NA
Percent Male/Female: 49%/51%
Percent Minority: 20%
Percent African-American: 4%
Percent Asian: 8%
Percent Hispanic: 4%
Percent Native-American: 1%
Percent in-state/out of state: 15%/85%
Percent Pub HS: 53%
Number of Applicants: 4,505
Percent Accepted: 25%
Percent Accepted who enroll: 41%
Entering: 458
Transfers: 5
Application Deadline: 1 Jan
Mean SAT: NA
Mean ACT: NA
Middle 50% SAT range: V 640-730, M 640-720
Middle 50% ACT range: NA
3 Most popular majors: political science, biology, English
Retention: 95%
Graduation rate: 89%
On-campus housing: 90%
Fraternities: NA
Sororities: NA
Library: 948,879 volumes
Tuition and Fees: $30,120
Room and Board: $7,670
Financial aid, first-year: 45%
Varsity or Club Athletes: 32%
Early Decision or Early Action Acceptance Rate: ED 29%

A polar bear for a mascot and a special program in Arctic studies? No, it's not just a cruel joke jibing those brave souls who venture to Bowdoin College in Brunswick, Maine, to study and live for four years. Traditions at Bowdoin, even those having to do with cold temperatures, run long and deep. With a list of alumni including some of the best authors, soldiers, and even Arctic explorers in American history, this small liberal arts college certainly has an illustrious past. Judging from the happy students seen around the bustling campus, though, the future of Bowdoin is looking pretty bright too. (And no, those smiles aren't simply frozen on their faces. . . .)

Striking a Balance

The strength and flexibility of Bowdoin's academic curriculum is just one of the college's features that keep students smiling. The college offers a surprisingly wide array of courses of study, boasting 38 majors and 41 minors, with programs ranging from environmental studies to the performing arts. Core distributional requirements do exist, but students report that it is "not difficult at all" to satisfy the mandatory two credits in the four distributional groups: natural sciences, social sciences, humanities, and non-Eurocentric studies. Likewise, freshmen are required to take freshman seminars, small, writing-intensive courses that range from "The Art of Winslow Homer" to "Mass Media in American Politics." One student described the core programs as "a good base" and noted that, even within the requirements, "at Bowdoin your education is very much catered to you."

Programs in the natural sciences are considered difficult, with physics being singled out by one student as "notoriously terrible." Government and legal studies are also regarded as quite grueling, yet students particularly praised Professor Bolbetti in this department for her stimulating lectures and kind manner. Indeed, personal relationships with teachers abound at Bowdoin, as all classes are small and led exclusively by professors. The administration, in fact, is making a concerted effort to continue to improve the student-to-teacher ratio and recently has downsized all introductory classes, the largest classes on campus, by cutting the maximum number of students from 75 to 50. Such actions, though, face mixed reviews from students who complained about "the scramble to get into the classes you want."

Top Honors

All Bowdoin students declare a major by the end of sophomore year, giving ample time to, as one student put it, "explore and think about how you can make the most of the amazing classes here." Bowdoin encourages periods of independent study, usually in the form of directed reading and supervised projects completed under the close instruction of a faculty member, and through which students earn regular credit for a semester's worth of work. The apex of such independent study is certainly the honors project in each major, an optional plan of study consisting of one or two terms during senior year that culminates in written dissertations, performances or creative works.

Bowdoin receives high praise from its students for its effort to satisfy the academic curiosities of all who study there. While everyone admitted to working hard at academics, or, as one student put it, "busting ass three or four days a week," most students describe the general workload as manageable.

Toga at Quinby? Luau at Ladd?

So just what are Bowdoin students busting the other days of the week? Similar to academics, students have a wide range of partying venues, all catered to personal taste, whether it be for food, drink or entertainment. The last of Bowdoin's fraternities were phased out in 2000, and the school has since taken over many of the houses to serve as "social houses." Upperclassmen apply to live in any one of the six houses, which are matched with the six freshman dorm buildings and thus are responsible for much of the social activity found on campus. The social houses "really stress community and you have to be really active to want to live there," one junior noted. Each co-ed house sponsors events throughout the year, such as barbecues, art exhibits, and community service events, as well as throwing the all-important weekend parties. The most popular house events are often annual themed parties, ranging from Quinby's spring Toga Party, to EuroJam at Baxter. Speaking of annual parties, Pinestock, fittingly on Pine Street, reigns as the biggest party of the year, when the senior residents of the street let loose and celebrate the end of the term. For those not interested in the hordes of freshmen that flock to the social houses, off-campus parties and those thrown in the college-owned apartments prove an entertaining alternative. "Basically, there are two scenes," one student noted, "the first being the social houses, which the freshmen get really into, and then there are the athletes in the apartments or off campus." A favorite spot of this junior, in fact, seemed to be a place lovingly referred to as The Crackhouse, an off-campus residence usually adopted each year by a sports team.

A Fling or a Ring

For those not interested in the houses (be they "Social" or "Crack"), students agree that there are plenty of alternative social scenes. On Thursdays students flock to Jack Magee's, a pub and grill located centrally in the student union. Smith Union also boasts lounges, a café, the student bookstore and a game room, making it a popular place to catch up with old friends or meet new ones. And how about that new friend met casually at the pub or perhaps a more formal event such as the popular Spring Gala? What is the dating scene like at Bowdoin? Well, as one student put it, "You are either hooking up or you are married." Students do complain about the lack of dating, but are quick to point out that, at formal events such as the popular Spring Gala and Junior/Senior Ball, there is ample opportunity to get dressed up and impress potential hook-ups . . . er, significant others.

"At Bowdoin your education is very much catered to you."

Maine Attraction

But what about off-campus fun in midcoast Maine? One student described Brunswick as "the perfect little (and I mean little) college town." Students rave about the cafés, Thai restaurants, and, most notably, the Sea Dog Brewery, the most popular off-campus spot for those looking to toss a few microbrews back. For those not satisfied by the options in Brunswick, Portland, Maine's largest city is not a far drive. Recommended heartily by a student who was "surprised by what Portland has to offer," the small city is home to the Maine Mall and many restaurants, bars, and clubs, as well as the Old Seaport, full of interesting shops. Freeport, the promised land of Northeast outlet shopping and more importantly, the holy site of the L.L. Bean outlet, is only a 20-minute drive. For campers and outdoor enthusiasts, it is truly a religious experience. For those not so interested in the great outdoors, hey, it's open 24 hours a day, 7 days a week and serves free coffee! Every good Bowdoin student makes the pilgrimage, sometimes at 4 A.M.

They Even Like the Food!

But why would anyone venture from a campus as idyllic as Bowdoin's? With all the red brick, ivy, and charm of a classic New England college, Bowdoin's combination of quaint architecture and modern facilities provide style, comfort and choice. After freshmen year, students can choose housing in a variety of forms. In addition to classic dorm-style living, in buildings such as 16-story Cole Tower, the tallest building on campus, upperclass students may live in social houses, university-rented apartments (such as the popular Brunswick Apartments) or live off campus. "The housing here is great," one student raved, "While at first I was confused by the many options, everything is nice, so I knew I would be happy!" Bowdoin students also are happy about the food. Known nationally for having some of the best college food in the country, students simply love the quality and variety offered at the two cafeterias, Thorne and Moulton, though one unhappy football player grumbled about Bowdoin's plan to "aim for more vegetarian options . . . blech."

New England Charm

So just what type of kids are living in these great dorms and eating this great food? One student described the typical Bowdoin student as "rich, preppy, and liberal; there are like four Republicans on campus." Almost all students noted that most of their colleagues hailed from the New England area and that lack of diversity is an issue on campus. In regard to increasing diversity, "the college is working hard," one student noted, "and there has been a noticeable rise in diversity" in recent years. Students also noted the lack of foreign students, and one such international noted that "Bowdoin doesn't understand international kids . . . the administration really needs to work out a better system of transfer credits and such things." Whether "from away" (as Mainers like to call everyone simply born outside the state lines) or a true-blue New Englander, the typical Bowdoin student is characterized as "someone excited to be in such a beautiful place, learning amazing things and meeting amazing people."

Student (Hard) Body

The majority of the students join the Bowdoin Outing Club, affectionately referred to as the BOC, a group that organizes trips ranging from whitewater rafting to hiking in beautiful Acadia National Park. Such groups also take advantage of Brunswick's ideal coastal location and one student gushed, "I love Bowdoin, but undoubtedly the best part about going to school here is the ocean." Not surprisingly, most of the active student body is also involved in athletics, whether competing on the Division III level, or simply playing intramurals and pick-up games around campus. A healthy rivalry exists with nearby Colby and Bates, and popular sports include ice hockey (where, of course, the Polar Bears reign supreme), women's basketball, and soccer.

Bowdoin College, tucked into the beautiful rocky coast of Maine, is truly a treasure with its flexible academics and happily challenged student body. Educating and inspiring such great Americans as Civil War hero Joshua Chamberlain, Harriet Beecher Stowe, Nathaniel Hawthorne, and Henry Wadsworth Longfellow, there is definitely something special about the ivy-covered brick halls and the close community they shelter. Simply put, Bowdoin College is breathtaking, especially in the New England fall with the bundled, still-smiling students kicking up leaves in the charming quads and the historic pines standing tall against the clear, cold sky. To borrow slightly from Maine's famous motto, this is truly the way life, and indeed, *college* should be. —*Marisa Benoit*

FYI

If you come to Bowdoin, you'd better bring "a shovel. It snows . . . a lot."

What is the typical weekend schedule? "Pub on Thursday; something low-key on Friday; social house parties on Saturday; and on Sunday we laugh about the things we did the night before."

If I could change one thing about Bowdoin, I'd "relocate it to a tropical island."

Three things every student at the Bowdoin should do before graduating are "go to L.L. Bean in the middle of the night, go to Pinestock (the biggest party of the year), and go out in the snow in sandals."

Colby College

Address: 4000 Mayflower Hill; Waterville, ME 04901-8840
Phone: 207-872-3168
E-mail address: admissions@colby.edu
Web site URL: www.colby.edu
Founded: 1813
Private or Public: private
Religious affiliation: none
Location: small city
Undergraduate enrollment: 1,830
Total enrollment: NA
Percent Male/Female: 47%/53%
Percent Minority: 16%
Percent African-American: 2%
Percent Asian: 5%
Percent Hispanic: 2%
Percent Native-American: 0%
Percent in-state/out of state: 16%/84%
Percent Pub HS: 58%
Number of Applicants: 3,873
Percent Accepted: 33%
Percent Accepted who enroll: 37%
Entering: 471
Transfers: 7
Application Deadline: 1 Jan
Mean SAT: NA
Mean ACT: NA
Middle 50% SAT range: V 620-700, M 640-710
Middle 50% ACT range: 27-30
3 Most popular majors: economics, biology/biological science, English literature
Retention: 94%
Graduation rate: 87%
On-campus housing: 94%
Fraternities: NA
Sororities: NA
Library: 350,000 volumes
Tuition and Fees: NA
Room and Board: NA
Financial aid, first-year: 45%
Varsity or Club Athletes: 33%
Early Decision or Early Action Acceptance Rate: ED 42%

What's not to love? For many students at Colby, this seems to be the popular sentiment. And with good reason—students rarely complain about Maine's cold winters and the remote location of their town, Waterville, but instead seek to make the most of their rural campus. Indeed, a feeling of enthusiasm pervades. Colby's 1,800 undergraduate-only student body seems to dismiss the notion that students on such a small campus would be left with little to do or get excited about. The result is a stimulating atmosphere in which to learn and have fun.

While Colby's tuition—like many other liberal arts institutions of its caliber—seems staggering to many students, the wealth of opportunities seems to make up for the rather hefty price tag. Indeed, students' $35,800 is, by all reports, well spent. Taking into account the wide range of academic offerings, extracurricular activities, and social events, there never seems to be a dull moment. Outside the walls of Colby's Georgian-brick buildings, the vast Maine landscape sustains skiers, hikers, and other outdoor enthusiasts. Nonetheless, some students find Colby's walls closing in on them, citing the need for a taste of "civilization," as one student identified the world outside Colby.

Fitting It All In

What Colby students praise most when it comes to their education is the faculty. Most note that "everyone is easy to approach and are willing to help"—just one of the benefits of the 10 to 1 student-to-faculty ratio. It is often the norm to "go over to professors' houses for dessert or class as a change of scenery." Of course, "there are always those one or two exceptions" when it comes to professor accessibility and interest. Students are quick to note that there is "definitely not" an overabundance of TAs, a problem that plagues other institutions. Among majors, the history and American studies departments are reportedly strong, as are the ever-improving sciences. Many students even identified the strength of the science departments as the main reason for coming to Colby. The Olin Science Center provides science majors and non-majors alike with the opportunity to study in state-of-the-art laboratories equipped with the latest technologies. The strength of the sciences notwithstanding, students occasionally find "easier classes that are very helpful if you are not a science person," such as "Rocks for Jocks" and "Clapping for Credit."

True to its liberal arts background, Colby requires students to sample one course in each of the following disciplines: history, social sciences, literature and English composition, natural sciences, language, diversity, art, and quantitative reasoning. While seemingly a daunting task, one junior noted that she had "no problems fulfilling my requirements." Apart from the requisites listed above, students must also complete a wellness requirement, aimed towards helping students overcome normal college struggles. The requirement can be met by attending weekly lectures, a hassle which many students nonetheless find "interesting." One sophomore's gripe that "as hard as I've tried to find an easy class to fill a requirement, I haven't found one yet" attests to the school's aim that all students receive a challenging, and innovative, liberal education. Students seem to hold up their end of the bargain—indeed, Sundays are reserved for studying and catching up. Unique to Colby is the Jan Plan, a month-long program formally sponsored by the school that allows students to dabble in non-traditional fields of interest. While freshmen are required to stay on campus during this period, upperclassmen are permitted to "pretty much do whatever and go wherever—within reason," and this can mean anything from "internships and research to pottery and EMT training." While most students relish the opportunity to try something different, some view the Jan Plan simply as an open invitation to take unrestricted advantage of the ski season.

Getting Serious About Not Being Serious

By all accounts, the student body is not very diverse, and cliques tend to form readily in such a close-knit community. However, one student was quick to point out that "pretty much everyone is welcoming and ready to meet new people." The self-containment of the campus permits students to "see familiar faces and get to know people in a neat setting." To be sure, not all students are so enthusiastic about their peers. One Maine native was surprised "to feel out of place sometimes because I don't have a lot of money and I'm not from Massachusetts or Connecticut."

> **"I didn't expect to love Colby as much as I do. There is so much about it that I have fallen in love with."**

Colby students have opportunities to meet new people not only in classes but also at parties, sporting events, and clubs. On the weekends, there is always "a ton going on." One student agreed, "I would definitely classify Colby as a school that likes to party." There are only a few small pubs in Waterville, and, as a result, "the activity is on campus." Colby-sponsored events such as dances and formals are reportedly well-attended, especially by freshmen, and give students the chance to go "all out" if for no other reason than because "there's nothing else to do in Waterville." Although there is always a party "until the wee hours of the morning," one student made note that "they have a tendency to go a little over-the-top." For students who don't drink (and they are well in the minority), there is still plenty to do. Jorgenson's, a local coffee house, serves as just one alternative to the room-party scene. "Late night trips to L.L. Bean" and movie nights round out the non-drinking options. When guys and girls get together at Colby, it is more in the form of hooking-up than dating. As one student put it, "for the most part, people kind of jump around."

When not taking advantage of the vibrant social scene, students at Colby take advantage of the wide array of extracurricular options. From clubs to community service, there are "lots of opportunities here." Whether making use of the Colby Volunteer Center or going out on their own for community service, "Colby students are super-involved and excited about being active." For those drawn to the outdoors, Colby even boasts a woodsman's team. Sports, too, are very popular and range from broomball to football. Those who do not partake directly in Division III action participate either through intramurals (called I-plays) or by turning out in droves to lend support to the hockey team. Even in the face of defeat at the hands of rivals Bates and Bowdoin, Colby students find solace in the dignity of their mascot, the White Mule.

When the Going Gets Cold, the Cold Go to L.L. Bean

Colby's campus garners nothing but enthusiastic reviews. Students come to Maine prepared for the bitter Maine winter and excited for the snowball fights that come along. The campus, a collection of Georgian buildings, "really is beautiful." One student alluded to Colby's winter wonderland appeal when he raved, "I feel like I am walking through some movie." Although upperclassmen get a wider selection of housing options, dorms are both grade-interspersed and co-ed, and so freshmen find themselves living next door to seniors, males next door to females. The dorms are divided into four commons, with activities directors allocating funds to be spent on the students. With this arrangement, "there is always enough going on. Fraternities, which were abolished in 1984, are not missed." Student affection for the living situation explains why many seniors do not bother with the process of applying for off-campus housing. Since "Colby likes to have everyone living on campus," on-campus senior apartments are made available for upperclassmen who prefer apartments to the dorm setting.

Dining halls serve students' needs just fine. There are three of them and "almost always one of them is open from 7 A.M. to 9 P.M." What's more, each dining hall caters to a slightly different taste, thus expanding the variety of students' meal choices. "There are always people passing through" the Student Center, which houses student mailboxes as well as the student activities office and the Spa, a late-night food store, "a great place to hang out and grab a cup of coffee or a shake." As for libraries, there are three. Many students venture to Miller, the largest, when the mood strikes them to study in one of the campus's hallmark buildings.

Administration Who?

Students have little to say about the administration. Indeed, they are so focused on everything Colby has to offer that they pay little attention to red tape. Most students are fine with the absence of fraternities: "It keeps things more united." As far as the administration's policy on alcohol, "pretty much, if they don't see it or hear it, it is not really an issue." Campus safety isn't a hot issue either. Residential and farming districts dominate much of the surrounding area and envelop students in a sense of security.

When it comes down to it, students' reasons for choosing Colby are as uniform as they are basic—a solid education, a small school size, and a fascination with the beauty of Maine all factor into their decisions. Students find that they must "put in the hours, but the reward comes out of it." Expressing a common Colby sentiment, one student noted, "I didn't expect to love Colby as much as I do. I am on 'leave of absence' for the semester, and I cannot wait to get back. There is so much about it that I have fallen in love with." *—Greg Hamm*

FYI

If you come to Colby, you'd better bring "a heavy winter jacket and boots."

What is the typical weekend schedule? "Pre-parties and dances Friday and Saturday nights, lots of studying on Sundays."

If I could change one thing about Colby, "I'd make it less expensive to go here."

Three things every student at Colby should do before graduation are: "sleep outside on Runnal's hill and overlook Waterville; drive to Freeport in the middle of the night just because you can; and experience the excitement of Colby a capella."

College of the Atlantic

Address: 105 Eden Street; Bar Harbor, ME 04609
Phone: 800-528-0025
E-mail address: inquiry@ecology.coa.edu
Web site URL: www.coa.edu
Founded: 1969
Private or Public: private
Religious affiliation: none
Location: rural
Undergraduate enrollment: 278
Total enrollment: NA
Percent Male/Female: 36%/64%
Percent Minority: NA
Percent African-American: NA
Percent Asian: NA
Percent Hispanic: NA
Percent Native-American: NA
Percent in-state/out of state: NA
Percent Pub HS: NA
Number of Applicants: NA
Percent Accepted: 73%
Percent Accepted who enroll: NA
Entering: NA
Transfers: NA
Application Deadline: 1 Mar
Mean SAT: NA
Mean ACT: NA
Middle 50% SAT range: V 570-670, M 550-640
Middle 50% ACT range: 25-29
3 Most popular majors: human ecology, marine biology, arts and design
Retention: 89%
Graduation rate: 61%
On-campus housing: NA
Fraternities: NA
Sororities: NA
Library: 35,000 volumes
Tuition and Fees: $22,469
Room and Board: $6,087
Financial aid, first-year: NA
Varsity or Club Athletes: NA
Early Decision or Early Action Acceptance Rate: NA

In 1969 a bunch of Harvard grads got together and decided that people would benefit by learning to understand the importance of how humans interact with their social and natural environments. The interdisciplinary approach they drew up boiled everything down to what they called Human Ecology. They chose the picturesque little seaside town of Bar Harbor, Maine, as the site for their project. Soon enough, they had created a small school of extraordinary opportunities that challenged students to rethink their roles in the world.

And the Meaning of Life Is . . .

Before graduation, every College of the Atlantic (COA) student is required to produce a thesis that answers the question "What is human ecology?" Human Ecology, the sole major at COA, introduces students to an interdisciplinary approach to defining the relationship between humans and the natural environment. Yes, it's a big topic to tackle, but when you are taking classes like "Agro-ecology of the Yucatan," "The Aesthetics of Violence," and "Shelter: Humans, Landscape and the Built Environment," somehow the answer tends to work itself out.

Although some struggle to find their area of focus, most say that COA "doesn't box you in with a major." Students can switch their focuses within the Human Ecology major. One senior reported that she had switched her focus from environmental law to Latin American studies to a pre-veterinary school track. However, with a student body of approximately 275 and faculty of approximately 30, COA is a "hard place to specialize when there is one professor who *is* the math department and another who *is* the philosophy department," according to one third-year student. The 55 classes offered per trimester also quickly fill up to their average limit of 18. Some students find it frustrating that the small school may not offer classes within their particular interest.

In turn, COA encourages students to pursue independent studies. One student explained, "If you're motivated, good, if not, you might have a hard time here. For example, most of my work in the last year and a half has been independent, outside of class. I did an internship, then a group study, followed by a residency (the equivalent of three interconnected independent studies), and when I get back from Yucatan I'm going to do my senior project." Graduation requirements also call for students to take time off from campus to do an internship.

On average, students take three classes per trimester—"four can be a lot." The workload focuses on class presentations and "intense" papers, as opposed to exams. A 9:1 student faculty ratio means that students get individual attention and know their professors well—everyone is on a first-name basis!

Classes also make use of research resources that include Mt. Desert Rock and Great Duck Island Lighthouses, Mt. Desert Island Biological Laboratory, Jackson Laboratory, a weather station, and a Global Monitoring System. "We may, for example, dissect whales or seals found on the coast and determine the cause of death," explains one student.

Housing: Converted Mansions, but Limited Space

COA guarantees housing, usually singles, for first-years only. The three-level horseshoe-shaped Blair-Tyson Dorm houses about 40 students. Around six to eight students share a kitchen and a bathroom, that features recycled toilet paper and no stalls! Seafox, a converted mansion, is "supposedly" substance-free, but really just a more quiet dorm of 12 students with spectacular views of the ocean. RAs are pretty easy-going about marijuana and alcohol and even bring their first-years to off-campus parties to bond with upperclassmen. One RA admitted, "I'm pretty loose about it. Although if someone is having a problem, I'd certainly confront him about it."

Most upperclassmen envy the first-years who get to stay on campus. "I had a blast!" claimed a former Blair-Tyson dweller. "But there's not enough room for us, which is a bummer." Upperclassmen find apartments in town about five minutes away or in more remote locations reached by bike or car.

The Grub—A Vegan's Paradise

The environmentally-conscious student body enjoys top-ranked cooking at its sole dining hall Take-a-Break, or TAB in local lingo. In 2002, the PETA (People for the Ethical Treatment of Animals) ranked TAB first out of 1,200 college dining halls for its vegetarian and vegan fare and gave it the privileged title of "Veggie Valedictorian." "The worst thing about the dining hall is its dining hours: dinner between 5:30 and 6:30 is kind of ridiculous," complained one student. Also, no meals are served on the weekends, so students make use of the many on-campus kitchens.

The food is all organic and mostly from local farms, including the COA's own Beech Hill Farm where students can participate in the work-study program or volunteer. All waste is disposed of in the school's compost garden. Being on the ocean, TAB features a lot of fresh seafood. "Basically, it's not McDonald's, so don't come looking for it," affirmed one senior.

The Weekend Chill

The illegal substance of choice is reportedly marijuana, "unsurprising" for the "chill" school that enrolls many "hippied-out" students. As opposed to hard liquor, beer is the choice beverage. "My buddies and I might throw back a couple of beers, but we don't often get rip-roaring drunk," reported a third-year student. Another student warned, "There are no crazy discos or mad party places, so if that's what you're looking for you might have a hard time here. It is Maine, after all." Students claim that hard drugs are pretty rare.

Because there are no Wednesday classes (due to Student Government meetings), "there are two weekends, Tuesday nights and Friday and Saturday nights." The scene starts, according to one student, "ridiculously early! Things get started around 8:00 and end by 11:30 or 12:00." Parties are held mainly at upperclassmen residences. The Thirsty Whale, Little Anthony's, and Nakorn Thai are popular town bars. "Only really good IDs work," complained one student about the strict drinking policy.

As for the dating scene, news travels fast. One senior lamented her days as first-year, when she "may have made one too many 'mistakes' that I couldn't escape. I saw them around nearly every day." Some students admit COA is a hard place to date because there are not a lot of new people to meet around. But the small size "makes random hookups a lot less random." COA is also very tolerant and accepting of homosexual relationships. Reportedly, "lesbians are usually more open than gay males."

Students Take Charge

The student government at COA is a remarkably powerful body. It has significant say in all major decisions of the school. Students even attend Trustee meetings. Classes do not meet on Wednesdays to accommodate Student Government committee meetings in which most students participate. Additionally, at 1 P.M. every Wednesday an All College Meeting to which all student organizations and committees report takes place. One student complains however, "It's always the same people that show up and, for the most part, say the same things, so reaching common decisions has less to do with compromise and more with tiring your opponent."

"I would *not* come here if I were a Republican."

The Student Activity Committee, a branch of the student government, brings about two or three bands per term to perform in TAB. The committee also sponsors coffeehouses, weekly Open Mike nights, the Winter Carnival, and Earth Day.

For the Outdoorsman in You

COA sports teams are completely nonexistent. But students are serious about outdoor activities, rain or shine. First-years pile all the essentials—boots, bikes, backpacks, cross-country skis, you name it—into the family car when they first arrive. With Acadia National Park in COA's backyard, students can be found scaling the island's mountains (at least ten!) on weekends and have often summited them all by graduation. Students have free passes to the local YMCA, can explore the miles of bike trails, catch a free whale-watching ride with the Allied Whale (a program for sea-mammal study and saving), or sit on the dock with their toes in the water and watch the sailboats float by.

Winter term is known as the trimester for hard work because sub-zero temperatures supposedly keep people inside. This hibernation is overstated, claimed one student. Even when Bar Harbor shuts down at the end of tourist season, COA students are still recreating outdoors with cross-country skiing, snowshoeing, Broomball, and even midnight dips in the ocean. With all these activities, TV is reportedly "*not* a big pastime." At COA, something like the campus tree swing *is* a big attraction.

Who You'll Meet

It may be telling about the kinds of people at COA that Earth Day is "the only day that we actually get off." COA attracts a certain kind of student. One student described the typical student as "someone who smells like tea-tree oil, has dreadlocks, wears Birkenstocks, and is environmentally-aware, politically-conscious, outdoorsy, pretty athletic, and earthy." Oh, and liberal. "There are maybe three Republicans here," warned one student, "I would *not* come here if I were a Republican." Although the school is often stereotyped, many students admit surprise at the diversity of opinion. One third-year student remarks, "I wasn't expecting anyone to challenge me." Another student determined the "dirty hippie" population to be less than a quarter of the school.

Students are generally from a middle-upper-class socioeconomic background, and though a substantial portion of the student body hails from Maine, students come from all over the United States. For such a small school, COA boasts a significant number of international students who are attracted by the special full scholarship package as well as the uniqueness of the school. In one student's words, "COA students usually have really strong beliefs about a lot of things, and like to voice them. I guess another way to look at it is that if you took the staple "weird kids" from any high school, most of them would fit in just fine at COA." *—Baily Blair*

FYI

If you come to COA you'd better bring: "a Nalgene, a backpack, and long johns."

What is a typical weekend schedule? "Go for a hike, do some reading, chill with friends, and lay low."

If I could change one thing about COA, I'd "move it to the tropics or a big city."

Three things every student should do before graduating are "join the Yucatan Program, go for a swim at Sand Beach on a night in January, and summit all the mountains on the island."

University of Maine / Orono

Address: 168 College Avenue; Orono, ME 04469
Phone: 877-486-2364
E-mail address: um-admit@maine.edu
Web site URL: www.umaine.edu
Founded: 1865
Private or Public: public
Religious affiliation: none
Location: rural
Undergraduate enrollment: 8,817
Total enrollment: NA
Percent Male/Female: 48%/52%
Percent Minority: 6%
Percent African-American: 1%
Percent Asian: 1%
Percent Hispanic: 1%
Percent Native-American: 2%
Percent in-state/out of state: 86%/14%
Percent Pub HS: NA
Number of Applicants: 5,249
Percent Accepted: 79%
Percent Accepted who enroll: 43%
Entering: 1,764
Transfers: 532
Application Deadline: rolling
Mean SAT: NA
Mean ACT: NA
Middle 50% SAT range: V 480-590, M 490-610
Middle 50% ACT range: 20-26
3 Most popular majors: education, engineering, business
Retention: 79%
Graduation rate: 49%
On-campus housing: 43%
Fraternities: NA
Sororities: NA
Library: 851,736 volumes
Tuition and Fees: $5,950 in; $14,650 out
Room and Board: $6,166
Financial aid, first-year: 75%
Varsity or Club Athletes: 7%
Early Decision or Early Action Acceptance Rate: NA

It is cold during the winter in Maine. But the arctic temperatures don't seem to bother the students at the University of Maine in Orono. In fact, they actively seek it out. Whether they are braving the chill outside by walking through the campus's extensive, forested grounds, or perhaps frosting their breath while screaming for their beloved hockey team in the Alfond Arena, UMO students know how to have fun . . . while wearing ski jackets.

"Maine" Focus = Academics

UMO students are adamant in proclaiming "this isn't the party school everyone thinks it is." In fact, UMO offers an extensive and rewarding honors program and actively seeks matriculation from the brightest high school students in the state. Students applying to University of Maine must choose between its five colleges: liberal arts and sciences, engineering, education and human development, and the natural sciences: forestry and agriculture. An early concentration on career-based majors demands both important decisions and hard work from the student body. Each school maintains its own specific requirements, but there is a set of university-wide core requirements including basic courses in English and math. Engineering is "by far the hardest school" many students reported, whereas the classes in the Education Department are rumored to be less demanding. Entering freshmen have the opportunity to enroll in the Academic and Career Exploration Program (ACE) instead of one of the baccalaureate degree colleges at the university. ACE allows students to explore the entire system for one year before narrowing their area of focus. ACE kids are also, as one student noted, "more likely to have a close relationship with their academic advisor." This same student lamented the fact that regular, department-based advisors at UMO are "distant" and "basically there to sign your schedule."

Of the general classes, "Human Sexuality" is known as the "go-to class" and is one of the biggest classes, with a headcount of about 350. Other than large general requirement classes, class size at University of Maine is reported to be small—"about 35 kids per class," reported one student. The professors enjoy a good reputation, and one student stressed that one must "try to develop relationships with the professors, not only as teacher to student, but as friend to friend. It is possible here but professors don't usually seek students out." While the professors receive passing grades from the students (and hopefully vice versa), the system for registering classes is reported to stressful for many students, especially freshmen. Upperclassmen receive priority in signing up for classes through either an online server or over the phone, and one freshman reported he "stay[ed] up all night to try to get the classes that [he] wanted. It was really frustrating and I feel that freshmen are left with little choice."

Grin and Bear It

The hockey team, the Black Bears, is a source of campus and state pride for all those who attend the games. With two national championships under their belts, (in '93 and '99), it is no wonder that UMO students keep coming to the rink in droves. The mischievous mascot Bananas the Bear is an adoring fan present at all UMO games and, to present an odd couple, so is the "Master of Horror" Stephen King. While they are physically in separate spheres at the games, King in his private box and Bananas on the sidelines egging on the massive crowd, both are in fact subject of popular legends. King is perhaps the university's most illustrious alumnus, having graduated with a degree in English from UMO in 1970 (just three years before the publication of *Carrie* made him famous.) He remains a visible presence on campus often giving lectures or donating money to various school and area organizations.

"Your community *is* here, but it's up to you to find it."

Bananas the Bear, although not a best-selling author, is famous in his own right. A popular legend states that the original mascot was a live black bear cub kept in one of the fraternity houses' basements when not making appearances at sporting events. The live bear, though, had to be replaced by a costumed performer after attacking the University of Connecticut husky at a basketball game.

Though hockey by far has the most loyal fan-base, the entire athletic department at UMO is very strong. Basketball is extremely popular, and the football team has improved greatly in the last couple of years. But UMO students don't spend all their time cheering from the sidelines. Whether it is intramural sports, music, drama, or even animation, UMO students are passionate about what they do outside the classroom. As one student said, "your own community *is* here, but it's up to you to find it." There are clubs and organizations to foster the interests of any and all students. Students are also known to take their own initiative and start their own interest groups. Recently, a group of students created "Cinefi" an organization that will host weekly screenings of independent and foreign films and has planned collaboration with various cultural groups in order to "unify students" using this particular medium. Likewise, there are sporting clubs, political organizations, religious groups, and, in true Maine fashion, even a "Woodsmen Team."

No Parking Anytime

UMO students come from all over . . . all over the state of Maine, that is. An overwhelming majority of students come from within the state, and they bring their cars and pick-up trucks with them. The campus is fairly large and spread out, as is the town of Orono. Bangor, a neighboring city, about a 10-minute drive away, is often a destination for students seeking escape from the isolated yet idyllic campus. Many students use their cars to work in various stores, restaurants, and bars in Bangor, or to simply go home for the weekend. Add up all these factors and consider the roughly 11,000 students who attend the university and you have a big problem with a capital "P": Parking. Public Safety is notorious for giving out parking tickets, and many students complain that there is simply not enough room for the multitude of cars around the campus. Public Safety at UMO can be rest-assured that all those scowls are simply for the tickets, as many students praise them on other, perhaps more important, facets of their jobs. The campus, once regarded as dangerous, has been greatly improved in terms of safety in recent years. Improvements include better lighting along pathways and also a walking escort service for students, though apprehensions remain as one female student confessed that she "wouldn't walk anywhere alone at night."

A New Union

The campus itself boasts a large number of facilities designed to enhance the student experience. Most of the dorms are said to be in "fair condition" and ones located on "the hill top," equipped with private bathrooms, are rumored to be the best. Recently, a new student union was built that houses recreational rooms, computer clusters, study areas, and a post office. Dining halls, known as "Commons," are rumored to be social centers—and the students gathered aren't even complaining about the food! While the cafeteria food is said to be "just plain cafeteria food" with "lots of cereal," students praise the dining options they are able to entertain. Students are able to purchase food from small stores located around campus, cafes, and even local restaurants and delivery services by using a "Maine Card" through which all expenses are charged to your account. Students praise the "Maine Card" yet seasoned delivery-fans warn of hidden costs demanded by local restaurants. Local eateries such as the Market Café, locally famous Pat's Pizza, and Margarita's (which doubles as a watering-hole) welcome students and compete with popular chains located in Bangor such as Olive Garden and, for those on a typical student budget, Taco Bell and Pizza Hut.

"Fill the Steins to Dear Old Maine"

Any school that references beer in its fight song has got to be a good time. UMO students would agree and indeed fill their beer mugs at frat parties and off-campus gatherings alike. The Greek system at UMO is quite strong, with frats such as SAE and Sigma Nu ruling the on-campus scene. Off-campus entertainment is also an enticing option for students, and clubs such as Ushuia's in Orono and various bars and pubs in Bangor draw many UMO students out on the weekends. While alcohol runs freely in the minds of UMO students, it does not run as freely on campus. Public Safety has been "really cracking down on underage drinking," one student noted.

UMO students enjoy the reputation of being a "relaxed and friendly community." While many students stated that they wished for a more diverse student body, others admitted that the campus was "pretty much as diverse as it gets in rural Maine." Due to its large and spread out student body (as many upperclassmen opt to live in off-campus housing after freshman year), one UMO student stated that he "could go for a day without seeing anyone [he] knew and got lonely," only to "see all my friends all over the place the next day."

UMO students have succeeded in creating an esteemed place of learning and living where individuals are excited to be a part of a club, a class, or simply a cheering crowd. Students, while happy with many aspects of the beautiful campus and strong classes, constantly strive to make UMO personally challenging and fulfilling all at once. The sense of community is reinforced by the actions of the bright, committed student body. One only has to attend a Black Bears game to view the enthusiasm of this strong community. —*Marisa Benoit*

FYI

If you come to the University of Maine, you better bring "a truck."

What is the typical weekend schedule? "Friday night, stay out doing bad things. Saturday, get up at 2 P.M. and go out again. Then on Sunday, you better sleep."

If I could change one thing about University of Maine I would "make it closer to the ocean and to Acadia National Park."

Three things every student at University of Maine should do before graduating are "go to a UMO vs. UNH (University of New Hampshire) hockey game, eat Pat's Pizza, and live in the dorms."

Maryland

Goucher College

Address: 1021 Dulaney Valley Road; Baltimore, MD 21204
Phone: 410-337-6200
E-mail address: admissions@goucher.edu
Web site URL: www.goucher.edu
Founded: 1885
Private or Public: private
Religious affiliation: none
Location: suburban
Undergraduate enrollment: 1,270
Total enrollment: NA
Percent Male/Female: 30%/70%
Percent Minority: 14%
Percent African-American: 6%
Percent Asian: 2%
Percent Hispanic: 2%
Percent Native-American: 1%
Percent in-state/out of state: 38%/62%
Percent Pub HS: 63%
Number of Applicants: 2,596
Percent Accepted: 68%
Percent Accepted who enroll: 21%
Entering: 365
Transfers: 22
Application Deadline: 1 Feb
Mean SAT: NA
Mean ACT: NA
Middle 50% SAT range: V 540-650, M 520-640
Middle 50% ACT range: 22-28
3 Most popular majors: education, psychology, English
Retention: 79%
Graduation rate: 68%
On-campus housing: 62%
Fraternities: NA
Sororities: NA
Library: 303,364 volumes
Tuition and Fees: $24,450
Room and Board: $8,200
Financial aid, first-year: 57%
Varsity or Club Athletes: 20%
Early Decision or Early Action Acceptance Rate: EA 76%

For students who enjoy both the beauty of a hilly campus and the convenience and excitement of living in a city, Goucher College may be the perfect school. A small liberal arts college located about eight miles from the center of Baltimore and an hour from Washington, D.C., Goucher is secluded by woods from the city, but close enough so that students have easy access to what city life has to offer. One student described the verdant, wooded campus as "absolutely beautiful . . . with the ability to escape if small campus life gets too overwhelming." With a relatively small student body of approximately 1,200 students, Goucher is able to provide a close-knit community with an ideal place to live and learn.

Small Classes, Better Learning

Although students at Goucher have to fulfill a number of requirements, many agree that this is essential for a well-rounded education. All students are expected to complete at least three semesters of a foreign language or test out of the requirement by showing proficiency on a placement exam. In addition, students must take one semester each of math, social science, a natural science, art, and two different half-semester physical education classes. Goucher students must also demonstrate "writing proficiency" and "computer proficiency in major" prior to graduation. Exploring New Frontiers is a one-course program that all freshmen must participate in. Since all Frontiers classes meet at the same time and all papers are due at the same time, the program provides an opportunity for the freshman to bond. In order to help students make the adjustments to college life, freshmen are also required to take a non-credit course, "Wellness and Transitions." It is more of a discussion course than a class, and topics include alcohol, sex, date rape, and other major issues on-campus. Consisting of about 15 to 20 freshman, the class meets three times a week for 50-minute intervals. Though some students complain about this requirement, many have found it beneficial in the end because it encourages student bonding and student awareness.

Perhaps one of the more enjoyable and beneficial requirements is the "off-campus experience," which can be satisfied by either studying abroad or obtaining an internship within a student's major. Students have the opportunity to participate in an exchange program with Exeter, a university in England, and one student per class is given a scholarship to study at Oxford for a year. Many students choose to intern in Washington or Baltimore as well as in the local community.

At this liberal arts school, learning takes place in an intimate environment where students call their professors by their first names. One student commented, "I've really been surprised about how much I enjoy the small classes and really getting to know your professor." Although some introductory courses or required courses may have up to 50 or 70 students, class sizes tend to hover around 15 students for most courses. As one student said, "They are just big enough so there is a diverse amount of people in the class, but small enough that you can feel comfortable expressing your views and opinions." Although there are no teaching assistants at Goucher, there are supplementary instructors (SIs)—undergrads who have already taken the class and done well.

"The people are great and the campus is beautiful. I would recommend this school to anyone."

The workload at Goucher is described as "steady," but the student's major and course selection plays a major role in this. Pre-med, and natural science majors are known for being relatively tough, whereas the communications and management majors give students a little more free time. Other popular majors include English, dance, and psychology. Some of the easier courses at Goucher include Math 100 ("Math for Plants") and several of the education courses (although they can be time consuming). Cell biology and expository writing, on the other hand, are "notoriously difficult." For students with a strong desire to learn, Goucher boasts an Honors college, the option to create your own major, and the 3 + 2 engineering program with nearby Johns Hopkins University. In the words of one satisfied student, "The academics are phenomenal at Goucher. Students should feel prepared to go out into the world if they used the education to the best of their abilities."

No Greeks at Goucher

When Goucher students are not busy studying, they have no trouble finding fun and interesting ways to occupy their time. One student remarked, "It is incredibly easy to get involved in activities, events and organizations on this campus. Therefore, it is incredibly easy to meet people." At Goucher, the students create a close community with no big divisions between classes. Although self-segregation and cliques exist on campus, the small size and liberal attitude of the school diminish the importance of cliques. One student remarked, "the population is very liberal and open-minded, which is really nice . . . although I wish there were minority students." Goucher students dress casually, with typical clothing ranging "from pajamas to Banana Republic."

Although the school is only 30 percent male, one girl says "I don't think it's a problem because there are plenty of other campuses around here and there are plenty of ways to meet people." Hanging out on campus, stopping by local malls and movie theatres, and visiting nearby schools such as John Hopkins University, Towson State, Loyola, and Morgan State are all popular options among Goucher students. Many are glad that there is no Greek system at the college, but those who are into frat parties can easily find them on neighboring campuses. On the weekends, students who have cars may head off to Washington, D.C., Annapolis, or Fells Point for concerts, mini-golfing, hiking, clubbing, bars, shopping, or just getting off campus for a little while. Other students have just as much fun hanging out in people's rooms on campus, having interesting conversations, and renting movies. There is also a shuttle that transports students to and from Towson where they can go to another popular hangout, the Gopher Hole. Also known as the "G-Hole," this hangout is a non-alcoholic pub that shows movies, has an open mike, and hosts live bands.

Activities abound on campus, and students can get involved in groups such as the "Bowling Congregation," a game show club, and a belly dancing club. Several respected organizations are B-GLAD (a gay/lesbian alliance), UMOJA (an African alliance), Lotus (which promotes Asian Pacific enrichment), Hillel (a Jewish community), *The Quindecim* (the student newspaper), and a capella singing groups. One of the larger and more active groups on campus is CAUSE (Community Auxiliary Service), which provides volunteers for Habitat for Humanity, local soup kitchens, and Parents Anonymous, a child abuse prevention program. Another option is the Student Activities Association, which helps to plan and organize campus activities and events. Recent speakers on campus include Hillary Clinton and Dorothy Allison.

Get Into Goucher Day (GIG) is one of the biggest events of the year at Goucher. On GIG Day, which takes places in the spring semester, classes are cancelled and there is a big carnival with faculty, staff and community members all invited for "rides, food and a good time." Another campus-wide event is the Pumpkin Bowl, a day of friendly competition between dorms, which follows Spirit Week on the weekend before Halloween. Several semi-formal dances are planned during the year, including The Blind Date Ball and Gala.

Renovated Dorms

With all of the activities and studying that Goucher do, they need somewhere to catch up on their rest. As one student put it, "The rooms all over campus tend to be big." Some of the newly renovated dorms, such as the Heubeck dorms, have air conditioning and are considered to be the best. The Stimson dorms, on the other hand, are not nearly as nice and are affectionately referred to as "the Ghetto dorms." There are also foreign language dorms, non-smoking housing, and 24-hour quiet housing available to students. Goucher provides an RA system for every house, but students do not have to worry about overly strict RAs. "The RAs are usually understanding. They don't want to write you up, but they expect you to help them achieve that," commented one student. Approximately 15 percent of the students choose to live off campus, either at home or in nearby apartments.

Those who do not live on campus can choose whether or not they want to sign up for a school meal plan, which has been described as "expensive and mandatory" for students who live in campus housing. However, the dining facilities are "very clean, with great hours" and "something is always open." "There are lots of happy vegetarians at Goucher," said one student who wishes that there were some additional meat dishes. The Kosher dining hall is also "a huge plus." When students get tired of the dining halls, there are plenty of choices for food off campus, including Paper Moon Diner, which has "good food, great service and is a really cool looking place." Louie's Café, Bubba's Breakaway, and Golden Gate Noodle House are other popular places to eat. As one student summarized, "The food is great . . . I've eaten much worse and of course better, but it was better than I expected."

The Goucher community can enjoy numerous renovations that include air conditioning in the dorms, new academic buildings, a new student center, and expansion of the alumni house. In addition, Gopher Stadium, a huge athletic facility capable of seating 1200 people, opened in the fall of 2001. The most popular teams on campus are the soccer, basketball, and lacrosse teams. Athletic facilities are good and a decent number of students participate in intramural sports.

A School for Anyone

As one student concisely put it, "I love Goucher. The people are great and the campus is beautiful. I would recommend this school to anyone." With classes that "really get you to become open-minded," Goucher is the picture of a liberal arts college that is "too beautiful not to enjoy." —*Robert Wong*

FYI

If you come to Goucher, you'd better bring "a car!"

What is a typical weekend schedule? "Thursday night is hanging out with friends at parties. Fridays and Saturdays are the same type of thing, but Saturday is always big for those who have a car and can go to other colleges or head to Fell's Point."

If I could change one thing about Goucher, I'd "increase the lack of diversity among the students and faculty."

The three things that every student should do before graduating from Goucher are "get involved in extracurriculars, study abroad, and go camping in the woods."

Johns Hopkins University

Address: 3400 North Charles Street; Baltimore, MD 21218
Phone: 410-516-8171
E-mail address: gotojhu@jhu.edu
Web site URL: www.jhu.edu
Founded: 1876
Private or Public: private
Religious affiliation: none
Location: urban
Undergraduate enrollment: 5,524
Total enrollment: NA
Percent Male/Female: 52%/48%
Percent Minority: 33%
Percent African-American: 6%
Percent Asian: 17%
Percent Hispanic: 3%
Percent Native-American: 0%
Percent in-state/out of state: 22%/78%
Percent Pub HS: 68%
Number of Applicants: 8,932
Percent Accepted: 35%
Percent Accepted who enroll: 36%
Entering: 1,127
Transfers: 7
Application Deadline: 1 Jan
Mean SAT: NA
Mean ACT: NA
Middle 50% SAT range: V 620-730, M 660-760
Middle 50% ACT range: 27-31
3 Most popular majors: biomedical/medical engineering, international relations, biology
Retention: 96%
Graduation rate: 87%
On-campus housing: 54%
Fraternities: 18%
Sororities: 19%
Library: 3,509,413 volumes
Tuition and Fees: $28,730
Room and Board: $9,142
Financial aid, first-year: 44%
Varsity or Club Athletes: 25%
Early Decision or Early Action Acceptance Rate: ED 60%

Johns Hopkins University carries the ring of East coast academic prestige, without the elitist stigma of the Ivy League.

Academics

At Johns Hopkins, all undergraduates are placed into either the School of Arts and Sciences or the George William Carlyle Whiting School of Engineering. The engineering school is very selective and many of the students are also pre-med. Course requirements are minimal since there is no core curriculum, however, students are required to take humanities, science, and math courses. "It's easy finding the English classes for science majors and the science classes for English majors. They tell you in the course description," said one junior pre-med. While getting into the classes of choice is easy, class size is a problem for many of the entry-level courses. One senior engineering major commented, "I was frustrated with the lack of personal attention my first two years, but now I'm taking upper division courses which have as few as 15 in a class." One aspect of academics Johns Hopkins students aren't afraid to complain about is grading. With an average grade of a low B, students feel they work far harder for their grades than students at other schools that experience grade inflation.

Living It Up in Baltimore

All freshmen and sophomores are required to live on campus unless they move into a fraternity or sorority. These dorms are small and unattractive, but by no means unbearable. "The dorms aren't perfect but [the set-up] provides a large number of potential friends in close proximity," explained one freshman girl. Some dorms are segregated by gender, but many have co-ed floors. About half of the buildings are regular dorms, while the rest suites with bedrooms branching off of a central common room. After sophomore year, students must enter the "rent market," which offers a wide range of off-campus houses not too far from campus. The most coveted apartments are passed down to friends by graduating seniors. "All you have to do is make friends with the seniors in the nice apartments," said one shameless junior. Most students claim the neighborhood is safe but still advise against living too far away. Muggings are not common, and the university provides campus security known as "Hop-Cops" to protect students.

"The weekends are great, but people are too serious mid-week."

The dining on campus does not receive rave reviews. "It's like eating at a five-star restaurant . . . Except the opposite," joked one jaded boy. Busy schedules make the dining experience eat-and-run for most students. But once liberated from the grasp of institutional dining, students discover that Baltimore presents a number of appetizing meal options.

Forget the Books

The majority of students are heavily involved in one or more extracurricular activity. These range from community service groups and a cappella groups to intramural and club sports. Varsity sports are somewhat low key given the Division III status of Hopkins. Lacrosse, however, the sole Division I sport, does draw a crowd. Up to four thousand students and local fans flock to the stands and sidelines to cheer on the winning team, which placed 2nd at the NCAAs last year. The student body shows a lot of support and the home games are always big social events. Besides sports and interest groups on campus, many students like to get off campus on the weekend and explore downtown Baltimore. Besides the nightlife, Oriels stadium provides a number of professional sporting events and concerts. Annapolis is also a fun day trip away for shopping and seeing men in uniform.

Pre-Meds Can Party Too

It is a common misnomer that schools with good academic reputations are lacking in the social realm. Indeed this is not the case at Johns Hopkins. Students describe a lively and social campus replete with a variety of weekend entertainment options. However many students think people are too academically focused the rest of the time. "The weekends are great, but people are too serious mid-week" said one freshman girl. The University helps out by sponsoring dances, concerts, and movie nights to bring students together in a safe environment. If this sounds tame, don't worry. "The frat parties are where it's at on the weekend," chimed one student. SAE and WaWa are the most popular, known for hosting outrageous parties like the foam party. Although the Greek scene does not dominate campus social life, frat row is the place to go on a Saturday night. One SAE sophomore boasted, "Rushing wasn't difficult. Everyone is out to make close friends and have a good time." Upper classmen not in the Greek system tend to go to parties at friends' apartments or to a strip of clubs and bars in downtown Baltimore known as "Fells Point." Other local colleges such as Layolla, Tawson, and Notre Dame of Maryland also party at Fell'\s Point. A more immediate hang out is PJ's Pub right near the dorms. And if you wake up next to a boy or girl after a late night, Peat's Diner is a must for breakfast.
—*Quinn Fitzgerald*

FYI

If you come to Johns Hopkins, you'd better bring "a calculator for the scary math and science classes, and something waterproof, like a bathing suit, for the foam parties."

A typical weekend schedule would consist of "working until 8:00, going to friend's house, visiting the local bars, then maybe out to Fells point for the clubs."

If I could change one thing about Johns Hopkins it would be to "make it more personable."

The three things you have to do before graduating are "go to Annapolis, eat at Peat's diner the morning after, and go to a Lacrosse game."

St. John's College

Address: PO Box 2800; Annapolis, MD 21404
Phone: 410-263-2371
E-mail address: admissions@sjca.edu
Web site URL: www.sjca.edu
Founded: 1696
Private or Public: private
Religious affiliation: none
Location: small city
Undergraduate enrollment: 477
Total enrollment: 537
Percent Male/Female: 55%/45%
Percent Minority: 8%
Percent African-American: 1%
Percent Asian: 3%
Percent Hispanic: 3%
Percent Native-American: 1%
Percent in-state/out of state: 15%/85%
Percent Pub HS: 68%
Number of Applicants: NA
Percent Accepted: 71%
Percent Accepted who enroll: NA
Entering: NA
Transfers: NA
Application Deadline: NA
Mean SAT: NA
Mean ACT: NA
Middle 50% SAT range: V 650-740, M 580-670
Middle 50% ACT range: NA
3 Most popular majors: no majors
Retention: NA
Graduation rate: 65%
On-campus housing: NA
Fraternities: NA
Sororities: NA
Library: 100,000 volumes
Tuition and Fees: $27,410
Room and Board: $6,970
Financial aid, first-year: NA
Varsity or Club Athletes: NA
Early Decision or Early Action Acceptance Rate: NA

"This school is a legend by itself. It is distinctly different," described one student. With a different purpose and a different method in education, St. John's, the third oldest college in the United States, has been teaching its students with the "St. John's method" since 1696.

Tutors and Fellow Students

St. John's has a different approach and a different language in education. The curriculum is "the Program," and the professors are "tutors." "We call our professors here 'tutors' because they guide us along a path as opposed to instructing us," explained a student. What makes the college different from others is its Program, which is based on the Great Books of Western Society. However, music, math, and science also constitute a major part of students' curricula. But, even math is taught through Great Books; "Reading Newton in the original text is how we learn calculus," described a student. The Great Books Program doesn't have any electives; it is all required: four years of mathematics, one-and-a-half years of Greek, one half-year of French, one half-year of Shakespearean poetry, one half-year of modern poetry, three years of Laboratory Science, one year of Music, four years of Seminar, one major essay at the end of each year, and one year of freshman chorus. All freshmen gather weekly to sing. However, there are also Preceptorials, or specialized classes on one particular work. Preceptorials can only be taken in junior and senior years, offering different subjects, from Aristotle to Joyce, Faulkner to William James.

No Grading

There are no tests and students' papers aren't graded. Students receive a grade for their work in a semester, which is a combination of papers and class. Class participation is considered "the quality and caliber of what one says, its tone, and how one treats confusion, difficulty in understanding himself and in others." Tutorials and Labs have around 14 students with one tutor, and seminars average about 20 students and two tutors. Students enjoy this method of education, though the reading load can be tremendous.

Everyone is called Mr. or Ms. in class, including the tutor. A student described the classes as "egalitarian," even with world-renowned tutors such as Eva Brann, Laurence Berns, A.P. David, and Joe Sachs. Also, the weekly Friday night lectures host visitors from philosophy departments of other schools such as Stanly Fish, Robert Pinsky, and Robert Fagles.

Students have a close relationship with their tutors: they play sports together, tutors are invited to student parties, and they have dinners together regularly. Students find the tutors interesting and "cool." One student noted that one of his seminar tutors was the first person to clone garlic. Even though all the classes have a tutor, some science and music courses also have assistants, who help with the technical set-up.

Older Students, Fewer Underage Problems

Parties are regularly organized and attended. The average student at St John's is older than at other colleges; therefore, underage drinking is less of a problem than elsewhere. However, underage drinking, if caught, is punished severely. Coffee-shop parties, which take place twice a month at the basement of McDowell hall, are very popular. The Great Hall, an 18th-century ballroom that doubles as the main classroom, hosts formal balls every month. Swing-dances, the Pink Triangle Society Cross-dress parties, and the annual Seducers and Corrupters party, make up a colorful social life for students. However, Lola's is probably the greatest theme party; a casino night. "There's live music, gambling (blackjack, poker, and roulette), dancing and a couple of bars. It's a great time. Some of our tutors will deal blackjack. It's a lot of fun," a student also describes Lola's; "We are allowed to hold this event because our school charter is older than that of the state of Maryland." Kegs are allowed on campus. The Senior Prank, which is based on kidnapping students from class and spending the evening drinking, is popular among students.

Reality Bites

Croquet Weekend, of Sports Illustrated and National Public Radio fame, is the weekend of the annual croquet match against the naval academy. A coffee shop party takes place the previous night. The day of the match itself is "an all-day lawn party with people wearing sun dresses and linen suits." A cotillion dance takes place after the match where Godiva chocolates with the St. John's seal on them are served with champagne. A student-run group, Reality, whose central activity is Reality Weekend, organizes Lola's, Croquet Day, and the coffee-shop parties. Juniors organize Reality Weekend as a celebration for graduating seniors. Beer, live music, a three-day film festival, and Spartan Madball are the key features of the Reality weekend. Rules of Spartan Madball are no shoes, no weapons, and no vehicles. The goal is to run the ball through the goal on a field with no boundaries. Spartan Madball, played once a year, resembles rugby.

Ideas Are What Counts

Even though there are some drawbacks of living in such a small community, St. John's students enjoy it. It is easy to get to know people since everyone is open and eager in discussing and sharing opinions. But, racially and ethnically, the student body is very homogeneous. "Our joke is that you can describe a third of the student body by saying 'oh, he's a tall, skinny, white guy.' But that matters very little, since the ideas are what count, and there is a huge range of ideas people here hold," is how one student described his peers. Another student related that even when they are drunk, students' discussion subject is most probably Aristotle.

"Reading Newton in the original text is how we learn calculus."

Most upperclassmen live off campus. All freshmen are required to live on campus, and the floors are single-sex except for two dorms on campus. "The Resident Assistants' main goal is to take care of you, not be a policeman." Humphreys, a freshman dorm, is well liked and Chase-Stone, an upper-class dorm, with its hardwood floors and high ceilings is also highly desirable. Another freshman dorm is Randall—famous for its clanking pipes and small rooms. Paca-Carroll is the "quiet dorm."

Historic Grounds

McDowell Hall, the main classroom building, is an 18th century colonial Governor's mansion. Lafayette danced in the Great Hall of McDowell Hall when he visited Annapolis after the American Revolution. The Liberty Tree on the front campus, which was cut down after Hurricane Floyd, was the meeting place for the Sons of Liberty of Maryland of the American Revolution. Humphreys Hall was a hospital and a morgue, and Pinkney Hall was a barracks during the Civil War. Much more recently built is the gym that houses a suspended track around the ceiling.

Overall, the campus is small and is characterized by its colonial red brick buildings. It is a safe campus, situated in a safe city, Annapolis. The quad is the place to meet on lazy Sundays. Even though there are some eating-out options in Annapolis, DC and Baltimore offer superior restaurants.

Students find the food on campus moderate. There are three meal plans: five, 14, or 21 meals per week and it is mandatory to be enrolled in one of them. The dining hall offers many options to vegetarian students. The Little Campus, now closed, was students' eat-out choice for over 30 years. Now, Harry Browne's is their new preference. Student also enjoy sushi at Nikko or Joss.

The Sports Triangle

People are engaged in many activities on campus; therefore, most stay in Annapolis rather than go to DC or to Baltimore. Some examples of popular student groups include Students in Project Politae work for Habitat for Humanity, St. John's Chorus sings, the elected Delegate Council distributes funds to student activities, and the Student Committee on Instruction discusses Program issues. Mabel the Swimming Wonder Monkey is a different organization that "watches and heckles bad movies." Melee is another organization where students are involved with medieval arts and crafts as well as rubber sword fighting.

Fencing, Crew, and Croquet are the only three varsity sports of the college, and students are proud of their success, and were the National Intercollegiate Croquet Champions for the third year in a row in 2000. All other sports are played as intramurals. Nearby golf courts and a swimming pool are available to students.

Students are proud to be a part of the St. John's tradition as well as of its history and are happy to study in a unique educational environment. "St. John's is totally incomparable. This place is unique, and it is what I always wanted." —*Yakut Seyhanli*

FYI

If you come to St. John's, you'd better bring "a formal dress. The formal dances and Croquet Weekend all require cotillion-style attire."

What is the typical weekend schedule? "Weekends are about relaxing. The campus is small enough that you pretty much recognize most people. That makes partying less important because you're not meeting new people unless you get off campus."

If I could change one thing about St. John's, I'd change "the fact that news travels fast! Everyone knows all the gossip on everyone else."

Three things that every student at St. John's should do before graduating are "go to a Coffee-shop party, pick a fight in Melee club and listen to a senior oral."

United States Naval Academy

Address: 121 Blake Road; Annapolis, MD 21402
Phone: 410-293-4361
E-mail address: webmail@gwmail.usna.edu
Web site URL: www.usna.edu
Founded: 1846
Private or Public: public
Religious affiliation: none
Location: small city
Undergraduate enrollment: 4,309
Total enrollment: NA
Percent Male/Female: 85%/15%
Percent Minority: 21%
Percent African-American: 6%
Percent Asian: 4%
Percent Hispanic: 8%
Percent Native-American: 1%
Percent in-state/out of state: 4%/96%
Percent Pub HS: 67%
Number of Applicants: 12,331
Percent Accepted: 12%
Percent Accepted who enroll: 83%
Entering: 1,214
Transfers: NA
Application Deadline: 1 Mar
Mean SAT: NA
Mean ACT: NA
Middle 50% SAT range: V 530-640, M 560-670
Middle 50% ACT range: NA
3 Most popular majors: economics, political science, systems engineering
Retention: 95%
Graduation rate: 86%
On-campus housing: 100%
Fraternities: NA
Sororities: NA
Library: 631,988 volumes
Tuition and Fees: none
Room and Board: none
Financial aid, first-year: NA
Varsity or Club Athletes: 36%
Early Decision or Early Action Acceptance Rate: NA

In 1845, the U.S. Naval Academy was established in Annapolis by the Secretary of the Navy George Bancroft. Today, over 4,000 "middies," or midshipmen, attend the Academy (which is located on the Severn River in Annapolis, Maryland), in preparation to become professional officers in the U.S. Navy and Marine Corps. In addition to free tuition, room and board, and medical and dental care, middies get $600 a month from which certain benefits are deducted. The USNA is truly unlike any other college. Said one senior, "I've met the most incredible people here and challenged myself beyond what I could have at any other college."

Major Discipline

Students at the Naval Academy are pushed to their limits not only in the physical sense, but also in academia. "They say a 3.0 here is like a 4.0 at a civilian college," noted one student. "It's tough here. But I do know people with 4.0s." The workload is very heavy and in addition to studying, middies are required to attend parades, training evolutions, special meals, pep rallies, and briefs, among other mandatory duties.

Students report that the hardest courses at the USNA are in the engineering and chemistry departments and the easiest are the ones taken freshman year, such as Naval Leadership. Although this school is known as a "conservative military school," it offers a variety of liberal arts courses as well. One junior, or "second-class middie," raved about her American Film and Society class where she had the opportunity to learn about history in the context of films produced in the 1930s.

The student-faculty ratio is among the best in the nation. "It's great when we need to talk to our professors. They will go out of their way to teach an extra study session at 7 in the evening before the day of a test just to make sure we succeed," remarked one "youngster" (sophomore). Most professors are either Ph.D. recipients or military officers and teach courses using textbooks they have written. "Many of the professors are well-published and have worked some pretty high-profile jobs." For example, in recent years the academy has had astronauts teaching in the Aeronautical Engineering Department.

When Will We Get Liberty?

It's thumbs down for alcohol at the Naval Academy. "You don't ever want to get caught drinking. There is absolutely no alcohol allowed in the dorms." Middies are expected to follow a strict honor code that applies to both their academic and personal lives. Social life at the USNA is pretty limited and students only have free time, or "liberty," on the weekends to venture out into the nearby towns or see their sponsor families—families in the Annapolis area who provide a surrogate home to middies during their four-year stay at the Academy.

The rules for liberty are very strict. According to class rank, middies will get a certain amount of time for liberty each weekend. Freshmen (plebes) have from 10:15 A.M. to 10:00 P.M. on Saturday, at which time they have to come back for "TAPS"—a process to make sure all middies are back on campus. Sophomores (youngsters) have from 10:15 A.M. Saturday to 1:00 A.M. on Sunday and then 8:15 A.M. to 8:00 P.M. on Sunday. Juniors (second class) have from their last military obligation until midnight on Friday, 10:15 A.M. Saturday to 1:00 A.M. on Sunday, then 8:15 A.M. to 8:00 P.M. on Sunday. Seniors (firsties) have the whole weekend unless they have watch or there is a home football game. In addition, students get overnight passes called "weekends." Youngsters get three, second classmen get five, and firsties get an unlimited number.

With less than 20 percent of its students being female, the "dating options are slightly limited for the guys," said one middy. Freshmen are not allowed to date upperclassmen and inter-company dating is also prohibited. "People date, but it's not popular to date within the school." According to one firstie, "We still have dances and concerts every once in a while with large turnouts from colleges all over Maryland. For once you feel like you're at a normal college."

The typical middy is a "4.0 high school student who did at least one sport and was a student-body leader," said one aerospace engineering major. Each middy is required to wear a uniform at all times. All 50 states and almost 20 foreign countries are represented by the student body. Because students are nominated for the Academy by the Senators and Congressmen from their home state, the geographic demography at the USNA is similar to that of the population breakdown in the United States as a whole.

As far as extracurriculars go, the multitude is amazing. Only at an institution like the Naval Academy could someone obtain a "private pilot's license and study astronomy." Among the other activities available are the Glee Club, Flying Club, Orchestra, Campus Crusade for Christ, as well as different intramural sports.

Beat Army!

There's no doubt that the largest sporting event for the USNA is the Army/Navy football game. Although all football games are required for middies, this is where they are the most spirited. During "Beat Army" week, when the football team plays rival West Point's United States Military Academy, "upperclassmen mix you a mystery drink filled with stuff like Bleu Cheese and Tabasco Sauce and you have to down it at a meal." Although the Naval Academy hasn't won any major championships in its recent history, they have won the past two football games against Army—which most consider just as important as a winning record.

> **"The caliber of men and women who come out of here is unmatched."**

An important part of attending the Academy is the physical fitness requirement for all midshipmen. "Everyone is required to play an intramural sport if they are not on a varsity sports team," explained one Plebe. The general consensus is that the sports facilities are decent, but not great. The more popular sports at the USNA are lacrosse, basketball, and soccer. For those who are not interested in varsity sports, club sports such as rugby, judo, powerlifting, and boxing are available.

Living with History

The campus is "modern, but mixed with some Gothic architecture." Most of the buildings on campus have been around since the Civil War, with some from even further back. All of the buildings have been remodeled on the inside and historically restored on the outside. While walking on "the yard," one will also notice many monuments. There have been a few recent additions such as the Glenn Warner Soccer Facility. "We have five multifunction gyms and one of the few nuclear labs in the world. Our science centers make up some of the most advanced centers in the country and in the Department of Defense," remarked one student.

Middies are all required to live on campus in the same dorm building called Bancroft Hall, also known as "Mother B." Bancroft Hall is split up into 30 company areas, each with its own identity. Although floors are co-ed, bathrooms are single-sex. Each student is provided with a personal computer and has a connection to a campus-wide data network. Yet there are many restrictions to life in Mother B. One plebe complained, "I wish they'd let us listen to the radio!"

Safety is not an issue at this school. "We have Marine guards at every gate and over 4,000 active duty sailors and marines living with us," explained one youngster. Besides an occasional sexual harassment incident, middies agree that the campus is very safe.

At a place like the Naval Academy, one needs all the energy possible to endure the "challenges faced every day." Middies eat together in "King Hall," where meals are served at the same time for all 4,000 students. Dinner is "buffet style" every night except on Wednesdays, when they have "sit-down meals and eat better food like lobster, crab, and fried chicken." Overall the Academy serves "very well-rounded meals with lots of options for other dietary needs. I think the food is exceptional."

One for Our Country

"The caliber of men and women who come out of here is unmatched," stated one middy. Not everyone can survive at this institution. Only those who are "physically, mentally, and emotionally prepared can endure the challenges at the Naval Academy." Traditions at this school dating back to the late 1800s still prevail today and make it even more unique than other colleges in the country. "If a girl puts on a midshipman's cover, the midshipman is required to give her a kiss. Another tradition occurs at the end of each parade season, where the freshmen throw the company commander in full uniform into the Severn River," laughed one student. When asked what distinguishes the U.S. Naval Academy from other colleges, the general conclusion is that "the unity in the student body is so amazing here. I feel so fortunate to have the opportunity to be here with others who want to serve our country." —*Jane Pak*

FYI

If you come to the USNA, you'd better bring a "good attitude and be ready to endure the challenges presented here."

What is the typical weekend schedule? "We're not like other schools. When we have liberty, we go to local cities or visit our sponsor families. But mostly, we just want to catch up on sleep!"

If I could change one thing about USNA, I'd "take away drill. We all hate drill."

Three things every student should do before graduating are "drink a Beat Army, fly in a T-34 training craft, and go sailing."

University of Maryland / College Park

Address: College Park, MD 20742
Phone: 301-314-8385
E-mail address: um-admit@uga.umd.edu
Web site URL: www.maryland.edu
Founded: 1856
Private or Public: public
Religious affiliation: none
Location: suburban
Undergraduate enrollment: 25,179
Total enrollment: NA
Percent Male/Female: 51%/49%
Percent Minority: 35%
Percent African-American: 12%
Percent Asian: 14%
Percent Hispanic: 5%
Percent Native-American: 0%
Percent in-state/out of state: 75%/25%
Percent Pub HS: NA
Number of Applicants: 23,117
Percent Accepted: 43%
Percent Accepted who enroll: 39%
Entering: 2,028
Transfers: 3,377
Application Deadline: 20 Jan
Mean SAT: NA
Mean ACT: NA
Middle 50% SAT range: V 570-670, M 600-700
Middle 50% ACT range: NA
3 Most popular majors: biology/biological sciences, criminology, speech
Retention: 91%
Graduation rate: 64%
On-campus housing: 39%
Fraternities: 9%
Sororities: 10%
Library: 2,956,648 volumes
Tuition and Fees: $5,898 in; $15,100 out
Room and Board: $7,241
Financial aid, first-year: 40%
Varsity or Club Athletes: 3%
Early Decision or Early Action Acceptance Rate: EA 55%

The University of Maryland, College Park, has been acknowledged as one of the nation's fastest-growing public universities. With its distinguished faculty, including Nobel laureates, National Academy members, and Fulbright scholars, the university offers an array of educational pursuits and social options. College Park, being a Division I NCAA Athletic school, is also known for its basketball and football teams, as well as its unmatched school spirit. Though the school is heavily involved in athletics, academics is a top priority, which is obvious by the school's wide range of special academic honors programs designed to challenge and enrich students' educational careers.

Academics

All students, regardless of their majors, are required to fulfill the CORE, about 30 credits of distributional requirements: nine credits in the humanities, ten in mathematics and science, six in behavioral science, and six in social science and history, with some further breakdown in each of these groups. One student described the CORE as being "diverse," giving students the "opportunity to learn about a lot of new things outside of your major." Many students advised against finishing the CORE requirements early on—"you'll regret it when you are drowning in upper levels in your junior and senior years."

At least 120 credits are needed to graduate with a single degree or a double major. The actual requirements vary, depending on the student's major. The most popular majors at College Park are Criminal Justice, Psychology, and Business. Computer Science, Biology, and Engineering are considered to be some of the school's most difficult majors. The university offers its students the chance to earn double, triple, and even quadruple majors, although it does not award them with minor degrees. Students have the option of creating their own Individual Studies major if the school does not offer one already in the same field.

The University of Maryland abounds with a wide range of special academic programs for its students. About 700 students enroll in the University Honors Program each year, a two-year program providing the students with smaller classes and stimulating seminars. Seminars allow students to explore and discuss topics in courses that may not be offered in the regular college academic program. Past seminar topics include an in-depth study of J.R.R. Tolkien's major works, an examination of the role of literature in identity and conformity, and applied ethics and public policy. College Park Scholars, CIVICUS, and Hinman CEOs are a few of the many special academic programs the school offers.

Classes are mostly taught by professors, although in large introductory-level classes TAs assist the professors in grading the students' work and lead small-group discussions. Students for the most part find TAs to be helpful, especially in such large classes, where the professors are often not available to answer specific questions students may have. Some students find that the TAs show more interest in the students and their understanding of the materials than the professors. One student commented, "They actually care if you understand as opposed to professors who just breeze through the day's lecture without you understanding a thing."

The faculty consists of many distinguished professors who are well-respected in their area of expertise. Maynard Mack, a Shakespeare Scholar, teaches English at College Park. An Emmy winner and numerous Pulitzer Prize winners can also be found teaching.

For the most part, students at College Park are satisfied with the education they are getting, although some have voiced a few grievances concerning class sizes and the lack of minors. In large introductory-level classes, students may find themselves in a large lecture hall with 500, or even as many as 1500, students. In such classes, it is difficult for the professors to get to know each individual student. One student commented, "The professors generally don't want to be there and neither do the students." Students find smaller, advanced classes with as few as 10 students to be more inspiring and conducive to learning.

Weekend Fun

The large campus, the diversity of its students, and its location provide the students with a spectrum of activities to engage in on the weekends. Parties and drinking go on in dorm rooms, and the school has a relatively lax policy on alcohol. "People party a lot on the weekends, but not serious hard partying," said one student. "Just partying to have fun and meet people." Oftentimes there are theme parties throughout the campus, such as the "Graffiti Party," where students wear white T-shirts and "write on each other with highlighters." Some other theme parties include Pimps and Hoes, foam parties, and Hawaii/beach parties.

"Find a place to make your own, whether it's a particular spot on the mall or step in front of a building. The campus is big enough that we all can have our own."

Dining out at nearby restaurants and eateries is another option. Restaurants on campus are mostly fast-food joints. If students want more variety, Applebee's, Chevy's, Smoothie King, and Chipotle are only a short walk away. Chipotle, a Mexican restaurant, is a particular favorite among College Park students; a student even commented that anyone who does not go there in their four years is a fool.

DC offers students with a gamut of cultural and off-campus activities—museums, shopping, restaurants, clubs, bars. With so many options to choose from, there is bound to be at least one activity to suit each student's interests.

Campus, "College Park"–Style

"The campus is gorgeous—it was the reason I decided to come!" exclaimed one student when asked to describe what the campus looked like. While it can be "a little sketchy" and "not especially safe late at night," the student remarked that it was surprisingly picturesque and romantic. The campus is huge, with "lots of trees and grassy areas to play Frisbee, lay out, read or chat with friends." Most of the buildings are red brick with white columns, and a beautiful multi-level fountain lies along the campus mall, at the heart of the school. "Find a place to make your own, whether it's a particular spot on the mall or step in front of a building," advises one student. "The campus is big enough that we all can have our own."

The administration is currently expanding and renovating its facilities to accommodate the growing number of students and their demands. Many of the facilities on campus are brand new, from an Olympic-sized swimming pool, to three new gyms, to a Performing Arts Center. A multi-million dollar Comcast Center was built for the Maryland basketball team, and the Student Union Building has just been renovated. In addition, new apartments are being built for upperclassmen due to the growing number of incoming freshmen each year. Old academic buildings are being remodeled as well.

Something for All of Us

Exclaimed one student, "Most people engage in an extracurricular activity—it is the only way not to get lost on campus!" Surely, in a campus as large and diverse as College Park, you can find at least one activity that suits your interest. Along with community service activities, career-related organizations, and other traditional student groups, Maryland offers some unique clubs. Several humor groups, such as Erasable, Inc., and Sketchup, are known for improvisation and sketch comedies, respectively. Maryland Cow Nipple is a parody publication with a mission to insult a different student group each week in its papers. Mockappella is the university's only comedy a cappella group. Getting to know other students may be difficult in such a large campus as College Park, so participating in an extracurricular activity makes it easier to make friends and to find people who share your interests. Said one student, "Most of the people in respective organizations are alike or have somewhat of a common interest—and they spend a lot of time together."

While College Park is a large campus, size and populationwise, it seems that students have found ways to make the experience and the place their own. —*Soo Kim*

FYI

If you come to University of Maryland, College Park, you'd better bring "an open mind."

What is a typical weekend schedule? "There are always tons of things to do on the weekends, but people are not going to be knocking on your door telling you about them—you have to be proactive and find stuff you like to do."

If I could change one thing about University of Maryland, College Park, "I would have smaller classes all the time."

Three things a student at University of Maryland, College Park should do before graduating are: "go to Chipotle (Mexican restaurant), find a place to make your own, and know the true meaning of freedom."

Massachusetts

Amherst College

Address: PO Box 5000; Amherst, MA 01002
Phone: 413-542-2328
E-mail address: admission@amherst.edu
Web site URL: www.amherst.edu
Founded: 1821
Private or Public: private
Religious affiliation: none
Location: small city
Undergraduate enrollment: 1,618
Total enrollment: NA
Percent Male/Female: 51%/49%
Percent Minority: 34%
Percent African-American: 9%
Percent Asian: 12%
Percent Hispanic: 8%
Percent Native-American: 0%
Percent in-state/out of state: 15%/85%
Percent Pub HS: 60%
Number of Applicants: 5,238
Percent Accepted: 18%
Percent Accepted who enroll: 43%
Entering: 408
Transfers: 11
Application Deadline: 31 Dec
Mean SAT: NA
Mean ACT: NA
Middle 50% SAT range: V 660-770, M 650-770
Middle 50% ACT range: 28-33
3 Most popular majors: English, psychology, economics
Retention: 97%
Graduation rate: 95%
On-campus housing: 98%
Fraternities: NA
Sororities: NA
Library: 960,189 volumes
Tuition and Fees: $29,728
Room and Board: $7,740
Financial aid, first-year: 47%
Varsity or Club Athletes: 27%
Early Decision or Early Action Acceptance Rate: ED 36%

What happens when you put 1,600 good-looking, "pretty darn athletic" students together in a sleepy northern Massachusetts town? All kinds of "extracurricular activities." From all-night cram sessions to watching athletic tournaments, to partying on the weekend, the students at Amherst College do it all and still manage to excel in "some of the most rigorous classes on any college campus anywhere." Situated in the beautiful landscape of Amherst, Massachusetts, this entirely undergraduate college boasts some of the most amazing sunrise and mountain vistas east of the Mississippi. But, if you want more from college than rolling hills and sporting events, have no fear. At Amherst, the possibilities seem endless.

A Liberal Education

The students of Amherst pride themselves on their liberal arts education. "A perfect balance between hard work and interesting professors," classes at Amherst prove both stimulating and challenging. With many majors to choose from and no specific academic requirements, students have time "to explore all their options." A seminar is required during freshman year, but "because there are over thirty to choose from, there are plenty that you [would] have found interesting anyway." Amherst academics are also notable for their intimate atmosphere—one freshman pointed out that the average class has about 14 people in it, while a knowledgeable sophomore was quick to point out that a "lecture" at Amherst usually consisted of only about 30 people. This, along with the ability to be able to take classes at some of the many surrounding universities, defines Amhers as a true "liberal arts" college.

For students seeking an easy ride, Amherst is not a good fit. Students say that there are no easy majors—"once you get in, you're in for a rigorous but extremely fulfilling academic experience, but the professors are really here to help you," commented one sophomore. Unique to Amherst College is the law, jurisprudence, and social thought (LJST) major, a popular fusion of political science and philosophy. Amherst's strong humanities and writing-based classes also attract many students. "We're really heavy on writing, and it prepares many people for other classes, as well as for graduate school," said one sophomore. For those students who prefer lab coats and giant plastic goggles, Amherst still offers plenty of science classes. Though the workload can be overwhelming at times, one student mentioned that he "never freaks out about it."

In addition to the highly personal in-class experience, students enjoy how easy and relaxed the registration process is. With advisors and professors there to give ample help and advice, registration at Amherst works smoothly. After a student preregisters for classes during the summer, he or she has two weeks in the beginning of the semester to officially decide what classes to take before handing in an official schedule. This flexibility helps to eliminate problems that might have been caused if "students and teachers had to deal with one another and they truly didn't want to be in the class," according to one freshman.

Extracurricular Activities

With plenty of extracurricular organizations to join, sports teams to watch, and parties to attend, the Amherst campus is alive with things to do. "Because the town can be really boring, it is up to us students to come up with various things to keep busy," said one sophomore. Amherst has groups built around almost every activity, be it singing, campaigning for animal rights, volunteering in the community, or listening to live music on a Saturday night. "Clubs and performance groups are pretty easy to get involved in. They're abundant enough to be a major part of Amherst society," said one student.

The campus center plays a major role in the lives of Amherst students. Housing a pool table, a coffee shop, and a recreation room with Ping-Pong tables, the center lives up to its name. "It's incredibly easy to relax and socialize at the campus center," said one junior. Catering to those who like more organized recreation, the group once known as The Amherst Party (TAP) puts on all kinds of productions, from formal and informal dances, to casino nights, to free movie nights every Friday. If all else fails, the students at Amherst still have four other local colleges in the area to socialize with—Smith, the University of Massachusetts at Amherst, Mount Holyoke, and Hampshire College.

Though some students enjoy partying at other colleges on the weekend, Amherst hosts its own share of parties. One student laughed that at Amherst drinking is "the most popular weekend activity by far." It is almost guaranteed that one of the athletic teams throws a party every weekend, and even some weeknights! "Everyone just kind of hangs out with their teams and drinks over at the team houses. Sometimes it can get pretty wild, but most of the time it's pretty kicked back," commented one sophomore athlete. Students reported a lax enforcement of the school's alcohol policies. The enthusiasm for partying makes Amherst a school "commonly visited by students from other schools in the area to party."

Though the town of Amherst is home to many college students, some complain that it is less than exciting. As one freshman said, there "sure isn't a whole lot to do. We have one stellar pizza place and a lot of crappy bars." However, many upperclassmen say that they like the bar scene in Amherst, which centers around a strip called Bar Row and is described as a great place to "paint the town." Many students at Amherst have their own cars, enabling them to visit either Springfield or Boston for a change of pace on the weekend.

The Amherst Dress Code: Horses and Alligators

"It seems as though everyone at Amherst has those darn Polo and Lacoste shirts that come in crazy colors like canary yellow, lime green, and salmon pink," said one frustrated sophomore. Students love the prep/jock look. "The point here is to look good without trying really hard," said one student who described the style of many Amherst guys as nice collared shirts and khakis. Amherst females tend to get dressed up to go out on the weekends, said one student who has "seen plenty of girls who are scantily clad at night, even though it gets down to about fifty degrees." While a lot of Amherst students look like they stepped out of a Ralph Lauren ad, many other students aren't "afraid to wear anything from designer jeans to homemade masterpieces." Amherst students tend to care about their appearance, but those who like to experiment with their clothing won't feel out of place.

"Because the town can be really boring, it is up to us students to come up with various things to keep busy."

Amherst Dorms: Some Beauties and Some Beasts

At Amherst, all dorms are not created equal. Some are spacious and comfortable, but others seem to be "lacking in a lot of things." Pratt is "by far the nicest dorm to live in," but James and Sterns are known as "The Ghetto." Other great dorms include Appleton and Valentine, which boast suites with their own bathrooms. The housing situation will be complicated the next four to five years while the school builds new dorms and renovates old housing complexes inside and out. Students have mixed opinions about the renovations and housing crunch. "While some get to stay in new dorms, most freshmen and sophomores have to stay in portable buildings that look like trailer homes," said one lucky freshman who lives in a nicer building. "I personally am against the reconstruction—some students are completely spoiled while others are stuck in the ghetto," grumbled one angry sophomore. In addition to dorm renovations, other reasons for the housing crunch include fewer students studying abroad and more students accepting admissions offers. Though some complain, many students feel that the dorms at Amherst are "way better than the average dorm at most other colleges" and most students end up happy with their living situations.

"The Total Package"

So what if Amherst is in the middle of nowhere and has a student body the size of most American public high schools? The fact is that students at Amherst feel they have nothing to complain about. "We live in a scenically gorgeous town, get a great liberal arts education, and are surrounded by good-looking athletic people," boasted one sophomore. "Now, if *that* isn't the total package, I don't know what is." —*Nate Puksta*

FYI

If you come to Amherst, make sure to bring "a warm pair of gloves and a winter coat."

A typical weekend at Amherst is "Drinking, sleeping, calling my parents, and studying on Sunday like it's my job."

One thing I would change about Amherst is "the poor transportation and the fact that freshmen can't have cars."

Three things you have to do before graduating are "watch the sunrise from the top of the Octagon, take a language course, and explore the surrounding-area colleges."

Babson College

Address: Admissions Office, Mustard Hall; Babson Park, MA 02457-0310
Phone: 781-239-5522
E-mail address: ugradadmission@babson.edu
Web site URL: www.babson.edu
Founded: 1919
Private or Public: private
Religious affiliation: none
Location: suburban
Undergraduate enrollment: 1,735
Total enrollment: NA
Percent Male/Female: 61%/39%
Percent Minority: 35%
Percent African-American: 3%
Percent Asian: 9%
Percent Hispanic: 4%
Percent Native-American: 0%
Percent in-state/out of state: 56%/44%
Percent Pub HS: NA
Number of Applicants: 2,402
Percent Accepted: 48%
Percent Accepted who enroll: 35%
Entering: 402
Transfers: 47
Application Deadline: 1 Feb
Mean SAT: NA
Mean ACT: NA
Middle 50% SAT range: V 550-630, M 600-690
Middle 50% ACT range: NA
3 Most popular majors: business management (100%)
Retention: 90%
Graduation rate: 83%
On-campus housing: 81%
Fraternities: NA
Sororities: NA
Library: 131,844 volumes
Tuition and Fees: $27,248
Room and Board: $9,978
Financial aid, first-year: 44%
Varsity or Club Athletes: 20%
Early Decision or Early Action Acceptance Rate: ED 60%; EA 67%

At Babson College, located in the affluent Boston suburb of Wellesley, Massachusetts, a concentration in some field of business management is requisite. This is not a school for the unmotivated or unfocused. In fact, one student labeled his peers a "cult of mavericks each ready to gun for millions" upon graduation, an exaggerated stereotype that nonetheless gives an accurate impression of the intensity with which Babson students approach their education.

Future CEOs of the World

From the moment freshmen arrive on campus, they enter a structured academic program geared towards their particular business interests. Freshmen must enroll in Foundation Management Experience, or FME. This program, which introduces students to concepts in accounting, marketing, and business and information systems, feeds into Intermediate Management Core (IMC), of which students must take three semesters into their junior year. IMC demands that students study the practical workings of a real-life company of their choice and prepare a presentation on their findings. While Babson takes care to school students in the liberal arts, only 50 percent of classes fall outside the realm of business-related fields. Though, as one student noted, "not everyone here is an aspiring entrepreneur," students understand that an intense business education is central to the Babson experience. What's more, students choose not from a variety of majors but rather from various concentrations in entrepreneurship. Among these, marketing and finance are most popular.

Class size averages roughly 25 students, and Babsonians appreciate the personal contact with professors that this small size affords. Students give their professors rave reviews, suggesting that perhaps professors deserve more credit than they are often given. One student referred to his professors as "war heroes," alluding to the experience in business management that members of the distinguished faculty bring to campus. Professors include the founder of Jiffy Lube and former CEOs of Digital Equip and Pizza Hut. The emphasis in the classroom is on the dynamics of teamwork and the relevance of working knowledge in any given field. TAs have no place at Babson; instead, upperclassmen "peer mentors" give freshmen support in the requisite introductory classes. Students complain about the heavy workload that often makes a Monday-through-Friday workweek necessary. Other students take issue with the curved grading system. Because grades are scaled down to meet a pre-determined average, the prevalent sense is that "anywhere else, it would have been an A."

Parties: Taking Advantage of Boston

Freshmen and upperclassmen at Babson do not tend to segregate when the weekend finally does roll around. Together, Babsonians of all years seek out the best parties, usually found in either suites or fraternities. About 10 percent of the student body identifies with a Greek organization although Greek parties are open to the greater college population. Although students estimate that alcohol and drug use are less prevalent here than at schools of comparable size, the party scene does play a strong role in the social plans of students. The administration takes a by-the-book approach to policing alcohol offenses, a stance which aggravates students who would prefer a more lax approach. Once a student accumulates three "strikes"—that is, three documented instances of violation of the alcohol policy—the student is no longer allowed to live on campus. As an alternative to alcohol-centered parties, the college hosts various theme parties throughout the year: fall weekend, Oktoberfest, Harvest, and the president's black-tie ball are among the most popular. The black-tie ball is not the only chance for students to dress up during the school year. On the contrary, professors regularly ask that students wear business suits to class in an attempt to give them a taste of a professional atmosphere.

"The standard-issue vehicle is pick-a-number-series BMW."

Despite the vibrant party scene, many students complain that random hookups are not as common as at other colleges. Perhaps for this reason, students often venture to Boston University or Boston College in search of a more diverse social environment. Students also seek out bars both around Wellesley and in the city. Although Boston is easily accessible via the T (Boston's subway system) and other means of public transportation, students find the hours of public transportation relatively inconvenient, thereby making cars the dominant mode of transportation. Parking, however, creates another problem, especially for freshmen, whose location on Lower Campus distances them from the parking lots available to students.

Common Breeds

Students come to Babson in hopes that the combination of their hard work and the college's program of study will make for a successful—and prosperous—future. Social concerns are of less importance. Indeed, one student described Babsonians as "hardworking, rich geeks." The student body is racially homogenous and politically and socially conservative. Students do not only segregate themselves by ethnicity; athletes, Greeks, international students, and those who live together freshman year often withdraw into their own cliques. The relatively high male-to-female ratio plays another important factor in student relations at Babson. Though the college has made an effort in recent years to correct this inequality, having approximately two guys on campus for every girl only increases the homogenous profile of Babson.

A Campus That Mimics Its Location

The Boston suburb of Wellesley, Massachusetts, houses the Babson campus. Students appreciate the safety and beauty afforded by this affluent town but complain that the area immediately surrounding their campus all but closes down by 9 P.M. The campus itself, like the student body, is small, with an architecturally distinct set of buildings. Students congregate at the Campus Center or Pub Reynolds for socializing; the library is better suited for serious studying. Of the dorms on campus, three in particular—Pietz, Vanwinkle, and Coleman—are consistently lauded as the most sought-after. While almost all freshmen live on Lower Campus, seniors have first choice in the room draw and often end up with singles and suites. Students seem, on the whole, happy with their living arrangements. An RA system is in place for all students to further ensure their comfort.

The quality of dorms, coupled with the high cost of off-campus apartments, accounts for the fact that 85 percent of students live on campus. For these students, a meal plan is required. Although dining on campus is met with student approval for both its taste and variety, the required meal plan for those living on campus frustrates those who would prefer to take advantage of the many Boston-area restaurants.

The Beaver Stays Home

At Babson, few organized activities outside of the classroom ever gain much popularity. Participation in community service, for example, is low. In spite of the fully equipped PepsiCo Pavilion Gym, athletics draw relatively small followings and do not elicit much school spirit for "the Beaver," Babson's mascot. Ethnic organizations and intramural sports, however, do draw in a relatively high percentage of students.

Students often come to Babson with lofty career goals in mind and, thanks in part to the school's efforts to distinguish itself as a top business school, they are not disappointed with the rigorous curriculum. Here, there is little evidence of diversity in ideals or background; as one student commented, the "standard-issue vehicle is pick-a-number-series BMW." For many, it is this common path that makes the Babson experience worthwhile. —*Greg Hamm*

FYI

If you come to Babson, you'd better bring a "business suit, a coffee maker, and an alarm clock."

A typical weekend at Babson consists of "Thursday night Pub Night, Friday exams and presentations, Saturday in Boston, Sunday studying and homework."

If I could change one thing about Babson, I'd "increase the school's overall population."

Three things every student at Babson should do before graduating are "attend a Knight Party, start at least one business, and intern at a company."

Boston College

Address: 140 Commonwealth Avenue; Chestnut Hill, MA 02467
Phone: 617-552-3100
E-mail address: ugadmis@bc.edu
Web site URL: www.bc.edu
Founded: 1863
Private or Public: private
Religious affiliation: Roman Catholic/Jesuit
Location: suburban
Undergraduate enrollment: 8,916
Total enrollment: NA
Percent Male/Female: 48%/52%
Percent Minority: 22%
Percent African-American: 5%
Percent Asian: 9%
Percent Hispanic: 6%
Percent Native-American: 0%
Percent in-state/out of state: 28%/72%
Percent Pub HS: 58%
Number of Applicants: 21,133
Percent Accepted: 32%
Percent Accepted who enroll: 34%
Entering: 2,315
Transfers: 69
Application Deadline: 2 Jan
Mean SAT: NA
Mean ACT: NA
Middle 50% SAT range: V 600-690, M 620-710
Middle 50% ACT range: NA
3 Most popular majors: English, communications, finance
Retention: 95%
Graduation rate: 87%
On-campus housing: 78%
Fraternities: NA
Sororities: NA
Library: 1,970,143 volumes
Tuition and Fees: $27,522
Room and Board: $10,207
Financial aid, first-year: 39%
Varsity or Club Athletes: 8%
Early Decision or Early Action Acceptance Rate: EA 44%

Mobs of Boston College students run around their beautiful campus every spring, tracing hidden clues to find their prize. The prize? It's not the prestige of winning some freshman orientation activity, nor a pot of gold (or scholarship money), but a much coveted ticket to one of the most popular dances at BC: Middlemarch. According to BC students, Middlemarch is "possibly the best college dance in the States." Only the lucky few who successfully complete the scavenger hunt gain entrance to this mysterious event.

Boston College, a Jesuit school located about six miles outside downtown Boston, offers its students a balance of popular parties, a rigorous core curriculum, and an open, suburban setting with the convenience of nearby Boston.

The Core on Academics

Boston College consists of several undergraduate programs: the College of Arts and Sciences, the Wallace E. Carroll School of Management, the Lynch School of Education, and the School of Nursing. Students enroll in one school, but can take elective classes from other schools. Some of the most popular majors and classes, such as Finance and Accounting, fall under the School of Management. English, Political Science, and Economics are popular in the Arts and Sciences. Students agree that classes in the pre-med arena, such as Organic Chemistry and Biochemistry, are exceedingly difficult.

All four colleges of Boston College share a core program that requires coursework in a myriad of subject areas. The College of Arts and Sciences, for example, requires 15 core courses including writing, literature, arts, mathematics, history, philosophy, social sciences, natural science, theology and cultural diversity. Many students complain about the stringency of the core requirements, even though one student confessed, "these classes are great for my personal development."

Students agree that the best part of BC academics is the teacher-student relationship. One student praised the professors for two of his favorite classes, Philosophy of the Person and Modern European History: "Both my teachers for these two classes knew the subject inside and out. They made learning the subject fun, they showed that they cared for their students, and were always available outside of class for any extra help." One freshman already had stories to tell about his professor, who threw a pizza party for the class at the end of the year. He lauds, "the good professor-student relationship makes BC an academically resourceful institution."

A Note on Being Catholic

When asked about the Catholic presence at the school, one student said, "I used to see the Jesuits on my way to classes last year." The Catholic influence seems to be felt more in the academics than the social life: one student felt that "some class offerings have Catholic undertones." Moreover, Jesuit priests teach some of the classes. One student claimed, "The school teaches students how to be a human through its Jesuit education."

Go Eagles! The Sports Scene at BC

As at many colleges, football is big at BC. During football season, there are "always tons of tailgates going on, parties left and right, parties at night." Notre Dame is BC's big rival, and some students make the trek out to Indiana for the big game. Hockey is also popular at BC, maybe "bigger than football," according to one student. Every year, the Eagles hockey team plays in the Fleet Center. One student recalls proudly one game from last season: "In the NCAA championship (Frozen Four), we had an adrenaline-rushing game against North Dakota, and although we couldn't bring the trophy back to the school, our patriotism to the team never cooled off." Basketball is also up there on the popularity list.

The athletic facility is complete and accessible for students who remain on the sidelines of the games. The Flynn Recreation Complex, affectionately called "the Plex," is fully equipped with treadmills, bikes, weights, track, tennis courts, squash court, swimming pool, and a basketball and volleyball court. Some dorms also have their own weight rooms.

Food and Living

When it comes to the living situation at BC, your luck depends mostly on your year. According to one student, "about half of the freshman class have to suffer the tragedy of living on the Newton campus." Although freshman get accustomed to living on the Newton campus and enjoy the benefits of a small and tight-knit community, one student complained, "Every student should know that if you live in Newton, it takes an extra hour in traveling time to get anywhere." One hour might be an exaggeration, but the students in Newton do have to take a shuttle bus to get to classes on Middle Campus. "The bus ride itself is only about five minutes long," said one student, "but they need to stand outside to wait for the bus to come—even when it's snowing heavily. Also, if you live on the main campus, you can go back to your room between classes, but otherwise, you'd have to bring all your books and be prepared to be out for the entire day."

"According to some students, Boston looks more like New England Clam Chowder (that is, white) than a melting pot, and many would say the same holds true for BC."

The rooms on the Newton campus are also notoriously small. Sophomore years and beyond, however, students may find themselves winning the lottery for comfortable rooms with kitchens and private bathrooms. Housing is usually guaranteed for three years, and many students choose to stay on campus. A fair number live off campus or study abroad their junior year. High-rise apartments with kitchens are available for upperclassman. Also popular are the "modulars," called mods for short. Mods are small townhouses located in the center of campus, famous for throwing popular parties.

Most BC students seem to be satisfied by the food. "Considering the amount they have to make, the food at BC is high quality," said one student. Students have a few dining halls from which to choose for every meal. The Lyons Dining Hall, called the Rat, is popular for lunch. Particularly popular plates are made-to-order steak and cheese, London broil, and dessert.

The Weekends

BC might not be known as *the* party school, but there is definitely enough partying going on. The school's social life centers around drinking and clubbing. The weekend starts on either Thursday or Friday, with partying on campus. The administration has announced a zero-tolerance alcohol policy and the BC Police Department is out on weekends to enforce the policy. Students nevertheless find it pretty easy to encounter bottles of liquor, usually through upperclassmen. One student even claimed, "I don't know if it's possible not to drink at this school, especially if you are on a sports team."

The spotlight of campus partying is in the mods. Students feel that the mods fill the social niche left open by the lack of a Greek system. One sophomore warned, "mod parties can be elitist." For the freshmen without IDs, however, "mod-hopping" is the ideal way of getting access to alcohol.

These parties may also be the ideal place for hooking up, which occurs frequently, according to some students. "People do date, but hook-ups are more popular," said one student. Another student added, "There is a lot of sex at this school. That's not even a question." When they get tired of campus, students take advantage of their proximity to Boston. Boston has a lot of clubs, according to BC students, but the bars are strict about the drinking age. The city also offers cultural activities, a wealth of shopping malls, movie theaters, and concerts. Students can also work at part-time jobs or internships in the city.

The Melting Pot Versus The Clam Chowder

According to some students, Boston looks more like New England Clam Chowder (that is, white) than a melting pot, and the same holds somewhat true for BC. One student who had grown up in a very diverse neighborhood said he experienced a "total culture shock when I came to BC because I had never been around so many white people before." These students stress, nevertheless, that racial problems or conflicts on campus are rare. Minority students can "make their voices heard to the community" through the school's cultural organizations. Activities such as the

Asian Caucus attract a lot of students. About BC, one student concluded—"It's fairly easy to meet people here if you go out there and try." —*Mariko Hirose*

FYI

If you come to BC, you'd better bring "a fun attitude."

What is the typical weekend schedule? "It depends on how much work you want to do. Popular activities are partying and going to football games."

If I could change one thing about BC, I'd "make it cheaper—a whole lot cheaper."

Three things every student at your school should do before graduating are: "scream and go wild at 11 P.M. during the finals week, go to Middlemarch, and learn the difference between the B and D lines on the T."

Boston University

Address: 121 Bay State Road; Boston, MA 02215
Phone: 617-353-2300
E-mail address: admissions@bu.edu
Web site URL: www.bu.edu
Founded: 1839
Private or Public: private
Religious affiliation: none
Location: urban
Undergraduate enrollment: 17,860
Total enrollment: NA
Percent Male/Female: 40%/60%
Percent Minority: 27%
Percent African-American: 2%
Percent Asian: 12%
Percent Hispanic: 5%
Percent Native-American: 0%
Percent in-state/out of state: 24%/76%
Percent Pub HS: 72%
Number of Applicants: 27,038
Percent Accepted: 58%
Percent Accepted who enroll: 29%
Entering: 4,560
Transfers: 133
Application Deadline: 1 Jan
Mean SAT: NA
Mean ACT: NA
Middle 50% SAT range: V 590-680, M 610-690
Middle 50% ACT range: 25-29
3 Most popular majors: business, communications, social sciences
Retention: 87%
Graduation rate: 73%
On-campus housing: 74%
Fraternities: 3%
Sororities: 5%
Library: 1,749,000 volumes
Tuition and Fees: $28,906
Room and Board: $9,288
Financial aid, first-year: 52%
Varsity or Club Athletes: 3%
Early Decision or Early Action Acceptance Rate: ED 47%

You walk out of your building, and are instantly transported from the confines of a dormitory to the heart of the largest city in New England. You walk to class along Commonwealth Avenue, one of Boston's main thoroughfares. You dodge traffic and businesspeople before making it to campus. You arrive at one of the many classrooms at Boston University and are again transported from the center of a major metropolitan city to a quiet classroom where Nobel Peace Prize-winner Elie Wiesel, among others, might be giving a lecture. This is Boston, and this is BU.

Watch Out for the T

BU is a university at the heart of Boston. As one student put it, "our campus is divided by a six-lane artery, Commonwealth Avenue, which is separated by the T, Boston's subway system. Try not to get run over by it." BU students have the opportunity to study in a school that offers not only a world-class education in the heart of an urban area, but also the chance to explore Boston, Massachusetts. BU is wedged in between the Red Sox's home at Fenway Park, and Newbury Street, the "Rodeo Drive of New England." The T has seven stops near BU's campus, putting the entire city at the fingertips of its students.

For the student who wants to spend his or her college years in the hustle and bustle of a big city, BU would be a wise choice. However, not everyone is suited to the urban lifestyle. According to one junior, the urban feel can be a drawback at times. "This school could use some more grassy areas; it just feels too urban sometimes, especially when you just want to relax, it is so fast-paced."

In a school with about 15,000 undergraduates, finding a niche can seem daunting at first, but, as one student notes, "you'll quickly find your place." BU has students from every state and about 50 countries. One senior said "when you're a freshman here, it is really easy to just sit down at the dining hall and talk to people, or just strike up a conversation with somebody."

Women feel challenged by finding an eligible man at BU. "You've got to remember that there are more girls than guys; then you take the guys and take into account that what seems like half of them are gay, then from the remainder, about half are jerks, so you end up with like one or two guys you are actually compatible with," said one freshman. Other students note that it is freshman year at BU where you have the most random love affairs. "You kind of begin settling down here after freshman year, that's when you know your people and where to find them," said a senior.

Know What You Want to Study? Good.

BU offers students the choice of which undergraduate college to enroll in. The university has 22 different schools, including the College of Arts and Sciences, School of Management, College of Communication, College of Fine Arts, and a college for nearly every other academic subject possible. An undergraduate at BU decides which college or school to belong to upon matriculation and registration. Students who aren't sure what they want to study enroll in the College of General Studies, which offers a core curriculum with a sampling of various disciplines during freshman and sophomore years. After that, General Studies students choose which specialty college to enter.

Each college has a unique culture, and students enjoy meeting people in their classes with similar interests and career goals. "I love the School of Fine Arts! I live in my Drama bubble, and I can't get enough of it," exclaimed one sophomore drama student. The College of Communications is among the best in the nation and is extremely selective. Students in the communications department have the benefit of Boston's many nearby radio and television studios when they look for internships and jobs. "Just knowing about everything out there, a T ride away, is really motivating to reach your ambitions," said one freshman in communications. The students in the College of Engineering are among the hardest workers on campus. Some students request to live on dormitory floors with other members of their college, and "the engineering floors are always the quiet ones," said one senior. Other schools have a more "relaxed" reputation. "Everybody knows that the hockey recruits will probably end up at the School of Hospitality Administration; that's the slacker school," said one sophomore.

Most students attend the College of Arts and Sciences, which offers a general liberal arts curriculum. "I had to take a lot of classes in order to complete the requirements for my majors, but there was never a class I had to take that I did not enjoy," said a U.S. history and biology double major. However, sometimes BU's academic requirements cramp students. One sophomore sociology major complained about having to take four semesters of a foreign language. "I just don't see the need for me to have to learn another language, especially in the direction I'm headed," he said.

Party Hard . . . Start on Thursday

Most BU students begin their weekend on Thursday night. After a four-day week, some students feel they deserve to take Fridays off. "I know plenty of people who make it so that they don't have to take classes on Fridays," said a senior. Most people over 21 head to Boston's happening nightlife, while those under 21 stay on campus for parties thrown in dorm rooms and try to hide their alcohol from the administration. Students complain about the administration's strict alcohol policies. "If you are under 21, you have to constantly watch out for RAs lurking in the hallway. Last year I got fined $250 along with four other friends for having four six-packs of beer," said a sophomore. On-campus students who are 21 are still subject to restrictions on their alcohol possession. Students who can legally purchase alcohol can only keep one six-pack and one liter of alcohol, without risking repercussions from the administration.

"I would never want to go anywhere else, it absolutely rocks here!"

Many underage students solve this drinking dilemma by partying at one of the many other colleges in Boston. "It is not strange to go to another school, like MIT or Harvard, to party at least once a month, if not more," said an underage student. Some drug use occurs on campus, but most students say that aside from some marijuana use, drugs aren't prevalent. Though a lot of social activity focuses on drinking, students reassure that "you don't need to drink or smoke pot in order to fit in." Most students say it's "perfectly cool" to show up to a party and decide not to drink.

High-Rises and Hotels

Most BU freshmen live in 18-story buildings around campus. The buildings overlook the city, meaning BU students occupy some of Boston's premier real estate. Thirteen floors of each building have student rooms, and the rest have amenities like dining halls. Students can eat at any one of the dining halls on campus and at the Starbucks or Jamba Juice at the student union. One upperclassman described the housing as "fine, but a little cramped, especially the first year. It gets a lot better after that."

Most BU students live on co-ed floors with single-sex bathrooms, though some females choose to live on an all-girls floor. Freshmen, for the most part, live with a roommate of the same sex. The bathrooms are "usually clean" and designed to handle an entire floor's needs. Due to a growing student population, BU recently purchased what used to be a Howard Johnson Hotel near campus and converted it into apartments. Students covet these rooms, as they are some of the only rooms on campus with air-conditioning and private bathrooms. BU upperclassmen also scramble for apartments in the new Student Village, which opened in the fall of 2001.

The guest policy at BU is "one of the largest drawbacks at this school," complain several students. Security guards man the doors of every building, and students visiting a different building after-hours have to fill out paperwork and sign them in at the guard station. This policy frustrates students; one female complained that while she "can see how it's beneficial for my parents' sanity, it really sucks." A male student grumbled that "it makes it difficult to have a girl in your room, because you have to sign them in with your security guard, and they only let you bring people in of your own sex." Overnight guests from outside BU must be registered with the administration and have a co-host if they intend to stay with a student of the opposite sex, and must report to the guard stations at 7 A.M.

No Football? No Problem!

While BU does not have a football team, "the little school spirit there is" focuses on the ice hockey team. The popularity of the team can be seen at T. Anthony's popular pizza restaurant, which has covered its walls in autographed photos of BU hockey stars dating back nearly a century. Everyone attends the game against neighbor and arch-rival Boston College. One student warned to "never ever be caught wearing a BC sweatshirt around campus, or things could get ugly."

BU's athletic department includes many other varsity sports such as lacrosse, wrestling, and rowing. Students also participate in club sports, which are well funded by the university. One such club is the Ice Skating Club. "The practices are a bit early, but it is a lot of fun to be able to disconnect and do something I enjoy," said a freshman on the synchronized skating team.

Some students say that the resources for club athletics are more plentiful at BU than at other schools, such as BC.

BU students think that they get the "true college experience." "We get a bit of everything," one student said. In addition to solid academics, BU students have an entire city at their disposal, waiting to be explored. One student summed it up, saying: "I would never want to go anywhere else; it absolutely rocks here!" *—Alberto Masliah*

FYI

If you come to BU, you better bring "a jacket because it will get really cold in the winter."

What is the typical weekend schedule? "Start partying early on Thursday night; Friday, chill out and then party more; Saturday, go do something fun in the city and then party even more; Sunday, just sleep and study."

If I could change one thing about BU, "I would change the guest and housing policy."

Three things every student should do at BU before graduating are "go to the BU/BC hockey game, try to hit every one of Boston's museums, and go to a Red Sox game at Fenway Park."

Brandeis University

Address: 415 South Street; Waltham, MA 02454
Phone: 781-736-3500
E-mail address: sendinfo@brandeis.edu
Web site URL: www.brandeis.edu
Founded: 1948
Private or Public: private
Religious affiliation: none
Location: suburban
Undergraduate enrollment: 3,057
Total enrollment: NA
Percent Male/Female: 44%/56%
Percent Minority: 21%
Percent African-American: 3%
Percent Asian: 9%
Percent Hispanic: 2%
Percent Native-American: 0%
Percent in-state/out of state: 25%/75%
Percent Pub HS: 75%
Number of Applicants: 6,080
Percent Accepted: 42%
Percent Accepted who enroll: 33%
Entering: 837
Transfers: 40
Application Deadline: 15 Jan
Mean SAT: NA
Mean ACT: NA
Middle 50% SAT range: V 627-710, M 630-710
Middle 50% ACT range: NA
3 Most popular majors: biological/biomedical science, economics, political science
Retention: 93%
Graduation rate: 84%
On-campus housing: 84%
Fraternities: NA
Sororities: NA
Library: 938,835 volumes
Tuition and Fees: $29,875
Room and Board: $8,323
Financial aid, first-year: 50%
Varsity or Club Athletes: 10%
Early Decision or Early Action Acceptance Rate: ED 72%

When people think of colleges in Boston, Harvard and MIT instantly pop into mind. However, what some people don't know is that the most exciting college town in the nation is also graced with the presence of a younger establishment named Brandeis University. Founded only in 1948, Brandeis has quickly earned an outstanding reputation as a university with great devotion not only to maintaining stellar undergraduate academics, but also to being a leading research university. Distinct from its Boston counterparts, Brandeis has also quickly earned the reputation of being the most Jewish college in the country.

Watch Out, Pre-Meds

Brandeis students seem to have few complaints when it comes to academics. There are a good deal of course requirements including freshman writing seminars, three semesters of language courses, and a gym class. Students have to take 32 hours of credit from "clusters" such as Medicine and Social Policy. However, students say that these requirements are "very open" and that it is "really convenient" to satisfy them. One freshman expressed that "it ends up just happening that you fulfill everything."

The majority of classes at Brandeis are relatively small in size. Aside from entry-level lectures in subjects such as chemistry that often top 300 people per class, students generally agree that most classes have approximately 20 students. Despite small class sizes, it is easy to be placed in the classes that you want; and even if you request to be in one of the higher-level, more popular classes, the school "will basically get you in." The small class size at Brandeis facilitates devout attention from professors, which in turn leads to academic rigor. However, intense schoolwork is a small price to pay for establishing relationships with some of Brandeis's faculty. Professors at Brandeis have included the late Eleanor Roosevelt, and Morrie Schwartz, who has been immortalized by the very successful book, *Tuesdays With Morrie.* The Brandeis faculty has included notables like women's rights activist Anita Hill and musician Leonard Bernstein.

Students at Brandeis feel that the typical class is often very difficult and demanding. While it seems that Economics and Political Science tend to be the "slacker" majors, students who are taking the pre-med sequence and are pursuing majors in science claim that it is "the hardest thing in the world" and that there is simply just a "ton of work." For example, one freshman interested in the pre-med program said that her introductory chemistry class probably lost about half of its students due to the intense workload. Fortunately, the students have a positive outlook on Brandeis's vigorous academics. Small class size, intimacy with world-renowned professors, and reasonable course requirements led one Brandeis student, when asked if she is pleased with the school's academics, to affirm wholeheartedly, "oh yeah, definitely."

Looking for Fun? Go to Boston . . . Or At Least Get Off Campus

While "the Deis," as it's known by students, is a haven in the world of academia, the campus's social atmosphere does not seem quite up to par. As one freshman said, "You've got to really search for something going on on-campus." Students tend to look toward Boston for weekend entertainment (which typically starts on Thursday night). The Deis is located in Waltham, Massachusetts, about 10 to 20 minutes from Boston. This proximity allows students to typically spend about one night a weekend there hitting up the clubs. However, underage students beware—it is common knowledge around campus that if you plan on dancing the night away at a club, you need an ID.

However, there is a lot more to do in Boston than go clubbing. Many students frequent Faneuil Hall or Harvard Square where it's easy to meet students from other colleges. The commute to Boston is easy for most to make because the majority of students in this predominantly wealthy student body have cars. Yet, students also note that those without cars needn't worry, because the "Bran-van" will be glad to take you into the city. The "Bran-van," aside from having a very cute name, is a school-funded vehicle whose purpose is to take students anywhere on or off campus. In addition, it saves students the trouble of choosing a designated driver.

What also drives students away from the grounds of Brandeis on weekends is the fact that a large percentage of upperclassmen live off campus. Moreover, fraternities are also not on campus—in fact, Greek organizations are not even recognized by "the Deis" (although, many disguise themselves as official clubs in order to receive funding from the university). Despite the lack of recognition from the university, fraternities play a large role in the social life at Brandeis. Not only do they throw parties such as formals and black tie events, but they also have their own tables in the dining halls and the members form strong cliques. As one student stated bluntly, "if you want a life and you're a guy, definitely join a frat . . . [it's] definitely not necessary for girls." Unfortunately, because Brandeis does not regulate frats, they also do not regulate hazing. While there are no hazing horror stories to report, it is well known that "pledging is a pain in the ass."

Fortunately, to say that there is nothing to do on the Brandeis campus on weekends would be an exaggeration. The school has also sponsored concerts for popular musicians such as Less than Jake and Tracy Chapman. Students also look forward to concerts by their own a cappella groups which are "amazing and award-winning." Students also partake in notoriously drunken parties in senior housing, although if a quieter, sober evening is more your thing, Cholmondeley's is great for a cup of coffee and an open-mic for local artists. All in all, students refer to weekends on campus as "hit or miss," but if it's a miss, there's always Boston.

"Brandeis Goggles"?

In reference to the girls at Brandeis, one male student jokingly said, "Nine out of ten Jewish girls are pretty, and the last tenth go to Brandeis." Brandeis girls have similar feelings for their male counterparts—as one female put it, "there are not a lot of attractive people here." This lack of hotties on campus has caused many students to wear, as they say, "Brandeis goggles." Similar to beer goggles, "Brandeis goggles" have the effect of reminding the wearer that beauty is relative, and therefore, he or she must lower his or her standards. It is these "Brandeis goggles" that students claim cause the great deal of hook-ups on campus.

If goggles aren't the reason, it could be the booze that leads to the large number of hook-ups at "the Deis." Moreover, students say that there is a significant presence of both marijuana and ecstasy on campus. All these substances are very easy to obtain, but students maintain that there isn't a serious drug abuse problem at the school, and drinking is far from a social necessity. However, at the same time, the campus and the Waltham police seem very indifferent to underage alcohol consumption, and one freshman noted that at parties she could just show any ID, no matter how old it said she was, and be allowed to enter a Brandeis party.

"It's not like I only see white, Jewish kids, but there are a lot of them."

Despite the school's relatively lax alcohol policy, freshmen are compelled to live in what are called "dry quads," where liquor is considered a no-no. Students are also not allowed to smoke cigarettes if they are within 25 feet of a dormitory. Failure to oblige by these rules leads to written citations which appear to many to be just a slap on the wrist, but students also say it is not a good idea to accumulate too many of these. These seemingly rigid rules for freshmen are not very strictly adhered to. One freshman pointed out that despite the dry-quad she lives in, "I have a bottle of Amaretto and Smirnoff in my closet right now."

Sweet Buildings

The physical aspects of "the Deis" are very popular amongst the students. The school is relatively small, which means it's never a "hassle to get around." Furthermore, the architecture is very interesting. For example, the theater building is shaped like a top hat and the music building looks like a grand piano. To represent the accepting religious policies on which Brandeis was founded, there are three separate houses of worship right next to each other. And interestingly enough, the sanctuaries have been constructed in such a way that at no time can any one of the buildings cast a shadow on another.

Perhaps the most dominant and "gorgeous" structure on campus is the university's first building, the Castle. Currently used as a residential building, the Castle's rooms are widely coveted by students. In particular, pre-meds desire rooms in the Castle because the university has deemed it a quiet building, where most residing students devote most of their time to their studies.

Students are also very proud of their gym, the Joseph P. and Clara Ford Athletic and Recreation Complex. This gigantic facility has recently served as a practice center for the Boston Celtics, and although sports are not a very prominent aspect of campus life, a lot of students do spend a lot of time at the gym either staying in shape or playing intramurals. Interestingly, there is no football at Brandeis, as demanded by the people who funded the construction of the gymnasium. With no football, the students typically cheer on the Brandeis Judges at baseball and basketball games.

A Jewish University

Although Brandeis has a predominantly Jewish population, the school is much more diverse than many people expect. Fifteen percent of students are minorities and this number seems to increase more and more each year, as evidenced by this year's freshman class, which has the greatest number of minority students and the fewest number of Jews in the school's history. Fortunately, students at Brandeis seem to avoid self-segregation, and as one student happily pointed out, "I hang out with totally mixed people." Furthermore, aside from the problems with looks, students are very happy with one another. One student confessed, "I wasn't really expecting to meet a lot of cool people here, but I really did." Another student added, "Everyone is just really friendly."

Despite Brandeis' increased efforts to diversify the student body, Judaism still plays a major role on the campus. As one student observed, "It's not like I only see white, Jewish kids, but there are a lot of them." Brandeis was founded upon the notions of tolerance, and the community is without doubt very accepting and liberal. This atmosphere allows the university to focus its attention on academics and maintain its growing reputation as one of the better research universities in the country. —*Jonathan Levy*

FYI

If you come to Brandeis, you'd better bring "an open mind."
What is the typical weekend schedule? "Head to the bars in Boston."
If I could change one thing about Brandeis, I'd "rework the athletics department."
The three things that every student should do before graduating from Brandeis are "drink the punch at a fraternity party, study abroad, and party at Pachanga, Brandeis' international style dance club."

Clark University

Address: 950 Main Street; Worcester, MA 01610-1477
Phone: 508-793-7431
E-mail address: admissions@clarku.edu
Web site URL: www.clarku.edu
Founded: 1887
Private or Public: private
Religious affiliation: none
Location: small city
Undergraduate enrollment: 2,167
Total enrollment: NA
Percent Male/Female: 39%/61%
Percent Minority: 17%
Percent African-American: 3%
Percent Asian: 4%
Percent Hispanic: 3%
Percent Native-American: 0%
Percent in-state/out of state: 38%/62%
Percent Pub HS: 71%
Number of Applicants: 3,694
Percent Accepted: 68%
Percent Accepted who enroll: 23%
Entering: 580
Transfers: 46
Application Deadline: 1 Feb
Mean SAT: NA
Mean ACT: NA
Middle 50% SAT range: V 540-650, M 540-640
Middle 50% ACT range: 22-27
3 Most popular majors: psychology, biology, political science
Retention: 86%
Graduation rate: 69%
On-campus housing: 76%
Fraternities: NA
Sororities: NA
Library: 289,658 volumes
Tuition and Fees: $26,965
Room and Board: $5,150
Financial aid, first-year: 57%
Varsity or Club Athletes: 13%
Early Decision or Early Action Acceptance Rate: ED 76%

Cluttering the Clark University campus are posters that display a large pea pod with different colored peas inside. Underneath it reads, "Categorizing people isn't something we do here." This diversity is what draws many students to Clark. Clark students, for example, enjoy music that ranges from Grateful Dead to country to the newest hip-hop. Clark also boasts the third largest population of international students.

Freudian Slip

In 1999, a statue of Freud was erected in Red Square, the center of campus. This statue inspired many debates among the students of Clark. But Clark students are proud that their university was the only campus where Freud ever spoke and his presence on campus brought attention to Clark's psychology department, a popular department with the students. Students also have the opportunity to explore many other departments, because they are required to fulfill a program consisting of classes in eight perspectives: aesthetic, historical, values, language, science, formal analysis, verbal expression, and comparative.

Other popular departments include the Center for Holocaust Studies, and the interdisciplinary Communications and Culture major. One very popular professor is Prof. Turner, who is one of the geography department's most respected faculty members. One of Turner's students said, "He is a big part of the reason I chose to minor in geography. Everyone should take a class with him." Students also gave good reviews to Creative Actor and Medical Ethics classes. Although non-art majors regard art as a slacker major, one art student reported that "art classes are much more time-consuming and demanding than any other classes I've taken."

The difficulty of classes is hard to generalize. Some lower-level classes are grueling while some upper-level classes seem quite basic. Some students, claim that academic variety is sacrificed due to Clark's small size. This small size, however, allows students to interact with their professors more intimately. Students say that professors are down to earth, very understanding, and incredibly approachable. Some professors even incorporate dinners into their classes. Students should be warned, however, that Clark has its share of professors with heavy accents. TA's do not teach classes, but they are there to help.

The Study Abroad Department at Clark is very popular; most students go away during their spring semester of junior year. Popular destinations include Scotland, London, Spain, Africa, and Japan. For those who want to try out being abroad for a shorter amount of time, Clark also participates with The College of the Holy Cross in a month-long May term in Luxembourg.

You Can Do What You Want To Do

Clark's social life is what you make of it. The weekend begins on Thursday since many students don't have class on Fridays. The Clark Student Activities Board brings entertainment on campus, ranging from bands and comedians to even hypnotists. The Clark University Film Society shows over thirty screenings each semester. Two theatrical groups, The Clark University Players Society and Clark on Drama, coordinate productions throughout the year. One of the most popular groups on campus is the improv troupe called the "Peapod Squad." Empty seats at their shows are hard to find! There are also two a cappella groups, the Counterpoints (all female) and the Clark Bars (coed), which perform on and off campus.

For such an academically motivated school, Clark has an inviting party scene. On weekends, underclassmen flock to crowded parties at upperclassmen-inhabited off-campus houses. Kegs are very common at these parties. Of-age and resourceful underage students frequent the local bars like Scarlet O'Hara's. One underclassman admits, "my social life is limited because I do not have a fake ID."

Clark's alcohol policy is relatively lenient. Freshman dorms are dry and no kegs are allowed in campus housing. While campus police enforce this policy, they are not as strict as the Worcester Police. One student said, "Due to the school's location, the school police seem to focus more on safety and less on alcohol policies."

The alcohol's presence at Clark is magnified on Spree Day. Spree Day is usually held in April as a celebration of the coming of Spring. The date is selected and kept secret by a committee of upperclassmen until that day when they interrupt students' slumber by banging on garbage cans and yelling. Classes are canceled, and students and staff flock to the Campus Green, which transforms into a carnival. Musical groups have played in the past, as well. By five o' clock, most students retire to their rooms to pass out.

Dorms

Campus housing is mandatory only for freshmen and sophomores, but two-thirds of the student body live on campus all four years. Freshmen usually live together in a first-year residence hall, yet some freshmen can live in dorms with upperclassmen. In general, freshmen halls are louder and more exciting than their upperclass counterparts. Rooms in the freshman halls, Wright and Bullock, are reportedly small but acceptable, and the better social life in these buildings make the cramped living worthwhile. A senior commented that living in a freshmen hall was "the highlight of my four years." Resident Advisors (RAs) in freshmen halls try to be your friend but often seem more like police that strictly enforce quiet hours.

Maywood Hall seems to be the most desirable of the upperclassmen dorms. Maywood is the newest residence hall, and its apartment-like 4 to 6 person suites consist of bedrooms, a common room, and private bathroom. Unfortunately for freshmen, they are not allowed in Maywood. In addition to the traditional dorms, students can live in theme houses like the Quiet House, the Year-Round House, and the Substance Free House.

> **"Among athletes, everyone is very close and dedicated and driven by a sincere love of the game."**

Freshmen and sophomores living in dorms must be on a meal plan. Students can eat either in the dining hall or at the Bistro, a deli that offers sandwiches, salads, and grill food made to order. Food in the dining hall is mediocre, but always suspiciously better when parents and prospective students are around. However, the variety of choices is good, and there is a special vegetarian/vegan section. The draw of the dining halls is not necessarily the food however; it's a great place to "sit with friends and talk and laugh a lot." Students are not rushed in and out, and meal times are considered a social gathering.

Little "Brick" Different

Clark's campus is very compact: a "far" walk on campus takes less than 10 minutes. Most of the buildings are fairly modern and constructed with brick. The Goddard Library (named after Robert Goddard, creator of the rocket) is a strangely shaped building, which supposedly looks like an open book from an aerial view. The library's strange shape makes for many interesting hiding places. According to Rolling Stone magazine, the Goddard Library was Jerry Garcia's favorite place to trip (an important consideration for any prospective student). At the center of campus is Red Square that, due to reconstruction, is no longer red. Right next to Red Square is the Campus Green, a very social place in warm weather where people read, lay out, or play frisbee.

Dana Commons is the student union and offers a place to e-mail, play Ping-Pong, shoot pool, watch movies, hold meetings, or eat at the Moonlight Cafe. The Moonlight Cafe is open late on weekends. The University Center (UC) is home to meeting rooms, the dining hall and Bistro, the mailroom, and the general store. The UC is at the center of campus and is a popular meeting place.

Wormtown

Worcester, is a sizeable industrial city in the middle of Massachusetts, and unfortunately, Clark sits in one of its less desirable areas. As in any big city, safety is a concern at Clark and thus students are encouraged to stay in groups and take advantage of the foot and car escort services. The key to staying safe at Clark is to use common sense and lots of caution.

While many students complain about Worcester, the city has its attractive points. The Worcester Centrum is a large concert arena, which hosts shows ranging from Eminem to Metallica. Worcester has many bars, a few dance clubs, and interesting international restaurants like Thai Cha Da, Dalat, House of India, Cactus Pete's and Tortilla Sam's. No trip to Clark would be complete without a trip to Tatnuck Bookseller and a meal at Wendy's Clark Brunch. Wendy's is a popular Clarkie social hang-out.

Worcester's location is close to nature trails, skiing, and Boston. Although Clark provides a shuttle to and from Boston, many students feel that cars are a necessity.

Extracurricular Activities

Clark prides itself on its abundance of clubs and extracurricular activities. Groups range from the Bisexual, Lesbian and Gay Association (BILAGA), Caribbean American Students Association, the Animal Rights Group, and MASSPIRG (an environmental group). Some clubs sponsor activities such as speakers and discussions. Religion on campus is not overly visible, but Hillel and the Clark Christian Fellowship do exist and help to create a religious community. Also, Clark students are fairly community service-oriented. MASSPIRG works closely with the community in environmental contexts, along with Rotoract, which is based solely on community service.

Many student athletes said that the Clark athletics are under-appreciated and under-funded. Clark is a Division III university that actively recruits athletes, but it does not offer sports scholarships. The men's basketball team and women's soccer teams are the most popular among fans. The softball team, the women's soccer team, and the men's soccer team have all received NCAA tournament bids. Clark has no football team, which tends to prevent any swelling of school spirit. Despite lack of outside appreciation, however, one junior athlete says that "among athletes, everyone is very close and dedicated and driven by a sincere love of the game."

Intramurals are popular, and sometimes becomes relatively competitive. Pick-up sports like basketball, soccer, and Frisbee bring out lots of Clarkies. The student body is fairly health conscious, making the fitness center (with cardiovascular equipment and weights) often very crowded.

Good Things Come in Small Packages

Whether it's a chat with the cook at Wendy's, a quiet evening hidden in Goddard Library, or a frolic on Spree day, Clark provides a small, but delightful, community. While sometimes the town of Worcester can be daunting, Clarkies find that their little peapod is a great place to spend their four years of college. *—Jessica Bondell*

FYI

If you come to Clark, you'd better bring "an accepting outlook to take in all our diversity"
What is the typical weekend schedule? "Check out local bars and chill with friends, catch up on sleep and work."
If I could change one thing about Clark, I'd "up the school spirit and lose Worcester."
Three things every student at Clark should do before graduating are "get something pierced, eat at Wendy's Clark Brunch, and take a nap on the green."

College of the Holy Cross

Address: 1 College Street; Worcester, MA 01610-2395
Phone: 508-793-2443
E-mail address: admissions@holycross.edu
Web site URL: www.holycross.edu
Founded: 1843
Private or Public: private
Religious affiliation: Jesuit
Location: small city
Undergraduate enrollment: 2,811
Total enrollment: NA
Percent Male/Female: 47%/53%
Percent Minority: 12%
Percent African-American: 3%
Percent Asian: 4%
Percent Hispanic: 5%
Percent Native-American: 0%
Percent in-state/out of state: 33%/67%
Percent Pub HS: 46%
Number of Applicants: 4,753
Percent Accepted: 43%
Percent Accepted who enroll: 35%
Entering: 694
Transfers: 20
Application Deadline: 15 Jan
Mean SAT: NA
Mean ACT: NA
Middle 50% SAT range: V 560-660, M 580-660
Middle 50% ACT range: NA
3 Most popular majors: social sciences, English, psychology
Retention: 94%
Graduation rate: 90%
On-campus housing: 78%
Fraternities: NA
Sororities: NA
Library: 561,970 volumes
Tuition and Fees: $26,440
Room and Board: $8,000
Financial aid, first-year: 57%
Varsity or Club Athletes: 24%
Early Decision or Early Action Acceptance Rate: NA

In the bustling college town of Worcester, Massachusetts, lies a small liberal arts school with strong Jesuit ties. Surrounded by other colleges in a "consortium," students at Holy Cross are able to get the close community feel and at the same time expand their horizons to a dozen other schools nearby.

Strong Core

The academic program at Holy Cross is meant to provide students a well-rounded liberal arts foundation. To this end, there is a core curriculum. In order to graduate, students must take one class in several departments including history, philosophy, religion, literature, art, math, and science as well as two classes in the social science department. However, the wide variety of classes offered by each department allows students to select courses that are interesting and applicable to them, so that no one is too far out of their academic comfort zone. For example, a student interested in biology may take a course in bioethics to satisfy the philosophy requirement. Though the core might seem daunting, most students do not see it as an obligation, but rather as a chance to leave college with a strong foundation in many different arenas.

Once students specialize, there are many fields which they may enter. Many choose a double major in economics and accounting. This is a difficult course of study, but the consensus suggests that the most demanding program at Holy Cross is biology with the premed concentration. A student in the program explains, "There are so many requirements for premed students, so it is challenging to manage your schedule when it comes time to take some core classes." The biological/premedical concentration is set apart by the fact that it requires about seven hours of lab work per week. At the other end of the spectrum, some social science majors, including sociology and psychology are generally considered easy. This does not mean they are "slacker majors," though. A Holy Cross junior laments, "If only Holy Cross had a slacker major!"

Academics at Holy Cross are challenging, and there is definitely a sense of competition among students. On average, students do about 25 to 35 hours of school work outside of class per week. Again, science majors bear a slightly heavier load and 40 hours of work per week is not out of the ordinary. The work is not easy. "I would say that the academics are very challenging at Holy Cross," adds a sophomore. "There aren't many 'easy A' classes if we have any at all." Though rigorous, the learning environment is tailored to the students. Many classes are discussion-oriented and consist of only a few students. In addition, professors are accessible outside of class for students who want extra help.

Students who attend one of "consortium" institutions may take classes at another, and transferring between them is easier than it might be from a university outside the program. Worcester Polytechnic is a notable member of this program.

On and Off Campus

Socially speaking, Holy Cross offers something for everyone. Options include school-sponsored social events, parties, Worcester clubs, and even opportunities to take advantage of the not-too-distant Boston shopping and nightlife scene. Weekends offer students a chance to take advantage of what is slightly farther away from campus. Boston, a forty-five minute drive or train trip, has much to offer, and the university conveniently provides a free shuttle on Friday and Saturday to either Boston or Solomon Pond Mall, a nearby shopping center that includes the popular Best Buy and outlet stores. Of the two, though, Boston is your best bet for anything trendy or fashionable. It's a good idea to check out the list of stores at SPM before venturing out there. Shopping is not the only thing to do, though. There's a great movie theater there as well.

There are options right at home, too, although a car is definitely a plus at this small school. While Worcester may not be the thriving metropolis one would hope, there are several nice restaurants nearby that cater to nights out with friends as well as the admittedly limited dating scene at Holy Cross. Worcester also has museums and the Centrum concert venue. Again, the bar scene in Worcester, which is the destination of choice on Thursday nights, is accessible only to those upperclassmen with cars, so there are a large number of off-campus parties at the residences that border the campus. The sports teams dominate many facets of life at Holy Cross, and the social scene is no exception. Most parties are hosted by members of one team or another. While this limits the options available to underclassmen, it does not mean that there is nothing to do.

Holy Cross makes a great effort to provide entertainment with a bevy of on-campus activities. There are concerts, and traditional annual parties such as the Senior Ball and the ROTC dance. Freshmen attend the Opportunity Knocks dance in the fall. A student who has attended in the past recounts, "It's a little different than your normal dance in that your roommate has to set you up with someone by calling his or her roommate, so the people going to Opp-Knocks together don't know until a day or two before the dance."

Underage drinking does occur but is difficult to get away with. Holy Cross has a strictly-enforced drinking policy and limits the number of people who can assemble in a room. Noise violations also lead to infractions. The university is dedicated to maintaining a safe and alcohol-free environment for minors, and Worcester police are tough on underage drinkers and those caught with fake ID's. Still, students report that it is possible to get alcohol with a fake ID and that establishments in the area aren't necessarily too critical. A senior who remembers his underage days well says, "For the underclassman, you can drink if you're brave enough, but you know you'd better not get caught."

One of the best features of Holy Cross is the ability to easily meet people and make friends. There is no Greek System, which makes the entire student body relatively cohesive. Still, there are cliques and small social groups. The best way to meet people is still through classes or in the dorms.

A typical Holy Cross weekend begins with an off-campus party on Thursday night. Friday is a time to recover, go to class, and go to a sports game. Saturday afternoons are a time to get busy with actual school work and before releasing stress at a bar or party at night. And on Sundays, resting and relaxing is key. Many opt to go to Sunday brunch before attending mass.

The social scene at Holy Cross, while more open to those with transportation and those who can legally drink, is hardly boring. There is something for everybody, both during the day and evening, and while some are initially put off by the lack of a dating scene, the ease of forming friendships and social circles seems to make up for that.

The Holy Cross Lifestyle

Holy Cross is a small campus built on Mount Saint James. It is very traditional, with red-brick buildings and "ornate" architecture that gives the campus an older feel. In the fall, the campus is covered with vibrant foliage that enhances the atmosphere. By contrast, Worcester, or "Wootown," leaves a lot to be desired. The majority of central Worcester seems rundown and unattractive. Few students venture out regularly, but those who do choose Shrewsbury Street (Exit 15 off East 290) for the selection of restaurants and its convenience to campus.

Campus life is extremely full at Holy Cross, and this may be attributed, at least in part, to the impressive amenities that the campus boasts. The facilities on campus provide opportunities for research and creative enjoyment. The science facilities and libraries are well-regarded and the art resources, too often overlooked, are notable as well. There are two gyms, one for varsity athletes and another, with an indoor track, for the general student body.

"For the underclassman, you can drink if you're brave enough, but you know you'd better not get caught."

At Holy Cross sports are king, though there are no historic rivalries. Basketball is the most popular, and school spirit pervades the entire campus during the season. "There is so much school spirit," says one student, "The games are so much fun and they're always so packed." Purple Pride Day, announced only a day in advance, is a campus-wide celebration of Holy Cross spirit. Although students often spend Thursday and Saturday nights partying, many reserve Fridays for supporting their teams at games.

With so many people living on campus, the dining halls are always busy social scenes. Kimball, the main dining hall, is buffet style, and most students can find something there. In addition, Lower Kimball, or "Lower," which is located below the main dining hall, offers quicker and more varied lunch options. Lower Kimball has a deli bar, a grill, ready-made meals, and Chinese food. Upperclassmen often opt to eat in Crossroads, a grill-style eatery with a wider selection.

Beyond the essentials, many students pursue their interests through extracurricular activities. The largest organization on campus is CAB, which organizes social events such as Opp-Knocks and brings in guests to speak and do comedy routines. Clubs on campus help foster the sense of community at this school. "Getting out there and trying your hand at any number of activities is really the easiest way to make friends here," noted one sophomore. Living together also helps cement this bond, as very few students live off campus. Now that new senior apartments have just been constructed, even fewer people are moving. The unity felt at Holy Cross is definitely felt through closeness of community and school spirit, but also through religion. The student body may be seen as white and homogenous, but it seems that the administration is trying to diversify and stimulate programs that minimize racial segregation or homophobia. Conservativism may pervade the steeples of Holy Cross, but so do the long-lasting traditions of education, liberal arts, and spiritual unity. —*Minta Nester*

FYI

If you come to Holy Cross, you'd better bring "a parka and running shoes."

What is the typical weekend schedule? "Thursday, off-campus party; Friday, athletic event; Saturday, study and go to a bar; Sunday, recover and study hard."

If I could change one thing about Holy Cross, I'd "make the student body more liberal."

Three things every student at Holy Cross should do before graduating are: "Slap Jesus' hand at the monument on the front steps of the main library, sled on a Kimball's tray, and attend the party on Caro Street on Saint Patrick's Day."

Emerson College

Address: 120 Boylston St.; Boston, MA 02116-4624
Phone: 617-824-8500
E-mail address: admission@emerson.edu
Web site URL: www.emerson.edu
Founded: 1880
Private or Public: private
Religious affiliation: none
Location: urban
Undergraduate enrollment: 3,518
Total enrollment: NA
Percent Male/Female: 36%/64%
Percent Minority: 10%
Percent African-American: 2%
Percent Asian: 3%
Percent Hispanic: 5%
Percent Native-American: 0%
Percent in-state/out of state: 35%/65%
Percent Pub HS: NA
Number of Applicants: 8,016
Percent Accepted: 52%
Percent Accepted who enroll: 32%
Entering: 651
Transfers: 248
Application Deadline: 15 Jan
Mean SAT: NA
Mean ACT: NA
Middle 50% SAT range: V 570-660, M 540-630
Middle 50% ACT range: 24-28
3 Most popular majors: performing and visual arts, journalism, media studies
Retention: 83%
Graduation rate: 66%
On-campus housing: 48%
Fraternities: 5%
Sororities: 4%
Library: 141,000 volumes
Tuition and Fees: $22,548
Room and Board: $9,858
Financial aid, first-year: 59%
Varsity or Club Athletes: NA
Early Decision or Early Action Acceptance Rate: 59%

If you are a budding artist looking for a diverse community that's as dedicated to liberal arts as it is to supporting creativity, then Emerson College combines the best of both worlds. As the only college in America dedicated exclusively to communication and the arts in a liberal arts context, Emerson attracts students who are united by one thing: a passion to learn, create, and perform in a vibrant, urban educational community.

Art School or Just School?

Located in the heart of Boston, Emerson is not your typical college. Providing both a liberal arts education and preprofessional art experience, the college prides itself on striking a balance between the two. The curriculum at Emerson creates unique synergy between the arts and academics by weaving them into a course of study that cultivates creativity and passion in its students.

Nearly all students declare their major freshman year, and upon doing so choose between the School of the Arts and the School of Communications. The School of the Arts includes the departments of visual and media arts, performance arts, and writing, while the School of Communications offers communication sciences, journalism, and advertising. The early declaration of majors does not, however, preclude certain core requirements. True to its foundation as a school of oratory, Emerson requires incoming students to take Oral Communication and Speech in their first year. While the class draws high marks for content, it is acknowledged to be one of the easier courses at Emerson. It is designed as a warm-up for later study—students are required to complete two semesters of history related to their major, many of which are described as "extremely challenging" for even the strongest students. While not all courses share this kind of academic intensity, there is no question that academics are taken very seriously at Emerson. As one student put it, "They don't mess around when it comes to liberal arts . . . they're often tougher than even the most intense arts courses."

Nearly every area of study at Emerson receives high marks from students. Particularly strong are the journalism, film (including television), and musical theater departments. Writing is one of the most rigorous majors and notably attracts the most driven and competitive students.

Otherwise, the only department consistently cited as "needing help" is radio, where a decline in the enrollment has disappointed students and faculty alike.

One of the few academic complaints regards the length of classes, which mostly run an hour and a half or longer. Class options and class size, however, are commended, as most students get their top choices, particularly within their major. With discussion classes limited to 16 students, and a recent move to limit lecture courses to 35, close interaction is in no short supply. Even the largest lecture courses, students point out, often include a fair amount of participation.

Presiding over small classes, Emerson's professors are considered a great asset. As one student recalls, "my first professor here was obsessed with exploitation films . . . he's silly, politically incorrect, and totally hilarious." While some required courses—especially certain writing core courses—are taught by graduate student TAs, few complain about them. "They go through like a year of training to teach a single course," one student points out, "so they tend to be pretty damn good at what they do."

While the pace at Emerson may seem to exclude those without a clear plan in mind, several students point out that simply isn't the case. Emersonians are driven, but a large percentage minor in a different field simply because they can't decide what they want to do. As one student put it, "everyone here knows what they want to do to some extent, but if they don't, they just take on two things." The workload, for those who do, is described as manageable and often helps students feel like they're getting the most out of their experience. And for those who truly can't decide on a single major, the "Planned Studies" major leaves flexibility for those who want to make their course of study truly unique. Remarkably, Planned Studies majors also needn't forfeit priority for class enrollment—they are given near-major preference in those fields relevant to their proposed course of study.

So Different, Yet So Similar

Every student has a different take on exactly who the typical Emerson student is. That is, perhaps, because the student body prides itself on just that—an amazing diversity of opinion on campus. Students are, according to one undergraduate, "all the overachievers and outcasts from high school," but each finds a place at Emerson. Woven into the undergraduate experience is a commitment to open-mindedness. Students celebrate their differences, and such universally supportive environment leads students to cheer, "you couldn't possibly feel uncomfortable about who you are at Emerson." This diversity, however, seems two-dimensional to some who complain "their personalities may be different, but everyone is white here. It's a school of misfits, but most of them are pretty well-off." Moreover, some students feel that all of the open-mindedness can become preachy; "if you don't come here with an open mind," says one student, "you'll have one beaten into you by sophomore year."

At Emerson, students are united by difference, "except," in the words of one undergraduate, "for the similarities most have, which include either homosexuality or an addiction to nicotine." While some students speculate that as much as 60% of the male population at Emerson is gay, an overwhelming sense of acceptance makes this fact seem commonplace. As one openly gay undergraduate put it, "I'm amazed with this place; it's a perfect world of respect and trust." Gay life is as much a part of student life as anything else at Emerson, a fact that only seems to disappoint women by severely limiting dating options. As one student says, "if you're a girl you come here to study. If you're a guy, you come here to date, especially if you're straight; then you'll be in the minority." However, it is not only this trend that characterizes the student body. First and foremost, Emerson students describe their peers as enthusiastic and consistently cite the creativity and diversity of their classmates as what makes their school stands out.

The intense creativity of Emerson students is reflected in the wide variety of extracurricular activities they immerse themselves in. Not surprisingly, the motivated and artistic student body finds that many of their activities relate to their major. Film students, for instance, often work their way into student productions and even professional projects throughout the year. "We have so many things to get involved in professionally, in addition to all the student-run things . . . seriously, how can you not love a school with its own record label?" gloats one Emersonian. The college, for instance, has one of the most popular college radio stations in the country, WERS, which attracts students from all corners of the campus. Additionally, the Majestic Theater—Emerson's own opera house—serves as a venue for a host of student performances and productions.

"You couldn't possibly feel uncomfortable about who you are at Emerson."

The college also provides incredible resources for students' creative endeavors outside of the classroom, including state-of-the-art filmmaking equipment. From lighting kits to cameras, students find that if they plan ahead, getting equipment is extremely easy. Moreover, unique study abroad opportunities, which include studying at Emerson's castle in the Netherlands, are also included in the list of "incredible things" the college offers.

Something Fun

As for parties, Emerson students know how to have a good time. Their location in the heart of a bustling Boston gives them a wealth of social opportunities, both on campus and off. Parties on campus seem to be mostly attended by upperclassmen, while local bars seem to be a popular choice for freshmen and sophomores. The college, however, does have a strict policy regarding underage alcohol consumption, and sometimes goes out of its way to shut down parties it deems inappropriate. Dorms, for example, are completely dry, or "supposed to be dry," and if students are caught by the administration twice, there is a mandatory suspension. This rarely happens, however, and simply prompts most of the social life to move off campus. Greek life exists, but is by no means the center of the party scene. Beyond parties, Boston offers a wide variety of movie theaters and shows that draw plenty of students. The student center is considered a popular hangout, and while not a party venue, it offers a central meeting place for a social scene that might otherwise be fragmented by the urban surroundings. In general, students express satisfaction with the social options available to them. One student notes that even on campus, "there is always something fun and interesting going on . . . you never feel forced to leave in order to enjoy yourself."

Living and dining facilities at Emerson comprise another of its most attractive features in the eyes of most undergrads. Housing is guaranteed for all freshmen, and most students choose to live on campus until the end of their sophomore year. Juniors and seniors often move off campus even though the dorms are described as anything from "very good" to "absolutely amazing." While housing options seem to quench students' thirst for luxury, the dining receives equally high praise. Emerson's primary cafeteria, housed in the "Little" Building (that is, in fact, extremely large), is billed as "wonderful . . . the selection is incredible," and special features such as a daily vegetarian selection make the food as diverse as it is appealing. The off-campus dining options encompass a multiethnic and affordable restaurant scene and reflect an overall sentiment among students: that the campus is inseparable from the Boston experience. Students feel that "the campus *is* Boston, so it makes everything more exciting," even if the urban location presents safety concerns. Students learn to deal with this environment, however, and a highly-praised freshman orientation makes the transition to urban life not just manageable, but exhilarating.

Finding Your Place

Emersonians feel as at home in Boston as they do on campus, and that feeling of support and comfort is what many feel makes the college truly unique. Their student body is as vibrant as their city, each member of the community able to express themselves fully in a supportive environment of trust and personal development. Students at Emerson feel like they can be academic and artistic, but above all, they can be themselves. The diversity of thought and the uniqueness of its curriculum make Emerson anything but your typical undergraduate institution, but as one student says "that's what makes this place so great. We're different, and we like it that way." —*R. David Edelman*

FYI

If you come to Emerson, you'd better bring "an open mind . . . or you'll have one beaten into you by sophomore year."

What is the typical weekend schedule? "Friday, movies for film students, party late; Saturday, go see a theater show, party late; and Sunday, sleep, study, do something creative."

If I could change one thing about Emerson, I'd change "the way you're informed about extra equipment for class. How am I supposed to know I'm going to need a 60GB hard drive for the first day?"

Three things every Emerson student should do before graduating are "reading on Boston Common, visit Anna's Taqueria, the best (and cheapest) taqueria in Boston, and participate in one of the off-campus programs—they'll send you to the Netherlands to live in a castle, or even L.A., it's your choice."

Hampshire College

Address: 893 West Street; Amherst, MA 01002
Phone: 413-559-5471
E-mail address: admissions@hampshire.edu
Web site URL: www.hampshire.edu
Founded: 1965
Private or Public: private
Religious affiliation: none
Location: rural
Undergraduate enrollment: 1,267
Total enrollment: NA
Percent Male/Female: 42%/58%
Percent Minority: 16%
Percent African-American: 3%
Percent Asian: 4%
Percent Hispanic: 5%
Percent Native-American: 0%
Percent in-state/out of state: 19%/81%
Percent Pub HS: NA
Number of Applicants: 2,094
Percent Accepted: 51%
Percent Accepted who enroll: 29%
Entering: 305
Transfers: 49
Application Deadline: 1 Feb
Mean SAT: NA
Mean ACT: NA
Middle 50% SAT range: V 600-700, M 540-660
Middle 50% ACT range: 25-29
3 Most popular majors: visual arts, social sciences, English
Retention: 81%
Graduation rate: NA
On-campus housing: NA
Fraternities: NA
Sororities: NA
Library: 110,000 volumes
Tuition and Fees: $29,392
Room and Board: $7,689
Financial aid, first-year: 53%
Varsity or Club Athletes: NA
Early Decision or Early Action Acceptance Rate: ED 72%; EA 73%

Whether judged on its academics, its professors, or its students, Hampshire College comes across as an incredibly unique and unconventional place to go to school. It combines a liberal atmosphere and "fun, open-minded students" with a demanding but uniquely individualized academic program.

Building Your Own Education

"The hardest thing about Hampshire," says one third-year student, "may be going home and being asked what your major is." Students at Hampshire College are in the curious position of not having an answer to that question, as Hampshire eschews the "traditional" academic system in favor of a unique program that is personalized to each student. The academic structure at Hampshire is composed of three divisions. Division 1 is intended to provide a broad base of knowledge and is spread among five schools: Humanities, Arts and Cultural Studies, Interdisciplinary Arts, Cognitive Science, Natural Science, and Social Science. Depending on a student's interest, Division 1 can consist of classes, individual projects, or some combination of the two. By the time a student enters Division 2, the work is more focused and involves projects in a student's selected field of study. The emphasis here is on building a portfolio and the work includes community service and multicultural components. Studying abroad is a common feature of Division 2 projects, and some students have even left for years before returning to "incorporate their experiences as part of the Division 2 process of self-discovery." Finally, Division 3 marks the culmination of a student's work at Hampshire. This is generally a major project, or "your masterpiece." Completion of a Division 3 project is celebrated with a party and the traditional ringing of a large bell at graduation.

Generally, students are pleased with the divisional system, but they note that it is not without its flaws. There's "lots of paperwork for everything, and lots of running around getting all the paperwork signed by half the faculty and staff and their uncles," said one student, adding that while "the requirements are unstructured, that doesn't mean better or unique." Another student noted that "freshmen often have a hard time with the Division 1 process," and that some professors don't know the system well enough. "But," he added, "the system is currently being revamped."

Another point many students stress is that Hampshire's lack of grades and tests does not make for an easier workload. There are many written papers, lots of reading, and "in classes you have to speak up all the time, and actually engage the material, not just take notes." Also, the written evaluations that students receive in place of grades can be "brutal," because they list weaknesses as well as strengths in great detail.

The professors at Hampshire are "insanely dedicated" and "extremely encouraging and helpful." They go by their first names and tend to build very personal relationships with the students, which is a good thing since students may find themselves working individually with their professors on entire Division 2 and Division 3 projects. "One of my professors wouldn't start class today until he gave everyone who wanted coffee a cup on him," said one student. Another professor is known to keep a sleeping bag in her office and sometimes spends the night there in case students need anything.

Classes at Hampshire tend to be small and oriented toward the arts and humanities. However, students are quick to point out that Hampshire is "pretty damned conducive to science-types as well," and that "the scientific instrument resources you will find here in many instances rival what you will find at a large public university." The most popular programs are in film, photography, and creative writing, and space in these classes can be limited. However, "95 percent of classes on campus are extremely easy to get into," and since Hampshire is part of the Massachusetts Five College Consortium, students can also take classes at Smith, Mount Holyoke, Amherst, and UMass at Amherst. The Five College Consortium is generally very useful and accessible by a bus that runs between the campuses every 15 minutes.

Party in the Valley: Drag Balls and Hampshire Halloween

Weekends at Hampshire "start Thursday afternoon," since most students don't have Friday classes. "You can do pretty much anything you want on the weekends and no one cares," be that partying, working, or just hanging out at the Hampshire Tree, a big old tree in the middle of a corn field. Concerts, movies, and poetry readings are frequent, and "there is some sort of party almost every weekend at Hampshire, often with some sort of theme such as 'glam rock,' or 'black lingerie.'" However, "people rarely know what all their options are, since many events are announced only at the last minute or by word of mouth." According to students, alcohol and pot smoking are very widespread at Hampshire, but most agree that there is little pressure to participate. "It is easy to be at the parties and not drink because there is good music and dancing." Finally, there are always parties at the other colleges within the consortium.

Hampshire is known for two big parties, Hampshire Halloween in October and the Drag Ball, which takes place in the spring. "Even if nobody chooses to go to school here, they should all plan on booking a flight to get to Hampshire Halloween." Another popular though "unofficial" event is the Easter Keg Hunt, for which several kegs are hidden in the pine woods and students search for them, cups in hand.

"We're Not All Hippies and Marxists"

Hampshire is certainly a liberal community, but most students resent being stereotyped as "Shaggy from Scooby Doo." One student confirmed that there is an "average amount of hippies" but notes that Hampshire students are very diverse and laid-back. "Hampshire is the only school where you can walk across campus wearing nothing but a pair of stiletto heels and have somebody look you straight in the eye and say, 'Those are great shoes, man, where'd you get them?'" Hampshire students tend to be friendly and outgoing and most have no trouble making friends: "You'd have to hide all the time to avoid making friends, and even when you did emerge, people would say, 'Hey, where have you been? Let's go pick apples!'" The dating scene, on the other hand, is virtually non-existent, and "most people either have casual sex, or are in serious relationships." Homosexual and bisexual couples are fairly common and are well-accepted.

> **"Hampshire is the only school where you can walk across campus wearing nothing but a pair of stiletto heels and have somebody look you straight in the eye and say 'Those are great shoes, man, where'd you get them?'"**

"There are a lot of complaints that Hampshire needs diversity," and some students feel that the atmosphere is unaccommodating to minorities. "There are a lot of rich white kids here," said one student, while another confirmed that "we see international students from the Middle East and such, as well as some blacks, but not as many as we would like to see." A minority student at Hampshire complained that there is "racism and negative energy" on campus, and that minorities may have a harder time adjusting to the college. Hampshire is implementing a mentoring program for minorities, however, and this should help the situation in the future.

Rolling Hills and "Ugly Buildings"

Hampshire freshmen generally live in dorms and then move to apartments called "mods" for their remaining three years of college. The dorms are mostly singles and are described alternatively as "dungeon-like" and "blessedly private." There are theme dorms, such as lesbian and gay, clothing-optional, substance-free, and study-intensive, colloquially known as "the morgue." The dorms are "very social," and all are co-ed, including the bathrooms. Interns live with freshmen to serve the role of RAs. However, they tend to be easygoing and friendly: "basically they're just here to give advice and make sure things are going well for you."

Hampshire students are also very fond of their campus, and though they universally deride the '70s-style buildings as "ugly," the idyllic setting makes up for many of the architectural deficiencies. Surrounded by farmland, fields, and woods, the Hampshire campus provides many beautiful spaces to bike, jog, or simply relax in nature. The campus also boasts several unique features, including a working farm with vegetables and animals, and the "Yurt," a Mongolian hut that started out as a student's Div 3 project and is now being turned into the campus radio station. Hampshire is also home to the Yiddish Book Center, and the Eric Carle Picture Book Museum, which will be the only children's book art museum in the country when it is completed later this year.

The SAGA Saga

SAGA, the campus dining hall, is rated anywhere from "good" to "I subsist on waffles," but includes a pasta bar, a salad bar, cereal, a lunchtime sandwich bar, and vegetarian and vegan choices. Other students are less optimistic, complaining about the lack of dining options. SAGA "is our only source of 'food' if one can call it that. They make us go, and we are never the same afterwards."

The surrounding towns of Amherst and Northampton offer plenty of fine restaurants and coffee shops, chief among these are the New India Restaurant, the Black Sheep sandwich shop, and Rao's coffeehouse, where "they play loud techno, but everyone studies to it." Finally, students can buy vegetables from Hampshire's own working farm or eat at "the Tavern," a student-run snack joint that serves great milkshakes but, lamented one student, "no longer serves alcohol."

Where the Frisbees Fly Leftward

Team sports and organized athletics are fairly lacking at Hampshire. "The only team sport worth anything is Ultimate Frisbee," said one student. "Our team is called The Red Scare and their motto is 'Are you, or have you ever been, a member of the Communist party?'" Hampshire also boasts a basketball team and a soccer team, and its athletic facilities include a full-size pool, an indoor track, indoor and outdoor tennis and basketball courts, a rock-climbing wall, and two sports fields. For the most part, however, Hampshire students tend to prefer individualized athletics; biking, rock climbing, kayaking, dance, martial arts, and yoga are all very popular.

Among other extracurricular activities, there are three major publications on campus: the Forward, a newspaper, the Omen, a free speech publication, and Macrocosm, a collection of student works. Political activism is very hot, and protests are common. But there is little pressure to join one group or another. Hampshire students "do their own thing," true to the freethinking atmosphere the college encourages.

Hampshire College offers students freedom to choose their education, supportive and caring professors, and a unique mix of "crazy, crazy people." Hampshire may not be for everyone, but "most people know before they ever set foot here." So if Hampshire College sounds like a place you'd enjoy spending the next four years, it probably is. —*Joseph Frenkel*

FYI

If you come to Hampshire, you'd better bring a "Nalgene bottle and a sense of responsibility."

A typical weekend consists of "a party on Friday, homework Saturday, going into town for a concert or something, and sleeping on Sunday."

If I could change one thing about Hampshire, I'd "like to see a student government that I could be inspired by. That and lowered tuition."

Three things every student at Hampshire should do before graduating are "get lost in the woods, discover the wonders of the farm center, and take a course in something you're completely not interested in."

Harvard University

Address: Byerly Hall, 8 Garden Street; Cambridge, MA 02138
Phone: 617-495-1551
E-mail address: college@fas.harvard.edu
Web site URL: www.fas.harvard.edu
Founded: 1636
Private or Public: private
Religious affiliation: none
Location: urban
Undergraduate enrollment: 6,649
Total enrollment: NA
Percent Male/Female: 53%/47%
Percent Minority: 40%
Percent African-American: 7%
Percent Asian: 17%
Percent Hispanic: 8%
Percent Native-American: 1%
Percent in-state/out of state: 16%/84%
Percent Pub HS: 66%
Number of Applicants: 19,609
Percent Accepted: 11%
Percent Accepted who enroll: 79%
Entering: 1,640
Transfers: 55
Application Deadline: 1 Jan
Mean SAT: NA
Mean ACT: NA
Middle 50% SAT range: V700-790, M 700-790
Middle 50% ACT range: 31-34
3 Most popular majors: economics, political science, psychology
Retention: 97%
Graduation rate: 96%
On-campus housing: 95%
Fraternities: NA
Sororities: NA
Library: 13,000,000 volumes
Tuition and Fees: $29,060
Room and Board: $8,868
Financial aid, first-year: 48%
Varsity or Club Athletes: 20%
Early Decision or Early Action Acceptance Rate: EA 19%

If you ask them, Harvard students will tell you that they are just like any other students at any other university. And they might be smiling when they tell you this, because the thing is, they aren't at just any other university. Harvard tends to get a bad rep for its egotistical, overly intellectual, even pompous student population, but in truth, the personalities of the students who flock to quaint and quirky Cambridge every September do not fit so simply into this 'Harvard type.'

If You Built It, They Will Come

At Harvard, the intellectual life of its students comes first. Boasting countless departments with top national rankings, scores of professors with prizes, titles, and books to their names, the university is able to provide its new undergraduates with a smorgasbord of educational choices. Freshmen begin their time at Harvard by structuring their schedules around the "Core Curriculum." This is entails a set of eight classes, selected out of 11 disciplines, and covers the sciences, foreign language, world cultures, and of course, the humanities. Students feel the Core "takes on the real liberal arts feel, and the core req's are pretty diverse." One junior reflected, "You come in knowing that you'll take lit and science no matter what your future concentration might be." The major complaint about the core classes among students is their consistently large size, as most are taught as large lectures and that "some of the classes end up being pretty narrow and specific, which can be tedious if you're not interested." However, by the end of their four years, most acknowledged an appreciation for the Core, as it provides the opportunity to take the "things you always wished you'd taken."

While just about all majors, or "concentrations," are strong, different areas attract attention among the undergrad population. Supported by the internationally renowned Kennedy School of Government, the undergraduate government concentration is very popular and though "Gov gets booked as 'jock' but it can actually be pretty challenging in the upper-level and tutorial-sized classes." Some students mentioned econ, or "Ec," as being considered pretty easy, because "Ec has less requirements than the other majors, so it can sometimes be looked at as kind of slacker, but if you're into it, it can be really interesting and worthwhile." Students have to apply to become concentrators in certain departments, including the interdisciplinary history and literature and social studies programs. Though just about all classes are "as challenging as you make them," the "21 Math series is really a killer," made up of the year-long sequence of multivariable calculus and linear algebra.

The workload at Harvard varies from concentration to concentration and from student to student. "People do a lot of work. Though they might not do it on time, pretty much everyone does the reading at some point in the semester," noted one student. "People are consistently very prepared." Students also recognize that what really makes a class is the high caliber of the professor who is lecturing. While there are many such profs across Harvard's many fields, Martin Feldstein, chair of the National Bureau of Economic Research and Harvard economics professor, is popular, as are Roger Porter and his "truly awesome" American Presidency class.

Students lament that large lectures are "a little too common," in most concentrations, and that "there are definitely more lectures than seminars because of the Cores—a lot of intro and intermediate classes are going to be lectures." Once students have passed the intermediate level, they can begin to engage more directly with peers and professors in smaller seminar and tutorial-sized classes. Because of the prevalence of large classes, the university is very dependent upon its graduate student population, who moonlight as TFs, serving as "a liaison between profs and your smaller section of the lecture." Students have accepted the system as the way it's going to be: "You learn the big concepts from the profs then TFs go over the nitty-gritty and important things, and they also read your papers." Students noted that this divide often increases the "deity status," of professors and though "everyone is very accessible by e-mail," "not a lot of people interact on a really personal level with lecture professors."

Harvard starts the semester off with "shopping period," when in the first weeks of the year students can attend a variety of classes before deciding which ones to register for. The university ends the semester, eschewing the calendars of its peer institutions, by having its "reading period," a week without classes to catch up on work and study, and finals after the winter vacation. The system gets mixed reviews from students, but they seem to "really appreciate the break before reading and finals." Harvard has recently come under fire for having "rampant grade inflation," which causes many students to laugh and remark, "I'd hate to see my grades with-OUT the inflation." The university has taken steps to combat this bad press and many students report that "professors try to curb grade inflation and are centering the classes on a lower average, which kind of sucks when you feel like you're really doing A work," and that "there's a definite momentum to push grades back down." This seems to stem from the general problem of the larger classes, where "there's no wiggle room or flexibility because in more quantitative classes, professors just need to calculate a number for your grade." In classes like Psych 1, where such grading was a complaint, students "totally loved" the class and "the lectures were always really engaging. Because they enter Harvard armed for an academic battle, students are able to meet the challenges of course selection and heavy workload.

Puritan Setting, Modern Fun

From freshman year forward, almost all Harvard students live on campus, and the system of 12 residential Houses is central to the college's social and residential life. Freshmen are housed on the storied "Harvard Yard," a beautiful quad lined with trees, statues and the classic red brick of "the typical New England College, because it is THE New England College." On the Yard, frosh bond with the other new kids in their entryways, each of which is monitored by graduate student proctors who "look out for you and hold weekly study breaks with snacks." The freshmen dorms are single-sex by room, and are "actually pretty nice, though it can vary a bit." There is a no-alcohol policy in Yard dorms which is "fairly strictly enforced, depending on your proctor." At the end of freshman year, students "block" together into groups of eight and are randomly assigned to a given house, where the groups of friends live for the next three years. As a result of the system's arbitrariness, there aren't set stereotypes for the different houses. A student observed that "the lottery can't effect the feel of a house, compared to back in the day when you'd get all athletes in one place and rich legacy kids in another because the House Masters would screen for candidates." Each house has its own set of amenities, from snack bars to computer labs to special features like a darkroom. These smaller communities "make the big university feel a lot more homey."

"I might say it's more of a 'Work Hard, Party Tentatively' sort of place."

The eating scene is also dependent on the houses. Freshmen eat in the large Annenberg dining hall, where "since the chefs have to cook for the whole freshman class, the food isn't that good." Most students can eat in any of the house dining halls, contained within each building. All the kitchens were recently renovated, and students have few complaints about the food, other than "it's a little bland sometimes, but there's always something to eat." Each house dining hall has a distinct feel, some of which are "warm old beautiful halls," while Mather House "feels very institutional." There is also a new chef on board who has been making some changes to the menu and is "being very creative—it's refreshing." When students get tired of the dining hall grub, Cambridge is waiting for them with open arms. Amid the clapboard houses along the twisty streets are some great places for grub of all kinds. Student-priced options abound, from "cool Mex food at Boca Grande," tasty and eclectic sandwiches in a delightful Sunday afternoon study spot at Darwin's Café, to "Henrietta's Table, which has great brunch, and the a cappella group the Krokodiloes serenade you there on Sunday mornings." One student mentioned that she "eats off campus a fair amount—more than I should!" Cambridge, especially the very close Harvard Square area, nestled into campus, provides a number of good study spots, and many chose to do reading in the Square's coffee and teahouses.

Walking around campus, you'll find traditional red brick mingling with neo-gothic and more modern forms of architecture. The university also meshes well with old Cambridge, which as a town is "very crunchy and offbeat." The locals are and always have been "very opinionated and politically boisterous." Harvard Square is host to a variety of shops which include the more mainstream Abercrombie and Fitch as well as more esoteric bookstores and independent movie theaters. Students feel safe on campus and in Cambridge because the University is diligent in its patrol of the area and in providing late-night transportation to any students who might need it. Especially on the weekends, Harvard students venture beyond Cambridge into downtown Boston, which is a short subway ride away on the local Red Line of the T, Boston's subway.

Finals? No, Not Exams . . .

The House system, in addition to academic and community resources, also acts as the hub of the after-hours Harvard social scene. On a given night of the weekend, freshmen will usually find themselves at parties hosted by the residential houses. The university often designates groups of rooms as the known 'party suites,' mentioned one student, "the major blocking groups that throw parties are definitely the 10-man in Currier House and the PhoHo Bell Tower." Alcohol is generally at the focus of these events, though in true Harvard fashion, it is not unusual to have "intellectual discussions late at night, under the influence of beer and pizza." The houses host annual formal dances as well as theme parties like Leverett House's annual 80s night. Harvard has a few fraternities and sororities, but these are very much under the radar, compared with the much "older-school Finals Clubs." These traditionally all-male groups have houses where members and their friends, as well as an array of freshmen girls, come to socialize on weekends. The clubs vary a bit in profile and penchant for activities: the Fly "is all the preppy boys," for example, and the Spee has bigger parties, including a yearly Chinese New Year Party that is "always an awesome time." Other popular clubs include the AD and the Fox. As an upperclassman, "you'll likely only visit the clubs where you or your friends are members."

Being underage and drinking is "really not an issue," said one student, "unless your proctor is really strict." Upperclassmen may also turn to the bar scene, and most often frequent Daedalus, Redline, and Grafton Street, right in Cambridge, though appropriate ID is necessary for these places. While drinking is a large part of the party network, drugs keep a rather lower profile, though "you know they're there, but you don't have to feel pressured or even see people doing them most of the time." For non-drinkers, there are options, though "a lot come out socially to dancing parties and have a good time." Students seem to stay as level-headed about their social activities as they are about their studies, remarking that "the weekend is definitely not a Wednesday through Sunday kind of thing here, I might say it's more of a 'Work Hard, Party Tentatively' sort of place."

There is also a constant succession of concerts, lectures, and debate forums flooding campus. Harvard frequently brings popular bands to campus to play—hometown Boston band Guster performed in the gym this past fall to a full house. There are also dollar-movie nights, when first-run films are shown, and though there is no central student center like at some schools, the house scene tends to make up for this. When it comes to love and dating, Harvard students feel that "there are a lot of random hook-ups, and a lot of couples, but not many people who go out on dates." Another joked, "I didn't know that people went on dates here." There are, however, "definitely enough attractive people." Harvard houses an active gay culture, and people feel that "the community is very open and accepting here, you see gay couples out in public all the time." In their other free time, students have essentially unlimited options. "We're mostly the type of overachievers that feel like we're not doing enough unless there's always something going on," laughed one student. The two most popular activities, on a list as long as the academic virtues of the University, are the House Committees, which organize social activities, and the variety of community service opportunities organized under the Phillip Brooks House. Also popular are the Women In Business Society, humorous groups like the Four Square Club, and the Hasty Pudding Club, whose renowned theatricals are nationally recognized. While some students feel that there is "no single stereotype of students at Harvard really except that we're all pretty driven academically," some students were more honest, admitting that "there is a lot of great diversity, don't get me wrong, but the majority of students are definitely upper-middle-class and above."

Crimson Pride

Harvard has a long tradition of high-level athletics, which is on a par with its dedication to first-rate academics. Students agree that football is the "most visible team," and lots of undergrads turn out for games, as well as for hockey and basketball games. There has been much athletic success in recent years, epitomized by last year's major rowing victories, which found women's openweight, men's heavyweight, and men's lightweight boats all national champions. Easily the biggest Harvard tradition, however, is the Harvard/Yale game, which annually attracts alums and spectators galore for raucous tailgating. Non-varsity athletes work out in the Malkin Athletic Center (the MAC), which is newly renovated and "a beautiful building," though reportedly lacking enough cardiovascular machines to service the huge number of students that come to workout. House IMs are very popular, and cater to competitive Harvard students battling it out on the playing fields for the sought-after Strauss Cup.

Harvard presents quite the package, first-rate academics, sports, and clubs, in a charming traditional New England setting, but students must consider whether they're ready for the challenge of forging their own way in a school that is "strictly fend-for-yourself." If you have the motivation to make the most of the many opportunities it affords, Harvard could be perfect for you. —*Charlotte Taft*

FYI

If you come to Harvard, you'd better bring "a pair of flip-flops for the ONE day it gets warm in the spring."

What is the typical weekend schedule? "Friday, see a movie; Saturday, hang out, go to a game, head to parties after 11; then Sunday brunch and work all afternoon."

If I could change one thing about Harvard I'd "reform the Core Curriculum so it is a little more flexible."

Three things every student at Harvard should do before graduating are "hook up in the Widener Library stacks, urinate on the John Harvard statue in the Yard, and run Primal Scream."

Massachusetts Institute of Technology

Address: 77 Massachusetts Avenue; Cambridge, MA 02139
Phone: 617-253-4791
E-mail address: admissions@mit.edu
Web site URL: www.web.mit.edu
Founded: 1861
Private or Public: private
Religious affiliation: none
Location: urban
Undergraduate enrollment: 4,178
Total enrollment: NA
Percent Male/Female: 57%/43%
Percent Minority: 55%
Percent African-American: 6%
Percent Asian: 27%
Percent Hispanic: 12%
Percent Native-American: 2%
Percent in-state/out of state: 9%/91%
Percent Pub HS: 76%
Number of Applicants: 10,664
Percent Accepted: 16%
Percent Accepted who enroll: 57%
Entering: 978
Transfers: 20
Application Deadline: 1 Jan
Mean SAT: NA
Mean ACT: NA
Middle 50% SAT range: V 680-760, M 740-800
Middle 50% ACT range: 30-34
3 Most popular majors: engineering, computer science, business
Retention: 98%
Graduation rate: 89%
On-campus housing: 96%
Fraternities: 26%
Sororities: 8%
Library: 2,667,215 volumes
Tuition and Fees: $29,600
Room and Board: $8,710
Financial aid, first-year: 66%
Varsity or Club Athletes: 25%
Early Decision or Early Action Acceptance Rate: EA 14%

During the month of January, the majority of MIT students return to campus for one of the activities that makes their university a unique one. Classes don't start until February, but few students miss the Independent Activities Period (IAP), where faculty and fellow students offer four weeks of fun, creative, and educational programs to the MIT community. Activities range from a workshop on how to create your own Bonsai to a lecture and tour of the Boron Neutron Capture Therapy (BNCT) at the MIT Research Reactor. According to one MIT underclassman, "IAP is one of the most anticipated events of the year." The program gives both students and faculty an opportunity to show off and to share their intellectual passions in a laid-back and enjoyable atmosphere.

Intense Academics

MIT has earned a reputation for intense academics, which is, by all accounts, an accurate one. Students here are passionate about math, science, and technology. Out of an undergraduate population of about 4,200, there were 1,813 students enrolled in engineering studies. Students are expected to test the limits of their abilities in the quest for new knowledge and in return, they are rewarded with an education that is "at the top in the world."

Students come from all over the world to Cambridge in order to learn from and do research with leaders in math and science. "There are famous inventors, Nobel Prize winners, and start-up owners in practically every field of study at MIT," said one student. The approximate 950 full-time faculty members include 10 Nobel Prize winners, four Kyoto Prize Winners, and two Pulitzer Prize winners. Professors teach most classes, so even freshmen have the opportunity to "listen to famous professors." TAs head smaller recitation sections, which meet once a week.

No student would call the workload light. "It will not be an easy four years here for you; the sooner you realize that the better off you will be," said one junior. Students complain about "lots of homework, especially problem sets," and all-night study sessions are not uncommon. All classes taken during the first semester of the freshman year are pass/fail in order to give students time to adjust to the level of work. Students are perpetually complaining about being "hosed," MIT slang for overwhelmed with work, which is derived from the analogy "getting an MIT education is like drinking from a fire hose." However, one student reveals "the workload is what you make it to be," and by choosing an easier major or settling for lower grades, student can lighten their burdens.

Every MIT student must take a core group of math and science classes, including two semesters of calculus, two of physics, one semester of biology, and one of chemistry, plus a lab requirement. One student says fulfilling these requirements has been "not bad at all," and many students get a lot of the core out of the way freshman year. Science and math requirements are, however, "just part of the bargain." Students are also required to take eight humanities, arts, and social science classes, four semesters of PE (Ping-Pong counts), and complete a writing requirement. MIT does its best to make humanities classes interesting and practical. "In my writing class, we put all the stuff we wrote into an online magazine," raved one freshman. Others complain that eight humanities classes are "a little constraining" and take up time that could be devoted to courses within a major.

All students are required to complete a major at MIT. The most popular areas of study are electrical engineering and computer science, with approximately one-fourth of all students. For students looking for the hard road, physics is said to be the most difficult major and management is reputably the easiest. Nevertheless, "you will be challenged regardless of the major you choose," and students warn that there are hard classes in every major. MIT students also have the option of double majoring, adding a minor or graduating in five years with a master's degree.

Introductory classes are usually large, around 200 to 400 students. Freshmen who want more individualized attention have the option of participating in the Experimental Study Group (ESG) program, where first-year students are taught in small groups by professors and upperclassmen and the format is either a discussion-based seminar or tutorial. Once introductory courses are out of the way, class size shrinks and can "range from two to 80 depending on the major." For classes that MIT does not offer, students have the opportunity to cross-register at Harvard or Wellesley.

"Contrary to popular media belief, most people on campus do not drink like fish."

One of the jewels of the MIT academic curriculum is the Undergraduate Research Opportunities Program (UROP). The program fosters research partnerships between undergraduates and MIT faculty, encouraging students to become involved at the forefront of developments in science and technology. "If you are interested in submersing yourself in cutting-edge research, MIT is the place to be," said one upperclassmen. Students participate for academic credit, pay, or as volunteers, and often work on UROP projects over the summer as well as during the school year. The program allows MIT students to apply what they learn in the classroom to real scientific problems.

Nights in the City

When it is time to put the books away, MIT students know how to have a good time. The Greek system on campus is very active, with 26 fraternities and six sororities. Usually there is a fraternity party "at least once a week," but these parties are often "by invitation only." Students also frequent the active club scene, dancing the night away with students from Boston's other universities. There are local bars, but you need an ID, and "everything closes at two in the morning." While in recent years techies have gained a reputation for heavy drinking, many students feel it is an unwarranted one. "Contrary to popular media belief, most people on campus do not drink like fish," said one student and non-drinkers are not ostracized or excluded from the social scene.

Both Boston and Cambridge provide a multitude of alternatives to the party scene. There are movies, restaurants, and coffee shops all accessible through Boston's system of public transportation, and students often venture out into the city. "People go off campus all the time to eat, especially on the weekends, " taking advantage of the restaurants in the North End or along Newbury street. In the beginning, many students do "a lot of touristy stuff," said one freshman, like visiting the Museum of Fine Arts or shopping at Quincy Market. Most students do not have cars because parking is hard to find in Boston and popular transportation makes them unnecessary.

How to Avoid Work: IMs and Hacking

Intramural sports are "very popular" at MIT, and each year hundreds of teams compete in everything from pool to water polo, with teams usually organized by living group. Intercollegiate sports are less popular, but about 20 percent of the campus participates at the varsity level in at least one sport. The rowing and fencing teams are "very strong," as are the pistol and rifle teams. Few people attend the football games, however, and "the opposing teams' fans often outnumber our fans."

MIT students traditionally show off their creativity and daring through performing hacks, "which are clever, non-destructive practical jokes on campus." Famous hacks of the past include placing a replica of a police car, complete with flashing lights, on top of the MIT dome and changing the inscription in lobby 7 to read "Established for Advancement and Development of Science, its Application to Industry, the Arts, Entertainment, and Hacking." Hacks are always performed with a spirit of mischief and fun, and students frown upon any prank that damages property or offends students.

The Housing Scene

MIT undergrads get to choose their housing starting freshman year. When new students first arrive, they are put in temporary dorm housing for orientation, which is followed by a four-day period when students can rush fraternities and sororities and attend events at the various dorms. Since MIT students choose where they live, each dorm is unique and it is the "personality that sets individual dorms apart," rather than location or setup. By the time classes start, students are set in permanent housing, either in fraternities and sororities or in a dorm through "a lottery system run by a computer."

The typical freshman dorm room is a double or a triple, and "most of them are very nice." All the dorms are co-ed, except for McCormick Hall, which is the all-girls residence. There is a residential advisor (RA), usually a graduate student, on every floor of the dorms. "RAs are generally very laid-back," said one student. Most students live on campus all four years, because "rent can be quite expensive in the area." On-campus living also means on-campus dining and the food rates range anywhere from "average" to "sucky." In the words of one freshman, "I've seen better and I've seen worse."

Passionate Students

When asked what sets MIT apart, many reply that the student body possesses a passion and intensity for learning found in few other places in the world. "The ultimate thing that differentiates MIT from other schools is that we are nerds, some of us big nerds, and we are proud of it." On a campus where students take science and math seriously, both buildings and majors are labeled with numbers (for example, computer science and electrical engineering is called course 6), and the words fun and math are not mutually exclusive. While many students profess a love/hate relationship with the university, they also say that if they could go back in time, they would choose MIT all over again. —*Pamela Boykoff*

FYI

If you come to MIT, you'd better bring "a graphing calculator."
What is the typical weekend schedule? "Go out on Fridays, but work the rest of the time."
If I could change one thing about MIT, I'd "upgrade the quality of the food."
The three things every MIT student should do before graduating are "develop a true love for calling things by numbers rather than names; hate school by taking 6.001, the Structure and Interpretation of Computer Programs; then, gradually learn to love it."

Mount Holyoke College

Address: 50 College Street; South Hadley, MA 01075
Phone: 413-538-2023
E-mail address: admissions@mtholyoke.edu
Web site URL: www.mtholyoke.edu
Founded: 1837
Private or Public: private
Religious affiliation: none
Location: suburban
Undergraduate enrollment: 2,191
Total enrollment: NA
Percent Male/Female: 0%/100%
Percent Minority: 35%
Percent African-American: 5%
Percent Asian: 10%
Percent Hispanic: 4%
Percent Native-American: 1%
Percent in-state/out of state: 35%/65%
Percent Pub HS: 64%
Number of Applicants: 2,936
Percent Accepted: 52%
Percent Accepted who enroll: 20%
Entering: 582
Transfers: 39
Application Deadline: 15 Jan
Mean SAT: NA
Mean ACT: NA
Middle 50% SAT range: V 600-700, M 580-670
Middle 50% ACT range: 26-30
3 Most popular majors: biology/biological science, English, psychology
Retention: 91%
Graduation rate: 80%
On-campus housing: 93%
Fraternities: NA
Sororities: NA
Library: 670,304 volumes
Tuition and Fees: $29,338
Room and Board: $8,580
Financial aid, first-year: 65%
Varsity or Club Athletes: 1%
Early Decision or Early Action Acceptance Rate: ED 65%

In the quiet town of South Hadley, Massachusetts, sits a small liberal arts college for women that is dedicated to its students' excellence. This tight-knit school allows women to form close bonds with other students and professors, as well as develop their own sense of independence and leadership. Mount Holyoke is also located within the Five-College Consortium that unites it with Smith College, Amherst College, Hampshire College, and the University of Massachusetts at Amherst, allowing students access to a wide range of academic and social opportunities outside of their college.

Small but Intense

Students find academics at Mount Holyoke to be extremely rigorous and challenging. The distribution requirements consist of three classes in the humanities, two in math or science (one with lab), two in the social sciences, one in a foreign language, one "multicultural" course, and six credits of physical education. Students describe these requirements as "a lot of work" but "flexible within reason," and most appreciate the diverse interests that the requirements help foster.

Some of the most popular majors at Mount Holyoke are psychology, English, chemistry, and biology. Although introductory classes can have as many as a hundred students, most tend to have only 20 to 30. Since there are very few teaching assistants, students generally deal directly with their professors. Sciences are considered the toughest classes, with one student describing the hardest classes as "'micro-anything." The classroom environment is considered "strong and interactive" because students are first lectured about "different perspectives" and then asked to develop their own. Students are also offered the option of staying on campus for "J-term," a period during the break between the fall and spring semesters when students can take courses, go on field trips or participate in internships.

Professors at Mount Holyoke are described as accessible and accommodating; one student claimed that her professors "are the best part of the school." Some famous faculty include author Beverly Tatum *(Why Are All the Black Kids Sitting Together in the Cafeteria?)*, Joe Ellis, Vincent Ferraro, and Anthony Lake, former security advisor to President Clinton. Students find these high-profile professors approachable and friendly, a factor that leads many high-school seniors to choose Mount Holyoke.

Women at Mount Holyoke can choose not only from the many classes offered as part of the college's 44 majors, but also from courses offered by any of the nearby colleges that comprise the Five College Consortium. A free bussing system connects all five of the colleges in the area, offering students a large range of academic opportunities. Students at Mount Holyoke can take classes for credit and participate in lectures or special events at any of the other four colleges. Within this system Mount Holyoke students can have all of the perks of a larger college while keeping the benefits of their own small school.

Living Among Women

Mount Holyoke is widely renowned for its campus, which students describe as "beautiful" and "pastoral," complete with brick buildings lined with stained glass, a river, and two beautiful lakes. One student described the campus as "a country club," while another praised its "peaceful, friendly atmosphere." The campus is self-contained and described by many as very safe, because of its location in tiny South Hadley.

"This is not the normal college experience. When you choose Mount Holyoke you are making a big decision: It's all girls all the time all living in the dorms all four years. That might be too much to handle for some people."

The women of Mount Holyoke are required to live on-campus for all four years unless they have special permission. The dorms are described as "very nice" and vary in size—while some students get large rooms in distant locations, others get "tiny rooms with a very central location." Most students prefer the older dorms, such as Pearsons and the Rockies, which are architecturally unique. Dorms consist mainly of double and single rooms, but all seniors and most juniors get singles. Guests are not restricted in the dorms, but a resident must escort them up and down the stairs or escalators. Each floor has one bathroom, and every dorm has at least one nonsmoking floor. There are also "quiet hours" between 11 P.M. and 8 A.M. on weekdays, and two official "quiet floors" exist for those who want general peace at all times.

Every dorm also has its own dining hall, and a full meal plan is included in tuition. Not only are there vegetarian and vegan options at every meal, but students can eat at the campus's kosher dining hall or showcase kitchen for a change of pace. Women at Mount Holyoke are generally happy with the food, with one student saying "you can always find something." On the weekends many students choose to sample local restaurants in the Five College area.

Outside of Class

Despite the heavy academic workload, most students at Mount Holyoke spend a good deal of time on extracurricular commitments, taking advantage of the many campus groups open to them. Students are especially interested in political organizations, working for undergraduate publications, and the very active Student Government Association. Musically oriented students can join the Glee Club, a number of instrumental ensembles, or the English Handbell Choir. The many community service organizations at Mount Holyoke range from work with the Campus Conservation Coalition to the Women's Center. Dozens of religious, academic and cultural groups are also available for students to join as well.

Sports are also a popular extracurricular option for Mount Holyoke students. Varsity teams face off against Mount

Holyoke's all-female rival, Smith College. The most popular and competitive teams are said to be field hockey, crew, lacrosse, and basketball. A huge amount of support is given to the very successful rugby team, a club organization with a large and vocal following on campus. Games are well attended and followed by lively parties. There are extensive athletic facilities open to all students that are used in popular intramural competition. Mount Holyoke also includes a huge equestrian center that one student called "one of the best in the country."

The social life at Mount Holyoke is very low-key compared to other schools in the area, which drives most students into the greater Five College area during the weekend. Many students take their cars or use the free bussing system to get to the fraternities at Umass Amherst or go to Amherst College for "TAP," where there are parties Thursday and Saturday nights. On campus, many students choose to hang out in small groups or watch movies, although there are some larger parties like Casino Night that attract students from other colleges. There is no Greek system at Mount Holyoke, which most students appreciate. Students say that the small size of their campus is enough to bring people together.

The Mount Holyoke administration has rules against having kegs in the dorms, although one student insisted that the "alcohol policies are very low-key." Many students say that drinking is not big on campus, and that nondrinkers definitely do not feel left out. One student summed up the party situation at Mount Holyoke by saying, "it's not a party school, but it's not restrictive either—you make it what you want." Most students report being very happy with the social alternatives.

Despite the lack of males, students report that the campus is fairly open to sexual or romantic relationships of any kind. Boyfriends off campus and girlfriends on campus are both commonly found. One student described Mount Holyoke's gay population as "very strong and out in the open," and it is quite clear that most students do not have a problem with homosexual relationships. Since guys are not a big presence on campus, girls find plenty of opportunity to visit one of the many nearby co-ed colleges during the weekends, although one student mentioned that it is still difficult to meet men "unless you are willing to make the first move." Another warned that "this is not the normal college experience. When you choose Mount Holyoke you are making a big decision: it's all girls all the time all living in the dorms all four years. That might be too much to handle for some people."

The student body at Mount Holyoke is described as incredibly diverse, consisting of women from all over the U.S. and the rest of the world, although most do come from the Northeast. One student said that Mount Holyoke is "way more diverse than most colleges," which allows students to learn from experiences with a wide variety of peers.

Students at Mount Holyoke appreciate their school's commitment to excellence and the great sense of balance it gives them. They find an extremely rigorous and personal academic program and diverse opportunities for extracurricular activity. They also find a small, supportive community of women conveniently located close to a large population of other college-age students. Lastly, they find a peaceful and contained college in a small town, with access to the social and academic resources of the Amherst/Northampton area. At Mount Holyoke, many women feel that they truly have the best of all worlds. —*Adrian Finucane*

FYI

If you come to Mount Holyoke, you'd better bring "a strong willingness to enjoy the fabulous company of women."

The typical weekend schedule is "get off campus and check out Amherst and North Hampton, or stay on campus and watch movies with pizza."

If I could change one thing about Mount Holyoke, I'd "encourage development around it to try to include it into the community."

Three things every student at Mount Holyoke should do before graduating are "stay for J-term, climb Mount Holyoke on Mountain Day, and go to Hampshire for Halloween."

Northeastern University

Address: 360 Huntington Avenue; Boston, MA 02115
Phone: 617-373-2200
E-mail address: admissions@neu.edu
Web site URL: www.northeastern.edu
Founded: 1898
Private or Public: private
Religious affiliation: none
Location: urban
Undergraduate enrollment: 14,144
Total enrollment: NA
Percent Male/Female: 51%/49%
Percent Minority: 25%
Percent African-American: 6%
Percent Asian: 7%
Percent Hispanic: 4%
Percent Native-American: 0%
Percent in-state/out of state: 37%/63%
Percent Pub HS: NA
Number of Applicants: 17,037
Percent Accepted: 61%
Percent Accepted who enroll: 28%
Entering: 2,974
Transfers: 798
Application Deadline: 15 Feb
Mean SAT: NA
Mean ACT: NA
Middle 50% SAT range: V 510-610, M 530-630
Middle 50% ACT range: 21-27
3 Most popular majors: business, engineering, health professions
Retention: 82%
Graduation rate: 50%
On-campus housing: NA
Fraternities: 4%
Sororities: 3%
Library: 710,843 volumes
Tuition and Fees: $24,467
Room and Board: $9,660
Financial aid, first-year: 67%
Varsity or Club Athletes: NA
Early Decision or Early Action Acceptance Rate: NA

Want to pack your college years with strong academics, real-life work experience, a lively campus, and all the resources Boston can offer? If so, maybe Northeastern and its five-year "co-op" program are for you. But beware: students warn that if the school sounds appealing but the intense program doesn't, you ought to look elsewhere.

Trimesters and the Co-op

If you attend Northeastern, get ready for the trimester system. The academic year is segmented into three parts, and as one student said, "I go to college later than everyone and I get out earlier," but "my vacations are shorter, so I don't get a lot of free time." Despite the short terms, classes do not feel rushed, and "the professors take their time when needed." Class sizes "differ depending on the class type," and can range from lectures of 90 or more people to writing classes of 13. Large lectures have corresponding labs or discussions of about 20 students, taught by TAs. Students seem to enjoy their instructors. Said a computer science major, "My comp sci professor is great. He is really funny and smart, and they use his curriculum at MIT." Majors applicable to the real world, such as engineering and criminal justice, are more popular than liberal arts tracks. This translates into the five-year "co-op" program, through which the vast majority of students gain work experience in their fields. The program places students in paid internships one trimester each year. If a student elects to start co-op in the freshman year, they will take an orientation class and typically begin work sophomore year. A co-op advisor will be there to help along the way. Many people arrive at Northeastern with a major in mind, but don't officially select a major until sophomore year. Because internships begin sophomore year, this flexibility still makes it possible for students to take co-op in their selected majors.

Northeastern is structured for the take-charge individual. The academic registration process is fairly simple to maneuver, and getting into classes is "easy as long as you register early; the longer you wait, the harder it is." The academic advising system puts responsibility on the student to get everything done, which can be stressful, depending on the individual. "There are about 13 or 14 advisors total and they all have office hours, so we can just go there. There is also a freshman advisor . . . You can go to whoever has [office] hours that day."

RAs and Apartment Hunting: Are You Feeling Lucky?

Most students feel that the on-campus freshman living situation at Northeastern is generally decent. Quality does vary, as some buildings have been recently renovated while others have not. White Hall is reported to be excellent, while Stetson East and West get less favorable reviews. Buildings are divided into single-sex wings, with an RA in each section. Students claim that some RAs are relaxed about alcohol policies, provided the students "are quiet and respect the rules, like no trashing the building and respecting quiet hours [after 11 P.M. Sunday through Wednesday and after 1 A.M. Thursday through Saturday] . . . but some other RAs write people up right and left." Special interest housing is available: Coe Hall is a "wellness" dorm, and there is also an honors dorm, as well as an international dorm. After freshman year, students of different classes can live together, and "sophomore dorms are VERY nice." After sophomore year a lot of students—over half—move off campus. Those who stay on campus might live in West Village Residence Halls or Davenport Commons, which opened in 2001 and features large rooms, kitchens, air conditioning, cable TV, and high-speed internet. Only freshmen and sophomores are guaranteed housing, and anyone considering a move off campus should be forewarned: looking for affordable housing in Boston is not for the faint of heart.

> **"I go to college later than everyone and I get out earlier, but my vacations are shorter, so I don't get a lot of free time."**

Students are satisfied with campus facilities. Northeastern is home to Matthews Arena, the oldest indoor arena in the world, where the hockey teams play. The Marino Recreation Center provides workout equipment for athletes and non-athletes alike, and one freshman said, "It's great. I go there every other day."

Students find themselves presented with a wealth of food options at and around Northeastern. The university provides a variety of meal plan options for their cafeterias, including the choice to put money on their Husky Card for use at local eateries. This is convenient, since one of the many advantages of being located in the hustle and bustle of Boston is the abundance of food. Student favorites include Chicken Lou's and Pizzeria Uno. In addition, with its several restaurants, pool tables, and plenty of comfortable chairs for reading, the on-campus Curry Student Center is a popular gathering place, as is the Cyber Café in Snell Library.

So Much to Do, So Little Time

Extracurricular activities abound at Northeastern, and "everyone is into something different." Freshmen have no trouble finding activities to join, because "groups come out. In the beginning of the year they set up tables for all the clubs, groups, frats, and sororities, so you get a good idea" of what is available. Students report that Greek life is present, but not a driving force on campus. Said one undergrad, "There are frats, but it's not the big thing here . . . not everyone is rushing to join them, like at some colleges." Other groups include the Student Government Association; the *NU Times New Roman*, a humor newspaper; and DownBeats, an a cappella group. Varsity sports are not particularly illustrious, but "football and hockey are popular here," and though the teams are "not that good" they are "still fun to support." The Homecoming football game yields an especially good turnout. The sport that gets the rave reviews is broomball, which is "like hockey, minus the skates." Co-ed teams flock to the ice at Matthews Arena to play with "a rubber-tipped broom, and a small ball for a puck . . . with shoes." The competition is intense, but it's all in fun. Said one broomball player, "Everyone kind of sucks. It's hard, a lot of falling down and bruises . . . one team's goalie dresses up in a frog costume."

Just as the activities on campus are diverse, so are the students. Though there are "a lot of people from New York, Massachusetts, and Connecticut," it is "not all white kids." The students do not self-segregate along racial lines, and one freshman said, "It's pretty socially integrated. My roommate is Puerto Rican, and one of my friends . . . is from Bridgeport, [CT]." Cultural organizations abound for students, including the African-American Institute and Latino/a Student Cultural Center.

Let's Party! . . . Hello, Officer

The social scene at Northeastern is alive on the weekends. For students with late Friday classes—or no Friday classes—the weekend begins on Thursday night. Drinking is prevalent, but the choice not to drink is accepted, too. Even for freshmen, students report that alcohol is easy to come by, and parties flourish in the dorms, but watch out: your RA might be cool about alcohol, but the police are not. Said one student, "NU is known for having the cops bust the parties." Some people party on, despite the threat, while the police presence leads others to "go clubbing or walking around instead." If campus parties aren't your scene, Boston offers a wealth of nightclubs and bars. Jillian's is a popular bar, and "the Roxy is an excellent dance club," according to one student. Local bars tend to be strict about carding, and trying to use a fake ID is risky, but there are still plenty of options—including a few bars that do not card if you have a college ID. Off campus, people from Northeastern mingle with other college students, especially those from nearby BC, BU, Emerson, and Simmons.

Beyond the clubs and bars, Boston offers innumerable resources. From shopping at Faneuil Hall or Quincy Market to Red Sox games at Fenway Park, recreation is everywhere. Boston's cultural attractions are also in close proximity, with the Museum of Fine Arts across the street from the Northeastern campus, and the Museum of Science just a "T" (subway) ride away. Since Northeastern is near three "T" stops, students have easy access to Boston, Cambridge, and the many other colleges in the metropolitan area.

The Total Package

Students at Northeastern love their urban campus, which delivers both a cohesive college feel and the excitement of Boston. Students are involved in campus life, joining groups and supporting the school at big events such as the annual Homecoming parade and football game. The co-op program distinguishes Northeastern from other universities; many students cite the opportunity to work in their field before graduation as the main reason they chose "NU." The extra year in school is well worth the expertise gained in real job experience for motivated, career-oriented students. Throw in respected professors and a diverse, active student body, and you begin to understand the exciting experience Northeastern affords. —*Katherine Lewandowski*

FYI

If you come to Northeastern, you'd better bring "a lawyer, to get you off all the alcohol fines you'll most likely get."

What is the typical weekend schedule? "Drink when and where you can, or go clubbing. Fit in a little work."

If I could change one thing about Northeastern, I'd "get rid of the police."

Three things every student at Northeastern should do before graduating are "do co-op, go clubbing, and play broomball."

Simmons College

Address: 300 The Fenway; Boston, MA 02115
Phone: 800-345-8468
E-mail address: ugadm@simmons.edu
Web site URL: www.simmons.edu
Founded: 1899
Private or Public: private
Religious affiliation: none
Location: urban
Undergraduate enrollment: 1,224
Total enrollment: NA
Percent Male/Female: 0%/100%
Percent Minority: 21%
Percent African-American: 7%
Percent Asian: 6%
Percent Hispanic: 3%
Percent Native-American: 0%
Percent in-state/out of state: 43%/57%
Percent Pub HS: 81
Number of Applicants: 1,753
Percent Accepted: 70%
Percent Accepted who enroll: 27%
Entering: 328
Transfers: 66
Application Deadline: 1 Mar
Mean SAT: NA
Mean ACT: NA
Middle 50% SAT range: V 500-600, M 490-590
Middle 50% ACT range: NA
3 Most popular majors: nursing, English, physical therapy
Retention: 83%
Graduation rate: 71%
On-campus housing: 59%
Fraternities: NA
Sororities: NA
Library: 235,431 volumes
Tuition and Fees: $23,550
Room and Board: $9,450
Financial aid, first-year: 67%
Varsity or Club Athletes: 15%
Early Decision or Early Action Acceptance Rate: EA 72%

Nestled in the bustling city of Boston rests the tranquil oasis of Simmons College. Roughly 1,300 young women attend Simmons for its liberal arts with a special focus on science. Students rave about the close-knit student body and excellent, approachable professors that combine to form a welcoming and laid back amosphere.

Science Anyone?

Simmons College offers a liberal arts education with special career preparation opportunities. The nursing program feeds student internships in the city, while the physical therapy major has a six-year doctorate program. Science at Simmons is especially strong. Nursing, biology, and chemistry are considered the most difficult majors, while communications and psychology are "not as demanding, but still difficult," according to one student. Class size is small, making it easy to enroll in most classes and enabling students to take a more active role in the classroom. Students rave about their professors. One student explained, "[The professors] give you their e-mail, cell phone number, home number, office number and office hours. They want you to come and talk to them. They are interested in helping their students."

Students must fulfill academic distributional requirements in six 'modes' to fulfill the graduation requirements for Simmons. In the process, students become more well-rounded and prepared for life after college. The requirements are surprisingly unrestrictive, though, and one student commented, "I found that I was able to experiment more during my freshman year than my friends at other schools."

An Escape from Beantown

The Simmons campus receives high marks from its students. Its peaceful green quadrangle in the middle of a busy Boston neighborhood serves as a quiet haven. One student exclaimed, "Our campus is beautiful. Most people come onto campus and forget they are in a city. When you walk through the gates, it feels very much unlike a city and a lot more like home." The campus is divided into an academic portion and a residential portion separated by one city block. The residential campus consists of a picturesque quadrangle bounded by the college's residence halls and Bartol Dining Hall. Also located on the residential campus is the Holmes Sports

Center that has an eight-lane swimming pool, suspended track, weight room, sauna, basketball court, dance studio, and squash courts. Next door is the Simmons Health Center which offers its comprehensive services to students.

"[The professors] give you their e-mail, cell phone number, home number, office number and office hours. They want you to come and talk to them. They are interested in helping their students."

Approximately five minutes' walk from the residential campus is the main campus. Here the college's main classrooms are located in the Main College Building (affectionately referred to as the "MCB") and the Park Science Building, where all science courses are taught. The main campus also hosts the Beatley Library and the newly constructed and unusually named One Palace Road Building. One Palace Road provides a number of student resources such as career services and counseling, as well as two graduate school departments.

Standard of Living at Simmons

The quality of dorm rooms differs at Simmons depending on renovations and specific buildings. Most freshmen live in doubles, but there are a few triples. There is an RA on every floor and one student said, "They're just there to help out, and are not too strict." Students are very pleased with their living situation. Recently renovated Evans Hall and Arnold Hall are "really nice and the only ones with elevators on campus," reported one student. Praise is not as free-flowing, though, when students are asked about the food at Simmons. Bartol Dining Hall is Simmons' main dining hall and students label the food as "fair." Luckily for hungry Simmons students, the best of Boston's restaurants, with its first-class seafood and ethnic fare, lie just outside the college's gates. Other dining options available to students on campus include the Quadside Café, serving as a snack bar and grocery, and Java City (Simmons' Coffee Kiosk) which doles out coffee and snacks.

Livin' It Up in Beantown

One student put it best by saying, "Basically, Boston becomes your campus." For this group of young women, the possibilities of the city are boundless. Students are able to take advantage of the city's many fabulous restaurants, go shopping on Newbury St., attend a Boston Red Sox game, and go to a concert at the Orpheum Theater. Boston offers anything and everything under the sun . . . and under the moon as well, as Simmons girls take advantage of the city's exciting nightlife.

Simmons is a dry campus and because of alcohol and noise restrictions; when students are in the mood for a more festive atmosphere, they go out to Boston clubs or to frat parties at BU and MIT. One student comments that because of this situation, "Simmons' girls have a lot of random hookups because they really don't know when the next chance will be." However, these meetings often develop into something more substantial, and students note that many of their peers are involved in serious relationships—both heterosexual and homosexual.

From Tea to Tennis

Students describe the student body as "intelligent" and "friendly." The small class size promotes unity and school spirit. According to one student, a tradition that has been going on for a few years now is the Friday Hall Teas where all the girls from each hall come together to "have tea or snack on goodies and just hang out and have fun."

Many Simmons students take part in sports and other extracurricular activities. The campus is described by one "as very active and involved." Simmons is home to eight Division III varsity sports and one student described Simmons sports as 'not awful'—basketball and soccer seemed to be one of the most popular sports among students. Other student organizations such as Simmons College Outreach, a student-run community service organization, and the Student Government Organization are just two of the many student activities and clubs in which students take part.

When John Simmons founded this college in 1899, his mission was to allow women to earn the 'livelihood' they deserved and to create a new generation of well-educated women. Today his mission continues to be realized as Simmons produces well-prepared independent women ready to enter the world. —*Kieran Locke*

FYI

If you come to Simmons College, you'd better bring a "Boston Red Sox hat."

What is the typical weekend schedule? "Hanging out, shopping, and eating in Harvard Square or on Newbury St. and going to an occasional party at a fraternity from a neighboring college."

If I could change one thing about Simmons, I would change "the dining-hall food."

Three things every student at Simmons should do before graduating are "visit the Isabella Stuart Gardner Museum, eat Ankara Frozen Yogurt, and go on the Swan Boats in Boston Commons."

Smith College

Address: 7 College Lane; Northhampton, MA 01063
Phone: 413-585-2500
E-mail address: admission@smith.edu
Web site URL: www.smith.edu
Founded: 1871
Private or Public: private
Religious affiliation: none
Location: suburban
Undergraduate enrollment: 2,647
Total enrollment: NA
Percent Male/Female: 0%/100%
Percent Minority: 28%
Percent African-American: 5%
Percent Asian: 10%
Percent Hispanic: 6%
Percent Native-American: 1%
Percent in-state/out of state: 24%/76%
Percent Pub HS: 65%
Number of Applicants: 3,047
Percent Accepted: 53%
Percent Accepted who enroll: 42%
Entering: 679
Transfers: 71
Application Deadline: 15 Jan
Mean SAT: NA
Mean ACT: NA
Middle 50% SAT range: V 590-700, M 580-670
Middle 50% ACT range: 24-30
3 Most popular majors: social sciences, biological/biomedical sciences, visual/performing arts
Retention: 90%
Graduation rate: 80%
On-campus housing: 87%
Fraternities: NA
Sororities: NA
Library: 1,296,828 volumes
Tuition and Fees: $27,544
Room and Board: $9,490
Financial aid, first-year: 61%
Varsity or Club Athletes: NA
Early Decision or Early Action Acceptance Rate: ED 70%

Walk around the picturesque town of Northampton, Massachusetts and you will inevitably spot a Smithie wearing a T-shirt that reads, "It's not a girls' school without men—it's a women's school without boys." This message of empowerment for women is one that clearly comes across when speaking with current students of the college. Although some miss the dynamics of coeducation, the general attitude is that what Smith lacks in males, it makes up for in excellent academics, varied activities, and a great campus experience.

Academics

One of the first things a Smith woman will tell you about life at the college is that studying is taken very seriously. One freshman commented, "I like the atmosphere here, which I feel is very conducive to studying." The reason for this might be the lack of distribution requirements, allowing students to explore and discover their academic interests. However, having no general education requirement does not necessarily make things easier; undergraduates still need 128 credit hours to graduate, half of which must come from outside their major. Also, having so much freedom puts pressure on students to make selections from a wide variety of course offerings. "It's hard to pick because there are so many interesting-sounding classes" a sophomore complained.

Another aspect of Smith academics that students truly appreciate is the small size of classes, which allows for close interaction with professors. According to one freshman, "The professors here are not afraid to give you lots of reading and work, but they are very open to questions. My professors were extremely helpful when classes first started and I didn't really know what I was doing." Although there is generally a positive feeling about the intimate discussions with professors and the absence of TAs, some students feel that the conversations can become "unstructured" because the emphasis is on ideas rather than background information. The level of difficulty at Smith seems to vary widely depending on the student and the particular class, but grade inflation tends to be a rumor rather than an actual issue.

Smith has strong departments in English, government, women's studies, and art history, which is partly due to its place in the Pioneer Valley's Five-College Consortium. Smith students, along with those from Hampshire College, Mount Holyoke College, Amherst College, and UMass-Amherst, can take a complimentary bus to attend class at any one of the schools. This provides both extended academic and social opportunities because Smith women can meet people at other campuses as well as partake of an even wider range of classes.

Living It Up in NoHo

In addition to access to all of the surrounding areas, Smithies have much available to them right in Northampton. A quaint shopping area offers a nice break from the dining hall with such options as the Fire and Water Vegetarian Café and Spaghetti Freddy's. NoHo, as it is abbreviated, can also be a source of social activity when there is nothing happening on campus. However, as one junior remarked, "coming from a major city, I miss the city. Northampton is too small for me." However, there are options should a student want to be in a bigger area, because Boston and New York City are both only a train ride away.

One of the many things Smith women appreciate about the small size is the safety and accessibility it affords. Students never feel uncomfortable walking around campus or the town because they know that a blue phone that provides direct access to security is always nearby. Also, it is quite easy to get around because everything can be reached easily on foot; neither a bike nor a car is necessary to travel around the campus.

"You'd be surprised at what some of those Smithies have thought up over the years!"

Smith's 125-acre campus has undergone many recent physical improvements, including a new student center and a Fine Arts Center. As one student said, "There's been a lot of renovating on campus in recent years, so Smith facilities are excellent." In addition to the "graceful buildings" in which classes are held, the Lyman Plant House holds the Botanic Gardens, an art gallery contains upwards of 24,000 works, and the Nielson Library houses the school's books. There are also extensive athletic facilities with 25 acres of playing fields, a boathouse, and the Ainsworth Gymnasium.

Crew and rugby are among the most popular of the 14 varsity athletic teams. Even a student who doesn't follow the sports teams on campus can appreciate the huge team spirit of the players. This is especially the case when playing against Seven Sister schools, such as Wellesley and Mount Holyoke, which tend to be the biggest rivals. In true sisterly fashion, a student commented, "I would say that I'm proud of my fellow Smithies who are part of a team and love being a part of the team."

Social Life and the Houses

Another one of the most beloved qualities of Smith College is the house system. Students never live in dorms. Instead, all women reside in old mansions that have been converted into housing for 90 to 100 students, each with its own kitchen and dining room. In addition to eating and sleeping, the houses are places for social interaction through afternoon teas and candlelight dinners. As one student commented, "the founders of Smith wanted to create a comfortable, home-like atmosphere for students to live in. I personally like the houses a lot because they foster a sense of close community." This strong connection to the house leads very few students to live off campus.

An integral part of the Smith experience is participation in on-campus activities, which include Smith Asian Students Association, Service Organizations of Smith (SOS), and the Smiffenpoofs, which is the oldest female a capella group in the nation. One student remarked that being part of an extracurricular activity is "the best way to become involved in the Smith community and it definitely makes your years at Smith so much more enjoyable." Smithies are known for their political awareness and activism, and the numerous cultural organizations indicate the diversity of the school. Yet, despite a large population of international students, one Smithie commented, "I think as far as numbers go, there are fewer women of color."

There are always tons of things to do on the Smith Campus that appeal to a wide range of interests. For those with political inclinations, there are lectures and debates open to the whole campus. As for the arts, the Rec Council at Smith shows bi-weekly movies and hires a musical artist to perform each semester. In the past, artists such as Pink, Fiona Apple, and Squirrel Nut Zippers have come to the concert hall. Despite all of these options, one student felt that, on a scale of one to ten, her satisfaction with the social options was a seven. "It is a small campus and it's not too close to a major city," she said, "but if you take the time out and actually give Smith social life a chance, you can enjoy it."

Traditions

When it comes to traditions, one student commented that, "you'd be surprised at what some of those Smithies have thought up over the years!" One of the most favored is Mountain Day, where the president of Smith randomly selects a day in October when there will be no class. Also, every year students celebrate Otelia Cromwell Day, which is the birthday of the first black student to graduate from Smith, by attending lectures and workshops pertaining to minority issues. Smith women also have been known to go a little crazy during events like Quad Riot (where personal-hygiene products are thrown out of rooms) and streaking during the first snow.

Smith is a college with a tradition for academic excellence, great friendships, a wonderful experience for a small, tight-knit group of women. Despite its lack of men and its location in a small town, it the women who attend Smith appreciate all that it has to offer. Through the multitude of activities, the house system, and small classes, Smithies can make lasting connections to their peers and to the school that will last far beyond graduation. —*Rebecca Ives*

FYI

If you come to Smith, you'd better bring "a nice warm down comforter because the winters here are cold!"

What is a typical weekend schedule? "Relaxing after class on Friday until tea at 4:00, followed by going out on the town at night. Saturdays are usually spent working or running errands during the day and partying in the evening. Sundays are definitely homework days."

If I could change one thing about Smith, I'd "move it closer to a big city."

Three things every student at Smith should do before graduating are "go crazy at Convocation, canoe on the Pond, and attend the Immortality Ball."

Tufts University

Address: Bendetson Hall; Medford, MA 02155
Phone: 617-627-3170
E-mail address: admissions.inquiry@ase.tufts.edu
Web site URL: www.tufts.edu
Founded: 1852
Private or Public: private
Religious affiliation: none
Location: suburban
Undergraduate enrollment: 4,910
Total enrollment: 8,465
Percent Male/Female: 45%/55%
Percent Minority: 36%
Percent African-American: 7%
Percent Asian: 13%
Percent Hispanic: 8%
Percent Native-American: 0%
Percent in-state/out of state: 24%/76%
Percent Pub HS: 60%
Number of Applicants: 14,307
Percent Accepted: 27%
Percent Accepted who enroll: 34%
Entering: 1,278
Transfers: 114
Application Deadline: 1 Jan
Mean SAT: NA
Mean ACT: NA
Middle 50% SAT range: V 610-710, M 640-720
Middle 50% ACT range: 26-31
3 Most popular majors: international relations, economics, biology
Retention: 97%
Graduation rate: 86%
On-campus housing: 75%
Fraternities: 15%
Sororities: 4%
Library: 1,613,000 volumes
Tuition and Fees: $29,630
Room and Board: $8,640
Financial aid, first-year: 36%
Varsity or Club Athletes: 14%
Early Decision or Early Action Acceptance Rate: ED 43%

With so many schools in the Boston area, you might expect that choosing one would be difficult. Not so for students at Tufts. Ask a student making the trek up or down the hilly campus whether he or she is happy, and you're bound to get an enthusiastic "I love it here!" With its charming and quiet campus within close range of the "quintessential college town" and an international student body, Tufts University offers its students the best of *all* worlds.

Time to Work

Students cite academics as one of the major reasons why they chose Tufts, describing the offerings as "excellent" and "exactly what I was looking for." Prospective students apply directly to either the College of Liberal Arts or the School of Engineering, and, upon arrival, face a rigorous set of academic requirements. Liberal arts students are required to take two courses in each of five main areas: fine arts, humanities, social sciences, mathematics, and natural sciences. In addition, they must complete a freshman writing requirement, a world civilizations requirement, and six semesters of a foreign language (one of the most rigorous foreign language requirements of any American university). These requirements are "demanding," but they often prove easier to fulfill than they seem at first appearance. As one student explained, "The requirements seem overwhelming when you first arrive, but they are really quite manageable. I'm a junior and I'm already almost done with all my requirements."

Classes at Tufts range in size from large introductory lectures to small upper-level seminars. Some classes, such as English and foreign languages, are purposely kept small to allow for maximum participation and interaction; however, there are occasions when "demand exceeds supply" for popular classes that are without extensive staffing, such as for certain non-Romance languages. Registration is based on both seniority and a first-come, first-serve basis, yet most students find it relatively easy to get into the classes they want. In addition to the normal course offerings, Tufts students have the option of taking a class in the Experimental College. These courses, which are taught by undergraduate or graduate students and change every semester, address such varied subjects as the history of the stock market, massage therapy, and active citizenship. The drawback? "A lot of the Experimental College courses are held at really strange times of night," one sophomore complained. The academic atmosphere also extends beyond the classroom to lectures delivered by prominent speakers—recent guests have included Al Gore and Colin Powell.

Among the most popular majors at Tufts are international relations, biology, psychology, and economics. The international relations program draws much of its strength from the prestigious Fletcher School of International Law and Diplomacy, where many international relations majors pursue graduate work. The international focus extends beyond the major, as approximately one-third of Tufts juniors choose to study abroad for at least a semester. Study abroad is actively encouraged; one junior urged, "Tufts makes it so easy, there's no reason not to go."

These adventures abroad provide a welcome break from Tufts' academics; in general, classes are "tough," and the workload tends to be on the heavy side. "They make you put in your time," noted one sophomore. Sciences at Tufts are notoriously difficult, with introductory biology classes referred to as "the pre-med, weed-out courses." But beware: the atmosphere for those students vying for medical school spots is considered "rigorous," "stressful," and "very competitive." This cutthroat attitude is not as evident in other majors, where students are "likely to share notes and study together in groups."

Living on the Hill

The Tufts campus, described by students as "gorgeous" and "well-kept," has buildings ranging in architectural style from modern to Gothic to Georgian. But be prepared for a good workout in exploring campus; one student warned that you will "need a good pair of sneakers, because you'll be doing a lot of walking up and down hills." The campus is informally divided into "uphill" and "downhill," with the upper area containing most of the academic buildings and the lower area housing the student center. Although the campus is relatively small—"everything is 15 minutes away"—uphill and downhill still become distinct communities. "People tend to stay in their area," remarked one sophomore. To students, the campus seems "very safe" and "quiet," with one student claiming that this tranquility can actually be "eerie" at times. For fun, people congregate on the President's lawn for sunbathing in warm weather and "great sledding" in the winter, while the "amazing" view of Boston from the roof of the library makes it another favorite Tufts spot.

"Tufts is an introduction to the real world's sociological politics . . . and it is a school that encourages thinking for the sake of thinking."

Freshmen are required to live on campus and are assigned to their living quarters by lottery. The school is said to be relatively good about matching roommates—that is, "as long as one does not lie on the questionnaire received in June." Dorms are co-ed either by floor or by room, with the exception of Richardson, the all-female dorm. Tilton, the all-freshman dorm, is a popular locale, as are the "more social" dorms of South, Miller, and Houston. Wren Hall is considered by many to be one of the worst places to live, with an "isolating" and "antisocial" suite structure designed "like a maze." Choosing a dorm after freshman year often requires some compromises, as "very few good dorms have good locations" and "what you trade off in size, you usually gain in convenience." Dorms are not air-conditioned, and students say there is "much room for improvement"; however, the friendships made in the current setup counteract many of the complaints. All dorms have RAs, who "tend to be pretty cool, though not about drinking if you're dumb enough to get caught doing it in the dorm." For those seeking an alternative to regular dorms, there are also cultural, theme, and Greek housing options.

The dining experience at Tufts draws mixed reviews from students. "Supposedly we have really good food," one sophomore mused. Freshmen are required to purchase a full meal plan, but after that students can switch to a combination of meals and "points," which can be used at on-campus stores and eateries as well as several local delivery places. Students complain that the general dining hall fare can be repetitive. "You may come to school loving it, but by the time you leave, you are pretty bored of it," one senior complained. As a result, "people eat out and order in a good deal." A popular coffee shop is Brown and Brew (named for Tufts' brown and blue colors), "a great place to grab a hot chocolate on a cold day or just hang out with friends and chat." When a change of scenery is desired, students venture into the local Davis Square area or Boston's North End.

Outside the Classroom

When Tufts students are not preparing for their rigorous courses, they spend their time in a myriad of extracurricular activities. "Most are devoted, if not fanatical," one sophomore noted about students' extracurricular involvement. One of the largest and most popular groups on campus is the Leonard Carmichael Society, an umbrella organization for student community service. "Even if they're not members, most people at Tufts help the group out a few times a year with their campus-wide events." In addition, many students write for humor magazines, ethnic publications, and literary journals such as Queen's Head. Performing arts groups are popular as well, but students admit that "it's hard to get into theater because it's small." Some more offbeat groups include the Monty Python Society and the No-Homers Club, "our resident Simpsons group."

Tufts participates in Division III sports, but students say that school spirit is for the most part "pathetic" in terms of athletics. "Supposedly Williams is our rival, but no one really cares about the rivalry," explained one student. One senior noted, "Tufts is by far not a school with school pride on the athletic front. We are good at what I like to call the 'preppy sports.'" Intramural sports, however, are very popular—"I recommend that everyone play one!" one student exclaimed. The most school spirit exhibited at Tufts happens first semester during the first week of reading period (the week before finals), when the campus gathers for the annual Naked Quad Run. "It is a very cheerful event," one senior said. "I go every year to cheer on my friends and make sure they don't fall."

Social life at Tufts draws mixed reviews. "When I first got to Tufts, I wasn't expecting much socially," one freshman remarked. There is a "small" Greek system that nevertheless "has a big influence on the campus." Those who decide to rush fraternities or sororities may find that "pledging is surprisingly hard-core considering the Greek system is so small." Fraternity parties tend to draw a lot of freshmen, while upperclassmen often attend house parties or go into Boston. Students complain that parties are "not always satisfying" and often "so crowded." In addition, there have been a lot of complaints about police breaking up parties early in the evening. "The Tufts University Police Department promised to stop crashing parties so early, but there seems to be no evidence of that," one student sighed. Alcohol and drug use are "pretty much the same as on any college campus," but there is "little pressure to drink." One of the loudest laments is that the dating scene "sucks" at Tufts. "People don't tend to be looking for relationships—most are just interested in random hook-ups," one student said.

For an alternative to the party scene, there are a variety of campus-sponsored events such as movies, concerts, and theatrical performances. Club Hotung offers alcohol-free entertainment in the campus center, complete with food and a D.J. on Friday nights. Boston is notoriously strict in enforcing carding policies, but Tufts upperclassmen still take advantage of the city's clubs, bars, and cultural attractions—all easily accessible by the "T" (subway) stop in Davis Square and a convenient shuttle. As one junior observed, "social life is equally centered between on- and off-campus entertainment."

The student body at Tufts is "diverse," a quality cited by one student as "one of Tufts' most attractive aspects." There is a sizable international population, due in part to the strength of the international relations program. On the whole, however, the student body is "pretty upper-middle class" and "preppy." According to one student, "it's OK to wear sweats to class once in a while, but people tend to dress pretty well—lots of J. Crew." The political bent of the Tufts population is "very liberal," leading one student to remark, "if I ever met a hard-core right-wing conservative, I'd be surprised."

Despite the professed lack of school spirit, the highly motivated students of Tufts are very proud of their school. They show it in their enthusiasm for classes, their commitment to extracurriculars, and even in their soft spot for Tufts' beloved mascot, an elephant named Jumbo. As one senior put it, "Tufts is an introduction to the real world's sociological politics . . . and it is a school that encourages thinking for the sake of thinking." Students who enjoy an intellectually stimulating environment coupled with access to one of the nation's greatest collegiate cities will delight in the experience offered by Tufts. —*Alison Schary*

FYI

If you come to Tufts, you'd better bring a "boyfriend/girlfriend."

What is the typical weekend schedule? "Parties, Boston, homework, sleep."

If I could change one thing about Tufts, I'd "increase school spirit."

Three things every student at Tufts should do before graduating are "watch (or participate in) the Naked Quad Run, explore Boston, and study abroad."

University of Massachusetts / Amherst

Address: 181 President's Drive; Amherst, MA 01003-9291
Phone: 431-545-0222
E-mail address: mail@admissions.umass.edu
Web site URL: www.umass.edu
Founded: 1863
Private or Public: public
Religious affiliation: none
Location: small city
Undergraduate enrollment: 18,606
Total enrollment: NA
Percent Male/Female: 49%/51%
Percent Minority: 17%
Percent African-American: 5%
Percent Asian: 7%
Percent Hispanic: 4%
Percent Native-American: 0%
Percent in-state/out of state: 82%/18%
Percent Pub HS: 90%
Number of Applicants: 20,449
Percent Accepted: 58%
Percent Accepted who enroll: 28%
Entering: 3,335
Transfers: 1,194
Application Deadline: 15 Jan
Mean SAT: NA
Mean ACT: NA
Middle 50% SAT range: V 500-620, M 510-630
Middle 50% ACT range: NA
3 Most popular majors: business, social sciences, communications
Retention: 83%
Graduation rate: 57%
On-campus housing: 60%
Fraternities: 3%
Sororities: 7%
Library: 3,089,191 volumes
Tuition and Fees: $7,482 in; $15,705 out
Room and Board: $5,748
Financial aid, first-year: NA
Varsity or Club Athletes: 5%
Early Decision or Early Action Acceptance Rate: NA

Nestled in the pleasant college town of Amherst, UMass is a public university that attracts athletes and bookworms alike. Despite what has for a long time been considered a party-school image, recently UMass Amherst has been gaining academically. UMass today boasts updated facilities and an award-winning faculty, enabling it to attract students who want both fun and academic promise.

Academics Please

UMass can accommodate a student's academic interests no matter where they lie. With bachelors degrees offered in almost one hundred areas, students enjoy a selection of almost every conceivable major, ranging from building materials and wood technology to business writing. One student touted the school as "a mix for both English and engineering majors." Those students who desire to pursue an uncovered subject are free to explore a self-designed major.

Whatever their major, students must fulfill general education requirements aimed at broadening their horizons. These requirements entail classes in disciplines including literature, the arts, history, the social and behavioral sciences, and the natural sciences. In addition, two courses focusing on non-Western cultures or the history of a minority group are also mandatory. Students also have certain writing requirements that must be met before graduation by enrolling in a college writing class freshman and junior years. The writing class taken junior year must be specific to a student's elected major. Although the requirements cover many subjects, most UMass students seem to feel that they are "easy enough to fulfill" and help them develop new interests.

"I am at a state school so I meet so many different types of people. Poor, rich, black, white, Americans, foreigners, non-English-speaking, and English-speaking students can all be found at this school."

Students generally feel that, while challenging, the work assigned at UMass is not impossible. Many students find that "the teacher makes the difference" in their classes, especially in math and science classes where some teachers "don't give you enough time to understand the material" while others "make the class." The main complaint students have about academics is that classes tend to be "big or huge," although they do get "smaller through the semesters, once you have a major."

For students who know where they want their college lives to take them, UMass provides many academically focused programs. Students who have particularly high test scores are invited to attend the Commonwealth College, which provides students with smaller class sizes and more rigorous course work. There are also residential arrangements called Talent Advancement Programs, by which students are grouped by major, and Residential Advancement Programs, by which students are grouped by class selection. Participating students are given the benefit of close interaction with like-minded peers.

For the students who want to explore a subject in which UMass does not specialize, there is the option of cross-enrolling in classes at other institutions. UMass is a member of the Five-College Consortium, an intercollegiate academic program that permits students from UMass, Smith, Mount Holyoke, Amherst, and Hampshire College to take classes at any of the other member schools. Many students take advantage of this opportunity to pursue their academic interests in a different setting. The other schools are accessible through a free bus system that connects the entire Amherst area. UMass also participates in more than 70 foreign exchange programs, giving students the opportunity to explore their interests abroad. Ultimately, there are many opportunities for UMass students that one might expect to find only in a small private university.

The College Town

Undergrads speak highly of Amherst, a "bustling college town" in the historic Pioneer Valley of western Massachusetts. Students report that they feel safe when walking around campus, but security still provides a bus that circles the 1,400-acre campus every 15 minutes. For no cost, the bus provides transportation to the neighboring schools, the mall, and distant parts of campus. The campus is described as "hilly" and "vast," and many say it is "beautiful in the fall and spring." The buildings at UMass are architecturally diverse, with Georgian and colonial styles characterizing the northern portion of campus, and more modern looking buildings on the southern half of campus.

All freshmen and sophomores are guaranteed on-campus housing, after which many choose to live off-campus. Freshmen like the fact that there is no distinct or separate freshman dorm, because they can learn from the upperclassmen with whom they are intermingled. Although other accommodations do exist, most floors are co-ed with single-sex bathrooms. Students are generally happy with their rooms, although they do warn against dorms in the overly quiet "Sylvan Area." Dorms tend to be tight-knit, with many students saying that they made most of their long-time friends on their floor freshman year.

In these dorms are DCs (Dining Commons) where students enjoy a wide variety of foods. Although the food is sometimes considered "a gamble," there are many options, including vegetarian and vegan selections. The DCs are close and convenient, especially those that have extended eating hours. Many students also choose to sample food from one of the many restaurants in the Amherst area.

Social Life

Living up to its image as a party school, any UMass weekend invariably includes parties at one of the 20 fraternities or sororities located on or near campus. Although attending fraternity parties is popular, non-Greeks report that they do not feel left out. The administration's tough policies strictly regulate underage drinking, but many students say that if they want to drink they are able to get away with it. The school also provides many alcohol-free activities for students to enjoy.

Generally students consider UMass to have a "very active" social scene. The campus hosts frequent concerts, movie showings, and performances, some in conjunction with one or more of the other colleges in the Five-College Consortium, giving students a chance to meet people from the other schools. Students tend to go to parties and spend time at other leisure activities during the weekend and then study on Sundays. One particularly favorite party is Bowl Weekend, a dance party in the Orchard Hill bowl.

Athletics and other extracurricular activities make UMass even more exciting. Sports traditionally play a key role on the UMass campus. Their particularly strong basketball and football teams are popular, and games are well attended. There are also plenty of unique organizations that students participate in, and ample opportunity to start a new organization if desired. One of the perks of UMass being a large school is its ability to bring many different types of students together. Many students feel that they learn not only from their classes, but also from their peers. One student praised the diversity at UMass, saying, "I am at a state school so I meet so many different types of people. Poor, rich, black, white, Americans, foreigners, non-English-speaking, and English-speaking students can all be found at this school."

Students attend UMass to take advantage of both the excitement and the academic rigor of the school. Academic opportunity, a variety of extracurricular activities, the symbiotic relationship of the Five-College Consortium, and a legacy for partying combine to make UMass at Amherst a rich and fulfilling school. —*Adrian Finucane*

FYI

If you come to UMass at Amherst, you'd better bring an "egg-crate pad for your bed."

The typical weekend schedule is "hanging out with your friends Friday and Saturday night, doing something fun Saturday and doing lots of homework on Sunday."

If I could change one thing about UMass at Amherst, I'd "make the buildings more architecturally pleasing."

Three things that every student should do before graduating from UMass at Amherst are "take advantage of the free and cheap offerings, go to a frat, and go to Bowl Weekend."

Wellesley College

Address: 106 Central Street; Wellesley, MA 02481-8203
Phone: 781-283-2270
E-mail address: admission@wellesley.edu
Web site URL: www.wellesley.edu
Founded: 1870
Private or Public: private
Religious affiliation: none
Location: suburban
Undergraduate enrollment: 2,300
Total enrollment: NA
Percent Male/Female: 0%/100%
Percent Minority: 44%
Percent African-American: 6%
Percent Asian: 26%
Percent Hispanic: 5%
Percent Native-American: 0%
Percent in-state/out of state: 13%/87%
Percent Pub HS: 63%
Number of Applicants: 2,877
Percent Accepted: 47%
Percent Accepted who enroll: 44%
Entering: 594
Transfers: 21
Application Deadline: 15 Jan
Mean SAT: NA
Mean ACT: NA
Middle 50% SAT range: V 620-720, M 630-720
Middle 50% ACT range: 27-31
3 Most popular majors: economics, English, psychology
Retention: 96%
Graduation rate: 89%
On-campus housing: 94%
Fraternities: NA
Sororities: NA
Library: 765,530 volumes
Tuition and Fees: $27,904
Room and Board: $8,612
Financial aid, first-year: 56%
Varsity or Club Athletes: NA
Early Decision or Early Action Acceptance Rate: ED 62%

With the likes of former Secretary of State Madeleine Albright and actress Elizabeth Shue hailing from its ivy-covered halls, Wellesley, a small all-women's liberal arts college, strives to maintain its reputation for turning women with potential into women with opportunities. Wellesley may be Lilliputian in size, but the same sense of community that connected the citizens of Swift's miniature fantasy-world also keeps the Wellesley family united and strong. "The great thing about Wellesley is how incredibly kind all of the staff is here," one frosh raved. "Everyone is all too willing to help." With such groups as First-Year Mentors, Big Sisters, and Academic Peer Tutors, Wellesley's "fantastic support system" creates "a nurturing environment" to ease the transition for incoming young women as they begin a four-year journey towards the future.

The Art of Academics, Dining and Sleep

When it comes to classes, the good news is that professors, rather than TAs, do the vast majority of the teaching. The bad news depends on your point of view. While hard-core majors such as economics, biochemistry, pre-law, and psychology definitely keep the upperclassmen on their toes, no one gets off easy. Thirty-two credits (four per semester) complete with distributional requirements, as well as the obligatory Writing 125, demands effort from all Wellesley women. Students point out that the professors are very approachable and accessible. "Every single professor I've met so far has made it a point to learn every student's name," one junior gushed.

"All the dorms have something unique." Dormitory arrangements at Wellesley consist of singles and doubles, housing approximately 30 to 35 women per floor, with a kitchen, laundry room, common living room, mass bathroom stall, and a private bathroom for male visitors. Each bedroom is supplied with all the basic furniture—bed, desk, bureau and/or closet, bookcase, and lamp. As far as individual dorms go, the "new dorms" tend to have more room and storage space than their older counterparts, yet suffer from being the farthest away from everything—except the Science Center and the "VIL" (the town of Wellesley). The most popular dorm is Stone Davis, which according to one student "is very nice."

The popular myth that the Wellesley dining hall is always open is apparently not to be believed. While "the quality of food could be better," students acknowledge that the college makes a special effort to offer a variety of food to suit everyone's needs. Sweet-toothed ladies rejoice—ice cream is always available!

Campus Highlights

Though Wellesley dorms feature channels in French, Spanish, and Italian for students with TVs, cable television is not provided in the dorms. Schneider's Student Center, the fast-food hub of Wellesley, is the only on-campus site where the women of Wellesley can sit back, scarf down Pizza Hut pizza and catch the latest episode of The Real World. Though the school has minimal home entertainment options, Wellesley is hardly short on scenery.

The campus is gorgeous. Period. "There are trees everywhere, and the sky seems 'bluer' here.'" One of the best places to study is by the lake, which has "a lovely breeze as well as a wonderful view" to distract the Wellesley scholar. While much of the campus exudes a deliciously creepy, Gothic aura, the most unique and contemporary structure may easily be the funky Science Center, which won the Halston Parker Prize for architecture in 1987. The orange carpet on the inside, glass walls, pillars, and outer-space feel make this building just as futuristic as the others are traditional.

Sport and Custom

Crew! No football here, girls. With the Charles River and Lake Waban integrally connected to the campus, crew is big as both a dorm and varsity sport. Athletics at Wellesley are important—students are required to take eight credits worth of physical education. However, for non-athletes there are plenty of fun classes to pick from. Yoga, it seems, rivals crew in popularity.

From Hoop Rolling to the extremely secretive event known only as Lake Day, Wellesley is steeped in traditions that get the college women out and about—and quite often dunked in the lake. When the first thick snow falls on the beautiful hills of Wellesley's campus, students grab their lunch trays and hit the slopes, or the rolling hills of Wellesley's golf course. On Flower Sunday, however, students take time to pause and reflect the Sunday before classes begin. With a campus-wide picnic, Flower Sunday offers another side of Wellesley life equal in importance to the others—except perhaps Tower Court, the huge last-night-of-freedom bash on the evening prior to the start of classes.

The Social Hitch: Not Just Boys

Wellesley can hardly be considered conventional in activity. Several years ago *Rolling Stone* covered the infamous Dyke Ball, a February dance paying homage to various sexual persuasions, where apparently around 1,300 guys tried to gain entrance. One Wellesley transfer junior debunked the myth that all Wellesley women are lesbians, though they are not all "guy-crazy" either. "Someone should really invent an MIT drunk frat boy repellent spray," she added. "They will really stick to you at Wellesley parties." One frosh pointed out, "some people find social life here lacking because of the absence of guys, but if you make an effort, you'll meet some sure enough."

"The sky is bluer here."

With the problem of young men out of the way, the next issue most plaguing Wellesley women regards the social scene, or lack thereof. In particular, trying to leave the small campus can cause its problems. "It takes 40 minutes by bus [to get to Boston], and if you're stuck standing on the bus, well, it's not fun." Even so, traveling to Boston is a popular destination, especially on the weekends.

As high as Wellesley is on parties, it is equally low on the use of drugs and alcohol. "I'm sure there are some," reported one upperclassmen, "I just haven't seen a lot." Considering that some students at Wellesley are employed by the town and college police, this is hardly surprising. Drinking and socializing off-campus occurs mainly on the weekends, in fact. "Frat Row," which consists of MIT and Boston University houses, is the scene of choice for underclassmen in particular. However since frosh are not allowed to have cars, they are trapped in Wellesley unless they take the Senate Bus (the name of the single mode of transportation bringing Wellesley women back and forth from the Boston/Cambridge area).

The Clincher

If New England boasts more colleges and universities than any other area of the United States, Massachusetts leads the pack. Wellesley participates in a 12 College Exchange with such schools as Mount Holyoke and Smith, the state's other all-female colleges, as well as with schools like MIT and Brandeis. With so many other colleges from which to choose, what sets Wellesley apart from the others? The answer lies in the fact that above everything else, the sisters of Wellesley College put each other first. "You meet all sorts of people here that you would never get to meet anywhere else! We watch out for each other. This, this is my family." *—Katherine Stevens*

FYI

If you come to Wellesley, you'd better bring "a supply of food."

What is the typical weekend schedule? "Friday: go to a society party on campus and come back to watch TV with your floor-mates; Saturday: bake cookies, party in Boston; Sunday: work all day and go see a movie at night."

If I could change one thing about Wellesley, "I'd make it co-ed."

Three things every student at Wellesley should do before graduating are "go traying, go to Tower Court, and dump a frat boy into Lake Waban."

Wheaton College

Address: East Main Street; Norton, MA 02766
Phone: 508-286-8251
E-mail address: admission@wheatoncollege.edu
Web site URL: www.wheatoncollege.edu
Founded: 1834
Private or Public: private
Religious affiliation: none
Location: suburban
Undergraduate enrollment: 1,521
Total enrollment: NA
Percent Male/Female: 36%/64%
Percent Minority: 11%
Percent African-American: 3%
Percent Asian: 2%
Percent Hispanic: 3%
Percent Native-American: 0%
Percent in-state/out of state: 33%/67%
Percent Pub HS: 61%
Number of Applicants: 3,534
Percent Accepted: 44%
Percent Accepted who enroll: 27%
Entering: 412
Transfers: 10
Application Deadline: 15 Jan
Mean SAT: NA
Mean ACT: NA
Middle 50% SAT range: V 590-670, M 550-650
Middle 50% ACT range: 25-27
3 Most popular majors: psychology, English, economics
Retention: 86%
Graduation rate: 69%
On-campus housing: 97%
Fraternities: NA
Sororities: NA
Library: 283,733 volumes
Tuition and Fees: $28,900
Room and Board: $7,430
Financial aid, first-year: 51%
Varsity or Club Athletes: 22%
Early Decision or Early Action Acceptance Rate: ED 66%

Each year at the end of freshman orientation, Wheaton's newest arrivals gather around picturesque Peacock Pond, as a crowd of upperclassmen look on, to each light a candle. The candles are floated on the water, illuminating the pond and symbolizing the entrance of the new freshman class into the community of Wheaton College. Senior year, just before graduation, these students once again gather at the pond to repeat the candle ceremony, marking their exit. One of Wheaton's oldest traditions, the ceremony also reflects the strong sense of community at this small, liberal arts college. Nestled in the sleepy town of

Norton, Massachusetts, Wheaton offers a personalized academic experience, a friendly and open student body, and a myriad of activities to suit every need. The college's proximity to both Boston and Providence proves to be a major advantage, with many students traveling to these two cities to pursue their interests, academic or otherwise, on a regular basis.

Making Connections

Students consistently cited their professors as Wheaton's biggest asset and the best part of their academic experience. One junior said, "The professors go above and beyond their jobs. They care about me outside of the classroom." Professors often invite students to their houses or challenge them to golf or tennis on the weekends. And in the classroom, they are just as amazing. The average class size at Wheaton is 20 to 30 students, but even in larger introductory or required classes (which often cap off at 100), professors make the effort to know each and every student. One student mentioned a professor who, in one of her larger classes freshman year, brought a video camera to class and taped the students saying their names. "He would watch it while he ran on the treadmill in the morning. He knew every student by the second week of class!" Though the workload at Wheaton is often tough, professors are not only very understanding when it comes to giving extensions, but are also always there to offer help outside of the classroom.

Wheaton is currently undergoing an overhaul of its general education and graduation requirements, to take effect with the class of 2007. General education requirements will be divided into "foundations" courses and "connections" courses. Required foundations courses will be English 101, a math course, two semesters of a foreign language, a class tentatively called "Beyond the West," and a first-year seminar. The first-year seminar has long been a required class for freshmen and offers students the chance to work closely with a group of about 20 other freshmen and a professor in a laid-back environment. It is offered in a variety of interesting and fun subjects each year and helps students adjust to the academic environment of college. New to the Wheaton academic experience will be the required "connections" courses, which will combine different academic disciplines to offer students a more integrated course of study. Students will be able pick courses to form connections that fulfill their interests. The school is also doing away with its "second transcript," a unique feature of Wheaton's education that required students to complete some kind of real-world learning experience such as an internship, job, club, or other activity in order to graduate. Students have mixed feelings about these changes, especially about the elimination of the second transcript requirement, but most feel that the general education changes are for the better and that the "connections" courses will make fulfilling the requirements more interesting.

Wheaton's academic offerings go beyond its campus, and there are plenty of opportunities to study abroad or at any of the schools in the 12-college consortium of which Wheaton is a part (these include Amherst, Bowdoin, Wellesley, and Dartmouth, to name a few). On or off-campus, students consistently praise the quality of their academic experiences and the personal attention they receive: "At Wheaton, you can make your education whatever you want it to be," said one senior.

One Big Family

Although Wheaton began accepting men in 1987, the number of women still exceeds the number of men by about 3 to 2. Although the benefits of being the only male on an all-female floor may seem obvious to any guy, one male student complained, "There's no such thing as guy time when you're surrounded by girls. You get used to dealing with cat fights and gossip on a daily basis." However, many male students do appreciate having a "good selection" of attractive girls on campus, and hook-ups are quite common. For the female students, the male to female ratio can be a problem when it comes to dating. One girl exclaimed, "It's hard because all the really good guys are already taken!" Nevertheless, Wheaton still boasts an active social life and a vibrant student body.

Students at Wheaton think highly of their peers, and endlessly praise the "friendly, outgoing, laid-back, and fun" student body. Because of Wheaton's small size, it is easy to get to know almost everyone, and cliques rarely form. One freshman gushed, "Everyone is just so friendly, even upperclassmen. It really feels like a family." Wheaton's size can have its drawbacks. "Rumors spread around campus fairly quickly," reported one student. However, most students feel that the size helps them get to know people and fosters a sense of community on campus.

Wheaton students are generally "preppy" and "fit" and tend to come from upper- or middle-class New England backgrounds. A few students suggested that there could be more racial and geographic diversity on campus. In an effort to bring such diversity to campus, Wheaton became part of the Posse Program, a national program that offers scholarships to high-achieving students from inner-city high schools and sends them as groups, or "posses" to schools like Wheaton. Although many of the posse students at Wheaton are from nearby New York and Boston, the program has helped to increase racial and socio-economic diversity on campus.

Students are involved in a wide variety of extracurricular activities. Student government is popular, as are community service groups like Habitat for Humanity and Backpacks for Mexico, the three a cappella groups, and Wheaton's newspaper *The Wheaton Wire.* Sports are also popular on campus. Wheaton's men's and women's soccer teams have been nationally ranked for the past few years, and their track teams boast national titles. Wheaton students often attend games and support their teams with spirit. Club sports and intramurals are popular activities and allow students to play everything from water polo to Ping-Pong. Wheaton gives students the opportunity to establish any organization they wish, and many take advantage of this each year. As with its academics, Wheaton allows students to make their experiences outside of the classroom whatever they wish them to be.

What to Do on the Weekends

Social life on campus usually revolves around dances at the Balfour-Hood Student Center and parties at the 11 student houses on campus, as well as the occasional dorm party. Well-attended theme dances take place in Balfour's Atrium, a large lobby-type space, almost every weekend. On nights when there isn't a dance, students flock to parties in student theme houses, which vary in size and distance from campus but almost always host a keg or two on the weekends. Parties and kegs must be registered under the assumption that no underage students will be drinking. In reality, though, the administration is fairly lax and drinking is common on campus. Although many social functions revolve around alcohol, non-drinkers don't feel pressured to drink, and there are non-alcoholic activities on campus.

Despite the busy social atmosphere, the town of Norton is one of Wheaton's more unpopular aspects and offers little in the way of student life. One student complained, "There's a CVS in Norton, and that's it." There are a few popular hangouts, though. The Loft, Wheaton's bar, serves beer, pizza, burgers, and sandwiches and often has live bands. The Lyons' Den is the campus coffee shop and is described by many students as "just like Central Perk in Friends." It boasts comfortable chairs and couches and a quiet room upstairs to study. But if students are looking for options beyond these, they usually travel to Boston or Providence. By car, Boston is about 40 minutes away and Providence about 20. Although there is a train to both cities, most students have cars, which many feel are necessary for life in Norton. One student cautioned, "If you don't have a car, Norton can kill you."

Dorms, Dining, and "The Dimple"?

Wheaton's campus is picturesque and woodsy with what one student described as "a wannabe Ivy League look." Two major motion pictures have used Wheaton as a look-alike for Harvard's campus—1986's *Soul Man,* and *Prozac Nation,* filmed in 2001. Yet students caution that only the area known as Upper Campus could ever be mistaken for Harvard Yard. The majority of upperclassmen reside on Upper Campus, as the dorms there tend to be nicer on the inside as well as on the outside, with ivy-covered brick walls and traditional collegiate architecture. It is also home to Emerson dining hall. Emerson offers a more formal atmosphere and shorter hours, making it a less popular choice for on-campus dining. Students more often prefer Chase dining hall on Lower Campus, which is open all day and offers a more relaxed atmosphere as well as a better selection of food, including wraps, stir-fry, sandwiches, hot food, and a grill. For many students, the school's meal plan is the worst thing about Wheaton. All students have the same meal plan which allows unlimited trips to the dining hall during operating hours. Many students complain that the system wastes money, especially for those who leave campus frequently, but the administration hopes that changes to the meal plan system will alleviate some of these complaints.

"You have to want to come to a small school where professors know who you are, and where you can't hide from people."

One student described Wheaton's dorms as "nice, when there's the proper number of people living there." One of Wheaton's biggest problems in recent years has been placing freshman in "forced triples," rooms of three students, originally meant for two. This problem has been somewhat eased with the addition of a new dorm, Beard Hall, which offers the unique opportunity to interact with a professor and his family who live in the dorm alongside the student residents. However, housing remains an issue. Freshmen and sophomores usually live on Lower Campus, in dorms that look like they're "straight out of the 70s," but which are near Chase dining hall and other campus buildings, and can be fairly nice on the inside.

One of the biggest adjustments for students new to Wheaton is dealing with co-ed bathrooms. Many say this was an issue at first, but eventually "everyone just gets used to it and it's not a big deal." All dorms have Student Mentors, or SMs, on each floor who organize dorm and floor events and help maintain the rules, although they can vary in levels of strictness. Keefe and Gebbie dorms are the exceptions. These are completely "self-governed," meaning that students organize their own events without SMs, and rely on themselves to enforce residence regulations. There are also wellness-themed, single-sex, and quiet dorms.

Students can also elect to live in one of 11 Wheaton-owned student houses on campus. Students apply for a house with a group of seven to 15 other students with common interests and, with the backing of a faculty or administrative advisor, establish a theme. Recent themes have included Music, Self-Esteem, or Environmental Awareness. The groups sponsor different events on campus and in the community, and also throw parties on the weekends. Getting a house can be a very competitive process. Because all students are required to live on campus, the houses are often the closest thing to an off-campus experience that a Wheaton student can get.

The center of Wheaton's campus is a quad known as "The Dimple" because of the big grassy area that slopes down in the center. Students congregate there to lounge on the grass on nice days; it is also the site of many campus-wide activities, such as the spring carnival. Surrounding The Dimple are classroom and administrative buildings, including Wheaton's new arts and humanities center—"a dream for art students"—and the remodeled science center. Wheaton is continually updating buildings on campus to better suit student needs.

Choose It for the Right Reasons

Wheaton students are overwhelmingly satisfied with their choice of college and are eager to rave about their Wheaton experiences. One student summed it up, "It's easy to be happy here. Those students who are not happy with Wheaton are the ones who chose it for the wrong reasons. You have to want to come to a small school where professors know who you are, and where you can't hide from people." Students who are looking for a sense of community will, without a doubt, find a vibrant one at Wheaton College. —*Jessica Lenox*

FYI

If you come to Wheaton, you'd better bring "a bathrobe because all the bathrooms are co-ed!"

A typical weekend at Wheaton consists of "school spirit on the athletic fields, dances at Balfour, parties at students houses, and hanging out with friends."

If I could change one thing about Wheaton, I'd "offer more options for the meal plan."

Three things every student at Wheaton should do before graduating are "swim (or get thrown into) Peacock Pond, go 'Dimple Diving' (sliding half-naked down the hill when it rains), and develop a personal relationship with a professor."

Williams College

Address: 988 Main Street; Williamstown, MA 01267
Phone: 413-597-2211
E-mail address: admission@williams.edu
Web site URL: www.williams.edu
Founded: 1793
Private or Public: private
Religious affiliation: none
Location: rural
Undergraduate enrollment: 1,988
Total enrollment: NA
Percent Male/Female: 51%/49%
Percent Minority: 30%
Percent African-American: 8%
Percent Asian: 9%
Percent Hispanic: 7%
Percent Native-American: 0%
Percent in-state/out of state: 20%/80%
Percent Pub HS: NA
Number of Applicants: 4,931
Percent Accepted: 23%
Percent Accepted who enroll: 48%
Entering: 539
Transfers: 6
Application Deadline: 1 Jan
Mean SAT: NA
Mean ACT: NA
Middle 50% SAT range: V 660-760, M 660-750
Middle 50% ACT range: NA
3 Most popular majors: economics, English, psychology
Retention: 97%
Graduation rate: 96%
On-campus housing: 93%
Fraternities: NA
Sororities: NA
Library: 888,504 volumes
Tuition and Fees: $28,090
Room and Board: $7,660
Financial aid, first-year: 45%
Varsity or Club Athletes: 32%
Early Decision or Early Action Acceptance Rate: ED 39%

On one Friday every October, the students of Williams College celebrate "Mountain Day." Roused in the early morning by the melody of their school song, throngs of Ephs (named for school founder Colonel Ephrain Williams) climb nearby Mt. Greylock instead of going to classes. A variety of pleasures await them at the summit, including a cappella performances, good food and hundreds of energetic peers.

Nestled in the scenic Berkshire Mountains, Williams College is a close-knit community of about 1,200 undergrads. Students at this small liberal arts school exhibit an appreciation for academics, athletics and the great outdoors. "The environment here is beautiful," said one student, "Fresh air, no pollution, and hardly any noise aside from college students."

Hitting the Books

Want to hear Williams' students praise their school? Ask them about the quality of their academic experience. Classes are "nice and small" and teachers "encourage learning." Professors are willing to go the extra mile to make academics enjoyable. One student related how her Chemistry 101 professor "plays the guitar and sings on Fridays," while another remembered an Introduction to the Novel course where "the class actually gave a standing ovation after a couple of the lectures."

Every Williams student is required to take at least three courses in each of the academic divisions: Languages and the Arts, Social Studies, and Science and Math. In addition, undergrads must take at least one "Peoples and Cultures" class and pass four quarters of physical education. PE classes range from beginning tennis to weight training and athletes at every level can use sports participation to place out of at least some of their requirements. Overall, the requirements "allow for a lot of freedom choosing classes," and are the subject of few complaints.

The most popular majors at Williams include English, economics, biology, and math. Chemistry and physics are among the most difficult. Students describe the typical workload as "quite a bit, with a few hours of reading or doing problem sets for each hour in class," but report that this "depends on the class." Adventurous Ephs can find academic opportunities beyond the Williams campus at the Williams-Mystic program, which allows students to pursue American maritime studies in Mystic, Connecticut, as well as the Williams-Oxford exchange with Exeter College in Oxford, England.

One of the most unique elements of Williams' academic life is the 4-1-4 system. Ephs take four classes during the fall and spring terms and take part in a month-long Winter Study in January. During Winter Study, professors offer "creative courses," like "Hologram Making" or "Reading Hamlet" and students enroll in one class that meets 3–4 times a week. Undergrads can also create their own courses, subject to committee approval, or go abroad. Many use this time to "bond with their entry mates, chill and have a good time." Since academic pressures are lighter than normal, undergrads take frequent trips to Boston, ski resorts, or local hiking spots.

Take a Look Around

While Williams students consider their setting "glorious—lots of open space, trees, old stone and brick buildings," they do admit that "the remoteness is not for everyone." The campus lies in picturesque Williamstown, Massachusetts, a small New England town best known for its summer theater festival. Boston, the nearest big city, is three hours away by car. Other than a handful of restaurants and a movie theatre, "there's not too much around." While a car is unnecessary for getting around campus, "it's wonderful for escaping Williamstown to go to Boston or New York City." In addition, Williamstown is not the right place for those easily intimidated by winter: "A distinctive feature here is the weather: very cold with a lot of snow."

All freshmen live either in the Frosh Quad or Berkshire Quad, nicknamed by students the "odd quad," since its non-freshmen dorms are "where the weird people live." Freshmen occupy either doubles or singles, which are arranged into entryways of about 20 students. Every freshman entryway has two Junior Advisors (JAs), who are "closer to the freshmen than the typical RAs." Entryways are also the site of a lot of social interaction, and students often form strong bonds with their neighbors. After freshman year, students enter in a school-wide lottery for housing.

On the whole, housing gets glowing reviews. "All upperclassmen have singles and common space as well," said one student. "They're generally nice; most of them have been recently redone." Dorms sometimes include common kitchens, laundry rooms, and living rooms with TVs and couches. The vast majority of students choose to live on campus all four years.

"In general, our facilities are not lacking," said one Eph. Due to a string of renovations, students now have a new science library ("very modern and cool") and a new student center with a coffee bar and performance space. One athlete raved, "the gym was just redone and is fantastic." Several museums are also located on campus, including the distinguished Clark Art Institute, "a jewel box in the middle of nowhere."

Parties and Practices

Weekends at Williams revolve around a mix of sporting events and on-campus parties. During the day, students usually spend their time either attending sporting events or catching up on work. "Sports are HUGE on campus," exclaimed one undergrad. The majority of Ephs play at least one sport, and football or soccer games can attract nearly the entire campus, especially if the Purple Cows are facing Williams' long-time rivals, Amherst. One student described the typical Williams game as "fans on the sidelines of a soccer game cheering wildly for their team against Amherst. Or folks at a hockey match: we scream and show our support and all those things." Track and Swimming are also popular varsity sports, while the

Williams Ultimate Frisbee Organization (WUFO) is one of the largest club teams.

"We are hardly a nerdy school in the middle of nowhere, and we are not a bunch of jocks either."

At the mere mention of Williams' athletics, most students will proudly boast of Williams' five-year streak as Sears Directors' Cup champions, an award given to the top NCAA Division III school in the country in terms of overall athletic excellence. Ephs also embrace their unusual school colors, as spectators and athletes alike deck themselves out in Williams' purple and yellow. School spirit flows through the entire campus, and even when students miss an amazing soccer game or track meet, they "enjoy talking about it afterwards."

When it comes to extracurriculars, no campus organization compares in size to the Williams Outing Club (WOC). WOC sponsors several trips every weekend, including hiking and camping in the spring and skiing in the colder months. Many students take advantage of these excursions, especially during Winter Study, when Ephs are known for "skiing all the time." In addition, WOC rents outdoor equipment to members and maintains both a cabin and a number of trails in the Berkshire area. Theater is also "very big on campus," as well as student government, Students for Social Justice, and the student symphony. Some of the more bizarre extracurricular activities include Killing As An Organized Sport, an annual game of simulated assassinations, and the Chocolate Lovers Association. Community service is also popular on campus and many students volunteer in the local school district.

The nightlife at Williams is very campus-centered. On Saturday nights, students often head to the "row houses," a group of upperclass dorms, where parties are held "in huge common spaces" and alcohol is served. Underclassmen do not seem to have trouble finding alcohol. In the words of one student, "the school appears to be strict, but security doesn't give a rip, and under aged students always have older friends." Most students also spend considerable time just chilling with friends. "Small group residence interaction is probably most prevalent over large party-type gatherings," said one Eph. Undergrads also venture into Williamstown for dinner at a local restaurant or to catch a movie.

The Ties That Bind

With a population of only 1,200 undergrads, Williams is, well, small. "You don't know everyone, but you recognize most people within a year or two," said one student. Weekend escapades and random hook-ups are hard to forget because "the place is so small here that everyone finds out." Students describe their classmates as a "hiking/enviro/Birkenstock/granola munching" population and many complain that "the school isn't the most diverse." Many also warn that most Williams stereotypes are completely off base. "We are hardly a nerdy school in the middle of nowhere and we are not a bunch of jocks either."

While most Ephs will admit to occasionally wishing that Berkshire weather were a little more like California's, or that commercial Williamstown looked a bit more like downtown Boston, few would ever choose to change their setting for the long haul. After all, their campus is "hilly and beautiful" and "surrounded by mountains and nature on all sides." Both the small size of the student body and the isolation of the campus help to establish the strong connections between students. As one Eph put it, Williams "is a community and it feels like a community." —*Mariko Hirose*

FYI

If you come to Williams, you'd better bring a "warm jacket."

The typical weekend schedule is "watch or play in a sporting event, party, and then work."

If I could change one thing about Williams, I'd "move Williamstown to a larger city."

Three things every student at Williams should do before graduating are "attend a football game," "hike to the top of Mt. Greylock," and "go to the art museums."

Worcester Polytechnic Institute

Address: 100 Institute Road; Worcester, MA 01609
Phone: 508-831-5286
E-mail address: admissions@wpi.edu
Web site URL: www.wpi.edu
Founded: 1865
Private or Public: private
Religious affiliation: none
Location: suburban
Undergraduate enrollment: 2,767
Total enrollment: NA
Percent Male/Female: 77%/23%
Percent Minority: 16%
Percent African-American: 1%
Percent Asian: 7%
Percent Hispanic: 3%
Percent Native-American: 0%
Percent in-state/out of state: 52%/48%
Percent Pub HS: 75%
Number of Applicants: 3,191
Percent Accepted: 76%
Percent Accepted who enroll: 29%
Entering: 718
Transfers: 51
Application Deadline: 1 Feb
Mean SAT: 1300
Mean ACT: 30
Middle 50% SAT range: V 550-660, M 620-710
Middle 50% ACT range: NA
3 Most popular majors: electrical engineering, computer science, mechanical engineering
Retention: 91%
Graduation rate: 73%
On-campus housing: 83%
Fraternities: 35%
Sororities: 25%
Library: 146,372 volumes
Tuition and Fees: $28,420
Room and Board: $8,984
Financial aid, first-year: 78%
Varsity or Club Athletes: 19%
Early Decision or Early Action Acceptance Rate: ED 83%: EA 95%

Welcome to Worcester Polytechnic Institute—or WPI—where learning is not the only objective. Located in Worcester, Massachusetts, WPI is the third-oldest engineering school in the country. A non-traditional learning environment combined with a quaint New England campus gives WPI students a top-notch technical education and a unique cultural experience.

Learning for a Purpose

Its unique curriculum—known as the "WPI plan"—makes WPI stand apart from other engineering and polytechnic schools. The WPI plan features hands-on, interdisciplinary learning projects, described by one student as "one of the best things about WPI." Three projects—to whose acronyms WPI students quickly become accustomed—are a large part of what defines a WPI education: Sufficiency, Interactive Qualifying Project (IQP), and Major Qualifying Project (MQP).

WPI classes are intense: many meet every day, some for up to 10 hours a week. In seven weeks, students cover roughly the same amount of material as would be covered in a thirteen- or fourteen-week-long semester. WPI has a unique academic calendar with four seven-week quarters, and an optional fifth summer session. Students generally take only three classes per quarter. "I like feeling as though you can start over in seven weeks should something go wrong," one student said. "If you have a bad professor, you don't have to worry about sticking it out for the whole semester."

Most WPI students major in science or engineering, but the school's philosophy is that humanities are still important. A required "Humanities Sufficiency Project" is conducted in an area in the humanities, after taking five courses in a related thematic concentration. Students usually complete the project by the end of their sophomore year. For students who major in Humanities, a "Technology Sufficiency Project" is required instead.

The Interactive Qualifying Project (IQP) is designed to bridge the gap between technology and society. Many choose to do these projects off campus, with approximately one-third of WPI students participating in the Global Perspective Program, allowing them to complete their IQP at many locations around the world. "The best thing is going away," reminisced one recent graduate. Recent projects have involved everything from studying the "Hydrodynamics of the Inner Canals of Venice," to "Computerizing the Catalog System for the National Museum of Bangkok," to "Improving Playgrounds in the London Borough of Merton."

The Major Qualifying Project (MQP) is a project conducted during senior year. Students can work in industry, independent off-campus research organizations, or with faculty researchers on campus. The research project is conducted at a professional level, with a written and oral presentation conducted by the student at the project's conclusion. The MQP gives students first-hand exposure to the cutting edge of current technologies and procedures, which can prove to be valuable experience when looking for employment or applying to graduate school.

For the most part, WPI students have very strong attachments to their professors: "WPI professors are their own breed. Many think of students as colleagues instead of as students. They work with you to solve problems, instead of saying, 'well, I taught you this in class.'"

Said one recent WPI graduate, "The bio professors were awesome. I was on a first-name basis with most of the members of the department." WPI professors possess a certain kind of attitude and persistence, which makes them not unlike the students themselves. Many hold help or review sessions at times when they will be most convenient for students, like in the evening: "They are very helpful, stay for an undefined period of time, stay until everyone gets it."

Science or Bust

The number of women at WPI is small, as seems to be the case at many engineering schools. But female WPI students report that there is "no extra pressure" placed on them, and several women have reported that "they never felt uncomfortable being a woman in a class consisting mostly of men." For some, it is something they "hardly ever even notice."

As members of the Colleges of Worcester Consortium, Inc., WPI students can take courses at any of the 14 other member schools. Students rarely take advantage of this option because it requires them to take semester-long—rather than quarter-long—courses. WPI students do, however, use the libraries at other schools.

Academics are certainly the name of the game at WPI, yet students report no cutthroat mentality between classmates. Instead, they often work together to solve problems. Introductory classes have "conferences," where "peer learning assistants"—older students who have taken the class and excelled—retake the class to help others.

Frats and Brats?

Much of WPI's social life revolves around the Greek System: there are 12 fraternities and two sororities. Even with so many fraternities on campus, students report feeling little pressure to drink. "Alcohol is available, but it's not forced down your throat," one student said. "You can always find a party on the weekend. I go to fraternity parties to meet people," a second student said. Reported another: "I think that the social scene is pretty decent. Remember—this is a technical school." To balance the guy-girl ratio, WPI men often depend on visitors for their romantic opportunities. The "majority of girls at fraternity parties are bussed in," said one student.

"WPI Professors are their own breed. Many think of students as colleagues instead of as students. They work with you to solve problems, instead of saying, 'well, I taught you this in class.'"

The campus feels safe to most students. WPI has its own police force, with officers who, in the words of one student, "usually just hand out parking tickets." Still, while on WPI's campus, students sometimes forget they are in a city with real crime issues. Students note that some caution is necessary when venturing out into the city.

The city of Worcester draws mixed reviews. Some students find interesting cultural activities and take advantage of the "quaint New England" environment. Others find Worcester "depressing," noting that it is a "dying industrial city." Basically, though, students agree that the city is what one makes of it.

Extracurricular opportunities abound. There are community service organizations, college chapters of national science and engineering societies, honor societies and numerous special interest clubs. In addition to varsity sports (NCAA Division III), WPI has numerous club and intramural sporting opportunities, which students describe as "a lot of fun."

On-campus university housing is guaranteed for freshman year only. Eighty-five percent of WPI students live off-campus after their first year. However, students enjoy "unbelievably reasonable rates" for apartments in the immediate vicinity of campus. The cost of living in Worcester is much lower than in Boston.

Freshman orientation is an excellent time to meet people. Having undergone renovations in the last three years, the campus dining hall, whose food used to "-really suck," has become "the closest thing to home cooking." It is so good, in fact, that students living off-campus like to come back and eat in the dining halls.

Goats of Fun

WPI certainly has its share of traditions, like the use of a bronzed goat's head in a series of year-long competitions in which each class tries to steal it for themselves. The victorious class gets its name engraved in a plaque on the goat's head.

In one competition between the freshman and sophomore classes, the two square off in a large-scale tug of war. It used to be played across a pond, with the losing class getting pulled into the water. Recently, water contamination has removed the pond from the picture. Now, the Worcester fire department hoses down a field for the event, creating a giant, artificially muddy mess.

Thinking of Applying?

Students recommend staying overnight in the freshman dorms, which can be arranged through the admissions office. This gives a prospective student a better first-hand perspective of the school. A sophomore electrical engineering major cautioned prospective students to "make sure you like engineering," citing that "students who don't often drop out or transfer." WPI is not the right school for everyone. It appeals to a certain type of student who likes challenges and enjoys learning, collaborative learning in particular. —*Andrew Read*

FYI

If you come to WPI, you'd better bring "a scientific or graphing calculator, not to mention a computer and time management skills."

What is the typical weekend schedule? "Cruising parties Friday night. Sleeping as late as possible . . . hanging out with friends, going to parties Saturday night; Sunday, doing homework."

If I could change one thing about WPI, I'd "add more women."

Three things every student at WPI should do before graduating are "hold, or at least see, the Bronze Goat's Head, go to Pricechopper at 3 A.M., and stomp on the WPI seal in the middle of the quad and see if the superstition about not graduating really holds water."

Michigan

Albion College

Address: 611 East Porter Street; Albion, MI 49224
Phone: 800-858-6770
E-mail address: admissions@albion.edu
Web site URL: www.albion.edu
Founded: 1835
Private or Public: private
Religious affiliation: Methodist
Location: small city
Undergraduate enrollment: 1,658
Total enrollment: NA
Percent Male/Female: 43%/57%
Percent Minority: 6%
Percent African-American: 2%
Percent Asian: 2%
Percent Hispanic: 1%
Percent Native-American: 0%
Percent in-state/out of state: 93%/7%
Percent Pub HS: 72%
Number of Applicants: 1,491
Percent Accepted: 85%
Percent Accepted who enroll: 41%
Entering: 526
Transfers: 24
Application Deadline: 1 May
Mean SAT: NA
Mean ACT: NA
Middle 50% SAT range: V 520-660, M 530-650
Middle 50% ACT range: 23-28
3 Most popular majors: economics, biology/ biological science, communications
Retention: 85%
Graduation rate: 68%
On-campus housing: 94%
Fraternities: 15%
Sororities: 34%
Library: 363,007 volumes
Tuition and Fees: $21,948
Room and Board: $6,262
Financial aid, first-year: 64%
Varsity or Club Athletes: 27%
Early Decision or Early Action Acceptance Rate: ED 88%

During their first night on campus, Albion freshmen sing Lo Triumphe, the school song. At least, tradition says they should. How many freshmen actually participate in this linguistically challenging tradition? Well, if not all of them, they'll have four years to figure it out. Besides learning Lo Triumphe, future graduates of Albion will have experienced going to school in a small town environment, with a close-knit student body, in a friendly, Midwest atmosphere.

Academic to the Core

Because of its relatively small student body, Albion provides an excellent opportunity for students to really get to know their professors. Class sizes average about twenty, and the largest lecture classes run about forty or fifty. TAs don't exist at Albion, although undergraduate student assistants sometimes lead the discussion sections. Most students at Albion find their professors to be challenging, but friendly, often taking their classes out onto the quad when the weather is warm. One student said, "I've gone to a couple of my professor's houses for dinner. They open their homes and it really helps you get in touch with your instructor." "Many [professors] become your friends and people you can talk to about stuff outside of academics," said another. One history major said, "The best class I have taken is Colonial American History because unlike a typical history, the structure of the class was different and a lot of fun. We had a variety of discussion groups, including one similar to the format of Jerry Springer." The administration pays attention to the attitudes of students toward their professor: at the end of each term, students evaluate nontenured professors, and the administration takes these evaluations into consideration.

Besides the classes required for their major, Albion students also need to get class credit in several different cores: a gender core credit, an environmental credit, a race credit, a lab science and a non-lab science. However, crafty students can choose classes that count towards both their core and their major. One communications major explained, "[I took] Race and Ethnicity, . . . a 300 level sociology class, which covered CORE for me. It really helped me to understand how race and ethnicity impact all of our lives, no matter what our background." But, of course even students taking core classes outside of their major still appreciate the idea behind the core classes, "to promote diversity and get students more in tune with all aspects of culture." Most undergrads will find the classes to be helpful and to provide a diversion from classes for their major. At the very least, said one student, "I didn't mind the core requirements at all."

Albion's Gerstacker Program in Professional Management and the Gerald R. Ford Institute for Public Service offer internships for political science and business majors. For those majoring in other fields, there are other people at Albion College who help students get started finding great internships. One female student exclaims, "Albion gives great internships! Most of my friends have spent a semester elsewhere, either in cities like NYC, Philly, New Orleans, or abroad in Vienna, London, Paris, or Heidelberg." These internships not only allow a brief escape into the real world but also build valuable resume experience; some students are able to parlay their internships into jobs after graduation.

Taking a Time-Out

Even the best students need a little time to relax; when asked about the coolest thing a professor had ever done in class, one student replied, "Canceled it!" After a week of demanding classes, Albion students know how to kick back and relax.

For some students, the weekend festivities start Wednesday night, when many Albion students can be found at one of the local bars. One student states, "Everyone goes out [on Wednesday] because typically there are not early Thursday morning classes. You don't have to be 21 to get into the bars, so there are people from all classes there . . . it's a good time. For the unfortunate souls who do have Thursday morning classes, there are parties on the official weekend, too. Fraternities throw theme parties: "Jimmy Buffet Bash, Hawaiian party, Toga night, Graffiti party are just some of them." How do you get into these fraternity parties? "Show up at the door!" says one partygoer. Unlike at some larger schools, most fraternity parties at Albion are open to everyone on campus. One sorority sister says, "People here are really friendly and always encourage underclassmen to go out to the frats/house parties. It is very easy to get to know people." Several organizations on campus try to get together formal dances, although most students agree these formal dances, except perhaps the Valentine's Day formal, are not very popular.

"We had a variety of discussion groups, including one similar to the format of Jerry Springer."

Aside from the fraternity parties, students say weekends in Albion are somewhat dull. Popular off-campus weekend destinations include the nearby city of Jackson (a popular place to go on dates), Michigan State or the University of Michigan (less than one hour from Albion), and home. Referring to the use of the student center, one fun-seeking student says, "The college is trying to encourage students to stay on campus during the weekends, but their attempts have not been popular among the students."

For those spending their weekends in Albion, the city has two bars, including the popular Cascarelli's (sometimes called "Relly's), a movie theatre that gives free admission on Wednesday, a big K, a grocery store and a couple restaurants. Many students also spend the weekends hanging out with friends in their room, watching movies, catching up on homework, or sleeping.

What's a Briton?

Many students come to Albion for the chance to play intercollegiate sports. Because it is a Division III school, almost anybody who wants to join the team can do so. While being a Division III school takes off a little bit of the stress of intercollegiate athletics, the competitive Briton spirit is still there. One volleyball player says, "It is stressful at the same time as fun."

Going to watch sports can be exciting at a smaller school, too. "It's great to go to sporting events here," says a student, "because you actually know a lot of the athletes! They are your friends, your classmates, or they live down the hall. Typical games have lots of students for that very reason." Another student says, "A typical basketball game is similar to those in high school. There is a student section with guys in matching T-shirts (known as Kresge Krazys) cheering on the team and aggravating the refs." Many athletes also participate in intramural sporting events, putting together teams of their sorority sisters, friends, or floormates.

Movin' On Up

All freshmen live in either Wesley Hall or Seaton Hall their first year, with the majority being housed in Wesley. Both residence halls have community bathrooms. One former Wesley resident describes her living experience: "The rooms are small and the furniture is old and not very good. But the dorm is clean and well taken care of." As sophomores, many students move into Whitehouse or Twin Towers, both of which have double rooms connected by a bathroom. All students must live on-campus, although options include living in one of the campus fraternity houses, or some college-owned apartments, in addition to the main dorms. Student RAs and Residence Hall Directors are available in every dorm to help students adjust to college life, and most students find the RAs to be friendly and knowledgeable.

Most hungry Britons take their meals at Baldwin, the only dining facility on campus. Few students complain about the quality of food, and some even enjoy the grilled chicken, vegetable soup, and homemade bread. Besides Baldwin, the only other place to get food on campus is at the Taco Bell eat shop, which also sells burgers and chicken tenders. But the dearth of places to get food isn't all that bad, considering the size of the campus: students report that walking to classes only takes five minutes. And for those who can't live without their store-bought junk food, the campus provides shuttle buses to downtown and to the bigger cities. Or, as an alternative, "There is always someone you know that has a car," says one student.

Comedy Central

As one female undergrad puts it, "Albion does a great job of keeping us entertained! They try really hard to bring in big name speakers, musicians, etc." Past visitors to campus have included singer Shawn Colvin, comedienne Paula Poundstone, authors Howard Zinn and Stephen Jay Gould, boxer Rubin "The Hurricane" Carter, and a hypnotist. In addition, students participate in over 120 student organizations, ranging from the school newspaper to community service groups to Section 41—the role-playing game organization.

Many students also participate in the Greek system at Albion. For interested students, one sorority officer explains, "[Getting into a sorority or fraternity is] not very hard. The recruitment structure is very open and allows for a variety of people to join." Her sorority sister adds, "If you make a point to hang out with the house you like and get to know them, it's not hard at all to get a bid." Many students who have joined the Greek system say being Greek gives them an opportunity to become more involved on campus and in the community.

But do not forget that students who choose not to pledge a sorority or fraternity can still get into the parties. One female student says, "If you choose NOT to go Greek, it's not a big deal. People intermix a LOT." And that feeling of people intermixing is everywhere at Albion. For some students, being at a small school can be stifling. "I don't like knowing a lot of people on campus," says one student, "and would rather have gone to a bigger school where I could meet someone new everyday." The relatively small student body also makes it harder to randomly hook up with people at parties. But for most students, the sense of community at Albion makes the difference. "I feel that it is perfect to get to know a lot of people and also it is easy to get involved in the activities available," says one senior, "If I don't know a person by their name, I almost always recognize them walking through campus, from a class or a job or something." One student says, "Everyone here is outgoing and friendly . . . people here say hi to you just because. I like walking around campus and seeing my friends and being able to call my professors at home to ask them a question about class." She goes on to sum up the Albion experience, "Small classes, good food, and a well balanced work/play ethic." *—Kenneth Tseng*

FYI

If you come to Albion, you'd better bring "a Brita water filter."

What is the typical weekend schedule? "Sleep in on Saturday morning, do homework, hang out with friends, go to parties, and attend church on Sunday if you're religious. There are also many other activities that different clubs offer. There are always things to do on the weekend if you're willing to look for them."

If I could change one thing about Albion, I'd "give us more off-campus housing options."

Three things every student at Albion should do before graduating are "go to a football game, go to a fraternity party, and participate in an event sponsored by a Greek organization."

Alma College

Address: 614 West Superior Street; Alma, MI 48801
Phone: 800-321-2562
E-mail address: admissions@alma.edu
Web site URL: www.alma.edu
Founded: 1886
Private or Public: private
Religious affiliation: Presbyterian
Location: rural
Undergraduate enrollment: 1,317
Total enrollment: NA
Percent Male/Female: 43%/57%
Percent Minority: 5%
Percent African-American: 1%
Percent Asian: 1%
Percent Hispanic: 1%
Percent Native-American: 1%
Percent in-state/out of state: 96%/4%
Percent Pub HS: 93%
Number of Applicants: 1,502
Percent Accepted: 79%
Percent Accepted who enroll: 28%
Entering: 333
Transfers: 31
Application Deadline: rolling
Mean SAT: NA
Mean ACT: NA
Middle 50% SAT range: NA
Middle 50% ACT range: 22-27
3 Most popular majors: business, education, biology/biological science
Retention: 85%
Graduation rate: 65%
On-campus housing: 85%
Fraternities: 25%
Sororities: 39%
Library: 246,649 volumes
Tuition and Fees: $18,854
Room and Board: $6,712
Financial aid, first-year: 74%
Varsity or Club Athletes: 32%
Early Decision or Early Action Acceptance Rate: EA 82%

The good-natured, comfortable campus of Alma College can feel isolated at times, but students report that the remote location often helps them more fully assimilate into "the college experience." Characterized by its small size and convivial atmosphere, Alma provides students with the opportunity to receive a well-rounded education and prepares them to venture into the professional world.

A Liberal Arts Tradition

One Alma student describes her school's philosophy as "a little bit of everything," and in keeping with the liberal arts philosophy, there are significant general education requirements needed to complete a bachelor's degree. Students must pass composition, math, and foreign language classes, as well as distributive requirements including humanities, literature, history, social, natural, and physical sciences, the arts, and more. Though one student says "it is a little hard to fit [all the requirements] in," most agree that they are a necessary component of a college education.

To graduate with a bachelor's degree, students are required to take a total of 136 credits. They also must complete two spring terms of enrollment. The spring term is a month from April to May when students are able to take classes in more creative and hands-on areas. One of these courses must be an "S" course, which draws on an international, interdisciplinary perspective and often includes travel.

The most popular majors at Alma are also some of its strongest, including business administration, biology, and health professions. All of these prepare students very well for graduate school in medicine or law, or for professional work right out of college, and are consequently accompanied by a significant amount of homework. The curricular options for fine and performing arts are very strong, especially for a school of Alma's size. Students appreciate the training though—as one said of the classes, "they are very challenging, but in a good way." Though work is difficult, they also report a low level of competition, and believe that the on-campus atmosphere is generally conducive to doing well.

Students appreciate that the small size of their school keeps class size down and allows for a lot more interaction with their professors, who are highly attentive and devoted to teaching. One student said she appreciated simply "being able to go see your professor and having them know who you are." Several professors also write their own textbooks, and students agree that because of the intimate atmosphere, science demonstrations are especially "cool." One biology professor routinely "throws balls representing molecules around the room to illustrate a point." A town the size of Alma also means that professors make up a large proportion of the population. "My professor for calculus, Nyman, is the mayor of Alma," said one student, "and he cracks a lot of jokes—while still getting enough information through to my brain that it hurts after class."

Inventive Activities

Although the small size of both the college and the surrounding town leaves students without a huge number of options for the weekends, most agree that those who are inventive will find plenty to occupy them. The student body mixes and freely associates amongst itself. With less than 2,000 students, one student said that in general it is "super easy to meet people, everyone is very friendly. Groups form but they are always open to new people." Although many students join fraternities or sororities, students agree that these "don't control social life," and the parties are attended by a variety of different people. However, the frats are limited by the administration to only one alcoholic beverage party per month, and kegs are officially barred from the campus. The President is actively trying to abolish the Greek system, but one student said that "if that ever happened, I think a lot of people would leave Alma, because of the fact that there would then be NOTHING to do." Students note that in general there is a lot of hooking up, but a lack of destinations make dating somewhat rarer.

"[It's] super easy to meet people, everyone is very friendly. Groups form but they are always welcoming towards new people."

In the rest of their free time, Alma students can see live shows at the Heritage Center, go shopping, and check out the restaurants in Mt. Pleasant (15 minutes away). Some students also choose to attend larger parties at nearby Central Michigan and Michigan State University. Students work out and play sports at the newly refurbished recreation center. And as one student noted, "Going to Wal-Mart is always an option."

Extracurricular groups and clubs also inspire devotion among the students, and many students come to be identified with the major things they do. One student estimates that she spends 15 hours a week with her dance company. Musical and dramatic groups are equally rigorous, and students extol the "consistently fabulous" performances. Community service is a common activity as well. Some students work on-campus jobs, but few work in the surrounding community.

Sports at Alma are strong for a small

school, although not usually a central part of student life. The volleyball team is especially good, and recently won a state championship. Football, soccer, and golf also fare well, and games are "decently attended." Many students take full advantage of the recreation center, and both varsity and non-varsity athletes play on the "tons" of intramural sports teams.

Living Cozily

Alma's pleasant brick campus makes its students feel "cozy." Although the buildings are not particularly unique architecturally, they are well maintained and the facilities are good. The campus' central location means that students often take full advantage of its proximity to neighboring cities and other schools. However, one student answers the question of whether there are enough things to do nearby the campus with a resounding "NO!"

Many students live in dorms all four years—only upperclassmen may move off campus, and their ability to do so is regulated by a lottery system. Some dorms are co-ed, some are not—"however you want it to be," said one student—and though "the underclassmen dorms are kind of old, that's not to say they're not spacious." Freshmen have residential advisors, who are "pretty good about handling things." Some students opt to live in themed dorms (athletic, band, etc.) and there is a service house, as well as Greek housing.

The dining options are cited as adequate, though some students have issues with the fact that they have to apply to different meal plans and can end up being denied. However, there are opportunities throughout the day for unused meal credits to be reclaimed. Vegetarian options are plentiful and the dining halls are clean and well-supplied. Some seating arrangements are fairly established but, Alma's amiable nature means that no tensions result from this stability. As one student described, "Sororities and athletic teams usually sit in the same spot, but they'd gladly move if you were there—or sit with you." For dates, students often go to restaurants in Mt. Pleasant, followed by bowling or ice skating.

Alma tends to attract a vast majority of its students from Michigan, many from the suburbs of Detroit or Grand Rapids. Although many fit the bill of "the general stereotype of a middle-class white kid," this doesn't mean that everyone brings the same viewpoint. As one student said, "though Alma isn't very culturally diverse, it is very diverse in personality." Students also believe that "there is a lot of mixing" among different social groups, and social marginalization or isolation is rare. One student noted, "[It's] super easy to meet people, everyone is very friendly. Groups form but they are always welcoming towards new people."

Overall, Alma students are at school there because it offers what they want from college academics, as well as an actively social and congenial student body. One student said that it was "the perfect place for me. I didn't expect how much I'd not miss home." Isolated though it may be, Alma offers students the chance to live and participate fully in the collegiate environment, and to learn skills useful for their futures. —*David Carpman*

FYI

If you come to Alma, you'd better bring "a car."

What is the typical weekend schedule? "Sleep until brunch at 11:30, rock climb, work, study, watch movies, play video games, party, and go to sleep around 2 A.M."

If I could change one thing about Alma, " I'd move it to a city where there are more things to do."

Three things every student at Alma should do before graduating are "go to Bar Night, go to a percussion performance, climb the rock wall."

Hope College

Address: PO Box 9000; Holland, MI 49423
Phone: 616-395-7850
E-mail address: admissions@hope.edu
Web site URL: www.hope.edu
Founded: 1847
Private or Public: private
Religious affiliation: Reformed Church
Location: suburban
Undergraduate enrollment: 3,035
Total enrollment: NA
Percent Male/Female: 36%/64%
Percent Minority: 5%
Percent African-American: 1%
Percent Asian: 2%
Percent Hispanic: 2%
Percent Native-American: 0%
Percent in-state/out of state: 77%/23%
Percent Pub HS: NA
Number of Applicants: 1,885
Percent Accepted: 90%
Percent Accepted who enroll: 38%
Entering: 725
Transfers: 59
Application Deadline: rolling
Mean SAT: NA
Mean ACT: NA
Middle 50% SAT range: V 540-630, M 540-650
Middle 50% ACT range: 22-28
3 Most popular majors: business administration, psychology, English
Retention: 87%
Graduation rate: 74%
On-campus housing: 84%
Fraternities: 6%
Sororities: 10%
Library: 320,000 volumes
Tuition and Fees: $19,322
Room and Board: $6,018
Financial aid, first-year: 66%
Varsity or Club Athletes: NA
Early Decision or Early Action Acceptance Rate: NA

Students at Hope College come together for many reasons. In the bleachers and on the sidelines, they all cheer on their remarkably successful athletic teams. Walking across their pine tree-lined campus, they live up to their reputation for Midwestern friendliness by saying "hi" to everyone they meet. And in chapel on Sundays, many students at this Christian Reformed college come together to celebrate their common religious values. Located near the shores of Lake Michigan in the heart of pretty downtown Holland, Hope College provides its students with solid academic programs, the personal attention only possible at a small school, and a warm social atmosphere, all structured around a core of Christian values.

Common Values

Spirituality is important to students at Hope, and religion influences nearly every aspect of campus life to some degree. Still, students maintain that non-religious students are not pressured to participate in religious activities. As one junior said, "at Hope you can be as strong or as loose in your faith as you want." One of the most popular religious events on campus is the Sunday night "singing-and-celebration" service called the Gathering. So many students pack the chapel for the Gathering that all the seats fill up and late-arrivers are left to sit in the aisles or stand in the back of the building. The Gathering is just one of the times when religion unites the student body. Groups of Hope students travel all over the world every spring break on mission trips; one junior who spent last spring break building homes for a deaf community in Jamaica described it as one of the "best experiences" of his life. A soccer player said that his coach sometimes uses faith in his coaching style, and a senior said "some professors do incorporate [religion] in their classes." While non-religious students are definitely in the minority at Hope, they are not excluded from campus life. A non-religious student commented that most students come from a Christian background and are "open and not afraid to profess their opinions. However, they are usually not that overbearing."

Students say that the typical Hope student is Christian, usually conservative, and often from Michigan or the greater Midwest. One student said she liked that Hope students are "generally well-rounded and geared toward future goals." The student body is predominantly white, which is ironic since the town of Holland is largely Hispanic. Attempts have been made to increase the school's diversity, and a senior said she was "surprised at how many students are from out of the state and even the country." However, a sophomore expressed frustration that because so many students have similar, religiously conservative backgrounds, they tend to "generate the same old boring views and stances on subjects." Despite this, he said that there are still a substantial number of "more open-minded" people on campus.

Hitting the Books

Students at Hope universally agree that the best parts of their academic experience are the close relationships they build with the professors who teach all their classes. One sophomore said that his favorite aspect of the school was the "intimate relationships" he had built with his teachers, and praised how "available and flexible" they were to student needs. Professors at Hope frequently go to sporting events to cheer on their students, and often invite their classes to their homes at the end of the semester for dinner parties. Many students become so close with their professors that they keep in contact even after their classes are over.

Part of the reason students and teachers are able to form such close bonds is the small size of classes at Hope. The average class has about 20 to 25 students in it. Many upper-level classes are even smaller, allowing students to get personal attention and sometimes even giving them the opportunity to get involved with their professor's research. One junior said that he liked Hope's small classes because they gave him the confidence to "be more bold to ask questions" of the professor in front of the group. The small class size does cause some problems, however, since it often becomes difficult for students to get into popular classes that quickly fill up. Students in popular majors sometimes have difficulty getting into courses that they need in order to graduate on time and end up needing to either plead to the Dean to let them in or stay on campus for a summer term in order to graduate on time.

Popular majors at Hope include biology and education, and both of these departments have excellent programs. Students majoring in education get to start doing fieldwork in local classrooms as early as their freshman year. One sophomore said that Hope "prides itself on its sciences," and the humanities majors are often less intense. Hope recently renovated its science buildings, and the premed program has a reputation for getting its students into selective medical schools. Biology is considered one of Hope's most challenging majors, as is religion. Students interested in studying religion benefit from the fact that the campus of the Western Theological Seminary is right next to Hope, and in fact, every year several students go to seminary there after graduation. A junior estimated that Hope students study about three hours a day; students in difficult majors put in a few more hours. Students who want a less intense academic experience typically major in communications. Academic requirements at Hope include taking several credits of religion, completing at least a 200-level foreign language class, a class on cultural diversity, and a class called "health dynamics," which one athlete said "is a joke. It's basically gym class, and even if you play a varsity sport, you still have to take it." Still, most students agree that the annoyance of some of their distributional requirements and the frustration of class registration are small prices to pay for the excellent education they receive at Hope.

Kicking Back

When they're not studying, students at Hope enjoy a wide range of social activities. Only a third to a half of the campus drinks, so while a more traditional "party scene" exists for those students who want it, nondrinkers have plenty of social options. The Student Activity Committee (SAC) sponsors two-dollar movie nights at Graves Hall, and brings in comedians, magicians, and bands to give performances open to the student body. The campus itself is dry, so technically no alcohol is allowed in the dorms. One junior said that while RAs can be "pretty strict" about this rule at times, people can generally get away with drinking in their dorms as long as it is quiet and hidden. A significant proportion of the student body is Greek, although there are few national frats or sororities on campus. Most of the Greek organizations are branches of smaller, local fraternities. They often hold theme parties, but not all of these are open to the whole student body—many are closed except to other Greeks. Parties are often also held in some of the off-campus houses, especially those where members of the soccer and football teams live. Upperclassmen who want to enjoy a beer in a slightly classier atmosphere favor the New Holland Brewery, especially on Wednesday "Stein Nights," when students who bring their own beer stein can get it filled up at a discounted price.

> **"The legend goes that you'll find your soulmate at Hope."**

Walking around campus on the average Saturday night, you'll probably see a lot of good-looking people. Hope students are an attractive bunch on the whole. As one student said, "whenever my friends come to visit from other schools they always say how hot the girls here are." Since Hope students are over two-thirds female, this seems like pretty good odds for the guys. But Hope isn't a school for someone looking for a lot of random hook-ups; many students are involved in serious relationships. "The legend goes that you'll find your soulmate at Hope," said one junior in a committed relationship, and reportedly a lot of Hope students end up marrying others from their school. Students say that Hope is a friendly place. "You could go up to anyone and say hello," according to one student. Partly because of the school's small size, there aren't many cliques, and people tend to have a lot of friends of different ages.

Housing in Holland

Hope students typically live in dorms for their freshman and sophomore years. Students live in double rooms on single-sex hallways and share common bathrooms. "The dorms are overall well-kept and comfortable," said one sophomore, although all the buildings have different reputations. In addition to the co-ed buildings, there are two all-male dorms and three all-female dorms, including Dykstra, "where all the guys go to scope for women," according to one male student. Kollen Hall is the most social dorm; "it's the party dorm, the loudest and craziest," said one former resident. Voorhees Hall houses "a lot of artsy-types," while international students tend to cluster in Scott. By junior year, most Hope students move into the "cottages." These are small houses on the perimeter of campus where groups of about six students live; they are still considered "on-campus housing" and have RAs, but they have their own kitchens and living rooms. The cottages are "a fun alternative to big-school living," according to one upperclassman. Seniors often move off campus, either to houses or to apartments in downtown Holland.

Hope's campus is small—"you can walk all the way around it in 15 minutes," according to a junior. Most academic buildings are in the center of this campus filled with pine trees, while the dorms and the cottages are around the perimeter. Many of the historic buildings are red-brick, while some of the newer buildings like the recently constructed science center are more modern. One senior raved that the campus is "so cute! Hope is big on preserving the old buildings it does have, but also on adding new buildings as the college expands."

Dining hall food is "pretty good" according to most students. Freshman often eat in Phelps Hall, which supposedly has the worst food on campus, but upperclassmen enjoy eating the much tastier food in Cook Hall, which typically serves a choice of several entrees every night, including vegetarian options. When students get bored of the dining halls, downtown Holland has a variety of unique restaurants less than a five-minute walk from campus. Windmill's is a favorite for breakfast, and students also enjoy relaxing and studying in coffee shops like Java Joe's (which has a stage where bands perform) and Lemonjello's (pronounced leMON-jello's by those in-the-know).

Sports and Spirit

Students leave campus and go into Holland for more than food and coffee, however. Faith-based community service is extremely popular at the school. One junior said that there are "a ton of opportunities to work in church soup kitchens or tutor kids or anything like that." Many students also spend their free time playing intramural sports ranging from inner-tube water polo to Ultimate Frisbee. When the weather is warm, students make the short trip down to the shores of beautiful Lake Michigan to hang out on the beach. Hope's Division III varsity athletic teams have had excellent records in the past few years. Both men's and women's basketball and soccer teams are extremely competitive, and draw massive support both from students and from members of the community who come out to watch, as well.

The large crowds are in large part due to the high level of school spirit at Hope. A combination of factors, including the small size of the student body and the commonly shared core of Christian values, bind students closely to their school. "If I could do it all over again I would definitely, definitely choose Hope," said one junior. "It's been a place where I can get a great education while strengthening my faith. I've gotten to meet some really great people, and made friendships I think are going to last for a long time." —*Katherine Kirby Smith*

FYI

If you come to Hope College, you'd better bring "a Nalgene bottle—everybody has one here."

What's a typical weekend schedule? "Friday, hang out with friends or go to a house party at night; Saturday, sleep until noon, study, go see a sporting event, then do something social or go to another party; Sunday, get up early and go to church, eat downtown at the Windmill, study, and go to the Gathering at night."

If I could change one thing about Hope College, I'd "loosen up the housing policy and make it easier to register for classes."

Three things every student at Hope College should do before they graduate are "attend Gathering, go on a mission trip for spring break, and go streaking on a Chapel Run."

Kalamazoo College

Address: 1200 Academy Street; Kalamazoo, MI 49006
Phone: 800-253-3602
E-mail address: admission@kzoo.edu
Web site URL: www.kzoo.edu
Founded: 1833
Private or Public: private
Religious affiliation: none
Location: small city
Undergraduate enrollment: 1,265
Total enrollment: NA
Percent Male/Female: 45%/55%
Percent Minority: 9%
Percent African-American: 2%
Percent Asian: 5%
Percent Hispanic: 2%
Percent Native-American: 0%
Percent in-state/out of state: 79%/21%
Percent Pub HS: 85%
Number of Applicants: 1,411
Percent Accepted: 73%
Percent Accepted who enroll: 33%
Entering: 337
Transfers: 4
Application Deadline: 15 Feb
Mean SAT: NA
Mean ACT: NA
Middle 50% SAT range: V 590-680, M 580-690
Middle 50% ACT range: 26-30
3 Most popular majors: economics, English, psychology
Retention: 88%
Graduation rate: 72%
On-campus housing: 75%
Fraternities: NA
Sororities: NA
Library: 342,939 volumes
Tuition and Fees: $22,908
Room and Board: $6,480
Financial aid, first-year: 58%
Varsity or Club Athletes: 25%
Early Decision or Early Action Acceptance Rate: ED 81%; EA 84%

When asked what their campus looks like, Kalamazoo College students joke about how the administration likes to describe the school, affectionately referred to as "K," as an "idyllic setting on an Arcadian quad." There is some truth to this poetic description, however. Nestled into a wooded hill near downtown Kalamazoo, Michigan, the strikingly beautiful campus provides an ideal environment for students looking to combine experiential learning and foreign study with an academically rigorous liberal arts education in a small, close-knit, and friendly community.

Life in the 'Zoo

K students often refer to the "K-bubble," the feeling that life on their campus is cut off from the rest of the activity in the small city in southwestern Michigan where the school is located. Entering Kalamazoo College truly feels a bit like entering a separate world. Nearly everything, from the streets to the dorms to the academic buildings, is made of red brick, giving the campus a sense of unity and consistency. The focal point of campus is the Quad, a large, sloping, rectangular courtyard surrounded by academic and administration buildings, dorms, the student center, and Stetson Chapel. In warmer months, K students can be found on the Quad reading, socializing, or playing one of Kalamazoo's favorite past-times, Frisbee golf. During the snowy Michigan winter afternoons, students grab their sleds and head for the steep hill. In all seasons, groups of students can be seen running naked across the Quad. "Streaking the Quad is one of those things almost everyone does at least once here," described one junior. "It's kind of what we're known for."

Most dorms are located either at the top or the bottom of the Quad, forcing most students to walk up and down the hill several times a day to attend classes and visit friends. One senior said that while the hill is pretty, "I have friends who won't come visit me because I live at the top of [it] and they live at the bottom, and they say the walk is too far." Regardless, its hillside setting makes Kalamazoo's campus visually appealing, though challenging for students with physical disabilities to navigate.

All K College students are required to live on campus until their senior year. Though Severn and Chrissey Halls are generally considered the nicest, while Hoben Hall is slightly more run-down, on the whole one sophomore raved, "The dorms are awesome!" Freshmen are randomly assigned to live in a suite with five other first-year students. These suites usually consist of two doubles, two singles, a common lounge, and a bathroom. In all buildings the suites are single-sex, and floors are co-ed. After freshman year, students enter a lottery for housing, and though one junior commented, "Sophomores get the worst rooms while freshmen get the best," even sophomores get to choose to live in suites or in more standard double rooms.

"If you really want to, almost anyone can be on a varsity team at K," but "there isn't as much enthusiasm for watching sports here as there is at other schools."

Living-Learning Housing Units are one of Kalamazoo's most unique features. An option for students after their freshman year, these "experiential learning centers" are freestanding houses on campus in which eight to ten students with an expressed common interest apply to live. Themes for these houses have in the past included the Service Learning House, the Women in Professional Fields House, the Wellness House, and the Men's Issues House. Other perks of "LLHU's," according to one junior, include "getting away from RAs, and getting off the meal plan." Though one senior joked, "the major 'Men's Issue' seems to be beer," these houses are designed to allow students to immerse themselves in one of their interests. Furthermore, this unique living structure serves as a resource for the college as a whole via the campus-wide educational events relating to their theme that each house is required to hold throughout the year.

Many seniors choose to live off campus in one of the nearby student neighborhoods. Off-campus housing proves much cheaper than living in the dorms, but even if seniors' apartments or houses have kitchens, they're still required to stay on one of Kalamazoo's meal plans. Students can purchase meal plans of various sizes, some of which allow students to transfer money to the Quad Stop, the on-campus grill and snack bar. Kalamazoo's one dining hall features many options, including a grill line, a vegetarian line, and an a la carte option. Though most students grumble about the quality of dining hall food, one sophomore admits, "We think the food is pretty bad here, but when friends visit from other colleges they think our food is really good."

Where Did All the Juniors Go?

Though students can't move off campus until their senior year, freshman and sophomores predominantly populate the dorms. Juniors are conspicuously absent on campus at K, because nearly 85% of students at Kalamazoo spend at least part of their third year on foreign study. Kalamazoo College's foreign study program was named best in the nation by *US News and World Report* in 2003, and many students cite the emphasis on travel as one of the best things about K. The college sponsors 26 different programs on six continents, allowing students to spend three to nine months anywhere from Ecuador to Thailand. A special endowment fund pays for students' overseas airfare. Programs exist for students with a range of language skills, and because credits from foreign study easily transfer, even students in rigorous programs like pre-med are able to study elsewhere. A sophomore said that Spain and Australia are "probably the easiest, and the biggest 'party places,'" but more adventurous students can live with families in Nairobi, Kenya, or Beijing, China. Another sophomore said that while it may seem strange that there are few juniors on campus at K, "it's normal to us because almost everyone here goes on foreign study."

A Studious Campus

Foreign study is just one aspect of Kalamazoo's unique academic philosophy, called the K-Plan. In addition to junior year study abroad, the K-Plan includes liberal arts curriculum, career development internships that nearly 80% of students participate in after their sophomore year, the Senior Individualized Project, or "SIP," which is a one or two credit final project in the subject of one's major, and an electronic portfolio or online resume. To graduate, seniors must take comprehensive exams, or "comps," in their major, which according to one student are "very stressful, and everyone dreads them." In addition to fulfilling requirements for their major, students must take a variety of liberal arts requirements, including written expression, oral expression, quantitative reasoning, computer literacy, and creative expression, as well as five terms of physical education. Most students enjoy this last requirement, since possible PE classes include bowling and indoor rock climbing, although one student complained that all the academic requirements "took up a lot of time I could have spent taking classes I would have enjoyed more." All freshmen are required to take a first-year writing seminar. These seminars have a diverse range of subjects, focusing on anything from the literature of King Arthur to road trips to science writing, and one computer science major said that he "liked the fact that there were freshmen seminars catered to non-humanities majors." Students also have to compete 25 LAC (language arts colloquium) credits by attending musical and dramatic performances or by listening to on-campus speakers.

Kalamazoo operates on the trimester system, so students start school in late September, have three ten-week terms during each of which they take three classes, and get out of school in mid June. Because each class only lasts for ten weeks, "we move very quickly through the material," said one sophomore, "and it can get very stressful." Another student observed, "We are a very studious campus." Students at K report spending hours a day keeping up with reading and other work. The workload at K is heaviest in subjects like biology and chemistry, which are two of the school's exceptionally strong programs, although majors in somewhat easier subjects like English and economics are also popular. "The science facilities are so nice," exclaimed one senior, "they get all the money!" The Dow Science building has indeed been recently renovated to update and improve laboratories and classrooms. The Light Fine Arts building has also had a major "facelift" in the past few years, and the Upjohn Library is scheduled to undergo a multi-million dollar renovation that will nearly double its current size.

Regardless of their major, students universally said that having small class sizes and close relationships with professors was one of the best parts of a K education. "I've never been in a class with more than 20 students," said one junior. Some introductory classes have up to 70 students in them, but as K students start taking more advanced classes for their major, they often find themselves in classes with ten students or fewer. "Because the classes are so small, you can really go in and talk to your professors when you need help," said one sophomore, "and the professors definitely love it when you do." Overall, students at Kalamazoo College enjoy the challenge and the opportunity presented by their academic environment.

After Class

Students at Kalamazoo College don't spend all their time on schoolwork. Despite the school's small size, a wide variety of social and extracurricular options are available at K. Though one junior reported, "about half the students go out and party, and the others stay in and study all the time," alcohol is readily available both on and off campus. Though technically students aren't allowed to have alcohol in their rooms if they're underage, the penalty for being caught drinking is "a slap on the wrist, and maybe some community service," according to one senior. Though a sophomore warns that "RAs can be pretty strict, and if you get caught drunk too many times you can get kicked out of school," this doesn't seem to deter most K students from partying on the weekends.

Dorm parties are infrequent and Kalamazoo does not have a Greek system, so most large weekend gatherings take place at seniors' off-campus houses, which one student says get "really packed because there are usually only a few parties a weekend." In addition to alcohol, a senior said that there's "a lot of pot" at K, but that most students tend to avoid harder drugs. The school sponsors some large parties, such as Monte Carlo night, and the Crystal Ball, where students traditionally dress in drag, but most social gatherings are more informal. Non-drinkers typically hang out in the dorms with friends on the weekends, watching movies or playing games, or attend one of the many cultural functions that take place regularly on campus.

Of the many extracurricular options available on campus, sports are by far the most popular. Students say that almost everyone plays either a varsity or an IM sport, and a senior said, "if you really want to, almost anyone can be on a varsity team at K." Though some varsity teams, like soccer, tennis, and swimming, are extremely successful, athletic participation doesn't seem to translate into athletic spirit because, as one sophomore commented, "there isn't as much enthusiasm for watching sports here as there is at other schools."

Frelon, Kalamazoo's dance company, is the school's largest extracurricular organization. "You don't have to have any previous dancing experience to be in it, and it's pretty fun," said one group member. Also popular is K's improv comedy group, Monkapult. "The shows are usually packed," said one sophomore. Kalamazoo College also has an active Habitat for Humanity chapter, and many cultural organizations. "You can pretty much find a group for whatever you want here," said one student.

Homogenous but Open-Minded

The typical K student, according to many, is white, upper-middle-class, and from a Detroit suburb. It's true that there's little ethnic or economic diversity at Kalamazoo College, and that most students are from Michigan, but one sophomore observed, "even though we are not very racially diverse, I feel we are open-minded." The students at this traditionally liberal institution are a close-knit group. "My favorite part about K is that I can walk down the street and see so many of my friends," said one student. Unified by a unique educational experience, students at Kalamazoo College learn to make the most of the resources of their school, their community, and the world. —*Katherine Kirby Smith*

FYI

If you come to Kalamazoo, you'd better bring "a water filter because the water in the dorms tastes terrible."

What is the typical weekend schedule? "Sleep till noon, do schoolwork in the afternoon, go to a party or watch movies with friends at night."

If I could change on thing about Kalamazoo, "I'd change the amount of academic stress put on students."

Three things every Kalamazoo student should do before graduating are "streak the Quad, go on study abroad, and steal something from the dining hall."

Michigan State University

Address: 250 Administration Building, MSU; East Lansing, MI 48824
Phone: 517-355-8332
E-mail address: admis@msu.edu
Web site URL: www.msu.edu
Founded: 1855
Private or Public: public
Religious affiliation: none
Location: small city
Undergraduate enrollment: 35,197
Total enrollment: NA
Percent Male/Female: 47%/53%
Percent Minority: 20%
Percent African-American: 9%
Percent Asian: 5%
Percent Hispanic: 3%
Percent Native-American: 1%
Percent in-state/out of state: 94%/6%
Percent Pub HS: NA
Number of Applicants: 25,210
Percent Accepted: 67%
Percent Accepted who enroll: 41%
Entering: 7,000
Transfers: 1,632
Application Deadline: 1 Aug
Mean SAT: NA
Mean ACT: NA
Middle 50% SAT range: V 490-610, M 520-640
Middle 50% ACT range: 22-27
3 Most popular majors: business, communications, social sciences
Retention: 89%
Graduation rate: 64%
On-campus housing: 44%
Fraternities: NA
Sororities: NA
Library: 4,420,208 volumes
Tuition and Fees: $7,088 in; $16,992 out
Room and Board: $5,272
Financial aid, first-year: 55%
Varsity or Club Athletes: 2%
Early Decision or Early Action Acceptance Rate: NA

You are standing in an oval-shaped stadium. You look all around and can't find a single empty seat. Thousands of people are on their feet, screaming for blood. At the bottom of the stadium, a chariot drives across the length of the field. A puffy man wearing green and white armor marches side to side in front of the stands. Soon after, you hear the crushing of bones and the yells of the people beside you. But you are not an extra on the set of *Gladiator* or *Ben Hur*. You are somewhere much more exciting. You are taking part in one of the greatest events in sports: you are at a Michigan State football game. When you turn to ask the guy standing next to you what he thinks about all of this, he responds, "The best, it's awesome."

The More the Merrier

Michigan State University is one of the biggest colleges in the country. Inevitably, students take the occasional large lecture class. However, being at one of the biggest colleges in the country provides for a lot of opportunities.

The university is divided into fifteen colleges, including the College of Education, the College of Engineering, and the College of Arts and Letters. For the aspiring politician, MSU offers James Madison College, a college dedicated to the study of politics and public affairs. For the aspiring teacher, MSU lets students apply to the College of Education as undergraduates. For the aspiring inventor, one computer science major warned, "The [engineering] classes themselves can be a little dull, but I think that's a result of engineering professors in general being dull." And for the people still looking for things to do, the College of Arts and Letters provides a great liberal arts education. Not surprisingly, many undecided MSU students choose to be in the College or Arts and Letters. As one student in the program said, "The College of Arts and Letters . . . seems to run smoothly, but it doesn't exactly have a small-school-within-a-big-school feel."

The honors college gives students the smaller school feel some prefer. As one student put it, "The honors college cuts through a lot of the red tape." An honors option TA invited her entire class to her apartment and cooked dinner for them. Students in the honors college also benefit from a guaranteed research opportunity with professors in their major. Most students will find their professors accessible and even fun-loving people. One student said the coolest thing his professor had ever done was to watch an English "football" game while lecturing, and another student said his professor "poured liquid nitrogen across the physics department halls." On a more normal day, students have dinner with their professors or meet them at other times of the day just to chat.

Many students find that they enjoy taking the occasional large lecture class. In an Intro to Psychology class, one male student said that he enjoyed doing an observational study: "groups monitored behavior in places like elevators and supermarkets—going to the place, introducing an unnatural element, and observing people's reactions." A female student said that the professor in the Intro to Psych made the really large lecture seem small. The best incentive for going to a big school like MSU seems to be the diversity of people. One student said, "I'm currently taking a teacher education class that is very thought-provoking. We talk about all these controversial issues and there are a bunch of really weird kids in my class, so it makes discussion extremely interesting."

Eat, Drink, and Be Merry

For the college students who come to MSU because of its party school reputation, they will likely be able to find what they are looking for. Typical of the party experiences of many a college partier, one wise sophomore said, "Most of the freshmen try to find these huge house parties where the kegs are always empty." According to another sophomore, most freshmen that drink go to off-campus parties and frat houses and dance clubs. Where do these ingenuous young freshmen go later on in their college career? "I think upperclassmen go to the same places that freshmen do, they just pretend that it's cooler."

Students say that only a small percentage of MSU students join frats or sororities. Unfortunately, getting into a frat party still isn't any easier than at other schools; to get into Greek parties, one guy said, "you either have to a) know someone in the frat or b) bring a lot of girls with you to the party." However, another undergrad pointed out, "Greek parties don't really go down like they used to." Students looking for the proverbial random hook-up, can usually find those. A female student reported, "My roommate last year was a big partier, and she didn't randomly hook up with anyone at all last year, but her friend hooked with like six guys in three months."

But an MSU social life does not have to revolve around drinking or random hookups. Every weekend, MSU opens up the Campus Center, where the school takes two or three buildings in the middle of the campus and hosts activities and free movies in some of the lecture halls. Students who want to go out to eat can choose from the multitude of chain restaurants in East Lansing. Mongolian Barbeque attracts many student diners, as well as El Azteco, Panchero's, Ruby Tuesday's, Beggar's Banquet, and others.

"Greek parties don't really go down like they used to."

For those looking for something a little more high-class (or someplace to go when parents are in town), the State Room at the Kellogg Center draws a lot of alumni. The Homecoming Ball gives students a chance to put on their formal wear, but other than that night, tuxedos and evening wear usually spend most of their time in the closet. The college also attracts many performing artists both collegiate and professional. One student remembered her experience with theatre at MSU, "I went to see Titanic [an off-Broadway non-MSU play] at the Wharton Center, which discouraged me from seeing any other plays. It was bad." But that student did have a good experience with some stars of a higher caliber, when she met Martin Sheen, Julia Louis-

Dreyfus, Alfrie Woodard and Rob Reiner at a Diane Byrum rally. Her male friends reported Julia Louis-Dreyfus is much better-looking in person than on television.

Like many college students around the country, MSU students also look forward to weekends as a chance to catch up on sleep and reading. And the undergrads have no problem with just relaxing. One male student said, ""I have the most fun at little 10-people shindigs where I know all the people there and we are all just kicking back and having fun."

Marry Me!

MSU legend has it that if you kiss someone near the Beaumont Tower, you'll get married to that person. Of course most college freshmen are not ready to take that plunge, and that's totally fine, since MSU offers great opportunities to meet people. Most of the freshmen live on campus during their first year. Experiences in each of the dorms differs. One female student that lived in Hubbard freshman year expressed great disgust at that Hall: "I hated Hubbard! The girls on my floor were totally anti-social, my roommate was an alcoholic, and my RA was never there." She said she enjoyed her new dorm—Wilson Hall—a lot more. A male undergrad reported that Mason Hall dorms were "nice" and a Bryan Hall resident said that he had a very large room. James Madison freshmen live in the very nice Case Hall, where they live in suites of four people, with two bedrooms connected by a bathroom.

Instead of resident assistants, MSU offers mentors for students living in the dorms. The mentors are MSU students, usually undergrads, who are responsible for keeping order on each of the floors. One dorm resident says, "Mentors are a good resource, and only enforce the 'rules' (with a few exceptions, like alcohol) when there's a complaint." People living in the dormitories usually take their meals in the cafeteria on the first floor of the residence hall, affectionately called the "caf." Caf diners enjoy the Vegetarian Vegetable Soup and the perennial college favorite, chicken fingers. Freshmen on the meal plan can usually also be found at the Union or the International Center, or they can get the cafeteria to go, at the Caf-II-Go.

Students who want to burn off the calories from the caf can exercise at any one of the three IM buildings on campus free of charge. They can also go to the weight rooms in the residence halls, although they pay a small maintenance fee for that convenience. For students who prefer jogging to running on a treadmill, one female student recommended going to see all the gardens on the far south side of the campus. "Most people don't even know they're there and they are so great! There is a children's garden with a bunch of fun colors and toys in it and a rose garden that is just amazing!"

Sparty

Michigan State boasts one of the best college sports programs in the country. The Spartans are perennial contenders for National titles and Big Ten titles. In addition to very successful teams, MSU students come out in force to support the MSU football, basketball, and hockey teams. The crowds can be counted on to be loud and energetic. One undergraduate football fan says, "The atmosphere is electric, especially during a game against a good opponent. I once gave high fives to three rows' worth of people I didn't even know after a touchdown." And every year students eagerly await the big game against cross-state rival University of Michigan (U of M). They even have a tradition of guarding Sparty—the MSU mascot—an entire week before the U of M game.

For the athletes that didn't make it onto MSU's Division I teams, they can always play any number of intramural sports, from soccer to volleyball to air force football. However, one male athlete warned, "Coed intramurals are pretty sweet for hanging out with the ladies, but if you are competitive, you should keep to the non-coed sports."

In addition to intramurals, students also participate in a lot of extracurricular activities, from community service to the Society for Creative Anachronism. Among the benefits of going to a big school is definitely the wide range of extracurriculars. One female student tutors a Chinese grad student in conversational English and gives campus tours through the Student Alumni Foundation. Another student helps seventh-grade kids in the local school district understand the importance of college and the potential they possess for the future.

Yes! Michigan!

Most MSU students hail from within the state, so they know what to expect when it comes to Michigan winters. What they might not expect is the size of the campus: it is big. One benefit to attending such a large school is the chance to meet lots of people; as one student said, "It is just a sweet all-around environment." One downside, though, is all the walking students say they have to do to get around campus. One upperclassman would still offer this little piece of advice for new Spartans: "The first year at college anywhere is the coldest winter anyone ever experiences because you have to walk everywhere and no one's used to that. The one thing I would recommend for anyone who plans on coming here is a good pair of tennis shoes, because you're gonna have a whole bunch of walking to do." —*Kenneth Tseng*

FYI

If you come to Michigan State, you'd better bring "comfortable shoes. Walks to and from class are perhaps the longest among all college campuses in the country."

What is the typical weekend schedule? "Like any college, there are always tons of parties going on at the frats. Some people go to the Campus Center for movies and other activities. Others just catch up on sleep and work."

If I could change one thing about Michigan State, I'd "make the campus smaller. It's such a pain to walk to places."

Three things every student at Michigan State should do before graduating are "attend a football game, eat at the Peanut Barrel, and walk on the Spartan stadium field."

University of Michigan

Address: 1220 Student Activities Building; Ann Arbor, MI 48109-1316
Phone: 734-764-7433
E-mail address: ugadmiss@umich.edu
Web site URL: www.umich.edu
Founded: 1817
Private or Public: public
Religious affiliation: none
Location: urban
Undergraduate enrollment: 24,472
Total enrollment: NA
Percent Male/Female: 49%/51%
Percent Minority: 30%
Percent African-American: 8%
Percent Asian: 12%
Percent Hispanic: 5%
Percent Native-American: 1%
Percent in-state/out of state: 68%/32%
Percent Pub HS: 80%
Number of Applicants: 25,108
Percent Accepted: 49%
Percent Accepted who enroll: 42%
Entering: 5,187
Transfers: 882
Application Deadline: 1 Feb
Mean SAT: NA
Mean ACT: NA
Middle 50% SAT range: V 570-670, M 610-720
Middle 50% ACT range: 26-30
3 Most popular majors: engineering, psychology, English
Retention: 96%
Graduation rate: 81%
On-campus housing: 37%
Fraternities: 16%
Sororities: 15%
Library: 7,484,343 volumes
Tuition and Fees: $8,650 in; $25,733 out
Room and Board: $6,620
Financial aid, first-year: 34%
Varsity or Club Athletes: 3%
Early Decision or Early Action Acceptance Rate: NA

Walking down State Street, U of M's main thoroughfare, it is impossible to forget where you are. Half the people on the street are happily wearing a blue or maize college shirt with Michigan boldly printed across the front. The other half probably wear their Michigan shirts underneath their top layers. This is the general attitude of the students at the University of Michigan—everyone has tremendous school pride and spirit and loves being there.

Wise Wolverines

Michigan is a rigorous academic institution, with scores of nationally-ranked programs and many notable professors. It offers thousands of classes and employs more than a thousand professors. At this stalwart of tradition, academics are surely at the forefront. For such a large school, Michigan has surprisingly modest class sizes. One freshman said that he "had no class larger than 75 people." There are huge lectures with hundreds of students for many introductory-level courses, but graduate student instructors are always accessible with regular office hours.

Most freshmen enroll in the College of Literature, Science, and the Arts (LSA), but there are other special tracks available to undergrads, such as the challenging honors program. With a fairly strict core curriculum that emphasizes reading the "Great Books," the honors program boasts its own alternative housing option, available only to its students. This fosters a very close-knit community in upscale dorms with extended quiet hours. "My best friends were other honors students," described one student in the program. Another popular program is the Residential College (RC), an offshoot of the LSA. The RC functions as its own small college for students who feel intimidated by the overwhelming size of Michigan. Consisting of a small group of about 900 students and 60 faculty members, all first- and second-year RC students live together on the East Quad, where most of their classes are held. Both the RC and the honors program are quite small and provide intimate settings with professors, and though the options for classes are more limited in each, cross-registration is quite common.

Michigan also offers a unique business program for upperclassmen, commonly known as the B-School. The Bachelor's in business administration is an intense program with an exceptional amount of requirements. Some, particularly Economics 101 and Accounting, are known as competitive "weed-out" courses. This competition is a product of popularity; as one applicant said, "Everyone you talk to wants to be in it."

A2

"I love campus life!" exclaimed one sophomore. This is the general consensus of Michigan's student body. Because of its complete integration with the city of Ann Arbor (often called A-Squared and written "A2"), students can find everything they need on campus. As one freshman put it, "There's everything here." This includes numerous shops, from both large chains to small independently-owned boutiques, and a vast selection of diverse restaurants. Popular eating choices include cheap midnight pizza slices from NYPD, bubble tea from Bubble Island, sandwiches and coffee from Amer's, and Stucci's ice cream. Gratzi is the famous "ooh-he's-taking-you-there" restaurant for classy dinner dates.

Like everything else at Michigan, the campus is huge, but well-landscaped, making long walks to and from classes less painful. One student described the campus as "absolutely beautiful" and enjoyable to trek through, even on bitingly cold winter days. Those not so keen on walking take advantage of the reliable bus system, whereas others use bicycles as their transportation of choice.

Hands-Down Diversity

Every year Michigan brings in new Wolverines from all over the country and all over the world. All 50 states are represented, along with more than 80 countries. One student commented that, "you can't avoid the diversity, not that you would try." Students have noted that while the population is diverse, many of the ethnic groups tend to group together and self-segregate. And as a state school, Michigan enrolls about one-third of its students from in state. "There are a lot of people pointing to their hands to show you where they live," noted one freshman on the "In-Staters" and the state of Michigan's uncanny resemblance to the human hand.

Many students make their friends through extracurricular activities, which are quite diverse. With more than 900 clubs, there is a group for anyone with any interest, though one freshman said that, "if you want to join a club, you have to put effort into finding it; it's not going to come to you." But after finding their match, members report the club/extracurricular experience to be enjoyable for both the activity and the social atmosphere.

Our Cereal Is Excellent

Almost all first-year students live on campus. A large number of dorms dot the campus, full of typical dorm rooms; there are some singles, many doubles, and a few triples. While they are not huge or luxurious, students find their dorms livable. Lots of freshmen are assigned to North Campus each year, which is a substantial bus ride away from the rest of campus. This separation is a mixed blessing for these residents. Some feel that it is good because "it's quieter and provides a strong sense of community within North Campus," while others dislike it because "you feel left out [of] the rest of the school." An enjoyable dorm life seems to characterize freshman year, however, and a good number stay in dorms as sophomores. By junior and senior years, though, off-campus housing becomes a popular alternative in the form of apartments, houses, co-ops, or frat and sorority houses.

"Wearing maize and blue is definitely something to be proud [of]."

The dining halls, on the other hand, did not receive any favorable reviews. As one student put it, "there's variety, but you end up eating a lot of cereal." It is at this point when Ann Arbor's great dining options come in handy. Shared undergrad wisdom says that "late night pizza is key."

Party Michigan-Style

Greek life rules at Michigan. There are scores of fraternities and sororities that always throw large, rowdy parties on the weekends, described as, "the kind of frat parties you see in the movies." For the freshmen, this is definitely the most accessible party scene; some freshmen feel that it is "hard to party without them." Pledging a fraternity or sorority is certainly considered important in order to be a part of the social scene. While non-members can always party, it can be hard for them to get into frat parties, and even when they do, they often feel "a little left out." For most upperclassmen and a few freshmen, house or apartment parties are another popular option. These are more low-key and intimate, and they do not involve the crush of random people you might find at a frat party. Ann Arbor has a wide selection of bars and clubs, which are frequented mainly by upperclassmen.

For those not thirsty for alcohol or debauchery, there are other options. These are harder to come by, but usually include hanging out in someone's room or going out to see a movie. Ann Arbor has a rich cultural scene, which provides another outlet; whether it is a performer coming through town or the art or music school putting on a show, there is always an event to attend. All students agree that you can find an alternative scene if you seek it out.

Michigan legend holds that if two people kiss under the arch leading to the Law Quad, they will end up marrying each other. And while such Michigan marriages do occur, it all begins with the active dating scene on campus. With a number of nice restaurants and movie theaters to encourage students, going out on a date is not a rarity like on many other college campuses. And for those non-committal types, there is always the random hook-up, which is also quite common. As one student put it, "it's a big school, and anonymity is key!"

Hail to the Victors!

The instant you step onto campus, you become a Wolverines fan. Michigan has a legendary college sports program, and all the students know this. Tremendous school spirit permeates all the well-attended sporting events. This is especially true of the football program. The Wolverines play in the "Big House," which despite holding more than 110,000 people still manages to have a thousand-plus waiting list for season tickets. Here you would be hard-pressed to find a student who was not wearing either bright yellow or blue. From jingling keys on third down and other "key plays" to singing the all-too-familiar fight song, students agree that going to a game "is an experience."

While football draws most of the attention, other Michigan sports are not left out; volleyball, basketball, and hockey are also popular. Michigan's hockey team is always a national contender, and many students find these games even more fun and action-packed than football games. Students love the school spirit at Michigan and appreciate how it brings their large community much closer together. One freshman summed up the Michigan experience by saying, "wearing maize and blue is definitely something to be proud [of]." —*Alex Chiu*

FYI

If you come to Michigan, you'd better bring a "bike for the long trek between classes."

What is the typical weekend schedule? "Friday, study, party, sleep; Saturday, football game, party, party; Sunday, sleep, study, party?"

If I could change one thing about Michigan, I would change "the food."

Three things every student at Michigan should do before graduating are "Go to the Big House, take a class with Professor Williams, and streak through the Diag (the quad in central campus)."

Minnesota

Carleton College

Address: 1 N College Street; Northfield, MN 55057
Phone: 507-646-4190
E-mail address: admissions@acs.carleton.edu
Web site URL: www.carleton.edu
Founded: 1866
Private or Public: private
Religious affiliation: none
Location: rural
Undergraduate enrollment: 1,932
Total enrollment: NA
Percent Male/Female: 48%/52%
Percent Minority: 20%
Percent African-American: 4%
Percent Asian: 8%
Percent Hispanic: 4%
Percent Native-American: 0%
Percent in-state/out of state: 23%/77%
Percent Pub HS: 75%
Number of Applicants: 4,170
Percent Accepted: 35%
Percent Accepted who enroll: 35%
Entering: 502
Transfers: 7
Application Deadline: 15 Jan
Mean SAT: NA
Mean ACT: NA
Middle 50% SAT range: V 640-740, M 640-720
Middle 50% ACT range: 27-31
3 Most popular majors: biology/biological science, political science, history
Retention: 95%
Graduation rate: 85%
On-campus housing: 83%
Fraternities: NA
Sororities: NA
Library: 662,871 volumes
Tuition and Fees: $28,527
Room and Board: $5,868
Financial aid, first-year: 56%
Varsity or Club Athletes: 20%
Early Decision or Early Action Acceptance Rate: ED 55%

At the northern reaches of Northfield, Minnesota sits the highly respected liberal arts school Carleton College. Besides being very small and very cold, Carleton prides itself on combining a top-notch, highly personal academic experience with a demeanor that refuses to take itself too seriously. Intramural sports, artistic interest groups, and political activism provide social outlets and break up academic rigors.

Hitting the Books

Carleton is known for its intensive but exhilarating academic program. The year is divided into trimesters, giving students more opportunities to choose new courses. Trimesters also make it easier for students to fulfill distribution requirements, which call for a minimum number of classes in four groups: arts and literature, math and science, social sciences, and humanities. For the most part students tend to appreciate the breadth of courses this program urges them to take. Regarding the distribution requirements, one junior said, "It makes you think more about your major rather than assuming that your high school ambitions are still what you want to do with your life." The most popular majors are biology, economics, political science, and American studies. Nearly all majors offer study-abroad programs which are highly encouraged and widely taken advantage of, particularly during junior year.

In addition, Carleton students seem to share a love of their professors. "Professors are very accessible and generally really interesting and cool," said a senior. "I've only had one professor in my three years here who didn't insist on being called by his first name." added a junior. Due to the small classes, students get to know their professors and often meet them outside of class. One professor requires everyone in the class to go out for coffee as part of "social credit" worth 5 percent of the grade.

Dorm Living

One of the benefits of a very small school is that everything is highly accessible no matter where you live. The dining hall is very close to the dorms, as are all the classroom buildings. The dorms themselves tend to be fairly large and comfortable. A unique aspect of the Carleton dorm system is that students of all graduating classes share the same floors. This lack of segregation creates a social environment with very little class hierarchy; freshmen are not hazed, but rather helped out by their upperclassmen floormates.

Usually floormates form close-knit groups of friends. Floors compete against each other for intramural sports and there is an ongoing rivalry among floors in everything they do. The floors are also co-ed and some of them have co-ed bathrooms. One freshman felt uncomfortable at first but warmed up to the idea: "I wasn't used to living with girls and sharing a bathroom. But I guess it's a good time to start and I've made a lot of friends in the process." The few complaints from students regarding dorm life center around noise pollution from the hyperactive radiators in the winter.

The food tends to be a bit more of an issue. Most Carleton students have a tremendous amount of school spirit and are reluctant to reveal any information that might reflect poorly on the school. However, when they do mention a drawback, it often involves the food. One junior remarked, "Well . . . It's not as bad as some. . . . They do have a decent salad bar and soup if all else fails." While the food receives lukewarm reviews, students rave about the brand new academic and dining building referred to as "linguistics and linguini."

Fun . . . Not in Class, Not in the Sun

Carleton students tend to keep busy despite the long winter. Division III varsity sports are a part of campus life, but the only boast made about the football team is that they have the highest GPA in the conference. The biggest sport at Carleton is Ultimate Frisbee and games are always well attended. Intramural sports are taken surprisingly seriously (in good fun, of course). They are organized by floor and include floor hockey, tennis, sailing, softball, and broomball.

> **"I've only had one professor in my three years here who didn't insist on being called by his first name."**

When students are not sporting, they are often getting involved in their community through clubs and organizations on campus. The outdoor enthusiast club is one of the biggest groups, and political clubs, which tend to be left-leaning, are quite popular. There are four a capella groups on campus who perform regularly, along with various theater groups who offer several plays each term.

Carleton also has fun with its traditions. One of the more notable traditional activities is the annual softball game with as many innings as years it's been played. Usually beer accompanies the 130-inning softball game, and more times than not a naked inning is played. A slightly more heart-warming tradition is the Dacie Mosses house. Dacie left her house to the university when she died on the condition that there would always be ingredients to bake cookies. "Any time I want, day or night, I can go to Dacie's and bake cookies with my friends. It's really fantastic," said an enthusiastic student.

Social Life

The nightlife at Carleton is not raging. That is not to say it does not exist. Carleton is not a state school, and it doesn't have fraternities. Nonetheless, Carleton students cannot be stopped from having a good time. Without a Greek system the student body is very open, without defined cliques. One junior girl explains that this means, "No more jocks! No more losers! And the wonderful thing about Carleton is we're all dorks!" The closest things to defined social entities on campus are the special-interest houses. These include a farm house, a culinary house, a yoga house, a canoe house, a green house, and a variety of cultural houses. The buildings usually only house about ten people, but they are not separated socially because they are required to put on regular campus-wide events.

Drinking on campus is very prevalent, but students note a lack of pressure to participate. Parties are very casual, and it would not be uncommon to see party-goers sporting sweatpants and T-shirts.

Northfield is a quaint town with restaurants and cafes. The Contended Cow is a popular pub with good music where students go when they want to get off campus. When students want to get farther away, a weekend trip to the Twin Cities is always an option. But for the most part there is a lot of activity on campus and students don't feel the need to leave. Many do not want to leave, as they find the small Carleton community cozy, supportive, and stimulating. If you value a snug environment, a fresh, frigid outdoors, and a challenging, personal education, then you will sure be happy at Carleton. —*Quinn Fitzgerald*

FYI

If you come to Carleton, you'd better bring "a sense of humor" and "a hat—Minnesota is cold."

What is the typical weekend schedule? "Procrastination, partying, and, inevitably, homework."

If I could change one thing about Carleton, I would change "the cold weather."

Three things every student at Carleton should do before graduating are "go streaking, go traying (sliding on the snow with trays), and go out to coffee with a professor."

Gustavus Adolphus College

Address: 800 West College Avenue; St. Peter, MN 56082
Phone: 507-933-7676
E-mail address: admission@gac.edu
Web site URL: www.gac.edu
Founded: 1862
Private or Public: private
Religious affiliation: Lutheran
Location: suburban
Undergraduate enrollment: 2,536
Total enrollment: NA
Percent Male/Female: 42%/58%
Percent Minority: 7%
Percent African-American: 1%
Percent Asian: 3%
Percent Hispanic: 1%
Percent Native-American: 0%
Percent in-state/out of state: 82%/18%
Percent Pub HS: 92%
Number of Applicants: 2,203
Percent Accepted: 77%
Percent Accepted who enroll: 39%
Entering: 662
Transfers: 42
Application Deadline: 1 Apr
Mean SAT: NA
Mean ACT: NA
Middle 50% SAT range: V 550-660, M 540-670
Middle 50% ACT range: 23-28
3 Most popular majors: biology, psychology, business
Retention: 90%
Graduation rate: 81%
On-campus housing: 85%
Fraternities: 27%
Sororities: 22%
Library: 281,761 volumes
Tuition and Fees: $21,535
Room and Board: $5,460
Financial aid, first-year: 71%
Varsity or Club Athletes: 25%
Early Decision or Early Action Acceptance Rate: ED 97%

The infamous winters of Minnesota might be expected to engender equally cold social environments, yet nothing could be farther from the truth at Gustavus Adolphus College. With excellent academics and a high rate of extracurricular participation, this liberal arts school has a lot to offer its Gustie population—not the least of which is an invitation to the Nobel Conferences held at the college each year.

Unique Curriculum

Gustavus requirements include a personal fitness credit, two human behavior/sociology credits, three writing credits, and one credit in religious studies. Students find the requirements one of the strong points of their college. The school runs on a 4-1-4 schedule, with four classes taken in the fall, one class during a short winter session called J-term, and four more classes during the spring semester. Incoming frosh select a first-semester class, described as a seminar-style "first step into college" course reserved strictly for first-year students. The professor of a student's seminar serves as his or her freshman faculty advisor.

Biology is reportedly the strongest and most popular major at Gustavus. Political science and psychology are popular as well. The biology department guards against overcrowding in introductory courses by splitting classes into two sections of approximately 80 people each (chemistry and psychology do the same). TAs assist students in lab classes, but professors do most of the formal teaching. Students relish the relationships with their professors, who often invite students over for dinner or organize opportunities to conduct research. Professors are also known to have saved students "out-registered" from a class. Registration usually works out for most people, although one undergrad said, "you may have to do a bit of finagling here and there." Frosh register over the phone before they arrive at school, while other students (with priority to upperclassmen) do so during a four-day period at the beginning of the semester. Academics are definitely competitive at Gustavus, but the "really good balance" that exists makes success an "achievable goal," one student said.

A Hilltop Campus

The self-contained campus is situated on top of a hill within the small town of St. Peter and includes a blend of older buildings and newer ones erected in the 1960s. Students in certain dorms enjoy a view of the Minnesota River Valley. The Arboretum, located on the west side of campus, attracts students looking for a "neat place to go watch the stars at night." St. Peter provides some off-campus housing but is "not much of a metropolis by any means," according to one student. Larger nearby cities include Mankato, a 10-minute drive away, and Minneapolis–St. Paul, less than two hours away. The Safety and Security department provides effective 24-hour security, Night Hosts guard the entryways from the hours of 8 P.M. to 3 A.M., and an escort service is available for students walking through campus at late hours. "I've never felt unsafe on campus," one female student said.

All first-year students are required to live on-campus. The North End is a reputed center for jocks and major party life, while those more interested in a quiet, academic, and artsy environment prefer the South End. The nine campus dorms are co-ed by floor or, in some cases, by section. Norelius Hall houses frosh and sophomores, and Wahlstrom includes students from all four classes. Dorms have "a lot of community to them," and are often the site of casual socializing or studying. The International House attracts international students and those interested in foreign studies. Collegiate Fellows and Head Residents (similar to RAs) offer a peer-support network. Off-campus houses are available in St. Peter and are close enough so that "off-campus students don't feel isolated."

The College Dining Room (CDR) is the central cafeteria on-campus. According to one student, "When you get the chicken strips, you realize someone loves you. When you get the tuna melt, you know Domino's is always a phone call away." The meal plan is mandatory for first- and second-year students, most of whom live on-campus. An additional option includes the flex plan, which gives students either $75, $100, or $200 to spend as they wish. Students looking for snacks find them at the campus Canteen shop.

The three-floor Gustavus Adolphus campus library, Folke Bernadette, is equipped with computer labs, audio-visual resources, a relatively broad selection of research materials, and an interlibrary loan connection with Mankato State University. Conference rooms also are available for social studying. The Jackson Campus Center and Johnson Student Union opened in 2000, and houses almost all the student organizations, a post office, the office of admissions, and even the campus radio station. Olin Hall is a center for math, computer science, and physics, and also has an observatory. The Nobel Hall of Science was renovated just a few years ago, and the King and Queen of Sweden were present during the opening of a new wing.

Golden Gusties

A large number of students participate in intramurals and form teams according to dorm or social group affiliations. Choirs and bands also draw large numbers of students. Future journalists and publishers write for the Gustavian Weekly, the primary school newspaper released every Friday, and the biannual Fire Thorne literary magazine. A number of students also support the Gustavian college yearbook. While students here generally shy away from political activism, they often engage in community service through the Meaningful Activities for Gusties in Community (MAGIC) student group, which connects undergrads with various community programs. Some students have worked with mental health patients, and the Study Buddies Program allows undergrads the opportunity to tutor area high school students. Less traditional groups include the Gustavus Sauna Society, which meets regularly in the athletic center saunas.

Gustavus Adolphus athletes maintain especially strong traditions in gymnastics and hockey, with the gymnastics team hosting this year's regional championship. The Lund Athletic Center houses all the athletic facilities, such as an ice arena, five racquetball courts, and an indoor track. One student mentioned how "people joke that Lund looks like a country club." The Golden Gustie mascot, Gus the Lion, inspires devoted fans (especially during hockey games) to dress in gold and black, including wigs. Many alumni return during homecoming, which features a dancing debut by the first-year hockey players during the football halftime.

The Campus Activities Board and the Student Activities Office organize most of the social activities on-campus, and the Peer Assistance group promotes parties that advocate "healthy lifestyles." Two big parties are the President's Ball, a formal held each year in a rented hall in the Twin Cities, and Earth Jam, a spring festival featuring multiple bands, which one student called "a very small version of Lollapalooza." Christmas in Christ Chapel attracts people interested in hearing seasonal music from the student choirs and orchestras. Gustavus provides a DJ in the Dive student center every Friday and Saturday night, and the Campus Activities Board also sponsors one or two concerts a year. Greek participation increases during rush time, but few students describe the Greeks as especially influential in campus social life, although they hold many of the parties on campus. In keeping with the casual social scene, dating is said to be fairly low-key and usually in the context of friendships. According to one student, "People would like to see dating happen more often."

"When you get the chicken strips, you realize someone loves you. When you get the tuna melt, you know Domino's is always a phone call away."

Most Gusties are natives of either Minnesota or the greater Midwest. Students describe their classmates as "not terribly diverse" and feel that a population of white, midwestern students "can get a little frustrating at times." In response to the limited diversity, the Diversity and Affirmation Committee holds an annual "Building Bridges" conference in March aimed at developing a more minority-friendly environment at Gustavus. The college has support groups for Asian and African-American students, but some report that the Hispanic support network is weak. The gay, lesbian, and bisexual students on-campus strongly promote Coming Out Week and dedicate time to increasing student awareness on-campus.

"Everyone has a lot of Gusty pride," one student said. Gusties proudly speak of their academic standing, competitive sports teams, congenial atmosphere, and prime access to the annual Nobel Conferences. Future Gustavus students not only need winter coats and flannel sheets, but also a "get-involved attitude" to maintain the strong Gusty tradition. —*Tahia Reynaga*

FYI

If you come to Gustavus Adolphus, you'd better bring a "warm coat."

What is the typical weekend schedule? "Homework, on-campus movie, Domino's, and more homework."

If I could change one thing about Gustavus Adolphus, I'd "have more weekend activities and more opportunities to get off campus."

Three things every student at Gustavus Adolphus should do before graduating are "participate in the Fun Run, fall asleep in the library, and spend quality time in Econo Foods."

Macalester College

Address: 1600 Grand Avenue; St. Paul, MN 55105
Phone: 651-696-6357
E-mail address: admissions@macalester.edu
Web site URL: www.macalester.edu
Founded: 1874
Private or Public: private
Religious affiliation: Presbyterian
Location: urban
Undergraduate enrollment: 1,840
Total enrollment: NA
Percent Male/Female: 42%/58%
Percent Minority: 27%
Percent African-American: 3%
Percent Asian: 5%
Percent Hispanic: 3%
Percent Native-American: 1%
Percent in-state/out of state: 27%/73%
Percent Pub HS: 67%
Number of Applicants: 3,713
Percent Accepted: 44%
Percent Accepted who enroll: 27%
Entering: 441
Transfers: 22
Application Deadline: 15 Jan
Mean SAT: 1343
Mean ACT: 29
Middle 50% SAT range: V 630-730, M 620-710
Middle 50% ACT range: 27-31
3 Most popular majors: economics, political science, psychology
Retention: 92%
Graduation rate: 82%
On-campus housing: 68%
Fraternities: NA
Sororities: NA
Library: 430,182 volumes
Tuition and Fees: $25,088
Room and Board: $6,874
Financial aid, first-year: 77%
Varsity or Club Athletes: 20%
Early Decision or Early Action Acceptance Rate: ED 54%

Leave no stone unturned, leave no establishment unquestioned. Macalester students are proud of their uncanny knack for questioning, injecting, inspecting, detecting, and selecting every possible establishment in society. Nearly every course from economics to Spanish to history is taught with a race, class, gender, or sexuality spin. As one student said, "even in the hard sciences, there are classes like 'biology and the female body/reproduction.'"

Small Class Sizes

Macalester uses its small size of 1,600 students to its advantage in the classroom. All the classes are small and one junior noted that her largest class still only had 27 students in it. Most classes have fewer than 20 students, and it is not uncommon to have fewer than 10. This small population fosters close student/teacher relationships, though the class size can be a problem for freshmen trying to get into classes.

Until very recently, Macalester offered a J-term: a time to take an exploratory class during the month of January between the two semesters. During this time, students could take anti-establishment courses like "Cursing and Swearing." Now students can use the time to pursue internships, conduct independent studies, or take courses at some of the other schools in the Twin Cities. Many students go home, and others simply relax and enjoy the free time.

As with many colleges and universities around the country, Macalester has its fair share of grade inflation. As and Bs abound, while Cs are "reserved for personal vendettas or total slackers." As one student said, "There's a few crusaders trying to curb it (grade inflation) but everyone just ends up hating them."

From Kosovo to Rothko

The Macalester campus does not remain faithful to a set building type. Situated over four blocks, it sports reminiscent, red brick buildings with white trim and chic, modern, glassy structures, creating an impressive skyline that complements the fall colors. The student union was finished in the spring term of 2001. The building includes a post office, a campus store, a lecture hall, and meeting rooms. Students are most thrilled, however, by the cafeteria with a variety of new food options. "It's really nice food, Asian and pasta and all kinds of stuff," mentioned one freshman. Along with the cafeteria is The Grill, where students get good food to go.

The students are enjoying the options the new dining area offers. Non-first year students can choose between 12 and 19 meals per week. Vegetarian and vegan options come with every meal, and the Hebrew House in Kirk Hall offers bi-weekly Shabbat dinners. The food drew poor marks from the students. Unfortunately, it is not even a matter of getting used to the Macalester cuisine: "The food was great my first year, but I detest it now because it is always the same," explained one student.

Macalester has a variety of housing options, ranging from the six-story Dupre Hall to the charming, antiquated Wallace to George Draper Dayton Hall, the newest building on campus. All freshmen and sophomores must live on campus. However, Macalester does not have enough housing for everyone. Seniors get first dibs on the remaining space and many juniors are left to fend for themselves in off-campus housing. Finding apartments is often difficult, and some people end up living far from campus.

One of the Twin Cities' wealthiest residential neighborhoods surrounds Macalester. A small shopping area with a mix of eclectic shops and coffee places is conveniently situated right off campus. Transportation is made easy with an excellent and inexpensive bus system. Since Macalester is located directly between Minneapolis and St. Paul, students can experience the best of both of cities. The Twin Cities have no lack of clubs and shows, and they are home to nationally renowned icons like the Mall of America and radio program Prairie Home Companion.

Internationalism

Macalester students say they're known for being "smart, but badly dressed" and are generally proud of this distinction. Because of the trend at Macalester to question everything that has to do with the establishment, women are often stereotyped as ultra-feminist: no make-up, no dresses. And everyone who is politically verbal is considered liberal. The few conservative students on campus are generally quiet. Macalester currently enrolls students from 76 different countries despite its small size. One famous alumnus is Secretary General of the United Nations Kofi Annan.

The student body is small, intimate, but some feel that this can get cliquish at times. Others disagree, saying the small atmosphere is a great way to get to know people well. Because of the size of the student body, news travels quickly. One student mourned that this "can be a real molestation when you do something stupid or get a bad reputation."

Hippie Holdout

Macalester students pride themselves in their political and social awareness. In many ways, wrote one student, Macalester is a "hippie holdout because students hold protests and vigils for darn near everything." Community service is especially big at Macalester. It has a program called MACTION, a popular community service group. MACTION organizes one-time community service events, but no continuing projects. The Queer Union (QU) is a "really awesome and high profile" group for gays, lesbians, and bisexuals. QU is involved with promoting HIV and AIDS awareness on campus. It reportedly used to organize a mass coming-out party on Parents' Weekend, but the administration convinced its members to change this tradition. Regardless of the group, people usually have some kind of issue. Other popular groups on campus include Macnaked, a group that holds random Frisbee tournaments at midnight, and Fresh Concepts, the "funniest improv group on campus."

Macalester is a "hippie holdout because students hold protests and vigils for darn near everything."

Although most people partake in activities, varsity sports are not as popular here as elsewhere. The football team never wins, and football players in general have a bad reputation. Students equate them with bad high school memories: "We were all oppressed by them in high school, and the tables are definitely turned here." The most popular team on campus is a toss up between men's soccer and women's soccer. At soccer games, bagpipes sound every time the soccer team scores a goal. Women's soccer made headlines when it won the NCAAIII championship in 1998.

For students who do not play sports or the bagpipes, there are plenty of "fun athletic cheers" to urge their team on and upset their opponents. Several students mentioned the cheer, "Drink blood, smoke crack, worship Satan . . . GO MAC!"

Colonial Rematch

Aside from varsity sports, intramurals abound. Soccer seems to be the most popular intramural sport. A favorite non-varsity event is the annual Colonial Rematch. Every fall at Macalester, the European students take on the African students in the ultimate payback for imperialism. The European students, varsity players from Denmark, Germany, or Spain gather in earnest, while the African team shows up, having never practiced, and delay the game half an hour while they "run around the field with flags, take pictures, yell a lot and practice other forms of quite amusing intimidation."

The Greek system has been banished from the Macalester campus, but students generally agree that the Greeks would feel left out anyway. For the Greek-seeker, sports teams often have houses off campus that act as similar communities. But for most students, the parties are quite sufficient without Greeks. Students rave about the bi-annual QU dances. One senior claims, "people get naked and dance on the tables long after the lights come on. Nothing like it." Another phenomenon on campus is the "progressive" floor-wide party, where each room offers a different kind of drink. Students go from one room to the next drinking, partying, and dancing in the various ambiences.

Drinking is big on campus, and visible, but most people feel that it is done in moderation. Alcohol is permitted, provided it is in a private room, but rumors now circulate that the administration wants to make Macalester a dry campus. Pot is definitely the drug of choice, but harder drugs are not accepted. Still, as one student put it, choosing not to drink is "generally respected, if you're an unrespectable person." The same applies for other drugs. Still, Macalester is not a party school. For better or worse, many people spend the entire weekend studying in the libraries.

Yet despite this, Macalester students are overwhelmingly happy with their college selection. When asked whether, knowing what she knows now, she would choose Macalester again, one senior said, "I would choose this school in a heartbeat." —*Nicole Jabaily*

FYI

If you come to Macalester, you'd better bring a "refrigerator."

What is the typical weekend schedule? "Movies, parties, and homework."

If I could change one thing about Macalester, I'd "increase the amount of housing on campus."

Three things every student at Macalester should do before graduating are "take classes outside their major, take advantage of being near the Twin Cities, and try doing a show for the radio station."

St. John's University / College of St. Benedict

Address: PO Box 7155; Collegeville, MN 56321-7155
Phone: 320-363-2196
E-mail address: admissions@csbsju.edu
Web site URL: www.csbsju.edu
Founded: 1857
Private or Public: private
Religious affiliation: Roman Catholic/ Benedictine
Location: rural
Undergraduate enrollment: 1,897
Total enrollment: NA
Percent Male/Female: 100%/0%
Percent Minority: 6%
Percent African-American: 0%
Percent Asian: 2%
Percent Hispanic: 1%
Percent Native-American: 0%
Percent in-state/out of state: 86%/14%
Percent Pub HS: 79%
Number of Applicants: 1,101
Percent Accepted: 87%
Percent Accepted who enroll: 49%
Entering: 468
Transfers: 37
Application Deadline: rolling
Mean SAT: NA
Mean ACT: NA
Middle 50% SAT range: V 510-660, M 580-680
Middle 50% ACT range: 23-28
3 Most popular majors: business, English, biology/biological science
Retention: 91%
Graduation rate: 78%
On-campus housing: 84%
Fraternities: NA
Sororities: NA
Library: 805,376 volumes
Tuition and Fees: $20,685
Room and Board: $5,788
Financial aid, first-year: 64%
Varsity or Club Athletes: NA
Early Decision or Early Action Acceptance Rate: NA

St. John's University for men and its sister campus, the College of St. Benedict for women, give the word "teamwork" a new meaning. Located in northern Minnesota, these two campuses are four miles apart, but are close in every other aspect. "Community" is the byword at St. John's/St. Ben's, beginning with academics. The faculty is approachable, and professors get to know students on a personal level. "If you are having a bad day, the professor will ask you why you're not being yourself," one St. Ben's sophomore said.

To graduate, students must satisfy many liberal arts requirements, including fine arts classes. In addition, all undergrads must take at least six "flagged" courses, which emphasize either writing, discussion, quantitative analysis, gender issues, or global topics. The theology department earns student praise, and courses emphasizing gender development and differences are also popular. The school enjoys a lofty reputation in Minnesota: "not that money's everything, but you see a lot of their graduates doing really well around here," one student proudly proclaimed.

The Benefits of the J-Term

Students are also quick to praise the "J-term," a three-week January semester during which they enroll in a single class. "It's a nice transition period, instead of jumping right back into things after Christmas break," one Johnnie said. Many use the J-term to study in other parts of the world. St. John's and St. Ben's offer programs in a broad range of locations, including Cairo, Rome, London, Spain, Greece, China, El Paso, and New York City. Those who opt to stay on-campus for J-term can choose from any number of unconventional courses, including Detective Fiction and Books You've Always Wanted to Read.

The town of "St. Joe" contains a number of popular bars, including Sal's and Loso's (aka "The Middie"). One favorite of many "Johnnies" is the LaPlayette (affectionately dubbed "The La"), known for its Taco Tuesday nights. For movies or a good meal, students usually head to the small city of St. Cloud, about a ten-minute drive from either campus. A car is not necessary for a social life; the "great" busing system, which runs until 2 a.m. every night, connects outing destinations to St. Joe. Campus hangouts include the pub in the Sexton Commons, a huge, recently built student center on the St. John's campus. The St. Ben's library is also quite a social scene on weeknights—a sharp contrast to the studious atmosphere of the St. John's library.

The Watab Mixer and Pine Stock

Both campuses are large, scenic, and secluded. With a definite sense of privacy, a small island in the middle of Lake Watab is host to the year's two biggest parties: the Watab Mixer and Pine Stock. The Joint Events Council, which sets up guest speakers and other campus programs, arranges for a band to play at these parties. Notable guests have included Soul Asylum, Blues Traveler, and the Jayhawks.

Unlike the celebrated "Dead Poets Society look" of St. John's, St. Benedict has modern architecture—with the noticeable exception of the library. "It sticks out like a sore thumb," said one Bennie, which is not to say Gothic architecture does not have its place on-campus; students affirm that Abbey Church at St. John's is "a beautiful, beautiful building. It's just breathtaking, really."

Catholic Influence, Not Rule

St. Ben's students say there is not a bad dorm to be found on their relatively young campus. Lucky seniors end up in the West Apartments, whose units feature a kitchen, large living room, and two spacious double bedrooms. Johnnies usually vie in the annual housing lottery for the Menton Court, site of 11 luxurious suites of four singles and a large bathroom. Dorms are the only place where Bennies and Johnnies live separate lives—but according to one Johnnie, "They don't do bed checks or anything." Students who live on-campus have a full meal plan, which allows them to eat in either the large commons or a smaller dining hall. Those who live off-campus or in the West Apartments can charge meals on a dining hall account if they wish.

A large number of the students are children of St. John's/St. Ben's alumni, which some say enhances the sense of community. Most students hail from Minnesota, and an overwhelming majority are Roman Catholic. Out-of-staters and non-Catholics are nonetheless welcome. "It's a very warm, supportive place—people readily accept you for who you are," one New Yorker said.

St. John's and St. Ben's are private schools in the middle of small college towns, and townsfolk repeatedly stereotype the students as "rich and preppy." Locals have griped about the late-night partying, but town-gown relations are reportedly "just fine. We don't have more quibbles than the next college town." If anything, they are on the upswing: VISTO, a student volunteer group, does a lot of charity work in the town, particularly around Christmastime. A core council consisting of town residents and students also works to improve community relations.

"It's a very warm, supportive place—people readily accept you for who you are."

VISTO is one of many strong extracurricular clubs and organizations at St. John's and St. Ben's. Both campuses have active student governments, and the Joint Events Council has members from both colleges. The schools support chapters of Greenpeace and ROTC, along with several bands, a cappella groups, and choirs. The radio station, KJNB, is popular among students and locals and often has listener call-in shows. Campus publications include the *Record* at St. John's and the *Independent* at St. Benedict's; both are biweeklies and they come out on alternate weeks. The Haehn Campus Center at St. Ben's boosts extracurricular life even more with its restaurants, intramural and varsity gyms, conference/banquet rooms, and a dance floor. Students consider themselves politically active, and although a sizeable liberal contingent exists, the majority of students at both schools have a conservative slant.

Football Fever

The most popular activities, in terms of sheer numbers and spirit, are without a doubt, home football games. A perennial Division III powerhouse, coach John Gagliardi is the subject of a new book, *Sweet Season*, about the philosophy of St. John's football. Students usually pack each game, but biggest is the game against the arch rival college of St. Thomas. "The St. Thomas games can be violent affairs," a senior quipped. Intramural sports, some of which take place in Warner Palaestra, are also popular. The Palaestra gym features an eight-lane pool, an indoor track, racquetball courts, and a sauna. Also the facilities at the Haehn Center are available to students.

Tradition thrives at St. John's and St. Benedict's. The week before Thanksgiving break, the campus sits down for a large turkey meal together, and before Christmas, students gather for the lighting of an enormous tree in the Great Hall. With generation after generation of families attending the schools, along with close interaction between the two campuses and a friendly face everywhere you turn, it's no wonder St. John's and St. Benedict's are a team to be reckoned with. Said one student, "Life here actually is a cliche—it's community-oriented, everyone really looks out for each other, and I cannot imagine going to school anywhere else." —*William Chen and Staff*

FYI

If you come to St. John's/St. Bens, you'd better bring a "hot pot."

What is the typical weekend schedule? "A movie and pizza night, a JEC dance, bowling, and recuperating and studying on Sunday."

If I could change one thing about St. John's/St. Bens, I'd "get more money for student employment."

Three things every student at St. John's/St. Bens should do before graduating are "walk to the chapel, swim at Lake Sag and go to Mass at St. John's Abbey."

St. Olaf College

Address: 1520 St. Olaf Avenue; Northfield, MN 55087
Phone: 507-646-3025
E-mail address: admissions@stolaf.edu
Web site URL: www.stolaf.edu
Founded: 1874
Private or Public: private
Religious affiliation: Lutheran
Location: rural
Undergraduate enrollment: 3,041
Total enrollment: NA
Percent Male/Female: 41%/59%
Percent Minority: 7%
Percent African-American: 1%
Percent Asian: 4%
Percent Hispanic: 1%
Percent Native-American: 0%
Percent in-state/out of state: 53%/47%
Percent Pub HS: 87%
Number of Applicants: 2,624
Percent Accepted: 73%
Percent Accepted who enroll: 41%
Entering: 779
Transfers: 40
Application Deadline: rolling
Mean SAT: NA
Mean ACT: NA
Middle 50% SAT range: V 590-690, M 580-690
Middle 50% ACT range: 25-30
3 Most popular majors: biology/biological science, economics, English
Retention: 93%
Graduation rate: 79%
On-campus housing: 96%
Fraternities: NA
Sororities: NA
Library: 654,950 volumes
Tuition and Fees: $23,650
Room and Board: $4,850
Financial aid, first-year: 60%
Varsity or Club Athletes: 22%
Early Decision or Early Action Acceptance Rate: ED 88%; EA 87%

A belief in the value of a strong and cohesive community suffuses St. Olaf's idyllic Northfield, Minnesota campus. Boasting a freethinking, committed student body, diverse academic programs (especially strong in the arts), and a good relationship with the town, St. Olaf offers every student "a chance to really fulfill your own potential."

Keeping Busy in the Cold

One of the simple realities of going to school in rural Minnesota is that the winters are, quite simply, freezing. Though the students don't seem to mind this—activities such as an extravagant Christmas Fest and traditions such as sliding down Old Main Hill on a dining hall tray necessitate winter weather—it is a defining characteristic of the campus life. However, there are plenty of distractions from the chilly environment, and on a compact campus like St. Olaf, it isn't difficult to find them.

The hilltop campus, comprised mostly of limestone buildings "built to look like Norway," is called "gorgeous" and "an absolute utopia" by students. One even says, "Our campus is even more beautiful than the pamphlets." The fall brings spectacular color to the trees, and the winter a significant amount of snow. In good weather, "Oles" congregate on the lawns to socialize or study; in the winter, they gather in the library or in the Fireside Lounge.

St. Olaf is internationally known for its arts programs, most notably in music. Both within and outside of the popular formal music major, a musical influence pervades the campus. One student says that although it seems that "everyone is in Ole choir (we have a nationally broadcasted concert every Christmas) it's not true. There actually ARE people here who are not musical." Many students come to St. Olaf for the excellent (though notoriously challenging) musical performance, theory, and education curriculum. There are also a plethora of concerts held by all different kinds of student groups on campus.

Students say that other extracurricular opportunities are strong and varied, with large numbers participating in political and social organizations, and religious groups. One student believes the Fellowship of Christian Athletes is "the biggest" activity but is also "becoming more and more of a cult." There are more eclectic organizations as well, including a Pirate Club. Many students work on campus jobs, as well, which one student said is "a great way to make friends."

Varsity athletic programs at Division III St. Olaf are strong, especially in cross-country (the women's team consistently wins their conference), swimming, and baseball. One students noted that the hockey team is also popular, and "a lot of people go to football games, but the team isn't actually all that good." In general, Oles turn out to support their teammates. "There's a fair amount of spirit," a junior said. "Since it's such a small school, it's just being faithful to your friends." Intramurals are extremely popular, and the on-campus sports facilities are well-kept. The newly constructed Tostrud Building houses an indoor track, weight rooms, and a climbing wall.

A Strong Foundation

In general, academics at St. Olaf are what one would expect from a school its size—small classes, lots of personal attention, and interesting professors. "I've been extremely pleased with all of my professors," said one senior, noting "their approachability and their genuine concern for my life as an academic and as a developing adult." One student recalled a professor who sent students in and out of the revolving doors of the student center as a way of demonstrating protein transport across cell membranes; another had an art class where the professor "jumped up on the table and started screaming profanities." Well-regarded physics professor Rober Jacobel recently had a glacier in Antarctica named after him.

Although academics are strong across the board, students agree that the St. Olaf atmosphere is more focused on the humanities. The strongest and most competitive major is music, while English also gets positive reviews. Some students say economics and psychology are weaker. The hard sciences are strong, but as one student said, "don't take organic chemistry unless it is absolutely necessary. If you do, be prepared to seek counseling for a loss in self-worth."

Students at St. Olaf are required to complete 35 full courses (each one worth approximately four semester credits) to receive their baccalaureate degree. They also must complete the general education distributional requirements, which are made up of three different areas. "Foundation studies" includes basic skills in writing, language, math, and a physical education requirement. "Core studies" covers more diverse areas, emphasizing history, literature, and natural science, which includes two courses on biblical and theological study. The third component is an "integrative ethics" course in which students pick from a variety of offerings. According to the course catalog this course area addresses "the questions of justice, morality, rights, and responsibilities, often in the context of a student's major." One student deemed the general education requirements "very reasonable," but another believed that they "change a little too often" and can be difficult to keep track of.

Every class at St. Olaf is taught by a full professor, and students report few problems getting into classes, especially after freshman year. The logistics of keeping classes small can be difficult—as one student said, "registration is a nightmare, but class size is great, usually about 20 to 30 students." There is also a well-connected and widely used study abroad program. One student called the school "very serious" about enabling students to spend a term or more in another country.

Music and Revelry

St. Olaf's campus is officially dry, which can mean different things to different students. While they generally agree that alcohol is easily obtainable, it also means that there are lots of alternatives, and the social scene is diverse. One student said, "I would compare it to high school. People do drugs here; some people do a lot. But I think that there is a 50/50 split between drinkers and non-drinkers. One never needs to feel left out. There are always people willing to not drink." Buntrock Commons, the student center, is the home of "The Pause," a student hangout that features pool tables, movies, concerts, and dances. Some students will also go into town to places such as the American Legion Club for live music.

The musical tradition of St. Olaf means that there are also many concerts happening all the time. The most famous is the annual Christmas Festival, when 12,000 people descend on Northfield to hear, among other things, five St. Olaf choirs and an orchestra. The Pause also has a weekly jazz night, and a cappella groups such as the all-male Limestones keep students entertained. Theater and improvisational comedy groups are also active and well supported.

Students live in co-ed buildings on single-sex floors, and the lack and price of nearby housing means that over 90 percent of students live on campus all four years. Freshman have RAs, who "can bust you for having alcohol" but who are also "pretty cool." Older students have the option of living in "honors houses." Some of these houses are themed, such as the French House, but a senior reported that "generally people will come up with a year-long service project and they will get a house." One student calls the main dining hall "a mecca for conversation and people watching," and the food is cited as "practically gourmet," with a large number of options for vegans and vegetarians. One student boasted, "We also have an awesome dessert selection. Try the white chocolate chip cookies!" In addition to the dining hall, there is a café called The Cage for snack foods and drinks.

> **"We live in a beautiful area with everything we could want; sometimes the real world is a shock when we graduate."**

St. Olaf was founded as a Lutheran college, and its official history declares that since its founding, "our Lutheran Christian perspective has remained at the very core of our identity." There are certainly non-Lutheran students at St. Olaf, but its religious spirit strongly influences the campus atmosphere, and some non-Christian students report feeling uncomfortable at times.

As one might expect from a Lutheran college in Minnesota, the student body tends towards homogeneity. Many are of Scandinavian descent, and a large number come from Minnesota and Wisconsin. However, a senior extolled the "huge international perspective. Oles have traveled the world and bring their experiences into their everyday lives. People are aware of the world, and in that sense we are diverse."

In general, Oles love the tight-knit community and close relationships their college provides. As one student said, "anyone can come here and find someone who shares their viewpoint or vision." One senior commented that since "we live in a beautiful area with everything we could want, sometimes the real world is a shock when we graduate," but even so, students' experiences at St. Olaf are not something that they would ever trade. —*David Carpman*

FYI

If you come to St. Olaf, you'd better bring a "Nalgene bottle, a musical instrument, and a heavy winter coat."

What is the typical weekend schedule? "Friday night, a little studying before the dances start; Saturday, going on little trips to the cities, or the apple orchard, or a coffee shop, then parties in the houses on Ole Ave; Sunday, church and then homework."

If I could change one thing about St. Olaf, I would "diversify the campus."

Three things every student at St. Olaf should do before graduating are "go to Christmas Fest, have lunch with your favorite professor, and try the lutefisk."

University of Minnesota

Address: 100 Church Street SE; Minneapolis, MN 55455
Phone: 800-752-1000
E-mail address: admissions@tc.umn.edu
Web site URL: www.umn.edu
Founded: 1851
Private or Public: public
Religious affiliation: none
Location: urban
Undergraduate enrollment: 32,457
Total enrollment: NA
Percent Male/Female: 47%/53%
Percent Minority: 17%
Percent African-American: 4%
Percent Asian: 8%
Percent Hispanic: 2%
Percent Native-American: 1%
Percent in-state/out of state: 74%/26%
Percent Pub HS: 90%
Number of Applicants: 14,746
Percent Accepted: 74%
Percent Accepted who enroll: 42%
Entering: 5,188
Transfers: 1,822
Application Deadline: rolling
Mean SAT: NA
Mean ACT: NA
Middle 50% SAT range: V 540-660, M 550-670
Middle 50% ACT range: 22-28
3 Most popular majors: social sciences, business, engineering
Retention: 83%
Graduation rate: 47%
On-campus housing: 22%
Fraternities: NA
Sororities: NA
Library: 5,700,000 volumes
Tuition and Fees: $6,280 in; $16,854 out
Room and Board: $5,696
Financial aid, first-year: 49%
Varsity or Club Athletes: 4%
Early Decision or Early Action Acceptance Rate: NA

Do you want to become part of a tradition of groundbreaking innovation and crowd-shaking victory? Students at the University of Minnesota attest to the variety of opportunities available at the university.

Go-pher it!

How does the University of Minnesota offer so many choices, opportunities and possibilities? One answer to this question is the size of the university itself. With four campuses—the Twin Cities campus standing as the largest—the university spans broadly across the center of Minneapolis. The urban setting of the university is one of its best aspects, says one freshman. It allows students to take hold of many metropolitan advantages, such as a major national center for business and the performing arts where many conventions, symposiums and exhibitions occur monthly. Also, students can attend the home games of many professional sports teams, including the Vikings, the Twins, and the Timberwolves. When sick of the busy activities in and around the university, one student reported that she goes to one of the national parks or lakes nearby to find some solitude and enjoy some time with nature. On campus, the University offers over 400 organizations, all of which give students yet another way to manifest their interests and fill their free time with interest.

Many students enjoy the areas around the university so much that they decide to move off campus. A large percentage of the student body makes this choice after freshman year. Off-campus housing is relatively cheap nearby and invites many students to consider Greek life at the university. Sororities and fraternities constitute a large part of the social scene at the university for many students. A majority of students who attend the university do not become members of the Greek system heritage, but a large portion of the student body admits to attending several Greek parties before they graduate from the University of Minnesota. "Frat parties are the thing to do, especially freshman year," says one sophomore.

For freshmen, dorm housing is guaranteed with the submission of a timely application. The university has eight residence halls and three apartment complexes, all of which provide suitable accommodations and locations proximal to classes. To make the walk to class more comfortable, the University of Minnesota is equipped with underground tunnels for student travel. Built between the major university buildings, these tunnels shield students against unwelcome cold or precipitation. Rumor has it that the University of Minnesota adopted the Gopher as its mascot as symbolic of the burrowing done by students in the tunnels everyday.

The university's mission is threefold: research and discovery; teaching and learning; and outreach and public service. The students who attend the university research and discover more than chemical and reactions and engineering innovations. The university helps them to find a sense of themselves within the twin cities of St. Paul and Minneapolis. With so many things being offered, what else could you need at a place like this? Students say some warmer weather would be a major plus at the university campus, but, then again, that's why the Gophers have their own tunnels.

A Tradition of Accomplishment

The University of Minnesota, founded in 1851, has hosted the inventions of the first heart pacemaker, the retractable seat belt for automobiles, the heart-lung machine, and the black box for aircraft. As the only major research facility in Minnesota, the university enjoys many federal grants for its hundreds of thrilling research projects. With a legacy of research achievements, the university particularly appeals to science-driven individuals. However, the University of Minnesota has much more to offer its incoming students than just science-based curricula. "The opportunities at the University of Minnesota run as rampant as the student spirit of the Gophers themselves!" says one freshman.

"The opportunities at the University of Minnesota run as rampant as the student spirit of the Gophers themselves!"

The university offers eight undergraduate colleges: the College of Agricultural, Food and Environmental Sciences; the College of Biological Sciences; the General College; the College of Human Ecology; the College of Liberal Arts; the Carlson School of Management; the Institute of Technology, and the College of Natural Resources. Student ability falls equally across the eight colleges. Each college holds a multitude of prestigious programs, fascinating lectures and hands-on opportunities. The range of offerings reflects the academic diversity fostered at the University of Minnesota. Whether a student wants to study forestry during a study-abroad program in Chile or take an online course to enhance his self-discipline and study skills at home, the possibilities all await everywhere he turns. Across the eight undergraduate colleges, a student has over 145 majors to choose from in his academic pursuits. One senior reports, "at first I was overwhelmed by the choices, but now I appreciate the freedom I have to choose." Many students choose a program that includes both a major and minor. The offered areas of study satisfy a wide range of interests that spans from agricultural education to computer science to finance to sport studies. And speaking of sport studies . . .

Maroon and Bold

The University of Minnesota boasts an impressive sporting legacy. Basketball and hockey seem to take the lead in most fan attraction. One student reported that "Sporting events are always fun; hockey games are great, and so is basketball, for both men and women." Basketball certainly brings an added dimension of excitement for the University of Minnesota student body as it grows in strength and success from season to season. The teams continue to attain thrilling victories, providing students with great entertainment on the weekends. Men's basketball at the University of Minnesota has had a history of turning players into NBA stars. Most recent graduates that have since played in the NBA include Bobby Jackson, Quincy Lewis, and Voshon Lenard. Women's basketball, likewise, has been an impressive squad for the Gophers, remaining a contender in the top 10 for many seasons.

The Mariucci Hockey Arena is also no stranger to huge crowds of rowdy, student fans. But the fans are not the only ones cheering loudly at the rink. In fact, the University of Minnesota is the birthplace of cheerleading. The first spirit squad was formed in 1898 by Johnny Campbell, a student disgruntled from three straight football losses for his team; today the cheerleading program at Minnesota is just yet another athletic legacy that proudly shows the school's colors of maroon and gold. Many fans enjoy the sporting tradition of their university by watching a basketball game, fencing competition, or gymnastics. They sometimes engage in the tradition rally cry, "Minnesota Rouser," as they support their classmates and friends. "Minnesota, hats off to thee! To thy colors, true we shall ever be" run the first two lines of the time-honored chant. Not all University of Minnesota undergraduates actively participate in sport playing or sport watching, but the sporting legacy at the university adds a sense of unity and pride for all. —*Aleksandra Kopec*

FYI

If you come to the University of Minnesota, you'd better bring "a bike."

What is the typical weekend schedule? "There's usually a sporting event to attend. The Superblock, a group of four dorms adjacent to one another, is also a great hangout for freshmen on the weekends."

If I could change one thing about the University of Minnesota, I "would make the campus smaller."

Three things every student at the University of Minnesota should do before graduating are "walk the bridge, sleep in the quad at the Superblock, and go to the state fair."

Mississippi

Millsaps College

Address: 1701 North State Street; Jackson, MS 39210
Phone: 601-974-1050
E-mail address: admissions@millsaps.edu
Web site URL: www.millsaps.edu
Founded: 1890
Private or Public: private
Religious affiliation: Methodist
Location: urban
Undergraduate enrollment: 1,158
Total enrollment: NA
Percent Male/Female: 45%/55%
Percent Minority: 16%
Percent African-American: 11%
Percent Asian: 3%
Percent Hispanic: 1%
Percent Native-American: 1%
Percent in-state/out of state: 50%/50%
Percent Pub HS: 65%
Number of Applicants: 913
Percent Accepted: 87%
Percent Accepted who enroll: 31%
Entering: 251
Transfers: 45
Application Deadline: rolling
Mean SAT: NA
Mean ACT: NA
Middle 50% SAT range: V 550-640, M 530-650
Middle 50% ACT range: 23-29
3 Most popular majors: business, social sciences, biological/biomedical sciences
Retention: 83%
Graduation rate: 67%
On-campus housing: 78%
Fraternities: 50%
Sororities: 50%
Library: 136,937 volumes
Tuition and Fees: $18,414
Room and Board: $6,768
Financial aid, first-year: 57%
Varsity or Club Athletes: 27%
Early Decision or Early Action Acceptance Rate: EA 94%

Isolated from the rough and tumble streets of downtown Jackson, Mississippi, one square mile of greenery peers out from behind an iron fence. The bustling campus of the much admired Millsaps College hides inside.

Majority Rules

At first glance, Millsaps might seem to be a haven for conservative, affluent, white Southerners—a closer look only confirms this view. The majority of the students come from Mississippi and the surrounding states, usually within reasonable driving distance from the school. The clothing ranges from Gap to Abercrombie, and the politics from moderately conservative to conservative, so some minority and liberal students admit to feeling a bit out of place. Most students, however, feel that the campus is friendly and generally accepting of everyone. "Most people are very receptive on campus if you share similar interests," said one student, and most students do share similar interests.

Aside from the common interest in fashion and the Greek system, the strongest link between Millsaps' students is a work ethic necessary to survive the college's academic rigor. Many students explain that staying afloat is simply a matter of knowing what work absolutely must be done and what can be set aside. Students made it clear that work comes before all else. This is especially evident when you consider that the most popular majors, biology and business, are also considered to be two of the hardest. Students also praise the small class sizes, usually under 30 students, the availability of professors, and classroom discussions. Most students attribute these benefits to the size of the school and also the size caps on classes.

Renovations Aplenty

Since most students spend the majority of their time at Millsaps living and eating on campus, the boarding and dining situations are crucial. One recent change to the living situation has been the "freshman side of campus." All freshmen live in the dorms on the north side of campus while everyone else lives on the opposite side. The purpose of this change is to allow the freshmen to bond as a class. Some upperclassmen, however, complain that under this setup, they don't get a chance to get to know incoming freshmen. Another grievance against the new freshman side is that one of the nicer dorms, formerly a reward to upperclassmen, is now for freshmen only.

Despite these complaints, upperclassmen are happy with their housing situations. All campus dorms are considered quite comfortable. Also, the most sought-after dorm, Goodman House, is still available to upperclassmen. Goodman is the only apartment-style dorm, featuring single rooms, kitchens, and private bathrooms—and seniors get top bids.

One student went so far as to say, "The Greek system is the entire social life on Millsaps' campus."

A second pleasant change to Millsaps' campus was the recent remodeling of the student center. At the center of campus, the student center houses a cafeteria with outdoor balconies, a coffeeshop, meeting rooms, a TV and pool table, and student mailboxes. Students use the student center regularly, mainly because of the cafeteria and mailboxes, but it also serves as a hang-out spot. The center is right next to "the bowl," a small, grass-covered valley. The bowl is also a frequent hang-out spot for studying and frisbee playing alike.

The dining at Millsaps seems to detract only marginally from the generally comfortable living arrangements. Students tend to rate the food itself as average by college standards. The main gripe is with the inconvenient cafeteria hours. The cafeteria closes for the day at 7 P.M. One student put it simply, saying "After 7, what do you do?" Although there are other places to eat nearby, they are mainly fast food. Most people would prefer longer dining hall hours to the alternatives in town, especially members of sports teams who don't want to eat a full meal immediately after practice.

A Greek for All Seasons

Certainly the most notable aspect of social and extracurricular life at Millsaps is the Greek system. One student went so far as to say, "The Greek system is the entire social life on Millsaps' campus." Because over half of the student body is in a fraternity or sorority, the system has a dominant role on campus. Some students feel that this segregates the social life, but others claim that Greeks and non-Greeks interact freely.

The weekend social scene is definitely centered around "the houses." The frat houses are most popular for underclassmen who can't get into the area bars. The common conception is that if you want to see people, Fraternity Row on Friday night is the place to do it. Upperclassmen also frequent the houses, but local bars like the Subway Lounge and CS's are also on their weekend agendas. A few students mentioned other weekend activities on campus, such as movies and concerts, but most students who aren't partying are heading home or on road trips to Ole Miss or New Orleans.

Greeks tend to be very active in the extracurricular scene at Millsaps as well. Community service-type activities are very popular, and when not affiliated with a religious group, are largely sponsored by sororities. Overall, the Greek system, being the campus social scheme, has made itself a necessity. Some students feel that the system is the only way to meet people. One student said, "The best way to meet people is to rush if you're not playing a sport." Other students say that being Greek isn't necessary; it is simply a matter of being outgoing and getting involved in activities.

However, Greek system might not reign supreme, as it has in the past. Both the new president and the new Greek advisor are making efforts to lessen the firm hold the Greek system has on campus. The primary change visible this year is the dry rush.

This new crackdown on the Greeks

won't put a damper on what Millsaps' students consider the best party of the year. Major Madness, a week-long, school-sponsored festival, features games, activities, performances and concerts by big name bands. Recent performances have included George Clinton, Reel Big Fish, and Better than Ezra.

The study-then-party atmosphere is a popular one, but Millsaps is known to lack real school spirit. While most people attest to being perfectly happy at Millsaps, players of varsity sports complain that, with the exception of a few faithful fraternities and sororities, very few students attend sports events or wear the school colors. In general, however, most students have nothing but good things to say about Millsaps. It provides a distinct atmosphere that satisfies the majority of its students. And while a few students feel the small size is a bit limiting, most agree that "the intimacy of 1,200 people confined to a square mile" is a perfectly comfortable and friendly situation. *—Lauren Rodriguez*

FYI

If you come to Millsaps, you'd better bring "a lot of paper, pens, and no-doz."

What is the typical weekend schedule? "Thursday night go to the frat houses, Friday night go out to the frat houses or out with friends, Saturday night go to the frat houses or out with friends, Sunday study all day long."

If I could change one thing about Millsaps, I'd "take it out of Mississippi."

Three things every student at Millsaps should do before graduating are "pull an all-nighter, dance on a pool table at a frat house, and get stressed out about comps."

Mississippi State University

Address: PO Box 6334; Mississippi State, MS 39762
Phone: 662-325-2224
E-mail address: admit@admissions.msstate.edu
Web site URL: www.msstate.edu
Founded: 1878
Private or Public: public
Religious affiliation: none
Location: rural
Undergraduate enrollment: 13,373
Total enrollment: NA
Percent Male/Female: 53%/47%
Percent Minority: 22%
Percent African-American: 19%
Percent Asian: 1%
Percent Hispanic: 1%
Percent Native-American: 0%
Percent in-state/out of state: 82%/18%
Percent Pub HS: NA
Number of Applicants: 5,000
Percent Accepted: 74%
Percent Accepted who enroll: 48%
Entering: 1,759
Transfers: 1,593
Application Deadline: 1 May
Mean SAT: NA
Mean ACT: NA
Middle 50% SAT range: NA
Middle 50% ACT range: 20-27
3 Most popular majors: business, education, engineering
Retention: 80%
Graduation rate: 47%
On-campus housing: 21%
Fraternities: 17%
Sororities: 18%
Library: 2,026,894 volumes
Tuition and Fees: $3,874 in; $8,780 out
Room and Board: $5,770
Financial aid, first-year: 71%
Varsity or Club Athletes: 3%
Early Decision or Early Action Acceptance Rate: NA

The college-bound student seeking a friendly environment should take a look at Mississippi State University. MSU is an increasingly challenging university that attracts students from within the state of Mississippi and across the nation. It's a school built on unity, friendliness, and, of course, education. Tucked away from the hustle and bustle of city life in quiet Mississippi State, Mississippi, students at MSU take great pride in their school and its athletic teams.

Bulldogs and Textbooks

MSU is divided into eight different colleges of undergraduate studies, ranging from the College of Education to the liberal arts-oriented College of Arts and Sciences. MSU also offers a variety of programs in agricultural, environmental, and forestry studies. At the College of Agriculture and Life Sciences, a student can major in anything from human sciences with an emphasis in interior design to food safety with an emphasis on management and production. MSU offers a wide range of pre-professional programs ranging from premed to poultry science, but freshmen are preoccupied with a core curriculum that covers a writing course, courses in the humanities, social and physical sciences, as well as computer literacy. Some freshmen, especially those going into the architecture field, find that they have much more work than other students. "I have 23 hours of work a week, models to build, but that's what happens at the best architecture program in the South," said one freshman majoring in architecture. Another freshman agreed, "The architecture program is great here. But, it is a little too demanding sometimes, although I love making all the models." MSU students note that the architecture, engineering, and biology majors provide the most challenging courses on campus. A sophomore noted that "architecture and engineering, hands down" are the most time-consuming. No matter what they major in, all MSU students are required to study a foreign language. A sophomore majoring in international business explained that it is "really a double major; business and a foreign language." A psychology major said that his foreign language requirement of four credits is "not that bad; at least I get to learn French."

Athletics *Are* the Weekend

MSU students feel Bulldog love flowing through their veins. The school is united by the common desire for the success of their athletic teams, particularly football, baseball, and basketball. "You have to be there if there is a game going on; it's what this place is all about," said a freshman. "We usually all go to the stadium, and if the game is going well, we will all stay until the end. Lately, the wins have been difficult to come by, but it will turn around," said a hopeful MSU senior. Since most of MSU's students are from within the state, many even go home if there's no athletic event to attend that weekend.

The biggest football game of the year is the Egg Bowl, which is usually on or around Thanksgiving Day. It pits MSU against archrival Ole Miss. "The Egg Bowl is something that I always look forward to. It is so much fun, and everybody comes out and shows some school spirit," said a sophomore. No one's quite sure how the Thanksgiving-season matchup got its name, but according to one freshman, "it doesn't matter what it's called, what matters is that we beat Ole Miss, and that's all." According to legend, many years ago a cow walked onto the field during the Egg Bowl, and MSU proceeded to win the game. Ever since, MSU students proudly ring cowbells at the game for good luck. One junior said that the administration has been trying to ban the cowbells because they're considered artificial noisemakers, but "we still find a way to sneak them in. I can't wait to do it this Thanksgiving."

Greek life dominates the MSU party scene. On football weekends and other big occasions, the fraternities always "make sure that there is a party to attend." Around 20 percent of the student population is involved in the fraternity and sorority system. One sophomore observed that Greek life is "pretty big deal here, especially if you want to party. You have to know someone in the frat if you want to drink." But a freshman who did not rush a fraternity because of his workload reassured, "I still party every weekend, and I can go to a frat if I want to. It is not frowned upon to not be a brother, or even if you don't want to drink. It's really great." Another non-drinking junior agreed that "people are friendly to you, regardless." Most MSU students are quick to note that there is very little drug use on campus. "We are very lucky to not have problems with extreme drug use or STDs or any of that other stuff that happens at other schools," according to one freshman. MSU students who indulge in the occasional drink feel constrained by the administration's alcohol policies, since MSU is a "completely dry campus." Students who drink admit that it is easy to get around the policy, and that if you "are just careful, you aren't going to get busted," although the strictness of enforcement "totally depends on your RA."

"That is the best thing about going to MSU: the people and the friendliness"

MSU students are known for their Southern hospitality. One sophomore raved "that's part of the magic here, everybody says hello to each other." A freshman commented that it's easy to make friends at MSU, and that "you find your niche faster than at any other school, it is awesome." Another freshman similarly said "that is the best thing about going to MSU, the people and the friendliness."

Southern Charm

Students love that their campus feels so "homely and cozy" and that people are "friendly wherever you go." The campus is literally the only thing in town; the borders of the school make up the borders of the city of Mississippi State, Mississippi, which borders the small town of Starkville. "It's so flat, so spread out, but everything feels so close together as time passes by," said one sophomore. Because of the campus's large size, however, many students feel that they "cannot make it here without a car." Though the school's administration has tried to introduce alternate transportation options, students often jump in their cars to get to far-away classes. "Most people just bring their cars to school, especially the people that live within driving distance. It is just something you need here," said one junior. Another reason for having a car is that most students go home for the weekend if there is "nothing going on." Cars are also helpful for the three-quarters of upperclassmen who choose to live off campus. "By the time you're a sophomore, you want to get together with your friends and move to an apartment," one junior said. There are plenty of apartment complexes in Starkville, but only a handful located within walking distance of the main part of campus.

For those students who do live in dorms, the facilities are satisfactory, though not luxurious. The standard freshman dorm "could be a lot worse," according to one freshman. All freshmen live in double rooms equipped with a sink and a refrigerator. Most freshman dorms are single-sex, and the co-ed dorms still segregate the sexes by hallway. Upperclassmen who decide to stay on campus usually live in suites, "which are a little ratty." One junior who lives on campus says that upperclassmen live in lackluster dorms because the "school has already made a good impression on the freshmen, and most people don't usually stay on campus for the rest of their years." Upperclass suites usually have four single bedrooms and a connected bathroom. A student who works in the university housing office mentioned that MSU is currently in the process of redesigning their dorms, and those renovations will be made soon.

At MSU, students feel like they are gaining more than a higher education. Not only are students learning, they feel "it is just so great here." They are quick to say that the best part about MSU is the friendliness of the student body and the faculty. One freshman said that "folks here are just good people—it is just that simple." As one senior put it, "it's just the good ol' South here, with good ol' people. I will be a Bulldog until the day I die." —*Alberto Masliah*

FYI

If you come to MSU, you'd better bring "a car. Things are all spread out."
What is the typical weekend schedule? "Wake up, study, visit friends, party, go to the game, party again."
If I could change anything about MSU, I would "make the buildings more attractive."
Three things every student should do at MSU before graduating are "go to the Egg Bowl with a cowbell, go to at least one game of every sport, get involved in an organization."

University of Mississippi

Address: PO Box 1848; University, MS 38677-1848
Phone: 662-915-7226
E-mail address: admissions@olemiss.edu
Web site URL: www.olemiss.edu
Founded: 1844
Private or Public: public
Religious affiliation: none
Location: rural
Undergraduate enrollment: 10,661
Total enrollment: NA
Percent Male/Female: 47%/53%
Percent Minority: 16%
Percent African-American: 13%
Percent Asian: 1%
Percent Hispanic: 0%
Percent Native-American: 0%
Percent in-state/out of state: 68%/32%
Percent Pub HS: NA
Number of Applicants: 7,603
Percent Accepted: 67%
Percent Accepted who enroll: 44%
Entering: 2,257
Transfers: 975
Application Deadline: 20 July
Mean SAT: NA
Mean ACT: NA
Middle 50% SAT range: NA
Middle 50% ACT range: 20-26
3 Most popular majors: education, accounting, marketing
Retention: 76%
Graduation rate: 52%
On-campus housing: 27%
Fraternities: 32%
Sororities: 34%
Library: 1,251,189 volumes
Tuition and Fees: $3,916 in; $8,826 out
Room and Board: NA
Financial aid, first-year: 63%
Varsity or Club Athletes: 4%
Early Decision or Early Action Acceptance Rate: NA

Students of the University of Mississippi affectionately call their school Ole Miss, reflecting how dear to their hearts this 155-year-old school has become. Indeed, Ole Miss quickly grows on a student, with its friendly atmosphere and traditional Southern feel. Yet at the same time, students find themselves immersed in an internationally aware institution, one that is quickly expanding not only physically but academically as well.

Academically Balanced

Students describe Ole Miss as academically well-balanced. The university offers seven undergraduate schools: the College of Liberal Arts and the Schools of Accountancy, Applied Sciences, Business Administration, Education, Engineering, and Pharmacy. The College of Liberal Arts and the School of Business Administration have the largest enrollments from the university's nearly 9,000 students. Students say that the Schools of Pharmacy and Engineering offer the most rigorous programs, while the School of Education is probably Ole Miss's biggest academic weakness.

At Ole Miss, as at any state school, class size is a concern. Indeed, although one student said that most classes are generally anywhere from 18 to 25 students, freshman core courses can get quite large and one history lecture course that she took had 175 students. The sophomore student insisted that she "never felt like a number, though" and that, despite the state school atmosphere, it's hard to feel anonymous at Ole Miss.

Moreover, Ole Miss offers several special programs tailored to provide closer attention for more specific, individualized needs. The university houses the McDonnell-Barksdale Honors College, an integral part of the university. Admitting just 120 freshmen in 2001, the Honors College selects students of higher caliber, with an average SAT score of 1350 and an ACT of 31.5. In addition, Ole Miss boasts an elite program known as the Croft Institute for International Studies that admits only 40 students and prepares them for international leadership. Ole Miss also offers several courses to all students from its Center for the Study of Southern Culture, which analyzes the less-studied yet "invaluable" tradition of the South. All freshmen are required to take what is called University Studies. University Studies is designed to help freshmen make a smoother transition from high school to college and occupies an hour credit for the first half of the first semester. "It really is a big help," said one sophomore, "especially because it is a great way to meet fellow freshmen."

The Good Ole Life at Ole Miss

Students at Ole Miss describe their dorms with a bit of ambivalence. As one student wryly said, "It's not the nicest place, but it's not the worst." The university is in a process of improving and modernizing its housing; students attribute the renovation of the dorms to the dramatic increase in enrollment in the past two years. For better or worse, the university adheres to a state-wide law that forbids any form of co-ed housing. As a result, undergraduates live in single-sex dormitories; the main freshmen buildings are Martin for women and Stockard for men.

Ole Miss students also must abide by strict rules. Guests must check in at a designated front desk and be accompanied by a host throughout the residential halls at all times. Moreover, Ole Miss dorms generally have rigid visitation hours: 11 A.M. to 11 P.M. on the weekdays, with late-night extensions to 1 A.M. on the weekends. The students of each dormitory, however, may vote to extend visitation hours during the first week of each semester.

The Mighty Greeks

When questioned about social life at Ole Miss, one marketing and communications major preferred to sum it up with statistics: "33 percent of our students are involved in Greek life—the largest percentage, I think, of any public university." Enough said. Indeed, fraternities and sororities play a prominent role in life at the University of Mississippi. While hazing is strictly forbidden on campus, Greek traditions are highly visible. During rush week in the fall, freshmen perform silly but otherwise innocuous stunts such as standing outside in the cold without a T-shirt and inventing creative chants in order to gain admittance to the Greek organization of their choice. Such activities can require the complete dedication of each rushee, and one freshman described rush as bringing the university to a halt, noting that "a lot of classes have been dismissed or cancelled."

Students insist, contrary to popular misconceptions, that the campus on the whole does not revolve around Greek life. "[Fraternities and sororities] aren't [all] we have to offer."

Belles of the Ball

Nonetheless, fraternity parties remain a popular choice on weekend nights. The exclusivity of these events depends largely on where they are held and which organizations are holding them. "Girls can get into any party," one undergraduate said, "but boys have to know someone in the fraternity to go." Yet even male students who don't get into these parties won't have trouble meeting beautiful people. "We have the finest women in the South . . . they're unbelievable," said one male student. Even a female student concurred, "Ole Miss is supposed to be known for having really pretty girls, which I personally don't notice."

"We have the finest women in the South . . . they're unbelievable."

At Ole Miss, dating is common, although often not in the conventional sense. Dates are often set up around football games, arranged specifically for having a companion to the Saturday event, and successful dates span from the night before a game to the night after. "You get a date for the football game," described one student, "They take you out for dinner, you go to a fraternity party together, and then you go to the football game." As odd a combination as dating and football may be, football's influence on Ole Miss life extends far beyond the social and dating scenes.

Getting into the Grove

When interviewed, one student simply captured the spirit of Ole Miss by proudly proclaiming, "We're a football school." Football games often become a focal point of life at Ole Miss, although one student conceded that the same applies at any school in the Southeastern Conference. Undergraduates at Ole Miss are especially given to watching games with a passion and reacting to results explosively. One student remembered a traumatic experience: "We really wanted to beat Texas Tech. A lot of people were disappointed because we were ahead. There was a lot of crying, a lot of throwing things."

Ole Miss prides itself not only on the games themselves but on the social events that stem from them. Tailgating at the Grove, a ten-acre grassy knoll at the center of campus, is a favorite pastime at Ole Miss. Students invest plenty of time and energy into making tailgating an elaborate festival; one student was quick to point out, "[There's] no actual tailgating, you don't stand next to your truck." Rather, she described the tailgate as an almost formal experience: "People bring in these nice tables, delicious food, they hang chandeliers, they bring candles and flowers, and sometimes they'll bring their good silverware." Students often come to football games and tailgates dressed up—it isn't uncommon to see boys in slacks and collared shirts and girls in sundresses. While intense, the amount of attention and planning that goes into these football events allows for many social opportunities. "You talk to people, you go from tent to tent, and you can eat everybody's food." Whether a football game is scheduled or not, Ole Miss students spend plenty of time at the Grove in general. Students laud the university and the student programming board for scheduling a variety of on-campus events, many of which occur at the Grove. Concert on the Grove is a favorite series, bringing artists like the Nappy Roots, Pat Green, and local bands to Ole Miss.

Controversy in Costume

Ole Miss's history is undeniably entwined in racial issues, and although the Civil Rights movement lies over four decades in the past, vestiges of that dark time in the school's history still remain. At the foremost is the Ole Miss mascot, Colonel Rebel, which was banned from the football sidelines in the 2003 season but is still an official trademark of the university. The mascot is controversial because, according to one African-American student, he resembles an old plantation owner. To some, Colonel Rebel is a reminder of Ole Miss's infamous past as a segregated university. Several students cited the historic integration case of 1962, in which Ole Miss's first African-American student, James Meredith, needed to be escorted by the U.S. military into the university's halls. Addressing the mascot controversy as a manifestation of the university's racial history, one student commented, "Our chancellor says it isn't a racial issue, but if you look at the big picture, you know it is." One student applauded the steps the administration has taken toward replacing the mascot, saying "Our current chancellor is really working hard to get over the stereotypes." The administration and the athletics program have decided to change Colonel Reb to a more positive image, but the transformation has been slow. In fact, the process has dragged on so long that a student movement to retain Colonel Rebel as the symbol of the school has gained momentum.

Ole Miss thus continues to tread the line between preserving tradition and identity, and accommodating the demands of a changing world. Students at the University of Mississippi find a school with a rich (albeit controversial) tradition but that's slowly changing in its policy, its physical plant, and in its people. —*Christopher Lapinig*

FYI

If you come to Ole Miss, you better bring a "rolling cooler for tailgating on the Grove."

What is the typical weekend schedule? "Stop by a fraternity party on Friday; wake up on Saturday, go to the Grove, go to a football game, come back to the Grove, and then go to the bar Library; and then rest all day Sunday."

If I could change one thing about Ole Miss, "I'd rewrite the negative history of segregation we have had."

The three things that every student at Ole Miss should do before graduating are "work on your tan at Sardis Lake, eat chicken-on-the-stick at 3 A.M., and road trip to Graceland Too."

Missouri

University of Missouri / Columbia

Address: 305 Jesse Hall; Colombia, MO 65211
Phone: 573-882-7786
E-mail address: mu4u@missouri.edu
Web site URL: www.missouri.edu
Founded: 1839
Private or Public: public
Religious affiliation: none
Location: urban
Undergraduate enrollment: 19,698
Total enrollment: NA
Percent Male/Female: 48%/52%
Percent Minority: 12%
Percent African-American: 6%
Percent Asian: 3%
Percent Hispanic: 1%
Percent Native-American: 1%
Percent in-state/out of state: 88%/12%
Percent Pub HS: NA
Number of Applicants: 10,215
Percent Accepted: 88%
Percent Accepted who enroll: 49%
Entering: 4,439
Transfers: 1,133
Application Deadline: rolling
Mean SAT: NA
Mean ACT: NA
Middle 50% SAT range: NA
Middle 50% ACT range: 24-29
3 Most popular majors: business, communications, social sciences
Retention: 84%
Graduation rate: 60%
On-campus housing: 53%
Fraternities: 20%
Sororities: 25%
Library: 3,111,319 volumes
Tuition and Fees: $7,278 in; $16,725 out
Room and Board: $5,770
Financial aid, first-year: 45%
Varsity or Club Athletes: 3%
Early Decision or Early Action Acceptance Rate: NA

Like many large state schools, the University of Missouri is defined by an active frat life and a relatively loose attitude toward academic life. At the same time, the sheer immensity of a state institution guarantees that students can find something to fit their interests. A closer look reveals some local color peeping through the State U mask.

Mizzou Curriculum

Students consider academics at Mizzou "average to moderately difficult." The undergraduate core curriculum includes a three-year language requirement and two writing-intensive courses, the hardest of the requirements to fill. Two of the more prominent academic programs are the Minority Achievement Program, which offers workshops to promote further education and teach effective study habits, and the extensive study-abroad program. The journalism school is the most recognized department that the university has to offer and is the main source of the small out-of-state diversity on campus. Undergrads report that along with the psychology department, the journalism school is the most popular. Some of the hardest classes are in the sciences, including University Physics, "the roughest course they offer here," one student said. One of the more popular courses is Human Sexuality, which has a more laid-back reputation. Professors teach lecture classes and TAs teach the smaller sections, but as one student explained, "many of the TAs are foreign and hard to understand, so you end up learning the most from books."

Academics are not a great source of stress for many Mizzou students. As one undergrad said, "Even during finals week, people don't seem very flipped out." People study in the two main libraries on campus, the law library and Ellis, which are some of the biggest libraries in the state.

Landscapes, Frats, Food

"The prettiest part of campus has to be the main quad with the pillars. There are always students out there having fun," another undergrad reported. The University of Missouri's huge campus is a big part of the surrounding town of Columbia. Students say it is a safe environment with "enough to offer," including a mall, restaurants, and the Blue Note, a local dance club and bar. The residents of this college town are friendly and take advantage of the facilities on campus. The town also plays an important role in student housing.

According to students, off-campus living is cheaper than staying in the dorms, and shuttles connect off-campus apartment buildings to different parts of campus. Off-campus residents say it is not necessary to have a car, although it is convenient for trips to the nearest big cities.

There is a lot of spirit behind the Tigers, especially the men's basketball team, which draws a full crowd for every game.

On-campus living is more convenient, with doubles and singles and community bathrooms. Suites of two bedrooms with a shared bathroom are also available, but these go mainly to the juniors and seniors. One student explained, "The rooms are boring, with thin cement walls and lofts or cots, but at least there aren't any bunk beds." Juniors and seniors get the best housing, and the best dorm is one of the only all-women dorms on campus—Johnston Wolpers—which one student said "looks like a hotel" and has air-conditioning. Most of the other dorms are co-ed with single-sex floors. Each floor of the residential halls has a residential advisor as part of a bigger advising system that first-year students find particularly helpful.

Other housing options include theme houses, language houses, and fraternity and sorority houses. The campus has a large Greek community, and their housing is, as one student described, "mansion-like."

Students who live on campus choose a meal plan of 7, 14, or 21 meals a week. Food can also be charged on student ID cards at the Brady Commons student union, which has Chik-Fil-A, Taco Bell, Pizza Hut, and Burger King outlets. The dining hall food does not get rave reviews, but is generally considered "acceptable," and there are always vegetarian options. Most students eat off campus in town a couple of times a week, with options from the cheapest and most favorite Taco Bell to the nicer and popular El Maguay Mexican restaurant. Some students find local coffee shops also offer a good place to study.

The university also offers an "E-Z Charge" to its students, which gives each student $400 of credit to spend each month. It is accepted at the bookstore, dining halls, campus convenience stores, Brady Food Court, and Memorial Union Food Court. "You end up buying everything you want on it at an extremely over-inflated price. Don't get it—it's very addictive," one student advised.

Athletics and Associations

Athletics play a big role in Mizzou life. There is a lot of spirit behind the Tigers, especially the men's basketball team, which draws a full crowd for every game. Kansas University is the rival that draws the most student animosity on campus. Intramural sports are popular among extracurriculars, and the athletic facilities are among the most heavily used on campus. One student called them "excellent, with at least six basketball courts and even a climbing wall." Options range from volleyball and basketball—which are some of the more popular—to the rock-climbing club that makes use of the climbing wall in the campus athletic complex. The meteorology club, the roller hockey club, and Peaceworks, an environmental awareness group, attract interest, as do many minority groups on campus, from the Asian American Association (AAA) to the Romanian Student Association to LUBRASA for Luso Brazilian students. Students do not consider Mizzou's undergraduate population diverse, although support networks for minority students include the ethnic clubs and other groups such as the Black Culture Center and the Black Collegiates. Another significant and controversial minority group on campus is the Triangle Coalition for gay and lesbian students. Most student groups are funded by the Missouri Student Association, MSA, the student government. The MSA, however, is "known as a joke rather than as an important student force," according to one student.

Campus Events

Students involved with the MSA work to organize movies, concerts, speakers, tutoring, rides, and advice opportunities. It has brought in such celebrities as George Stephanopoulos, and organized barn dances—including its own version of the popular MTV program Singled Out for Valentine's Day. Other big social events revolve around basketball games, such as big pep rallies before the games and other parties put on by the fraternities. One of the biggest events of the year is homecoming for the big football game each fall. The university has rules against kegs on campus, but the administration has a reputation for being relatively lax with the frat houses. There are also rules about drug use on campus, but some students say they are not well enforced. Other activities include the yearbook, the *Savitar*, and the *Maneater*, the bi-weekly newspaper. Performance opportunities on campus also abound, with theater, singing, and orchestral student performing groups.

The student body is considered rather conservative by many undergrads, more so than the surrounding town. Diversity continues to be an issue for students on campus, as the majority are white Missouri natives. Different programs have been introduced to promote diversity and raise the academic level of the school. The Bright Flight program and the Curator Scholarships both offer opportunities to students with good ACT scores and class rank. The Conley Scholars Program is also a unique academic opportunity for incoming students. It guarantees four years in the University of Missouri Medical school without taking the MCATs. In general, the campus, while large, is full of what students agree are "friendly" people. *—William Chen and Staff*

FYI

If you come to U of Missouri, you'd better bring "a planner."

What is the typical weekend schedule? "Going out on Friday and Saturday, doing all your studying and work on Sunday."

If I could change one thing about U of Missouri, I'd "make more parking spots."

Three things every student at U of Missouri should do before graduating are "get active, have fun, and do well in school."

University of Missouri / Kansas City

Address: 5100 Rockhill Road; Kansas City, MO 64110
Phone: 816-235-1111
E-mail address: admit@umkc.edu
Web site URL: www.umkc.edu
Founded: 1929
Private or Public: public
Religious affiliation: none
Location: urban
Undergraduate enrollment: 8,870
Total enrollment: NA
Percent Male/Female: 40%/60%
Percent Minority: 29%
Percent African-American: 14%
Percent Asian: 6%
Percent Hispanic: 4%
Percent Native-American: 1%
Percent in-state/out of state: 81%/19%
Percent Pub HS: NA
Number of Applicants: 2,480
Percent Accepted: 78%
Percent Accepted who enroll: 39%
Entering: 763
Transfers: 1,386
Application Deadline: rolling
Mean SAT: NA
Mean ACT: NA
Middle 50% SAT range: NA
Middle 50% ACT range: 21-28
3 Most popular majors: liberal arts/sciences, business, education
Retention: 73%
Graduation rate: 27%
On-campus housing: 14%
Fraternities: NA
Sororities: NA
Library: 1,241,084 volumes
Tuition and Fees: $5,575 in; $14,726 out
Room and Board: $5,100
Financial aid, first-year: 78%
Varsity or Club Athletes: 4%
Early Decision or Early Action Acceptance Rate: NA

Despite the stereotype, "University of Missouri at Kansas City is not a hick school." In fact, Kansas City is one of the fastest growing cities in America. Located in the heartland of America, UMKC offers an affordable education in an urban setting.

Known as the "artsy" of the UM universities, UMKC may not draw as many out-of-state students as some other state schools, but it still offers a diverse student body. What it lacks in geographical diversity, it makes up for in its students' wide-ranging backgrounds and interests. A large percentage of UMKC students are part-time or returning students, many of them having to balance their studies with jobs or families.

Ambitious Academics

As can be expected with an older student body, UMKC is known for its excellent pre-professional programs and tends to attract students who are career-oriented. Specifically, the dual-degree programs that offer a B.A. or B.S. degree in conjunction with a degree in medicine, law, dentistry, or education, cater to ambitious and focused students.

The College of Arts and Sciences is comprised of 15 departments ranging from traditional majors such as English and history to more unusual departments such as military science. Computer science and psychology are two of the most popular departments. Requirements vary according to major. Overall, the requirements for B.S. and B.A. degrees are similar except that a B.S. degree requires a total of 60 hours in math and science credits. In general, students must complete a minimum of 26 semester hours and a minimum of 12 semester hours in their respective majors. Double and combined majors are also available.

UMKC students must comply with a unique Missouri law that requires students to complete courses about the U.S. Constitution and the Missouri State Constitution. Though most appreciate the former requirement, some out-of-staters complain about the latter.

Students who wish to intensify their academic experience can participate in a special honors program that encompasses much more than their requisite honors classes. Honors students have their own publications—*The Undergraduate Review* and *The Onner's Gazette*—and have access to special honors facilities. The program itself centers on a weekly one-hour colloquium offered every semester. Honors in all classes meet with the faculty and distinguished guest lecturers to discuss a wide range of subjects.

With a professor to student ratio of 12:1, UMKC prides itself on its small class sizes. Hence, though UMKC is a research institution, students are not bogged down in huge classes with little student-professor interaction. "At UMKC you don't feel like a number. The professors I have encountered are extremely accessible," one student said. The one complaint students did have concerned the intensity of work. "I didn't expect my American Studies course to be so intensive. I am enjoying it though," one freshman said.

Kasey the Kangaroo

How UMKC came to have a Kangaroo as its mascot is a question that has been pondered for years. Although UMKC officially got the idea for its mascot from two kangaroos adopted by the Kansas City Zoo back in 1936–37, the kangaroo was probably adopted largely because of Disney's "Kasey the Kangaroo's" popularity. Apparently, "Kasey" seemed the perfect mascot for a school called "KC."

The kangaroo is a prominent symbol. First-years arriving in the fall are greeted by organizations at the Roo Fair, a one-day activities fair that introduces students to UMKC's more than 200 organizations. Some of the many organizations range from *U-News*, the weekly student newspaper, to *KCUR*, UMKC's public radio station, one of the first educational radio stations in the state. But even with the wide range of activities, students wishing to start new organizations will find the Student Life Office extremely helpful. With over a dozen fraternities and sororities, Greek life undoubtedly plays a role on campus as well. But, according to students, "if Greek is not your thing, that's okay too."

For the athletically inclined, UMKC is a NCAA Division I affiliate. Part of the Mid-Continent Conference, the school offers a wide range of varsity teams for both men and women. Women participate in basketball, golf, tennis, volleyball, cross-country, track and field, and softball. Men compete in basketball, golf, tennis, cross-country, track and field, rifle, and soccer.

Even if they don't take part in varsity athletics, most students come out to cheer for their favorite teams. Among the biggest events of the year is the basketball game against Kansas State University, one of UMKC's traditional rivals. During this game, the UMKC stands are often packed, and the Kangaroos go wild. For less hardcore athletes, UMKC offers a wide range of intramural sports at Swinney Recreational Center.

Campus Living or Apartment Style?

Despite the bustling on-campus extracurricular life, less than 10 percent of students actually live on campus. The one on-campus dorm is "Residence Hall" with approximately 330 students living within its walls. The rest of the student masses live off campus. For non-Missouri natives, the availability of cheap local housing is one of UMKC's greatest draws. "Coming from out of state I was worried at first about finding a place. It turned out to be the easiest part of coming to college," one student said.

"Coming to UMKC from New York City, I was shocked to see how friendly Kansas City is. People on the street will stop to say hello or good morning."

To facilitate student searches for off-campus housing, UMKC has its own real estate office. It helps students find nearby university-owned rentals while the Welcome Center has listings of non-university-owned property. Students describe the rentals as relatively inexpensive and extremely convenient. The Twin Oaks Apartment complex is popular among students.

Located on the west side of campus, its proximity to UMKC makes it a favorite.

Small-Town Friendliness

Contrary to popular belief, Kansas City is truly a bustling city with the friendly atmosphere of a small town. "Coming to UMKC from New York City, I was shocked to see how friendly Kansas City is. People on the street will stop to say hello or good morning," one student said. Located in one of Kansas City's most happening neighborhoods, UMKC offers its students a lively off-campus social life. Close by are the popular 51st Street Coffeehouse, Main Street eateries, and area parks and museums. Less than a 15-minute walk from campus is the Country Club Plaza shopping and restaurant district. With its Mexican architecture and numerous fountains, the Plaza area is quite a "site." For students wishing to splurge, the Plaza houses such upscale stores as Ralph Lauren and Tiffany's. Lots of students also frequent Abercrombie and Fitch, the Gap, and The Limited. Also nearby is the Cheesecake Factory, a popular restaurant among UMKC students. Within minutes of campus, Westport has many bars featuring live bands, and is the place to be for nightlife. Students would agree that social life in Kansas City is great because it is safe as well as relatively inexpensive. Unlike students at other urban schools, UMKC students report that they don't have to worry so much about safety during a night out on the town.

With its abundance of activities on and off campus, it's no wonder UMKC students have so much school spirit. They rave about UMKC life both inside the classroom and out. As one student said, "I just hate the thought of graduation." —*Alyssa Blair Greenwald*

FYI

If you come to U of Missouri, you'd better bring "a sense of humor."

What is the typical weekend schedule? "Friday and Saturday, go to bars or go out to eat, and sleep in on Sunday."

If I could change one thing about U of Missouri, I'd "make it more geographically diverse."

Three things every student at U of Missouri should do before graduating are "explore haunted Epperson House Hall, be Kasey the Kangaroo, and attend a UMKC-KSU game."

Washington University

Address: Campus Box 1089, 1 Brookings Drive; St. Louis, MO 63130
Phone: 800-638-0700
E-mail address: admissions@wustl.edu
Web site URL: www.wustl.edu
Founded: 1853
Private or Public: private
Religious affiliation: none
Location: suburban
Undergraduate enrollment: 7,219
Total enrollment: NA
Percent Male/Female: 47%/53%
Percent Minority: 26%
Percent African-American: 8%
Percent Asian: 10%
Percent Hispanic: 3%
Percent Native-American: 0%
Percent in-state/out of state: 11%/89%
Percent Pub HS: 61%
Number of Applicants: 19,514
Percent Accepted: 24%
Percent Accepted who enroll: 29%
Entering: 1,342
Transfers: 199
Application Deadline: 15 Jan
Mean SAT: NA
Mean ACT: NA
Middle 50% SAT range: V 640-730, M 670-750
Middle 50% ACT range: 28-32
3 Most popular majors: business, engineering, psychology
Retention: 96%
Graduation rate: 87%
On-campus housing: 80%
Fraternities: 27%
Sororities: 21%
Library: 1,565,626 volumes
Tuition and Fees: $29,053
Room and Board: $9,240
Financial aid, first-year: 42%
Varsity or Club Athletes: 8%
Early Decision or Early Action Acceptance Rate: NA

Undergrads dot the grassy quad with notebooks in their hands and smiles on their faces. Few landscapes are more picturesque, but at Washington University, this is the daily scene. There is an incredible energy in the air as students seize every opportunity to explore life from the safe-haven of their St. Louis school. Like the city that hosts the college, Wash U is a lively, stimulating place that combines Midwestern values and intellectual curiosity.

Pre-Med—Everyone?

According to its students, "Wash U is tough—really tough." Prospective students apply to one of five undergraduate colleges: The College of Arts and Sciences, The School of Engineering and Applied Science, The School of Art, The School of Architecture and the John M. Olin School of Business. The School of Business is notoriously easier than the other four schools, while students in the School of Engineering and Applied Sciences and the School of Architecture reportedly "never sleep." Despite these discrepancies, a comprehensive set of distributional requirements and rigorous programs of study in all five colleges require "a lot of work in order to do well." Math and science are known to be the most difficult and biology and psychology the two most popular majors.

With such a reputable medical school, it seems that "everyone and their brother comes into Wash U pre-med" but they are quickly scared off by the difficulty of the introductory chemistry classes. Popular classes include "Cultural Anthropology" and "Intro to Biological Evolution," and students often recall giving standing ovations to their "phenomenal professors" for lectures in these classes.

Although Wash U may be difficult, students generally feel that the extensive support system will prevent anyone from falling through the cracks. "The University genuinely wants us to do well and there is so much support; it is unbelievable." Professors teach all classes with the exception of the Freshman Writing Class, for which graduate students lead sections. Undergrads claim their TAs are "helpful," but one student said that there's "little point getting help from the TAs when I can go visit my professor just as easily. The staff is absolutely astounding."

The flexibility of the Wash U academic departments is cherished by its students. Frequently, undergrads will complete a major in one school while minoring, double minoring or even triple minoring in subjects directed by other schools. The variety of majors and classes is "almost overwhelming," and it is extraordinarily easy for students to design their own major if the standard fare does not satisfy expectations. One senior reported that the "opportunities and facilities continually amaze me and everyone's enthusiasm is so encouraging, you want to do well for more than just a grade."

Over-Commitment and General Enthusiasm

"I think you'd be hard pressed to find a student who is not involved in at least one extra-curricular," claimed one student at Wash U. With hundreds of clubs and student organizations ranging from "Skydiving" to "Chess," Wash U students are overwhelmed with opportunities to get involved, and almost all students seize this opportunity. In fact, freshman must quickly learn how to say no because, according to one student, "If you did a tenth of everything you could possibly do, you'd never sleep."

The most popular activities include intramural sports (although on the collegiate level women's basketball is the only sport that catches attention), Campus Y (the community service organization), several a cappella and improv comedy groups, and the Congress of the South 40 (the student governing body). Extensive student involvement in all activities is what makes Wash U's extracurricular programs so dynamic. Furthermore, the city of St. Louis provides many opportunities for internships and work. In such an energetic environment, the "possibilities are endless."

Play Hard on Frat Row

"Very wet on weekends and dry as a bone on weeknights," Washington University is best described as the quintessential work-hard, play-hard environment. New students quickly learn that frat row is the place to be every Friday and Saturday night—for everyone. Given their proximity to the headquarters of Anheuser Busch, Wash U students claim a fondness for a certain golden brew, and report no difficulty in obtaining alcohol at any age—however, they are also quick to defend the right to abstain. One student observed that "many underclassmen, particularly guys, do a lot of drinking at the frats," but, when questioned, another male underclassman hailed the fraternities for the amount of respect they give to those who choose not to drink. Dry parties are also known to be well-attended frat events.

In a school where 30% of the student body belongs to one of 11 fraternities or five sororities, Wash U maintains a fun environment that is open and inviting. Deferred rush gives students the chance to relax into Greek life before joining, and one underclassman praised the sororities' inclusiveness. "They are great! They don't haze at all and have a genuine focus on philanthropic work—unlike so many other schools I know."

Frat parties are known to be hook-up events, but many students were surprised at how many committed couples there are. "I get the impression that people are looking to meet someone special," said a female freshman. Homosexual and interracial couples are not commonplace at Wash U, although no one seems to object to them in principle.

Off frat row, popular parties include W.I.L.D., Walk-In Lay-Down, a campus-wide party held on the first and last Friday of the year featuring both local and nationally recognized bands. The Spin Doctors, Outkast, and They Might Be Giants have been recent performers. W.I.L.D. is one of "the few times almost all students socialize together"—beginning around noon and going until late in the night. Additionally, The School of Architecture hosts a biannual "Bauhaus" party that is another popular event, and Thursday night at the Rat (short for Rathskeller—an underground bar and restaurant) is the kickoff to every weekend for fun-seekers.

You Go to School Where?

Once students discover that Washington University is in Missouri, not a pacific northwestern state, they learn to love the city of St. Louis. The clubs, bars, and music of downtown lure upperclassmen who own cars, and even those who depend on public transportation find St. Louis incredibly accessible and appealing. A fifteen-minute walk from campus, "The Loop" is known for it's inexpensive shops and restaurants, and as an "off beat, college-town-like" section of St. Louis. Forrest Park, one of the nations largest public parks, borders campus and provides students with bike trails, wide open greens and outdoor attractions.

"Everyone is involved in everything and incredibly energetic about what they are doing."

Getting people to leave campus tends to be a problem, however. Known as "the most beautiful campus anywhere," and the only school that actually looks like its brochure, Wash U is the place where students want to be. Its gothic architecture and "incredible quadrangles" are often the site of pick-up football games, picnic lunches and study sessions.

Hotels and Turkey Sandwiches

Located on the South 40 (the center of student activity on campus), the dorms of Wash U are considered to be "just as beautiful as the rest of campus." However, housing crunches during the past year have resulted in two new dorm buildings that students say are "more hotel-like than a college dorm should be." Air-conditioned, carpeted rooms and "maid service for the bathrooms" make the decision to leave campus a difficult one for upperclassmen, and the university has had to offer "incentives" including free telephone and Ethernet service to lure students away from the crowded housing system.

Washington University's dining services are praised by some, while others consider the food "pricey" and "lacking in variety." "I have had more turkey sandwiches here than I ever expected to eat in my life," claimed one sophomore. Generally, it is believed that "the food could be better, but no one is starving" and it is possible to get good cheap food.

Abercrombie and Fitch Poster Children

Esteemed as a "moderate to very attractive" student body, Wash U prides itself on having well-dressed students. Although, in general the population is upper-middle class, Wash U is too big to be defined by one stereotype, and students genuinely appreciate the diversity on campus. There are a number of students from metropolitan areas like Chicago and New York, but Wash U also attracts students from other parts of the country and the world—creating an extremely diverse, sophisticated atmosphere. "The people" are universally hailed as what makes Wash U so special. Surprising to many new students, "everyone is involved in everything and incredibly energetic about what they are doing." Students, faculty and neighbors are all "so unbelievably friendly," that even with its other strengths, most students believe that Wash U's greatest asset is its Midwestern charm. —*Emily Barton*

FYI

If you come to Wash U, you'd better bring "an open mind and a daily planner because you will meet so many different types of people from so many places."

What is the typical weekend schedule? "Most people go out either Friday or Saturday night, and go to Frat Row or in to St. Louis' Central West End or to the clubs downtown. During the day we study or go shopping or just hang out with friends and look at the day wasting away."

If I could change one thing about Wash U, I would change "THE NAME!!! Washington University is a pretty generic name."

Three things every student at Wash U should do before graduating are "go to Walk In Lie Down (WILD) . . . go see a St. Louis sporting event, and visit the Loop."

Montana

University of Montana

Address: 32 Campus Dr; Missoula, MT 59812
Phone: 800-462-8636
E-mail address: admiss@selway.umt.edu
Web site URL: www.umt.edu
Founded: 1893
Private or Public: public
Religious affiliation: none
Location: small city
Undergraduate enrollment: 10,193
Total enrollment: NA
Percent Male/Female: 47%/53%
Percent Minority: 9%
Percent African-American: 0%
Percent Asian: 1%
Percent Hispanic: 1%
Percent Native-American: 4%
Percent in-state/out of state: 79%/21%
Percent Pub HS: 70%
Number of Applicants: 3,987
Percent Accepted: 96%
Percent Accepted who enroll: 51%
Entering: 1,968
Transfers: 897
Application Deadline: rolling
Mean SAT: NA
Mean ACT: NA
Middle 50% SAT range: V 490-600, M 460-570
Middle 50% ACT range: 20-25
3 Most popular majors: business, education, conservation
Retention: 70%
Graduation rate: 37%
On-campus housing: 22%
Fraternities: 6%
Sororities: 6%
Library: 952,279 volumes
Tuition and Fees: $4,260 in; $11,860 out
Room and Board: $5,292
Financial aid, first-year: 59%
Varsity or Club Athletes: 4%
Early Decision or Early Action Acceptance Rate: NA

From the center of campus, the top of Mt. Sentinel can be seen peaking out behind the tower of Main Hall, giving visitors a good notion of the two main factors in an average University of Montana student's life: extreme outdoor activities and some academics to go along with them. "The outdoor opportunities here are unbeatable; you can do a different sport everyday if you want: skiing, hiking, fishing, rafting, snowshoeing, rock climbing . . ." Montana Grizzlies all claim that "Big Sky is where it's at."

Schooling

Even with the incessant temptations posed by the amazing natural environment surrounding them, Montana students still know how to balance a serious academic schedule. The university's general education requirement for liberal arts majors requires that all complete 120 course credits and achieve "competency" in three major areas: English/writing composition, math, and foreign language. Students must also take 39 upper-division credits in addition to their major requirements. While some students grumble that the general education requirement covers some of the same material as high school, in general, students view the requirements as beneficial to their undergraduate experience. "Even if you walk into school freshman year thinking that you know what you want to do with your life, the academic requirements force you to take another look around. And hey, when you're 18, that's probably not a bad idea."

Majors at UMontana range from wildlife biology to marketing and management. "The easy majors are the ones in the Business School," one junior explained. More challenging majors include forestry, philosophy or physics. UMontana also has more specified schools under the umbrella of undergraduate studies including the School of Pharmacy and Allied Health Sciences, the School of Education, the School of Forestry, the School of Journalism, and the School of Business Administration. Some students apply for courses at these schools during the admissions process.

The Davidson Honors College is another, more specialized train of study for serious students. Classes in the honors college are small, ranging from 20 to 25 students, and to qualify for admission a student must have finished freshman year, maintained a high GPA, and participated in volunteer service.

"The outdoor opportunities here are unbeatable; you can do a different sport every day if you want: skiing, hiking, fishing, rafting, snowshoeing, rock climbing . . ."

In the larger scope of the university, class sizes range from large lectures of over 300 students down to 25-person seminars. One student remarked that some of the big lectures are notoriously boring. Almost all classes are taught by professors, except a few introductory classes such as math, English and psychology, which are sometimes taught by teaching assistants. Some students made a complaint typical of many schools—that they have trouble communicating with some TAs in the math department since English is not their first language.

One major perk that this state university boasts over many is Dial-BEAR, the class registration process. "It makes registering less of a hassle and gives you a pretty good chance of getting into the classes that you want," explained one student. The process entails students meeting with their faculty advisor before registering, then calling in to find out if they have gotten into the classes they wanted. The priority of last names switches from the first to the last half of the alphabet every other semester, too.

Another facet of undergraduate education at Montana is the study abroad programs. Many students who come from in-state and want to get a diverse perspective on the world—and even some from out-of-state who get tired of the freezing winter temperatures—choose to travel with UMontana faculty to countries such as France, Germany, Australia, Mexico, New Zealand, or other East-Asian nations where they can live with host families.

Bunking Up for a Long, Cold Winter

All the dorms on campus are located within a ten-minute walk of major classroom buildings, "which, trust me, is a major plus in the middle of winter," one junior commented. All freshmen are required to live on campus, which is anything but a dreaded experience, since every dorm is equipped with laundry facilities, game rooms, and lounges for studying, hanging out, or watching TV. One student recalled, "I met most of my best friends in the dorms freshman year; it's the place where you interact with the largest mix of people on campus."

There are upperclassmen RAs living on each floor, enforcing dry campus policy, acting as student counselors and liaisons with the administration. Students contend that "they aren't too strict though." At the beginning of the year, the RAs, along with Peers Reaching Out, a student organization, offer students pertinent information on topics such as sex, drugs, drinking, assault, and stress management. Some dorms have substance free floors or floors reserved for students in the Honors College. Pantzer, a dorm built in 1995, offers students suite-style living while Lewis and Clark Village, a dormitory set to open in the fall of 2004, will soon be available for single students with sixty or more credit hours. Jesse and Aber are the two high-rise dorms, and single-sex housing is offered in Turner (all female) and Elrod (all male). There is also housing for married couples living on campus.

After freshman year, many Grizzlies choose to move off campus into Missoula where there are many affordable housing options within good proximity to campus. The majority of students bring a car to school, but many also get around on bikes or the public bus system, which is free with a student ID. There's also the option of living in a fraternity or sorority house, although it is not hugely popular and numbers are quickly falling off as the administration's ban on booze has tightened significantly over the past few years.

On-campus dining "ain't too shabby" either, students claim. While the food is labeled "decent" or "takes some creativity," dining facilities are "clean and nice," and students can spend their meal plan money anywhere on campus. Trading their meal credits to eat at campus restaurants such as Café Bistro, instead of the main dining hall or "the Zoo" as students affectionately refer to it, is a popular option. Missoula also offers students some excellent restaurant options. Food for Thought is located right across the street from campus, and Finigan's, the Depot, and Pizza Pipeline are also hot spots to grab a bite. If Indian Food is your thing, make sure to check out Tupus Tiger (it's vegetarian, too!). Favorite coffee shops include Cybershack, where you can check your email while enjoying a hot drink, and BoJangle's, which also has live entertainment and poetry readings.

Students spend more than just meal time in Missoula though, adding to the strong relationship between the town and university. Students often see shows at the Montana Repertory Theater or visit the Southgate Mall, and Missoula residents come to see theater and dance productions at the university theater or sporting events at the Adams Center. It is also not uncommon for students to stick around for rafting, kayaking and hiking during the summer.

Grizzlies Got Game?

Sports are popular year-round at UMontana. Students receive special discounts at the nearest ski area, which is 15 to 30 minutes away by car. Other popular winter activities include snowshoeing or trips to indoor gym facilities for climbing walls, weight rooms, basketball and racquetball courts, and exercise rooms. In the more temperate fall and spring seasons, students enjoy hiking, biking and jogging outside. Intramural softball and basketball are popular throughout the year. Some of the most popular varsity sports are the football, women's basketball and soccer teams. Every year, students anticipate the Montana/Montana State football game, where the 20,000 capacity Washington-Grizzly Stadium is packed. Homecoming weekend also draws a huge crowd. Another event not to be missed by U of M students is the Forrester's Ball. For this theme party, the gym is decorated to look like a mining town. Upon entering through the "mining shaft" food and drinks may be purchased for the price of a kiss.

On normal weekend evenings, students either hit up parties off campus, head to the bars downtown, or check out the alcohol free Nite Kourt events sponsored by Residence Life, a student organization that promotes alternatives to the bar scene. In the past, these events have included comedy acts, the free use of a game room, a Velcro obstacle course, laser tag, and mix and mingle gatherings. For a university that is repeatedly rated one of the best party schools in the country, the administration has really tightened drinking regulations on campus over the past few years, starting in 1996 when the campus became officially dry.

As for extracurricular activities, some of the most popular include ASUM (the student government), the student band, Peers Reaching Out, Advocates (a group of student ambassadors to the University), Greek activities, dance and theater productions, and writing for a literary publication or the Kaimon (the university paper which comes out twice a week).

The Beauty of "Big Sky"

UMontana boasts some amazing new and renovated facilities. In 1999, the Field House was renovated and changed into the Adams Center, which included the building of an auxiliary gym, new seating, new weight and training facilities, and the Jacobson Academic Center. Renovations in the University Center included the addition of more eateries, study lounges, student organization offices, a game room, the women's center, a bank, a post office, a hair salon, a computer store, a travel agency, and a ballroom. One student described the greatly improved campus hub as "real sweet."

At the heart of Montana's campus is a large green known as the "oval." In the fall and spring, students draw to the lawn to throw Frisbees, draw, read and socialize;

a good example of how the people at U of M create an intimate and welcoming atmosphere on such a huge campus. One student summarized, "we've got a lot of the long-haired, peace-lovin', hippie thing going on." So if the great outdoors is a necessity and a big school with big spirit is enticing, then U of M in BigSky Montana might just be right for you. *—Susanne Kenagy*

FYI

If you come to U of M, you'd better bring "a warm coat, preferably Patagonia or Northface, unless you want to stick out from the crowd."

What's the typical weekend schedule? "Booze. Outdoors. Booze. Chill . . . homework. Substitute any other activity for a football game!"

If I could change one thing about U of M, I'd "import more non-white folks."

Three things every U of M student should do before graduating are "ski at Snowbowl, drink at Charlie B's, and go to the Forrester's Ball!"

Nebraska

Creighton University

Address: 2500 California Plaza; Omaha, NE 68178
Phone: 800-282-5835
E-mail address: admissions@creighton.edu
Web site URL: www.creighton.edu
Founded: 1878
Private or Public: private
Religious affiliation: Roman Catholic/Jesuit
Location: urban
Undergraduate enrollment: 3,607
Total enrollment: NA
Percent Male/Female: 40%/60%
Percent Minority: 16%
Percent African-American: 3%
Percent Asian: 8%
Percent Hispanic: 3%
Percent Native-American: 1%
Percent in-state/out of state: 50%/50%
Percent Pub HS: NA
Number of Applicants: 2,605
Percent Accepted: 90%
Percent Accepted who enroll: 34%
Entering: 802
Transfers: 95
Application Deadline: 1 Aug
Mean SAT: NA
Mean ACT: NA
Middle 50% SAT range: V 550-640, M 550-660
Middle 50% ACT range: 24-29
3 Most popular majors: nursing, psychology, finance
Retention: 86%
Graduation rate: 70%
On-campus housing: 44%
Fraternities: 22%
Sororities: 28%
Library: 481,848 volumes
Tuition and Fees: $19,348
Room and Board: $6,984
Financial aid, first-year: 51%
Varsity or Club Athletes: 7%
Early Decision or Early Action Acceptance Rate: NA

When asked to name their favorite aspect of Creighton, students agree on one: the size of the school. They say the small size of the campus and classes make it "easy to get to know your professors and people around you." One student remarked, "When you're in a smaller situation, you're more apt to work in teams." Thanks to its size, a student choosing Creighton can expect a warm atmosphere to go along with a rigorous academic program.

Close Interaction

The relatively small enrollment at Creighton makes small classes and close faculty-student interaction possible. Freshman introductory classes like chemistry and psychology hold between 40 and 60 students, while upper-level classes rarely enroll more than 20. Students say the abundance of personal attention from the faculty is one of Creighton's strong points and many delight in the fact that their professors actually know their names.

Creighton has three undergraduate schools: the College of Arts and Sciences, the Business School, and the Nursing school. The Business School attracts many students, and the nursing school is said to be "excellent and pretty demanding." Within the College of Arts and Sciences, biology, chemistry, psychology, and education are the most popular majors—each gets high praise. Students have a hard time naming "worst departments," and besides complaints about the lack of a music program, they say they are generally "pretty satisfied" with Creighton's existing majors and departments.

Those interested in the health fields are particularly satisfied at Creighton. According to one student, "If you're interested in health professions, this is the school for you." A great number of students are interested in medicine, dentistry, and nursing. One student praised the concentration of the student body in the sciences, saying that it allowed him to be "surrounded by people with the same focus, which is important." Many of those who don't go on to medical or dentistry school do graduate work in the sciences.

Academics are described as "competitive" and "challenging, but nothing overly demanding." One student said there are "definitely not any [guts] in the sciences, and most classes are writing-intensive anyway." Another mentioned a gymnastics class as a gut, but on the whole students seem to agree that there are few easy courses.

A Demanding Core Curriculum

A rigid core curriculum exists in the arts and sciences school, which one student said provides "a good base in just about anything." One drawback is that "you're not going to like all the classes you're going to take." To graduate, students must complete 128 credit hours, with 64 of them going toward the core. The core itself is comprised of six classes in theology, philosophy, and ethics; six in culture, ideas, and civilizations; two in the natural sciences; two in the behavioral sciences; and five in skills (English, math, communications). In addition, two intro-level language classes or one higher-level language class is required. The business and nursing schools have different requirements, but all Creighton students, regardless of school, must complete the theology requirement. Some students felt six classes devoted to religion is "a little excessive," while others criticized some of the views taught as "really biased and lame." Defenders of the requirement point out that other religions besides Catholicism are covered and maintained that "religion is never forced on anyone."

One disadvantage of Creighton's small size is its small library. A frustrated student complained that "for major research, you have to go elsewhere." To supplement its limited collection, the three-story Reinhart Library participates in an interlibrary loan system, allowing students to gain access to any book in any college within a week or two. Students also praised the librarians for going out of their way to help.

All freshmen and sophomores must live on campus. Of the four dorms, three are co-ed by floor and the fourth, Deglman, is all-female. One student recommended Deglman to incoming first-year women because "people really get to know each other there." Swanson, "the loudest and dirtiest" dorm, is also the biggest and is known as the party dorm. Another housing option is the small Creighton House, where everyone has his or her own room and takes turns cooking meals. Students also can request to live in specified floors known as the Wellness Community or the Study Community. Study Community floors are meant to be quieter than normal floors, while Wellness Community floors are supposedly substance-free. One freshman living there described the policy as a "joke," however, "because people have beers in their fridges."

For the first two years, undergrads must buy a meal plan. Students eat either in the two main cafeterias or in the Student Center, which houses some fast-food places such as Taco Bell and Godfather's Pizza. When Creighton students want to escape what some feel is the "gross" on-campus food, they frequent such off-campus eateries as Austin's Steakhouse, the Garden Café, and T.G.I. Friday's.

Filling Those Extra Hours

Also at the Student Center are fireside chats, held weekly by school president Father Schlegel, and Java Joint, coffeehouse sessions where students play blues and drink coffee. On warmer days the grassy mall in the center of campus replaces the Student Center as the main hangout. The mall, which still has train tracks on it from the days trains ran through the campus, is the site of one of the biggest parties of the year. During the first week of the fall term, a stage is set up and a reggae band is brought in for Jamaican Jam. Another popular event is called Dim Wand, the name of a hypnotist who comes to hypnotize the students in his audience. A third unusual, popular activity is The Price Is Right, for which Creighton buses students to the nearby Civic Center to compete in their own version of the television game show. Prizes include trips to New York City, mountain bikes, and color TVs.

Regarding social life, one student reported that "there is always something to do," while another added the corollary that "there's not much to do if you're under 21." Off campus, students like to frequent the historic part of Omaha known as Old Market, where bars, restaurants, and shops line quaint cobblestone streets. Other things to do on a weekend include going to the movies, the bowling alley, or frat parties.

About one-third of Creighton students participate in the Greek system, but students report there is no pressure to join and no stigma against the non-Greek. Most frat parties are open to all, so independents do not feel excluded. Although some students say Omaha has a high underage drinking rate, the school administration upholds a strict alcohol policy.

"Some students felt six classes devoted to religion is 'a little excessive,' while others criticized some of the views taught as 'really biased and lame.'"

Many students also participate in community service activities, especially Habitat for Humanity. With organizations such as Habitat, students take service trips across the country during their vacations. Students also go on weekend spiritual retreats. Those interested in journalism write for the weekly newspaper, the *Creightonian*, or work for JTV, the student-run television station. Those with a literary bent work on *Windows*, a quarterly literary magazine.

Students also participate in Division I sports and intramurals. Creighton has no football team, but as one student said, "soccer and baseball rock here." The women's softball team and the tennis team also do well. Creighton Blue Jay athletes practice and play in the Kiewit Athletic Center, while non-athletes use the Fitness Center connected to the Student Center. "Practically everyone does intramurals," said one undergrad, with volleyball, basketball, and soccer among the most popular.

Many undergrads do not consider Creighton's student body diverse; most people come from the Midwest and only a small percentage come from foreign countries. One student saw the homogeneity as a boost for campus clubs: Multicultural activities are a "big thing just because the school is not very diverse." Regarding the political scene, one undergrad said the campus is "not a political hotbed," adding that views were largely right-leaning. The lack of a pronounced lesbian/gay community at Creighton is consistent with this assessment.

When asked what they would tell high school students thinking of applying to Creighton, students advised a visit to the campus, "because if you don't like Omaha, you will be miserable for a while." Undergrads say the city is boring, and some lament that the campus is "not really pretty because it's in downtown." One good thing about the campus is that it's safe. Students say they feel very safe on campus because "Creighton spares no expense" on security. Guards are said to be "always driving around looking for things to do," and will even drive students anywhere within reason at night. In general, however, students said they would tell high school seniors to apply to Creighton simply because "you get your money's worth" through its tough academic program and lots of personal attention. —*Santosh Aravind and Staff*

FYI

If you come to Creighton, you'd better bring "a car."

What is the typical weekend schedule? "Watching movies and chilling with friends. There's really not much else to do here at night because everything closes before midnight. We usually do our homework on Sunday night."

If I could change one thing about Creighton, I'd "bring in more school spirit. We're definitely lacking in that area."

Three things every student at Creighton should do before graduating are "go to a basketball game, volunteer with one of the organizations on campus, and attend at least one church service."

University of Nebraska

Address: 14th and R Streets; Lincoln, NE 68588
Phone: 800-742-8800
E-mail address: nuhusker@unl.edu
Web site URL: www.unl.edu
Founded: 1869
Private or Public: public
Religious affiliation: none
Location: small city
Undergraduate enrollment: 18,118
Total enrollment: NA
Percent Male/Female: 52%/48%
Percent Minority: 10%
Percent African-American: 2%
Percent Asian: 2%
Percent Hispanic: 2%
Percent Native-American: 0%
Percent in-state/out of state: 86%/14%
Percent Pub HS: NA
Number of Applicants: 7,631
Percent Accepted: 78%
Percent Accepted who enroll: 61%
Entering: 3,653
Transfers: 901
Application Deadline: 6 June
Mean SAT: NA
Mean ACT: NA
Middle 50% SAT range: V 500-640, M 520-660
Middle 50% ACT range: 21-27
3 Most popular majors: business, engineering, education
Retention: 81%
Graduation rate: 48%
On-campus housing: 25%
Fraternities: 15%
Sororities: 17%
Library: 1,184,824 volumes
Tuition and Fees: $4,684 in; $12,064 out
Room and Board: $5,207
Financial aid, first-year: 67%
Varsity or Club Athletes: 4%
Early Decision or Early Action Acceptance Rate: NA

At the University of Nebraska, football comes right after a warm winter coat on the list of biological necessities. "You can't go two minutes on this campus without hearing someone mention the football team or seeing a sweatshirt branded with Cornhusker paraphernalia," a junior declared. With five National Championships to their name and arguably the most devoted throng of fans, Cornhusker spirit runs deep in this part of the country, with the university's Memorial Stadium holding the all-time record for 220 consecutive sold-out games. As a freshman summed it up proficiently, "We don't mess around when it comes to football."

Making the Grade

While students don't always speak with the same vitality about studying as they do about last Saturday's football game, they seem to be satisfied with the academic program. The university offers a total of 149 majors, creating a niche for just about everyone in the academic domain. The majors are divided between nine academic colleges: the College of Agricultural Sciences & Natural Resources, the College of Architecture, the College of Arts & Sciences, the College of Business Administration, the College of Engineering & Technology, the College of Fine & Performing Arts, the College of Human Resources & Family Sciences, the College of Journalism & Mass Communication, and the Teacher's College. Workload varies tremendously depending on the major, class, and number of credit hours taken per term. One student summarized, "Basically, if you take a lot of science classes, your workload will be more difficult." Organic Chemistry and Genetics were noted as two of the most grueling classes. The toughest majors and academic programs are Pre-Law, Pre-Med, Anthropology, "and almost any science."

For students seeking a challenging academic schedule, UNL offers the University Honors Program. Students are accepted to the program before freshman year based on high school academic records and standardized test scores. They have access to some of the university's best professors, smaller classes, honors computer centers, and live in special housing in Neihardt Hall. For those willing to reserve most of their energy for the football games, "Generally, most people here are pretty laid-back, and I'd say business majors and English majors are the least difficult," a sophomore explained.

Most classes take place in lecture halls and cater to around 150 students. However, if you're not big on standard lecture classes, "English classes and others similar to that are usually smaller, with about 30 people in them," as an English major commented. No matter the number of students enrolled, however, professors are friendly and willing to work with students' schedules to set up out-of-class meetings. TAs generally serve as helpful guides through complex subject matter. Although one student warned, "You can't count on the TAs in the science department to speak English very well, so while they're always willing to help, sometimes they just don't understand your question."

Living and Eating: the Good, the Bad and the . . .

Students are required to live on campus freshman year, and while many live off campus after that, they generally view the requirement as beneficial to their college experience. "You meet a lot of people that you might otherwise never get to know, some of whom become your best friends." Several of the dorms are co-ed, although bathrooms are single-sex. These dorms, like Abel, are said to be messier and nosier than single-sex dorms like Sandoz, a women's dorm. Love Hall, where residents share household responsibilities and costs, is another on-campus living option for women. Cather and Pound are two upperclassmen dorms that offer their residents laundry facilities and computer clusters on every floor.

All of the first year dorm rooms are fairly similar. Most are doubles and have a basic set of two beds, desks, shelves and closets, as well as a high speed Internet connection and cable. The rooms are air-conditioned, too, which is a major plus on those humid Nebraska days. Freshman dorms are staffed by upperclassmen RAs to keep the dorms a place conducive to studying and sleeping as well.

UNL is a dry campus, and one of the RA's major responsibilities is to help enforce the policy, taken quite seriously by the administration. A sophomore clarified the conditions, "There is no alcohol allowed on campus at all, and the administration has really been cracking down on offenders in the last two years." At a place where, "weekends start of Thurday," and the primary social options are sorority and fraternity parties or the bars on 'O' Street, drinking is a focal point. While a typical Nebraska student may be a pre- and post-gamer (football games are other drinking fests), the administration's position on alcohol makes socializing without booze more fun and feasible for those Huskers who aren't hardy partying types.

> **"You can't go two minutes on this campus without hearing someone mention the football team or seeing a sweatshirt branded with Cornhusker paraphernalia."**

Most of the students move off campus after freshman year due to both the dry campus policy and the abundant availability of inexpensive housing near campus. "Rent is about $250–350 per person and most people really like the idea of finding a group of friends to live with and setting up their own place." Other common housing options are fraternity and sorority houses. While students insist that there is no stereotype for the sort of person who thrives at UNL, one student observed that, "Greek men and women seem to hold more leadership positions on campus." Statistically, the average Greek GPA is higher than the overall university average, as well.

The dining halls are very clean and never too crowded. Speaking to the food's quality, a student commented, "It's decent. Most people complain, but it's a buffet and you can always find soup, salad and sandwich stuff." On the up side, meal plans allow students to eat in any of the dining halls, and their ID cards also serve as charge cards to pick up snacks and meals on the run.

The Layout

The Husker's campus is divided into two sections, City Campus and East Campus. Students agree, "It would be quite a walk between the two, but it's only about a five minute drive." Shuttle buses run between the sections for students without cars. City Campus houses most departments, while the home economics and agriculture schools are on East Campus. As for the favorite buildings on campus, some agree that the Nebraska Union, the campus's social center, is top of the list, while others call for Memorial Stadium, standing for the Husker's passion for football. The Nebraska Union houses the University Bookstore, a convenience store, auditorium, copy shop, game room, food-court and big-screen television lounge. Memorial Stadium also recently underwent renovations in 1999 when $40 million was invested in the addition of new skyboxes.

Something for Everyone

Other UNL teams boast impressive records in addition to football. Some notables are the men's gymnastics team with eight national titles, women's indoor track and field with three, and the women's volleyball team which won the national championship in 1995 and 2000. Intramural sports are the most popular extracurricular activity, offering students an outlet for physical activity as well as a great way to meet new people. Most popular events are flag football and softball. Active students also take full advantage of the Lee Sapp Recreational Center, housing two indoor tracks, a climbing wall, basketball and racquetball courts, and a weight room.

Outside of academics and athletics, students keep busy with an array of other activities including community outreach volunteer programs, various on-campus publications such as the *Daily Nebraskan*, and the performing arts. 'Scarlet and Cream', a men and women's singing and dance group, is among the most prestigious of the performing groups. Many UNL students add a job to their busy schedules, as well. One student predicted that, "about 70 percent of the student body works at least a few hours a week to make extra spending money."

The Greek houses are known for throwing some of the best parties of the year. If you like to get dressed up, each frat and sorority has two formals a year. Every house has theme parties, too. Some recent themes were the '70s, cowboys, disco, doctors and nurses, beach party, and Catholic school. "You name it, and we've done it," a student declared.

Other places to spend evenings out are the bars on 'O' street, frequented by many upperclassmen. The city of Lincoln offers university students more than just a place to bar hop though. There are some great places to catch dinner with a group of friends such as Lazlos, Old Chicago, Ruby Tuesdays, and Applebee's. The Haymarket, a quaint section of town near campus, is a popular place to go on dates, and if you're into movies, there are several theaters down town.

Home football games are all-day events not to be missed. A typical game day begins at the tailgate, reaches its crescendo with students painted red from head to toe, trickling into the evening as students make their way back home to catch a televised game before heading out for some more partying in the evening.

The University of Nebraska, with its celebrated football tradition, array of academic opportunities, laid-back atmosphere and enthusiastic student body presents Huskers with the chance to have some the best four years of their lives. —*Susanne Kenagy*

FYI

If you come to the U of Nebraska, you better bring "a warm winter coat, you usually have to walk a little ways to class and it can get very cold."

What's the typical weekend schedule? "Go to a frat party on Thursday and Friday nights, prime before the football game on Saturday, get pizza after, wake up late on Sunday and do homework in the afternoon."

If I could change one thing about the U of Nebraska, "I'd get rid of the train tracks that run through campus. You have to wait on your way to class while trains pass."

Three things every student should do at the U of Nebraska before graduating are "swim in the fountain in front of the Union, pass library class, and go to a football game."

Nevada

University of Nevada / Reno

Address: Mail Stop 120; Reno, NV 8957
Phone: 775-784-4700
E-mail address: asknevada@unr.edu
Web site URL: www.unr.edu
Founded: 1864
Private or Public: public
Religious affiliation: none
Location: urban
Undergraduate enrollment: 11,752
Total enrollment: NA
Percent Male/Female: 45%/55%
Percent Minority: 20%
Percent African-American: 2%
Percent Asian: 7%
Percent Hispanic: 7%
Percent Native-American: 1%
Percent in-state/out of state: 82%/18%
Percent Pub HS: NA
Number of Applicants: 4,144
Percent Accepted: 90%
Percent Accepted who enroll: 56%
Entering: 2,107
Transfers: 1,019
Application Deadline: rolling
Mean SAT: NA
Mean ACT: NA
Middle 50% SAT range: V 470-580, M 480-590
Middle 50% ACT range: 20-25
3 Most popular majors: education, business, health professions
Retention: 77%
Graduation rate: 39%
On-campus housing: 13%
Fraternities: 8%
Sororities: 7%
Library: 1,082,941 volumes
Tuition and Fees: $2,925 in; $10,195 out
Room and Board: $7,275
Financial aid, first-year: 31%
Varsity or Club Athletes: 3%
Early Decision or Early Action Acceptance Rate: NA

At the heart of the "Biggest Little City in the World" and the base of the Sierra Nevada mountain range lies the University of Nevada Reno. Home to renowned academic facilities, experienced faculty members, a variety of extracurricular activities, and an active social scene, UNR offers it's students "a state university where you can get an Ivy League education."

From Shake Tables to Western Traditions

The undergraduate academic programs at UNR consist of the College of Agriculture, Biotechnology, and Natural Resources; the College of Arts and Science; the College of Business Administration; the College of Education; the College of Engineering, the College of Human and Community Services; the Mackay School of Mines, and the Reynolds School of Journalism. Of the 12 total schools and colleges, the Mackay School of Mines is internationally recognized and the School of Engineering houses the second-largest shake table in the country (used to test roadside structures under earthquake conditions); the Reynolds School of Journalism boasts Pulitzer Prize-winning professors and alumni.

The smaller class sizes available at UNR allow students to develop personal relationships with the school's talented faculty members. Aside from getting to know the reigning experts in areas from terrorism to Chinese studies, one journalism student says, "I can call my Pulitzer Prize-winning professor's home phone number with a question when I'm copy editing for the *Sagebrush* [UNR's student newspaper]."

The UNR honors program draws raves from students. "You're in smaller classes and you get to register early so you can get into any class at any time," says one freshman of the honors program. The only drawback, according to one student, is that "the whole point of the honors program is to get into really good classes your freshman and sophomore years, because after that there aren't any honors classes offered in most majors." Another student agreed, saying that "it's one of those school secrets that everybody knows about."

Students find the workload at UNR manageable, though most agree with the opinion of one senior: "The workload's what you make it. The more priorities you have and the more things you're involved in, the harder the workload seems." Many students find engineering courses to be among the hardest, although many find Western Traditions (WT), part of the core curriculum requirements at UNR, to be difficult as well. Completing the WT requirements, which include philosophy, literature, and history, "includes a lot of reading from primary sources, a lot of writing, and a lot of lectures."

High School All Over Again

Nearly 85 percent of all UNR students come from their home state, Nevada. Of these, 60 percent come from high schools in and around Reno. Like one freshman student, many feel as though "UNR is like an extension of high school. Most of the people I see are either from my high school or from another high school in Reno."

For many native Nevadans, the biggest draw of UNR is the Nevada Millennium Scholarship, which provides generous financial aid to students who meet certain eligibility requirements and graduated from a Nevada high school. As one UNR student said, "How could I turn down the Millennium Scholarship? I'm basically getting paid to go to school here." Some of the out-of-state students and those without the Millennium Scholarship express feelings of resentment toward the "Reno kids going to school for free," but on the whole, the local students and those from outside Nevada find that "it's an easy place to meet people and make friends quickly."

It's All Greek to Me

The majority of UNR's social scene takes place at the fraternity and sorority houses surrounding the campus. Although the fraternity constitutions were recently amended so that they are no longer allowed to serve alcohol, as one students says, "UNR's like any other college campus—there's definitely alcohol here and people definitely have no trouble finding it if they're looking." Of the nine fraternities and four sororities found at UNR, Sigma Nu reportedly throws the best parties and Delta Delta Delta is the most popular sorority. While many students choose to rush fraternities or sororities, those that aren't involved usually agree that they are always welcome at Greek parties.

Students can also find house parties in nearby areas, whether thrown by the intramural rugby team or partiers living off campus. For students 21 and over (or those with fake IDs), downtown Reno offers drinking and gambling at infamous casinos, nightclubs, and bars like The Wall and Beer Barrel.

"It's an easy place to meet people and make friends quickly."

While reportedly some UNR students use drugs, one student assures that "there's no pressure to do anything you don't want to do." Another student agrees, saying, "Everyone is just here to have a good time and have some fun. If you don't drink or do drugs, you'll find the people who don't do that either. If you do drink or use drugs, you'll find people that do the same." Most students agree that marijuana is the most widely used drug on campus.

Something for Everyone

Many UNR students are involved in some type of extracurricular activity. Student Orientation Staff, a group in charge of welcoming incoming freshman to UNR, is one of the largest groups on campus, while the Campus Greens, a liberal organization, and the Feminist Leadership Majority Alliance are also popular clubs. The campus newspaper, the *Sagebrush*, is written and produced entirely by students, and intramural sports are a common way for students to participate in athletics at a less competitive level than varsity sports.

In addition, the student government organization and the student union bring in cultural events and entertainment for UNR students. From concerts to lectures to movie showings, students rarely find themselves with nothing to do on campus.

Battle for the Cannon

Football games are always well attended by UNR students, alumni, and much of the Reno community, but no game can compare with the annual "Battle for the Cannon." Each year the football teams from the University of Nevada Reno and the University of Nevada Las Vegas compete for possession of the coveted Fremont Cannon. The game is held at UNR every other year, when students from both universities pack into Mackay Stadium proudly wearing their respective "FUNR" and "FUNLV" shirts.

While football remains the largest sport on campus, other sports are growing in popularity as well. Volleyball draws a consistent devoted crowd, while soccer and softball are consistently gaining more and more viewers.

Students of All Ages

Most students at UNR (about 75 percent) live off campus and commute to and from school every day. For these students, most agree with one engineering major that "a car is an absolute necessity." Many of these students are older; they hold proper jobs and sustain families. Although not your typical college scene, these older students pepper classes with their life experiences and anecdotes. There is something to be said about age-old wisdom, and younger students actually enjoy the companionship of the older students.

Those who choose to live on campus find themselves in either the Manzanita, White Pine, Lincoln, Canada, Juniper, Nye, or New Hall. While Nye Hall is the oldest and generally has smaller rooms, it is the most actively social dorm on campus. Incoming students hope to find themselves in New Hall, which, as its name suggests, was completed in 2003. As one student describes it, "New Hall has huge, luxurious dorms with vaulted ceilings and private bathrooms in each dorm room." Most halls are co-ed and RAs live with freshman in the halls to ensure that rules are enforced and to provide support for the transition from high school to college. Visitors must sign in and out at the entrance to each hall, and alcohol is prohibited unless all residents are over 21.

Whether for its exciting social scene, its renowned academic departments and programs, its reasonable tuition, or its extracurriculars and athletics, UNR's reputation is growing. More and more out-of-state students find themselves at UNR, while local students continue to enjoy the benefits of the Millennium Scholarship and being able to live at home. As one student said, "At first I was only interested in the Millennium, but now, given the choice, I'd choose UNR again even without the scholarship money. I love it here!" —*Sarah Newman*

FYI

If you come to UNR, you'd better bring "good luck in case you decide to try the casinos."

What is the typical weekend schedule? "Try to do something fun on Friday night; head to an extracurricular meeting Saturday morning; go to a football game Saturday night; and try to get some work done on Sunday."

If I could change one thing about UNR, I would "make the campus level instead of on that hill."

Three things every student at UNR should do before graduating are "watch UNLV lose the cannon, go to a frat party, and figure out what you're really interested in."

New Hampshire

Dartmouth College

Address: 6016 McNutt Hall; Hanover, NH 03755
Phone: 603-646-2875
E-mail address: admissions.office@dartmouth.edu
Web site URL: www.dartmouth.edu
Founded: 1769
Private or Public: private
Religious affiliation: none
Location: rural
Undergraduate enrollment: 4,079
Total enrollment: NA
Percent Male/Female: 51%/49%
Percent Minority: 32%
Percent African-American: 6%
Percent Asian: 12%
Percent Hispanic: 7%
Percent Native-American: 3%
Percent in-state/out of state: 3%/97%
Percent Pub HS: 62%
Number of Applicants: 10,193
Percent Accepted: 21%
Percent Accepted who enroll: 51%
Entering: 1,068
Transfers: 19
Application Deadline: 1 Jan
Mean SAT: NA
Mean ACT: NA
Middle 50% SAT range: V 650-750, M 680-770
Middle 50% ACT range: 27-33
3 Most popular majors: economics, political science, psychology
Retention: 96%
Graduation rate: 93%
On-campus housing: 83%
Fraternities: 24%
Sororities: 22%
Library: 930,500 volumes
Tuition and Fees: $29,145
Room and Board: $8,625
Financial aid, first-year: 51%
Varsity or Club Athletes: 19%
Early Decision or Early Action Acceptance Rate: ED 34%

On the edge of New Hampshire, bordering Vermont, lies a small college town along the Connecticut River. The students at this college in Hanover have access to more outdoor recreational activities than one can imagine. Students can be routinely found canoeing, kayaking, and swimming on the river during the spring and summer months, and ice-skating on the pond during the winter. Surrounded by beautiful mountains to the north, this college even has its own ski lodge and slopes, open to its students. In the autumn, leaf-peepers flock here to admire the colorful foliage and hike along the Appalachian Trail. With so much beauty in their world, one wonders how these students are able to take it all in and still have time to study. To outsiders, this picturesque setting may appear to be an unlikely location to host an institution of higher learning. To those who've been here and who've studied here, this is the *perfect* place.

Welcome to Dartmouth.

Green Ivy

You know how everyone you know in high school—guidance counselors, teachers, parents, and the like—all tell you that college is going to be easier than high school? Well, the students at Dartmouth College don't seem to agree. Many students commented that classes are rigorous and fast-paced, and the "workload is pretty steep," since each quarter is only 10 weeks long. This unique academic schedule is known as the Dartmouth Plan, which divides the school year into fall, winter, spring, and summer quarters. Students choose to study during any three of the four terms each year, and are required to remain on campus for three terms during their first and last years, as well as during their sophomore summer. One perk of the system, however, is that they only enroll in three courses per term.

All of the classes at Dartmouth are taught by professors, and students praise the "close interaction" and attention they receive. However, some lament the fact that the administration under President Wright has recently placed a greater emphasis on professors to research rather than teach. The result is that "newer profs really suck in comparison to the older profs, who still believe that they are teachers first and researchers second." Teaching Assistants (TAs) are usually students who have previously enrolled in a particular class and help the professor grade papers. The quality of the TA can vary greatly; luckily, many classes don't even make use of them.

Several students singled out Education 20: Educational Issues in Contemporary Society as a "life-changing" course, "one of those hardest classes you'll ever love." It is enormously popular every year, drawing over two hundred students and a waitlist for enrollment. Guest speakers from all facets of education are invited to lecture on various issues; past speakers include inner-city teachers, school superintendents, and even the student-body president of a local high school. The education department faculty are known for holding "lively and fun, interactive courses." Professor Andrew Garrod impressed his students by learning the names of all 200 students in his lecture and ran the class like a "discussion seminar, calling on students by name."

Other prominent professors include psych professor Rogers Elliott, who has "been here forever," English professor Peter Saccio, who can "make anybody love Shakespeare," Thomas Cormen, a popular and "brilliant computer scientist," and psych professor Robert Kleck, whose experiments have been repeated on *Oprah.* John Rassias in the French and Italian departments is well known for developing new methods of teaching language, in which students meet in a small group with a professor or TA, during a "drill" session, a "fast-paced daily speaking practice session" that promotes quick thinking.

One biology major commented that "it's a lot harder to get an A in science and math courses than in English and history." A history major corroborated this claim by admitting that "there is some grade inflation in the humanities." Though Dartmouth academic departments are strong all-around, international relations, biology, chemistry, dance, and foreign languages are one of the tops in the nation.

One of the strengths of Dartmouth academics is its commitment to study abroad programs. To fulfill the foreign language requirement, students can opt to go on a LSA (Language Study Abroad), in which they take classes abroad, studying with both Dartmouth and local professors, while living with host families. Another option is to participate in one of over 40 different FSPs (Foreign Study Programs), where students will explore a particular field in an ideal location for study. For instance, there are programs in Coral Reef Ecology in Jamaica, Rainforest Ecology in Costa Rica, and Colonial Literature in Trinidad, to name just a few.

Life's a Party, Drink It Up!

In Hanover, "people tend to drink at the frats on weekends. Aside from that, they do whatever it is that people do," observed one student. The college sponsors various social alternatives to partying on Webster Avenue (a.k.a. Frat Row), such as dance parties, fun fairs, and fake casinos, but with poor attendance, these "haven't exactly been all that the administration had hoped." There are few bars in Hanover, though it does have a dance club called "Poison Ivy," which students don't seem to care for. There's no doubt about it—the social life at Dartmouth revolves around the Greek system, which became the inspiration for the 1978 film *Animal House*, co-written by Dartmouth alumnus Christian Miller '62. Today, Theta Delta Chi hosts a toga party each spring.

"The whole *Animal House* rep is not entirely false," noted one student, "a lot of people drink a lot of alcohol every weekend," though another is quick to claim that "we're no better or worse than any other college in the nation." At Dartmouth, 60 percent of the eligible undergraduate population (non-freshmen) are members of a Greek house. Underage drinking is prevalent on campus and never a problem for those who wish to drink, though they may encounter a limited selection—"you must like beast from the keg," one senior warned. With regard to peer pressure to drink, one sorority member said, "If you're willing to hang out with drinkers and just not drink, people love you. If you aren't comfortable being around people who are drinking, though, I could see there being problems." A male student corroborated this claim by observing, "non-drinkers may feel out of place." In addition to the traditional all-male fraternities and all-female sororities, there are three co-ed fraternities and two co-ed undergraduate "societies" on campus. The undergraduate societies differ from fraternities in that they are non-exclusive and have no pledge period.

A few years ago, the administration launched the Student Life Initiative, an attempt at "reimagining the campus environment" in terms of social and residential life. So far, in an effort to reform the Greek organizations, permanent taps and large refrigeration units have already been eliminated, while stricter drug and alcohol policies are still under consideration. The college hopes to de-emphasize Greek life by organizing and building new residential dorm "clusters," groups of dormitory buildings connected by common areas, which they hope will foster a sense of community and continuity as the center of a student's residential life experience.

Perhaps these clusters will also help revive the dormant love lives of Dartmouth students. "When you don't have time to sleep, do you really think you are going to have time to date?" asked one senior. Most students agree that not a lot of dating goes on. Granted, there are a few successful relationships and "virtually married couples," but the majority of students don't go out on dates. Even if they wanted to go out, the fact that they live in Hanover doesn't help their cause. "There really isn't anywhere to go unless you have a car, because the closest activities are 20 minutes away," one student complained.

Students also blame the Greek system because it fosters the kind of environment where guys are able to just stay at their house, and wait for the girls to go to their parties. "Then, these little nerdy high school boys never learn about asking girls out, the girls get frustrated, and everyone just vents their sexual frustration through random hook-ups" a senior said. Random hook-ups are so prevalent that students often describe relationships on campus as "six degrees of hook-up," meaning everybody knows everybody else through, at most, six different hook-up connections. Residents in the various co-ed houses report having no difficulty meeting members of the opposite sex, though traditional dating still tends to suffer.

The college hosts four big weekend events each year, one during each semester. In the fall, during Homecoming weekend, freshmen build a 70-tier bonfire in the center of the Green, and then take part in the Freshmen Sweep, where they run around the fire the same number of times as their class year—the Class of 06 will run 106 laps. Winter term brings Winter Carnival, and along with it comes free ski days at the Dartmouth Skiway, sledding on the golf course, a polar bear swim at Occum Pond, and the construction of a snow sculpture on the Green.

The Green Key Society, an organization which works on various community service projects at Dartmouth and in Hanover, hosts Green Key weekend in the spring term, when bands will often come to campus for an all-day party. Summer term has Tubestock, which is the highlight of the sophomore summer. During this event, the Connecticut River gets filled with students in inner tubes, floats, or whatever inflatable devices they happen to have.

Students say dance troupes and a capella singing groups are quite popular, although the Dartmouth Outing Club (DOC) has the most members of any student organization on campus. Some project that approximately 80 percent of the undergraduate population have gone on a trip with the DOC. After spending so much time with the natural world, it's no wonder that these students often find themselves streaking and swimming au natural. "People are very open about nudity and sexuality, but not really in a disgusting way," said a biology major. The Ledyard Challenge consists of jumping into the Connecticut River at the Ledyard Canoe Club, swimming across to Vermont, and running back across the bridge back to the club—all done naked, and without getting caught.

Closet Nerds

At Dartmouth, "the thing everyone is always remarking on is how smart they never guessed their classmates were." To an outsider, the students here never appear to study much, and yet still do well in their courses. But the students know that this is because all the studying is done independently, behind closed doors. "They don't engage in boasting games of who has more work to do, but rather act like the 300-page of dense science reading and the 20-page paper they did last night was nothing. It's poor form here to complain about how much work you have to do," warned a senior.

Students describe the typical Dartmouth student as a white, upper-class prepschooler from "just outside of Boston," who wears a North Face jacket over an Abercrombie shirt and Gap jeans. A sophomore observed that "there is a BIG line between [socio-economic] classes here, noticeable in who joins the Greek system," and to which house they belong. In terms of diversity, a history major commented, "It's somewhat homogenous, but not really, probably whiter than most Ivies." Indeed, three-quarters of the student population is Caucasian, though students say the school has been actively recruiting more Native American and international students recently. One complaint voiced by students is that "there is a lot of conformity once students arrive here. Everyone comes in with lofty aspirations and unique traits, but leaves 'Dartmouthized.'"

For a school full of "nerds in high school who tried to cover for being smart by being jocks," sports don't seem to attract much fan support at games, except for the football games during Homecoming weekend. The administration keeps pushing Harvard as the principal rival, though students say that "you can never get a seat at a Dartmouth-Princeton game, and the biggest hijinks always occur at these games." The most popular and well-attended games are for Dartmouth's ice hockey team, which is one of the best in the country. Women's ice hockey, field hockey, and lacrosse also fare well in their leagues.

For the rest of the students, the Kresge Fitness Center is, as one student put it bluntly, "surprisingly bad." The facility does not have adequate equipment or machinery to accommodate the enormous demand by students, strange in light of the fact that Dartmouth requires its students to pass a swim test in order to graduate, and also has a mandatory three-term physical education requirement. Many students also participate in intramurals, putting together teams made up of groups of friends, club members, or frat brothers.

The Big Green

Students describe the Dartmouth campus as "classic New England—red brick buildings" covered in ivy, situated among open green spaces and lots of trees. All of the buildings are centered around the town Green, enclosed by Baker Library at one end, and the Hopkins Arts Center at the other. Also noteworthy are Kiewit, the nine-story underground computer center, and Berry Library, a new addition to famous Baker Library. Berry contains a large collection of books, as well as "a lot of great study spaces," and a media center capable of creating all types of interesting projects.

The "River" dorms and the Choates (which students refer to as the "Chetto") house most of the freshmen, since they have smaller doubles and an ugly facade, which makes them undesirable to upperclassmen. The "River" dorms in particular are the farthest from central campus, forcing students who live there to "walk twenty minutes uphill every day just to eat." In terms of location, one upperclassmen said, "Mass Row is where it's at"—step outside these dorms and you're in front of the dining hall and classrooms. Others flock to the East Wheelock cluster, which is Dartmouth's experiment to replicate the residential experience found in Harvard's House system and Yale's Residential Colleges. To promote bonding among students, the cluster hosts special activities, panel discussions, and even trips to Boston and Montreal throughout the school year. Though farther from the dining halls, the cluster features its own snack bar, which serves the "full range of grill food as one of the dining halls." The rooms in East Wheelock are much larger, with 2 to 4 singles attached to a common room and a private bathroom.

The thing everyone is always remarking on is how smart they never guessed their classmates were.

All of the dorms at Dartmouth are co-ed, a few have single-sex floors, but most floors are co-ed (with single-sex bathrooms). Students say that only about 10 percent of the population chooses to move off campus, and most off-campus housing is so close that "they're practically still on campus." One alternative to Dartmouth housing is to live in one of the fraternity, sorority, or co-ed houses. Because Hanover is a small town, you won't find any apartment complexes near campus, although students will often rent a house with a group of five or six friends, the cost of which is comparable to what they would pay for boarding at Dartmouth otherwise. One bonus, however, is that they get to give their house a cool name like the "Love Shack" or the "River Ranch."

Safety on campus has generally never been an issue. Being in such a rural location, "you're more likely to be attacked by a rabid squirrel than be the victim of a crime." Another student echoed these feelings by adding, "there's hardly any crime, and when there is, it's usually on big weekends when tons of people pour into Hanover and it's harder to keep track of outsiders." This mindset, as well as safety procedures, may be about to change. In 2001, two Dartmouth professors were the victims of a double homocide that took place in their home, just four miles from the center of campus. Still, students appear confident that this is not the beginning of a crime trend of any sort. The last murder that occurred in Dartmouth was in 1991, the one before that, in 1948.

The on-campus meal plan received relatively high marks from students, who, after freshmen year, have a choice of meal plans ranging from $450 to $1200 (with $750 as the typical plan). The four main dining halls (each with a different atmosphere and focus) are cafeteria-style, so that you pay only for what you eat. "It's great because you're not restricted to eating during certain hours and food is available from 7 A.M. to 1 A.M. every day," raved a sophomore. Among students, Homeplate, where healthy food is served, is a favorite. In addition to the dining halls, students are welcome to use their cards to eat at various other smaller cafés on campus, such as Collis Café, which serves excellent homemade fruit smoothies, stir fry, omelets, and baked goods, and The Big Green Bean, a coffeehouse. Despite this, one student felt that "we do not have enough places to eat—every night the dining halls are packed." For off-campus fare, EBAs (Everything But Anchovies) pizza is a late-night staple which delivers until 2:15 A.M. Students also recommend Panda House, which is relatively inexpensive for going out with friends.

The Good Life

Oh the places you'll go after Dartmouth. Theodor Geisel graduated in 1925 and went on to become a popular children's book writer, under the pseudonym "Dr. Seuss." Dr. Seuss is remembered on the freshmen outdoor orientation trips sponsored by the DOC, when the Moosilauke Lodge crew serves green eggs and ham for breakfast on the last day. The college also counts Daniel Webster, poet Robert Frost, former Vice-President Nelson Rockefeller, and former U.S. Surgeon General C. Everett Coop among its notable alumni. Today, Dartmouth graduates can be found involved with government, law, medicine, banking, and consulting. A diploma from Dartmouth is a ticket to the good life.

Students at Dartmouth bleed green. One student lamented, "Four years is not enough time to do all there is to do here. I'm a senior, and the mere thought of leaving makes me want to break down and cry." In the famous Dartmouth College Case argued before the United States Supreme Court, Daniel Webster remarked, "It is but a small school, sir, and yet there are those who love it . . ." And love it, they do. —*Christopher Au and Staff*

FYI

If you come to Dartmouth, you'd better bring "a warm jacket."

What is the typical weekend schedule? "Eat dinner in the food court with friends, tails with a frat, some sort of party, sleep on Saturday, do some work, do something outdoors, cook or order in with friends, go out to a room party or hang out at a frat and play pong. Sunday, we sleep, do a lot of work and watch *The Simpsons*."

If I could change one thing about Dartmouth, I'd "make the administration less strict and intrusive."

Three things every student at Dartmouth should do before graduating are "do the rope swing (if it hasn't been cut down yet), sled down freshman hill, and run around the bonfire."

University of New Hampshire

Address: Thompson Hall; Durham, NH 03824
Phone: 603-862-1360
E-mail address: admissions@unh.edu
Web site URL: www.unh.edu
Founded: 1866
Private or Public: public
Religious affiliation: none
Location: rural
Undergraduate enrollment: 11,496
Total enrollment: NA
Percent Male/Female: 43%/57%
Percent Minority: 5%
Percent African-American: 1%
Percent Asian: 2%
Percent Hispanic: 1%
Percent Native-American: 0%
Percent in-state/out of state: 57%/43%
Percent Pub HS: 79%
Number of Applicants: 10,376
Percent Accepted: 77%
Percent Accepted who enroll: 34%
Entering: 2,709
Transfers: 493
Application Deadline: 1 Feb
Mean SAT: NA
Mean ACT: NA
Middle 50% SAT range: V 500-590, M 510-610
Middle 50% ACT range: NA
3 Most popular majors: business, social sciences, health professions
Retention: 85%
Graduation rate: 68%
On-campus housing: 51%
Fraternities: 5%
Sororities: 5%
Library: 1,101,469 volumes
Tuition and Fees: $8,664 in; $19,024 out
Room and Board: $6,234
Financial aid, first-year: 55%
Varsity or Club Athletes: 6%
Early Decision or Early Action Acceptance Rate: EA 62%

Nestled in one corner of the country among the White Mountains, nature trails, and quaintness of small-town Durham, the University of New Hampshire boasts an intricate balance between a laid-back environment, approachable professors, a marquee hockey program, and many free-spirited people who like to have "lots of fun and drink lots of beer."

Take Action in Academics

Academics at UNH are based on a student's effort and enthusiasm. Many students feel that though "the academic reputation of the institution among the public is perhaps not stellar," the quality of education is certainly strong and the resources are in place for motivated students to attain a top-notch academic experience. As one student explained, "If one is willing to take advantage, UNH has the resources, structures, and professors to provide an excellent broad-based education. Most people end up being very much pleasantly surprised."

UNH has a plethora of majors, including many departments and programs unique to a few colleges and universities around the nation. These include a degree in Water Resources Management and the Dairy Management major in which students have the opportunity to train and study at UNH's own dairy farm. Business is the most popular major on campus, while psychology, philosophy, and communications are considered relatively easy majors. Many students consider the natural and physical science programs the most difficult yet most rewarding concentrations. The English department is also well praised.

Regardless of major, all students are required to fulfill General Education (GenEd) requirements in eight different academic areas. Students feel that, for the most part, the GenEd requirements force students to interact with departments that they normally may have ignored. UNH requires three courses in biological sciences, physical sciences, or technology; and one course each in writing skills, quantitative reasoning, historical perspectives, foreign culture, fine arts, social science, and philosophy, literature or ideas. As one undergrad put it, "The GenEds are key to providing a broad-based education. Granted they may be a pain to complete at times, but they are certainly worthwhile, and most people don't have too much difficulty with them." Be sure not to get your hopes up on finding easy science classes, though: "There are legends of extremely easy, almost fourth-grade-level science courses. No one seems to find these classes though. Most of the science classes, even for GenEd purposes, are challenging," commented a psychology major. GenEd classes tend to be fairly large, but class size, especially in language and upper-level classes, is in general, not perceived as a major problem by most students.

Teaching Assistants help provide "supplementary support and in the sciences, oversee labs," but most teaching is conducted by professors, who students feel are very accessible. "Professors, even in larger classes, definitely want you to get to know them, through office hours or e-mail. However, as with most academic things at UNH, it is up to the student to take the initiative and make it happen."

The Essentials: Sleep and Food

The campus is described as "extremely picturesque," "very New England-like," and "beautiful until the snow turns to mud in the winter." UNH is set on over 200 acres in the mountains, and the campus has plenty of greens and courtyards, and "even [has] a stream though the middle of it."

Dorms run the whole range from "pretty small and dingy" for freshmen to "large-apartment or suite-style for lucky upperclassmen." Most freshmen are assigned to the all-freshmen dorms, Williamson and Christensen. These dorms are reputed for fostering close-knit bonds among students on a floor. Most have "Okay" sized doubles and a number of forced triples. Freshmen, as well as upperclassmen, who seek other options may request to live in the mini-dorms, smaller communities based on themed living. Mini-dorm themes include health living in Marston House, theater and performing arts in Eaton House, and science and engineering in Sackett House. All students also have the option of living in substance-free Engelhardt Hall, which is considered "quiet," though one student felt that the substance-free policy could be "better enforced." Stoke Hall is the largest dorm at UNH, and "where students are stuck living. No one chooses to live in Stoke."

After freshman year, students enter the "haphazard" housing lottery in which seniors are given preference. Gables, Woodside, and Forest Park Apartments offer suites or apartment-style living and are usually inhabited by juniors and seniors. Sophomores, for the most part, live in the centrally located part of campus called "Lower Quad," with popular sophomore dorms being Hunter and Gibbs. The newest dorm, Mills, opened in November 2002.

The food at UNH is described as "varied" in quality. Students have the option of eating at traditional all-you-can-eat dining halls or in more restaurant- and fast-food-style atmospheres. Philbrook, Huddleston and Stillings are the three main dining options. One sophomore said, "The food is pretty average on a day-to-day basis, but the brunch on weekends is absolutely amazing. It's unbelievably good." Another student agreed, adding, "Stillings is supposed to be a bit better than Huddleston or Philbrook, but I can never tell the difference." In October 2003 the university opened Halloway Commons, a two-level dining hall which features an amazing plethora of dining options. From breakfast until its closing time at 9:30 P.M., students can enjoy Halloway's Euro kitchen, Asian station, brick oven pizza, salad bars, delicatessen, grill, and café.

Students can also eat at other locations, including the MUB (Memorial Union

Building) Food Court. Students use their meal plan to get $5.65 towards food at one of the fast-food places within MUB. Options include Taco Bell, Chinese cuisine, a pizza place, a burger joint, and more.

Durham? I Didn't Even Know Him

With their school's location in rural Durham, University of New Hampshire students often fantasize about having more of a big-city life. "Durham has little besides the university," said one student, who quickly added, "I must admit that you get used to it, though it may take a bit of time." Students' favorite hang-outs in Durham include The Licker Store, an ice cream and coffee shop, as well as Mike Libby's Bar. To get more of a variety than the few restaurants and stores that Durham offers, students often make the 20-minute trip to Portsmouth. Wildcat transit, the university-sponsored shuttle system, runs buses to different parts of Portsmouth on a regular basis. A popular destination is the major shopping center with many "affordable, suburban-type restaurants" in the outskirts of the city.

A number of students also have cars on campus. However, parking is reported to be an extreme problem, and "you almost always get a ticket if you park anywhere near anything." Students are also frequent visitors to the mountains. In the more temperate months, many students are active hikers and campers, while skiing rules during the winter. UNH is located near some of the nation's best ski resorts. Killington, Loon, Cannon, and countless others are all potential day-trips.

> **"If one is willing to take advantage, UNH has the resources, structures, and professors to provide an excellent broad-based education."**

On campus, students find entertainment at MUB, the large student center, and at the on-campus movie theater, which plays three or four movies a week. The Whittemore Center Arena, the $30 million stadium complex in Durham, is also well frequented by students. Typical of rural schools, another extremely popular on-campus student activity is drinking. Frat parties are usually "rather raucous and loud but always well attended." For more "laid-back" parties people stick to Gables or other on-campus apartments and houses. Drinking is also extremely prevalent in the dorms, but RAs and other authorities are rather strict about large parties in residence halls. Most students do not find being underage a problem, but some non-drinkers feel excluded from much of the social scene.

Fish on the Ice?

There is "something for everyone" extracurricular-wise, and "almost everyone tries to do something." Members of the student newspaper, *The New Hampshire*, the Outing Club, the radio station, and especially, the athletic teams are all well respected. "Regardless of everything and everyone else, however, hockey players rule this school," said one student. And indeed, hockey games are UNH's most unifying experience, and even non-sports fans attend games. The Wildcats are routinely among the nation's top teams competing for the NCAA and Hockey East titles. Before games, there are huge bonfires and pep rallies, while during games, UNH often leads the Hockey East in attendance. Mayhem breaks loose at all games, especially after UNH's first goal, when one of the frats throws a fish onto the ice. Origins of the tradition are not known to most students, but the tradition is a signifying mark of UNH's school spirit.

One of the most repeated criticisms of UNH is the lack of diversity in its studentbody. There are very few non-Caucasian students, and it seems that everyone hails from a similar background. As one student said candidly, "We have a bit of diversity among white students, but almost no diversity among ethnic or racial groups. I find this a problem, though most students don't seem to notice." At the same time, however, a typical student stereotype is hard for students to describe, although one undergrad was able to offer, "A typical UNH student drinks a lot and is extremely good-looking. It's amazing the number of attractive students we have."

UNH and Durham, New Hampshire may not be for the student looking for a bustling city life or huge department stores. However, for a student searching for a school with lots of school pride, a picturesque campus, and a relaxed atmosphere, the University of New Hampshire fits the bill. —*Nirupam Sinha*

FYI

If you come to the University of New Hampshire, you'd better bring "a thick winter jacket."

What is the typical weekend schedule? "Thursday Night: Hit the frats or Gables. Friday: Make it through class, chill out, and then head back to the frats. Saturday: Go into Portsmouth to the mall and for dinner, go back to the frats. Sunday: try to do some work."

If I could change one thing about the University of New Hampshire, I'd "locate it near more of a city."

Three things every student at the University of New Hampshire should do before graduating are "get a smoothie, go to a hockey game, and watch a movie on T-Hall lawn."

New Jersey

The College of New Jersey

Address: PO Box 7718; Ewing, NJ 08628-0718
Phone: 609-771-2131
E-mail address: admiss@vm.tcnj.edu
Web site URL: www.tcnj.edu
Founded: 1855
Private or Public: public
Religious affiliation: none
Location: suburban
Undergraduate enrollment: 5,961
Total enrollment: NA
Percent Male/Female: 41%/59%
Percent Minority: 16%
Percent African-American: 6%
Percent Asian: 5%
Percent Hispanic: 5%
Percent Native-American: 0%
Percent in-state/out of state: 95%/5%
Percent Pub HS: 65%
Number of Applicants: 6,323
Percent Accepted: 48%
Percent Accepted who enroll: 41%
Entering: 1,232
Transfers: 211
Application Deadline: 15 Feb
Mean SAT: NA
Mean ACT: NA
Middle 50% SAT range: V 570-660, M 580-690
Middle 50% ACT range: NA
3 Most popular majors: business, psychology, English
Retention: 94%
Graduation rate: 81%
On-campus housing: 60%
Fraternities: 41%
Sororities: 59%
Library: 550,000 volumes
Tuition and Fees: $7,443 in; $11,640 out
Room and Board: $7,416
Financial aid, first-year: 47%
Varsity or Club Athletes: NA
Early Decision or Early Action Acceptance Rate: ED 39%

Students from New Jersey have something to smile about. The College of New Jersey, or TCNJ to those from the Garden State, is one of the country's best educational deals. Originally developed as a school for teaching professionals (New Jersey Teachers' College), TCNJ now offers an affordable, world-class education to students from both in and out of state.

No Slacking Allowed

Students at TCNJ are quick to point out the rigor of their academic schedule. From freshman year, students at TCNJ are required to take a number of core courses that span all academic disciplines and modes of thought. Rhetoric I and II deal with writing and public speaking and are required for all students. Other required courses are "Society, Ethics, and Technology" and "Athens to New York"—an intense cultural study of the city requiring 10 hours of community service. One freshman remarked that "Athens to New York" has been the highlight of his year, crediting his "great" professor with his love for the course. Other students were not as quick to praise their instructors. Because professors from all disciplines teach core courses, getting into a good section can be a hit-or-miss process. The rest of the core curriculum is composed of courses in the humanities, natural sciences, and cultural studies. Students at TCNJ are required to be proficient in a foreign language and must also take three semesters of classes that explore non-Western culture.

Founded as a college for teachers, TCNJ still serves as a training ground for future educators. Education is the most popular major, while biology and communications also attract many students. The science majors are considered the hardest majors at TCNJ, although every major seems to have one or two classes that "everyone fears," according to one junior. Many classes are available at the honors level, which is open to all students. TCNJ has an honors program as well as an honors dormitory.

Classes at TCNJ are generally small and personally taught. "It's almost like being in high school," remarked one student who is very pleased with the camaraderie that comes from smaller classes. Classes are always taught by professors, and professors are easy to reach. All faculty hold office hours, and professors respond promptly to e-mails from students. Registration for courses at TCNJ is done exclusively online. Students complain that this registration process is inefficient. "You need to have five different plans, because registration is a pain," lamented one junior. Most students, however, get into classes they enjoy.

Party On

Students at TCNJ agree that the social life at the college revolves around the weekend party scene. One student remarked that, "You would have to live in a hole not to hear about the weekend parties by Thursday or Friday." Most students trek to weekend parties with their respective groups of friends. Parties generally take place at the homes of upperclassmen or off-campus fraternities. Partying in dorms is also very popular, but dormitory rules can be strict. Alcohol is not officially allowed in the dorms, and students can get kicked off campus for three drinking violations. Most students insist, however, that if people are careful and responsible about drinking it is unlikely to get into too much trouble.

"You would have to live in a hole not to hear about the weekend parties by Thursday or Friday."

When students aren't partying on the weekends, they usually drift toward one of the local clubs. Although TCNJ has no real college town, Trenton is only a short drive from campus. Many upperclassmen have cars and routinely leave campus on weekend nights to explore the surroundings. There are also campus-wide events that draw students from their regular party schedules. Bands play at TCNJ "all the time" according to one sophomore, and school-wide formal and semi-formal dances are very popular. Although the college has attempted to provide an alternative to the party scene, some students feel that there is still a lack of activity for those who do not drink regularly. "One comedian came to campus, but everyone left because he sucked," complained one disappointed freshman. Upperclassmen recognize, however, that the administration at TCNJ has worked hard over the past several years to provide alternatives to the party scene.

Despite the wealth of weekend activity on campus, many still consider TCNJ a "suitcase" school. Because most of the students at TCNJ come from New Jersey, it is not difficult to travel home on weekends, and many students do go home every weekend. Even those who like to party often tire of the repetitive scene and drift home or off campus for the weekends.

Living with Friends

Housing is guaranteed for freshmen and sophomores at TCNJ. Most freshmen live in Travers and Wolfe, the only high-rise towers on campus. Most rooms are doubles and have plenty of space for two people. One freshman recommended that all incoming students "bring a rug to make your room feel homier." Adding to the home-like feeling in the freshman dorms are the many residential assistants who live with freshmen. Community Assistants (CAs) live with freshmen and serve as hall organizers. Peer Advisors (PAs) also live with freshmen and help to foster a sense of community among the new students. CAs and PAs plan floor-wide events, and students insist that their best friends become the people on their freshman floor. Floor activities range from study breaks to extracurricular information sessions.

Upperclassmen who receive on-campus housing are thrilled to find themselves living in beautiful townhouses. About ten people live in each gender-by-floor townhouse. Those living off campus often find it difficult to find a place to live, as the area surrounding TCNJ is a residential neighborhood that doesn't cater to college-age students and their budgets. Most upperclassmen bring cars to school, so living a little further from campus is not a huge problem.

People and Places

The TCNJ campus gets mixed reviews from students. Impressions of the campus layout range from "beautiful" to "creepy." Most of the architecture at TCNJ is colonial, grand red-brick buildings with large white columns. TCNJ students love the fall, as the foliage in New Jersey is incredible. Spring finds TCNJ covered in beautiful flowers. Newer, modern buildings are also prevalent on campus, as are construction projects. New social science and biology buildings have been constructed as part of a project to renew many of the facilities at TCNJ. The older facilities at the college, however, still maintain their mystique; Kendall Hall, the music building, is even rumored to be haunted.

One complaint that students often voice is that TCNJ has no real college-town atmosphere. Nearby Ewing is a small residential town with no real commercial area. Trenton and Princeton are both short drives away, so many students find themselves heading for these bigger cities in search of excitement. Philadelphia and New York are both only an hour away, so these cities are also available to all students.

There are plenty of resources for fun on campus, however. The Brower Student Center houses student activity offices and the campus bookstore. Also in the student center are a food court, an arcade, and a billiards room. The Rathskeller, or "The Rat" to TCNJ students, is the only bar on campus, and it is in the student center. The Rat is a popular hangout for students over the age of 21, and this bar often features local bands and singers.

The food at TCNJ, according to students, often leaves something to be desired. Even though the college switched food companies recently, students maintain that the food is not very good. Vegetarian students find themselves with very few dining options, and there are no dining facilities open after 8 P.M.

Active Minds and Bodies

The student body at TCNJ lacks a bit in diversity. Most students are from white, middle-class families. One sophomore insisted, "If you don't own clothing from Abercrombie & Fitch, then you don't belong here!" The college has, however, been making attempts at diversifying its campus. More minorities are attending TCNJ than ever before, and student-led ethnic groups are popular on campus. The Asian American Association produces a huge show every year, and both the Black Student Union and the Jewish Student Union are very active. Extracurricular activities at TCNJ number in the hundreds, with student government organizations being among the most popular.

Sports are also a big part of life at TCNJ. "A lot of the people here are the smart jocks from your high school," reflected one junior. Intercollegiate athletics are very competitive, as TCNJ's Division III sports teams often fare well against Division I teams. Field hockey and soccer are among the most popular sports. Club sports are also very popular, with rugby and lacrosse being the most popular of the club sports teams. There is also an on-campus recreation center with a gym, racquetball courts, and other sports facilities. In addition, several other gyms are scattered around campus to make athletic participation more convenient.

TCNJ students agree that their college offers many opportunities to get involved and have a good time. This New Jersey school always ranks highly among the country's state schools, and TCNJ is quite a bargain for in-state students. TCNJ students are very involved in their college community, and they have a fun time while getting a great education. "I love it, because it's such a fun school," said one freshman. "Who can ask for more than that?" —*Justin Cohen*

FYI

If you come to The College of New Jersey, you'd better bring "your own food."

What is the typical weekend schedule? "Nap until parties on Friday, drink Friday night, sleep late on Saturday, party again, and do all of your homework on Sunday."

If I could change one thing about The College of New Jersey, "I'd make the campus more diverse."

Three things everyone at The College of New Jersey should do before graduating are: "get lost in Ewing; go to a toga party; order from Cluck U Chicken at 3 A.M."

Drew University

Address: 36 Madison Ave, Madison, NJ 07940-1493
Phone: 973-408-3252
E-mail address: cadm@drew.edu
Web site URL: www.drew.edu
Founded: 1867
Private or Public: private
Religious affiliation: Methodist
Location: suburban
Undergraduate enrollment: 1,558
Total enrollment: NA
Percent Male/Female: 39%/61%
Percent Minority: 16%
Percent African-American: 4%
Percent Asian: 6%
Percent Hispanic: 5%
Percent Native-American: 0%
Percent in-state/out of state: 59%/41%
Percent Pub HS: 69%
Number of Applicants: 2,587
Percent Accepted: 72%
Percent Accepted who enroll: 21%
Entering: 397
Transfers: 39
Application Deadline: 15 Feb
Mean SAT: NA
Mean ACT: NA
Middle 50% SAT range: V 560-670, M 540-640
Middle 50% ACT range: NA
3 Most popular majors: psychology, economics, political science
Retention: 85%
Graduation rate: 75%
On-campus housing: 89%
Fraternities: NA
Sororities: NA
Library: 491,489 volumes
Tuition and Fees: $27,906
Room and Board: $7,644
Financial aid, first-year: NA
Varsity or Club Athletes: 21%
Early Decision or Early Action Acceptance Rate: ED 97%

Hailed more than once by the Princeton Review as one of America's "Top Ten Most Beautiful College Campuses," Drew University breaks the stereotype of "ugly New Jersey and its turnpike." With its majestic trees and winding paths, the school has earned the nickname "University in the Forest." Students say stepping on campus is like entering a different world, leaving all kinds of urban ugliness and commercial eyesores behind. Yet Drew offers the best of all worlds, occupying a prime location in Madison, New Jersey, just 30 minutes from the skyscrapers of New York City and less than an hour from the sands of the Jersey shore.

Academic Breadth and Depth

In an effort to ensure both "breadth and depth" in education, Drew University requires its students to complete both a major and a minor. General requirements include two courses in four distribution groups: natural and mathematical sciences, social sciences, humanities, and arts and literature. In addition, there is a writing and foreign language requirement. Most students agree that fulfilling them is "not too much of a chore." Another student remarked with regret, "At first they [the requirements] seem really annoying, but now that I'm done with them, I wish I had taken the time to enjoy them more."

True to the school's liberal arts roots, popular majors at Drew include theater, psychology, and English, but students refrain from sticking their school into a mold. "It's a good mix of arts and sciences, not just a science or English school." Indeed, science majors report "excellent facilities," and one physics major went so far as to say "Drew's physics department is the reason I came here."

Students of all majors praise their school's "warm and caring" faculty. As one student boasted, "Here the professors are concerned about each student—they care about you instead of their master's degree or their book publishing. You're a name to them, not a number." Another student simply said, "Academically, I have no complaints."

Special Stuff

Although the majority of students do come from the New York/New Jersey area, Drew offers a number of special academic programs that draw students from beyond the bounds of metro New York.

Particularly popular is the school's seven-year accelerated medical program, conducted in conjunction with the University of Medicine and Dentistry School of New Jersey. Students accepted to this program complete college in three years and proceed directly onto medical school without having to go through the hassle of the application process. Similar pre-professional programs are available in the fields of law, business, and teaching. The school has a highly developed study abroad program, as well. One student estimated that roughly half of the student population participates in these international seminars, month-long programs in January and June that allow students to study in places from Ireland, to Egypt, to France.

Specifically for freshmen, the First-Year Seminar Program offers students the opportunity to study a topic in depth with small classes consisting of 12 to 16 people. The professors leading these seminars also serve as the students' faculty advisors, giving frosh a head start on building relationships with their instructors. Student feedback on the seminars ranged from good to bad: one first-year described the selection of topics as "anything a kid would ever want to know," while another grumbled that they "only seem interesting until you get to class." In recent years, seminar topics have included the History of New York City, the NCAA and the Student Athlete, and Images of Women in Quebec Literature.

Another very popular Drew program is the Computer and Knowledge Initiative Program through which all students receive a free personal computer, software, and printer upon entering Drew as a freshman. Students praise the free stuff as "awesome—the best!"—an enthusiasm compounded by the fact that these computers are the students' to keep after graduation. Network access in the dorms adds convenience to students' lives and makes for a well-connected student body.

Small School Living

Most students live on campus for all four years, since decent housing in surrounding Madison tends to be expensive and hard to find. But there are few complaints since dorms are generally livable. Housing options range from single-sex suites to co-ed floors of singles. Every dorm has a Residential Adviser (RA) on every floor (usually an undergraduate), and a Residential Director (RD) in charge of everything (usually a graduate student). Students can also opt to live in one of seven theme houses. Among the more popular are La Casa, a Hispanic-American dorm; The Earth House, concentrating on environmental concerns; and Umoja House, the African-American house.

Drew University breaks the stereotype of "ugly New Jersey and its turnpike."

Campus food is described as "pretty good." The vegan line, though repetitive, is edible, and there is a grill room and stir-fry bar for students tired of regular lunch-line fare. Students can either eat at Commons, the only campus dining hall, or use "points" to buy munchies at the snack bar or The Space, both located in the University Center. The Other End is another well-frequented campus eatery. On weekends, the coffee shop-type establishment hosts bands, and students can sit and sip coffee while enjoying the mellow ambiance.

"More than Its Fair Share of Weirdoes"

Students count their school's small size as both a blessing and a curse. As one student explained, "It's great because you get to know people, but it's ridiculous—if there's someone new on campus, you'll know." Though small, however, the student body reportedly does not lack variety. Said one student, "It is a liberal arts school, so you get more than your fair share of weirdoes, but it's still a college so you get every type of person." Apparently the variety works though—different types of people are generally said to "mix pretty well." "There are definite groups, but they're not really exclusive," observed one student. One area in which the school's size can hurt, however, is the dating scene. "There are so few people, so there's not much choice," complained one sophomore male.

The school's small size takes its toll on the social life in other ways, as well.

"There's always something happening—it's just hard to find it sometimes," said one student. Added to the fact that the school has no fraternities and sororities, upperclassman dorms are the primary sites for bacchanalian blowouts. Recent changes in the administration's alcohol policy are reportedly hindering dorm party success, however, as the school cracks down on campus drinking. Thus far, it seems its attempts are working. Many students report that nowadays, parties are often moved to off-campus venues in an effort to dodge the new university regulations.

The Roads of Jersey

Students describe Madison, New Jersey, as "not a college town at all." "Small and quaintly residential," it offers students little more than basic necessities, like a supermarket, a movie theater, and CVS Pharmacy. Sweet Dreams coffee shop is a notable exception, named by student after student as the best place to take a date near campus. Nearby Morristown, with its wider selection of eateries and bigger movie theater, is a fast 5-minute drive for students with cars or friends with cars. On weekends, too, many students with cars will head for New York City, 30 miles west of campus. But since only juniors and seniors are allowed to have cars on campus, underclassmen often have to find their own fun around campus.

Drew students report that there is no shortage of school-sponsored events. Drama tends to be very popular, and student productions are well-attended. Most non-student plays are held at the recently rebuilt S. M . Kirby Shakespeare Theater, while most student performances take place in the Commons theater. Drew is also home to the annual New Jersey Shakespeare Festival, celebrating the Bard and his greatest works. Visitors flock from all over the state to attend this May event. Drew students take a lot of joy in the prestige the event brings to their school. "It's great because a lot of times students can get really involved in planning and preparations for it," said one student.

There's More to Life . . .

Drew athletics are a popular extracurricular activity, thanks to what one student called the school's "phenomenal" facilities. Although Drew has no football team, other sports like soccer and those on the intramural level draw considerable student support and substantial participation. For the not-so-athletically inclined, Drew offers a host of musical, literary, and service groups. Popular a cappella singing groups include On a Different Note and 36 Madison Avenue, or "MadAv." Campus publications like the literary magazine, *Insanity's Force*, and the weekly newspaper, *The Acorn*, give students the opportunity to display their journalistic talents. Community service organizations, especially environmental concerns groups, also enjoy high student participation.

As one student concluded, "Many people are here because they have to be—they don't really think about it and just go through the motions, and because Drew's a very liberal school with lots of freedom, it's easy to just stay that way. But I'd warn everyone not to squander the experience—there's just too much out there to waste time. And what better place to spend your four short college years than Drew?" —*Jane H. Hong*

FYI

If you come to Drew, you'd better bring "a car. There's nothing to do around here on the weekends so you either want to bring a car your junior year or be friends with someone who has one."

What is the typical weekend schedule? "Those with cars usually drive off campus to New York City for their fun. Otherwise, you're pretty much stuck in this boring town relaxing and studying."

If I could change one thing about Drew, I'd "bring in some Greek life to the college."

Three things every student at Drew should do before graduating are "go to Sweet Dreams Café with a date, study abroad, and take a road trip to New York City."

Princeton University

Address: Box 430; Princeton, NJ 08544
Phone: 609-258-3060
E-mail address: NA
Web site URL: www.princeton.edu
Founded: 1746
Private or Public: private
Religious affiliation: none
Location: suburban
Undergraduate enrollment: 4,779
Total enrollment: NA
Percent Male/Female: 52%/48%
Percent Minority: 35%
Percent African-American: 8%
Percent Asian: 12%
Percent Hispanic: 6%
Percent Native-American: 1%
Percent in-state/out of state: 14%/86%
Percent Pub HS: 57%
Number of Applicants: 14,521
Percent Accepted: 11%
Percent Accepted who enroll: 73%
Entering: 1,164
Transfers: NA
Application Deadline: 1 Jan
Mean SAT: NA
Mean ACT: NA
Middle 50% SAT range: V 680-770, M 700-780
Middle 50% ACT range: NA
3 Most popular majors: history, English, political science
Retention: 98%
Graduation rate: 97%
On-campus housing: 97%
Fraternities: NA
Sororities: NA
Library: 5,315,332 volumes
Tuition and Fees: $28,540
Room and Board: $8,109
Financial aid, first-year: 51%
Varsity or Club Athletes: 23%
Early Decision or Early Action Acceptance Rate: NA

Every year crazy Princetonians are known to swallow live goldfish, serenade upperclassmen with love songs, and streak through campus. But unlike at other schools, these wild acts are not performed in the name of school spirit, nor are they for fraternity pledging—students are trying their hardest to make their way into the elite of the elite, the crème de la crème, the eating clubs of Princeton University.

Bicker All You Want

Eating clubs were established at Princeton in the 1800s with the dual purpose of replacing the Greek system and providing students a place to dine while the refectory grew more and more crowded as admission rates climbed. From the outset these clubs were picky; only after a lengthy period of interviews and scrutiny do the successful students gain membership. This process of evaluation that takes place during the second semester of sophomore year is called "bicker."

This time-honored tradition, once referred to by alumnus F. Scott Fitzgerald as an "orgy of sociability," has been controversial from its inception, primarily because of its unnecessarily exclusive nature. University President Woodrow Wilson noted in 1906, "About one-third are left out in the elections; and their lot is deplorable. They go forward to their graduation almost like men who are in the University but yet not of it."

Although today more than half of the eleven eating clubs are sign-in clubs that skip the bicker process and do not cut applicants, the process has always garnered criticism from students. At times, this elite process of selection has even been spotlighted by the national press. Four years ago *The Wall Street Journal* published a series of articles that essentially accused the most prestigious eating club, Ivy, of discriminating on the basis of religious affiliation and race, although many students argue this is not the case.

In spite of the exclusivity, the bicker clubs have enjoyed increased popularity in recent years, seeing a 20 percent increase in the number of students who bickered the selective clubs, making it close to 80 percent who enter the process each year. However, one junior in a sign-in club explained, "Much of the old school glory associated with [bicker] clubs has deteriorated . . . This is largely due to the changes they underwent when they became co-ed." In addition to Ivy, Cottage, Cap and Gown, Tiger Inn, and Tower go through the bicker process. Each club has a distinct identity. While Tiger Inn is "all about alcohol," Cap and Gown is athletic, and Terrace F. is "artsy." Students tend to become identified by their eating club. Although one freshman maintained, "the snobbiness is pretty bad," another noted that the exclusivity "isn't always a negative," because it enhances the eating club experience "for those lucky enough to reap its benefits." One Cottage member stated, "The aura of elitism and mysticism surrounding the eating clubs is . . . grossly exaggerated. The real problem is not so much elitism, but more the resultant segregation of groups on campus. Yet with all their faults, the clubs offer a great sense of community and a relatively safe social scene." Another maintained, "I have friends in all eleven clubs, friends who are independent, friends who are members of co-ops, and friends who continue to live in the residential colleges. I'm frustrated that I see less of these people than when we all ate in the same dining hall, but I also have a huge number of friends in my club who I get to eat with every day."

Housed in former mansions equipped with dining rooms with long banquet tables and spacious areas for social events, the clubs are big enough only to provide living quarters for the officers. Meals are prepared by chefs, and the food is reported to be "exceptional," particularly when compared to dining hall fare. The more ritzy clubs, like Ivy, even have waiters. Prospect Avenue, dubbed "the Street," is the site of all 11 clubs and the heart of Princeton's social life. While some of the clubs will have bouncers or be "member's only" on a given night, there are almost always clubs that are open to everyone.

Day by Day

A "Gothic paradise," Princeton University has one of the most striking campuses in the nation. "We even study it in our Intro Architecture class," noted one junior. Stretching 500 acres of immaculately manicured lawns, the campus, "looks like it was taken out of a movie." Located in a suburb of New Jersey, the campus combines a safe and enclosed ambiance with an artistic and antique style. Ivy (the plant, not the eating club) creeps up the walls of the stone buildings and the large gates make it feel like its own community within a larger town. Although the towns surrounding Princeton are not particularly exciting, it is close enough to large cities that students don't feel isolated. Nonetheless there is much more to Princeton than its pretty façade and grounds of grandeur.

Unlike many universities, Princeton guarantees housing for all undergraduate students. Freshmen and sophomores are required to live on campus and spend their first two years in one of five residential colleges—Rockefeller, Mathey, Butler, Wilson, and Forbes. Each college has its own dining hall, common room, and computer cluster, as well as its own master, dean, resident assistants (RAs), and faculty advisers. Although slightly removed from the other colleges, Forbes is said to have the best double rooms as well as the best food on campus. However, getting good housing in this college is simply the luck of the draw: a number of freshmen in Forbes are assigned to run-down rooms known as "Freshman Slums." After freshman year, most students move into upperclassmen dorms and a small handful move off campus.

"I feel like I'm having the quintessential collegiate experience."

Overall, students report that the food served in the college dining halls is decent, although one freshman commented, "The menu is so redundant you get really sick of the cuisine really fast." It features grill items, vegetarian and vegan options at every meal. If you're hoping to avoid the monotonous rotation of meat loaf, freshman and sophomores can use their meal plan at Frist (the campus center) for late meals, which are so tasty that Frist was ranked number one in a national survey on college dining. Upperclassmen, however, do not eat in the college dining halls. This is why they may join an eating club or else a co-op where students prepare meals for each other. If these options are unappealing, they can declare themselves "independent" and cook alone. The most popular off-campus eateries include Hoagie Haven, PJ's Pancake House, and

Chilis, while T. Sweets, which has "the most phenomenal ice cream with mix-ins," is not to be missed.

The Academic Intrigue

Princeton's distinguished faculty alone has drawn many a student into New Jersey territory. Lecturers include acclaimed journalists, Nobel laureates and prominent politicians—even a former president of France. Those who help give Princeton its academic claim to fame include writers Toni Morrison and Joyce Carol Oates, historian James McPherson and philosopher-historian Cornell West. In addition to being respected and renowned, professors are also surprisingly accessible. Students of all majors unanimously agree that close relationships with faculty members are easy to maintain. With less than half as many grad students as undergrads, the university's graduate program is relatively small, so many professors actively pursue undergraduate teaching. Even freshmen entertain close relations with professors and faculty advisors. However the larger courses do have mandatory sections, called "precepts," in which students interact with TAs, not professors.

In addition to being proficient in a foreign language, completing a one-semester writing class, a junior essay, and a senior thesis, students must take a minimum of 30 courses in seven distributional areas: Epistemology and Cognition, Ethical Thought and Moral Values, Historical Values, Literature and the Arts, Social Analysis, Quantitative Reasoning, and Science and Technology. Much to the dismay of humanities-oriented students, one semester of math and two semesters of a lab science are also mandatory. Those who dread the sciences, however, can work around the requirement by taking statistics-oriented social sciences, like election statistics.

Freshman seminars, usually of ten to 15 students, offer the opportunity to work in a small group setting and discuss innovative topics. More than 60 different seminars are offered each year, and recent topics have ranged from Blasphemy and Pornography to Extraterrestrial Life and Literature. Some Princetonians feel that the rigor of academics combined with the elite reputation fosters a ruthless environment. One sophomore said, "The general atmosphere at Princeton is too serious. People need to lighten up and realize there is more to life than getting *the* Princeton degree." She added, "A lot kids here are almost too focused and miss out on a lot of the good things Princeton has to offer." However, a junior disagreed, "Everyone has interests outside of studying. I've found the environment to be surprisingly laid back."

Most courses are reading-intensive, but the workload varies depending on your major. While a junior history major cited an average of 20 to 25 hours per week, another student claimed it was much less, only eight to ten hours per week. Students agree that the most strenuous majors are engineering and molecular biology. For those whose interests lie beyond a single field, "certificate" programs that are like minors are offered. Courses at Princeton range from elementary to overwhelming. "Shake and Bake" (Earthquakes and Volcanoes), "Nuts and Sluts" (Abnormal Psychology) and "Rocks for Jocks" (Introductory Geology) are notoriously easy, while a course on The Divine Comedy is described as "Dante's next level of Hell."

Bright College Nights

Weekends at Princeton begin Thursday night at "the Street" with parties at the eating clubs. For the most part these events are not members-only, although some clubs distribute a limited number of tickets when featuring particularly popular bands or DJs to prevent overcrowding. Even if you can't get in to a party, "you'll still bump into all your friends along the way and have a good time." One freshman observed, "The street itself feels like a night club!"

Alcohol is easily attainable at these parties, but students agree that there is no pressure to drink. Kegs are tapped in the appropriately named "tap rooms" in the basement of each club and are therefore separated from the dance floors upstairs. One senior noted, "It's nice how they are kept separate so that you can have a sober-free, wild night and not feel awkward about not drinking." However another student pointed out that "there's pretty much nothing outside of 'The Street,'" and wishes "there was more of a bar scene or that kids threw more room parties." Because fraternities and sororities don't have houses, their activities are limited to meetings, room parties, and the occasional off-campus formal. Coupled with the fact that only ten to 15 percent of the student body is Greek, this means that Greek life does not significantly contribute to nightlife. In fact, fraternities have had such problems with recruitment and financing that Beta Theta Pi demoted its status from "fraternity" to "social club" in fall of 2002. One student noted that the only reason the system at all visible is because certain frats and sororities are prevalent in certain eating clubs. For example the SAEs and Pi Phis dominate Ivy, while Thetas and KAs fill Cottage, etc.

Fridays at Princeton are noticeably tamer and referred to as "culture nights." On these evenings students head for the a cappella concerts, improv shows, or theatrical productions. The more ambitious trek to nearby New York City or Philadelphia (both less than an hour away by train) to visit friends, see the sites, or tag along with college-sponsored excursions to Broadway shows. Saturdays are much like Thursdays, and students head to "the Street" until the wee hours of the morning.

The "weekend of the house parties," a three-day-long extravaganza hosted by the various eating clubs, is unanimously cited as the biggest event of the year. One student explained, "It's like a three-day-long prom," involving a semiformal, a formal, and a day of lawn parties, for which students stick with the same date. One sophomore recalled, "It's so stressful finding a date, everyone starts getting frantic more than a month before."

Diversity University?

Although Princeton recently instated a "need blind" financial aid policy and over half of students receive some form of financial aid, many nevertheless insist that the university has a very upper-crust feel. This may be surprising considering that students hail from every class and background, from all parts of the U.S. and from over 60 different countries. However one junior observed that the student body is more diversified in terms of nationality than race. Another argued that these similarities are "not really focused on since we all have different niches." The wide array of student interests helps to counterbalance the homogeneity that exists within the student body. "The most wonderful thing about being here," one student explained, "is that each person is amazingly talented." She explained that she is constantly surprised "by the depth of people's interests—it's really cool to discover that my next-door neighbor is not only a Westinghouse scholar, but also an amazing poet, or that a girl in my history class used to dance with a professional ballet company." Yet in spite of this diversity, one junior complained, "Everyone here is a little too cliquish." Another lamented, "I'm frustrated a little by the cliquishness. The fact that I know there are a ton of amazing kids I'll never meet just because we run in different circles is really disappointing."

Students can channel their interests into any of the 200 some odd student-run organizations that span from intramural sports to science-fiction discussion groups to student government. The Student Volunteer Council (SVC), which has the largest membership of any club at Princeton (more than 70 percent of the student body), serves as an umbrella organization for community service projects. It places students into various community service projects in the neighboring cities of Trenton and Newark. Additionally, for the musically and theatrically inclined, performance groups abound: there are 11 a cappella groups, a glee club, several large bands and smaller ensembles, and an orchestra. Favorites among thespians and audiences alike include, improv comedy groups (the most renowned being Quipfire!), the Princeton Shakespeare Company, and the Triangle Club—a one-of-a-kind musical comedy ensemble.

Although some complain that support for the varsity sports teams is really lacking, hundreds grab their furniture and head to the fields to add it to the bonfire lit when the Tigers defeat Yale or Harvard's football team. Another annual ritual is the Cane Spree, a day of passionate competition between the freshmen and sophomores that culminates in mud wrestling. Sadly, one of Princeton's most famous traditions, the Nude Olympics, was banned by the administration in 1999. With all of these opportunities, the average student is "really happy to have the privilege of attending Princeton and partaking in all of the wonderful activities and academics." Asked to describe the best thing about Princeton, one junior concluded, "I feel like I'm having the quintessential collegiate experience." —*Amanda Stauffer*

FYI

If you come to Princeton, you'd better bring "preppy clothes—something lacoste or polo."

What is the typical weekend schedule? "Thursday night party 'til 1:00, Friday no class (unless you're a freshman), then movie / date night, Saturday go to a basketball game then party until 3:00, 4:00 or 5:00 A.M.—most students are out at the Street, but many pregame in dorm rooms from 10:30 to midnight, Sunday sleep in, eat brunch, work."

If I could change one thing about Princeton, "it would be the excess of big lectures. It seems that so many of the great professors find themselves teaching 300 person lecture classes rather than 12 person seminars."

Three things every student should do before graduating from Princeton are "tailgate at the Yale / Princeton game, swim naked in the Woody Woo (Woodrow Wilson School) fountain, and do the 'Prospect 11' when you drink a beer at each eating club."

Rutgers University

Address: 65 Davidson Road #202; Piscataway, NJ 08854-8097
Phone: 732-932-4363
E-mail address: admissions@asbugadm.rutgers.edu
Web site URL: www.rutgers.edu
Founded: 1766
Private or Public: public
Religious affiliation: none
Location: suburban
Undergraduate enrollment: 28,070
Total enrollment: NA
Percent Male/Female: 47%/53%
Percent Minority: 39%
Percent African-American: 8%
Percent Asian: 20%
Percent Hispanic: 8%
Percent Native-American: 0%
Percent in-state/out of state: 92%/8%
Percent Pub HS: NA
Number of Applicants: 26,678
Percent Accepted: 55%
Percent Accepted who enroll: 35%
Entering: 5,086
Transfers: 1,328
Application Deadline: rolling
Mean SAT: NA
Mean ACT: NA
Middle 50% SAT range: V 530-630, M 560-670
Middle 50% ACT range: NA
3 Most popular majors: social sciences, psychology, biological sciences
Retention: 88%
Graduation rate: 65%
On-campus housing: 47%
Fraternities: NA
Sororities: NA
Library: 4,737,147 volumes
Tuition and Fees: $7,927 in; $14,441 out
Room and Board: $8,027
Financial aid, first-year: 50%
Varsity or Club Athletes: 3%
Early Decision or Early Action Acceptance Rate: NA

Rutgers is a school with many faces. While the name Rutgers may refer to one university, it encompasses multiplicity of experiences. More a system of schools than one institution itself, Rutgers University, New Jersey's public university, is comprised of three campuses across the Garden State—the oldest and largest at New Brunswick and two smaller locations at Newark and Camden—as well as schools within these campuses.

As different and distinct as they are, each campus and school offers a unique academic, social, and extracurricular experience of its own. Rutgers is a university of commuters and dorm-dwellers, of hardworking academics and tireless party-goers. Indeed, you can sample every flavor of college lifestyle and take advantage of a vast selection of exciting opportunities at such an expansive state school—as long as you're willing to brave the nuisances of Rutgers life.

Cows and the City

With over 50,000 students system-wide, Rutgers is a behemoth of a university. The university spans three separate campuses: Camden in South Jersey, Newark in the North, and the largest, New Brunswick-Piscataway, which is the physical and figurative center of the system. What's more, each location houses several subordinate colleges: while Camden encompasses a College of Arts and Sciences and undergraduate business school, Newark is home to its own liberal arts college, in addition to schools for business, nursing, and criminal justice. As home to over half of the Rutgers population, New Brunswick offers a whopping ten undergraduate colleges: Cook College for Agricultural and Environmental Studies; Douglass College, the Women's College at Rutgers; Livingston College (a "progressive and contemporary" school that offers socially relevant programs); Rutgers College (New Brunswick's oldest and largest liberal arts college); the Edward J. Bloustein School of Planning and Public Policy; the Ernest Mario School of Pharmacy; the Mason Gross School of the Arts; the Rutgers Business School; the School of Communication, Information, and Library Studies; and the School of Engineering. All three campuses offer university programs for adult students.

Each school has its own academic focus, and, fittingly, its own personality and look. One Cook College student proudly proclaimed the beauty of her campus. "Cook Campus is probably one of the nicest campuses—very green, many open spaces, but plenty of trees and lots of squirrels. We have an outdoor roller rink and volleyball sand pits, and barbecue grills everywhere. And a swing set." Nonetheless, students agree that the buildings around campus leave much to be desired. "The architecture is not overly impressive. Most of it is utilitarian and brick, built 30 years ago or so," one freshman said.

Between the urban streets of Newark and the more suburban area of New Brunswick-Piscataway, Rutgers University boasts both rural and urban campuses. One freshman said that one of the defining features of the New Brunswick campus is "the smell on a rainy fall afternoon. We have horse stables next to the freshman dorms, cows further down the road, and a 'piggery.'" Meanwhile, Newark students enjoy a "campus" integrated into New Jersey's largest city with all the trappings of a cosmopolitan cultural center. Students cite Newark resources such as the recently completed New Jersey Performing Arts Center as invaluable to Rutgers-Newark students.

Despite the marked schism between the urban landscape of Newark versus the quieter areas of Camden and New Brunswick, one issue—campus safety—concerns Rutgers students university-wide. "Outside of campus, it can get pretty dangerous," one Newark student said. "Inside the campus it's pretty safe. There are police cars all over the place." New Brunswick students expressed a similar concern, despite their campus's more suburban location. "We were warned during orientation that some parts are like the 'hood, and we were also actually warned that some parts *are* the 'hood by [a] security officer." But New Brunswick students are quick to add that, "Once you get past that area, there is a decent downtown area."

Excruciating "Expos"

According to Rutgers students, the academic requirements do force some people to take classes that they might never have considered before. "Just like most other colleges, you have to take some sciences if you're a fine arts major and dance if you are a bio-tech major," one student said. "All that we are missing is mandated physical education classes." Students insist, however, that fulfilling these requirements is not very troublesome. "Everyone tries to cover all areas by choosing classes that overlap like 'Writing Papers in the Biological Sciences' to cover an English and a science course."

Yet there is one dreadful gauntlet of a course that all freshmen are forced to endure. "Expository Writing," not-so-affectionately known as "Expos," is universally hated among Rutgers students. "Basically, they choose two readings and tell you to make some kind of connection," one sophomore recalled. "You would have to analyze the two readings really closely and try to find some common ground between them, like one reading on potatoes and another on military groups. You would have to B.S. a lot, but it would have to make sense." Students profess that the class is a lot of work and not very gratifying. "I used to stay up all night writing my papers," said one student.

"Since it is a state school, a significant fraction of people go home on the weekends."

With so many schools under its canopy, Rutgers offers academics that cover the spectrum of difficulty. Each college and campus has its own personality: Livingston, for example, is widely considered the easiest to get into and graduate from, while the School of Pharmacy, while prestigious, is renowned for being rigorous.

Dealing with Numbers

Rutgers offers several unique programs that prepare students for less popular, yet fruitful careers in fields such as veterinary medicine and pharmacy. The School of Pharmacy, in fact, offers a well-respected 2+4 Program. Students spend two years at either the Camden or Newark campuses and upon completing that "preprofessional" phase move on to study for four "professional" years at the New Brunswick practice. This accelerated program allows students to receive their Pharm. D diplomas within six years, yet it does so at a cost. "You really have to love pharmacy in order to stick with the program," one student said.

Students say that large class sizes and poor TAs are significant problems at Rutgers. One freshman commented, "The worst thing is the size of Rutgers as a whole, because it means enormous classes, like 3000 biology students in eight classes, or getting stuck with recitation grad students who can barely speak English or don't know what they're doing." A Cook College student, however, insisted that these problems vary from college to college. "Cook College is relatively small, so we receive a good deal of individual attention in certain classes and with academic advisors." However, the same student concluded, "It's hard to go from a close-knit high school to being a number."

The Commuter Experience

For 90 percent of Rutgers-Netwark College of Arts & Science students, college life does not involve a dorm. While convenient for some who live in the area, complaints about the commuter lifestyle are common among Newark students. "It's really hectic because you have to get up early and go to class early and if you have lecture you have to get to class early to get a good seat," said one student. Moreover, students say that, especially in a school as large as Rutgers, commuting makes it hard to meet people. "If you drive to school, you don't get as much interaction with people, so I guess you miss out in a way."

Even on the New Brunswick campus, people find themselves off campus often. "Since it is a state school, a significant fraction of people go home on the weekends," said one New Brunswick freshman. For people that do stay on campus for the weekend, though, students say there's plenty to do. Greek life, especially on the mainly residential New Brunswick campus, offers the majority of the parties, where "lots of people go to party and drink." However, one student insisted, "If you're not interested in frat parties, there are also many clubs you can join. In fact, Rutgers offers clubs like the Medieval Club. One student said of the organization, "They tried to recruit my friend as a member, asking if she know how to sing, dance, or sew because they have no women in their club. No wonder they have no women."

"Rutgers Brings People Together"

Although the prospect of attending such a densely packed university may seem overwhelming, students insist that meeting people often comes naturally. One New Brunswick sophomore said, "My hallmate would be friends with some guy I met online a long time ago—it's just a lot of connection everywhere." According to students, Rutgers can help your love life, too. "People from all over New Jersey come here, and it's good to get to know people from the South when you're from the North," said one student. "My boyfriend is from Lebanon, New Jersey, and I'm from Jersey City. I never would have met him if I didn't come to Rutgers." Indeed, as one sophomore happily concluded, "Rutgers brings people together." —*Christopher Lapinig*

FYI

If you come to Rutgers, you'd better bring "readiness to deal with Expos—they're the worst."

What is the typical weekend schedule? "Party on Thursday; hangover Friday morning; go out with friends Friday night; sleep in until noon on Saturday; chill and do some homework on Saturday night; and then catch up on readings on Sunday."

If I could change on thing about Rutgers, I would "make the food better."

Three things every student at Rutgers should do before graduating are "accidentally hit on a cute professor or TA, mistaking them for a student in your class; buy food from one of the grease trucks; and go to any game—even if the team loses—because at least they give you free stuff to lure you in."

Seton Hall University

Address: 400 South Orange Ave, South Orange, NJ, 07079
Phone: 973-761-9332
E-mail address: thehall@shu.edu
Web site URL: www.shu.edu
Founded: 1856
Private or Public: private
Religious affiliation: Roman Catholic
Location: suburban
Undergraduate enrollment: 5,080
Total enrollment: 10,000
Percent Male/Female: 48%/52%
Percent Minority: 30%
Percent African-American: 11%
Percent Asian: 8%
Percent Hispanic: 9%
Percent Native-American: 0%
Percent in-state/out of state: 79%/21%
Percent Pub HS: 70%
Number of Applicants: 5,575
Percent Accepted: 85%
Percent Accepted who enroll: 25%
Entering: 1,165
Transfers: 288
Application Deadline: rolling
Mean SAT: 1062
Mean ACT: 24
Middle 50% SAT range: V 480-590, M 490-600
Middle 50% ACT range: 22-27
3 Most popular majors: business, education, social sciences
Retention: 79%
Graduation rate: 53%
On-campus housing: 42%
Fraternities: NA
Sororities: NA
Library: 506,042 volumes
Tuition and Fees: $21,580
Room and Board: $8,550
Financial aid, first-year: 71%
Varsity or Club Athletes: 6%
Early Decision or Early Action Acceptance Rate: NA

At Seton Hall University, two traditions dominate the school: Catholicism and men's basketball. Despite the large number of commuters, students at the Hall enjoy a sense of community and a busy social life. Between hanging out on the campus green and spending weekends in New York City, students can enjoy the best of both worlds.

Academic Life

Seton Hall comprises six undergraduate schools—the College of Arts and Sciences, W. Paul Stillman School of Business, College of Education and Human Services, College of Nursing, School of Theology, and School of Diplomacy and International Relations—to which students must apply individually. Besides being the largest undergraduate division, the College of Arts and Sciences features Seton Hall's popular communications program, which boasts such successful alums as sportscasters Dick Vitale and Bob Ley. Communications majors take advantage of state-of-the-art studio facilities, including those for Pirate TV and WSOU, the popular student television and radio stations.

The "internationally renowned" School of Diplomacy and International Relations draws many applicants and has brought to campus such speakers as UN Secretary-General Kofi Annan. Other popular undergraduate programs include nursing, secondary education, and business, while the sciences attract fewer majors. "Must take" classes include "Zen and Yoga" and "Scuba Diving."

Though Seton Hall retains strong ties to its Catholic tradition, one student emphasized that "there are people here of every race, creed, and religion—our diversity is part of our strength." Undergraduates are required to complete two religion courses, though "they can cover any religion, not just Catholicism," noted a senior. Priests often teach courses on both religious and secular subjects.

Academic requirements vary by school and program, though for most undergrads "the core curriculum is long—at Seton Hall it can be tough to graduate in four years." Many students must take summer classes or enroll in as many as six classes in a term, though AP credits from high school can fulfill many of the requirements and help to lighten the academic burden.

Classes are generally very small. Although some freshman intro classes approach 100 students, half of Seton Hall's classes enroll fewer than 20. Undergrads rave about the accessibility of the faculty, noting that most professors keep regular office hours and will give students their home phone numbers. Though teaching assistants reportedly help run science labs, a senior recounted "I never had a TA in my four years at Seton Hall."

"Technology plays a huge role both in and out of the classroom at SHU," reported a communications major. Seton Hall provides inexpensive IBM laptops for all undergrads, and students praise the university's online course registration system. *Yahoo Internet Life* magazine recently ranked Seton Hall as the nation's #1 most "wired" Catholic university.

Location, Location, Location

Seton Hall's location in South Orange, New Jersey (except the Law School, which is in Newark) is a major factor in some students' decision to attend. A majority of undergrads are from the Northeast and like the school's closeness to home, especially since approximately 40 percent of the students are commuters.

What sets Seton Hall apart from comparable schools, according to one undergrad, is the University's proximity to New York City: "within 15 minutes, you're in the greatest city in the world. New York is our place to hang out." Students are less willing to praise the town of South Orange, which according to one student is "not really a college town. There are two or three bars, and that's it." Though the university "SHUttle" provides transportation to local towns, students agree that New York is the preferred weekend destination.

Although students feel safe on campus, some noted that one side of campus approaches Newark, which can be dangerous. Students describe campus security as "effective." There are pedestrian escorts, gatekeepers at the two entrances, and constant patrols. Students carry ID badges that they must show at the front desk of any dorm, and must sign in visitors.

A Mix of Old and New

A mix of old and new buildings, the Seton Hall campus is small and self-contained. The Bishop Dougherty Student Center is the social hub of the campus, and houses the cafeteria, student organizations, and Pirate's Cove—a "dark and comfortable" coffee house that sponsors musical performances and poetry readings. With the arrival of spring, students migrate outdoors onto the large, central green. Some even "live and sleep on the green in spring," according to a senior.

Students generally praise Seton Hall's on-campus food options. At the Galleon Room, the main dining facility, undergrads can sample from national chains such as Kentucky Fried Chicken and Taco Bell, an "authentic" family pizzeria, a "homestyle" sandwich shop, and other traditional dining hall options. Although the cafeteria remains open until 1 A.M., students often order take-out from El Greco's pizzeria, Cluck U. Chicken, and local Chinese restaurants.

When students aren't grabbing a quick bite late at night, they are usually hitting the books. "The jewel of the Seton Hall campus" according to one student, the $20 million Walsh Library is the preferred destination for studying. Students take advantage of the 400 study carrels and many group-study rooms on the library's third and fourth floors, though some wish that the library would extend its hours and remain open past 11 P.M. on weeknights and 5 P.M. on weekends.

"Technology plays a huge role both in and out of the classroom at SHU."

All Seton Hall students have free access to a weight room, Olympic-size swimming pool, indoor track, and multipurpose courts in the massive Brennan Recreation Center. The facilities are reportedly in good condition, though one senior complained, "the weight facility is lacking."

Seton Hall has no on-campus residency requirement, and many students either move off campus or commute from home. Nevertheless, those who reside on campus feel that living in the dorms exposes them to a more vibrant social life and fosters a stronger sense of community with their fellow students. Xavier is reportedly the best dorm, featuring private bathrooms (shared by two doubles) and wall-to-wall carpeting. Older halls, such as Boland Hall (the freshman dorm) and Aquinas Hall, are less popular. Options in dormitory living include nonsmoking floors, substance-free floors, and Ora Manor—university-owned apartments for upperclassmen a few blocks from campus. Although the university does not permit official fraternity houses, many Greeks opt to live together in off-campus housing.

The Social Scene

Seton Hall undergrads get involved in a wide array of activities. Popular extracurricular activities include intramural sports, the weekly student newspaper, *The Setonian*, the yearbook, *The Galleon*, the campus radio station, gospel choir, the Student Government Association (SGA), and a pep band for basketball games. The diverse student body participates in many special-interest organizations, including the Women's Resource Center, Black Student Union, African Student Leadership Coalition, the Latino organization Adelante/Caribe, and the Filipino League. A Student Activities Board sponsors movies, while many undergrads are involved in community service projects organized through DOVE, Seton Hall's Division of Volunteer Efforts. Popular campus events include the Pirate Queen and King Contest, the Senior Formal, and University Day, a fall Saturday when Seton Hall opens its doors to parents and the community.

Commuters have little trouble participating in extracurricular activities, since most organizations meet during the afternoon. The university has established a commuter lounge and a commuter council, which raffles off a great parking space each month. Nevertheless, one undergrad said that being a commuter makes it "a little more difficult socially—it's not as easy to meet so many people."

Sports and More

Seton Hall's Division I men's basketball team dominates the university's sports program. Come winter, students flock to Continental Airlines Arena to watch their Pirates face arch-rival Rutgers and out-of-state competition like St. John's and Georgetown. The Midnight Madness pep rally before the first basketball practice also draws a huge crowd. Since Seton Hall does not have a football team, men's and women's soccer rule during the fall. The baseball team also attracts a loyal following, with many students watching the games while partying atop the university parking garage.

Beyond basketball, Greek life is a significant social force. "For the size of the campus, we have a pretty high percentage of students who are Greek," observed one student. Big events include formals and the fall Greek Week competition between the fraternities and sororities. Although the Greek parties and activities are not exclusive events, one student admitted that it is difficult to know where and when these events are if you are not part of the Greek system.

Nevertheless, plenty of social opportunities are available to those who don't rush. Commuters and residents alike come out for Pirates basketball games, participate in campus organizations, and take advantage of the "incredible" social and cultural life of New York City. As one senior summed it up, "If you like being in the middle of everything, Seton Hall might be just the place for you." —*Justin Albstein*

FYI

If you come to Seton Hall, you'd better bring a "map of Manhattan, our weekend playground."

What is the typical weekend schedule? "Thursday night—go to bars or a frat party; Friday—date night; Saturday—go clubbing in NYC; Sunday—recover."

If I could change one thing about Seton Hall, I'd "bring back the football program, which was discontinued in 1982."

The three things that every student should do before graduating from Seton Hall are "go to a Pirates basketball game, explore New York City, and party on top of the parking garage during a Pirates baseball game."

Stevens Institute of Technology

Address: 1 Castle Point Terrace; Hoboken, NJ 07030
Phone: 201-216-5194
E-mail address: admissions@stevens.edu
Web site URL: www.stevens.edu
Founded: 1870
Private or Public: private
Religious affiliation: none
Location: urban
Undergraduate enrollment: 1,757
Total enrollment: NA
Percent Male/Female: 75%/25%
Percent Minority: 46%
Percent African-American: 4%
Percent Asian: 25%
Percent Hispanic: 9%
Percent Native-American: 0%
Percent in-state/out of state: 65%/35%
Percent Pub HS: NA
Number of Applicants: 2,049
Percent Accepted: 50%
Percent Accepted who enroll: 38%
Entering: 390
Transfers: 53
Application Deadline: 15 Feb
Mean SAT: NA
Mean ACT: NA
Middle 50% SAT range: V 560-650, M 640-710
Middle 50% ACT range: NA
3 Most popular majors: engineering, computer science, biochemistry
Retention: 88%
Graduation rate: 57%
On-campus housing: 75%
Fraternities: 30%
Sororities: 33%
Library: 61,536 volumes
Tuition and Fees: $26,960
Room and Board: $8,500
Financial aid, first-year: 70%
Varsity or Club Athletes: 19%
Early Decision or Early Action Acceptance Rate: ED 47%

What makes Stevens different from other schools? "Laptops," said one student. "Freshmen get their own laptops for free." Other perks? Internship programs, a happening Greek frat scene, and frequent trips to New York City. Stevens Institute of Technology offers a diverse, stimulating environment for students with a strong interest in the sciences. Because of its relatively small undergraduate population and its location just across the Hudson River from Manhattan, Stevens provides the atmosphere of a small college with the resources of a throbbing, energetic city.

Work at the Core

Academics at Stevens are both rigorous and thorough. Depending on the major, schedules are determined by a preset course track that students follow from the start of freshman year. As the school name suggests, students do not come to Stevens to major in English. "We see the same 30 students every day in all our classes," one student said. "We travel around together." But some students find that the course track is "very annoying, because we have to take a lot of classes we don't need."

The most popular major at Stevens is engineering, even though the core for engineering is "much harder" than that of science majors. Some other popular majors are computer science and chemical biology. Like every school, Stevens also has a major for the so-called "slackers"—business technology. However, students at Stevens hesitate to call any of their peers by that name. "There really are no slackers here; everyone has to work hard. But the course load for biz tech compared to engineering is very, very light." Biz Tech, includes a "watered-down version" of calculus and a lighter core.

Stevens' professors are knowledgeable, but many students have trouble following them in class. As one student stated, they "know a lot, but can't teach, and you end up having to teach yourself." However, another student said, "The professors are always there, there's always someone to contact if you don't understand something." There was mixed opinion about the TAs. One student said, "The TAs are not always helpful, because many have limited English experience," while another said, "Some of the TAs can't really speak English, but, overall, they are good."

Because students must take 19 to 21 credit hours a year, which is an "abnormally high number for a regular college," they usually end up doing work "deep into the night," as one student said. "If you can't work on your own, you won't survive," warned one student. "You have to have independent study habits. If you know how to study, you'll do fine." "We have too many classes," one student complained. "They are quite a bit of work," another student agreed. "It was an academic shock."

Stevens has several special programs: the seven-year doctorate program, the seven-year dentistry program, the Co-op program, and the Reduced Load program. The Reduced Load program allows students to graduate in five years with a tuition-free fifth year, allowing students an easier time with their classes. The Co-op program offers students a five year plan in which they pick three out of the ten semesters to work at a company instead of taking classes. Companies such as Johnson and Johnson, Colgate, Merck, and Lucent come on campus and conduct interviews. Students are paid about $7,000 a year for the internship. Most students enjoy their experience, but some students complain that their job consists solely of "running errands." Other students, however, are able to conduct chemical experiments during their internships. "It's really great because you alternate between working and going to class. What you learn in the classroom you bring to your internship and what you learn during your internship you bring to the classroom," one student said.

It's All Greek to Me

The Greeks are "involved with every organization on campus," one student stated, making them a ubiquitous presence at Stevens. They also hold parties such as the popular Halloween weekend party, Christmas parties, and weekend parties. To the chagrin of many students, this past year the school declared a "dry period," during which any frats or sororities caught serving alcohol to underage students were forced to shut down. At parties, girls generally have their choice of dance partners—the guy-to-girl ratio at Stevens is a staggering 7 to 2. As one student said, "Girls are treated like queens." One female student said, "It's a lot easier to meet guys here—the majority of my friends are guys."

As most students are from New Jersey, many freshmen go home on weekends. But those who stick around on campus have plenty to do. As one frosh said, "There's lots to do, you just have to be motivated to do it." For the non-partier, the largest lecture rooms in Buchard Building, which are converted into movie theaters on weekends, offer an attractive alternative. Jacobus Hall, the student lounge, is equipped with couches, a large-screen TV, billiards table, and climbing wall, and popular clubs such as Exit, Hammerstein Ballroom, Bahama Mamas, and Planet are right around the corner in Hoboken and New York City. Hoboken, according to one student, has "more bars per square mile than any other city in the world." Being underage is an inconvenience, but not a big problem because of all the other activities students can take part in. Another popular location is Washington Street, which is described as being the "main hangout," complete with "everything you need—clothes, restaurants, food, groceries, and ATM machines."

Typical Stevens Students

The self-described stereotype of Stevens students is "nerdy," "dorky and always sitting in front of the computer," or "very math-oriented." But is this stereotype really accurate? Some students agree: "For the most part it's true; if you go here, you're gaining a lot of math background. People spend a lot of time in their rooms in front of the computer." But other students disagree. As one student said, "Most people aren't really like that; people like to have a good time here."

Stevens students tend to form cliques according to ethnicity, Greek affiliation, or which sport they play. "People tend to self-segregate here," one student said. Another said, "I'd like to see a little bit more diversity—Stevens is very lacking in that respect."

Students spend a fair amount of time on extracurricular activities at Stevens, "between five and seven hours a week." And "if people hold office in the Greek organizations, they are much more active," one student said. Some of the most popular activities are: ethnic groups like the Chinese Student Association, Black Student Union, and Latin American Association; the co-ed service fraternity, Alpha Phi Omega; and the weekly newspaper *The Stute*. About 80 percent of the students at Stevens are part of the work-study program.

"Girls are treated like queens."

As a Division III school, athletics at Stevens generate much enthusiasm within the athlete population. For instance, it is common for volleyball players to watch soccer matches, and for lacrosse players to rally behind the volleyball team. However, team spirit is distinctly lacking within the "non-jock" population. Although there is no football team, both men's and women's lacrosse teams, as well as the women's soccer team, have performed very well in the past. For those who do not want to play varsity sports but still wish to keep in shape, the Charles V. Schaefer Jr. Athletic Center, renovated just two years ago, offers a gym and a pool, as well as basketball, squash, and tennis courts. Intramurals are very popular, and so are spontaneous games of ultimate Frisbee, volleyball, and lacrosse on the spacious lawns.

Setting and Sustenance at Stevens

Freshmen are guaranteed housing—men live in Davis Hall and women in Humphrey Hall. Although there is no air-conditioning, the double rooms are "livable" and no more than five to ten minutes away from classes. With all the freshmen living together, groups form pretty quickly. "Most people meet their closest friends in the hall they live in," one student said. After freshman year, there's a "big fight" for the best dorm rooms. Seniors and juniors get first pick for a room in one of the five dorms on campus. The most expensive residences are Castle Point Apartments, which have rooms equipped with a kitchen, bathroom, and two rooms.

The campus itself is "beautiful. It's right on the waterfront; the location is extremely good." Said one student: "There's lots of grass, lots of trees, you have the city right next to you and when you look across the river, you see Manhattan." Parking is a problem, even though freshmen and sophomores are not allowed to park their cars at Stevens unless they commute. According to one student, "the security is not that great, but you don't really need it. People think Hoboken is ghetto, but nothing's going to happen to you."

One student said bluntly, "the food really sucks, but they're trying to make it better." A recent effort to "make it better" was renovating Pierce Dining Hall, the main eatery on campus. "They added more types of food, like Asian and Italian; it's roomier, more convenient, and everything looks a little more appetizing," a student said. Besides Pierce, there are fast-food joints and late-night cafés around campus.

A Degree with a Good Reputation

When asked whether they would return to Stevens if given a second chance, most students were thoughtful but generally answered affirmatively. "I'd probably choose the school again because it's close to home and it's small," one student said.

So what kind of person is right for Stevens? As one student put it, "If you're looking for the typical college experience, our campus life isn't rich enough. If you're not sure about what you want to do, don't come here. But if you're looking for good engineering experience and a degree with a good reputation, this is the school for you." *—Frances Cheng*

FYI

If you come to Stevens, you better "bring a jacket, because the school's a wind tunnel."

What is the typical weekend schedule? "The weekend doesn't start until Friday night, and most frosh go home, but some students go to the city, hang out with friends, or eat in Hoboken. Sunday is saved for studying."

If I could change one thing about Stevens, "I'd improve campus life quality."

Three things every student at Stevens should do before graduating are "enjoy the fireworks displays from Castle Point, go bar-hopping on Washington Street, and get internship experience."

New Mexico

New Mexico State University

Address: Box 30001, MSC 3A; Las Cruces, NM 88003-8001
Phone: 505-646-3121
E-mail address: admissions@nmsu.edu
Web site URL: www.nmsu.edu
Founded: 1888
Private or Public: public
Religious affiliation: none
Location: small city
Undergraduate enrollment: 12,531
Total enrollment: NA
Percent Male/Female: 46%/54%
Percent Minority: 52%
Percent African-American: 3%
Percent Asian: 2%
Percent Hispanic: 44%
Percent Native-American: 3%
Percent in-state/out of state: 82%/18%
Percent Pub HS: NA
Number of Applicants: 5,706
Percent Accepted: 81%
Percent Accepted who enroll: 44%
Entering: 2,049
Transfers: 520
Application Deadline: 28 Aug
Mean SAT: NA
Mean ACT: NA
Middle 50% SAT range: NA
Middle 50% ACT range: 18-23
3 Most popular majors: criminal justice, elementary education, accounting
Retention: 72%
Graduation rate: 46%
On-campus housing: 18%
Fraternities: 4%
Sororities: 3%
Library: 4,000,000 volumes
Tuition and Fees: $3,216 in; $10,788 out
Room and Board: $4,422
Financial aid, first-year: 60%
Varsity or Club Athletes: 6%
Early Decision or Early Action Acceptance Rate: NA

Less than an hour north of Mexico, in the middle of the desert, lies the oasis of New Mexico State University. The town of Las Cruces charms most with its Southwestern Navajo style and hospitable feel. With its strong agricultural and applied sciences programs, a spacious campus, a varied and lively social scene, and its abundance of cultural diversity, NMSU is the place for those looking for a quality education with a relaxed atmosphere.

Viewing a Wider World

New Mexico State University students enjoy a wide variety of majors under the six undergraduate Colleges of Business Administration, Education, Human and Community Services, Arts and Sciences, Agriculture, and Engineering. While some majors, like communication studies or family and child science, are considered easier than others, most students agree with one senior in that "the workload is challenging, but rewarding at the same time."

Many students rave about the "Viewing a Wider World" program, in which students are required to take six credits in departments other than the one they are majoring in. In the words of one communication studies major, "You really find out a lot about other areas that you otherwise wouldn't have even thought about learning about."

One opinion that all NMSU students seem to be able to agree on is the accessibility and helpfulness of the faculty. One student offered, "All of the professors I've had here have been really approachable and willing to help in any way they can. Most of them are always asking students to come to their office hours, even if it's just to talk to them for a little while."

From El Paso to Mexico

NMSU students enjoy a social setting as diverse as their student body. The large university is home to an active and popular Greek system, not to mention that El Paso is less than an hour away with its restaurants, movies, theater, and other entertainment. The college often sponsors activities, such as the well-attended homecoming bonfire and a variety of cultural events. Meanwhile, the local night clubs sometimes sponsor college nights for students of all ages, and, of course, in the words of one student, "There's a lot of partying going on." Many underage students, particularly freshman, prefer to cross the border into Mexico to party, where it's more difficult to get into trouble for underage drinking. Greek life does exist, and although frats only attract a small percentage of the student body, they do throw parties almost every weekend.

"Our student body is really amazingly diverse. I had expected a lot of Caucasian or Latino students, but now I've got friends from Japan, Kuwait, and Thailand."

The dating scene at New Mexico State University is variable as well. In the words of one student, "There are definite random hook-ups. There's definitely dating. There are some homosexual couples and definitely some interracial couples. Some people find their future husband or wife here. It's such a big system that there's a lot of everything going on."

Forego Food and Embrace Diversity

Most agree that dining out is superior to the meal plan at school, which the majority forego. In the words of one senior, "I think they've made some improvements in the food here since my freshman year, but back then, even the people who paid for their meal plans wouldn't eat that stuff." Instead, students prefer a number of on-campus restaurants that serve everything from Mexican to Chinese to pizza.

While all its students love NMSU for different reasons, an overwhelming majority agree that the school's diversity is one of its best features. As one family and child science major puts it, "Our student body is really amazingly diverse. I had expected a lot of Caucasian or Latino students, but now I've got friends from Japan, Kuwait, and Thailand."

In addition to student appreciation for all the different cultures represented at NMSU, the school administration and the Union Program Council (UPC) host regular cultural events to celebrate the different customs of all the students.

"The Horseshoe"

New Mexico State University is one of the nation's largest campuses. Much of the space comes from the school's renowned Agriculture Department, but all NMSU students can enjoy their wide, spread-out campus. Some of the favorite spots on campus include "The Horseshoe," a wide ring of buildings spread out in the shape of its name. There, students can find everything from athletic facilities to ROTC practice fields to student services and the financial aid office. One senior, however, enjoys the Horseshoe for one of its less well-known features, "I love the duck pond! It's my favorite place on campus." What's more, the Horseshoe is just outside of the student dorms, making it a convenient place for students to visit.

Whether it is New Mexico State University's highly regarded academic programs, the great cultural diversity, the warm and sunny weather, or just the duck pond that strikes your interest, NMSU students would agree with the advice of one communication studies major, "This is a really great place to go to school. I'd choose to come here again without a doubt, and, in fact, I only wish I'd known about it earlier." —*Sarah Newman*

FYI

If you come to New Mexico State University, you'd better bring "a pair of sandals."

What is the typical weekend schedule? "Do some sort of on-campus activity, hang with friends, get some sleep in, and do some work."

If I could change one thing about New Mexico State University, I'd "stop raising the tuition fees."

Three things every student at New Mexico State University should do before graduating are "go to El Paso, go see the *mariachis*, and visit the duck pond."

University of New Mexico

Address: Student Services Center 150; Albuquerque, NM 87131-2046
Phone: 505-277-2446
E-mail address: apply@unm.edu
Web site URL: www.unm.edu
Founded: 1889
Private or Public: public
Religious affiliation: none
Location: urban
Undergraduate enrollment: 17,166
Total enrollment: NA
Percent Male/Female: 43%/57%
Percent Minority: 46%
Percent African-American: 3%
Percent Asian: 3%
Percent Hispanic: 33%
Percent Native-American: 7%
Percent in-state/out of state: 88%/12%
Percent Pub HS: NA
Number of Applicants: 6,232
Percent Accepted: 76%
Percent Accepted who enroll: 59%
Entering: 24,821
Transfers: 966
Application Deadline: 15 June
Mean SAT: NA
Mean ACT: NA
Middle 50% SAT range: V 510-630, M 480-600
Middle 50% ACT range: 19-24
3 Most popular majors: business management, health professions, education
Retention: 72%
Graduation rate: 46%
On-campus housing: NA
Fraternities: NA
Sororities: NA
Library: 1,800,000 volumes
Tuition and Fees: $3,169 in; $11,436 out
Room and Board: $5,300
Financial aid, first-year: 49%
Varsity or Club Athletes: 7%
Early Decision or Early Action Acceptance Rate: NA

Comprised of sprawling green lawns and adobe buildings in Albuquerque, New Mexico, the University of New Mexico is a college that gives students the opportunity to be what they want. Among its 30,000 enrollees are recent high school graduates, preprofessionals, and continuing-education students returning to college. This diversity offers undergraduates a unique college experience in the heart of a Southwestern city.

Academics: Lost Among Many, but Not Lost in Life

Many students enter UNM with a good idea of their career paths. Thus, although there is a significant percentage of students in pursuit of their bachelor's degrees in the liberal arts, many opt to take the preprofessional route. "Everyone is pre-something," said one student, "and the premedical and prenursing tracks are huge because UNM is a great medical school." According to students, this can make the environment "very competitive," especially in the larger "weed-out" introductory science courses. Some students report that because of the high number of students, getting into classes can sometimes be tricky, especially for undergrads who want to take graduate-level courses. Students having trouble with the material can, however, seek help from the free tutoring program offered by the library.

Despite the dominance of preprofessional programs, students also noted that the geology and photography departments are quite good. Classes are largely taught lecture-style at UNM and sometimes number 300-plus students, with the smaller math and English courses numbering 20 to 30. Some students complain about the large class size, but note that if a student is motivated, closer, fulfilling professor-student relationships are easy to come by. Academic facilities are outstanding, with six libraries, and a number of good study and social centers, including the Student Union Building (SUB) and the Cellar.

Looking for a Party?

The UNM party scene is dominated by fraternities and sororities. According to students, the more popular fraternities are Kappa Sig and Sig Ep and the most notable sorority is Kappa Kappa Gamma. The biggest campus parties of the year are the fall and spring "Crawls," during which the city and Greek houses team up to close off the streets around campus. There are a number of activities for attendees, including cardboard mazes set up in the fraternities for students to crawl through. Older students say they prefer the "nicer" 21-and-over clubs downtown. Although UNM is officially a dry campus, most students agreed that alcohol was "easy to find," even for those underage. Several described the campus community as very "tightly knit," saying that "everyone knows everyone through someone else." Most agreed that it is relatively easy to meet new people at parties and other extracurricular gatherings.

> **"Everyone is pre-something . . . the premedical and prenursing tracks are huge."**

UNM also sponsors a number of concerts and social events. Towards the beginning of the year, there is a "Welcome Back Night," where students are invited to watch a movie screened on the school's sports facility, Johnson Field. Another notable event is the "Balloon Fiesta," at which hot air balloons are launched from campus on a Friday evening in the fall. UNM also attracts a number of headlining bands throughout the academic year. One recent event featured indie rock band The Donnas.

Off Campus and Off Hours

The city of Albuquerque offers UNM students a "fun and interesting place to live." A famous local restaurant called Frontier is a popular local hangout—"everyone is there at two in the morning on Friday nights," one sophomore said. Another favorite is the Student Union Building, the SUB, which reopened after renovation this fall, and contains a number of restaurants and a computer center.

For students with cars, there are numerous recreational opportunities in the area. Several malls in the nearby area offer shopping, and many students leave campus on weekends to explore the greater Albuquerque area. Parking, however, is described as "very difficult," and campus parking has been alleged to overfill its lots.

Dwelling and Dining

There is a lot of variation in the quality and pricing of on-campus housing. Students apply for a particular building and are later placed according to their ranked preferences. Many attested to the superior accommodations found in the Student Residence Centers, which consist of suites of six bedrooms connected by a common kitchen and living room area. An alternative housing option is Coronado, which has been described both as the worst of the spectrum with "a billion rooms sharing just one bathroom," and the best: "a great place to party because there are so many people in it."

The residence halls have an RA system, which can be "a pain if your RA is strict." Despite the fact that housing is available all four years, most students choose to move off campus after freshman year. Housing is easy to find in the surrounding area, especially because "many students are from nearby." Students still advise living on campus at least one year, however, because it is a good way to meet people.

Students living on campus are automatically placed on a meal plan. Meals can be redeemed at the cafeteria, which stacks three floors of cafeteria-style options and is open continuously between 7 A.M. and 7 P.M. Several students affirmed that the cafeteria food was extremely unpopular. For those who can't stomach the cafeteria option, meal plan "point" alternatives are redeemable at the SUB, the bookstore, and the on-campus Pizza Hut stand.

What Makes a Lobo

While a couple of students complained about a lack of campus cohesion and student involvement, UNM boasts several hundred undergraduate organizations that one student noted "includes almost anything you could think of to do." Club and intramural sports are also "very popular," and it's "typical" to find students working out in the Johnson Center, the athletics center, late into the evening.

Varsity sports events, particularly football and basketball games, are well attended. The annual football game against New Mexico State University draws a large crowd, and festivities include a pregame bonfire and lots of tailgating. The school's mascot, El Lobo, is the inspiration for the signature cheer, in which fans howl at opponents before basketball games.

Students describe the student body as mostly middle-class, and "very culturally diverse." UNM is also remarkably ethnically diverse, and many report the feeling that white students are more of a minority on campus than ever before. There is a support network for minority students which includes a number of student centers and the school's dedication to bilingual education. While there are student jobs aplenty, obtaining on-campus employment involves meeting a financial aid requirement; consequentially, many students hold part-time jobs in the surrounding area, which are reportedly easy to find in the commercial districts.

As one student put it, your experience at University of New Mexico is what you make it. In a university of 30,000 students, it is possible to get lost in a sea of preprofessionals, but it is also possible to take advantage of unmatched diversity and resources. Students who understand this principle and are prepared to optimize their college experiences for themselves will find an outstanding value at the University of New Mexico and an extensive wealth of educational opportunities. —*Stephanie Teng*

FYI

If you come to University of New Mexico, you'd better bring "your old school notes, your skis, and an attitude to work."

What is the typical weekend schedule? "Friday, frat parties, clubs, or campus events; Saturday, sleeping in or leaving campus, finding a party or concert at night; Sunday, doing homework or going to work."

If I could change one thing about University of New Mexico, I would "improve the food."

Three things every student at University of New Mexico should do before they graduate are "try to meet a lot of new people, attend the pre-NMSU bonfire, and join a student organization."

New York

Adelphi University

Address: 1 South Avenue; Garden City, NY 11530
Phone: 800-233-5744
E-mail address: admissions@.adelphi.edu
Web site URL: www.adelphi.edu
Founded: 1896
Private or Public: private
Religious affiliation: none
Location: urban
Undergraduate enrollment: 3,746
Total enrollment: NA
Percent Male/Female: 28%/72%
Percent Minority: 23%
Percent African-American: 11%
Percent Asian: 4%
Percent Hispanic: 7%
Percent Native-American: 0%
Percent in-state/out of state: 91%/9%
Percent Pub HS: NA
Number of Applicants: 4,027
Percent Accepted: 70%
Percent Accepted who enroll: 24%
Entering: 686
Transfers: 520
Application Deadline: rolling
Mean SAT: NA
Mean ACT: NA
Middle 50% SAT range: V 480-580, M 480-590
Middle 50% ACT range: NA
3 Most popular majors: business, education, social services
Retention: 76%
Graduation rate: 49%
On-campus housing: 23%
Fraternities: 4%
Sororities: 5%
Library: 631,000 volumes
Tuition and Fees: $17,800
Room and Board: $8,400
Financial aid, first-year: 92%
Varsity or Club Athletes: 6%
Early Decision or Early Action Acceptance Rate: 59%

Located on Long Island, with a student body composed primarily of commuters, Adelphi offers a unique college experience geared mostly toward students who reside nearby and plan to either live at home or to visit home often. One enthusiastic student claimed that "even as a commuter, you can still get a full college experience from Adelphi, spending long hours at the library, or just hanging around campus." And if your idea of a full college experience is an intimate environment, both socially and academically, where you can cheer for a great basketball team, experience a level of independence, and still be able to go not so far for a home-cooked meal, Adelphi may be just the place for you. If, however, you want to go further from home, and stay on campus during weekends, enjoying yourself at Adelphi might require a little bit of an adjustment and frequent trips into New York City.

Intimacy and Choices

Adelphi consists of several different schools for undergraduates. Besides the College of Arts and Sciences, there are also individual schools for education, business, nursing, social work, and psychology. Students must indicate which college they are applying to on their college application. Requirements vary depending on the college and major of choice. Students in the College of Arts and Sciences must fulfill General Education requirements, which force students to take at least six credits in arts, natural sciences and mathematics, humanities and languages, and social sciences. However, one student admitted that although the requirements were "a pain in the neck, and I complain about them now," the skills acquired in the classes will likely help in the future, "so it all pays off in the end."

One student cited the "small classes and personal attention" as the best aspect of Adelphi academics. However, this intimacy has recently been jeopardized by an increase in enrollment, which has led to overcrowding in some classes and sections. This overcrowding tends to be significant only in introductory classes and classes with especially popular professors. Many of Adelphi's classes are still small enough to foster "great group discussions," even if they are not quite so intimate. Overall, students reported that they were happy with professors. Dr. Salvadore Primeggia, a sociology professor, received especially rave reviews for being enthusiastic, "talking to students as equals," and for getting everyone involved in class discussions. As one student enthusiastically exclaimed, "I have never been in a more exciting class!" Although not all professors inspired such praise, students agreed that the professors were fairly accessible, and that they "make an effort to accommodate students" even if their office hours are "few and far between."

Students cited nursing, business, and education as the most popular majors. The theater department is reportedly also large. Business, social work, education, and theater are considered by some to be the most competitive and intense of the majors. Science classes, especially biology, tend to be dominated by premed students, and are therefore considered to be difficult and competitive as well. However, if you are considering a major in one of these areas, you need not be intimidated by their reputations. Speaking about her education classes, one student said that although they were sometimes very time-consuming, they were "enjoyable," and "don't necessarily feel like work." And students can always make use of Adelphi's "excellent resources to obtain help," which, besides professors, includes a learning center and tutors. Said one student, "[Adelphi] has a lot to offer, including direction if you don't know what you want to do with your life." Advisors, professors, and other staff are always readily available for advice, "plus there are so many electives that if you don't know what you want, you can take a course that may spring some interest."

And You Thought Your Menopausal Mother Had a Hormonal Imbalance . . .

One notable aspect of Adelphi is the disproportionate number of female to male students. In certain classes, notably those in education, nursing, and English, there may be no males at all. One student felt that the ratio was a major disadvantage to the school, stating that, although "the guys love it, because there are so many girls to choose from, the girls hate it because all the guys you meet, you either become friends with and aren't attracted to, or you are attracted to but find out they are attracted to someone else." However, these difficulties must work themselves out somehow, because, according to students, "there is a lot of random hooking up," and even some dating.

Another aspect of Adelphi social life that one should take into consideration before applying is that, of those undergraduates who live on campus, many go home on weekends, leaving the school "a ghost town come Thursday nights." One student lamented that "there is nothing to do on the weekends." However, with a large mall nearby, students can find solace and drown their sorrows and boredom in the latest Banana Republic and Kenneth Cole fashions. There is even a shuttle bus that goes back and forth to the mall and bus terminals. And if shopping fails, New York City is also only a 30-minute train ride away. Adelphi bar nights can also provide a break from weekend boredom. These fraternity or sorority sponsored events are held at various bars, which are primarily populated by Adelphi students for the night, allowing students to interact with "the same people you see in your classes all week, only now they're drunker." However, according to one student, even these "get tiring after awhile" since you are constantly seeing the same people.

Constantly seeing the same people is a natural product of the small undergraduate population. Another negative consequence of Adelphi's small size is that "*everyone* knows your business." Although it is officially a dry campus, one student explained that people often drink in dorms anyway, and that alcohol plays "a major role" in the social scene. Although students are put on probation if they get caught, this is rarely an issue. Being underage is reportedly "not a problem" either, because the bouncers at the Adelphi bars will usually let you in. Light drug use plays a small role in the social scene as well. According to one student, "people smoke and drink in the dorms and no one really cares."

Don't Judge a School by Its (Long Island) Accent

The majority of Adelphi students come from the tri-state area, especially Long Island, and they are primarily white. However, it would be wrong to stereotype the school based on these demographics. While some complain that lack of diversity is a problem, others claim that Adelphi is "very diverse," and that there are "a lot of foreign students." One student claimed that although many minority groups tend to hang out together, "it is not because they don't get along with other white people." Whether the diversity is great enough may be a matter of opinion, but as one student said, "diversity or no diversity, Adelphi is a very inviting place to all races and genders." And apparently, to all sexualities as well, since the attitude towards homosexuals is reportedly "pretty accepting," although one student admitted that it may be difficult to hide one's homosexuality for long because, due to the small size of the campus, "news travels fast."

"Adelphi has a lot to offer, including direction if you don't know what you want to do with your life."

A sense of community is strongest among residents at Adelphi. However, commuter students feel ties to Adelphi as well. This sense of community and school spirit stems mostly from a common sense of pride in Adelphi's basketball and lacrosse teams, which draw big crowds, and are a major component of student life. Basketball even sparks a tradition known as Midnight Madness, which involves students participating in silly games to win prizes up until midnight, when the basketball teams come out, marking the official start of the basketball season. According to one student, midnight madness "shows school unity because everyone is there."

Students report that there is not much extracurricular involvement outside of sports. While sororities and fraternities are the largest organizations, Greek life is not really that big, and some students complain that Greek pride is something that is conspicuously lacking in the Adelphi community. Besides sororities and fraternities, students may also choose to become involved in student government, or publications such as the *Delphian*, a weekly newspaper, or *Ascent*, a literary magazine. However, many students are too busy working to pay for their Adelphi education to become too heavily involved in other pursuits.

For the most part, students are happy with the campus and housing. Campus is described as small and homey, allowing students to travel across campus to different buildings in very little time. The campus is also very "floral," which makes it especially beautiful in the springtime, as one student enthusiastically pointed out. Garden City, the wealthy suburban town in which Adelphi resides, also got positive reactions from students. It is described as "beautiful," and has much to offer students, including nearby malls, restaurants, bars, and close proximity to Manhattan. Students also agree that they feel very safe at Adelphi, and have "no problem walking across campus alone at night." If someone did feel unsafe, there are blue security lights posted around campus that students can press to notify security. One major complaint, however, is that there are inadequate parking spaces, a major inconvenience at a school where many students commute. Overcrowding has also become a problem in dorms lately due to a rise in enrollment.

Many students are satisfied with their experience at Adelphi. They enjoy the intimacy of the academic and social environment, and the beauty of their suburban campus. Others really appreciate the school's close proximity to home. However, students admit that Adelphi is not for everyone, and that those who live far from Adelphi, or who do not wish to go home on the weekends, should carefully consider their choice before deciding on Adelphi. —*Elyssa Berg*

FYI

If you come to Adelphi, you'd better bring a "car."

What is the typical weekend schedule? "Most people go home, others go to NYC, local bars, or shopping at the local mall."

If I could change one thing about Adelphi, I'd "change the party scene."

Three things every student at Adelphi should do before graduating are "go to Midnight Madness, attend the Adelphi Bar Night, and make a weekend trip to NYC."

Alfred University

Address: Saxon Drive; Alfred, NY 14802-1205
Phone: 800-541-9229
E-mail address: admwww@alfred.edu
Web site URL: www.alfred.edu
Founded: 1836
Private or Public: private
Religious affiliation: none
Location: rural
Undergraduate enrollment: 2,080
Total enrollment: 2,450
Percent Male/Female: 48%/52%
Percent Minority: 12%
Percent African-American: 5%
Percent Asian: 2%
Percent Hispanic: 4%
Percent Native-American: 1%
Percent in-state/out of state: NA
Percent Pub HS: 89%
Number of Applicants: 1,951
Percent Accepted: 73%
Percent Accepted who enroll: 33%
Entering: 473
Transfers: 124
Application Deadline: rolling
Mean SAT: NA
Mean ACT: NA
Middle 50% SAT range: V 490-600, M 490-610
Middle 50% ACT range: 23-28
3 Most popular majors: fine arts, engineering, business administration
Retention: 80%
Graduation rate: 66%
On-campus housing: NA
Fraternities: 12%
Sororities: 6%
Library: 250,000 volumes
Tuition and Fees: $20,192
Room and Board: $9,012
Financial aid, first-year: 87%
Varsity or Club Athletes: 17%
Early Decision or Early Action Acceptance Rate: 93%

"If you want a bustling city life, Alfred University is not the place to be. But for everything else a college student needs, its great," boasted one Alfred student. True to his words, Alfred University, located in upstate New York, is small-town school. Yet, what it lacks in big-city glamour, it makes up for with rolling pastures and a close-knit community. Its nationally recognized ceramic engineering department doesn't hurt, either.

Not Your Typical Curriculum

Academics at Alfred are truly unique and diverse. Popular majors range from the less common, such as athletic training, to more typical offerings such as computer science and mechanical engineering. Students at Alfred tend to have a wide array of academic interests. Classes are described as challenging, and students agree good grades are not so easy to come by, although requirements and difficulty do vary by major. The only course all students are required to take is physical education. "I guess they want us all to be fit," one student said, trying to rationalize this requirement.

One of the strongest and most popular majors at Alfred is ceramic engineering. Not only is Alfred nationally recognized for its faculty in this department, but the school also makes available many co-op opportunities for majors to pursue their interests in this field. Indeed, the program is so good, many students say they came to Alfred because of it. Other strong departments include the arts, computer science, business, English, and history. The music department, on the other hand, tends not to receive such rave reviews due to its limited course selection.

In addition to its regular academic programs, Alfred offers a special honors program for qualified students. This program provides academically ambitious students more access to the best professors at the university. Honors students have the opportunity to delve into certain fields in more depth than they would have studying under the normal program.

As a small school in a small town, it is not surprising that Alfred gets good reviews for its small class sizes. The average class enrolls only about 15 students, and professors teach not only all lectures, but conduct all discussion sections as well. The small-scale learning environment fosters a supportive environment, and many students note that they felt close to their professors. The close-knit community also proves advantageous in that it allows for students to participate more confidently in their education. In fact, it is not unusual to find professor-student interactions even outside the classroom. Professors and students are often seen meeting for a meal or coffee in a local eatery. At Alfred, learning is not confined to the classroom.

"If you want a bustling city life, Alfred University is not the place to be. Yet for everything else a college student needs, it's great."

The two libraries on campus also receive acclaim from students. Of the two, Herrick Memorial tends to be the more popular study place, and is often crowded. The other library, Scholes, has the largest ceramic engineering research collection in the world.

In addition to these excellent libraries, Alfred boasts many new classroom buildings. Olin is a fairly recent business building, and the Miller Performing Arts Center and Glass Science Laboratory are both new additions to the campus. Binns-Merrill Hall and Kanakadea Hall, housing the ceramics and human studies departments, respectively, are also being renovated. This is not unusual for Alfred, which tends always to be on the cutting edge. "Our campus is constantly being remodeled—it's great!" boasted one student.

Northern Exposure

Most students would agree that life in the boonies is part of the Alfred experience. First-year students at Alfred live in special freshman dorms, usually in doubles, coed by floor. Barresi is one popular freshman dorm, whereas Tefft tends to be less popular. Upperclassmen select rooms by lottery and have a wide array of choices open to them ranging from suites to campus apartments with full-size kitchens. In addition, a large number of students live off campus in sorority or fraternity houses.

The food is not horrible, and students may eat in either of the campus's two dining halls—Powell, located in the campus center, or Ade. Alfred changed its dining services a few years ago, and students say they are benefiting from it. Many students opt to eat at off-campus eateries, as well. Popular spots include the Collegiate, The Dill Pickle, Little Sicily's, and Alfred Pizza and Sub Shop.

Extracurricular Life in the Boonies

Alfred University is an extremely health-conscious school, so it is no surprise that sports are very popular. Alfred is a Division III school and cannot offer athletic scholarships, but the school still manages to have great athletic competition. The lacrosse team is very good, having made the Division III NCAAs twice in the last four years.

School spirit at athletic events is extremely high, as many an Alfred student comes out to support the Saxon Warriors. The school's athletic facilities are described as "fairly good" and are open to all students free of charge. These include squash courts, basketball courts, a swimming pool, and a weight room. For those not as athletically inclined, intramurals are popular, including everything from squash to basketball.

In addition to sports, other popular campus activities include participating in the college newspaper, the *Fiatlux*, which is distributed bi-weekly. Other journalistic venues include literary magazines such as the *Alfred Review* and the *Poasis*. Students describe both of these magazines as "bizarre but interesting." Other popular extracurriculars include the school radio station and a world-traveled jazz band. Greek life also holds a strong presence on campus, and according to students, is the "begin-all- and-end-all" of campus social life. Alcohol is also big, and binge drinking is perceived as a problem by some. However, despite the predominance of alcohol, students say they do not feel pressure to drink.

Located in such a rural community, Alfred sponsors many on-campus activities. One in particular is Hot Dog Day, the campus's biggest weekend of the year featuring parades, non-stop partying, live bands, and "a lot of fun."

Although many of the students come from New York, Alfred draws in a wide range of students from all sorts of backgrounds. In this small town, these students band together and experience what has been described as "a great four years." Said one student, "Although Alfred isn't for everyone, if you can handle small town life, do give it a try. You won't be disappointed."
—Alyssa Blair Greenwald and Staff

FYI

If you come to Alfred, you'd better bring "your CD collection, your school bag, and a camera."

What is the typical weekend schedule? "Friday: hang out with friends and get pizza from Alex's; Saturday: work out and watch a movie; Sunday: enjoy the small-town life while doing your homework."

If I could change one thing about Alfred, "I'd make it a Division I school."

One thing I'd like to have known before coming to Alfred is "how small a town Alfred really is."

Bard College

Address: PO Box 5000; Annandale-on-Hudson, NY 12504
Phone: 845-758-7472
E-mail address: admissions@bard.edu
Web site URL: www.bard.edu
Founded: 1860
Private or Public: private
Religious affiliation: none
Location: rural
Undergraduate enrollment: 1,333
Total enrollment: 1,440
Percent Male/Female: 44%/56%
Percent Minority: 13%
Percent African-American: 3%
Percent Asian: 4%
Percent Hispanic: 5%
Percent Native-American: 1%
Percent In-state/out of state: 25%/75%
Percent Pub HS: 60%
Number of Applicants: 3,118
Percent Accepted: 36%
Percent Accepted who enroll: 31%
Entering: 343
Transfers: 32
Application Deadline: 15 Jan
Mean SAT: NA
Mean ACT: NA
Middle 50% SAT range: V 650-750, M 590-690
Middle 50% ACT range: NA
3 Most popular majors: social sciences, visual and performing arts, language and literature
Retention: 86%
Graduation rate: 70%
On-campus housing: 85%
Fraternities: NA
Sororities: NA
Library: 280,000 volumes
Tuition and Fees: $28,808
Room and Board: $8,544
Financial aid, first-year: 60%
Varsity or Club Athletes: NA
Early Decision or Early Action Acceptance Rate: 55%

With no core curriculum and minimal distributional requirements, small classes and extracurricular activities like "The Surrealist Circus," Bard College is a haven for the artistic and academically focused. Nestled in the stunning Hudson River Valley, Bard offers its students a liberal arts education in a small, safe environment.

Make Your Own Major

The academic environment at Bard is challenging, but rewarding. "There's a lot of work . . . but everyone's intelligent and

I've grown so much as a student and a person here," said one junior. There are distributional requirements, including at least one science class, but students agree that these are easily managed, and one can "get them out of the way quickly to move on to what you really want to study." Class sizes tend to range from 4 to 25, with only a few classes having over 30 students. This creates a cozy setting, although a common complaint is that some students get *too* comfortable. "There are a lot of people here who are . . . eager to get their ideas out there, and they can be really long-winded."

The two most difficult and competitive majors at Bard are photo and film, offered by the well-respected art department. These "high-demand majors" take up a lot of time, and involve an extensive series of workshop classes where students criticize each other's work. While the art classes are difficult to get into, many students find that the science classes are "hard to pass." A fair number of students choose interdisciplinary majors, such as integrated arts, or create their own majors. "The school's selling point is that you make your own curriculum, and make your own program; it takes initiative," commented one sophomore. While first-year students sometimes find this prospect daunting, teachers are always available for help.

Because Bard is such a small school, courses can sometimes be difficult to get into. During the registration period, teachers sit in their different classes while students "scramble" from room to room, trying to see where there is space available. "Registration is horrible," according to some; but others say that it is fairly easy into get the classes you want if you plan ahead and contact some of the teachers in advance. "Get there early, and try to get [the professors] to know your face," advised one student; "It definitely takes some strategy." Outstanding classes include James Chase's political science class, and Gregory Moynahan's history class.

Chill Weekends

Due to Bard's fairly remote location, most people "hang out and have parties in their dorms" on the weekends. There are no fraternities or sororities at Bard, nor any social or theme houses, which makes the party scene more diffuse. Although students frequent nearby bars and "are definitely into costume and theme parties" such as the Silk Party and the Drag Race, many people spend their free time with close friends, attending cultural activities, shows, or concerts. The Bertelsmann Campus center boasts a 100-seat cinema for movies, as well as lounge areas, public e-mail terminals, and a multi-purpose room. There is definitely a drinking scene on campus; smoking is also common. While one Bard student suggested that "non-drinkers and non-pot-smokers feel weird about the party scene," another student asserted that it was very easy to have a substance-free social life. Having a car is a great way to improve the social scene at Bard; it gives students the opportunity to travel to Redhook and Tivoli, as well as more dynamic areas like Rhinebeck or even New York City. Many freshmen do not have cars, but by sophomore year "almost everyone at least has access to a car."

The Victorian Hudson

The Bard campus is located next to the Hudson River. Many students have a beautiful view of the Catskill Mountains from their rooms, as well as outlooks onto the old mansions that surround central campus. Notable spaces on campus include the Anna Margaret Jones Meditation Garden, which is "a nice place to study when the weather's good," and the newly built Richard B. Fisher Center for the Performing Arts, whose two theaters, four rehearsal studios, and professional support facilities "bring visitors to Bard who know nothing about the school, but have just heard about this cool state-of-the-art theater." Other important places to check out are some of the older buildings which are "rumored to be haunted—they used to be elderly homes or homes for the mentally insane."

Vassarification?

Bard is traditionally known for its "hipsters, hippies, punks, creative-writery-looking kids with green hair and eyebrow rings." Most students are from New York, Boston, and LA, and have a strong, artistic, free-spirited bent. The student body is fairly homogeneous, "rich and rastafarian," which can "sometimes get suffocating." Some students commented that they wished there was more diversity, not only racially and culturally, but also politically and ideologically. However, there is reportedly a new kind of student appearing at Bard because of the administration's desire to "make the school more prestigious." Though the particular traits of this new breed are hard to pinpoint, "they just have a different feeling from the older classes," said one student. The general consensus among older students is that "they are trying to Vassarify, to create a more clean-cut image." In concordance with this shift, the administration has been toughening up some of its policies, particularly with respect to smoking and drinking. "You used to be able to smoke almost anywhere, and nobody cared, but things are kind of different now."

High-Class Living

Although freshmen must live on campus, many students move off after their first year. While Tewksbury, considered by some to be the least appealing dorm, is "like a 1960s motel, creepy and gross and made with cinderblocks," the dorms vary in size and style and can often provide "a cozy sense of community." Cruger and Keen, for example, are more modern dorms, while Ward Manor is a beautiful old mansion, whose residents often have private bathrooms and balconies overlooking the Catskills. Most of the floors are co-ed, and peer counselors live with the freshman to offer advice. "They can get you in trouble, too, but for the most part they're pretty chill," said one sophomore.

"Bard is traditionally known for its hipsters, hippies, punks, creative-writery-looking kids with green hair and eyebrow rings."

Students living on campus must have a campus meal plan, which includes daily meals at either Kline Dining Hall or a small café. Meal-plan money can also be transferred to an on-campus store, which has easy-to-make dorm food, such as canned soups and microwave popcorn. There are plenty of vegetarian and vegan options, including a separate co-op for vegans with its own food service hall—but the overall consensus is that the campus food leaves something to be desired. The vegan co-op, called Feitler House, is a residence hall for 13 students, chosen by application, who are then personally responsible for all of their cleaning and cooking decisions. "Basically, it's where the really belligerent vegan kids live," one student quipped.

Many students eat off campus regularly at restaurants in Redhook or Tivoli, as there are frequent shuttles from Bard to these towns. "The campus is beautiful, but it's in the middle of nowhere," one student reported. "We're right on the Hudson River, and there are gorgeous old mansions . . . but we're really very secluded. It can get stagnant."

Beyond Academia: on the Fields and in the Clubs

Many Bard students take part in one of the approximately 60 clubs at the college. These groups range from religious and cultural groups to activist and political groups, the latter of which are "mostly leftist." Anyone can start a club and receive school funding, and this results in creative and unusual organizations such as the "Beerology Club" and the "Bard Chainmail Club," which is dedicated to teaching the Bard community "how to make their own chainmail armor and jewelry."

Students who are interested in more athletic endeavors can play either varsity or intramural sports. Bard is not really a "gung-ho athletic school," as one student explained. "There are no homecomings, and people don't really go watch games, except maybe to see their friends play." However, the students on the teams are very active, and many of them are tri-varsity athletes. Though the school does not have a football team, they do have a rugby squad that attracts some spectators. "Lots of people work out and do intramurals," one student assessed, "but it's all mostly non-competitive."

Bard College offers a stimulating academic environment set in a picturesque landscape. Art, music, and the humanities flourish in this creative student body, and academic freedom gives every student the chance to design his or her own education. "If you're ready to self-motivate and take initiative," commented one student, "Bard is the perfect place to pursue your academic passions." —*Diana Dosik*

FYI

If you come to Bard College, you'd better bring "a bike."

What is the typical weekend schedule? "It starts on Thursday night and consists of partying, chilling, sleeping, whatever."

If I could change one thing about Bard College, it would be "the fake open-mindedness."

Three things every student at Bard should do before graduating are "go to a soccer or rugby game, play four-square, and have cheese and wine at an art opening."

Barnard College

Address: 3009 Broadway; New York, NY 10027
Phone: 212-854-2014
E-mail address: admissions@barnard.edu
Web site URL: www.barnard.edu
Founded: 1889
Private or Public: private
Religious affiliation: none
Location: urban
Undergraduate enrollment: 2,297
Total enrollment: 2,297
Percent Male/Female: 0%/100%
Percent Minority: 31%
Percent African-American: 5%
Percent Asian: 19%
Percent Hispanic: 6%
Percent Native-American: 1%
Percent in-state/out of state: 36%/64%
Percent Pub HS: NA
Number of Applicants: 3,686
Percent Accepted: 34%
Percent Accepted who enroll: 43%
Entering: 543
Transfers: 87
Application Deadline: 1 Jan
Mean SAT: NA
Mean ACT: NA
Middle 50% SAT range: V 630-710, M 620-700
Middle 50% ACT range: 27-30
3 Most popular majors: English language and literature, psychology, political science
Retention: 94%
Graduation rate: 86%
On-campus housing: 88%
Fraternities: NA
Sororities: NA
Library: 201,566 volumes
Tuition and Fees: $26,528
Room and Board: $10,264
Financial aid, first-year: 41%
Varsity or Club Athletes: NA
Early Decision or Early Action Acceptance Rate: 45%

A supportive all-women's college located in the greatest city in the world with access to caring, famous professors and an Ivy University across the street? Yep, that's Barnard for you.

Located in the neighborhood of Morningside Heights in New York City, Barnard has been educating women for more than a century. With a top-notch curriculum and a diverse student body, Barnard continues to educate modern women for the twenty-first century.

Core Curriculum with a Barnard Twist

Academics at Barnard are taken seriously. As one student said, "if you are a slacker, you don't really go here. Or you do and leave." As an independent affiliate of Columbia University and as a liberal arts school with a hefty core curriculum, students are fully aware of their academic responsibilities. The core requirements, more individualized and woman-oriented than Columbia's counterpart, introduce students to a variety of topics, aiming to create well-versed women who can tackle a math problem as well as remark on the fine details of a Rembrandt painting. The core includes an interdisciplinary First-Year Seminar, First-Year English, physical education, and courses fulfilling the nine Ways of Knowing which includes topics such as historical studies, languages, and visual & performing arts, as well as laboratory sciences and quantitative & deductive reasoning. Students have varied opinions on the core classes. Some wish the requirements did not exist, while others are thankful for the opportunity to take "classes which you might otherwise shy away from. Frequently, you end up finding your major in one of those requirements you wouldn't have otherwise taken." The reported hard majors at Barnard are natural sciences, economics, and political science. Film and art are difficult time-wise, and women's studies, dance, and English receive high marks. Class sizes vary and can consist of 20 to 200 people depending on the subject and type of class (lectures versus seminars and colloquiums). One fact that students are very enthusiastic about it that "TAs simply don't exist." To keep class sizes small and TAs out of the picture, students report some difficulty trying to get into popular classes. One Barnard student described "waiting in line for hours just to get your name on a list for class is somewhat hopeless," but well worth it if the effort succeeds. An added benefit of belonging to Barnard College is that one can go across the street and take classes at Columbia University. While "you could basically go all four years and take no classes off of Barnard's campus," says one student, the reverse is also true and frequently done. However, one junior did admit that "being a Barnard student in a joint class that happens to meet at Columbia can be difficult" due to the fact that "some Columbia students are not comfortable with the idea of Barnard girls in their classes. After all, they applied to Columbia, and we did not." While the workload can be whatever you choose to make it, students say that academics are competitive and most people do a lot of work, but that's what college is supposed to be about. The academics can be described in three sentences. As one student said, "It's Barnard. It's topnotch. It's great."

Social Life

For a college student, New York City is a great backyard. Students gravitate towards downtown on weekends for shows, museums, and club and bar hopping. "Most places here or downtown don't card," said a student. Favorite haunts for Barnard students include Starbucks, the West End, and the Abbey. Non-drinkers, however, do not feel left out of the social scene. In fact, one student says, "One-third of students don't ever drink." Women at Barnard do go out on dates and attend semi-formals a few times a year as guys can be found at one of the numerous colleges around town including Columbia, Julliard, Fordham, Marymount College, and the Manhattan School of Music. However, according to one senior, students mostly go out in groups as opposed to dating. A student center helps create a centralized place of interaction for students where they can go to the snack bar, lounge, student store, music practice rooms, and a bowling alley. There is a very small Greek population at Barnard. The Greek situation is "pathetic," as one senior describes it. While not absent, students report that alcohol and drugs on campus do not seem to be a problem. Many Barnard women are active in clubs, sports teams, artistic endeavors, and they report that most of their good friends come from these outside activities.

"It's all women who care about the world and care about succeeding in even the most male-dominated professions. It's very empowering."

Living on the Edge

More than 90 percent of Barnard students live on campus due to the exorbitant rents for Manhattan abodes off campus. Students can choose to live in a Barnard/Columbia dorm, off campus, or at Barnard's dorms. However, living off campus isn't something students suggest. One said, "Twenty and alone in a big city? Harlem? No." Students complain that the dorms are very small, especially on the Quad, where most freshmen live and where one is required to have a meal plan. One aspect that Barnard students enjoy is the special housing options available. "You can find a house for basically whatever your heart desires, or you can make your own and get special interest housing with your friends," one student said. Students warn that rooms should be kept "very, very clean" due to pest problems in New York City buildings. However, as one student assured, "exterminators are easily reachable." As far as counseling goes, an RA system allows students to get advice and guidance. Students report that the RAs are not strict and want to be friends as opposed to authority figures.

Students speak highly of Barnard's four-acre campus. Barnard's beautiful architecture, steps, and green space in the middle of a bustling city are a welcome change from the usual city high-rises. In fact, one student mentioned that "the main walk through campus is called 'College Walk.' It was 116th street . . . and is this gorgeous brick walk now lined with tall trees." Students report that they feel safe at Barnard, "more so than elsewhere," one student commented, "even though there have been some instances of sexual assault in the campus area."

Where to Chow Down and Chill Out

Students have no major complaints about the dining hall food, besides the fact that there are only a limited number of places to eat, including two dining halls on campus and one at Columbia. Vegan and kosher options are readily available, and students boast of the abundance of ethnic food offered. Many people, though, cook in their apartments or out to eat at local restaurants-Le Monde for French food, the West End for Burgers, Tomo for Japanese and Sophia's for Italian.

While people are very dedicated to community service and extracurriculars at Barnard, sports do not seem to draw such a large crowd. There are intramurals that people can participate in, but students report that not much interest is put into sports due to the fact that "all Barnard athletes compete on Columbia's teams . . . but Columbia's teams in general are really bad, so it's a touchy issue," said one student.

The Skinny

Students report that one of the greatest aspects about the school is that it's all female. "It's all women who care about the world and care about succeeding in even the most male-dominated professions. It's very empowering," said one senior. At Barnard, students obtain the tools to continue changing the world, while the world of New York City continues to change around them as well. As one junior commented, "What happened here? American Revolution. Manhattan Project. Riots of '68. What didn't happen here?" —*Lisa Siciliano*

FYI

If you come to Barnard, you'd better bring "black pants and a MetroCard."

What is the typical weekend schedule? "Fridays are usually filled with labs, sections, or office hours. On weekend nights, most people go out around campus or head downtown to have fun. But pretty much you can find people working all of the time."

If I could change one thing about Barnard, I'd "change the lack of community."

Three things every student at Barnard should do before graduating are "go to midnight breakfast where the deans serve breakfast in the gym the night before finals start, learn the school song, and have a debate with a Columbia student on why Barnard is better."

The City University of New York System

The City University of New York (CUNY-pronounced "kyoony"), underwent radical revision on November 22, 1999 that its Chancellor Matthew Goldstein hopes will "redefine and substantially broaden the view of the role and promise of a public urban university." On that date, New York State Board of Regents approved CUNY's Master Plan Amendment proposal to remove remedial courses from the baccalaureate curriculum and demand demonstration of basic skills through the SAT, ACT, or Regents Exams. It also revamped its intra-system transfer policies and received a $97 million boost from the 1999-2000 state budget. Through these changes, CUNY has improved its academic image, strengthened its offerings, and yielded a high retention rate of its students.

Variety and Different Focus

CUNY is the third-largest university system in the world with 200,000 students on twenty-one campuses (ten undergraduate, six community colleges, one technical, four graduate) throughout the five boroughs of New York. An additional 150,000 part-time and continuing-education adult students attend a CUNY school. Its student body reflects the city's ethnic diversity: 32 percent of students are black, 31 percent white, 25 percent Hispanic and 12 percent Asian. Although the differences among colleges are immense, nearly all the students interviewed by the *Insider's Guide* mentioned the word "bureaucratic." As one student said, the colleges are "run by the city of New York, so basically . . . anyone you deal with at the administrative level gives you the same attitude you would expect at the Department of Motor Vehicles."

A Good Deal

Despite the dissatisfaction with the administration, however, most CUNY students feel they're getting a good education and a good deal. The huge variety of night courses attracts a large population of students who work during the day. All of this is available at a price made more reasonable by the fact that most students are from New York and can live at home, which is "a big reason" many students choose CUNY schools. According to one undergrad, "Most students I know here work and are from families where that's necessary." Understandably, most students take up to six years to graduate and the graduation rate is low.

Each school has its individual strengths. "[Each college] has different concentrations," one student said. "Hunter has a big nursing school; at Queens, it's English; at Baruch, it's business; and The City College covers the technical areas: engineering and computer science." According to students, these individual strengths help them decide which school to attend. "If a student lives in Brooklyn, and wants to be an English major, it's not that big a commute—he'll go to Queens," one student explained.

Grab Bag

Campus environments vary as well. Students describe the colleges in Manhattan as more fast-paced and urban than those in the other boroughs; they are also considered "more liberal" and "free." According to one undergrad, some students from suburban Long Island "come to Queens and are in awe of it—if they went to Manhattan, they'd have a heart attack. The culture is different in Long Island: you really don't see anyone with a shaved head and nose ring walking around the other campuses." Students in Manhattan say, "It's Manhattan"—in the middle of everything, creating an extremely diverse and exciting environment.

"[The colleges are] run by the city of New York, so basically . . . anyone you deal with at the administrative level gives you the same attitude you would expect at the Department of Motor Vehicles."

Admissions criteria depend on the individual school. Spaces in the community colleges are guaranteed to New York students who have earned a high school diploma, while the four-year schools maintain more selective admissions policies. Students are required to have a cumulative academic average (CAA) of 80, a measurement that incorporates grades only from "academic" subjects such as math, English, science, foreign language, and history.

Overall, students praise the faculty as one of the CUNY system's greatest assets. "We have a lot of really fine teachers here," one student said. Others described their professors as "gifted people as well as gentle and giving teachers," and "excellent, and nationally renowned."

New York City serves as both CUNY's campus and its source of extracurricular activities: A CUNY ID can get a student discounts at many museums, galleries, and theaters around town. One student even claimed that "if you make arrangements, there's hardly a museum in the city that won't let you in for free." However, this does not prevent some CUNY schools from having strong extracurriculars, including newspapers, clubs, and student government.

Students generally agree that the CUNY system provides a solid education for people of all ages, interests, schedules, and backgrounds. General Colin Powell and Jerry Seinfeld are two of many distinguished alumni of the CUNY system as is the current Chancellor Goldstein. The colleges are reportedly "malleable to the individual student's ambitions" and meet the changing needs of a remarkably diverse population. According to one student, "Overall, the administration is pretty unpopular, but the teaching is informative if you choose the right courses—it's a good education." —*Seung Lee and Staff*

City University of New York / City College

Address: 160 Convent Avenue; New York, NY 10031
Phone: 212-650-6977
E-mail address: admissions@admin.ccny.cuny.edu
Web site URL: www.ccny.cuny.edu
Founded: 1847
Private or Public: public
Religious affiliation: none
Location: urban
Undergraduate enrollment: 8,638
Total enrollment: 11,136
Percent Male/Female: 49%/51%
Percent Minority: 81%
Percent African-American: 33%
Percent Asian: 15%
Percent Hispanic: 33%
Percent Native-American: 0%
Percent in-state/out of state: 93%/7%
Percent Pub HS: 85%
Number of Applicants: 5,537
Percent Accepted: 36%
Percent Accepted who enroll: 51%
Entering: 1,011
Transfers: 1,070
Application Deadline: rolling
Mean SAT: NA
Mean ACT: NA
Middle 50% SAT range: V 390-540, M 430-590
Middle 50% ACT range: NA
3 Most popular majors: computer science, engineering, architecture
Retention: 77%
Graduation rate: 27%
On-campus housing: 0%
Fraternities: NA
Sororities: NA
Library: 1,413,641 volumes
Tuition and Fees: $3,384 in; $6,984 out
Room and Board: NA
Financial aid, first-year: 82%
Varsity or Club Athletes: NA
Early Decision or Early Action Acceptance Rate: NA

What's it like to go to college in the heart of Harlem? Just ask the students of City College of New York (CCNY). About ten street blocks in length and two avenues wide, the campus of CCNY is at the center of a vibrant neighborhood. Everything from local restaurants to annual festivities projects the community's diversity and invites exploration by CCNY's eager and adventurous students.

A Cultural Hotbed

At CCNY "everyone's different and has their distinct personalities," said one freshman who was amazed by the diversity of the student body and their active involvement on campus and in the Harlem community. Located in the heart of one of the most diverse cities in the world, CCNY attracts students who are open to learning about others: "there's a mixing of cultures here; you won't see a black table or an Asian table in the cafeteria." CCNY students are, as a rule, very involved in extracurriculars. "There are so many clubs, and people are always outside the cafeteria encouraging people to join," commented one student. These clubs can be both serious in focus, like the AIDS- and

Cancer-Awareness organizations, or more recreational in nature, like the Jackass Club that gets together to perform "stupid stunts" or the Game Club, "for dweebs who get together to play the latest video games." Community service activities are among the most popular, as students frequent local soup kitchens and help out with toy drives. While most agree that there isn't a "stereotypical CCNY student," all seem to share the ability to multi-task. Most students work part-time and attend classes full-time. For example, one particularly busy student attended classes full-time, worked in the student government, helped with the History Club, was very involved with his church, tutored children two days a week, and helped coach a youth football team.

Students enjoy the resources in the city around them and the "awesome variety of food and cultures in Harlem." According to one junior, "the culture is so rich in Harlem, you can easily find food from every culture from West Indian to Asian." Currently, New York City is investing a lot of money in the area to build shopping centers and to draw public attention to the neighborhood's rich history. As another junior noted, "Harlem is going to be one of the premier shopping districts in New York City. People who once looked to midtown [Manhattan] as the place to shop will soon discover Harlem."

Making the Rent

CCNY is distinctive because, unlike most colleges, there are no dormitories for students. Without on-campus housing, most opt to live at home or rent apartments near campus. One student who lives at home reported that most CCNY students come from the five boroughs of New York City, though a few commute in from the surrounding suburbs. A convenient CCNY bus picks students up every 15 minutes from the nearest subway station and drops them off at campus. Another freshman reported that while he takes three subways to get to school each day, "the difficult commute is not really a problem, since the subway is right by the college."

While the school does not own any of the apartment buildings in the area, a campus agency does provide some assistance in the search for affordable housing. One sophomore commented that this service isn't too helpful, though; "a lot of people apply for housing, but most are still waiting." A freshman warned, "I'm telling you, it's not cheap." Harlem's economic resurgence, while great for the neighborhood and for the overall City College experience, is driving up real-estate prices in the area, so rents are high. Students reported paying no less than $1,000 a month for small, one-bedroom or studio apartments in nearby brownstones. To help pay for the rent, many CCNY students take part-time jobs after classes and on the weekends. The work-study program offers students great opportunities to learn and make some money at the same time. According to one student, "It's not a problem to find work, I always see students working in the library and various offices."

Not Exactly Social Butterflies

Without dorms to structure campus living, the weekend experience at CCNY is different than at most schools. Since most students head home after their classes and extracurricular commitments are finished and stay off campus for the weekends, CCNY "is not too big on social life." The school does sponsor a Kick-Off party at the beginning of each semester, and another party every month, usually held in Shepherd Hall or the gym. Turnouts for these events vary; the first party of the semester reportedly had so many people that it was shut down, while in other cases students admitted being "too lazy to go back to campus for the parties." At CCNY, according to one junior, "weekends usually don't revolve around the school, except for doing school work."

> **"There's a mixing of cultures here."**

Despite the mostly non-existent party scene, there is a plethora of daytime on-campus activities to enrich the City College experience. The school organizes many free concerts and has hosted a number of motivational speakers. Recently, concert pianist Jeni Slotchiver visited and entertained students from CCNY and other area colleges with several pieces. Luncheons and dinners with well-recognized authors, poets, and other speakers also draw large crowds. Last year, Walter Cronkite, who used to teach at CCNY, came and spoke, and currently students are eagerly awaiting the visit of Secretary of State (and alumnus) Colin Powell. Other notable speakers have included Russell Simmons, the producer of Def Jam Records, as well as New York State Senator Charles Schumer and Governor George Pataki.

Students agree that there is a strong sense of school spirit. According to one junior, "because of City College's 150-year history, everyone feels proud of the school." Walking around New York City, you'll see people wearing their City College sweatshirts, and the sense of community and camaraderie is nothing new—this is "the way the college has always been."

Climbing the Educational Ladder

The self-proclaimed "best of CUNY," City College students are generally very satisfied with the education they receive. According to one history major, the toughest major offered is "without a doubt electrical engineering, though biochem is also rough." Although it may be difficult, the strongest program at CCNY is engineering, and in recent years this and the other sciences have grown quickly. CCNY also offers a variety of special premed options, including the Sophie Davis program, a seven-year track that partners with the State University of New York's Downstate Medical Center. For those students who don't want to struggle through years of hard classes, CCNY students report that there is one easy major; "psychology [is] the prettiest major to have, everyone ends up with a high grade."

In order to smooth the transition to college life, a block system was recently instituted for CCNY freshmen. In this system, 20 to 30 first-year students are grouped together and attend the same classes with the same professors their first semester. One block participant raved that this is a "great way for freshman to get to know some faces and gives them a set schedule for their first semester, so that they'll be ready to pick their own classes second semester." Students are placed in blocks based on their intended major, but most of the block classes are in the liberal arts. By pairing three liberal-arts courses with one course for their major, the block system gives freshman "a fuller view of what the school has to offer" and what another student calls "a community feel." In addition, all freshmen have to take a "freshman seminar," which teaches time-management and study skills, encourages them to explore the city, and offers general counseling services. While students receive no credit for freshman seminar, most are glad to have it. As one freshman noted, "in high school you're stressed [by teachers] about doing this and doing that; here it's up to you. You can go to class or not—you decide whether to take the education for granted. They don't take attendance here, so you're really responsible for yourself."

CCNY professors recognize that learning takes place in and out of the classroom. Art and music professors, in particular, like to send their students to the Metropolitan Museum of Art and to the Museum of Natural History for projects. At CCNY, all grades given are whole letters; there are no pluses or minuses to be found. According to one junior, this motivates students to work harder, as they will not be complacent and settle for a B+ when they could put in a little more work and earn that A.

And there are certainly a number of good places to work or to hang out on campus. Many CCNY students bring their laptops to the library and cafeteria, where they can work and eat at the same time. The cafeteria offers deli sandwiches, rice and beans, and other fast food at a reasonable price. The Hungry Minds Café is also another good place to lounge in between classes. Students will often kick off their sneakers and take a little nap, and "occasionally you'll hear a little snore." Students also named Shepherd Hall and the Game Room as good places to unwind—"you see a lot of guys in the Game Room, so if you're a single female, that's definitely where you want to go."

For anyone looking for a good education in an urban setting—at a fair price, no less—City College is definitely worth checking out. The students are friendly, active, and as diverse as the Harlem area itself. CCNY students don't miss having "a cute little dorm room," because they have a whole city to explore. —*Jenny Zhang*

FYI

If you come to City College, you'd better bring a "planner to keep up with all the things going on" and "a cell phone, because you'll get a lot of numbers from all the cute girls."

What is the typical weekend schedule? "Sleep in on Friday, work, then party on Saturday, and work and sleep on Sunday."

If I could change one thing about City College, I would "add dorms."

Three things every student at City College should do before graduating are "visit every building, go to a jazz concert, and do something dramatic."

City University of New York / Hunter College

Address: 695 Park Avenue; New York, NY 10021
Phone: 212-772-4490
E-mail address: admissions@hunter.ccny.edu
Web site URL: www.hunter.cuny.edu
Founded: 1870
Private or Public: public
Religious affiliation: none
Location: urban
Undergraduate enrollment: 15,494
Total enrollment: 20,516
Percent Male/Female: 30%/70%
Percent Minority: 55%
Percent African-American: 18%
Percent Asian: 15%
Percent Hispanic: 22%
Percent Native-American: 0%
Percent in-state/out of state: 96%/4%
Percent Pub HS: 74%
Number of Applicants: 10,550
Percent Accepted: 29%
Percent Accepted who enroll: 49%
Entering: 1,491
Transfers: 1,296
Application Deadline: 15 Mar
Mean SAT: NA
Mean ACT: NA
Middle 50% SAT range: V 470-570, M 480-580
Middle 50% ACT range: NA
3 Most popular majors: psychology, English, social sciences
Retention: 80%
Graduation rate: 32%
On-campus housing: 1%
Fraternities: 2%
Sororities: 1%
Library: 760,000 volumes
Tuition and Fees: $3,369 in; $6,969 out
Room and Board: NA
Financial aid, first-year: NA
Varsity or Club Athletes: 1%
Early Decision or Early Action Acceptance Rate: NA

Located in the heart of a great cultural center, Hunter College in New York City has an extremely diverse undergraduate community, dedicated professors at the top of their fields, and solid educational opportunities.

Academic Opportunities

Students cite nursing, education, and the performing arts as the best departments at Hunter, with English and communications also garnering high praise. The honors program offers interdisciplinary courses to qualified students, which allows them to devote less attention to core requirements and more to their majors. Hunter also offers study-abroad programs in Europe, Africa, Asia, South America, and the Caribbean, with Europe the most popular destination.

The college's distribution requirements include lab science; several courses in the humanities; music, sociology, or economics; and four semesters of a language. Few students complain about these requirements. Classes can be as large as 300 in the sciences and introductory lectures, and as small as ten in the upper-division and honors classes. Evening sessions are popular at Hunter, especially among the many students holding day jobs.

Students say professors are supportive and "treat us as human beings." At least 50 percent of the staff are adjunct professors, whom students say are outstanding. Students don't have as much access to these professors, however, because adjuncts have neither on-campus phone numbers nor offices. For the most part, students say they must make appointments to see their professors. "The professors are there but students have to make the effort to get help," claimed one undergraduate. TAs do not lead sections or teach classes.

Commuter School

Hunter's main academic buildings are uptown, on East 68th Street, but the only dorm is on 25th Street. A shuttle bus runs from the dorm to the campus every hour, and public transportation is abundant. First- and second-year students generally remain at the school for the whole day. Between classes, they hang out or study in the cafeterias, hallways, lounges, or club offices. Although Hunter is primarily a commuter school, students say it's easier to meet classmates and become involved in campus life if they live in the dorm, which houses about 400 people. Most of the dorm residents are in the nursing, physical therapy, athletics, or honors programs. With no meal plan, students are forced to dine in the neighborhood's numerous eateries or, as most prefer, prepare food for themselves in the kitchens located on every dorm floor. Each dorm room has the added convenience of a sink. Many undergrads go to Hunter's library to study. As one sophomore put it, the silence is "like a cemetery." Commuter students generally opt to study at home.

New York City provides students with countless options for entertainment including, but hardly limited to, world-famous theaters, restaurants, and museums. Campus parties are rare, and students say drinking is rare as well. Sororities and fraternities play a minor role in campus life, occupying no houses and performing charity work as their main activity. Cultural clubs organize some social events such as dances and rallies. RAs on each floor of the dorm sponsor activities each month, ranging from a papier-mâché night to a game night.

Politically Active

The fact that most Hunter students hail from New York, New Jersey, or Connecticut does not at all imply a homogeneous student body. According to one student, "It's incredible; everyone's completely different, yet they live together in harmony." Another student called Hunter a "mini-NYC." Many students are politically active, especially concerning issues of racism, feminism, abortion rights, the environment, gay and lesbian rights, and AIDS. The student branch of New York Public Interest Resource Group (PIRG) gets students involved in both environmental and campus issues. The active student senate represents academic departments, school interest, and students at large. One student said anyone can join the senate, although not everyone gets to vote. The teachers involved are said to be "top-notch."

> **"It's incredible; everyone's completely different, yet they live together in harmony."**

Although sports are not a big priority on campus, both basketball games and wrestling matches are well attended. Intramurals such as volleyball are also quite popular. Hunter's athletic facilities receive positive reviews despite the complaint that, as one student put it, "they're hidden in the basement." Students read the *Hunter Envoy*, a biweekly newspaper, as well as other student publications. Ethnic organizations (such as the Asian-American, Caribbean, Greek, Puerto Rican, and African-American clubs) are very popular, as are dance groups, choir, jazz band, and theater clubs. The student-run Shakespeare Society also produces a full play and a collection of scenes once a semester. No classes are held during Dean's Hours every Tuesday from 2 to 3 P.M. and Wednesday from 1 to 3 P.M., so that student clubs and organizations can hold meetings.

The City

The Hunter campus is truly part of the city. According to one student, "At times it's good because you're involved with the real world, but you also miss out on the things a private university in the city can offer, like a campus and unity." One undergraduate said there's "not really a campus, just some buildings together, and the dorm is by itself." Many students work full-time and consider school a "part-time thing." The city provides easy access to work and job openings.

"The school is involved with the community, and the community is involved with the school," one student said. The area around Hunter is a commercial district, so it's busy, and students assert that they "blend in." The school has taken measures to ensure student security, including emergency phones and guards that "roam around a lot." Each dorm resident is generally allowed no more than two guests at a time.

According to one student, "The teachers are at the top of their fields and really want to teach, but they're not teaching under the best conditions." Students are managing all the same, however. As one undergraduate pointed out, "It is a city school, and the tuition is still low."

One student warned incoming freshmen to "make sure you're on top of your education and getting what you want. No one's going to help you unless you ask for help." Another student suggested that if you're looking for a structured program and lots of guidance, Hunter might not be the best choice. But Hunter students seem satisfied. "We get a much richer experience because of the huge diversity in terms of nationality and also in terms of age," one said. "This diversity gives a unique flavor to Hunter College." In fact, many undergrads see Hunter as a working model of the real world. —*Andrew Hamilton*

FYI

If you come to Hunter, you'd better bring "a map—the city and buildings can be confusing."

What is the typical weekend schedule? "A lot of people participate in student government and political activities on the weekend. Also, many like to go downtown or to midtown. The options are endless in the city."

If I could change one thing about Hunter, I'd "change the career advisor system. It is very impersonalized now and things can get overwhelming."

Three things every student at Hunter should do before graduating are "see a student drama production, eat from a street vendor, and walk across the third-floor bridge from the outside (all the buildings are connected by bridges)."

City University of New York / Queens College

Address: 65-30 Kissena Blvd, Kiely Hall, Room 217; Flushing NY 11367-1597
Phone: 718-997-5614
E-mail address: NA
Web site URL: www.qc.edu
Founded: 1937
Private or Public: public
Religious affiliation: none
Location: urban
Undergraduate enrollment: 12,012
Total enrollment: 15,061
Percent Male/Female: 37%/63%
Percent Minority: 45%
Percent African-American: 9%
Percent Asian: 10%
Percent Hispanic: 19%
Percent Native-American: 16%
Percent in-state/out of state: 99%/1%
Percent Pub HS: 67%
Number of Applicants: 6,280
Percent Accepted: 40%
Percent Accepted who enroll: 48%
Entering: 1,233
Transfers: 1,684
Application Deadline: rolling
Mean SAT: NA
Mean ACT: NA
Middle 50% SAT range: V 440-550, M 480-590
Middle 50% ACT range: NA
3 Most popular majors: accounting, sociology, psychology
Retention: 84%
Graduation rate: 42%
On-campus housing: 0%
Fraternities: 1%
Sororities: 1%
Library: 985,550 volumes
Tuition and Fees: $3,561 in; $7,161 out
Room and Board: NA
Financial aid, first-year: 89%
Varsity or Club Athletes: 1%
Early Decision or Early Action Acceptance Rate: NA

Take 76 acres of gently rolling grassy hills, plop down a handful of student-filled buildings and some fountains, roll in the famed skyline of the largest and busiest city in America, and you have the basis for Queens College. Students claim that Queens College has the finest professors and the nicest campus of any CUNY school. Just as the college uniquely accommodates both city and nature lovers, it also stretches to fit a wide range of academic needs, from honors seminars with renowned professors to catch-up work in algebra.

Academic Options

Queens College offers majors in dozens of academic fields. Among the most popular are political science, psychology, media studies, and an array of science programs populated with pre-meds. Many students apply directly to the famed Aaron Copland School of Music, which offers special undergraduate programs in music education and performance. Through the Freshman Year Initiative program, first-year students can enroll in a special sequence of courses taught by the college's most sought-after professors. Undergrads rave about the accessibility of the faculty: "At the first class, a famous professor gave us his home phone number," one junior recounted. According to one senior, "there are so many must-take professors at Queens College, I can't even attempt to name them all."

All Queens College undergrads must fulfill the Liberal Arts and Science Area Requirements (LASAR), which divides the college curriculum into seven areas. Students take introductory courses in each area, many of which are large lecture classes. According to a senior, "the LASAR requirements aren't too hard to fill—they're mostly classes you'd want to take anyway." Outside of introductory courses, students can expect an average class size of 20 to 40 people.

Student opinion varies widely when it comes to Queens College's course registration system. Undergrads may preregister for classes within their major, and generally do not have trouble enrolling in required courses. Nevertheless, some students report having had difficulty gaining admission to seminars outside of their majors. The actual registration process, which one student described as "relatively hassle-free," takes place either by phone or online. Professors post syllabi, class readings, and discussion forums on Queens College's online "Blackboard" server, demonstrating the strides Queens College has made to keep its technology up-to-date.

"The college has so much potential, it's mind-blowing."

Talented and motivated Queens College undergrads can pursue an honors track in one of six broad fields: Business and Liberal Arts, Journalism and Liberal Arts, Humanities, Mathematical and Natural Sciences, Pre-Engineering, and Pre-Health Profession Studies. "There is an honors track to fit every student's academic interests," reported an anthropology major. Extremely popular among undergrads, the Business and Liberal Arts (BALA) track "has a strong community feel," according to a senior. Extra-small classes and close contact with professors characterize Queens College's honors programs: "The most I've ever had in a class is 20 people," reported one BALA student.

Queens also makes an effort to reach out to students who have fallen behind in their studies, not just to its academic elite. Its SEEK program (Search for Education, Elevation, and Knowledge) is designed for students who might have missed a few essential high school courses or who aren't ready for a standard college curriculum. SEEK provides personal academic counselors who help students schedule the necessary college prep classes that will enable them to begin the LASAR sequence and eventually earn a bachelor's degree. According to one student, "If it weren't for SEEK, I wouldn't be in college."

Campus Life, Commuter School

Since Queens College is a commuter school (there are no dorms; most students live with their parents), many students leave campus directly after classes. To encourage undergrads to spend a little extra time on campus, the administration schedules "free hours" in midday, during which no classes are held. The student union serves as headquarters for more than 175 extracurricular clubs and organizations, along with Thursday-night club-hosted parties, frequent guest lectures, and several wide-screen TVs. Popular extracurriculars include the Student Association, the campus newspaper *The Knight News*, and cultural groups such as Hillel and the International Club. Undergrads also turn out for campus movie screenings, student drama productions, and concerts at the Colden Center for the Arts.

Queens College undergrads have many dining options. Students can sample from pizza, Chinese food, and kosher cuisine in the cafeteria. Students report that the quality of the food is better than average. Also, an array of fast-food restaurants just off campus allow a quick and greasy meal to break up the cafeteria routine.

Queens College students take pride in the beauty and prime location of their campus.

"You can see the skyline from anywhere on campus—it's breathtaking," described one student. Undergrads can reach the heart of Manhattan within half an hour via bus or train. One popular on-campus destination is the library, where students study among "lots of gorgeous lounges and expensive computer labs," according to a senior. For students driving to school, campus parking facilities are reportedly adequate.

Athletics do not occupy a central place in Queens College's campus life. While there is no football program, the softball, soccer, and swimming teams attract many participants. Low spectator attendance is a problem, however: "If we get 20 people to come see a game, that's a great turnout," reported one team member. Even if few actively support their Queens College Knights, all students can take advantage of the campus gym and athletic facilities.

Student opinion is mixed when it comes to Queens College's social life. One senior lamented, "Since Queens College is a commuter school, people want to go home. It takes initiative to get involved in social life." Nevertheless, many undergrads stick around after classes for campus parties, which often take place in the student union's fourth-floor ballroom. A number of fraternities and sororities exist, offering students another opportunity to interact after classes, though none of them have houses.

Even though most Queens College students are from the New York area, undergrads are quick to mention the diversity of the campus: "It's one of the most diverse campuses in the country—it's wonderful to interact with people of every background," described one senior. A large population of international students further enhances the diversity of the student body. Not surprisingly, this mirrors the diversity in the New York community of Flushing that surrounds the college.

Because the state has imposed various budget cuts affecting Queens College (and the entire CUNY system), students have rallied to preserve and expand the unique resources of their school. From a wealth of attentive professors to a vast selection of specialized academic programs, the Queens College experience offers an inexpensive, flexible education to students of all backgrounds and interests. Students hope that Queens College will continue to pursue these goals in the future because, as one senior articulated, "the college has so much potential, it's mind-blowing." —*Justin Albstein*

FYI

If you come to Queens College, you'd better bring "an open mind, because the campus is so incredibly diverse."

What is the typical weekend schedule? "Thursday night: party on campus, Friday/Saturday: chill with friends or go into the city, Sunday: catch up on schoolwork."

If I could change one thing about Queens College, I would "give it a larger budget."

Three things that every student should do before graduating from Queens College are "go bar hopping in the city, go to a Broadway play, go to a few campus parties."

Clarkson University

Address: Box 5605; Potsdam, NY 13699
Phone: 800-527-6577
E-mail address: admissions@clarkson.edu
Web site URL: www.clarkson.edu
Founded: 1896
Private or Public: private
Religious affiliation: none
Location: rural
Undergraduate enrollment: 2,756
Total enrollment: 2,902
Percent Male/Female: 75%/25%
Percent Minority: 7%
Percent African-American: 2%
Percent Asian: 3%
Percent Hispanic: 1%
Percent Native-American: 1%
Percent in-state/out of state: 77%/23%
Percent Pub HS: 86%
Number of Applicants: 2,556
Percent Accepted: 81%
Percent Accepted who enroll: 28%
Entering: 725
Transfers: 89
Application Deadline: 15 Mar
Mean SAT: NA
Mean ACT: NA
Middle 50% SAT range: V 520-620, M 580-670
Middle 50% ACT range: NA
3 Most popular majors: mechanical engineering, civil engineering, multi/interdisciplinary studies
Retention: 87%
Graduation rate: 73%
On-campus housing: 75%
Fraternities: 15%
Sororities: 12%
Library: 272,204 volumes
Tuition and Fees: $23,500
Room and Board: $8,726
Financial aid, first-year: 80%
Varsity or Club Athletes: 12%
Early Decision or Early Action Acceptance Rate: 89%

Nestled in the small college town of Potsdam, NY, Clarkson is a thriving undergraduate university primarily dedicated to the teaching of engineering and business. With approximately 2700 undergraduate students, and with class sizes averaging only 20 students per class, Clarkson is a closely knit community where students and professors come together to solve real-world problems in a hands-on manner.

And You Thought the SATs Were Hard . . .

One thing that all students at Clarkson can attest to is the rigorous and demanding workload. As one senior put it, "Clarkson is a fast-paced school where professors have high expectations." However, few students find their worldoad unmanageable, with most students agreeing that what they gain from their courses is well worth the work they put in. Some of the things that students liked best about classes at Clarkson include the emphasis on interdisciplinary learning and team-based approaches to problem solving.

Although the workload might be hard at Clarkson, most students agree that their "professors are great." Not only do most professors have flexible office hours, some even make the effort of visiting students or holding study sessions in student residence halls. In addition to academic interactions however, some professors also interact with students socially through intramural sports or other extracurricular activities. It seems that the only negative thing students had to say about teaching at Clarkson was the inevitable presence of TAs and professors with strong accents.

Since Clarkson is mainly an engineering and business school, most students major in those two areas, although majors in the sciences, humanities, and liberal arts are available as well. Popular majors at Clarkson include mechanical engineering, interdisciplinary engineering and management, and e-business. Regardless of what the major is, however, each student at Clarkson must complete a common set of distributional requirements. These include courses in the humanities, social sciences, natural sciences, engineering, computers, and math. Clarkson is renowned for its strong emphasis on "learning by doing" in which students are encouraged to apply the skills that they gain in classrooms to solving practical, everyday problems. For example, a program called Venture@Moore House allows a group of sophomores to design and market a new product while living together. Indeed, this is representative of the Clarkson academics atmosphere where "rather than being a competitive environment, Clarkson is more of a cooperative learning environment in which students are encouraged to work in collaborative group projects."

Living and Dining

All freshmen at Clarkson live in well-furnished doubles with "good heating." For freshmen, these rooms are located in a cluster of residence buildings (the Quad) that house approximately 60 students per floor. After freshmen year, students can also choose to live in themed houses, Greek houses, or townhouses, which one junior considered "the cream of the crop." Most students at Clarkson live on campus for all four years and permission must be obtained to live off campus. However, off-campus housing is not too difficult to come by and is usually available within a ten-minute walk from campus.

An RA system does exist in the Clarkson dorms, although for the most part, RAs are generally viewed as fair. As one RA put it, "just don't be stupid and you'll be fine, but if you feel the need to be stupid, at least be nice to the RA who catches you."

Food at Clarkson received mixed reviews. As one student summed it up, "the food used to be bad, but it has really improved in the past few years. For the most part they [now] have something for everyone, and if they do not, they are more than willing to work with you on the issue." For the occasions when dining hall food simply will not do, Potsdam offers many great restaurants serving different national and international cuisines. Some of the more notable spots include The Cantina, Lobster House, and Little Italy, any of which would be "great spots for a nice date."

Filling up Free Time (As If Such a Thing Exists at Clarkson)

Although Clarkson is not a dry campus, partying in residence halls are forbidden, so most of the alcohol-related activities occur in either the various fraternity houses on and off campus or the local bars. A typical freshman weekend generally includes at least one such party and most students agree that being underage does not pose a large problem. However, one student complained that "these parties serve just beer" and that "only a few themed parties each semester serve something besides beer." Just how freely does the beer flow at these parties? When asked if drinking ever gets out of hand, one student thought that Clarkson "has a problem of not being harsh enough" about alcohol and that "problems [occur] every weekend." Another thought that most people were "very responsible" about their drinking. For students not into the party scene, Clarkson organizes movies, guest speakers, and other events for students each week.

Other extracurricular activities also play a large part of life at Clarkson. Some of the more popular activities include the Outing Club, Clarkson TV, Clarkson Radio, and the Clarkson Senate. Devotion to extracurricular activities varies. While some students are "involved in way too many things," others concentrate just on a few. Overall, extracurriculars are "pretty much what you choose to make of them."

Golden (K)nights

The Greek scene at Clarkson, consisting of ten recognized fraternities and two recognized sororities, plays a large role in the lives of many students. There is delayed rush at Clarkson, which is "great because you get to know other students well before you pledge, so you don't end up picking the wrong house." Fraternities and sororities live together in recognized Greek houses that offer their own optional meal plans. Apart from throwing the various weekend parties mentioned above, fraternities and sororities play an important role in the Potsdam community by raising money for charities and performing countless hours of community service. It is interesting to note that Clarkson recently held the honor of having the highest fraternity and sorority average GPA in the Northeast.

But what do students do on Saturday nights, before the kegs are tapped at the frats? Why, go watch a hockey game, of course. At Clarkson "Hockey is #1." As the only Division I teams on campus, the men and women's hockey teams are extremely important to school spirit—games against arch-rival and neighbor, St. Lawrence University always sell out quickly. In order to maintain the level of their hockey team, Clarkson actively recruits players from around the country. This practice has created some resentment among students, one of whom disliked "the money wasted on athletics when many parts of the campus need fixing."

Not a varsity athlete? No problem. "If you want to play a sport but not on a school team, there are over 100 intramural teams to play on." Furthermore, Clarkson boasts a top-notch indoor recreation center that houses a long list of facilities including a gym, a pool, a weight room, and several basketball courts.

In and Around Campus

Clarkson students come from predominantly Northeast middle-class families. Ethnically, the student body is largely white, though as one student said, "a proud black community" exists on campus. Unfortunately, as one female student noted, because Clarkson is an engineering school, "the guy to girl ratio is so off that there are a lot of single guys out here."

The Clarkson campus is situated on 460 wooded acres and consists of 49 buildings. Although many of the buildings on campus house state-of-the-art facilities, most students find Clarkson's buildings aesthetically "boring." What Clarkson lacks in architectural beauty, it makes up for in natural beauty, especially during the fall. However, don't forget your boots—being buried under snow for four months of each year is yet another endearing characteristic of the university.

> **"Clarkson is a fast-paced school where professors have high expectations."**

Potsdam is a typical college town that bustles during the school year and hibernates during academic breaks. It is not unusual to hear some students complain "there is nothing to do in Potsdam." One junior countered that such people "need to get out of their rooms more, and see what [Potsdam] has to offer. [The city] may not be a metropolis but there are definitely things to do, and places to see."

When the need to get away from Potsdam arises, many options exist, most of which are within a few hours' drive from campus. These include Syracuse and Albany in New York, as well as Cornwall, Ottawa, and Montreal in Canada. Montreal, one of the renowned party cities of North America, is especially popular. Many students, however, are satisfied with the campus life at Clarkson and the small (but promising!) local community of Potsdam. Watch some hockey, play in the snow, and you'll be fine. —*Anthony Xu*

FYI

If you come to Clarkson University, you'd better bring a "warm coat" and a "computer."

What is the typical weekend schedule? "Saturday, sleep in, have brunch with friends, go watch the Men's Hockey game, and then party; Sunday, sleep in, do homework all afternoon, and then catch up on TV with friends."

If I could change one thing about Clarkson University, I'd change "the male to female ratio and the fact that it snows all year long!"

The three things every student at Clarkson should do before graduating are "cheering on you Golden Knights to victory, making 'creative' snow sculptures at night, and going clubbing in Canada."

Colgate University

Address: 13 Oak Drive; Hamilton, NY 13346-1383
Phone: 315-228-7401
E-mail address: admission@mail.colgate.edu
Web site URL: www.colgate.edu
Founded: 1819
Private or Public: private
Religious affiliation: none
Location: rural
Undergraduate enrollment: 2,827
Total enrollment: 2,827
Percent Male/Female: 49%/51%
Percent Minority: 11%
Percent African-American: 4%
Percent Asian: 4%
Percent Hispanic: 3%
Percent Native-American: 0%
Percent in-state/out of state: 33%/67%
Percent Pub HS: 65%
Number of Applicants: 6,268
Percent Accepted: 34%
Percent Accepted who enroll: 35%
Entering: 731
Transfers: 11
Application Deadline: 15 Jan
Mean SAT: NA
Mean ACT: NA
Middle 50% SAT range: V 610-700, M 630-710
Middle 50% ACT range: 27-31
3 Most popular majors: English, political science, economics
Retention: 95%
Graduation rate: 88%
On-campus housing: 67%
Fraternities: 35%
Sororities: 32%
Library: 1,110,309 volumes
Tuition and Fees: $29,940
Room and Board: $7,155
Financial aid, first-year: 49%
Varsity or Club Athletes: 39%
Early Decision or Early Action Acceptance Rate: 49%

Colgate was founded in 1819 by 13 Baptist men with $13 and 13 prayers. Despite having the lucky number 13, Colgate is a school with a lot working in its favor. Located in Hamilton, New York, Colgate has grown from its humble beginnings into a school with close to 3,000 undergraduates and numerous opportunities for students. If you are looking for a small school with a great community and strong academic tradition, then Colgate is the place for you.

"Gym and Swim Test . . . Could Do Without"

There are 49 concentrations at Colgate with the most popular being English, Economics and Psychology. All freshmen choose a seminar class from a huge variety of choices including everything from

Global Change to Philosophy. This small class gives students the opportunity to interact closely with their 20 classmates as well as their professor. Their seminar professor then becomes the student's advisor until the spring semester of their sophomore year, when students select their major. Most students seem to like the system because it allows them to get to know their advising group as well as their advisor both in and out of the classroom. However, as one sophomore complained, "There are a lot of good teachers here. It just seems that all of the not-so-good ones are assigned to be academic advisors."

Colgate requires 32 classes to graduate, which include four core classes, two classes in each of the three distribution areas (social sciences, natural sciences, and humanities), four gym classes, and a swim test. As one student described, "The core, distribution, and language requirements are great . . . That's how I picked my two majors. Gym and swim test . . . could do without." Colgate also offers various study abroad programs that students love. These include short-term options, where a student can go to a foreign country and study in a typical classroom setting for just a month.

Students seem to find that "the workload isn't smothering, but [that] it takes time." Most classes have approximately 15 to 30 students, with the 175 students in Introductory Psychology being the largest class at the school. Most students find that the more difficult classes are in the natural sciences, while Sociology and Education tend to be easier. Generally, students love their professors and find them very approachable and intelligent. As one freshman said, "All of the classes I have taken so far have been great."

An Ideal Campus

When asked what they think of their campus, Colgate students have the same response: "it is absolutely gorgeous." The only complaint seems to be the large hill upon which it is situated, known as Cardiac Hill. One student commented, "Walking up and down the hill really isn't fun . . . especially in the winter." Most of the freshmen dorms are on top of the hill, while upperclassmen housing, fraternities, and restaurants are at the bottom. Students say Moraine Lake is the most noteworthy aspect of the beautiful landscape because, as one senior commented, "it would be the perfect place for a fall wedding." For this purpose there is also the chapel, which is the most prominent building seen from the quad. Another architectural beauty on campus is Persson Hall, which gives the best view of Colgate from its glass walkway.

Due to the strong on-campus life, the small town of Hamilton doesn't have much to offer students. As one student commented, "Downtown Hamilton . . . has enough to sustain day-to-day life. People don't leave campus too often; only every once in a while." With this on-campus emphasis, students note feeling "completely safe at Colgate."

"Pretty Good Rooms"

There is a good amount of variety in housing at Colgate, which begins right from freshman year. There are approximately seven freshman dorms that all have slight variations. West is considered to be the best, but it is co-ed by floor as opposed to Drake, which is co-ed by room. East is substance-free, while West is thought to be the party dorm. Most people are very happy with where they were placed freshman year and find that their best friends are their roommates or other people from these dorms. There is a Residential Advisor program, which places a group of students with an upperclassman, who helps with moving in, roommate issues, and maintaining the university alcohol policies. The RAs can be strict, but students generally don't find the program to be much of a problem.

After freshman year, there are a number of different options for upperclassmen. Some students opt to live in theme houses like the Asian Interest House or the Ecology House. Sophomores usually continue to live in dorms, juniors tend to go for on-campus apartments, and seniors often enter a lottery to live off campus. As one student remarked, "All classes have pretty good rooms and a variety of set-ups."

Homogeneous

The consensus among Colgate students is that the student body is very "homogenous." However, no one seems to be overly concerned about this fact because most students anticipate this before deciding to attend the university. As one freshman commented, "The vast majority of students are rich, good-looking white kids who like to go out and play sports." The evidence for this appears in a variety of different ways ranging from the cars students drive to the clothes they wear. Many people do have cars, although there is a good shuttle system for those who don't. As far as apparel, most students make an effort to look nice before they head off to class. J. Crew, Polo, and Abercrombie & Fitch are brands of choice and more generally, students will wear "something pretty preppy or something very designer."

Despite the lack of diversity, students seem to be very happy with their classmates. As one junior commented about the student body, "I absolutely adore it!" People think that they are more comfortable with the students they have found at Colgate than if the school were composed differently. There is a small portion of minorities, but people find that they generally stick together rather than integrate with the rest of the student body. The accepted stereotype is that Colgate students are "highly intelligent underachievers who enjoy an active social life."

"Everybody Works Hard and Plays Hard"

One of the most unusual aspects of the Colgate social scene is that students party Wednesday through Monday. Students find that their partying revolves around the extensive Greek system and local bars. Upperclassmen can be found in one of the three most popular bars, which are the Jug, Risky Business, and the Hour Glass. Each provides a different atmosphere. Provided they have a fake ID, freshmen can be found in these bars as well. This tends to be a preferred option for those who do not enjoy the on-campus party scene that primarily consists of fraternity parties.

At Colgate, the Greek system is quite popular, although people who do not rush don't find it to be a problem. The parties are open to all and rush does not start until sophomore year, so that people can form connections during the previous year. Students really like the opportunity to rush because it opens them up to a whole new group of people. The most popular frat is Sigma Chi and the most popular sorority is Kappa Kappa Gamma, but no matter which they end up in, students find that they form strong bonds with their brothers and sisters. Frats tend to have many theme parties, ranging from the Reform School Party (with the Catholic school girl look) to Beta Beach (everyone dresses in beachwear). The sororities also throw mixers with themes such as Rubik's Cube, where people wear all of the colors and end up wearing one color by switching clothes.

> **"Even though there are only 3,000 kids and we are in a town that is basically one block long, there is always something to do."**

There is not a very strong dating scene, but rather students experience random hook-ups. Essentially, people at Colgate like to have a good time and, as one freshman said, "Everybody works hard and plays hard."

Extracurriculars

Some of the most popular student organizations at Colgate are Outdoor Ed, Student Government, the Link program (where juniors and seniors help advise freshmen), and Sidekick, in which Colgate students tutor elementary school children. There are many community service options and people often volunteer through their sorority or fraternity. There are also some comedy and a capella groups, as well as the CUTV station (which is on Channel 13 as part of the school's lucky number). Many students work on-campus jobs and according to students, "everyone is involved in something."

"Sports Are Very Intense"

One of the most common extracurricular activities at Colgate is athletics. The most popular sports are football, basketball and hockey, which tend to draw the greatest number of people. People are proud of their teams and enjoy going out to the games to show school spirit. The gym facilities are also quite extensive, including one of the best golf courses in the entire country. People make use of the gym with great frequency, especially the weight room and tracks. The Greek system also organizes intramural games that many people can participate in. Students say that even though Colgate is a small school: "sports are very intense."

To sum up the Colgate atmosphere, one sophomore commented, "Even though there are only 3,000 kids and we are in a town that is basically one block long, there is always something to do. It never gets boring or old." If you are looking for an academically strong school with a relaxed atmosphere and beautiful campus, then you should put Colgate down as an excellent option. *—Rebecca Ives*

FYI

If you come to Colgate, you'd better bring "a warm jacket."

What is the typical weekend schedule? "Friday night, go out; Saturday, brunch at Frank Dining Hall, work; Saturday night, go out; Sunday, work all day."

If I could change one thing about Colgate, I'd "pick it up and move it to the Caribbean."

Three things every student at Colgate should do before graduating are "kiss someone on Willow Path (that's the person you are supposed to marry), get rowdy at a hockey game, and wait in line at the Jug."

Columbia University

Address: 212 Hamilton Hall; New York, NY 10027
Phone: 212-854-2522
E-mail address: ugrad-admiss@columbia.edu
Web site URL: www.columbia.edu
Founded: 1754
Private or Public: private
Religious affiliation: none
Location: urban
Undergraduate enrollment: 6,988
Total enrollment: 21,857
Percent Male/Female: 52%/48%
Percent Minority: 28%
Percent African-American: 7%
Percent Asian: 14%
Percent Hispanic: 7%
Percent Native-American: 0%
Percent in-state/out of state: 25%/75%
Percent Pub HS: NA
Number of Applicants: 14,129
Percent Accepted: 12%
Percent Accepted who enroll: 63%
Entering: 1,041
Transfers: 17
Application Deadline: 2 Jan
Mean SAT: NA
Mean ACT: NA
Middle 50% SAT range: V 660-760, M 660-750
Middle 50% ACT range: 27-33
3 Most popular majors: English, social sciences, visual and performing arts
Retention: 98%
Graduation rate: 93%
On-campus housing: 98%
Fraternities: 15%
Sororities: 9%
Library: 7,200,000 volumes
Tuition and Fees: $28,206
Room and Board: $8,546
Financial aid, first-year: 44%
Varsity or Club Athletes: NA
Early Decision or Early Action Acceptance Rate: 31%

There aren't many colleges that offer students both an Ivy League education and the opportunity to live in a city alive with culture. Located in the Upper West Side of New York City, Columbia allows students to have the best of both academia and social life. "Columbia has a great mix of urban, intelligent people who are capable of so much," said one student. The students here not only learn from Nobel Laureate professors, but also get an education in street smarts while living in "the heartbeat of the U.S."

A Liberal Education

One thing many students find surprising about Columbia is that they don't have to declare a major, but can instead decide to concentrate in a specific area of study. This makes the school very appealing to those who desire variety in their liberal arts education. Nonetheless, there is a mixed reaction to the core curriculum that students are required to complete before graduation. Some students find the core to be a good way to get to know professors and fellow students because of the small class sizes, while others think that it is "too restrictive" and prevents them from taking the courses they really want to take.

"Come to Columbia only if you're willing to work hard. This place isn't easy," said one junior. Students here are competitive and know what it takes to succeed. "I've seen many sunrises while doing problem sets or studying for tests." Most students agree that although "the workload is high, it's definitely manageable." One pre-med student said that "the biggest mistake I made was taking Orgo freshman year." Students in the School of Engineering reportedly have more work than those in the College. As far as grade inflation is concerned, it "can't be that bad if the average GPA at the School of Engineering is a 3.0," although that might sound like grade inflation to most.

Most core classes have sizes of approximately 20 people. However, if you want to take Kenneth Jackson's "The History of the City of New York," be prepared to sit in the aisles if you're late to class because all the seats will be taken. Projects in Jackson's class are "a wonderful combination of the intellectual and the fun," requiring students to sign-up for various organized expeditions throughout New York City, exploring the different boroughs, the financial district, the old tenement houses, etc. and even offering an overnight bike tour with your classmates. Clearly the "largest and most popular class on campus," this class's enrollment is typically restricted to only juniors and seniors. Another popular class is introductory economics with Xavier Sala-Martin, though this course is also known to be one of the easier ones.

For the most part, students are very satisfied with their professors. "I have friends whose professors take them out for drinks at the end of the year," said one student. The relationships that students build with their instructors at Columbia "will often develop into great mentorships." Despite complaints about TAs who couldn't speak English well and professors who were caught up with their own research, one student said, "for the most part, professors at Columbia are excited to interact with their students."

From Clubs to Clubbing

In Morningside Heights, Columbia students never complain about not having anything to do. "There's a subway stop right on campus making it easy for us to venture out into the city," said one undergrad. The downside to this is that there isn't much of a campus life. To improve the situation, the university recently built a student center called Lerner Hall. However, as long as Columbia is in Manhattan, students agree that "we will never have the campus life other college students experience."

The general consensus is that "on-campus parties are a drag." Most people tend to frequent bars like The West End, Cannon's, 1020, A.M. Café, and The Heights in the vicinity of the campus for their nightlife fun. "There's just so much going on in the city that the campus is usually deserted on weekend nights," said one senior.

"New York is a drinking town," said another student. The university's stance on alcohol on campus seems pretty lenient to most students. Columbia has a voluntary ambulance service called CAVA that takes students to the hospital if they're sick or have passed out. It is used by the university to promote safety without disciplinary repercussions. Notwithstanding, students who don't drink can definitely take advantage of the other opportunities present in the City. "This is New York! You can always find something to do and people to hang out with if you work hard enough at it. There's a niche for everyone at this school." From the community service clubs on campus to the clubs in the city, the social alternatives at Columbia surpass those of most other schools simply because of its location.

Something for Everyone

"People come here from so many different places with so many different cultures and ideas," said one sophomore. Although the bulk of students come from the Tri-state area or California, there is no "typical" student at Columbia. One student commented that many people in the college are "liberal, proactive, and opinionated," explaining the presence of numerous organizations on campus. Columbia offers over 300 student groups that serve to expand religious, cultural, and political horizons for its diverse student body. One of the more widely known organizations is the marching band. "The weirdest, yet cleverest band in the world," the marching band is known for its timely performances such as its famous march through the library the night before the Organic Chemistry Final. The Columbia Community Outreach program is another popular organization that brings students to community service projects within Manhattan.

Sports are not Columbia's forte. When asked who their rival is, most students are in the dark. Students make use of the extensively renovated gym facilities (featuring basketball, squash, and racquetball courts, an indoor track, and an Olympic-size swimming pool) and the sports fields uptown from campus. Among the club sports available at Columbia are water polo, kayaking, rugby, sailing, volleyball, and skiing. One thing you can't forget if you're going to Columbia is your swimsuit: "You can't graduate without passing the swim test!"

Don't Be Fooled . . .

Even though Columbia is in the midst of bustling New York City, it's amazing how "you can forget that you're in a city" when walking through the campus. "The architects who made our campus did a good job of trying to fool us," said one freshman. Mostly made up of red brick and "classical college architecture," Columbia is always undergoing renovations. One of the newest additions is Lerner Hall, which most students agree to be an "eyesore" because of its glass walls and modern design. Students agree that the best part of their campus is "accessibility to everything" within a three-block area. One thing they wish were more common was large, open fields of grass. "There's not much room in the city, so we don't get the grassy areas to lounge around in," said one student.

One might be worried about safety at a school like Columbia, but students agree that there is no need. "The campus security is great. I walk around in my PJs at three in the morning and I don't feel threatened at all. There's always someone else up at this place," said one student.

"New York is one of the greatest cities in the world. Columbia is one of the greatest universities in the world. Put them together and you get something you can't achieve at any other college."

"A great thing about Columbia is that you're guaranteed housing all four years you're a student," explained a junior. Because reasonably priced housing in Manhattan is almost impossible to find, students agree that "you're better off staying in the dorms." East Campus is considered the nicest on-campus dorm because of its four- to six-person suites equipped with bathrooms, kitchens, and lounge areas, and views of the East and West Rivers. Wien Hall is known by far as the worst dorm, with its "nasty tiles, bad paint jobs, and rickety doors." River Hall, which was recently added back into the housing lottery, is considered the more "chill dorm" because of its co-ed suites made for 10 to 12 people, practical for large group gatherings.

The food at Columbia is "better than your high school cafeteria, but worse than your mom's cooking." First-year students are required to purchase the on-campus meal plan. Finding an eatery on campus is easy and the hours are accommodating. Columbia students can get dining points to put on their cards in order to eat at other eateries on campus, including some "good delis, a Taco Bell, and a Pizza Hut Express." Because it's in the City, students can always find a multitude of restaurants to satisfy their taste buds elsewhere as well. Some favorite restaurants off campus include Tomo for sushi, Koronet's for pizza, Taqueria y Fonda la Mexicana, and Sofia's Bistro.

What They've Got

Attending Columbia is a great experience for most students. "New York is one of the greatest cities in the world. Columbia is one of the greatest universities in the world. Put them together and you get something you can't achieve at any other college," said one student. The opportunities to participate in cutting-edge research and make connections to the business world are remarkable. Instead of looking at Monets and van Goghs in books, you can go straight to the museums and check them out in real life. But nothing will really be handed to you at Columbia. As one undergrad summed up, "You have to go and get what you want yourself. Your life here will depend on your own actions and what you make of the plentiful resources here." —*Jane Pak*

FYI

If you come to Columbia, you'd better bring a "credit card. It's expensive to live in the city."

What is the typical weekend schedule? "The weekend starts on Thursday night with lots of parties and drinking. Friday night is more of a homework or chilling-with-friends night. Saturday night is more up in the air with movies, parties, or bars."

If I could change one thing about Columbia, I'd "make it more affordable and change the relationship between students and the administration."

Three things every student at Columbia should do before graduating are "eat at Tom's Diner at 5 A.M., go to Orgo Night, and hit every bar in Morningside Heights."

The Cooper Union for the Advancement of Science and Art

Address: 30 Cooper Square; New York, NY 10003
Phone: 212-353-4120
E-mail address: admissions@cooper.edu
Web site URL: www.cooper.edu
Founded: 1859
Private or Public: private
Religious affiliation: none
Location: urban
Undergraduate enrollment: 917
Total enrollment: 917
Percent Male/Female: 67%/33%
Percent Minority: 36%
Percent African-American: 5%
Percent Asian: 16%
Percent Hispanic: 5%
Percent Native-American: 1%
Percent in-state/out of state: 56%/44%
Percent Pub HS: 60%
Number of Applicants: 2,041
Percent Accepted: 14%
Percent Accepted who enroll: 70%
Entering: 201
Transfers: 27
Application Deadline: 1 Jan
Mean SAT: NA
Mean ACT: NA
Middle 50% SAT range: V 620-710, M 690-790
Middle 50% ACT range: NA
3 Most popular majors: fine/studio arts, electrical engineering, chemical engineering
Retention: 92%
Graduation rate: 75%
On-campus housing: 15%
Fraternities: 15%
Sororities: 2%
Library: 100,000 volumes
Tuition and Fees: $27,250
Room and Board: $9,000
Financial aid, first-year: 35%
Varsity or Club Athletes: NA
Early Decision or Early Action Acceptance Rate: 20%

There is always room for Jell-O at Cooper Union. That's because school founder Peter Cooper invented the tasty treat in the 19th century. Cooper also established one of America's most unique schools. All students at the Cooper Union for the Advancement of Science and Art are provided with scholarships covering their tuition. Many important innovators, such as Thomas Edison and Andrew Carnegie, have passed through Cooper on their way to greatness.

Working Hard in the Big Apple

Cooper is located in the heart of the city that doesn't sleep, and many of the students expect to stay up late doing work. The academic course load is strenuous, with required classes including calculus, physics, chemistry, and the humanities. One student described the work as "enough for six oxen, seven work horses, and eight mules to haul from about here to the end of the hall." Physical Properties of Chemistry and Data Structures are two tough courses, but according to one student "most of the classes tend to be really hard. The professors allot more hours each week for homework, studying, or class time than you physically have." There is little grade inflation at Cooper; the average grade is a C.

Class size typically ranges from 6 to 23, but classes can be difficult to get into because size is capped at 30. "The ones required for your major are guaranteed, but the electives are the ones we line up at 4 A.M. to register for." Emphasis is placed on creative problem solving in real-life experiences. The result is that "companies know that Cooper students are hard workers and have a good foundation in their field." Many students also work on intensive research projects in their concentrations before they graduate.

Freshman year, schedules "are pretty much picked for you." While Cooper is not a liberal arts college by any measure, students of all concentrations (majors) are required to take four years of humanities. This shift from solely science-centered programs to a more diverse broad-based education dates from 1997 and was the result of student demands.

Another unique aspect of Cooper is that it consists of three mostly self-contained schools—Art, Architecture, and Engineering—each having its own requirements for graduation. Engineering is the largest and most famous school. The humanities classes provide an opportunity for students in the three schools to interact. Although intermingling between schools is limited after freshman year, one junior in engineering said that "three of my best friends here are architects."

Although overworked, students rave about the academics. "I am really happy I came here. I have learned a ridiculous amount in my short time here, and every day is a tremendous learning experience. I don't think I could have gotten that anywhere else."

Profs Who Interact

Most students rave about the professors, who are "all brilliant." There are no TAs at Cooper, ensuring that students know their professors well. Many students benefit from this close relationship, although "they'll know when you're not in class." Another student added: "I like teachers' command of the subjects. Famous (and tough professors) include Emanuel Kondopirakis (mathematics), Fred Siegel (humanities expert on American cities), John Bove (organic chemistry), Toby Cumberbatch (electronics), and Irv Brazinsky (thermodynamics). "Cooper has a very interactive environment between students and professors, who are more like your contemporaries. You really learn about what it's like to use the information they teach you in the classroom and apply it in life," said one junior.

"Others perceive us as geeks. They are right but we don't exactly walk around with pocket protectors."

A number of upperclassmen agreed that they have had awe-inspiring discussions in classrooms and with professors in which all their years of learning at Cooper seemed to "just come together and fit perfectly like a jigsaw puzzle. It was amazing." Although students think they get a lot out of their professors, some wish they would lighten the workload. One student added, "popular classes are those sections with easy professors."

Campus Life?

When a junior was asked about Cooper's campus, she replied, "what campus? You mean the five buildings within a four-block radius?" While the physical plant of Cooper is extremely small, students can use the entire city as their campus. The centralized location makes moving around campus a cinch. Few students have a problem with the condition of the buildings, but renovations are taking place anyway. "The Foundation building is still in the process of being cleaned up, and the Hewitt and Engineering buildings will be torn down and rebuilt really soon."

Living at Cooper is another unique experience. Housing is guaranteed only for freshman year, and there is only one dorm. Cooper charges students a rooming fee comparable to the price of local apartments, but living conditions are very good—some say even luxurious. One sophomore commented, "the average freshman suite is a single-sex apartment with its own kitchen and bathroom. All the buildings and suites are air-conditioned and are pretty well kept by the Cooper custodial staff."

After freshman year, most students move off campus into their own apartments. Although some students would like to live on campus for another year, the lack of housing "makes the students more independent quicker than students at other schools." Housing options vary considerably; "some students live 2 blocks or 20 blocks away. It depends on the person and what's available."

Room and board are not covered by the Cooper scholarship, and there is no meal plan. Students can get a meal plan from NYU, but most students choose to find their own food. Frankie's Kitchen is located on campus, and serves cafeteria-style food. Popular local places include Ray's Pizzeria, Around the Clock, Paul's, Teriyaki Boy, and Veniero's for pastries and deserts. Numerous ethnic foods are also available in the neighborhood. Since almost all students live in apartments or dorms equipped with kitchens, eating in is always an option.

Students believe that Cooper has a lot of cultural and geographic diversity for a small school, but one junior commented, "there are many people from different countries, but Asian, Jewish, and Anglo-Saxon seem to predominate." The idea of a student stereotype varies by school. Said one junior, "you can definitely tell the engineers from the artists by the way they dress." Another student added, "others perceive us as geeks. They are right but we don't exactly walk around with pocket protectors. We wear anything we want."

Life After Books

Cooper's downtown location in a cultural mecca helps students forget their limited campus. With so many opportunities, one senior said, "your social life is what you make it. Some kids would go to frat parties, other kids would rather experience all New York City has to offer."

Cooper has two fraternities and one sorority. Although all three are academically grounded, one of the fraternities has tried to become more party oriented, with mixed results. A sorority member commented, "we're not the typical sorority where girls get humiliated to join. We're a genuine sisterhood." The NYU Greek system and local dance clubs are options for students looking for a more traditional party scene.

Dating is not big on the Cooper campus, due largely to the lopsided male-to-female ratio among students. Many students look to the city for romance. One junior said, "there's something like three couples out of about 170 people. Many people try to maintain relationships outside of school."

The lack of centralized residency discourages many on-campus parties. One student commented, "I once went to one. Let's say I'd never go back again. But other people have told me that some are nice." The administration is somewhat lax about alcohol enforcement. A junior described the administration's policy as being of the "very lightly policed no drunk freshmen are allowed to be falling down the stairs in the dorms kind." Drugs are unpopular on campus. "Those who do drugs are no longer attending the school."

The variety of organizations at Cooper is just as abundant as at any other college. Groups such as Renaissance, the Chinese Student Association (CSA), the African-American student organization (Onyx), and the Jewish student organization (Kesher), regularly sponsor trips to concerts at Lincoln Center, movies and lecture events, and other social activities.

Professional societies on campus are more co-curricular in nature, and somewhat more important than regular extracurriculars. "Everyone belongs to a professional society, even if they don't go to the meetings," commented a junior. Respected societies include SHPE (Society of Hispanic Professional Engineers), AICHE (American Institute of Chemical Engineers), and IEEE (Institute of Electrical and Electronic Engineers).

Cooper actively recruits athletes. The basketball team was recently featured on

ESPN and HBO, though most other sports are run on a more limited basis. Ultimate Frisbee is a popular club and intramural sport on campus, but other intramurals suffer from lack of participation. There is a gym, consisting mostly of free weights for student use, but it is mostly used by male students. "Females tend to join other local gyms."

On the whole, CU students advocate that "there aren't that many other places that offer one of the best undergraduate experiences in engineering, art, or architecture. If you really do know what you want, and your parents have no problem with a free education, Cooper is the place to be." —*Matthew Gross*

FYI

If you come to Cooper Union, you'd better bring a "thousand-pack Excedrin Migraine bottle."

What is the typical weekend schedule? "Physics homework, calculus homework, the lab, new project design, chemistry homework, engineering design homework, and lastly the humanities paper."

If I could change one thing about Cooper Union, I'd "have everyone expect a little less from the students so that people could be more social and better grounded."

Three things every student should do before graduating from Cooper Union are: "get laid, get drunk, and go on a date."

Cornell University

Address: 349 Pine Tree Road; Ithaca, NY 14850-2488
Phone: 607-255-5241
E-mail address: admissions@cornell.edu
Web site URL: www.cornell.edu
Founded: 1865
Private or Public: private
Religious affiliation: none
Location: rural
Undergraduate enrollment: 13,725
Total enrollment: 20,141
Percent Male/Female: 51%/50%
Percent Minority: 27%
Percent African-American: 5%
Percent Asian: 17%
Percent Hispanic: 5%
Percent Native-American: 0%
Percent in-state/out of state: 40%/60%
Percent Pub HS: NA
Number of Applicants: 21,502
Percent Accepted: 29%
Percent Accepted who enroll: 49%
Entering: 3,003
Transfers: 555
Application Deadline: 1 Jan
Mean SAT: NA
Mean ACT: NA
Middle 50% SAT range: V 620-720, M 660-750
Middle 50% ACT range: 25-30
3 Most popular majors: engineering, business management, social sciences
Retention: 96%
Graduation rate: 90%
On-campus housing: 51%
Fraternities: 25%
Sororities: 24%
Library: 6,800,000 volumes
Tuition and Fees: $28,754
Room and Board: $9,529
Financial aid, first-year: 50%
Varsity or Club Athletes: NA
Early Decision or Early Action Acceptance Rate: 43%

At Cornell, students are surrounded by a perfectly manicured landscape and have their very own student-run hotel to boot. Cornell students are content with their environment, where tough classroom academics meet real-life application every day to produce a variety of fun and novel ideas.

The Pressure Cooker

At Cornell, the academic pressure is intense, to say the least. "It's a competitive atmosphere," said one student, "I definitely feel the crunch." All the hard work does pay off however, as the "academic opportunities are tremendous."

Cornell truly has something for everyone, with seven distinct undergraduate schools that range from architecture to hotel management. While more than one of Cornell's schools are regularly considered among the best in the country, the School of Arts and Sciences and the School of Engineering are generally considered the most rigorous programs at the University. The Hotel School, on the other hand, while very well-regarded in its field, is said to be the least difficult school: "Hotellies have one paper to write a semester and spend the rest of the time getting dressed up and eating cookies." This is not to say that many students get off easy at Cornell: Students are quick to remind you that "Cornell is the easiest Ivy to get into, and the hardest to graduate from." Psychology, biology, and government are said to be some of the most popular majors at Cornell.

"Cornell is the easiest Ivy to get into, and the hardest to graduate from."

Like their counterparts at many other schools, students at Cornell are required to fulfill a number of distributional requirements. Students in the Arts and Sciences program take a range of classes from social sciences, history, humanities, arts, and physical and biological sciences. Students must also be proficient in a foreign language—most are able to fulfill this with AP credits from high school. Some students bemoan the physical education requirement, but with the variety of classes offered in that department, students can generally find something that fits their interests.

Cornell's size has its benefits and drawbacks. For example, intro classes tend to be enormous, often filling lectures with hundreds of students. The situation isn't always improved through the help of TAs. One student complained, "Half the time I don't think my TA speaks English." As you move through the school and get past the huge introductory lectures, classes get smaller and more personalized. This may be as much a product of being savvy and finding the smaller classes as it is about prioritizing the upperclassmen above the freshmen. If you look hard enough, you can get lucky: "Out of my four classes, three are under 20 students, and I'm only a freshman."

There are about 15 libraries to choose from on campus, including something for everybody. While "the Law Library is so quiet, breathing is loud," there are also outlets for less hardcore studiers. Students love the view from Uris, "a good place to pretend you're studying," while Olin is also popular. It's lucky there are so many library options available, as students find themselves studying for more time than they would like. "Sometimes, I feel like I can barely keep up. The work just never stops."

Loving the Food

Cornell has 33 residence halls on campus. Of these, there are ten "program houses," or theme dorms, that cater to students of different interests. There are also co-op options for students who are interested. Freshmen all live together in the recently renovated North Campus, while mostly sophomores call the lively and "crazy" West Campus their home. Although West Campus has a tradition of being wild, and a "non-stop party," there are a significant number of students who still choose to live in a Greek house or nearby in Collegetown, which also boasts a lively reputation.

Those who move off campus, however, despite help from the off-campus housing office, often miss some of the on-campus amenities. It is rare that college students can actually rave about dorm food, but the hotel school definitely creates bragging rights for the entire university: Students love Cornell's "unbelievable" food service that is run by the Hotel School. One student even said that, Sunday brunch "is probably the best meal I've ever had in my life."

Greek Is Chic

Cornell has 45 fraternities and 18 sororities that include about 30 percent of the school's population. Although some frats like to claim that there is no pressure to rush, the Greek presence pervades the school's social life. From the annual Green Eggs and Kegs homecoming party to after-hours fiestas that do not even begin until the wee hours of the morning, Cornell students are certainly never without a party. Despite some recent regulations regarding alcohol, drinking still lies at the heart of the weekend party scene.

For those who are less interested in Greek life, there are plenty of other things to do around campus. Students can take in a movie at the Cornell cinema, or visit one of Collegetown's bars and dance clubs such as Republica and The Palms. Slope Day is the biggest party of the year; it's replete with live music, food, and alcohol, and, according to one student, it's the "one day the administration looks the other way with regard to drinking." Cornell students say they do drink a lot, but "it's totally your option."

Living It Up

Most students at Cornell take part in at least one of the myriad extracurricular opportunities at the school. The *Cornell Daily Sun* is very popular, along with working at any number of other student publications. Theater performances, a capella groups, and improv and sketch comedy groups are all popular as well. Community service groups also attract large numbers of students to work on any number of different projects.

Sports are very popular at Cornell. While only some students brave the weather to cheer on Big Red football in the fall, come hockey season you'll find students camping out for tickets. Intramurals are well attended by all sorts of students who aren't members of varsity teams. The school's climbing wall is also a popular spot for student recreation.

Some students find the homogeneity of the school somewhat disappointing, as many students hail from New York. Cornell is a half-public, half-private institution that entices many locals to apply and attend. One student complained, "More than half of my classmates must be from Long Island!" While students may feel there's a disproportionate New Yorker population, the university's size and international reputation ensures a feeling of diversity. One recent alum brushed off critics, noting that "there are students and professors from all over the world."

You'd Better Like Snow

While Cornellians are certainly surrounded by some of the best landscaping at any university, some complain that the campus is "beautiful, but isolated." The many feet of snow dropped in winter, however, make the campus somewhat less inviting. Winters are long and cold, maybe "God's revenge on someone!" The students have even developed their own lingo for the weather in Ithaca—"Ithacating [means] some sort of rain, snow, or sleet, with constantly gray skies."

Despite the unfortunate weather, Cornellians refuse to stay indoors. Perhaps because the campus is set away from big cities, students are confident that security is never a problem. If students are still concerned, however, the university does offer a late-night escort service to walk students home, as well as security phones throughout the campus.

Cornellians love their school. "I came here and fell in love with the campus" said one student. Another gushed, "The mix of work and play here is outstanding. I couldn't imagine myself anywhere else in the world." *—Zane Selkirk and Staff*

FYI

If you come to Cornell, you'd better bring "intellectual curiosity and snow gear."

What is the typical weekend schedule? "A slow night watching a movie on Thursday, a frat party on Friday, and catching up on all your work on every other day!"

If I could change one thing about Cornell, "I'd change the weather."

Three things every student at Cornell should do before graduating are "camp out for tickets to a hockey game, go to Slope Day, and take plenty of time to enjoy the beautiful campus."

Eastman School of Music

Address: 26 Gibbs St., Rochester, New York
Phone: 585-274-1060
E-mail address: admissions@esm.rochester.edu
Web site URL: www.rochester.edu/Eastman
Founded: 1921
Private or Public: private
Religious affiliation: none
Location: suburban
Undergraduate enrollment: 500
Total enrollment: 800
Percent Male/Female: 45%/55%
Percent Minority: 30%
Percent African-American: 3%
Percent Asian: 6%
Percent Hispanic: 2%
Percent Native-American: 0%
Percent in-state/out of state: 17%/83%
Percent Pub HS: NA
Number of Applicants: 1,950
Percent Accepted: 29%
Percent Accepted who enroll: 47%
Entering: 145
Transfers: NA
Application Deadline: 1 Jan
Mean SAT: NA
Mean ACT: NA
Middle 50% SAT range: V 500-650, M 510-650
Middle 50% ACT range: 22-28
3 Most popular majors: music performance, music education, jazz studies
Retention: 89%
Graduation rate: 86%
On-campus housing: 73%
Fraternities: 16%
Sororities: 15%
Library: NA
Tuition and Fees: $23,800
Room and Board: $11,900
Financial aid, first-year: 70%
Varsity or Club Athletes: NA
Early Decision or Early Action Acceptance Rate: NA

Do you love music? Not just as a hobby, but as your life? Do you love music enough to practice until you get calluses from playing your instrument for so long? Enough to sing not just in the shower, but for hours at a time? If you do, you probably already know about this world-renowned music school. At the Eastman School of Music, serious musicians can immerse themselves in an environment where everyone thinks about, listens to, or plays music 24 hours a day.

Learning About Music

Eastman provides its students with a rigorous and thorough musical education as well as a solid humanities background. Most students are performance majors (the technical name is "applied music"). The next most popular majors are music education, composition, and theory. The performance major requires three years of theory, two years of music history, covering everything from Gregorian chants to contemporary music, and, of course, weekly lessons. Performance majors must be competent piano players regardless of their chosen instrument. All performance majors must take Piano 101 and 102, or test out of this requirement. Eastman also has a humanities requirement, which can be filled with courses in literature, history, languages, philosophy, or a combination of these. Eastman students are serious about their humanities classes as well as their music, and classes are not easy. As one undergrad explained, "It seems like either you do really well or you completely fail." By senior year, most of Eastman's requirements are out of the way, and students have more flexible schedules that allow them to audition for jobs or graduate school.

Because Eastman is part of the University of Rochester, students have access to the university's libraries and other facilities. Some of the humanities classes are held on the U of R campus, although as one student said, "You can make it all four years without leaving this campus." The reason many like to stay on the Eastman campus is the 15- to 20-minute bus ride to the U of R.

Students who apply to Eastman can ask to work with a particular professor, and many apply to the school primarily to do just that. One student, for example, said he met his cello teacher at a summer music camp and decided to go to Eastman so he could continue to study with her. Some popular professors include clarinetist Kenneth Grant, pianist Barry Snyder, and flautist Bonita Boyd. The members of the Cleveland String Quartet also teach at Eastman and attract many to their classes and concerts. Students have substantial contact with faculty members, both in lessons and in other contexts like chamber groups.

Living and Breathing Music

Everything at Eastman revolves around music. The musical motif on campus is inescapable; the snack bar is called the Orchestra Pit and the newspaper is called *Clef Notes*. Students rave about their "access to music on hand anytime." They can go to concerts every night if they want to; Eastman's calendar is filled with student and faculty performances by soloists and groups in the Eastman Theater, concerts every other week by the Rochester Philharmonic Orchestra (Eastman students get free tickets), and limitless other performances. Eastman's Sibley Library also has an enormous music collection (the second-largest in the nation), including books, manuscripts, and recordings of "just about everything," one student said. Whenever undergrads want to listen to music but just can't find a concert to go to, they can always listen to their favorite symphony or opera at the library. Students who want to participate in athletics, student government, and other nonmusical extracurricular activities can journey over to the University of Rochester campus.

"It's not like a big old party school."

For those with the energy to play for more than the three to six hours they're expected to practice each day, there are plenty of opportunities to perform. Some students give several recitals a year, while others only do one in their four years at school. Many undergrads participate in chamber orchestras, quartets, or other small ensembles, either for credit or for fun. Jazz bands and string quartets are in constant demand at local restaurants and bars. Traveling Broadway shows that come to Rochester sometimes need a player to fill in and look to Eastman students for help. Students also have many chances to play at church services, weddings, and other special events.

Few Distractions

The Eastman campus is small, with just three buildings located in the heart of downtown Rochester: Eastman Commons, a classroom building, and Sibley Library. The food at the cafeteria is "pretty normal," according to one student. "You know, it's got a salad and pasta bar, burgers and fries, and a frozen yogurt machine." In the dorm, freshmen live in doubles, and all upperclassmen have singles. Moving off campus is a popular option for juniors and seniors, but freshmen and sophomores are required to live on campus. Many students prefer the dorm because the surrounding neighborhood reportedly "isn't the greatest." Dorm life exposes students to an environment where everyone knows everyone else and has the same interests, so life can get a little boring. For those who need to get away, popular options include the Rochester Club, which features jazz every Friday night, and the Spaghetti Warehouse. Students also like to hang out and "go crazy" at nearby dance clubs in downtown Rochester.

Campus social life is somewhat limited. As one student explained, "It's not like a big old party school." For those who favor the Greek scene, there is one all-male fraternity, one sorority, and one coed fraternity. The all-male and all-female groups each have a floor of the 14-story Eastman Commons to themselves. The all-male fraternity sponsors most of the parties, while the other Greek groups focus on community service work. Eastman has two annual formals, one in the fall and one in the spring. Small parties in the dorm are common; one student remarked that the delivery truck from a local liquor store is frequently spotted outside the dorm. Students don't seem to mind the low-key social scene; as one sophomore pointed out, "The fewer distractions, the easier it is to concentrate on practicing—which is good, I guess."

Freshmen typically arrive at Eastman from all corners of the world with visions of their names in lights. Each dreams of being the next great viola player, soprano soloist, or jazz pianist. These dreams become transformed over the next few years into more realistic aspirations. One junior explained that it doesn't matter to her whether she ends up as the soloist with a major symphony or a player in a community orchestra: "As long as I'm playing, that's cool with me." —*Susanna Chu and Staff*

FYI

If you come to Eastman, you'd better bring, "a lamp, because the dorms don't have overhead lighting."

What is the typical weekend schedule? "Practice and go to concerts."

If I could change one thing about Eastman, I would "change the weather!"

Three things every student at Eastman should do before graduating are "attend a seminar by a world-famous musician, play every instrument once, and go see Niagara Falls."

Eugene Lang College of the New School University

Address: 66 West 11th Street; New York, NY 10011
Phone: 212-229-5665
E-mail address: lang@newschool.edu
Web site URL: www.newschool.edu
Founded: 1919
Private or Public: private
Religious affiliation: none
Location: urban
Undergraduate enrollment: 4,926
Total enrollment: 7,692
Percent Male/Female: 34%/64%
Percent Minority: 23%
Percent African-American: 5%
Percent Asian: 12%
Percent Hispanic: 16%
Percent Native-American: 0%
Percent in-state/out of state: 36%/64%
Percent Pub HS: NA
Number of Applicants: 2,812
Percent Accepted: 49%
Percent Accepted who enroll: 45%
Entering: 624
Transfers: 807
Application Deadline: 1 Feb
Mean SAT: NA
Mean ACT: NA
Middle 50% SAT range: V 580-690, M 510-610
Middle 50% ACT range: 21-27
3 Most popular majors: humanities, design and applied arts, visual and performing arts
Retention: 78%
Graduation rate: 50%
On-campus housing: 21%
Fraternities: NA
Sororities: NA
Library: 4,137,000 volumes
Tuition and Fees: $24,130
Room and Board: $10,810
Financial aid, first-year: 64%
Varsity or Club Athletes: NA
Early Decision or Early Action Acceptance Rate: 76%

Situated in the heart of New York City, Eugene Lang College is the undergraduate, liberal arts college of New School University, formerly known as the New School for Social Research. Founded in 1973 as the Seminar College of the New School for Social Research, Lang acquired its current name when philanthropist Eugene Lang and his family donated $5 million to the school in 1985. Despite the name change, seminars that range in size from 5 to 15 students remain the basis of the educational experience at Lang.

It's All Up to You

Lang is a small college that enrolls over 500 students and offers a strong liberal arts education. The New School University is comprised of Actors Studio Drama School, Eugene Lang College, Graduate Faculty, Mannes College of Music, Milano Graduate School, The New School, and Parsons School of Design. It also has affiliated programs with Benjamin N. Cardozo School of Law, Dial Cyberspace Campus, Educated Citizen Project, Jazz & Contemporary Music/New School University BFA Program, and Joffrey Ballet School/New

School University BFA Program in Dance. It is obviously a bit confusing to try to make sense of how all these schools interact, but students can take classes at the other schools to a certain level.

Courses at Lang itself are divided into five broad areas of concentration: literature, writing and the arts; social and historical inquiry; mind, nature and value; urban studies; and cultural studies. Students use these areas as the basis for designing their own majors. "You don't actually design your major all by yourself; there are certain paths you can take like gender studies, queer theory or education under cultural studies" said one student. Since most classes at Lang are interdisciplinary, students say that they get exposed to many different subjects rather than sticking with a single one.

Lang's strength is in the social sciences. Students looking for hardcore science courses and lab facilities have to enroll in courses at Cooper Union and transfer their credits. Many students also take classes at Parsons School of Design that is also under New School University. Juniors and seniors can also take graduate classes at the Milano Graduate School. Seminars, often taught by famous professors or by published authors in the case of the writing program, can be very demanding and usually involve several writing assignments. Administration has taken steps to enforce an attendance policy, giving professors rights to fail students who miss three classes throughout the semester; however, as one student commented, "This is not the way it works in practice. The professor usually lowers your grade instead of failing you."

Students complain about the small number of full-time faculty members and the big "turnover of professors." Since most professors are only "visiting," they are "here for one term and disappear the next." Overall, students have praise for their professors: "I have had some incredible professors who have helped me make important decisions affecting my life." Students see their interactions with professors as one of the major benefits of attending Lang. "I can call all of my professors at home," on student exclaimed. Students are also positive about the advising system: "My advisers did really advise me—about academic issues as well as about my personal life." One student went as far to say, "I probably would not be in New York right now if it wasn't for my advisors. That's how close you can get to them." Lang has a study abroad program with the University of Amsterdam, but that is the "only official study abroad option." Many students still go to different countries for a term or an entire year.

New York, New York

Most Lang students are self-defined urbanites. For those who aren't, adjusting to life in New York City is the biggest challenge. Social life centers on clubs and cafés in Greenwich Village as well as other parts of the city. "Parks are also great in the spring," said one enthusiastic junior. Most students agree that "You can either fall through the cracks or benefit from everything the area has to offer."

Students think of the student body as a reflection of New York City: diverse, liberal and composed of strong individuals. "One thing we don't have at Lang are conservatives—we are a fairly progressive bunch," noted one sophomore. However, despite the progressiveness, "the political activism of the Seminar College days has faded away."

Formal extracurricular activities and sports programs do not exist at Lang. "There are not many sports fans here." Those who are into sports can participate in Cooper Union's small intramural sports program. Lang in the City is a college-sponsored program that offers students discounted tickets to performances, movies and art events, but "is not used by many students." One student explained, "You don't go through the school, you create your own independent life." Lang's Internship Coordinator helps place students in internships with employers in the city. Professors' connections also help in getting high-quality internships. "We even get credit for internships; they are an incredible experience. They allow you to bring theory and practice together," said a senior.

A Single Building

Eugene Lang is situated in a five-story building that contains classrooms, study rooms and a small cafeteria. One student said, "we, at least, don't have to walk for miles to get from one class to the other." However, students taking classes at Parsons or at the Milano Graduate School have to walk "a couple of streets." Lang's library is part of a three-school consortium with the libraries of Cooper Union and New York University, giving students access to nearly 3.3 million volumes.

"Survival in New York City is a big part of the Lang experience."

One housing option for Lang students are the three residence halls within walking distance of the school building: Loeb Hall, Marlton House and Union Square. Rooms vary in size and type depending on the building. The dorms do not belong entirely to Lang; students share them with students from Parsons School of Design and Mannes College of Music, which are also schools under the New School University. Space is guaranteed to freshmen and first-year transfer students but others are often forced to enter the painful search for apartments in New York city: "I would not recommend the dorms, but then, I would not recommend looking for an apartment in your first year in New York either," noted one student. "The moment you move to an apartment, your social life is totally independent from the school." These "New Yorkers" do have to commute to school.

Lang combines a strong liberal arts education and small seminars with the opportunities of the most urban setting possible. This combination leads Lang students to build their potentials in their time here and leave Lang as independent thinkers and as "individuals." —*Engin Yenidunya*

FYI

If you come to Eugene Lang, you'd better bring "a readiness to adjust to life in New York City."

What is the typical weekend schedule? "Everyone does their own thing in the City because we don't have formal extracurricular activities or sports programs. Most people do go to clubs and cafés in Greenwich Village, though, and during the spring—we hang out in the parks nearby."

If I could change one thing about Eugene Lang, I'd "make it so the dining halls are not non-existent."

Three things every student at Eugene Lang should do before graduating are "enjoy New York City, do an internship (which you get credit for), and take advantage of Lang in the City—a program that offers students discounted tickets to performances, movies, and art events."

Fordham University

Address: 113 W. 60th St., New York, NY 10023
Phone: 800-367-3426
E-mail address: enroll@fordham.edu
Web site URL: www.fordham.edu
Founded: 1841
Private or Public: private
Religious affiliation: Catholic
Location: urban
Undergraduate enrollment: 7,228
Total enrollment: 14,600
Percent Male/Female: 40%/60%
Percent Minority: 23%
Percent African-American: 6%
Percent Asian: 6%
Percent Hispanic: 11%
Percent Native-American: 0%
Percent in-state/out of state: 61%/39%
Percent Pub HS: NA
Number of Applicants: 11,380
Percent Accepted: 57%
Percent Accepted who enroll: 27%
Entering: 1,728
Transfers: 295
Application Deadline: 1 Feb
Mean SAT: NA
Mean ACT: NA
Middle 50% SAT range: V 530-630, M 530-630
Middle 50% ACT range: 23-27
3 Most popular majors: psychology, business management, communications
Retention: 89%
Graduation rate: 73%
On-campus housing: 39%
Fraternities: NA
Sororities: NA
Library: 1,900,000 volumes
Tuition and Fees: $24,647
Room and Board: $9,700
Financial aid, first-year: 68%
Varsity or Club Athletes: NA
Early Decision or Early Action Acceptance Rate: NA

With a whiff of countryside, a hint of suburbia, and a dash of metropolis, the three campuses of Fordham University combine the best of what New York City and its bordering communities have to offer. If you're seeking a mix of academics with cultural and outdoor opportunities, Fordham might be for you.

A Boom, No Bust

Recent changes at Fordham have been so rapid that to many it seems like a whole new school, and most agree that the new version is much better than the old.

The $230 million endowment which, according to one student, is "approaching half the GDP of Sierra Leone" has made possible major renovations at Fordham's Lincoln Center campus in Manhattan. During the summer of 2003, the Fordham administration dedicated funds to a video production facility, a new computer lab, a general facelift in Quinn Library, a new White Box Theater, the expansion of the Pushpin Gallery, a gallery for student work, on-campus wireless Internet capabilities, and several new classrooms and faculty offices. A music professor at the Rose Hill campus discussed long-term plans to build a new performance space dedicated solely to the arts, as now the only sufficiently large space available is at the adjacent Fordham High School.

One junior cites major improvements in the Lincoln Center campus dining hall: "the Fordham Cafeteria has gone out of its way to reinvent itself," now serving grilled chicken wraps and fresh smoothies. Despite their low ranking as one of the worst college dining halls less than five years ago, a Rose Hill campus senior agrees that the cafeteria has "gotten much better" and offers "more options." The 1998 merger of the all-women's Marymount College with Fordham University added exciting new elements to Fordham academics, social life, and resources.

Three Are Better than One

Fordham's eleven undergraduate and graduate schools are divided into three campuses: Rose Hill in the Bronx, Lincoln Center in midtown Manhattan, and Marymount, 25 miles north of the city in Tarrytown, New York. Each campus provides a unique vibe so that students can choose which best meets their liking while benefiting from the diverse resources of three distinct campuses. Students apply for admission to one, but can transfer once they matriculate and often cross-register. One student claims that the Rose Hill campus was voted "the greenest" location in all of New York City. "In addition to the very picturesque gardens and trees that you can sit under while reading," she says, "there's this huge field in the middle of campus (Eddie's Parade), that's perfect for playing on. Some people break out the soccer ball or softball gloves or lacrosse sticks; I prefer Frisbee." Rose Hill focuses on a classic liberal arts education and includes an undergraduate College of Business Administration. In the spirit of healthy rivalry, one student insists that Rose Hill is the "much cooler campus" compared to Lincoln Center—"except for being in Manhattan." And being in Manhattan is key. Known for its excellence in art, media, and the performing arts, the Lincoln Center campus provides students ideal access to the city's thousands of cultural resources.

More than 70 percent of Fordham students live on campus in traditional college residential halls. Some dorms offer special features, like kitchens in a senior dorm and Queens Court, which holds daily debates and public speaking events, as well as other cultural events and dinners with faculty. While the "dorms are pretty nice," with fitness centers, 24-hour security, and apartment suites for two or three, many upperclassmen choose to live off campus.

"[Fordham has] 8 million opportunities to open new horizons."

For typical extracurricular opportunities other than those in the performing arts, Lincoln Center students go to the Rose Hill campus and participate in activities and club sports. In turn, Rose Hill students visit Lincoln Center for its cultural events and use it as a "starting-off point" for a night out on the town. The Ram Van comes regularly to take students from campus to campus for free, about a half-hour ride.

While the bulk of activity may seem to be in full force at its original campus locations, the all-women's Marymount campus in Tarrytown, NY, clearly holds its own. Female students looking for more of a sense of family with smaller, more intimate classes choose the Marymount campus. Marymount students experience all the benefits of an empowering women's college, while associating with a larger, co-ed community.

A Three-Headed Academic Beast

Fordham is increasingly becoming more selective and competitive. Students commend small class size and award-winning professors as demonstrating the excellence of a Fordham education. Except for the biology department, there are no teaching assistants, which means that professors themselves lead discussion groups. Professors reportedly make themselves available to talk with students and are approachable.

Fordham features a true liberal arts education, requiring its students to take classes in literature, philosophy, theology, history, math, natural science, social science, fine arts, and a foreign language. Students commence their Fordham careers with a freshman seminar and complete it with a senior seminar in Values and Moral Choices. Students must also take classes that fulfill their global studies and American pluralism (which focuses on issues of ethnicity, race, and class) requirements. The extensive core curriculum is not especially popular among freshmen daunted by "seemingly endless" requirements, but seniors "appreciate" the core curriculum for exposing them to fields of study that they otherwise would have overlooked.

Your Roommate

When asked what the typical Fordham student is like, one student responded, "white, from Long Island and a communications major." Many are Catholic and "over-privileged," coming from private schools in the tri-state area (New York, New Jersey, Connecticut), Massachusetts, and Ohio. As a result, many students complain about the lack of diversity in ethnicity, religion, and geography.

Commuter students make up a large percentage of the student body (at the

Lincoln Center campus, it's a 1:1 ratio of residential to commuter students. One student says that commuters are stereotypically "total metrosexuals" from Westchester who are "always dressed up" and "all drive BMWs."

Out and About

The bar scene typifies Fordham nightlife. Rose Hill students can be found flooding the bars on Arthur Avenue of the Bronx's Little Italy. Lincoln Center students scatter among bars and nightclubs all over Manhattan, though many frequent nearby favorites. Because of the hassle of registering parties and the requirement that all suitemates hosting a party must be at least 21, on-campus nightlife generates little support. One student wishes Fordham held "more events, more concerts" and would "like to see a bar on campus" in order to generate a sense of community.

The bar-scene social life means alcohol is the substance of choice for most students and contributes to the fact that there are more drunken random hook-ups than relationships. But the influence of the school's Jesuit tradition attempts to mitigate these facts. The student organization Prevention PARty hosts alternatives to alcohol-infiltrated social events. Moreover, there's the co-habitation policy, which is sometimes a point of contention. Fordham enforces a 3:30 A.M. curfew for students visiting members of the opposite sex. One incensed student declares, "How arbitrary. One can visit but not spend the night. A 3:30 curfew, however, allows individuals plenty of time and room to engage in behavior the church would find shameful."

Fordham sports aren't anything to go crazy about. Athletic teams are "OK to good," but "Fordham doesn't usually have great school spirit." Rose Hill has decent facilities, including a "typical university fieldhouse." But the Lincoln Center campus has only a fitness center and doesn't support any teams.

Fordham's strong ties to religion are expressed in a well-developed Campus Ministry, though one student reported, "Nobody complains about the theology requirements." For all the talk about Catholicism, students insist that Fordham is open to people of all religious traditions.

The City That Never Sleeps

And what do you *think* college kids smack-dab in the center of the world would do for fun? With restaurants, museums, nightlife, cultural events, and little nooks and crannies just waiting for discovery, New York City defines the Fordham experience. Exploring New York is a "major part of the Lincoln Center campus," reports one senior. Among one Lincoln Center student's favorite activities are hanging out in Central Park, people-watching along Mulberry Street in Little Italy, celebrity-watching at key restaurants, and going to talk shows, like David Letterman, for free.

With summer internship opportunities sometimes literally just across the street, the city provides unbelievable resources. Internship programs at major corporations and media outlets attract many Fordham students. The Lincoln Center campus also offers a Bachelor of Fine Arts in dance through its joint program with the Alvin Ailey Dance Center only a few blocks away. With its "8 million opportunities to open new horizons," New York City offers Fordham students an invaluable resource. As one student put it, "it's why *I'm* here." —*Baily Blair*

FYI

If you come to Fordham you'd better bring "a Frisbee!"

What is the typical weekend schedule? "Wake up at 3 P.M., do nothing until dinner at 8 P.M., and go out again at 1 A.M. to party."

If I could change one thing about Fordham, I would "make it more diverse."

Three things every student should do before graduating are "go to Alumni Court at least once, go see a show in New York City, and be at school for Spring Weekend."

Hamilton College

Address: 198 College Hill Road; Clinton, NY 13323
Phone: 315-859-4421
E-mail address: admissions@hamilton.edu
Web site URL: www.hamilton.edu
Founded: 1812
Private or Public: private
Religious affiliation: none
Location: rural
Undergraduate enrollment: 1,851
Total enrollment: NA
Percent Male/Female: 48%/52%
Percent Minority: 13%
Percent African-American: 4%
Percent Asian: 5%
Percent Hispanic: 4%
Percent Native-American: 0%
Percent in-state/out of state: 42%/58%
Percent Pub HS: 57%
Number of Applicants: 4,565
Percent Accepted: 35%
Percent Accepted who enroll: 31%
Entering: 491
Transfers: 2
Application Deadline: 15 Jan
Mean SAT: NA
Mean ACT: NA
Middle 50% SAT range: V 600-700, M 610-700
Middle 50% ACT range: NA
3 Most popular majors: social sciences, languages, psychology
Retention: 93%
Graduation rate: 84%
On-campus housing: 96%
Fraternities: 34%
Sororities: 20%
Library: 558,000 volumes
Tuition and Fees: $30,200
Room and Board: $7,360
Financial aid, first-year: 51%
Varsity or Club Athletes: 30%
Early Decision or Early Action Acceptance Rate: 49%

Looking for a beautiful campus, a close community of spirited, involved, and just plain nice people with small classes that are only taught by professors? Well, Hamilton College, located in the picturesque Adirondack area of Clinton, New York, might be the school for you. Having witnessed numerous changes over recent years, including physical improvements, major changes in the curriculum, and a new president, Hamilton is an exciting and welcoming place to be.

The Curriculum: New and Improved

As of this year, Hamilton has done away with distributional requirements in an effort to encourage students to design their own curriculum. Still essential to a Hamilton education, however, is the writing requirement, which requires that students take three writing-intensive classes in any subject by the end of their sophomore year. While this may prove difficult if you don't plan your schedule well—"last semester was pretty bad because I took *all* writing classes, so it got a bit monotonous, always writing papers," bemoaned one freshman—Hamiltonians undoubtedly graduate with a strong foundation in writing skills. "My writing has definitely improved since I was a freshman; I thought that I had learned to write well enough in high school, but there is always room to grow in that area," commented a junior.

It's no surprise, then, that Hamilton's English department is very strong, and that English 150, a survey of Western literature, is the most popular class among freshmen. There is also a writing center where other students are available to edit papers and talk out ideas. Other popular majors include government, economics, and psychology, while the language departments are considered weak. Hamilton's academic offerings are strengthened across the board by the wide supply of study support. Such aid is not limited to the liberal arts at the writing center—if you need some help with math, you can always head over to the Q-Lit center to meet with a tutor.

Classes run small at Hamilton, ranging from around 40 in freshman classes to 6 in some upperclassmen courses. This can make some classes very difficult to get into, but if the professor is understanding or if you are a major in that subject, your chances are greatly improved. Students praise the interaction with their professors, who are "very personable," and feel that small classes allow for a wealth of intellectual opportunities. "The professors are incredible and so willing to meet with and help you. Almost every professor I've had has extended office hours if needed and given us his or her home telephone number," gushed a junior. In terms of Hamilton's workload, it depends on what classes you take, but one junior says that "most students are very focused throughout the year, and it gets a little more hectic during finals."

Sports, Greeks, and . . . the Dog Pound?

While there is no pressure to drink, alcohol is important to the social life for many—"you're in the middle of nowhere, what else is there to do?" pointed out one student. Hamiltonians generally drink one to four nights a week, though there aren't many "four-nighters." This year, however, with the arrival of the new president, Hamilton has been cracking down on its alcohol policy and underage drinking has reportedly decreased a little. "There are ways around the strictness, but it's not really worth it," said a freshman. "However, if you want something you can get it." With or without alcohol, Hamiltonians are not lacking in fun. About 30 to 35 percent of students go Greek, so fraternities and sororities contribute greatly to the party scene by hosting most of the on-campus parties. Everyone is always invited to their themed parties that are reputedly "always fun," from '80s night to "farm party." Societies sometimes host parties off campus, but those are sometimes invite-only because partygoers must be shuttled.

If you're not into the frats, there are other options. Non-Greek events, like acoustic coffee-houses, do occur, but as one sorority member pointed out, "it's hard to attract athletic and Greek types to stuff like that," and at Hamilton that's a large percentage of the student body. Groups like the Campus Activity Board (CAB) and the Inter-Society Council, however, try to provide a variety of gatherings like Alexander Hamilton weekend, during which there are relay races and a carnival day.

Sports are undoubtedly a big part of the social scene—Friday nights are pretty dull, for example, because athletes don't go out in preparation for Saturday games. Even though all of Hamilton's sports are Division III and academics always come first, students love their teams. "School spirit has increased since I came here," claimed one junior. Sporting events are popular, and Hamilton has great hockey, basketball, and lacrosse teams. The football team is not too fantastic, but Hamiltonians still come out to cheer, especially since the basketball fans' tradition of the "Dog Pound" has spread to other sporting events. This tradition consists of group of exceptionally fanatical guys dressed up in costumes cheering and going crazy in a roped-off area of the field or gymnasium.

Play a Sport or Wreak Some HAVOC

Hamilton's extracurriculars are dominated by sports, and if you're on a team, that obviously takes up a lot of your free time. The less intense types play IMs (intermurals), which are very popular. Beyond the playing field, a lot of Hamiltonians are involved in HAVOC (a student-run community service organization), yearbook, and the Hamilton Outing Club, from which you can rent just about any outdoors equipment. While extracurriculars are not as popular here as at other institutions, "after freshman year, when you don't do too much, you start wanting to get more involved," noted an upperclassman.

The Campus: Old, New, and Improving

Hamilton was once made up of two colleges: Hamilton College for men and Kirkland for women. Now it's one, but Hamilton, the north side, and Kirkland, the south side, have very distinctive architectural tones. The north side's buildings are old and "feel very New-England, very prestigious," while Kirkland, built in the '60s, has "imposing" and "cold-looking" modern architecture. The two campuses are close and small enough that commuting between the two is not a problem. While there isn't a whole lot around the campus, "it's less isolated than I thought it would be when I came here," said a freshman. You need a car to get anywhere, and though freshmen cannot own cars, there is a jitney service that runs to nearby malls and to various places on campus. Clinton itself "is a beautiful town, and there are no issues with locals coming on campus—it's an open campus," noted one student. Hamilton has two main dining halls, as well as a diner and a pub that are part of the meal plan. As at any college, it's easy to get sick of the food, but there are a variety of options offered, from sushi to stir-fry. As a part of the college's dedication to its physical plant, Hamilton's science buildings are now undergoing major renovation: there will be a new part added, and all the labs will be brought up to date.

Hamilton's dorm options are well liked, especially since Greek houses were taken away and made into dorms for upperclassmen in 1996. "While a lot of frat members were very upset about that," said a junior, "I love it. I'm around so many different people. It's a great way to meet people by not having them segregated by societies in different houses." There is a lottery system for all students except freshmen, who live amongst upperclassmen. Other options are available in terms of housing; you can opt for single-sex floor or for a substance-free dorm that is located in Kirkland. Off-campus housing is available to only a small number of seniors, and the administration is trying to eliminate it completely.

A Typical Hamiltonian . . .

Hamilton is not known for its ethnic diversity; most students will probably tell you that a diverse campus was not their priority when they chose their school. The student body is quite homogenous, "it's pretty much white kids from Connecticut who wear J. Crew," and there is considerable self-segregation, from races to fraternities, which are generally divided by sports. Despite the modicum of diversity that the lack of Greek houses fosters, upperclassmen often room with members of their own society or sports team. "The administration is trying to pass a rule that will bar students in societies from living together, but that is a long way from happening," said a freshman. There is a definite conservative political presence on campus: "Hamilton's academics are liberal, but the student body is quite conservative. I thought that I would find more liberals here because of the academics," noted a junior.

"The professors are incredible and so willing to meet with and help you. Almost every professor I've had has extended office hours if needed and given us his or her home telephone number."

According to one junior, "the dating scene is so weird:" there are a lot of random hook-ups, and then couples who are all but married. There are some drugs on campus: Hamilton has a zero-tolerance policy for narcotics like cocaine, but "study drugs" like Ritalin are present. The small student population has its curses and its blessings. News travels fast in such a small institution: "everything gets passed around so quickly and you sort of know everyone's name or face. Sometimes it can feel a bit like high school, but in a good way," said a freshman.

Hamilton's close-knit community is, in fact, what students really love about it. Its small size especially allows freshmen to feel at home from the start: "all the upperclassmen are really nice and welcoming," lauded a freshman. "I was very attracted to the small, intimate campus," said one student. "And it sounds clichéd, but everyone here is so friendly. People just hang out and spend a lot of time together, and they don't really leave on the weekends. When I got here, it felt like camp." Hamilton may be small, but Hamiltonians' love of their campus, their professors, and their community is immense.

—*Samantha Wilson*

FYI

If you come to Hamilton, you'd better bring "a warm jacket for the winter."

What is the typical weekend schedule? "Friday, hang out, dinner and a movie; Saturday, party, then to the bar (which is "downtown", i.e. down the hill); Sunday, homework all day.

If I could change one thing about Hamilton, I would "put it in San Diego. Everyone's so much happier when it's nice out."

Three things that every student at Hamilton should do before graduating are: "go to a Bundy party, go for a walk in the Root Glen, and dance at the diner late-night."

Hobart and William Smith Colleges

Address: 337 Pulteney St.; Geneva, NY 14456
Phone: 315-781-3622
E-mail address: admissions@hws.edu
Web site URL: www.hws.edu
Founded: 1822
Private or Public: private
Religious affiliation: none
Location: small city
Undergraduate enrollment: 1,893
Total enrollment: 1,893
Percent Male/Female: 45%/55%
Percent Minority: 10%
Percent African-American: 4%
Percent Asian: 2%
Percent Hispanic: 4%
Percent Native-American: 0%
Percent in-state/out of state: 50%/50%
Percent Pub HS: 65%
Number of Applicants: 3,108
Percent Accepted: 66%
Percent Accepted who enroll: 26%
Entering: 532
Transfers: 24
Application Deadline: 1 Feb
Mean SAT: NA
Mean ACT: NA
Middle 50% SAT range: V 540-620, M 530-620
Middle 50% ACT range: 24-27
3 Most popular majors: English, economics, psychology
Retention: 86%
Graduation rate: 72%
On-campus housing: 90%
Fraternities: 17%
Sororities: NA
Library: 370,000 volumes
Tuition and Fees: $28,948
Room and Board: $7,588
Financial aid, first-year: 59%
Varsity or Club Athletes: 23%
Early Decision or Early Action Acceptance Rate: 81%

Located on exquisite Seneca Lake, Hobart and William Smith Colleges (HWS) offer students a unique package of comfort and academics. Both Hobart, the men's college, and William Smith, the women's college, have their own deans, masters, athletic teams, student governments, and admissions staffs, but the two colleges share a single campus, faculty, classes, and dorm system.

Together but Apart

This "coordinate system" of different administrations but common experience mainly draws praise from students. Many women consider the numerous support groups, the women's studies program, and the general focus on women's issues "empowering." However, some males felt that the coordinate system benefits only women, and some are convinced that HWS should place "more emphasis on the coming together of the sexes than on each sex finding its own strength." But regardless, Hobart men admit to leaving college sensitive to women's issues and problems.

Carefully Groomed Grounds

Nature has endowed HWS well with Seneca Lake, and HWS administrators have carefully built and maintained the campus. The appearance of Hobart and William Smith Colleges is "addictive" and "breathtaking." One student explained, "I knew I was coming here as soon as I set foot on campus." Not only is the campus beautiful, but it is also "incredibly well kept."

> **"[On Deviance Day] each student does something deviant. Last year, one girl ate an earthworm, lots of people did stripteases, and some guy stole a fire hydrant and brought it to class."**

How picturesque is Seneca Lake? According to legend, all the buildings that have been built between the "Lady of the Lake" statue and Seneca Lake have burned to the ground because the Lady of the Lake will not allow any object to obscure her gorgeous view.

Geneva, New York, home of HWS, is not a college town. One student joked, "Hobart would be perfect if it were in Ithaca." The Seneca Lake area does, however, have its benefits: there are numerous wineries in the area that offer wine tasting to those who are of age.

Living

In general, students like their dorms. Yet, one senior complains that "the housing situation sucks" because of Hobart and William Smith's strict limitations for off-campus living. But students are generally happy with on-campus options. Freshman live in standard, comfortable dorms, but upperclassmen can now live in luxurious condominiums. According to one pleased student, "The condos are nicer than my house!" Other options, including theme houses and the field house, where students till their own land, offer unique living arrangements.

Hobart and William Smith students like their dining hall food, in general. The quality is mediocre, but "the variety is amazing," said one senior. Outside of the dining halls, students can snack at The Cellar, Café Cabana (downtown), or Just Cookies and Pies—which, paradoxically, serves top-notch sandwiches also. Spinnakers and Ports offer more upscale, gourmet meals.

Typical Students?

Two traits characterize the typical students at Hobart and William Smith: "well-off" and "friendly." Yes, "80 percent of the campus dresses in J. Crew," said one student, but the other 20 percent feel little pressure to conform. Most of the students are Caucasian and hail from New England and the Mid-Atlantic suburbs. Some feel that "Hobart is not as diverse as it could be," but Hobart is now making a large-scale effort to attract and support minority students. Minorities comprise approximately 20 percent of the student body. While some say that students still segregate themselves to some degree, one senior said, "Your group changes from where you come from [and what ethnic group you are] to where you are or where you are going." However, one Hispanic freshman believes, "Some people here can be so closed-minded at times it is not even funny." The gay and lesbian population is small, but accepted. The Gay, Lesbian, Bisexual Friends network provides support to homosexual students and awareness to others.

Greek life at Hobart plays a major role in social life. Also, the condos provide more than enough space for room parties. In general, alcohol is readily available, and HWS can reportedly be a "real weed-fest," though most feel that drugs are no more or less prevalent at HWS than at other colleges. Random hookups are common, but "long-term relationships are difficult."

In Class and Out

With regard to extracurriculars, students range from "apathetic" to "fanatical," with the mean skewed towards the "apathetic" end of the spectrum. However, student government, especially William Smith's Congress, affects life directly and powerfully. "Geneva Heroes' brings Hobart and William Smith students together with area eighth graders to perform community service.

Academics at Hobart are what one makes of them. The year is divided into three trimesters, allowing students to take few classes at once. Hobart and William Smith excel in political science, English, women's studies, and biology. Students rave about the accessibility and excellence of their professors. Jack Harris, one well-loved professor, spices his sociology class with Deviance Day, when "each student does something deviant. Last year, one girl ate an earthworm, lots of people did stripteases, and some guy stole a fire hydrant and brought it to class."

A new science building provides science majors with excellent facilities. Physics, however, is a weak point. Additionally, Hobart and William Smith send hundreds of students abroad each trimester. The destination list is huge for such a small school, and professors accompany students to some foreign locations.

Hobart and William Smith seem to attract "a lot of kids who had all the opportunities in the world in high school, but only took advantage of a few of them." HWS changes most of these people, but nevertheless fails to inspire some. —*Brian Abaluck and Staff*

FYI

If you come to HWS, you'd better bring "the foresight that there's a lot of emphasis placed on gender differences."

What is the typical weekend schedule? "Party at the frats or in rooms, sleep, relax."

If I could change one thing about HWS, I'd "add more activity options outside of school—there's a lack of anything constructive to do."

The three things that every student at HWS should do before graduating are "piss off someone of the 'opposing' gender, tell a tourist the "Lady of the Lake" legend, and throw a party in your condo."

Hofstra University

Address: 100 Hofstra University; Hempstead, NY 11549
Phone: 516-463-4700
E-mail address: hofstra@hofstra.edu
Web site URL: www.hofstra.edu
Founded: 1935
Private or Public: private
Religious affiliation: none
Location: suburban
Undergraduate enrollment: 9,469
Total enrollment: 13,140
Percent Male/Female: 46%/54%
Percent Minority: 20%
Percent African-American: 9%
Percent Asian: 4%
Percent Hispanic: 7%
Percent Native-American: 0%
Percent in-state/out of state: 78%/22%
Percent Pub HS: 70%
Number of Applicants: 11,741
Percent Accepted: 72%
Percent Accepted who enroll: 21%
Entering: 1,790
Transfers: 757
Application Deadline: rolling
Mean SAT: NA
Mean ACT: NA
Middle 50% SAT range: V 50-600, M 520-610
Middle 50% ACT range: 23-27
3 Most popular majors: marketing operations, information science, psychology
Retention: 76%
Graduation rate: 55%
On-campus housing: 41%
Fraternities: 6%
Sororities: 7%
Library: 1,600,000 volumes
Tuition and Fees: $16,542
Room and Board: $8,450
Financial aid, first-year: 58%
Varsity or Club Athletes: 7%
Early Decision or Early Action Acceptance Rate: NA

If you enjoy the peace and quiet of suburbia, the bustling and hectic life of New York City, *and* have a car, then Hofstra is the place for you. Whether you plan on commuting or living on campus, the best of both city and suburbs is easily accessible at Hofstra, a small, affordable sanctuary just a short train ride away from the city.

Progressive Learning

Academics at Hofstra cover a broad spectrum of topics, with 2,000 classes and 98 majors to choose from. Majors are often chosen based on how much one is willing to put into their studies. For example, a Chemistry major will have a far different workload than a Physical Education major. One student said that Hofstra's academics were "not very challenging" yet diverse in the sense that they gave opportunities for exploration into new subjects.

Despite the core requirements in math, social studies, natural science, humanities, foreign language, and cross-cultural studies, most students find a unique path in the many classes offered. Hofstra is divided into the Hofstra College of Liberal Arts and Science, the Saturday School, the New College of Hofstra, the University College for Continuing Education, and the Honors College.

The progressive style of learning, especially in the New College and the Honors

College, gives students flexibility in their schedules. However, it is also a big responsibility to make wise choices about their education. Many students enthusiastically say that a great advantage to Hofstra is its small class sizes. The largest class size is 65 students, while the average class has 20 or fewer. "Professors help incite our curiosity in different subjects by giving us a lot of personal attention," said one economics major. Another student commented: "they really respect everyone's needs and limitations. Sometimes a prof. will let you into a capped class if you show interest and motivation."

Traditional Minds

One of the biggest strengths of the Hofstra learning experience is its wide variety of options for every person and every interest, which Hofstra calls its progressive style. Ironically, the student body does not seem to parallel Hofstra's progressive view on education. Although socioeconomic and racial diversity is reflected in the statistics, students comment that the undergraduate population can seem homogenous—"rich preppy kids from Long Island," as one student put it. Another commented that "everyone goes overdressed to class—like they're going to a nightclub," though another certainly didn't mind that so many female students look their best for early morning classes. Hofstra may be a great fit for those students who enjoy updating their wardrobe every season.

> **"Everyone goes overdressed to class—like they're going to a nightclub."**

Intramural, club, and varsity sports are definitely popular on campus, but they are not necessarily community events. The most popular sports include football, lacrosse, and basketball. Many student athletes, however, travel on weekends with their teams and many go home. One student described a Hofstra game as "an empty stadium with potential."

Student organizations are another one of the many things to do outside of the classroom. For journalists, there is *The Chronicle* and *Nonsense Magazine*, for politicians there is student government, and for performers there are various theater and music groups. A popular hangout is the Hofstra Recreational Center, which has sports facilities such as ball courts, a track, a pool, and space for the many gym classes offered.

Free Spirits

Hofstra's social scene has lots of free spirits, literally. Its active Greek life, composed of 14 sororities and 18 fraternities, provides a strong party scene for students to let loose on weekends. Bar hopping at the hip Bogarts, Monterrey's, and McHebes is also popular. Some of the annual campus parties include the Freak Formal every Halloween and Homecoming. "The Freak Formal is one of those things you have to go to at least once," raved one student.

The University makes an effort to bring popular music groups to campus for student enjoyment. Plays put on by students and movie specials are also frequent events. The campus isn't actually as dead as it would seem with half the student body (those who commute) gone. Some people complain, however, that they have a hard time meeting people and making friends and that it's easier to meet people off campus than on campus. Others say they feel that they fit right in, indicating that perhaps Hofstra is a place for specific people with similar interests.

Ins and Outs

The influx and out flux of students at Hofstra varies by the hour, as commuter students rush to class, chill at cafés, hit the books at Axinn Library, and go home once again. Half of the student body commutes, as most live in the near vicinity. Many also live on campus and go home on weekends. Despite the mass exodus, Hofstra students tend to be satisfied on campus. Residential life is characterized by dorms that are "Okay" with "average RAs [who] don't really do anything." The setting has lots of "trees and statues and squirrels." Most agree that Hofstra has an exceptionally beautiful campus, which one student described as not only gorgeous, but "conveniently divided into classes, sports, and dorms facilities."

The area around Hempstead, however, is not the nicest—"it's ghetto," one student commented. Safety is not a major concern for those on foot, but most students learn to walk in pairs, drive, or take public transportation at night. Apparently the town of Hempstead isn't the hippest place to be, but it houses enough shopping establishments and restaurants to attract many people nonetheless. Those who drive complain that parking "can be an absolute nightmare."

More than a few students express dissatisfaction with the food on campus, which they deem expensive and bland: "it should be better for the price we pay." Most students eat at the Student Center, where wraps seem to be very popular. Those who might want to dine out for some spice go to the popular restaurants Bits n' Bytes or Kate's and Willis.

For the more outgoing student, excitement can be found only a short drive or train ride away in New York City. After the intense personal attention from the school, students rave that proximity to New York is Hofstra's second-best asset. "It makes up for Hempstead and definitely sets Hofstra apart from other schools," said one student. Students at Hofstra live in an ideal location and have the privilege of a liberal and flexible education. Although not so liberal themselves, most students at Hofstra extol their school and enjoy their college experience. *—Carolina Galvao*

FYI

If you come to Hofstra, you'd better bring "cash and a fake ID."

What is the typical weekend schedule? "Study all weekend long . . . yeah right! Go home, sleep, chill with friends, go into New York, and wait for the night to start up to go to bars and parties."

If I could change one thing about Hofstra, "I would [keep] a dining place open 24/7, providing coffee."

Three things every student at Hofstra should do before graduating are: "Eat at Sbarros at least 100 times, and regret each time saying 'Okay, this was the last time,' suffer from three fire alarms a day, and go to McHebes' happy hour!"

The Julliard School

Address: 60 Lincoln Center Plaza; New York, NY 10023-6588
Phone: 212-799-5000
E-mail address: admissions@julliard.edu
Web site URL: www.julliard.edu
Founded: 1905
Private or Public: private
Religious affiliation: none
Location: urban
Undergraduate enrollment: 488
Total enrollment: 778
Percent Male/Female: 48%/52%
Percent Minority: 29%
Percent African-American: 10%
Percent Asian: 13%
Percent Hispanic: 6%
Percent Native-American: 0%
Percent in-state/out of state: 22%/78%
Percent Pub HS: NA
Number of Applicants: 1,806
Percent Accepted: 8%
Percent Accepted who enroll: 83%
Entering: 116
Transfers: 25
Application Deadline: 1 Dec
Mean SAT: NA
Mean ACT: NA
Middle 50% SAT range: NA
Middle 50% ACT range: NA
3 Most popular majors: music, dance, drama
Retention: 94%
Graduation rate: 75%
On-campus housing: 48%
Fraternities: NA
Sororities: NA
Library: 80,793 volumes
Tuition and Fees: $21,250
Room and Board: $8,440
Financial aid, first-year: 67%
Varsity or Club Athletes: NA
Early Decision or Early Action Acceptance Rate: NA

They say if you can make it in New York, you can make it anywhere. If a quick peek at the alumni of the Julliard School—including world-renowned artists such as Yo-Yo Ma, Robin Williams, and Patti LuPoneis—is any indication, the saying is true. High above busy Manhattan streets, students at Juilliard work to perfect their talents and live up to their school's stellar international reputation. The school's 850 students are selected to be the next generation of great performers, and they pride themselves on a devotion to the arts that colors every aspect of student life at this prestigious conservatory.

The Arts Are Not a Luxury

There's no such thing as being "undeclared" at Julliard. All students at the college level are accepted into one of three divisions: music, dance, or drama. Each division is "like its own community" and "truly becomes your family," reported a dance student. Since students work on dozens of performances and productions with other classmates from their same year and division, "closeness is inevitable." "We eat, breathe, and sleep the same material for four years. I know these people like I know my siblings," explained one student.

Schedules vary greatly by division, although all agree that studies here are demanding. As a fourth-year music student noted, "although music students may spend fewer hours a day formally training than the actors or dancers, we are expected to use that free time to practice." Music students report practicing their instruments four to six hours a day, while students in the drama and dance divisions may be on stage or in the studio from nine in the morning until ten at night. Everyone appreciates the opportunity for intensive training with some of the legends in their fields. As one musician said, "Since most of the students are at the top in their age level, they are used to the long hours. It's really the elite faculty that makes the experience worth it."

Besides classes and training within their division, all Juilliard students must complete a two-part liberal arts sequence. During the first two years, students enroll in a "core curriculum," a series of humanities seminars focusing on classic texts. Third and fourth years select from a variety of electives, including art history and foreign languages. While some say they appreciate the break from performing, most describe the humanities courses as "very, very lame." One student complained, "no one does the reading and the teachers try to make you relate the text to you own life rather than studying it on its own, a technique that is more corny than it is enlightening." Yet he admitted, "People don't come here for the [liberal arts] classes," and praised teachers' efforts and enthusiasm despite general "student apathy." Those desiring more intense academic courses may choose to fulfill the liberal arts requirements with classes at Columbia or Barnard, but few actually take advantage of cross-registration due to scheduling difficulties and the "pain-in-the-neck commute uptown."

Yes, Virginia, Juilliard Students *Do* Have a Social Life!

In between rehearsals, lessons, and memorizing lines, Julliard students of all divisions manage to "squeeze in some social interaction." The sense of community is strong here, stemming in part from the mandatory on-campus housing for first-year students. Students from other years may choose to live on campus, but most choose to move into apartments after the first year. Up to 350 students are housed in the school's single dormitory, the Meredith Willson Residence Hall, which occupies the top 12 floors of the Samuel B. and David Rose Building, next to the academic building. While students from other Lincoln Center institutions, including the School of American Ballet, also live in the dorm, Juilliard students have several of their own floors and live only with one another. Students typically live in "big and dirty" suites of eight, and freshmen always have double rooms. Although some complain about rooms "no bigger than a shoe box" and the "non-functioning air and heat," students praise the availability of soundproof practice rooms, "the spectacular view" of the Hudson, and the "ridiculously convenient" location. Roommates are generally assigned randomly, though the school makes an effort to pair up students from different divisions. Several students claim to have made great friends through the rooming process, but most agree that "students here tend to self-segregate" by division. Each floor has a "very committed and accessible" RA who is chosen through a "very difficult" selection process. A fourth-year dancer said the RAs as "aren't strict. They're just looking out for you" and would "rather be your friend" than turn you in. But another student remembers the "vehement" RAs on the Quiet Floor. "They would come by and shush you if people came over. It actually ended up being very anti-social."

"To able to train under the greats of today while studying with the greats of tomorrow is an experience I could have only found here."

With its prime Lincoln Center location in the heart of midtown Manhattan, New York City is truly Julliard's backyard. Students take full advantage of the city, attending professional shows, visiting museums, and heading downtown to party at "exotic-looking clubs." The area right around campus is "extremely safe" and also a popular location to hang out. "The bars around here frequently don't bother to card, so younger students often don't venture very far," explained one third-year student. Those living on campus also throw parties of their own, which "may or may not" be broken up by the RAs. As one second-year musician recounted, "One suite usually has the 'big' party and everyone just goes there." Drinking and pot-smoking on campus are "rampant," according to one student. For those looking for some more organized activities, the Office of Student Affairs holds ice cream parties, movie screenings, and other social events. But one student warned that the OSA's attempts seem "too much like forced socialization. It feels like we're in kindergarten with the constant activities."

The dating scene at Juilliard is "limited." Students' time constraints and the school's small size make "relationships difficult to keep up" according to a second-year musician. While long-term relationships may be rare, there are a handful of students who are "practically married." The campus atmosphere is "extremely tolerant" of all sexual orientations, according to one student. Overall, students tend to socialize and date other students in their division and report that "you have to make the effort if you want to branch out."

Complaints about the dining hall food unite students in all three divisions. All on-campus students must purchase a meal plan, which one lamented as "the worst part about living in the dorms." The food is "typical cafeteria fare," with pasta the main option for vegetarians. Students protest over the high prices and small portions, but note the social advantages of a central dining hall. Still, one student said the dancers "eat very little because of the lack of variety of healthy options." Students also voice mixed feelings about the small on-campus health center. While they find care to be adequate overall, "the lack of weekend hours" is a frequent complaint, particularly since a doctor's note is necessary to excuse a student from weekend rehearsals and events.

Here Today, Famous Tomorrow

Despite its cutthroat reputation, students claim the atmosphere to be "generally supportive" at Julliard. Pressure and competitiveness vary among divisions and instruments, but "for the most part, you compete against yourself. Most pressure is self-motivated," according to one musician. Still, some admit there can be "a certain amount of jealousy" within a division, "especially of the more well-known students." Several commented that there is an adjustment when one first comes to Juilliard. "Of course, everyone was the best back at home. But now you're with the best of the best. It's just not possible to always be number one anymore, and that can take some getting used to," explained one student. The intensity and focus of the program also requires some adjustment, because "there is a sense here that everything you do should be professional, which at times can be stressful." Still, one dancer said that was the reason she came to Juilliard: "To study here is to have the opportunity to achieve greatness. There is a preprofessional feel to the campus because we are training to become professionals."

Not every student will become world

famous, and not every student wants to. Juilliard prides itself on creating "artists, not simply performers," and technical perfection and creativity is valued above "fame and fortune." No matter what the future may hold, Juilliard provides extensive career counseling to all its students. The Office of Career Development is an "excellent resource," helping students create press kits, write resumes, and find summer programs. The International Advisement Office also provides assistance to the school's large number of students from overseas and helps them adjust to life in New York. Students rave about the alumni connections, claiming that the "strong connection among Juilliard graduates" is a huge asset when seeking a job. Actors in particular are noted for helping each other find parts after graduation. But one student lamented the heavy concentration of alumni in New York, explaining, "if you choose to leave the city, the support system almost disappears."

Juilliard is not for the undecided. The focus is intense, and "students need to know that this is what they really want" before deciding to enroll in the one of the nation's most competitive art institutions. "You can't expect to come to Juilliard and have a typical college experience. It just won't happen," reminded one student. But students here don't feel that they've missed out on anything. As one student raved, "to able to train under the greats of today while studying with the greats of tomorrow is an experience I could have only found here." —*Amelia Page*

FYI

If you come to Juilliard, you'd better bring "shower shoes, because we clean our own bathrooms."

What is the typical weekend schedule? "Catch up on practice, attend rehearsals and/or electives, then chill out for the new week. Go see as many New York shows as possible."

If I could change one thing about Juilliard, "I'd integrate it with another university."

Three things every student at Juilliard should do before graduating are "leave Manhattan and go to one of New York's other boroughs, visit the city's major art museums, and see another division's performance."

Manhattanville

Address: 2900 Purchase Street; Purchase, NY 10577
Phone: 800-328-4553
E-mail address: admissions@mville.edu
Web site URL: www.mville.edu
Founded: 1841
Private or Public: private
Religious affiliation: none
Location: suburban
Undergraduate enrollment: 1,618
Total enrollment: 2,400
Percent Male/Female: 31%/69%
Percent Minority: 22%
Percent African-American: 6%
Percent Asian: 3%
Percent Hispanic: 13%
Percent Native-American: 0%
Percent in-state/out of state: 69%/31%
Percent Pub HS: NA
Number of Applicants: 2,330
Percent Accepted: 55%
Percent Accepted who enroll: 32%
Entering: 415
Transfers: 72
Application Deadline: 1 Mar
Mean SAT: NA
Mean ACT: NA
Middle 50% SAT range: V 480-590, M 470-560
Middle 50% ACT range: 22-26
3 Most popular majors: business management, psychology, art
Retention: 78%
Graduation rate: 55%
On-campus housing: 71%
Fraternities: NA
Sororities: NA
Library: 280,000 volumes
Tuition and Fees: $23,040
Room and Board: $9,380
Financial aid, first-year: 67%
Varsity or Club Athletes: 35%
Early Decision or Early Action Acceptance Rate: 44%

In the small town of Purchase, New York, close student-teacher relationships are the most valuable selling point of Manhattanville College. Personal attention is received by all students, who study hard to acquire a well-rounded liberal-arts education.

Only a Hop and a Skip Away

Manhattanville is like an island: a small, self-contained and comfortable community. However, only a short distance away is one of the grandest and most energetic cities in the world—New York. Manhattanville's size and its proximity to New York City are two more reasons most students attend. While campus is essentially a bubble, isolating students from the everyday hassle of cities, frequent trips to New York allow students a chance to get away from the small-town feel of this school. Besides the ability to take trips into the city, many students live in the tri-state area and go home frequently. According to one student, "I like that I live close enough that I can go home when campus gets too stifling."

Subject Matter

Manhattanville College may be small in size, but it has a relatively large scope of majors and programs from which to choose. Students report that its strengths lie in the humanities and social sciences, and according to one student, "the journalism program is awesome and amazing." Reportedly, its weaker programs are in the sciences, and students even mention sometimes finding difficulty in taking science classes. Students also have an overwhelming series of distributional requirements to fulfill in their four years: six courses in the arts, eight in math and science, three in humanities, six in global perspectives, and three in the social sciences. In addition, all students take a mandatory writing intensive course, and all freshmen take a year-long preceptorial class, which encompasses many different types of world literature. One student claimed the requirements "got in the way of classes I would rather have taken." However, the general sentiment is that everyone suffers together.

Following the general trend of "smallness," class size is usually limited to 20 students, with review and help sessions led by student instructors (Sis). This creates a tight bond between students and professors, who are all easily approachable and available. Professors are also instrumental in finding and writing recommendations for internships, which many students apply for at nearby companies such as IBM and Pepsi. Many others study abroad for a semester—especially language majors—in one of the college's overseas programs. However, as one student commented, "it's difficult to go away for a term with all the requirements. Most people who go abroad graduate late."

"The personal attention we get here is amazing."

The "portfolio" system is another manner in which personal attention is given at Manhattanville. In this system, students meet with academic advisors at the beginning of their freshman year to form a tentative list of courses to put in their portfolio. They then meet again every spring to see how closely they are following or deviating from their plans; they also submit a sample of their work from that year, along with a written self-examination. Portfolios are then reviewed by a board of faculty to assure that students are succeeding academically.

The Bubble

While this small environment is conducive to close relationships with faculty and staff, it is somewhat isolated from the outer community. True, students frequently hang out in New York City, but, said a senior, "we sort of forget about interacting with our own community and almost avoid it." Indicative of this is the low participation in community service or outreach activities. Furthermore, most students either commute or live on campus. There are four dorms, all of which are said to be comfortable and homey. Spellman is a dry hall that houses freshmen, while Tenney is a multicultural dorm. Both have been recently renovated. Also, to the surprise (and delight) of many, floors and suites are all co-ed. As for dorm food, students generally regard the food on campus as decent. There is one main dining hall that one student commented "tries hard to serve variety," and a café, which serves "junk food and coffee," and is open late.

Since a large portion of the student body comes from nearby areas, some commute and many go home on weekends. This reportedly damages the prospects for exciting on-campus social events on weekends, though students make an effort, particularly through the Clubs Council, to make do. The Council organizes weekend events such as the Spring and Fall Formals, the Quad Jam, movie marathons, and performances. In-suite parties are common, but difficult to organize because of strict administrative rules: alcohol policies are less than lax and prohibit kegs on campus. The Pavilion is the name of the student center and serves as a popular hangout spot. It hosts the traditional Monday Night Football screenings where students can "eat, drink, and be merry," one student joked. Other popular weekend options are hitting the city or checking out nearby pubs.

During the week, students engage in extracurricular activities. There are about 50 clubs on campus, and intramural and club sports are popular, as is writing for school publications, such as the newspaper, the *Touchstone*.

With all their activities, students are often overwhelmed by opportunities and things to do. Ultimately, said one senior, "the personal attention we get here is amazing, more than I ever expected in college. It's been great to be able to get so close to my professors and make such good friends along the way." —*Carolina Galvao*

FYI

If you come to Manhattanville, you'd better bring "a word processor and a spirit willing to be shared."

What is the typical weekend schedule? "Depends, either go home or hang out on campus and party or go into the city."

If I could change one thing about Manhattanville, I'd "make more people stay on campus over the weekends."

Three things every student at Manhattanville should do before graduating are "go to Monday Nights at the Pavilion, spend time in New York with friends, and break one of the administration's strict rules!"

New York University

Address: 70 Washington Square North; New York, NY 10011-9191
Phone: 212-998-4500
E-mail address: admissions@nyu.edu
Web site URL: www.nyu.edu
Founded: 1861
Private or Public: private
Religious affiliation: none
Location: urban
Undergraduate enrollment: 19,490
Total enrollment: 37,134
Percent Male/Female: 40%/60%
Percent Minority: 28%
Percent African-American: 6%
Percent Asian: 15%
Percent Hispanic: 7%
Percent Native-American: 0%
Percent in-state/out of state: 49%/51%
Percent Pub HS: 70%
Number of Applicants: 30,101
Percent Accepted: 33%
Percent Accepted who enroll: 42%
Entering: 4,169
Transfers: 640
Application Deadline: 15 Jan
Mean SAT: NA
Mean ACT: NA
Middle 50% SAT range: V 600-700, M 610-710
Middle 50% ACT range: 27-32
3 Most popular majors: business management, drama/theater arts, film/cinema studies
Retention: 91%
Graduation rate: 78%
On-campus housing: 56%
Fraternities: 4%
Sororities: 2%
Library: 4,644,000 volumes
Tuition and Fees: $28,496
Room and Board: $10,910
Financial aid, first-year: 61%
Varsity or Club Athletes: 10%
Early Decision or Early Action Acceptance Rate: 51%

Located near the Greenwich Village, NYU provides students the opportunity to frequent myriad nightclubs and cafés, walk right through the scene of a movie being filmed, or just hang out and listen to music in Washington Square Park. "The city is within us," one student proudly proclaimed.

Diversity Sums It All Up

Mention NYU, and instantly you hear of NYC, which everyone simply refers to as "the city." Often regarded as the college's best feature, the city is about as diverse as they come. Anything you're looking for, the city's got. NYU dorms and class buildings are integrated into the city—providing easy access to the theatre, the arts, the world's leading business center (Wall Street), and hundreds of restaurants. "It's the real world, with all types of people with various backgrounds and interests," remarked one student. Added another, "New York City will challenge the way you think and view the world. As they say, 'if you can make it here, you can make it anywhere.'"

NYU has a student body representative of the city's diversity. Students come from all over the U.S. and the globe. With six separate undergraduate schools ranging from traditional academic areas to colleges devoted to the arts, social work, or music, NYU reflects the multitude of cultures represented in the Village. Each maintains its own personality and academic requirements. NYU's version of the small liberal arts college, the College of Arts and Sciences, requires students to take courses under the Morse Academic Plan (MAP) with the intention of providing a well-rounded liberal arts education. Requirements are not universally loved. "They take a long time to wade through," remarked one undergrad. "And with the amount of money we're paying, we should be able to take what we want."

The Gallatin Division of NYU takes a different approach, however. Referred to as the "create your own major" division, work is self-paced and credits are earned as academic work is completed. Professional schools include the Stern School of Business; the School of Education, Health, Nursing, and Arts Professions; and the School of Social Work. Among these, the most selective are the Tisch School of the Arts and the Film School. As one student put it, "they have excellent education in drama, film, and dancing. They have Academy Award winners working there." NYU also offers a wide range of study abroad options. An example is the "Freshman Year in Florence" Program that allows students to spend their first year in Florence, start their college lives in a smaller community, and to study the Renaissance at its origin.

> **"It's the real world, with all types of people with various backgrounds and interests . . . anything you want, it's got."**

As one of the largest private universities in the nation, NYU is inundated with lecture courses that are inordinately large. Little personal attention is provided "unless you *really* make an effort to track someone down" and graduate students teach many classes, including most of the freshmen writing courses. The close-knit, pleasant atmosphere of smaller, enclosed campuses is absent here. "You can get lost in such a large university," said one student.

Living in the City

While NYU is concentrated in one of the nicer and safer areas of NYC, there is no clear delineation between campus and Greenwich Village. The quality of dorms vary, but residents are generally pleased. Some are apartment-style and have private bathrooms, and "although you have to clean them, they are a huge advantage." Many are renovated apartment buildings and residential hotels. Others—including Rubin, Weinstein, and Hayden—are more traditional, and house many freshmen. The Weinstein cafeteria has TVs playing, and students can touch the TV screen to request a video from the NYU music video station. Hayden Hall is located right on Washington Square Park and is known as a bit of a "creepy dorm" because it is so old. Third Avenue North is a dorm that is considered "in between" the good and the bad, though its dining hall "kind of has a fifties twist to it." Carlyle is considered good because of the apartment-style rooms, but it is bit of a walk from campus. Although Goddard is traditional, many students like it for its proximity to most classes. Broome Street is "supposed to be huge in terms of space, but 10 or 11 people share one kitchen and two bathrooms." One of the noisier dorms is Brittany, which houses many students from Tisch.

Regarding food, one freshman admitted, "It started off great, but now it gets kind of boring." At meals, cereal, a salad bar, hamburgers, hot dogs, turkey burgers, and three entrees are always present. But whatever cuisine you crave that the dining halls cannot provide, you can find in the city. "There's at *least* a couple eateries anywhere you walk." One area, referred to as "the Four Corners," has a café at each corner, including the Café Figgaro—a vegetarian place popularly known for its falafel. One student admitted, "it can be very, very expensive to attend NYU—there are numerous forms of financial aid, merit scholarships, and work-study programs, but living in the city can put a hole in your pocket."

Events Actually *on* Campus

There are many activities on campus, but like the academics, "it's easy to get lost in the shuffle here." Students said that being part of an organization helps to ease the feeling. Popular on campus are the Political Spectrum, Peers' Ears, and the Sexual Health Advisory. A daily newspaper, the *Washington Square News*, is also continually seeking writers, as are literary magazines and cultural publications. Students for Social Equality, a political group, is also popular among students. But if none of the existing organizations particularly strikes one's interest, creating a new one is not regarded as a difficult task. "If you have an idea and you have people willing to do it, NYU will give you funding," one undergrad pointed out.

NYU's Cantor Film Center hosts several film screenings and festivals every year that bring acclaimed directors, writers, and film critics to campus. Recent examples include *Rendez-vous with French Cinema 2001* and the screening of Ang Lee's *Crouching Tiger, Hidden Dragon.* Despite all the efforts to bring activities on campus, NYU's social life revolves around the city. Students frequent local clubs, from jazz clubs like Blue Note and The Bottom Line to dance clubs like the Spa and Twilo. With no major Greek life, few parties are actually held on campus grounds. In fact, no place on campus is really large enough to throw a traditional dance or party. However, the offerings are plentiful off campus, and many students choose to spend much of their leisure time there. You can find parties with non-stop action until 4 A.M. You can find dimly lit, quaint little coffee shops. You can find comfortable outdoor cafés with views of the New York masses walking by.

But with no clear definition of a campus and with undergraduate students spread far apart, there is little school spirit. There is very little focus on organized athletics, though club sports include ballroom dancing and racquetball. "Just look at the name," one student point out, referring to the NYU Violets, "and you can tell why." For those seeking to work out, however, the Jerome S. Coles Sports Center maintains stellar facilities, including an Olympic-size pool, an additional dive pool, a track, and tennis courts. The Coles Center also organizes classes for the NYU community that range from golf to martial arts, belly dancing to indoor climbing, and fitness to ballroom dancing.

Given its location, security is tight in campus buildings. Students use their ID cards to get into campus buildings, and 24-hour security guards monitor all dorms. But most feel safe in Greenwich Village and the East Village. The increased activity at night around the NYU neighborhood also provides security in anonymity, giving the impression that the areas around campus are a safe place to walk. "The lights come alive at night," one student remarked. Although undergrads sometimes complain about losing IDs and consequently being locked out of their own dorms, one explained that "it's just important to be alert and to use common sense when living in New York City as in any place!" Doing so opens many doors—the city is at the students' fingertips, and all recommend that good use be made of this opportunity to melt into the country's most populous and most vibrant city. —*William Chen and Staff*

FYI

If you come to NYU, you'd better bring, "money—lots of it!"

What is the typical weekend schedule? "Go to a club or go to theater . . . parties are held at bars so there aren't any dorm parties."

If I could change one thing about NYU, I would "improve communication between the administration and students."

One thing I'd like to have known before coming here is "that the city is not as dangerous and 'scary' as many believe it to be."

Parsons School of Design

Address: 66 Fifth Ave, New York, NY 10011
Phone: 877-528-3321
E-mail address: parsadm@newschool.edu
Web site URL: www.parsons.edu
Founded: 1896
Private or Public: private
Religious affiliation: none
Location: urban
Undergraduate enrollment: 2,400
Total enrollment: 2,800
Percent Male/Female: 25%/75%
Percent Minority: 30%
Percent African-American: 4%
Percent Asian: 19%
Percent Hispanic: 7%
Percent Native-American: 0%
Percent in-state/out of state: 51%/49%
Percent Pub HS: NA
Number of Applicants: NA
Percent Accepted: 44%
Percent Accepted who enroll: 48%
Entering: NA
Transfers: NA
Application Deadline: 1 Mar
Mean SAT: NA
Mean ACT: 24
Middle 50% SAT range: V 450-600, M 490-620
Middle 50% ACT range: NA
3 Most popular majors: communication design, fashion design, illustration
Retention: 85%
Graduation rate: 55%
On-campus housing: 22%
Fraternities: NA
Sororities: NA
Library: NA
Tuition and Fees: $23,900
Room and Board: $9,896
Financial aid, first-year: 75%
Varsity or Club Athletes: NA
Early Decision or Early Action Acceptance Rate: NA

In the heart of New York, in downtown Greenwich Village, students are finding their way through the challenge of Parsons and the excitement of the city. One student says, "We have access to all kinds of facilities and events in the city that has offerings from all over the world. Even beyond what the city can give us, the university offers information and facilities for those interested in learning."

The City as Campus

New York City is one of the most dynamic cities of the world, offering many centers for culture, design, communications, architecture and business. The campus, located in Greenwich, is at the heart of Manhattan's artistic life. Parsons has a main building along with three residence halls in walking distance of the Greenwich Village campus. Loeb Residence Hall houses mostly freshmen and provides its residents access to an art studio, a reading room, a lounge and laundry room. The other two residence halls, The Marlton House and Union Square, are for those above 19 years of age. These two halls offer singles, doubles and some suites.

As for other resources, Parsons provides its students with links to New York University's and Cooper Union's libraries. Many students also take an advantage of the Parsons study abroad programs. France, Israel, the Netherlands, Great Britain and Sweden are destinations offered to students, and many choose to go to Paris. The Paris campus consists of a couple of dorms within the walking distance of the main building.

Not Only Fashion Design

Parsons also offers different areas of study. There are three four-year undergraduate art and design degree options: BFA, the Bachelor of Fine Arts, BBA, the Bachelor of Business Administration and the five-year BA/BFA degree. The Bachelor of Business Administration requires the completion of a specific curriculum in design marketing. The five-year dual degree offers students a complete studio art or design major along with a liberal arts education.

Since Parsons is a part of the New School system, students always have the option of choosing electives from the New School for Social Research. The first year is the "Foundation Year" and the courses offered, which are basics of drawing and design, are the "Foundation

Courses." The Foundation program is also offered as a part of non-degree programs. The freshmen take classes in small sections, with 15 to 20 students, often taught by professionals in the field of the class. The class offerings are constantly evolving and new programs are being added as a result of changing trends and job opportunities in the design world.

Parsons challenges all students and weeds out slackers. "The workload is too heavy. Many people drop out the first year and some more drop out the following years," comments a student. Fashion and product design are considered the hardest majors. Design marketing isn't as challenging as fashion and product design.

"The workload is too heavy. Many people drop out the first year and some more drop out the following years."

There also are four affiliate schools that offer two-year programs and whose graduates continue their education at Parsons to complete their bachelor's degree. One is in Paris, France, the others are in the Dominican Republic, Kanazawa, Japan, and Seoul, South Korea. Students studying in France take French Language classes, a part of the core curriculum. The aim of this core curriculum, which also includes Liberal Studies courses that offer classes on the intellectual and historical aspects of France, is to help students become more independent in their environment.

It Takes Two to Tango

The students enjoy their time in the city but many have money issues. "You have to pay a lot to either rent an apartment or live outside Manhattan and take the subway. Parsons is a very expensive school," a student says. This may explain another comment of students. Students find Parsons to be always concerned with teaching about marketing your designs and making money. Students say that it is a "School of Design" and not a "School of Art." One student explained, "Anyone who doesn't like to make money upon graduation or anyone who is really interested in fine arts and learning skills and crafts should stay away!"

The social life for Parsons students is not on campus or at school but rather in the city. Being underage can cause great problems since it narrows down many of the clubbing options. However, almost all have found ways to solve the problem. The social life takes place outside of school, and since there is no campus, people have other lives. "I feel like a working adult here, because I live in an apartment and go to school everyday like my office and come home and I have a completely different social life."

Designers Lead the Way

Many famous and successful designers, artists and employers of huge companies live in New York and visit Parsons all the time. The teachers are all professionals in their fields and many are working designers in Manhattan. "They just teach part-time which is very cool." Students have great connections through their savvy teachers, which allow many students to obtain outstanding and competitive internships.

As long as managing to find the balance between the New York City life and the work, students are happy to be a part of the lively, energetic city, with its Museum of Modern Art, the Guggenheim, the Whitney and many other art shops. But since art has been said to imitate life, New York and Parsons are guaranteed to produce many complex masterpieces. —*Yakut Seyhanli and Staff*

FYI

If you come to Parsons, you'd better bring "lots of money and a tolerance for diversity."

What is the typical weekend schedule? "Going clubbing, going to art museums—basically anything goes in New York City."

If I could change one thing about Parsons, I'd " change the heavy workload."

Three things every student at Parsons should do before graduating are "study abroad, wander around New York City, and get an internship."

Rensselaer Polytechnic Institute

Address: 110 8th Street; Troy, NY 12180-3590
Phone: 518-276-6216
E-mail address: admissions@rpi.edu
Web site URL: www.rpi.edu
Founded: 1824
Private or Public: private
Religious affiliation: none
Location: suburban
Undergraduate enrollment: 5,139
Total enrollment: 9,630
Percent Male/Female: 75%/25%
Percent Minority: 21%
Percent African-American: 4%
Percent Asian: 12%
Percent Hispanic: 5%
Percent Native-American: 0%
Percent in-state/out of state: 53%/47%
Percent Pub HS: 79%
Number of Applicants: 5,480
Percent Accepted: 70%
Percent Accepted who enroll: 27%
Entering: 1,049
Transfers: 165
Application Deadline: 1 Jan
Mean SAT: NA
Mean ACT: NA
Middle 50% SAT range: V 580-680, M 640-720
Middle 50% ACT range: 24-28
3 Most popular majors: engineering, computer science, management
Retention: 91%
Graduation rate: 78%
On-campus housing: 55%
Fraternities: 35%
Sororities: 20%
Library: 488,000 volumes
Tuition and Fees: $28,496
Room and Board: $9,133
Financial aid, first-year: 70%
Varsity or Club Athletes: 35%
Early Decision or Early Action Acceptance Rate: 83%

Imagine going to a school that boasts alumni from the likes of Washington Roebling, who designed and built the Brooklyn Bridge, George W. Ferris, creator of the Ferris Wheel, to National Hockey League players Adam Oates, Daren Puppa, and Joey Juneau. Not only known for being a great technology school, Rensselaer Polytechnic Institute is also well recognized for its Division I Hockey team.

A Ton of Work

Undergraduates at RPI are able to choose their majors from among the Schools of Architecture, Humanities & Social Sciences, Management & Technology, Engineering, and Science. The school also offers a degree in information technology (IT), a relatively new degree which was created in response to the industry's need for IT professionals. Although the five schools of RPI offer a diverse range of strong academic programs, Rensselaer does have a primary focus on engineering, which is generally considered the toughest major, while "management and information technology are the slacker majors." The difficulty of the engineering major can be partially attributed to the tough requirements, among which Differential Equations ("Diffy Screw"), Introduction to Engineering Analysis, and Data Structures and Algorithms are reportedly the toughest. Regardless of major, all students must fulfill the distribution requirements that include courses in humanities and social sciences.

Class sizes vary between 30 and 40 people, although there are some larger intro classes. While getting into classes is not usually difficult, there are sometimes problems with overcrowded computer science and engineering classes. Another complaint involves students not being able to understand their TAs' foreign accents. Students always feel that they have a "ton of work," but as one sophomore said, "academics are quite good; they are what made me choose RPI."

De-stressing

Besides knowing how to work hard, students at Rensselaer also know how to fraternize and have a lot of fun. There are 30-plus frats and four officially recognized sororities that are popular on campus, though students report that they do not feel the pressure to rush. Although alcohol is not supposed to be present in the dorms, and kegs are not allowed on campus, the administration is reportedly not very harsh on alcohol. Being underage is not generally considered an issue: "The frat boys stamp that you are underage on your hand when you walk into parties, but you can still get drinks." Some of the best parties are the annual frat parties including Phi Kappa Alpha's "Shoot the Dog" which has the slogan: "If you don't come to this party, we'll shoot this dog." And Alpha Epsilon Pi's golf party, where "you go through different rooms and each room is a different 'hole'—serves a different drink, and if you get through the 18 drinks you finish with a Jack Daniels."

If downing alcohol or going to parties is not your idea of relaxing, the campus hosts movie nights three times a week that show films currently in theaters or, occasionally, before they are even released—an "awesome and cheap alternative." And there is always something going on at the Student Union, which is a popular hangout with wireless Ethernet. Those interested in theater can go to the Playhouse to see plays, while those eager to see famous performers head to the Field. RPI has a history of great concerts with big performers such as Pearl Jam, Alanis Morisette, Korn, and Third Eye Blind. After a long week, however, many students prefer just to chill with their friends. As expressed by one freshman, "I love the people on this campus most—they make it what it is . . . nothing else. RPI isn't in the best place, but as a student body, we make do with what we have."

Sleeping and Eating, When Time Permits

Freshmen, unless they are commuters, are required to live in dorms, but most report satisfaction with this situation: "I feel the general on-campus living situation is pretty good," remarked one freshman. The average freshman dorm has two students per room, a lounge, a computer lab, and a laundry room. Upperclassmen dorms are nicer and have air-conditioning and heating. While some floors are co-ed, bathrooms are always unisex. Suite situations are also unisex. The best freshman dorm on campus is Barton Hall—"It's like a Hilton there literally, it cost over a million dollars to renovate." Otherwise, there is not much difference between the freshman dorms except that Cary Hall is all male. RAs live on every floor of every freshman dorm and get along well with the students. After freshman year, many students live off campus due to lower costs of living. Off-campus housing costs approximately one-third to one-half the price of living on campus, and many apartments are only a short walk from campus.

Although the five schools of RPI offer a diverse range of strong academic programs, Rensselaer does have a primary focus on engineering.

The campus meal plans are very versatile and try to suit the individual student. Based on their choice of meal plan, students may have unlimited visits to the dining hall. They can also get RADs or MADs (Rensselaer or Marriott Advantage Dollars) to use their dining cards for food at some of the mini-stores on campus. Besides the three largest dining halls, Commons, Bar-H, and Russell-Sage, there are many fast-food options at the Student Union. There is even a Ben and Jerry's on campus.

Some undergrads recommend that you buy your own food after freshman year from the local Price Chopper, which can save half the amount spent on meal plans. Also a couple of blocks away from the campus are a Friendly's, a Popeye's, and a Taco Bell. For good but cheap pizza, two favorites of RPI students are NY Pizza and Hoosick Pizza. There are also plenty of restaurants in downtown Troy. For a meal with that special someone, there is both an Olive Garden and The Macaroni Grill, about a 15-minute drive away in Albany.

Attention, Females

The student stereotype of RPI is "that we are all computer-loving nerds." "On one level," one student admitted, "it is true for the most part." Students have greatly differing opinions about campus diversity.

Some students feel that there is a "good racial/ethnic mix," while others call the student body "homogeneous and disappointingly normal and cliquey and preppy." However, most males agree that the 3:1 male to female ratio "really sucks." Females, on the other hand, have a great time taking advantage of this: "Because there are three or four guys to every girl, girls who wouldn't normally have a lot of guys after them suddenly get a ton of attention from guys." Another related comment is that there is not enough sex. An interesting T-shirt on campus says, "Sex Kills—Come to RPI and Live Forever."

More than Classes and Parties

Many students at RPI also find time to be involved in various extracurriculars and sports. This involvement comes in different forms, ranging from writing for the *Poly*, the daily newspaper, and joining the *X-Files* Club to driving for the RPI ambulance and waltzing away with the Ballroom Dance Club. All types of extracurricular clubs exist at RPI, from those of community service such as APO and Circle K, to those of ethnic groups such as the Black Students' Alliance and Alianza Latina.

Although the school actively recruits for hockey, football, and basketball, hockey is the most popular sport because it is the only Division I team at RPI. There is a lot of spirit for the hockey team; even before school starts in the fall, students line up by the hundreds, if not the thousands, around the Student Union to get the best seats for the year's hockey season. Rensselaer's very active pep band also does special cheers for the hockey team. The "Big Red Freakout," where "everybody dresses up and paints their faces and everything in red" is the biggest hockey game of the year, and one of the biggest annual school-wide events. For students who want to do more than cheer but don't play on a team, there is a gym students call the "iGym" because it is made out of clear blue glass like the popular Apple computer. Intramurals are also extremely popular at RPI.

If you decide that RPI is the school for you, just watch out for West Hall. Rumored to be haunted, the building, which has a morgue in the basement, used to be a civil war hospital. Apparently, "it's falling down the hill that it's on." But that's the only thing about the school that seems to be falling down. As one freshman remarked, "The school's only going to get better . . . so I guess I'm in the right place. After all 'why not change the world' is a motto of students here at RPI." —*Victoria Yen*

FYI

If you come to RPI, you'd better bring "a smile!"

What is the typical weekend schedule? "Go out Friday and Saturday night. During the day, you sleep in, do random stuff like laundry or clean the room. Sunday night is the mad rush to do homework due on Monday!"

If I could change one thing about RPI, I'd "have a better male/female ratio."

Three things every student at RPI should do before graduating are "walk around campus at night (it's really pretty), go sledding down the library hill, and see an RPI hockey game!"

Rochester Institute of Technology

Address: 1 Lomb Memorial Drive; Rochester, NY 14623
Phone: 585-475-6631
E-mail address: admissions@rit.edu
Web site URL: www.rit.edu
Founded: 1829
Private or Public: private
Religious affiliation: none
Location: rural
Undergraduate enrollment: 12,279
Total enrollment: 12,279
Percent Male/Female: 69%/31%
Percent Minority: 15%
Percent African-American: 5%
Percent Asian: 7%
Percent Hispanic: 3%
Percent Native-American: 0%
Percent in-state/out of state: 60%/40%
Percent Pub HS: 85%
Number of Applicants: 8,697
Percent Accepted: 69%
Percent Accepted who enroll: 39%
Entering: 2,342
Transfers: 880
Application Deadline: 15 Dec
Mean SAT: NA
Mean ACT: NA
Middle 50% SAT range: V 540-640, M 570-670
Middle 50% ACT range: 25-29
3 Most popular majors: engineering, computer science, design and applied arts
Retention: 87%
Graduation rate: 55%
On-campus housing: 60%
Fraternities: 7%
Sororities: 5%
Library: 400,000 volumes
Tuition and Fees: $20,802
Room and Board: $7,833
Financial aid, first-year: 72%
Varsity or Club Athletes: 56%
Early Decision or Early Action Acceptance Rate: 81%

"Brick, brick, brick, brick, lots of brick." That's how most students describe RIT's campus. No wonder why the family, alumni and student weekend is known as the Brick City festival. Every building is made of red brick at this university, which offers a strong education combined with valuable training for the workplace.

Academics You Can Actually Use

The single word that describes RIT academics best is "pre-professional." The main focus here is on life after graduation. As one student described it, "We actually learn stuff that we'll use later on in life." Upon application, students choose to enroll in one of the six colleges that focus on applied science and technology, business, science, engineering, imaging arts and sciences, and liberal arts. Students may also choose to enroll in the National Technical Institute for the Deaf (NTID). Because they must make this commitment so early on, "most freshmen arrive with their majors and even careers in their minds."

Both the photography department and the engineering programs receive high praise from students while NTID is the world's largest mainstream college program for the deaf and hearing-impaired. This institute provides sign language interpreters in every classroom and in laboratories to give 1,100 students with impaired hearing a first-rate, fully integrated college experience.

The academic requirements at RIT consist of "a general core of classes and a core of classes inside the major." Although some engineering and science majors say that "liberal arts is an easy major," in general most agree that "no major is particularly easy." Class size varies depending on the level of the course. Students say the majority of classes tend to be 40 students or less with some larger intro classes. Laboratory classes are "usually around 10 or so."

Although the majority of students seem to be happy with most professors and describe them as "extremely knowledgeable about their subject areas" and "more than willing to help out their students," one student did confess that "there are always a few not so good ones around." Most professors are "easy to contact and get along with." There are "hardly any TAs," and they are "used primarily for grading."

RIT's quarterly system creates a fast-paced schedule. Generally, undergraduates think that "RIT provides great academic instruction." In most majors, students combine classroom education and work experience through RIT's very popular co-operative education program (Co-op). These students take five years to complete their degrees, and in their last two years they spend four of the eight quarters working full-time in a firm. Students describe the benefits of Co-op as "gaining valuable experience in the workplace, being able to apply what you learn in your courses, having an advantage over other job candidates, and helping finance your education." The company assignments for Co-op are based on students' interests and career choice with companies such as AT&T, General Motors, Texas Instruments, Xerox and IBM as employees.

Residential Life—Many Options to Choose From

Freshmen are required to live in the dorms, which students say are "in good shape" and are coed either by floor or by door. Most have doubles, and some have singles. Most of the dorms have recently been renovated and the new rooms have full air conditioning and heating, more closets and floor space, and jacks for phone, cable and network connections. After freshman year, the three housing options are living in the dorms, living in on-campus apartments, and going off campus. A number of hearing students also choose to live in the NTID dorms, specifically designed for the deaf and hearing impaired. Four on-campus apartment complexes all have the convenience of bus service and the advantage of an active social scene. RIT also has special-interest housing options consisting of Art, Community Service, Computer Science, Engineering, Photo, Unity and International Houses, where students with similar interests live together on a designated floor. The Greeks also live together in either the dorms, the apartments, or their own houses.

Where Do They Eat?

There are three places to eat on campus. Gracie's, the "all-you-can-eat buffet-style dining hall" with a wide range of options; the Commons, a restaurant-style dining hall; and the Student Alumni Center cafeteria. The RITskeller, beneath the cafeteria, has a full bar that serves alcoholic drinks to staff, faculty and students who are over 21. The Commons also houses a coffee stop called the College Grind. When going off campus, Nick Tahoe's in Rochester, which is open 24 hours, is a student favorite. The restaurant is known as "the home of the original Garbage Plate." According to one student, these plates make "a good 2 A.M. I-need-to-study meal." There are also "corner stores" in the tunnels under the dorms where students can buy snacks. These tunnels are also favorite places to socialize because they have pool tables and arcade games. "Crossroads" has a dining area as well as a market.

Who Are These People?

"Deaf, hearing, white, black, Asian, Indian, foreign, musician, artist, engineer—we've got it all," commented one undergraduate about the student body. "The only stereotype is that we don't have any school spirit," another one added. There is a wide enough variety of students on campus that anyone should be able to find plenty of people with similar interests. While some groups form right away and remain constant, most students find their groups changing throughout their years at RIT. One point that all students agreed on is that the student body "needs more women," although they admit the male-female ratio has been improving . . . slowly. Despite these extremes in the student body, one student claimed that "people start to look and act alike at the end of senior year, as if they were coming from the same factory."

Which Way Is the Party?

The Greeks throw parties, and there are smaller parties in the dorms in addition to apartment parties. Alcohol is completely banned from dorms and frat houses and may only be served in apartments. Nondrinkers say they do not feel excluded at any of the parties. Fraternities and sororities are not dominant in the social scene and their parties are open to nonmembers. Their houses are located on the "Quarter Mile," the famous path from the dorms to the academic buildings. One student referred to how there are "lots of random hookups among frats and sororities."

"We are good at grades, not sports."

Most other social events are held at the Student Alumni Union. The College Activities Board shows current movies on the weekends; "concerts and lectures are also common." As one student said, "You do have to know where to look, but the events are out there." Upperclassmen also go off campus to local bars like the Creek. About ten minutes from campus, Rochester offers bars, clubs, restaurants, concerts and movies. Having a car or knowing someone with a car helps a lot when someone wants to go off campus. Although many students consider cars essential, "they are by no means required to have fun at RIT."

When They Are Not Studying!

The Rochester Wargamers Association and Guild (RWAG) is the largest student club on campus "because they count anyone who comes to their meetings as members." The members play role playing games and different card games. The RIT Formula SAE Team is another popular organization that designs, builds and then races its own cars. In 1998, the Rochester Cannabis Coalition was a controversial club; they were denied official recognition and use of the Student Government funds because they supported education about cannabis, an illegal drug. Although some students use soft drugs, the drug scene is not extremely popular at Rochester.

RIT's varsity teams do not attract huge crowds. Men's and women's hockey are the most popular teams with "very, very enthusiastic fans." The basketball teams follow the hockey teams in terms of popularity. One student stated that "the general RIT population couldn't care less about how the sports teams are doing." Another undergraduate said, "We are good at grades, not sports." Despite this lack of support for varsity sports, intramural sports are often played and attract large participation.

RIT is for the career-oriented who has already made certain decisions about the future. And this planning pays off. Firms are ready to grab RIT students upon graduation because of the high quality of their education and their workplace experience that they have already gained through Co-op. What most of these career-oriented students discover, though, after four or five years, is that "they didn't actually expect to enjoy RIT so much!" —*Engin Yenidunya*

FYI

If you come to RIT, you'd better bring a "computer and a warm coat."

What is the typical weekend schedule? "Do homework or work on whatever projects need to be completed until dinner time, eat dinner, usually go back and continue to work on projects and homework, and then maybe sometime around 9 P.M. or so, if everyone feels up to it, we might watch a movie, or perhaps leave campus to find something to do."

If I could change one thing about RIT, I'd "want it to have a better sense of culture, not only a better sense, but actually a better sub-culture . . . [There's] nothing as exciting, enticing, and extravagant as some of the major events and activities that constantly go on at other schools."

Three things every student at RIT should do before graduating are " lick the RIT tiger statue on the famous RIT 'quarter mile' walk from the dorms to the academic buildings, make an effort to really get to know the resources that are on campus, and visit the RIT Red Barn."

Sarah Lawrence College

Address: One Mead Way; Bronxville, NY 10708-5999
Phone: 914-395-2510
E-mail address: slcadmit@sarahlawrence.edu
Web site URL: www.sarahlawrence.edu
Founded: 1926
Private or Public: private
Religious affiliation: none
Location: suburban
Undergraduate enrollment: 1,226
Total enrollment: 1,226
Percent Male/Female: 26%/74%
Percent Minority: 15%
Percent African-American: 5%
Percent Asian: 5%
Percent Hispanic: 4%
Percent Native-American: 1%
Percent in-state/out of state: 21%/79%
Percent Pub HS: 65%
Number of Applicants: 2,667
Percent Accepted: 40%
Percent Accepted who enroll: 30%
Entering: 323
Transfers: 10
Application Deadline: 15 Jan
Mean SAT: NA
Mean ACT: NA
Middle 50% SAT range: V 610-710, M 530-650
Middle 50% ACT range: 24-29
3 Most popular majors: liberal arts
Retention: 91%
Graduation rate: 72%
On-campus housing: 87%
Fraternities: NA
Sororities: NA
Library: 193,000 volumes
Tuition and Fees: $30,824
Room and Board: $10,394
Financial aid, first-year: 46%
Varsity or Club Athletes: NA
Early Decision or Early Action Acceptance Rate: 46%

For those students who feel they never quite "fit in" in high school, Sarah Lawrence offers a safe learning environment in a peaceful suburb of New York City. They can explore their individuality with others who "are just like them" through creative projects and self-directed study. This educational philosophy prepares each student to leave the small liberal arts school in four years ready for "everything and nothing," as one senior said. If you can "handle learning for the sake of learning," Sarah Lawrence may be the ideal college for you.

Self-directed Study

The curriculum at Sarah Lawrence College consists of three courses per semester, each of which requires an independent project. Course registration requires an interview process: students interview teachers during the first few days of campus life to find out about the course material and expectations, while professors decide whether the students are right for their class. By graduation, all students must have taken one course in three of the following four disciplines: humanities, creative arts, social sciences and history, and natural sciences and math. Aside from these requirements, students are free to choose from a diverse course list. Since the requirements for the B.A. degree are so loose (there are no majors at Sarah Lawrence, only concentrations), students can feel both liberated and overwhelmed with a new sense of responsibility. According to one student, "You decide if you want to slack off. It's up to you to take intermediate and advanced courses. No one is going to make you do it." The endless possibilities for a course of study make the atmosphere at Sarah Lawrence anything but dull. As one student said, "One of the things I love about SLC is that no two people are studying the same thing. Two people in the same class could be working on totally different conference topics so the class means something different to each of them." Although diversity in interests is key, popular concentrations include theater and writing. Some students come to Sarah Lawrence intending to focus on one area of study, but according to one sophomore, most students usually receive a "relatively well-rounded education." Another sophomore commented that students "are pushed to a point where the lines between academic categorizations start to blur. There is a heavy emphasis on viewing topics within the vast context which they exist in." Therefore, no matter what classes you choose, you will graduate viewing the world in a "more sophisticated way, as a conscientious and critically thinking citizen."

In their first two years at Sarah Lawrence, students choose a faculty advisor to help them design their program of study. Students meet with their advisor, or "don," once a week during their freshman year and biweekly thereafter. Close relationships with professors are common around campus. According to one student, "Most of the professors don't treat you as if you are their student, but rather as if you are a colleague." This strong relationship is bolstered by the small seminar courses that dominate the departments at Sarah Lawrence. Seminar sizes generally range from 12 to 18 students. The college does offer some lecture courses, however, and students are required to take two before they graduate. While professors teach seminars, there are some TAs who are available primarily for students needing extra help.

Students at Sarah Lawrence say they are "passionate about learning," and they appreciate the college's emphasis on the learning process instead of on grades. Unless students ask for letter grades in their courses, they receive only written evaluations detailing their performance. The evaluations foster a noncompetitive spirit among the students. One senior said that he "never had a conversation with peers about grades." Another student explained that the "result in the form of a letter grade is not as important as why that result happened." Special academic programs at Sarah Lawrence include independent-study projects, study abroad, and a continuing education program for students of nontraditional age—demonstrating that the overall academic program is both diverse and unique.

Living at SLC

The Sarah Lawrence campus is self-contained and situated within a quiet suburb of New York. Students call the campus "very beautiful"—it is surrounded by trees, rocks, and lots of hills. On one end is the city of Yonkers, a "lower-middle class" neighborhood which doesn't even know Sarah Lawrence exists, according to one student. At the other end of the hill is Bronxville, "one of the richest communities in the country." The relationship between the college and the affluent, rather conservative community of Bronxville is sometimes strained. "We don't go over well in Bronxville," said one undergrad. Another student stated that the stereotypical Sarah Lawrence student ("artistic, weird, liberal, and flakey"), is the exact opposite of the school's wealthy neighbors. The benefit of living in such a wealthy enclave is that crime is minimal. Security guards patrol the area, but security measures are generally unobtrusive. The school also provides emergency phones and escort services. One student said that security measures were recently increased, making her feel even safer than before.

Some students live off campus, but most choose to live on campus because living off tends to be expensive. There are no "average" dorms at this college, according to one student. Options range from a single room with its own bathroom to a converted pantry in an old mansion. Single rooms used to be guaranteed for upperclassmen, but in the past few years, more people have decided to attend the college, causing a housing crunch. To amend the crowded situation, Sarah Lawrence purchased an apartment building off campus which students say is comfortable. Frat and sorority housing is nonexistent due to the absence of any type of Greek life. As one student blatantly stated: "I wouldn't have come here if there had been a Greek system. It goes against the core values of people who attend the school."

"Sarah Lawrence is not strong on tradition. It's hard to maintain it in a school that fundamentally questions tradition itself."

Dining options for students are also varied. First-year students are required to eat on the school's meal plan, either in the main cafeteria or the health-food bar (which reportedly has the best food around). A third dining option is a fast-food restaurant, the Pub, which serves fried and grilled items. Many people who petition to have kitchens as upperclassmen even cook for themselves, said one student.

Diversity on campus is improving in several areas, said students. One undergrad said that Sarah Lawrence is still a white-dominated campus, but recently the number of minorities within the school community has grown. Students also report a large Jewish presence on campus. Geographically speaking, most students come to Sarah Lawrence from New York, California, and Texas, although several countries and many other states are represented. Economically speaking, students report that people come from all backgrounds, although one student said that she thinks people shy away from applying to the school due to its heavy price tag.

Originally a women's college, SLC went co-ed in 1968. In general, males in the college say that they benefit from the "alternative woman's perspective" that comes with Sarah Lawrence. The college has a reputation for a fairly large and accepted gay and lesbian population, pushing gay issues into the forefront of discussion. As for relationships on campus, one student said that couples are not very visible due to cliques and to the individualistic pursuits of the general population. However, despite Sarah Lawrence's unique student body, most undergraduates agreed that the dating scene was typical for most colleges.

Extracurricular Activities

Extracurricular activities at Sarah Lawrence reflect a wide range of student interests. Activism is a high priority for many students. Some recent activism has surrounded the anti-sweatshop movement and anti-globalization, said one student. Theater, dance, writing, and art are always popular on campus. Students can participate in an ensemble performance or create their own work to exhibit around the campus.

On weekends, students tend to go into New York City to visit an art museum or attend a Broadway show. On campus, there are movies and a dance every Saturday night. All campus parties are initiated by students and must be registered with college administrators. According to one student, while Sarah Lawrence has formerly had a reputation for drug use, the administration has recently become harsher and harsher on the use of illegal substances.

Some other activities that students rate highly are gay/lesbian/bisexual Coming Out Week, and the Deb Ball, which began as a debutante ball for the prim Sarah Lawrence women of decades past, but has since become a less "proper" tradition. The annual Bacchanalia, a spring festival of bands, beer, and dancing, also earns student praise. Other traditions for the school are virtually nonexistent. Said one student, "Sarah Lawrence is not strong on tradition. It's hard to maintain it in a school that fundamentally questions tradition itself."

Campus response to sports is close to apathetic. None of the students interviewed for this article even knew which sports teams their college sponsored. In fact, Sarah Lawrence has men's and women's tennis, crew, cross-country, swimming and equestrian teams. Students can now enjoy the new Campbell Sports Center and the announced construction of Leckonby Football Stadium, but they tend to use it like everything else at their school, in a very individual capacity.

For students entering Sarah Lawrence, word from the campus is that if you're eager for a "unique educational experience" where you will truly get educated and learn "stuff," Sarah Lawrence is the place for you. The next four years at SLC will expand your mind and help you to explore your individuality to its fullest. —*Lisa Siciliano*

FYI

If you come to Sarah Lawrence, you'd better bring a "bottle of hair dye, a sexy outfit, an open mind, and a sense of humor."

What is the typical weekend schedule? "A small intimate party with a few friends, a jaunt to New York City to see a show or visit an art museum, and hours spent in the library on Sunday."

If I could change one thing about Sarah Lawrence, I'd "change the way people act towards one another."

Three things every student at Sarah Lawrence should do before graduating are "attend the Coming Out Dance, do performance art on the main lawn, and volunteer at schools in the neighborhood."

Skidmore College

Address: 815 North Broadway; Saratoga Springs, NY 12866
Phone: 518-580-5570
E-mail address: admissions@skidmore.edu
Web site URL: www.skidmore.edu
Founded: 1802
Private or Public: private
Religious affiliation: none
Location: suburban
Undergraduate enrollment: 2,506
Total enrollment: 2,506
Percent Male/Female: 40%/60%
Percent Minority: 12%
Percent African-American: 3%
Percent Asian: 5%
Percent Hispanic: 4%
Percent Native-American: 0%
Percent in-state/out of state: 29%/71%
Percent Pub HS: NA
Number of Applicants: 5,606
Percent Accepted: 46%
Percent Accepted who enroll: 25%
Entering: 636
Transfers: 30
Application Deadline: 15 Jan
Mean SAT: NA
Mean ACT: NA
Middle 50% SAT range: V 580-670, M 580-660
Middle 50% ACT range: 25-28
3 Most popular majors: visual and performing arts, business management, social sciences and history
Retention: 91%
Graduation rate: 75%
On-campus housing: 77%
Fraternities: NA
Sororities: NA
Library: 400,000 volumes
Tuition and Fees: $29,630
Room and Board: $8,300
Financial aid, first-year: 40%
Varsity or Club Athletes: NA
Early Decision or Early Action Acceptance Rate: 57%

Looking for a school where you can get a liberal arts education by day and have a great time at night? Look no further than Saratoga Springs, New York, home of Skidmore College. Skidmore students rave about the town, their professors, and the social scene. Except for a few grumbles about the heavy snowfall every winter, Skidmore students have no complaints about their school.

It's All About Liberal Arts

Students appreciate the freedom and wide range of academic options they have at Skidmore. In picking classes, students "have a lot of flexibility and choices, but the requirements get more specific within your major." The main requirement for freshmen is LS1, an introductory liberal studies course covering a wide range of disciplines including philosophy, religion, gender and race issues, and class separation issues. By the end of sophomore year, students are expected to complete LS2, a continuation of LS1 but "more broad in its coverage of the various topics," according to one sophomore enrolled in it. There are additional natural science, social science, math, art, language, non-Western history and lab science requirements. Though all these requisite classes may seem exhaustive, as one sophomore girl insists, "The overall breadth of the requirement is pretty flexible."

Classes are tough at Skidmore. One sophomore business major cited art history and English as two majors "with a fair amount of work." He added that "business majors start out with a lot of work," but another student contended that "there are some aspects of the business major which are pretty easy." Other students say the anthropology/sociology major is difficult, as well. General agreement is also that Skidmore lives up to its reputation for having tough science classes.

Skidmore classes tend to have creative, interesting assignments. An environmental studies major enjoyed her "fun project in Medieval Europe where we showcased medieval armor in a six-minute film." Two business majors reported a lot of group projects, including a semester-long one where students are asked to invent a product, create a marketing strategy for their product, and present their work to real business executives who then grade the students on their overall performance.

One junior said that some students don't like group projects "because they are a lot of work," but that they are the "best intro into what you're going to learn."

Students have only positive comments about their professors. One girl was so impressed with her professor in an introductory class in social work that she decided to major in the subject. Because of Skidmore's small size, there are no TAs, so professors teach every class and grade every paper. "You get a lot of one-on-one attention" from the professors, said one senior. Professors feel comfortable having fun in class—one Spanish professor brought his dog, who he always talks about in lecture, to class "just for a change of pace." An economics professor had all of his students keep news journals and held weekly discussions to make sure that his students were able to relate what they learned in class to the real world. Another advantage to Skidmore's small size, according to a freshman, is that "you can find at least one friend who has taken some professor's class and can give you the low-down."

Work Hard, Play Hard

Skidmore students are challenged by their classes, and reward themselves for their hard work with a great time on the weekends. At a small school like Skidmore, students of all classes socialize together. The parties "generally aren't exclusive," said one freshman, so it is easy to meet people. Drinking is a popular weekend option, especially during the cold winter months when students tend to stay indoors. Despite the fact that Skidmore dorms have an RA system, students report that few underage students get in trouble for alcohol consumption. As one sophomore said, "the school acts like it's trying to crack down on drinking, but unless you're really obnoxious, they'll look the other way." There are no fraternities or sororities at Skidmore, and many students think that is a good thing. "It makes social groups less segregated," commented one sophomore. Skidmore students tend to hang out in smaller groups in their dorms or apartments in the winter, but when the weather is nice students living off campus host big house parties where everyone is welcome and "half the school goes." One party animal admits "I have plenty of fun, but the social life gets old at times. The same dorm rooms can only be so exciting." Luckily, Saratoga has an active downtown bar scene for students who tire of the house party routine.

"If you're . . . into preppy, pink-shirt-wearing guys, you're not going to find many of those. But if you're into the hippie type, you're in luck."

While many students agree with a junior who said that "non-drinkers are not ridiculed," most students at Skidmore do drink. For sober students, there is a substance-free dorm. The school also provides non-alcohol-related weekend activities, like movie nights, dramatic productions, or weekend hiking excursions. Skidmore also has two annual formal dances: Morbid, a Halloween dance, and the springtime Junior Ring. Downtown Saratoga also boasts a wide variety of restaurants catering to the college crowd. The food at Skidmore "is not outstanding. I've visited schools where the food was significantly better. Here it's not horrible—it just gets kind of monotonous," said a sophomore who dines out at least twice a week. A junior agreed that "the dining hall gets boring, so you have to get really creative in order to survive. I eat downtown all the time, which is sad because it's so expensive." Popular restaurants include Scallions (famous for its crab cakes) Lillian's, Sperry's, Chianti's, and the Brew Pub.

Love and Lust in Saratoga Springs

Students agree that predominately white Skidmore is "not the most diverse school by any means." What the school lacks in ethnic diversity, it makes up in geographic diversity, according to one sophomore who has met people from all over the country attracted by Skidmore's strong academics and active social scene. The stereotype of a Skidmore student is "the liberal, artsy types from rich families." One junior girl claimed, "You're either a hippie or daddy's rich girl. And since there aren't any jocks here because there are no sports teams worth coming to Skidmore for, most guys fall into the artsy and hippie category." Skidmore has a reputation for its beautiful female students, but some girls complain that the male population isn't quite as good-looking. One single girl complained, "depending on your type, there are some cute guys here. If you're like me and into preppy, pink-shirt-wearing guys, you're not going to find many of those. But if you're into the hippie type, you're in luck." The campus "dating" scene consists mainly of random hookups on the weekends. While a few students are able to find significant others, one senior observed that "it's really hard to go out and meet someone and have it turn into something."

Quality Dorm Life

"Our dorms are really nice. They are far bigger than any other dorms I saw when I visited schools," raved one freshman. Freshman dorms are organized in suites, with combinations of several double and single rooms all connected with a common bathroom. All suites are single-sex. An all-female floor is available by request, but most students choose to stay on co-ed hallways. The dorm rooms in the South Quad area are notoriously smaller than those in North Quad, but every dorm has its advantages. One sophomore guy insists that Wilmarth has the best location, while others point to Wait as Skidmore's best because it offers the biggest dorms for freshmen and sophomores. Juniors and seniors either live off campus or in Scribner, and the school is scheduled to build a new Scribner village within the next two years. The campus itself is very compact, and students "love that everything is close together." Academic buildings lie on a large quad surrounded by dormitories. When the weather is warm, students can often be found playing Frisbee or lying out on the quad. "But," one junior warned, "in the winter you'll be lying in five feet of snow." As one student pointed out, "it gets so cold and so snowy—by the end of the winter you want to sue someone."

Skidmore students agree that they love their school enough to brave the cold winters. One girl commented that though she originally chose Skidmore because it was close to home, no matter where she lived, "I would choose it all over again." —*Jenny Zhang*

FYI

If you come to Skidmore, you'd better bring "a warm down jacket, a scarf, a hat, and gloves for the cold winter."

What is the typical weekend schedule? "Go out on Thursday night; pregame and hit the bars on Friday; watch a movie or party Saturday night; and work on Sunday."

If I could change one thing about Skidmore, I'd "make the dining hall food better."

Three things every student at Skidmore should do before graduating are "hit up the downtown bar scene, get to know your professors, and go to Morbid."

St. Bonaventure University

Address: Route 417; St. Bonaventure, NY 14778
Phone: 800-462-5050
E-mail address: admissions@sbu.edu
Web site URL: www.sbu.edu
Founded: 1858
Private or Public: private
Religious affiliation: Franciscan
Location: rural
Undergraduate enrollment: 2,229
Total enrollment: 2,710
Percent Male/Female: 46%/54%
Percent Minority: 0%
Percent African-American: 0%
Percent Asian: 0%
Percent Hispanic: 0%
Percent Native-American: 0%
Percent in-state/out of state: 77%/23%
Percent Pub HS: 72%
Number of Applicants: 1,704
Percent Accepted: 88%
Percent Accepted who enroll: 39%
Entering: 584
Transfers: 75
Application Deadline: 15 Apr
Mean SAT: NA
Mean ACT: NA
Middle 50% SAT range: V 480-570, M 480-580
Middle 50% ACT range: 20-25
3 Most popular majors: journalism, business, education
Retention: 83%
Graduation rate: 69%
On-campus housing: 76%
Fraternities: NA
Sororities: NA
Library: 287,000 volumes
Tuition and Fees: $17,925
Room and Board: $6,594
Financial aid, first-year: 74%
Varsity or Club Athletes: 17%
Early Decision or Early Action Acceptance Rate: NA

Far, far away in the little town of Olean in upstate New York, one big, happy family lives nestled among the picturesque Allegheny Mountains. You just need to put a smile on your face and get ready to have a good time to fit right into the St. Bonaventure community. Students here are "really down to earth," according to one student; "outgoing and fun-loving," claims another.

One Big, Happy Family

Students mostly hail from nearby: upstate New York, New Jersey, Long Island, and Ohio. Many even know each other from high school. But even though students' homes are nearby, they rarely travel home on the weekends—the family feel is strong on campus. Contributing to the family atmosphere, everybody seems to have brothers, sisters, and cousins as fellow students, and parents, aunts, uncles, and grandparents in whose footsteps they are following. "Family and alumni weekends are huge," says one student. She adds that alumni networking is strong: "alumni are always looking for 'Bona' kids to work for them."

Academics

The benefits of a small university stand out when it comes to the St. Bonaventure education. Class sizes are small, ranging from 10 to 35 and averaging at about 20. There is one big lecture hall, but most students never enter it with the exception of freshmen orientation. Despite the small class size, registering is rarely a problem. If one occurs, there is a designated night in which students can meet up with professors whose classes they did not get into and try to work something out.

The small class size provides an atmosphere in which "after the first week, everyone is comfortable speaking up in class." One student mentioned a professor she had who videotaped short interviews with his students, so that he could get to know the entire class. Professors often invite students to their houses for dinner and try to promote class unity. They are also "extremely understanding" and will accomodate students bogged down by work or recovering from the flu. A downside to small classes is that professors know who is in class and who skips, so it's a good idea to drag yourself into class on Friday morning even after a night of a little too much fun.

The core curriculum, referred to as Clare College, requires that students take 12 specific classes—history, theology, sociology, science, two English, etc.—before graduation. While underclassmen begrudge having to fulfill these rigid requirements, especially the theology classes, seniors appreciate having received a well-rounded education.

Franciscan values are "huge here." Because St. Bonaventure is a Catholic school, and theology pervades all aspects of education. Professors smoothly fit Franciscan values into the curriculum, not just in theology classes. There is also an on-campus friary, where the friars are reportedly friendly. Students even see the friars out on weekends, throwing back a beer alongside them at the bar. Father Dan, a beloved Bona icon, seems to know each and every student by name and always gives out a big smile and "Hello!"

Bona Fide Essentials: Sleep and Eat

Freshmen and sophomores live on campus in typical college dorms, with long hallways, RAs, singles, doubles, triples. Sexes are separated by floor. Most students consider the dorms small but decent, though one student described her freshman year room as having that "jail cell feeling." Students never have to wait in line to use the dorm toilets and showers because there are plenty. Students tend to form lasting friendships with their freshman year neighbors, who often remain the base of their social groups for all four years.

Juniors and seniors get to live in on-campus garden apartments or highly desirable townhouses (townhouses are restricted to seniors), while others choose to live in off-campus housing. Off-campus houses have descript names such as, the Club House, Caddy Shack, Boat House, Beach House, Buffalo House, Mad Dog, Doll House, The Morgue, etc. Each house has a distinct personality that varies from year to year as the group of residents change. One downside to these frat-like dwellings is that the old Victorian houses are "disgusting," having been battered by partying Bona students for years. Most off-campus students drive the five minutes it takes to get to the main campus buildings, although they complain that parking is impossible.

With regards to food: "Horrendous—I mean absolutely horrendous," exclaims one Bonaventure student. The main Hickey Dining Hall and four on-campus cafés are notorious among students for serving bad-quality and boring meals on a four- or five-day rotation. One student insisted that "salad, bagels, and cereal are the safest things." In recent years the dining management has changed, but students complain that it hasn't gotten any better. "Here, you *lose* weight." Despite the unappetizing food, the dining hall and cafés, especially the Rathskeller Café in the Reilly Center (the closest thing Bonaventure has to a student union) are still good places to meet up with friends between classes.

When the Going Gets Tough, Leave Campus

When life becomes too busy and stressful, students can take advantage of Mt. Irenaeus, an invaluable student retreat and beautiful escape only 20 minutes away. Many of the friars live up on the mountain, and they always welcome any Bona visitors with a home-cooked meal and hours of chatting, advice, and comfort. Students visit by themselves, in groups of friends, as a religious group, as a team, or with other extracurricular groups. The friars hold all-girls and all-boys nights. One girl exclaims that the all-boys nights claim all her guy friends. "The guys just rant and rave about their mountain nights." She reasons that it takes them out of their element, away from video games, and provides them with a place where it's cool to talk.

A Party Town

"The weekend starts on Wednesday!" exclaims one student. When Wednesday night rolls around, students can be found kickin' back at The Burton, one of the four bars in Olean, for the $6 all-you-can-drink special. Thursday night the rest of the school comes out flooding to all four bars: The Burton (where everybody goes), The Hickey, Foster's (newly opened in 2003), and The Other Place (a senior hangout). On Friday nights some eager students meet up at the bars as soon as they get out of classes at around 3 P.M. Friday and Saturday nights are big house-party nights. Then, at around 11 P.M. or whenever the kegs are kicked, students head out again to the bars and hang out until 2 A.M., when they close. For safe transportation, a bus operates regularly between the town and campus from 11 P.M. to 3 A.M.

For such a small school, there seems to be a plethora of nighttime activity. Many students boasted that Bonaventure was ranked the #9 party school in the nation (though they were unaware of the source). To curtail binge drinking, the university has attempted a new academic excellence program that encourages professors to have tests on Fridays.

Random hook-ups, as opposed to long-term relationships, seem to be the popular mode of sexual expression. Although when people do get together, they "seem to get together for a very long time." Friendships are also fostered: one senior explained that she doesn't find her guy friends attractive anymore. "I see my guy friends as my brothers," she says. One male senior described the girls as, "really chill girls who like to party and can drink like the guys."

Students describe the student body as generally white, Catholic, and laid-back. One student mentioned that, "there's a lot of rich kids, but there's not a lot of flaunting of the richness." Despite recent attempts by the admissions office to recruit minorities, Bonaventure is not known for its diversity. The few African-American students "tend to hang out with each other," reports one student. The athletes also tend to separate themselves because of their rigorous Division-I practice schedule that prevents them from going out most nights.

Bona Pride

"The Bona pride is ridiculous!" cries one sophomore. Students insist that one must-do for anybody nearby is to attend one of the men's basketball games, which sell out quickly. The Bona Rowdies section at the Reilly Center (which seats 6,000 at the main basketball court), seats die-hard fans who dress up, lead the cheers, and "get crazy!" In January 2001, Jay Bilas of ESPN ranked the Reilly Center one of the nation's top five "Hostile Homes," along with Duke's Cameron Indoor Stadium, Kansas' Allen Fieldhouse, Arizona's McKale Center, and Michigan State's Breslin Center. The Richter Center, a new $5 million field house, will supposedly be completed in Fall 2004.

> **"The weekend starts on Wednesday."**

The very successful men's club rugby team gets great support, too. Other teams usually just attract friends of members of the team. Many students lament the large amount of money allocated to the basketball team when compared to the budgets of smaller, but more successful teams.

The Bubble Effect

Besides the bars, the poor town of Olean (population 15,400) offers little in the way of entertainment. There's a Wal-Mart—"Wal-Mart runs are a big deal." There's a mall—"if you can call it that." Other than that you can drive the hour it takes to get to Buffalo, the nearest city. Says one student, "You have to make your own fun here."

So isolated, students feel they live in a bubble where everybody knows everybody, and sometimes since childhood or high school. One student observes, "A portion of this community doesn't know what's going on outside of here. We live in a bubble." Everybody knows everybody's business. Laughs one junior, "My friends and I have a saying: 'If you kick a rock, it echoes for three weeks.'" While students find the rumor mill frustrating, they also appreciate the closeness and knowledge that they have many intimate friends who will support them. This invaluable family feeling keeps the community strong. —*Baily Blair*

FYI

If you come to St. Bonaventure you'd better bring "a fake ID."

What is the typical weekend schedule? "Bars, bars, bars, house parties, bars, recover, study, gossip over the weekend's happenings."

If I could change one thing about St. Bonaventure, I would "change the weather—it's constantly just dark and it rains a lot. The first snowfall is around Halloween and it doesn't stop until April."

The three things every student at St. Bonaventure should do before graduating are "go to the mountain, go to a b-ball game, and hike to Merton-Heart where there's a clearing in the shape of a heart."

St. Lawrence University

Address: 23 Romoda Dr, Canton, NY 13617
Phone: 315-229-5261
E-mail address: admissions@stlawu.edu
Web site URL: www.stlawu.edu
Founded: 1865
Private or Public: private
Religious affiliation: none
Location: rural
Undergraduate enrollment: 2,150
Total enrollment: 2,150
Percent Male/Female: 47%/53%
Percent Minority: 5%
Percent African-American: 2%
Percent Asian: 1%
Percent Hispanic: 2%
Percent Native-American: 0%
Percent in-state/out of state: 54%/46%
Percent Pub HS: 71%
Number of Applicants: 2,867
Percent Accepted: 65%
Percent Accepted who enroll: 33%
Entering: 620
Transfers: 27
Application Deadline: 15 Feb
Mean SAT: NA
Mean ACT: NA
Middle 50% SAT range: V 520-620, M 520-620
Middle 50% ACT range: 21-27
3 Most popular majors: social sciences and history, biology, psychology
Retention: 85%
Graduation rate: 72%
On-campus housing: 95%
Fraternities: 15%
Sororities: 23%
Library: 533,000 volumes
Tuition and Fees: $28,185
Room and Board: $7,755
Financial aid, first-year: 70%
Varsity or Club Athletes: NA
Early Decision or Early Action Acceptance Rate: 80%

Tucked into a corner of the Adirondacks, in a small town in New York near the Canadian border, sits St. Lawrence University, just small enough to fit into the little town, but big enough for its students to call it home. The relatively small size of SLU allows the formation of a close-knit community, both within the student body and between the students and faculty. The rural location affords opportunities for outdoor activities and gives the campus its beautiful backdrop, the pride of many a SLU student. Even though many students complain about the huge piles of snow in the cold winter months, most agree that the warmth of the friendly people around them more than makes up for the weather.

Studying at SLU

Academics at St. Lawrence are described as difficult at times, but, as one student said, "you don't have to be doing work ALL the time." Some of the most popular departments include economics, psychology, and biology, with geology cited as a less popular subject. Because of the small size of SLU, students benefit from small class sizes and they enjoy close contact with professors right from the start of their freshman year; students reported that essentially all classes enroll between 20 and 25 students, are taught exclusively by professors, and have a TA or two to give extra help to students who need it. Small class size rarely results in students being shut out of classes they want to take, though. One student said, "registration usually is pretty hectic . . . students line up in front of the registrar's office and wait for hours to get classes, but then everybody usually gets the ones they want in the end."

St. Lawrence's academic program includes a fair number of required courses: undergrads must take courses in two out of three groups: modern languages, math or computer-related, and fine arts or music. They also are required to take at least one class each in the humanities, social sciences, and lab science, and one class which relates to a non-Western culture. Opinions of these requirements vary from "a hassle" to "a good way to get us to start exploring different departments." In addition, freshmen participate in the First Year Program, a year-long course devoted to developing oral and written communication skills, taken with other students from the same dorm. While many students acknowledge the benefits of FYP, others complain about how the course runs the whole year and often conflicts with other desired courses.

When students at St. Lawrence want to study, they often head for Owen D. Young library, the main library on campus. ODY is a fairly modern building; and although its aesthetic merits are often debated, most agree that the recent renovation has made the atmosphere on the inside cheerful and stimulating. However, the lively atmosphere also frequently inspires conversation, and many students describe ODY as more of a social place than a studious one. For hardcore, serious studying, Madill, the science library, is your best bet.

Living and Eating

Housing at SLU is mainly in dorms, although there are also off-campus options such as Greek and theme housing and athletic suites. The dorms are mostly set up in traditional singles and doubles, and are co-ed, but some dorms also offer the option of suites with kitchens, mostly for upperclassmen. Students cite Sykes as one of the best dorms, with Whitman as the best dorm for freshmen. On the other hand, Lee and Rebert halls are said to be the worst, although even in those less desirable dorms, rooms are reportedly spacious and nicely furnished. Almost universally, students praise their dorms, whether they live in the best or worst location, for the sense of community fostered there.

As upperclassmen, students at St. Lawrence have more housing options, although finding an off-campus apartment isn't really one of them, since available apartments are extremely scarce in Canton. However, many upperclassmen choose to live in Greek houses, which lie just at the edge of campus; one student living in her sorority house described her experience by saying it is "very home-like, and there is always something to do." Theme housing is another alternative to dorms available after freshman year, and such houses include a house for environmentalists, for people who enjoy outdoor activities, and for cultural groups and international students.

SLU students tend to give their meal plan and dining options high ratings. There are three on-campus eating establishments: Dana Dining Hall (a traditional cafeteria), Northstar Pub, and Jack's Snack Shop (a deli). The pub has more of a relaxed atmosphere where students go to hang out and relax, and the food there is considered the best of the options on campus, particularly the chicken wrap sandwiches. Jack's Snack Shop, on the other hand, is the place to go if you need to pick up a quick bite, and is frequented by students in between classes. There are two meal plans available to students, the 21-meal plan, which is only accepted at Dana, and a declining-balance plan which is accepted at all three on-campus locations. While students favor the declining-balance plan because of its flexibility, most agree that it is impossible not to run out of money before the end of the semester, and so that plan is better for students who are not eating all of their meals on campus.

"You don't have to be doing work ALL the time."

When students get tired of the places to eat on campus, or just want to treat themselves, they look to the restaurants in the town of Canton. For quick meals, there are the standard chains: McDonald's, Burger King, and Pizza Hut, and also A-1 Oriental Kitchen, which is a popular delivery choice. Other restaurants in Canton include Sergie's Pizza, which has pizza and Italian food, Jerek Subs, and The Lobster House; the Cactus Grill, a Mexican restaurant located in nearby Potsdam, is also frequented by many St. Lawrence students.

Life After Studying

Students at St. Lawrence spend a lot of time on extracurricular activities, and there is "always something to get involved in." One of the most active groups on campus seems to be the Outing Club, which goes on lots of trips and does other activities together. A recently founded karate club, which is student-run and student-taught, is growing rapidly, an example of the ample opportunity to start new organizations if you are interested. Many students also spend their time working for *The Hill*, the main weekly publication of St. Lawrence.

Sports are also an option at St. Lawrence, both for fans and athletes. Varsity soccer and hockey are the most popular, with rugby and lacrosse games also drawing crowds. School spirit peaks at the time of the Clarkson-SLU hockey game, and the long-time rivalry draws huge crowds. Students say that you have to get tickets at least a week in advance if you don't want to stand up to watch the game, but that it is one of the highlights of the year that cannot be missed. Sports are not limited only to varsity athletes, though, as St. Lawrence has a wide variety of intramural teams, which allow people of all levels the opportunity to play. In addition, the athletic facilities are described as "great, and always available to everybody." All of the sports facilities have been recently renovated and according to one student athlete, "facilities at SLU are in tip-top shape."

Unfortunately, the social life and weekend plans are definitely limited by the small student body and the school's rural locale. Some things that students do when they are hanging out or partying include shooting pool, going to see a movie (with a discount for showing a student ID), going to see a band playing at Java House, or going to a frat party. However, students complain that campus security and Canton police strongly frown upon student alcohol use, which is not allowed on campus. On top of that, on-campus and off-campus parties alike tend to get shut down soon after they begin. Thus, most students say that they spend a lot of time hanging out in bars in Canton with their friends, or taking trips on the weekend to Ottawa, the capital of Canada, or to Syracuse, both of which are within a few hours driving distance.

Even though there may be downsides to living in a remote, rural town, students at St. Lawrence agree that the beauty of their campus and the surrounding area is worth it. The architecture of the university, a mixture of old and modern buildings, the quaintness of the town of Canton, and the beauty of the mountains and forests make St. Lawrence a scenic and pleasant place. If you are looking for a school with a fast-paced, urban environment and a restaurant and club for every night of the week, SLU may not be for you; however, if you want a school with a tightly-knit community of professors and students, set in a beautiful landscape offering a place to hike or just sit and contemplate, St. Lawrence University is the one. *—Lisa Smith*

FYI

If you come to St. Lawrence, you'd better bring "a jacket. It's really cold out."

What is the typical weekend schedule? "There are two groups on campus. For one group, the weekend starts on Thursday nights, and they go to bars. The other group is the outdoorsy group. They go to the Adirondack Mountains to go hiking, backpacking, skiing, and kayaking."

If I could change one thing about St. Lawrence, I would "make it so that the clubs could be completely student-run."

Three things every student at St. Lawrence should do before graduating are "streak the Candlelight Freshman Experience, ring the bells in the chapel, and take a faculty member out to lunch."

State University of New York System

The State University of New York System is one of the largest state university programs in the United States, consisting of 64 individual campuses and over 410,000 students. SUNY offers a variety of degrees, ranging from the one-year certificate programs designed to prepare students for specific employment at the system's 30 community colleges to the advanced doctorate degrees offered at the four university centers in Binghamton, Buffalo, Stoneybrook and Albany. Other campuses are scattered around New York, and are represented in Brockport, Brooklyn, Canton, Clinton, Erie, Farmingdale, New Paltz, Old Westbury, Onondaga, and Syracuse. Aside from the community colleges and the university center programs, the remaining SUNY schools are divided into schools focused on cultivating different specific academic interests, including technology, veterinary medicine and forestry studies.

To simplify the process of applying to such a diversity of schools, prospective students may apply to up to eight campuses at once. Fifty-one of the 64 SUNY schools accept this common application.

Like many state university programs, the SUNY system is almost completely comprised of in-state students. Almost 90 percent of SUNY's enrollment comes from New York, and these students pay a heavily discounted price for their education. Although this makes college significantly more affordable, when combined with the increasing number of students the SUNY system admits each year, students say it also creates large lectures and low levels of attention for undergraduates.

Many SUNY students agreed that the SUNY system is not one to pamper its students. In order to get involved on campus or find direction either academically or with extracurricular activities, a student must be self-motivated. According to one student, the isolated locations of most SUNY campuses make it difficult to maintain a social life and get off campus.

Despite these challenges, however, the SUNY system boasts a wealth of opportunities at a very affordable price. With over 6,650 degrees available and a niche for any student willing to make an effort to find it, SUNY provides the magnitude of resources only possible with such a broad range of campuses and students. Following are articles about the SUNY campuses located in Albany, Buffalo, Binghamton and Stonybrook. —*Stephanie Teng*

State University of New York / Albany

Address: 1400 Washington Avenue; Albany, NY 12222
Phone: 518-442-5435
E-mail address: ugadmissions@albany.edu
Web site URL: www.albany.edu
Founded: 1844
Private or Public: public
Religious affiliation: none
Location: suburban
Undergraduate enrollment: 11,953
Total enrollment: 16,867
Percent Male/Female: 50%/50%
Percent Minority: 22%
Percent African-American: 9%
Percent Asian: 6%
Percent Hispanic: 7%
Percent Native-American: 0%
Percent in-state/out of state: 95%/5%
Percent Pub HS: NA
Number of Applicants: 17,667
Percent Accepted: 56%
Percent Accepted who enroll: 22%
Entering: 2,276
Transfers: 900
Application Deadline: 1 Mar
Mean SAT: NA
Mean ACT: NA
Middle 50% SAT range: V 500-600, M 520-610
Middle 50% ACT range: NA
3 Most popular majors: social sciences and history, business management, psychology
Retention: 84%
Graduation rate: 63%
On-campus housing: 58%
Fraternities: 4%
Sororities: 5%
Library: 1,192,000 volumes
Tuition and Fees: $4,820 in; $9,720 out
Room and Board: $7,052
Financial aid, first-year: 54%
Varsity or Club Athletes: NA
Early Decision or Early Action Acceptance Rate: NA

SUNY Albany lies at the heart of the state's SUNY system. Located in New York's bustling capital city, the school provides a sound academic environment that will not strain the student budget.

Unforgiving Requirements

Strict course requirements, however, do strain students' schedules. All undergraduates must take two courses each in humanities and arts, social science, and natural science, as well as two writing-intensive classes. "It's those writing classes that are particularly annoying," one junior said, complaining about the number of assignments. Other requirements include a cultural and historical perspective class and a class in human diversity. These interdisciplinary classes combine the social sciences and the humanities. Particularly driven students can also participate in the General Education Honors Program, which centers on small discussion sections with more individual attention from professors.

Although upper-level courses usually enroll around 30 students, introductory lectures max out at 400. Professors are not inaccessible, however, and undergraduates remain the school's focus. Students apply to a particular school after their freshman year. The schools of business and criminal justice tend to be the most selective. Applicants must take a placement test, submit a writing sample, and meet a minimum grade-point average. Albany features many strong academic departments, most notably in psychology and English. Students also say the political science program, assisted by the backdrop of the state government scene in Albany, is excellent.

A Divided Campus

"Campus" is a misnomer of sorts for SUNY Albany. The university actually has two campuses, one uptown and one downtown. The uptown campus is the school's true center, containing most of the student housing and academic buildings. Four quads—Dutch, Colonial, State, and Indian—form the corners of the uptown campus's square design, enclosing an open area around a fountain known as "The Podium."

Various dorms and special-interest halls are contained within the quads.

Students insist that despite the dorms' identical appearance, each has its distinct personality. Perhaps this is because students are free to live with peers who share their interests. Wellness Hall, for example, stresses health and exercise and has Nautilus machines. One of the quads is reserved for first-year students only. "It's comforting knowing that everyone you live with is entering the same situation," one freshman said. Other special-interest options include Math Hall, Science Hall, and Substance-Free Hall. Those few undergraduates living on the uptown campus often complain about the accommodations, which generally take the form of either suites with private bathrooms or doubles with hall bathrooms. Downtown campus, about a ten-minute walk away, wins in the looks category with ivy-covered brick buildings as opposed to the "gray and dreary" structures of uptown. Many students move off campus after their first or second year. The school owns off-campus housing called Freedom Quad, where many graduate students reside.

A New York Crowd

So many New Yorkers make the trek upstate for school that a Long Island-based rock radio station, WDRE, now broadcasts its signal in Albany. Because a large portion of the undergraduate population comes from the melting pots of New York City and Long Island, the campus is ethnically if not geographically diverse.

Albany offers much more than a great educational bang for your tuition buck.

According to students, the nearly 30 frats and sororities are a significant force at SUNY Albany. Rushing is a popular undergraduate activity, although students generally do not feel pressured to participate. The Greeks are the primary campus source of parties and alcohol. "I'm glad you don't have to be a full-fledged member to attend their parties," said one sophomore. Albany's several bars and pubs provide an alternative to the Greek night life for the 21-and-over crowd—the Lamp Post, Peabody's, and Washington's Tavern are perennial student favorites.

Albany students report feeling content with the school's food policy—mainly because they can charge purchases at Taco Bell, Nathan's, and Pizza Hut to their meal accounts. When students spend time in the city, it is mainly for food or to socialize at the bars.

Despite the popularity of political science as a major, the school student government reportedly lacks mass student appeal. The Student Association organizes some annual social events, such as the year-end "Party in the Park" and Fallfest, both of which feature live music, dancing, and plenty of food. The student newspaper, *The Albany Student Press*, comes out twice a week and draws enthusiastic undergraduate participation. Unfortunately, the same cannot be said for varsity sports, but students have glowing praise for the school's recently built "tremendous" sports complex, where many work out in their spare time. Students also have no complaints about the security and safety of the school. An escort service and shuttle van serve as alternatives to late-night walking. Abundant emergency phones throughout campus also work to put students at ease.

All things considered, Albany offers much more than a great educational bang for your tuition buck. Its satisfied student body and sound academics would make it a great deal in any state of the union. *—Ann Zeidner and Staff*

FYI

If you come to Albany, you'd better bring "snow shoes."

What is the typical weekend schedule? "Frat parties, bars on Friday and Saturday, sleeping on Sunday."

If I could change one thing about Albany, I'd "change the food."

Three things every student at Albany should do before graduating are "go to Fountain Day, visit Lake George, go to Party in the Park, explore Albany."

State University of New York / Binghamton

Address: PO Box 6000; Binghamton, NY 13902-6001
Phone: 607-777-2171
E-mail address: admit@binghamton.edu
Web site URL: www.binghamton.edu
Founded: 1946
Private or Public: public
Religious affiliation: none
Location: suburban
Undergraduate enrollment: 10,378
Total enrollment: 12,820
Percent Male/Female: 47%/53%
Percent Minority: 28%
Percent African-American: 5%
Percent Asian: 17%
Percent Hispanic: 6%
Percent Native-American: 0%
Percent in-state/out of state: 95%/5%
Percent Pub HS: 87%
Number of Applicants: 18,315
Percent Accepted: 42%
Percent Accepted who enroll: 27%
Entering: 2,077
Transfers: 691
Application Deadline: rolling
Mean SAT: NA
Mean ACT: NA
Middle 50% SAT range: V 550-640, M 590-690
Middle 50% ACT range: 24-29
3 Most popular majors: business management, psychology, English
Retention: 91%
Graduation rate: 80%
On-campus housing: 57%
Fraternities: 10%
Sororities: 10%
Library: 1,787,000 volumes
Tuition and Fees: $4,717 in; $9,617 out
Room and Board: $6,412
Financial aid, first-year: 44%
Varsity or Club Athletes: 4%
Early Decision or Early Action Acceptance Rate: NA

Over their four college years, SUNY Binghamton students learn to appreciate Binghamton life's small pleasures—jaunts through the rain, midnight food runs, good movies on free cable. And although many upperclassmen admit their school can get pretty monotonous—"there's nothing to do out here in the middle of nowhere!"—most would agree that it gets better as it goes. Even those students who reported loathing the school their freshman year would now offer this caution to their predecessors: "If you want to transfer out of this place, transfer out quick because this school really grows on you. Everything—the place, the people, even the never-ending rain—it all gets better as time goes on. Trust me, if you stay here, you'll hate your first year but love the rest."

The Ivy of the SUNYs

Binghamton is widely recognized as one of the most academically competitive SUNYs, attracting many of New York's best with its affordable quality education. The University comprises five undergraduate schools catering to a wide range of interests: the Harpur College of Arts and Sciences, the Decker School of Nursing, the School of Management, the School of Education and Human Development, and the Thomas J. Watson School of Engineering and Applied Science.

Graduation requirements vary with school and program. Generally, though, most majors have to fulfill one course credit in each of four core areas: the arts, pluralism, global interdependencies, and communications. In addition, all students must earn two phys-ed credits and satisfy a writing requirement. Many students agree with the general education requirements and think them great in theory but typically hate them in practice. Said one senior, "Requirements are good in the sense that they encourage students to get a broad view of things, but they're kind of a waste of time too."

And if there's one thing Binghamton students lack, it's enough time in the day. One student emphasized, "Binghamton may be easy enough to get into, but it's really hard to stay in." Students of all majors claim to grapple with "substantial" workloads, but engineering, management, and science (especially pre-med) majors reportedly suffer the heaviest loads.

Class sizes at Binghamton follow traditional college patterns—huge introductory courses of up to several hundred students with numbers generally shrinking as classes become more specialized in the upper levels. Teaching is generally rated as average. One student remarked, "Some professors don't even really seem to like teaching, but then there are those that make you really love your classes. I guess it's that way at most schools." TAs often co-teach and lead discussion sections for lower-level courses, becoming fewer less present at the higher levels.

Students conveniently register for classes via computer, a process which one sophomore described as "very easy and great in that I can register from home if I wanted to." Because class availability follows a pecking order dictated by seniority and major, frosh sometimes find themselves having a hard time getting into the classes they want. But, according to one experienced senior, "If you know what you're doing, you can pretty much petition and beg your way into any class." In several instances, though, the classrooms themselves have lacked the space to accommodate enrollees. Faced with a shortage of seats, many students ended up sitting through class without desks or chairs. One student voiced his concern: "It's like you're paying money to sit on the floor. That's just not right."

In years past as well, students have had to deal with similar shortages in housing. One year, in fact, the situation was so bad that some freshmen were forced to take up temporary quarters in floor TV common rooms because there were no permanent rooms available. Despite occasional problems, however, most students seem pretty content with their on-campus housing. One student described the dorms as "totally decent" with "relatively big and clean" rooms.

Community Life

Undergrads live in one of five "communities," each of which includes several coed dorms and a central building housing a dining hall. Each community has a distinctive character and stereotype attached to it. Newing College is the Greek-dominated party dorm. Hinman is the quiet haven for hardcore studiers. Dickinson is racially and ethnically diverse, while College-in-the-Woods (CIW) is notorious for abundant drug use. The fifth dorm, the graduate community, is restricted to juniors and seniors. The summer before freshman year, incoming frosh are asked to indicate their first and second community choices on a preference sheet, and in most cases, they are assigned to one of the two. After freshman year, students can choose to remain in their communities, move to another, or move off campus. Apartments are generally "cheap and easy-to-find," but students without cars may find transportation a problem.

Most communities have libraries where students can do work, but the main Bartle library is also a popular study spot. Late-night studiers seeking a quiet atmosphere can find it in the "tombs," a popular nickname for a scary tomb-esque section of Bartle's main lobby.

In Pursuit of the Freshman 15

After stressful study sessions, Binghamton students grab much-needed sustenance at Snax or the Night Owl, open until midnight and 1 A.M. respectively. Students can charge these purchases to their meal plans.

At mealtimes, Bing students have the option to eat in the community dining halls or at the mini-mall, which sells typical food-court fare like Taco Bell, Chinese food, pasta, and char-grill. School food was described as "decent, but pretty repetitive" with the same entrees offered again and again. "How many ways are there to prepare chicken?" wondered one student. "And amazingly, no matter how they make it, it all tastes *exactly the same.*"

For students looking to escape campus food, Binghamton's main throughway, Vestal Parkway, is a hungry man's heaven. Dozens of eateries ranging from dirt-cheap grease to pricier four-star cuisine dot this long asphalt strip. Perennially popular options include T.G.I. Friday's, Olive Garden, Denny's. and Tony's—great food at a bargain. No. 5 was said to be a good place to take a date. Local Binghamton also attracts students with its many sports bars and handful of clubs. Some clubs will periodically hold "SUNY nights," which one student described as "a good way to meet other people in the university."

The Self-Contained Brain

Seen from the air, the Binghamton campus is arranged in a circle, which students have affectionately dubbed "the Brain." Wooded mountains enclose the campus, creating a valley of sorts; this valley tends to keep clouds in above school grounds, resulting in lots of rain and snow. "Don't forget to bring an umbrella," advised one student.

Just a short walk from campus is a nature preserve spanning 117-acres. "It's a great place to take a date," said one sophomore guy. Other students flock there to escape the noisy campus construction currently in process. "I mean, it'll be great when the campus union is renovated and those new dorms are done, but for now, I'm just looking to get away from the racket," said one student.

"For a school without a football team, we have a ton of really big and buff guys."

Because Binghamton's campus is so isolated and self-contained, most students would agree that cars are a necessary evil for off-campus treks. "Cars are great because of the freedom they give, but parking is a drag," said one car owner. Not only are parking spaces on campus limited, but the lots are often inconveniently located. Newing College's three parking lots are commonly referred to as "heaven," "purgatory," and "hell," with "hell" being the farthest and "heaven" the closest distance away.

Cars also prove convenient when Bing students just want some "away time." While New York City, a three-hour drive, may be a bit far for a road trip, major college-towns Syracuse and Ithaca are both less than an hour away, making for a good day or weekend getaway.

Weekend Fun

Back on campus, Greeks tend to dominate social life. The party scene revolves around the frats, which regularly throw weekend bashes. Alcohol abounds at these events; for $3, attendees can drink as much as they want. Considering the abundance of inebriated guys and girls in attendance at these parties, it is not surprising that here are where most random hook-ups occur. Some people will go with dates, but it's less common.

For students not into the partying and drinking scenes, the university offers a host of other social options. Movie showings, student productions, guest lectures, and dances are just a few of the alternatives. The campus pub is also another fun hangout, with a bowling alley, arcade, and billiards.

Surprising Diversity

Binghamton has no football team, a reality that undoubtedly contributes to the general absence of school spirit among the student body. Despite that empty pocket, however, intramurals or "co-recs" are pretty popular, especially soccer and rugby. The university athletic facilities are divided between the East and West Gymnasiums. East Gym is generally considered the better of the two, but unlike West Gym, it is not free. Remarked one student, "For a school without a football team, we have a ton of really big and buff guys."

In addition to intramurals and recreational sports, lots of students report heavy involvement in campus extracurricular groups. The Student Association, Binghamton's answer to student government, is generally recognized as pretty popular. Cultural organizations also enjoy high student participation, not surprising in light of the school's diverse student makeup. Music-minded students can perform in school musical groups like the orchestra and wind ensemble, and journalistic or literary minds can write for one of the many campus publications. Binghamton students hold a variety of interests, and club offerings reflect this wide range.

Indeed Binghamton's student body can be surprisingly diverse and eclectic considering Binghamton is a state school full of mostly New Yorkers. Even within the state, though, certain regions are said to be over-represented—Long Island in particular. For some this can be a drawback, as one student complained, "There are too many students from Long Island, Westchester, and New York City. There aren't even that many from upstate New York!"

But all things considered, Binghamton would qualify as a wise college choice for Yankee and non-Yankee alike, offering an excellent education for the money and a diversity rarely found at state institutions. —*Jane H. Hong and Staff*

FYI

If you come to Binghamton, you'd better bring "a winter coat and a fake ID."

What is the typical weekend schedule? "Drink with housemates, stop by other friends houses for a couple of drinks, go to the bars downtown, come home and make food, wake up and go to Rolando's Diner for inexpensive breakfast and coffee, nap, start the whole process over again. On Sunday, you do all the work that you should've done during the past two days."

If I could change one thing about Binghamton, I'd "make it warmer."

Three things every student at Binghamton should do before graduating are "Eat at Pepe's at 3 A.M., get wings at Sportsman's, and cut your hair in a mullet to pay homage to the local townsfolk."

State University of New York / Buffalo

Address: 3435 Main St.; Buffalo, NY 14222
Phone: 716-645-6900
E-mail address: ubadmission@buffalo.edu
Web site URL: www.buffalo.edu
Founded: 1846
Private or Public: public
Religious affiliation: none
Location: suburban
Undergraduate enrollment: 17,054
Total enrollment: 24,000
Percent Male/Female: 54%/46%
Percent Minority: 21%
Percent African-American: 8%
Percent Asian: 9%
Percent Hispanic: 4%
Percent Native-American: NA
Percent in-state/out of state: 98%/3%
Percent Pub HS: NA
Number of Applicants: 1,657
Percent Accepted: 61%
Percent Accepted who enroll: 31%
Entering: 3,059
Transfers: 1,337
Application Deadline: rolling
Mean SAT: NA
Mean ACT: NA
Middle 50% SAT range: V 500-600, M 520-630
Middle 50% ACT range: 21-27
3 Most popular majors: business management, social sciences and history, engineering
Retention: 85%
Graduation rate: 56%
On-campus housing: 21%
Fraternities: 1%
Sororities: 1%
Library: 3,200,000 volumes
Tuition and Fees: $4,850 in; $9,750 out
Room and Board: $6,512
Financial aid, first-year: 66%
Varsity or Club Athletes: NA
Early Decision or Early Action Acceptance Rate: 63%

In 1846, the University at Buffalo was a private medical school consisting of a few lecture rooms in an old church. As the years went by, the university steadily expanded by adding a school of pharmacy, a law school, a dental school, a school of arts and science, a school of management and numerous other offerings. After becoming part of the SUNY system in 1962, the school grew rapidly and split into a North Campus and South Campus and became the largest public university in all of New England. With their school offering the largest faculty in the SUNY system and the greatest number of degree programs, students at SUNY Buffalo can be found exploring a wide variety of studies and interests.

Options, Options and More Options

"This school has just about every single major you can think of." Buffalo offers a wide variety of majors to meet the tastes of its large student body, but if you can't decide on one there's always the option of double-majoring or minoring in another subject. According to one student, "You would be amazed by the number of students who choose to take on a second major or minor." Those who do not wish to follow a traditional major program have the freedom of designing their own major, but students agreed that this is rarely necessary and that "it is hard enough just trying to decide on which major to choose amongst all of the ones that are already there."

When asked about the academic environment at Buffalo, one student said, "It is a big science and engineering school." The engineering and pharmacy departments in particular are highly regarded as ranking among the best in the SUNY system. Students agreed that science, engineering, and computer science courses, as well as premed classes, tend to be on the more difficult side. However, the campus is by no means dominated by science lovers. Widely considered easier than the sciences, communications is a strong and popular major. When asked about premed courses at Buffalo, one communications major said, "I don't see the premed students often . . . I think they spend most of their time studying in the health and science library." The general feeling among undergraduates is that "Your workload depends on which classes you take," and that it is possible to challenge yourself to whatever extent you are motivated.

Registration is probably the biggest source of complaints with respect to academics at Buffalo. The large student body can make it "extremely hard to get the classes you want." There is an online registration system in use, but classes close out quickly, and that is when the trouble begins. One junior said "getting closed out of two classes isn't uncommon" and this means waiting on the end of a telephone in an attempt to get into classes. One glimmer of hope is for students to see their advisors, who can occasionally get them into a class.

Buffalo does require students to take certain core, or general education classes their freshman year. These classes range from math to social studies, and according to one student, "nobody wants to take them." You can expect these and other introductory classes to have as many as 300 to 400 students in them. Although developing a relationship with a professor is harder in such lecture classes, students can get to know them by visiting during weekly office hours, which every teacher holds. Students can also receive help by attending the smaller recitations led by graduate student TAs. Students are happy with the majority of their professors, however, "sometimes you will come across a teacher or TA [who is] difficult to understand or doesn't know English all that well—especially in the math department." Regarding the overall academic environment, one student said, "I hate work, but I love to learn."

Social Life

When the week of classes is over, students have fun by doing almost whatever they want. The bars on Main Street are some of the most popular destinations for a night out and according to one student, "You could show them a library card and you would get in." Only about ten percent of students are involved in Greek life, but the fraternities and sororities make up a large part of the social scene. Parties in dorms are also popular among students. There are plenty of other options, such as the movie theater, the symphony orchestra, concerts, or just hanging out with friends. After a hard week, friends never hesitate to "just stay in and watch a movie or some TV."

Buffalo's big social events each year are Fall Fest and Spring Fest, when popular bands perform at North Campus for the students. Students can easily attend local Buffalo Bills or Sabres games or travel about 20 minutes north to Canada. As one student said, "There is always something to do, but it's up to you to take advantage of it."

The large student body at Buffalo makes it possible for almost anyone to find a group of friends that shares their interests. A sophomore member of a sorority spoke not only of her close ties with her sisters, but also of having met some of her best friends in classes and in her dorm. Students agreed that it is very easy to meet people in all different parts of the campus. One negative aspect of the size of UB is that people must make a conscious effort to keep up contacts. With so many students, "groups form right away, but can change in an instant."

Never Go Outside

Since UB is part of the SUNY system, nearly all of the students are New York State residents. The school has a reputation for having a large number of middle-class students from Long Island and Rochester, but students agreed that you are still "able to meet all kinds of different people from very different parts of the state."

Buffalo is the only SUNY school that does not require freshman to live on campus, but the majority of underclassmen choose to do so while upperclassmen tend to move off campus. Said one student, "the rent is decent, and the proximity is not bad either." Those who live on campus get to take advantage of the university's underground walkway system that allows students on North Campus to get to most dorms and classes without ever stepping outside to brave the harsh, snowy winters of Buffalo. "I don't think I would ever make it to class in the winter if it weren't for those tunnels," one student said. Some students are also lucky enough to live in the Hadley Village Undergraduate Apartments or the newer South Lake Village Apartments, which come furnished and are considered to be very nice. There are RAs for everyone living in dorms regardless of year. When asked about their level of strictness, one student offered, "You can do pretty much anything you want in the dorms, but there are some limits."

"You can do pretty much anything you want in the dorms, but there are some limits."

For the most part, students feel safe while on Buffalo's large campus, but some girls said that they were not crazy about parts of South Campus and certain other areas around campus. Although there were mixed opinions about needing a car, there was a general consensus that having wheels is helpful. Most freshmen tend not to have cars, but many decide to bring them when they return sophomore year. As one student said, "there's everything here, but you have to be able to get to it."

I'm Getting Very Hungry

Buffalo students enjoy eating out once in a while and can pick from a large number of choices, including a nearby Olive Garden and Red Lobster. Said one student, "there are lots of really good lesser-known restaurants around, but you need a car and someone who knows how to get there." There are plenty of fast food options close to campus as well, which always make for "quick meals or great late-night snacks." Of course, Buffalo wings are a favorite among many UB students. As multiple students said, "It's Buffalo. How can you not eat Buffalo wings? They're just that good!"

While eating on the university's meal plan, students have several places they can enjoy all-you-can-eat dining hall food. There are plenty of vegetarian options available and the meal plan is flexible, allowing hungry students to use credit at other locations. The new food court on North Campus is said to have great chow and a lot of options. The dining halls and food court are more than just a place to grab a quick bite. Students can often be found chatting in noticeable cliques long after they have finished their meals.

Taking Sports into Their Own Hands

Basketball and football are big sports at UB. Even though the Division IA football team does not have a winning reputation, one spirited student remarked, "I don't miss a home game." On campus, there is much more to sports than the varsity teams. Each year, over 9000 UB students take a break from their work and participate in club sports or intramurals. The athletic facilities are good and mostly open to all students. "There are all the gym facilities you could [ask for]," the football stadium is only a few years old, and the natatorium has hosted the World University Games and the Empire State Games in the past.

The city of Buffalo has much to offer to the university and its students. The size of the school allows people to choose their own education and have a great time along the way. When approached with the idea of going back and choosing a college again, one undergraduate enthusiastically replied, "I would definitely choose UB. I love it!" —*Brett Youngerman*

FYI

If you come to SUNY Buffalo, you'd better bring "a heavy winter jacket."

What is the typical weekend schedule? "Watch some movies and hang out in the dorms with friends by day; go out to the bars or a party by night."

If I could change one thing about SUNY Buffalo, I'd "move it to Florida where it is warm."

Three things every student at SUNY Buffalo should do before graduating are "go to the Steer, eat wings at the Anchor Bar, and go to Canada."

State University of New York / Stony Brook

Address: Stony Brook, NY 11794
Phone: 631-632-6868
E-mail address: ugadmissions@notes.cc.sunysb.edu
Web site URL: www.sunysb.edu
Founded: 1957
Private or Public: public
Religious affiliation: none
Location: suburban
Undergraduate enrollment: 14,224
Total enrollment: 20,855
Percent Male/Female: 52%/48%
Percent Minority: 42%
Percent African-American: 10%
Percent Asian: 24%
Percent Hispanic: 8%
Percent Native-American: 0%
Percent in-state/out of state: 97%/3%
Percent Pub HS: 85%
Number of Applicants: 16,864
Percent Accepted: 54%
Percent Accepted who enroll: 26%
Entering: 2,415
Transfers: 1,506
Application Deadline: 10 July
Mean SAT: NA
Mean ACT: NA
Middle 50% SAT range: V 500-590, M 550-650
Middle 50% ACT range: NA
3 Most popular majors: psychology, computer science, business
Retention: 84%
Graduation rate: 55%
On-campus housing: 50%
Fraternities: NA
Sororities: NA
Library: 3,199,000 volumes
Tuition and Fees: $4,358 in; $9,258 out
Room and Board: $7,346
Financial aid, first-year: 58%
Varsity or Club Athletes: 5%
Early Decision or Early Action Acceptance Rate: NA

Looking for a belly-dancing club? Sweatshop protests? A vegan club? SUNY's Stonybrook campus has enticing offerings for every kind of student. Just east up Long Island, close to Port Jefferson, Stonybrook is two hours by train into the city, far away from the clean, tree-covered suburban campus. While the city of Stonybrook might be "far from everything," as one student complained, its proximity to Manhattan is a major selling point for students who like to get into the city for its cultural, artistic, culinary, and entertainment options.

Location, Location, Location

One undergraduate said life at Stonybrook meant having "the best of both worlds," because the town is "pretty clean, you're out in the 'burbs kind of thing—but it's not that rural." The train station on campus lets students pop over to New York whenever they want. Few students stay on campus over the weekend because the city features so many things to do. The majority of students who hail from Long Island make a mass homeward exodus weekly. Some even live at home, though others choose to live in university housing. For the first year, this means being doubled or tripled (two or three students to a bedroom), but upperclassmen get nicer room arrangements in suites of four to six with a common room and a shared bathroom. One freshman said being tripled can be really trying, but "if you tough it out for the first year it [housing] can get pretty good afterwards." Stonybrook also has a brand new apartment complex for its undergraduates, and off-campus apartments are always an option.

On DEC

All Stonybrook students have course requirements known as "DEC requirements," short for Diversified Education Curriculum. These requirements, falling in categories A through K, are "assigned classes in order to make you a more well-rounded student." They include courses in writing, history, engineering, and a foreign language. While one student found DEC requirements "kind of annoying" because they "make you learn a lot of stuff not really [relevant] to your major," others say DEC requirements are helpful. One senior attested, "I came into Stonybrook thinking I wanted to be a chemistry major, but then I changed my mind. As I went through my DEC classes, I found out what I wanted to do."

Big Pond, Lots of Fish

Students say class size at Stonybrook can be a problem, especially in introductory classes. Professors split large classes up into TA sections, but students say TAs can be difficult to track down and somewhat unresponsive to student needs. "It's really hard to get help, because it's a big school. You have to educate yourself." Some of the teachers are not that helpful and classes are too big." Going to professors' office hours and getting to know your department advisor helps individual students stand out among a sea of faces.

One student said that at first at Stonybrook she "felt like I was all by myself." To get out of the slump, Stonybrook mans their dorms with Resident Advisors (RAs), who are there to give advice and bring some college experience to the table. The RAs are "cool" and "if you have problems they'll help you out," advisees say. Part of the RA's job, as always, is discipline, but students say "They're not there to prevent you from having fun; they're just there to make sure everything stays in check. It's not prison-ish."

Students also recommend living with other students in your area of study, so that you get to know others with similar interests. Another great way to meet people and distinguish yourself from the others around you is to be part of a club or organization. With an array of extracurriculars ranging from belly-dancing to political protest groups, everyone is sure to find their niche. "This is a very diverse campus, so there's not one look or one way" to be, dress, or act. Joining a sorority or fraternity "definitely makes you active in stuff on campus," one upperclassman said, "but it's not the only way to get involved." The unique thing about Greek life is it's something you can only get in college. If going Greek is for you, don't hold back. But don't feel pressured if that's not your style. One non-Greek said "the school is so big you can get away from" being Greek, and it's "not as rowdy as it seems on TV." Greek life is just one of many other possibilities at Stonybrook, there for the taking. Students say they appreciate that they have "people who are into this and people who are into that. It's like you have lots of little worlds going on."

"It's like you have lots of little worlds going on, because you have people who are into this and people who are into that."

That's Delivery

While one freshman said that food options at Stonybrook were great, offering variety and flexibility, upperclassmen were less enchanted. Stonybrook's campus is divided into four quads, each of which offers its own meal options, including buffet and home-style dining as well as restaurants and fast-food chains like Taco Bell and Pizza Hut. If the offerings are less than delectable, students say they "must give them props for having a lot of different options." "They have delivery too!" one student added, saying that the ever-popular college staples of Chinese and pizza were available among the delivery options. First-year students are required to have a meal plan—hardly an inconvenience when even delivery is paid for this way—but after that year students are welcome to fend for themselves. One deli in the student union offers not only meals, but also a grocery store. Every dorm on campus has a kitchen on each floor, though there are no in-suite kitchens. There is also a cooking building for students who plan on making all their own meals.

Another way of getting fed at Stonybrook offers educational and cultural experiences on the side. Many groups, like the popular Caribbean Student Organization (CSO), throw parties and host workshops and lectures for their fellow students. Students come to learn about international relations and cultural differences, and for the chow. Don't look for alcohol at these gatherings and parties, though. Students say the administration is strict about keeping alcohol off campus and unavailable to those under the age of 21.

Who Reigns in the Parade?

Homecoming week brings out the spirit of Stonybrook's Sea Wolves in full force. The Friday parade features floats built by teams of students representing their quads and organizations. Students make banners and enter them in competitions with each other, and every building on campus decorates a bulletin board to display their creative efforts. As if that weren't enough, Stonybrookers also make boats every year for the Roth Regatta. So named for the quad on which the Stonybrook pond is located, the event brings out all Stonybrook's would-be boat makers and has them race their boats on the pond. Spirit Week, an event much like Homecoming, takes place every spring. Residence halls compete in trivia and Olympic-style competitions in the gym to win glory for the Stonybrook name.

When Stonybrook students aren't competing for spirited titles, you might find them at the Wang Center, a new Asian center at the university where students can find sushi and a whole lot of information about Asian history. The Staller Center, another cultural location on campus, offers workshops and art in its theaters and galleries, or you can stop by on a Friday night to see chic in action at one of Stonybrook's fashion shows. —*Stephanie Hagan*

FYI

If you come to Stonybrook, you'd better bring "a laptop."

What is the typical weekend schedule? "Thursday's a big party night at clubs like Rumba Skies; Friday night, go to a movie on campus or take the train, go into the city, and hang out with friends; Sunday, go to the library and study."

If I could change one thing about Stonybrook, I'd "change the dorms. Some of them are really old!"

Three things every Stonybrook student should do before graduating are "realize that Manhattan is so close and actually go do something in the city, join an organization, and go to the Staller Center."

Syracuse University

Address: 201 Tolley Administration Building; Syracuse, NY 13244
Phone: 315-443-3611
E-mail address: orange@syr.edu
Web site URL: www.syracuse.edu
Founded: 1870
Private or Public: private
Religious affiliation: none
Location: urban
Undergraduate enrollment: 12,645
Total enrollment: NA
Percent Male/Female: 42%/58%
Percent Minority: 16%
Percent African-American: 7%
Percent Asian: 5%
Percent Hispanic: 4%
Percent Native-American: 0%
Percent in-state/out of state: 44%/56%
Percent Pub HS: NA
Number of Applicants: 13,644
Percent Accepted: 69%
Percent Accepted who enroll: 31%
Entering: 2,916
Transfers: 254
Application Deadline: 1 Jan
Mean SAT: NA
Mean ACT: NA
Middle 50% SAT range: V 550-640, M 570-660
Middle 50% ACT range: NA
3 Most popular majors: communications, business management, social sciences and history
Retention: 91%
Graduation rate: 77%
On-campus housing: 73%
Fraternities: 12%
Sororities: 16%
Library: 3,115,000 volumes
Tuition and Fees: $25,130
Room and Board: $9,600
Financial aid, first-year: 55%
Varsity or Club Athletes: 57%
Early Decision or Early Action Acceptance Rate: 65%

Everything about Syracuse University, it seems, is big. In addition to the large student body (roughly 11,000 undergraduates and 4,000 graduates attend), the University boasts 12 undergraduate colleges as well as the gigantic 50,000-seat Carrier Dome. Even the weather—with a winter season that begins in November and extends into March and April—speaks to the larger-than-life quality of this nationally recognized research institution. For students who can navigate their way through all that Syracuse has to offer, though, the experience can be unparalleled.

Choosing Early

Where students applying to other schools often need not declare their majors, students who intend to come to Syracuse must apply to one of the 12 undergraduate colleges: architecture, education, arts and sciences, engineering and computer science, human services and health, university, information studies, law, management, citizenship and public affairs, public communications, and visual and performing arts. Although they do have the option of applying to a plurality of colleges at the time of application, students must choose one upon matriculation. In order to encourage a diverse course of study, the administration allows students to sample courses outside their colleges. For those students who prefer grounding in a liberal arts education, the College of Arts and Sciences offers a more interdisciplinary, less pre-professional, program of study. Freshmen in this college receive an introduction to their school through Freshman Forum, a seminar-style class that pairs a small group of undergrads with a professor in an intimate setting. Among the other colleges, the S. I. Newhouse School of Public Communications enjoys the most national renown among peer institutions. Admission to the communications school tends to be more competitive and selective. The schools of architecture and management consistently top the list of Syracuse's most rigorous schools.

Appropriately, class sizes and academic requirements vary by college. Popular classes—macroeconomics, for example—and general educations classes ("gen eds") typically draw upwards of 200 students, though classes tend to get smaller, and, as one student notes, "more comfortable," each year. Students deem the workload "time consuming, but nothing too difficult," and report spending "three hours a night" studying on average. Although they give their professors favorable marks for knowledge, lecture presentation, and accessibility, students are more divided with regard to teaching assistants, who lead outside-of-class "recitations." While some acknowledge that TA's are helpful because of the experience they bring to their particular field, others cast them off as "useless."

Frats and Bars

Students do not deny that theirs is a party school—on the contrary, they are proud of the balance of academics and busy social calendars. Given the cold weather for which their school is notorious, the social scene "is the only thing that gets us out in the winter." Syracuse is home to a large Greek system, and the many fraternities and sororities take advantage of their influence and presence on campus to host well-attended keg parties and the occasional formal. Those in the drinking crowd who tire of frat parties often take a walk down Marshall Street to check out the bar scene or seek out the house parties around campus. Students find that the party scene becomes more manageable each year; as one student put it, "freshmen look for parties, upperclassmen are rocking the parties." The only problem in all this, it seems, is overcrowding at parties, which has the effect of detracting from the experience. Apart from alcohol, pot is prevalent, though "nothing is forced on anyone." In an effort to crack down on the amount of underage drinking, the university maintains a three-points-and-you're-out policy, strictly forbidding alcohol in underage rooms. The university also sponsors events that aim to draw students away from parties. Despite these efforts, students easily circumvent the administration's policies.

Big and Small

In spite of Syracuse's large size, stereotypes persist. One student characterized the typical student as "rich, drunk, and Northface-wearing." Nonetheless, students are quick to defend the heterogeneity of their school and add that, at Syracuse, it is easy to make friends, "especially in the first few weeks or so" before cliques begin to form, generating a feeling of community within the greater student body. Considerations of diversity aside, students rally around their nationally ranked basketball team and their mascot, Otto the Orange, named by MasterCard as one of the nation's best mascots. The Carrier Dome, located on campus, regularly draws capacity crowds for football and basketball games; it has also attracted big-name acts such as Elton John and U2 to Syracuse. Because only a small portion of students actively participate in sports, many students take advantage of intramurals, which offer everything from basketball to broomball. Many extracurricular activities are also widely popular, among them learning-based service programs, the Student Association, and student radio and TV stations. Still others seek employment from the University.

"[The social scene] is the only thing that gets us out in the winter."

Syracuse: City and Campus

Syracuse University is set on a hill overlooking the city of Syracuse, giving students the unique opportunity to experience campus and city life simultaneously. It is rumored that if two students share a kiss on a particular bench on campus, they will marry. Such is the charm of the campus. Students appreciate the mix of modern and classical buildings that surround them, particularly on the Quad, which serves as the geographic center of campus. Although the various colleges have their own buildings, no walk across campus takes more than fifteen minutes. The 120-step climb from the Quad to the Mount (home to several frosh dorms), on the other hand, requires a little more stamina, especially in the icier months. Dorms, especially during freshman year, provide the formative social experiences that allow students to develop close relationships that last into senior year. Most freshmen live in either open or split doubles. Options for on-campus housing become more attractive as students get older, though many sophomores still opt to live off campus. The food at Syracuse draws so-so reviews in terms of quality and variety, although dining halls vary considerably across campus. To get away from the monotony of the meal plan, students venture into the city to such original restaurants as the Pita Pit, the Acropolis, and Dinosaur BBQ. Another diversion is the huge Carousel Mall, although Syracuse offers little else in the way of entertainment and culture. Nor does it have a completely clean safety record, and robberies are not unheard of. Back on campus, though, blue lights everywhere assure students that their administration does not take a passive approach to policing the area.

Thanks to its size, Syracuse University is in a unique position to offer its undergraduates a richly diverse academic and social experience even as it asserts its position as a premier research institution. And just in case they become too wrapped up in college life, the town of Syracuse, located at the foot of the college, offers an appropriate dose of the "real world." —*Greg Hamm*

FYI

If you come to Syracuse, you'd better bring a "Gore-Tex jacket, because you'll need it by the end of October."

A typical weekend at Syracuse consists of "Up at 2 P.M., bum around until night, out at 10, back at 3. And do it all over again."

If I could change one thing about Syracuse, I'd "increase the average daily temperature and create a better city."

Three things every student at Syracuse should do before graduating are "rush the court/field at the Dome, sled down one of the streets during a blizzard, and enjoy all the opportunities to meet people and hear interesting speakers."

Union College

Address: Union Street, Schenectady, NY 12303
Phone: 888-843-6688
E-mail address: admissions@union.edu
Web site URL: www.union.edu
Founded: 1795
Private or Public: private
Religious affiliation: none
Location: small city
Undergraduate enrollment: 2,147
Total enrollment: 2,147
Percent Male/Female: 53%/47%
Percent Minority: 12%
Percent African-American: 3%
Percent Asian: 5%
Percent Hispanic: 4%
Percent Native-American: 0%
Percent in-state/out of state: 46%/54%
Percent Pub HS: NA
Number of Applicants: 3,828
Percent Accepted: 45%
Percent Accepted who enroll: 33%
Entering: 573
Transfers: 23
Application Deadline: 15 Jan
Mean SAT: NA
Mean ACT: NA
Middle 50% SAT range: V 550-650, M 590-680
Middle 50% ACT range: 23-30
3 Most popular majors: political science, economics, psychology
Retention: 93%
Graduation rate: 84%
On-campus housing: 80%
Fraternities: 21%
Sororities: 25%
Library: 304,348 volumes
Tuition and Fees: $28,928
Room and Board: $7,077
Financial aid, first-year: 50%
Varsity or Club Athletes: NA
Early Decision or Early Action Acceptance Rate: 74%

At the small liberal arts institution called Union College in Schenectady, New York, graduation means more than wading through the general curriculum and completing the twelve trimesters. Union's uniqueness is captured in the "unofficial" graduation requirements: the "campus crawl," which involves having a beer at each of the fraternities all in one night; painting the Idol, a stone statue on campus; running naked around the Nott Memorial, and throwing oranges onto the ice following Union's first hockey goal against RPI.

General Education

There is a general education curriculum that all majors take. Freshmen take two history, two science, one math, one social science, and two literature/civilization classes, as well as the Freshmen Preceptorial, a class that includes a lot of reading, and "basically teaches you how to write." Students give a positive rating to this: those that come to the school undecided will be exposed to a wide range of subjects, while those already declared will graduate with a well-rounded education. The class sizes are small, with approximately 40 students in introductory courses and 10 in upper-level classes. "Professors are extremely accessible and even in large classes, you get to know your professors very well," said one student, who also praised Union for its "near-perfect balance between a rigorous workload, low average class size, and professor accessibility." Students enjoy their classes, for the most part. "A seminar professor took our entire class out to dinner at a great Indian restaurant, and then to a movie," said one student.

Union runs on a trimester system, giving students three distinct segments of study as opposed to two in the traditional semester system. School starts two weeks later than most schools in the fall, and includes a Christmas break of over six weeks, though school does not finish until the middle of June.

Students often take three classes per semester, which often meet only on Monday, Wednesday, and Friday. The trimester system, however, means that there are only 10 weeks to complete a course that usually requires 15 weeks. In total, students must complete 36 courses in 12 terms. The course load is generally tough, with upper-level courses expecting around five to seven hours of homework or reading per week. One course, Congressional Politics, had over 24 hours of work per week.

Students identify the popular majors to be Political Science, Biology, and Economics; the hardest majors are reputed to be chemistry and any of the engineering sciences. Some slacker majors are political science, English, and history.

> **"The people are friendly, the profs are amazing and really nice, always willing to help."**

There are many opportunities for studying abroad. Students can study in England, through a program sponsored by the English department, as well as in Vienna, where one student took his best class walking around the city, touring museums: "it was in Vienna, had no homework, and was very hands-on."

Greeks and Alcohol

Greek life and alcohol dominate the social life at Union. With 13 frats and three sororities, is "the mother of the fraternities," in the words of one student. However, Union recently enacted a plan that may result in some Greek organizations losing their traditional houses. Social life is centered on the fraternities providing the entertainment and alcohol for the students. "If you like to drink and party, Union is the place for you," said one student. "If you don't like to drink, you could be bored." Students agreed that the school tries to be strict on their alcohol policy, but many underage drinkers still manage to find alcohol easily. Frat parties are usually free and open to all, which prevents non-Greeks from feeling excluded. The dating scene consists almost exclusively of hook-ups; no one dates. One student put the number at "five hook-ups a year."

Students often feel that the social life is centered on how much money each student has. "The parking lots are filled with BMW's, Land Rovers, Merecedes, etc," one student noted. Students often feel as if they have stepped into a J. Crew catalog, as dress is important to the students. Many students come from wealthy backgrounds, often from the Northeast, especially New York and Massachusetts. Few students come from outside the Mid-Atlantic and New England states, and even fewer are internationals. Union can be difficult for students on financial aid since most packages do not cover the expenses of academic materials, which can be expensive at the school.

You Come to Schenectady for Union

An admissions staff member once said to a student, "you don't come to Union for Schenectady, you come to Schenectady for Union." The campus is very beautiful and well kept. "The students take great pride in the gardens, the buildings, and the overall atmosphere," said one student. "The compact nature of the campus keeps everything within easy reach and view . . . the gardens are a miraculous and wonderful place to spend a spring afternoon." The off-campus area has improved over the last few years, but students will often choose not to leave the campus on foot at night. The school has a trolley service, which students find very accessible and useful. Although freshman may not have cars on campus, over 80 percent of upperclassmen have their own vehicles in order to take advantage of the surrounding areas, according to students. Albany is a half-hour drive from Union, which is home to many bars, clubs, and a great deal of shopping.

Students find the dorms to be satisfactory. "Generally, the conditions are good: there are few complaints." Union is constantly improving the living conditions through renovations, though there are many other options available. Some students live in apartments that Union leases right across the street from campus. Some buildings, West, Fox, and Davidson have the reputation as party dorms. Other dorms that provide calmer living arrangements include Webster, the co-ed, substance-free dorm, Richmond, the all-female dorm, and South, the all-male dorm. Members of Greek societies can choose to live in their respective houses. Others may choose to live in a theme house, where students share similar interests. Housing is guaranteed only through junior year, causing some students to utilize the nearby apartments.

Students generally have no complaints about the food. There are two dining halls on campus, which offer a wide variety of foods. The "Rathskellar" sells greasy foods, but not much else. Students agreed that, even though some may not care for the dish of the day, there is such a wide variety that everyone is content. Most students eat on campus in the main dining halls.

Choice of Activities

Union students have the choice of over 70 clubs to participate in: ballroom dancing, a capella singing groups, *Concordiensis* (the weekly newspaper), the *Idol* (a literary magazine), the Minerva Committee (bringing speakers to campus), and many more. Drama students may choose to participate with the Mountebacks, a popular theater troupe.

Hockey and football are the school's biggest sports. Each hockey game attracts at least a quarter of the undergraduates to home games. Pre-game parties are often well attended, and "pride runs high for hockey in particular." Union's biggest rival is RPI, both in hockey and football. Although turnout may be high, few students care to wear Union clothing. "There is not a whole lot of shouting unless people are drunk," said one student. There is cheering but it comes mostly from the alumni and faculty. Union kids are very apathetic."

Students are proud that their school is set apart from others both by the small size of the student body and the beautiful campus, "which is just amazingly picturesque and unique." "I am extremely happy here," said one student. "The people are friendly, the profs are amazing and really nice, always willing to help, and I love the area." *—Andrew Hamilton*

FYI

If you come to Union, you'd better bring "a warm hat and gloves."

What is the typical weekend schedule? "Parties both Friday and Saturday nights. Otherwise, hockey games (winter) or time outside (spring and fall) with work Sunday evenings are popular pastimes."

If I could change one thing about Union, "I'd build a new gym and fieldhouse."

Three things that every student at Union should do before graduating are "paint the Idol, take a term abroad, and try something new."

United States Military Academy

Address: 600 Thayer Road; West Point, NY 10996-1797
Phone: 845-938-4041
E-mail address: admissions@usma.edu
Web site URL: www.usma.edu
Founded: 1802
Private or Public: public
Religious affiliation: none
Location: rural
Undergraduate enrollment: 4,041
Total enrollment: 4,041
Percent Male/Female: 84%/16%
Percent Minority: 0%
Percent African-American: 0%
Percent Asian: 0%
Percent Hispanic: 0%
Percent Native-American: 0%
Percent in-state/out of state: 8%/92%
Percent Pub HS: 86%
Number of Applicants: 10,843
Percent Accepted: 13%
Percent Accepted who enroll: 84%
Entering: 1,197
Transfers: NA
Application Deadline: 21 Mar
Mean SAT: NA
Mean ACT: NA
Middle 50% SAT range: V 570-660, M 600-690
Middle 50% ACT range: 26-30
3 Most popular majors: liberal arts, science studies, humanities
Retention: 86%
Graduation rate: 84%
On-campus housing: 100%
Fraternities: NA
Sororities: NA
Library: 600,000 volumes
Tuition and Fees: none
Room and Board: none
Financial aid, first-year: NA
Varsity or Club Athletes: NA
Early Decision or Early Action Acceptance Rate: NA

There is no wussy orientation program for incoming "college" freshmen of the United States Military Academy. The opening weeks of training for cadets, affectionately known as the "Beast," are mandatory for all incoming students and future military officers. Students endure long hikes, target practice, and the gas chamber. One student reminisced, saying, "the Beast was the most intense six weeks of my life." It is during this time that the most cadets are apt to drop out. For the 90 percent or so who do survive, the United States Military Academy, known as West Point, is four years of free "education with a purpose" that ultimately requires the cadet to pledge allegiance to the flag for several years after graduation in exchange for this world-class training.

GI Joe Hits the Books

Academics, above all else, are the top priority for cadets at West Point. The course load, while including such traditional subjects as writing skills, psychology, foreign language, economics, politics, and geography, also includes, in the later two years of studying, focus on such subjects as math and science while giving the cadets a bit more leeway in terms of electives.

Far and away the most popular major on campus is engineering. Engineering math courses are rigorous in terms of both workload and grading. Civil and mechanical engineering top the list as the most popular of the engineering sub-specialties and earned high marks from the cadets. Slacker majors at West Point are nearly non-existent. While the political science and history departments are routinely praised, science and engineering, being the main focus of study, cause the most consternation and exasperation. One cadet stated that his physics and chemistry courses were "ludicrously hard." Some of the least favorite of West Point's requirements are the physical education classes that include such fear inspiring names as "boxing." According to one cadet, who put it quite succinctly, "PE just sucks."

But fear not future cadets, for the academy provides a Center for Enhanced Performance that improves cadets reading skills, speaking abilities, and study habits.

Professors are also readily available to help upon request. One student recalls meeting with a physics professor for a late-night study session the night before an exam.

Class sizes, ranging from 16 and 20 students, are as small and accommodating as the most prestigious American liberal arts institutions. Smaller class sizes facilitate open discussion and help encourage cadets to ask questions when the material presented is particularly difficult.

The library, although disparaged by some students, underwent renovations for West Point's bicentennial.

"This Ain't No Party, Soldier"

Perhaps the most drastic change that comes with military life is the alteration in the social lives of the cadets. The main credo of any nascent cadet is, "Get the hell away from Post," Post being the affectionate term for the academy. Life at the academy is strictly regimented with designated times for everything from extracurriculars to movie times. Intramurals are popular options with most cadets since the campus is chock full of sports enthusiasts. However, waking up at 6 A.M. everyday for roll call tends to drain the cadets.

Dining hall food at this verdant redoubt on the Hudson tends to draw mediocre reviews from most students. A perk of the experience, at least for upperclassmen, used to be the fact that first years, a.k.a. "plebes," must serve their elders. The first two meals of the day were nerve-wracking for plebes as they were generally expected, at these meals, to remain at the beck and call of the other cadets. Dinner was generally more relaxed (and was optional), allowing cadets time to kick back and gossip about the day's events. The potentially angst-ridden plebe would also be happy to know that breakfast and lunch are optional on weekends, providing a brief respite from the upperclassmen. There has been a recent push on campus and by the administration to reduce the level of hazing that occurs at the academy. "The way plebes were treated changed a few years ago into a more orderly and professional method parallel to the Army's structure that involved each class being assigned a rank and responsibilities instead of the three upperclassmen just hazing the plebes like it was before," said one cadet.

On-campus dating is sparse thanks in part to the fact that strict regulations exist concerning male/female interactions. Another possible factor contributing to this paucity of "lovin'" may be the fact that, according to one cadet, the women at West Point "ain't nothing to rave about." However, according to some female cadets, being in the minority, they can always find a date on campus. Unfortunately for the sexually deprived senior, West Point forbids seniors from dating plebes. Some cadets attempt to maintain their relationships from high school. The other cadets provide them with the moniker, "2 percent Club." Simply put, of those who attempt to maintain their relationships from high school, only about 2 percent are successful.

Obviously, at West Point, no Greek system exists. The camaraderie provided for students by the Greek system at other universities is fulfilled by the military regimentation—"training, sleeping, eating, learning together"—the sense that everyone is in it together.

Character development and education are what inspires most cadets. "Not everything about this place is great, but everything helps to make us better leaders, no matter how much it may suck. I'm glad I'm here." While this may sound a bit contrived, West Pointers insist that they are not brainwashed. "You just have to accept the fact that this lifestyle is nothing like that of the typical college student."

The typical college lifestyle? We all know that means raucous binge drinking, right? Not at West Point. The administration keeps a tight ship allowing only those legally able to drink to do so on Post. So for you 18-year-olds who love "alky shoot" or the "beer funnel," you'd better stay away.

Dorm lifestyle at West Point is also somewhat different from the typical college experience. The rooms, of course, are small and all basically look alike. Cadets must keep their rooms in tiptop condition owing to the frequent inspections that occur throughout the year. Companies, a military type unit, are comprised of around 120 cadets. Throughout the year these cadets work to overcome and adapt to the hardships of military lifestyle. As a result, close friendships are formed. One cadet's advice is to "quickly adapt." Those slow to adapt to the military lifestyle are often left feeling lonely and abandoned.

"The camaraderie is fulfilled by the sense that everyone is in it together."

As previously mentioned, leaving Post is a popular option for cadets. Only seniors can leave on weekends but everyone, with permission, can head into town on the weekends. Popular destinations, outside of the local region, include Boston, New York City, and in some isolated instances, Washington, DC. However, the majority of cadets remain on campus during the weekends. Frequently, movies are shown in academy halls throughout the weekend at specified times.

Sports are also extraordinarily popular on campus. Varsity games are frequently attended by cadets and pick-up games can always be found on campus. Attendance at football games is mandatory. The Academy has a 40,000-seat stadium. Mandatory attendance is not a problem for cadets because, simply put, everyone is into athletics. Personal fitness is a virtue on this campus and encouraged by the administration—hence the popularity of sports. The Army, in fact, requires that cadets participate in intramural activities. Clubs are also popular on campus and range from martial arts to film forums.

The campus itself is dominated by Gothic architecture with a smattering of renovated buildings for West Point's 200th birthday in 2002. Construction has dominated campus in recent years, but most cadets are not fazed, believing the renovations have greatly improved the efficiency of the campus.

Nach der Schule

During the first two summers of their West Point careers, cadets must attend Camp Buckner. The level of training is intense and prepares them well for future combat. After that, they may be stationed at any location within the United States. Again, adjustment and adaptation is the key to success at West Point.

After graduation, West Point cadets are required to serve six years in the United States Army. Many graduates generally look forward to this period of growth and maturation, calling it an incredible learning experience. The cadets are commissioned into the army as second Lieutenants.

Overall, the benefits of a West Point education are tremendous but the adjustments numerous. Graduates wax romantic about their days at "The Point." The academics are rigorous but only for those who successfully navigate the extraordinarily competitive appointment and acceptance progress. This institution forever changes the hearts and minds of its graduates. —*Sean McBride and Staff*

FYI

If you come to West Point, you'd better bring "a flexible mind-set. You're going to need it to get through the loads of physical and mental work here."

What is the typical weekend schedule? "It varies for the different classes. Seniors get a lot more leeway as far as leaving the Post whereas the plebes are stuck with a limited number of times to venture away."

If I could change one thing about West Point, I would "get rid of the mandatory wake up call for everyone at 6 A.M."

The three things that every student should do before graduating from West Point are "go bar-hopping in town, attend an Army-Navy Game, and get an awesome post."

University of Rochester

Address: Wilson Boulevard; Rochester, NY 14627-0001
Phone: 585-275-3221
E-mail address: admit@admissions.rochester.edu
Web site URL: www.rochester.edu
Founded: 1850
Private or Public: private
Religious affiliation: none
Location: suburban
Undergraduate enrollment: 4,675
Total enrollment: 8,296
Percent Male/Female: 53%/47%
Percent Minority: 20%
Percent African-American: 4%
Percent Asian: 12%
Percent Hispanic: 4%
Percent Native-American: 0%
Percent in-state/out of state: 50%/50%
Percent Pub HS: NA
Number of Applicants: 8,682
Percent Accepted: 56%
Percent Accepted who enroll: 19%
Entering: 934
Transfers: 90
Application Deadline: 20 Jan
Mean SAT: NA
Mean ACT: NA
Middle 50% SAT range: V 590-690, M 620-720
Middle 50% ACT range: 26-31
3 Most popular majors: economics, biology, psychology
Retention: 94%
Graduation rate: 81%
On-campus housing: 80%
Fraternities: 26%
Sororities: 19%
Library: 3,276,000 volumes
Tuition and Fees: $27,430
Room and Board: $8,818
Financial aid, first-year: 59%
Varsity or Club Athletes: 28%
Early Decision or Early Action Acceptance Rate: 58%

Do you like cold weather? Do you like music? How about participating in a class-wide community service project the first day of each school year? If you answered yes to any of these questions, then the University of Rochester is a potential school for you! With a little more than 4,000 undergraduates making up its very diverse student body, the University of Rochester prides itself on providing its students with a balanced and personalized scholastic experience. Located in upstate New York on the banks of the Genesse River, the University of Rochester boasts some of the strongest math and science departments in one of the snowiest regions of the country. But don't worry—the entire university is connected by underground tunnels that are often filled with student advertisements and fun-loving graffiti, and which provide a warmer way to get from class to class in the middle of February.

The Truth About Academics

Students at the University of Rochester, or UR for short, take their studies very seriously. In addition to requiring 128 credit hours to graduate, the UR curriculum demands that students focus on different academic areas in an attempt to encourage a well-rounded educational experience. At UR, all majors and their respective courses are assigned to one of three categories: humanities, social sciences, and math/natural sciences/engineering. After declaring a major by the beginning of the third year, all students must also take "cluster" courses in the remaining two categories. UR students love these clusters because of the flexibility they afford. One junior explained, "You can even make up your own clusters if you cannot find exactly what you want. It makes you feel like you are learning all sorts of things without being bound by a core curriculum."

These cluster courses, like all other courses at UR, can range in size and format from large lectures to smaller seminars. While the majority of classes have about 20 students, some science lectures can have as many as 300, while some seminars can have as few as 10. A student who prefers smaller classes might elect to take "Quest" courses—a popular option for the past few years. These small courses generally have very focused topics, and work to foster interaction between students and their teachers. Additionally, most UR students work one-on-one with a professor to develop a specialized field of research for their major. Overall, students find that their professors are not only very accessible, but that they are also more than willing to answer questions, set up appointments, and reply to e-mails.

UR is also able to offer its students some very special academic opportunities. Firstly, UR students can take music courses at the world-renowned Eastman School of Music because of its close proximity to the central campus. UR students can also participate in various combined undergraduate/graduate programs, such as the Rochester Early Medical Scholars Program, which is known around campus as "REMS." Lastly, UR offers a "Take Five" Scholars Program. Students apply to this program in their senior year to qualify for a fifth year of study, tuition-free! About 125 students enroll in the "Take Five" program each year in hopes of enhancing their academic experiences at UR.

Most students find the science-oriented environment of UR very rewarding. Although they spend anywhere from two to five hours in the library each day, students like the academic atmosphere. The most popular majors are biology, chemistry, computer science, and political science. As one UR junior noted, "It's pretty competitive here, and most people are pretty serious about their work."

The Buzz About Housing

Besides academics, URers find many other things to fill their time. The weekly campus newspaper, *The Campus Times*, brings attention to happenings on campus and events around the world. For quick updates, students rely on *The Buzz*, a two-sided flier that appears twice each week. In addition to appearing in print, these publications also maintain Web sites for up-to-the-minute news.

UR students are also very involved in musical endeavors. From the U of R Symphony and Symphonic Wind Ensemble to their a capella groups, the Yellowjackets, Midnight Ramblers, Swingshot!?, and Vocal Points, musicians are always active on campus. Drama and theater are popular among students, too. Most productions go up on the famous stage of the Todd Theater, and UR produces about three major productions each semester.

URers place the utmost importance on community service as well. Community service groups are the most popular extracurricular organizations on campus, and upperclassmen encourage freshmen to get involved on Wilson Day, an all-day community service event for first-year students.

Lastly, UR plays host to a number of fraternities and sororities—18 and 11 respectively. Although the university claims that only 20 percent of its students are affiliated with a Greek organization, one student proclaimed, "It seems like everybody is in one house or another." While frats and sororities may be a major force, they do not all have their own housing because of the strict space issues on campus. Instead, they have certain floors in specific residence halls.

"It's pretty competitive here, and most people are pretty serious about their work."

When it comes to housing at UR, most undergraduates live on the River Campus, the central campus of the university. Although only freshmen and sophomores are required to live on campus, most people live on for all four years in the coed residence halls. New for this year, freshmen now live together in Quad Housing. Freshmen are assigned to one of six residence halls, all of which have been recently renovated and equipped with kitchenettes and lounge areas. Freshmen may choose to live in affinity housing—housing groups based on common interests. Similarly, upperclassmen may choose to live in Special Interest Housing (SIH)—choosing from interests such as community service, music, foreign languages, international populations, Greek life, and drama. In all of these residence halls, people can choose to live on substance-free or smoke-free floors. When asked about the housing on campus, a junior replied, "Why live off campus? The dorms are quite nice, and you're surrounded by your friends. Plus, it's just easier."

From Crazy Tuesdays to D-Day

Despite the fact that UR students take their work very seriously, they also find the time to relax and have fun. Surprisingly, Tuesday nights, also called Crazy Tuesdays, are a huge party night on campus. Tuesday nights aren't the only night to go out; Thursday, Friday, and Saturday nights are also busy times for people looking to have fun. Students with cars often go into the city of Rochester to sample the multitude of restaurants, bars, and coffeehouses. Many URers, however, tend to stay on campus. Most fraternities throw campus-wide parties in addition to their formals, semi-formals, date parties, and invitation-only mixers. Although the university is trying to enforce stricter policies with regard to drinking, students say that alcohol is definitely prevalent on campus.

For those students who aren't partygoers, hanging out at Wilson Commons can be an excellent alternative. Wilson Commons is a six-story glass atrium designed by I.M. Pei, the architect most famous for his pyramid outside the Louvre in Paris. The Commons is actually supposed to look like a pinball machine and contains game rooms, restaurants, and lounge areas. Most students like to use Wilson Commons as a meeting area, and you commonly see people waiting outside the building for friends.

In addition to weekend options, a few special days during the year are favorites among URers. The absolute best day of the year, according to many, is Yellowjacket Day. The Yellowjacket is the mascot of this Division III school, and is also the namesake for the first day of the school year. On Yellowjacket Day, all upperclassmen get together and relax for the first time since leaving campus the previous spring. Students also love Dandelion Day. D-Day, as it is commonly known, is usually one of the first nice days in the spring after the terribly cold, dreary winter. The entire River Campus is filled with rides, activities, and a fun, festive atmosphere. Unlike the Winter Carnival, an indoor event in the Wilson Center, D-Day is completely outdoors, and it isn't uncommon to see people running around dancing and yelling all day long. So despite the fact that UR is, in the words of one student, "definitely an academic school," students certainly know how to have fun, too—especially when it's not too cold! —*Shira Tydings*

FYI

If you come to the University of Rochester, you'd better bring "mittens!"

What is the typical weekend schedule? "go to frat parties, attend a concert, hang out with friends, and sleep really late."

If I could change one thing about the University of Rochester, I'd "make it more school-spirited in terms of athletics."

Three things every student at the University of Rochester should do before graduating are "go to D-Day really early and party, sled on a food tray, and tag the tunnels."

Vassar College

Address: Box 10, 124 Raymond Avenue; Poughkeepsie, NY 12604
Phone: 845-437-7300
E-mail address: admissions@vassar.edu
Web site URL: www.vassar.edu
Founded: 1861
Private or Public: private
Religious affiliation: none
Location: suburban
Undergraduate enrollment: 2,472
Total enrollment: 2,472
Percent Male/Female: 39%/61%
Percent Minority: 18%
Percent African-American: 5%
Percent Asian: 8%
Percent Hispanic: 5%
Percent Native-American: 0%
Percent in-state/out of state: 28%/72%
Percent Pub HS: NA
Number of Applicants: 5,733
Percent Accepted: 31%
Percent Accepted who enroll: 35%
Entering: 634
Transfers: 18
Application Deadline: 1 Jan
Mean SAT: NA
Mean ACT: NA
Middle 50% SAT range: V 650-730, M 630-700
Middle 50% ACT range: 28-32
3 Most popular majors: English, psychology, political science
Retention: 94%
Graduation rate: 88%
On-campus housing: 95%
Fraternities: NA
Sororities: NA
Library: 830,000 volumes
Tuition and Fees: $29,540
Room and Board: $7,665
Financial aid, first-year: 55%
Varsity or Club Athletes: NA
Early Decision or Early Action Acceptance Rate: 49%

Once a women's college where pearls and gloves were required at daily tea, Vassar has undergone many radical changes, though many of its traditions remain intact. Consistently ranked among the top liberal arts schools in the nation, Vassar is celebrated for its educational endeavors and academic caliber, for its history of curricular innovation, and for the aesthetic of its campus. Vassar became co-educational in 1968, but traces of its early days can still be found in the hallways of the original dorms, which were built seven feet wide to accommodate the hoop skirts characteristic of 19th-century women's fashion. Nearly 150 years later, Vassar's strong commitment to academics and the idea of open-mindedness and tolerance endures.

Surveying the Grounds

Ranging from Gothic to modern, the architecture at Vassar can best be characterized as eclectic. The campus is self-contained and separated from Poughkeepsie, New York by a guarded gate, which creates an isolated atmosphere. Students generally feel safe, and security is well enforced: all buildings are locked and an ID is required for entrance. Students are generally happy with Vassar's facilities, especially Thompson Library, which is "beautiful and amazing—it looks like a cathedral."

Almost all Vassar students (98 percent) spend their four years living on campus in one of the nine dorms. The most popular dorms are Cushing and Jewitt; however, the largest dorm, known for its distinctive tower and ideal central location, is Main, which was the first building on Vassar's campus. All dorms are co-ed except one—Strong, an all-female dorm. Although students can request to live there, many female students are placed there randomly because not enough girls request a single-sex dorm. However, one Strong resident explained that although she was initially unhappy when she received her dorm assignment, she "can't think of anyone living there now who doesn't like it once they get used to the idea of it." The most unpopular dorm is Noyes, which one student said "is really a Motel Fifty," less comfortable than most and "pretty ugly."

Each dorm is equipped with a parlor, TV room, game room, and laundry room. In addition, because a member of the famous Steinway family was once a student at Vassar, a Steinway grand piano can be found in every dorm. Many juniors and seniors live in the coveted on-campus Terrace Apartments (TAs) or Town Houses (THs), which can be either single-sex or co-ed. "Each dorm fosters a sense of community," reported one junior. This community, which includes Student Fellows (advisors to freshmen who provide support rather than discipline) and House Fellows (professors who live in the dorms, offering guidance and study breaks to undergrads), facilitate the formation of lasting relationships and adaptation to college life.

Vassar's All-Campus Dining Center, referred to as the AC/DC, garners criticism from the student body. Despite the fact that there are many options, especially for vegetarians and vegans, most students were apathetic about Vassar dining. One student lamented that the menu repeats itself on a weekly basis, while another complained about the point system for meals, which requires you to weigh your food, "even your salads," and check out with your items rather than have unlimited self-service. All students living in dorms are required to be on the meal plan, and most venture into Poughkeepsie to eat out only on rare occasions or when parents visit. When they do, favorite eateries include the Saigon Café, which serves tasty Vietnamese cuisine, the Acropolis Diner, which is open 24 hours a day, and The College Deli right around the corner from campus. Students also grab snacks and hang out in "Juliet's," a billiard hall off campus.

School Days

By and large, Vassar professors receive uniformly high marks and elicit much praise. One philosophy major assessed that the "quality of the professors is the most attractive feature of Vassar." Given the small size of the school, there is a great deal of student-faculty interaction, and almost all professors are highly accessible—in fact, the majority of them live on campus. Classes at Vassar generally enroll fewer than 30 students, though some popular lectures, like Introduction to Art History, have several hundred students. Registration for classes is done on the Internet, and most students find it to be "a breeze." Some do complain however, that because many classes have capped enrollments, it becomes difficult and often impossible to get into them. But one sophomore psych major noted that "professors will try to go out of their way for you . . . so if you want to get into a full class or get a new type of field work approved, or even get into a different dorm, it just takes a little leg work and you can get what you want."

Vassar offers a wide array of academic programs. English and psychology are named among the best departments at Vassar, and most believe there are no standout gut courses, though Music as a Literature has been known to give out easy "A's." Many students take advantage of the opportunity to do field work—an internship arranged through a specific academic department. Junior Year Abroad is also popular among students, as one-third of juniors take a semester or a year away. Established Vassar programs, several of which are co-sponsored by Wesleyan College, are located in many European countries, but students have the option to choose their own (often exotic) destination and create an individualized program of study.

Party Hardy

Although Vassar lacks Greek organizations, students say alcohol is both accessible and widely consumed. After all, Vassar was founded in 1861 by a brewer, Matthew Vassar, who made the hallways of one dorm exactly wide enough to roll kegs down, so that if the college failed he could turn it into a brewery. Making their founder proud, students agree that keg parties are the most frequent form of weekend entertainment. While students note that the on-campus security's enforcement of drug and alcohol laws is, in a word, "lax" (one student recalled that when drinking in her hallway, an officer told her: "go drink that beer inside your room") the administration has recently begun to crack down on campus parties. As an alternative to such parties, students often frequent Matthew's Mug, the on-campus bar and dance club.

The party scene is stimulated by each dorm throwing a "campus party" during the year—another indication of the strong residential community at Vassar. The most popular campus-wide parties all tend to require costumes: the biggest party is the Halloween Party, followed by the "Pimps and Hoes" party and "Heaven and Hell."

Non-partiers and students looking for a mellower weekend can attend the weekend Blodgett film series, a play or concert on campus, or a movie in town; or they can ride the two-hour train to New York City. One junior did comment, "If I could change one thing, it would be that there would be more places to hang out at night, especially on the weekends. Sometimes there's nothing to do and you have to get creative." This can be hard to do since many students feel that the city of Poughkeepsie is basically dead: "There's not much to do in town, there's no culture; all you can do is go to the mall." One student expressed concern that the town is a little dangerous and advised prospective students to "never ride the city buses," though she added, "getting away is easy if you or a friend has a car."

Outside the Classroom

Athletics are definitely not the first thing that comes to mind when thinking of Vassar College. The mascot, not surprisingly, is the Brewer. While students do participate in an extensive co-ed intramural system, varsity athletes and school spirit are in short supply. The exception to this is the men's rugby team, which does extremely well in their division. In a recent series of campus-wide renovations, also including a new drama space, Vassar has expanded its athletic facilities with a new wood-floored gymnasium and new playing fields.

But if athletics are not Vassar's strong suit, the arts certainly are. According to one student, "a significant number of the students here are 'drama-ramas': artsy and dressed in black, sort of like beatniks." Consequently almost every weekend a new production goes up. Vassar also has a wide variety of musical performers, ranging from a cappella singing groups (Vassar has more than any other college its size) to a Renaissance singing group called Matthew's Minstrels. In addition, Vassar has an active polo club, and a variety of environmental and cultural groups that promote campus events.

Despite strong arts and cultural programs, political activism is virtually nonexistent—even though most students are liberal. Nevertheless, a strong sense of social activism prevails on topics such as gay rights, reproductive rights, and women's issues. The campus weekly, called the *Miscellany News*, often publishes politically oriented articles, and students can keep up-to-date nationally with their small-scale daily newspaper, the *Daily Brew*.

"Vassar's probably one of the most liberal colleges you'll find . . . anywhere."

Town-gown relations are strained and there is "resentment in the Poughkeepsie community," one student explained, "due to the fact that we tend to perpetuate the uppity, spoiled stereotypes they hold about us by avoiding the town and rivaling with other nearby schools." In spite of the efforts of a select few Vassar students to foster a positive relationship between the school and town, students agree that the school is very separate from the surrounding area due to the "general sense of apathy at this place."

Diversity University?

Vassar students hail from almost every state in America and several foreign countries, but the majority are from New York, New Jersey, and California. Many students specifically note a lack of cultural diversity, and label the student body as "pretty homogeneous." Minority students at Vassar have a strong support network in ethnic organizations and the ALANA (Asian Latino African American Native American) Center. Like many other small liberal arts colleges, Vassar battles what one senior referred to as the "'Vassar bubble': you have to look hard to find news and information about the outside world, but gossip around the campus spreads like wildfire." One sophomore added, "Everybody knows everyone else's business and you begin to feel trapped."

Another common complaint (especially on behalf of the female student body) is that the male to female ratio is noticeably unbalanced. Vassar is approximately 35 percent male, 65 percent female, and next year is expected to be even more uneven. Students believe that this results from a lack of qualified male applicants. The result, as one sophomore commented, is that "Vassar's probably one of the most liberal colleges you'll find . . . anywhere." Another boasted that the best thing about Vassar is "that you feel very much at home. You grow into Vassar, find friends you've always wished you had, and fit in with many different groups of people. You can't characterize a 'Vassar student,' and in that regard, everyone can find a place."

Vassar students are proud of their school's genuine commitment to academics, the beauty of their secluded campus in Poughkeepsie, and the feeling of acceptance and freedom that pervades their environment. "People here are passionate not only about their classes but about their beliefs," reported one student. "That's what I love about this place." Vassar College is tightly knit but eclectic. In step with its lasting sense of tradition, afternoon tea is still served in Rose Parlor, but pearls and gloves are no longer required. —*Amanda Stauffer*

FYI

If you come to Vassar, you'd better bring a "a Bob Marley poster so that you gain acceptance, a tapestry to get the Vassar feel in your room, and the *Communist Manifesto*, because you'll need to read it at least twice during your college career."

What is the typical weekend schedule? "Attend sporting events, visit New York City, go to the town houses for a party or dance all night at the Mug."

If I could change one thing about Vassar, "I would change the lack of men on campus. This is no place to find your husband, let alone a date."

Three things every student at Vassar should do before graduating are "ring the bell on top of Main building, streak during Primal Scream, and take a mini-course in knitting, salsa dancing, Swedish massage, or wine tasting."

Wells College

Address: 170 Main St.; Aurora, NY 13026
Phone: 800-952-9355
E-mail address: admissions@wells.edu
Web site URL: www.wells.edu
Founded: 1868
Private or Public: private
Religious affiliation: none
Location: rural
Undergraduate enrollment: 437
Total enrollment: 437
Percent Male/Female: 0%/100%
Percent Minority: 13%
Percent African-American: 5%
Percent Asian: 4%
Percent Hispanic: 4%
Percent Native-American: 0%
Percent in-state/out of state: 73%/27%
Percent Pub HS: 85%
Number of Applicants: 404
Percent Accepted: 86%
Percent Accepted who enroll: 31%
Entering: 109
Transfers: 36
Application Deadline: 1 Mar
Mean SAT: NA
Mean ACT: NA
Middle 50% SAT range: V 50-650, M 500-590
Middle 50% ACT range: 22-26
3 Most popular majors: social sciences and history, psychology, English
Retention: 75%
Graduation rate: 63%
On-campus housing: 84%
Fraternities: NA
Sororities: NA
Library: 140,000 volumes
Tuition and Fees: $14,292
Room and Board: $6,830
Financial aid, first-year: 71%
Varsity or Club Athletes: NA
Early Decision or Early Action Acceptance Rate: ED 96%; EA 90%

Students at Wells, an all-female liberal arts school, are enthusiastic about their small community in Aurora, New York. Fairly compact and surrounded by Cayuga Lake and rolling hills, the rural campus boasts waterfalls, hiking trails, and small gardens. Students describe the campus as "wooded and peaceful." They rave about their interaction with professors, the history and traditions of Wells women, and the strong alumnae support.

Stellar Interaction

Students cite interaction with faculty as one of the best things about Wells. "They teach brilliantly and interactively. The faculty make the college experience worthwhile," one senior said. Students describe Wells as a tight-knit community where students are treated "with respect and understanding by professors." Undergrads report that they get to know their professors quite well, and it is not uncommon to go over to their houses for dinner, to babysit, or just hang out in their offices.

The range of academic possibilities is extensive and students have the option to create their own class or major. All students must fulfill distribution requirements by enrolling in courses in foreign language, formal reasoning, arts and humanities, natural and social sciences, wellness, and physical education. In addition, as part of the liberal arts curriculum, students must take a group of courses whose theme is "Learning for the 21st Century." Priority for registration is given by class, beginning with seniors. With the exception of creative writing and computer classes, students report that there is usually no problem getting into classes. Notoriously popular classes include Human Sexuality and Women and Sex in Early Modern Europe. Courses are described as rigorous, and one senior said, "Classes are rough and getting an A is getting tougher." Another student called the grading "tough, but fair."

Small-Town Living

The town of Aurora is about 25 minutes north of Ithaca, and students wanting a change from the typical Wells social scene generally go to Cornell University or Ithaca College on weekends. Students also go to Syracuse for women's studies lectures or other campus events. "Many first-years start at Wells thinking that it's going to be like a huge school. They see all the images of what a college is like and when Wells doesn't fit all that, they freak out," said one student. As one student explained, the people that Wells are right for are the ones who see that, in fact, Wells is different—a small, all-female community, who "because of our location in the middle of nowhere are forced to come up with our own fun, thus creating very strong friendship bonds." Some activities Wells students create includes organizing dances such as Mainly '80s or Disco Dodge, playing sports on campus, and going to the Morgan Opera House in Aurora for plays. There are no sororities on campus and while students say alcohol is not hard to obtain, they also advocate there is no pressure to drink.

A Place for Self-Expression

Students describe Wells as a great place for self-expression and exploration. In speaking of student support for the lesbian and bisexual students on campus, one undergrad described the campus community as "very supportive of people's lives." Wells' minority population is small. Many students at Wells are from in-state or the Northeast. Further, there are minority clubs and cultural activities on campus for support and learning, such as the United Women of Color and the American Indians in Science.

Home Is Where the Heart Is

Many dorms are actually old homes, each with their own unique feel. There are five residence halls. Glen Park is the old home of Henry Wells, who founded Wells Seminary in 1868 for the "gift of female education." Students say it has a "homey feel," with a large, central kitchen, three floors of rooms, and a spiral staircase winding through the middle. Each room is different, but many have high ceilings and wooden floors. Leach is a more typical dorm, with three floors of rooms and a large central lounge. Dodge, a dorm built in the 60s, draws the most complaints for its age, but also inspires fierce loyalty from those who live there. Although it has smaller rooms, upperclasswomen can obtain singles in rooms meant to be doubles. Dodge hosts one of the biggest campus events, the Disco Dodge, in the fall.

Almost all students live on campus, since they need special permission to live off campus. First-year students are assigned "sisters" from each of the three other classes to provide guidance and friendship. There is also an RA system in the dorms. Renovations to the ever popular Weld House, a dorm used by students of all years, has provided Wells students with expanded Internet access, two 24-hour computing labs, and a network connection in every room. The renovations to Weld are part of a general $2.4 million dollar technology upgrade that give Wells' students the most up-to-date computer software and hardware with a student-computer ratio of 3:1.

"Students describe Wells as a great place for self-expression and exploration."

Students must buy a meal plan of 19 meals per week. During the week, meals are served in one dining hall, though the Somner Student Center provides weekend brunch and Saturday dinner. Somner Center is open daily until midnight and the meal plan allots each student $50 a semester to spend there (they can also pay cash). Students say the dining hall has a huge salad bar, a deli bar, and for hot food, a meat line and a wellness/vegetarian line. Undergrads report that vegetarians usually have no problem finding something to eat.

Active Women

Sports at Wells have been improving. Wells recently joined the All Women's College Conference (AWCC) and now offers students the opportunity to participate on the field hockey, lacrosse, swimming, and soccer teams among others. Other athletic options include intramural basketball and volleyball, and there is a golf course on campus for student use, as well.

Rife with Tradition

Wells is famous for its traditions. Students are divided into odd/even classes depending on year of graduation for such events as the Odd/Even basketball game. Other traditions include the Junior Blast, where first-years hide the juniors' beds and leave clues about where to find them. Fall and spring weekend festivities feature bonfires and concerts, which in the past have drawn such acts as the Spin Doctors. Other traditions include a countdown of the last hundred days of senior year; seniors mark the first day of the countdown with a champagne breakfast and wear of their graduation robes. Bells are rung from Main tower to celebrate everything from the first snowfall to the marriage of a Wells woman.

Wells is noted for its consistent and strong alumnae support, and students praise the opportunities this support provides for leadership and internships. Wells offers a leadership week where alumnae help match students with internships in January for credit. One student said, "Our alumnae network is really amazing and it's one of the things that I think makes Wells women so successful. Alumnae feel indebted to the school and give by way of internships, which I think is one of the reasons why Wells women have such high graduate school acceptance rates."

Wells is not right for everyone, but for the student who seeks a school with strong academic roots and many opportunities to participate in tradition and form lasting friendships, Wells is a strong community. One student said, "This tiny school has a unique all-female environment. The atmosphere on campus is supportive and open—people can be who they want to be. I wouldn't trade my Wells experience for the world!" *—Laura Chaukin and Staff*

FYI

If you come to Wells, you'd better bring "a pair of good shoes. You'll need them to keep your feet warm and dry in the weather here."

What is the typical weekend schedule? "People hang out with friends usually. There are some parties that go on, but most people take the laid-back route and do some light studying and relaxing."

If I could change one thing about Wells, I'd "relocate the school to a place with more things to do off campus."

Three things every student at Wells should do before graduating are "jump in the lake, take advantage of an internship, and develop a relationship with a professor."

Yeshiva University

Address: 500 West 185 Street; New York, NY 10033-3201
Phone: 212-960-5277
E-mail address: yuadmit@ymail.yu.edu
Web site URL: www.yu.edu
Founded: 1886
Private or Public: private
Religious affiliation: none
Location: urban
Undergraduate enrollment: 2,798
Total enrollment: 5,906
Percent Male/Female: 56%/44%
Percent Minority: 0%
Percent African-American: 0%
Percent Asian: 0%
Percent Hispanic: 0%
Percent Native-American: 0%
Percent in-state/out of state: 40%/60%
Percent Pub HS: 4%
Number of Applicants: 1,793
Percent Accepted: 77%
Percent Accepted who enroll: 65%
Entering: 907
Transfers: 20
Application Deadline: 15 Feb
Mean SAT: NA
Mean ACT: NA
Middle 50% SAT range: V 580-670, M 590-680
Middle 50% ACT range: 25-30
3 Most popular majors: psychology, business, biology
Retention: 86%
Graduation rate: 88%
On-campus housing: 85%
Fraternities: NA
Sororities: NA
Library: 654,000 volumes
Tuition and Fees: $19,654
Room and Board: $6,980
Financial aid, first-year: 47%
Varsity or Club Athletes: NA
Early Decision or Early Action Acceptance Rate: NA

Picture this—a sociology class begins with an admitted gang member lecturing on the hardships of daily life on the street at a school that also requires its students to participate in programs of Jewish studies in the original Hebrew and Aramaic. Not possible, you say? Take the Sociology of Deviance at Yeshiva University and one day you may have one of the head gang members of the "Latin Kings" presenting the lecture.

A Rigorous Combination

As undergraduates, students at Yeshiva University pursue a full program of Jewish studies while taking college courses in the liberal arts, sciences, and business. Divided into Yeshiva College for men and Stern College for women, the university also includes the undergraduate Sy Syms School of Business, The Belz School of Music, Isaac Breuer College of Hebraic Studies, Irving I. Stone Beit Midrash Program, James Striar School of General Jewish Studies, and Yeshiva Program/Mazer School of Talmudic Studies. Most freshmen do not begin their years as Yeshiva students on campus in New York City. Instead, with the S. Daniel Abraham Israel Program, freshmen who want to spend a year in Israel and concentrate on Jewish studies take courses at any one of more than 30 Israeli institutions. Upon their return sophomore year, however, the students must satisfy the university's requirements in three years instead of four—however this does not seem to be much of a problem. As one student said, "I feel that the requirements are interesting and they help serve in providing a well-rounded education."

The Programs and Classes

Students explore diverse interests within 40 majors and may tailor their studies through concentrations and joint degree programs, or by adding a minor. Yeshiva University is for all majors—from engineering to English. The school has a very respectable honors program stressing writing and critical analysis, cultural enrichment, research, internships, and individual mentoring, along with a joint program with Columbia Engineering. Workload varies depending on your major, but overall "it's not too bad—except if you are pre-med."

Some classes are held very late in the day, and because Yeshiva is such a small school, popular classes close out very quickly. However, this limited class size leaves little room for complaints about student-faculty relationships. Students are able to have very personal relationships with their professors. "I am very happy with my professors; they all love to teach," comments one student. And from another, "Professors are always willing to help a student strive for more knowledge." Such an enriching experience with faculty may be difficult to find elsewhere, but is hard to miss at Yeshiva.

A Prime Location

While the campus is very small, Yeshiva has some beautiful buildings ranging in style from gothic to modern. Being smack in the middle of Manhattan gives the campus a different feel from the classic "grass and trees" atmosphere of many other schools. As evidenced by one student's complaint that "I wish there was more grass . . . all we have is one patch of grass," greenery is at a minimum, however students also note that New York City's Central Park is a favorite destination. And of course, on those freezing cold, snowy days of winter, "walking to a class is never a problem."

New York City offers the best of everything: from Broadway Theater to kosher dining, from Manhattan's museums to the richest resources in Jewish history and culture outside of Israel. For the motivated and career-oriented students of Yeshiva, unsurpassed opportunities for internships and jobs on Wall Street and in the offices of the world's leading corporations and international organizations are just minutes away. The midtown Manhattan area where Stern College is located has all the attractions of downtown New York City literally at its doorstep. The Washington Heights area of Yeshiva College, however, has some crime problems. Campus security is known to be tight though, and a van escort service operates nightly.

Not Just Religion

Most students have part time jobs, but they still find time to "do everything on the weekends . . . concerts, clubs, bars, sporting events, chill in Central Park". Undergraduates on the main campus participate in intercollegiate and intramural sports and physical education classes in the Max Stern Athletic Center, which houses a gym, the six-lane Benjamin Gottesman Pool, exercise and steam rooms, a track, areas for fencing and wrestling and a lounge-recreation area. Intercollegiate sports include basketball, cross-country, fencing, golf, tennis, volleyball and wrestling, while intramural athletics include basketball, floor hockey, karate, softball and running.

Though school spirit could be stronger, most students are proud of their school's athletics. "The facilities are great and are always open, almost everyone plays on intramural teams, and there are tons of pick up sports games." There are also over 30 clubs and organizations, ranging from chess club and environmental society to philanthropic society and student government. Community service is also big at YU, where many students visit the sick in a neighboring hospital, and the chess club runs good-will events to help those who are less fortunate.

Live Somewhere, but Eat?

The average freshman dorm at Yeshiva is a nicely sized square, and most students are happy with their living conditions with the exception that they are "shoved in the middle of nowhere land." After freshmen year, students can stay in the dorms (where there are RAs on each floor who are "awesome—they are very friendly and easy going") or get an apartment. For those who remain in the dorms, Rubin dorm is *the* place to be. It is not only the newest, but also "smack dab in the middle of campus," making it close to all the main student attractions on campus: the cafeteria, gym, pool, sauna, steam room, track, and cafeteria store.

> **"The school has a closeness—all students feel as one not only because they are all Jewish, but also because they are always ready to lend a hand to each other."**

The harshest criticism of dorm life by the students comes as a result of a terrible meal plan "that we don't want but there is no other option—we can't eat pizza or order out every day." Many students feel that they are ripped off for non-nutritious, over-priced food. One exasperated sophomore explained the dearth of dining choices by noting "Vegetarians would not be able to survive—they are better off eating the tables for fiber." While the dining halls are clean, the hours are not suitable for many: "whenever you actually need the store to be open, it isn't."

The best thing about not wanting to eat in the dining halls, however, is the desire and the opportunity to explore the whole city for other dining options. Manhattan has thousands of wonderful, easily accessible restaurants. A place often frequented by Yeshiva students is Timeout, "the official YU pizzeria." And it seems that everyone at Yeshiva and Stern has been to Dougies and Pizza Cave.

The Down and the Dirty

The student body at YU is composed of middle class to wealthy students who wear very preppy clothing. Abercrombie & Fitch, J.Crew, Gap, Structure, and Banana Republic are the common brands found on the campus where "most students are fit and sexy." Although virtually all students are Jewish, many enjoy the diversity found within this homogeneous group. As one student noted, "the school has a closeness—all students feel as one not only because they are all Jewish, but also because they are always ready to lend a hand to each other. There are many different types of Jews from all over the world; all these cultures come together to form a melting pot known as Yeshiva University." This very friendly campus where people are always willing to be your friend does not have a problem with drugs. "You can honestly say that drugs are not found on campus," said one student. Of course, because Yeshiva and Stern separate the men and the women, there are no random hook-ups on campus, though dates are very common. There is also "no sex, no STDs, no alcohol, no kegs, and no Greek anything." This makes for some nice clean fun, although students at Yeshiva still pride themselves on great private-apartment parties. —*Victoria Yen*

FYI

If you come to Yeshiva, you'd better bring "a Kippa—this is a Jewish Orthodox University."

What is the typical weekend schedule? "Weekends are chilled out. Students party all over the city and study all day on Sunday. We may be an all-male campus, but we party like no other school."

If I could change one thing about Yeshiva, I'd "like to have more diverse courses."

Three things every student at Yeshiva should do before graduating are "take part in a Shabbat Tisch, have some cookies from Grandma's Cookie Jar, hit up Kaffeine (a café) for after-hours."

North Carolina

Davidson College

Address: PO Box 1737; Davidson, NC 28036
Phone: 704-892-2230
E-mail address: admissions@davidson.edu
Web site URL: www.davidson.edu
Founded: 1837
Private or Public: private
Religious affiliation: Presbyterian
Location: suburban
Undergraduate enrollment: 1,644
Total enrollment: 1,644
Percent Male/Female: 50%/50%
Percent Minority: 10%
Percent African-American: 5%
Percent Asian: 2%
Percent Hispanic: 2.8%
Percent Native-American: 0.4%
Percent in-state/out of state: 22%/78%
Percent Pub HS: NA
Number of Applicants: 3,387
Percent Accepted: 34%
Percent Accepted who enroll: 40%
Entering: 468
Transfers: 11
Application Deadline: 2 Jan
Mean SAT: NA
Mean ACT: NA
Middle 50% SAT range: V 620-710, M 630-720
Middle 50% ACT range: 27-31
3 Most popular majors: English, biology, economics
Retention: 96%
Graduation rate: 89%
On-campus housing: 92%
Fraternities: 42
Sororities: NA
Library: 422,000 volumes
Tuition and Fees: $25,903
Room and Board: $7,371
Financial aid, first-year: 29%
Varsity or Club Athletes: NA
Early Decision or Early Action Acceptance Rate: 58%

If a "quaint, brick-laden paradise" strikes your fancy, come to Davidson. If you're looking to be stretched to your cognitive limits, come to Davidson. If you're looking for a small, Southern school, quietly nestled in a small, yuppie town, come to Davidson. If you're the friendly type who doesn't find striking up a conversation with a perfect stranger in the least bit weird, come to Davidson. If you're looking for that quintessential "work hard, play hard" school, come to Davidson. If any of these scenes appeal to you, then Davidson College in Davidson, North Carolina, just might be the place for you.

Hardcore Academics

The academic atmosphere at Davidson cannot be described as anything less than "intense." Students across the board wholeheartedly agree that academics at Davidson are a priority. As one student simply said, "We work a ton!" The coursework is rigorous, the pace intense. "This is not a laid-back school," one sophomore noted.

Students also agreed that the professors are friendly, down-to-earth, and willing to help their students achieve. "The professors are really amazing. I was not anticipating the challenge. The courses are extremely demanding but really interesting. Professors are passionate about what they teach and extremely willing to spend hours with you outside of class to provide extra help or just to talk," noted one student. One junior said, "The professors aren't afraid to be real people . . . most of them are more liberal than the students, so they challenge us to think outside of our somewhat sheltered lives." At Davidson, classes generally range from 20 to 30 students. There are no lectures and no TAs. Students appreciate the fact that their professors aren't just in "auto-lecture" mode, thinking about their newest book or latest research; they are genuinely interested in teaching.

Davidson prides itself in giving its students a true liberal arts education. The school requires students to complete a core curriculum, with courses in literature, fine arts, history, religion and philosophy, natural sciences, math, social sciences, as well as a physical education requirement. Some students praised the requirements, saying "the school got me to study stuff I never would have studied otherwise," while others complained, saying, "There is a lot of pressure to get all of the requirements done before senior year." Although some students feel the pressure to complete all of the requirements, students agree that there is plenty to choose from when completing the required courses. For the P.E. requirement students can even learn to water ski!

This small Southern school offers a wide variety of majors and minors, including several interdisciplinary studies. Economics and Chemistry are two of the most popular majors. And one senior English major noted, "There are an insane amount of pre-meds here!" The school is known for its excellent pre-medical program. Among the hardest majors are Chemistry, Physics, and Economics. As one student described, "Chem and Physics majors are nutty pre-meds, Econ majors are brutal future bankers, and Sociology and Anthropology majors are slackers."

All in the Family

"This is the most friendly place I have ever been to," one student said. "It is overwhelming your first week here because everyone *wants* to meet you." The students definitely cherish their family-like community. A conversation about life at Davidson will inevitably include the honor code and the Southern hospitality. Central to the Davidson community is the school's honor code, which states that students will not lie, cheat, or steal, and promise to report anyone who does. Entering students sign a pledge that they will live under the system, knowing that a disciplinary infraction will lead to either a suspension or expulsion from the college. "The honor code isn't some archaic utopian idea put in place by the founders," one senior said. "It's a way of life here. I can leave my room unlocked and not have to worry that my laptop is going to get stolen." While the code may be strict, it comes with its advantages—students can schedule their own exams.

Some students complain that the student body lacks diversity. As a student simply commented, "It needs work." Another student followed up by saying, "It seems as if everyone is white, middle- to upper-class, and is from the South."

Despite this fact, the college is not lacking in diversity in terms of activities and extracurricular opportunities. With the recent construction of the Knobloch Campus Center, the hub of campus activities, students can find a lot to do outside of hitting the books. There are a myriad of clubs and organizations students can join, ranging from *The Davidsonian* and *Libertas* campus publications, to various performing arts and religious groups. Recently, groups such as the Counting Crows, Ludacris, and even the Royal Shakespeare Company have visited Davidson.

"Chem and Physics majors are nutty pre-meds, Econ majors are brutal future bankers, and Sociology and Anthropology majors are slackers."

Sports at Davidson are, in the words of one freshman, "not the reason I came here." One student said, "Sports aren't huge at Davidson because we just don't have that tradition." However, the student body rallied behind the basketball team as it had a near-appearance in the Sweet Sixteen. Davidson is the smallest Division I school, but it is competitive in its 11 varsity sports for men and ten for women.

Because Davidson is affiliated with the Presbyterian Church, most students are in some way religious. However, students feel that the Christian nature of the school isn't domineering and the administration doesn't try to "make you be Christian."

Patterson Court

The houses and fraternities centered on Patterson Court are the focal point of the social scene at Davidson. Although the fraternities only claim 35 to 40 percent of the male population, about 60 percent of women join one of the six eating houses. Fraternities still choose new members by the pledge system, and the administration has cracked down to make sure there is no hazing. For women, the eating house membership is chosen by lottery, a system which the students regard as fair. Transferring between eating houses is reportedly easy if a student wishes to do so.

One, however, must not feel as if he has to join a fraternity to have fun at Davidson. "The frats and eating houses provide a lot of the entertainment on the weekends; however, the parties are open to the entire campus so it's not crucial to be a member in order to have fun." On the alcohol issue, students commented that drinking isn't really a big issue on campus. Students who are comfortable drinking do drink, and those who aren't comfortable, don't. In terms of an alcohol policy, "The school has to be nominally strict, but if you can find a Solo cup into which you can place your beer, there's no problem," said one upperclassman. On weekends, students can be found partying on Patterson Court and in the senior apartments.

Only a 20-minute drive away, nearby Charlotte provides even more social and cultural opportunities. "Even though the town of Davidson is really small, there is more than enough to do in Charlotte," notes a sophomore. "You can easily hitch a ride with a classmate who has a car."

Southern Living

Several students raved about freshman year housing. "Even though the rooms are a little tight, the dorms weren't as bad as some of the colleges I visited," one freshman said. Most freshmen live in Richardson Hall on five single-sex floors. Other freshmen live in Belk Hall. Sophomores live in "Sophomore City," comprised of three identical dorms. About 95 percent of students live on campus. "You learn to live with what you have. It's not that bad." A junior noted, "Most dorms are very nice, freshly renovated and large. The senior apartments are amazing!" Seniors live in suite-style dorms, all with kitchens and living rooms. There is no special-interest housing, and the fraternity houses are non-residential. Students note that there is a lot of variety in the cafeterias, but nothing beats the home-cooked meals that are available in the eating houses. —*Scott Rodney Woods*

FYI

If you come to Davidson, you'd better bring "a work ethic."

What is the typical weekend schedule? "Parties on Friday nights, do homework on Saturday, party Saturday night, maybe do something in Charlotte, and work on Sunday."

If I could change one thing about Davidson, "I would have the administration care just a little less about appearance and spend that money instead on the faculty."

Three things every student at Davidson should do before graduating are: "Find and get to know a quality member of the faculty, go late-night swimming at the Lake Campus, and buy a cup of coffee at Summit Coffee."

Duke University

Address: 2138 Campus Drive; Durham, NC 27708
Phone: 919-684-3214
E-mail address: askduke@admiss.duke.edu
Web site URL: www.duke.edu
Founded: 1838
Private or Public: private
Religious affiliation: none
Location: urban
Undergraduate enrollment: 6,206
Total enrollment: 11,752
Percent Male/Female: 51%/49%
Percent Minority: 29%
Percent African-American: 11%
Percent Asian: 12%
Percent Hispanic: 6%
Percent Native-American: 0.41%
Percent in-state/out of state: 15%/85%
Percent Pub HS: 63%
Number of Applicants: 15,047
Percent Accepted: 25%
Percent Accepted who enroll: 44%
Entering: 1,636
Transfers: 35
Application Deadline: 2 Jan
Mean SAT: NA
Mean ACT: NA
Middle 50% SAT range: V 650-740, M 670-770
Middle 50% ACT range: 29-33
3 Most popular majors: economics, biology, psychology
Retention: 97%
Graduation rate: 93%
On-campus housing: 81%
Fraternities: 29%
Sororities: 42%
Library: 5,234,471 volumes
Tuition and Fees: $29,345
Room and Board: $8,210
Financial aid, first-year: 42%
Varsity or Club Athletes: 24%
Early Decision or Early Action Acceptance Rate: 32%

Known for its excellent academics, athletics, and party scene, Duke offers "an incredibly well-rounded experience." Sometimes referred to as the "Ivy of the south," Duke offers the same rigorous academics and distinguished faculty as many of its northern cousins but "with a better basketball team and better weather." Although intense about their academics, students mostly mutually support one another. This intensity and camaraderie is carried over to basketball, the second passion of Duke students. At Duke, students push themselves to the limit both in terms of academics and in terms of school spirit, making the most of their time in the "Gothic Wonderland" that is Duke.

Y2K, Duke Style

Duke changed its curriculum in 2000; it requires that students take at least three classes in each of four areas of knowledge, which include Arts and Literatures, Civilizations, Social Sciences, and Natural Sciences and Mathematics. At least two of these classes must offer exposures to two different Modes of Inquiry and three Focused Inquiries. Students must also fulfill a writing and research requirement, and must prove competency in a foreign language. Some of the freshmen affected by these new requirements were "not big fans" of the changes. One student said that the curriculum forces you to take classes you do not really want to, and allows much less flexibility. However, another freshman pointed out that even with the more restrictive curriculum than before, there are no classes that are required, so the options are pretty open.

One area where options definitely abound is in picking a major. Students can choose from 38 existing majors, or, if they cannot find something that matches their interests, they can opt for the alternative Program II. Program II allows students to pick their own topic and design an individualized curriculum with the help of a faculty advisor. Freshmen may also choose to apply to the FOCUS Program, a first-semester program that takes an interdisciplinary approach to one of about 20 themes. The students are in small seminar classes of about 10-15 students, with some of the university's most distinguished professors. One freshman said that while it was a rewarding experience, prospective applicants to the program should "know what they're getting into. It's a lot of work, and you have to be very dedicated."

For the most part, the workload depends on a student's major. For the many premed students, or those majoring in engineering, the workload can be pretty demanding, even "overwhelming." However, those in other majors, especially such "slacker" majors as sociology, history, religion, or cultural anthropology, generally find the workload much more reasonable. Yet even premed students can balance their schedules by taking such gut courses as Introduction to Jazz, Introduction to Geology, or even Social Dancing.

Despite Duke's reputation as a distinguished research university for graduate work, undergraduates do not feel marginalized. Professors generally get rave reviews from students. Said one student, "the professors make everything come to life, even in lecture classes." The legendary James Bonk, a professor of chemistry for over 40 years, is reportedly so great that students go to Chem 11L (a.k.a. "Bonkistry") lectures even though students claim it is possible to learn the material without going to class. The professors are "extremely accessible." They are eager to get to know their students, and encourage students to meet with them, even outside of office hours.

Abercrombie, Fitch, and Duke

So you may wonder what Duke students are like. While most agree that there is no "typical" Duke student, there are some characteristics that seem to apply to the population as a whole. For one, the students are passionate about what they do, fully embracing the motto of "work hard, play hard." "In everything, whether it's in classes, in debates, or at basketball games, everyone here is always intense," said one student. Another student stated that the student body was "overwhelmingly very attractive." Or, as a more modest student put it, "I'm not grossed out when I look around or anything." The reality of the situation may depend on personal opinion, but there is at least a consensus on one thing: most people at Duke care about their appearance. As one student commented, "everyone looks like they walked out of an Abercrombie & Fitch ad." The gym gets a lot of use, since everyone is "ridiculously healthy." Most people get dressed up to go to classes; girls generally wear skirts and sweater sets, and guys don khakis and button- down shirts. However, do not mistake a concern for appearance with superficiality, a characteristic that is not at all common to the Duke population. Students are routinely surprised with how "incredibly impressive" their peers are. Many people have rare and special talents, and you "constantly meet people who have done things that blow your mind."

Some students complain that Duke is a little *too* much like an Abercrombie & Fitch ad, with its homogeneity, but others praise the school for its attempts at recruiting people of diverse ethnic and socioeconomic backgrounds. While there may be a stereotype of "wealthy white kids who drive expensive cars," one student asserted, "Duke is not a school full of snotty little rich kids. A lot of students are on financial aid and work study." The geographic, ethnic, and socioeconomic diversity "make [the school] a lot more interesting." However, despite the improved diversity, many still find that self-segregation is a problem. Although students say there is a lack of racial or ethnic tension, there is also a lack of interaction. This segregation even extends to housing, with many minority students choosing to live on Central Campus. However, people do defy this stereotype, choosing to interact with people of all ethnicities, so "it really depends on the person."

What Would You Do for Basketball Tickets?

Another thing that Duke students have in common is "amazing school spirit," which stems mostly from Duke's highly successful basketball team. Said one student, "if you're not at a game, you're watching it in your room." Students take their basketball seriously, which is manifested by Krzyzewskiville, or K-ville, a yearly tradition. Named after the basketball coach, K-ville refers to the tent city that springs up as students camp out to get tickets to choice home games. Students come days before school reopens to pitch their tent, and they camp out, or "tent" for weeks, enduring snow, 20-degree weather, and frequent "tent checks," in the middle of the night, which ensure that at least one person is in the tent at all times. The tenters are so hard-core that one student recalled receiving death threats after moving to the front of the line after discovering a loophole in the rules. At basketball games, the energy is "like nothing you've ever felt before." Some paint their bodies from head to toe in blue and white (the school colors) and others dress only in saran wrap. Basketball helps create a sense of community among Duke students. As one student said, " you just warm up when people mention Duke. When you're away from school, and you see someone who goes to Duke, you just get a flood of emotion." Another student expressed similar sentiments, claiming "we all love each other by association with Duke." (Just as long as you don't try to steal someone's tent spot, that is!)

Here a Greek, There a Greek . . .

The social scene is, for the most part, dominated by the Greek system. However, the excitement of toga parties and other such fraternity sponsored theme parties is not limited to members of the fraternity. The organizations generally have a welcoming attitude, so those who are not in a fraternity or sorority do not feel left out. A student who does not wish to go to a frat party may opt instead to go to one of the bars on campus, which include Tap House and Hideaway, the latter of which "you can get served at with an ID that says you're 38." However, one student commented that Duke "does not exceed its reputation as a party school." This is due, in part, to a recent crackdown on underage drinking. East Campus, where freshmen live, is now completely dry. Distribution of alcohol has also become more tightly controlled. Kegs must be purchased through the university, and parties must have university-approved bartenders. However, despite these new regulations, it is "not at all" difficult for underage students to obtain alcohol. You just have to be "a little bit quieter" about it, and not walk around with open drinks. Students often drink in their rooms before going out, or get other people to get them drinks.

Joining a fraternity or sorority is not essential for making friends either. Most people tend to stick by their friends from freshman year. One student said that 90 percent of his friends were from his freshman dorm. People tend to form a close circle of friends that can be cliquish at times. However, according to one student, "everyone's open to meeting new people," although it may be easier to meet people in classes than it is in a social setting. Those who do choose to join a fraternity or sorority may find that it governs their social life. There are strong ties to fraternities, and some students commented that there is limited mixing between guys in different fraternities, and between the Greeks and non-Greeks. While the fraternity members are very accepting at parties, they tend to be aloof from the general population otherwise. Sorority members however, are not as exclusive, partially because the sorority members do not live together as do the frat brothers.

OK, so you have friends, but what if you need something more? One lonely freshman lamented that a lot of girls come to Duke with boyfriends from back home, while the guys are notably unattached. However, this student, and prospective Duke students may be relieved to know that commitments are hardly a problem among the upperclassmen. In fact, the scarcity of them might be the only concern. Because of the intense commitment that Duke students have to their academics and extracurricular obligations, there is, "unfortunately," little time left over for dating. Casual hook-ups seem to be the only alternative to serious relationships. As far as same-sex relationships go, one student commented that there does not seem to be a large population of homosexuals at Duke, but that the general attitude is accepting.

At Home in a "Gothic Wonderland"

Duke's sprawling campus, with its Gothic architecture, beautiful stonework, set in the middle of acres of forest, have earned it the title of "Gothic Wonderland." One student said that the campus gives you "a spiritual feeling, whether you're religious or not," and that the "gorgeous" campus alone was enough to make her come to

Duke. All freshmen live on East Campus. The housing is "decently sized," although only a couple of dorms have air-conditioning, and you have to pay a lot extra for it. Upperclassmen live either on Central Campus or West Campus, which is coveted for its close proximity to classes, and also because it is party central. A majority of seniors tend to move off-campus. One of the advantages of being in a fraternity is guaranteed housing on West Campus, in the section of a dorm that is designated for the particular fraternity. A student may also choose to rush Selective Housing groups, which are co-ed and have certain themes, such as the Arts Dorm, Woman's Studies Dorm, or the multicultural Prism dorm. This also guarantees housing on West Campus. Most freshmen like the arrangement, claiming that the all-freshman East Campus makes the atmosphere "less intimidating." The only real complaint about the campus is that, because it is so spread out, it is necessary to take a bus or car to get to classes, and both parking and the bus system are "major issues."

"In everything, whether it's in classes, in debates, or at basketball games, everyone here is always intense."

Students generally feel safe on campus, although they do not say the same about the surrounding city of Durham. What does Durham have to offer college life? Well . . . "plenty of opportunities for community service" as one student said. And although the beauty of the campus allows you to "walk around without a care in the world," many students do not do this, instead choosing to involve themselves in such activities as Habitat for Humanity and tutoring in public schools. Other popular extracurricular activities include student government, a cappella groups, and intramural sports. Protest groups, such as Students Against Sweatshops, are also prevalent, and one student complained about them, stating "a lot of it is protest just to protest."

Students do occasionally head off campus to see a movie, eat dinner, or go to a bar on weekends. Especially popular is Satisfactions, or "Satties" as it is also known, a restaurant/bar that is a big Thursday night hangout. Also popular are Parizade and Georgia's, restaurant/bars that are also major party destinations. Although these places are strict about carding, you only need to be 18 to get in. Those with cars may also take a short ride to Chapel Hill, which is a more active college town.

Although the bars of Durham may offer a change of pace from the frat-dominated social scene, many students do not find it necessary to go out to eat. With a flexible meal plan that allows students to use points to buy food from such places as McDonalds, Breyers, or The Loop, students can often satisfy their cravings on campus. And if a student can't find what they want from any of the several options on campus, they can get food delivered from almost any restaurant in the vicinity of Duke.

All in all, Duke students tend to be well rounded, and although they are intense about their academics, they do not let it consume their lives. They are able to find a balance between studying, partying, and extracurricular interests. The unique combination of rigorous academics, extraordinary school spirit, abundant parties, all encased within the beautifully lush Duke campus creates "an incredible experience" which cannot be replicated in other schools. —*Elyssa Berg*

FYI

If you come to Duke, you'd better bring "money and a computer."

What is the typical weekend schedule? "Study, study, study, and then hang out at night."

If I could change one thing about Duke, I'd "change the dining system. The food is okay but the food-point system could use a little work."

Three things every student should do before graduating from Duke are "tent, fool around in Duke Gardens, and climb the dome on top of Baldwin Auditorium."

North Carolina School of the Arts

Address: 1533 South Main Street; Winston-Salem, NC 27117
Phone: 336-770-3291
E-mail address: admissions@ncarts.edu
Web site URL: www.ncarts.edu
Founded: 1965
Private or Public: public
Religious affiliation: none
Location: small city
Undergraduate enrollment: 738
Total enrollment: 738
Percent Male/Female: 59%/41%
Percent Minority: 15%
Percent African-American: 10%
Percent Asian: 3%
Percent Hispanic: 2%
Percent Native-American: 0%
Percent in-state/out of state: 48%/52%
Percent Pub HS: NA
Number of Applicants: 744
Percent Accepted: 46%
Percent Accepted who enroll: 59%
Entering: 200
Transfers: 64
Application Deadline: 1 Mar
Mean SAT: NA
Mean ACT: NA
Middle 50% SAT range: V 540-640, M 500-620
Middle 50% ACT range: 20-25
3 Most popular majors: visual and performing arts
Retention: 75%
Graduation rate: 48%
On-campus housing: 60%
Fraternities: NA
Sororities: NA
Library: 190,000 volumes
Tuition and Fees: $3,555 in, $14,155 out
Room and Board: $5,530
Financial aid, first-year: 64%
Varsity or Club Athletes: NA
Early Decision or Early Action Acceptance Rate: NA

A haven for talented and dedicated young performers, aspiring filmmakers, and theater production buffs, North Carolina School of the Arts (NCSA) is anything but a traditional college. With its highly selective admissions policy and hard-core artistic atmosphere, artists who end up at NCSA have to be intensely devoted to their fields. With no sports and no time for extracurriculars, NCSA is virtually all arts, all the time.

Lights, Camera, Acting!

NCSA is divided into six schools: Modern Dance and Ballet, Drama, Filmmaking, Music, Theater Design and Production (known as D&P), and Visual Arts. Students can apply to and enter only one of the six schools. All six have excellent reputations and get rave reviews from students: dance students praise the drama program, acting students can't stop talking about the dedicated D&Pers, and so on.

Along with courses for training in their field of art, first-year students have to take classes from a general curriculum known as General Studies, or GS, but the classes are helpful since, as one D&Per explained, "they relate to your major. An art student will take history of art, or a drama student will find it helpful to take English classes, whereas a scene-builder is better off taking math." If the mention of the M-word invokes chills in your scene-building body, never fear. GS classes are "pretty easy," according to a second-year D&P major who is not a big fan of mathematics.

Most students find the faculty in GS to be good, but as one student observed, "some of them just don't want to be there. They'd rather be where people care more about regular academics, because students here don't really care about general studies classes. They want to be completely focused on their art." Other students described GS classes as "disappointingly unchallenging" and "not very worthwhile." A first-year acting student, however, said that he at least enjoys the classes as "a good change of pace."

Academic classes may take the back seat at NCSA, but don't be fooled—they may not be cracking textbooks and pulling all-nighters for papers, but students are worked to the bone in their artistic training and are expected to dedicate themselves seriously to their art. In fact, during the second year, the faculty "cuts" or dismisses any students they judge to be unprepared for the level of dedication required for success at the school. If you ever wanted a chance to test your dedication as an artist, NCSA is it, and there is no warm-up period—it's intense from day one. "It's hard to get in, and hard to stay in," said a D&P Lighting Design major. "Freshman year especially they hammer you with a lot of work. It's tough." Dancers typically have classes from 8 A.M. to 5 P.M., and actors train from 9 A.M. to 6 P.M. If you think that's bad, check this out: D&Pers often pull "triple crews," working from 8 A.M. to 11 P.M. on a set. For NCSA students who are this passionate about their art, the intensity of the training is a heaven of hell.

Weak-Ends: Dead on Arrival

With the heavy workload during the week, NCSA students look forward to a more relaxing weekend schedule. Partying happens mainly off campus, since the school's alcohol policy is fairly strict and most students choose to live off campus after their first year because of cheap rents and lackluster dorms. Like the overall social scene, parties are pretty chill. D&P students have a traditional Friday night party called "Beers": each year, two to four off-campus houses volunteer to alternate hosting the parties. A drama student described them as "the same people at the same houses drinking. Basically everyone who goes out drinks." There are also a few theme parties every once in a while, such as a recent 80s party. Students with ID hang out at the 1st Street Drafthouse, which a fourth-year D&P student described as "*the* hangout—the only place you can go every night and find people out." Every student stresses that a car is a must-have, if possible, in Winston-Salem.

"Everyone has the notion that people here are super-artsy fartsy . . . and they are."

The Student Activities Committee does plan some events, such as a recent first-attempt at a Winter Ball, but they're generally not very popular. "Student Activities doesn't work at all, because it's really badly run," criticized one student. One successful school-organized event is Beaux Arts, a weekend-long party the week before graduation. It includes special events and bands during the week, a carnival on Saturday, and a semiformal dance at the end of the week. One student described it as "a lot of fun. We get to dress up, though it seems like the point is to wear the least amount of clothes possible." In addition to Beaux Arts, there are roughly 200 student performances each year.

Sketchy Meat

A common sentiment among students is that on weekends, the NCSA campus itself is dead. "A lot of people leave, since half the students are from North Carolina," said a fourth-year student. "There's no incentive to stay, so people just pack up." Winston-Salem also earns less-than-ecstatic reviews. "There's not a whole lot to do there," said one student. "It's a typical small, Southern city." Students describe Winston-Salem as "sketchy" and "shady," though the NCSA campus is described as safe. People usually venture off campus to eat, another activity for which a car comes in handy. Despite a snack bar in addition to the cafeteria and constant vegetarian options, "the food here is nasty. I don't eat the meat they cook here—it doesn't look right," said one student.

Artistic Integrity, Artistic Intensity

Because students spend so much time working with people in their schools, they also tend to socialize primarily with students in their fields. Each school definitely has a stereotype, and there isn't much mixing between them. Also, with only about 700 undergrads, NCSA is "*very* small," adding to the competition within the schools, which one dance student described as "pretty intense. Even if you're all friends, in the arts, you have to compete for parts, and in the end, for a job." Despite the competition, students are impressed with their classmates. "There's so much talent here, it's amazing," said a second-year student. "I never expected it." One student added, "everyone has the notion that people here are super-artsy fartsy . . . and they are. But it's not a bad thing. There are so many different types of people here, and it's OK to be different. That's the best thing about it." Students agree that the student body at NCSA is notably diverse.

Hot Student Bodies

The student body at NCSA is also above-average in terms of looks, partly because of the inherent attractiveness of dancers and actors. "Every single dancer is beautiful," said a ballerina, "and drama guys are hot." Even with the abundant hotties, one student admitted, "it's hard to date somebody and work with them, and also since it's such a small school, nobody wants to date. They'd rather be good friends." Another student said that despite the dating shortage, "there is probably more sex than usual here. There are also a lot of gay people. It's a very good environment for someone who's gay—kind of like a gay oasis in the middle of the city."

Students have mixed reactions to the younger faces that sometimes appear on campus, those of the seventh through 12th graders who attend NCSA high school. "They try to keep us as separate from them as possible, but generally people don't like it," said a dance student. Another student said, "at times it's pretty awful, but they're not allowed in our area at all. There are some benefits, like in our productions—there's a wider range of talent." A first-year drama student who happens to be dating a girl at the high school added, "at first I thought it was kind of stupid, but now I think it's all right."

The annoying high schoolers and the usually lifeless weekend scene are a small price to pay for the NCSA experience. As one actor put it, "my classes are really what's keeping me alive. They've given me a new respect for the art of acting, and this school has really improved me as a person. It's really exhilarating." Other students agree that the high level of professionalism and talent in this select community of dedicated artists makes NCSA as worthwhile as it is unique. *—Patricia Stringel*

FYI

If you come to NCSA, you'd better bring "a microwave, a fridge, and a blender."

What is the typical weekend schedule? "Practice, practice, practice."

If I could change one thing about NCSA, I'd "end the construction—there's always too much renovation going on."

The three things every student should do before graduating from NCSA are "go see other departments' performances, go to Beaux Arts, and have a beer at 1st Street Drafthouse."

North Carolina State University

Address: Box 7103; Raleigh, NC 27695
Phone: 919-515-2434
E-mail address: undergrad_admissions@ncsu.edu
Web site URL: www.ncsu.edu
Founded: 1887
Private or Public: public
Religious affiliation: none
Location: urban
Undergraduate enrollment: 22,780
Total enrollment: NA
Percent Male/Female: 58%/42%
Percent Minority: 18%
Percent African-American: 10%
Percent Asian: 5%
Percent Hispanic: 2%
Percent Native-American: 1%
Percent in-state/out of state: 93%/7%
Percent Pub HS: 90%
Number of Applicants: 12,133
Percent Accepted: 59%
Percent Accepted who enroll: 50%
Entering: 3,628
Transfers: 1,116
Application Deadline: 1 Feb
Mean SAT: NA
Mean ACT: NA
Middle 50% SAT range: V 530-630, M560-670
Middle 50% ACT range: 23-28
3 Most popular majors: engineering, business management, biology
Retention: 89%
Graduation rate: 64%
On-campus housing: 31%
Fraternities: 10%
Sororities: 9%
Library: 986,000 volumes
Tuition and Fees: $3,829 in; $15,113 out
Room and Board: $5,918
Financial aid, first-year: 39%
Varsity or Club Athletes: NA
Early Decision or Early Action Acceptance Rate: NA

If you're looking for science and technology, serious parties, and die-hard school spirit, North Carolina State University might just be the place for you. With almost 30,000 students, NC State also offers tons of different people, perspectives and opportunities. The campus is located next to downtown Raleigh, the capital of North Carolina. Both in-state and out-of-state students consider NC State to be quite a deal: the university is the largest research institution in North Carolina and fourth in the nation in attracting corporate research. And students are eager to point out that, in spite of its size, campus doesn't feel that big, and can be walked across in 15 minutes. Additionally, Raleigh offers an ample selection of museums and events, though most students stay close to campus to participate in the vibrant campus life.

"Not Just a Cow College"

Although originally an agricultural school, NC State students are quick to point out that their school is now best known as a technical school. The design, textiles, and engineering programs in particular are popular. In the words of one student "there's no question that there are a lot of engineers." This reputation has reached the point where students majoring in humanities complain that the humanities don't get as much funding—meaning that it can be harder to get into the popular non-science classes, which are "more fun." In general, registering for classes can be really frustrating because of the sheer numbers of students at NC State, but "it does all get worked out in the end."

Before freshman year students apply to the individual college within the university that contains their major. But if you really don't have a clue about what you want to do, don't worry—there's the First-Year College, which requires you to take specific classes and specialized tests designed to help you settle on the right major. Students suggest, though, that if you have any idea what you want to do, it's better to go ahead and try it out since each college has faculty advisors to help you plan your academic career.

Students generally don't talk about their grades, a fact that contributes to NC State's laid-back atmosphere. Some assignments are actually optional, which also helps perpetuate this attitude among students. Optional tests are to the advantage of self-motivated students, but help disguise how much work there can be.

Introductory classes are usually very large, but you can find yourself in smaller classes, as well. Despite the larger classes being taught by professors, there are many teaching assistants as well, some of whom don't speak English well. Not all of these professors are the most personable, but students do have the opportunity to talk to them, especially if they're willing to put forth some effort. Many of the majors, particularly the sciences, are demanding and leave little room in a student's schedule for exploration, sometimes only allowing one free course per semester outside of that major. Freshmen in particular have trouble getting into "fun classes" like Physical Education or Mythology.

Cheers, Beers, and Wolfpack Pride

School pride is without a doubt a fundamental part of the NC State experience. With a history of nationally successful varsity basketball and football teams, students flock to games. As expected, tailgates for home football games are a major event, with up to 55,000 fans barbecuing, drinking, and hanging out. At the games, which are "the most fun in the entire world," fans are clad in red (the school color), and are notably "obnoxious, loud, fun, and hilarious," particularly at games against rival UNC Chapel Hill. It isn't all about winning though; win or lose in the regularly sold out stadium, NC State fans go to celebrate and party, and they celebrate the losses just as loudly.

There aren't many school-wide, school-sponsored social events other than athletic exhibitions at NC State. As one student put it "the administration assumes we can find ways to entertain ourselves." NC State students seem more than up to the challenge, hosting their own cultural and social events "all the time." There is a movie theater on campus, and you can go to a play or concert every other night if you want to. The administration even provides free tickets to students in the Honors or Scholars program. While there is no drinking at school-sponsored events, students definitely party hard every weekend. Typically people party off campus in friends' apartments, and students report that practically everyone drinks underage. One girl commented that "I think there are people who don't drink, but I don't pay attention." NC State has its fair share of frats and sororities, but students don't feel pressured to be involved with them. One girl in a sorority noted that Greek life "can still be interesting even if you don't drink."

(A Few) Girls Gone Wild

While NC State's guy to girl ratio has been dropping, you "can still definitely notice that there are more guys." Unfortunately for wannabe Don Juan's, this gives girls the advantage. However, don't let this hinder your plans for romance; tons of students are dating, and there is plenty of hooking up. There is a very active Gay, Lesbian, Bisexual, and Allies association, probably because campus is not a particularly accepting place. "It would be a rough place to be gay," one student reported. With more than 90 percent of students from in-state, you might expect the student body to be homogenous, but there are also students from all 50 states and 100 countries. While NC State has the demographics of a culturally diverse environment, some students complain that their school isn't very socially integrated. At the same time, one out-of-state student said he had expected more racism, but has found it to be a non-issue. While most students are physically active, making good use of the gym, one girl admitted, "You might find some beer guts" due to the hard partying.

"The administration assumes we can find ways to entertain ourselves."

NC State has an enormous variety of extracurricular clubs for students, ranging from political groups to club sports to community service groups. For example, the school has an enormous Habitat for Humanity chapter that meets each weekend and builds its own house every year. Religion also tends to be a "big force" at NC State: Campus Crusade for Christ is one of the largest student organizations. "But it is OK not to be religious," one student is quick to mention. Club sports are really competitive, often with serious tryouts, and if you just want to enjoy a casual game, intramural athletics is the place for you. Ultimate Frisbee and touch football are two of the more popular intramural sports. NC State also has a really popular outdoor adventures program through which you can learn how to rock climb, hike, or backpack. Not everyone at NC State cares about extracurricular activities, but those that do tend to pick one or two and get involved pretty seriously.

Sick of Brick

Campus architecture is dominated by red brick; the buildings and walkways are all brick and there is even a large open area called "The Brick Yard." One student jokingly insisted that the university receives a donation of brick every year and is obligated to use it. Just because campus looks like a brick factory doesn't mean it is ugly. On nice days, people flock to the open areas to sunbathe and play Frisbee. On the flip side, students warn that the brick walkways flood and overflow when it rains, so invest in a good pair of galoshes! Probably the most unique building on campus is Harrellson Hall, a round concrete building. Students report being surprised when they went to their first class because all the classrooms are shaped like pie slices, "mak[ing] the blackboards really weird."

Most freshmen live on campus in a variety of different styled dorms. There are freshman-only, single-sex dorms, and suites or halls. The administration does a pretty good job pairing up roommates, but for those who really don't get along, it's not that difficult to change housing.

One thing that students living in dorms praise is the chance to meet many new people and sleep more because they're closer to class. The dorms are grouped into three campuses: East, West and Central. West Campus is the most popular, probably because it houses several special academic programs such as the Honors Program, University Scholars, and the First-Year College. One dorm, Alexander, has a system where every American student is paired with an international roommate.

Most upperclassmen, however, live off campus in apartment complexes and houses. The school provides transportation between apartments and school (known by many as "the drunk bus"). Lots of students have cars and consider them important for their social life, since public transportation in Raleigh is a "joke." Students living off campus don't usually buy meal plans but instead cook at home or eat at the many nearby restaurants and cafes. Hillsborough Street, which runs through campus, is a favorite strip of eating and watering holes.

With one dining hall on each side of campus, students get tired of eating the same food. An on-campus food court with fast-food chains like Chick-fil-A and Taco Bell helps to break the monotony. Dining halls are not very social, but more like places to take care of business; students say they "get by" on the food there. If you want to watch sports with your meal, the Wolves Den is the place to go—a student center where you might also go for a club meeting. Campus is very casual, including classes, and many students seem to be comfortable showing up in sweatpants and old T-shirts.

Although it has strong roots in agriculture, NC State is not just a "cow college" (although it does have a large share of good ol' country boys). Among the huge student population is every type of person imaginable. With a lively social scene and countless activities available, you won't have trouble keeping yourself busy. And on top of that, one student reported, "I feel like I'll have a really strong background to do whatever I want when I graduate." —*Alistair Anagnostou*

FYI

If you come to NC State, you'd better bring "red clothes and a Frisbee."

What is the typical weekend schedule? "Take a nap and party with friends Friday night; go to a sports event Saturday; party again Saturday night; and then catch up on work Sunday after sleeping in or going to church."

If I could change one thing about NC State, I'd "add a lot more parking."

Three things every student at NC State should do before graduating are "attend every football tailgate in a season, work for Habitat for Humanity, and drink a pint in Mitch's Tavern on Hillsborough Street."

University of North Carolina / Chapel Hill

Address: Campus Box 2200, Jackson Hall; Chapel Hill, NC 27599
Phone: 919-966-3621
E-mail address: uadm@email.unc.edu
Web site URL: www.unc.edu
Founded: 1789
Private or Public: public
Religious affiliation: none
Location: suburban
Undergraduate enrollment: 15,961
Total enrollment: NA
Percent Male/Female: 40%/60%
Percent Minority: 20%
Percent African-American: 11%
Percent Asian: 6%
Percent Hispanic: 2%
Percent Native-American: 1%
Percent in-state/out of state: 82%/18%
Percent Pub HS: 18%
Number of Applicants: 17,141
Percent Accepted: 35%
Percent Accepted who enroll: 56%
Entering: 3,460
Transfers: 649
Application Deadline: 15 Jan
Mean SAT: NA
Mean ACT: NA
Middle 50% SAT range: V 580-680, M 600-690
Middle 50% ACT range: 24-30
3 Most popular majors: communication, social sciences, business management
Retention: 95%
Graduation rate: 80%
On-campus housing: 43%
Fraternities: 12%
Sororities: 12%
Library: 2,573,000 volumes
Tuition and Fees: $4,165 in; $16,606 out
Room and Board: $6,516
Financial aid, first-year: 31%
Varsity or Club Athletes: NA
Early Decision or Early Action Acceptance Rate: 41%

If you're looking for a school where there's tons of tradition, intelligent and fun-loving people, awesome athletics, and high-quality education, the University of North Carolina at Chapel Hill is the place for you. In the middle of a friendly town, and distinguished by "gorgeous grassy quads, oak trees, and red-brick buildings," UNC entices students to fall in love with its campus and easy-going atmosphere. Said one student: "It's something you have to come to Chapel Hill and experience–it brings a smile to your face!"

Learn it All

Students at UNC–Chapel Hill get a broad education, regardless of what they choose to major in. "I think it's wonderful to be able to learn about things outside your concentration," said one student, when asked about the General College Requirements. In the spirit of a liberal arts education, students have "perspectives" to fill from different disciplines (i.e. math, science, philosophy, art, etc.) during their freshman and sophomore years. "They're a great way to expose students to a broader range of knowledge," according to one business major. Students must then declare their majors by the end of their sophomore years. Business and all science majors are competitive at UNC. Psychology is also popular, Journalism and Business are known to have good departments, and Communication Studies has labeled an easy major by students.

Class sizes vary according to level and subject. An introductory biology or economics course might enroll as many as 400, while English, foreign language, and math classes will generally never have more than 30 students. Larger classes usually meet for weekly recitations in classes of 15 to 20 students. "Getting into a class has never been a problem for me. Any student who demonstrates genuine interest in the course should have no trouble getting into it."

Even though UNC students may seem to be all fun and games, you'd be surprised at the amount of studying they have to do. "The workload is pretty challenging and there's a lot of pressure to do well." But the key is to take on a manageable course load. Tar Heels learn to "break it up over the semester and keep their work balanced with play. People here work hard *and* play hard!"

Professors and TAs at UNC are "knowledgeable and interesting." One journalism major said, "I've had terrific professors and TAs during my time here." There seems to be a consensus among the students that if you seek the instructors out, they can be very resourceful. They're quite personable as well. Deb Aikat, professor of Electronic Information Sources "uses a digital camera to capture everyone's face at the beginning of the semester. From then on, he knows everyone's name." Another well-known professor at Chapel Hill is Chuck Stone in the journalism school. He was the first nationally syndicated black columnist and was also a White House correspondent for ABC News.

Grade inflation has been an issue of concern at UNC recently. Some students say "professors are generally reluctant to give out A's" while many professors claim that inflation definitely exists. Although some attribute the higher average GPAs to the rising quality of the entering classes, many professors think that it's no excuse and feel that they should raise the standards. However, many Tar Heels feel that any A's they get "are definitely well deserved."

As far as special academic programs, "there are tons!" The Honors Program, the Burch Fellows Program, and the numerous study abroad programs are just a few. The Burch Fellows Program sends students to do self-designed research around the world. Some fellows of the past have worked with "flying doctors" in Kenya, traveled to Northern Ireland to study conflict resolution, and worked at a camp for the deaf in Minnesota. "You can find so many different programs that provide the chance to study in a place you never dreamed of going to before at Chapel Hill."

It's Time to Get Your Groove On!

You'll never have a problem finding something to do at this school. Students, whether part of the Greek scene or not, "have a great social life." Although only 20 percent of the student body is Greek, they still have a visible presence on campus. Said one sorority sister: "I think it's partly because of the fact that Greeks are so active, involved, and inclusive of the rest of the campus." Indeed, non-Greeks say that they don't feel left out of the social scene: "I'm not Greek and my social life is perfectly fine," said one student. Drinking is just as common as at most other colleges, although there has been a recent move to reduce it. The ALE is a prominent force at UNC to enforce drinking rules and catch fake ID users. "If you're not 21, it's hard to get into most of the bars uptown, unless there are mixers or special 18 and up nights . . . but that's not really a big deal because the uptown scene is focused on upperclassmen anyway."

Students at Chapel Hill get dressed up for the annual fraternity and sorority formals. In addition, there are theme parties throughout the year like the 70s, 80s, toga, beach, and luau parties. And you can't forget the infamous Halloween bash all along Franklin Street. People come from all over the state for this happening party.

But parties aren't everything at Chapel Hill. Students will often just use the weekends to "hang out with friends, sleep, and catch up on work." As far as campus-wide organized activities go, you'll find movies at The Union, lots of lectures with the different organizations all over campus, and tons of bands playing at the local concert hall. Dating is a big part of UNC social life, but the 60 to 40 female to male ratio makes it an interesting challenge for the men. "Way too many gorgeous people around!" and "There are a lot of beautiful girls here," are just a couple of the comments students at UNC make about the attractiveness of the student body.

The Tar Heel

There seem to be mixed feelings about the diversity of the students at UNC-Chapel Hill. One student commented that "ethnically and personality-wise, the school is very diverse." Others think that the minority presence on campus is lacking. The school has been getting an increasing percentage of minority students each year, but some students also feel that "ethnic polarization exists." Since UNC is a state school, "so many people are all from the same geographical area . . . the South," commented one out-of-stater. With more than 80 percent of the undergraduate population from in-state, some out-of-state students say that it's hard to rush for the frats and sororities just because they "didn't have the connections the in-staters had."

The typical Tar Heel is "intelligent, involved, social, and incredibly friendly." Students come from both wealthy and middle-class homes and usually wear jeans and T-shirts to class. Most people participate in organized activities, with community service being one of the more popular extracurriculars.

"I love Carolina . . . the people, the atmosphere, the classes, Chapel Hill, just life in general!"

The Sports Authority

Sports are also a very important part of the Tar Heel life. "This is a sports-crazed school," said one student. With 75 percent of undergraduates participating in intramural sports, numerous club sports, and Division I varsity sports, UNC students are on the whole "very fit." Students are great about attending games and cheering their teams on, especially when they're playing archrival Duke. Men's basketball and Women's soccer are among the more popular teams at UNC, with basketball consistently among the top ten and soccer winning the national championship recently. After basketball victories, the tradition is to have "huge, raging bonfire parties on Franklin Street." Sports at this school aren't just for the jocks, however. The gym facilities include tennis courts, swimming pools, and golf courses, and are available for even the non-athletes who just want to stay fit and have some fun.

Living at Chapel Hill

Most students at Chapel Hill feel safe on campus. "Usually the only crime we have is theft that occurs when students don't lock their dorm doors," said one student. Tar Heels love the gorgeous homes, inviting streets, and friendly neighborhoods surrounding the campus. Movie theaters, restaurants, and shops draw students to Franklin Street. Some popular local restaurants are Cosmic Cantina, Hector's, Time Out Chicken, and Pepper's Pizza. As far as on-campus dining, students seem to be pretty satisfied with its services. Freshmen are not required to have a plan, but most do since eating in the dining halls is a good way to socialize with others. Students are "OK" with the system and say that the dining halls are clean, although some "wish that they were open later."

UNC has a North, Middle, and South campus. South campus is relatively isolated, but since it's home to almost 50 percent of the on-campus residents, "it's a great setting to meet other people." North and Middle campus predominantly house upperclassmen, transfers, and graduate students. Freshman suites are "pretty small, but adequate." RAs watch out for all of the freshmen, and "it really depends on who you get, but for the most part they're pretty cool." Some students live on co-ed floors, and undergrads can also choose to live in one of the Theme Houses, such as the Spanish House or the Women's Issues House. Many upperclassmen move off campus after their sophomore years, but "it's not abnormal to stay on campus all four years." Off-campus housing is "affordable and within walking distance," said one student. But regardless of where you live, there's a "real sense of community here at Chapel Hill."

Sweet Carolina

As the first state university in the U.S., UNC–Chapel Hill has many traditions. One student recounted the myth about "The Old Well," which stands in the heart of the campus. "It's said that drinking out of The Old Well on the first day of classes will earn you all A's." Another landmark at Chapel Hill is the tree called "Davie Poplar." Students say that the tree has been around almost as long as the University and "as long as this tree stands, so shall the University!" Having been struck by lightning, today it is held up by a rod. "And just in case it does come down, there is always Davie Poplar, Jr. and Davie Poplar, III!"

Many students at UNC say they "wouldn't trade going to UNC for anything." With never-ending parties, hardcore academics, some of the best athletes in the nation, and the "friendly Carolina smile," Chapel Hill students know how to balance their fun with work. "There is no place I would rather be than here," said one enthusiastic Tar Heel. "I love Carolina . . . the people, the atmosphere, the classes, Chapel Hill, just life in general!" —*Jane Pak*

FYI

If you come to UNC, you'd better bring "lots of ramen noodles and a computer."

What is the typical weekend schedule? "Party all weekend long, with short breaks for sleeping and doing homework."

If I could change one thing about UNC, I'd "change the honor code. It's very oppressive and limits the enjoyment of students."

The three things every student should do before graduating from UNC-Chapel Hill are "go to the UNC-Duke basketball game, spend Halloween on Franklin Street (the wildest party in the state!), and climb the Morehead-Patterson Bell Tower during your senior year."

Wake Forest University

Address: Winston-Salem, NC 27109
Phone: 336-758-5201
E-mail address: NA
Web site URL: www.wfu.edu
Founded: 1834
Private or Public: private
Religious affiliation: none
Location: suburban
Undergraduate enrollment: 4,045
Total enrollment: NA
Percent Male/Female: 48%/52%
Percent Minority: 11%
Percent African-American: 7%
Percent Asian: 3%
Percent Hispanic: 1%
Percent Native-American: 0%
Percent in-state/out of state: 29%/71%
Percent Pub HS: 63%
Number of Applicants: 5,995
Percent Accepted: 41%
Percent Accepted who enroll: 41%
Entering: 1,007
Transfers: 50
Application Deadline: 15 Jan
Mean SAT: NA
Mean ACT: NA
Middle 50% SAT range: V 600-680, M 620-710
Middle 50% ACT range: NA
3 Most popular majors: business, communication, psychology
Retention: 93%
Graduation rate: 87%
On-campus housing: 75%
Fraternities: 37%
Sororities: 50%
Library: 1,734,000 volumes
Tuition and Fees: $26,490
Room and Board: $7,600
Financial aid, first-year: 38%
Varsity or Club Athletes: NA
Early Decision or Early Action Acceptance Rate: 55%

Buried away in North Carolina with the likes of UNC-Chapel Hill and Duke is another, smaller university that prides itself on both academic and social intimacy. With an undergraduate population of about four thousand, students at Wake Forest University feel that they receive a level of personal attention missing at their larger counterparts. Rallying behind their nationally renowned basketball team, Wake Forest students, despite their small numbers, make a lot of noise and are known to be one of the most spirited student bodies around.

Get Ready to Work

Wake Forest's small size provides its students with wonderful perks. Class sizes typically range from 20 to 40 students, and even the largest introductory lectures rarely enroll more than one hundred people. These small classes allow professors to develop personal relationships with their students, and students love the attention. This is not hard to believe considering these small classes have been taught by professors such as Maya Angelou. Teaching assistants instruct very few classes, and teaching seems to be the main priority among all of the professors. One enthusiastic freshman exclaimed, "the teachers here are awesome, and I feel like I've really connected with a lot of them." When the weather is nice, as it often seems to be in North Carolina, many professors opt to get out of the classroom and hold class outside on the grass of what has been called, "a nice and landscaped, green campus."

To enjoy the benefits of having such intimate classes taught by wonderful professors, Wake Forest students put forth a lot of effort to be prepared for class. Professors usually know their students personally, and demand a lot of them. Participation is a must, and as one frustrated student said, "you just can't get away with stuff like not doing the reading, because of the small classes." However, Wake Forest students agree that they'd much rather get to know their professors than hide away in a large lecture hall. Moreover, many students say that if you want to avoid Wake's academic rigor, you should major in either politics or economics. You can also take off from Wake Forest for a term and participate in one of their many abroad programs in London, Tokyo, Venice, or Vienna. Conversely, students warn that to major in philosophy, chemistry, or biology is to "move your dorm room to the library."

The only real complaint that Wake Forest students have about academics pertains to course requirements. Students have to take three classes in each of the following four areas: literature and arts; natural sciences, and math; history, philosophy, and religion; and social and behavioral sciences. Freshmen must also take first-year seminar courses, but have a variety of topics from which to choose. While the Wake Forest curriculum does ensure a liberal arts education, some students find these requirements to be excessive. One freshman feared that she would "be filling divisionals even after sophomore year." However, in general, students are in love with academic life at Wake Forest and revel in developing relationships with devoted professors who are experts in their fields.

Thank You, Sir. May I Have Another?

The social scene at Wake Forest revolves around the Greek system. As one sorority sister exclaimed, "Greek life is simply huge." Another student remarked that "athletes don't pledge, but pretty much everyone else does." In actuality, 50 percent of the student body pledge either to a fraternity or a sorority, and an estimated 85 percent at least rush one of the organizations. Interestingly, fraternities at Wake Forest do not actually have houses. Instead, they have what are called "lounges," or halls located in the basement of the dormitories. Weekends usually consist of what are called "hall crawls," where groups of friends go drinking and partying from one fraternity lounge to another.

"This is a work-hard, play-hard type of place."

Students feel that if you do pledge a sorority or fraternity, it is tough to avoid alcohol. One pledge stated, "Drinking is just a big aspect of Greek life." It is because of this drinking, one female noted, that "Wake Forest is not so much of a dating school as it is a drunken hook-up school." However, the university does have a "kind of tight" alcohol policy which students say resulted from a drunk driving accident. If caught drinking underage, students can be fined, and repeat offenders can be kicked off campus. Yet, students feel it is very difficult to get in this kind of trouble, as the majority of resident advisors "don't typically care about drinking." Others note that there are many social alternatives to Greek life. Intramural sports and community service groups occupy a lot of students' time, and although many say the city of Winston-Salem is not too exciting, it hosts many popular restaurants. Furthermore, concerts, comedy shows, and plays are constantly being shown on the campus itself.

Surprisingly, for a school that is so academically demanding, many students often begin to "go out" on Wednesday nights. Yet students do not spend much time recuperating from "hall crawling," as they are up early studying the next morning. As one student said simply, "This is a work-hard, play-hard type of place."

Good Southern Living

The majority of students are pleased with their style of life at Wake Forest. Freshmen rooms are described as "tiny, but big enough" and are scattered among the on-campus dorms. Many sophomores remain on campus, but make an effort to live in the dorm of their particular fraternity lounge. Students are very enthusiastic about dorm life and say "it creates great friendships."

Juniors and seniors are more likely to live off campus in one of the many condominium complexes that surround the university, or in one of Wake Forest's theme houses. However, the majority of students are so content with campus housing they live there for all four years. Adding to this happiness is the fact that students are allowed cars for all four years, and while many do have automobiles, others note that it is easy to get by without one. Furthermore, campus athletic facilities are all top of the line, and the new Benson Center provides a great place for students to hang out.

The food at Wake Forest is considered good, but students do complain about the lack of variety in dining. Unfortunately, just as the food at Wake Forest lacks assortment, so does its student body. While students do not tend to form cliques or self-segregate, diversity is an issue on campus. One freshman characterized the majority of her student body as being "preppy, white, and Republican." The university does recognize this as one of its faults and is making concerted efforts to attract minority students. In the meantime, however, Wake retains what one student called "a 'WASPy' reputation."

The Spirit of the Demon Deacons

Perhaps the most exciting time of the year at Wake Forest is basketball season. Known as the Demon Deacons, the Wake Forest basketball team is consistently ranked in the top twenty-five in the nation and can boast of NBA star and alumni Tim Duncan. Such a high level of competition brings the students out to cheer on their Deacons in mass. One avid fan said, "Hoops is just awesome and everyone has extreme team spirit." After victories, students run back to their campus and do what they call "rolling the quad." This consists of covering Wake Forest's absolutely gorgeous campus with rolls of toilet paper. However, even when the basketball team is not in season, Wake Forest provides constant excitement for its students, and its high academic standards make it one of the best universities in the country. —*Jonathan Levy*

FYI

If you come to Wake Forest, you'd better bring "a work-hard, play-hard attitude."

What is the typical weekend schedule? "The weekend starts on Wednesday night here. People go Hall crawling from lounge to lounge for the frat parties, but during the day, you'll find people studying like crazy."

If I could change one thing about Wake Forest, I would "move it to a more exciting city. Winston-Salem is boring."

The three best things about attending Wake Forest are "home basketball games, the small class sizes, and Hall Crawling."

North Dakota

University of North Dakota

Address: Enrollment Services, Box 813; Grand Forks, ND 58202
Phone: 701-777-4463
E-mail address: enrolser@sage.und.nodak.edu
Web site URL: www.und.edu
Founded: 1883
Private or Public: public
Religious affiliation: none
Location: small city
Undergraduate enrollment: 10,277
Total enrollment: NA
Percent Male/Female: 52%/48%
Percent Minority: 6%
Percent African-American: 1%
Percent Asian: 1%
Percent Hispanic: 1%
Percent Native-American: 3%
Percent in-state/out of state: 58%/42%
Percent Pub HS: NA
Number of Applicants: 3,628
Percent Accepted: 72%
Percent Accepted who enroll: 77%
Entering: 2,020
Transfers: 920
Application Deadline: 1 July
Mean SAT: NA
Mean ACT: NA
Middle 50% SAT range: V 470-570, M 500-590
Middle 50% ACT range: 20-26
3 Most popular majors: education, aeronautics, nursing
Retention: 77%
Graduation rate: 49%
On-campus housing: 26%
Fraternities: 9%
Sororities: 9%
Library: 1,118,259 volumes
Tuition and Fees: $4,205 in; $9,878 out
Room and Board: $4,234
Financial aid, first-year: 47%
Varsity or Club Athletes: NA
Early Decision or Early Action Acceptance Rate: NA

Students at the University of North Dakota praise the varied offerings of their school, such as the strong aeronautics program, as well as praising the safe campus conditions. However, many complain about one item that even school officials would rather choose to ignore as they attempt to build a nationally diverse student body—harsh winter weather. Each year the winter months bring frigid temperatures and endless inches of snow to the UND campus. The school, according to one senior, has few underground tunnels to provide protection from the elements and only a limited number of "plug-ins" that students can use to prevent their cars from freezing in the parking lot.

Strong Technology Programs

Although UND offers a number of liberal arts majors and reputable pre-professional programs, the aeronautics and engineering departments are reportedly the most highly regarded and attract students from all over the country. One student said the nearby Center for Aerospace Science adds to the school's reputation and has helped make both aviation and aeronautical studies two of the most popular majors on campus. Other popular programs include communications, nursing, and physical therapy. All students must take courses in the humanities, social sciences, and natural sciences in order to fulfill general education requirements, which one engineering student said are "pretty easy" to fulfill.

Class size, as one student described, reaches nowhere near the size of other major state universities. Introductory courses in the sciences enroll about 150 students in each section while upper-level courses have fewer than 10 students. Consequently, few students find themselves shut out of a classroom: "I sometimes might not get the particular section and time period, but I've never not gotten into a class I wanted to take," one undergrad said. Students register over the phone in order of most credit hours and highest grade point average during days specifically assigned by the registrar's office. The same phone system also allows students to change classes and check their grades and financial aid status.

The size of the university allows for strong interaction between professors and students. "Most professors teach a lot, but they don't bog you down with so much work; they're more concerned with students learning," one junior said. Only professors teach actual classes, but TAs do lead lab recitations and review sections. Students interested in advanced work may qualify for the general honors program of the university or for more specific honors work often found within the major. UND also offers free tutoring in all subjects as well as free counseling through the student counseling center.

Comfortable Campus

After the spring thaw each year, the groundskeepers at UND are said to plant an "awesome amount of flowers," which gives the campus a very "green" feel during the warmer months. Self-contained and located at the edge of town, UND is a small campus and includes some newer facilities intermixed with the older buildings that are prevalent. "Some buildings are very old, but they're still very clean and comfortable, and the school has been upgrading classes with multimedia equipment," one junior said. The Chester Fritz Library provides an adequate collection of publications, but one student described the online system as "hard to use" and some of the material as "outdated for some subjects like engineering." The librarians, however, are "very helpful" in addressing student requests. Many students head to the library of their particular department for serious and uninterrupted study. Other study locations include the second floor of Memorial Union Student Center, the Burger King, and the study rooms located in each dormitory.

A large percentage of students at UND choose to live off campus; many students are "older and/or married people putting themselves through college." As such, the university offers on-campus single and married student apartments at "affordable" rates. Students can also choose to live in the regular dorms. Although only available to juniors and seniors, students consistently mention Swanson as the most popular and comfortable dorm. Swanson has a glass elevator, bathrooms in every room, and a system that allows residents to buzz in guests. Other students often choose to live in fraternity or sorority housing.

"A large percentage of students at UND choose to live off campus; many students are 'older and/or married people putting themselves through college.'"

Wilkerson Hall houses the main cafeteria, which provides a wide variety of entrees and a salad bar. Students opting to live in campus dorms must purchase a meal plan, which they can redeem at either Wilkerson or the dining hall in the student union building. The town of Grand Forks offers limited food options as well: the 42nd Street Eatery, a deli-style place with sandwiches and coffee, and Speedway, which has cheap entrees.

Limited Social Opportunities

The University Program Council works to provide quality social activities on campus, and sponsors performances at the Chester Fritz Auditorium by musicians such as country music entertainers Travis Tritt and Reba McEntire. Council members also sponsor movie nights and a coffee bar at the Memorial Student Center, which also includes several game and recreational rooms, the popular Burger King, and comfy chairs to "just hang out with friends." Limited social opportunities exist in Grand Forks (especially for those under 21), but many students of age frequent Bucks Down Under for cheap pitchers and the Antique bar. The university strictly enforces a "no alcohol" rule on campus, but fraternities may sponsor parties (since their houses are off campus) if they hire security guards to prevent underage drinking. As such, many students feel the party scene at UND lags behind those at other colleges and universities.

Most students at UND are either from Canada or the northern United States. One student felt the university does not take enough measures to ensure geographic and ethnic diversity on campus, and that "students are about as liberal as you can be in North Dakota, which doesn't say very much, and most aren't politically active." A recent controversy on campus involved Native American students, who protested the school's use of the "Fighting Sioux" as the UND mascot. Negotiations are still in progress to find an alternative symbol.

The Hyslop Sports Center attracts a number of students looking to unwind after a hard day of class, and includes everything from dance and aerobics classes to an indoor track, Olympic-size swimming pool, and modern exercise equipment. The Division I hockey team usually plays to sellout crowds, since students enjoy free admission to all games. Other successful teams include men's and women's swimming and basketball, which attract the most spectators when facing rivals North Dakota State University or the University of Minnesota at Minneapolis. A large group of students also participates in intramural sports, such as tennis, soccer, basketball, and volleyball.

Other popular pastimes include writing for the *Dakota Student*, which is a biweekly campus newspaper with a weekly arts and entertainment section. Others participate in the student government or the University Program Council, which plans entertainment and social activities for students. The highest student involvement, however, reportedly occurs in the various clubs associated with majors, such as the Engineer's Council, Psychology Club, or Medical School Club. In fact, there are so many extracurricular clubs and organizations that students say they often have trouble attracting enough members to sustain themselves.

UND provides a police force for the school, emergency phones, and an escort service, but the hometown atmosphere that characterizes the Grand Forks community causes few students to worry about issues of safety on campus. The close-knit feel, according to several students, is one of the most attractive qualities of UND. Despite the daunting North Dakota weather, students say the academic and social environment at UND more than compensate for the discomforting winter temperatures. —*Marti Page and Staff*

FYI

If you come to UND, you'd better bring "a car and some really warm clothes."
What is the typical weekend schedule? "Party, go to bars, and just hang out."
If I could change one thing about UND, I'd "give more funding to the arts department."
Three things that every student should do before graduating from UND are "visit Turtle River State Park, check out the Icelandic State Park, and go fishing in the Red River."

Ohio

Antioch College

Address: 795 Livermore Street; Yellow Spring, OH 45387
Phone: 937-767-6400
E-mail address: admissions@antiochcollege.edu
Web site URL: www.college.antioch.edu
Founded: 1852
Private or Public: private
Religious affiliation: none
Location: rural
Undergraduate enrollment: 715
Total enrollment: 715
Percent Male/Female: 52%/48%
Percent Minority: 13%
Percent African-American: 6%
Percent Asian: 1%
Percent Hispanic: 5%
Percent Native-American: 1%
Percent in-state/out of state: NA
Percent Pub HS: NA
Number of Applicants: 504
Percent Accepted: 75%
Percent Accepted who enroll: 41%
Entering: 157
Transfers: NA
Application Deadline: rolling
Mean SAT: NA
Mean ACT: NA
Middle 50% SAT range: NA
Middle 50% ACT range: NA
3 Most popular majors: political science, multi/interdisciplinary studies, communications
Retention: 77%
Graduation rate: 43%
On-campus housing: NA
Fraternities: NA
Sororities: NA
Library: 300,000 volumes
Tuition and Fees: $23,275
Room and Board: $5,664
Financial aid, first-year: 76%
Varsity or Club Athletes: NA
Early Decision or Early Action Acceptance Rate: NA

Antioch College is an anomaly in the middle of Ohio. This small school is known for rejecting mainstream America. Ironically, students experience life outside college for half their years with required off-campus academic programs called co-ops. The ambiguity resonates in its student body. Vaguely summed up by one student, "This place is not normal." Intrigued? Confused? Antioch students wouldn't have it any other way.

More than Just a Year-Round School

Perhaps one of the most unique aspects of Antioch College is its cooperative education programs, "co-ops," in which students leave campus to explore internships and employment—all for college credit. The co-op program is fully integrated into the basic academic schedule and requires students to take co-ops for two of the four terms (fall, winter, spring, and summer). Freshmen generally stay on campus for their first fall and winter and then participate in co-ops during alternating terms through the rest of their years. The college offers a special co-op office with advisors, ideas, information, and documentation of past co-op experiences to be utilized by students (most often by freshmen). After freshman year, students are allowed to design their own co-op experience and the chosen programs generally agree with the student's major but are not required to. Students are very enthusiastic about the co-op programs, saying that it gives them hands-on experience in fields that they are interested in. Past co-op experiences have included working for the circus, writing for major publications, filmmaking in New York City, Web site design, and domestic and international travel to name a few. Antioch requires that one co-op involve studying a culture other than one's own. The college is always there to support and help students design experiences, but many upperclassmen say that they don't really use the co-op office.

Are there downsides to this unique and interesting opportunity? Yes. It does require "going to school all-year round," a fact that many Antioch students admit can be a source of isolation from their friends both at home and at school. "It's hard to make relationships because people are always leaving," said one student, and the flux state of the campus can be felt on many different levels. Also, the co-op program can lead to new opportunities and experiences, or as one student said, "Someone could go off and do pottery in Vermont, and really find their niche, and then never come back"—a fact that perhaps contributes to Antioch's low retention rate. On campus, the academic departments are regarded as small and strong. General requirements involve a language and quantitative reasoning, both of which students are able to pass out of by taking placement exams. Academics at Antioch are said to be intense, a fact that should not be lost on those individuals drawn to the school by the absence of tests and grades. Instead of grades, students receive narrative evaluations from teachers, although grades can be provided on request (for students wishing to transfer, etc.) "The philosophy behind Antioch academics is that you learn it because you want to learn it," explained one student. However, stress levels are still said to be extremely high. Class size is small (generally 10–20 students) and the teachers are extremely talented. One student made sure to differentiate between the new teachers and Antioch's long-time professors, saying that new teachers often don't understand the philosophy behind Antioch's academics.

Old Facilities

The facilities at Antioch are generally regarded by students as being simply "old." Dorms are described as "run-down and shabby." But in typical Antioch fashion, the students would much rather speak about the communities of students within the dorms than the buildings themselves. Housing is characteristically lax, with a mix of all classes occupying most dorms and even floors. Floors are co-ed and some dorms even have co-ed "couple" rooms (though, there are also single-sex dorms and floors available). Housing, like the student population, is extremely flexible and there is no crowding for space. The dorms vary in respect to size and character: North houses mostly first-years, does not have Internet access, and was summed up by one student as "certainly not a palace." Many of the dorms do not have phone lines to individual rooms and instead the residents must share hall phones. There seems to be a dejected acceptance of the living conditions at Antioch, yet most students continue to live on campus for all four years.

Like the dorm buildings, many academic and administrative buildings on campus are also in need of renovation. The Olive Kettering Library boasts a large periodical collection and a "very helpful staff," yet many students complain that the library is in need of new resources. Above all, Antioch students are painfully aware of their school's difficult financial situation. When asked about the facilities, one student stated, "This school needs to be brought into the 21st century," and that "Antioch's biggest shortcoming is its constant need for a larger endowment." While the antiquated buildings may be frustrating for some, others enjoy the atmosphere and the activities that accompany the old campus. One student delightfully mentioned exploring the underground tunnel system as a "must-do activity" and also disclosed that many of the college and historic buildings of Yellow Springs (a nearby town) are haunted. The town of Yellow Springs, described by one student as "unlike anywhere else in Ohio," maintains a strong relationship with Antioch students. First-years are introduced to the town during their first week on campus by dining in the homes of the residents of Yellow Springs. While the local businesses are often viewed as "tourist traps," some inexpensive restaurants, such as Ha Ha's Pizza and Subway, offer a welcome haven to Antioch students fleeing from the unpleasant food in the college's cafeteria.

Ah, yes, "The Caf." Perhaps the only thing that Antioch students agree on is the poor quality of the food. Although there is plenty of choice in dining at Antioch: a meat, vegetarian, and vegan selection is available at every meal at the Cafmost students still cannot stomach it. Instead, snacking is popular at the student-run coffee shop (the C-shop); and for the most desperate, there are kitchens in some of the dorms around campus.

"Anything Goes Here"

If there is one thing that unites Antioch students, it is being different. "It's like the freaky school" one student explained. Indeed, the campus is alive with different groups supporting different causes such as SPROUTS, a student group which stands for "Supporting Plants Requires On Us Together and Separately"—an organization that seeks to gain rights for plants. The Community Government is a student organization that, in addition to organizing themed dances for every Friday and Saturday night, also has some say with the administration regarding hiring and firing of teachers and creation of policies. The dances are highly attended and alcohol is available. There are also many chem-free activities available for students who prefer not to drink—bonfires, weekly shows, and movies sponsored by various student groups are always going on somewhere on campus.

"This place is not normal."

There are no intercollegiate sports teams at Antioch. In fact, women's rugby is the only competing sport, though many club sports such as Ultimate Frisbee are popular. Students also take advantage of Glen Helen, a 1000-acre nature preserve that borders the campus, where many go hiking or biking during the weekends. Following that health-conscious trend, an important organization at Antioch is the student-run Wellness Center. It is dedicated to supporting the physical, emotional, and spiritual needs of Antioch students.

The gay and lesbian population at Antioch is extremely vocal, with its own center in the Student Union and its own social events. "If you are not bisexual at Antioch, you are in the minority," said one student. One girl said simply, "There is no gender here—you love who you love and no one bothers you." It is generally agreed that Antioch students are incredibly accepting of different lifestyles, all of which come to a head with the annual spring student-run "Gender Fuck" dance which requires attending naked or as the opposite sex. Cross-dressing is apparently a common occurrence at Antioch. "All parties guarantee at least five boys in drag, at least," said one first-year. Indeed, all forms of sexuality are openly discussed at Antioch, due in part to the controversial SOPP (Sexual Offense Protection Policy.) Though jokingly referred to as the "hooking up policy," students do abide by it. It requires verbal consent between two people before any sexual activity and serves to promote a dialogue between individuals on campus. "There's lots of sex, it's a big part of life here," explained one third-year.

There are also a lot of parties. Antioch students describe the typical weekend as starting on a Thursday night with organized parties on both Friday and Saturday nights. Alcohol is easy to come by and being underage doesn't seem to matter at Antioch. One student mentioned smoking pot and tripping in Glen Helen to be a favorite pastime of many students. Campus security is present yet relaxed, say most students. One student recounted a conversation with a security guard who explained, "I don't bust. It's paperwork, and I hate paperwork." For the most part, social life revolves around the campus due to the fact that Antioch students are "stuck in the middle of nowhere."

The typical Antioch student is hard to pinpoint because the students "are all about NOT being typical." Consider the much-loved student-run annual bike-race known as "Camelot" during which Antioch students collect and throw "all imaginable forms of human waste" at each other. Why? At Antioch, many things defy definitions and answers. Yet as many Antioch students will tell you, sometimes the questions are more important. —*Marisa Benoit*

FYI

If you come to Antioch, you'd better bring a "bike, a bong and lots of food because The Caf sucks."

What is the typical weekend schedule? "Thursday night: BYOB to hang out, Friday: party, Saturday: theme party, Sunday: catchup on work and sleep."

If I could change one thing about Antioch I'd "change the economic status—we need more money."

Three things every student at Antioch should do before graduating are "ride in Camelot, dress up as the opposite sex, and get a piercing."

Bowling Green State University

Address: 110 McFall Center; Bowling Green, OH 43403
Phone: 419-372-2086
E-mail address: admissions@bgnet.bgsu.edu
Web site URL: www.bgsu.edu/welcome
Founded: 1910
Private or Public: public
Religious affiliation: none
Location: rural
Undergraduate enrollment: 15,703
Total enrollment: NA
Percent Male/Female: 43%/57%
Percent Minority: 8%
Percent African-American: 5%
Percent Asian: 1%
Percent Hispanic: 2%
Percent Native-American: NA
Percent in-state/out of state: 93%/7%
Percent Pub HS: NA
Number of Applicants: 10,128
Percent Accepted: 91%
Percent Accepted who enroll: 39%
Entering: 3,605
Transfers: 702
Application Deadline: 15 July
Mean SAT: NA
Mean ACT: 21
Middle 50% SAT range: V 460-560, M 450-560
Middle 50% ACT range: 19-24
3 Most popular majors: education, speech, psychology
Retention: 77%
Graduation rate: 59%
On-campus housing: 44%
Fraternities: 8%
Sororities: 11%
Library: 2,416,000 volumes
Tuition and Fees: $7,086 in; $14,044 out
Room and Board: $5,996
Financial aid, first-year: 59%
Varsity or Club Athletes: NA
Early Decision or Early Action Acceptance Rate: NA

While for one weekend each year, it is the internationally revered home of the World Tractor Pulling Championships, the town of Bowling Green is perhaps best revealed through its offering of a solid and dynamic liberal arts education to the students of Bowling Green State University.

An Academic Myriad

With over 160 majors including everything from Glass, Popular Culture, and Fiber/Fabric to the more commonly seen Humanities, Arts, and Sciences, it is rare to find a student who cannot find a personal course of study at BGSU. While almost every academic program is regarded as strong and marketable, the most popular majors among undergraduates are biology, psychology, and the renown and competitive education program. Several options are available to fulfill each student's needs, including self-designed majors, double majoring, an honors program, and several pre-professional programs. Getting into classes is not typically regarded as a problem. One student noted that being shut out is particularly unlikely "if you get on waiting lists immediately and actually talk to people to get strings pulled." Another student liked the fact that he could easily take classes outside his major, such as dance and theater. Students generally praise most of their professors, even when they have problems communicating with them. "My English teacher barely speaks English," said one undergraduate. "We are always asking him to repeat what was said and say it slower, but he's a good sport about it." Another undergraduate was impressed by the fact that her professors "remembered [her] name, and who I was." Students noted several creative assignments, including everything from "stand in front of a mirror naked and watch yourself" to "just relax for the weekend."

The Living Experience

The rules at BGSU dictate that freshman and sophomores are required to either live on campus or with their parents, although the general consensus is that "everyone gets around them." Almost 60 percent of BGSU students live off campus, as apartments are widely available close to campus. Rent can be rather high, though students say the experience is worth it. For those students who live on campus, co-ed dorms of single and double rooms are the norm. However, special housing for honors students, musicians, and other special interest groups are available, as well as housing in any of the 35 fraternities and sororities. Every dorm has its definite set of rules, and while some halls strictly enforce these regulations, others barely acknowledge their presence. Each student living in a residence hall is required to purchase a meal plan (students in the Anderson or Bromfield halls are exempted) which can be used at any dining hall on campus, as well as at a local convenience store. But as one student observed, "A box of Lucky Charms costs over five bucks!" The Sundial has been noted as "the best place to eat, but it's mass chaos at mealtime."

Students tend to be pleased with the overall experience and appearance of campus. The trees and landscape are frequently praised, and while the weather is notorious for being bitter cold, students note that the fall and winter seasons enhance the natural beauty of the area. The student union, a main center of activity on campus, is being closed as a new, improved facility is to be opened soon that will accommodate the massive growth the school has experienced since the original building was built in 1958. An old cemetery marks the middle of campus, a landmark which most students find interesting and compelling. There is a myth regarding the ghost of a woman who haunts Hanna Hall, "Supposedly," one student reported, "the ghost must be invited to every theater production or something bad will happen during the play, so every year they personally invite her."

"Supposedly," one student reported, "the ghost must be invited to every theater production or something bad will happen during the play, so every year they personally invite her."

The town of Bowling Green integrates with parts of the university, and undergraduates say that the relations between the town and school are comfortable and friendly. Most students work, be it on or off campus, which when combined with the great number of commuters makes for definite frustration with the lack of space in the parking lots. One student noted that sometimes it takes him over half an hour to get to his car from his residence hall. Students who work exceptionally late hours can apply for special permits that allow them to park near their dorm. During the nighttime hours, some tend to be wary of the apparent lack of security and lighting while others commented that they did indeed feel safe on campus.

When Friday Comes

For BGSU students, weekends can mean almost anything: partying at a frat or private apartment, clubbing in either Bowling Green or nearby Toledo, working out at the gym (a greatly acclaimed facility) or playing intramurals, going to a football or hockey game, seeing a show, going home, taking a road trip, working, or most likely, a mixture of many of the above. While Bowling Green is a dry campus and the residential halls strictly enforce the rules, undergraduates observe that being underage isn't really a problem, with the help of a fake ID or an older friend.

The Greek system tends to be somewhat prominent, as one student noted, "God, if I see another toga I'll scream!" But, students repeat that it is definitely not an overpowering social force. Many students are involved in Bowling Green's 180 registered student organizations, which include everything from religious and cultural groups to honor societies, music groups, political and public speaking forums, and drama. Marching band and Greek activities are regarded as the most popular extracurriculars. BGSU actively recruits athletes, with football, basketball, and hockey as the most popular sports. "There is a good amount of school spirit, and it's nice to see it," one undergraduate noted. "However, it's not overdone." Most students attend the annual football game against rival school University of Toledo, where one student insists "You must get your picture taken with Freddy and Freida Falcon!"

When describing the student population, most regard their peers as laid back and typically friendly. "There is a stereotype of the khaki wearing prep here, but honestly, no one really cares," noted one undergraduate. Diversity is "present, but very minor," although multicultural organizations on campus thrive. Bowling Green is a high quality university with a great number of opportunities, be it academic, extracurricular, social, or just plain everyday living. "Our colors may be poop and orange," exclaimed one student, "but we're really cool, I promise!" —*Amanda Ambroza*

FYI

If you come to Bowling Green, you'd better bring "a thick jacket! It's freezing here in the winter!"

What is the typical weekend schedule? "People party at night, work out and study during the day, and some even venture off campus to go home or take road trips."

If I could change one thing about Bowling Green, I would "create more parking spaces."

Three things that every student should do before graduating from Bowling Green are "ride the elevators in University Hall and try to make it out alive, go to football and hockey games, and walk on the right side of the seal."

Case Western Reserve University

Address: 103 Tomlinson Hall, 10900 Euclid Avenue; Cleveland, OH 44106-7055
Phone: 216-368-4450
E-mail address: admission@po.cwru.edu
Web site URL: www.cwru.edu
Founded: 1826
Private or Public: private
Religious affiliation: none
Location: urban
Undergraduate enrollment: 3,457
Total enrollment: NA
Percent Male/Female: 60%/40%
Percent Minority: 21%
Percent African-American: 5%
Percent Asian: 14%
Percent Hispanic: 2%
Percent Native-American: 0%
Percent in-state/out of state: 60%/40%
Percent Pub HS: 70%
Number of Applicants: 4,428
Percent Accepted: 78%
Percent Accepted who enroll: 24%
Entering: 836
Transfers: 83
Application Deadline: 15 Jan
Mean SAT: NA
Mean ACT: NA
Middle 50% SAT range: V 590-710, M 630-730
Middle 50% ACT range: 26-31
3 Most popular majors: biology, psychology, business
Retention: 91%
Graduation rate: 76%
On-campus housing: 78%
Fraternities: 36%
Sororities: 15%
Library: NA
Tuition and Fees: $24,742
Room and Board: $7,260
Financial aid, first-year: 63%
Varsity or Club Athletes: 66%
Early Decision or Early Action Acceptance Rate: 86%

Case is a place that "makes you proud of being nerdy and allows you to explore interests you never knew you had." It is a small community of some of the most hardworking students in America, who play just as hard. It is in many ways "your traditional geeky tech school." Yet, nestled near America's Rock and Roll Hall of Fame, Case has a dynamic character that distinguishes it from its other "geeky tech" counterparts.

Sleep? What's That?

Prospective students, be warned: "This just isn't a place for people who are looking for a constant party." *Forbes* rated Case as having the second-hardest workload of any school, surpassed only by famously workaholic M.I.T., and this rating was validated by the students as "absolutely true." If you're interested in Case, be prepared for four rigorous years, filled with many late-night study sessions and serious cramming. One student claims that 3 A.M. is the earliest he ever goes to bed. This is most often true in the engineering and hard-science majors.

Engineers, premed students, and hard-science majors constitute a whopping 66 percent of the undergraduates at Case. Nurses and small pockets of arts and humanities majors make up the rest of the 3500 undergraduates. Engineers are expected to fulfill many requirements, including as many as ten specific classes, such as thermodynamics, which is "worthless, if you're a civil engineer." Some students feel that there are too many requirements for certain engineering majors. The arts and humanities departments are reportedly much more liberal in terms of requirements.

Although the students are of high caliber and are very hardworking, they do not report feelings of competition among themselves. "Everyone's competing to do well, but you don't get the sense that people are out to do better than everyone else," says one student.

Students at Case are generally happy, but "it's also pretty common to hear people complaining," frequently about the workload. "This isn't a school where you'd be able to find a scene if you wanted to go out on a Tuesday night, and not that most of our students want to, but not having the option to makes people a little cranky at times."

Teachers at Case received mixed reviews from "great" and "accessible" to "never available" and "too into their research." One student claims that he "never had a bad teacher," while another says that he's "had some good ones and some arrogant ones." One student says that "the freshmen teachers are phenomenal, very energetic and very accessible." No other teacher embodies this description more than the extraordinary Dr. Ignacio Ocasio, better known as Doc Oc, who teaches intro chemistry. He has the entire freshman class send in pictures of themselves upon acceptance to the school and puts them on his screen saver along with their names. "Before we even get to campus, regardless of whether or not you're in his class first semester, he knows your name." Besides trying to know each of his 350 students, he draws on technological resources to be accessible and helpful to all his students, like having his lectures videotaped and available on the Internet, along with snapshots of the chalkboard to capture class notes. Although Doc Oc is an extraordinary rarity, at Case approachability and helpfulness are traits particularly found in the first-year lecture halls. However, one junior notes, "As you get into higher level courses, there seems to be a lack of personality." Still, "The teachers are very helpful, if you seek them out yourselves," and at Case there does not seem to be any prevalence of foreign professors who do not speak English well, with the exception of some Physics TAs.

Interested in the Greek Scene?

Beyond classes and long hours of grueling studying, there indeed lies a vibrant social scene, which revolves largely around the fraternities and sororities. Beware, however, if frat parties and Greek letters don't get you enthused, you might feel a bit left out. Although "Greeks" constitute only 30 percent of the student body, "Greek life severely dominates the social scene on campus, even though the number [of participants] is relatively low." One of the biggest events on campus is Greek Week, which is described as "an intra-brotherhood bonding experience, which promotes a competitive atmosphere between different Greek houses." The week-long event is filled with many lighthearted activities, such as a human pyramid, egg toss, can castle for charity, an obstacle course, and the biggest event of all, the rope pull, which is played with trenches and a human weight limit of 1700 lbs. There are many different fraternities, each with different personalities, and "people end up generally where they fit best." For instance, Phi Delta and Sigma Alpha Epsilon are known to have predominantly athletes, while Zeta Psi and Sigma Nu have more of the "involved and fun guys." Different sororities have their own stereotypes as well, but many find that "while the stereotypes exist for a reason, they aren't always true." The Greek parties, which are pretty much the dominating parties, seem to be a good time, until they get busted. "Most houses get in trouble for stupid things." Greek house parties are not permitted to have kegs or hard alcohol, but it is reportedly still relatively easy to find alcohol, especially if you know a fraternity brother.

"[Case] makes you proud of being nerdy and allows you to explore interests you never knew you had."

With the exception of Homecoming games or any match against Carnegie Mellon, the Spartans teams generally do not draw a huge crowd. Some of the highly ranked women's teams like swimming and soccer seem a bit more popular, but typically the sports teams receive little attendance to their games. On the other hand, intramural sports are hugely popular with 75 percent of undergraduates participating at one time or another, the most popular sports being soccer, flag football, basketball, and softball.

For off-campus entertainment, Case is fortunately located on University Circle, a one-mile-square area that offers students a multitude of cultural opportunities at incredibly low prices ($10 tickets to plays). Although Cleveland as a whole is not as exciting as one might expect, between downtown and University Circle is a vibrant area that is very accessible and cordial towards students. During the whole first week of school, there is a big street carnival for the feast of the Assumption. In addition, one can visit the Cleveland Museum of Art, admire the city's botanical gardens, watch a performance in Cleveland's impressive theater district, or listen to the famous Cleveland Orchestra in Severance Hall. Then one can head down to Little Italy for dinner and late-night doughnuts. Beyond the downtown area, however, is "fairly ghetto" and not particularly receptive towards students.

The Dating Scene: The Good, the Bad, and the Geeky

With the female-to-male ratio hovering at around 40:60, one would think that the Case women have somewhat of an advantage in the dating scene. However, considering that "a large portion of the guys are already in serious relationships with their video game consoles," the number of eligible men and women are much more even than expected, or perhaps disadvantaging to the females. "We lost tons of men to video and computer games," says one female student.

The dating scene at Case seems to favor more serious dating and long-term relationships rather than random hook-ups. "The 'hey, I met someone cute last night' scenario just doesn't come up very often," says one junior, with the exception of some freshmen girls being pursued by single upperclassmen. All in all, the dating pool is very limited. Case is a small enough community in which one would be familiar with all the eligible men and women in very short time. Have no fear, though. The dating scene does serve its purpose. One upperclassman says that she knows of four girls already engaged, and over half of her friends are in serious relationships. "People usually complain about how awful the dating scene is, but when they finally land a relationship, they're the kind that last."

Living at Case

Students are required to live on campus all four years. Freshmen primarily live in doubles or sometimes singles on single-sex floors on the north side of campus. The rooms run a bit small, "but hey, they're dorm rooms." Sophomores then move onto either fraternity or sorority houses, or into suites on co-ed floors on the south side of campus with the rest of the non-Greek student body. Suites have six 8' by 10' bedrooms, a common room, and bathroom, all of which are not particularly roomy. South-side dorms are seen as "severely lacking, both in residence life and general facilities." An ongoing project to replace the south-side dorms with a brand-new residence village will be completed in 2005.

A huge plus about living at Case is that it caters to each student's personal needs. There are many living arrangements available including priority housing for gay students and married couples. As for dining at Case, it is "nothing to write home about, but enough variety to not make it mundane and horrible," serving your traditional non-spectacular, yet fulfilling college meals.

With top-notch academics, a thriving social scene and a plethora of extracurriculars to keep them busy, students agree there's never a dull moment at Case. If you're the "work hard, play hard, or even the party hard type," explained one student, "you can be sure you'll find your niche here." —*Margaret Scotti*

FYI

If you come to Case, you'd better bring a "computer—it's required."

What is the typical weekend schedule? "Friday, get drunk and party; Saturday, sleep late, attend a study session, then party at night; Sunday, go to review sessions, study, and do homework."

If I could change one thing about Case, it would be "the five months of snow."

Three things every student at Case should do before graduating are "explore University Circle, participate in Greek Week, and attend the Brain Bowl, Case vs. Carnegie Mellon."

College of Wooster

Address: Galpin Hall; Wooster, OH 44691
Phone: 800-877-9905
E-mail address: admissions@acs.wooster.edu
Web site URL: www.wooster.edu
Founded: 1866
Private or Public: private
Religious affiliation: Presbyterian
Location: small city
Undergraduate enrollment: 1,856
Total enrollment: 1,856
Percent Male/Female: 47%/53%
Percent Minority: 7%
Percent African-American: 5%
Percent Asian: 1%
Percent Hispanic: 1%
Percent Native-American: 0%
Percent in-state/out of state: 56%/44%
Percent Pub HS: 73%
Number of Applicants: 2,392
Percent Accepted: 72%
Percent Accepted who enroll: 30%
Entering: 517
Transfers: 16
Application Deadline: 15 Feb
Mean SAT: NA
Mean ACT: NA
Middle 50% SAT range: V 550-650, M 550-650
Middle 50% ACT range: 23-29
3 Most popular majors: English, communications, history
Retention: 86%
Graduation rate: 65%
On-campus housing: 97%
Fraternities: 7%
Sororities: 8%
Library: 581,000 volumes
Tuition and Fees: $25,040
Room and Board: $6,260
Financial aid, first-year: 65%
Varsity or Club Athletes: 35%
Early Decision or Early Action Acceptance Rate: 84%

"The best kept secret in America." That's how many College of Wooster students describe their school. A small liberal arts school of almost 2,000 students nestled in a rural northern-Ohio town outside of Cleveland, the College of Wooster is proud of its academics, Scottish heritage, and "Pipe Band," though many students feel the college does not receive the attention and respect it deserves.

A+ Academics

The College of Wooster is extremely proud of its capstone program called independent study (IS). All juniors and seniors are required to complete this requirement within their major. During junior year, students devote one semester to IS, while all of senior year is spent researching, writing, and creating "the mini thesis." English, music, biology, and international relations all receive good reviews, while theater, philosophy, and communications are viewed as some of the slacker majors. Requirements for majors fluctuate between seven to 13 credits. Some have a required study abroad component—a popular option among students—which is usually fulfilled through a larger American university.

In addition, Wooster requires its students to complete a set of core requirements that are rather lengthy, but for which "there is plenty of choice, and you can finish by the end of first semester sophomore year." First-year students complete small writing-intensive seminars (FYS), which are taught by the students' academic advisors for the year. One student felt that a writing seminar is "great because it teaches you to think and write at the college level."

The harshest academic criticism is heaped on the registration process. Students are randomly given a number (in a lottery-style process) and according to the number, allowed into the registration building. "At this point, we run around like crazy signing up for classes. If a class is full, it's full, and you can't take it. Poli sci and religion classes are usually the first to go."

Once actually enrolled in classes, students cannot say enough about their professors and the academics. As one international relations major put it, "The professors are what make this school." Another student described professors as "very approachable and extremely willing to help. Without grad students at the college, professors can focus 100 percent on undergraduate teaching in small class settings. It's wonderful." The average class size is 15 to 20 students, while "large" classes tend to have no more than 30 to 35 students. Some classes have TAs, but they are not a large part of the academic structure at the College of Wooster. Students certainly must work hard, but "the work load is adequate; nothing more than you can't handle."

Where's the Town? Let's Climb the Chapel and Take a Look

The campus is described as pretty and fairly large for the size of the student body. One student summed it up: "the administration seems to love fresh brick." Others like the green and the tree-lined paths "of a picturesque college." One student was quick to point out McGaw Chapel as one of Wooster's most interesting buildings. McGaw Chapel, with a seating capacity of 1,600, is built partly underground and partly above ground; the construction was half-completed when bedrock was discovered, and construction could not be completed as planned. The "oddly shaped" building is loved by some and hated by others, but almost everyone admits that the views from its roof are worth a glimpse.

Dorms are considered "fairly nice" in general. Armington and Stevenson are both all-freshmen dorms, but students warn that rooms in those buildings "are like closets." Freshmen also have the option of living in all but four of the other dorms on campus. Many of these other dorms are program dorms, with some harder to get into than others. Examples of programs dorms include science and humanities, international, smoke-free, chemical-free, and quiet dorm. The recently renovated Kenarden Hall, which features beautiful interior and exterior architecture, and Luce Hall, the campus's newest residence hall, are both favorites of many upperclassmen. Besides having the option of entering the standard room draw or applying to one of the special program dorms, upperclassmen are able to apply to live in one of the small houses owned by the university. These houses also have program designations, such as Common Ground or Greenhouse, which are usually more specific than the program dorms. In general, most students live in doubles, with a few getting singles and even fewer sharing triples.

When asked about food, one student enthusiastically revealed, "It is good, surprisingly." There are two main dining halls on campus. Kitteredge is considered the "No-Fry Zone," while Lowry Hall has more of the traditional stations and staples, including pizza, burgers, and fries. Dining Halls are open from 7 A.M. to 7 P.M., though students would certainly welcome more options. To break the monotony, students often are forced to look elsewhere. Matsos, a Greek restaurant, is a favorite of students; it is recommended to save time for a talk with Spiro, the owner, because "he loves students." The Old Jaol and Woogle's are also popular spots.

Students, however, do feel the effects of Wooster's small-town character, and complain about the lack of off-campus eateries. As one student said, "Besides a couple of tattoo parlors downtown, the town is dead." Most everything also closes by 9 P.M., though one freshman said, "C.K. (Country Kitchen) is good for late-night snacks, though you have to watch out as to what you order sometimes."

Something for Everyone

What the rural town of Wooster lacks, students feel the campus makes up for socially. The Greek system exists, but many students feel that its influence represents only one segment of the school's population. Many of the most enjoyable parties are thrown in various rooms, houses, and dorms—being underage is not considered a major problem. One student, however, commented that "drinking is not as prevalent as I thought it would be. There are many non-drinkers, and there is no pressure at all." There are plenty of campus-wide activities ranging from parties such as the 70s / 80s Dance, Spring Fest, and 20s Prohibition Party, and for those who wish to volunteer and contribute to the community, blood drives and campus clean-ups.

Many students are also frequent visitors to Cleveland. Though parking can be a problem, cars remain the easiest and most accessible form of transportation.

"Almost everyone has at least one friend who has a car on campus, so it's not at all a problem," said one freshman.

There are many active organizations and groups on campus and virtually every student takes part in at least one extracurricular activity. Some of the campus's favorite groups include Amnesty International, Peace by Peace, College Republicans, The Volunteer Network, and the student newspaper, *The Voice.* Wooster's most famous and respected student group, however, remains "the Pipe Band." Representative of the school's proud Scottish tradition, the Pipe Band is a group of Bagpipe players who, clad in kilts and knee socks, can be seen playing at various functions and at random spots across campus. "They're very cool and so good. The campus can rally around them and is extremely proud," said one student. The band also plays during half-time at football games.

"The professors are what make this school."

Wooster's sports teams compete in Division III of the North Coast Athletic Conference. Athletics aren't a huge part of the Wooster experience, but football and baseball usually post winning records. The gym is well-frequented by students, and was recently renovated. Intramurals are also a big draw and favorite method of relaxation for many students.

"More Diversity, Please"

The biggest criticism of the College of Wooster is a lack of diversity in its student body. There are very few non-Caucasian students, and almost everyone hails from a similar background. As one student said candidly, "We have a whole lot of diversity among white people, but almost no diversity among ethnic or racial groups. This needs to change." While there are some international students, most students come from Ohio and the Northeast. Interestingly, however, in the midst of this lack of diversity, it is hard to describe a typical College of Wooster student. "Jocks, freaks and geeks, tree-huggers and nerds, you'll find them all here, and all are comfortable here," one student reported.

The College of Wooster is nestled in small-town USA and boasts a hard-working student body and an excellent teaching faculty. For small classes and individual attention, the College of Wooster is certainly recognized, but students warn "you have to be prepared to get to know the cows well." —*Nirupam Sinha*

FYI

If you come to the College of Wooster, you'd better bring "air freshener for the carpets in the dorms."

What is the typical weekend schedule? "Go to Common Grounds on Friday to hear music and drink coffee, sleep in on Saturday, do a little homework, watch movies at night, or hang out with friends; Sunday sleep even later, procrastinate some more, finally do more homework and try not to get depressed about going back to class on Monday."

If I could change one thing about the College of Wooster, I'd "bring more diversity to campus."

Three things every student at the College of Wooster should do before graduating are "eat at Matsos, fill up Kauke Arch with snow, and look at the stars from the golf course."

Denison University

Address: Box H; Granville, OH 43023
Phone: 740-587-6276
E-mail address: admissions@denison.edu
Web site URL: www.denison.edu
Founded: 1831
Private or Public: private
Religious affiliation: none
Location: suburban
Undergraduate enrollment: 2,096
Total enrollment: 2,096
Percent Male/Female: 43%/57%
Percent Minority: 9%
Percent African-American: 5%
Percent Asian: 2%
Percent Hispanic: 2%
Percent Native-American: 0.3%
Percent in-state/out of state: 45%/55%
Percent Pub HS: 70.5%
Number of Applicants: 3,289
Percent Accepted: 61%
Percent Accepted who enroll: 31%
Entering: 633
Transfers: 10
Application Deadline: 1 Feb
Mean SAT: NA
Mean ACT: NA
Middle 50% SAT range: V 550-650, M 560-670
Middle 50% ACT range: 24-29
3 Most popular majors: economics, communication, English
Retention: 86%
Graduation rate: 76%
On-campus housing: 98%
Fraternities: 28%
Sororities: 41%
Library: 728,000 volumes
Tuition and Fees: $25,760
Room and Board: $7,290
Financial aid, first-year: 50%
Varsity or Club Athletes: NA
Early Decision or Early Action Acceptance Rate: 70%

Located on a hill in the middle of Ohio, surrounded by hills and big trees, full of squirrels running about, harboring a bioreserve, Denison inspires descriptions of "peaceful" and "beautiful." Aside from their spectacular surroundings, Denison students describe a demanding courseload and a social life dominated by Greeks.

Broadening Horizons

Students say Denison offers a broad but comprehensive liberal arts education. The General Education Requirements (GER) include two years of a foreign language and distribution courses that span a range of categories including philosophy, math, and science. "The requirements can be a burden, especially if you want to have a double major," a student commented. Environmental studies, biochemistry, computer science, and biology are considered to be the hardest majors, while political science, music and economics are relatively easy. Still, many students find themselves overwhelmed with work, and don't report any lazy Sundays. Even though pre-professional students don't have their own majors, programs are offered to these students that include special advisors and related clubs. These include the pre-med, pre-vet and pre law clubs.

Students usually find it easy to get into classes, even though most classes are capped at 15 to 20 people, but "some studio art classes are hard to get in," one student complained.

Pleasing Professors

Students are pleased with their professors, noting that many of them are well-known in their fields: "The microbiology professor worked on the Viking program to determine if there was life on Mars." "I had a class of ten people and towards the middle of the semester, people stopped participating and the discussions weren't very good, so the professor had us over to his house for dinner and a "therapy session" so we could make the class better," recalled a student. Another said, "We had a medieval feast in my Anglo-Saxon English class. An English professor invited our class to his house for a movie and dinner." Students emphasize that professors try to make students think constantly and not memorize in "everywhere but the chemistry department." Also, the speakers that visit the school are enjoyed by many Denison students. Among recent visitors was scientist Keith Campbell, who cloned "Dolly" the sheep. TAs are useful for students in that "they add to professors' help but don't replace it." The biggest complaint about academics is that "grading is harsh."

Greeks and Their Beer

"If you are not obnoxious, then being underage is not a problem," commented one student. Upperclassmen parties are common, but not as popular as the fraternity and sorority parties that take place off campus. The two bars in Granville are also popular with upperclassmen. "D-Day (Derby days) is a great activity," students say, complimenting their drinking festival. At keg parties, everyone pays for a mug and is bussed out to a field where there are many kegs waiting for them. Drugs are not as common as drinks: "Marijuana is popular, but there are strict rules against it. Beer rules here." There are two formal parties per year which are the only occasions people get dressed up for, unless you are part of the Greek system. As for relationships, "There is a lot of sex, but homosexuals and interracial couples are frowned upon," says one student.

Besides Beer . . .

Non-drinkers, characterized as mostly "sports people," also find things to do. Other social activities on campus include lectures, movies, and dances. Students feel "you have to search out the fun activities but they do actually exist." Student organizations like the juggling club add color to the social life on campus. Community service is also very popular. Nevertheless, many find the life outside the university "dull." There aren't many options for dining or shopping in Granville. Pizza Hut and Taco Bell are the most common dining places to go to outside of the Denison meal plan, which students must purchase. "I would never recommend anyone attending Denison University unless you like to live in the same room eating the same horrible food for four straight years," one student said. The cafeterias are noted for their crowded lines although "the cafeteria people are some of the nicest people you have ever met." The limited public transportation to any nearby cities like Columbus makes cars a must for many.

Inn Denison?

The freshmen dorms aren't a big complaint at Denison; students note that "the nightmare starts later," when you realize that you are phased out of off-campus housing. Students feel stranded by these kind of restrictions: "Their reasoning is that they believe on-campus living is a significant determinant in having a fruitful Denison career while in reality it is to force all students into paying the school for residential expenses as well as the costly meal plan." Also, a housing lottery results in many juniors staying in freshmen dorms. Shorney is known as "the Ghetto" while the Sunset dorms are apartments, air-conditioned, and the biggest dorms on campus. Students believe that instead of building new dorms, the administration should allow more off-campus housing.

Wealthy and Homogeneous

Many complain of the cliques that form right away. However, "it's still true that a couple bottles of beer always open up the way for new friendships." The typical Denison student is characterized as rich and preppy. Abercrombie, J. Crew, and North Face are the uniforms of many. "Wealth is prevalent," is a common comment, and most of the students seem to have come from "wealthy east-coast boarding schools."

Abercrombie, J. Crew and North Face are the uniforms of many.

Students report geographic, but not ethnic, diversity. The student body is very athletic. Swimming and lacrosse recruit heavily while "football doesn't matter that much. The lacrosse team made the final four a couple years ago and men and women's swim teams are strong competitors for the national championships."

Enjoy the Peace

Despite the difficult class-work, students seem to be happy with their choice of college. With its peaceful campus and wild Greek parties, Denison is indeed a place to be enjoyed. —*Yakut Seyhanli*

FYI

If you come to Denison, you'd better bring "your J Crew gear."

What is the typical weekend schedule? "Students like to hang out with their friends drinking or just watching movies. Greek parties are big here on the weekends, too. But we all know that we can't put off our homework and just play on the weekends. There's way too much here to do that."

If I could change one thing about Denison, I would "make the grading easier."

Three things that every student should do before graduating from Denison are "walk up the hill from Mitchell center in the middle of winter, get lost in the library stacks, and do at least one May Term internship."

Kent State University

Address: PO Box 5190; Kent, OH 44242-0001
Phone: 330-672-2444
E-mail address: kentadm@admissions.kent.edu
Web site URL: www.kent.edu/admissions
Founded: 1910
Private or Public: public
Religious affiliation: none
Location: suburban
Undergraduate enrollment: 18,813
Total enrollment: NA
Percent Male/Female: 40%/60%
Percent Minority: 10%
Percent African-American: 8%
Percent Asian: 1%
Percent Hispanic: 1%
Percent Native-American: 0%
Percent in-state/out of state: 93%/7%
Percent Pub HS: NA
Number of Applicants: 10,056
Percent Accepted: 90%
Percent Accepted who enroll: 41%
Entering: 3,729
Transfers: 952
Application Deadline: NA
Mean SAT: NA
Mean ACT: NA
Middle 50% SAT range: V 450-570, M 460-570
Middle 50% ACT range: 19-24
3 Most popular majors: business marketing, education, health sciences
Retention: 72%
Graduation rate: 46%
On-campus housing: 33%
Fraternities: 4%
Sororities: 4%
Library: 1,120,369 volumes
Tuition and Fees: $6,374 in; $12,330 out
Room and Board: $5,570
Financial aid, first-year: 67%
Varsity or Club Athletes: 13%
Early Decision or Early Action Acceptance Rate: NA

Kent State University will live on forever as the site of intense Vietnam War protest, which exploded into the shooting of four students on May 4, 1970. Kent State, however, doesn't try to keep the event under wraps. In fact, the University just inaugurated a memorial for the four students. Additionally, students at Kent are able to study conflict management and dispute resolution. This non-traditional subject matter is representative of the various academic opportunities that surround the Golden Eagles.

Academics Abounds

Students at Kent State have a wide range from which to choose a course of study. Aside from a traditional College of Liberal Arts and Sciences, Kent State also hosts the College of Fine and Professional Arts, the School of Nursing, a College of Education, and a College of Business Administration, among others. The College of Education and the Fine Arts program are considered quite strong. Regardless of major, however, students are allowed to take classes in any of Kent's colleges. As part of the Kent experience, students are required to fulfill Liberal Education Requirements (LERs), which consist of courses from all fields, including humanities, fine arts, social sciences and basic sciences. Student opinion is split on these requirements. One sophomore said that "we have to take 39 LERs, which are supposed to make us well-rounded students, but that means I have to take a lot more of these annoying classes when I really would like to delve into my major." Another student, however, said that "they can be kinda fun and relatively easy, so I don't mind them too much." Students are cautious about the nursing and architecture programs, both of which have notorious reputations for being difficult.

For those who seek a greater academic challenge, there is an Honors College, which allows students to take more advanced classes as a freshman. One freshman said, "instead of having to go through basic English 1 and 2, I was able to jump right into a more in-depth literature class." Being part of the Honors program, as another student described, "affords more attention from the professors. You're not as anonymous." Freshmen in the Honors College get to take smaller classes, although class size does not appear to be a major problem at Kent. Most classes range from 25 to 30 students, while larger classes, as one senior said "rarely exceed 75 students or so." TAs are definitely present on campus, but rarely teach classes above the introductory level, particularly in the English, Foreign Language, and some science departments. The academic options at Kent are quite varied and as one student put it, "if you choose the right classes, academics are great. There are a lot of classes offered."

Where to Go for a Good Time

Kent not only offers plenty of classes, but there are many social options as well. Though many join fraternities, one junior explained that "life is still pretty balanced. There's no real pressure to go Greek." Aside from Greek life, the Student Center serves as a social center, housing a concert hall in the basement, pool tables, and plenty of restaurants. Additionally, as one student stated, "A lot of the student organizations are based there, so it can get really social." Various departments organize lectures open to students of any discipline and there is a pretty lively music scene. The University recently had George Clinton and the Psychedelic Funk play at its Homecoming. Students on campus find it quite easy to meet each other. As a freshman said, "this school is pretty large, which can be an adjustment for some people, but it's easy to meet people from all sorts of backgrounds." As for off-campus fun, there is a "big strip one block away with bars and restaurants," described one senior. There, students profit from the food at Ray's Place and the $3 pizzas at The Loft. On the weekends, students generally stay on campus, even if they are from nearby Cleveland.

Why Leave?

Students have good reason to stay on campus since it is, simply put, "very beautiful." The campus covers several blocks with "several hills, nice landscaping, and these wonderful trees that are naturally there. Front Campus is one the prettiest spots and is right by the fashion museum," described one freshman. The campus boasts a new wellness center, where students partake in aerobics, yoga, and various fitness classes. Students can get around campus very easily thanks to KSU Bus service, which one student called "a very intricate and efficient system." Safety on campus is a minor issue; students are quick to mention the security escort service, which students find particularly useful on late nights coming home from the library.

"If you choose the right classes, academics are great."

Coming home, however, does not necessarily mean returning to the lap of luxury. As one student described the dorms, "If you're in a double, it's pretty small; if you're in a single it's really, really small." Freshmen are not required to live on campus, although most do. Freshmen generally choose from Terrace Dorm, which is co-ed, or the single-sex dorms, Prentice and Dunbar, for women and men respectively. Students in the Honors College get to live in Honors Housing, which tends to be better. There are strict visitor policies; officials emphasize that visitors must be escorted at all times. Students who might not want to deal with these policies move off campus. There are many apartment complexes in the surrounding area, most of which are served directly by the Kent bus system, making them extremely convenient.

On-campus dining is described as "pretty good. We have a lot of options here." All students are given a Flash Card from the beginning, which then serves as a debit system for all the food establishments on campus, which includes a McDonald's and Friendly's in the Student Center. For those in search of a more fancy meal, Mario's is one of the few restaurants where students can sit down and be waited on. Kent State has not been described as terribly vegetarian friendly, but it has, according to students, improved its selection in recent years. While on campus students rarely go off campus to eat, one student cited The Pufferbelly as "very worth going to."

Socially Conscious Students

The Kent State student body is very involved in social causes, mostly through community service. The strong Greek system recently staged a Build-a-Playground Campaign, in which they went to a local elementary school and built a playground set in one day. The school also has a strong America Reads program. Students can find pretty much anything at Kent, ranging from the Christian Coalition to the Neo-Pagan Coalition, or the more prominent chapter of Amnesty International and the Lesbian, Gay, Bisexual Union. Students can get involved in physical activity either through personal workouts at the wellness center, or else join intramural and club teams, among which the Green Dragon Kung Fu Club is quite popular. Varsity sports do not play a central role in student life. As one student described it, "There is plenty of school spirit, although that doesn't mean our teams are that great. Our football team just won its first game and the season's almost over." Regardless, the male and female basketball teams are both well regarded, especially due to recent success in NCAA tournaments.

Kent State offers its students many academic and social opportunities. Furthermore, the school strongly emphasizes diversity and has been attempting to improve its racial diversity. The school also fosters many artistic endeavors. For example, a large community of published writers live and work at Kent, a situation which one student described as being "a great opportunity if students take the initiative to do something with it." Kent, while still greatly tied to its past history, has evolved since May 4, 1970, and maintains a very dynamic and socially minded student body. —*Shu-Ping Shen*

FYI

If you come to Kent State, you'd better bring "a phone—you'll use it a lot."

What is the typical weekend schedule? "Partying and catching up on the sleep lost during the week."

If I could change one thing about Kent State, I'd "upgrade the dining hall food."

Three things that every student should do before graduating from Kent State are "go to Brady's Café, visit the Fashion Museum, and check out some musical event."

Kenyon College

Address: Ransom Hall; Kenyon College; Gambier, OH 43022
Phone: 740-427-5776
E-mail address: admissions@kenyon.edu
Web site URL: www.kenyon.edu
Founded: 1824
Private or Public: private
Religious affiliation: none
Location: rural
Undergraduate enrollment: 1,576
Total enrollment: 1,576
Percent Male/Female: 46%/54%
Percent Minority: 8.4%
Percent African-American: 4%
Percent Asian: 3%
Percent Hispanic: 2%
Percent Native-American: 0%
Percent in-state/out of state: 26%/74%
Percent Pub HS: 51%
Number of Applicants: 2,838
Percent Accepted: 52%
Percent Accepted who enroll: 30%
Entering: 439
Transfers: 16
Application Deadline: 1 Feb
Mean SAT: NA
Mean ACT: NA
Middle 50% SAT range: V 620-720, M 610-690
Middle 50% ACT range: 27-32
3 Most popular majors: English, social science, visual and performing arts
Retention: 91%
Graduation rate: 83%
On-campus housing: 99%
Fraternities: 23%
Sororities: 8%
Library: 371,000 volumes
Tuition and Fees: $30,330
Room and Board: $5,040
Financial aid, first-year: 39%
Varsity or Club Athletes: NA
Early Decision or Early Action Acceptance Rate: 80%

Why would anyone want to go to a small liberal arts college in the middle of Ohio? Well, ask any Kenyon student and they will be more than happy to tell you. Kenyon College creates a friendly and peaceful community within the rural village of Gambier. Amid beautiful valleys and hills, Kenyon students live on a 1,200-acre campus with their closest friends. Strong academics, sports, arts, and students who know how to throw parties are all just part of Kenyon's charm.

Academic Attention

With a student-teacher ratio of 9:1, an average class size of less than 20, and nary a teaching assistant to be found, Kenyon students benefit from the individual attention they receive from their professors. While students admit they are more inclined to have their work done because it's hard to hide in a class with six people, they don't seem to mind the extra effort. It is not uncommon for a student to build a strong relationship with their professor both in and outside of the classroom. One student enjoys visiting with her professors at their homes, and "couldn't imagine being taught by a graduate student if Kenyon had them." Although the classes are small, students do not seem to have a problem getting into their top choices. One senior noted that "only a couple of classes are competitive." Kenyon students agree that the academics can be very challenging depending on your schedule. One Dance and Spanish double-major admitted that while her dance course did require reading, it was: Literature and Popular Culture in Latin America that made her work the hardest.

Kenyon puts a twist on the classic set of core classes usually demanded of undergraduates and instead requires that every student complete nine "units" (two semesters) in courses beyond their major. One or more of these units must be in each of the four academic departments: fine arts, natural sciences, humanities, and social sciences. One student mentioned that while you cannot get around these requirements, they can "be fulfilled without having to take many painful classes." This framework is another example of Kenyon's dedication to the individual education of its students, as it ensures a broad education while still giving students freedom when picking courses. Kenyon students choose their majors from 38 departments, with the additional option to double major, or complete either a minor or concentration in another department. Students describe all of the majors to be "solid," with English, religion, philosophy, and the natural sciences noted as exceptionally strong. Kenyon offers five interdisciplinary majors, such as international studies, which are popular among those students up for the challenge. A senior described the benefit of these programs, as they "provide a unique and refreshing perspective on traditional majors." In place of a senior thesis, Kenyon requires that everyone complete a "senior experience" within their major before graduation. Students display the culmination of their individual education in a project, presentation, performance, exhibition, or paper.

After Class

Looking for a Kenyon student after class? They might be writing for the weekly newspaper the *Kenyon Collegian*, working for the campus activist group, or serving on student government. Kenyon students describe themselves as "involved," and often give back to Knox County through community service. Each year ten students are chosen to write for the internationally renowned *Kenyon Review* published by the English department. Students gain valuable experience working for a professional publication. In addition, the college hosts readings by visiting authors several times a year. Students choreograph and perform in dance performances, act in plays, and speak their minds at open mic nights. Kenyon students also enjoy just taking a walk around their "really spectacular" campus. You can find them playing Frisbee when it's warm, and sledding at the environmental center during the winter. One senior often visits nearby waterfalls just beyond campus, and many raft down the Kokosing River.

Dorms Galore

On-campus housing is mandatory for all Kenyon students for all four years. Freshmen live together in the "quad" or in one of two dorms across the street. These close quarters help freshmen make friends and create a community. Freshmen do live with Residential Advisors, but say that RAs "don't limit activity too much and provide a good balance between being cool and making sure the shit doesn't hit the fan" said one student. Freshmen live with roommates on co-ed floors, but single-sex halls. All Kenyon dorms are non-smoking. There are no "typical rooms," and one junior complained that despite seniority, she had a "huge" room the year before and a less spacious one as an upperclassman. Beyond freshman year students still live on campus but it is "not a problem" as they "block off dorms and live with friends." The south part of campus is older and has "a lot of character and a homey feel," says one student. The newer dorms and Kenyon apartments are on the north part of campus, and tend to host most of the parties. Students describe campus buildings to be very nice and "state of the art," including new science facilities and athletic center.

Dorms mean dining halls, and that's pretty much the only eating option at Kenyon. With two main dining halls and two restaurants, Kenyon students do get a little "bored" when its time for dinner. However, students have an unlimited meal plan, and find that the dining halls are open "virtually all day long and into the night." One student felt that "the food is improving and no longer a problem on campus." The Gambier Grille offers a classic American menu, and students go there when they get tired of putting their food on a tray. Some make the effort to drive five miles to Mount Vernon for chain restaurants and local eateries. The Kenyon Inn also has a restaurant with "really good food," but it's a little pricey for most students.

Size Matters

Kenyon's 1,551 students share their market, post office, bank, and bookstore with the rural village of Gambier. One student joked that Gambier was actually "on campus," but most enjoy this close connection. Kenyon students agree that everyone is town is "super friendly" and that their close-knit community has a "nice little feel to it." Though Gambier does leave some students wanting a little more, like "at least one sushi restaurant," there are shuttles to the slightly larger town of

Mount Vernon, and more urban Columbus is only an hour's drive. While students travel to Columbus for good meals, plays, or concerts, most are content staying on campus for the weekends.

"The campus is very accepting and laid-back."

One student explained that while Kenyon might be in the middle of nowhere—yes, an Amish horse and buggy can been spotted in the parking lot on occasion—the student body more than makes up for it. Though Kenyon students describe themselves as diverse in "interest and opinion," the majority of the student body is undeniably upper-middle-class and white. Despite this uniformity, one student explains that "no one is left out; the campus is very accepting and laid-back." Students do not judge one another based on race or sexuality, and if Kenyon were to become more diverse it would not present a problem. Kenyon's students are not cliquey despite the campus' small size, but instead are friendly to everyone. Students do not find that they are defined by being in a fraternity, playing a sport, or by what clothes they wear. "You are accepted around campus whether you dress up or just wear sweatpants and a T-shirt," said one student. People say hello when they pass each other on the walkways, and one sophomore says that if you "haven't seen one of your friends in two days, you start to wonder."

Making a Splash

Beginning in 1980, the men's swimming and diving team has won 25 consecutive national championships. The women's team follows closely, currently holding 19 national championships. All told, Kenyon's Lords and Ladies are unstoppable in the water. As a Division III school, Kenyon competes in the North Coast Athletic Conference against schools like Denison and Oberlin. Basketball is by far the biggest spectator sport on campus, and the lacrosse and track programs are also very strong. If you aren't quite ready to swim the 200 Medley Relay in one minute and 28 seconds, Kenyon has the traditional assortment of intramural and club sports. Most non-varsity students enjoy the opportunity to play flag football, rugby, snowboarding, chess, and Ultimate Frisbee with friends. Kenyon students will find a new home for all of their athletic needs when the new $60 million dollar Center for Fitness, Recreation, and Athletics opens in the fall of 2005, designed to rival Division I athletic centers. Kenyon students are very excited to try it out.

We Make Our Own Fun

From "Shock your Mama" to "Summer Send-Off," Kenyon is never at a loss for on-campus entertainment. Campus parties kick off the weekend on Wednesday and continue until Sunday. Students take a midweek break joining their friends in other dorms, apartments, or at the fraternities. Greek life at Kenyon is "substantial, but not overwhelming" says one student, and the fraternities throw some of the best parties. Unlike many big schools, all are welcome at the campus frats—brothers and non-brothers alike. In fact, most Kenyon parties open their doors to all students. The apartments on north campus throw the most parties and serve alcohol to all. Kenyon students find that security is pretty relaxed about parties, but if you are underage and "you walk around with an open container, you're going to get written up." Security and RAs can "write up" students for underage drinking, but the first offense is not usually a big deal. One sophomore joked that she couldn't think of any of her friends who "haven't been written up." The Gambier Grille becomes a bar during the evenings, but only for those students who are of the legal age. "You really have to be 21; they check your school ID, too." Even those old enough to buy a pitcher choose to follow the crowds of people headed to on-campus parties. Many non-alcoholic activities are also sponsored by the college, including movies, dinners, and scavenger hunts. Most parties are casual, but there are occasional semi-formals and one formal dance each year. While students certainly experience the college hook-up at Kenyon, one student claims it's just "too small to sleep around." Many people date, and because of the small size, find themselves in serious relationships. From professors to boyfriends, Kenyon students seem quite pleased to know everyone on campus, and if you came to visit, chances are they'd say hi. If you're in the market for an intellectual community of friends nestled in the charming Midwest, Kenyon may be just for you. —*Megan Ferguson*

FYI

If you come to Kenyon you'd better bring a "smile—people are pretty friendly here."

What is the typical weekend schedule? "Start the weekend on Wednesday; when Friday rolls around, go out to dinner and go to a swim meet; Saturday, sleep in, work, and make the rounds of the on-campus parties; then crash and work on Sunday."

If I could change one thing about Kenyon I'd "expand the eating options near campus."

Three things every student at Kenyon should do before graduating: "Raft down the Kokosing, do the Freshman Sing, and use the new athletic center."

Miami University

Address: 201 South Campus Avenue Bldg.; Oxford, OH 45056
Phone: 513-529-2531
E-mail address: admission@muohio.edu
Web site URL: www.muohio.edu
Founded: 1809
Private or Public: public
Religious affiliation: none
Location: suburban
Undergraduate enrollment: 15,384
Total enrollment: NA
Percent Male/Female: 45%/55%
Percent Minority: 9%
Percent African-American: 4%
Percent Asian: 2%
Percent Hispanic: 2%
Percent Native-American: 1%
Percent in-state/out of state: 73%/27%
Percent Pub HS: NA
Number of Applicants: 12,204
Percent Accepted: 77%
Percent Accepted who enroll: 37%
Entering: 3,549
Transfers: 308
Application Deadline: 31 Jan
Mean SAT: NA
Mean ACT: NA
Middle 50% SAT range: V 55-640, M 580-660
Middle 50% ACT range: 24-29
3 Most popular majors: business management, social science, biology
Retention: 90%
Graduation rate: 80%
On-campus housing: 45%
Fraternities: 24%
Sororities: 27%
Library: 2,697,000 volumes
Tuition and Fees: $8,353 in; $18,104 out
Room and Board: $6,680
Financial aid, first-year: 34%
Varsity or Club Athletes: 10%
Early Decision or Early Action Acceptance Rate: 68%

As one college sophomore at Miami University reflected on her college applications, "when I imagined college in high school, Miami is what I thought it'd be like. It's a traditional college town." Located in Oxford, Ohio, with picturesque red brick campus buildings surrounded by the countryside, Miami University is the ideal college for people who take pride in academics, still want to savor the college life of a thriving Greek system and experience a well rounded liberal education in a safe, yet daring atmosphere.

Academics

This "Public Ivy" takes education seriously. Every student at Miami University must complete the Miami Plan for Liberal Education which consists of foundation courses in the humanities, social sciences, fine arts, and formal reasoning, in addition to a thematic sequence of courses which provides an in-depth look into a subject other than your major. Culminating a student's program of study is the Senior Capstone Experience—a workshop, seminar, creative work, or project that is designed to meld a broad, liberal education with the specialized knowledge of a major. Miami boasts of nationally recognized programs in engineering, business and accounting. Students say that pre-med and business are the harder majors and that slackers tend to lean towards the education major. Architecture majors also handle a tough course load and actually bring "refrigerators, cots, and sleeping bags into the studio because they practically live there when projects are due." The difficulty of classes depends on how hard one wants to make his or her schedule. One student explained that "only crazy people take 18 credit hours." Students appreciate the small class sizes (other than the large introductory classes) that Miami offers with a student faculty ratio at 17 to 1; however, students complain about the difficulty of getting into classes. It's a "huge problem" one student stated. Another student explained that "your scheduling priority for classes is by credit hours, so it only gets easier to get into classes." In-season athletes, graduate students and honor students have first choice for classes, followed by seniors, then juniors and so on. The best way to get into a class, one student explained, is "to stay for a week. A number of students will be discouraged that there is no room and someone will drop the class, leaving a spot open to you." Students do receive close attention from their professors, with only a limited number of TAs around the school. Miami also ranks among the top 10 schools in the country for the number of students who study abroad. The school has a European Center for students to attend in Luxembourg, but will accept nearly any other study abroad program from other colleges, as well.

Living Large (and Clean)

An adjective that students consistently use to describe their school is "clean." As one student commented, "The dorms reflect the campus. The cleaning system is amazing. Everything is clean." The self-contained college campus consists of colonial red brick buildings making up south, east, north, west, and central quads. "It's pretty," said a junior of the campus. "If you closed your eyes and thought 'college,' you would picture Miami." Dorms vary across the board from "big, but pretty dismal" to the all-girls' dorms which are like "posh hotels." Some dorms have air-conditioning, but for the most part dorms are typical, but clean college rooms. After sophomore year, most students choose to move off campus. As one sophomore said, "It's definitely rare for a senior to be in dorm." Fifty percent of students live on campus in dorms and Greek houses. The Greek system dominates student activities on campus with a third of the school involved in a sorority or fraternity. "Everyone goes through rush," one student stated. While the Greek chapters "do party and have a good time," they each have their own philanthropy which supports "a higher cause." The Greek system also supports popular theme parties and the only semi-formal and formal events on campus. One student said her Greek life is "enriching my experience. I don't think I would have met so many people had I not joined. The different sororities all live together and interact with one another." If not part of a Greek chapter, students may tend to feel left out. "If you're not in a Greek chapter and you're a business major, you don't have any friends," said one student. Western campus offers an alternative for the "hippie, artsy and eclectic people." Western Campus is a place to live and learn, separated from the main campus stereotype, said one architecture student.

Dining received rave reviews by students and is rated one of the best systems in the country. Students reported the dining halls were "immaculate" and easy to use. "The meal plan works perfectly," said a sophomore, "we can get snacks and eat whenever we want." While dining halls tend to close around seven, a convenience store located in the student center caters to a late night attack of the munchies. Students say that bars and restaurants uptown, including Kona, Mary Jo's Cuisine, The Alexander House, and the classic Bagel and Deli, offer good dining alternatives.

Social Life Seekers

One has to actively search and carve a social life out of Miami's surroundings. Drinking is prevalent on campus. "We live in the middle of a corn field—what else is there to do but get hammered and pass out every weekend? Not much," said one student. Another student agreed with that sentiment, "It kind of sucks for non-drinkers. If you don't have a party to go to, you feel like a big loser." Students speak of freely flowing alcohol. For those who do not drink, Miami does offer an after dark program that "gives kids something to do every Friday night from 10 P.M. to 2 A.M.," said a junior. The college also sponsors concerts and movies for the non-drinkers on campus. Students also make the occasional drive to Cincinnati or Dayton to encounter a larger social life. Dating is relatively nonexistent at Miami due to the fact that there's nowhere to go, but students did attest to the frequency of random hook-ups.

"It's just the ideal environment to spend four years screwing up, having successes, and complaining about authority."

Sports play a varied role on campus. Intramurals are a big draw, especially broomball, a game that Miami students invented, played on ice without skates. The only team most Miami students turn out in droves to support is the hockey team. "Usually the games are standing room only," said one student.

The Skinny on Miami

The typical Miami student stereotype has been described as "the beautiful blonde, anorexic, wealthy, conservative, who wears Abercrombie, drives a black SUV, went to a Catholic high school, and got good grades in AP classes." Known to some as the "J. Crew University," most Miami students tend to dress with class for class. One student commented that "college students are supposed to come to class in pajamas. Well, not at Miami." Most students at the college come from white, upper-middle class, conservative backgrounds. Diversity on campus is definitely lacking, students report, even though the administration has tried to diversify the student body. Students also comment on the "health-craze" nature of the population. One student stated that "there are very few obese students. You will stick out if you do not at least *appear* athletic, in shape, or thin." Another student said that there are actually "lines in the recreation center to get onto exercise machines." Many students commented on the prevalence of eating disorders in the community.

Most students said that they would attend Miami again if given the chance due to its good reputation, its price, and the college-town feel of the campus. As one student said, "Most people think Miami, a midsize public university, is actually private and that can go a long way when you're out in the world. It's the ideal environment to spend four years screwing up, having successes, and complaining about authority." —*Lisa Siciliano*

FYI

If you come to Miami of Ohio, you'd better bring "khakis and sandals, for winter, summer, spring, and fall."

What is the typical weekend schedule? "Start getting drunk on Thursday and don't let up 'til Sunday when studying and laundry take over."

If I could change one thing about Miami, I'd "change the homogenous nature of everyone."

Three things every student at Miami of Ohio should do before graduating are "explore Uptown at night, play broom ball, and walk through the hub in the fall when the leaves are changing."

Oberlin College

Address: 101 North Professor Street; Oberlin, OH 44074
Phone: 440-775-8411
E-mail address: college.admissions@oberlin.edu
Web site URL: www.oberlin.edu
Founded: 1833
Private or Public: private
Religious affiliation: none
Location: rural
Undergraduate enrollment: 2,848
Total enrollment: 2,848
Percent Male/Female: 44%/56%
Percent Minority: 18%
Percent African-American: 7%
Percent Asian: 6%
Percent Hispanic: 4%
Percent Native-American: 1%
Percent in-state/out of state: 11%/89%
Percent Pub HS: 63%
Number of Applicants: 5,934
Percent Accepted: 33%
Percent Accepted who enroll: 37%
Entering: 747
Transfers: 57
Application Deadline: 15 Jan
Mean SAT: NA
Mean ACT: NA
Middle 50% SAT range: V 630-740, M 610-710
Middle 50% ACT range: 26-31
3 Most popular majors: music performance, history, English
Retention: 89%
Graduation rate: 76%
On-campus housing: 72%
Fraternities: NA
Sororities: NA
Library: 1,541,000 volumes
Tuition and Fees: $29,688
Room and Board: $7,250
Financial aid, first-year: 56%
Varsity or Club Athletes: NA
Early Decision or Early Action Acceptance Rate: 75%

A liberal arts college paired with a Conservatory of Music in northern Ohio seeks students who value diversity and "weirdness." Creativity and enthusiasm a must. Conformists need not apply.

Experimental Education

As the first college to admit women and African-American students over a century ago, today Oberlin continues its tradition of welcoming a diverse student body to attend the College of Arts and Sciences and the Conservatory of Music. Placing value on creative thought and cultural awareness, all kinds of people flock to Ohio in order to spend four years completing a major and nine credit hours in each of three divisions (humanities, social science, and natural science) in addition to nine credits of cultural diversity courses. Students agree that the requirements are "easy to fill" and are "beneficial to anyone pursing a liberal arts degree." Reported hard majors include biology, neuroscience, psychology, and creative writing. Slacker majors consist of theater, dance, and cinema studies. Competitive majors include creative writing, for which one has to apply to every class "even after you've been accepted as a major." With famous professors like writer Dan Chaon, who was recently in the running for the National Book Award, no wonder students are eager to take part in Oberlin's thriving literary world.

Students enjoy their relatively small classes without any TAs. While registering for classes can be difficult online, students say that to get into a class, "show up to the first few classes and the professor will almost always let you in." Special programs at Oberlin include Winter Term, ExCo, and Semester Away. Winter Term, spanning the four weeks of January allows students to study a subject intensively either on or off-campus. Some students line up internships while others write poetry books, or create their own CDs. ExCo (Experimental College) is a student-run organization that sponsors for-credit courses taught by students, faculty, and townspeople. Recent ExCo classes have included performing Gilbert and Sullivan, grassroots organizing, Norwegian, scuba instruction, and storytelling. Students can spend a semester abroad in one of Oberlin's programs in England, Italy, France, the Netherlands, and various other countries. At the Oberlin

Conservatory of Music, students prepare for a career in performance or teaching while being exposed to the liberal arts institution that surrounds them.

Chillin' at Oberlin

Oberlin students find themselves attending small parties in dorm rooms or big flier parties in off-campus houses for a good time during the weekend. Drinking is the norm on campus, though Greek life on campus is simply non-existent. While the school does not host any formals or semi-formals, Oberlin still knows how to throw a good party. Safer Sex Night and Drag Ball are huge college-sponsored parties where most everyone attends. Other hangouts include the dance club, the 'Sco, and the Feve, Oberlin's bar. Besides a few good Chinese restaurants, students complain of the lack of dining and entertainment options directly around the college. After a few years, some students report that campus becomes claustrophobic. The best solution is to get out to the nearest city, Cleveland, if you can find someone with a car. Extracurricular activities tend to be how people "describe themselves, define themselves, and how they often make their friends," says one student. Cliques don't often exist on-campus people say, but after freshman year, "you move on to friends you really like." The dating scene is almost non-existent on campus, students say, and random hookups are the norm.

> **"We're weird. We value weirdness. We're kind of a stage for dialogue between these groups and the overarching American culture."**

Most people tend to think of Oberlin students as a bunch of hippies. "We do have our fair share of hippies," says one student, "but we also have the Indie-rock kids and various other poster children from the 'I Wasn't Cool in High School Club.'" However, people seem to think that the campus runs the gamut of diversity in every category. "There are a lot of wealthy people . . . to very low-income, but somehow everyone seems to think they're poor." People usually wear casual clothes to class, students say, but some unique individuals cultivate their own fashions, like "the bathrobe guys, the leg-warmer girls, the guy who wears the bear suit every Friday, the guy who wears no shoes and the same tie-dyed shirt every day and runs everywhere he goes, and the girl with the tail pinned to her pants . . ."

Most students are non-athletic and do not attend games or play on varsity sports teams; however students love the popular Ultimate Frisbee intramural team. The football team is reported as "terrible," having not won a game for several years. The school does boast an 115,000-square-foot gym facility that is used for basketball, volleyball, and intramurals.

Two Needs: Eat and Sleep

Living options include on-campus housing in 11 traditional dormitories, apartments, co-ops, and themed houses. A typical freshman dorm room is a divided double—two small rooms with a wall and door down the middle. RAs and rules for living (besides some quiet hours) aren't strict unless you live in a program house that, like the French House, has language rules. Seniors usually live off campus in small houses where the rent is reportedly very cheap. About one-third of Oberlin students decide to live in co-op housing where they take responsibility for all aspects of day-to-day operations and use a democratic approach to solving disputes.

Dining hall options aren't particularly spectacular, but they're not bad either. Students can go to traditional all-you-can-eat dining halls or the food court–style Dascomb. Students with meal plans can purchase food from the DeCafe which makes salads and sandwiches. Cafeterias are usually crowded and people tend to eat and run without staying too long.

Look Around!

Oberlin's campus makes a picturesque landscape full of beautiful brick buildings (among "weird modern buildings that don't fit") all organized around a park called Tappan Square. A walk around the college gives a person the sense of what Oberlin students are all about. With a world-renowned art gallery, the Allen Memorial Art Museum, and an environmental science building that is working towards being completely self-reliant (and that was completely designed by students), the grounds of Oberlin are continuously being updated to forward educational advancement while still encouraging the traditional values of a sound liberal arts education. Oberlin students flock to the college because they value diversity and because "We're weird. We value weirdness," says one student. "We're kind of a stage for dialogue between these groups and the overarching American culture." *—Lisa Siciliano*

FYI

If you come to Oberlin, you'd better bring "an open mind. You won't get away with much prejudice here, and pretty much anything goes inside the Oberlin bubble, so you better be ready to accept it."

What is the typical weekend schedule? "School work, paid work, sleep late, dinner out, maybe a party or a movie, breakfast and the fourth meal on Sunday night."

If I could change one thing about Oberlin, I would change" the amount of talking that occurs before anything happens. It seems like you have to meet with a panel of 35 students, ten professors and three deans before you're allowed to do anything around here that affects any change."

Three things every student at Oberlin student should do before graduating are "shop at the Super-K at 4 A.M., dance in the cage at the 'Sco, and come in full costume to Drag Ball."

Ohio State University

Address: Third Floor Lincoln Tower, 1800 Cannon Drive; Columbus, OH 43210
Phone: 614-292-5995
E-mail address: oafa@fa.adm.ohiostate.edu
Web site URL: www.osu.edu
Founded: 1870
Private or Public: public
Religious affiliation: none
Location: urban
Undergraduate enrollment: 36,855
Total enrollment: NA
Percent Male/Female: 52%/48%
Percent Minority: 15%
Percent African-American: 8%
Percent Asian: 5%
Percent Hispanic: 2%
Percent Native-American: 0%
Percent in-state/out of state: 89%/11%
Percent Pub HS: NA
Number of Applicants: 19,563
Percent Accepted: 74%
Percent Accepted who enroll: 41%
Entering: 5,982
Transfers: 2,047
Application Deadline: 15 Feb
Mean SAT: NA
Mean ACT: NA
Middle 50% SAT range: V 520-620, M 540-650
Middle 50% ACT range: 23-27
3 Most popular majors: psychology, family resource management studies, English
Retention: 85%
Graduation rate: 59%
On-campus housing: 24%
Fraternities: 5%
Sororities: 6%
Library: 5,600,000 volumes
Tuition and Fees: $5,658 in; $15,741 out
Room and Board: $6,781
Financial aid, first-year: 52%
Varsity or Club Athletes: 9%
Early Decision or Early Action Acceptance Rate: NA

Looking for that Big Ten college experience, replete with an enormous student body, endless academic possibilities, and tons of school pride? Ohio State University, located in Columbus, Ohio, might be just the place for you.

Size Matters

With an undergraduate population of over 42,000, there is no denying that OSU is HUGE. With 177 possible majors and over 10,000 course offerings, the school offers something for everyone. Engineering, history, and business are all described as being good majors, with psychology and business described as the easiest. "Everyone who's a sucker takes Psych," said one sophomore. Organic Chemistry is almost unanimously declared the toughest class at OSU, with statistics, economics, and honors science classes also considered difficult. All students must complete the General Education Curriculum, or GEC, which varies from major to major. Most majors require a combination including a foreign language, physical science, and a biology sequence. While some students appreciate the liberal arts approach, others are not so thrilled. "It's hell!" griped one student. Students are generally happy with the quality of their professors, though many complain that their Teaching Assistants (TAs) have "English issues."

"I didn't expect how easy it would be to make the school feel small. I'm not a faceless, nameless number. I'm a person!"

OSU students also have the opportunity to apply to the Honors Program, a rigorous program for academically competitive students. Students in the Honors Program receive priority in scheduling, smaller class sizes, and generally a more intimate environment within the University. While scheduling is no problem for athletes and honor students, it can sometimes be a problem for others, depending on the class. In an attempt to make registration easier, OSU has implemented an online course registration system, where students may also view course availability and waiting lists.

Living and Eating

All freshmen at OSU must live in the dorms unless they are living at home. There are three main areas of campus in which students can choose to live, each with its own personality. South Campus is the social end of campus, with older dorms and two-person suites. North Campus is quieter and the dorms are generally thought to be nicer, with air-conditioned, two- and four-person suites. West Campus contains the two Towers, Lincoln and Merrill, which reputedly house "jocks and honor students." Housing can be either co-ed or single sex, depending on floor and dorm. For students looking for an alternative to normal dorm life, there are many different types of theme housing. Humanities, Engineering, Agriculture, International, and Arts are just a few of the possibilities. Another option is Steeb Hall, which houses freshmen who wish to participate in a "First Year Experience" leadership program.

All three main areas of campus contain their own cafeteria. Most students seem to agree that the food is just plain "bad," and many choose not to have a meal plan at all. Those that do can choose a plan with eight, 10, 14, or 19 meals per week. Sprouts, in South Commons, is the only vegetarian dining hall, and few other on-campus alternatives exist. The University is attempting to expand the meal program, though they have not met with success so far. Most juniors and seniors choose to live off campus and take advantage of the plethora of restaurants up and down High Street. Ample housing exists in the areas surrounding Ohio State, and students say to "expect to pay more the closer you are" to the middle of the sprawling campus.

Buckeyes and Booze

Make no mistake about it, Ohio State Buckeyes like to party. With over 50,000 total students, you can bet that there is always something going on. Underclassmen tend to frequent the clubs and bars on High Street such as The Spot and Not Al Too's. Frat parties are another popular diversion, as OSU supports an active Greek scene. Being underage is not perceived as being a problem by most students, and as one student stated, "If you want alcohol you can get it." For those looking for alternatives to the party scene, there are plenty. With over 500 registered student organizations, "everyone's in something." From environmental groups to Starfish, the Jewish Center's community service organization, the options are as diverse as the student body. Each dorm, as well as many clubs and groups, has its own intramural teams ranging from basketball to inner tube water polo. The Wexner Center for the Arts, located on campus, frequently has performances and exhibitions and the Ohio Union, OSU's student center, often sponsors speakers, as well as providing space to study and places to eat.

Buckeyes do not generally limit themselves to just the "Campus" area, but take advantage of nearby shops, restaurants, and movies. Downtown Columbus and the Short North are only a short ten-minute bus ride away straight down High Street. With the inaugural season of pro-hockey in Columbus in 2000-2001, Blue Jackets games attract large crowds of students and Columbus residents alike to the new Arena District in the heart of downtown. Bucca de Beppo, Lemongrass, and Haiku are all popular downtown restaurants. Closer to campus, the Lennox Town Center boasts a 24-screen movie theater, several restaurants such as Don Pablo's, Champs, and Johnny Rockets, as well as a Barnes and Noble, Target, and an Old Navy.

An Urban Campus

Although for years the stretch called High Street near campus was rundown with seedy bars and riddled with graffiti, recent efforts by the Gateway project to revive the area have proven to be successful. The smaller stores are disappearing and giving way to Starbucks, Urban Outfitters, and Steak and Shake, and the overall safety and appearance of the area is greatly improving. Most students say they feel safe on campus and as one student commented, "OSU does a good job at trying to keep people safe."

Though there is no true stereotype for a student body so large, most say it is mostly middle class, and over 90 percent of the students are from Ohio. As one student said, "OSU could be more diverse for having so many people." With its sprawling, flat campus, getting around without a car is easy, though for students living off campus, a car is almost a necessity. The University is centered around the Oval, a large, grassy open space in the middle of campus. For some, it is their favorite hangout to play Frisbee, read, or socialize. However, for those making the trek across the Oval to get to class, it also becomes a big pain. "Sometimes it pisses me off it's so big!" complained one student.

"Rabid Football Fans" and TBDBITL

Ohio State Students are not just passionate about their football, they're "rabid," commented one student gleefully. "The Game", the annual football contest between Ohio State and Michigan, their bitter Big Ten rivals to the north, inspires an entire week of partying and spirit activities. The OSU Marching Band, an impressive group of several hundred musicians, is widely hailed among Buckeyes as "The Best Damn Band in the Land," or TBDBITL, as a popular bumper sticker reads. Their formation of the Script Ohio during half-time is a widely lauded Buckeye tradition. However, OSU is not just about football. The men's basketball team made a Final Four bid in 1999 and has boasted winning seasons since, playing in the brand new Schottenstein Center. The women's gymnastics, synchronized swimming, and rowing teams have also met with successful seasons recently. But Buckeyes need not be varsity athletes to participate in athletics. Intramurals are popular, and Larkins Hall is a huge recreational facility open to all students. Containing five swimming pools, multiple gymnasiums and weight rooms, the facility has become outdated and plans are in the works to raze the entire thing and build an all new, state-of-the-art center.

Though most students who choose to attend OSU are well aware of its immense size, many are still shocked at how big it really is. However, size does not always mean anonymity. Said one student: "The diverse opportunities, people, and points of view are available because it's such a big place. I didn't expect how easy it would be to make the school feel small. I'm not a faceless, nameless number. I'm a person!" —*Melissa J. Merritt*

FYI

If you come to Ohio State, you'd better bring "a bike—this is a huge campus."

What is the typical weekend schedule? "Football!!!"

If I could change one thing about Ohio State, I'd "make it a little smaller—the red tape here is amazing."

The three things every student should do before graduating from Ohio State are "jump into Mirror Lake the Thursday before the Michigan game, go to a Michigan game, go to at least one really wild party."

Ohio University

Address: 120 Chubb Hall; Athens, OH 45701
Phone: 740-593-4100
E-mail address: frshinfo@ohiou.edu
Web site URL: www.ohiou.edu
Founded: 1804
Private or Public: public
Religious affiliation: none
Location: suburban
Undergraduate enrollment: 17,342
Total enrollment: NA
Percent Male/Female: 45%/55%
Percent Minority: 5%
Percent African-American: 3%
Percent Asian: 1%
Percent Hispanic: 1%
Percent Native-American: NA
Percent in-state/out of state: 91%/9%
Percent Pub HS: 84%
Number of Applicants: 13,195
Percent Accepted: 75%
Percent Accepted who enroll: 37%
Entering: 3,703
Transfers: 508
Application Deadline: 1 Feb
Mean SAT: NA
Mean ACT: NA
Middle 50% SAT range: V 500-600, M 500-610
Middle 50% ACT range: 21-26
3 Most popular majors: business management, English, education
Retention: 85%
Graduation rate: 70%
On-campus housing: 44%
Fraternities: 12%
Sororities: 14%
Library: 2,405,000 volumes
Tuition and Fees: $6,972 in; $14,142 out
Room and Board: $7,320
Financial aid, first-year: 47%
Varsity or Club Athletes: NA
Early Decision or Early Action Acceptance Rate: NA

According to legend, Athens, Ohio, is one of the most haunted cities in the United States. Superstition holds that Athens, home to the Ohio University Bobcats, lies at the center of a pentangle formed by five cities where witches were hung in the 1700s. This geographic peculiarity supposedly causes the campus to be inhabited by a variety of spooks and spirits in addition to its 17,000 students. Some Bobcats report lying in bed while no one else is in the room and hearing phantom typing on their computer keyboards. Others note that on the fourth floor of one Wilson dorm, the grains of wood on one door form a demon's face—this room has had so many reports of haunting that the university no longer assigns students to live there. Ghoulish stories, however, have certainly not scared students away from this school. Combining a well-deserved party school reputation with solid academic programs and a picturesque campus, it's no wonder that neither the ghosts nor the students want to leave OU.

Bobcats Hit the Books

OU, as one sophomore observed, is "more than just a party school; the academics are really good, too." Regardless of major, all OU students have to complete a series of requirements known as "tiers." Tier One consists of freshman English and math, Tier Two involves 30 credit hours-worth of classes in a cross-section of academic subjects, and Tier Three requires a junior-level English composition course. Students have mixed opinions about the tier system, some saying that they appreciate the opportunity to take classes outside of their major, while others complaining that "the extra classes are a waste of tuition money."

Luckily for those who don't enjoy completing their tiers, students only have to put up with each class for two and a half months. OU operates on the quarter system, so students enroll in three ten-week terms per academic year instead of two longer semesters like at most universities. As a result, school starts in late September, finishes in June, and provides a six-week break between the fall and winter terms that lasts from Thanksgiving until after New Years. Because of the short terms, classes meet either every day or in two-hour, twice-a-week sessions. One junior commented that a perk of the quarter system is that "we're on campus for the really nice weather in spring," while a sophomore said she liked the schedule because "if you've had a bad term, you get a fresh start in just a few weeks."

With ten different colleges and an assortment of well-respected programs, there's something at OU to satisfy any academic interest. Boasting such standout graduates as *The Today Show*'s Matt Lauer, journalism is unanimously cited as OU's best program, and one of the most selective. Other strong majors include business, engineering, and pre-med, while majors in retail merchandising and in sports administration are considered somewhat less challenging. In order to begin taking upper-level classes, students must apply to the college in which they want to major. Most upper-level classes have about 20 or 30 students whereas intro classes can enroll up to 300 students. One sophomore cited this as a problem for freshmen undecided about their major, since the application process only takes place in the fall and "it can be hard to fit all your classes in four years, and lots of students end up staying for extra terms."

While students looking for an easy term can take guts like Health 101, Engineering Technology 280, art, or a "University College" class that teaches study skills and research techniques, science classes are said to be more challenging. Chemistry 151 is known to be the hardest class at OU, and rumor has it that nearly a third of students fail the first time they take it. Despite a few particularly hard classes, OU academics are generally found to be manageable. One junior described his course load as "moderate; it's not really easy but I can get my work done." Though some grumble about TAs who speak poor English, or annoying system backups during the online course-registration procedure, on the whole students are more than pleased with the quality of academics.

Good Dorms, Bad Eats

Despite occasional reports of poltergeists, most OU students are satisfied with their living arrangements. Students are required to live in the dorms for both freshman and sophomore years, in their choice of either single-sex or co-ed buildings. All the dorms have air-conditioning, and most rooms are doubles with common bathrooms on each hall. One of the major perks about living on campus is that each dorm room comes furnished with a computer with high-speed Internet access, so students don't necessarily have to purchase a computer of their own. Although dorms on the West Green quad are generally considered nicer than those on the New South quad, most students like living on campus in general because "it gives you the chance to meet people you'd never think to talk to otherwise," according to one sophomore. Most students move into off-campus housing for junior and senior years. These houses are in "student ghettos" where college students rent most of the houses, and none are more than a ten-minute walk from campus. "I love living off campus; it's cheaper and more relaxed," chimed in one student.

The rooms may be popular, but the dining halls are not. The major complaint about living on campus is the dining hall food. "It's horrible," said one sophomore, "I think they put laxatives in it because it just runs right through you." A senior commented that dining hall food is "really redundant, and you can't really eat healthily at all." Others complain about the dining halls' limited hours of operation. On-campus dining does have a few perks though. The super-20 meal plan option allows students to get cash for the meals they don't use, and the Grab-n-Go café lets students use their meal plan to purchase packaged food to take back to their rooms.

Life of the Party

The best aspect of OU, according to one student, is that "everyone goes out, and every night there's something to do." While the social scene caters to partygoers, there are enough options to ensure that every Bobcat has a great time. About a third of students join a fraternity or sorority at OU, making the Greek scene a powerful social force on campus. In addition to Friday- and Saturday-night frat house parties that draw large crowds, Greeks sponsor some popular annual parties. One such party is Derby Days, a party held in a cornfield one Saturday during spring term where bands play and kegs flow from morning until night. With the exception of a few invite-only parties, most Greek events are open to the general student body, although one sophomore noted that "girls are pretty much always welcome at frat parties, but sometimes they're stricter about non-Greek guys." Students agree that there's no pressure to rush. One male junior observed that "it's not like you're considered un-cool if you're not in a frat," and a female student agreed that "you don't feel obligated to be in a sorority." There's no real social division between Greeks and non-Greeks, since "you have to live in the dorms for two years regardless, so you make a lot of friends both in and out of the Greek system."

"The Halloween Party is insane; it's like nothing I ever expected!"

OU has an equally vibrant non-Greek party scene. Upperclassmen enjoy hanging out at Athens bars, of which there are more than 20, especially during the Cork Street Shuffle, when on the Saturday night of Mom's Weekend, students go from bar to bar with their mothers and have a drink at each one. House parties are frequent and open to everyone. According to one sophomore, "you can basically walk into any party even if you don't know anyone and have a great time; everyone's so cool and friendly." Every year, streets populated by student houses throw huge parties like Palmer Fest, Oak Fest, and High Fest, where the streets are closed off and filled with students while each house hosts a party.

Given the supernatural legends surrounding OU, it is appropriate that the biggest of these block parties is the annual Halloweenfest. Cork Street, the main street in Athens, shuts down completely as more than 30,000 students descend on OU from universities all over Ohio. "Everyone dresses up and gets trashed. It's a mile-worth of kids standing shoulder to shoulder," explained one sophomore. Another student raved, "the Halloween party is insane; it's like nothing I ever expected!" Clearly, drinking is an important part of the OU social life. Despite recent administrative attempts to crack down on campus drinking, including increases in the police force patrolling the streets on weekend nights, alcohol is readily accessible to those who want it. Non-drinkers need not feel excluded from OU social life however. As one sophomore said, "I didn't drink much at all my freshman year, and I still went to all the parties and had a great time."

Another remarkable feature of the social scene at OU is the friendliness of the student body. "Everyone is pretty close knit here," commented one junior. A senior described the average student as "preppy, but not stuck up, really down-to-earth, friendly, good people." About 90 percent of the student body hails from Ohio, which does lead a lot of students to hang out with high school friends at first, but most upperclassmen agree that by the end of freshman year they've met most of their friends through classes or the dorms. One sophomore summed it up best: "students here are really chill; they're serious about school during the week so they can go out and party with their friends on the weekends."

A Red-Brick Beauty

Located in the wooded hills of Ohio, Athens was originally a manufacturing town that produced a large proportion of the country's bricks. Though most industry has since left the area, the legacy of the town's past is clearly visible on OU's campus, which many students name as their favorite feature of the school. One sophomore described the campus as "something you'd see in a movie," with large, tree-lined quads surrounded by beautiful, red-brick, colonial architecture. Students take advantage of their surroundings during the warmer fall and spring quarters by studying under a tree, sunbathing, "folfing" (Frisbee golfing), or just hanging out in the courtyards outside the dorms. Although the architecture remains old-fashioned, recent additions and renovations to science and political science buildings keep the campus updated. The Hocking River runs through the center of the hilly grounds, and the brick streets and sidewalks visually tie the campus and the city together.

The city is a "good mix between urbanism and trees," commented one junior, who added that one of the things he liked best about the small-town environment "is that Athens is basically a walking town—you can get anywhere in 15 minutes without a car." Though some students lament that Athens' small size makes them feel like they live in "the middle of nowhere," most are enthusiastic about the options available downtown. Since Athens is primarily a university town, many of the restaurants and bars cater to college students. In addition to the multitude of bars and clubs, popular late-night destinations include restaurants like the Pita Pit, Goodfellow's Pizza, Burrito Buggy, and a calzone restaurant called D.P. Dough, all of which are open until the wee hours of the morning so that students can grab a late-night meal. Policemen on horseback ensure the safety of the campus, and the mass of student housing surrounding the downtown area makes students feel at home off campus as well as on.

Athletics and Extracurriculars

After dividing their time between academics and partying, many students say they don't have much energy to devote to dozens of extracurricular interests. For those students who do wish to get involved in extracurriculars, OU offers a variety of opportunities. Many organizations relate directly to students' majors, like the business fraternity, the newspaper run by journalism students, or the radio station run by telecommunications majors. Other popular organizations include the Ski Club, which takes an annual trip to Colorado during winter break and a whitewater rafting trip in West Virginia during spring break, and the student government groups in every dorm. Many students opt to work, often in on-campus jobs in the library or dining halls. "The jobs start at minimum wage," said one sophomore dining hall employee, "but you get raises quickly and a discount on your meal plan." Intramural sports, or "IMs," are one of the most popular extracurricular options. With IM leagues in everything from flag football to Ultimate Frisbee to table tennis, students sign up in teams with friends, dorm mates, or members of their fraternity or sorority to engage in friendly competition once or twice a week.

In addition to participation in IM sports, athletically inclined OU students have the opportunity to make use of one of the finest student gyms in the country. The Ping Recreation Center, over 168,000 square feet, houses everything you could possibly want, from weights to tennis courts to a swimming pool to aerobics classes. Although the Ping Center is one of the most popular and heavily used resources on campus, attendance at varsity sporting events is much more sparse. As one junior observed, "the football team sucks, so no one goes to the games." Though the basketball, baseball, and club hockey teams are somewhat more popular, on the whole "there's not much school spirit in terms of athletics," as one senior described.

In spite of the lack of sports fans, OU students love their school and hardly mind the shoddy performance of the Bobcat athletic teams. One junior said that students enjoy being on campus so much that "no one wants to go home when classes are over in the spring!" From its wild parties to its beautiful campus, from the friendly students inhabiting it to the ghostly legends surrounding it, OU is a unique institution that inspires enthusiasm in its students. One sophomore said, "I feel at home here. It's a great atmosphere to learn in, and everyone makes you feel so comfortable. I wouldn't want to go anywhere else." *—Katherine Kirby Smith*

FYI

If you come to OU, you'd better bring "a beer bong, a fake ID, an iron stomach to handle the dining hall food, and a warm coat for the frigid winter quarter."

What is the typical weekend schedule? "Friday: pre-game in the dorms, go out to a house party or frat party, hit up the bars, get some pizza at Goodfellow's, go home and sleep until mid-afternoon. Saturday: do it all again. Sunday: sleep all day, try to do some work."

If I could change one thing about OU, I'd change the "strictness of the campus police."

Three things every student at OU should do before graduating are "party at Halloween, go to Derby Days, and do the Cork Street Crawl on Moms' Weekend."

Ohio Wesleyan University

Address: 61 South Sandusky Street; Delaware, OH 43015
Phone: 740-368-3020
E-mail address: owuadmit@cc.owu.edu
Web site URL: www.owu.edu
Founded: 1842
Private or Public: private
Religious affiliation: Methodist
Location: suburban
Undergraduate enrollment: 1,935
Total enrollment: NA
Percent Male/Female: 46%/54%
Percent Minority: 8%
Percent African-American: 5%
Percent Asian: 2%
Percent Hispanic: 1%
Percent Native-American: 0%
Percent in-state/out of state: 60%/40%
Percent Pub HS: 75%
Number of Applicants: 2,212
Percent Accepted: 80%
Percent Accepted who enroll: 30%
Entering: 546
Transfers: 39
Application Deadline: rolling
Mean SAT: NA
Mean ACT: NA
Middle 50% SAT range: V 540-650, M 540-650
Middle 50% ACT range: 23-28
3 Most popular majors: business, psychology, zoology
Retention: 80%
Graduation rate: 66%
On-campus housing: 81%
Fraternities: 44%
Sororities: 34%
Library: 500,000 volumes
Tuition and Fees: $25,440
Room and Board: $7,110
Financial aid, first-year: 60%
Varsity or Club Athletes: 37%
Early Decision or Early Action Acceptance Rate: 95%

While it's a little bit too cold for some, students at Ohio Wesleyan University always have good things to say about their school. Located in small-town of Delaware, Ohio, OWU offers a challenging academic program as well as a lively Greek life to counterbalance all the work.

The Right Stuff

Students praise the small classes and caring environment that OWU offers and OWU students are very quick to note the dedication of their professors who seem to be there for them whenever students need help. Don't get the wrong idea, though. OWU is not an easy school. One student commented, "OWU is a lot of work. It's easy to get in, but it's very hard to stay in."

OWU has some core requirements for graduation. While some students are not ecstatic about the guidelines, many think that the requirements are a helpful tool to direct their education. One student described the academics as "challenging, but not too much that you can't handle it. The distribution requirements make you experience things you wouldn't normally learn, and it makes for a well-rounded education." OWU requires a freshman English class, two semesters of a foreign language, and classes in non-European culture, fine arts, social sciences, and natural sciences. The school also requires students to take 15 courses numbering 110 or above.

There is an incredible number of academic resources at OWU to help students through their difficult classes. One of the most popular is the Writing Resources Center. Open every weekday, students come with the sole purpose of becoming "more confident, effective writers." The WRC is only one of many different resources that are designed specifically to help students excel.

While there are some school-wide resources outside of the classroom built for students' needs, students rank their classes and professors very highly. One student noted, "All intro science classes are capped at 50, and almost every class only has 20, 12, or as few as 4 students in them." Compared to many schools where huge, introductory classes are prevalent, these numbers are certainly boast-worthy. Students couldn't be happier with their dedicated professors. The personalized attention they give helps to make every class worthwhile. Students find that all of these things help contribute to their good experiences with the graduation requirements. There are enough courses offered that every student can find something that is both interesting and that fulfills a requirement although some student report missing some of the more diverse opportunities available at larger research institutions.

Behind the Scenes

Although students are kept busy by their classes, most note having plenty of time to kick back and get to know their peers. Most students point first to the fact that they have too much work to go out during the week, although on some days students will socialize a little bit with their friends, watch movies in their rooms, and generally hang out. Real partying is more or less entirely restricted to the weekends.

Many students point to the Greek life at Ohio Wesleyan as one of the key elements of their social life. A little less than half of the men, and slightly fewer women, associate themselves with the fraternities or sororities. Many students find themselves walking up the hill on Friday and Saturday nights to the frats and sororities that are almost always throwing parties. One girl commented, "glittery, tight tops that show cleavage and tight jeans are a must." While each of the parties take on slightly different personalities, everybody can find a good night on the hill. Additionally, in the small town of Delaware, Ohio, there are a couple of student-frequented bars that offer an alternative to students who are of age.

Some students find Delaware life a little dull. As one student says, "There just aren't many places to hang out in Delaware, Ohio." There are a few shops and a movie theater in the town, but in order to really go out and find something interesting, students often say that they like to drive to larger towns nearby. During the few days a year when it is warm, many students enjoy hanging out on the green lawns of campus and playing Frisbee.

One complaint from many students is the lack of diversity at OWU. When asked what they might want to change about their school, answers ranged from the high cost of the school to the apathy of the student body. One student simply said, "they need to increase the number of non-white students."

The energy of OWU students seems to be dampened by the cold weather during the Ohio winters.

The energy of OWU students seems to be dampened by the cold weather during the Ohio winters. Many end up inside, watching movies and studying instead of being as active as they might like in more community-oriented activities. One student expressed her frustration with the inactivity of students and professors alike, and the carelessness that can come with it: "Too many people, students and faculty both, couldn't care less about the appearance of our school. There is trash everywhere. Once, an entire pot of spaghetti was overturned on a sidewalk outside the campus center—it stayed there for four days before someone cleaned it up."

While some OWU students seem too involved in their work to care much about what's going on around them, others describe themselves as very involved in extracurricular activities. OWU certainly has opportunities for every interest. Additionally, the administration does a stellar job of planning open events for all students to attend. OWU students often comment on the incredible number of events, from parties to lectures that are held on a regular basis. Students recognize the Campus Programming Board as lying at the core of student life, planning and hosting "too many events to list."

Sports, too, are for everybody at OWU. The University organizes intramural sports for people with little experience, and at the varsity level OWU has had recent success with several of its Division III sports. While OWU is not entirely focused on its sports program, many students mention that watching games is a lot of fun.

While students seem to be pretty active outside of the classroom, many agree that little exists during the week except for their work. OWU students point to the Mean Bean Coffee House as a cool place to have some coffee (as well as the only coffee shop in Delaware) and get some work done. Students also like the Delaware Public Library as well as the on-campus libraries for quiet places to settle down to read.

Living and Eating

OWU offers a wide selection of dorms to choose from. There is an all-female dorm, an honors dorm, and four other co-ed dorms. Students seem to be happiest in Smith, a co-ed dorm that is the only air-conditioned dorm on campus. RAs are present on each floor of the dorms, and their attitude seems to vary a lot. While one RA claims that she is "as strict as can be," other students say that they are generally "pretty laid back, not very strict" and "for the most part, invisible." There are study rooms on each floor where students sometimes convene to hang out. Generally, parties appear to be fairly restricted to "The Hill," where all of the frats are located.

While students seem generally happy with their living conditions, the university's food doesn't garner such good marks. One student even says, "The dining hall food is horrible, I often get food poisoning from it." Although feelings are clearly quite strong regarding some of the dining halls, there do seem to be some good eating havens on campus. Smith dining hall is centrally located and all-you-can-eat, and the Bishop Café in the Hamilton-Williams Campus Center is widely recognized as having the best food on campus.

Is OWU for You?

OWU students are hard working and dedicated to their studies. They put up with the freezing temperatures of Delaware, Ohio, to take advantage of small classes and caring professors. But, it's not all work. When they need some time off they enjoy taking down time to watch movies, or going out to experience the standard, drunken Greek party life up on "The Hill." If you're not afraid of the cold, love to work, and enjoy the odd party, OWU is the place for you. —*Zane Selkirk*

FYI

If you come to OWU, you better bring a "Frisbee," a "big coat," and a "cookbook so you can make your own food."

What is the typical weekend schedule? "Driving in to Columbus, hanging out with friends, and sleeping."

If I could change one thing about OWU, I would "move the school to a bigger city."

Three things that every student at OWU should do before graduating are "slide down The Hill on a mattress, work hard, and go to at least one soccer game."

University of Cincinnati

Address: PO Box 210063; Cincinnati, OH 45221-0091
Phone: 513-556-1100
E-mail address: admissions@uc.edu
Web site URL: www.uc.edu
Founded: 1819
Private or Public: public
Religious affiliation: none
Location: urban
Undergraduate enrollment: 19,204
Total enrollment: NA
Percent Male/Female: 51%/49%
Percent Minority: 18%
Percent African-American: 14%
Percent Asian: 3%
Percent Hispanic: 1%
Percent Native-American: 0%
Percent in-state/out of state: 93%/7%
Percent Pub HS: NA
Number of Applicants: 9,899
Percent Accepted: 88%
Percent Accepted who enroll: 45%
Entering: 3,983
Transfers: 1,269
Application Deadline: 31 July
Mean SAT: NA
Mean ACT: NA
Middle 50% SAT range: V 460-590, M 470-610
Middle 50% ACT range: 19-26
3 Most popular majors: business marketing, engineering, visual and performing arts
Retention: 73%
Graduation rate: 49%
On-campus housing: 14%
Fraternities: NA
Sororities: NA
Library: 1,800,000 volumes
Tuition and Fees: $6,936 in; $17,310 out
Room and Board: $6,744
Financial aid, first-year: 58%
Varsity or Club Athletes: 12%
Early Decision or Early Action Acceptance Rate: NA

Looking for "hands-on-based knowledge" that gives you that extra edge with job placement? Look no further than Cincinnati. This "not-that-spread-out" campus located in scenic downtown Cincinnati has everything a student could want . . . at least it will after the construction is finished.

More Songs About Buildings

Trying to overcome its reputation as a commuter school, UC is a campus marked by rapid change and construction intended to promote campus unity and spirit. Said one engineering student "UC stands for 'Under Construction' forever." She further explained that although the head of the University has attested that there are no plans for future projects, it was apparent that certainly the campus would be under construction for some time to come. However, the construction is not all bad. Another student remarked that "they are really trying to improve and create a nicer atmosphere for the students." To create a more central gathering place for students, a new recreational center is being built, as well as some more on campus dorms. Currently, though, the best housing on campus are Turner and Schneider, which are only a couple of years old. These two dorms have suite-style rooms with bedrooms adjoining a shared common space connecting them all. However, most students still live off campus in the Clifton area across the street from campus.

How 'bout Dem Bearcats?

What is a Bearcat? Well, it's one hell of a basketball player. Sporting events, as any good Ohioan could tell you, are events that bring the community together and instill a sense of belonging and school pride. While at other schools in Ohio, football is the main sport, the Bearcats actually have a strong tradition of basketball and are ranked seventh in the country by ESPN. One might wonder if it is difficult to get tickets to the games. Absolutely. One student reported camping out overnight to buy tickets to a game that was three weeks away, understanding full well that student tickets to the game would be sold out in a matter of hours. So be sure to get a spot in line early if you want to root for the rowdy Bearcats.

Day by Day

How's the weather? Schizophrenic. According to one student, Cincinnati "doesn't like to make up its mind what season it's supposed to be." One day in winter it may be raining and the next there might be a wind-chill of -15 degrees Fahrenheit. Be prepared for anything.

While the food is reputedly "decent for dorm food," there are plenty of different stations with different types of food in the dining halls. Meals are conveniently located within the dorm buildings so hungry students don't have to brave the unpredictable weather. And if you crave something more ethnic (or just plain better) and don't mind heading off campus, you're in luck. Dining options are plentiful and good in Cincinnati. Indian, Chinese, Japanese and Italian restaurants are just a hop, skip, and jump away. Make sure you have a car, though, because you will need it if you want to do anything off campus.

"Diverse people like to do diverse things, and the people at UC are diverse," noted one student. This makes for an entertaining and full social scene. There is a strong Greek presence at the school, but there is also a large contingent of GDIs (God-Damned Independents). And actually, the two groups are fairly fluid so don't feel too pressured to join if you don't think frats are your scene. House parties are generally held in the Clifton area. There are also plenty of bars and clubs in downtown Cincinnati that students frequent. Aside from partying, according to one student, "there are so many clubs and activities that it's impossible not to do something." Students are very active around campus doing everything from club sports to community service, although the former is a bit more popular than the latter. Also, there are on campus alternatives to parties, such as "Friday Night Live," at which several comics from the show *Whose Line Is It Anyway?* recently performed.

If you're wondering where you can take a date, the answer's actually Kentucky. Just across the border of Kentucky, there is an area called Newport on the Levee. This area has a lot of non-franchise, family-owned restaurants that lend themselves to the romantic atmosphere of a date. Another popular Kentucky destination is the Cold Stone Creamery in that same area.

"There are so many clubs and activities that it's impossible not to do something."

On campus, be sure to check out McMicken Hall's stone lions that supposedly growl when virgins walk through them, the "haunted" Cincinnati Observatory Center, and the Crosley Tower, which was reportedly created from one continuous pour of concrete

Class? Oh, Yeah! Class!

UC students have classes, and depending on the program they are in, most get their money's worth on their education. "While other schools may have one thing, there are three huge things that our campus has that others don't. CCM, DAAP, and the Engineering School are all awesome programs." The first two stand for the College Conservatory of Music and Design, Architecture, Art, and Planning. These three programs are the most competitive at UC, while the Business Program (CBA) and the Nursing Program, one student reported, are accorded less prestige among the students. However, the most interesting aspect of the academic program at UC is its co-op programs. Co-op is designed to give students real world experience in their program of study reinforcing what they have learned in class. This experience renders students better equipped to handle their future jobs as well as gets their foot in the door with respect to potential employers and therefore "really helps with job placement" after school.

Fortune Telling

The University of Cincinnati does not have the school spirit of some of its other Ohio university brethren but may get there soon. The University of Cincinnati is doing a lot to improve itself and should offer more well-rounded college experience as soon as they finish construction. —*Ashley Elsner*

FYI

If you come to the University of Cincinnati, you'd better bring a "campus map. It's confusing with all the construction going on."

What is the typical weekend schedule? "Thursday through Saturday evenings are spent out and about, and the rest of the weekend is spent putting off work to Sunday."

If I could change one thing about the University of Cincinnati, "I'd have better parking and make it less expensive. Even if you have a pass, that doesn't guarantee you'll get a spot in your assigned lot."

Three things every student at the University of Cincinnati should do before graduating are "go to Skyline on Ludlow for chili, talk to people, and get involved."

Wittenberg University

Address: PO Box 720; Springfield, OH 45501
Phone: 937-327-6314
E-mail address: admissions@wittenberg.edu
Web site URL: www.wittenberg.edu
Founded: 1845
Private or Public: private
Religious affiliation: none
Location: small city
Undergraduate enrollment: 2,182
Total enrollment: NA
Percent Male/Female: 42%/58%
Percent Minority: 9%
Percent African-American: 6%
Percent Asian: 2%
Percent Hispanic: 1%
Percent Native-American: 0%
Percent in-state/out of state: 53%/47%
Percent Pub HS: NA
Number of Applicants: 2,524
Percent Accepted: 85%
Percent Accepted who enroll: 30%
Entering: 636
Transfers: 39
Application Deadline: 15 Mar
Mean SAT: NA
Mean ACT: NA
Middle 50% SAT range: V 510-677, M 518-683
Middle 50% ACT range: 25-29
3 Most popular majors: business marketing, English, biology
Retention: 83%
Graduation rate: 70%
On-campus housing: 90%
Fraternities: 22%
Sororities: 33%
Library: 259,000 volumes
Tuition and Fees: $24,948
Room and Board: $6,368
Financial aid, first-year: 71%
Varsity or Club Athletes: 28%
Early Decision or Early Action Acceptance Rate: ED 74%, EA 97%

At Wittenberg University, the freedoms of a liberal arts education are combined with a conservative background based in Wittenberg's Evangelical Lutheran Church affiliation, a mix that students at Wittenberg find "supportive" and "just plain perfect."

Wittenberg's small student population is an asset in the eyes of most students. "Our size really makes it easy to get to know people. In fact, you can't escape it. From my first day on campus people I didn't know were saying hi to me," one student said. Other students were slightly less enthusiastic about the fact that their classmates knew all the details of those inevitable freshman-year mistakes. As one student put it, "Word travels fast, real fast."

Wittenberg Wisdom

Deadlines approach even more quickly. "We aren't some Ivy League, but we're no slackers either. I'd say we're as East Coast, academically, as an Ohio University can get." Wittenberg grants scholarships based on academic merit, but not athletic ability. Students whose grades fall below 2.3 are given a semester to repair their grades before the administration suspends them.

Some students describe the course offerings at Wittenberg as "run of the mill," but the individual attention students receive is "truly above average." "I've never had a teaching assistant teach any of my classes," said one student, "and I've found my professors extremely approachable when it comes to scheduling appointments." Class sizes cater to this same idea, with a class of 40 students occurring "rarely, and even then only in the premed and intro science classes." Most classes enroll fewer than 20 students.

Prelaws, Premeds, Prerequisites

Popular departments at Wittenberg include biology, geology, and psychology, with numerous pre-med and pre-law students as well. The Wittenberg education is founded on prerequisites in each of seven areas: Integrated Learning; Natural World; Social Institutions; the Fine, Performing, and Literary Arts; Religious and Philosophical Inquiry; Western Historical Perspectives; and Non-Western Cultures. Students also have to fulfill requirements in the two co-curricular areas of physical activity (which can be fulfilled through either intercollegiate athletics or various health and fitness courses) and community service, which requires sophomores to complete 30 hours of community service over the course of one term.

The campus facilities vary from "newly renovated and modern" to "built in the sixties and seventies and definitely showing it." Myers Hall, the original Wittenberg building of 1846, still stands and today houses Wittenberg's honor students. Dorms are coed, but floors are single-sex, and students can visit the opposite-sex floors only until 12:30 A.M. Students are required to live on campus for the first two years, after which time all but a few move off campus. Students complain that the dorms are surrounded by low income housing, making the off campus housing a more attractive option.

BYOB

Fraternity and sorority members, who make up approximately one-third of the campus population, live off campus in one of Wittenberg's 11 Greek houses (six sororities and five fraternities), where much of the school's nightlife is centered. Alcohol is allowed only in the rooms of students 21 and over, and fraternity parties, instead of providing kegs, are BYOB. Keg parties can be found at private student houses off campus and out of the jurisdiction of university policy. The Ringside Cafe, which has a weekly college night, is a popular student hangout and many students say they drink, on average, four times per week. The town of Springfield "kinda sucks," one candid student remarked, because "we are the fast-food mecca of America." Students who want to find some serious grub often have to hunt long and hard before they find a cool hangout like Springfield's Mike and Rosey's Restaurant.

> **"From my first day on campus people I didn't know were saying hi to me."**

The student union, however, with its Marriott-catered food and flexible meal plans, is a popular hangout for the social studier and hungry student. The second floor of the union has a la carte food service open until 1 A.M., as well as a bar.

Students are heavily involved in a wide range of extracurriculars. Intercollegiate sports, especially against rivals Denison, Ohio Wesleyan, and Oberlin, are popular draws, as are various intramurals, rock climbing, spelunking, and water skiing on the nearby Springfield reservoir. To get away from campus, students often visit the "neat little hippie town" of Yellow Springs, a 15-minute drive from campus. When students want to relax on campus they head to the Hollow, a grassy vale that is filled with sledders throughout the winter. Warm weather invites sunbathing, picnicking, and Frisbee-tossing to the Hollow.

When spring approaches, the Hollow is also home to a weekend of music, drinking, and general stress relief called Wittstock. Past Wittstock performers have included Hootie and the Blowfish and 10,000 Maniacs, while some students "just go for the carnival aspect of it."

Recent changes to campus life have been minimal. Wittenberg switched from a trimester to semester system, and the new university president, Baird Tipson, "runs things pretty smoothly," one student said. Perhaps the homogeneity of the university is responsible for the smooth aspect of campus life. The population is predominantly Caucasian, and alternative lifestyles, such as homosexuality, are "kept on the down low . . . we don't discuss it much, and perhaps it's better that way."

Regardless of general student attitudes toward minority groups, undergrads described the atmosphere as "supportive," "intensely friendly," even "homey." Just one warning before you decide to make "Sprinklefield" your home away from home: "be prepared for the wet."

—Vladimir Cole and Staff

FYI

The three best things about attending Wittenberg are "small class size accompanied by personal attention by professors, friendly and aesthetically pleasing campus, and off-campus housing for junior and seniors in the immediate campus area."

The three worst things about attending Wittenberg are "the new parking lot that eliminated the Frisbee golf fields, some outdated residence halls and inadequate parking, and no paper towels in the bathrooms."

The three things that every student should do before graduating from Wittenberg are "go abroad, visit the Career Placement and Development Office, and take advantage of exit meetings."

One thing I'd like to have known before coming here is "that tuition increases four percent every year."

Oklahoma

Oklahoma State University

Address: 324 Student Union; Stillwater, OK 74078
Phone: 405-744-6858
E-mail address: admit@okstate.edu
Web site URL: www.okstate.edu
Founded: 1890
Private or Public: public
Religious affiliation: none
Location: small city
Undergraduate enrollment: 18,043
Total enrollment: 21,872
Percent Male/Female: 51%/49%
Percent Minority: 16%
Percent African-American: 3%
Percent Asian: 2%
Percent Hispanic: 2%
Percent Native-American: 9%
Percent in-state/out of state: 88%/12%
Percent Pub HS: 98%
Number of Applicants: 5,639
Percent Accepted: 92%
Percent Accepted who enroll: 63%
Entering: 3,265
Transfers: 1,651
Application Deadline: rolling
Mean SAT: NA
Mean ACT: NA
Middle 50% SAT range: V 500-610, M 500-610
Middle 50% ACT range: 21-26
3 Most popular majors: management, engineering, agriculture
Retention: 83%
Graduation rate: 55%
On-campus housing: 39%
Fraternities: 14%
Sororities: 18%
Library: 2,409,000 volumes
Tuition and Fees: $3,898 in; $10,324 out
Room and Board: $5,168
Financial aid, first-year: 40%
Varsity or Club Athletes: 7%
Early Decision or Early Action Acceptance Rate: NA

When you think of Oklahoma State University, what's the first thing that comes to mind? Cowboys? Wrong! Contrary to the commonly held perception, students at OSU come from diverse backgrounds, and agriculture is perhaps the last thing uniting the student body. Ranking as one of the top accounting schools in the nation, OSU has shed its agricultural image and offers its students a wide selection of academic, extracurricular, and social activities. The school's small-town atmosphere attracts many students, and its proximity to Oklahoma City and Tulsa provides additional venues for recreation and cultural activities.

Academics

Students are generally pleased with their academic experience at Oklahoma State University. Like many other colleges, OSU has academic requirements students must fulfill in order to graduate. The requirements vary within each major; however, every student must take courses in political science, English, American history, and American government. Hard majors include "anything that requires chemistry or physics," such as engineering and premed. Marketing and education are considered to be easy majors at OSU. Depending on the level of the course, the class size can vary. Most general education classes range from 20 to 75 students, but some science classes can have up to 250 students. In addition to classroom learning, students at OSU frequently have the opportunity to participate in projects and research conducted by professors and other staff members. "Freshman year I was involved in a research scholars program where I actually got to be in a lab with a professor after having little to no training. I got to do a lot of hands-on stuff that I would not have otherwise been able to do," recalled one student.

From time to time, OSU invites celebrities, politicians and other renowned figures to speak on campus. Recent speakers include Felicia Rashad, Suzanne Somers, and Magic Johnson. Students praise the faculty for their availability outside of class and are mostly satisfied with the quality of education at OSU. "I am most thrilled about the information I am learning in my classes, and my only grievance is that there is not enough time to do everything I need to be doing," said one student.

The Campus Experience

So what kind of students attend OSU? "The stereotype is that we are all hicks from small towns, but that is not the case at all!" said one student. In fact, the student body at OSU is fairly diverse. Students from both large cities and small towns attend OSU. The majority of the student body is Caucasian, with a moderate mix of minorities and international students. However, students agree that the student body is accepting of diversity and respects each other's beliefs.

The Greek system is of great significance at OSU—one-third of the student body belongs to a fraternity or sorority. There are currently 11 sororities and 20 fraternities at OSU. "Most of the time when you go somewhere, one of the first questions people ask you is, 'Are you in a house?'" said one student. Often, the best parties on campus are organized by fraternities, but in order to attend these events, you must either be a member of a sorority or fraternity, or be invited by a member. The Frontier, Destination, and Plantation Balls are a few of the parties hosted by fraternities.

For students who are not members of a Greek house, there are still a wide range of weekend and social activities to select from. "Though Stillwater is a small town, it is college-oriented, so there is always something going on and if not, there is always the option of going out to eat in the city or Tulsa," said one student. For the most part, freshmen and upperclassmen do the same things on the weekends. Some people drink and party; some people hang out with friends; and for those who live nearby, there is always the option of going home. The drinking scene is fairly big at OSU. However, students are not pressured to drink, and non-drinkers can fit in any social event.

OSU has many student organizations that are respected by both students and faculty. From intramurals to student government to community service projects, students can find just about any activity to suit their interests and passion. Many students agree that involvement in extracurriculars is a great way to make friends and to contribute to the school.

The Student Activities Board is considered one of the premier leadership organizations on campus. The Board has sponsored visits from various prominent figures, such as former first lady Barbara Bush and sex therapist Dr. Ruth Westheimer. Many students are involved in committees for Homecoming festivities, which are said to be the third-largest in the nation. Two campus-wide community service projects are held every year, one in the fall and one in spring. Called Into the Streets and The Big Event, respectively, these projects require students to give up one day each semester to provide community service to those in need throughout Stillwater. Every year before the first home football game, students put on a big show called Orange Peel. Celebrities such as Bill Cosby, Faith Hill, and Sinbad have taken part in this event in the previous years. Depending on the organization and the student's interests, time commitment to extracurriculars can range from as few as five hours to as many as 30 hours a month.

The sports scene has a significant presence on OSU's campus. Basketball and football are perhaps the school's most popular sports, but the school is also known for its wrestling team, which won the national wrestling championship in 2003. Referring to OSU's athletes, one student said, "Our guys are unbeatable." For those who are not on sports teams, intramurals and recreational activities in the fitness center are available.

Grubbin' and Cribbin' Options

OSU students unanimously describe the campus as beautiful. "All of the architecture is modified Georgian architecture, so all the buildings look the same," said one student. Another student said, "Our school is so pretty, I feel like I can be comfortable anywhere on campus." The student union building is the largest in the nation, and many of the campus's facilities are under renovation. A new football stadium is in the works, and the fitness center is fairly new. The Wellness Center and the Colvin Center are two athletic facilities open to the students. There are restaurants, dance clubs such as Tumbleweed and The Ozone, and a movie theater in the campus's vicinity. Students also have the option of traveling to Tulsa or Oklahoma City, which are each an hour away from OSU. The majority of the students have cars, but not having one should not preclude one from taking full advantage of all that the campus and its vicinities have to offer.

> **"The Greek systems offer long lasting friendships, the campus activities provide leadership opportunities, and international study programs broaden our view of the world."**

Students are required to live on campus or in a Greek house their freshman year, unless their parents live in Stillwater and they want to live at home. Most freshmen live in standard dorms, which, according to many students, are "fairly nice." Freshman student housing is actually undergoing change as dorms are being replaced with apartment-type housing, and the new system should be completed within the next few years. Most dormitories are air-conditioned and have a lot of storage space and enough room to be comfortable. Campus housing is available to all students, but most students choose to move to an apartment or a Greek house after freshman year. Marriage housing and honors dorms are a couple of the special housing options offered by OSU. "We also have a Spanish floor at one of our dorms, where student can only speak Spanish. I think it's a great idea!" said one student. RAs are present on every floor but are reportedly lenient and easy-going, for the most part.

Students at OSU are satisfied with the various dining options OU offers. "The cafeterias and places to use your meal plan are excellent. I never had a problem with not liking the food," said one student. Most students eat at the non-cafeteria concessions on campus, which offer pizza, sandwiches, hamburgers, and "anything and everything you could possibly want." There are also a lot of restaurants in Stillwater. The most famous is Eskimo Joe's, which used to be a bar and is now a restaurant by day, bar by night. Thursday nights are big for Joe's—the place is almost always packed after 11 P.M. The Hideaway offers great pizza, Joseppi's offers Italian food; in addition, you have the typical Red Lobster, Chili's, Applebee's, and other small restaurants.

When asked to choose one thing that differentiated OSU from other schools, students replied that the student body is worthy of distinction. "The people at OSU are very friendly and down to earth!" remarked one student. Many students said they would choose to attend OSU again in a heartbeat. "OSU has opened up so many opportunities for me to excel. The Greek systems offer long-lasting friendships, the campus activities provide leadership opportunities, and international study programs broaden our view of the world. I never expected to walk away from OSU having had so many great experiences and memories." —*Soo Kim*

FYI

If you come to Oklahoma State University, you'd better bring a "desire to meet new people. If you leave OSU without meeting the people, you've missed out on one of the campus' best assets."

What is the typical weekend schedule? "Parties usually start on Thursday night and occur on Friday and Saturday night too. On weekends in the fall when we have football games, students tailgate and celebrate before and after the game."

If I could change one thing about Oklahoma State University, I'd "change the university's policy on bad weather. OSU never closes or cancels class, regardless of the weather."

Three things every student at Oklahoma State University should do before graduating are "go to all the athletic events possible, get involved in one of the many student organizations on campus, and participate in Homecoming festivities."

Oral Roberts University

Address: 7777 South Lewis Avenue; Tulsa, OK 74171
Phone: 918-496-6518
E-mail address: admissions@oru.edu
Web site URL: www.oru.edu
Founded: 1963
Private or Public: private
Religious affiliation: none
Location: suburban
Undergraduate enrollment: 3,041
Total enrollment: NA
Percent Male/Female: 41%/59%
Percent Minority: 25%
Percent African-American: 16%
Percent Asian: 2%
Percent Hispanic: 5%
Percent Native-American: 2%
Percent in-state/out of state: 36%/64%
Percent Pub HS: NA
Number of Applicants: 1,337
Percent Accepted: 67%
Percent Accepted who enroll: 65%
Entering: 589
Transfers: 241
Application Deadline: rolling
Mean SAT: NA
Mean ACT: NA
Middle 50% SAT range: V 480-600, M 470-590
Middle 50% ACT range: 20-26
3 Most popular majors: religious education, theological studies, mass communications
Retention: 80%
Graduation rate: 50%
On-campus housing: 71%
Fraternities: NA
Sororities: NA
Library: 216,000 volumes
Tuition and Fees: $13,970
Room and Board: $5,900
Financial aid, first-year: 71%
Varsity or Club Athletes: 10%
Early Decision or Early Action Acceptance Rate: NA

Glistening in gold and silver, the Oral Roberts University Prayer Tower rises 250 feet toward heave, exemplifying the school's commitment to religious excellence and perseverance. People worship inside the tower 24 hours a day, 365 days a year, and a prayer line receives telephone calls from across the nation. From the tower's observation deck, visitors behold a panorama encompassing all of ORU's other architectural wonders, including the 45,000-seat Christ Chapel and 50-foot sculpture of prayer hands.

Religious Rules

In 1963, Oral Roberts claimed to receive a vision from God calling for a university to be built in Tulsa. Roberts promptly obeyed and founded Oral Roberts University. Not surprisingly, religion influences student life, both in and out of the classroom. The university holds mandatory chapel services twice a week for all students. The campus dress code stipulates with exceptions for Fridays and Saturdays, shirts and ties for males, and modest skirts for females (in recent years, however, the code has relaxed to allow casual but appropriate attire for both sexes after 4 P.M.). When students apply, they must sign a statement agreeing to follow an honor code that forbids drinking, smoking, cheating, and premarital sex. All female students have a midnight curfew and male students must observe the same curfew for their first two years.

ORU requires students who are not living with their families to live on campus, but few students see this requirement as a burden because the dorms provide pleasant accommodations. Extensive renovations of the dorms are currently underway, and a food court including fast-food restaurants is also planned. Students live in single-sex wings that serve as social substitutes for sororities and fraternities. Although dancing remains forbidden on campus, each wing hosts clambakes and other events. Most students who choose to attend ORU do not mind the rules; in fact, one undergrad explained that "living a Christian life here has made me stronger, and frankly, I wouldn't want to live amidst the grease of secular life."

Academic Resources

Academically, many students gain communications experience by working for ORU's television station or for the national Abundant Life Prayer Group. The

Learning Resources Center is the primary academic facility on campus, with 4.5 acres of libraries, classrooms, and labs. The Center, like all the dorm rooms, is hard-wired with a closed-circuit TV system so students can watch different educational programs as well as 26 channels offered on cable. The administration blocks out some channels, such as MTV, because they are deemed inconsistent with ORU's religious spirit. Sermons are also occasionally shown, which give the observer a taste of what one student called ORU's specialty—"Charismatic Christianity." Many students report that the theology program is excellent, despite one undergrad's complaint that "there's not much serious questioning or confrontation." In recent years, the education department also has earned praise from students. The business school, located in a building that one observer described as "futuristic in a sixties sense," is popular because it instructs young capitalists on how to combine morality and economics.

In pursuit of excellence in mind, body, and spirit, ORU requires all students to participate in sports. Many play intramurals, and attendance at varsity games is high. Last year, in an effort to invigorate the sports program, ORU changed the name of its teams from the Titans to the Golden Eagles. All ORU teams play in Division I, and the basketball and golf teams usually bring the most victories. The Tulsa community uses ORU's basketball arena, the Maybee Center, for everything from the local sports to graduations and concerts. Major performers such as Garth Brooks have performed there in recent years.

"In pursuit of excellence in mind, body, and spirit, ORU requires all students to participate in sports."

Students generally agree the ORU has changed for the better. Four years ago, the 75-year-old Oral Roberts stepped down as president of the university and passed the post on to his son, Richard Roberts. Students describe the younger Roberts as highly approachable and popular on campus. Enrollment continues to increase and if you are seeking a spiritual, as well as an academic, collegiate experience, you may be one of the growing number of applicants considering Oral Roberts University. —*Brian Abaluck and Staff*

FYI

If you come to ORU, you'd better bring "the knowledge that you won't be able to watch MTV because television channels are censored."

What is a typical weekend schedule? "Mandatory chapel services, intramurals, perhaps an excursion into Tulsa."

If I could change one thing about ORU I'd "improve upon the lack of extracurricular opportunities."

The three things that every student should do before graduating from ORU are "play intramurals, go to prayer group regularly, and take advantage of the city of Tulsa."

University of Oklahoma

Address: 1000 Asp Avenue; Norman, OK 73019-4076
Phone: 800-234-6868
E-mail address: admrec@ou.edu
Web site URL: www.ou.edu
Founded: 1890
Private or Public: public
Religious affiliation: none
Location: small city
Undergraduate enrollment: 20,193
Total enrollment: NA
Percent Male/Female: 50%/50%
Percent Minority: 23%
Percent African-American: 6%
Percent Asian: 5%
Percent Hispanic: 4%
Percent Native-American: 8%
Percent in-state/out of state: 79%/21%
Percent Pub HS: NA
Number of Applicants: 7,248
Percent Accepted: 89%
Percent Accepted who enroll: 60%
Entering: 3,833
Transfers: 2,557
Application Deadline: 1 June
Mean SAT: NA
Mean ACT: NA
Middle 50% SAT range: NA
Middle 50% ACT range: 23-28
3 Most popular majors: marketing, management information systems, business
Retention: 82%
Graduation rate: 54%
On-campus housing: 21%
Fraternities: 17%
Sororities: 25%
Library: 4,107,132 volumes
Tuition and Fees: $2,929 in; $8,078 out
Room and Board: $5,030
Financial aid, first-year: 48%
Varsity or Club Athletes: 9%
Early Decision or Early Action Acceptance Rate: NA

"My schooner is going to plow your longhorn, Boomer Sooner!"—these are words not often heard at most universities, but then again, the University of Oklahoma, or OU, is not most universities. Two storied groups, the Boomers, or pioneers who agitated to bring about the opening of Oklahoma to settlers before 1889, and the Sooners, the settlers who slipped in to stay before the gun was fired, demonstrate how OU students come to college with an eagerness and dedication to partake in the rich tradition, academic, and social realm that OU strives to provide. But what about the schooner plowing the longhorn? Well, the Sooner schooner, a Conestoga wagon, is the official OU mascot, and is pulled by horses Boomer and Sooner. The longhorn in the raucous cheer belongs to OU's arch-rival, the University of Texas. This rivalry is played out in the "Red River Shootout" or more commonly referred to as "OU-Texas!" The trek down south to the game in Dallas is a college must—if not to fill the Cotton Bowl Stadium with the call-response cry of "Boomer, Sooner!" then to make a quick run-through of the Texas State Fair for a funnel-cake. The OU-Texas game has become such a long-standing, important tradition that "the president of the University cancelled school for a day one year when OU won." As such, the students and faculty, including President Boren (a former Oklahoma governor and senator), take much pride in the traditions of the university, especially that of sporting upside-down longhorn decals on their cars and other merchandise.

Big Fat Greek World

Greek life and athletics are the two most popular on-campus activities among students at OU. With 39 current fraternities and sororities in tow, it is only logical that 50 percent of the students sport Greek letters. Because the 12 sororities hold their rush the week prior to the beginning of school, the on-campus housing allows these freshman co-eds to venture up to school early and get settled in prior to beginning the rush process. As with most selection processes, there is some competitiveness, though recently, President Boren has organized the rush system to make sure that everyone who rushes the entire week will receive a bid to at least one house. Normally, "because there are so many sororities, to continue to attract new members the houses have each developed their individual strengths and interests, and consequently girls almost always discover a house that they feel they belong in." In just the last year, three new sororities have taken up residence on the OU campus, so if a students are willing to spend a week viewing cleverly choreographed shows and 10,000-square-foot, "flawlessly furnished," houses, going Greek could be going right up their alley. Though such a large Greek system might seem overwhelming, it proves a premium for the party scene. The festivities include many theme parties, where attendees don everything from rock-star attire to the 80s prep look. And of course, the Greeks also realize the importance of philanthropy, hosting numerous fundraisers, including dance marathons where they work up a sweat jiving to good tunes. It is also important to note that there is life outside of Greek—"no one is disparaged if they don't like the idea of housing with 100 girls." Though the party scene is decidedly Greek-oriented, those who choose not to rush don't find themselves left out of the fun.

While the dating scene is often non-existent at other colleges, OU students "date well and date often." Often, dates include a trip to Classic 50s Drive-In, a Sooner institution, where the menu is tasty, offering everything from "candy in any drink, amazing hamburgers, potato boats, and the Crimson and Cream Slush" (OU's colors). A Greek favorite seems to be the "date-parties" thrown by both fraternities and sororities. These gatherings normally involve the members of the fraternity, all with their dates, traveling on a charter bus to clubs or other wild venues to dance the night away. A particularly favorite of these date parties is the Lambda Chi's "Destination Unknown," where they round everyone up on a bus a take a weekend excursion to a far-away and exotic party locale (such as Memphis). Because these excursions require a date, students are accustomed to intermingling and asking each other out.

The Weekend Comes Sooner

While technically the weekend starts on Friday, to the Sooners of the University of Oklahoma the weekend comes, well, sooner. Thursdays can be jam-packed with house parties or the many frat parties and Fridays and Saturdays can consist of movies at the Student Union, taking a trip to Oklahoma City for some shopping and restauranting at Bricktown, catching an OU Drama School production, playing basketball outside, sleeping, reading in the grass, working out at the Huffman Gym, or . . . partying! Though "many freshman feel that alcohol is necessary in order to have a good time on weekends," it is possible to find groups that just want to "hang low-key style." In fact, that tactic might be a smart idea, as the OU administration has been cracking down on underage drinking, increasing the budget for undercover cops to appear at parties as normal college kids. Nonetheless, it has been said that the town of Norman is nestled "smack-dab in the midriff of the bible belt," so with a strong spiritual presence on campus, finding non-party groups is not difficult.

Aside from these activities, the weekends can be broken down into two types: football weekends and non-football weekends. If there is an OU football game that Saturday, "the whole day is consumed . . . by the game." Tailgaters arrive a day in advance to stake a claim to a prime tailgating position. The main road into campus becomes a one-way street, literally, as before games traffic only flows towards the stadium and afterwards it only flows towards the highway. The competition for the traffic flow is the horde of people, especially the returning alumni who come to revel in reliving their college days. By the time Sunday rolls around, all are "generally recuperating" and Norman finally lays still.

Brains and Brawns

Sooners understand that a healthy mind is just as important as that healthy bod. Currently, 600 National Merit Scholars are enrolled at OU, ranking the university at the top among public universities in National Merit Scholars enrolled per capita and in the top five in Rhodes Scholars graduated. In one student's opinion "Boren is successfully getting to the point of dressing a private school in public-school clothing." Another noted that the "Honors College is so hot right now." To be accepted into the Honors College, applicants must meet higher admissions standard which require both higher test scores and high school GPA.

If accepted, the hard work is definitely compensated. Students in the Honors program have the opportunity to enroll in the small sections consisting of 22 students or fewer, compared to normal OU lecture classes of many hundreds. Honors students are also encouraged to study abroad or try out summer study at Oxford University. They have easy access to research internships with faculty in science laboratories or on humanities projects, and students can only graduate with honors if enrolled in the Honors College. One of the best perks, besides getting to line up end-zone-to-end-zone during a football game, is the early-enrollment process, which for Honors students practically "guarantees the lucky dogs whatever classes they want."

"OU students date well and date often."

Even the students who feel that "going summa cum laude is just a little summa too much" enjoy the array of blossoming academic prospects at the university. All classes are taught by professors, including the infamous "Dr. Indestructo, who once cut off his finger for the advancement of science" (a.k.a. a hot dog covered in liquid nitrogen) and "dabbled in the drinking liquid nitrogen business." Business management seems to be the most popular major, with communications sliding in as the "most painless." A unique major, visual communications, combines art and business "for all those art majors who understand the importance of not starving" and meteorology, though highly demanding, is one of the university's strongest fields. TAs lead the discussion sections and labs, and except for maybe the physics department, all are easy to understand.

Sooner Sighting

One student felt that "We have everything here—cowboys, preps, sluts, cool people, jocks, white trash, punks, you get the point," but to the naked eye, the school still remains highly homogenous. Community life fosters a combination of "an abundance of Southern hospitality" and the heavy efforts of the active Student Life program, which offers New Student Week and Winter Welcome. When planning one's attire for the next day, most students go for the "T-shirt/jeans combo" but it is commonplace to catch "the occasional trendy or occasional slob in the sweats and even the occasional tuxedo for, you know, Greek life." In fact, when one first enters an OU dorm, he or she might be "blown away by the attractiveness—and I am not talking about the sofas." It seems to be a fact that Sooners value the benefits of staying healthy and fit. Whether they are motivated by the success of the finely tuned athletic teams or just love to compete themselves, intramural sports have become the number-one extracurricular activity among students. Most of traditional sports are included in the intramural season: football, basketball, softball, and baseball, plus the additions of the ever-popular ooze-ball and pickle ball (the former is a type of volleyball played on a muddy court "accompanied by a friendly hosing down by the local Norman Fire Department," and pickleball is a type of co-ed touch football). Also, Homecoming is an event in which all participate. Almost all student organizations enter a float into the annual parade, which they design and create before filling the overflowing stadium with fans for the game.

(Okla)Homa Away from Home

Most OU students, if they are not living in a sorority or frat house, live in the dorms all four years. In fact, freshmen who do not live at home are required to live on campus. Housing consists primarily of two double bedrooms, connected by a bathroom, and is assigned on a first come, first serve basis. Couch and Walker are the dorms in demand due to their refreshment conveniences: the Couch Express in Couch sells miscellaneous foods and has a grill, and Walker has Etcetera, a convenience store for random stuff. Adams Tower "is okay (people who live there like it)—it has a Burger King/Baskin Robbins, but the halls are a lot smaller and it just seems a little more institutional." A student is fine as long as he or she does not live in Cross, the oldest and farthest dorm from campus, a "double whammy." Freshmen year dorms are co-ed by floor, while upperclass rooms can be co-ed by suite.

Co-ed visitors must be out of freshmen rooms by midnight on weeknights and 2 A.M. on weekends. Most freshmen "expect and respect the rules" and think it is a decent trade for "the opportunity to meet so many people and become involved on campus." All freshman floors have RAs who work hard to organize social events for the floor and be available to any other needs their freshman may have. Each room can control its own air and "thanks to spraying rooms, students are going bug-free for a few months now!"

Are You Going to Eat That?

Many believe the OU on-campus dining options are "pretty good" while others feel "the food is great . . . off campus." The cafeteria offers Sooner Sports Grill's hamburgers and wings and make-your-own stir-fry along with an assortment of daily specials. Couch Express has eat-on-the-go options with "gooey grilled cheese," yogurt, pizza, and drinks. The Student Union offers a basic food-court atmosphere with Wendy's, Chick-fil-A, Sbarro, Mexican and Chinese food.

Surrounding campus, Norman is your typical, safe college town, catering to college students. The off-campus dining and shopping are first-class, and everyone in town "seems to understand that OU is what it is because of the community, the tradition," and works diligently to keep the special spirit alive. Most students are from in-state or the Midwest, and many were preceded at OU by their parents or grandparents, coining the phrase "Sooner-born and Sooner-bred and when I die, I'll be Sooner-dead." The love for athletics and creating social bonds only enhances the intense school spirit, which can make a trip to the Oklahoma Memorial Stadium rather intimidating for visitors—especially once the rumbling of Boomer . . . Sooner begins. —*Jocelyn Ranne*

FYI

If you come to OU, you'd better "NOT bring anything orange, the color of both of OU's rivals: Texas and Oklahoma State."

What is the typical weekend schedule? "Tons of frat parties with the opportunity to go to plays put on by the OU School of Drama. Then, of course, we cannot forget OU football, when Saturdays in Norman become a completely different world."

If I could change one thing about OU, I'd "add more parking spaces! With each year's freshmen class growing, parking is becoming a larger and larger problem."

Three things every student at OU should do before graduating are "attend an OU football game, go for a Coke date at Classic 50s Drive-In (especially during Happy Hour for half price drinks), and study in the Great Reading Room."

The University of Tulsa

Address: 600 South College Avenue; Tulsa, OK 74104
Phone: 918-631-2307
E-mail address: admission@utulsa.edu
Web site URL: www.utulsa.edu
Founded: 1884
Private or Public: private
Religious affiliation: Presbyterian
Location: urban
Undergraduate enrollment: 2,691
Total enrollment: 4,119
Percent Male/Female: 47%/53%
Percent Minority: 18%
Percent African-American: 8%
Percent Asian: 2%
Percent Hispanic: 3%
Percent Native-American: 5%
Percent in-state/out of state: 65%/35%
Percent Pub HS: 79%
Number of Applicants: 2,077
Percent Accepted: 73%
Percent Accepted who enroll: 36%
Entering: 552
Transfers: 200
Application Deadline: rolling
Mean SAT: NA
Mean ACT: NA
Middle 50% SAT range: V 540-700, M 540-700
Middle 50% ACT range: 22-30
3 Most popular majors: management, engineering, visual and performing arts
Retention: 79%
Graduation rate: 63%
On-campus housing: 52%
Fraternities: 21%
Sororities: 23%
Library: 1,103,000 volumes
Tuition and Fees: $15,736
Room and Board: $5,610
Financial aid, first-year: 49%
Varsity or Club Athletes: 11%
Early Decision or Early Action Acceptance Rate: NA

People come to the University of Tulsa for the same reason they come to Tulsa itself: TU offers diversity, beauty, and opportunity in the heartland of America. TU's relatively high rate of acceptance does not mean the curriculum lacks vigor; in fact, students say the university offers a challenging, world-class education.

A Top Priority

TU's commitment to academic excellence reaches many programs. The College of Engineering and Applied Sciences is considered preeminent worldwide, particularly for its petroleum research and chemical engineering programs. The English department is recognized nationally as a center of James Joyce scholarship. The department publishes the *James Joyce Quarterly*, an academic journal with international circulation, and the McFarlin Library houses a special collection that features Joyce's writings along with 20th-century Anglo-Irish, American, and Native American literature.

Students consider the university's commitment to a strong academic program a top priority. The university curriculum, called the Tulsa Curriculum, provides a solid foundation in the liberal arts. The Tulsa Curriculum is divided into three parts: the core curriculum, the general curriculum, and the major area of concentration. The core curriculum focuses on reasoning, writing, math, and language courses. In order to fill the general curriculum requirements, students must take two courses in each of four blocks: Artistic Imagination, which includes literature and art courses; Social Inquiry, which studies the nature and behavior of the individual and group; Comparative and Historical Interpretation, which includes classes on religion, politics, economics, and culture; and Scientific Investigation, which consists of classes in the experimental and natural sciences.

Undergraduates note the strength of many of TU's departments. The School of Business is particularly impressive, with strong programs in marketing and communication. Additionally, with the current emphasis on computers and technology, TU's Management Information Systems (MIS) program is very popular among undergraduates. Students do say, however, that programs in music, theater and economics are lacking, and the TU Honors program also gets mixed reviews: some students find it rewarding, while others believe it needs improvement. All agree, however, that the small class size and personal attention given to students by professors makes Tulsa's academic program attractive. One senior said, "I have been here for four years and have never been taught by a teaching assistant and have never been in a class with more than 35 students."

All Work and No Play?

Of course, life at TU is not all work and no play. There are a number of activities in which to get involved and meet other people. The largest organization at TU, the Student Association, is responsible for coordinating various student activities and community service projects. Undergraduates also enjoy writing for TU's newspaper, *The Collegian*, or managing the student-run radio station, the Underground. Students also spend time in many of the different ethnic organizations on campus.

Perhaps the best way to meet other people at TU is through the Greek system. Fraternities and sororities host parties almost every weekend. While drinking is officially forbidden, enforcement is lenient and most would describe TU as a wet campus. By going Greek, freshmen have an easy way to go to great parties such as Snake-in-the-Grass and Pike Fest, meet a lot of new people quickly, and make many new friends. If the Greek scene is not for you, however, don't worry. There are plenty of other alternatives. When the Student Association is not sponsoring a dance or party, you can find them throughout the dorms. As one student puts it, "TU students love to have fun, finding a party is never a problem." Also, it is quite common to hang out with friends at JR's or at the Hut.

Students also take advantage of the city's entertainment. The city boasts a nationally renowned ballet corp, an opera company, a philharmonic, and several theater groups. The Gilcrease and Philbrook are popular museums. Reportedly, the Gilcrease Museum has the largest collection of Western American art in the world. Tulsa also boasts several festivals during the year, including Oktoberfest, Reggaefest, and Mayfest.

Students take their dates out to one of the city's restaurants, such as the Metro Diner, or they frequent malls such as Woodland Hills, Promenade, and Southroads. Free university shuttle service provides transportation to all of these places as well as to movie theaters around the city; one of which is close to campus, featuring 20 screens.

Where We Hang

When students hang out on campus, they usually spend time in the Allen Chapman Activities Center (ACAC), one of the university's two libraries, or their dorms. ACAC features the Hurricane Hut (a restaurant that serves as a center for beer guzzling), as well as meeting halls and study rooms. Many undergraduates like to study on the green lawns surrounding the church-like McFarlin Library or inside the law library, which is open 24 hours.

Although housing is reportedly comfortable, with dorm rooms including air conditioning, cable, and computer connections, a large percentage of the student body chooses to live off campus or in fraternity or sorority houses. Many believe the food, which some diners call "unappetizing" and "monotonous," has driven students off campus.

"TU students love to have fun, finding a party is never a problem."

There are five dorms on the TU campus: Lottie Jane, John Maybee, Twin Towers, Tower West, and Lafortune. Tower West and Lafortune are coed by suite, while Lottie Jane and John Maybee are single-sex. Twin Towers offers newer, smaller rooms, and is coed by floor. Housing in the area can be found cheaply, including the University Square Apartments for those wanting the benefits of apartment living without having to move off campus. While most agree housing at TU is not a problem, they complain about a lack of parking. And although the new shuttle service is helpful, most students agree a car is very important.

What students at the University of Tulsa really enjoy about their school is its size. The approximately 4,200 undergraduates are just enough to establish a diverse community while keeping a family-like environment. Tulsa is also known for its commitment to athletics. Sports are popular, although some students think TU places too much emphasis and funding on the sports program. Men's basketball is thought to be the biggest sport, and a new Convocation Center is being built for the basketball games. The football team plays in Skelly Stadium and is usually heavily supported at games. TU has a wide variety of men's and women's sports in everything from tennis to golf. Students not wanting to play a varsity sport take advantage of the popular intramural program.

A small, private school in America's heartland, the University of Tulsa is proud to provide its students with a solid liberal arts education. Prospective students are encouraged to take advantage of Tulsa Time, the University's program for prospective students to visit the campus, ask questions, and experience life at TU. As one student said, "When you have a degree from TU, people pay attention." If you are looking for a beautiful, active, and fun university in a great city with a strong academic program, then the University of Tulsa is definitely for you. —*Brian Abaluck and Staff*

FYI

If you come to TU, you'd better bring "money and a large-screen television."

What is the typical weekend schedule? "Go to the movies or a party at one of the fraternities, and try to work in some study time."

If I could change one thing about TU, I'd "enlarge the dorm rooms—man, are they tiny!"

Three things every student should do before graduating from TU are "take at least one class from Dr. Joseph Kestner, visit the Alexander Hogue Gallery, and do an internship at one of the publications."

Oregon

Lewis and Clark College

Address: 615 SW Palatine Hill Road; Portland, OR 97219
Phone: 503-768-7040
E-mail address: admissions@lclark.edu
Web site URL: www.lclarke.edu
Founded: 1867
Private or Public: private
Religious affiliation: none
Location: suburban
Undergraduate enrollment: 1,763
Total enrollment: NA
Percent Male/Female: 40%/60%
Percent Minority: 12%
Percent African-American: 2%
Percent Asian: 6%
Percent Hispanic: 3%
Percent Native-American: 1%
Percent in-state/out of state: 13%/87%
Percent Pub HS: NA
Number of Applicants: 3,223
Percent Accepted: 68%
Percent Accepted who enroll: 23%
Entering: 504
Transfers: 56
Application Deadline: 1 Feb
Mean SAT: NA
Mean ACT: NA
Middle 50% SAT range: V 600-690, M 580-670
Middle 50% ACT range: 25-29
3 Most popular majors: social sciences and history, English, foreign language
Retention: 81%
Graduation rate: 63%
On-campus housing: 63%
Fraternities: NA
Sororities: NA
Library: 477,423 volumes
Tuition and Fees: $24,686
Room and Board: $7,030
Financial aid, first-year: 54%
Varsity or Club Athletes: 30%
Early Decision or Early Action Acceptance Rate: 74%

Not far from the city of Portland, Oregon, students at Lewis and Clark College carry on blissfully on a wooded estate with a spectacular view of Mt. Hood in the distance. Small classes, a close-knit community, and a love for the great outdoors draw a diverse student body to this oasis in the Pacific Northwest where outdoor activities are never too far away.

Attentive Academics

Lewis and Clark is known for its strong academic departments that lavish students with personal attention. Favorite majors include international affairs, biology, business, English, and sociology/anthropology. Classes generally enroll around 20 students, although some introductory courses can enroll between 40 and 60 students. Small class size allows undergraduates the opportunity to "become closer with professors," who are known to take keen interest in their students. One student described her professors as, "approachable, friendly, and involved in the academic careers of their students." Another student added, "Professors at LC do not try to push their ideas onto you. They are well educated and want to see you grow with the expertise they can provide in their field." There are no TAs at Lewis and Clark. Students feel that academics are "challenging." However, one undergrad explained that students "enjoy the challenge because they respect the professors and feel intellectually rewarded by their classroom experience."

As part of the liberal arts requirement, incoming freshmen are required to take Inventing America, a survey course covering American history and philosophy. The class is apparently "hated by most freshmen." However, one undergrad explained that "Inventing America can be an amazing class with the right professor, which is pure luck because all different types of professors teach it (including psychology, biology, math, etc.)."

Many students flock to Lewis and Clark for its renowned international affairs and language departments. Students also report these departments as being the "most demanding academically." Many students double major with whatever language they are taking. Students praise the extensive study-abroad programs, which allow them to travel and implement their newly acquired language skills. Over half of all Lewis and Clark undergrads go abroad before they graduate. They can choose among programs in Germany, France, and England, as well as those in more exotic places such as India and Argentina. Lewis and Clark also allows students to study in Washington, D.C., while completing an internship with a government bureau or private company. For one student, working in Washington "provided me with work experience while I went to school at the same time."

Students feel that they are "mostly liberals, who are upstarts seeking change and newness in the world."

When Lewis and Clark students need to hit the books, they use the "totally awesome" Watzek Library. Watzek has a wide array of resources including an interlibrary exchange program, which allows students to borrow from other libraries if their own does not have what they need. There are study rooms for group study, long tables, and private carrels with computer hookups that allow students to check their e-mail from a laptop instead of waiting in line at the computer center. "Everyone goes" to the library, said one student, "which makes it a pretty social place."

Since the mid-1990s, a number of construction projects have revamped the Lewis and Clark campus. The size of Watzek Library was doubled and a center for the humanities and arts was finished in 1996. The Templeton Center was restructured, bringing the "headquarters for student activities closer together, which is a plus," according to one undergrad. Students also rate the weight room as "a step up." A new arts and humanities building and music building were completed in 1998.

No Greek Scene? Thank God

There is no Greek system at Lewis and Clark, but students do not seem to miss it. One student explained that it was "a big part of why people come to LC." The Greeks were removed from campus in the early 1970s with a donor's amendment. Apparently, the donor would not give the school her fortune unless they promised to prohibit Greek houses, install an all-women's dorm, and serve ice cream at every meal!

Despite the lack of a Greek scene, Lewis and Clark is not lacking in social events on the weekends. Although this is not a "major party school," many students partake in a drink or a joint or two over the weekend. Dating does occur at Lewis and Clark, though how often depends on which student is asked. Random hookups also occur frequently; students do warn that with a small campus, the social scene can seem "filled with rumors" at times, but people are "mostly laid-back about romance here."

Lewis and Clark is technically a dry campus, but apparently this policy does not stop anyone from drinking. Although students report that campus police will "write up" students and repeat offenders may find themselves before a peer review committee, it does not happen very often. However, due to this policy, most large parties are held off campus. Lewis and Clark students are lax when it comes to drugs and alcohol. One student explained that "it is easy to drink and smoke here, though it is not done in excess too often." Marijuana is the most prevalent drug found on campus, although drugs like LSD and mushrooms are also in use to an extent.

Students report spending their weekends doing numerous activities on and off campus. Popular hangouts on campus include two student-run cafes, the Rusty Nail and the Platform, which host music events regularly. Many students enjoy the big-screen movies presented every Saturday night in Council Chambers by the Students Organized for Activities (SOFA). Many students report they enjoy just "relaxing with friends on-campus." Since Lewis and Clark's campus is located in a suburban neighborhood (which means there is nowhere to go "just off campus"), many students venture into Portland for nighttime activities. Undergrads describe Portland as "a great city where the people are always friendly despite all the rain." There are numerous clubs, pubs, bars, and restaurants that students enjoy going to, including Fulton Pub, Buffalo Gap, and Seges. In addition, Powell's is also a popular Portland gathering spot for Lewis and Clark students. It is the largest independent bookstore in America and apparently has "good readings on Friday nights." Portland also has a growing swing and rave scene as well. However, students complain that fun in Portland only lasts so long because "everything closes very early, like 10 P.M. on the weekends."

Many a Rainy Day

Fortunately or unfortunately, depending on whom one asks, there are many rainy days on the Lewis and Clark campus. The LC campus is not a place to be without an umbrella, which drives some students nuts. Yet, other students appreciate the weather because campus is like "a huge, wet garden." Green is certainly the most appropriate adjective for the campus, which has a rose garden, lots of trees and grassy lawns, and cobblestone paths, not to mention the "spectacular" view of Mt. Hood. The charm of a lush campus "makes students love Lewis and Clark despite the impossible rain."

Freshmen and sophomores are required to live on campus, although many students consider this requirement restrictive and overly expensive. Some go so far as to equate living on campus to "hell on earth." Although others feel that "it is hard to meet new people when you move off campus and you are closer to the campus facilities on campus." Students who live on campus are usually housed in dorm rooms in groups of two, four, or six (known as a "six-pack"). Room size and amenities vary from dorm to dorm. Most dorms are coed by floor (because residents of each floor share a bathroom) and some have language theme floors. While students rate Copeland as the best dorm, Platt-Howard (also known as "the projects") is consistently called the worst. Copeland is known across campus for throwing parties and is generally acknowledged as the most social dorm. Hartzfeld, which offers some suites, is preferred by upperclassmen who remain on campus; the atmosphere is peaceful, which allows for better studying. For those who do not mind the walk, the luxurious Stewart dormitories, about 10 minutes from the center of campus, have walk-in closets and large rooms, although they reportedly lack the social atmosphere of Copeland. Lewis and Clark has one all-female dorm, commonly referred to as "the convent."

The main dining hall at Lewis and Clark is in the Templeton College Center, nicknamed "the Bon" (pronounced as "Bone") for the catering company, Bon Appetit. Students living on campus must purchase a meal plan that includes at least 14 meals per week. The food is considered "pretty good," for college food. Students say that Bon Appetit, which is considered the best food service in the Northwest, offers a variety of options for each meal. Pizza, salad, and sandwiches are popular choices. Several vegetarians, of whom there are many at LC, reported that they cater well to their needs. Students who have Flex points, which are purchased at the beginning of the school year, can use them at the Trail Room, a grill on the floor below the Bon. Students rarely venture off campus for a meal, as there is little choice in the residential neighborhood surrounding the school. Domino's Pizza does deliver, but most students save their money for quality meals in downtown Portland.

It is generally agreed that there is a "big schism" between people who live on and off campus after sophomore year. Since the campus is surrounded by a suburban residential area, housing is often more affordable off campus than on. A large number of upperclassmen choose to move out of the dorms and into "cheap and plentiful" apartments or houses with friends. For those who live farther away from campus there are shuttle buses run by the college. Many students have cars, but caution that one has to be careful to avoid parking tickets.

Trail Blazers

Many students fear that Lewis and Clark will soon be stereotyped by their most famous graduate, Monica Lewinsky. In reality, students say that "there are a lot of rich kids rebelling" at LC. The school does make up for its "nonexistent" racial diversity with a good number of international students and a diversity within the students' backgrounds and interests. Students feel that they are "mostly liberals, who are upstarts seeking change and newness in the world." However, others pessimistically believe that "everyone here pretends to be hippie and liberal while content to buy their Tommy gear and be apathetic to global and environmental causes." Generally, undergrads feel that "most students accept people for who they are and are supportive of people of different races, religions, and sexual orientations."

The student body of Lewis and Clark has low school spirit. What spirit there is for varsity athletics is "mostly athletes supporting their friends and other athletes." This does not mean, however, that Lewis and Clark students swear off athletics altogether. In fact, intramural sports are some of the most popular activities on campus, especially volleyball, skiing, soccer, crew, rugby, lacrosse, and sailing. Students who aren't as into school-sponsored athletics enjoy taking advantage of their natural surroundings by participating in outdoor activities. Hiking, rock climbing, mountain biking, and skiing are popular sports. One student suggested that Lewis and Clark students are passionate about "outdoorsy" activities since "the Nalgene bottle clipped onto a backpack with a carabiner is the biggest fashion statement here." Students can reach the Oregon coast in two hours and the Columbia River Gorge in about an hour's drive. Both are apparently "breathtaking, even on a drizzly day." For the non-athletes, there is the campus TV station, LCTV, and radio station, KLC. Various green clubs are also reportedly popular. Aspiring writers can join either the *Pioneer Log* or *Sacajawea's Voice*, the two campus newspapers.

Even at a college without tremendous school spirit, the Lewis and Clark mascot, the Pioneer, is an appropriate representative of the school. An attitude typical of Lewis and Clark is apparent in one of the school's mottoes: "Do not follow where the path may lead, go instead where there is no path and blaze a trail." Although students rally around the fact that their school is actually a close-knit community, "people here like to do their own thing, and Lewis and Clark's free-minded attitude encourages this." Students at Lewis and Clark are individuals who "blaze their own trails," but who will come together to support their community. Many students believe that Lewis and Clark offers them the best of all worlds—a solid liberal arts education in a community of outdoors lovers. *—Alison Pulaski and Staff*

FYI

The three best things about attending Lewis and Clark are "the small classes, the fact that professors listen to you, and that everything is green."

The three worst things about attending Lewis and Clark are "the isolation of being off campus, that everyone thinks that kids here are like Monica Lewinsky (alumna), and that Monica Lewinsky no longer attends."

Three things that every student should do before graduating are "go to Portland, hike around Mt. Hood, and go somewhere weird to study abroad."

One thing I'd like to have known before coming here is "how many inches ice cream can add to your waist-line."

Oregon State University

Address: 10 Kerr Administration Building; Corvallis, OR 97331-2106
Phone: 541-737-4411
E-mail address: osuadmit@orst.edu
Web site URL: osu.orst.edu
Founded: 1868
Private or Public: public
Religious affiliation: none
Location: suburban
Undergraduate enrollment: 15,413
Total enrollment: NA
Percent Male/Female: 53%/47%
Percent Minority: 13%
Percent African-American: 1%
Percent Asian: 8%
Percent Hispanic: 3%
Percent Native-American: 1%
Percent in-state/out of state: 88%/12%
Percent Pub HS: NA
Number of Applicants: 5,811
Percent Accepted: 75%
Percent Accepted who enroll: 69%
Entering: 3,058
Transfers: 1,037
Application Deadline: rolling
Mean SAT: NA
Mean ACT: NA
Middle 50% SAT range: V 470-580, M 480-610
Middle 50% ACT range: 20-26
3 Most popular majors: business marketing, liberal arts, human development/ family studies
Retention: 80%
Graduation rate: 59%
On-campus housing: 22%
Fraternities: 13%
Sororities: 12%
Library: 1,403,000 volumes
Tuition and Fees: $4,014; $14,898 out
Room and Board: $5,976
Financial aid, first-year: NA
Varsity or Club Athletes: 6%
Early Decision or Early Action Acceptance Rate: NA

Oregon State University is like your perfect date: it has beauty, intelligence, and a laid-back, fun-loving attitude. Nestled in quiet Corvallis, OSU offers its nearly 19,000 students solid academic programs complimented by lively social life and picturesque surroundings.

A Natural High

OSU is situated in the middle of the stunningly beautiful Willamette Valley of Oregon Trail fame. For the outdoor enthusiast, a plethora of exciting activities abound: hiking and camping in the nearby woods, "little running trails" which wind through campus and cross "rarely used back roads," fly fishing and water sports on the many Oregon rivers, even snowboarding and skiing in the Cascade Mountains. If this is not enough, Corvallis is a mere 45-minute drive from the majestic Oregon coast. The Willamette Valley gives campus its "always green and beautiful" appearance, framed by mountains and trees. Students rave about "gorgeous red brick" architecture and spacious, grassy quads. Students praise Corvallis, a subdued town of just 32,000 permanent residents, for being "super safe." Students comprise about 40 percent of the total population in this university town, and campus buildings occupy much of the city. Because the university attracts a large international population, the city is remarkably diverse despite its relatively small size. What Corvallis lacks in big-city hustle and bustle it delivers in peaceful charm; there are "tons of flowers in planters" and students say the recently redone waterfront is "absolutely stunning." Town-gown relations range from "decent to good." There are occasional bouts of friction, but differences are forgotten when it comes time to cheer for Beaver sports teams.

Making a Beaver Outta You

School spirit runs deep, "especially during football season." The rivalry between OSU Beavers and their archrival, the Ducks of the University of Oregon, is so intense that their annual football matchup has been nicknamed the "Civil War." In addition to the numerous pep rallies in the week leading up to the War, one dining hall serves duck for dinner every night so that students can eat their rival's mascot as they prepare to devour them on the field. Orange and black, the school colors, are "everyone's favorite" during Civil War week as students go public with their Beaver pride—one recent graduate even remarked that she intends to use orange and black as her wedding colors. But you don't have to be a huge football fan to fit in at OSU. Even though it seems intense, "in practice," a sophomore explained, "school spirit is fairly muted" except during the Civil War. Despite the fact that OSU football has had a weak record against the University of Oregon in recent years, students continue to name Civil War week as a highlight of each year.

Academic Buffet

When they're not cheering on their football team, Beavers are "very satisfied" with the academic offerings at their school. Boasting a staggering array of more than 200 academic programs and classes in everything from "crop and soil science" to "Japanese language" to "apparel, interiors, housing and merchandising," OSU has something for both the serious studier and the student looking for an easy A. The engineering and prepharmacy programs widely considered OSU's best and most challenging. Communications, twentieth-century studies, and sociology are great majors for the "very lazy," and one engineering student joked that the business department is the "shameful destination of most failed engineers."

All students have to fulfill a set of academic distributional requirements called the Baccalaureate Curriculum, more commonly known as "Bacc Core." One sophomore was frustrated that he had to take so many "easy and stupid" Bacc Core classes. Other students said they appreciated the educational diversity required by Bacc Core, and could "understand the thinking" behind receiving a "well-rounded education." A junior praised the unusual classes available in Bacc Core, and strongly recommended a "very interesting" class that focused on food in non-Western cultures.

Impersonal, gargantuan intro classes are a common cause of complaint for freshmen. Though recognized as somewhat "unavoidable" due to the university's size, these classes were assailed for lacking class participation and for having professors "who are more interested in their own research than in teaching a class." Fortunately, students report, by the beginning of sophomore year, students have a better grasp of their interests, and as they take more advanced classes, "class head counts thin considerably."

For students looking for challenges beyond the standard undergraduate curriculum, the University Honors College (UHC) was founded in 1995. With about 500 students, the comparatively small UHC has a unique identity, with access to all the benefits of a large university. Many students working toward their Honors Baccalaureate Degree live together in the McNary—or "McNerdy," as it is sometimes referred to—Complex and have to complete an additional thesis project. The "very intelligent" members of the UHC are highly respected by their peers, even though some are perceived to be "a little snooty."

Day In, Day Out

When not in their dorms, apartments, or classes, Beavers spend a significant amount of time in the "awesome" Dixon Recreation Center. This recently renovated rec center is equipped with a full gym, exercise rooms, and courts for games of basketball, volleyball, and raquetball. For slightly less athletic endeavors, the basement of the beloved MU building houses a popular bowling alley and game rooms. A senior recommended that students enroll in some of the "really fun" classes offered at the rec center, like "step aerobics, pilates, bowling, fly fishing and country-and-western dancing."

"We've even got a 'hick' frat!"

Though many universities require freshmen to live in on-campus housing, OSU has no such rule. Even so, most freshmen opt to spend their first year living in traditional dorm-style housing, complete with "cramped" quarters and long hallways of identical double rooms. Upperclassmen who choose to live on campus find "stellar options" available, including well-lit spacious suites with several single rooms attached to common kitchen and living areas. Still, by sophomore year most Beavers elect to move out of the "expensive, mostly crappy" dorms into off-campus housing, which is readily available though, according to one junior, "still not exactly the lap of luxury." One freshman found the dining hall food "surprisingly" edible, but most students agree that cereal becomes a diet staple once the novelty of buffet-style meals wanes. Fast-food chains in the Memorial Union student center building accept meal plan points and offer a popular alternative to the dining hall. Otherwise, a grocery store and an array of coffee shops close to campus provide students with the sustenance to fuel their busy lives.

Animal House, Beaver Style

Many OSU students choose to live in one of the 25 fraternity or 12 sorority houses on Greek Row, and Greek life is an important part of the campus social scene. The "always packed" frat parties are a "great way to meet people" according to one social student. OSU frats are famous (or infamous, depending on your perspective) for their "Thirsty Thursday" parties, the weekly blow-outs that end each academic week. Some students head to these parties as early as 3:00 on a Thursday afternoon, and don't stumble home until the wee hours of the morning. Each Greek house has such a distinct personality that one student joked that it is easy "to judge a Greek by their letters." He said that each house has so "carefully purified its strain over the years" that it is like "some sort of convergent Darwinism run amok." A junior agreed that there is a Greek organization for nearly every type of person at OSU; "we've even got a 'hick' frat!" she exclaimed. Those who decide to go Greek are very attached to their houses. One sophomore described his fraternity as "a brotherhood based on friendship and acceptance." Non-Greeks have a less rosy view of the system. One particularly vehement junior described the overwhelming majority as either "inconsiderate Neanderthal frat rats or stereotypically dumb sorostitutes." Other students simply ignore Greek row; "it's just not my style," said one freshman girl, who didn't feel at all pressured to join a sorority. Everyone has an opinion about the Greek system at OSU, and its merits and demerits come under heated debate in the pages of student newspapers like the *Barometer.*

OSU has a long-standing reputation as a party school, and merry-making is an activity both Greek and non-Greek students have in common. Beyond frat parties, every weekend features dozens of house and apartment parties for students looking to have a good time. For the over-21 crowd, a lively bar scene close to campus includes lots of student favorites like The Peacock and Platinum. Escape, an alcohol-free on-campus nightclub, opened in 2002. It emerged from an administrative effort to curb underage and binge drinking but was quickly deemed a "dismal failure" by much of the student body. Many students agree that "with the lack of ready-made things to do" in Corvallis, thought and creativity are often needed to find enjoyable alternatives to partying. Those students with a car find access to the many things to do in the nearby metropolis of Portland. Popular school traditions like Mom's Weekend and Dad's Weekend also help to break the study-party-sleep routine.

Just Chillin': A Lesson for Life

At OSU, where dressed up means "something other than jeans and a school sweatshirt" and professors "allow or even prefer students to address them by first name," the campus attitude can best be described as "laid-back." "People here are friendly," observed one senior; it's "a very cheerful place." Disputes over politics and school policy create "remarkably little tension" and generally remain confined to the "entertaining and enlightening arguments" in campus publications. Despite a "very diverse campus . . . ethnically, nationally, and linguistically," political beliefs which encompass "every point on the spectrum," and "clothing and hair that run the full gamut of possibilities," everyone here "just gets along," said a junior. OSU manages to maintain unity while promoting understanding, and many feel that is the hallmark of its education. —*Claire Gagne*

FYI

If you come to OSU, you'd better bring "an industrial strength umbrella and an orange Beavers sweatshirt."

What is the typical weekend schedule? "Drink, sleep late, study. In that order."

If I could change one thing about OSU, I'd "make the break between classes longer. Ten minutes isn't enough with a campus this large!"

Three things every student at OSU should do before graduating are "go to Thirsty Thursday, cheer for the Beavers at a Civil War game, and spend lots of time at MU."

Reed College

Address: 3203 Southeast Woodstock Boulevard; Portland, OR 97202-8199
Phone: 503-777-7511
E-mail address: admission@reed.edu
Web site URL: www.reed.edu
Founded: 1909
Private or Public: private
Religious affiliation: none
Location: suburban
Undergraduate enrollment: 1,363
Total enrollment: 1,420
Percent Male/Female: 46%/54%
Percent Minority: 11%
Percent African-American: 1%
Percent Asian: 5%
Percent Hispanic: 4%
Percent Native-American: 1%
Percent in-state/out of state: 21%/79%
Percent Pub HS: 65%
Number of Applicants: 1,847
Percent Accepted: 55%
Percent Accepted who enroll: 31%
Entering: 314
Transfers: 33
Application Deadline: 15 Jan
Mean SAT: NA
Mean ACT: NA
Middle 50% SAT range: V 660-760, M 620-710
Middle 50% ACT range: 29-32
3 Most popular majors: social sciences, biology, English
Retention: 86%
Graduation rate: 67%
On-campus housing: 57%
Fraternities: NA
Sororities: NA
Library: 480,925 volumes
Tuition and Fees: $27,560
Room and Board: $7,380
Financial aid, first-year: NA
Varsity or Club Athletes: NA
Early Decision or Early Action Acceptance Rate: 70%

If you're an athlete, Reed College probably isn't going to suit your lifestyle. On the other hand, if you are interested in a stimulating academic life, an offbeat, intellectual student body and a political climate that would make Karl Marx feel at home, then Reed could be the place for you.

Wanna See a Naked Professor?

Reed is not an academic cakewalk, but the professors' sense of humor and adventure are the subject of much student praise and often make the "nuts" workload worth it. C.D.C. Reeve is known for his popular lectures, Nigel Nicholson for his online nudity antics (see http://academic.reed.edu/classics/faculty/nigel/nigel.html) and Wally Englert for his lyrical recitation of Homer's *Iliad* in Greek. Professors and students are on a first-name basis. "Most students don't even know their professors' last names," one student said.

Students consider academics at Reed to be generally tough. They report the workload to be challenging, but not overwhelming. Students issue a warning to people who want to slide their way to good grades: "Slackers generally don't make it to their junior year to even declare a major," admonished one senior math major. Two of the school's toughest classes—the writing-intensive freshman humanities course and the senior thesis—are required, and these bookend the first and last years of the Reed experience. However, Reedies who want a less arduous program can opt for classes in the psychology department, reported by some students to offer the easiest major on campus. But beware, even the "slacker" majors are, according to one student, "just insanely difficult instead of ludicrously difficult." Students have an easier time during the intersession, called Paideia, when they can take 10 day courses in scuba diving, basket weaving, bagel making, and a multitude of other not-entirely-academic classes.

At Reed, students are not just another number in class. Except for a few large lectures, classes are generally small, most with no more than 30 students, and all are taught by professors—you won't find any TAs at Reed. However, some students complain that the small class size makes it difficult to get into some of the more popular courses. Another common complaint is that courses for the major don't count for general distribution requirements.

Students unanimously report that a Shakespeare scholar would feel more at home than an up-and-coming scientist—Reed does not even offer an engineering major. Students who want it all—the Reed experience and an engineering program—study for three years at Reed and then transfer to another institution for two years. While the student body seems more artsy than science-oriented, "the left brain and the right brain are equal here," a political science major commented.

Blast from the Past

Much of the culture at Reed seems to be left over from the Sixties. The Reed Kommunal Shit Kollective speaks for itself. The student operators of this organization rent, among other things, kiddie bikes to students who want a cheap, silly-looking and environmentally friendly way to get around.

"Silly," as well as "zany" and "wacky," are some of the adjectives that Reed students use to describe themselves. "People who wouldn't fit in anywhere else fit in at Reed," said one student. "Everyone's wacky here—and most people are wonderful." Because of this, students warn that prospective Reedies should visit the campus to get a sense of the student body before they commit to attending the school. But for those who do choose Reed, a laid-back social atmosphere awaits. "There aren't any real groups here or class distinctions," said one student. "Everyone is pretty cool." Cliques don't dominate the social scene. Jocks can't be popular because Reed does not participate in intercollegiate sports—although intracollege rugby teams are a perennial favorite for participants and fans alike—and no one worries about getting into the best fraternity, because there is no Greek system.

Substance abuse among students is reportedly widespread. One student said "everybody" drinks and a lot of students do drugs. However, those who choose not to use drugs or alcohol do not feel out of place. "They're cool, like me," said one freshman, while another said, "Do non-drinkers and non-drug users feel out of place? Not really, but you have to be comfortable around them." Reedies, or, as they are sometimes called, Weedies, report that the student union is one of the most popular places to do drugs, although it also sponsors a lot of non-drug-related activities. According to students, the school does not bust students for drug or alcohol use unless they cause harm or embarrassment to another student, per the school's liberal Honor Principle. Kegs are allowed on campus if they are registered, a senior said, and one dorm is substance-free for those who want to escape the boozing.

> **"Slackers generally don't make it to their junior year to even declare a major."**

Students complain that the student body is not sufficiently racially diverse. "Reed's a pretty white school," said one sophomore. Said another, "We're not ethnically diverse enough to have many interracial couples." Despite the racial homogeneity, students compliment their school on its efforts to attract students of all financial means. "A lot (of students) are on major financial aid, but some people are on none whatsoever and are from a rather comfortable socioeconomic status," said a senior.

Please, Sir, Could I Have Some More?

While the well lit dining halls receive kudos from students, the meal plan is less satisfactory, and even "hotly contested" by some accounts. "You start with a certain number of points at the beginning of the semester, and each food item costs a certain number of points," a senior explained. "You get to budget the food yourself." Problems begin when students pile on the food at the beginning of the semester and find themselves point-less at the end. "People run out of points before the end of the semester," a student complained. They also run out of time to eat, as many students say they would like to see longer dining hall hours. But for those who can manage to conserve their points and hit the dining halls when they're open, the cafeterias offer a vast array of "pretty damn good" food. "We have vegan everything all the time," gushed a sophomore.

And since the school is within biking distance of downtown Portland, students also go there to find nourishment, although they cannot use their dining hall points in any of the downtown restaurants. Students who eat at Montage, which offers "good food for decent prices," will have their leftovers wrapped in tin foil that is molded into representational forms like ducks and other animals.

Put 'Em in the Asylum

Students give positive marks to the campus and dorms, "an island of Vermont in Oregon," according to one. Another added, "It's really beautiful, especially the cherry trees during spring." Indeed, many Reedies like to spend their Sundays stretched out on the lush campus lawns, reading and napping the day away.

Reed's dorms are popular, although by one student's count, only about half of the student body lives on campus. For the brave souls who make their way out into the real estate market, apartments can be found as close as across the street from the Reed dorms. For campus-faring types, housing is more than adequate. Old Dorm Block, home to students and centipedes alike, is one of the most popular dorms. "My room is so sweet," said a house adviser who lives in ODB. "It is a single with a working fireplace, a bay window, closet, built-in-bookcase, the works." Two of the dorms have elevators, and several offer theme housing, including language houses, the Outhouse, which has an outdoors theme, and the cat dorm, where students care for Oskar the cat.

Dorms are not segregated by grade, and students report that this integration facilitates friendships. Some students are also designated as house advisers, who are like RAs, but aren't there to bust students for doing "bad" things. Students refer affectionately to one dorm as The Asylum, and they either love it or hate it. One student noted that views on the Asylum are analogous to life at Reed as a whole—"if you like the people here, you're really going to have the time of your life. If not, you really should think about going someplace else." —*Sarah Pearce*

FYI

If you come to Reed, "you'd better bring a sense of humor."

The typical weekend schedule "involves a lot of studying, a lot of partying and some jogging and laundry thrown in for good measure."

If I could change one thing about Reed, "I'd decrease the stress culture."

Three things every student at Reed should do before graduating are "write a thesis; sneak into the rhododendron gardens; and Pict (a mysterious ritual which students are not at liberty to discuss with non-Reedies)."

University of Oregon

Address: 240 Oregon Hall; Eugene, OR 97403
Phone: 541-346-3201
E-mail address: NA
Web site URL: www.uoregon.edu
Founded: 1876
Private or Public: public
Religious affiliation: none
Location: urban
Undergraduate enrollment: 16,041
Total enrollment: NA
Percent Male/Female: 46%/54%
Percent Minority: 12%
Percent African-American: 2%
Percent Asian: 6%
Percent Hispanic: 3%
Percent Native-American: 1%
Percent in-state/out of state: 75%/25%
Percent Pub HS: NA
Number of Applicants: 9,889
Percent Accepted: 86%
Percent Accepted who enroll: 39%
Entering: 3,317
Transfers: 1,296
Application Deadline: 15 Jan
Mean SAT: NA
Mean ACT: NA
Middle 50% SAT range: V 500-610, M 500-610
Middle 50% ACT range: NA
3 Most popular majors: business, broadcast journalism, sociology
Retention: 83%
Graduation rate: 59%
On-campus housing: 21%
Fraternities: 10%
Sororities: 10%
Library: 2,420,000 volumes
Tuition and Fees: $4,794 in; $15,990 out
Room and Board: $6,981
Financial aid, first-year: 41%
Varsity or Club Athletes: 8%
Early Decision or Early Action Acceptance Rate: NA

Set by the Willamette River and the Cascade Mountains, the University of Oregon's 250-acre campus offers its students the vast resources of a public university along with the individual attention given by a midsize institution. The combination of well-regarded academics, diverse extracurricular opportunities, and lush, green surroundings make Oregon an amazing place to spend four years.

Academics

In addition to major requirements, most students find the general distribution requirements, or academic "clusters," to be very rewarding. By taking classes outside his major to fulfill the requirement, one student said, "I never would have taken some of the classes I ended up really enjoying." Although most introductory courses are large, students say that professors are very accessible. "You just need to make an effort and the professor would be happy to meet with you," said one freshman. To contrast this large size, all English and math courses are capped at 30 students per class. Classes become much smaller in upper division courses; some classes have no more than four students. Although the majority of majors offered at UO are respected, the pre-professional programs are particularly well regarded; Business, Journalism, and Architecture boast superb faculty and strong reputations. One academic option for freshmen is the Clarks Honors College, a liberal arts program for first year students, which offers small classes, individual attention from top-notch professors, and a work load emphasizing writing, verbal skills, and critical thinking. With the best professors of the university at their disposal (including UO's president), honors students say it is most definitely worth the work.

Extracurriculars Abound

With ferocious spirit, the Ducks are a force to be reckoned with on the track, field, or elsewhere. Varsity athletics play an important role for students, with track and field, basketball, and football teams drawing the biggest crowds. Besides going to the soon to be renovated Autzen Stadium to see the Ducks fight it out against archival Oregon State, students are heavily involved in intramural sports, community service, and political action. "We don't just talk, we do something," one student said about activism on campus. As the sixth-largest college source of Peace Corps volunteers, UO also boasts over 250 active student organizations ranging from the *Oregon Daily Emerald*, the daily newspaper, to a variety of political interest groups heavily involved in local and national politics. The community internship program, which entails working in Eugene for academic credit, is a combination of community service and work experience. "There is something here for everyone. It is just a matter of finding your thing," one student noted, showing the diversity of the UO campus.

". . . it will not be long before UO reclaims its rank as the most wired college by Yahoo!"

A Social Niche for Everyone

Besides extracurricular activities, UO students like to party. The Greek scene is prominent with 15 fraternities and 11 sororities. In contrast to the Greeks, there is a high contingency of alternative or hippie crowds, sometimes referred to as the granolas. Drug use is apparent, although marijuana is predominant, mushrooms and LSD are present as well. Many students, however, have no problem finding a niche between these two extremes and, in the end, everyone has a group of friends. Sometimes students go to Eugene for the weekend because it is a "fun, liberal place," but apparently "dead" at night, encouraging some to stay on campus. Students are extremely happy with campus security; with good lighting, call boxes, and Safe Rides program, students have no problem walking around late at night.

Dorms and Dining

Freshmen who choose to live on campus stay in either in Bean Hall, Hamilton, or Walton Dorms. Bean, known for being "small and dark," exclusively houses freshmen, while Hamilton and Walton house a mixture of freshmen and upperclassmen. Students have the choice of single-sex, coed, athletic, or "academic pursuit" dorms, allowing students of all lifestyles to live comfortably. In addition to meeting fellow students through dorms and classes, Freshman Interest Groups (FIG) led by upperclassmen bring students together in groups of 15 to 30 students who share the same academic interests. "It was a great way to meet people and see if other people are going through the same thing you are academically or otherwise," one student said.

Many sophomores remain on campus living in Hamilton, Walton, or Carson. Because Carson also houses graduate students, undergraduates claim it is a much quieter area of campus. Another option is Riley dorm, where 75 percent of the residents are international students. "It's a great place to live. You get to meet and hang out with people from all over the world," one American student said. While students who live on campus must have a meal plan, the variety of places to get food makes it "doable." As junior year rolls around, the majority of students move off campus to nearby apartments. Rather than having a meal plan, many upperclassmen eat at the Erb Memorial Union (EMU), the student center, between classes. There, students can use their meal plan to purchase food from Subway, Jamba Juice, and Pizza Hut, or specialty food at the "Market Place," which offers different types of food every day. "Without fail, I go to the EMU on Tuesdays for Indian and Wednesdays for Mexican," one student said.

Getting a Face Lift

While UO is already a well respected institution, its campus is still changing for the better. The science research buildings, home to two American Cancer researchers, were recently renovated, while the gym has just undergone the first phase of remodeling. Now equipped with a new fitness center, indoor rock climbing wall, and astro turf field, students can now utilize the new facilities for intramural and physical education classes. In addition, more renovations of the gym will soon be completed, as well as the stadium and Gilbert Hall in the near future. Great strides are also being made with the computer system on campus. With the purchase of new Internet servers, and Internet connections in every classroom and dorm, it will not be long before UO reclaims its rank as the most wired college by Yahoo! By bringing together a great faculty, developing facilities, and a smaller student body in comparison to other public institutions, UO is a well regarded school offering a solid liberal arts education. *—Jessica Morgan*

FYI

If you're coming to University of Oregon, you'd better bring "an umbrella!"

What is the typical weekend schedule? "Work, eat out, go to a sporting event, party a bit, work some more."

If I could change one thing about the University of Oregon: "rain, um, rain, and, um, rain."

Three things that every student should do before graduating are, "go to a football game, do a community internship, and play an intramural sport for a season."

Willamette University

Address: 900 State Street; Salem, OR 97301
Phone: 503-370-6303
E-mail address: undergrad-admission@willamette.edu
Web site URL: www.willamette.edu
Founded: 1842
Private or Public: private
Religious affiliation: none
Location: small city
Undergraduate enrollment: 1,650
Total enrollment: NA
Percent Male/Female: 49%/51%
Percent Minority: 15%
Percent African-American: 2%
Percent Asian: 7%
Percent Hispanic: 5%
Percent Native-American: 1%
Percent in-state/out of state: 46%/54%
Percent Pub HS: NA
Number of Applicants: 1,640
Percent Accepted: 83%
Percent Accepted who enroll: 26%
Entering: 353
Transfers: 70
Application Deadline: 1 Feb
Mean SAT: NA
Mean ACT: NA
Middle 50% SAT range: V 560-680, M 560-660
Middle 50% ACT range: 25-30
3 Most popular majors: English, political science and government, psychology
Retention: 88%
Graduation rate: 80%
On-campus housing: 71%
Fraternities: 32%
Sororities: 32%
Library: 333,000 volumes
Tuition and Fees: $25,432
Room and Board: $6,600
Financial aid, first-year: 64%
Varsity or Club Athletes: 30%
Early Decision or Early Action Acceptance Rate: 83%

In the heart of downtown Salem, Oregon, surrounded by office and state government buildings, one finds the oasis of Willamette University. The campus, with its lush greenery, historic red-brick structures, and a stream crossing through it, complements a unique university where academic fervor mixes with an intimate, friendly, and fun student body.

Professors Who Care

Willamette University, the oldest university west of the Mississippi, has a reputation for strong academics. With Oregon's seat of government right across the street, it's no surprise that political science is one of the most popular majors. However, following the completion of the Olin Science Center, more and more students are choosing to specialize in the natural sciences, especially biology and chemistry. Other strong departments at this liberal arts institution include economics, psychology, and English.

Students across the board rave about the quality of the academic experience here. The average class size is about 25 students, and one undergraduate commented that a 35-student lecture constitutes "a really big class." As many seminars and upper-division classes enroll only eight to ten students, undergraduates report that "we can do so much more within our classes," such as long discussions, special projects, guest speakers, and even field trips. Classes are challenging but not overwhelming, and students are able to adjust to the rigorous atmosphere after their first year. For a university of its size, Willamette offers an incredible number of courses, and students can only complain they don't have the time to take all the classes they would like.

One of the most remarkable features of the university is the degree to which professors care about and are involved with their students. For better or worse, professors keep track of undergrads and follow their progress. As one student explained, "If the professor notices you have missed a few classes or that your grade is slipping, he will definitely take you aside to talk about what's going on with you and try to find a solution." Professors reportedly "know their stuff well," and one student reverently referred to his history professor as "ferocious—the smartest guy I've ever met." In general, professors are both very well respected and well liked.

"Drying Out" the Campus

Dominating the social scene is the administration's move to make Willamette a completely dry campus. Suddenly, alcohol is no longer served at on-campus functions and students risk punishment if they are caught with alcoholic beverages. Even the fraternities, which are located on campus, now host dry parties.

However, this administrative action has not halted the social life at Willamette. More parties are now thrown off campus, in the apartments or houses of students, and upperclassmen frequent the handful of bars in close proximity. Occasionally, undergraduates make the trek to Portland, 45 minutes away, to hit the bar and club scene there. On campus, the university sponsors one to two formal dances per semester, new release films played in school auditoriums, and events such as Art Attack, a weeklong celebration of the arts, and Wustock, a popular homecoming celebration. Five fraternities and three sororities are located at Willamette, but non-Greeks report that they do not feel excluded. Salem, a town of about 90,000, is not known for a "bumpin'" weekend scene. Besides the few bars immediately around campus, students say entertainment in Salem is limited to the movies and bowling but praise the quality of nearby movie theaters and bowling alleys.

Students at Willamette are serious about their extracurricular activities as well. At such a small school, almost every student plays some kind of sport, with a surprising number involved at the varsity level. Football, soccer, basketball, and track are popular among undergraduates, but a wide range of varsity sports are available. School spirit "depends on the season," although the men's basketball team recently won an NAIA division championship. At every basketball game, fans fill the auditorium to sing the favorite "Ooh aah Bearcats" song. A plethora of other extracurricular activities are also available, with most students participating in some club or group. The debate team, outdoors groups, and volunteer organizations are most popular, and students note that sports and volunteering are the most popular activities.

Campus and Facilities

Students say it's easy to get hooked on what many people considering Willamette's greatest attribute: its "picturesque," "stunning," "quaint and beautiful" campus. Some undergrads also describe the campus as "red and green—there are red bricks and green trees and lawns." The grounds are so well kept that students wonder how just how much money the University spends on groundskeeping. Squirrels abound, and ducks paddle around Mill Stream, which runs right through campus.

The other university buildings and facilities are a source of pride for students and administration alike. Students hit the books in 24-hour study rooms at the Mark O. Hatfield Library or in open classrooms around campus. When they feel like taking a study break, they drag their books to the Bistro, a student-run coffee shop. Many students, especially those who live in the West Campus, "away from frats," find it quiet enough to study in their dorm rooms or in the student lounges.

"If the professor notices you have missed a few classes, or that your grade is slipping, he will definitely take you aside to talk about what's going on."

Students name Doney the best dorm because it's quiet, but other dorms are considered comfortable as well. Kaneko, a new dorm built by Willamette's sister school, the nearby Tokyo International University of America, is equipped with tennis courts, a swimming pool, air-conditioning, and tinted windows; the dorm is a "regular Hilton." Freshmen and sophomores are required to live on campus, but about half of juniors and seniors choose to move off campus to nearby West Salem. Of them, most are very satisfied with the apartments and houses available, the safety of the neighborhood, and the increased opportunities "to find something to do."

Willamette students are from mostly conservative, white, upper-middle-class backgrounds, although in recent years the campus has become increasingly diverse. Students realize that the student body is fairly homogeneous but do not report that this takes away from their overall experience there. One undergraduate reported that the campus was "pretty diverse" compared to the state of Oregon itself, but Japanese students from TIUA add an international perspective both in and out of the classroom.

How Do You Say "Willamette"?

Students all agree that the intimacy between students, the faculty, and the administration distinguishes Willamette from other universities. There is a "close camaraderie" between students in the small school, and everyone else feels like they know a lot of their classmates, "but in a good way." Professors genuinely care about the students in their classes, and even the administration exudes a feeling of intimacy and compassion toward undergraduates.

Willamette students generally are very content with their college choice. Students only really complain about the price of attending the school, which indicates something of the happiness of students there. Just listen to a Willamette student's spirited cry when an outsider mispronounces the school's name: "It's Wil-*lam*-ette, dammit!" —*Johnny Swagerty and Staff*

FYI

If you come to Willamette, you'd better bring "a raincoat. It pours in Oregon all year round."

What is the typical weekend schedule? "Do something outdoorsy like hike, hang out with friends, eat, and sleep."

If I could change one thing about Willamette, I'd "even out the ratio of girls to guys since there are far more females than males right now."

The three things that every student at Willamette should do before graduating are "visit the Star Trees, take rhetoric class, and be "Mill-Streamed"—where you are thrown in the Mill Stream fully clothed on a special occasion."

Pennsylvania

Allegheny College

Address: 520 N. Main Street, Meadville, PA 16335
Phone: 814-332-4351
E-mail address: admiss@allegheny.edu
Web site URL: www.allegheny.edu
Founded: 1815
Private or Public: private
Religious affiliation: United Methodist
Location: rural
Undergraduate enrollment: 1,924
Total enrollment: 1,924
Percent Male/Female: 47%/53%
Percent Minority: 5.4%
Percent African-American: 2%
Percent Asian: 2%
Percent Hispanic: 1%
Percent Native-American: 0%
Percent in-state/out of state: 68%/32%
Percent Pub HS: NA
Number of Applicants: 2,612
Percent Accepted: 80%
Percent Accepted who enroll: 97%
Entering: 539
Transfers: 13
Application Deadline: 15 Feb
Mean SAT: 1200
Mean ACT: 25
Middle 50% SAT range: V 550-650, M 550-650
Middle 50% ACT range: 23-27
3 Most popular majors: biology, psychology, economics
Retention: 84%
Graduation rate: 66%
On-campus housing: 73%
Fraternities: 26%
Sororities: 29%
Library: 279,648 volumes
Tuition and Fees: $24,400
Room and Board: $5,880
Financial aid, first-year: 74%
Varsity or Club Athletes: 48%
Early Decision or Early Action Acceptance Rate: 97%

Do visions of smart, beautiful students rushing off to small science classes quicken your heart rate? Do you long for a green, pastoral setting that one student described as "beautiful . . . picturesque, very distinguished . . . and very much like out of a movie"? Can you cope with an administration that is "pretty ridiculously strict" on its alcohol policies? If so, you should give Allegheny College a closer look.

Classes: Small on Size, Big on Work

Students universally praise the intimate academic system at Allegheny, but warn that it is "extremely challenging." Class sizes are small: there are generally fewer than 30 people in any given course. One student noted that "the classes are personable and you're not just one in a thousand students, which is great. But that can be a downfall as well, because there is no easy way to skip class. People notice." Students also noted the accessibility of their professors: "You never feel like you can't go to them. In fact, they respect you more if you admit to them you have a question instead of suffering alone in your dorm. They have office hours, but their doors are usually open all day to students with questions or problems."

Along with the small size there comes a heavy workload. Classes at Allegheny are "time consuming and hard." A communication arts major noted, "I have time to myself on the weekends a little, but I don't think I could ever have one day and not do any work." Allegheny also boasts a demanding set of graduation requirements. All freshmen choose a Freshman Seminar from a list of roughly 30 offerings. Course titles range from Anthropology and Dance to Creativity and Problem Solving to Biotechnology. These class sizes are particularly small (15 to 20), and the professor of each class serves as the students' academic advisor for at least the next two years. All sophomores choose a Writing in the Liberal Arts seminar such as Films of Ingrid Bergman and Woody Allen, Political Economy, or The Revolutionary Mind. Juniors must choose both a major and a minor, pursue the necessary credits for each, take a Junior Seminar, and begin to devise a Senior Project in their major field. Seniors must finish the course requirements for their major and minor, complete their Senior Project (which involves extensive research), and present an "oral defense" of that project. Throw in requirements in the Humanities/Arts, Natural Sciences, and Social Sciences, and top it all off with a physical education requirement, and the road to graduation can become rocky indeed.

The road is worth traveling though, particularly for those interested in the sciences. Students agree that this is "definitely a school for science people." One student crowed, "All of our natural sciences are very good. Our pre-med program is excellent." Often, these natural science classes are also the most difficult. "Chemistry, calculus, organic chemistry, and some psychology courses" were mentioned as particularly tough. Nor can students look to a lenient grading policy for help: there's "not really" any grade inflation.

Students seem less enthusiastic about the Humanities/Arts and Social Science programs. Fields such as communications, political science, and history are dubbed "slacker majors." Students note that a pro-science bias seems to have surfaced over the past 10 years at Allegheny. The college recently constructed a new science building, while budget cuts led to the elimination of such humanities majors as Classics, Greek, and Sociology/Anthropology.

"Everyone Is like Family"

Because of its small size and intimate classes, the atmosphere at Allegheny is "incredibly friendly." Even the professors get into the act. One freshman mentioned that her science teacher "helped us all study for our test at night—when he could have been doing *anything* else!" A sophomore recalled how her professor "took us on a picnic and paid for all the food!" One senior gushed, "I think there is a tremendous sense of pride and loyalty that accompanies being a student here. We make this place our home for the four years that we are here, and everyone is like family. There is a sense of bonding because we share this special place."

There are both benefits and drawbacks to such an intimate campus. Students note that "you have to try exceptionally hard *not* to meet people," and "it's weird if there is no one you know in the dining hall at any given time." On the other hand, social groups can be "very cliquey," and the "gossip mill" is pointed to as a source of occasional angst. One sophomore called Allegheny's social scene "high schoolish."

As for the student body, what a body it is! Maybe it's the mandatory physical education classes, but students universally proclaimed, "There are both incredibly attractive men and women here—plenty of singles to go around!" Allegheny's typical student is a "middle- to upper-class Pennsylvanian who wears Abercromie & Fitch, Aeropostale, and The Gap." According to one student's observation, people from the local town of Meadville often refer to Allegheny students as "the rich kids on the hill," although one student who said this also believed this to be "not true."

Student reactions to Meadville vary. One student described it as "pretty boondocks." Another disagreed, calling Meadville a "fairly good surrounding town. There's a WalMart, Kmart, Giant Eagle, Valumart, Peebles, and plenty of other stores as well as a grand assortment of restaurants." All students agreed that Meadville is a safe town, and no one could recall any incident in which they or a friend had ever felt in danger.

To Greek or Not to Greek, That Is the Question . . .

Students neither love nor hate the dorms at Allegheny. A typical freshman dorm was described as "small, two to a room, no A/C." Some private bedroom setups become available to upperclassmen. Students must remain on campus through their sophomore year, and are then free to move off campus. Those who choose to move off have mixed reactions. "I liked living in the dorms because I felt more a part of campus, but I like the freedom of living off campus."

"The people down in town call us 'the rich kids on the hill' but that's not true."

Students find all sorts of different things to do with their time. Many become involved in activities like student government, community service, GAP (Gator Activities Programming: a group that sponsors movies and events), Orchesis (a student-run dance company), church groups, and sports (both varsity and intramural). One freshman felt that "everyone is a part of some thing or another. Everyone here was involved in something in high school, and wouldn't feel right not getting involved now."

Greek life also consumes a great deal of time for those who choose to participate. Fraternities and sororities host many parties, formals, and other activities throughout the year. Students agree that there is no hostility between Greeks and non-Greeks, and feel that non-Greeks "really don't feel left out." On the other hand, those who choose Greek life find that it has a strong impact on shaping their social lives. A senior said that she did "something pertaining to Greek life one night each weekend."

As for partying, a resourceful freshman will not be at a loss for something to do on the weekends. One freshman said, "I'm not going to lie. There is alcohol on campus, but there will be no matter where you go. Not everyone is going to check your ID so if you are looking for alcohol, you can find it." Those who do not want to drink won't have a problem, either. Fraternity parties are not allowed to have alcohol (though a few manage to sneak it in every once in awhile), so those are good places for non-drinkers to go and dance. There are also film, stage, and concert offerings available almost every weekend for those who find party life to be tiresome.

Regardless of how they choose to spend their time outside of class, Allegheny students agree that "Allegheny is a college on too much caffeine. It's always buzzing—there is always a class to take or homework to do. With so many opportunities it is hard to stop yourself." For those freshmen in search of a great science education in an intimate setting, Allegheny's opportunities could be well worth grasping. —*Betty Wolf*

FYI

If you come to Allegheny College, you'd better bring "anything you use as stress relief so you don't go crazy!"

What is the typical weekend schedule? "Saturday: wake up late, have lunch, drive with friends to Pittsburgh, come back and work, go to a party. Sunday: do homework."

If I could change one thing about Allegheny, I'd "put it in a different place. This town is really beat."

Three things every student at Allegheny should do before graduating are "uphold the tradition of kissing someone on the "Thirteenth Plank," come back early in the fall and party during 'Camp Allegheny,' and participate in 'Kegs and Eggs' during Homecoming."

Bryn Mawr College

Address: 101 North Merion Avenue; Bryn Mawr, PA 19010-2899
Phone: 610-526-5152
E-mail address: admissions@brynmawr.edu
Web site URL: www.brynmawr.edu
Founded: 1885
Private or Public: private
Religious affiliation: none
Location: suburban
Undergraduate enrollment: 1,322
Total enrollment: 1,322
Percent Male/Female: 0%/100%
Percent Minority: 20%
Percent African-American: 3%
Percent Asian: 13%
Percent Hispanic: 3%
Percent Native-American: 0%
Percent in-state/out of state: 20%/80%
Percent Pub HS: NA
Number of Applicants: 1,743
Percent Accepted: 50%
Percent Accepted who enroll: 64%
Entering: 306
Transfers: 11
Application Deadline: 15 Jan
Mean SAT: NA
Mean ACT: NA
Middle 50% SAT range: V 630-730, M 600-690
Middle 50% ACT range: 26-30
3 Most popular majors: mathematics, English, biology
Retention: 91%
Graduation rate: 77%
On-campus housing: 98%
Fraternities: NA
Sororities: NA
Library: 1,089,120 volumes
Tuition and Fees: $27,520
Room and Board: $9,370
Financial aid, first-year: 64%
Varsity or Club Athletes: NA
Early Decision or Early Action Acceptance Rate: 62%

Right outside of Philly, easily available profs that actually care about undergrads, a party scene that covers four colleges, and traditions to boot. There's only one college that meets these exciting criteria: Bryn Mawr. Located on Philly's swanky Main Line, Bryn Mawr College combines a healthy social life with an incredibly intense intellectual life. Being a single-sex university doesn't faze Bryn Mawr women: "At Bryn Mawr we're a community of women—empowered, beautiful, and intelligent."

No Slackers

Academics at Bryn Mawr are described by one sophomore as a "ton of work"and are the number one priority for Byrn Mawr students. Bryn Mawr stresses a core set of academic standards that include a Freshman Liberal Studies Seminar sponsored by the English department, three humanities requirements, two social science courses, and three courses in the natural sciences. Unfortunately for students not inclined to the sciences, this includes two labs. The Freshman Seminar focuses, as most universities like to do, on the students writing. According to one student, there are no "gut" majors. Every field of study is challenging in its own unique way. But those classes with particularly mean reputations include Organic Chemistry and Elementary Greek and Latin. Greek students, according to student legend, "eat, sleep, and dream Greek."

Class size at Bryn Mawr is generally small. The intro courses tend to be larger, but generally class size runs between 20–50 students. Classes also include some students from surrounding schools such as Haverford. Pre-registration is key and students have a ten-day shopping period during which they decide their upcoming semester schedule. Upperclassmen are not given preference in registration. Bryn Mawr uses a lottery system to determine whether or not students make it into the class of their choice. Bryn Mawr registrars try to accommodate students and are generally described as "helpful, courteous, and accommodating." Seniors, however, do receive preference if the course is a requirement for their major.

Professors here are "awesome." "I once had a major test coming up. I didn't feel prepared at all so I called up my professor. She sat down with me and went over the work. It was wonderful." This kind of faculty dedication is not uncommon at a small school such as Bryn Mawr. Professors readily hand out their home phone numbers and e-mail addresses. Often, they burn the midnight oil long past office hours to accommodate a student in need. Lucky students have even set up lunch dates with their professors to discuss the latest math theorem or that Byron poem that was difficult to understand. As for the TAs, so often feared by students at large research universities, they are present on campus and do assist in teaching. All classes are, however, taught by professors.

With such stress placed on academics at Bryn Mawr, one would think that there is an intense feeling of competition. According to one student, "Competition is not a problem at Bryn Mawr. We're all in this together." The Honor Code also helps to discourage competition. The Honor Code prevents students from discussing tests and grades outside of class. The code also allows for unproctored exams and plays an integral role within the school community.

Slackers, although lacking at Bryn Mawr, will be happy to know that grades are not sent home to parents. Every student's academic file is kept confidential. This adds to the feeling of "independence" that many freshman say, "they absolutely love."

Social Life: Crazy, Sexy, Cool

Thanks to brother school Haverford, Bryn Mawr women do enjoy the "traditional" college experience. Although there are some parties at Bryn Mawr, Bryn Mawrians often head into Philly (UPenn, Drexel), Swarthmore, and Haverford to party on the weekends. Haverford, the main party locale, is a mere mile away. It is easily within walking distance of the campus and a bus runs between the two schools every fifteen minutes. A lot of individuals head into Philly for "College Day" which is sponsored by other Philadelphia area colleges in addition to Bryn Mawr and includes parties, concerts, and general merriment.

Bryn Mawr's alcohol policy follows Pennsylvania Law. If you're 21 you can have a wet party or alcohol in the room. Nevertheless, underage students who desire alcohol can easily aquire it. In general, Bryn Mawr students are fairly responsible drinkers. As for the non-drinkers, the school sponsors several bashes annually including the Fall Bash and the semi-formal Pallas Athena.

Beyond the normal party scene, Philadelphia offers a myriad of activities for the culturally-minded student. The Ben Franklin Parkway in Philadelphia has a ton of museums and other cosmopolitan activities for the burgeoning aesthete. The Society Hill Area, including South Street, is also a popular destination for the Bryn Mawr student. The Hill offers several artsy movie theatres and South Street is known for its trendy shops and restaurants.

On campus hangouts include the "Campus Center." The Center boasts a small café where students frequently congregate. It also sponsors a Performing Arts Series along with dances and little concerts.

Dating at Bryn Mawr received mixed responses. While dating certainly isn't the dominant form of social activity, students do "see" other students from neighboring Haverford and Penn. Some girls have serious boyfriends off campus and at home. There is also an active Rainbow Alliance on campus and issues of sexuality are freely discussed at Bryn Mawr. As one student puts it, "single sex doesn't mean no sex."

Incoming students to the college are welcomed at the beginning of the term with freshman orientation. Each freshman is assigned to a Customs Group during "Customs Week," known at other colleges as Orientation Week. Two sophomores lead these inchoate Bryn Mawr groups and act as valuable resources for the new students. The Customs Groups established during the first week provide a social foundation for the incoming class. Freshmen can often be seen with their group heading to meals or other activities.

Living It and Loving It

Living at college is probably one of the major concerns of incoming students. Bryn Mawr's campus is full of beautiful old Gothic dorms, in a style that rivals Princeton and Yale. The rooms themselves are fairly large by college standards and 70 percent of them are singles that are "greatly appreciated" by freshman looking for a nap after a particularly trying test. The school guarantees housing for all four years. Nevertheless, some upperclassmen choose to live off campus. There has been a recently built facility known as Glen Meade that was once a house owned by the school, which now serves as student housing. Although the large majority of students do live on or near campus, Bryn Mawr also has a few commuters.

What about the individuals whom you'll be sharing your lives with for the next four years? Students at Bryn Mawr, unlike other schools, are not cliquish. While some in the country characterize Bryn Mawr as a bastion of liberalism and feminism, most students are quick to discount that myth. There is a definite ethnic and geographical diversity present on campus that helps to combat stereotypes present in the media and the society at large.

> **"Students at Bryn Mawr, unlike other schools, are not cliquish."**

Bringing guys into this community, specifically the dorms, has never been a problem. Male visitors are expected to abide by the Honor Code and students are, of course, responsible for the behavior of their guests. It is expected that roommates will notify each other when a guy spends the night. It is the students themselves who decide on the co-ed status of the bathroom on their floor at the beginning of the year. In other words, many choose to have co-ed bathrooms to accommodate boyfriends and friends.

The social lives in the dorms are enhanced by the presence of upperclassmen in all dorms. No dorms at Bryn Mawr are specifically reserved for freshman. Hall Advisors help to monitor the girls but are there only in an advisory capacity.

The campus itself is verdant and quaint. Everything is confined to a large rectangular area and all buildings are contained within this area. Bryn Mawr, the town, is a wealthy suburb of Philadelphia that contains numerous coffee shops and small commercial outlets. Town/gown relations are positive as the town actively supports Bryn Mawr students in their social outreach efforts.

Students are apt to hang out in their dorm rooms but do often venture into the town proper to socialize at Starbucks or Xandos. During most of the weekdays students are either studying or shopping in the city. While some students do dine off campus the food on campus is "really good, especially the all beef hamburgers." There are four dining halls on campus including one in Brecken Dorm. A lot of Haverford boys also eat at Bryn Mawr. On weekends, however, students tend to venture into Philadelphia to eat or they can easily order pizza and Chinese food from local restaurants.

Extracurriculars and Traditions

Students are often dedicated to extracurriculars and Byrn Mawr is no exception. The Student Self-Government Association is a popular and well-respected organization on campus. Students also actively participate in Christian Fellowship, Jewish Fellowship, as well as cultural and academic groups.

But perhaps what makes Bryn Mawr what it is today is its Traditions—Traditions with a capital "T." The Traditions are four events conducted each year. They are mostly for the freshman but are heavily attended by upperclassmen as well. Parade Night is the first of these traditions, designed to welcome freshman into the Bryn Mawr community. Lantern Night is also an all-school extravaganza. Each class holds up a lantern of a distinct color used to identify the class. Rumor has it that the girl whose lantern burns out first will be the first in the class to earn her PhD. Hell Week, a time honored parody of sorority rushes, is also wildly popular among sophomores and freshmen. "The Hellers" (the sophomores), are each assigned a freshman. For the remainder of the week the freshman must do every bidding of the sophomore. Luckily for the freshmen, sympathetic juniors rescue them from the nefarious grip of the sophomores by providing them with little treats and respites during the week. Lastly in May, the college president rides into campus on a horse to open up May Day celebrations. The President then delivers a speech, which is then followed by a Maypole Dance. The girls then proceed to buckle down for final exams.

A Final Word

Students rave about the benefits of having a single-sex education. Single-sex education "provides girls with an opportunity to gain confidence" and students tend to "feel a lot more confident in [their] academic abilities" after only a year. —*Sean McBride*

FYI

The three best things about attending Bryn Mawr are "the Traditions, friends, and the professors."

The three worst things about attending Bryn Mawr are "the massive amount work, the lab requirements for science courses, and the stress."

Three things every student should do before graduating from Bryn Mawr are "to ring the Taylor Bell, go abroad, and party in Philly."

One thing I wish I knew before coming here is "there are so many vegan dishes in the dining hall!"

Bucknell University

Address: Freas Hall; Lewisburg, PA 17837
Phone: 570-577-1101
E-mail address: admissions@bucknell.edu
Web site URL: www.bucknell.edu
Founded: 1846
Private or Public: private
Religious affiliation: none
Location: rural
Undergraduate enrollment: 3,439
Total enrollment: 3,439
Percent Male/Female: 52%/48%
Percent Minority: 11%
Percent African-American: 2.9%
Percent Asian: 6%
Percent Hispanic: 2%
Percent Native-American: 0.4%
Percent in-state/out of state: 32%/68%
Percent Pub HS: NA
Number of Applicants: 7,760
Percent Accepted: 39%
Percent Accepted who enroll: 52%
Entering: 917
Transfers: 21
Application Deadline: 1 Jan
Mean SAT: NA
Mean ACT: NA
Middle 50% SAT range: V 590-670, M 620-700
Middle 50% ACT range: 25-30
3 Most popular majors: management, economics, English
Retention: 94%
Graduation rate: 88%
On-campus housing: 89%
Fraternities: 39%
Sororities: 43%
Library: 710,985 volumes
Tuition and Fees: $28,960
Room and Board: $6,302
Financial aid, first-year: 55%
Varsity or Club Athletes: 38%
Early Decision or Early Action Acceptance Rate: 52%

One student praised Bucknell as "mostly everything I could want in a place of education." Indeed, Bucknell students all seem to agree on the high quality of their educational experience. Even with this unconditional appreciation for their college, they are quick to caution that some might not fit the typical Bucknell mold. The beauty of the campus, the idyllic setting in Lewisburg, Pennsylvania, and the small size of the student body have the combined effect of alienating some while creating a close-knit atmosphere for others.

Liberal Arts Learning

As is typical of students at small liberal arts colleges, Bucknellians enjoy close interaction with faculty. Students describe professors as "eager" and "accessible," their lectures "interesting" and "engaging." Many enthuse that, even in larger lecture courses, professors make an effort to know their names and encourage one-on-

one discussions over coffee or during office hours. There is always a lot of work to do, but students have an optimistic attitude towards their workload: "Isn't that what college is about?" Teaching assistants, a common cause of student frustration at most colleges, are appreciated here. Because only professors teach classes, TAs at Bucknell exist only to supplement what students learn in class. They are, as one student pointed out, "nice and really know how to help you out if you don't understand a concept." With the exception of introductory lecture courses, class sizes average around 20 to 30 students. Students also happily note that classrooms are well equipped to handle a variety of learning needs.

Bucknell runs on a two-semester academic calendar. Traditionally strong majors include engineering and business, although economics and biology majors also have good reputations among students. Required classes for freshmen include one English and one math, as well as a "foundational skills" class designed to give freshmen a comprehensive grounding in the liberal arts traditions of writing and arguing; sophomores must complete two lab sciences. More generally, students must take four humanities courses, two courses in the social sciences, and three writing courses—but there is no specific language requirement. Aside from the "foundations" class, Bucknell also gives freshmen the opportunity to apply to a Residential College seminar program, the acceptance into which allows them to live in one of the nicer dorms on campus on floors divided by program: the Environmental College, Humanities College, Social Justice College, etc. Freshmen also praise the quality of the orientation programs, which provide them with opportunities to meet their peers in a setting that also welcomes them to the school.

The Wednesday-Friday-Saturday Weekend

Bucknellians are quick to admit that "drinking is big here; everybody gets drunk," and for many students, the Wednesday-Friday-Saturday party schedule is common. It seems that the only distinction that can be made in terms of alcohol is *where* students drink. Since students are not allowed to rush frats and sororities until sophomore year, freshmen generally drink in their rooms; upperclassmen have the advantage of going to frats and sororities to party. The majority of upperclassmen, in fact, belong to one of the Greek houses, and that seems to suit everyone just fine. The administration, however, has a strict take on the issue. A point system for drinking increases the punishment with each incidence of drinking. One student complained, "I wish the administration could just accept the fact that we get drunk on the weekends and leave us alone." All in all, the students are able to find ways to elude the point system.

In contrast to alcohol use, drug use is not very prevalent, although one student claimed that his classmates do "abuse things like Ritalin to help them study." As an alternative to drinking, Bucknell sponsors concerts, speakers (Toni Morrison is one recent notable speaker), and movies, but students tend to stay away from these in search of the party scene. As one junior pointed out in what could be the school's unofficial motto, "At Bucknell, we work hard, and we play hard. We know our limits, and we know that you've got to let yourself loose sometimes, or else the academic demands here will end you." The intense party scene facilitates an environment where random hook-ups are common, and where dating is less often the norm. One freshman candidly remarked, "Oh yeah—hook-ups are definitely popular. I've hooked up with six people already and it's only been a month and a half!"

Playboy Ranks Bucknell the #3

The dominant student stereotype at Bucknell is that of the "rich, white, good-looking" prep-schooler. Students are not so quick to dismiss this label. Rated third in a *Playboy* survey of the most attractive student bodies, Bucknellians seem proud of this distinction. However, with these preppy good looks comes a lack of diversity, which Bucknell seems to be trying to change, albeit with little success. Student comments suggest that the lack of diversity is not limited to appearances. One noted, "There is hardly any diversity in ideologies," while another said, "There really is a lack of diversity in backgrounds and ways of thinking and projecting oneself." Though most students seem to have bargained for this lack of diversity when they applied, others see it as detrimental to college life. Some students may try too hard to fit the homogenous mold. One student claimed, "Based on sight alone, I would say that nearly 40 percent of the girls on this campus have an eating disorder and unnaturally wear a size 2 or below; it's absurd."

"We know that you've got to let yourself loose sometimes, or else the academic demands here will end you."

In the Middle of Nowhere, Close to Everywhere

Students love the beauty of their campus and the fact that it is surrounded by "wide open grass fields everywhere." Lewisburg, Pennsylvania, is praised as much for the beauty of its Victorian homes and its popular eateries as for its proximity to both New York City and Philadelphia. Several students remarked that a walk through the town has a calming effect and is a good break from the intensity of the campus. Popular dorms on campus include Smith Hall, home to the residential college programs, and Hunt Hall, which houses mostly juniors. These are all kept clean and, along with about half of the other residences, are air-conditioned. Student opinion on the subject of dorm life varies: some students are happy with their draw, while others are stuck in a "dingle" (a single with two people). Dorms, halls, and now, even rooms are co-ed. One dorm is substance-free, while another is equipped with kitchens and family rooms.

When it comes to dining on campus, students praise everything from the taste of the food to the cafeteria ladies: "They are more like friends than people that are there to feed many hungry college kids." Students choose from four on-campus locations for their meals: the Bison, Larison Dining Hall, the Terrace Room, and the "Caf," Bucknell's main dining hall. Each caters to different tastes. Since a meal plan is required, however, and since most students stay on campus for their four years at Bucknell, few students complain.

On the Playing Field

By one estimate, most students spend ten to 15 hours a week on extracurricular activities. Sports and political groups are the most popular activities; community service is less so. A new gym facility opened in the 2002 much to the appreciation of student-athletes. School spirit is most evident at soccer and basketball games, where Bucknellians take to the playing field as members of the Patriot League. For those to whom inter-college sports do not appeal, intramurals "are great—like high school sports all over again!"

For all the shortcomings that come with being a small, homogenous student body, students here are content with their academic experience. Cliques actually tend not to form because of the school's size, and students take advantage of the close-knit community to form close bonds with their peers. One soon-to-be-graduating senior looked back on her experience at Bucknell with satisfaction, saying, "I don't have anything but good things to say about my experience." —*Greg Hamm*

FYI

If you come to Bucknell, you'd better bring a "good self esteem; every student on this campus is amazingly talented, and I still hold that Bucknell chooses students at least 50 percent based on looks."

A typical weekend at Bucknell consists of "procrastination, and a lot of it . . . even if you think there's nothing to do one weekend, by some miraculous turn of events, you find yourself socially booked until at least midnight on Saturday."

If I could change one thing about Bucknell, I'd "diversify it! I'm not just talking race or religion. These people are all the same!"

Three things every student at Bucknell should do before graduating are "go to the Freeze and the Campus Theatre, walk around downtown Lewisburg, and go wild at least once!"

Carnegie Mellon University

Address: 5000 Forbes Avenue, Pittsburgh, PA 15213
Phone: 412-268-2082
E-mail address: undergraduate-admissions@andrew.cmu.edu
Web site URL: www.cmu.edu
Founded: 1900
Private or Public: private
Religious affiliation: none
Location: urban
Undergraduate enrollment: 5,475
Total enrollment: 5,475
Percent Male/Female: 61%/39%
Percent Minority: 42%
Percent African-American: 5%
Percent Asian: 23%
Percent Hispanic: 5%
Percent Native-American: 0%
Percent in-state/out of state: 24%/76%
Percent Pub HS: NA
Number of Applicants: 14,271
Percent Accepted: 38%
Percent Accepted who enroll: 49%
Entering: 1,365
Transfers: 38
Application Deadline: 15 Dec
Mean SAT: NA
Mean ACT: NA
Middle 50% SAT range: V 590-700, M 680-770
Middle 50% ACT range: 27-32
3 Most popular majors: engineering, social sciences, computer science
Retention: 94%
Graduation rate: 82%
On-campus housing: 72%
Fraternities: 14%
Sororities: 10%
Library: 999,798 volumes
Tuition and Fees: $28,986
Room and Board: $7,845
Financial aid, first-year: 54%
Varsity or Club Athletes: 14%
Early Decision or Early Action Acceptance Rate: 49%

It is midnight at Carnegie Mellon, and groups of students creep out of the libraries, computer clusters, and art studios. They are going to "paint the fence," a legendary activity in which students are allowed, between midnight and dawn, to paint the metal fence at the center of campus. The fence is used to advertise everything from frat parties, to memorials, to any of the range of activities hosted by the school's interesting mix of students, affectionately referred to as "the freaks and geeks."

Academics for Artists and for Techies

Carnegie Mellon is comprised of five undergraduate schools: the Mellon College of Science, the Carnegie Institute of Technology, the College of Fine Arts, the College of Humanities and Social Sciences, and the School of Computer Science. Each school and major has different requirements. "The requirements suck when you have to do them, but are great for applying to grad school," said a recent graduate. Students enjoy the wide range of courses offered. "It's hard to find such a good business program, as well as computer science and theatre arts school all in one school," mused one senior. Said another student, "I have taken art and dance courses as well as engineering, computer science, and robotics courses." There is even a bagpipe major, which sets the school apart from others.

Undergraduates agree that the academics, though intense, are excellent preparation for further study. The most prestigious and the most difficult majors are generally in the arts, engineering, and computer schools. Classes are difficult and fast-paced, but the work often produces tangible results very quickly: "We learned how to build robots within the first three weeks of class, and then built a robot every week after that," said a student. On the other hand, some students refer to the School of Humanities and Social Sciences as "H & Less Stress." Students considered English, psychology, and modern languages to be the slacker majors.

Class sizes range from below 20 for seminars and electives to about 100 people for introductory classes, although the size of some popular lecture classes can be in the 200s. A senior, having taken computer programming classes and humanities classes, identified the best part of CMU as having "such a diverse and good faculty."

Diversity in the Social Life

The diversity at CMU extends outside the classroom. Freshmen find numerous ways to meet each other. A list of activities includes cruises, clubs, and "a crazy and silly night called Play Fair where everyone runs around making fools of themselves in attempts to meet people." Freshman year is the best, according to a student, because "by sophomore year, a lot of people keep their doors shut." The social groups that form during freshman year often stay together over the four years. One junior said that Carnegie Mellon "is very cliquish—especially among the ethnic groups."

One way in which CMU lacks in diversity is gender. About two-thirds of the population is male. Although this might seem encouraging for females, students attest that "in terms of attractive people, the campus is limited," and they complain that a large percentage of the guys lack social skills. Nevertheless, those who want to randomly hook up have the opportunity to do so.

Frats and sororities are easy to rush and are an integral part of the social scene on campus, according to students. Parties are regularly held at the frats and sororities—especially, Kappa Kappa Gamma, Phi Kappa Theta, and Theta Xi. Unfortunately, students claim that parties are often little more than crappy beer and bad music, except for the occasional beach party, jungle party, and foam party. "You can avoid Greek life if you just join other activities," said one student. However, according to some, freshmen usually only have the option of frat parties because they don't know enough people to go to other parties.

Underage drinking is officially not allowed on campus, and those caught doing it will be punished. However, "it's pretty easy to get alcohol if you want it," said one girl. "As long as no one sees it and you're not being stupid, there haven't been many incidents involving underage drinking busts." Kegs are allowed on campus in the non-dry Greek houses, but no alcohol is allowed in student rooms.

"I have taken art and dance courses as well as engineering, computer science and robotics courses."

Some students could ask for more from the social life. "Some weekends go by where there's not a lot to do," said a recent graduate. Outside the party scene, however, there are plenty of options. Movies play five nights a week in the University Center for $1. Over a hundred student clubs meet throughout the week. The drama school produces several plays that are given high ratings by students. Last, but certainly not least, for those looking for video games, there are late-night gaming sessions in the computer clusters.

Suburbs of Pittsburgh

CMU is a small campus, with patches of grass and yellow brick buildings with copper roofs that have turned green over the years. "This is a beautiful and safe campus," said one pleased freshman. The art building is especially notable. One student commented, "every time I walk in the art building I see some new—usually odd, but amazing—work of art." "It's very pleasant here," said one student of the campus, but with a caveat: "unless it's a really nice day, you won't see anyone hanging out outside—we're notorious for hanging out in computer clusters."

CMU is located in the suburbs of Pittsburgh where it is considered safe, although "like any big city there are some shady areas." Students give Pittsburgh high ratings, and one student happily commented, "I love the fact that I am in a city but at the same time feel that I have an actual campus." Said another student, "there are many restaurants, bars, and museums within a mile of campus."

The food and the dining halls were given negative reviews in general. Upperclassmen warn future freshmen to get as small of a dining plan as possible. Those in the dining hall are either "cliques or loners," said one sophomore. People instead choose to eat off campus, at the Trucks, the Union Grill, or the numerous cheap restaurants near campus. For dates, students often leave campus and head over to Station Square, an area with nice restaurants.

Most students thought that their freshman housing was adequate. Students rated RAs in the dorms as considerate, helpful, and nice. Mudge, a converted mansion, is the students' favorite dorm, with suite-style, spacious rooms, and a gorgeous courtyard. Donner, on the other hand, is "a dungeon, with small dingy rooms and shared bathrooms." Some dorms have air conditioning and CMU is always renovating to keep their dorms up-to-date. Despite the good reviews given to dorms, many students opt after the first year to live in the cheaper apartments off campus.

Computers versus Athletics

The late night gaming sessions in the computer clusters is more popular than the athletics at CMU, according to students. "People are too lazy. Only about five people go to football games," said a freshman. Even at the homecoming game, the stands don't fill up. Non-campus sports, such as the Super Bowl, also do not catch the attention of many CMU students. However, intramurals, where students compete in teams according to their school and major, are popular among the students.

If you prefer building robots to football, and if cutting-edge technology is as important to you as a great arts program, then CMU is the place to be.

—*Andrew Hamilton*

FYI

If you come to Carnegie Mellon, you'd better bring "a warm coat and a computer."

What's the typical weekend schedule? "Friday night, party; Saturday, sleep until noon, do homework until dinner, party; Sunday, work."

If I could change one thing about Carnegie Mellon, "I would lessen the influence that Greek life has on campus."

Three things every student should do before graduating from Carnegie Mellon are "paint the fence, step away from a computer, and see a strange experimental play."

Dickinson College

Address: PO Box 1773, Carlisle, PA 17013
Phone: 717-245-1231
E-mail address: admit@dickinson.edu
Web site URL: www.dickinson.edu
Founded: 1783
Private or Public: private
Religious affiliation: none
Location: suburban
Undergraduate enrollment: 2,261
Total enrollment: 2,261
Percent Male/Female: 42%/58%
Percent Minority: 8%
Percent African-American: 2%
Percent Asian: 3%
Percent Hispanic: 2%
Percent Native-American: 0%
Percent in-state/out of state: 40%/60%
Percent Pub HS: NA
Number of Applicants: 4,095
Percent Accepted: 51%
Percent Accepted who enroll: NA
Entering: 574
Transfers: 30
Application Deadline: 1 Feb
Mean SAT: NA
Mean ACT: NA
Middle 50% SAT range: V 580-670, M 570-650
Middle 50% ACT range: NA
3 Most popular majors: foreign languages, political science, English
Retention: 89%
Graduation rate: 79%
On-campus housing: 92%
Fraternities: 21%
Sororities: 23%
Library: 305,272 volumes
Tuition and Fees: $28,615
Room and Board: $7,210
Financial aid, first-year: 53%
Varsity or Club Athletes: 47%
Early Decision or Early Action Acceptance Rate: 63%

One student summed up her experience at Dickinson by noting that "Dickinson truly tests your desire for your diploma." A school built on tough academics, Dickinson also boasts small classes, a close-knit community, and a thriving Greek scene. Located in suburban Pennsylvania, its programs in political science, international business, and foreign languages have made it the choice destination of many an aspiring international globetrotter.

You'd Better Get to Class

Many students praised small class sizes at Dickinson as one of the school's best attributes. The average class at Dickinson has only 15 to 30 students, and all classes are taught by professors. Lectures are almost unheard of, with the exception of a few introductory science courses. Many students agree that these small classes lead to close student-professor relationships. "The professors are all great here. They're very, very good about making time to talk to their students or help their students with whatever they need," said a junior. One unique aspect of Dickinson is that the professors actually live on campus. Because of this, students will often be invited over for meals or get-togethers outside of class. One student even reported that a few professors have been spotted at college parties.

There is a price to be paid for such academic intimacy. Students groaned about Dickinson's strict attendance policy. A senior reported that "15 to 20 percent of your grade is based on attendance," so cutting class is not an option for those concerned about their GPAs. The workload at Dickinson also receives complaints. "You have to work hard in all your classes," one student reported. "Dickinson has a lot more course work than a lot of other schools." Added another student, "I think a lot of students come here not expecting Dickinson to be as challenging as it is. I know that's how it was for me."

In order to graduate, students must fulfill distribution requirements outside their majors. These courses consist of philosophy, religion, environmental studies, the social sciences, the natural sciences , foreign language, comparative civilizations, physical education, and literature. "Fulfilling the distribution requirements is not that hard," said a student. "The hard part is fulfilling the requirements of your major." Students must take 10 to 15 classes in their major for 32 credits overall. All freshmen must also take a Freshman Seminar. These seminars provide a practical introduction to skills that incoming students will need at Dickinson—such as library and research skills—in the context of learning about a topic they enjoy.

Beyond the classroom, many students are drawn to Dickinson for its extensive study abroad programs. Students may study for a semester or a year abroad at a wide variety of affiliated programs around the world. Programs in most European countries, Africa, Asia, and South and Central America offer the opportunity to take classes pertaining to a major or "to integrate themselves into an entirely different culture." Noted one junior, "our study abroad programs are different because they aren't in big cities. They're in small towns, often with host families so you don't get a lot of English-speaking tourists running around." Most students praise Dickinson's study-abroad program, with one student calling it "the shining jewel in Dickinson's crown." A few students, though, express complaints that the Global Education Office can be disorganized. "They claim it's one of the best, but it really doesn't help," complained a senior. "They're not organized and they lost my application. I never got to go abroad."

It's Toga Time!

Much of the social life at Dickinson centers around Greek life. Even people who don't wish to join a fraternity or sorority generally join the rush process simply because "it's a good way to meet people." Frat parties make it particularly easy for freshmen to join the social world of Dickinson. "During my first few weeks, a lot of the frats had open parties," said one sophomore. "I found it very easy to make friends at frat parties. You know, you get up to the front of the line and talk to the guy at the keg for awhile. It's just very easy to meet people." Despite this comment, other students report that the administration takes a fairly hard line with regard to alcohol on campus. "No kegs allowed on campus," said a fraternity member. "If you get caught with a keg, you'll lose your house. You're not supposed to serve alcohol at all." A junior girl noted that the administration's policy on drinking could get "pretty weird." "Kegs are not allowed because they promote binge drinking. You should have cans. Glass bottles can break when people are drunk. You've got to have food, too, to mitigate the effects of the alcohol."

Fraternities find ways around the restrictions. "A lot of the fraternities will have cocktail parties," said one student. "Every Thursday night, my fraternity has a cocktail lecture, and a party following," said another. "It's very formal. We once turned guys away at the door because they weren't wearing jackets and ties." Such get-togethers are co-ed and by invitation only. Generally speaking, alcohol and Greek life seem to go hand in hand here. "They don't call it 'Drinkinson' for nothing," laughed a student.

An Extended Family

Students report that the small size of Dickinson's student body has a major impact on their social lives. "It's a communal feeling. I can't walk to class without seeing people I know. It sounds sappy, but I like the extended-family feeling."

The small size of the campus also has an effect on the dating and hook-up scene at Dickinson. "Freshman year is an all-out orgy pretty much. After that, everyone settles down." According to most students, it is hard to "get around" at Dickinson because it's such a small campus. "You'll get a reputation." People seem to start dating more and hooking up less as they move into sophomore and junior year. "It's hard to find a second-semester sophomore without a boyfriend or girlfriend," said one senior.

Besides drinking and dating, Dickinson offers a wide variety of extracurricular activities. "A lot of the students here like to get involved in *everything*. It is the diversity of the programs that draws people to Dickinson." Many Dickinsonians are involved in athletic pursuits, be they varsity sports, club sports, or intramurals. Soccer, basketball, and volleyball draw the most participants." Students also enjoy activities such as student government, literary magazines, choir, drama club, student senate, an improv comedy group, and foreign language clubs. Students note though, that campus offerings are low on political activism and volunteer activities. "The campus is apolitical," said one student, "which is weird since so many students are studying social sciences." "One thing we really need here are volunteer programs," said another.

> **"There is a good amount of forests and green rolling hills. It's very calming. We have little parks and fields everywhere."**

Students agree that the typical Dickinsonian is female, more on the preppy side (J. Crew and Abercrombie & Fitch are popular clothing brands), and went to a private school. Many had high SAT scores, and hail from upper-middle-class backgrounds. Most students are from Pennsylvania or New Jersey. Students disagree on the overall "hottie ratio" of the school. One young man said, "there are enough hot girls, but the guys are . . . I dunno . . ." Another disagreed, saying, "I think the guys are better looking. Attractive girls are few and far between. In fact, my friends even have a running joke that they ought to have a photo requirement for female applicants."

The Limestone That Binds: Facilities at Dickinson

Dorms at Dickinson "are pretty decent," said one student. Campus housing is divided into quads and traditional dorms. While the dorms have kitchens and are coed, quads are smaller and have new carpeting. Quads, as Student Directed Learning Centers, allow for theme housing including multicultural groups, ROTC, language houses, and fraternities and sororities. Students generally feel that the traditional residence halls "give more sense of community than other housing options. They're louder and more fun." Students are required to live on campus for their first three years, and must apply to live off-campus if they wish to do so senior year.

Most dorms have weathered the strain of college students fairly well over the years, and those that have not are currently undergoing major renovations. "Most of the dorms are nice" said a sophomore, "however, my freshman dorm was horrendous! It was old cinder blocks, and kind of dirty. It's being renovated, though." The extensive renovation project has led to a housing crunch, leaving many students temporarily reassigned to apartments just off campus. "It's pretty sweet," said a sophomore resident. "It's clean and nice, and the building manager doesn't care what we do as long as we're quiet."

As for student life, most Dickinsonians can be found at the Hub at least once a day. The Hub building holds the cafeteria, the mail room, the dean of students' office, the bookstore, and the office on residential life. Dickinson's cafeteria food is often highlighted in guidebooks for its award-winning food, but students gave it more mixed reviews. "They say it's really good, but it's not all it's cracked up to be. You pretty much get chicken, burgers, and pasta," said one student. Another added, "Dickinson's food is very predictable. The salad bar and the 'other side' stuff are the same every day. The hot bar is the only thing that changes. It seems like they rotate the same hot bar menu over and over every couple of weeks."

All students praised Dickinson's campus as "beautiful." "Most girls come here because they say the campus is pretty," said one student. "The buildings are predominantly limestone. They're old. There is a good amount of forests and green rolling hills. It's very calming. We have little parks and fields everywhere." Unfortunately, the town of Carlisle is not as much to the students' liking. "Two bad malls and a bowling alley that closes at 5 P.M.," reported an undergrad. "I'm used to having entertainment right at my fingertips, and coming to Carlisle was a shock to me," added another.

Crime has become a more visible problem on Dickinson's campus. "A lot of weirdos from the town wander onto campus . . . It's something to watch out for," said one undergrad. One female undergrad noted that "if you invite danger, it'll come your way, but basically I think it's a pretty safe campus." The administration is working to keep it safe with electronic key tags for accessing buildings, and a student patrol system. Dickinson even provides a shuttle from the campus to one of the most popular bars to "make sure all the drunk kids make it home safely."

Upon graduating, Dickinson students traditionally march through the front door of the oldest building on campus. Students see this as a sign that Dickinson has opened the door to the world for them. In that world, Dickinson's sons and daughters can reminisce about four years at a close-knit college that challenged them to high standards of academic excellence. *—Betty Wolf*

FYI

If you come to Dickinson, you'd better bring "a computer. There's only one computer lab open all the time, and the facilities are inadequate."

What is the typical weekend schedule? "Thursday night party, Friday night watch a movie, Saturday night party, Sunday do nothing."

If I could change one thing about Dickinson, I'd "change the no keg rule."

Three things every student should do before graduating are "rush, go abroad, and make friends with somebody who's not like you."

Drexel University

Address: 3141 Chesnut Ave, Philaldephia, PA 19104
Phone: 1-800-2DREXEL
E-mail address: enroll@drexel.edu
Web site URL: www.drexel.edu
Founded: 1891
Private or Public: private
Religious affiliation: none
Location: urban
Undergraduate enrollment: 11,585
Total enrollment: 11,585
Percent Male/Female: 60%/40%
Percent Minority: 26%
Percent African-American: 9%
Percent Asian: 14%
Percent Hispanic: 2%
Percent Native-American: 0%
Percent in-state/out of state: 64%/36%
Percent Pub HS: NA
Number of Applicants: 11,697
Percent Accepted: 60%
Percent Accepted who enroll: NA
Entering: 2,110
Transfers: 659
Application Deadline: 1 Mar
Mean SAT: NA
Mean ACT: NA
Middle 50% SAT range: V 520-620, M 550-660
Middle 50% ACT range: NA
3 Most popular majors: informational science, engineering, management
Retention: 85%
Graduation rate: 57%
On-campus housing: 26%
Fraternities: 12%
Sororities: 8%
Library: 443,597 volumes
Tuition and Fees: $21,075
Room and Board: $6,400
Financial aid, first-year: 74%
Varsity or Club Athletes: 8%
Early Decision or Early Action Acceptance Rate: NA

Where can you find a top-notch engineering and science school in a world-class city that gives you the opportunity to receive on-the-job training while still being in school? One place would be Drexel University, located in the City of Brotherly Love, Philadelphia, where students set the only limits to what they can learn and experience.

The Curriculum

The co-op program is the most defining and attractive feature of Drexel. Officially known as the Drexel Co-op and as "The Ultimate Internship," it gives students the option of doing up to three six-month internships in almost any field. A junior said, "I know a lot of people like myself who have had co-ops with research labs in the school and worked on really cutting-edge projects. I also know people who've gone to companies and done interesting work. Some people I know interned in R&D labs at chemical companies where they were involved in developing new products."

Major corporate employers of Drexel students in the co-op program include GlaxoSmithKline, Comcast Corporation, Verizon, Sunoco, Inc., and Bristol-Myers Squibb Company. The co-op program provides numerous benefits for Drexel students. In addition to practical on-the-job training, which teaches skills students may use in their future careers, co-op internships also help students figure out exactly what it is they want to do—or do not want to do—post graduation. Also, "if you land a really cool co-op job," you might end up working there after graduation.

Drexel is divided into six colleges: the College of Arts and Sciences, the College of Business, the College of Media Arts and Design, the College of Engineering, the College of Information Science and Technology, and the College of Evening and Professional Studies. In addition, three schools offer undergraduate B.S. degrees: the School of Biomedical Engineering, Science, and Health Systems; the School of Education; and the School of Environmental Science, Engineering, and Policy.

Drexel has a strong emphasis on science and engineering at the undergraduate and graduate levels. In addition to science, however, Drexel also has a liberal arts educational component. According to a Drexel student, "one would think that since the school is more or less an engineering school it would have sub-par liberal arts classes, but that's simply not true. Artsy departments actually have some excellent faculty—in part because even though there are not many history or literature majors, everybody has to take at least some courses in those areas."

One course, University 101, a requirement for all freshmen, has received mixed reviews. The program serves the dual purpose of acclimating students to Drexel and Philadelphia, and of getting students involved in a community-service oriented program.

Social Scene

As on most college campuses, much of the social life on the Drexel campus does involve alcohol. According to one student, "alcohol is disgustingly present on campus. You can't walk through even a small group of people without hearing someone making plans about getting drunk or talking about how drunk they got last night."

Fraternities and sororities are certainly a large part of the party scene on campus, but there are many other options. Some students report that parties are "always going on." And while some students may drink alcohol to extremes, especially freshmen, drugs seem to play a much smaller, more limited role in campus life.

If for some reason the parties on campus are not enough to satiate some students, there are always the many off-campus dance clubs. Still, many students find just hanging out with friends and watching a movie in a dorm perfectly enjoyable, and a respectable alternative to going out.

The Streets of Philadelphia

A frequent complaint among Drexel students is that there is no "real campus." This reflects the fact that Drexel is an urban school. But, this does not mean it's a boring place. Said one student: "since Drexel's located in the core of the city, all of the attractions like the zoo, museums, parks, and restaurants are within walking distance. The school also does a pretty good job of organizing trips to different places, especially for incoming students who aren't familiar with the city."

As an urban school, prospective Drexel students are often worried about crime. However, there are phones located strategically across campus, putting students in immediate contact with the police if need be. One freshman reported feeling "perfectly safe" walking around campus alone at night.

> **"I know a lot of people like myself who have had co-ops with research labs in the school and worked on real cutting-edge projects."**

Drexel has long prided itself on being ahead of its competition in terms of accepting new technologies and applying them. Drexel was the first university in the country to require students to have personal access to a computer, in 1983. After finishing near the top in the "most wired" campus rankings in *Yahoo! Internet Life*, Drexel has also turned its sights to developing a wireless network to service the entire campus. According to a computer science major, "the school's put a lot of effort into establishing the wireless network. It covers most of the campus, including all the school buildings and dorms."

What's On in Philly?

Drexel students contend that though some outsiders may have a negative opinion of Philadelphia, their host city is actually a wonderful place to go to school. The city has many great neighborhoods, and there is never a shortage of things to do: visitors can hear the Philadelphia Orchestra, watch an Eagles, Flyers, Sixers, or Phillies game, or catch a musical or play at one of the many theatres on the "Avenue of the Arts."

For the student whose palate desires more than just cafeteria food, there are many great restaurants on and around campus. For ethnic foods, University City is the place to go, and is home to the excellent Thai Singha House, Tandoor India buffet, and, while a bit on the pricey side, Zocalo's, for just the right mix of Tex-Mex. One will find no shortage of famous and upscale restaurants in Center City, but a truly reasonably priced gem is "Rangoon," a Burmese restaurant, with excellent lunch specials and very friendly owners.

One student reported that "there are also lots of places to visit, like the museums, and the public library system in the city is excellent. The Philadelphia Zoo is my favorite place to go."

For a city that has been called "the #1 fattest city in America" by *Men's Health* magazine, much has been done by the city to improve Philadelphians' fitness, including making the city more bike-friendly. According to one student, whose "favorite thing to do around the city is to go out riding," there are many "places to bike, either on road or off."

Student Body

For a city as diverse as Philadelphia, Drexel's student body seems to some to be lacking sufficient representation by Black and Latino groups. Many of the students are from the Philadelphia region. One student observed that "it seems like most people are from Delaware, New Jersey, and the whole of Pennsylvania." However, "there are a great deal of international students."

Beyond the Classroom

Sports teams at Drexel do not consume campus life as they might at a larger state school. However, there are many athletes, and some intramural sports get a good showing. Says one student: "the recreational/athletic department here is fabulous. We have a well-run, up-to-date gym with facilities for basketball, swimming, and just plain working out. It's as good as most private gyms or fitness clubs." Beyond the gym, the athletics department "also organizes a lot of intramural activities each term, including soccer, basketball, lacrosse, softball, and football. Generally, these get a lot of people involved."

For the most part, students at Drexel are satisfied with their school, yet there are numerous complaints about the administration. Said one student, "any time you have to work with the administration be prepared for a hassle and lots of frustration. Paychecks are never on time if you work within the school, financial aid packages and bills are always wrong, the residential living administration is obtuse at best, and it always seems like the administration is out to get you."

Extracurricular opportunities abound. If there is something you are interested in, chances are you can find a group of people that share your interest. If not, you can go elsewhere in Philadelphia and find a group. Students at Drexel believe themselves lucky to have the benefit of their co-op program and the advantages of the surrounding city. —*Andrew Read*

FYI

If you come to Drexel, you'd better bring "a towel, a smile, a pillow, and a sense of humor. A pair of nice shoes, a nice shirt, and nice pants don't hurt either."

The typical weekend schedule involves "going out Friday and Saturday nights, sleeping late Saturday and Sunday."

If I could change one thing about Drexel, "it would be the school administration."

Three things every student at Drexel should do before graduating are: "run up the art museum steps, stay in the computer cluster through 'til dawn breaks, and go to South Street."

Franklin and Marshall College

Address: PO Box 3003, Lancaster, PA 17604
Phone: 717-291-3953
E-mail address: admission@fandm.com
Web site URL: www.fandm.edu
Founded: 1787
Private or Public: private
Religious affiliation: none
Location: suburban
Undergraduate enrollment: 1,926
Total enrollment: 1,926
Percent Male/Female: 52%/48%
Percent Minority: 9%
Percent African-American: 3%
Percent Asian: 4%
Percent Hispanic: 2%
Percent Native-American: 0%
Percent in-state/out of state: 35%/65%
Percent Pub HS: NA
Number of Applicants: 3,425
Percent Accepted: 62%
Percent Accepted who enroll: 70%
Entering: 534
Transfers: 16
Application Deadline: 1 Feb
Mean SAT: NA
Mean ACT: NA
Middle 50% SAT range: V 570-660, M 590-680
Middle 50% ACT range: NA
3 Most popular majors: government, business, English
Retention: 91%
Graduation rate: 84%
On-campus housing: 67%
Fraternities: NA
Sororities: NA
Library: 435,771 volumes
Tuition and Fees: $28,860
Room and Board: $7,070
Financial aid, first-year: 43%
Varsity or Club Athletes: 55%
Early Decision or Early Action Acceptance Rate: 70%

If enthusiasm is what you are looking for, Franklin and Marshall is the place to find it. Students dedicate themselves to all aspects of college life. Many chose the college for a challenging course load, and that is what the school delivers. But their dedication extends far beyond the classroom. From helping in the community to enjoying themselves on the weekends, F&M students enjoy keeping themselves busy. Nestled in the picturesque town of Lancaster, this small liberal arts college prides itself on both academic excellence and rigor, combined with a healthy taste for amusement.

STUDY, STUDY, STUDY!

"Classes are hard," F&M students unanimously chime. When asked what an easy major is at F&M, one senior replied "I don't think that there is one." But, F&M is a college designed to be tough, and the students rise to the challenge posed by their inspiring professors. "I have tons of reading to do every night. Some people don't do all of the reading . . . but those are the students who only get average grades."

A self-proclaimed liberal arts college, F&M's focus has long been on the sciences. "The school has pretty good facilities for being [so] small," one senior reported. Students say F&M's computer facilities are excellent, with Ethernet connections available in all public areas, such as libraries and classrooms, and in most of the dorms—"my whole life is on the Web," one student boasted. While the science complex was renovated recently, the school is currently trying to help the arts programs with renovations and expansions. The arts "deserve better," one student said.

Many students choose F&M for the premed program. Students "don't always survive the pre-med program, but that's what they come for," said one undergrad. "I have sympathy for the pre-meds," one junior commented. "They hammer themselves." Students report that departments such as English, Classics, and Psychology are also quite strong.

Distribution requirements consist of courses in at least three different areas, such as Knowledge and Belief, Foreign Study, and Social Science. Two semesters of foreign language also are required.

Class sizes are small at F&M, topping off at around 20 to 25 students, so some freshmen have trouble getting into the classes they want. Many feel that the close rapport with professors and the small, discussion-intensive sections far outweigh any problems with registration. F&M professors, including Howard Kaye and Carol Auster in sociology, Sanford Pinsker in English, and Curtis Bentzel in German, earn student praise for their dedication and desire to teach. They "seem to want to be here [and] . . . treat you like you're smart," one student said. By the time you graduate, one student was happy to report, you're "close to one if not close to a bunch." It is not unusual for students to eat dinner or baby-sit at their professors' houses. Many students remain in close contact with professors even after graduation. One junior exclaimed in praise of his profs, "If you give them an inch, they'll give you a ton!"

Franklin and Marshall students are quick to point out that their college is not entirely a machine that grinds their faces into the books. Instead, they characterize the college as a place "that is really academically rigorous and then parties like at any other school." Extracurriculars provide the main chance to meet other people, and if "one is not involved, it makes it harder," one student reported. Popular activities to which students devote a great deal of time and energy include the drama society, known as the Green Room; the weekly newspaper, the *College Reporter;* the radio station, WFNM; the Student Congress; Minority Integration Program; and the College Entertainment Committee. Various community service programs connected with F&M's new Community and Public Service Institute and the America Reads Program also attract wide participation. Students involved in these campus activities, as well as in work study programs, consider themselves "some really dedicated individuals."

Outside the Classroom . . .

Much of the F&M social scene is dominated by Greek societies, which although not officially recognized by the college, involve the majority of the student body. Weekends consist of "frat parties, frats, and more frats," according to one senior. Although much town-gown tension stems from the Greek houses' loud parties and initiation rituals, which one member said get "pretty rough," students seem to find that the independence of the Greek societies from the college has pulled a lot of the tension away from the school. At the same time, students agree that membership or non-membership defines them. Campus cliques center on Greek membership and reportedly turn the dining hall experience into a "'Dining Hall Culture." One student warned, "You don't just sit anywhere . . . like high school."

For those who dislike the Greek system and the many parties dominated by drinking, "there really isn't much left to do [but] . . . sit around and complain," one senior groaned. Another summarized the F&M college work ethic as "kill yourself working during the week and kill yourself drinking on the weekend."

To provide an alternative for those uninterested in Greek activities, the school sponsors parties, such as the Blizzard Bash and Around the World, movies, lectures, and an occasional comedian. Guests have included Kwaisi Infume, Maya Angelou, John Updike, Newt Gingrich, Billy Joel, and the Dave Matthews Band. A popular campus hangout is Ben's Underground, which has a pub-like atmosphere where students can eat snacks and play pool or versions of supermarket bingo and The Dating Game.

As for real dating, one experienced senior reported that "there isn't really much to do in Lancaster, so the dating scene is very limited." Frat parties are the center of social life on weekends, and "the parties are a lot of drinking and some dancing and hooking up. That's about it." Another student agreed that the social scene was "hookup central," with very few steady couples populating the campus.

The town of Lancaster gets mixed reviews from students. Some like its quaint affability while others lament that "Lancaster sucks . . . nothing to do." The town has a dance club for students over 18, a 24-hour bowling alley, as well as many restaurants and coffeehouses, such as the popular Fred and Mary's and the Cafe Angst. Philadelphia and Baltimore, as well as the closer malls and outlets, offer more excitement for students who have cars, but some claimed that there was too much work to allow frequent excursions.

Food at F&M gets the same sort of tempered criticism as it does everywhere. In the dining hall, suggested one grumpy student, avoid everything. Another exclaimed, "Some of their creations are just amazing!" such as the orange cheese sauce and "ratatouille." The options for vegetarians are mainly salad and pasta, and according to one student "it's bad, it's bad pasta." But, students gladly use their meal credit for snacks and sandwiches at the college Common Ground, and food in Lancaster is rated highly, with many pizza spots, chain and local restaurants, and a Farmer's Market for fresh vegetables.

Dorm life at F&M is almost universally praised. First-year students and sophomores are required to live in the dorms, with mostly co-ed floors, although students can request single-sex housing. Dorm life is supervised by RAs—residents call them "tools of the administration"—but this does not seriously hamper social life. The dorms are reported to be very spacious and convenient, with phone and Internet connections, but many juniors and seniors move off campus, where the housing is "pretty good," although security is less tight outside the perimeters of the campus security patrols. As for safety, walking at night "could be dangerous if people are stupid," but students generally walk in groups, especially to and from off-campus locales.

"The parties are a lot of drinking and some dancing and hooking up. That's about it."

Enthusiastic participation in athletics or attendance at sporting events are not priorities at F&M. The football and basketball teams are popular and their games are fairly well-attended, especially by certain Fummers who paint their faces blue and do push-ups for every Diplomat touchdown. But overall, the teams are not a central rallying point for school spirit, which, on the whole, is rated very low—"people are really negative about the school . . . very cynical in general."

F&M is a Division III college and does not give athletic scholarships. For those not on teams, club sports and intramurals are popular. The state of the art Athletic Sports and Fitness Center (ASFC) is good for many exercise-hungry students.

While F&M students generally think of themselves as nonpolitical and "pretty apathetic," many are also fairly conservative in their views on social issues. The student population is "more diverse than people give it credit for," but one student admitted that racial minorities are seldom fully integrated into the mainstream of the student body. However, the small minority groups are active and outspoken, with the Black Student Union acclaimed for being the only really politically active forum on campus.

While the challenges of the social environment make some F&M students "a little bitter," the intelligent cynicism of the student body seems to fit well with the mission of the school as a place of devotion to rigorous academics. Franklin and Marshall is a perfect fit for those students with an enthusiastic desire to educate themselves, to better their community, and to make time for a healthy social life as well. The requirements for students both in and out of the classroom are intense, and the process of rising to meet these challenges breeds a healthy dedication to all aspects of college life. —*Erik Weiss and Staff*

FYI

The three best things about attending Franklin and Marshall are "good classes, crazy partying, and air-conditioned dorms."

The typical weekend schedule involves "going out to the Friday and Saturday nights, sleeping in and hanging out, then doing a little homework on Sunday."

If I could change one thing about Drexel, "it would be the habit of being judged by your fraternity or sorority."

Three things every student at Franklin and Marshall should do before graduating are: "have Chinese food at that place in the student center, go to the Farmer's Market, and make a stir-fry."

Gettysburg College

Address: 300 N. Washington Street, Gettysburg, PA 17325
Phone: 717-337-6100
E-mail address: admiss@gettysburg.edu
Web site URL: www.gettysburg.edu
Founded: 1832
Private or Public: private
Religious affiliation: Lutheran
Location: suburban
Undergraduate enrollment: 2,377
Total enrollment: 2,377
Percent Male/Female: 48%/52%
Percent Minority: 6%
Percent African-American: 3%
Percent Asian: 1%
Percent Hispanic: 1%
Percent Native-American: 0%
Percent in-state/out of state: 28%/72%
Percent Pub HS: NA
Number of Applicants: 4,573
Percent Accepted: 50%
Percent Accepted who enroll: NA
Entering: 687
Transfers: 25
Application Deadline: 15 Feb
Mean SAT: NA
Mean ACT: NA
Middle 50% SAT range: V 580-650, M 590-660
Middle 50% ACT range: 26-29
3 Most popular majors: business, political science, English
Retention: 88%
Graduation rate: 76%
On-campus housing: NA
Fraternities: 44%
Sororities: 26%
Library: 351,848 volumes
Tuition and Fees: $28,474
Room and Board: $6,972
Financial aid, first-year: 53%
Varsity or Club Athletes: 45%
Early Decision or Early Action Acceptance Rate: NA

Some Gettysburg students, though they hesitate to admit it, are at first drawn to the small liberal arts college solely by the famous battlefield. But when they get to campus they soon realize that there is more to the college than its rolling green hills speckled with bullets and stories from one of the most definitive battles of the Civil War. Indeed, the college is rooted deeply in the culture of this major historical site. As many Gettysburg students will tell you, however, the college is a place that is home to thoroughly modern facilities, students, and social life—you won't find battle reenactments here on Friday nights!

Small and Strong

The classes at Gettysburg are regarded by one student as simply "small and strong." The class size, even for the introductory courses, is relatively small. Virtually all of the upper-level classes have only 10 to 15 students. All classes are taught by professors, though there are TAs available to supplement the lectures in the form of individual help or as leaders of study group sessions. One student commented that the classes are "challenging, yet not overbearing." Many students, when asked about academic stress levels, responded that the workload is entirely self-motivated and that "kids take what they want from it and *that* shapes their experience." The emphasis on general requirements shapes Gettysburg's strong liberal arts core with requirements existing in all of the fundamental areas such as foreign language, math, English, science, and physical education. Students strongly assert that the fulfillment of requirements does not entirely shape their academic experiences, but rather gives them a broad intellectual base from which to begin their concentration. Popular majors at Gettysburg include business, political science, English, and (who would have guessed it) history. management is also an extremely popular major and is also regarded as one of the easiest. Students are required to declare their major by the beginning of junior year, yet most declare much earlier in order to fulfill both general and major requirements in an orderly fashion. The workload is generally major and student-specific, but some students estimate that they spend at least three hours a night doing schoolwork.

Facilities

The most popular place for students to be spending those three hours studying would probably be the well-liked Musselman Library, regarded by the students as a "great facility that is open 24 hours." Almost the same amount of enthusiasm can be noted when students are asked about the dorms at Gettysburg. Residential facilities "improve dramatically as you get older," one student explained, and there is much diversity among the different buildings. Freshmen are usually given the smallest rooms, described by one student as "cinderblock squares," but were rated by one freshman as "around 7 on a scale from 1 to 10." To expand upperclassmen housing, the school purchased two old motels in an attempt to compensate for a housing shortage on campus. Perks of this housing include close parking (a major plus since most Gettysburg students have cars on campus) and private bathrooms. Gettysburg also offers suite-living in the new dorms named The Quarry Suites, which are reserved for juniors and seniors. In addition to dorms, many male students opt to live in their respective fraternities that maintain prominent locations on campus. Students are generally happy about their living conditions, and opportunities abound for getting out of your dorm room to hang out with fellow students. One such gathering place is the College Union Building, a student center with a coffee shop, bookstore, sitting areas, and the popular café "The Bullet Hole," which provides students with made-to-order subs, pizza, and various alternatives to the cafeteria—not that Gettysburg students are actively searching for alternatives. Students are enthusiastic about the food from the cafeteria, known as the Servo. There is a lot of selection and flexibility in the meal plans, and, for the pickiest of eaters, there is always the option of eating off campus. Gettysburg offers a plentitude of off-campus eating options. Everything from local establishments—Pizza House, located close to campus, is highly recommended—to take-out, to popular fast-food chains such as Friendly's and Perkin's. Anything a hungry college kid could want is located fairly close to Gettysburg's campus.

Little Men on Horses (We're Talkin' About Polo, not Cavalry)

When asked to describe a typical Gettysburg student, variations on a common theme were shot back with rapid speed at the interviewer: "Gorgeous . . . Beautiful . . . Impeccable . . . Perfect." Sound good after spending four years bemoaning the lack of attractive specimens at your high school? Surprisingly, the students admission that the campus is an apparent Abercrombie & Fitch breeding ground was in fact a negative aspect of the school. The typical student is described as being white, conservative, upper-class, wearing Polo, and from the Tri-State Area. As one student said, "This is a George W.–type school." Some students long for diversity in all forms, though most admit that there is some economic diversity. The homosexual community is not vocal at Gettysburg, and some students admit to never having met an openly gay person at the college.

"The cultural atmosphere at Gettysburg can accommodate everyone's interests by providing a broad spectrum of things to do."

There are, however, many opportunities to socially interact with a diverse group of people. Despite the apparent flawlessness of the student body and the strong Greek system, students say that it is very easy to meet people at Gettysburg. "There are cliques, well the entire Greek scene is all about cliques, but you get to know some really cool people in your classes," commented one student. Likewise, there are numerous clubs, service organizations, and intramural sports that bring the student body together. Intramural sports are popular at Gettysburg, as are the Division III varsity sports. The men's soccer and lacrosse teams are currently very strong, and the majority of Gettysburg students are apt to attend games to root their "Bullets" on.

Greeks and Ghosts

You thought the battle was rough? Try getting into a frat party if you are a freshman guy not surrounded by a posse of freshmen girls! Ok, so it isn't that bad, but the Greeks are known to virtually rule the social scene at Gettysburg. There are currently ten fraternities and four sororities to which about half the student body belongs. Students say that it is not imperative to belong to a frat or sorority, but most admit that the weekend social scene is almost entirely taken up by Greek parties even if you yourself are not a member. As one student said, "There is basically a frat party every night of the week." Some popular frats include ATO, TKE, and FIJI. Students tend to agree that the social scene is alcohol-oriented, but assert that they never have felt pressure to drink at Gettysburg. Chem-free (or Greek-free) alternatives include off-campus parties and also campus-organized events such as performances, concerts, etc. There is a student-run Campus Activities Board that is responsible for planning group trips to Baltimore (only an hour away), Washington, DC, and Hershey Park to provide a change of scenery and activity for restless Gettysburg students. As one student explained, "The cultural atmosphere at Gettysburg can accommodate everyone's interests by providing a broad spectrum of things to do."

The common complaint of most students involves the rural location of the college. "There is nothing to do here—that is why we stay on campus!" explained one student. The surrounding town of Gettysburg is described as "touristy" but also has restaurants and a movie theater for entertainment. However, the campus itself is described as "beautiful." The school is on the edge of the historic battlefield and is home to some Civil War-era buildings. Pennsylvania Hall, one of the oldest buildings on campus dating from 1837, acted as a field hospital during the famous battle, and now is rumored to be haunted by the ghosts of patients and nurses. Likewise, many of the old buildings, along with the grounds of the battlefield, are regarded as having restless spirits. Many Gettysburg students claim to experience chilling rendezvous with local favorites such as The Blue Boy and the Sentry on the Tower.

Gettysburg College is an institution that values tradition while providing bright futures for its talented students. The classes are small and personal with a strong concentration on the particular needs of the students, and the social scene is inclusive and filled with classic college fun. A beautiful school filled with beautiful people? Even the ghosts don't want to leave . . . —*Marisa Benoit*

FYI

If you come to Gettysburg you'd better bring "Natty Light and Gap clothes."

What is the typical weekend schedule? "Party on Friday night; sleep 'til noon on Saturday; go to the frats on Saturday night; then sleep and do work on Sunday."

If I could change one thing about Gettysburg, I'd "make it more diverse."

Three things every student at Gettysburg should do before graduating are "go to a party at every frat, eat at Pizza House, and tour the battlefield."

Haverford College

Address: 370 Lancaster Avenue; Haverford, PA 19041-1392
Phone: 610-896-1350
E-mail address: admitme@haverford.edu
Web site URL: www.haverford.edu
Founded: 1833
Private or Public: private
Religious affiliation: none
Location: suburban
Undergraduate enrollment: 1,105
Total enrollment: 1,105
Percent Male/Female: 47%/53%
Percent Minority: 27%
Percent African-American: 5%
Percent Asian: 15%
Percent Hispanic: 7%
Percent Native-American: 1%
Percent in-state/out of state: 20%/80%
Percent Pub HS: NA
Number of Applicants: 2,598
Percent Accepted: 32%
Percent Accepted who enroll: 55%
Entering: 311
Transfers: 4
Application Deadline: 15 Jan
Mean SAT: NA
Mean ACT: NA
Middle 50% SAT range: V 640-740, M 640-720
Middle 50% ACT range: NA
3 Most popular majors: biology, history, political science
Retention: 95%
Graduation rate: 91%
On-campus housing: 98%
Fraternities: NA
Sororities: NA
Library: 497,784 volumes
Tuition and Fees: $28,880
Room and Board: $9,020
Financial aid, first-year: 42%
Varsity or Club Athletes: 74%
Early Decision or Early Action Acceptance Rate: 55%

How many parts of the body can you think of that have three letters? Better think on your toes, because at Haverford you'll be visiting the university president's house in the middle of the night to wake him up for this little pop quiz. It's a little weird, but somebody has to do it.

'Fordian Slips

'Fordians are welcomed to campus as part of Customs Group, a group of freshmen led by an upperclassman in orientation activities like the one mentioned above. "They really hold your hand," one freshman said. She claimed that Haverford is more like camp than college, and warned that nothing at Haverford is what you might call normal. "It's the kind of place where no one is the same, but you understand perfectly . . . why they're here," one student explained. "I'll meet kids who look like total hoodlums, and they're econ philosophy double-major genius kids; they will always surprise you."

The Naked Truth

One student claimed that there seems to be a lot of "awkward nudity" on campus. "Every once in a while, a [sports] team will show up at a party and take off all their clothes." The track team is the most notorious for spontaneous stripping: "They're big on it, running naked in nothing but shoes," a junior noted. "But they're national champions, so you can't really say it's bad for them or their success."

Fortunately for the modest, you don't have to be naked to be a spectator. "Lots of people will come out to most of the sporting events," one athlete said. "It feels like a very low-level, high school kind of function, mostly because of the mellow atmosphere." Football fans will find themselves disappointed however, because the Black Squirrels at Haverford (unofficially the 'Fords) have no football team. Luckily they do play lacrosse and boast a winning track team, in addition to offering a strong line-up of intramural sports.

The 'Fordian Mind

Academic distributional requirements at Haverford demand that students sample classes in natural science, social science, humanities, and math. These requirements don't appear to be too rigorous for those who go to a liberal arts college to get away from science and math. "They offer easy courses that take care of your distributions," one junior said, adding that students can select courses as difficult or as easy as they like, depending on their interests. Overall students are in favor of the requirements. One sophomore asserted, "It's good that you're forced to take science or math. It keeps you honest and well-rounded." There's also a physical education and wellness requirement, which can be circumvented by playing in intramural leagues, or students can have fun with it by taking a badminton or night bowling class.

Haverford also requires students to enroll in one social justice class. "It's a very valuable requirement, in my mind," one sophomore said. "It's a good way to balance all the orthodoxy that you get from studying the classics of academia." As for studying abroad and other curriculum and programs, Haverford offers an array of options, but as one student explained, "They don't really push anything."

"You can't be a jerk. If you come in with a bad attitude, you get a reputation because it's a small school."

Students say that the small size of the school allows Haverford to provide "a lot of what they advertise, which is the intimate, personal contact with the professors." Special guests invited by professors offer day-long workshops open to the entire campus, as well as "Work In Progress" sessions, where they bring a paper they're working on and invite comments and questions from students. Last year professor Mark Gould—a "big time sociologist" and "really brilliant megalomaniac" whose classes are highly recommended in spite of the fact that "he's given *an* A in the last ten years"—brought Justice Richard Posner to campus. Speakers and special guests, in addition to the open-enrollment policy with nearby Swarthmore, the University of Pennsylvania, and Bryn Mawr, keep the small school from having limited resources or too few offerings. Students say that there is a good amount of overlap between the three universities, particularly Bryn Mawr, which is the most popular of these options because shuttles run between the campuses every ten minutes. One student said, "You can eat at Bryn Mawr, you can major at Bryn Mawr, you can even dorm at Bryn Mawr." There's a little less involvement at Swarthmore because "it's not terribly convenient, and that's where the rivalry is."

Life, Liberty . . .

According to one Haverford sophomore, "The dorm living is pretty dope." In addition to on-campus dorms that provide a large number of singles, Haverfordians have the option of living in Haverford College Apartments (HCA). HCAs offer two-bedroom apartments with a kitchen and bath. They are a little farther from campus than the dorms, but are the most popular housing option. There are no fraternities or sororities, although there are some houses predominately occupied by members of sports teams. Students say these are like "semi-frats; they're the un-frats we have."

On weekends some students venture into the surrounding towns or into Philadelphia. Haverford also offers student-run concert series, a cappella performances, improvisational comedy troups like The Throng and The Lighted Fools, and "sometimes hokey school-sponsored dances." A group called "'Fords Against Boredom" plans events like movies, Phillies games, and nightclub outings that are open to the whole campus. "The parties, they're sporadic," one student revealed. Because of the size of the school, he said, "It's hard to get a critical mass." Some blame it on the athletes: "Nobody parties on Friday because the only people who party are people on sports teams, and they don't party on Fridays because they have games on Saturdays." Students say there's usually one main party each weekend, but they warn, "We party more like a nerd school than you'd think."

. . . And the Pursuit of the Honor Code

If "the party scene is generally subdued," it is certainly not because rules prevent wild parties. "The alcohol policy here explicitly encourages drinking in moderation," one senior said. Students emphasize that there are no rules at Haverford, but because of the Honor Code and good sense, "Everyone understands the boundaries and is smart enough to know that if lines are crossed in the future we'll be punished." The Honor Code is a general agreement among students, re-ratified and amended by the student body at the beginning of each semester, that insists upon honesty and respect in academics and social life. Due to the efficacy of the Honor Code, many tests are take-home, and professors trust their students to spend the allotted amount of time on them without eliciting help from classmates. Moreover "people just leave their doors unlocked left and right," one sophomore said, because "there is a social aspect to [the Code] as well, which governs the way you behave towards people." Another added, "You can't be a jerk. If you come in with a bad attitude, you get a reputation because it's a small school. There's no football team, there are no frats, so there's no meathead jerk guys like that. That's the biggest positive about the bad social scene here."

Students tell a story—the accuracy of which has not been verified—to illustrate these loose rules and "earthy" feel of the school. A student was growing marijuana in his closet using halogen lamps as a light source, and failed to turn them off before leaving on a long break. The student, who was punished with community service hours and required to attend a fire safety course, "was not admonished for the growing of marijuana whatsoever," but for breaking safety codes by having halogen lights in his room and leaving them on over break. This story represents the relaxed atmosphere that makes Haverford such a unique college. —*Stephanie Hagan*

FYI

If you come to Haverford, you better bring "an open mind. Kids who have one do well. Kids who don't . . . flounder at the beginning."

What is the typical weekend schedule? "The weekend pretty much starts on Thursday; Friday kind of dies, for lack of something to do; Saturday during the day people will go out to most of the sporting events, though a surprising number of people sit in the library all day; Saturday night they always manage to have something, usually school-sponsored; Sundays, work."

If I could change one thing about Haverford, "I'd definitely say athletic facilities, the gym is miserable."

Three things every student at Haverford should do before graduating are "spend the night in the library, swim in the faculty pool and the duck pond, and find the underground tunnels."

Lafayette College

Address: 118 Markle Hall, Easton, PA 18042
Phone: 610-330-5100
E-mail address: admissions@lafayette.edu
Web site URL: www.lafayette.edu
Founded: 1826
Private or Public: private
Religious affiliation: Presbyterian
Location: urban
Undergraduate enrollment: 2,300
Total enrollment: 2,300
Percent Male/Female: 51%/49%
Percent Minority: 8%
Percent African-American: 4%
Percent Asian: 2%
Percent Hispanic: 2%
Percent Native-American: 0%
Percent in-state/out of state: 28%/72%
Percent Pub HS: NA
Number of Applicants: 5,504
Percent Accepted: 36%
Percent Accepted who enroll: 66%
Entering: 590
Transfers: 8
Application Deadline: 1 Jan
Mean SAT: NA
Mean ACT: NA
Middle 50% SAT range: V 560-650, M 610-700
Middle 50% ACT range: 25-29
3 Most popular majors: social sciences, engineering, biology
Retention: 94%
Graduation rate: 85%
On-campus housing: 98%
Fraternities: 24%
Sororities: 45%
Library: 525,000 volumes
Tuition and Fees: $27,328
Room and Board: $8,418
Financial aid, first-year: 58%
Varsity or Club Athletes: 48%
Early Decision or Early Action Acceptance Rate: 66%

Once described as a sleepy and traditional small liberal arts college, Lafayette is challenging those conceptions. Lafayette students take advantage of popular engineering and business programs, while the campus is glimmering with beautiful dorms, labs, and the massive Kirby Sports Complex. The extremely athletic student body comes alive to see their Lafayette Leopards compete with archrival Lehigh, while almost everyone on campus takes part in a variety of intramurals. A vibrant social life and a park-like campus in Easton, Pennsylvania, add to the Lafayette experience, and more than anything else, Lafayette students value the "family atmosphere" their school offers.

The Core Curriculum

Academics at Lafayette are by no means a free-for-all. All first-semester freshmen must complete a core class called a First-Year Seminar (FYS), a writing intensive class capped at 16 students. FYS topics cover a wide and untraditional variety of subjects: recent offerings have included Popular Culture, Women Detectives, and The Appeal of Evil in Western Culture. All students also must take College Writing (English 110) either freshman or sophomore year, while second-semester sophomores are required to enroll in a Values and Science/Technology (VAST) seminar. VAST seminars explore issues in modern science in a writing-intensive format: recent courses have included Computers and Society, Science in Literature, and Technology and the City. In addition to completing requirements for one's major, all students are required to meet distribution requirements in humanities/social sciences, natural sciences, mathematics, and writing, while many are required to take a course dealing with a foreign culture. While engineering and science students are reputed to have the most difficulty meeting all their requirements, most students feel that meeting their requirements and taking the required courses within their major is manageable. Most Lafayette students carry a load of four courses per semester, though many engineering and science students must enroll in five classes at once.

The Academic Picture

Perhaps the aspect of academics that students at Lafayette College value most is the small class size and close contact with approachable, supportive professors. Classes generally enroll around 15 to 20 students, while popular introductory-level classes can enrol 60 or 70. Professors teach all classes; TA's only supervise labs. Students rave about the accessibility of their professors. A junior recounts, "I was going to drop my electrical engineering class, but a professor who didn't even teach the course offered to help me. He tutored me for two hours every other night, and with his help, I made it through the class." Students say that they value getting to know their professors well, but complain that as a result, they cannot go unnoticed when absent from class.

Lafayette offers a traditional liberal arts curriculum with about 40 individual majors from which students can choose. Setting Lafayette apart from many similar liberal arts institutions is the exceptionally strong and popular engineering program. Students praise the "outstanding" engineering faculty and the "state-of-the-art" facilities. Another popular field of study is Economics and Business, which is well-known for its large selection of courses relevant to the "real world." Chemistry, physics, and biochemistry students can take advantage of the multimillion-dollar Hugel Science Center. One undergrad warns that only those who are "seriously into programming" should consider the Computer Science major. Students generally describe grading as "fair," while a junior complains that professors of more advanced courses tend to phase out any beneficial curve. Courses considered easy include Elementary Public Speaking, A Chemical Perspective ("Baby Chemistry"), and several basic music classes ("Clapping for Credit"). Organic chemistry and certain physics offerings are reputed to be among the most difficult classes at Lafayette. Students report experiencing little trouble registering for and getting into their desired classes, and many Lafayette juniors take advantage of a growing number of opportunities to study abroad.

Campus Distractions

Students describe the Lafayette campus, sitting atop a hill overlooking the convergence of two rivers, as "incredibly picturesque." Many new and renovated buildings provide comfortable, luxurious spots for students to live, study, and hang out. Of the dorms, Keefe Hall garnered praise for its air-conditioning and "hotel-like" atmosphere, while South College is known as a big party hall. Many undergrads rush fraternities and sororities, but freshmen must wait a full year before they may rush.

The main library on campus, Skillman Library, is a serious place for everything from nightly course work (which students say averages 2 to 4 hours) to cramming for finals. Though Skillman closes at midnight, the library contains an all-night study lounge.

"I was going to drop my electrical engineering class, but a professor who didn't even teach the course offered to help me. He tutored me for two hours every other night, and with his help, I made it through the class."

In addition to the post office and activity rooms, several dining options exist in Farinon, the student center. The upstairs dining hall is popular for meals, while students fulfill their junk-food cravings in the downstairs snack bar. Gilbert's, a popular new coffeehouse, is a big draw thanks to its late-night food, nice atmosphere, and open-mike nights. Outside of Farinon, the dining room in Marquis Hall is praised for the made-to-order Asian food. Most undergrads describe the food as "fair to okay," while a junior complains that the menus are "annoyingly repetitive." Domino's Pizza is always a phone call away, but for the more adventurous, popular off-campus eating destinations include Campus Pizza, Morici's (Italian), Don Pablo's (Mexican), and The Olive Garden. For those over 21, Porter's is a popular hangout. Many Lafayette students have cars, and the college also operates a weekend bus system to and from the Lehigh Valley Mall (a 20-minute drive from campus).

Since tiny Easton has little entertainment to offer, undergrads generally spend their time on campus. The Lafayette Activities Forum (LAF) sponsors films, concerts, and other activities, while the Williams Center for the Arts brings in many performers throughout the year.

The student government and the daily newspaper (*The Lafayette*) are among the most popular extra-curriculars. Many students also join the Lafayette Investment Club, a haven for budding Wall Street tycoons that invests a small portion of the college's endowment.

Social life generally centers on frat parties, and although Lafayette retains its reputation as a "party school," students report that Greek life plays a less important role on campus than it has in the past. Lafayette's alcohol policy has become stricter in recent years, and includes a ban on kegs. Fraternities dominate the social scene, but all students are welcome at most parties, and undergrads generally don't feel pressure to rush.

As for dating, both men and women at Lafayette agree that, "there are nearly as many people dating as there are people randomly who are just hooking up on a one-time, no-relationship basis . . . I think we're pretty big into committed relationships." One disadvantage of the small student body is that there just are not that many new people to meet and date after a while.

An Athlete's Paradise

Lafayette undergrads unanimously describe the student body as "athletic." Varsity sports attract a large following, with the football and men's basketball teams drawing the largest crowds. The most anticipated sports event of the year is the football game that pits the Lafayette Leopards against their arch rivals from nearby Lehigh. At a less competitive level, intramurals are extremely popular, and include, in addition to the usual sports, activities such as chess, mini golf, croquet, and card games. Teams are drawn from fraternities, residence halls, and groups such as the International Students Association. Athletes and non-athletes alike take advantage of Lafayette's impressive Kirby Sports Complex. An undergrad explains that "If you want to meet someone in the afternoon, go to the gym. Everyone's there." Students have free access to Kirby's facilities, including the basketball, squash, tennis, and racquetball courts, swimming pool, and hockey rink, and the gym, which stays open until 2 A.M. on weeknights, truly serves as "one of the social centers of campus."

The Student Body

Lafayette students describe their classmates as generally white, Christian, straight, middle-class preppies from Pennsylvania, New Jersey, or New York who wear clothes from Abercrombie & Fitch, The North Face, and The Gap. There are few minority students at Lafayette; however, a junior reports that the campus is becoming more diverse. The African Black Cultural Club (ABC) and the Hillel House attract a number of undergrads. Many students say that the lack of diversity is their main complaint about Lafayette.

According to one undergrad, "Lafayette's small size really made the transition from high school a lot easier. It's so easy to meet people here, and soon, everybody knows each other." Everyone at Lafayette seems to form a tight web of social bonds, from fraternities, to sports teams, to members of a First Year Seminar who are still friendly after two years. While some see the college's small size as an obstacle to meeting new people, most students agree that the intimate feel of Lafayette unites them and gives rise to an overwhelming sense of school spirit. Add to that spirit a stunning campus and a group of caring, supportive professors, and you can see why most Lafayette students wouldn't think of being anywhere else. —*Justin Albstein*

FYI

The three best things about attending Lafayette are "the people are really friendly, the professors are totally open to talking about anything, and classes prepare you for the real world."

The three worst things about attending Lafayette are "administration and paperwork, it's impossible to find parking, and there's never enough time to do everything you want to do."

If I could change one thing about Lafayette, I'd "try and eliminate some of the masses of administrative paperwork."

The three things every student should do before graduating from Lafayette are "rush fraternity, visit the Crayola Crayon factory—you can see it from campus, and go to a Lafayette-Lehigh football game."

Lehigh University

Address: 27 Memorial Drive West, Bethlehem, PA 18015
Phone: 610-758-3100
E-mail address: admissions@lehigh.edu
Web site URL: www.lehigh.edu
Founded: 1865
Private or Public: private
Religious affiliation: none
Location: urban
Undergraduate enrollment: 4,685
Total enrollment: 4,685
Percent Male/Female: 60%/40%
Percent Minority: 11%
Percent African-American: 3%
Percent Asian: 6%
Percent Hispanic: 3%
Percent Native-American: 0%
Percent in-state/out of state: 30%/70%
Percent Pub HS: NA
Number of Applicants: 8,254
Percent Accepted: 44%
Percent Accepted who enroll: 84%
Entering: 1,144
Transfers: 110
Application Deadline: 1 Jan
Mean SAT: NA
Mean ACT: NA
Middle 50% SAT range: V 580-660, M 630-710
Middle 50% ACT range: NA
3 Most popular majors: finance, marketing, mechanical engineering
Retention: 93%
Graduation rate: 84%
On-campus housing: 65%
Fraternities: 33%
Sororities: 43%
Library: 791,194 volumes
Tuition and Fees: $27,430
Room and Board: $7,880
Financial aid, first-year: 43%
Varsity or Club Athletes: 28%
Early Decision or Early Action Acceptance Rate: 84%

On the side of a mountain in the town of Bethlehem lies Lehigh University, with the fraternities at the top of the hill and the classrooms at the bottom. Some students wonder if this configuration says something about their priorities. Although Lehigh has a very active Greek system, students are more than satisfied with the academics as well. According to one student, "The most unique quality of Lehigh is that students party hard and study hard."

Academics

Lehigh, whose team name changed recently from the Engineers to the Hawks, is known for its excellent engineering school; however, the university also has fine schools of business and arts and sciences. Each school has its own set of requirements, but all first-year students are required to take English 1 and English 2. First-year students in the engineering school also must take physics, chemistry, and one elective. Class size ranges from 200 to 300 people in introductory lecture courses to around 30 people in upper-level classes. All courses are taught by professors, with TAs leading only weekly recitation sections. For an "easy A," some students recommend "religion courses" and Human Sexuality.

For students looking for a challenge, Lehigh offers special programs such as the Five-Year Plan, in which engineering students can earn a bachelor's and a master's degree in five years. In addition to this opportunity, any undergraduate may take classes in the graduate school by petitioning the graduate committee and gaining permission from the instructor.

Dorms and Surroundings

Students at Lehigh say they are quite satisfied with their housing options. Only freshmen are required to live on campus, but the majority of undergraduates remain on campus all four years. The most desirable places to live include campus apartments in Trembley and the freshman dorm known as "M&M" (McClinton and Marshall). Most dorms are co-ed by floor. For upperclassmen who do choose to live off campus, fraternity and sorority houses are popular options.

As for the food, students are as satisfied as they can be with food that isn't home cooking. Lehigh has five dining halls, including three traditional cafeterias, a food court with a Burger King and a deli, and a shop where students can take out bag lunches. For breakfast they can make their own omelets or waffles every day of the week. When dinner rolls around, many students would suggest forgoing the meat in favor of the safer pasta.

Social Life and Student Body

"When you are not studying, you are drinking. And when you drink, you drink a lot," said one Lehigh student. Undergrads say Greek life is basically the be-all and end-all at Lehigh; about half of them join one of the 26 fraternities and eight sororities. Students look forward to the annual Greek Week, which occurs in the spring, and is a week filled with toga races, eating contests, and other competitions. The Lehigh/Lafayette game is one of the biggest rivalries, providing the occasion for some of the best parties. "During Lehigh/Lafayette they have sunrise cocktails every morning before classes; even the teachers are trashed the whole week. There are huge parties every night," one student said. The administration has recently made an unpopular move to regulate the size of parties. One freshman explained, "There is a new regulation limiting the number of people attending parties. Before 12 you must be on the 50-person guest list, and then an extra 50 people are allowed to enter after 12, but they have to sign an 'uninvited' guest list."

"When you are not studying, you are drinking. And when you drink, you drink a lot."

When life on the Hill becomes monotonous, students attend campus comedy acts, movies, and concerts. If students need to get away, they do not have far to go to find the big city; New York is only a two-hour drive, and Philadelphia is just 90 minutes away.

Lehigh students participate in all sorts of extracurriculars, ranging from varsity sports to community service to drama. Popular sports include football, wrestling, crew, and basketball. Students say that football is not only the dominant sport, but also dominates the social atmosphere. Games prompt an array of tailgates and early morning cocktail parties, and foster a healthy school spirit.

For students who are less athletically inclined, intramurals offer competition without the pressure of organized varsity sports. Beyond the sports fields, Lehigh offers choir, drama, the Brown and White (a biweekly newspaper), an orchestra, and many opportunities for community service.

Through its community service programs Lehigh has been making an attempt to improve relations with the neighboring towns of Bethlehem and Allentown. For example, with STAR Academy, a popular tutoring program, Lehigh students act as mentors for local middle school and high school students. Although the programs are slowly making progress, students say that they don't go to town much and still yearn for more to do outside of the university.

Most Lehigh undergrads come from the tri-state region of Pennsylvania, New Jersey, and Delaware, and some students feel that the student body could be more diverse—geographically, racially, and economically. One sophomore said, "I wish it were more diversified. There are very few minorities and very few 'different-looking' people. It is very much of a 'clone campus,' I think." Yet Lehigh students are a very satisfied bunch who enjoy the university's close-knit, self-contained community.

Lehigh is a school with a lot of pride and spirit, and its students enjoy the strong academics and social life. As one student said, "My friends at other schools think I always have about 10 times more work than they ever do, but I also have 20 times more fun than they do!"

—Katherina Payne and Staff

FYI

If you come to Lehigh, you'd better bring "sweaters—lots and lots of sweaters."

What is the typical weekend schedule? "Go to a frat, sleep late, hang around and watch TV, go out, go out."

If I could change one thing about Lehigh, I'd "make the social life more than just frats."

Three things that every student should do before gradating from Lehigh are "take Human Sexuality, party like a madman/madwoman, and take a daytrip to Philadelphia or New York."

Mulhenberg College

Address: 2400 West Chew Street, Allentown, PA 18104
Phone: 610-821-3200
E-mail address: admissions@ muhlenburg.edu
Web site URL: www.muhlenberg.edu
Founded: 1848
Private or Public: private
Religious affiliation: Lutheran
Location: suburban
Undergraduate enrollment: 2,470
Total enrollment: 2,470
Percent Male/Female: 44%/56%
Percent Minority: 8%
Percent African-American: 2%
Percent Asian: 3%
Percent Hispanic: 3%
Percent Native-American: 0%
Percent in-state/out of state: 37%/63%
Percent Pub HS: NA
Number of Applicants: 3,822
Percent Accepted: 35%
Percent Accepted who enroll: 60%
Entering: 548
Transfers: 9
Application Deadline: 15 Feb
Mean SAT: NA
Mean ACT: NA
Middle 50% SAT range: V 550-640, M 560-650
Middle 50% ACT range: NA
3 Most popular majors: business, psychology, biology
Retention: 93%
Graduation rate: 81%
On-campus housing: NA
Fraternities: 27%
Sororities: 22%
Library: 271,260 volumes
Tuition and Fees: $24,945
Room and Board: $6,540
Financial aid, first-year: 43%
Varsity or Club Athletes: 40%
Early Decision or Early Action Acceptance Rate: 60%

Students at the small Mulhenberg College in Allentown, PA, enjoy both the academics and the atmosphere of their school. Its small size provides a close-knit, friendly environment, in which the students can live and learn.

Inside Victorian Academic Buildings

Students may complain about their heavy course load, but most enjoy the academic challenge. As one said, "I like going to class each day. I have interesting courses and like to learn from them." Students must take 34 courses before they graduate. The core requirements are literature, religion, philosophy, three semesters of language, two sciences, reasoning, history, two courses in behavioral science (psychology, anthropology, sociology etc.), culture, and a first-year seminar. Many students wind up enjoying these required courses, adding that they wouldn't have taken such classes if not required. However there are some who find some of the requirements too strict. "Religion and philosophy should be electives, regardless that it is a Lutheran campus," believed one student, whereas another said, "we have to take two sciences, which is very disturbing to us non-science people." Every major has a set curriculum, which fills up most of the schedules. Students face some scheduling hurdles, like once-a-year course offerings and conflicting class times.

Biology, premed, chemistry, and theater arts are considered the toughest and the most competitive majors. Philosophy and communications are "very popular" among students, along with English, business, and psychology. Muhlenberg sponsors several combined undergraduate/graduate programs: a three-year undergrad/four-year grad dental program with University of Pennsylvania, a three-two forestry and environmental studies program with Duke University, a three-two engineering program with Columbia and Washington University, as well as a four-four medical school admission with MCP/Hahnemann University. Students may participate in honor programs such as the DANA Scholars and Muhlenberg Scholars programs, and create their own majors or take courses at other schools.

Few classes have over 25 students, except for labs, and students are fond of the "personalization and attention" this brings. However, some complain that the small number of classes also makes it harder to get into them, especially in freshman and sophomore years. This problem decreases as students declare their major because at that point professors sign the students into classes. Students are pleased with the proficiency of the faculty and believe that they are "accommodating and care a lot about their students." One student said: "I run into them [my professors] at the grocery store and it's like running into a friend." Since there are no student teaching assistants at Muthenberg, students have the opportunity to work in classes instructed by professors who are eminent in their fields like Dr. Daniel Klem, "a world leader on why birds fly into windows. People from all over call him up for help in designing bird-safe buildings," is how one of his students described Dr. Klem.

Smashmouth and Much More

Besides well-known professors, students also benefit from and enjoy the guest speakers that come to campus. Chie Abad, who was on a national tour about sweat shops, stopped at Muhlenberg with the help of students organizations such as Amnesty International and PAT. The alternative band Smashmouth also visited campus and gave a spectacular concert. Besides Smashmouth, Citizen King, Jim Breuer, the Wallflowers, George Clinton, Blues Traveler, and Bob Cat have also been known to come to Muhlenberg in the past.

"I run into them [my professors] at the grocery store and it's like running into a friend."

Being underage has not prevented students from drinking since fraternity parties reportedly offer alcohol to all. However, the administration has become stricter about alcohol, students report, and forces students to sign in when they enter certain parties. Kegs are not allowed on campus, and students say, "frats have been temporarily closed down because of alcohol problems." Many lucky enough to be over 21 prefer going to the bars in nearby Allentown.

The non-drinkers also find a lot of things to do. Events like the West Side Dance, senior balls, semi-formals, and fraternity or sorority formals have an important role in the school's social life. The shuttle running to the malls, shopping centers, and to theaters are useful for freshmen since they are not usually permitted to have cars on campus. Besides the Muhlenberg Activities Council (MAC), which provides most of the programs on campus, other popular and respected student organizations are the radio station (WMUH), Hillel, APO (a community service fraternity).

Homogenity Among Preppy Muhlenbergers

A typical Muhlenberg student is chic, wearing J. Crew, Gap, and Abercrombie outfits, and driving a nice car. Students say that there are cliques, and even though groups aren't formed right away, people do tend to stick with those whom them meet during the first months of school through dorm life or organizations. Students find their peers homogeneous and classify a typical Muhlenberg student as "white" and "preppy."

Living in the 'Berg

When its time to get in shape, the gym offers a great weight-lifting room with up-to-date equipment. Tennis courts and a swimming pool provide other athletic options. Football, men's and women's soccer, and basketball are among the most popular sports. Many students participated in intramural and club sports, and in the annual Scotty Wood Basketball tournament.

Muhlenberg students tend to live on campus all four years. Freshman dorms such as Prosser and New West have been renovated recently, but the worst dorm, East Hall, is notorious for its bugs, which are known as "Eastle Beastles." After freshmen year, students enter the housing lottery, and the upperclass rooms are considered much nicer and more spacious than the rooms assigned to freshmen. All dorms are co-ed except for Brown, and the women who choose to live in this all-female building enjoy huge rooms with higher ceilings than any other dorm on campus. Pets are not allowed anywhere on campus. Though the dorms can get noisy on the weekends, quiet hours exist during the week to help those who are studying or sleeping. These hours are strictly enforced during exam periods.

When not in their dorms, Muhlenberg students often socialize at Seegers Union, which includes the campus eateries, student mailboxes, and meeting rooms. There are many different meal plans, and most students prefer the most inclusive option. Chefs cooking in front of students assure students of the hygiene of the kitchen. There is always a pasta bar and decent vegetarian options. Banana flambé is a specialty of the dining halls. There are two dining halls on campus; one offers grab-and-go options and the other is a traditional sit-down cafeteria.

Safe and Sound in Allentown

Students enjoy the safety and beauty of their school. The campus is composed of Victorian, stone buildings and tree-lined, green open spaces. Its proximity to local parks and forests provides another option for those who love the outdoors. Safety call boxes scattered around campus provide a hotline to security staff, whose members patrol on foot, bicycle, and car to give Muhlenberg an atmosphere of safety. Students can go into nearby Allentown to shop the Lehigh Valley Mall or to visit popular bars, coffee shops, and various restaurants. On lazy Sundays and when the weather is nice in the spring, however, students are happy to stay on campus. They take a blanket, their radio, and their tons of reading, sit down outside one of the school's picturesque buildings, and take advantage of Muhlenberg's many academic and nonacademic offerings. —*Yakut Seyhanli*

FYI

If you come to Muhlenberg, you'd better bring "a musical instrument."

What is the typical weekend schedule? "Eat, sleep, and do homework—there's usually a lot of work."

If I could change one thing about Muhlenberg, I'd "update the bookstore—they never have the required text books."

Three things that every student should do before graduating from Muhlenberg are "walk through the rose garden of the campus, go to a candlelight carol, and go to a soccer game."

Pennsylvania State University

Address: 201 Shields Building, University Park, PA 16802
Phone: 814-865-5471
E-mail address: admissions@psu.edu
Web site URL: www.psu.edu
Founded: 1855
Private or Public: public
Religious affiliation: none
Location: urban
Undergraduate enrollment: 34,829
Total enrollment: 34,829
Percent Male/Female: 54%/46%
Percent Minority: 13%
Percent African-American: 4%
Percent Asian: 5%
Percent Hispanic: 3%
Percent Native-American: 0%
Percent in-state/out of state: 76%/24%
Percent Pub HS: NA
Number of Applicants: 27,604
Percent Accepted: 57%
Percent Accepted who enroll: NA
Entering: 5,929
Transfers: 366
Application Deadline: rolling
Mean SAT: NA
Mean ACT: NA
Middle 50% SAT range: V 530-630, M 560-670
Middle 50% ACT range: NA
3 Most popular majors: business, engineering, education
Retention: 92%
Graduation rate: 80%
On-campus housing: 36%
Fraternities: 13%
Sororities: 10%
Library: 3,117,880 volumes
Tuition and Fees: $8,382 in; $17,610 out
Room and Board: $5,660
Financial aid, first-year: 50%
Varsity or Club Athletes: 5%
Early Decision or Early Action Acceptance Rate: NA

To those at Penn State, one question is constantly tossed their way: What exactly is Nittany? Furthermore, what is a Nittany Lion? While outsiders struggle to find a meaning to this word, it seems that most Penn Staters have given up and accepted that, as one junior put it, "I have no freakin' clue what a Nittany is, so stop asking." The infamous Penn State mascot has long been a mystery to all. It surfaced in 1907 when a student claimed that it was the "fiercest beast of all." Time, though, has since obscured the meaning and at the same time created one of the most unique and lasting mascots ever.

What's in a Name?

Strange mascots aside, Penn State—with its gigantic alumni base and long history—has become a world-renowned university with a tremendous endowment that attracts top-notch professors. While some complain that these professors are too consumed in their own research to care about students, others are inspired by them. As one student said, "my business law professor made class so interesting that everyone always went, in a 300-person class." Among other things, the university can boast top-ranked undergraduate programs in architecture, business, and engineering. Generally, these programs are more competitive and more demanding than others, which are by no means cakewalks.

Academics are of great importance to Penn State students. Most of them agree that classes are hard and intense, but not overwhelming. According to one sophomore, "academics are very serious, yet it isn't hard to do well if you really try." Generally, students take rigorous schedules that demand a lot of energy to sustain. As one student put it, "even the dumb try to be smart." For freshmen and sophomores, classes tend to be large, and professors can be quite removed. Like most other schools though, profs are more than willing to meet with students if they put in the effort. TAs at Penn State are a toss-up. Not many students show enthusiasm towards their TAs, and some were even turned off by some TAs' lack of English skills, particularly in engineering and science courses.

For those looking for a more rigorous academic program, Penn State offers Schreyer Honors College. Open to select applicants, it offers special honors classes much smaller than ordinary classes, consisting of only 15 to 25 students. The program also offers enhanced study-abroad and research opportunities. Those accepted get to live in their own honors community including special housing open to only them, which is considered the nicest on campus. The prestigious program is open to students of all majors, though it is capped at 1800 students a year, a very small percentage of the total population. On top of all these perks, all students who graduate from the Honors College receive a nice shiny medal. Seriously.

Rustic Lions

Enclosed by mountains, University Park gives off a rustic and backcountry feel. This adds up to a beautiful campus enjoyed by all. Students disagreed which season was the prettiest in University Park. One junior said that, "Campus is gorgeous in the fall with all the leaves and the mountain surroundings," while a sophomore claimed that, "campus is so pretty in the winter because there is snow and lights covering everything." Apart from its beauty, campus is also quite expansive. Getting across campus can take a long time on foot, and many own cars or bikes to get around.

All freshmen get the pleasure of living in dorms their first year. Though the rooms are "like boxes" everyone seems to enjoy their first-year dorm experience. Students all have great stories of their stay, and meet lots of their close friends there. RAs were said to be not so strict or interfering, even though they could get "annoying at times." Almost all freshmen live on East Hall which provides a social atmosphere, as it is right by the Quad which is perfect for sunbathing, volleyball playing, and general hanging out, weather permitting.

Dorms get nicer for upperclassmen, athletes, and honors college students. Nonetheless, upperclassmen generally move out of the dorms after freshman or sophomore year and into apartments or frat houses. There is plenty of off-campus housing available at an affordable price, which means no more dorm food and fending for yourself. Luckily, University Park offers more than enough to make this easy, with tons of restaurants available to students in the campus area. Most are quick, cheap places tailored to the essentials for every student: burgers, pizza, tacos, and wings.

The Very Happy Valley

Perhaps even more famous than their mascot is their football coach Joe Paterno. He has become synonymous with the school and is himself an institution, having coached at Penn State for more than half a century. Walk down any street, and his picture will surely be on every corner and his cutout in every window. He is a legend. While the football program and Joe Pa himself have drawn criticism because of below average performances these past few years, football is still a major aspect to student life. Saturdays in the fall are devoted to games at the 100,000-plus capacity Beaver Stadium, America's second-largest college stadium. At the immense student tailgates, which completely surround the stadium on game days, you would be hard-pressed to find someone not wearing blue and white. As one sophomore said, "Football is the biggest thrill. So much school spirit goes into the games."

As most Americans know, football goes hand-in-hand with beer consumption. Penn State provides no exception. An old saying goes that College Park is, "A drinking town with a football problem." Drinking and parties are both rampant at Penn State, which constantly lands itself as a top-ranked party school. A major part of this is due to the large role fraternities and sororities play in the social scene. Those looking for a party can easily find one at a frat any night of the week starting on Wednesday. Equally popular are apartment parties, which most students gravitate to after they tire of the frat scene.

"Football is the biggest thrill. So much school spirit goes into the games."

All these parties lead to a lot of drinking, which in turn leads to a lot of hooking up. The general attitude is, as one sophomore put it, "There's 20,000 of the opposite sex; I think most people are trying to live it up while they are here." Because of this, most people stay single and the random hookup has become a common occurrence. This is not surprising, considering the overall "hotness" of the student body. It is often described as "a moving Abercrombie & Fitch catalogue," which means a few things: great looking people, perfect bodies, expensive clothes, and a homogeneous feel.

While drinking is prevalent, drug usage is reportedly a little less widespread. Students say that marijuana is somewhat commonly encountered, and harder drugs, while they are available, are "kept on the DL" and are much less common. One student commented, "There are always people who do it, but drugs are definitely not a big thing at Penn State."

For those who do not drink, the university offers Late Night Penn State. These are alcohol-free, school-sponsored events that take place every weekend. Activities include screening of movies, open mics, scheduled performances, and arts and crafts. While well-attended, the majority of students consider Late Night Penn State, "for people who need the school to help them with improving their social skills." In addition, major musical acts frequently pass through, providing yet another alternative to the party scene. Finally, students can always get caught up in their extracurriculars to pass the time. There are hundreds of clubs, allowing students to easily find others with similar interests. Many times these groups hold their own functions, which are alternatives to the regular parties.

One great example of this is THON, a charity event that raises money for children with cancer. It is the largest student-run philanthropic event in the world, raising over $3 million annually. THON is a 48-hour dance marathon that thousands of Penn Staters participate in. It has become one of the most popular events of every year, while being the most benevolent at the same time. THON basically sums up the experience one might expect at Penn State: if you are willing to work for it, there is a lot of fun to be had. —*Alex Chiu*

FYI

If you come to Penn State, you'd better bring a "strong liver."

What is the typical weekend schedule? "Party, recover, party, recover, cram."

If I could change one thing about Penn State, I'd "make it smaller."

Three things every student at Penn State should to before graduating are "go to a football game, go to THON, and listen to the Willard Preacher."

Susquehanna University

Address: 514 University Ave, Selinsgrove, PA 17870
Phone: 570-372-4260
E-mail address: suadmiss@susqu.edu
Web site URL: www.susqu.edu
Founded: 1858
Private or Public: private
Religious affiliation: Lutheran
Location: rural
Undergraduate enrollment: 1,995
Total enrollment: 1,995
Percent Male/Female: 42%/58%
Percent Minority: 6%
Percent African-American: 2%
Percent Asian: 2%
Percent Hispanic: 2%
Percent Native-American: 0%
Percent in-state/out of state: 65%/35%
Percent Pub HS: NA
Number of Applicants: 2,411
Percent Accepted: 63%
Percent Accepted who enroll: 72%
Entering: 504
Transfers: 27
Application Deadline: 1 Jan
Mean SAT: NA
Mean ACT: NA
Middle 50% SAT range: V 530-620, M 530-630
Middle 50% ACT range: NA
3 Most popular majors: business, communications, psychology
Retention: 88%
Graduation rate: 77%
On-campus housing: 80%
Fraternities: 26%
Sororities: 24%
Library: 279,149 volumes
Tuition and Fees: $23,480
Room and Board: $6,510
Financial aid, first-year: 67%
Varsity or Club Athletes: 56%
Early Decision or Early Action Acceptance Rate: 72%

Located in rural Pennsylvania, Susquehanna University can be easy to overlook. Prospective students who find out about it will see, however, that Susquehanna provides a close-knit atmosphere with small classes and quality education.

The school attracts many of its students from the Northeast, especially New Jersey, Pennsylvania, and New York. While the student population once consisted mainly of white middle- and upper-class undergrads, recent outreach efforts and scholarship programs have increased the number of minority students and programs.

A recently initiated merit aid program called Assistantships offers promising incoming freshmen an annual scholarship as well as an opportunity to obtain work experience under the supervision of a faculty or staff member. Another unique program is the Write Option: students in the top one-fifth of their class and enrolled in a college-preparatory program at their high school are allowed to submit two graded writing samples in place of SAT or ACT scores.

Name Games

Although the name of the school implies otherwise, there are no graduate students at Susquehanna. Many undergraduates are attracted to Susquehanna's highly rated biology and music programs. The business department, accredited by the American Assembly of Collegiate Schools of Business, is also popular; acknowledged as outstanding by business and non-business students alike, it is one of only a few schools of its size to be accredited.

The school's curriculum requires students to take courses from three broad categories: perspectives on the world (history, literature, and fine arts), intellectual skills (math, logic, writing seminars, and foreign languages), and contemporary world (social science, hard science, and technology). Few students complain about the requirements; many say that this diverse grounding adds to their educational experiences at Susquehanna. Special programs enhance Susquehanna's standard curriculum. Students can create their own major with the help of a faculty member, or can elect to travel abroad. Students seem pleased in general with the student-faculty interaction as well as with the small class sizes. Classes usually have about 20 to 25 students, and the teaching is done by professors rather than TAs, who are "practically unheard of."

Service

Community service is a popular option at Susquehanna. In recent years, over half the student body has participated in volunteer services, including the Habitat for Humanity program, the Student Association for Cultural Awareness (SACA), the university's Study Buddy program with students from local schools, the Ronald McDonald House for hospitalized children, and the Pennsylvania Service Corps. Other extracurricular activities are popular as well, and the university's Degenstein Center Theater and Lore Degenstein Gallery, both with state-of-the-art equipment, provide major new showcases for student musicians, artists, and actors.

Susquehanna has a lot of school spirit, as many of the athletic teams are nationally ranked in NCAA Division III. Students frequently show support not only for their football team but also for the basketball, volleyball, and soccer teams. Intramural sports are also important at Susquehanna, and many students take advantage of the newly remodeled gymnasium. Because of Susquehanna's location in Selinsgrove, Pennsylvania, where "there's practically no downtown," social life is limited to campus activities sponsored by SAC (Student Activities Committee) and the Greek system. Most upperclassmen also own cars for trips to nearby cities for shopping, clubbing, and other diversions.

Greek Life and Beyond

Some students feel that the Greeks divide the campus, but most Greek activities are open to everyone. The two biggest social events of the year are Greek Week, which consists mostly of fraternity- and sorority-sponsored partying, and Spring Weekend, a festival held before final exams. Students report that, while both events are widely attended, Greek Week is more exclusive to Greeks, and Spring Weekend better involves the entire campus. Another popular campus event is the annual Thanksgiving dinner, where professors serve students special holiday food in the cafeteria, which is decorated with candles.

Classes usually have about 20 to 25 students, and the teaching is done by professors rather than TAs, who are "practically unheard of."

While everyone at Susquehanna University is guaranteed campus housing, incoming students have complained in the past about the crowded freshman dorms, which consisted of mostly triples. Three residence halls have been added, and a fourth updated, and there are also high quality apartment-like dorms and suites, making housing more spacious. Students can also choose to live in the University Scholars House, which includes study areas, a seminar room, a resident assistant's quarters, and a visitor's apartment that allows special university guests to interact informally with students. Some of the most popular dorms include Hassinger Hall, which features newly installed air-conditioning; also known as "Hotel Hassinger," it houses a small theater and several computer labs.

Students report that security is "good and reliable" on the Susquehanna campus, due in part to such security measures as the Walk Safe escort service.

Susquehanna offers intimate classes, a strong sense of community, and great athletics. "You can walk across campus and know everybody's face," one senior said, "but you can also go away from everyone you know and be by yourself for a while."
—*Seung Lee and Staff*

FYI

If you come to Susquehanna, you'd better bring "lots of sweaters."

What is the typical weekend schedule? "Sleeping, eating, going to parties, and studying on Sunday."

If I could change one thing about Susquehanna, I'd "change how crowded the cafeteria is."

Three things every student should do before graduating from Susquehanna are "swim in the Susquehanna River, go to the Lewisburg Theater, and take Rock Music and Society."

Swarthmore College

Address: 500 College Avenue, Swarthmore, PA 19081
Phone: 610-328-8300
E-mail address: admissions@swarthmore.edu
Web site URL: www.swarthmore.edu
Founded: 1864
Private or Public: private
Religious affiliation: none
Location: suburban
Undergraduate enrollment: 1,479
Total enrollment: 1,479
Percent Male/Female: 48%/52%
Percent Minority: 32%
Percent African-American: 7%
Percent Asian: 16%
Percent Hispanic: 9%
Percent Native-American: 1%
Percent in-state/out of state: 17%/83%
Percent Pub HS: NA
Number of Applicants: 3,886
Percent Accepted: 24%
Percent Accepted who enroll: 43%
Entering: 371
Transfers: 5
Application Deadline: 1 Jan
Mean SAT: NA
Mean ACT: NA
Middle 50% SAT range: V 670-770, M 680-760
Middle 50% ACT range: NA
3 Most popular majors: economics, biology, political science
Retention: 96%
Graduation rate: 92%
On-campus housing: 93%
Fraternities: 6%
Sororities: NA
Library: 567,875 volumes
Tuition and Fees: $28,802
Room and Board: $8,914
Financial aid, first-year: 48%
Varsity or Club Athletes: 45%
Early Decision or Early Action Acceptance Rate: 43%

Students at Swarthmore share a passion for true learning; this is manifested in their dedication to the rigors of academics and the pursuit of knowledge. Unlike at many higher-level institutions, Swarthmore's students do not dwell on grades. Swarthmore is also one of the few colleges that provide international students with financial aid. Its truly need-blind admission policy attracts many underprivileged students and accounts for the socio-economic diversity found on campus. The school is also smaller than most other colleges, offering students the chance to develop close relationships with their schoolmates.

A Protestant Work Ethic

Swarthmore students are expected to fulfill 32 classes in order to graduate. Some of these requirements can be fulfilled with acceptable scores from the Advanced Placement exams. At least three classes must be taken in each of the humanities, social sciences, and natural sciences. The most popular majors at Swarthmore are economics, biology, and english. Engineering and chemistry are considered to be some of the more difficult majors at Swarthmore, though one student commented, "There are no slacker majors here!" All students must take Primary Distributional Requirements, or PDCs, which are writing-intensive introductory courses.

Both students and faculty take academics seriously at Swarthmore. The workload is pretty intense, but many students give reassurance that it is quite manageable if one uses his time efficiently. "If you come to Swarthmore, you'd better bring a Protestant work ethic," commented one student on Swarthmore's rigorous academic program. A typical workload at Swarthmore is about 500 pages of reading each week, and about one or two ten-page papers each week. "A lot of professors don't entirely expect all the work assigned to be done," said one student, "and most students don't do it all. Annoyingly, getting an A often requires doing all the work assigned and more."

One advantage of attending Swarthmore is its flexibility in accommodating students in creating their own academic programs. There are a few special academic and honors programs available to students, but if students should not find any of these appealing to their academic interests, they may be able to design their own program.

Classes at Swarthmore provide students with an enriching and intellectually stimulating academic experience. "Contact Improvisation Dance opened up a body awareness I never had before—and that most people in the world lack—and Playwright's Lab reintroduced me to art in all forms after I had been estranged from it after an intellectual high school experience," said one student about two interesting classes he had taken at Swarthmore. Fictional Writers' Workshop, a small class with a lot of student-student teaching, is another one of the many intellectually eye-opening courses offered at the school.

It is quite common for students to call their professors by their first names, thus showing the close relationships students are able to form with their instructors. The faculty-to-student ratio is fairly low, due to the small size of the school. Courses are taught entirely by the professors themselves, and in other cases, the classes are taught by visiting professors.

We Don't Just Study!

When asked about the typical weekend schedule of a Swattie, one student replied, "Contrary to popular notion, Swatties part with their books and have fun. Some students partake in the party scene, which consists of drinking and dancing. Some students relax and hang out, while some travel to Philadelphia," which is only 15 minute train ride from the school. Still, there are plenty of things to do at the school, so many students choose to stay on campus on weekends.

Students remark on having relative freedom with alcohol, they are treated as adults and are expected to act accordingly. The lenient policy on alcohol seems to work well, for it allows students to take care of each other in order to keep police out of the party scene.

Freshmen tend to go to Philadelphia via train or car or attend parties hosted by campus groups. Oftentimes parties have themes, such as the Black Light Party, Masquerade Ball, and the '80s Party, giving students the chance to dress appropriately for the respective themes. Most upperclassmen go out to local bars or private parties. They are less likely to attend big parties, and if they have cars, some upperclassmen go to Philly.

> **"What I love about campus life is how intimate and close-knit of a community this is."**

The campus's small size enables students to develop closer relationships with their schoolmates. Though small in size, the campus is fairly diverse. Said one student about the diversity of the campus, "What I love about campus life is how intimate and close-knit a community we have. You meet interesting people from Alaska, Hawaii, Puerto Rico, Jamaica, Sri Lanka, etc. And since there are only about 1,400 students, and about 350 new faces every year, you get to meet a lot of people." The small size of the campus seems to give students the advantage of getting to know a larger number of people beyond the level of mere acquaintances. "It is really easy to meet people because people are generally very friendly and approachable. Everyone is accepted here, and a lot of it goes back to the Quaker philosophy of tolerance," said one student about the school's social atmosphere.

Outside the Classroom

Swatties are equally serious about their extracurricular activities as they are about their studies. There is a wide variety of organizations to choose from, including community service groups, arts and theater, and athletics. For the most part, the athletic scene is not that big in Swarthmore, since it is a Division III NCAA school. However, the school has been increasing athletic support in recent years. The most widely respected organizations in Swarthmore are political groups and community service activities. Tutoring is quite common among students; some go to nearby towns, such as Chester and Chinatown, or local schools to tutor children. Others volunteer at the Children's Hospital or the local homeless shelters.

The arts scene is of significance at Swarthmore, with around ten a cappella groups, dance classes, and a Drama Board that promotes and funds productions. SWIL (Swarthmore Warders of Imaginative

Literature) is a humorous science fiction and fantasy organization. Swarthmore's paper, *The Phoenix*, demands a great deal of time and dedication from its board.

Many Swatties agree that students are not identified by the activities in which they participate; however, joining an organization provides a good chance to meet people like oneself, whether as part of a sports team, a religious organization, or an ethnic group. Said one student, "People are very devoted to their activities and the trick is managing these along with your academic and social life."

The "Ville"

Fairly isolated from the city, the college town is sometimes called the "ville," with a few small shops within walking distance. The campus is a nationally recognized arboretum, with buildings that are old and preserved, surrounded by the woods and a creek. The school is constantly rebuilding and renovating. One of the oldest and most noteworthy buildings is Parrish. It consists of dorms, classrooms, and administrative offices.

Most of the students are satisfied with the dorms at Swarthmore. Students say that compared to most colleges, the rooms are fairly large. Upperclassmen mostly get singles, and underclassmen are roomed in doubles, triples, or quads. For the most part, students stay on campus; very few people live off campus.

Sharples, a buffet-style dining hall, is where most students eat. The Tarble snack bar serves food that is predominantly deli-style, while the Kohlberg coffee bar offers drinks. There is also a student-run café, called Paces, which is slightly nicer than the dining hall. A few restaurants are available in the ville, including a Chinese restaurant and a pizzeria. For some fancy dining, students can always drive or take a train to Philadelphia.

Swarthmore's small student body, its isolated campus location and rigorous academic program attract intellectually voracious individuals and put them in a close-knit environment so that they may be able to foster deep, intimate relationships among students and faculty alike. —*Soo Kim*

FYI

If you come to Swarthmore, you'd better bring "a desire not to be competitive or compare yourself to other people. No one does it."

What is the typical weekend schedule? "Some students partake in the party scene, which consists of drinking and dancing. Some students relax and hang out, while others travel to Philadelphia."

If I could change one thing about Swarthmore College, "I'd bring in some conservatives because it is such a liberal campus."

Three things every student should do before graduating are: "walk through the Crum woods, visit Chester (a city only five minutes away) and take advantage of the study abroad option."

Temple University

Address: 1801 North Broad, Philadelphia, PA 19122-6096
Phone: 215-204-7200
E-mail address: tuadm@mail.temple.edu
Web site URL: www.temple.edu
Founded: 1888
Private or Public: public
Religious affiliation: none
Location: urban
Undergraduate enrollment: 21,429
Total enrollment: NA
Percent Male/Female: 42%/58%
Percent Minority: 34%
Percent African-American: 23%
Percent Asian: 8%
Percent Hispanic: 3%
Percent Native-American: 0%
Percent in-state/out of state: 77%/23%
Percent Pub HS: NA
Number of Applicants: 15,316
Percent Accepted: 78%
Percent Accepted who enroll: NA
Entering: 3,496
Transfers: 2,617
Application Deadline: 1 Apr
Mean SAT: NA
Mean ACT: NA
Middle 50% SAT range: V 480-580, M 480-580
Middle 50% ACT range: 19-24
3 Most popular majors: education, psychology, finance
Retention: 79%
Graduation rate: 47%
On-campus housing: 27%
Fraternities: 1%
Sororities: 1%
Library: 5,086,211 volumes
Tuition and Fees: $8,062 in; $14,316 out
Room and Board: $7,112
Financial aid, first-year: 69%
Varsity or Club Athletes: 8%
Early Decision or Early Action Acceptance Rate: NA

With campuses in Philadelphia, Japan, and Rome, and a wide variety of liberal arts and preprofessional programs, Temple University caters to the interests and diversity of its students. The university's organized academic system and commitment to being a public research university draw large numbers of students from local and international backgrounds each year.

Learning from "The Core" Out

Temple's general education requirement, known as the "Core Program" has a comparatively large portion of academic coursework in fairly specific arenas, some of which are very unique to Temple. These include one year of race studies, several additional writing-intensive courses, and coursework in a foreign language or international relations. Students are in disagreement about the value of these requirements: some felt that they were a good way to diversify the academic program in a structured fashion. "I don't think I would have taken a class like the American culture class I took two years ago," remarked one reminiscent Temple senior. Others, however, said they felt the core requirements deteriorated the quality of academic life at Temple. "It seems like I'm taking a number of courses that I'm not very interested in just to fulfill requirements," noted one sophomore.

Temple's business administration, journalism and psychology programs are particularly popular, and a number of undergraduates in the business major are also members of the numerous business-related registered student organizations. These groups include the Accounting Professional Society and the Business Honors Student Association. Still, with the number of undergraduate resources available at Temple University, students find it easy to major in almost any of the academic subjects of interest to them.

In comparison to previously inefficient and frustrating processes of course registration, the relatively recent addition of the OWLnet system allows students access to their records online, making registration and various administrative tasks significantly easier. "I heard that signing up for classes used to be extremely difficult," said one Temple student, "but online registration has been really important in streamlining the process."

What Owls Do with Free Time

Student leadership and varieties of business management are a large part of Temple extracurricular and social life. The on-campus movie theater and one of the on-site cafés, housed in the recently renovated Tuttleman Center and the SAC (Student Activity Center), are completely dependent upon the students who organize and run them. "The Owl Cove provides a good, cheap alternative to the cafeteria menu," said one Temple sophomore, "but I wouldn't recommend eating all of your meals there." The movie theater plays second-run movies at discount prices, and schedules for its shows and show times are available on the regularly updated student activity Web site. Students also said that they check the calendar frequently to find out about other events on campus, such as roller skating, trips to see community theater, and on-campus comedy shows.

For those that aren't involved in the student-run on-campus restaurants or entrepreneurial efforts, Temple boasts over 120 undergraduate organizations catering to a plethora of different student interests, including ethnic groups, the film society, and "Déjà Vu," an organization dedicated to planning organized events for undergraduates. "I haven't met anyone that doesn't participate in at least one extracurricular activity," said one Temple student. Another noted that work is often the extracurricular, as most students are devoted to a job when not taking classes.

The campus also boasts a healthy Greek community, and there are a number of university recognized fraternities and sororities. These organizations host parties with different themes each weekend, and several students cited Greek events as being central to their nightlife at Temple. Another popular option is to leave campus for the weekend to explore the Philadelphia area, where students have sought out a number of excellent theater and restaurant venues to frequent. Students say that the bars and cuisine offered on South Street are quite good, while others mention that seeing a show at the Wilma or Walnut Street Theaters is a must.

Living There and Loving It

Unlike many four-year universities, Temple does not require its students to live on campus all four years. Consequently, the shortage of rooms and the affordable "but not cheap," real estate prices in the greater Philadelphia area cause a number of students to live in off-campus apartments. Students say that this is not a hindrance to their social or academic lives, however, because campus life is not dependent on residential location. For those who choose to live on campus, the New Residence Hall is generally regarded as the best place to live, while Peabody falls to the less desirable end of facilities. Students live mostly in shared doubles but there are also on campus apartment units that include kitchen and dining room facilities. Student residential life is monitored by Residential Advisors, who are upperclassmen selected both to advise and discipline undergraduates living on campus. In addition to the general tussle of lottery draws, Temple also offers themed housing for students of different academic interests or cultural backgrounds.

"It seems like I'm taking a number of courses that I'm not very interested in just to fulfill requirements."

There are several on-campus dining venues available for eating depending on where students are or what type of meal they desire. The Johnson/Hardwick Complex is home to the Esposito dining court, which is the primary dining hall. Students said that it serves "slightly better than normal cafeteria food," with "sheer quantity of different options" in its favor. Students choose from menu items offered at multiple stations and the cafeteria is filled with different decorations and food depending on the season. Still, most recommend that prospective students consider eating at the other on campus dining facilities, including "Fresh Bytes," a small eatery in the Tuttleman Center, to escape from the monotony of mass-produced food. Most students also agreed that the lunch trucks that appear on street corners are a must-visit for any student at Temple, because they "offer great food at affordable prices."

Tradition in Diversity

The athletic program at Temple is particularly rich with tradition. The university is competitive in a number of varsity sports and, and students regularly paint their faces with Temple colors, red and white, to support their athletic teams and the festively dressed Temple Owl that attends each game. Students find one of the more popular sports to be basketball, and they cluster in the Apollo Arena to watch numerous games during the season. Aside from its athletes, Temple has a diverse student body with varying interests. The cultural diversity is noticeable, with the percentages of African-American and Asian-American populations rising to double-digit figures in the last decade. While the majority of the undergraduate population is "local"—of Pennsylvanian descent, there is still a large number of out-of-state students in attendance.

With so many people to meet, activities to participate in and culture to explore in Philadelphia, students say lots of Temple undergraduates find themselves torn about whether to spend a semester at a Temple campus abroad or in one of their academic programs in other countries. Still, that option is there, and many students do choose to spend a semester in Tokyo or Rome during their undergraduate careers.

The availability of academic and social opportunities adds to the diversity of the Philadelphia campus whose international flavors, both imported and exported, epitomize the Temple experience of interactive learning to achieve goals. Temple University provides its students with a rich educational and extracurricular undergraduate experience that keeps enrollees and alumni coming back for more, year after year. —*Stephanie Teng*

FYI

If you come to Temple University, you'd better bring "a train ticket and an imagination."

What is the typical weekend schedule? "Friday, go see a movie at the SAC, visit a Greek party afterward; Saturday, check out Philadelphia or go to some off-campus parties; Sunday, catch up on schoolwork."

If I could change one thing about Temple, I'd "eliminate some of the many requirements of the Core system."

Three things every student at Temple should do before graduating are "watch a men's basketball game, eat a cheesesteak, and visit Museum Row."

University of Pennsylvania

Address: 1 College Hall, Philadelphia, PA 19104
Phone: 215-898-7507
E-mail address: info@admissions.ugao.upenn.edu
Web site URL: www.upenn.edu
Founded: 1740
Private or Public: private
Religious affiliation: none
Location: urban
Undergraduate enrollment: 9,742
Total enrollment: NA
Percent Male/Female: 51%/49%
Percent Minority: 40%
Percent African-American: 6%
Percent Asian: 18%
Percent Hispanic: 6%
Percent Native-American: 0%
Percent in-state/out of state: 19%/81%
Percent Pub HS: NA
Number of Applicants: 18,784
Percent Accepted: 21%
Percent Accepted who enroll: 39%
Entering: 2,450
Transfers: 230
Application Deadline: 1 Jan
Mean SAT: NA
Mean ACT: NA
Middle 50% SAT range: V 650-750, M 680-760
Middle 50% ACT range: 28-32
3 Most popular majors: finance, economics, history
Retention: 97%
Graduation rate: 92%
On-campus housing: 96%
Fraternities: 31%
Sororities: 22%
Library: 5,152,960 volumes
Tuition and Fees: $29,318
Room and Board: $8,642
Financial aid, first-year: 44%
Varsity or Club Athletes: 19%
Early Decision or Early Action Acceptance Rate: 39%

One of the members of the Ancient Eight, the University of Pennsylvania was established in 1740 by a group including Benjamin Franklin to educate future leaders of America. Nearly 300 years after its founding, UPenn continues to produce many of the nations best and brightest. Unlike other Ivy League schools, UPenn offers undergraduate degrees from four schools, of which three are career oriented. As one junior put it, "we work like crazy here, but UPenn will put me in a great place career-wise when I graduate."

The Business of Learning

When you apply to UPenn, you apply to one of four undergraduate schools: The College of Arts and Sciences, the world-renowned Wharton School, The School of Nursing, or The School of Engineering and Applied Sciences. Most undergraduates apply to the College of Arts and Sciences, which offers the classic liberal arts education that is associated with a Bachelor of Arts (BA) degree. In fact, students in this school complain that UPenn focuses so much on assuring that you study everything that it is difficult to focus on a subject that interests you specifically. In order to graduate, students are required to take 20 elective classes in addition to the classes in their major—usually 12, but some majors require as many as 14. Of those 20 elective classes, 10 are required "distributional classes" taken in each of the seven academic areas of study that the university has determined to be of significance. According to one sophomore, "the distribution classes are OK because AP credits count toward fulfilling them, but it's really confusing to figure out what classes you have to take each semester with so many different groups and random classes in each group." However, the university is currently testing out a new set of requirements in the so-called "Pilot Program." This program requires only four core classes and is meant to give students more freedom to control their own education while working closely with an academic advisor to ensure a diverse education. Besides schedules being limited by course requirements, classes are capped and fill quickly, so many freshmen report difficulty gaining admission into certain classes. "UPenn has a strange way of registering for classes. You used to have to call to register, but now you can either call or go online. However, everyone tries to register at the same time so the servers get jammed or you can't get through on the phone. It's a mad dash to get classes unless you are super-organized and call a week early," reported one junior.

Besides the College of Arts and Sciences, UPenn is home to the Wharton School, arguably the most prestigious graduate business school in the country, which lends its resources to a select group of highly motivated undergraduates. To graduate from Wharton, one must take 37 classes, any two of which must be taken outside of Wharton. All undergrads take such classes as Management 100, Law and Legal Processes, Accounting, Finance, and Human Resources Management. According to one Whartonite, "the intro classes like Macro- and Micro-economics and Management 100 are the worst classes. Everything else is great and I will feel very lucky to have a degree from Wharton on my resume." The third school open to undergraduates at UPenn is the Nursing school, which like Wharton requires extra classes to graduate—28 classes in medicine and the rest to be taken in the College of Arts and Sciences. Finally, the School of Engineering and Applied Sciences, known as SEAS to the students, is much like majoring in engineering at most colleges across the country. The curriculum is highly structured, and students must be dedicated from the beginning. As one SEAS freshman noted, "I think if I was anywhere else, I would be taking the same engineering classes. However, I came to UPenn because I wanted to be in a city and the people seemed really great when I visited." Ultimately, across all four schools, it is universally noted that "people study all the time!" The reason for all this studying, stated one student, is that "the curves in most of the classes are scary. Basically, the policy is to curve the class average to 80 percent, so that even if you get a 90 percent and everyone else gets a 95 percent, you get a C as your grade." Others noted that curves were generally only applied in math, science, and business courses.

Togas Abound

With everybody studying, one might wonder what the students of UPenn do to kick back, relax and take a break from the stress of classes. According to most Quakers, as students are known, the key to social success is through fraternities and sororities. According to one sophomore, "you've got to be in a frat or a sorority if you want a social life." Why the frats and sororities? The answer seems to be that in recent years UPenn's on-campus alcohol policies have become very strict. These rules apply to the fraternities and sororities too, but students report that the houses seem to get away with more than do the dorms. Others noted that the Greek party scene has also taken a hit in recent years. Still, according to one student, frats are still the place to live: "UPenn has dorms that are called 'college residences' because they want to seem very Ivy League, but basically they are dorms in high rises and the RAs [resident advisors] are very strict about noise and alcohol. It's great to be in a frat because the housing is nice and the people are cool."

"UPenn is a bubble. You feel so isolated from real life when you're at school."

Besides Greek parties, students also go into Philadelphia for its clubs, or hang out on South Street, where one student noted "you usually see people you know. South Street has a very college atmosphere to it even though it isn't on campus." Otherwise, parties are kept fairly small and are at people's off campus apartments—where many upperclassmen live. Most freshmen, however, live on campus and stick to the frats when they want to party. It seems at UPenn that partying is ultimately what you make of it. Many choose not to party much, but for those who do the tendency seems to be more about hanging out with friends than going to a universally "cool" spot.

Ivy-Covered Walls or the City of Brotherly Love

Besides partying, Quakers also don their red and blue to support their many varsity sports teams. The most watched sports are men's basketball and football. As for the women's teams, one female athlete complained that "the women are pretty much ignored by the crowds." UPenn students are also involved in a plethora of extracurricular activities. As one junior put it, "what Penn lacks in parties and school spirit, it makes up for with its clubs." Students at UPenn are involved both on campus and off. The most popular student organizations are in the community service sector with *Kite and Key* being the biggest of the service organizations. "In Philly community service just happens. There are so many opportunities that at some point in your four years at UPenn, you'll do at least one community activity."

Many Quakers do more than volunteer in the community, they live there. Although freshmen live in the dorms, many upperclassmen choose to live in apartments surrounding campus as a cheaper and more comfortable environment. For those who do live on campus, there are a wide variety of living options. Most freshmen live in dorms around the Quad, which is meant to resemble the Oxford-Cambridge system of living. Each of these dorms has about 400 students and has a dining hall close by. As for eating on campus, there are three main dining halls and a kosher kitchen offering students a variety of meal plans, as well as an a la carte food court. Dining halls are open Monday through Friday and offer up to 15 meals a week to students. According to one student, "the dining halls are fine and usually less greasy than the food carts around campus. However, the food carts are great for lunch when it's not snowing or raining, and the food is cheap too." If food carts don't interest you, there are also a number of restaurants close to campus. Also, by sophomore year most student housing has some sort of kitchenette in it.

Anybody Lose a Button?

While there are many opportunities for students to interact with the community that they live in, most students find themselves in what is affectionately deemed the "Penn bubble." According to one junior, "you feel so isolated from real life when you're at school. Honestly, I hear more about drunken exploits at the Button than I do about what's in the news!" The Button? What on earth you may ask, is the Button? It turns out that the Button is a large sculpture in the center of campus of a broken button. As legend has it, all UPenn students hope during some time in their four years to have sex under the Button. However, most students only note using it as a shield in the inevitable snowball fights that accompany the first snowfall of the season.

Ultimately, most students describe life at UPenn as being an intense four years of learning that "may be hard at times, but offers no regrets." Although the student body at UPenn isn't huge, the number of activities available to all allows students to explore anything they choose during their college years. "If you want to do something at UPenn, there is always someone who will do it with you. People at Penn do everything from football to basket weaving." As one senior put it, "I didn't really know what I was getting into when I chose to come to UPenn, but I don't think I would have been any happier anywhere else." —*Sophie Jones*

FYI

If you come to UPenn, you'd better bring "a tube top and a lap top."

What is the typical weekend schedule? "Frats, friends, clubbing in Philly, and studying a lot!"

If I could change one thing about UPenn, I'd "eliminate the tough curves that make people so stressed about classes."

Three things every student at UPenn should do before graduating are "go to a frat, eat a Philly Cheesesteak, and take a class at Wharton."

University of Pittsburgh

Address: 4200 Fifth Avenue, Pittsburgh, PA 15260
Phone: 412-624-PITT
E-mail address: oafa@pitt.edu
Web site URL: www.pitt.edu
Founded: 1787
Private or Public: public
Religious affiliation: none
Location: urban
Undergraduate enrollment: 17,910
Total enrollment: NA
Percent Male/Female: 48%/52%
Percent Minority: 14%
Percent African-American: 9%
Percent Asian: 4%
Percent Hispanic: 1%
Percent Native-American: 0%
Percent in-state/out of state: 86%/14%
Percent Pub HS: NA
Number of Applicants: 15,888
Percent Accepted: 55%
Percent Accepted who enroll: NA
Entering: 3,112
Transfers: 461
Application Deadline: rolling
Mean SAT: 1189
Mean ACT: 25
Middle 50% SAT range: V 540-650, M 560-650
Middle 50% ACT range: 23-29
3 Most popular majors: business, social sciences, English
Retention: 87%
Graduation rate: 63%
On-campus housing: 42%
Fraternities: 10%
Sororities: 7%
Library: 3,807,550 volumes
Tuition and Fees: $9,274 in; $18,586 out
Room and Board: $6,800
Financial aid, first-year: 59%
Varsity or Club Athletes: 7%
Early Decision or Early Action Acceptance Rate: NA

According to one student: "If you can get over trudging up and down The Hill all day, Pitt's a wonderful place." Students at the University of Pittsburgh, situated on a hill just a few miles from downtown Pittsburgh, rave about accessible professors, a bursting social scene, and the inevitable physical fitness gained from hiking to class.

Well-Rounded, Rigorous, and Rewarding

"Whether a film major or pre-med," Pitt students are all exposed or, some might say subjected to, a list of requirements that can take up to one-third of their schedules. Graduation requirements include general education classes in such areas as the humanities and social and natural sciences. As well as general education, students must fulfill skills requirements, which consist of composition and quantitative/formal reasoning, a broad category that can be fulfilled through a math, computer science, or philosophy course. Students can elect to test out of these requirements through scores on the SATs or AP tests. Though the framework is the same for everyone, students have a broad selection of courses to choose from to fulfill their requisites, and most students agree that the obligations are generally not cumbersome, with many enjoying the well-rounded education they feel it promotes. Popular majors include both sciences and humanities, such as mathematics, English literature, psychology, and communications.

As with any school, there is the usual assortment of "joke classes." Freshman Studies, an orientation class, is said to be "a waste of time," while business calculus or statistics lighten the workload for some. Beware of a certain science professor, though, who likes to make students in "Rocks for Jocks" earn their course credits. However, even those with rigorous schedules consider their workload to be fair. "It's a lot of work, but I'm managing okay," said one freshman. Another adds that schedules can be "very rigorous but extremely rewarding."

Professors teach all classes while recitations, smaller sections with more personal interaction and frequent quizzes, are taught by graduate teaching assistants. Pitt students agree that the professors work hard to supplement the coursework by giving the material a living face. Professors often arrange field trips for their students, with history classes visiting the battlefields at Gettysburg and German language students embarking on a seven-day trip to Germany. The professors are described as "approachable and competent" educators who continually try to make the students feel more comfortable and to offset the serious work with a little play. One biology teacher plays "Bio-jeopardy," while a calculus professor is known to play relaxing classical music before the start of each class.

Living in a Can of Comet

A point of pride for the University of Pittsburgh is the Cathedral of Learning, a 42-story-tall structure in Gothic style which is "the second tallest education building in the world." It houses a variety of classrooms and offices, as well as the Nationality Classrooms, themed rooms each scaled to a different culture. However, in contrast to the Cathedral of Learning, students describe the rest of the campus's modern architecture as rather "blah."

Parties are often free, especially for good-looking freshman girls.

Freshmen usually live in one of three tall, round dorms known as Towers, which look like "big cans of Comet." Two of the towers consist of doubles and one houses singles. While some students claim that freshman housing is "decent," others declare that it's "horrible." The rooms are air-conditioned and 24-hour quiet floors are available, though even on the regular floors a tight reign is kept on late-night noise. Housing is co-ed by floor, and about 30 students live on each floor. Rooms are pie-shaped and are "way too small" in general. The size of the desks are also a big complaint, and one student grumbled that because his desk is so tiny, he has to put his keyboard on his lap to type. Students are assigned Resident Associates, who help the freshmen make the transition to college and also enforce the bans on candles, halogen lamps, smoking of any variety, and other fire hazards. After freshmen year, students usually live in suites or off-campus apartments.

The meal plan is arranged in blocks. Students on the meal plan are allotted six blocks a day, each worth $4.85. While they are free to spend them either in the traditional dining halls or at various participating restaurants, unused blocks are deleted at the end of the week and students complain about the inevitable loss of money. Many end up going on a Starbucks spending-spree at the end of the week to get their money's worth. Students enjoy the variety of places to eat, but some complain that dining hall hours on Friday and Saturday nights are a problem. "The dining hall operates on the assumption that this is still a commuter campus. They ignore the fact that there has been a recent boom in on-campus living."

You've Gotta Do Something Besides Study!

Students agree that one of Pitt's main attractions is the diversity of entertainment the city offers. One student said, "I honestly can't think of anything this campus can't offer." Another student added, "Pitt students are intelligent and think that academics are important, but not all-consuming. We know how to get out and have a good time." Dance clubs are popular, but students also spend their weekends at playing football on the Cathedral lawn, going to parties, or just hanging out with friends. While there's a sizable amount of drinking, students who choose not to drink don't feel left out of the social scene. Many students also take advantage a variety of school-sponsored activities, such as weekend trips to Niagara Falls and local productions of the musical *The Lion King*. Others choose to attend the abundant parties, usually hosted by students living off-campus or the Greeks. According to one student, some frats do charge an admission of about five dollars, but the parties are often free, "especially for good-looking freshman girls."

In addition to entertainment options, there is a huge variety of student clubs and organizations; most students are involved in some type of extracurricular activity. Especially popular is the Outdoors Club, which goes skydiving and rock-climbing. Many students also participate in community service projects, such as Habitat for Humanity. Some choose to manage the stress of the academic life by joining the Campus Fools and learning to juggle or ride a unicycle. Another popular option is the Pitt Pathfinders, a student group that is paid to lead tours of the campus. "It's so hard not to find something you can participate in and be passionate about," one student explained.

Sports are an integral part of the Pitt experience. Football gets especially high marks, boosted by Pitt's triumph last year over Penn State. Pitt actively recruits its football players, and the recruiting tent has a presence at most football games. For those who don't join the varsity teams, intramurals are a popular alternative and there is always someone playing sports on the lawn.

Many students come to the University of Pittsburgh expecting to get lost among the thousands of undergraduates, but most are pleasantly surprised. One freshman explained, "It's a lot more personal than I thought it would be." Pitt's large, urban campus can be intimidating, but below the surface is "a very close, tight-knit university." —*Tracy Serge*

FYI

If you're coming to Pittsburgh, you'd better bring "your dancing shoes so you can tear up the floor at the many local night clubs."

What is the typical weekend schedule? "Work, party, eat, sleep . . . not so different from anywhere else."

If I could change one things about Pittsburgh, I'd "eliminate The Hill—it's such a pain to walk up every day."

The three things that every student should do before graduating from University of Pittsburgh are "go to a football game, have fries at the O, and live a year in the Towers"

Villanova University

Address: 800 Lancaster Avenue, Villanova, PA 19085
Phone: 610-519-4000
E-mail address: gotovu@villanova.edu
Web site URL: www.villanova.edu
Founded: 1842
Private or Public: private
Religious affiliation: Roman Catholic
Location: suburban
Undergraduate enrollment: 7,375
Total enrollment: NA
Percent Male/Female: 50%/50%
Percent Minority: 14%
Percent African-American: 3%
Percent Asian: 5%
Percent Hispanic: 5%
Percent Native-American: 0%
Percent in-state/out of state: 27%/73%
Percent Pub HS: NA
Number of Applicants: 10,897
Percent Accepted: 47%
Percent Accepted who enroll: 54%
Entering: 1,584
Transfers: 119
Application Deadline: 7 Jan
Mean SAT: NA
Mean ACT: NA
Middle 50% SAT range: V 570-660, M 590-690
Middle 50% ACT range: 25-29
3 Most popular majors: business, engineering, communication
Retention: 94%
Graduation rate: 85%
On-campus housing: 70%
Fraternities: 11%
Sororities: 40%
Library: 1,049,011 volumes
Tuition and Fees: $26,168
Room and Board: $8,640
Financial aid, first-year: 48%
Varsity or Club Athletes: 19%
Early Decision or Early Action Acceptance Rate: 54%

How would you like to win a cruise or a brand new Mustang for shooting a couple hoops at school? If this sounds appealing to you, you might find yourself in good company among the basketball-crazy Villanova wildcats. "Hoops Mania" isn't just the season opener where the basketball team is introduced—it's a Villanova fever that has been contagious since the school was founded. While football's not much of a big deal, Villanova students "go crazy over basketball."

Players, Greeks, and Saints

Basketball is just one of Villanova's many traditions. A Catholic university located only about 15 minutes away from Philadelphia, Villanova boasts an exciting night life and a Greek system devoted to perpetual partying. Forty percent of the student body belongs to one of their 16 fraternities or sororities. The Greeks are particularly prevalent on campus during rush when "all the rushes have to build chariots and race them around; that's always fun to watch." While students say that anyone can survive without belonging to a fraternity or a sorority, an active social life is a must. One student confessed, "As important as our grades are to us, [partying] is a really important aspect of our school."

But fraternities and sororities are not all about drinking and dancing the night away; they also avidly promote philanthropy. Each fraternity and sorority is affiliated with a different community service organization and organizes two events per year to raise money for these chosen charities. The service-based Greek life yields events like the Special Olympics on Villanova's campus, as well as a number of projects in Philadelphia city schools, shelters, and soup kitchens. "Habitat for Humanity is huge on our campus," one senior said, recommending that everyone go on mission trips during fall or spring break to build houses. "I know for some of my friends who go to big universities, it's not the cool thing to get involved in community service," she explained. "But here, it's the cool thing to do."

The Holy Grounds

For entertainment on college grounds, students go to Connelly Center, where free movies are shown on weekends. Many also venture into Philadelphia. Railways line either side of campus and make it possible for freshmen and sophomores, who are not allowed to have cars, to explore the city. Weekend shuttles also run into the heart of Philadelphia and to the nearest mall. On the first Friday of every month, art galleries and museums are free for the public, and students often take advantage of this and swarm into the city. Philadelphia offers clubs like "Shampoo" and "Envy" that host college nights for students. One sophomore recommended the popular South Street: "Shopping is fun because there are lots of random boutiques, but it's even fun just to sit and watch the people go by and the random happenings." Another student agreed: "The people there are very different from what you see on campus; it's a breath of fresh air." Also downtown are Pat's Cheesesteaks, frequented by most students, and a bar called Brownie's. "When you turn 21," one senior said, "it's the rite of passage—you go to Brownie's."

Villanova hosts a handful of annual campus-wide events. The St. Thomas of Villanova Day parade is "basically this huge party," held in the fall when students return from summer vacation. A similar carnival, NovaFest, is hosted at the end of the year. However, do not expect to obtain easy access to alcohol at these parties or at any other social gatherings; Villanova has a strict alcohol policy that is enforced by Resident Advisors. No alcohol is allowed for students under age, and students over 21 are only allowed to keep a certain amount of alcohol in their dorm room. Students say the RAs are "pretty strict on it. They make themselves very friendly, and very approachable, but we know that they're the arm of the law."

As for food and sustenance, Villanova offers a number of dining options in addition to regular dining hall meal plans. Meal plan points pay for items at the convenience store, the Italian kitchen, and the grill. Coffee shops like "The Holy Grounds" can be found all over campus, in libraries and in classroom buildings. There's also a traveling coffee cart that tries to capture customers from the nearby Starbucks.

Holy Wisdom

Villanova's quest for a liberal arts education for its students entails a number of distributional requirements. "They try to make you as well-rounded as possible," one senior said, listing the requirements in science, math, theology, history, foreign language, English, and ethics. Applicants apply to one of Villanova's four colleges: Arts and Sciences, Commerce and Finance, Engineering, or Nursing. Students have the option of changing their college program once they are enrolled and are not required to declare a major until the end of sophomore year. "Our school is very much broken up by the college you're in," one senior said. "Academic-wise, you're very segregated." The freshman core, however—a survey of Western Literature and history from the ancient medieval period through the Renaissance and the Enlightenment to the present—is required of all freshmen and is "a big mixing pot."

Goin' to the Chapel

One amorously-minded sophomore noted the beauty of Villanova's on-campus church. "It's the most gorgeous chapel," she said, noting that couples are married there every weekend. "Freshman year you're supposed to put your name on the list because there's a four-year waiting list to get married there." While no one actually signs up to be married that far in advance, you might be able to arrange a marriage in a different way: couples who kiss under the arch in Coor Hall as freshmen are said to be destined for wedding bells in this chapel.

"Basically everybody at this campus is out of an Abercrombie & Fitch catalog. But there are still some people who throw everybody on campus for a loop."

When it comes to other chapel-going, students say the Catholic tradition of the school is more like background noise than an omnipresent affiliation. "I was expecting it to be a whole bunch of Catholics," one freshman said, "But only some go to Mass." He soon discovered that Villanova was "more religiously diverse" than he had expected. The majority of students on campus are in fact Catholic, but as one sophomore noted, "they are not necessarily stringent Catholics; it is present, but I wouldn't say it pervades social life."

Feel free to walk into Coor Hall or the chapel as you please, but watch your step at St. Mary's on West Campus. Not only do students tell great ghost stories about this and other buildings, they also warn that if you step on the seal in the floor there, you won't graduate in four years.

Posterchild for Preppy

"Basically everybody at this campus is out of an Abercrombie & Fitch catalog," one sophomore confessed. "But there are still some people who throw everybody on campus for a loop." Students describe the typical Villanova student as "upper-middle class white—just your basic kid who grew up in the suburbs and whose parents are together . . . and they have brothers or sisters who go here or who've graduated from here; there's a lot of legacy at Villanova." Another sophomore explained, "I guess you could say that most of the people here have a lot of money because a lot of them come from New Jersey and drive BMWs. But there are a lot of people who don't go with that crowd and who don't really care about that stuff." The homogeneity of the student population is a widespread complaint, although one sophomore optimistically reported, "The incoming class was far more diverse than ours," and "a lot more cultural clubs have popped up on campus recently."

Overall, students say the size and atmosphere of Villanova help make everyone feel at home. One sophomore remarked, "Villanova's big on community, and I think that's one of the things that really attracted me: leaving home I'd kind of have a new family as soon as I got here." Another student appreciated that Villanova is "not so big that you get lost in the masses, but not so small that everybody knows everything about everyone else; it makes for a comfortable feel." Remember, though, whether headed towards class, the chapel, or Philadelphia—watch out for those seals. —*Stephanie Hagan*

FYI

If you come to Villanova, you'd better bring "a good work ethic, black party pants, and a fake ID."

What is the typical weekend schedule? "Friday nights party, Saturday sleep in, do some work during the day or watch football, Saturday night more parties, Sunday lots of people have meetings, and then lots of work."

If I could change one thing about Villanova, "I'd change the lack of diversity."

Three things every student at Villanova should do before graduating are "go to the basketball games, watch the chariot races, and get involved."

Rhode Island

Brown University

Address: Box 1920; Providence, RI 02912
Phone: 401-863-2378
E-mail address: admission_undergraduate @brown.edu
Web site URL: www.brown.edu
Founded: 1764
Private or Public: private
Religious affiliation: none
Location: small city
Undergraduate enrollment: 6,030
Total enrollment: NA
Percent Male/Female: 45%/55%
Percent Minority: 33%
Percent African-American: 6%
Percent Asian: 14%
Percent Hispanic: 6%
Percent Native-American: 1%
Percent in-state/out of state: NA
Percent Pub HS: NA
Number of Applicants: 14,612
Percent Accepted: 17%
Percent Accepted who enroll: 53%
Entering: 1,458
Transfers: NA
Application Deadline: 1 Jan
Mean SAT: NA
Mean ACT: NA
Middle 50% SAT range: V 640-750, M 650-750
Middle 50% ACT range: 26-32
3 Most popular majors: biology, history, international relations and affairs
Retention: 97%
Graduation rate: 95%
On-campus housing: 80%
Fraternities: 5%
Sororities: 1%
Library: 3,191,502 volumes
Tuition and Fees: $29,846
Room and Board: $8,096
Financial aid, first-year: 44%
Varsity or Club Athletes: 29%
Early Decision or Early Action Acceptance Rate: 27%

Combining academic freedom with a strong liberal arts foundation, Brown University is not your typical Ivy League school. The lack of general requirements and an unlimited pass/fail option demonstrate Brown's commitment to intellectual freedom. Set upon a hill overlooking Providence, Rhode Island, the university also has a good relationship with its urban neighbors. Finally, the student body—though quite diverse—shares a vision of open-mindedness and a passion for the arts. In classes, in the city, and on campus, one can sense Brown's commitment to—as one student phrased it—"its own definition for a liberal arts education."

Brown Academics—Choose Your Own Adventure

Unlike all other Ivy League schools, Brown has no core requirements. Each student must choose a "concentration" in which they must take approximately 12 courses (although some concentrations can require as few as eight or as many as 20). The only other requirement is that students take 30 course credits by the time they graduate, leaving a workload of about four classes per semester. Although this system allows Brown students to "take classes you want to take," some freshmen commented that it left them "disoriented" at times. To remedy this, Brown offers "a lot of advising systems to guide freshmen through the academic process." By taking advantage of their advisors, students felt that they were able to make the most of their academic freedom.

All classes at Brown can be taken pass/fail. Although a popular rumor on campus has it that a student once took all 30 of his classes pass/fail and still got hired by a top investment bank, most students use the option more prudently. However, this allows many academic options that adventurous students can undertake, such as independent study, group study courses, and work in interdepartmental fields. Also, since failed classes don't appear on a student's external transcript, students are encouraged to take "random classes for pure interest." Brown follows the typical pattern of large introductory classes and smaller upper-level classes, but the humanities tend to shrink down faster than the sciences. Students recommend concentrations in economics, English, and education.

"There is no typical Brown student. Our only similarity is being open to the many different things Brown and its people have to offer."

Students stress the importance of liberal attitudes in shaping their work habits. Although Brown students are often stereotyped as "too liberal," one student explained that they are simply "not as aggressive" as at other schools. Many students take semesters or years off, and "personal leaves are very popular and encouraged" by the administration. Some programs even offer credit to students for embarking on internships—leading a large portion of the junior class to study or work abroad. Just as the small number of graduate TAs encourages direct engagement between professors and students, Brown's loose requirements encourage students to be "willing to help each other."

Work Together, Play Together

Although most students appreciate the unique academic system, most agreed that "the people really make Brown special." Brown students described themselves as being "really independent," "self-motivated," "chill," and even "fashionable." However, there is a sense that the "typical Brown student is one who doesn't like to be called the typical Brown student." As one put it: "There is no typical Brown student. Our only similarity is being open to the many different things Brown and its people have to offer." Nonetheless, many students find themselves dealing with stereotypes that Brown is either "grungy" or full of "nerds and jocks." Students deny this misconception, instead focusing on their hard work ethic, knowledge of the world, and "desire to do things." At Brown, no matter what someone is interested in, whether it is politics or partying, they will probably be very dedicated to it.

The social life at Brown revolves around a diverse scene, since "people have their own ways of partying." For most freshmen and some sophomores, the "small" yet "visible" frat and sorority houses in Wriston Quad dominate the party scene. As students get older and "the frat parties start to get old," upperclassmen often go to house parties or take the 15-minute walk or five-minute drive to bars in downtown Providence, which reported let in underage students with regularity. In general, international students tend to find their own party scene in clubs such as Viva. For the most adventurous, Boston is also only an hour-long car ride away.

Brown also has its share of special events. The biggest dance, Sex Paragod, put on by the Lesbian, Gay, Bisexual and Transexual Alliance (LGBTA), is known for its cross-dressing and general craziness. For the more conservative, Brown also has two large formal dances that give students a chance to wear tuxedos and gowns. Spring Weekend, a festival before finals each year, is well known for the big-name bands that come play each year. Brown's dating scene is typical of most Ivy League schools, featuring "couples living like they're married" and some "random hookups"—but not much in-between. One male student admitted, "the chicks aren't the most attractive in the world, but they are getting better." Drugs definitely are present on campus, especially "huge, but controlled" pot use, but there are reportedly few serious problems because students "don't go over their limits." For students not into drugs or alcohol, Brown offers many social opportunities through its ubiquitous arts organizations. Brown male a cappella is known as some of the best around, giving students the option of concerts and performances to round out their nightlife.

The Campus on the Hill

Brown's 140-acre campus is all within a 10- or 15-minute walk from its center—the "beautiful" main green, a large open space around which all of Brown's largest classrooms are clustered. Students like the fact that their campus is small enough to feel unified, but large enough to attract bars and clubs. The buildings provide a good mix of old-brick architecture and unique, modern buildings. A great view of Providence is available from Prospect Park, and the campus bar, the Underground, is very popular with undergraduates. Thayer Street houses an assortment of cafes, restaurants, and even a movie theatre to allow students a break from their studying. Providence residents "like students in general," and since students often go into Providence, there are close ties between the city and university.

Brown recently changed its requirements so that undergraduates must now live on campus at least six semesters. This rule did not go over well with students, given that evaluations of the dorms ranged from "alright" to "not what you would expect from an Ivy League school." One freshman complained that the freshmen dorms, which are mostly doubles, were "old" and "dirty," but the housing for upperclassmen seems to improve a lot. Freshmen are all assigned to a unit, comprising of 20 to 30 students living in the same hallway or section of the dorm. This system works well, because freshmen get to know the people in their grade before moving off into program houses such as the literary house, or mixed living conditions. After three years of on-campus living, about half of seniors choose to live in off-campus apartments, rounding out their diverse housing experience at Brown.

Sports, Arts, and Other Fun

The three big extracurriculars at Brown seem to be "sports, writing, and arts." Brown has a large population of students who play a sport, estimated at 30 percent, but most students do not have much school spirit, leaving most games without many fans. One athlete complained, "We do well, but students just don't know about it." This atmosphere creates tight-knit sports teams that tend to spend a lot of time together. Brown is also known for its "controversial" newspapers, such as *The Brown Daily Herald.* One student explained, "It seems like we have some wacky extremists, but Brown isn't out of the mainstream. People are just encouraged to just say what they believe in; this is the place to do that." Most students, however, focus on Brown's many theatre, comedy, and singing groups as the center of campus events. Comedy groups like Improvidence and the highly acclaimed a cappella group Brown Derbies are considered "talented" and "always go over well." Brown also benefits from its proximity to the Rhode Island School of Design (RISD), which shares many joint organizations with its Ivy neighbor.

Getting Your Grub On

Brown students gave a mixed reaction to their dining halls. Most liked the flexibility of the point system—whereby if you miss a meal during the day, you get credited for a late meal or snack that night. Brown offers a few different eating venues in which to spend these points, including two main cafeterias, The Gate (pizza) and Joe's (burgers and fries). One freshman said, "The food sucks, but everyone probably says that about their college food," while another said that the cafeterias are good places to hang out with friends. One other concern was that one of the dining halls closes on weekends, often leading to large crowds in the other. Luckily, students can find plenty of dining options in Providence—one junior recommended Federal Hill, Providence's "Little Italy," for a good Italian meal.

When asked how to describe Brown, one student exclaimed, "You will meet amazing people and make incredible friends." Most students echo this view, claiming that despite its faults—such as a lack of school spirit and questionable housing—Brown more than makes up for it through the quality of its academics and student body. Brown students may be liberal, but the student body is diverse enough to elude the description of a typical student. For those looking for modern ideas of intellectual freedom contained within the seventh oldest university in the country, Brown may be the right place. —*Adam Rein*

FYI

If you come to Brown, you'd better bring an "open mind to a lot of different people."

What is the typical weekend schedule? "Movies, ice cream, and party hopping on Friday and Saturday; cramming on Sunday."

If I could change one thing about Brown, I'd "change the rule that you have to live in the dorms your first three years."

Three things every student at Brown should do before graduating are "go to Louis' for Sunday Brunch, cross-dress at Sex Paragod, and party during Spring Weekend."

Rhode Island School of Design

Address: 2 College Street; Providence, RI 02903
Phone: 401-454-6300
E-mail address: admissions@risd.edu
Web site URL: www.risd.edu
Founded: 1877
Private or Public: private
Religious affiliation: none
Location: small city
Undergraduate enrollment: 1,882
Total enrollment: 2,119
Percent Male/Female: 36%/64%
Percent Minority: 31%
Percent African-American: 2%
Percent Asian: 12%
Percent Hispanic: 5%
Percent Native-American: 0%
Percent in-state/out of state: NA
Percent Pub HS: NA
Number of Applicants: 2,524
Percent Accepted: 32%
Percent Accepted who enroll: 55%
Entering: 392
Transfers: 119
Application Deadline: 15 Feb
Mean SAT: NA
Mean ACT: NA
Middle 50% SAT range: V 540-650, M 550-650
Middle 50% ACT range: NA
3 Most popular majors: fine and studio art, commercial and advertising art, industrial design
Retention: 93%
Graduation rate: 82%
On-campus housing: 43%
Fraternities: NA
Sororities: NA
Library: 84,587 volumes
Tuition and Fees: $26,199
Room and Board: $7,368
Financial aid, first-year: 42%
Varsity or Club Athletes: NA
Early Decision or Early Action Acceptance Rate: NA

People live, breathe, and dream art at the Rhode Island School of Design, affectionately called "Rizdee." Its students purportedly have the greatest workload in the country, surpassing even MIT. If you can make it through the 'grueling' freshman year, the rest of your time will be spent working creatively with renowned professors, many of who are accomplished artists, and you will graduate with a diploma from one of the top art schools in the country. But it's not all work: from dressing up for the Artist's Ball, to cheering "Go Nads!" life is a little crazy and always unusual at RISD.

Art Is Life

RISD offers every imaginable artistic discipline, from illustration, architecture, and graphic design—the most popular majors—to the more unconventional glass-blowing courses. Freshmen must take two English, two art history, and three studio courses both semesters, choosing from history, philosophy, and science classes second semester. Also, to graduate, students need studio credits, which consist of the creative core classes that "everyone spends hours and hours working on." The liberal arts courses are "informative and pretty good," and supplements, groups of 15 to 20 students from lecture courses, are "great because you can speak, have discussions about what you're learning in class, and can voice your questions." One girl complained, however, that the lectures were too large and disjointed, and that the schedule was too limited. But those who come to RISD are not looking for the typical liberal arts curriculum.

The workload at RISD is heavy, with students spending seven hours a day in the studio; says one student, "my roommate pulls all-nighters at least one night a week, every week." The first year is "one of the hardest workload-wise because you are fulfilling assignments, whereas later you are doing your own work and it is more specific for major requirements." In the imaginative environment of RISD, students say "it's easier to do the work because you are surrounded by other people doing it too, your peers motivate you."

Architecture majors are the hardest-worked of all; "you don't see them the first year," and many even sleep in the studio, emerging after 24-hour work sessions. The illustration major, on the other hand, "is very broad—you can do a lot of media, and people want to try their hand at a lot of different things." Those interested in double-majoring in some fields like printmaking and textile design will find that they are required to stay five years, yet the quality of the professors make it worthwhile for some.

RISD professors are not the usual bunch of tweed-jacketed scholars with thick-rimmed glasses sitting behind desks; many of them have made their names on the New York art scene, and eccentricity seems to be a requirement. One student divulged the story of a certain heartbroken professor who broke into the Providence sewer system, where he put all of his belongings, cast an exact replica of himself, left it there with everything he owned, and moved on. "It was a huge art piece, but there was no publicity, only people who had heard about it from others went to see it. He really made it for himself, it was a cathartic experience." Tom Mills is a professor famous for his exceptional drawing foundation class, and, like many professors at RISD, has studios in New York City. He also gives "mini art history lectures to supplement work in class to help his students."

Because of its focus on the arts, RISD does not have any major science facilities. Science classes can be taken in the Nature Lab, although some students take advantage of RISD's cross-registration program to take classes at Brown. The science requirement is very basic and no math is required, and one student confided that the Nature Lab was probably used more frequently for artistic purposes, as "the stuffed animals kept there make better models than live ones—they hold still."

The art facilities are stellar, as is to be expected from a school of RISD's prestige. Not surprisingly, "there are studios for anything you want to do, open 24 hours a day." Art supplies are conveniently located in the RISD store on campus.

Party, Anyone?

There are plenty of options to choose from when deciding how to spend your meager free time at RISD. Thayer Street is the local hangout for many students, only two blocks from quad, and has a wide variety of restaurants and bars to choose from. Whether you crave Italian food, Thai food, or cheesecake, it can be found on or near Thayer, home to Pizzeria Uno, O-Cha (meaning 'delicious' in Thai), The Cheesecake Factory, Paragon, the Greek Andrea's, a crepe place, and the upscale seafood restaurant, Hemingway's. Thayer is the place to see and be seen for freshmen and upperclassmen alike.

There is also the mall, an enormous complex with a cinema within walking distance of campus. Many students go to private parties at RISD and Brown, and though RISD has no Greek system, students can still enjoy Brown's frat parties, which host the wildest nights around. For those looking to dance, there are clubs, Viva being the most popular, and other venues that have themed events such as goth night, fetish night, and '80s night, by far the most popular: "'80s is a really big deal here."

For those without real over-21 IDs, there is still plenty to do—there are always concerts (Enrique Iglesias, Britney Spears, Le Tigre, Rilo Kiley, and Three Doors Down have played), dances, Broadway shows such as *Hairspray,* and art openings, as well as visiting speakers like the fashion designer Todd Oldham and Martha Stewart, among others. The highlights of the year are the three formal events thrown by the school. The Artist's Ball in first semester is "really, really crazy, everyone goes all-out on costumes, some people end up naked, and one girl, dressed as Sailor Moon from 'Anime' won a national contest for best costume and a trip to Cancún for two." Electroflow has a more 'rave-like' atmosphere, and is held in a parking garage with DJs on each level, and Beaux Arts is held in the springtime down by the river. New York City and Boston are just a train ride away, and some professors organize trips for the class to look at shows in the cities. Ski trips are another option.

"It would be weird if you were normal."

The school's alcohol policy is "supposedly strict, but most can get away with drinking. There are Public Safety people on patrol living in dorms who will look through your stuff if they suspect drinking and confiscate any substances, but it doesn't occur that often." Non-drinkers are equally comfortable, as there is no pressure at all to drink.

At RISD it is incredibly easy to meet people, and "everybody is pretty nuts; there are different personalities, and everyone is talented." The male to female ratio is "very weird," said one girl, "that's why we go up to Brown." Students report that many of the guys at RISD are gay, and that combined with the enormous workload makes having a love life difficult.

The Look and the Life

Students love the old New England-style buildings and the nice, cozy little town just across the river from Providence. The campus is situated on top of College Hill, which can be "kind of treacherous in winter," so bring your snow boots! All freshmen live in dorms around Lower and Upper Quad, which are conveniently linked so "you can walk around the whole thing to visit friends (or go to the cafeteria) without venturing out into the cold." Each floor has a common room where people can hang out, as well as a work room where "you can paint big paintings, draw, or do big sculptures." Freshman year guarantees decent housing, usually singles or doubles. Due to lack of housing, half the student body moves off campus after their first year to live with friends, though there is a new dorm with a 500-person capacity. In addition, projects for a new student center, museum, and library are underway to house the school's growing collection.

The main places to eat are the Met, which has a vegan bar, salad and sandwich bar, and the popular panini maker, as well as Carrhaus, which is "like a coffee shop with couches," and the Pit, a grill serving hamburgers and veggie burgers. The food at RISD is good, and the veggie options are particularly popular as they cater to the school's large vegetarian population.

Go Nads!

Sports are not taken too seriously at RISD, and this is reflected in the choice of team names: the hockey-playing Nads draw the biggest crowd, and one girl described the game as "hilarious—a lot of drunken people yelling and a large penis (the team mascot) skating around." The basketball team is the Balls, the swimming team the Strokes, and the school cheerleaders are known as the Jockstraps. To keep students fit, RISD has a gym and a small fitness center offering classes ranging from modern dance to yoga and the Brazilian dance *capoeira*, and students can always use the Brown facilities, which boast an Olympic pool, a huge gym and a skating rink.

The emphasis at RISD is more on school spirit than sports prowess, and "people here are nuts, basically. We are all in our own little art bubble, we work a lot and don't mind the work, and we know that we can't party 24/7." One student raves, "you feel a part of everything, everybody is really different but nobody judges you for it. Everyone has their own style and personality . . . it would be weird if you were normal." —*Serena Hines*

FYI

If you come to RISD, you'd better bring "an incredibly open mind."

What is the typical weekend schedule? "Friday, you are usually tired from the week's work so you go out for a drink or to the movies; Saturday and Sunday, sleep in, spend the rest of the day in the studio, and later go down to Thayer Street, walk around, go to a party."

If I could change one thing about RISD, I'd "remove the hills."

Three things every student at RISD should do before graduating are "go to a Nads hockey game, go to the Artists' Ball, and try being a poor artist for a little bit."

University of Rhode Island

Address: Kingston, RI 02881-2020
Phone: 401-874-7000
E-mail address: uriadmit@uriacc.uri.edu
Web site URL: www.uri.edu
Founded: 1892
Private or Public: public
Religious affiliation: none
Location: rural
Undergraduate enrollment: 10,784
Total enrollment: NA
Percent Male/Female: 44%/56%
Percent Minority: 11%
Percent African-American: 4%
Percent Asian: 3%
Percent Hispanic: 4%
Percent Native-American: 0%
Percent in-state/out of state: 62%/38%
Percent Pub HS: NA
Number of Applicants: 11,072
Percent Accepted: 69%
Percent Accepted who enroll: 31%
Entering: 2,383
Transfers: NA
Application Deadline: 1 Mar
Mean SAT: NA
Mean ACT: NA
Middle 50% SAT range: V 490-590, M 500-610
Middle 50% ACT range: NA
3 Most popular majors: communication studies, psychology, human development and family studies
Retention: 79%
Graduation rate: 58%
On-campus housing: 33%
Fraternities: 7%
Sororities: 11%
Library: 1,205,038 volumes
Tuition and Fees: $5,858 in; $15,324 out
Room and Board: $7,402
Financial aid, first-year: 72%
Varsity or Club Athletes: 14%
Early Decision or Early Action Acceptance Rate: NA

Did someone say par-tay? At URI everyone seems to be saying "party." However, the once top-ranked party school has apparently started to lose some of its party-animal charm. According to one student "URI isn't the party school it used to be." That is welcome news to an administration that has tried, in recent years, to quell the "Animal House" and focus more intently upon academics.

Hardcore Curriculum

Party animals: don't pack your bags just yet. The University of Rhode Island does require its students to meet graduation requirements by taking courses in the natural sciences, fine arts, mathematics, languages, and social sciences. While this subject load may seem daunting, prospective students should not distress. The requirements, according to one sophomore, are "fairly easy if you pay attention in class and take semi-decent notes."

But be forewarned, introductory classes, especially at large state universities, can be ridiculously large. Some courses at URI enroll as many as 500 students. However, according to students, the average class size is 40 to 50 students. Certain majors also require its participants to take specific classes. Students rave about the Chemical Engineering and German departments in particular and URI has long been known for its marine biology programs.

Again, a common problem at major universities is the glut of TAs teaching classes. While URI does try to ensure that courses are taught by professors, some students complained about the high number of TA taught lecture courses. However, when the professors are present, and that is the majority of the time, they are easily approachable when the students make the effort.

For the more academically inclined graduate of the Rhode Island public school system, the University offers a rather impressive and prestigious honors program. The class sizes are generally smaller and the course load more rigorous. Students can apply directly after high school or after their freshman or sophomore years. Like most other universities, URI extends to its students the possibility of study abroad that, for some Rhode Island weary scholars, is a great chance to "escape and have a blast." URI also offers a "Centennial Scholarship" for motivated and qualified students that can provide the lucky few with a full ride. You know what that means freshmen? More disposable income and leeway with the parents!

In terms of academic upgrades, the University of Rhode Island recently committed itself to building a new $9 million environmental studies center on the Kingston campus. The price tag includes a whopping $1 million federal grant.

URI also sponsors numerous academic lectures. Recent talks have centered on such topics as "Genetic Diversity of Life", "Global Youth Cultures", and "Vietnam". Lectures are popular options for academically inclined students.

Home Sweet Home

The campus of URI is a random smattering of gothic, colonial, and modern architecture. The Quad, at the center of campus, is picturesque and, at least according to one student, a great place to "do homework or have sex." The Quad is surrounded by academic buildings, while the Greek houses are relegated to the outskirts of the sprawling campus. Campus dorms, the student center, and the library were recently renovated. "The campus feels like it's brand spankin' new!! I absolutely love it!!"

The dorms at Rhode Island get mixed reviews. However, one enthusiastic student stated that her dorm "had a large common room, which we can easily veg out in." All dorms, save one, are coed by floor. There is an all female dorm for those interested. For the non-substance using students there is a "Wellness Dorm" that prohibits smoking and drinking. Sorority and Frat houses are also popular options for upperclassmen. Many upperclassmen complain about the inadequacy of on-campus housing. However, one of the best options available for upperclassman housing are the apartments along the nearby beach. Surf's up!

After a hard days night in the library students can chow down at one of URI's three main dining rooms or the oft praised "Ram's Den." Several meal plans are available to URI students, including a 10-, 15-, or 20-meal plan. At the Ram's Den students use food points purchased at the beginning of the semester to buy the delectable goodies offered at "by far the best food joint on campus." The other dining halls vary, with some serving fast food and others serving actual entrees. The Den offers some well liked grilled entrees. The university has made strides recently in helping to provide for the needs of its vegetarian students. Despite the improvements in dining students still complain about the lack of weekend service.

"As a sophomore, I'm already dreading having to leave here."

One student described the town of Kingston, "It's like Disney World without the rides and wonderful Florida climate." Drinking is the only thing that seems to dull the monotony of this one horse town nestled in the vast wilderness of Rhode Island. Yet, some students relish in the small town setting, describing it as "the ideal little college town!" But where do students crash after a hearty night of hard drinking and wild fun?

Getting Soaked on a Dry Campus

The official administration policy is one of "no alcohol." But according to most students on campus the university is wet to the point of deluge. As with most large state universities, Greek life is the dominant form of social activity on campus. All parties must be registered with the university police but this has not drastically altered the availability of alcohol. One student loudly exclaimed, "Rams party more than study." This, of course, results in the non-drinkers feeling ostracized from the mainstream and has spurred animosity between Greek and non-Greek students. Luckily for those not interested in the frat scene, the University does have an entertainment committee that brings in speakers, theatrical productions, and concerts to campus.

Extracurricular activities are also major parts of student's lives here on campus. Basketball and football games are particularly popular draws especially when URI is playing cross state rival Providence College. Other notable sports teams are the baseball, volleyball, soccer, and sailing team. The sailing team has earned numerous national and international distinctions.

Student senate and the student-run

newspaper, *The Five Cent Cigar*, also garner favorable attention on campus. One of the more fascinating clubs at URI is the Experimental Art Society that sponsors such activities as film production and instrument production. The perennial favorite Surf Club also holds September lessons for surfing novices.

The political atmosphere on URI's campus is one of liberal toleration. Racial issues do occasionally surface on campus as a result of several racially self-segregated dorms. Student groups are attempting to combat this problem. A large part of the student body is also comprised of commuters who live nearby and drive to school.

Overall, despite academics playing second fiddle to social life, many students say that URI offers its motivated students a healthy learning experience and for all students a positive college experience. "As a sophomore, I'm already dreading having to leave here. I *love* this place—and it was actually my last choice in high school. Give URI a chance, you won't regret it." *—Sean McBride and Staff*

FYI

If you come to URI, you'd better bring "good walking shoes—it's a large and hilly campus."

What is the typical weekend schedule? "Friday, hang out locally; Saturday, party or go see a movie; Sunday, study."

"If I could change one thing about URI, I'd build more dorms—they're too cramped and distant."

Three things everyone should do before graduating from URI are "take part in Homecoming, run naked across the Quad, and change their major at least once."

South Carolina

Clemson University

Address: 105 Sikes Hall; Clemson, SC 29634-5124
Phone: 864-656-2287
E-mail address: cuadmissions@clemson.edu
Web site URL: www.clemson.edu
Founded: 1889
Private or Public: public
Religious affiliation: none
Location: rural
Undergraduate enrollment: 12,805
Total enrollment: NA
Percent Male/Female: 59%/41%
Percent Minority: 11%
Percent African-American: 7%
Percent Asian: 2%
Percent Hispanic: 1%
Percent Native-American: 0%
Percent in-state/out of state: 70%/30%
Percent Pub HS: NA
Number of Applicants: 11,315
Percent Accepted: 52%
Percent Accepted who enroll: 45%
Entering: 2,474
Transfers: NA
Application Deadline: 1 May
Mean SAT: NA
Mean ACT: NA
Middle 50% SAT range: V 540-640, M 570-670
Middle 50% ACT range: 24-29
3 Most popular majors: business marketing, engineering, education
Retention: 87%
Graduation rate: 72%
On-campus housing: 46%
Fraternities: NA
Sororities: NA
Library: 1,126,431 volumes
Tuition and Fees: $6,934 in; $14,532 out
Room and Board: $5,038
Financial aid, first-year: 39%
Varsity or Club Athletes: 8%
Early Decision or Early Action Acceptance Rate: NA

To the casual observer, it might appear that there are many ways in which a student at Clemson would be prevented from graduating. Take, for example, Calhoun Mansion. Legend has it that any student who takes a tour through it will never receive his or her degree from the university. Another calls to mind the plaque on the statue of Thomas Green Clemson. It is said that if a student reads this, he or she doesn't stand a chance at graduating. Yet another points to the names of previous graduates etched on campus sidewalks, saying that if a student steps on his or her own last name, he or she is destined never to graduate. Despite these terrors, Clemson is attracting a lot of bright young minds and was even named *Time Magazine*'s Public School of the Year in 2000.

From Farms to Foreign Languages

Clemson offers its students a wide variety of academic options, from the very popular, yet reputedly challenging computer science and engineering majors, to Parks, Recreation, and Tourism Management, which is also known by students as Party Right Through May. Students are required to fulfill general education requirements, including a certain amount of class hours in most general subjects, which include oral communication, writing and computer skills. The requirements aren't too limiting and, as one student simply put it. "Yes, there are academic requirements. They are fair."

Clemson students are placed in one of five colleges according to major. Two of the more popular are the College of Engineering and Science, and the College of Architecture, Arts and Humanities. Engineering and computer science are traditionally large majors, while agriculture retains a strong following due to the university's original purpose as an agricultural school. Other majors, however, are capped each year.

Clemson students also have something else in common: as one student put it, "my blood runneth orange."

Most Clemson students offer few complaints when it comes to academics. Being a large state university, Clemson offers many options academically. Some students do say, however, that it is sometimes difficult to get into certain classes. Others note that some "professors can't speak English" and that this precludes any possible relationship, especially when many classes are taught by TAs. Still others praise the ability of their professors, and one commented that "all professors give out their home phone numbers in case you have questions."

Eat, Drink, and . . . Drink

The typical Clemson student, most students will tell you, can be described as "a flat-out conservative Southerner." The city of Clemson, South Carolina, is definitely a college town, and most students agree that "the town wouldn't be here if it wasn't for the students." Many students head into town on Friday and Saturday nights, generally choosing to stay on campus during the week. Bars in downtown Clemson, however, close at midnight due to Blue Laws. There are two private bars that close at two, and "they are packed after midnight." Most students generally have parties after the bars close downtown, fondly known as Twelve-Oh-Ones. One student comments that Clemson has an "affinity for ticketing underage drinkers," and most drinking occurs off-campus, though there is an on-campus bar. Many Clemson students do have cars, although most complain about the significant lack of parking. According to one student, anyone with a car "more than likely already has one or two parking tickets this year."

While many students choose not to live on campus, there are a variety of on-campus dorms. The average freshman dorm is "single-sex . . . and you can loft the beds," said one student. Another commented, "I lived in the crappiest dorm but had the best time and met the greatest girls." Others agree, saying that dorms are where students often meet their best friends. All dorms have RAs, but students report that female dorms tend to have stricter visiting policies and rules. There are also many co-ed dorms, most of which are divided by floor. Additionally, honor students may live in their own dorm, known as Holmes Hall, which comes complete with a kitchen in each four-person suite.

Clemson is currently undergoing a "building period," including a renovation of older buildings, the construction of three new dorms and a student union. The campus itself is very large, and as one student commented, "Be prepared to build up your legs—it's a big campus and there are a bunch of hills." Clemson has a variety of food choices for students and a recently improved meal plan. There are two dining halls, a restaurant-type dining hall, a canteen, two cafes and a food court. Students agree that there are many options, "even for those with a vegetarian bent." One student especially praised the desserts in the cafeterias, saying "Clemson makes its own ice cream, and it's awesome!"

Orange-Blooded Greeks

Ask the average Clemson student what he looks forward to the most, and you will almost always get the same answer: football. Tiger football is not only huge on campus, but is well respected across the country. Besides being "very friendly and willing to help anyone with anything," Clemson students also have something else in common: as one student put it, "my blood runneth orange." During the fall, claimed one student, "it's all about football." Said another: "When there are 86,000 people in Death Valley (the stadium) and the football players come running down the hill, you can't hear the person next to you." As football players enter the stadium, they rub Howard's rock, originally from Death Valley, California. When players rub the rock, "they are pledging that they will give 110 percent during the game."

The athletics program at Clemson is such a strong force that it is also heavily supported financially. Most Clemson students are familiar with IPTAY Collegiate Club. Begun in 1934 when Dr. Rupert H. Fike organized the first athletic support group, IPTAY has grown into the largest athletic support group in the nation. It stands for "I Pay Ten (Dollars) a Year," and while the figure of contributions has risen significantly, IPTAY has continued to be a powerful force on campus, developing an athletic scholarship endowment and rebuilding athletic facilities.

Although athletes are an important force on campus, most students say that with the large student population, they do not overpower campus life. "You always have classes with athletes and they are treated the same as students," one person commented. There are also a lot of opportunities for non-varsity sports, including intramurals and clubs. In general, most students say there is little division among students. There are cliques, most say, but everyone can find their own niche. One student describes Clemsonites as "aware of image, but not slaves to it." One also said that while the school is furthering diversity, there are still "too many white Southerners." Others disagree, saying that the most important factor on campus is that students are "Tiger fans and extremely proud to be at Clemson."

There is a significantly large Greek life on campus, which, according to campus publications, involves about 25 percent of the student body. "Rushing is time-consuming, but not really difficult or embarrassing," said one student. The Greek system includes business fraternities, community service sororities and large social fraternities and sororities. There are Greek houses on each end of campus, although technically sororities cannot have houses thanks to "a really ignorant state law that a house with more than four girls living in it is considered a brothel." As one student put it, "Greek life is hugely integral to Clemson life."

In sum, Clemson provides it students with an accommodating academic program, a nice campus and lots of school spirit. So much, in fact, that many students would agree that never graduating may not actually be so bad a fate. —*Jessamyn Blau*

FYI

If you're coming to Clemson, you'd better bring, "your tailgate gear."

What is the typical weekend schedule? "Go to parties, go watch football, and go to football parties."

If I could change one thing about Clemson I'd "renovate the dorms—they're a bit sub-par."

The three things that every student should do before graduating from Clemson are "have a night they do not fully remember, attend a Greek life function, and learn how to love independence."

Furman University

Address: 3300 Pointsett Highway; Greenville, SC 29613
Phone: 864-294-2034
E-mail address: admissions@furman.edu
Web site URL: www.engagefurman.com
Founded: 1826
Private or Public: private
Religious affiliation: none
Location: small city
Undergraduate enrollment: 2,654
Total enrollment: NA
Percent Male/Female: 46%/54%
Percent Minority: 10%
Percent African-American: 6%
Percent Asian: 1%
Percent Hispanic: 1%
Percent Native-American: 0%
Percent in-state/out of state: 32%/68%
Percent Pub HS: NA
Number of Applicants: 3,866
Percent Accepted: 58%
Percent Accepted who enroll: 33%
Entering: 739
Transfers: NA
Application Deadline: 15 Jan
Mean SAT: NA
Mean ACT: NA
Middle 50% SAT range: V 590-690, M 590-680
Middle 50% ACT range: 24-29
3 Most popular majors: political science, business administration, biology
Retention: 92%
Graduation rate: 74%
On-campus housing: 95%
Fraternities: 30%
Sororities: 35%
Library: 453,211 volumes
Tuition and Fees: $22,712
Room and Board: $6,264
Financial aid, first-year: 48%
Varsity or Club Athletes: 28%
Early Decision or Early Action Acceptance Rate: 77%

"If I could change one thing about Furman, I'd make Wednesday a day of rest," wished one student. Furman University, idyllically set in a suburb of Greenville, South Carolina, boasts a stunning campus as well as challenging academics, leading students to request such respites. Uniquely combining the traditions of the old South with interpersonal attention, Furman takes pride in its reputation as one of the South's prime sources of a liberal arts education.

What's a TA?

When asked about the prevalence of TAs at Furman, a sophomore commented, "TAs? I've never seen one." Personal interaction with professors is a key facet of the Furman education. Class size is extremely tiny by most standards—even some popular introductory courses may contain only 20 or 30 students. In the words of one sophomore, the small size creates a "more personal relationship with your professor." In the chemistry department, undergrads can get involved in actual research with professors after fulfilling a basic lab requirement; last year, a professor took a group of students to Los Alamos National Laboratories to help him conduct research.

With an education centered on direct professor-student communication, students praise their professors as "quirky, but good" and "genuinely good people to get to know." Students rave about the amiability and sense of humor of their professors as well. As one freshman noted, "my Latin teacher spent half an hour of class time explaining how the Berenstein bears are vehicles of a godless, fascist regime." The workload is commonly described as "substantial" or even "heavy" in some courses, especially in upper-level classes. One student complained, "The professors often forget that you have two other classes to study for besides theirs." Still, the sheer number of compliments outweighs any complaints about professors. "Professors are great about moving tests and papers to fit your schedule," one student commented.

The semester-system must have seemed too blasé for the creative minds at work in Furman's administration. In its place lies another unique feature of the Paladin education: the trimester system. Students take three courses in the spring and fall terms and two in the winter term, with each class meeting every weekday. A junior commented, "I personally enjoy the trimester system. It allows you to focus on the few classes you take. It's not any easier though! You're cramming a lot into a short duration of time, especially in the winter term." A common complaint concerns Furman's "spring break." The trimester system, also known as the 3-2-3 system, causes spring break to fall at the end of February, preventing many students from being able to plan vacations with family or students from other colleges. Still, overall acclaim for the system is high.

> **"Furman tries to make you as much at home as possible."**

Furman's liberal arts curriculum, called General Education Requirements, obligates students to expand their knowledge on a variety of topics including English, mathematics, arts, religion, culture, and the humanities. However, most students agree that the requirement is easy to fulfill since many of the courses can be fulfilled with AP or IB credits. The Cultural Life Program mandates that students attend eight culturally enriching events involving speakers or presentations on such varied subjects as religion and the ecosystem.

Students also praise the general quality of the courses. One student remarked, "I love the diversity of thought and the breadth of each course." Although most students agree that Furman's "well-balanced, sound academic program" stands out among many universities, most lament the grading situation and report that grade inflation is almost non-existent. Still, according to a sophomore, the challenging academics make "a degree from Furman mean so much to employers and graduate programs."

Life in the Park

"Beautiful, lush, photogenic, awe-inspiring, tall trees with thousands of leaves, beautiful fountains"—anyone would agree that Furman's campus is a masterpiece of natural artistry. Described as "gorgeous and always kept clean," Furman's "totally safe" central campus and its four academic buildings are flanked by fountains, a library, and a chapel. "Our chapel and library are across the way from each other with two gorgeous fountains in between. It's an amazing sight that adds to the already amazing beauty of our campus," said one student. During the fun of orientation week, freshmen go "fountain-hopping," frolicking in each of the seven fountains on campus. According to myth, those foolish few who choose not to participate will flunk out. Trees grace the buildings, including a new home for the business department, and woodlands surround Greenville and the campus. Students hang out by the lake, where they sunbathe or just relax, often gazing at the nearby picturesque bell tower, "the trademark of our school." Legend has it that lovers who kiss under the bell tower are destined to marry.

Although students admit that they live in the "Furman Bubble," off-campus activities are still enjoyed. After many renovations, the city of Greenville now boasts many restaurants and bars that are popular with students, who generally view the dining hall food as only "decent." Monterrey's is known for delicious Mexican food, the Peddler is highly praised for its overall excellence, and the Rice Bowl is also greatly acclaimed. Coffee Underground remains a popular place to hang out and talk over a cup of joe.

Despite any lingering popularity, off-campus housing has been abandoned. Starting with the class of 2004, on-campus living was required of every student. Freshmen and sophomores occupy the on-campus dorms, and juniors and seniors have the privilege of living in Furman's on-campus apartments, which are "amazing in space and cleanliness." All dorms were once single-sex, however, now there are five co-ed dormitories. Each dorm hall has its own theme, but students have the opportunity to live in special themed housing geared toward learning a foreign language by immersion.

Southern Comfort

"There's more pressure to go to church than to drink here. Non-drinkers aren't out of the loop." On Furman's officially dry campus, wild nights filled with large, liquor-filled parties are virtually unknown.

Parties generally move around wherever particular frats rent space or take place at the frat houses themselves off-campus. Furman has seven fraternities and six sororities, comprised of around 30 percent of the student body, one student estimated. Frat rushes are monitored closely under a no-hazing rule that allows them to be "more social and less stressful."

The non-Greek side of Furman offers many social alternatives. The university puts on several campus-wide events a year, including concerts hosting such artists as the Dave Matthews Band and Blues Traveler, and themed dances are also extremely common. Recent themes included a "Dukes of Hazzard" party, and a '70s party. The college throws a major food, game, and music event a few times a year called "Thursday Alive," designed to bring the student body together. A food court in the student center known as "Paladen" is a popular place to munch and chat. Furman's small size makes it almost impossible not to meet a group of friends. As one freshman put it, "even antisocial students meet people. You can't avoid it." Students most often hang out on campus because Furman is "pretty self-sufficient and almost entirely enclosed."

Drugs are used very rarely. In the words of a freshman, "the only drugs on campus are nicotine and alcohol." Also absent is the dating scene, along with sex in general. One student estimated that the number of hook-ups compared to the number of dates was relatively even. A junior attests that "no one on Furman's campus dates, but everyone seems to get engaged by graduation." Overall, however, there is "pretty widespread social satisfaction."

"Quasi-Diversity"?

As one student attested, Furman is "geographically diverse, ethnically quasi-diverse, and religiously homogeneous." With most students adhering to some form of Christianity in this formerly Baptist-affiliated college, "Evangelist Christian" remains a strong stereotype. Most students are middle-class, but "the wealthy kids are easier to spot." Still, "on the whole, people tend to mix pretty well."

Most students thrive in the realm of extracurricular activities, especially in volunteer jobs. CESC, the Collegiate Educational Service Corps, is the umbrella organization responsible for 70 different volunteer groups. Although most people are a part of CESC in one way or another, those not involved often play a role in MayDay PlayDay, a fair held for the whole community. Other activities draw students of many diverse interests. One group dedicates itself to Western European sword fighting, "where you get to swing around PVC piping at each other."

Sports are not particularly popular at this small university, and many lament the absence of a large football program. Still, Furman's soccer program is top-notch, enthusiasm for major sports is relatively high, and intramural sports such as flag football, soccer, and softball are widely enjoyed.

One undergrad summed up Furman for his classmates when he said, "the campus is gorgeous, the people are great, and I've made awesome friends here." *—Robert James*

FYI

If you come to Furman University, you'd better bring "a Bible approved by one of the major Protestant denominations."

What is the typical weekend schedule? "Wake up at noon, eat, work until sunset, and party until dawn."

If I could change one thing about Furman University, I'd "lighten up religious intolerance."

Three things every student at Furman University should do before graduating are "go fountain hopping, throw someone in the lake on their birthday," and "stay up all night fueled on No-Doz and coffee."

University of South Carolina

Address: Colombia, SC 29208
Phone: 803-777-7700
E-mail address: admissions-ugrad@sc.edu
Web site URL: www.sc.edu
Founded: 1801
Private or Public: public
Religious affiliation: none
Location: small city
Undergraduate enrollment: 16,567
Total enrollment: NA
Percent Male/Female: 46%/54%
Percent Minority: 23%
Percent African-American: 17%
Percent Asian: 3%
Percent Hispanic: 1%
Percent Native-American: 0%
Percent in-state/out of state: 87%/13%
Percent Pub HS: NA
Number of Applicants: 12,016
Percent Accepted: 70%
Percent Accepted who enroll: 37%
Entering: 3,561
Transfers: NA
Application Deadline: 15 Feb
Mean SAT: NA
Mean ACT: NA
Middle 50% SAT range: V 500-610, M 510-620
Middle 50% ACT range: 21-26
3 Most popular majors: experimental psychology, business adminstration, marketing
Retention: 82%
Graduation rate: 60%
On-campus housing: 47%
Fraternities: 17%
Sororities: 17%
Library: 3,333,764 volumes
Tuition and Fees: $4,984 in; $13,104 out
Room and Board: $5,064
Financial aid, first-year: 43%
Varsity or Club Athletes: 6%
Early Decision or Early Action Acceptance Rate: NA

If you were asked to find a cocky student at the University of South Carolina, you'd be hard-pressed to do so. You would, however, have no trouble finding "Cocky," the big red mascot that leads the South Carolina Gamecocks in spirit at the football games. Football is, without a doubt, the most popular sport on campus, attracting a stadium full of fans for each game. But USC is not a university that's just about football. "Oh no," one senior promised, "there's so much more to this splendid university." With its campus set in the heart of Columbia, South Carolina, the University of South Carolina provides its students with nearly everything one could ask from a large university. These benefits include a wide range of impressive academic programs, a well-deserved reputation as a party school, the perks of living in a city while still maintaining a quintessential campus atmosphere, a vast array of extracurricular activities, and, of course, a passionate student body that will forever be loyal to the Gamecock. It's no wonder that students at USC love their school.

Academics 101

With 17 different colleges at their fingertips, each offering a variety of programs of study, students seem pleased with the variety of academic opportunities. "I feel challenged, yet still comfortable and confident in my work," said one sophomore. Along with the traditional majors offered by the College of Liberal Arts and the College of Science and Mathematics, USC also gives students the opportunity to pursue more career-orientated endeavors in schools such as the College of Education, College of Hospitality, Retail, and Sports Administration, and the Moore School of Business. "Business is probably the best program here," remarked one student, and USC's undergraduate international business program has consistently been named the best in the country in recent years. Depending on their majors, students at South Carolina can for the most part choose how rigorous their schedules will be. One student studying public relations explained, "The course load is pretty manageable," while a finance student disagreed, claiming "I have yet to have an easy class." In addition to business, pharmacy and chemistry are considered hard, while education is thought to be relatively painless.

Although academic requirements vary from college to college, every USC student must fulfill general education requirements, including one full year of English, basic science, social sciences, and humanities. Close to 80 percent of freshmen elect to enroll in University 101, South Carolina's unique class that orients freshmen to college life, although this class is not a requirement. The class is designed to help freshmen learn to make the most of the resources at USC and involves research projects on current events, workshops on how to develop better study habits, and tours of the campus—all of which ease the transition from high school to college.

Though sections of University 101 have only about 25 students, class size for other courses ranges "anywhere from 20 to 300 people," according to one sophomore. Most classes are taught by professors, while TAs run labs and discussion groups that are "by and large really helpful" for larger lecture classes. While most introductory classes tend to be large lectures with hundreds of students, students seem happy with the quality of instruction. The professors include several famous stand-outs, like Don Fowler, the former chairman of the Democratic National Committee, and students report that their professors are generally enthusiastic, accessible, and helpful.

Having Fun, Gamecock Style

While USC has a reputation as a "party school," socially, the campus is diverse enough to allow every kind of student to have a great time. The large Greek community and prevalent bar scene are balanced out by on-campus social events and off-campus outdoor activities, creating an environment where students say there is always something to do. One sophomore explained, "The social options keep me busy . . . I don't think anyone's ever bored." Five Points, a downtown bar and restaurant district within walking distance of campus, is generally considered the "biggest hangout spot." Thursday nights are "college nights" at Five Points.

With 12 sororities and 16 fraternities, Greek life plays a huge part in the social scene. Though a lot of on-campus partying revolves around frat parties and Greek "mixers," one student said, "There is no pressure to rush, and you can make just as many friends not being in [a fraternity or sorority]." Despite the prominent party scene, USC administration does attempt to regulate drinking. Kegs must be registered and approved for entrance onto campus, and SLED officers, undercover cops who attempt to catch underage drinkers, are fairly strict. However, this does not seem to pose much of a threat, because although drug use is not prevalent at USC, most students do drink. One student pointed out that non-drinkers do not feel excluded, "but that would be hard to prove since I don't know too many non-drinkers."

Outside of drinking, USCers have plenty of social alternatives. Russell House, the student center, sponsors on-campus activities such as the Battle of the Bands and frequently screens movies on the weekends. Additionally, many South Carolina students take advantage of the great outdoors surrounding them. On weekends, students head to Charleston to go to the beach, camp in the mountains in Virginia, or take advantage of the yearlong warm weather in other ways by playing Frisbee or hiking.

The dating scene at South Carolina is a blend of steady relationships and random hook-ups, because, as one junior explained, "going on dates just doesn't happen that much." One happy male raved, "there are a great many good-looking people here; I'm very pleased about that!" Indeed, with an approximately 55 to 45 female-to-male ratio, the men do have a larger pool to choose from. Since most students are from within the state, some continue to hang out with their high school friends, although many make new friends in their dorms or through extracurriculars. Most students seem to agree that "it's very easy to meet people here." In spite of the majority of the student body—approximately 67 percent—originating from the South, one student observed, "there are people from all over here, even from other countries." South Carolina, in fact, houses students from over 100 countries and is diverse not only in terms of its students' geographic origin but also in terms of wealth and ethnicity.

Home Sweet Home

Most students tend to live on campus, although a variety of living options are available in Columbia. On the whole, "dorms are so-so," said one freshman. For the most part, freshmen live on campus in Freshman Centers, dormitories equipped with double rooms, common bathrooms, and common rooms to promote a social atmosphere. Students can choose between single sex and co-ed dorms, though co-ed dorms still separate men and women into different entryways of the building. Most dorms have policies that restrict visiting hours between males and females, although one male student reported having "snuck girls into the room a couple of times." One student described the co-ed Towers complex, where many freshmen live, as "horrible," although other buildings for freshmen, like Bates, are "on the whole, pretty nice."

"The biggest campus-wide tradition would have to be tailgating for football. Enough said."

After freshman year, those who continue to reside on campus typically live in apartment-style buildings. Every dormitory is air-conditioned, a major perk during the intense heat of the South Carolinian spring and fall. Off-campus living offers apartments and houses. Students in the Greek system now have the option to live in the "Greek Village," a complex of more than a dozen multi-million-dollar fraternity and sorority houses located just outside of campus, which was recently constructed. Whatever students choose, off-campus living is "at its farthest about 10 minutes away" from campus, and "isn't too expensive." Many students have cars to get from off-campus houses to class, creating one of the most frustrating problems on campus: parking. Finding parking is unanimously cited as the worst part about living off campus, but the perks of being able to drive seem to outweigh the troubles of parking.

Since the campus is located in the city center, "it is in walking distance to just about anything" and "people frequently go into town to shop, see movies, or eat." Favorite off-campus eateries include El Burrito and Courthouse Coffee. However, feelings about on-campus dining halls are mixed. While some students maintain that the food is quite tasty, others complain: "Dining on campus is rather horrible; the food runs right through you." Unfortunately for those dissatisfied, students living on campus are required to purchase a meal plan, which allows them to eat at a variety of on-campus locations such as Gibbs Court—which calls itself a Tuscan-style bistro—or the Grand Marketplace. The student center also houses a Chic-Fil-A, Taco Bell, and Pizza Hut. If nothing else, students agree that USC has an assortment of dining options.

Campus: A True Southern Belle

Despite parking problems, USC students love their campus and the surrounding city. "It's certainly a beautiful campus, but really too spread out," lamented one senior. Built into a hill in the heart of Columbia, the architecture is a mix between old-fashioned and modern. The Horseshoe—the oldest part of the University and the most popular hangout on campus—is a long, open, grassy quad surrounded by many of the school's most beautiful buildings, some of which pre-date the Civil War. Currently much of the campus is under construction as the university renovates its older facilities and builds new ones.

Tailgating, and Other Extracurriculars

Students at the University of South Carolina are generally active both on campus and in the community. According to one student, "about half the students work either on campus or in downtown Columbia." Intramural and club sports are also very popular among students. "The sport facilities and gyms are all pretty nice," one student noted, and a new physical fitness center was erected not too long ago. At a school as big as USC, students can find an organization to meet almost any interest, from writing for the daily newspaper, *The*

Gamecock, to working for WUSC, the campus radio station; from volunteering to tutor with Carolina for Kids or building houses with Habitat for Humanity, to joining a political organization like the College Republicans or the College Dems. Most of the residence halls additionally have student governments set up, and, of course, being active in the Greek system is always a popular pastime.

However, it is tailgating that is the one activity in which almost every student participates. The Williams-Brice Stadium fills to capacity every game as fans pour in to cheer on their beloved Gamecocks at the football game, which is by far the most popular sport on campus (although baseball and basketball are close seconds). "Football is the *best* part of USC!" exclaimed one student. "We tailgate for five hours before the game starts; school spirit is a must!" Another student agreed, "the biggest campus-wide tradition would have to be tailgating for football; enough said."

After spending several hours eating and drinking under the brilliant Carolina sun before kickoff, it's no wonder that so many students cite football games as their favorite part of USC. The enthusiasm at the Williams-Brice Stadium is indicative of the general feeling at the University of South Carolina, where students truly love their school. With a vast array of academic and extracurricular options to choose from, students at USC have the opportunity to make exactly what they want of their four years in Columbia. *—Katherine Kirby Smith*

FYI

If you come to USC, you'd better bring "a good pair of tennis shoes because the campus is so spread out, your John Deere hat, and a cooler for tailgating, of course."

The typical weekend schedule consists of "Eat, party, bar, party, pass out, do it again. Or, go somewhere in nature and do the complete opposite!"

If I could change one thing about USC, I'd "change the lack of parking."

Three things every student at USC should do before graduating are "go to Five Points, road trip up to football away games, and run through the campus naked."

Wofford College

Address: 429 North Church Street; Spartanburg, SC 29303-3663
Phone: 864-597-4130
E-mail address: admissions@wofford.edu
Web site URL: www.wofford.edu
Founded: 1854
Private or Public: private
Religious affiliation: Methodist
Location: small city
Undergraduate enrollment: 1,085
Total enrollment: 1,107
Percent Male/Female: 50%/50%
Percent Minority: 11%
Percent African-American: 8%
Percent Asian: 2%
Percent Hispanic: 1%
Percent Native-American: 0%
Percent in-state/out of state: 66%/34%
Percent Pub HS: NA
Number of Applicants: 1,349
Percent Accepted: 78%
Percent Accepted who enroll: 31%
Entering: 297
Transfers: 16
Application Deadline: 1 Feb
Mean SAT: 1212
Mean ACT: 25
Middle 50% SAT range: V 550-660, M 580-670
Middle 50% ACT range: 22-27
3 Most popular majors: business economics, biology, political science
Retention: 88%
Graduation rate: 75%
On-campus housing: 88%
Fraternities: 54%
Sororities: 61%
Library: 209,804 volumes
Tuition and Fees: $20,610
Room and Board: $6,100
Financial aid, first-year: 55%
Varsity or Club Athletes: 48%
Early Decision or Early Action Acceptance Rate: NA

When the Reverend Benjamin Wofford of Spartanburg, South Carolina, passed away, he left money to found a college "for literary, classical and scientific education." One hundred and fifty years later, Wofford College still stands as a bastion of solid education in an environment designed to nurture personal growth and experience.

A Select Education

Founded in 1845 and still affiliated with the United Methodist Church, Wofford has remained small by choice. The administration reportedly has no plans to expand enrollment but instead plans to concentrate on providing a select group of students with a strong education in the humanities, arts, and sciences. Professors are accessible and maintain an "open-door policy," according to students. Undergrads are required to take courses in the humanities, English, fine arts, foreign language, science, history, philosophy, math, physical education, and religion. These general education requirements are meant to ensure that by the end of their first two years, students have taken classes they normally would not have considered. Students are also required to complete four interim projects. The month of January is Interim, when students can research, travel, take an internship, or work on an independent project. Among the most popular majors at Wofford are biology, business, chemistry, English, and history. The science department is reported to be particularly strong, with "most students getting into their first or second choice of medical schools," according to one undergrad. Students also recommend the philosophy and zoology introductory courses.

Wofford's active student body puts their full support behind their impressive athletics program. As part of the deal, Wofford built a brand-new athletic complex, the Richardson Physical Activities Building, which opened in the summer of 1995. Wofford basketball, football, and soccer games already draw crowds, especially when the Terriers play rivals Citadel or Presbyterian College. "Student interest tends to drop off a bit when one of the teams is not performing well," one student said, "but overall, we are very proud of our sports teams."

Using New Technology

The F. W. Olin Building is one of Wofford's most prized possessions. Designed as a model for integrating technology in teaching the liberal arts, this state-of-the-art academic building houses high-tech audiovisual equipment, ultramodern language labs, computer science facilities (including the computer center for the school's network), and classrooms. Plans for a new science building are also in the works. "The older buildings on campus are always kept in good shape," one student said.

Students seem content with Wofford's living conditions, and few of them choose to live off campus. A new all-female dorm gets good reviews for its two-room suites, and Dupree is considered one of the best and most social dorms for upperclassmen. Many students consider Marsh dormitory to be Wofford's least popular: it houses first-year male students, and the lack of privacy (especially in the huge bathrooms) is the biggest complaint. "The guys who live there get rowdy a lot and the place usually ends up getting trashed after a while," one student said. The fraternity houses are not residential.

Social Life

The Greek system is strong at Wofford, although kegs are banned from campus. Students say they usually have no problem finding parties off campus if there isn't anything happening on fraternity row. "There is some pressure to join a frat, but that's only because rush period starts three weeks into the fall semester," one student said. Pressure to rush is reportedly heavier among Wofford men than women.

"No one here is just a number."

Wofford students tend to describe their classmates as "interesting and colorful." Although the majority of Wofford students are from South Carolina, a large percentage come from other southeastern states. Before the school went coed, its name brought to mind the image of the "Wofford Man," which one student said was a "cultured, well-liked individual—a Southern gentleman." Today Wofford students preserve their traditions, but they point out that the school now "prides itself on progressive thinking." Not too progressive, however: Wofford students and administrators alike tend to be politically conservative, although one undergrad said the administration is "liberal enough to let the students do what they want." "Clashes at Wofford don't last very long. There isn't a lot of activism here," one senior reported. Life at Wofford is best described as "mellow"; life moves a bit slower than in big cities, and the atmosphere on campus is relaxed. "Wofford students are not afraid to look a campus visitor in the eye and say hello," one student said. "The school is small enough so that you know almost everyone. No one here is just a number." One student reported that it is not unusual for undergrads to "give the president of the college a high-five as he walks by."

Living in the South

The city of Spartanburg, which students describe as a "blue-collar town," offers a reasonable variety of restaurants and entertainment at low prices. It is a place where you can "find a K-mart very easily, but not a Banana Republic," one student said. The city is no bustling metropolis, but one student predicted that a new BMW manufacturing plant has the potential to "turn Spartanburg into another Raleigh."

According to undergrads, Wofford offers a friendly southern environment and a solid education, particularly for those considering a career in law, medicine, or the ministry. "Wofford transcends the classroom in many ways," one student said. "It does have the potential to be too personal due to its atmosphere and size, but I'd have to say that the positive effects outweigh the negative ones." Another student added, "If you want an outstanding overall college experience, come to Wofford, but if you want to spend four years with your nose buried in a textbook, don't." —*Jeff Kaplow and Staff*

FYI

If you're coming to Wofford, you'd better bring, "your Southern hospitality."

What is the typical weekend schedule? "Frat parties and chill hang out time, interspersed with work time, too."

If I could change one thing about Wofford, I'd "make Spartanburg a much hipper, more hopping town."

Three things every student should do before graduating from Wofford are "go to a frat party, attend a basketball game against Citadel, and take a road trip to the beach."

South Dakota

University of South Dakota

Address: 414 East Clark Street; Vermillion, SD 57069
Phone: 605-677-5434
E-mail address: admiss@usd.edu
Web site URL: www.usd.edu
Founded: 1862
Private or Public: public
Religious affiliation: none
Location: rural
Undergraduate enrollment: 5,769
Total enrollment: NA
Percent Male/Female: 39%/61%
Percent Minority: 6%
Percent African-American: 1%
Percent Asian: 1%
Percent Hispanic: 1%
Percent Native-American: 2%
Percent in-state/out of state: 77%/23%
Percent Pub HS: NA
Number of Applicants: 2,539
Percent Accepted: 86%
Percent Accepted who enroll: NA
Entering: 1,126
Transfers: 620
Application Deadline: rolling
Mean SAT: NA
Mean ACT: NA
Middle 50% SAT range: V 450-630, M 450-610
Middle 50% ACT range: 19-25
3 Most popular majors: business marketing, education, health sciences
Retention: 77%
Graduation rate: 48%
On-campus housing: 19%
Fraternities: 20%
Sororities: 12%
Library: 335,757 volumes
Tuition and Fees: $4,205 in; $8,917 out
Room and Board: $3,504
Financial aid, first-year: 59%
Varsity or Club Athletes: 26%
Early Decision or Early Action Acceptance Rate: NA

One might say that the University of South Dakota has a split personality: Monday through Friday the college whirls and bustles, while over the weekend it seems like a ghost town that dawdles and yawns. During the week the college offers exotic extracurricular activities, small classes led by attentive professors, and a thriving Greek scene. But on the weekends, you will find that most of the students have either gone home, or to nearby Sioux Falls, South Dakota, and Sioux City, Iowa.

Premeds Study Together

Most students at USD are enrolled in the College of Arts and Sciences, which features traditional majors, including chemistry, mathematics, and English. Core requirements here usually account for about 10 of the courses that the students take. Among the requirements are at least one course in the humanities, one in the social sciences, one in math or computer science, and one in health and wellness. Students identified the biology department of the College of Arts and Sciences as particularly strong. Many of those who major in biology go on to med school at the University of South Dakota. According to several students, the pre-meds are grade-conscious, but not deathly competitive; in spite of their desire to succeed, said one student, most of "the pre-meds still study together."

Undergrads at the university may enroll in other colleges, including the School of Business, the School of Education, and the College of Fine Arts. Students cited the nationally-accredited School of Business as especially good, and many involved in campus media find advisors in the Mass Communications department of the College of Fine Arts.

USD offers few colossal-sized classes. Even the lectures are tiny by state-school standards. The largest lectures might enroll about 250 students, but lectures average about 100. By junior year, classes range from about 20 to 30 students. Lectures and seminars alike are usually led by professors; TAs are a rare sight at the university. "Just about all my classes have been taught by professors," said one student, "and just about all my professors have known my name." Students work reasonably hard at USD, with many claiming to spend upward of 20 hours a week on their studies, but conceded that it is possible to get by with as little as six. The business, mathematics, and education majors were cited as burdening their students with much work.

Weekday Fun, Weekend Boredom?

Social opportunities abound Mondays through Thursdays. On Tuesdays, a local movie theater (one of two in Vermillion) offers discount movie night. Thursdays, the student association brings in a comedian to perform at Charlie's After Dark, an on-campus club. Famous speakers also appear during the week; some speakers have included Larry King and Tom Brokaw. Promised one student, "There's a lot going on, if you pay attention to the posters." There are also plays put on through the theater department, which offers cheaper tickets to students, and several art galleries both on campus and downtown.

Thursday evenings also feature frat parties, widely attended in part because the campus is dry. You cannot miss the Greek presence on campus. According to one independent student, people in frats and sororities are often invited to more parties and make more friends. The benefits of being in one of them are not just social; one independent student lamented that students in Greek organizations seemed to have more leadership opportunities, as they have an identity and a network in campus organizations. However, not every independent student complained about the Greek scene; one student commented that she never felt at all hindered by being independent. While Greeks may have an edge in terms of leadership opportunities and social connections, other networks like residential life, student government, and activities run through the Student Activities Center are equally open to all students.

"Just about all my professors have known my name."

Vermillion, according to students, has little to offer in way of fun. While there are a few bowling alleys, two movie theaters, and fast-food restaurants, most students see Vermillion as little more than a place to live, shop, and drink. There are a fair number of bars, and during Dakota Days, the annual homecoming game, which is often against South Dakota State, they may open as early as 6:30 A.M. Housing is plentiful, although students must stay on campus for at least two years before they can move into an apartment off campus. There are only a few stores in town, so finding what you want can be difficult. Complained one student, "Vermillion doesn't even have a Wal-Mart nearby," although another claimed that there was one 25 miles away in Yankton, which "to a South Dakotan is 'nearby,'" in part due to South Dakota's higher speed limit of 75 miles per hour on the highway.

And so on the weekends, students leave campus. Many go home to work and earn money for college, even if home is many hours away. "To people here, every city in South Dakota is close," explained one student. But, many also go to Sioux Falls, Sioux City, or even Minneapolis, to find the kind of fun that most college students take for granted: plays, rocks concerts, and exotic restaurants, to name a few. This weekly exodus is not a very widely advertised fact; said one a USDer, "I was really surprised to see how quiet it is here on the weekends." Other students, however, say that despite the number of students who leave campus on the weekends, "if one is creative, it really isn't that hard to find something fun to do" and can find "many activities to fill the weekends."

Getting Involved

Extracurricular opportunities for students abound at USD. Students can work at the *Volante*, the weekly paper founded by *USA Today* creator Al Neuharth, and

KAOR, an alternative radio station that broadcasts 24 hours a day. Those who choose to major in mass communications can also work for the campus television station, KYOT, Monday through Friday. News broadcasts are watched in homes and dorm rooms all around Vermillion. Cherry Street Promotions, a student-run advertising agency, handles marketing for campus and local businesses.

The Coyote (pronounced "Cah-yoat" here) Student Center is a popular hangout for students during the day, and also houses the Program Council, an umbrella organization of student agencies, and a student film society that shows free films on campus once a week. Community service opportunities abound in Vermillion, and many students are very proud of how much their time can be used to aid those in the surrounding areas. In fact, there are so many service options at USD that an umbrella organization called SERVE (Students Enriching the Vermillion Environment) broke away from the Program Council, and now includes programs like Adopt-a-grandparent, Big Pal/Little Pal, Into the Streets, Vermillion Heroes, and Adopt-a-school.

For the more athletically inclined, USD offers a vibrant intramural program. Students form their own teams; games are played once or twice a week. Among the more popular intramural sports are flag football, softball, and volleyball.

The dorms at USD receive praise from many students. Four of the dorms on the north side of campus, Beede, Mickelson, Olson, and Richardson, are attached to one another, and the complex has its own dining facility. The dorms on the south side, including Julian, are reputed to be more party-oriented. Students can also request to live on a quiet floor, where loud music and socialization are strictly forbidden, or a single-sex, smoke-free, or substance-free floor. Most rooms are one-room doubles, with the occasional quad and triple. Rooms are not spacious, but certainly adequate and are generally in good repair. Still, many students choose to move off campus as soon as they are allowed, in large part due to the dry-campus policy and in order to have kitchens.

Dining hall facilities were recently privatized, and one student swears the food has vastly improved as a result. Another student appreciated the dining halls' attempts to make food healthier and less greasy, but wished for greater variety in the dishes offered. Off-campus options include The Silver Dollar for steak and Chae's Chinese food.

Leaning Left

Stepping onto the University of South Dakota's three-square-block campus is a bit like dropping down the rabbit hole; the Vermillion university is not your typical state school. The classes are small. The professors get to know you personally. There is no alcohol on campus. And on the weekends, the university is desolate. But if taken full advantage of, the academic and extracurricular opportunities just might be to one's liking. *—William Chen and Staff*

FYI

If you come to the University of South Dakota, you'd better bring "a ridiculously insulated winter coat."

What is the typical weekend schedule? Study, sleep and party.

If I could change one thing about the University of South Dakota, I'd "eliminate the negative stereotypes of on-campus weekends—they are really quite fun."

Three things that every student should do before graduating from the University of South Dakota are "visit a reservation, find the river and walk the trails, and stay on-campus at least one weekend and discover how many things there are to do."

Tennessee

Rhodes College

Address: 2000 North Parkway; Memphis, TN 38112
Phone: 800-844-5969
E-mail address: adminfo@rhodes.edu
Web site URL: www.rhodes.edu
Founded: 1848
Private or Public: private
Religious affiliation: Presbyterian
Location: urban
Undergraduate enrollment: 1,541
Total enrollment: 1,536
Percent Male/Female: 44%/56%
Percent Minority: 10%
Percent African-American: 4%
Percent Asian: 3%
Percent Hispanic: 1%
Percent Native-American: 0%
Percent in-state/out of state: 29%/71%
Percent Pub HS: 63%
Number of Applicants: 2,345
Percent Accepted: 70%
Percent Accepted who enroll: 27%
Entering: 442
Transfers: 14
Application Deadline: 1 Feb
Mean SAT: NA
Mean ACT: NA
Middle 50% SAT range: V 610-710, M 600-690
Middle 50% ACT range: 26-30
3 Most popular majors: social sciences, biology, English
Retention: 89%
Graduation rate: 73%
On-campus housing: 75%
Fraternities: 51%
Sororities: 58%
Library: 270,761 volumes
Tuition and Fees: $22,938
Room and Board: $6,382
Financial aid, first-year: 44%
Varsity or Club Athletes: 43%
Early Decision or Early Action Acceptance Rate: 83%

Quietly nestled among trees and Gothic stone buildings, Rhodes College is home to a small, close-knit community of students and faculty. Ask any Rhodes student what they like (or dislike) most, and you'll likely hear, "the Rhodes community." Set in a small residential section of Memphis, Tennessee, students live and learn with a unique group of students and professors.

Extra Small, Extra Tight

Rhodes has all of the benefits one would expect from a small, liberal-arts school: a small student body, close interaction with professors, and intimate class sizes. However, what many students would hail as Rhodes's greatest strength, others would say is Rhodes's greatest weakness. One sophomore noted, "most of the time, it's great seeing the same people over and over again, then again, sometimes it's not." When students come to Rhodes, they are really surprised at just how tight-knit the community is. It is not out of the ordinary for a professor to invite his or her students over for dinner at their home, or even give their home telephone number out to their students. The students become a sort of family away from home over the years. However, there are some drawbacks to the college's size: just like high school, gossip spreads quickly through the grapevine, and like a small town, everyone knows what everyone else is doing. Despite these drawbacks, many students said that if they had to do it all over again, they would choose Rhodes.

Most classes have less than thirty students, and it is common to find upper-level classes with fewer than ten students. Of course, there are large lecture classes, too. However, these are mostly introductory courses, especially those in the sciences. Students stress that these large lecture classes are rare, and often do not have more than one hundred students in the course. "The accessibility to professors is incredible," said one freshman. Indeed, students find that their professors make themselves available for their students and are generally willing to help in any way they can. "The conversations I've had with my professors over meals have been some of my most memorable experiences at Rhodes," recalled one senior. The close contact with professors also means that there is little opportunity to hide in classes, and participation is essential. "I've found that I've really grown into someone who can defend my ideas and participate in a lively dialogue about anything from Shakespeare to religion," said one junior.

Like many liberal arts colleges, Rhodes has a core curriculum, constructed in such a way that students are exposed to the Humanities, Social Sciences, Natural Sciences, Mathematics, and the Fine Arts. Rhodes has religious ties with the Presbyterian Church, but many say that the religious atmosphere is not divisive. However, there is a course requirement in religion; students can either elect to take a course in Search or Life. Search is primarily concerned with the integration of history and religion and Life focuses on individual religious traditions, examining sacred literature and traditions. Another key aspect of life at Rhodes is the Honor System. Even before students set foot on campus, they become aware of how seriously the College takes the Honor System. In fact, it is the only campus tradition that requires 100 percent participation. An all-student Honor Council maintains the Honor System.

"I've found that I've really grown into someone who can defend my ideas and participate in a lively dialogue about anything from Shakespeare to religion."

Most departments at Rhodes are well regarded, especially the Biology and English departments. "One thing I've found is that the small size of the school somewhat limits my course selection," noted one sophomore. To supplement its course offerings, Rhodes offers cross-registration programs with Washington University in St. Louis and students can take study abroad courses with other colleges and universities.

"Walking in Memphis"

Perhaps one of Rhodes's greatest assets is the fact that it is located in Memphis, Tennessee, the 15th largest city in the country, and a vibrant cultural and entertainment center. The city's Beale Street is a haven for blues music. The renowned musical atmosphere—noted by Marc Cohn's "Walking in Memphis" and Bob Dylan's "Stuck Inside of Mobile with the Memphis Blues Again"—attracts students to clubs and restaurants. One freshman said, "I was so surprised that there was so much in Memphis!" Every weekend, you can find Rhodes students along the streets of Memphis, enjoying the sites and sounds. "Memphis in May," three days of outdoor concerts, is a popular event.

Although Memphis boasts a lot of off-campus activities, there is certainly more than enough to keep one occupied on campus. The Greek scene is extremely popular, setting the social scene on campus. Over half of the student body belongs to a fraternity or a sorority. One junior said, "The Greek scene is great here even though it's a small college." Students commented that those who aren't interested in joining a frat or sorority don't feel excluded on campus. All the parties are open, but Greek life tends to dominate the social atmosphere. Rush for the fraternities and sororities envelope freshmen as soon as they arrive on campus, and new members are tapped by the end of the first week of classes. Greek ties are significant but students say they do not overcome one's connections to the college as a whole.

Giving Back

Beyond Greek life, social opportunities on campus can be lacking. "Sports aren't particularly big here," noted one senior. Students commented that community service plays a large role in the life of the College. "Being in a large city like Memphis provides for a lot of community outreach opportunities," said a Rhodes sophomore. Whether working at soup kitchens, Habitat for Humanity, or volunteering at St. Jude's Children's Hospital, Rhodes students can always be found giving back to the community. Most of these community service groups are encompassed within the Kinney Volunteer Program, which includes all kinds of options for community service. The sense of community at Rhodes does not stop at its gates but includes the city of Memphis as well.

Rooming at Rhodes

Residential life at Rhodes is yet another area of student life that is community-based. Suites are common in the freshmen dorms and most dorms have only fifty residents each, so students end up knowing a whole dorm full of people. All freshmen and sophomores are required to live on campus, and many upperclassmen do so as well, causing a housing crunch in recent years.

With encouragement from Rhodes's President, the College is aiming to create a more diverse student body and a greater appreciation for multiculturalism. The Rhodes Townhouse Selection Committee and the Residence Life Office recently developed an opportunity for six students to live with one another and create a project. Diverse groups of six students were invited to apply for an opportunity to work on a series of diversity initiatives focused on the residential community. These initiatives involved townhouse programming, consulting with student organizations and campus offices about their programs, developing methods by which communities discuss issues, or other original ideas from the townhouse members.

On-campus meal opportunities are limited to the cafeteria, affectionately titled "the Rat." Students also have the choice of dining at the "Lynx Lair," a fast-food-style alternative to the Rat. Commenting on the food, a freshman said, "The food isn't fabulous, but it's better than starving."

From small classes that facilitate involved class discussions to life-changing a kickin' Greek scene, Rhodes College is the perfect place to be if you are looking for the best of both worlds: a top-notch liberal arts college located in a vibrant, big city. Students at Rhodes are close-knit and many said they would choose Rhodes again. "The combination of small class sizes with superb professors as well as being located in a large city like Memphis is the best," said one senior. "Rhodes is my home away from home. I knew I had made the right decision my first day on campus," said one freshman. *—Scott Woods*

FYI

If you come to Rhodes, you better bring a "desire for a small school atmosphere."

What is the typical weekend schedule? "On Friday watch a basketball game, then go to a frat party or head downtown to Beale St. On Saturday, community service during the day, then party that night. Sundays are for church, homework, and intramural games."

If I could change one thing about Rhodes, I would "make it slightly bigger."

Three things every student at Rhodes should do before graduating are, "spend a night experiencing Beale St., take a class with Professor Arce, and go to Memphis in May at least once."

University of Tennessee

Address: 800 Andy Holt Tower; Knoxville, TN 37996
Phone: 865-974-2184
E-mail address: admissions@tennessee.edu
Web site URL: www.tennessee.edu
Founded: 1794
Private or Public: public
Religious affiliation: none
Location: urban
Undergraduate enrollment: 19,956
Total enrollment: NA
Percent Male/Female: 49%/51%
Percent Minority: 12%
Percent African-American: 7%
Percent Asian: 3%
Percent Hispanic: 1%
Percent Native-American: 0%
Percent in-state/out of state: 86%/14%
Percent Pub HS: NA
Number of Applicants: 9,724
Percent Accepted: 58%
Percent Accepted who enroll: 60%
Entering: 3,682
Transfers: 1,372
Application Deadline: 15 Jan
Mean SAT: NA
Mean ACT: NA
Middle 50% SAT range: V 500-600, M 500-610
Middle 50% ACT range: 21-26
3 Most popular majors: psychology, English, accounting
Retention: 77%
Graduation rate: 58%
On-campus housing: 32%
Fraternities: 15%
Sororities: 20%
Library: 9,773,775 volumes
Tuition and Fees: $4,450 in; $13,532 out
Room and Board: $4,580
Financial aid, first-year: 38%
Varsity or Club Athletes: 6%
Early Decision or Early Action Acceptance Rate: NA

True to the words of one sophomore, "Football owns UT." Attending a football game in Neyland Stadium will convince any doubters—a sea of over 100,000 cheering fans don their bright orange jerseys and produce deafening roars of approval at the sight of their beloved Volunteers. At a school of over 26,000 undergraduates, UT's large-scale features seem to dominate more than just the football stadium. However, in conjunction with a close-knit Southern tradition, UT often succeeds in shrinking down some potentially huge aspects of student life into something more manageable and comfortable.

Solid Studies

Overall, most students appreciate UT's academics. As many people would suspect in a university as large as UT, some classes tend to be rather large. Freshman introductory classes often have 100 or more students crammed into lecture halls, and one junior mentioned taking an intro biology course with over 400 classmates, saying, "the classes are too big. There are too many people, and that makes it hard for professors to meet everyone in their classes." Lectures like these tend to be the exception rather than the rule, however, as the majority of classes hold 20 to 30 students.

With the question of workload, a junior responded, "It's not easy, but it's not a ton. All classes require some time and effort, but it's fairly steady." TAs are subjects of both complaint and praise at UT. A sophomore commented that students "rarely have professors teaching labs or discussions" and that "TAs do all the grading and relating to students, so we have to meet them." A junior expressed that there weren't too many TAs, just "too many bad TAs." One sophomore complained, "Some can barely speak English!" The ineptitude of some TAs is another factor sparking controversy, as one sophomore lamented that there are many "TAs who don't know how to explain things." Still, students report overall confidence that most TAs know their subject matter.

Professors garner more praise than complaint at UT. Professors seem "quite knowledgeable about their subjects and are always willing to help the students." Students also notice the care professors have for their students. Engineering, architecture, computer science, and biochemistry are rumored to be among the most difficult majors, while sociology, Spanish, and business top the list of the easier ones. Accounting is known to be a top program, and sports management can be rather competitive.

UT's Honors Program offers the benefit of special honors classes, priority registration, and personalized advising. In the words of a junior, the program "presents many opportunities that you would never have known about or had the opportunity to do."

Some students are dissatisfied with the process of registration, mentioning that "with low funding, there are fewer professors to teach; thus there are fewer classes. It makes it hard to get into the ones you need. Once you do get into those classes, they are huge."

The Greek Empire

"If you like to party, you are pretty satisfied." UT has established itself as a party mecca, an opinion partly attributed to the university's dominating Greek scene. Many students use fraternities and sororities to give themselves "a second family in a school of 26,000 plus." Phi Gamma Delta, Sigma Chi, and Kappa Sigma are noted as being particularly hip frats, with Alpha Chi Omega and Kappa Delta rounding out the most popular sororities, although numerous others of each abound. Formals, date parties, toga parties, and the like happen throughout the Greek system, so non-Greeks who enjoy these activities could be left out. All-Sing and Carnicus are two Greek-based events displaying the singing, dancing, and acting talents of members. Rushing is easy "if you are willing and there is a group out there for you." Many students admit that they met their best friends through Greek membership.

As for substance availability, a sophomore commented, "drugs are prevalent but not as much as alcohol. I guess it's a Southern thing." Still, one student commented, "non-drinkers are definitely able to fit in—we have 26,000 people so there's a place for everyone." This observation comes in spite of the administration's official dry campus policy. Students say that after the university was named the number-one party school in a recent national publication, university officials have worked to crack down on alcohol, though without much success.

However prominent the Greek scene remains, alternatives do exist for non-Greeks. The university itself plans and coordinates special events for the entire student body. Homecoming boasts student-made floats, a soap-box derby, and an ever-popular football game. The city puts on a popular fireworks show on Labor Day called Booms Day. Freshmen are introduced to the university through a special orientation called Torch Night. The university regularly arranges presentations involving special speakers, some of whom have included everybody from Dr. Patch Adams and Tennessee Governor Don Sundquist, to *Survivor* winner Tina Wesson.

Home-Southern Sweet-Home

UT's campus is described as "very large with lots of hills." "The Hill" dominates the central part of campus, where many trees flank academic and residential buildings and harbor thousands of squirrels. Hodges Library, Neyland Stadium, and Thompson-Boling Arena remain some of the most prominent campus buildings. Scenic views add to the campus's allure as students can see the Great Smokey Mountains from taller buildings. Although its large overall size may seem daunting at first, "most everything day-to-day is in walking distance," so a car is not required, although bicycles are recommended since parking for cars is expensive and often difficult to find.

For all the beauty of the area, one senior lamented Knox County's reputation as one of the worst counties in the United States for pollution, and what was thought to be the university's lackluster commitment to taking better care of the campus. Recycling programs are still in the fledgling stages, and many buildings are falling into disrepair, a junior asserted.

Most students enjoy the proximity to Knoxville, but the city's lack of under-21 clubs remains an unresolved issue. The Strip fairs better in terms of popularity; students benefit from its long row of restaurants and places to hang out. Coffee shops are popular on the Strip, and the Copper Cellar is a top spot to take a date.

Dorms receive mixed reviews. Presidential, whose courtyard is the hanging-out center for freshmen, is a three-dorm complex that consists of a male dorm (Reese), a female dorm (Humes), and a coed dorm (Carrick). These three dorms are generally considered the overall best, with Gibbs also getting a high rating. Students unanimously agree that Hess, nicknamed "the Zoo," is the worst, having no air-conditioning for the Southern heat, a communal bath, and run-down rooms. Morrill, a dorm for upperclassmen, is considered decent. Some dorms are connected with particular fraternities and sororities.

For those choosing to forgo the dorm route, off-campus housing is a popular option. Although freshmen are not allowed to live off campus, many people do to take advantage of the relatively cheap prices for decent accommodations.

> **"It's supposed to be a dry campus—key word is 'supposed to be.'"**

The food situation is neither embraced nor hated. Many students complain about the expensive price of meal plans and prefer to eat off campus. However, the dining halls do provide good vegan options, besides having available a grill and fast-food restaurants like Chick-Fil-A. The plan includes the option of munching at an all-you-can-eat buffet, along with "bonus bucks" to be used at various other places. Most students prefer to swing through the dining halls quickly, rather than using them to hang out. The Hermitage Room in the University Center is a big dining room that boasts real china and silverware, unbeknownst to many students.

Homogeneous Home-Sweet-Home

As one junior jokingly remarked, "we're stereotyped as big, stupid rednecks." However, the "partier" stereotype does often emerge among a group of admittedly homogeneous students. Many scholars do regret that the school is made up of mostly "middle-class Southern ladies and gentlemen," rather than having a good mix of minorities. Still, students praise the inclusion of many international students in their student body.

A sophomore testified to the prevalence of cliques when she said, "there are 20,000 people on campus . . . you have to have a clique. Everyone has a clique, even if it's just three people." Students agree that self-segregation is both a blessing and a problem in the midst of such a vast student body.

Cliques may have the effect of breaking up such a large group of undergraduates into small isolated sectors, but athletic fervor tends to unite all. Football remains the most popular spectator sport. UT boasts Neyland Stadium, one of the country's largest, in which over 100,000 "Volunteers" go wild when the band forms UT's traditional "Power T" and blasts out "Rocky Top" to inspire a football team that won a National Championship in 1998. Women's basketball is also popular among students. Tickets are easy to obtain if a student really wants to attend an event.

Among extracurriculars, intramural sports remain the most popular type of activity though various activities span a wide range of interests. Organizations wishing to advertise their meetings literally "Paint the Rock"—students paint messages on a rock positioned in a central part of campus. *The Daily Beacon* dominates the publication scene; the Student Government Association, a group devoted to addressing campus problems, and NORML, students working to legalize marijuana, are among the other groups on campus. Student employment is also plentiful: one sophomore estimated that just over half of UT's students work a "real job" on the side.

At first glance, UT might seem overwhelming with its bigger-than-life size, fanatical athletics, and dominating Greek scene. Nevertheless, students are able to find their own niches to create a smaller, more comfortable sense of community. A sophomore summed it up for her fellow Volunteers when she said, "I would not dream of being anywhere else but UT. Any school that can gather 100,000 people in a stadium united by one bond—how can that place be bad?" —*Rob James*

FYI

If you come to UT, you'd better bring "a tolerance for the color orange."

What is the typical weekend schedule? "Friday: go to dinner and hang out with friends; Saturday: get up and go to the game, party after the big UT win; Sunday: recover from the previous two nights and study during the afternoon and evening."

If I could change one thing about UT, I'd "make parking easier."

Three things every student should do before graduating are: "see an away football game (especially Florida), go to a party, and Paint the Rock."

University of the South (Sewanee)

Address: 735 University Avenue; Sewanee, TN 37383-1000
Phone: 800-522-2234
E-mail address: admiss@sewanee.edu
Web site URL: www.sewanee.edu
Founded: 1857
Private or Public: private
Religious affiliation: Episcopal
Location: rural
Undergraduate enrollment: 1,340
Total enrollment: 1,360
Percent Male/Female: 47%/53%
Percent Minority: 9%
Percent African-American: 5%
Percent Asian: 1%
Percent Hispanic: 1%
Percent Native-American: 0%
Percent in-state/out of state: 24%/76%
Percent Pub HS: 54%
Number of Applicants: 1,669
Percent Accepted: 71%
Percent Accepted who enroll: 32%
Entering: 367
Transfers: 13
Application Deadline: 1 Feb
Mean SAT: NA
Mean ACT: NA
Middle 50% SAT range: V 560-660, M 550-650
Middle 50% ACT range: 24-28
3 Most popular majors: social sciences, English, visual and performing arts
Retention: 88%
Graduation rate: 76%
On-campus housing: 92%
Fraternities: 45%
Sororities: 43%
Library: 648,459 volumes
Tuition and Fees: $24,135
Room and Board: $6,720
Financial aid, first-year: 38%
Varsity or Club Athletes: 51%
Early Decision or Early Action Acceptance Rate: 76%

"What's a TA?" The University of the South, called Sewanee by all its students and neighbors, offers a place where teaching assistants just don't exist and a large class is hard to find.

Small, but Not a Melting Pot

This small school fosters a community that is suffocating to some and liberating to others. "It's definitely a bubble," one student said. "It's really backwards too. You get sucked in. I want to change the world, and I'm starting to forget what's important and what's just Sewanee." Another student said, "I think it's small enough and isolated enough that we get to know each other." She believes this helps cultivate an environment in which the honor code is upheld. "There's an amazing sense of community and trust. I've never locked my door and I leave my backpack lying around." It's also easy to develop a relationship with a member of the faculty or even the administration. Each student is assigned a faculty advisor, and on the second Sunday of every month, the university vice chancellor holds a "porch light." He or she leaves the porch light on, and students are welcome to stop by for a visit that evening.

Some undergrads complain that the mixture of students at Sewanee is far too homogeneous. The standard dress, say students, looks like a private school uniform, with some adaptations: "It seems like every guy wears a blue blazer and khakis with tennis shoes, an old messed-up baseball cap, and a bow tie. I've never seen so many bow ties in my life!" Students say the school is mostly made up of "Southern rich people." There are approximately 12 international students and 60 minority students on campus. One minority student called race an "insidious" problem, saying it was difficult to maintain a sense of security about his identity. "If I were a white person I think I'd have a profoundly different experience," he said. To address such concerns, Sewanee's administration assigns an additional faculty member to all minority students to help them become adjusted to campus life and to assist them with specific concerns.

Goin' to the Chapel

Sewanee is known for its Episcopalian tradition. One upperclassman said most of her friends go to church on Sunday morning. If you do set foot in the chapel, be sure to avoid the seal in the floor. Legend says anyone who steps on the seal will not graduate from Sewanee, unless they streak across the quad. Sewanee also has a tradition with angels. "A legend says that since this place is so beautiful, angels lived here before people did," said one upperclassman. "Every member of the Sewanee community has their own angel, so when you leave campus you touch the roof of your car to let your angel know to come with you so you can return safely to campus."

Though most people walk or bike to class, students say cars are a must. "Most people have cars, even freshmen, except international students," said one student from Ghana. "Sometimes you need to go to Walmart and things like that, and a car is a huge help." Also within a short driving distance is "a nice Mexican place" and some nearby Chinese buffets to supplement the cuisine from McClurg, Sewanee's dining hall. The fare now includes a stir-fry kiosk where students can order and have food cooked in front of them. "It's quite an improvement," said one student, "I try to stop by as often as possible."

Sewanee doesn't have freshman dorms. Instead, each dorm is interspersed with members of all classes. Freshman housing is assigned, while upperclassmen enter a lottery to get their top-pick rooms. Members of the "Order of Gownsmen," a society of students with high GPAs, are given preference in the room picks, as are proctors and assistant proctors, who function as RAs in the dorms to keep quiet hours and enforce rules. Students choose co-ed or single-sex dorms, and most rooms are doubles. Freshmen are required to live on campus, and there seems to be an unwritten rule that only seniors live off campus, though few choose to do so.

"You can still have a good time if you don't like alcohol, you just need to be a little more creative with your activities."

If you expect to be a member of the Gownsmen, students say, don't be an economics major. "Econ and math majors are like death—you don't see those people at parties." Political science is the most popular major at Sewanee, due to what students see as a swiftly improving department. Religion and art history are viewed as "slacker majors," though "some people take them seriously." Good grades are hard to come by in virtually all majors, however, as grade inflation is reportedly nonexistent.

The Great Outdoors

Students take advantage of their 10,000-acre campus to commune with nature and all its offerings. "You've got to spend time outside here, and the campus is huge," one student said. "The outing-programs office is very active," said another. A sample weekend's events include a hiking trip around the campus perimeter, a canoeing trip, mountain biking, and rock climbing. You can also get involved in intramural sports, which are "big, but pretty casual." Varsity athletics are not central to campus life, though students say they have spirit, especially when it comes to football and basketball.

Mud Wrestling, Anyone?

One student estimated that 70 percent of undergrads at Sewanee belong to a fraternity or a sorority. "I came up here with the mentality that I would never be in a frat, and now I'm the president of my fraternity," said one brother. "All my tight-knit male relationships have come as a result of my fraternity friends—either from my frat or others," he said. "Shake day" begins the annual pledging activities. "All the pledges and brothers jump into a pile of mud and wrestle each other, and at the end of the day you shake hands with members of the frat you want to pledge" said one member of Gamma Sigma Phi. Hazing doesn't seem to exist at Sewanee, but there is a "pledgeship" term that lasts six weeks for upperclassmen, eight for freshmen. "During this time, you're a little brother being groomed to be a big brother—learning what the fraternity stands for." The sorority rush process works a little differently from its male counterpart. "Women pair off with their first-choice sorority, and those who aren't selected then move to their second choice, so that no one gets left out," said one student. Fraternities and sororities are the source of most of the social activities on the Sewanee campus, but even those who aren't Greek are welcome at parties, even formals and cocktails, free of charge.

Along with the Greek system comes lots of drinking at Sewanee. "Being underage is absolutely no problem," said one upperclassman. "As long as you have a pulse you can buy alcohol." Another student said, "On any given Friday night, you're going to be given six beers by random people. It seems we share alcohol more than we share wisdom." Those who don't like to drink agree that "you can still have a good time if you don't like alcohol, you just need to be a little more creative with your activities." Going bowling or to the movies rank as popular weekend alternatives to the party scene, as does making the most of Sewanee's outdoor opportunities. Whether it's indoors or out, Sewanee students seem to be happy with their school. "If you want big-city living this is definitely not the right place for you, but if you like to chill out in the woods, you'll probably like it here."
—*Stephanie Hagan*

FYI

If you come to Sewanee, you'd better bring "a bow tie and a good pair of trail shoes."

What is the typical weekend schedule? "Frat parties Friday and Saturday nights, sports events Saturday morning and afternoon, and library all day Sunday."

If I could change one thing about Sewanee, I'd "try to make the campus a little more diverse."

Three things every student at Sewanee should do before graduating are "hike Perimeter Trail, see a sunset from Green's View, and go to a professor's house."

Vanderbilt University

Address: Nashville, TN 37203
Phone: 800-288-0432
E-mail address: admissions@vanderbilt.edu
Web site URL: www.vanderbilt.edu
Founded: 1873
Private or Public: private
Religious affiliation: none
Location: urban
Undergraduate enrollment: 6,146
Total enrollment: NA
Percent Male/Female: 48%/52%
Percent Minority: 19%
Percent African-American: 6%
Percent Asian: 6%
Percent Hispanic: 4%
Percent Native-American: NA
Percent in-state/out of state: 20%/80%
Percent Pub HS: 60%
Number of Applicants: 9,836
Percent Accepted: 46%
Percent Accepted who enroll: 34%
Entering: 1,582
Transfers: 52
Application Deadline: 1 Jan
Mean SAT: NA
Mean ACT: NA
Middle 50% SAT range: V 610-700, M 640-720
Middle 50% ACT range: 27-31
3 Most popular majors: social sciences, engineering, psychology
Retention: 94%
Graduation rate: 84%
On-campus housing: 84%
Fraternities: 34%
Sororities: 50%
Library: 1,812,869 volumes
Tuition and Fees: $28,440
Room and Board: $9,457
Financial aid, first-year: 41%
Varsity or Club Athletes: 10%
Early Decision or Early Action Acceptance Rate: 50%

Set in the hip "Music City" of Nashville, Tennessee, Vanderbilt University is one of the top colleges in the South. Its Southern flavor and energetic students make it thrive with activity on all fronts. Vanderbilt is a good place for both challenges and fun.

School Time

Students at Vanderbilt need to be on top of their game in terms of time management, as the rigorous academics take up a lot of time and energy. Most students are up for the challenge; "It's tough and I like it, " said one student. Vanderbilt has four undergraduate colleges: Engineering, Arts and Sciences, George Peabody College for Education and Human Development, and the Blair School of Music. Most freshmen enroll in the school for Arts and Sciences. Many students complain about the Core Program for Liberal Education (CPLE) requirements, which are required classes that cover a broad range of subjects and require taking a foreign language. Some students describe it as "synonymous with classes that you hate," while others praise it because it is "much more flexible than core requirements at other schools." The university has indicated that these requirements are under revision and may change considerably in the near future.

On the positive side, almost all students boast about the small class size and the personal attention they get from their professors. One senior said that he had never been bumped from a class and that he had formed a personal relationship with each of his professors. With 95 percent of Vanderbilt's classes enrolling fewer than 50 students, Vanderbilt students certainly cannot complain.

The course load at "Vandy" is demanding. Some of the most difficult majors are engineering, economics, and biology, while generally some of the easier classes are taught in the Peabody College. But, as one student put it, "nothing at Vanderbilt is for slackers." There tend to be plenty of premeds on campus and students brag that the new science facilities are "amazing." In spite of all the premeds, students enjoy the relaxed environment at Vanderbilt in which they report virtually no academic competition. "We would never decline notes to a friend, like some people would at a more cutthroat school."

Play Time

One of the aspects students emphasize the most when talking about their school is the incredible dynamic balance between the academics and the social life. "The defining characteristic of Vandy is the balance between work and the active social scene. It is definitely a very social campus," commented one student enthusiastically.

The social life at Vanderbilt is also characterized mostly by Greek life, with 50 percent of girls in sororities and 35 percent of guys in fraternities. Frats and sororities guarantee to have at least one party each weekend. Many of the social events on campus center around rush, which lasts for about four months.

"The defining characteristic of Vandy is the balance between the work and the active social life. It is definitely a very social campus."

Most frat parties, which often host live bands, take place on Fridays and Saturdays, while Thursdays are usually reserved for going downtown to bars and clubs. Some nearby bars are Havana and Buffalo Billiards, your classic honky-tonk dives. Most students, even those with cars, take cabs at night because it is safer. One student admitted that having a car on campus was "more of a burden than anything else." Saturday is game day. Although Vanderbilt is not the best in its conference, students get dressed up for football games and take dates to the tailgates.

The alcohol policies on campus are pretty strict, according to one senior, especially regarding minors. However, even underage students can find alcohol if they want it. Frosh suites and the upperclassmen Tower Suites are alternative party locations. Partying isn't everything though: One student said, "there are so many great alternatives that partying doesn't have to be your only option."

Needless to say, the music selection at Vanderbilt is incredible. Nashville's reputation as the "Music City" comes into play when artists like Dave Matthews, Guster, OAR, Weezer, Afro Man, Counting Crows, Nelly, and John Mayer come to homecoming or Rites of Spring, the annual spring festival that takes place before finals. Its location in downtown Nashville also leaves Vanderbilt students plenty of options.

Keeping Busy

When Vanderbilt students are not working hard or playing hard, they are engaged in some sort of extracurricular activity. Football games are popular, but the really good sports teams are men's and women's basketball. Most students on campus play a sport of some sort, be it intramural, club, or varsity. The Rec Center receives a lot of praise for its facilities and its outdoor spring break trips. "Our Rec Center is second to none: large indoor pool, indoor climbing wall, basketball, volleyball, racquetball, squash courts, and fitness facilities, with great programming. I got my SCUBA certification in the pool, and also learned how to roll a kayak there." Student organizations are also very prominent on campus–400 organizations for 6,000 undergrads. The enormous list encompasses student publications, theater groups, major volunteer and community service organizations, and ethnic group associations.

Who's Where

Despite all of the bustle, life seems to be tranquil enough on the Vanderbilt campus. Vanderbilt is actually a national arboretum. Because of this it is easy to forget that the gorgeous campus is in the middle of Nashville—hence the nickname "Vanderbubble." "You can be 20 feet from the road and all you hear is the wind in the trees and birds chirping. I don't know how they do it," said one student. The area just beyond the tranquil campus is conveniently tailored to students. A Blockbuster Video, as well as various shops, restaurants, and plenty of low-key coffee shops to hang out or study in are all within a short walk.

Rand Dining Hall food did not receive such laudatory comments. Students are not very enthusiastic about the food, saying that it's "ehh, okay." The Pub stays open late hours and is the best source of edible food on campus. The wide array of nearby off-campus restaurants like SATCo, Las Palmas, Rio Bravo, and Bread and Co. offer up good food for everybody's tastes when on-campus dining just won't do.

Dorms, on the other hand, are mostly renovated and in great shape. Each suite has cable TV (with HBO), Ethernet, and a phone line for every student. Singles are also available, some even with kitchens. As one student described the dorms, "Some are plush and some are more institutional, but it's a trade off for the tone of the dorm and its location." Because the residential conditions are excellent, students very rarely live off campus. Vanderbilt is implementing a new "residential college" system in 2006 that will help promote an even stronger sense of community.

Community, however, doesn't seem to be lacking at all on this campus. The student body is known for its friendliness and willingness to meet new people. Although Vanderbilt has an image of being a homogenous school made up of rich Southern belles, this is rapidly changing. The admissions office has made a huge effort to recruit students of different backgrounds, and this has been reflected recently with an increasing visibility of minorities on campus.

Vanderbilt definitely still does have a Southern feel to it. One senior commented on the attractiveness of the student body, "the girls are almost notoriously good looking," he said, explaining that some feel uncomfortable in such a socially competitive environment. Overall though, students seem satisfied with the high-quality academics and the active social life at Vanderbilt. "I honestly see very few ways in which I could be more challenged or more educated, even in comparison with more prestigious schools. Overall, I could not have picked a better college." —*Carolina Galvao*

FYI

If you come to Vanderbilt, you'd better bring a "nice set of clothes and a taste for the South."

What is the typical weekend schedule? "Alternating between work and play, depending on what's going on. It is *always* a tradeoff. Thursday hit up the bar/club scene downtown, Friday parties on campus, Saturday football game and frat parties. Sunday is all business, study, study, study."

If I could change one thing about Vanderbilt, "I would create more parking and make items/food on campus less expensive."

Three things every student at Vanderbilt should do before graduating are: "go for an entire football game, head to a frat party, and take a kayaking or climbing trip exploring Tennessee with the Outdoor Rec Center."

Texas

Baylor University

Address: Waco, TX 76798-3435
Phone: 800-229-5678
E-mail address: admission_serv_office@baylor.edu
Web site URL: www.baylor.edu
Founded: 1845
Private or Public: private
Religious affiliation: Baptist
Location: small city
Undergraduate enrollment: 11,987
Total enrollment: NA
Percent Male/Female: 42%/58%
Percent Minority: 21%
Percent African-American: 6%
Percent Asian: 5%
Percent Hispanic: 8%
Percent Native-American: 1%
Percent in-state/out of state: 84%/16%
Percent Pub HS: NA
Number of Applicants: 7,431
Percent Accepted: 81%
Percent Accepted who enroll: 48%
Entering: 2,620
Transfers: 437
Application Deadline: rolling
Mean SAT: NA
Mean ACT: NA
Middle 50% SAT range: V 530-630, M 550-650
Middle 50% ACT range: 22-27
3 Most popular majors: management, teacher education, business marketing
Retention: 84%
Graduation rate: 72%
On-campus housing: 29%
Fraternities: 13%
Sororities: 17%
Library: 2,252,780 volumes
Tuition and Fees: $18,430
Room and Board: $5,434
Financial aid, first-year: 50%
Varsity or Club Athletes: 7%
Early Decision or Early Action Acceptance Rate: NA

In the heart of Waco, Texas, Baylor University shines. More than just another Southern, Baptist-affiliated private institution, Baylor students are proud of their education and traditions. Whether they're studying biology or volunteering their time to improve the surrounding community, Baylor Bears make the most of their time at school. As one student summed it up: "The best thing about Baylor is the multitude of things to which you can devote yourself. You can always find something that interests you at this school."

The Cores

Baylor is wonderful for keeping students slightly more well-rounded than they might care to be. Students are required to take two semesters of Chapel Forum, a seminar where guest speakers lecture students twice a week. In addition, there are other degree regulations including minimum number of semester hours and residence requirements. Students believe that the academic requirements are "fair and understandable." There are some who complain about having to take courses in fields unrelated to their track of study, but most agree that because of today's ever-changing job market, the requirement is "very useful."

Biology is regarded as the hardest major at Baylor, which is well known for its pre-med program. Professors use the program to weed out those who won't be able to handle the pressure. As far as easier majors go, business and education are known to be less stressful. "A class on how to make a billboard? PLEASE!" remarked one student about the education major. However, because of the high-achieving students at the school, the environment is still cutthroat. "I'm not aware of any majors that aren't competitive—this is Baylor!" said one senior.

For those students who are looking for even more of a challenge, there is the Baylor Interdisciplinary Core (BIC) which takes the top professors in each discipline at Baylor to create classes that teach more than one subject at a time. Students enter the highly selective program as freshmen and continue it through their senior year. One participant says that "it is vastly more interesting, memorable, and ultimately more practical than the regular basic courses required for the major of your choice."

Coors Light Anyone?

The social life is pretty limited at Baylor. Approximately half the students are in a frat or sorority. Parties revolve around the Greek system and are often the best in frats. Drinking is present at this school even though it is Baptist-affiliated. However, students think "there's not a lot of pressure to drink if you don't want to. Most parties will serve canned sodas as well as alcohol." As far as rushing these frats and sororities, Bears say that some cruel things go on. One student said that she's "had to help clean up guys smeared in excrement by frats they rushed and weren't wanted at" and "help girls who had been drawn on in permanent pen on their naked bodies as to what they needed to improve on their figures before getting a bid."

If Greek life isn't your thing, don't worry. A popular and well-respected group on campus is The Baptist Student Union. It's known for not letting non-Baptists lead the various ministries, even if they are Christian. Mission Waco is another religious group on campus that is highly respected for its work with the homeless and needy. However, if you're not religious, there are over 250 other organizations at Baylor, from singing groups to ethnic associations. A popular volunteer group is Steppin' Out. Students in this group set aside a day to help the Waco community with various service projects. One student said extracurriculars are "the best way to meet and make friends."

Appearance Only Goes So Far

The students are downright beautiful at Baylor. One student commented that there are enough "attractive people, but not beyond the physical aspect." One problem students at this school seem to deal with is appearance. "There's a lot of bulimia and anorexia here," said one girl. "People try to look wealthy, but a majority are from middle-class families." However, one student stated that people are very casual and wear jeans and t-shirts. Dating is a rarity at Baylor. One student said that people "just get laid or engaged." But do not fret, because people are reported to be "really friendly and easy to get to know." Whether it be in class or through activities, you're sure to find some people you click with.

Two if by Land, Green if by Victory

Sports are pretty dry for the Baylor Bears. Although most people go to the football games, it's just to "hang out and pretend to support the team." But there is one team that Bears do "hate with a passion"—the Texas A&M Aggies. Although they have not won any championships lately, students are still shooting for glory.

As the oldest university in Texas, Baylor definitely has many traditions. Bears know when their athletic teams have won a game or not. It's a tradition to light up the tower of Pat Neff Hall with green floodlights for victories and with white floodlights for losses. Another tradition is the Homecoming bonfire, which was originally set around the campus for protection against Baylor's opponents. And even for non-athletes, the gym facilities are excellent. One student proudly stated, "We have the best gym in the south." Intramurals are a part of many students' lives, explaining the "athletic-look" of most Bears at this beautiful Southern school.

Living in the Comfort of Protection

"It's an attractive and typical college campus with brick buildings and nicely manicured lawns and gardens," said one student about Baylor. The campus is spread out with many great hiding spots. Students enjoy spending time in Cameron Park or Lover's Leap, either reading or sleeping on a blanket. There are also some coffee shops people go to hang out or just relax. "There are so many little nooks to run away to when you just want to spend some time alone." Crime is not an issue at Baylor. Students feel safe on campus because of "the Baylor DPS. They're wonderful!" With no recent issues in crime, it's no wonder why people feel able to leave their doors unlocked without a threat.

Baylor students aren't very fond of the dining options at the school. The food is "gross, but bearable," said an off-campus student. Another student said that he gets "filled up, so it's good." The food in the SUB is reportedly the only "good stuff" by most students. The SUB includes chains like Chik-Fil-A, Subway, Dunkin Doughnuts, and Starbucks. People like eating off campus more than in the dining halls at restaurants like Crickets, Ninfa's, and Outback Steakhouse.

"The best thing about Baylor is the multitude of things to which you can devote yourself. You can always find something that interests you at this school."

One thing that might distinguish Baylor from many universities are the visitation hours for its on-campus residents. All dorms at this school are single-sex and have residential advisors to regulate visitation hours from members of the opposite sex. There are only several hours a week when visitation is allowed, a policy many students think to be "too restrictive, but understandable." Another downer is that the rooms are a "bit on the small side." Dorms are nevertheless clean and lively, with different personalities for different dorms. The women's halls—there are eight—are a good example. North and South Russell are for non-Betty freshmen girls. Alexander Hall is labeled as the dorm with the "smart and beautiful girls." For the men, there are three residence halls, with Penland Hall as the largest and most diverse. Many students go off campus after their frosh year for privacy and quietness, but the rent is usually expensive and the lifestyle not as exciting as dorm life.

Baylor Bears enjoy the unity they have through the strong Christian presence on campus. Many students take pride in their traditions and beautiful campus. With its beautiful Southern atmosphere and world-class education, Baylor is a university full of opportunities for people interested in many different things. "As with any college, your experience at Baylor depends on your attitude towards everything around you," said one junior. "It's a matter of whether or not you take advantage of the awesome prospects Baylor has to offer." —*Jane Pak*

FYI

The three best things about attending Baylor are "the student life center, the multitude of things to get involved in, and its closeness to Dallas and Austin."

The three worst things about attending Baylor are "Waco, the fakeness about a lot of people, and rushing."

The three things every student should do before graduating from Baylor are "have a frozen mochaccino at Common Grounds, have a water fight at the fountain in the center of campus, make fun of the newspapers on campus."

One thing I'd like to have known before coming here is "how there's absolutely nothing to do in Waco."

Rice University

Address: PO Box 1892; Houston, TX 77251-1892
Phone: 713-348-7423
E-mail address: NA
Web site URL: www.rice.edu
Founded: 1912
Private or Public: private
Religious affiliation: none
Location: urban
Undergraduate enrollment: 2,787
Total enrollment: NA
Percent Male/Female: 53%/47%
Percent Minority: 36%
Percent African-American: 7%
Percent Asian: 14%
Percent Hispanic: 11%
Percent Native-American: NA
Percent in-state/out of state: 54%/46%
Percent Pub HS: NA
Number of Applicants: 7,079
Percent Accepted: 24%
Percent Accepted who enroll: 40%
Entering: 700
Transfers: 48
Application Deadline: 10 Jan
Mean SAT: NA
Mean ACT: NA
Middle 50% SAT range: V 650-750, M 670-770
Middle 50% ACT range: 28-33
3 Most popular majors: economics, electrical engineering, biology
Retention: 96%
Graduation rate: 92%
On-campus housing: 73%
Fraternities: 0%
Sororities: 0%
Library: 2,100,000 volumes
Tuition and Fees: $18,253
Room and Board: $7,880
Financial aid, first-year: 32%
Varsity or Club Athletes: 24%
Early Decision or Early Action Acceptance Rate: 32%

Seventeen Magazine is a fan of Rice University in Houston, Texas. The magazine voted the university the "coolest school in the land" in their October 2002 issue, which featured the "50 Coolest Colleges." Luckily, Rice's appeal expands beyond the world of teeny-bopper magazines, though *Seventeen's* praise for Rice's "community-minded residential college system," "Big 10–type extracurriculars," and "great shopping" doesn't stray too far from the mark.

"We Study a Lot"

"We study a lot," was how one student described a typical Rice undergrad. "Some people study a lot all the time, even on weekends and nights, but if you want, you can be out Monday through Sunday having a good time." Even for those who choose the latter route, the university's academic requirements must first be met, which can vary in intensity depending on major and the number of AP credits an individual has coming in. There are three areas of distributional requirements—humanities, social sciences, and natural sciences. Students point out that the requirements have their "ups and downs" but one student said it is beneficial since "taking classes outside of your major really helps to open your mind." Most students take a lot of science courses anyway, and it seems like "half of the school is premed," to some students. In fact, it is common for students to continue their research at Rice over the summer. One of Rice's most well-known programs is the Rice-Baylor program, which basically means you have "guaranteed acceptance to medical school." Unfortunately, many premed students do not have the luxury of going abroad—a hefty sacrifice considering that about half the university's students do so for at least a semester.

In terms of getting into classes, freshmen often have the most difficulty procuring a spot for the more coveted lectures. The upside for freshmen is that core courses tend to be smaller in size, ranging from 20 to 30 people, than upper-level courses. One Rice freshman bragged that, "My smallest class is an amazing Introduction to Theater class, which only has about ten students."

While most Rice students "study a lot," electrical engineering majors study more. Most students would agree that the electrical engineering major is the hardest. "People who do that are crazy," one student said. "My roommate is that major and one of the classes he takes [is] three classes worth of credit at any school other than Rice!" Stress is usually at its peak during midterm exams and finals, "which is where the hardest assignments tend to lie." But students warn that the number of classes you take is *not* proportional to the workload.

The workload is more bearable when students have the opportunity to take classes from famous professors such as Dennis Houston, a humanities teacher famous for lectures where "he spits out obscenities left and right." People actually camp out in front of the registrar's office to ensure a spot in Houston's public speaking class. Bombs and Rockets, a class about the politics of American national security, is another hot ticket. Luckily, the class assignments are often as interesting as the lecturers. One premed student was assigned the task of creating artificial blood for one of his science courses.

Grade inflation doesn't seem to be a prominent concern at Rice, although some classes, such as chemistry, do have what are called "redemption points." In this system, if a student's score on the final exam is better than that of a test from the beginning of the year, the earlier test score is replaced with the higher grade. For more difficult classes, recitation sessions taught by the TAs are offered. Students seem to have mixed feelings about TAs, some complaining that they only muddle the information and that it can be "really hard to understand" those with foreign dialects. However, one student praised the grad students at Rice; "This year I am taking a class taught by a TA and she's better than the professor." Whichever the case, "between the office hours of the TAs and professors, you can always get help if you need it."

Rice Lets Loose

Rice isn't all brains and no beer (despite its Greek-free status). Although most parties serve up alcohol, there are "ALWAYS other things to do" one student emphatically pointed out and "there's no real split socially between drinkers and nondrinkers." Plus, "you could always go to parties and just not drink." The residential colleges throw a lot of the parties. Well-known bashes include the Annual Night of Decadence "which is basically a nude party," Disorientation (at the end of orientation week), and the Tower Party. Late-night games of Powderpuff Football and chilling "with the guys, playing some poker, and watching a movie," are options for those students who just want to veg out. The dating scene (or lack thereof) at Rice is often blamed on the common stereotype that "most of us guys tend to be shy," one male Rice student explained. And the males' shyness only works to their disadvantage, since "there's a good amount of cute girls on campus."

Residential Colleges: Instant Family

The social life at Rice is greatly supplemented by the university's residential college system. About 400 people (100 from each grade) live in each of nine colleges, providing an instant family atmosphere ingrained in freshmen from the start of "a great orientation week." But not all students are as enthusiastic about what they call "O-Week." Freshmen from each college are divided into groups of five. "You're really tight with them from the start and you do all your activities with your group," a student explained. Some students complain that the downside to this system is that "you're already lodged into your college social group." And yes, the residential colleges definitely do have different personalities students said, which "are all brainwashed into us during our orientation week." But there are many positive things to be said for the residential college system, too. One student put it aptly, saying, "It's the best parts of a fraternity and a dorm all put together." And don't worry about meeting people outside of your residential college. Classes, parties, or common friends are all ways to extend your circle of friends, although it does "take a little bit more effort."

Each college has its own Master and staff of Associates. The Master is a tenured professor at the university and handles academic and personal matters, in addition to organizing social events. He or she lives and eats with the students in the residential college. The Associates are faculty members, most of whom live outside of Rice, except for the two Associates who reside in each college. They provide academic advice and help direct students' career choices.

> **"Some people study a lot all the time, even on weekends and nights, but if you want, you can be out Monday through Sunday having a good time."**

Dorms vary from college to college, but most students would agree that none are shamefully terrible. They range from singles to quads, most of which are located on co-ed floors and share single-sex bathrooms. There are more singles in the newer colleges, but there's no reason to fear being lonely—usually four singles comprise a suite, with its own common room and bathroom. And don't worry about playing your music too loudly: the RA system is fairly lenient and the RAs "tend to be really cool here and enjoy hanging out with us."

Ode to Houston

What's green, flat, and pretty all-around? Why, of course, the campus of Rice University. The campus has "lots of great facilities and big open quads" which students said "people are actually encouraged to walk on," although some prefer to utilize the plush grass for napping. The main local attraction is Rice Village, an outdoor mall with a mix of franchises and independent retailers that is "packed with restaurants." But who wants to walk when you can hitch a ride with any of the estimated 40 percent of Rice students who have cars on campus? Beyond campus, Houston has so much to offer, including the Theater District, Chinatown, and the Galleria (a "really famous really large mall"), that "sometimes groups go on Houston drives in the middle of the night until about three or four in the morning" just to explore, one student said. And if you get bored of the on-campus scene, venture to Houston for some "pretty good" clubbing or to catch a concert at The Engine Room. Favorite Rice bar hangouts include Bar Houston, Brian O'Neil's, Brock's Bar, and Two Rows. Luckily for students not blessed with the luxury of wheels, a new rail system has been put in place that many hope will make "getting places a bit easier."

Get Your Grub On: More than Just Rice

Each college has its own dining hall, and the quality varies greatly, although overall the food at Rice is "good by college standards." Most seniors tend not to eat in the dining halls, opting instead to cook their own food or eat out. On Saturday nights, the servery is closed for all students—a mixed blessing because "it forces one to go off campus." And there are more than enough places to choose from, with a great range in price and quality. When the clock strikes 2 A.M., Taco Cabana, "a better, cheaper version of Taco Bell," is the place to be for post-party munchies. House of Pies is another Rice novelty.

Salsa and *The Thresher*

"People game, take salsa lessons, play ultimate Frisbee" and do anything to "enrich themselves," one student said of the extracurricular scene at Rice. Although some organizations are more "official" than others, "as long as you have a group of people with a common shared idea, it can be made into an official club." The Cabinet, the residential college student government, is a popular activity, even more so than its counterpart, the university student government. Future journalists can take a stab at writing for Rice's widely read newspaper, *The Thresher*. High participation rates show more than just an interest to beef up the resume. "Everybody does their own thing," one student explained.

Although Rice's athletics are not the pinnacle of the university, "baseball here is huge." The school's baseball team won the College World Series in 2003. Rice students don't just cheer for the champs, though. A surprisingly large number of people attend the football games "even though we're quite pathetic," one student said. College sports are another popular option—teams from various residential colleges compete against one another for the President's Cup. Although there are separate workout facilities for varsity athletes, the general public facility "is more than good enough to work out in" and is "well-kept." —*Dana Schuster*

FYI

If you come to Rice you'd better bring a "sense of humor, good work ethic, lots of shorts, and an umbrella."

What is the typical weekend schedule? "Every weekend here is different than the next if you make it that way."

If I could change one thing about Rice, "I'd create a better on-campus transportation system."

Three things every student at Rice should do before graduating are "jump in Gillis's (the President's pool); climb Willy's statue; and climb 180, 90, and 45 (giant stone statues in the engineering quad)."

Southern Methodist University

Address: PO Box 750181; Dallas, TX 75205
Phone: 800-323-0672
E-mail address: enrol_serv@mail.smu.edu
Web site URL: www.smu.edu
Founded: 1911
Private or Public: private
Religious affiliation: United Methodist
Location: suburban
Undergraduate enrollment: 6,210
Total enrollment: 10,064
Percent Male/Female: 46%/54%
Percent Minority: 26%
Percent African-American: 5.8%
Percent Asian: 6%
Percent Hispanic: 8%
Percent Native-American: 0.5%
Percent in-state/out of state: 74%/36%
Percent Pub HS: 66%
Number of Applicants: 6,152
Percent Accepted: 66%
Percent Accepted who enroll: 34%
Entering: 1,380
Transfers: 327
Application Deadline: 15 Jan
Mean SAT: NA
Mean ACT: NA
Middle 50% SAT range: V 540-630, M 550-650
Middle 50% ACT range: 23-28
3 Most popular majors: business, communications, social sciences
Retention: 85%
Graduation rate: 70%
On-campus housing: 48%
Fraternities: 37%
Sororities: 38%
Library: 2,577,345 volumes
Tuition and Fees: $23,588
Room and Board: $8,391
Financial aid, first-year: 37%
Varsity or Club Athletes: 14%
Early Decision or Early Action Acceptance Rate: NA

Located in the upscale Dallas neighborhood of Highland Park, Southern Methodist University is frequently perceived as a safe haven for rich, Texan sorority girls and their preppy boyfriends. In reality, however, SMU provides a comprehensive education with big city benefits for a broad spectrum of students.

More than a Country Club

The red brick and white columns of the SMU campus evoke feelings of colonial-style schools of the northeast, although students appreciate the warmer weather. While the central fountain and tree-lined walkways might suggest otherwise, the campus is more than just a country club where students coast from high school to Daddy's firm. The academic requirements aim to produce well-rounded, educated individuals. Each student is required to take two Cultural Formations classes as well as courses in five out of the six Perspectives categories, which include the arts, history, literature, religion and philosophy, politics and economics, and behavioral sciences. All freshmen are also required to take Wellness, a class that seeks to educate students about themselves, which many consider to be relatively easy. A variety of honors programs have their own requirements and offer students a challenging curriculum.

At SMU, students receive a lot of personal attention from a variety of sources. Professors, TAs, and even a Learning Enhancement Center, which features tutors and a writing center, are easily available to help anyone who might be struggling, or just looking for an extra edge. As one student said, "lots of people are trying to help you out." The student even relayed an account of freshmen English professors canceling class to have individual conferences with each student. This one-on-one attention is the result of classes that are often capped to ensure small size. Enrollment in the largest classes is rarely above 100 and many classes are 30 people or less. Students do admit that they don't get into every class that they would like, but also say that early registration helps to avoid this problem.

Students attest that the workload can depend heavily on your major or honors program, but everyone works at some point. Some people say that the work comes in spurts unless you have a class that happens to be heavy on reading. Many students are pre-professional, making the business major one of the most competitive. One honors student said, "when you work, you work hard." But SMU students also know how to have fun and enjoy their surroundings when they get the chance.

Weekend: Campus or Dallas?

When the weekends come, SMU students know how to have fun on campus and in Dallas. Greek life is popular on campus and nearly half of all SMU students are affiliated with the Greek system. Fraternities and sororities regularly have parties at their houses or at local clubs. Some fraternities are known to hold parties at undisclosed locations and hire buses to drive students from the frat house to the party and back in order to avoid the possibility of drunk driving.

The Greek system plays a large role in SMU social life. All freshmen girls are considered potential rushees and are thereby banned from sorority parties until rush begins in the spring. However, Greek life does not completely overpower social life, and some students have no problem not rushing. Students do say that it might be harder for people who aren't in the Greek system to find other people to befriend, but that they can be found. Some students are adamant that most people are really friendly and open and try not to be exclusive. Fraternities and sororities do sometimes have their own private parties.

For non-Greek events, most students get all dressed up and head to clubs in nearby areas like Deep Ellum and the West End. Students say being underage is no problem because most clubs are 18 to get in, 21 to drink. This means that underclassmen and upperclassmen can easily party at the same spots. When students have had their fill of weekend partying, many spend their evenings in the same popular areas checking out the great restaurants and hitting a movie.

Even though Dallas is a sprawling city and many students bring their cars, students without cars have no trouble getting by, on and around campus. The student center is a popular hangout and houses all the necessities, including the post office and a small grocery store. It also features a deli, a Chick-fil-A, a Blimpie's, and other popular eateries where students can use meal plan flex dollars. Some students have no problem eating regularly in the cafeterias, or at least on campus, but others note the monotony of dining hall food. Luckily there are a number of popular restaurants, like the student favorite Snuffer's, within walking distance of campus. Those who dare to venture even farther have all the restaurants of Dallas to choose from, as long as they have a friend with a car to give them a ride.

There are even some reasons for students with cars to hang out on campus from time to time. At the beginning of the year a screen is set up outside for outdoor movies. Many individual dorms will have cookouts or other fun activities. The school also puts on a variety of movies, concerts, and lectures throughout the year. The Tate Lecture Series draws a huge number of students and local Dallas residents, who gather to see famous faces like Sidney Poitier, John Irving, Chris Matthews, and even Vice President Dick Cheney.

Wellness Says "Get Involved!"

At SMU, almost everyone is involved in some sort of extracurricular organization. In fact, during Wellness, freshmen take a field trip to the Student Activities Center in order to stress the importance of being involved in student organizations. Some of the most popular groups involve activities planning, leadership, and a variety of campus ministries. Campus Crusade for Christ draws in the neighborhood of 100 students to weekly meetings. Other well-respected organizations include the service group Student Foundation and the Program Council, which is responsible for student programming and sponsoring activities.

SMU is one school that defies the popular reasoning that off-campus students don't spend time on campus. All freshmen are required to live in the dorms unless they are commuters. The freshman dorms, Boaz and McElvaney, are considered the loudest and craziest. Other halls, most of which are newly renovated, are more likely to be set up in suites, with a bathroom attached to each suite.

"The majority of the people are a lot nicer than I expected, but there is a lot of money around here."

After freshman year students have several options. Some choose to remain on campus, a popular choice for some honors students who love Virginia-Snider Hall, the honors dorm. A large number of upperclassmen choose to live in their fraternity or sorority houses. Many others choose to move into nearby apartments. Because Highland Park is such a nice area, the apartments can be on the expensive side, but students say that small ones are reasonably priced. Another popular option, particularly for sophomore girls who will potentially be moving into sorority houses their junior year, is the Panhellenic House, an old Greek house that is now open to all sorority members.

Despite the fact that students tend to spread out after their freshman year, student activity on campus and school spirit remains an important part of SMU. Even though the football team is known to be less than outstanding, many people head out for the games. Before each home football game students and alumni gather for a tailgate on the Boulevard, the main road running through campus. Shirts and ties and cocktail dresses are common football game attire for most students, in traditional Southern fashion. Win or lose, SMU students are proud of their team.

SMU students feel that they are very friendly and open and are a diverse crowd. Like most small, Southern, Christian-affiliated schools, however, they can be accused of lacking ethnic and geographic diversity. As one student said, "it's still a Southern school, and you can tell." Almost half of the students are from Texas and a large number of the other half are from the Midwest, California, and Florida. But the varieties of extracurricular activities prove that not every SMU student is exactly alike. Some students even feel that the school is relatively liberal, or, as one said, "more conservative than UT but more liberal than A&M." Said one freshman, "The majority of the people have been a lot less snobby and a lot nicer than I expected, but there is a lot of money around here." —*Lauren Rodriguez*

FYI

If you come to SMU, you'd better "bring a lot of money. Dallas is expensive."

What is the typical weekend schedule? "Thursday night begins the weekend. Class attendance on Friday is often quite sparse. Friday night, we party all night again, and sleep most of the day Saturday until the evening. Then most people go out with some friends, or find something different to do for amusement. Sunday is a day of laundry, sleep and homework."

If I could change one thing about SMU, "I'd have them take away the Methodist part."

Three things every student at SMU should do before graduating are "take an art history class with Professor Comini, go to Snuffers and get the cheese fries, and drive around, lost, in the West End."

Texas A&M University

Address: College Station, TX 77843-1265
Phone: 979-845-3741
E-mail address: admissions@tamu.edu
Web site URL: www.tamu.edu
Founded: 1876
Private or Public: public
Religious affiliation: none
Location: small city
Undergraduate enrollment: 36,775
Total enrollment: NA
Percent Male/Female: 51%/49%
Percent Minority: 16%
Percent African-American: 2%
Percent Asian: 3%
Percent Hispanic: 9%
Percent Native-American: 1%
Percent in-state/out of state: 97%/3%
Percent Pub HS: NA
Number of Applicants: 17,284
Percent Accepted: 68%
Percent Accepted who enroll: 60%
Entering: 6,949
Transfers: 1,769
Application Deadline: 1 Feb
Mean SAT: NA
Mean ACT: NA
Middle 50% SAT range: V 520-630, M 550-660
Middle 50% ACT range: 22-27
3 Most popular majors: business, engineering, agriculture
Retention: 89%
Graduation rate: 75%
On-campus housing: 27%
Fraternities: 4%
Sororities: 6%
Library: 2,923,964 volumes
Tuition and Fees: $4,748 in; $11,288 out
Room and Board: $5,893
Financial aid, first-year: 32%
Varsity or Club Athletes: 4%
Early Decision or Early Action Acceptance Rate: NA

There's no tradition like Aggie tradition. Students go to Texas A&M to get mugged, dunked, and mustered. And that's just the beginning. "We have so many traditions, and the student body is united because of those," one freshman said. "Everybody who lives here is really supportive of the school."

For starters, there's Midnight Yell, a cheer practice at midnight on Fridays. "It's basically like a big pep rally," one student said. If A&M wins the football game, the next day the yell leaders, who are elected by the student body, are tackled by a group of freshmen, or "fish," as Aggies say, and dunked in the "Fish Pond." The first Tuesday of every month greets a more somber tradition, called Silver Taps or Muster. "We honor Aggies that have passed away. They call off their names, and someone in the audience yells or says 'here.' It's like a roll call for the dead, to remember them." The spirit continues at mugging down, when dates are kissed after the stadium lights go down at Midnight Yell. And upperclassmen meet at the Chicken, a local bar, to dunk their rings, each filling a pitcher with beer, dropping their class rings in, and chugging the pitcher to the bottom.

Many of these traditions center around football, as they might at any Southern school. One student, disappointed with A&M's record, said the school should recruit more heavily and play to win. "Everybody wants football at A&M."

Conservatism is another part of the long-standing inheritance of Texas A&M. "To be serious, this is a pretty conservative school," one student said. "We have the George Bush library and everything." One student pointed out the typical Aggie look: "pretty clean-cut, no piercings or tattoos, a clean-cut haircut. The picture I have in my head is just a student with shorts, tennis shoes, an A&M shirt, and a backpack. Conservative."

Students claim drinking is done in moderation, in keeping with what is mostly a Christian atmosphere. "A lot of students drink, a lot of students don't," one student said. The administration keeps drinking "kind of controlled. I would say they're pretty on top of things."

Come On, Aggie, Light My Fire

Among the many Texas A&M traditions is the annual bonfire. Students cut and chop wood, stack it, and make plans for an enormous bonfire the weekend of the football game against the school's biggest rival, Texas University. Preparations begin at the start of the semester, and two weeks before the game, students begin working around the clock to make sure everything is in place. "The bonfire is the greatest example of teamwork that you can imagine. It's the only thing that I've ever heard of where you work towards the same goal, because most everybody who cares about the school does something for Bonfire," one student said. "The heat from it is unbelievable and it burns for three days. It's an amazing thing to see and know that you were a part of it."

"There aren't many schools where you can just walk by and hear somebody say howdy."

The bonfire was put on hold in 1999, when 12 students died and others were injured in a bonfire-related accident. "It's a very complex issue, but it meant a lot to a lot of people around here. And the families of some of the Aggies who got killed are some of the biggest supporters of its return," one sophomore said, who had not yet gotten to take part in it since joining the A&M community. As of yet, the tradition has not be reinstated.

At the "Corps" of the Spirit

At the head of the spirit at A&M is the Corps. "It's a military-like organization with a fraternal atmosphere," said one Corps member. "We're keepers of the spirit and we carry on all the traditions." A&M started out as a military school (among other things), as the student explained, and "it was in the '50s or '60s when it got integrated. The Corps stayed alive, though it's still mostly male."

With over 800 student organizations, including the Corps, students feel little need to form many fraternities or sororities. "I'd say maybe two percent of the student body is in a frat or a sorority," one upperclassman said. "I think one reason is all the organizations," another suggested. "It's already so easy to find friends." Another noted that, "Sororities are more popular [than fraternities], because the girls don't have the Corps."

Students say they don't feel lost at their college in spite of its large population, because "there's a lot of unity here. There aren't many schools that you can just walk by and hear someone say 'howdy.'"

Fields and Forests of Academic and Residential Life

While students warn against engineering and biomedical majors as some of the more difficult academic programs, they suggest parks and recreation for a breezy time. "If your GPR (grade point ratio) gets too low you can get kicked out of your major. Then parks and rec is all that's left." Students are divided into colleges according to major. Underclassmen can choose to take the general studies track, getting basic requirements down at the start of their college careers, yet must declare a major after two years.

Large classes are the norm, at least at the intro level. "My introductory accounting class was the smallest class I've ever had, and it had about 60 people in it. My other classes have 100 to 200 people in them," one student said, although he speculated that "once you get into your upper-level classes I heard that they're a lot smaller." Honors classes are also generally smaller.

Housing is "pretty much mixed" at A&M, with both upperclassmen and freshmen in the dorms. While students can choose to live in a co-ed dorm, all floors are single-sex. Two Resident Advisors on each floor at A&M enforce the rules and just hang out with students. "I've heard of some being real pains, but my RA's totally cool," said one freshman. The consensus is that they're "not strict, as long as you follow the rules."

A number of different housing arrangements are possible, from singles to modulars, which are doubles that include a bathroom. Other dorms offer community baths. While every dorm has "a lot of pride," each has its own personality. Northside is a spirit-oriented dorm described as being "kind of on the left side of A&M." All in all, the dorms are "kind of cool," though some options are less glamorous than others. One student in the Corps (which offers housing for all its members) described his freshman room's "white-tiled floor with white walls and two desks. No luxuries." Whether you end up in a cozy room or a palatial suite, you won't find it hard to get housing. There's plenty on campus, though some students—including freshmen—choose to live off campus.

For your appetite, Texas A&M serves up three dining halls. "I recommend breakfast," said one freshman. Other buildings of import include the recreational center. "It's state-of-the-art. It has a rock-climbing wall and I don't know how many basketball courts," said one athlete. "A lot of the buildings are really new," he said, pointing out that on the whole the "campus is really nice. It's really green and well-kept." —*Stephanie Hagan*

FYI

If you come to Texas A & M, you'd better bring "spirit—we've all got it here."

What is the typical weekend schedule? "Friday night Midnight Yell, Saturday morning football game at Kyle Field, relax in the afternoon, go out Saturday night, and Sunday is errands and getting ready for the week."

If I could change one thing about Texas A&M, I'd "put elevators in the dorm."

Three things every student at Texas A&M should do before graduating are "get mugged, go to Midnight Yell, and dunk your Aggie ring."

Texas Christian University

Address: 2800 S. University Drive; Fort Worth, TX 76129
Phone: 817-257-7490
E-mail address: frogmail@tcu.edu
Web site URL: www.tcu.edu
Founded: 1873
Private or Public: private
Religious affiliation: Christian
Location: urban
Undergraduate enrollment: 6,851
Total enrollment: NA
Percent Male/Female: 41%/59%
Percent Minority: 18%
Percent African-American: 5%
Percent Asian: 2%
Percent Hispanic: 6%
Percent Native-American: 0%
Percent in-state/out of state: 77%/23%
Percent Pub HS: 72%
Number of Applicants: 6,137
Percent Accepted: 71%
Percent Accepted who enroll: 39%
Entering: 1,451
Transfers: 382
Application Deadline: 15 Feb
Mean SAT: NA
Mean ACT: NA
Middle 50% SAT range: V 510-620, M 520-630
Middle 50% ACT range: 21-27
3 Most popular majors: business management, communication, education
Retention: 82%
Graduation rate: 64%
On-campus housing: 46%
Fraternities: 34%
Sororities: 38%
Library: 1,299,875 volumes
Tuition and Fees: $17,630
Room and Board: $5,780
Financial aid, first-year: 42%
Varsity or Club Athletes: 14%
Early Decision or Early Action Acceptance Rate: NA

Texas Christian University (TCU) is a college that was *made* for viewbooks. With its lovely campus, beautiful, sunny weather, and good-looking student body, its attractiveness is hard to beat. Just as attractive are TCU's academic offerings and plentiful student organizations. TCU's fine reputation is clearly well-founded.

P.E. for Big Kids

Most students agree that TCU's academics have a lot to offer. The required core curriculum makes sure that entering students take classes in many disciplines. All students must complete nine hours of Foundation courses (writing and math), six hours of languages and literature, 36 hours of Exploration classes (physical and life sciences, religion, history, philosophy, and fine arts), and, interestingly, two hours of physical education. "P.E. is fun. They have cool classes, like fencing, bowling, scuba diving, and stage combat," said one sophomore. "You also have to take a health class. I took one on prescription drugs, and it was really interesting." TCU is also known for its 3-2 program, which allows students to get a bachelor's degree and MBA in five years.

There are slackers at TCU, as with any college, but for the most part, TCU students take their academics seriously. "It's all what you put into it," said a criminal justice major, "so if you put in the work, you get a lot out of your classes." According to one freshman, opportunities for work are definitely not lacking. He reported, "They work you pretty hard. I'm still just in the basic freshman core requirements, and I have massive amounts of reading for every class." Popular majors include nursing, business, communications, and psychology, which is known as one of the easier "athlete" majors. The honors program gets mixed reviews. Honors students do have a lot more work and get to take a few of the smaller honors classes each semester, but some students say there isn't much of an advantage to being in it. "It's a bunch of crap," said one business major. "When you graduate, you're recognized with maybe a stamp, but other than that, there's not much."

Professors at TCU are accessible and earn praise from students. "They work hard, they really know their stuff, and they expect students to, also," said a freshman. Many students cite the individual attention from professors as one of TCU's greatest strengths. "They listen to you and keep track of you . . . if you're absent a few times, they'll give you a call, stuff like that," explained one sophomore. Barring your standard huge lectures, class size at TCU is small, usually around 30–40 students at most, and gets no complaints.

Let's Go, Eyeball-Blood-Spitting Lizards!

With over 160 registered student organizations including *The Daily Skiff* newspaper, *The Image* magazine, dance, music, and theater groups, religious organizations, and a radio station, TCU has an impressive array of extracurriculars that offers students great opportunities for leadership. TCU also has a variety of intramural sports that are popular, as well as student government.

Varsity athletics at TCU are Division I. Football games, featuring not just cheerleaders, but also 'showgirls' "that are really pretty to look at," said one male student, are especially popular with students and alumni. In addition, the tennis team, which recently went to Stanford in the NCAA Championship, is always in the top five in the nation, and basketball usually does well. Despite the strong football following, though, "there's not a lot of school spirit, since nobody stays on campus," said one sophomore. The school mascot is the hornfrog. "It's actually a lizard, but it's called a horn *frog*," explains a business major. "It's not a good mascot because it's not very intimidating. It spits blood out of its eye or something like that." Ooh, scary.

Animal, er, Dorm

Some of the most visible organizations at TCU are the fraternities and sororities. With ten each of national fraternities and sororities, there is no way around the fact that going Greek is big at TCU, for better or for worse. Students in the system get designated dorms instead of houses, which they say has its perks. Besides nicer furnishings in the dorms due to alumni donations and other funds just for Greek groups, they enjoy theme parties, mixers, formals, and an instant niche. They also do volunteer work. "Each group has their own philanthropy. Ours works with Alzheimer's, so we volunteer at a nursing home and do stuff like that," said one junior sorority member.

"It's not a good mascot because it's not very intimidating. It spits blood out of its eye or something like that."

Students who are not involved in the system tend to be either disgusted by it or indifferent to it. Whatever their attitude, there seems to be some separation between Greeks and non-Greeks on campus. "They are perceived as really snobby by people who aren't in them," admitted one sorority girl. In fact, one non-Greek sophomore said he decided not to rush fraternities because "the frat guys I talked to were rich little pieces of . . . uh, jerks, that were stuck-up and conceited. I didn't want to hang out with those kinds of guys." Still, some Greek parties are open to all students, and as one student said, "If you bring girls, you don't have to pay."

Dude, Where's Your Car?

Regardless of the strong Greek presence at TCU, there are plenty of other opportunities to socialize and party. TCU has a dry campus, with RAs that do rounds in dorms to enforce the rules, including a rule forbidding students of the opposite sex to be in each other's rooms after a certain time, and a campus police force known as the "Froggy Five-O." One student confirmed, as one might expect, that "a lot of people break the rules."

Not surprisingly, most partying happens off campus. With downtown Fort Worth only one exit away, going downtown to bars and clubs, like Longhorn's, Cowboy Cats, Neon Moon, and City Streets is also popular. The clubs usually have 18 and over nights with regular dance music on weekends, though most of the bars are strict about carding before serving alcohol. A lot of students leave campus to eat, since food at The Main, the TCU cafeteria, is "really expensive and pretty awful." Popular restaurants include steak houses like Texas De Brazil and Del Frisco's, and a "gourmet hole-in-the-wall thing" called Michael's. Dallas-Fort Worth has a lot of cultural attractions as well, such as art museums and concert centers. With all there is to do downtown, students report that a car is "a must."

Two Cute Girls for Every Boy?

The overwhelming majority of students at TCU are from Texas, and the homogeneity doesn't end there. There is very little racial and ethnic diversity, and the stereotype of the Kate-Spade-bag-toting TCU student going to class dressed in Banana Republic is very much a reality. Still, students agree that TCU "is a really friendly campus. Everybody is so nice, which really surprised me because we're supposed to be snobby," said a junior. "Walking around, everybody says hi to each other." The campus, which takes ten minutes to walk across, is also beautiful. It's covered with Southwestern cream-colored brick buildings with red Spanish-style roofs and "pretty flowers everywhere," an idyllic scene with the year-round Texas sunshine.

TCU is also a hottie haven—there is no dispute that it's "a very, very pretty school," said one happy freshman boy. "It's what the guys talk about all the time," he laughs. "Our girls are really pretty," agreed one sophomore, "and they dress up a lot. Most people make an effort to look nice." With the nearly 3-to-2 girl-to-guy ratio, it's safe to say that TCU is pretty much crawling with cute chicks. "Because of the ratio, I'm sure we girls do try to look nicer so we can be noticed," said a sorority girl. Not a bad deal, especially for the males of the student body. As one of the lucky guys admits, "We can't complain." —*Patricia Stringel*

FYI

If you come to TCU you'd better bring "friendliness and good looks."

What is the typical weekend schedule? "If you stay on campus: go out to dinner, party at a frat, study and nap on Sunday."

If I could change on thing about TCU, "it would be the desertion on the weekends."

Three things every student at TCU should do before graduating are "eat at Texas De Brazil, take a fun P.E. class, and play an IM sport."

Texas Tech University

Address: Box 42013; Lubbock,TX 79409
Phone: 806-742-1482
E-mail address: nsr@ttu.edu
Web site URL: www.ttu.edu
Founded: 1923
Private or Public: public
Religious affiliation: none
Location: urban
Undergraduate enrollment: 22,768
Total enrollment: NA
Percent Male/Female: 54%/46%
Percent Minority: 18%
Percent African-American: 3%
Percent Asian: 2%
Percent Hispanic: 11%
Percent Native-American: 1%
Percent in-state/out of state: 96%/4%
Percent Pub HS: NA
Number of Applicants: 13,101
Percent Accepted: 69%
Percent Accepted who enroll: NA
Entering: 4,531
Transfers: 2,218
Application Deadline: rolling
Mean SAT: NA
Mean ACT: NA
Middle 50% SAT range: V 480-590, M 500-610
Middle 50% ACT range: 21-26
3 Most popular majors: Business marketing, interdisiplinary studies, human sciences
Retention: 80%
Graduation rate: 52%
On-campus housing: 26%
Fraternities: 13%
Sororities: 18%
Library: 2,234,274 volumes
Tuition and Fees: $4,745 in; $11,825 out
Room and Board: $6,023
Financial aid, first-year: NA
Varsity or Club Athletes: 6%
Early Decision or Early Action Acceptance Rate: NA

Other than being the home of terrible dust storms and the birthplace of Buddy Holly, the West Texas city of Lubbock is most notable for Texas Tech University and its Red Raider traditions. This unassuming school, with its Spanish mission-style architecture and suspicious lack of live trees, is actually a proud and spirited rival of Texas A&M, on the opposite side of this large state.

The Texas Alternative

Texas Tech's founding marked the beginning of a long history of rivalry between Texas Tech and Texas A&M. The original plan to found a college in West Texas was made with the intention of making it a second branch of A&M. Instead, an unaffiliated college with the same focus on agriculture and technology was founded in the small town of Lubbock. Though the town has grown and the curriculum has become more diverse, Texas Tech still considers itself a prominent alternative to the size and location of A&M.

Texas Tech has developed into a completely comprehensive academic environment, housing an undergraduate school, a law school, a graduate school, and a medical school—all on one campus. The undergraduate school is divided into eight academic colleges: Agricultural Sciences and Natural Resources, Architecture, Arts and Sciences, Business Administration, Education, Engineering, Human Sciences, and the Honors College—each with its own academic requirements. While the engineering and architecture majors are considered the toughest and most competitive, education, business and agriculture are also held in high regard.

Classes are large (about 300 people) in popular introductory classes in political science and the hard sciences, but the size decreases to around 30 or 40 in upper-level courses. One student mentioned that the workload is "not so much that I can't handle it," reflecting the general consensus that the amount of work is moderate. A few students do complain about the seemingly large number of professors in the math and science departments with relatively incomprehensible accents. A second complaint is simply that lack of communication between different departments tends to make things harder than they should be. Overall, though, students feel that they are receiving a high-quality education in a capable environment.

Living Texas Style

Texas Tech's campus is simply another detail that contributes to the unity and spirit of the university. Although the campus is large and near the center of Lubbock, it is an isolated unit. The entirety of the campus is in one area, the only division being a highway that separates the medical school from the rest of the university. Some of the buildings are Spanish style with red terra cotta roofs, others are classic red brick, and still others are described as "ugly, yellowish buildings." Students maintain that the campus is well cared for, but also mention that all of the planted trees and plants seem to die quickly.

"It doesn't matter where you're from, you can come here and find a place to fit in."

Living at Tech is somewhat conservative in nature. With one exception, all of the dorms are single sex. In most cases, a male and female dorm are connected by a common eating area and lounge. Chitwood/Weymouth and Coleman, which is co-ed by floor, are the freshman dorms and are similar to high-rise apartments. These three have a reputation for being loud. Horn/Knapp, the all women's dorm, is quiet and laid-back, while Sneed/Bledsoe, the all men's dorm, is said to be loud and out of control.

Outside of the common lounge areas, the place to study or just hang out is the new University Center, which is said to get pretty crowded. The next most popular study spot is the main library, which, although it is supposed to look like a stack of books on its side. One student described it as looking "like a giant radiator."

The student population at Tech, while leaning towards cultural homogeneity, is considered comfortable by most students. Students do point out that people at Tech come from a multitude of different lifestyles and situations and that everyone has a different point of view. Conversely, the two campus stereotypes are "prep" and "cowboy." One student even specified that the "cowboys" are mostly found around the agriculture buildings while everyone else is more preppy. As one student said, however, "It doesn't matter where you're from, you can come here and find a place to fit in."

Play, Play, and More Play

Even though both the campus and the city of Lubbock are officially dry, the social life at Texas Tech is far from alcohol-free. Most students agree that the Tech weekend is for partying, with a short break for football on Saturdays. Both upper- and lowerclassmen flock to the weekend frat parties and house parties. Parties in dorms are less frequent due to relatively strict enforcement of the alcohol policy. For off-campus partying, students head to the Depot District, a social area near campus packed with bars, clubs, and restaurants. Tom's Daquiris is considered a must-visit for all Tech students. Students say that getting alcohol at local bars and clubs, not to mention frat parties, is easy enough, but a popular trip is "the Strip," a row of liquor stores just outside of town made to look like Las Vegas. Weekend alternatives to parties and clubs include seeing minor league hockey games at the Coliseum, a sports arena on campus, or catching concerts at the local venue, the United Spirit Arena.

These Raiders don't spend all of their non-class hours partying and watching football. Extracurriculars are extremely popular on campus simply because there are so many possibilities. Fraternities and sororities are popular, and the Greek scene maintains an active role in community service. There are over 300 student organizations, including sports clubs and clubs related to each academic major. Some especially prestigious groups include the Student Government Association and the University Select. The SGA, made up of elected representatives, is a well respected group because "they have quite a bit of clout in the administrative decision-making process on issues relating to campus life." The University Select is a group of outstanding students who serve as ambassadors for the president and the dean, give campus tours, and run the orientation program.

Intramurals are also extremely popular

on campus. Students can be on teams with their fraternity, sorority or other organization, or just form a team with a group of friends. Many cite football and volleyball as being two of the most popular, but the competition is fierce in virtually every sport.

The Mighty Red Raiders

If Texas Tech students have nothing else in common, they do share an overwhelming Raider team spirit. Football and basketball games are packed on a regular basis, plus several student groups are devoted entirely to supporting Texas Tech athletics. One of these groups, the all-male Saddle Tramps, decorates the campus with red streamers before every home football game. This includes wrapping the famous statue of Will Rogers on his horse, Soap Suds. This statue, whose rear end faces the rival campus of A&M, is dedicated to Will Rogers because of his generous contributions to another group of Red Raider football supporters, the "Goin' Band from Raiderland." Along with the streamers and the band, "tortilla tossing," where fans toss tortillas every time the team scores, is a long-practiced tradition. Homecoming week is yet another ritual related to Raider football. The weeklong celebration includes pep rallies, various concerts and a bonfire.

But football isn't the only esteemed and celebrated Tech team. Due in part to famous coach Bobby Knight, box seats at the basketball arena sell out early in the year and all home games are well attended. The entire Tech campus also knows when any Raider team wins a conference championship, because the bells in the administration building ring for 30 continuous minutes in celebration.

Students praise Texas Tech for its unity and spirit along with the quality education it provides. Many students also include the friendly campus atmosphere as one of the things that makes them most confident that Texas Tech was the right choice.
—Lauren Rodriguez

FYI

If you come to Texas Tech, you'd better bring a "hairbrush, because you'll never be so windblown."

What is the typical weekend schedule? "Friday, party. Saturday, football then party. Sunday, sleep."

If I could change one thing about Texas Tech, I'd "change Lubbock."

Three things every student at Texas Tech should do before graduating are "experience everything you can, live in the dorms, and live somewhere other than the dorms."

Trinity University

Address: 715 Stadium Drive; San Antonio, TX 78212-7200
Phone: 210-999-7207
E-mail address: admissions@trinity.edu
Web site URL: www.trinity.edu
Founded: 1869
Private or Public: private
Religious affiliation: Presbyterian
Location: urban
Undergraduate enrollment: 2,406
Total enrollment: NA
Percent Male/Female: 49%/51%
Percent Minority: 20%
Percent African-American: 2%
Percent Asian: 6%
Percent Hispanic: 11%
Percent Native-American: 0%
Percent in-state/out of state: 70%/30%
Percent Pub HS: 73%
Number of Applicants: 2,949
Percent Accepted: 69%
Percent Accepted who enroll: 34%
Entering: 683
Transfers: 40
Application Deadline: 1 Feb
Mean SAT: NA
Mean ACT: NA
Middle 50% SAT range: V 580-680, M 610-190
Middle 50% ACT range: 27-30
3 Most popular majors: business management, social sciences, English
Retention: 87%
Graduation rate: 75%
On-campus housing: 78%
Fraternities: NA
Sororities: NA
Library: 898,527 volumes
Tuition and Fees: $19,176
Room and Board: $7,290
Financial aid, first-year: 43%
Varsity or Club Athletes: NA
Early Decision or Early Action Acceptance Rate: 82%

Amidst the rolling lawns and perfectly manicured oak trees in San Antonio sits Trinity University, a country club by any gardener's standards. But don't let this atmosphere fool you. Besides having a "practically 2-to-1 student to gardener ratio," and a special endowment just for landscaping, Trinity offers a solid liberal arts education with motivated students and a top-notch, dedicated faculty.

Common Curriculum

Trinity has consistently ranked high in a variety of publications like the *US News and World Report*, *Money* magazine, and the Princeton Review as one of the best small liberal arts universities west of the Mississippi—and it is not hard to see why. Since classes rarely enroll more than 50 and can be as small as five, and because there are very few TAs, professor-student interaction is said to be "fabulous" and "a cornerstone of a Trinity education." "I don't think there even are TAs here," said one junior. Besides small classes, Trinity offers a top-notch faculty, all of who have PhDs in their respective fields. "They are really there to help you learn inside and outside of the classroom" with extensive office hours, mentoring programs, and countless opportunities for undergraduates to do research with professors.

Trinity has the Common Curriculum, which emphasizes the seven Understandings including World Culture, Judeo-Christian Culture, and Cognitive Thinking. "The requirements do fill up a lot of your schedule the first couple years unless you have AP credits, which can be a pain, but its still worth taking a wide variety of classes if not to learn about a few topics outside your major, to find a major which really interests you," said one senior who changed his major six times in the course of his first two years. All the majors are reputable with the sciences, business, and education programs being the strongest. "We have great placement success with education graduates and students bound for medical school," boasted one student.

Facilities of a Country Club

The Trinity campus has been described as nothing less than "beautiful." The buildings are made from 'Trinity Red' brick and sit among the lush landscape. Dorms are considered very decent. "I lived in Prosths last year which is not considered to be the best dorm on campus, but it's still luxurious by most standards with big rooms, and a great view of the skyline of San Antonio," said one student. Students can choose to live in quiet, dry dorms, or for the more rowdy, more social dorms where alcohol is allowed. Yet, there are some complaints about some dorms, like Herdon, being isolated from the rest of the campus.

"Everyone here says 'y'all.'"

Safety is a non-issue for Trinity students. "I always feel safe when I'm walking around campus alone, day or night," a female student said. With campus phones and 24-hour police patrol, students say crime is really rare and students rarely feel the need to use the free escort service that is available to any students who don't feel safe walking around campus alone.

Social Life

The social life at Trinity circles around the Greek system. Approximately 30-35 percent of the students are members of a fraternity or sorority. "I love my sorority because it gives a great structured social life, but I'm able to have friends outside my sorority too," one student said. For those who don't wish to be a frat brother or sorority sister, they are welcome to most Greek events, but many are disappointed with the social life outside the frat parties. There are 10 bars in San Antonio on St. Mary's Strip, including Crazy Horse Saloon and Tycoon Flats, but "good luck getting in as a freshman because they card practically all the time." Additionally, there are some good clubs for blues and other places for country western dancing. San Antonio also offers a Sea World, the Alamo, Hemisphere Park, and River Walk, a mall, for some daytime fun as well. For the dance club bound, Austin offers some "fun places" which are much less strict about checking IDs than places in San Antonio.

There are two places to go for food on campus: C and Maybee. Since at least one is open until 12, students can always get a snack. C offers food for student on the go, while Maybee offers sit down meals with several different themes. "The quesadillas from the Mexican food line are the best," said one energetic student. People say Airmark, the food company responsible for the cafeteria cuisine, does a fair job making sure everything is edible and the food is sometimes actually pretty good.

Outside the Classroom

As a division III School, Trinity does not give its athletes scholarships, but "we still hold our own on the fields," said one football player. Saturday foot ball games bring in a good crowd of around 2,500. "We put on our cowboy hats and cheer like crazy," according to one football fan. Other solid teams include men and women's tennis, soccer, and volleyball. While Trinity's athletics is not quite at the level of UT/Austin, it has enjoyed a solid showing in the SCAC (Southern Collegiate Athletic Conference) in the last few years in particular.

For those who are not up to the commitment of varsity sports, "intramurals are huge!" exclaimed one student, summing up feelings toward the program. Teams made up of fraternities, sororities, and independents come together to play ferocious games against each other from inner tube water polo to pole vaulting. Besides intramurals, there are a tremendous number of activities for students to get involved in, like the *Trinitonian*, the student daily newspaper, although it is said that students tend to be apathetic when it comes to active student organizations.

The Students

Although Trinity is Presbyterian affiliated, one student said, "I don't feel like it's a particularly religious school." However, Christian religious groups have a strong presence on campus. "But there is something here for everyone. Almost everyone can find a niche here," said one student. That said, students agree that the population is relatively homogenous. "Everyone here is white, upper middle class and says 'ya'll'," said a student. Yet, the school administration has admittedly taken tremendous strides to diversify the student body. A higher and higher proportion of students hail from out of state. However, the amount of ethnic diversity still lags and continues to be a high priority of the admissions office. As a consequence, the campus tends to be fairly conservative although tolerance toward all viewpoints is also understood.

With an administration dedicated to consistent improvement on academic and social fronts, it is no doubt that at Trinity, undergraduates receive a top-notch education in a community of "tightly knit" students, enthusiastic faculty, and incredible gardeners. —*Jessica Morgan*

FYI

If you come to Trinity you'd better bring "a cowboy hat."

What is the typical weekend schedule? "Go to a football game, the Crazy Horse Saloon and to church on Sunday."

If I could change one thing about Trinity, I would "make it a little bigger."

The three things every student should do before graduating from Trinity are "go to a football game, play an IM sport, and get thrown in the fountain."

University of Dallas

Address: 1845 East Northgate; Irving, TX 75062-4799
Phone: 972-721-5266
E-mail address: undadmis@acad.udallas.edu
Web site URL: www.udallas.edu
Founded: 1956
Private or Public: private
Religious affiliation: Catholic
Location: suburban
Undergraduate enrollment: 1,218
Total enrollment: NA
Percent Male/Female: 45%/55%
Percent Minority: 27%
Percent African-American: 2%
Percent Asian: 7%
Percent Hispanic: 15%
Percent Native-American: 0%
Percent in-state/out of state: 59%/41%
Percent Pub HS: NA
Number of Applicants: 1,183
Percent Accepted: 90%
Percent Accepted who enroll: 31%
Entering: 308
Transfers: 70
Application Deadline: 15 Feb
Mean SAT: NA
Mean ACT: NA
Middle 50% SAT range: V 520-670, M 520-640
Middle 50% ACT range: 22-29
3 Most popular majors: social sciences, English, biology
Retention: 82%
Graduation rate: 63%
On-campus housing: 60%
Fraternities: NA
Sororities: NA
Library: 232,472 volumes
Tuition and Fees: $18,104
Room and Board: $6,494
Financial aid, first-year: 68%
Varsity or Club Athletes: NA
Early Decision or Early Action Acceptance Rate: 83%

The study of the traditional western canon dominates the University of Dallas—students are exposed to it in many forms, and almost all choose to study abroad in Rome. The core curriculum, paired with small classes and the "Rome program," makes the University of Dallas a small, Catholic, liberal arts university that stands out from its peers.

The Core Curriculum

One of the things that many UD students say drew them to the university is the core curriculum. It includes four courses in English, mathematics, and the fine arts, two in the sciences, American civilization, Western civilization, and theology, and one in politics and economics. In addition there is a language requirement. One student commented that the core "broadens students' horizons and challenges them to become even more well-rounded people." Some students wish that one of the four philosophy classes were replaced with another politics class, citing that they felt four philosophy classes was overkill. UD has a strict policy on attendance—miss four classes, and you are automatically dropped from the course. This policy draws mixed reviews from students, some saying that it makes sure everyone is committed, others that the policy could stand to be more lenient, and that they are 18 years old and can take charge of their own lives.

UD has many strong programs. The biology department is considered one of the strongest, especially the premed track, which boasts a high percentage of students accepted to top-tier medical schools. Students also say that the English and classics majors are very strong. Classes with English Professors Dr. Davies and Father Maguire often top lists of favorite classes at UD, with students commenting on Father Maguire's amazing guidance. Students agree that classes at UD are challenging, with a few notable "guts" like the Fundamentals of Biology course. Many students feel that the resources at UD need to be enlarged. There is only one small library, but those in the bio field seem happy with the lab facilities. Other favorite facilities include the Haggerty Art Village, a center that houses an auditorium often used for art history lectures, a gallery, and many studios.

Teachers Going Beyond the Classroom

UD students are very happy with their professors. One student commented that although the faculty is small, they are all very talented. Professors at UD are described as being extremely approachable, and always willing to talk. There is even a senior-faculty happy hour, where seniors and faculty have time to meet in a nonclassroom setting. Another student favorite is the Last Chance Lecture series, in which professors are picked to speak to students as if this were their last speech ever and could talk on anything they wanted.

Housing Options Galore

Students at UD are required to live on campus until they are 21 unless they live with their families in the Dallas area. Housing at UD ranges from dorms to apartments. Most of the dorms have been renovated. The dorms are all single sex—in the past there have been one or two coed dorms, but most students say that they prefer single-sex living. The dorms have strict rules about visits by members of the opposite sex, which some students complain are too severe. After freshman year, students can choose their dorm and roommates. Another on-campus housing option for upperclassmen are the apartments run by the university, which come fully furnished, each with its own porch and reasonable rent, an option that entices many students. All on-campus rooms have ethernet connections, allowing students to easily connect to the network from their desks. About half of UD students live off campus, many of them living in the Tower Village apartments right across from UD. Students living in the dorms are required to have either a 14- or 19-meal plan. Students report being happy about the improvements made by the dining halls.

Social Scene

On weekends many students head off into Dallas—which is full of museums, shops, movie theaters, clubs, and good restaurants. Most students say that it is helpful to have a car since the university is "a bit isolated; the only food store nearby is the PDK convenience store." Students rave about Dallas, saying that it is an easy escape from the UD campus if you want to get away. Those who stay on campus find themselves with a wide array of options to choose from. Every weekend the student programming board has at least one event, which varies from an Indiana Jones trilogy night to Mallapalooza, a concert in which all the campus bands perform. Students' views on the alcohol policy at UD differ greatly. Some say that it is very strict, citing that if you are under 21, you cannot be in a room with alcohol, even if it is in a closed container. Others say that there is alcohol available to underage drinkers if they want it, yet everyone agrees that drinking does not play a large part in the UD social scene. There is a casual dating scene at UD, but it does not dominate social interactions.

One of the largest events of the UD year is Charity week. During this fall week, students participate in events such as a karaoke contest, a "jail" they can have their professors put into to prevent class, and a family day, all to raise money for local charities. Also during charity week, a big-name speaker comes to campus to address the student body. This past year the speaker was Jane Goodall, the world-renowned chimpanzee expert. Another interesting program is the "Dinner and Discourse" program, where once a week a speaker comes to campus to give a guest lecture and to eat dinner with students.

What To Do When Not Studying Philosophy

Although one senior commented that often students get caught in the "UD bubble and they don't always know what is going on in the real world," she also noted that "when students do indeed look out of the UD Bubble, they get really involved." One of the largest service groups on campus is the "Best Buddies" program, which pairs students with mentally and physically handicapped people. Students then run trips and do various activities with their buddies. The UD chapter was recognized as the best one in the region this past year.

Students also participate in intercollegiate sports, although athletics are not a main focus. UD has 14 varsity teams and is a Division III member of the NCAA Though there is no football team at UD—an anomaly at a Texas school—its soccer team is a stand-out.

Andiamo!

One of the main programs attracting students to UD is the Rome program. Almost every member of each year's sophomore class spends at least one semester in Italy. UD owns a small campus in the Alban Hills, 20 minutes from central Rome. This campus among the idyllic olive groves provides the perfect background for a unique semester. Students take classes from UD professors in subjects such as Roman art and architecture, and weekends provide time for class trips with professors to sites discussed in classes. Students find that this program is especially rewarding since "you are in the midst of everything you have been reading and studying." The emphasis on the western tradition is one of the things that sets UD apart from other similar schools. While on the Rome program, students are given 10 days off to travel, and students take advantage of it, going to places such as England, Germany, the Czech Republic, Greece, and Spain, just to name a few.

Students find the Rome program especially rewarding since "you are in the midst of everything you have been reading and studying."

The student body is generally described as conservative. Diversity is somewhat lacking, with only a small percentage of minority students and not many openly gay or lesbian students.

It is the mix of strong classes, interaction with professors, an emphasis on Catholic values, and the Rome program, that makes UD the school that it is. Although some of the rules may seem a bit harsh to students, most seem to agree that after spending four years at UD, they leave with a strong base of knowledge and a real interest in learning—an amazing experience they will remember forever.

—*Sarah Coleman*

FYI

If you come to UD, you'd better bring "an umbrella for the Texas 'winter.'"

What is the typical weekend schedule? "Stay up late, sleep in, do work, go out, sleep in, go to the snoozers and boozers mass at 7:30 Sunday night."

If I could change one thing about UD, I would "enlarge the library."

Three things every student at UD should do before graduating are "go to Rome, try to spend the night in the library, and stargaze with Dr. Olenick."

University of Houston

Address: Houston, TX 77204-2161
Phone: 713-743-1010
E-mail address: admissions@uh.edu
Web site URL: www.uh.edu
Founded: 1927
Private or Public: public
Religious affiliation: none
Location: urban
Undergraduate enrollment: 26,283
Total enrollment: NA
Percent Male/Female: 48%/52%
Percent Minority: 57%
Percent African-American: 15%
Percent Asian: 21%
Percent Hispanic: 21%
Percent Native-American: 0%
Percent in-state/out of state: 98%/2%
Percent Pub HS: NA
Number of Applicants: 8,175
Percent Accepted: 78%
Percent Accepted who enroll: 59%
Entering: 3,457
Transfers: 2,433
Application Deadline: 1 May
Mean SAT: NA
Mean ACT: NA
Middle 50% SAT range: V 450-560, M 470-590
Middle 50% ACT range: 18-23
3 Most popular majors: business management, psychology, social sciences
Retention: 77%
Graduation rate: 37%
On-campus housing: 9%
Fraternities: 3%
Sororities: 3%
Library: 2,123,257 volumes
Tuition and Fees: $3,348 in; $9,888 out
Room and Board: $5,694
Financial aid, first-year: 45%
Varsity or Club Athletes: NA
Early Decision or Early Action Acceptance Rate: NA

Looking for a big Texas school that still provides a great liberal arts education? The University of Houston, with a new image, a new logo, and a recent $5 million campaign to encourage you to come, is on its way up.

Diversity in Academics

UH is a gigantic, diverse campus in every way. It houses more than 30,000 students, yet manages to maintain an academic program that seems to satisfy everyone. Fourteen colleges make up the UH system, each one with a specialty, such as the College of Education; of Business Administration; of Natural Sciences and Mathematics; or of Humanities, Fine Arts, and Communications. Students choose from classes in any of these colleges, allowing departmentalized studying over a wide range of topics. One of the most respected colleges is the Conrad N. Hilton School of Hotel and Restaurant Management, which has an on-campus hotel to give students handson experience.

Though a large university, UH takes its role as a liberal arts school very seriously. Core requirements make up a large portion of the underclassmen's schedules. The requirements include a total of 42 class hours, consisting of six hours in communication (English), three hours of math or logic and reasoning, three hours of humanities, three hours of visual or performing arts, three hours of natural sciences, three hours of social sciences, three hours of history, and six hours of government. While some students feel "bogged down" by these requirements, most are simply "indifferent." The requirements, while often tedious, provide students with a solid background in subjects one would otherwise avoid.

Of the 120 different concentrations undergrads have to choose from, the most difficult are considered to be the math-based ones, including engineering and architecture. While there are no definite "slacker" majors, one student believed that geology would be a safe bet "because when I took that class I skipped the second half of the semester (except the tests) and still got an A." Majors with good reputations are optometry (for which there is an entire college), engineering, and journalism. The sciences wields its own reputation, as well, offering impressive resources such as the Texas Center for Superconductivity Research, now known simply as "Paul's House" in honor of Paul Chu, a

UH professor who did early research in superconductivity. The theater department boasts the Pulitzer Prize–winning playwright Edward Albee, who teaches and works to produce entertaining shows for the entire student body.

Every year 300 hard working students go through a thorough application process in order to join the Honors College. This college—the only interdisciplinary college at UH—gives selected students the opportunity to have a small liberal arts college atmosphere within a huge university setting. Members of this elite group must maintain a high GPA. In exchange for their efforts, honors students enjoy other perks including the chance to live in the best dorms on campus, access to smaller classes, and priority registration.

For the other students at UH, there is not too much about which to complain. They register for classes through a phone system, and are rarely unable to get the classes they want. While some lectures in the core system can have up to 600 students, most upper level courses enroll no more than 30 students.

A Diverse Crowd

Despite the decent dorms, good food, and quiet atmosphere, UH remains a commuter school. Less than a fifth of the students live on campus and despite all the racial and ethnic diversity, about two-thirds of the student body is from the same county in Texas. Students often live in off-campus apartments, or, more commonly, choose to stay at home and drive to school. The average age of UH students is significantly higher than that of other colleges, and many students are adults taking classes part time, or returning to school after time out in the real world.

> **"Commuters do things that they have to and then go home."**

But campus residents are fairly happy with the UH culture. Because of the distance between housing complexes, solidarity develops from the four different residence halls: Cougar Place (lots of varsity athletes and a suite setup), Moody Towers ("the dorms that suck the most . . . with cramped rooms and communal showers"), the Quadrangle, and Cambridge Oaks (privately run on-campus apartments). Students living on campus have the opportunity to know one another better, as they are often the only ones around during weekends, without a home to "zip back to and do a load of laundry."

The UH meal plan actually allows students to eat and pay for what they want. Instead of specified meal costs, the card works like a debit card, taking money out of an account set aside for food. This allows students to eat all over campus in places from the Horizon's Café, with a Pizza Hut, Fresh Grill, and Little Kim Son, to the new Millennium 2000 Café, with a Wendy's, a Taco Bell, and a coffee shop. In addition, students can use their "meal money" to shop at any of several convenience stores and make food on their own. In the past, students have protested the food, but the administration is making efforts to improve it, with the addition of fast food and convenience store options.

Hanging Out off Campus

Houston is the fourth largest city in the country and has much to offer UH students. Unfortunately, UH is not in the best area of Houston. Ten minutes from downtown (by car or the Metro, Houston's public transit) and right off the interstate, as one student put it, "UH is in the middle of the ghetto, you have to go over to Rice for things like cool coffee shops." But again, the administration is looking to change all that. With an on-campus police department and a multitude of emergency phones, crime is at a low. Nevertheless, students remind you that just as you should not walk around anywhere late at night, "you don't want to walk around alone on the campus perimeter late at night." As long as students use common sense, UH is a safe campus.

Students maintain that having a car is almost essential, as there is little campus nightlife. Hence, many students, even those who live on campus, own cars. In Houston itself, students hang out in clubs like Numbers, which has live alternative music, and Rockefeller's. Coffee shops are ever popular with the college crowd, and in the city many frequent the new Magic Bus, a combined bar and coffee house.

During the daylight hours students can go to the museum district and learn about natural history, science, or art, or shop in the Galleria, a mall complete with an ice skating rink. For a day trip, many students choose to go to the beaches at Galveston or to Freeport for a change of pace.

Staying on Campus

On-campus life is relaxed between classes and schoolwork. A typical UH student wears jeans and T-shirts, and is "way casual." Unless you are one of the few in a Greek organization or in an academic honor society, the chances to get dressed up are few and far between. But diversity, in dress and attitude, is abundant.

The campus itself is fairly compact, yet "very beautiful," with the country's largest sculpture garden, and plenty of grassy areas and trees. One student stated, "you keep on discovering new areas of the campus every day." The beautiful opera house/music building also makes seeing performances that much more enjoyable.

There are over 250 student organizations at UH, and they range from the Cattle Rustler, to the Young Socialists, to the Shotokan Karate Club, to the National Leadership Honor Society. The Student Program Board oversees all student social activities. In mid-April, the annual Frontier Fiesta and Cook-Off rouses school spirit with a weekend of "Broadway-like" performances, cultural dances, and food—all in a carnival-like atmosphere.

Without any exceptional sports teams, school spirit has waned in the past few years, and is, according to one student, "not so healthy," while another comments that "I have better things to do than go watch the football team lose." Others, however, say support for the sports teams is increasing. With past athletic greats like Carl Lewis and NBA MVP Hakeem Olajuwan as UH alumni, the athletic department definitely has the potential for greatness.

UH is a large, diverse school with plenty going on to suit anyone's taste. Every option is available both academically and culturally in this growing and changing institution, led by an administration set upon improving in the new millennium. —*Kyla Dahlin*

FYI

The three best things about attending UH are "the honors program, Frontier Fiesta, and downtown Houston."

The three worst things about attending UH are "the parking, the lack of school spirit, and the fact that so many students commute."

Three things that every student should do before graduating from UH are "to study by the Cullen Spring fountain on a nice spring day, to hear a concert in the new opera house, and to join a club!"

One thing I'd like to have known before coming here is that "'advisors don't usually know how to help you."

University of Texas / Austin

Address: Campus Mall Center D0700; Austin, TX 78712-1111
Phone: 512-475-7440
E-mail address: frmn@uts.cc.utexas.edu
Web site URL: www.utexas.edu
Founded: 1883
Private or Public: public
Religious affiliation: none
Location: small city
Undergraduate enrollment: 39,611
Total enrollment: NA
Percent Male/Female: 48%/52%
Percent Minority: 34%
Percent African-American: 3%
Percent Asian: 17%
Percent Hispanic: 14%
Percent Native-American: 0%
Percent in-state/out of state: 95%/5%
Percent Pub HS: NA
Number of Applicants: 22,179
Percent Accepted: 61%
Percent Accepted who enroll: 58%
Entering: 7,935
Transfers: 2,137
Application Deadline: 1 Feb
Mean SAT: NA
Mean ACT: NA
Middle 50% SAT range: V 540-650, M 570-680
Middle 50% ACT range: 22-28
3 Most popular majors: social sciences, business management, communication
Retention: 91%
Graduation rate: 71%
On-campus housing: 17%
Fraternities: 10%
Sororities: 14%
Library: 4,346,398 volumes
Tuition and Fees: $3,950 in; $10,490 out
Room and Board: $5,975
Financial aid, first-year: 47%
Varsity or Club Athletes: NA
Early Decision or Early Action Acceptance Rate: NA

Life at the University of Texas has something for everyone. With 48,000 students, this flagship state school is a world unto itself. Not only is there an enormous range of quality course offerings, but students can enjoy a vibrant social life as well. In addition to the wealth of resources offered by the university, students can take advantage of the exciting scene in surrounding Austin. And, of course, there's nothing like a football game to get the weekend going. Life at UT is full of possibilities—according to one student "if you make an effort to talk to people at the gym, on campus, at gatherings, you could have 47,999 friends."

Charging into Classes

UT's size affords a wide variety of course offerings. While many introductory classes have Teaching Assistants, upper-level courses can have as few as 15 students. If you're in a popular major, signing up for courses can be difficult. UT anticipates that this can be a challenge to incoming freshman, and provides an orientation program to ease the transition to life at UT and help students navigate the class registration process.

All students must fulfill certain graduation requirements, including a foreign language requirement, writing proficiency, and a course on Texas history. Like most universities, classes at UT can range from "awesome to absolutely awful." The education major is generally regarded as one of the easiest; students in math and science departments tend to have the most rigorous academic programs. A small and select group of students enroll in "Plan 2": a multidisciplinary liberal arts major offering small classes taught by some of the University's best professors. Students applying for this competitive program must fill out a secondary application in addition to their general application to UT. Plan 2 students live in separate dorms in the "Honors Quad" for their four years as an undergraduate. As a result, students in Plan 2 tend not to meet as many students outside their small program.

Most undergrads agree that one class everyone should take before graduation is Interpersonal Communications taught by

Dr. John Daly. "The class is a blast," explained one student.

Longhorn Life

Though most freshmen live on campus, UT's large size necessitates that some students move off campus. Many high school seniors send in a housing application and deposit even before they are accepted to the school. Indeed, housing is limited, and competition for on-campus housing can be fierce. Jester, the largest dormitory—and often cited as the "worst" dorm—is a high-rise building housing almost 3,000 students. Jester even has its own zip code! All dorms, however big or small, have air-conditioning; and students can elect to live in co-ed or single-sex dorms.

Most upperclassmen live off campus and seem to enjoy the opportunity to get to know the city of Austin a bit better. Off-campus housing options range from reasonable to costly; those students living particularly far away make use of a UT-operated shuttle service.

"You won't find a more exciting city to go to school in."

Although most Longhorns live off campus, there are extensive dining hall and eating options on campus. On-campus students usually purchase meal plans, allowing them to eat at any on-campus dining hall. Students cite the food as decent, but tire of the options as the "choices are the same throughout the year." Nonetheless, they praise the convenient dining hall hours, which are open late to accommodate a range of schedules.

Awesome Austin

Nestled in the heart of Austin, UT thrives on its location in the midst of a vibrant and exciting city. While some students complain that the campus "feels scrunched" and "lacks the big quads you see at Northern universities," there are "tons of activities" happening off campus. Many Longhorns enjoy Sixth Street for its nightclubs, bars, and trendy restaurants. "A slice of pizza from one of the street-side places on Sixth Street will even cure a hangover," said one UT senior. Known as "The Live Music Capital of the World," Austin also affords endless opportunities for listening to music. With a range of high-tech firms in the city and the State Capital building just steps from campus, students are constantly in the midst of activity. "One thing that differentiates UT from other schools is Austin" said one student. Indeed, after graduation, many students elect to remain in Austin claiming that "you won't find a more exciting city to go to school in on the face of the planet."

For those Longhorns who crave outdoor activities, Austin's weather is nearly ideal. Many students enjoy going to lakes and swimming areas like Hippie Hollow, Lake Travis, Lake Austin and Canyon Lake. Since school is out before the summer really heats up and winter temperatures rarely drop below freezing, students can take advantage of the outdoors for much of the school year. Students feel safe on campus and regularly venture off campus for "camping, running, fishing, hiking, and mountain biking."

Longhorn Pride

"Texas is football, no ifs ands or buts." Athletics is huge at UT—and why not? The football team is consistently ranked in the top 15 and the school invests heavily in its athletic facilities. "The gym is gorgeous, albeit busy," said one student. "There are more than enough machines and weights to keep you busy and sweating."

Athletics are not the only things that unite students. The large Greek system also provides ample opportunities for socializing. Though many students "go Greek," those who don't can still attend the parties. Frat parties occur frequently, however, and some students feel that too much of the campus social life centers on such Greek-hosted social events.

Some students work paying jobs either on or off campus, but many spend time in extracurricular activities. Students participate in service, volunteer and faith organizations of all sorts. And since Austin is the state capital, students interested in politics can easily seek internships in government offices.

Being a UT student means having a lot of energy and pride—UT students are nothing if not spirited. With so many different opportunities at their fingertips, students can have an educational experience characterized by both breadth and depth. While the school's size may seem overwhelming at first, students agree that freshman should jump right in and get involved: "The community is a welcoming one." According to one student, "If I had to choose again, I'd definitely take UT over any other school." *—Lucinda Stamm*

FYI

If you come to UT Austin, you'd better bring "a cowboy hat. If you're a guy, this is standard attire."

What is the typical weekend schedule? "Thursday is pretty low key; Friday and Saturday nights students tend to go all out. During football season, Saturday is 'game-day' and most students start the day drinking with the masses of people at the game. By Sunday students are back to work."

If I could change one thing about UT Austin, I'd "make the social life less dependent on the Greek System."

Three things every student at UT Austin should do before graduating are "swim in the campus fountains, take John Daly's Interpersonal Communications class, and take advantage of the music scene in Austin—they don't call it the 'Live Music Capital of the World' for nothing."

Utah

Brigham Young University

Address: A-153 ASB; Provo, UT 84602
Phone: 801-378-2507
E-mail address: admissions@byu.edu
Web site URL: www.byu.edu
Founded: 1875
Private or Public: private
Religious affiliation: Church of Jesus Christ of Latter-Day Saints
Location: urban
Undergraduate enrollment: 29,379
Total enrollment: NA
Percent Male/Female: 50%/50%
Percent Minority: 7%
Percent African-American: 0%
Percent Asian: 3%
Percent Hispanic: 3%
Percent Native-American: 1%
Percent in-state/out of state: 30%/70%
Percent Pub HS: NA
Number of Applicants: 8,588
Percent Accepted: 72%
Percent Accepted who enroll: 79%
Entering: 4,924
Transfers: 1,132
Application Deadline: 15 Feb
Mean SAT: NA
Mean ACT: NA
Middle 50% SAT range: V 540-650, M 560-670
Middle 50% ACT range: 25-30
3 Most popular majors: education, business, social sciences
Retention: 92%
Graduation rate: 73%
On-campus housing: 20%
Fraternities: NA
Sororities: NA
Library: 2,511,155 volumes
Tuition and Fees: $3,150
Room and Board: $4,874
Financial aid, first-year: 20%
Varsity or Club Athletes: 4%
Early Decision or Early Action Acceptance Rate: NA

Nestled amongst the majestic mountains of Utah, Brigham Young University unites young members of the Church of Jesus Christ of Later Day Saints from across the country. Students come to BYU seeking a top-rated education as well as a community in which they will be able to find a future mate of common faith. The ever-present reminders of the religious nature of the school further this community atmosphere as the rules of The Book of Mormon are followed without need for much enforcement.

Hittin' the Books

Although the first reason many students choose BYU is religious dedication, the academic side of BYU is an advantage as well. The rigors of academics at BYU are apparent from the outset. Before graduation students must complete a set of general education requirements that include classes in mathematics, biology, the physical sciences, American Heritage, Wellness (physical education), and the History of Civilization as well as at least 14 credit hours of religious study. With so many requirements, freshmen find themselves attending most of their classes with other freshmen, which "serves as a means to get to know other freshmen even though classes are usually huge." However, the large class sizes of freshman and sophomore year decrease rapidly once students choose their areas of concentration.

With a large undergraduate population of nearly 30,000, freshman year can be quite daunting. However, the BYU administration strives to make the transition from high school to college as smooth as possible. One way in which they do this is through the "Freshmen Academy." Some freshmen elect this option in which all involved live near each other and take three classes in common (a math class, a writing class and a foreign language class) for their first semester of school. One student reports that, "the Freshmen Academy is great because you really feel a sense of community with other freshmen. Especially since you all live together."

For the most academically and religiously focused students, BYU offers an honors track open to all students upon matriculation to the university. The honors program requires that students take specified honors classes and maintain a GPA above 3.5, but it also goes beyond the classroom. To graduate with honors, students must also complete a study of 16 great works of literature/cinema/performance in a self-directed program, as well as complete courses in advanced languages (either foreign or mathematical), show commitment to the community through service activities, and have faculty sponsors to support their bid for an honors degree.

Beautiful Utah

The only way to describe the atmosphere of Provo, Utah, is awe-inspiring. With many buildings on campus designed with reflective glass, the Utah scenery is reflected throughout campus and a brilliantly inspired atmosphere abounds. The sprawling, modern, architecturally innovative campus gets rave reviews from students. As one student puts it, "It is so refreshing to walk to class on a clear day and breathe in everything. I feel very inspired here and know that this place is where I am meant to be."

Living the Book of Mormon

So how, amongst all this beauty, do students live? Students are not required to live on campus at any time in their years at BYU. This is especially key, because the older you get, the more married couples you will find as well as the number of people returning to school after their mandatory two-year missions. However, the school does follow a strict code of housing that students living both on and off campus must adhere to. This includes restrictions as to when students may have members of the opposite sex in their rooms (always with the doors open and usually not after midnight) as well as modesty of dress (no bikinis allowed by the pool). Although these rules are strict, they do not often have to be rigorously enforced because the student body is relatively self-enforcing. As one student notes, "We are at BYU because we want to live as Mormons and follow the Book of Mormon. If we wanted to have random sex and party all the time we would've gone somewhere else."

"Students look forward to meeting a future mate and all the fun before that."

All These Rules

Because of the religious nature of the school, students at BYU find themselves inundated with religion in all aspects of their lives. However, to BYU students this is not at all a negative. Although Mormonism is one of the fastest growing religions, it is still relatively uncommon in many parts of the country. Thus, for many Mormons, BYU is a haven. Within the school, students are very active within their wards (church congregations) as well as in community service and the many other activities around campus. Also, upon matriculation to BYU, students sign an honor code of both an academic and religious nature. Besides things like agreeing to be honest and not cheating, students also agree to avoid mood-altering substances (including caffeine and alcohol). This means no chatting at a coffee shop and no indulging in chocolate bars, for example. However, growing up with Mormon backgrounds makes these restrictions nothing new to students.

Finding "The One"

Due to the strict laws of the Book of Mormon, Mormons must marry within their religion. Where better to find a Mormon spouse than at a Mormon school? Thus, upon coming to BYU, finding a future mate is one of the main focuses of most students. This focus on marriage rather than random hook-ups is further encouraged by the school administration with policies against couples alone in dorm rooms together. Students are often found going out on group dates and according to one student, "most kids date around quite a bit" in their quest to find that perfect person they will spend the rest of their lives with. As one student said, at BYU people "look forward to meeting a future mate and all the fun before that." Also, it is not uncommon to see young, newly married couples on campus. Partying rarely occurs. As one student puts it, "there are no problems getting beer if you really want it, but most don't." The parties that students tend to go to are dances sponsored by the school. However, the most popular form of dating tends to be going to dinner in groups of couples. Many students can be found on dates at the Skyroom (an on-campus restaurant on the sixth floor of the Wilkinson Student Center, the Wilk).

Cougar Pride

If you're not up for going on a dinner date, what about attending a football or basketball game? As one student puts it, "the stands are packed for football games, basketball games and devotionals." The BYU Cougars are Division I and a member of the Mountain West Athletic Conference. They have a nationally ranked football team with many televised games. With such a sense of community unity at the school, it is no surprise that students rally so fervently behind their mascot, Cosmo the Cougar.

In all aspects of life, BYU is a place of community. "It is so gratifying to be able to practice your faith and to feel the presence of God in our lives as we strive to become spiritually fulfilled adults," notes one student. And nothing could be more of an inspiration towards a fulfilled life than being amongst members of your own faith in the majestic Utah surroundings. —*Engin Yenidunya*

FYI

The three best things about attending BYU are "the great friends, the unity of faith, and beautiful Utah skiing."

The three worst things about attending BYU are "the large size of the school, all the general education requirements, and the curfew rules."

Three things that every student should do before graduating from BYU are "eat at the Skyroom (a restaurant on campus), hike to the Y on the hill, and most importantly . . . get married."

One thing I'd like to have known before coming here is that "the pressure to find a mate is everywhere."

University of Utah

Address: 201 South 1460 East Room 250S; Salt Lake City, UT 84112-9057
Phone: 801-581-7281
E-mail address: NA
Web site URL: acs.utah.edu
Founded: 1850
Private or Public: public
Religious affiliation: none
Location: urban
Undergraduate enrollment: 22,648
Total enrollment: NA
Percent Male/Female: 51%/49%
Percent Minority: 10%
Percent African-American: 1%
Percent Asian: 4%
Percent Hispanic: 4%
Percent Native-American: 1%
Percent in-state/out of state: 84%/16%
Percent Pub HS: 95%
Number of Applicants: 5,802
Percent Accepted: 90%
Percent Accepted who enroll: 54%
Entering: 4,455
Transfers: 2,150
Application Deadline: 1 May
Mean SAT: NA
Mean ACT: NA
Middle 50% SAT range: NA
Middle 50% ACT range: 20-26
3 Most popular majors: sociology, finance, communications
Retention: 75%
Graduation rate: 53%
On-campus housing: 7%
Fraternities: 5%
Sororities: 5%
Library: 2,991,692 volumes
Tuition and Fees: $3,647 in; $11,293 out
Room and Board: $5,036
Financial aid, first-year: 28%
Varsity or Club Athletes: 8%
Early Decision or Early Action Acceptance Rate: NA

The University of Utah is a commuter-based school set in Salt Lake City at the base of the Wasatch Mountains. On weekdays, students participate in a wide array of classes and activities, whereas on weekends it is common for students to head to their Utah homes.

Quality Education

Students were generally happy with the quality of education, praising the "wide range" and "good selection" of classes. Professors were described as "helpful" and "accessible," with a student noting that some professors go out of their way to provide students with connections to various internships and community-service positions. While one student cited that "easier" classes with "multiple-choice tests," most students agreed that the pace and level of difficulty of classes was substantial and adequate. The English department in particular was praised for its "good faculty." Some of the most common majors at the University of Utah include communications, finance, psychology, political science, and economics.

Commuters and Community

Students generally go to class wearing jeans and T-shirts. While "there is the occasional girl in high-heels," most people dress in a "relaxed" fashion. The dating scene is not very active the University of Utah. Students report that while people do go on dates, the social scene mostly consists of "different groups of people hanging out" and "not really dating." There are a number of married couples, and some of the on-campus housing is allocated to them. In general, however, students feel that the "number of attractive people" on campus was "pretty good," potentially a contributing factor to what one student observed as "a lot of random hook-ups going on."

While the Greek system is present at the university, most people found that there is "not much pressure" to be part of it, citing classes and dorms (for those who live on campus) as potential spots for meeting close friends. As the University of Utah is largely a commuter-based campus with a large number of students coming from in-state, it is common for students to head home on the weekends. One student complained that it is "hard" to form lasting friendships because most people commute, despite people's propensity to be "pretty friendly." "It would be good if people could spend more time on campus and get to know people of different backgrounds." Students also report that it is common for students to hang out mainly with a circle of close friends from high school. Although students describe the ethnic background as "homogeneous in that it is predominantly white," they also feel that the student body's diversity is increasing: "You get to see minority and international students around." In fact, the Utah Opportunity Scholars Program awards 20 four-year scholarships covering tuition, books, and fees to underrepresented, first-generation college students entering the university from high schools in the greater Salt Lake area.

"It would be good if people could spend more time on campus and get to know people from different backgrounds."

Those students who do not live at home and commute to school daily, get to enjoy "generous" and "nice" on-campus housing conditions, which are generally spacious and "very comfortable." However, students were not as thrilled about on-campus dining, which they deemed as "overpriced" and "repetitive." One student added that, "If you're vegetarian, the options are severely limited." French fries, pizzas, and grilled cheese sandwiches were mentioned as foods that students "had to live on." One student disparagingly remarked, "It's pretty impossible to mess up grilled-cheese sandwiches, but somehow they did." Students also noted that it is common to see people eating by themselves in the dining halls, since "people aren't too good about sitting with people that they don't know."

The options for off-campus dining are great, with "many fantastic restaurants" just a few minutes away from campus. Students can get downtown easily via the bus and train system, and enjoy substantial discounts at restaurants simply by presenting their student IDs.

The Grounds

Students described the campus as "fairly nice," with "grassy areas" and buildings of varied architectural styles. In particular the President's Circle was mentioned as an aesthetically pleasing spot, while the Union Building was praised as "a great place to hang out on a lazy Sunday afternoon."

In general, most students agreed that if they could choose all over again, they would still choose the University of Utah because of its range of classes, its proximity to home, and the number of cultural opportunities in Salt Lake City. While some students remarked that ethnic and religious diversity could use some improvement, most considered the University of Utah a "great and enjoyable place to be." —*Wenshan Yeo*

FYI

If you come to the University of Utah, you'd better bring "a readiness to work hard."

What is the typical weekend schedule? "Clubbing, drinking and partying—period."

If I could change one thing about the University of Utah, I'd "have people spend more time on campus."

Three things every student at the University of Utah should do before graduating are "get to know the professors better, do some internships, try some of the great restaurants off campus."

Vermont

Bennington College

Address: Bennington, VT 05201
Phone: 800-833-6845
E-mail address: admissions@bennington.edu
Web site URL: www.bennington.edu
Founded: 1932
Private or Public: private
Religious affiliation: none
Location: rural
Undergraduate enrollment: 508
Total enrollment: NA
Percent Male/Female: 34%/66%
Percent Minority: 4%
Percent African-American: 1%
Percent Asian: 1%
Percent Hispanic: 2%
Percent Native-American: 0%
Percent in-state/out of state: 5%/95%
Percent Pub HS: NA
Number of Applicants: 701
Percent Accepted: 69%
Percent Accepted who enroll: 35%
Entering: 172
Transfers: 34
Application Deadline: 1 Jan
Mean SAT: NA
Mean ACT: NA
Middle 50% SAT range: V 580-690, M 500-630
Middle 50% ACT range: NA
3 Most popular majors: visual and performing arts, interdisciplinary studies, English
Retention: 81%
Graduation rate: 83%
On-campus housing: 95%
Fraternities: NA
Sororities: NA
Library: 128,413 volumes
Tuition and Fees: $28,770
Room and Board: $7,140
Financial aid, first-year: 64%
Varsity or Club Athletes: NA
Early Decision or Early Action Acceptance Rate: 86%

"When you come to Bennington, you are not handed an education," commented one student, "you create one." This desire to create is the general attitude pervading this small New England college set upon a hill.

A Different Philosophy

Bennington is unique in many ways, one being that it does not have a set core curriculum—students must take eight classes a year and complete a senior project. This allows students the freedom to take classes in various disciplines without having to worry about completing core or required courses. In addition to typical college courses, Bennington also offers several unusual interdisciplinary courses such as Anatomy through Movement. Many students find this freedom daunting. One student commented that this curriculum (or lack thereof) has "forced me to think long and hard about why I'm here in the first place." Students meet with faculty advisors and create their Plans of Study. Many students say that these meetings require a great deal of confidence, and that "students have to feel comfortable discussing their plans with faculty, or marching into a professor's office to request a tutorial." The benefit of this method is that students find that their work is "personal, not imposed." Students at Bennington also do not receive grades. Letter grades can be requested to supplement written evaluations, however, the system emphasizes the fact that students should be learning for the love of knowledge, not being competitive and working solely for a good GPA.

Student-faculty interaction is part of the core of a Bennington education. Small classes lead to students really developing close relationships with their teachers. Students rave about their professors, including literature standout April Bernard and Psych Professor Ron Cohen. Bennington encourages faculty members to continue their work while teaching, leading professors to be called "teacher-practitioners."

Real-World Experience

Another unique aspect of Bennington is its Field Work Term, a seven-week period during the winter in which students pursue various paths in off-campus environments. During the FWT students get experience as well as make important connections for jobs after graduation. Projects range from working at a Buddhist elementary school in Canada, to working at a small publishing company, to leading trips in a youth leadership training program in Australia. Students give rave reviews of the FWT program, which is a requirement for graduation, saying that it teaches you how to apply for jobs and "to find out whether what you think you want to do is what you really want to do." Furthermore, Bennington students pride themselves on graduating with a resume as well as a diploma.

One of the things that many students take an active role in is the creation of art. Students at Bennington have access to a myriad of art resources right at their fingertips. The Visual and Performing Arts Center is open 24 hours a day, seven days a week, and comes complete with private studio spaces for advanced students. The dance performance space, "Martha Hill," is 10,000 square feet and is one of the biggest springboard performance floors in the western hemisphere. The library draws mixed reviews—most humanities students seem to be happy, but some students feel that the social science and science resources are lacking. Extensive research is often hard to do, although the interlibrary loan program with Williams College is farily good.

Students at Bennington are assigned to one of 12 houses that surround the commons lawn. About 30 people live in each of these white, colonial-style clapboard houses with green shutters. As one student described, "The houses feel cozy—each house has a living room with a piano and a fireplace. Each house has its own personality and reputation, and there are a variety of quiet and loud houses that students pick and choose between. The rooms are decently sized, and upperclassmen are pretty much guaranteed a single room. Every Sunday the House Chairs hold a Coffee Hour, which is used to bring together the house community and raise house and campus issues. The House Chairs "act as informal resident advisors—responding to house issues, keeping an eye on freshmen, and acting as role models for younger students." One advantage (or sometimes a disadvantage) of the house system is that you really get to know the people you are living with. With the exception of one off-campus vegan co-op house, virtually all students live on campus.

"Individuals are part of a dialogue with the larger community, and it is a very challenging and potentially rich conversation."

Students at Bennington are not only well housed, but they are very well fed. Students gave a good review of the college's food. One student estimated that 60 percent of the student body is vegetarian, so there are always vegetarian options. Students really appreciate the "Napkin Notes" they can send to "Dining-Hall Dave," who responds in order to make improvements in dining-related issues. Also popular is the way the community at Bennington comes together at special events like the midnight breakfast. Every term during final week, the administration schedules a surprise "midnight breakfast" announced by fire trucks driving through the center of campus. All students leave what they are doing and go to the dining hall where they are served breakfast by the administration, faculty, and staff. The midnight breakfast is "a nice way to chill out for a few hours in the middle of a really hectic week."

A Community like No Other

Bennington's social atmosphere resembles that of its academic world: small and intimate. There are always tons of performances at Bennington and the school brings in such notable lecturers as Jamaica Kincaid and Frank Bidart. There are a lot of parties at Bennington, but they are heavily monitored by security, and thus there is little underage drinking at school-sponsored events. Minors still find ways to drink though, although most students would not say that there is a big drinking problem on campus. There are no frats at Bennington; most of the parties are thrown by the houses or by the campus activities board. Some of the best social events are the parties thrown by the campus activities board with varied themes such as Andy Warhol, Transvestite Nite, Bowlerama, Sunfest, and Swing Night, to name a few. These parties are generally well attended and the college usually brings in good bands to enliven the atmosphere. The student body at Bennington is about 65 percent female, so "the dating scene, if there is one, is weird to say the least." The student body was described by another student as being "an open-minded and a diverse bunch," and students say that being homosexual or bisexual is never an issue. Some people feel that the student body "lacks ethnic diversity to an extreme," but they "have a large array of international students who contribute a lot to the on-campus culture." Students at Bennington are often stereotyped as being "wealthy, flighty, druggie," and "angsty artist types," but other students vigorously disagree, saying "there are lots of people with varied interests here."

Students relax at Bennington by taking advantage of the growing outdoor program and the beautiful scenery that surrounds the college. The Appalachian Trail lies four miles away, and there is great skiing in the area during the winter. There are no formal sports at Bennington; however, there is an intramural soccer team that plays other teams in the area. There is also a two-on-two basketball and a badminton tournament each term. Students at Bennington are very happy with the addition of a fitness center complete with a rock-climbing wall, a sauna, an aerobics room, weightlifting equipment, and cardiovascular equipment. Also offered are free kickboxing and yoga classes.

Escaping Bennington

When students start to feel a bit claustrophobic, they usually head to New York City, Boston, or Burlington, which are each about three hours away by car. The bus station is close to campus and buses leave to these destinations regularly. For a shorter trip, Williamstown and North Adams, Massachusetts, are nearby and offer the closest access to culture, good restaurants, and art. About half the students at Bennington have cars, and they are "useful, but not necessary; you can get anywhere by car-pooling or using the campus van."

One thing that students at Bennington cannot rave enough about is its wonderful sense of community. As one student said "there is nothing artificial about it, so the ideal of 'community' isn't just administrative nonsense. It's something that you live with (and in) every day." At Bennington, as one student summed it up, "individuals are part of a dialogue with the larger community, and it is a very challenging and potentially rich conversation." —*Sarah Coleman*

FYI

If you come to Bennington you'd better bring "a free spirit."

A typical weekend schedule would be "11 A.M.: wake up, shuffle up the hill to brunch in your pajamas. Noon: go to a movie, walk to the lake or go shopping in town. 5 P.M.: dinner. 10 P.M. until you fall asleep: sometimes a party, sometimes a spontaneous drive to Lake George or Albany, or just a cozy marshmallow roast around the fireplace in your house."

If there were one thing I could change about Bennington, "I'd make it affordable to everyone who wants to and deserves to study there."

Three things everyone should do before graduating are "go swimming at Lake Paran, dress up for Transvestite Nite, and sleep all night on the lawn."

Marlboro College

Address: Marlboro, VT 05344
Phone: 802-258-9236
E-mail address: admissions@marlboro.edu
Web site URL: www.marlboro.edu
Founded: 1946
Private or Public: private
Religious affiliation: none
Location: rural
Undergraduate enrollment: 303
Total enrollment: NA
Percent Male/Female: 40%/60%
Percent Minority: 4%
Percent African-American: 1%
Percent Asian: 0%
Percent Hispanic: 2%
Percent Native-American: 1%
Percent in-state/out of state: 10%/90%
Percent Pub HS: 64%
Number of Applicants: 229
Percent Accepted: 82%
Percent Accepted who enroll: 40%
Entering: 78
Transfers: 19
Application Deadline: 1 Mar
Mean SAT: NA
Mean ACT: NA
Middle 50% SAT range: V 590-690, M 500-620
Middle 50% ACT range: 24-29
3 Most popular majors: visual and performing arts, social sciences, cultural and gender studies
Retention: 68%
Graduation rate: 42%
On-campus housing: 78%
Fraternities: NA
Sororities: NA
Library: 58,106 volumes
Tuition and Fees: $21,630
Room and Board: $7,425
Financial aid, first-year: 58%
Varsity or Club Athletes: NA
Early Decision or Early Action Acceptance Rate: 75%/90%

The intimate quality of the college experience at Marlboro College extends beyond its rustic surroundings into the social lives of students both inside and outside the realm of academics. According to students, the tightness of the community is one of Marlboro's most attractive qualities, but also one of the "most challenging" aspects of being a student.

Rigorous Academics

Students call Marlboro academics "rigorous," often featuring one-on-one tutorials with professors. These tutorials are very popular with undergrads. Most introductory classes enroll 15 to 20 people, while the higher-level seminars are even smaller. Literature and the social science departments are reportedly strong at Marlboro, with the former ranking as one of the more popular majors. Religion, Literature, and Philosophy is considered the most difficult and rewarding course. As one student said, "It's the history of Western thought in one year: *The Iliad* in one week, *The Divine Comedy* the next."

Marlboro has few academic requirements. Regardless of their major (or "field of concentration" in Marlborian terms), students must fulfill a writing requirement before their sophomore year and submit a 20-page portfolio of their writing at the end of the semester, which is judged by the faculty. If the instructors view a submission unacceptable, the student has two more opportunities to pass the requirement. If a student fails to pass after three tries, he or she is asked to leave the college, regardless of previous academic achievements. The requirement can sound intimidating to incoming freshmen, but students describe it as a "good thing" that pressures them into writing clearly and concisely. One of Marlboro's most interesting opportunities is its World Studies Program where students focus on International Relations as an academic discipline often study and work abroad during the first semester of their junior year. Students are required to write about their experiences upon their return.

Marlboro undergrads consider themselves "extremely lucky" to have strong relationships with the faculty. Teaching assistants are relatively non-existent, although some students often choose to co-teach a course with another student as their final "Plan of Concentration," a cumulative interdisciplinary effort of their last two years of study. Otherwise described as a "senior thesis times ten," this final work is relatively flexible—some opt for writing a 120-page paper while others produce a play. The intimacy students and their professors enjoy is a highlight of Marlboro, and it is not uncommon for students to enjoy dinner at any one of their professors' homes. Marlboro has one centrally located cafeteria, which encourages both students and faculty to enjoy one another's company at mealtimes.

Although upperclassmen receive priority during class registration, one student said that he "never heard of anyone not being able to take a class because it was full." The average class size is seven or eight students, and class-sizes of three or four are not uncommon, which "makes it awfully hard to hide if you haven't done your work," remarked one student. The professors, for the benefit of the students, provide 20-minute introductory lectures during the first two days of each term. Although courses are described as "demanding," faculty advisors make sure their advisees keep up with the course load. The lack of organized athletics at Marlboro encourages students to focus on their schoolwork, "so what you do here is study," one student explained.

Beside dorm rooms, places for students to hang out on campus are limited, and those not interested in going to the Campus Center find themselves seeking a ride into Brattleboro, a small town popular for its "cultural and liberal" atmosphere, about 15 minutes from campus. The Campus Center functions as a campus coffeehouse, alternate cafeteria (with limited hours), game room, post office, and general location for all campus-wide events. For those who want a more sociable study place, the center is the place to meet.

Marlboro Living

All Marlboro undergrads are required to live on campus freshman year, though most students live on campus all four years. Students praise the dorm rooms, some of which have balconies. The rooms are favorably sized, and usually only frosh live in triples. The priority for housing selection is based on how many credits a student has earned. All the Way is one of the more popular dorms because of its large kitchen, while Howland is generally the least favorite due to "dumpy" conditions and higher noise levels. The thin walls in Howland "really affect your love life," one student moaned. Resident advisors (RAs) live in each dorm and organize meetings to vote on "quiet hours" and other inter-dorm issues. One student remarked, "Unlike other colleges, the RAs at Marlboro are more like advisors and less like police." Dorm halls are co-ed, and only one dorm, Half Way, is reserved for women. Each year, one building is designated "substance-free" and one is "smoke-free." Security reportedly is not an issue at Marlboro, and some students do not worry if they forget to lock their doors.

Marlboro's isolated location limits the availability of off-campus housing. College-owned cottages are designed for students who desire a close-to-campus location and independence from typical dorm living. Each cottage, usually occupied by juniors or seniors, consists of four bedrooms. Renting houses in the woods from townspeople is another option, and Brattleboro, despite the commute, attracts many looking for alternatives to dorm housing.

The Grub

Dining hall food at Marlboro is reportedly decent. Many students complain about the lack of variety, although vegetarian and vegan options are available at every meal. There is freshly baked bread every day, which one student described as "fantastic." Student workers do the cooking, and accept suggestions by their peers. Dining hours are limited, but those who miss a meal can find snacks at the Campus Center. According to one undergrad on the meal plan, "You can eat as much as you want, and you don't have to pay per item." Every Sunday is Ben & Jerry's Night and both on- and off-campus students are welcome to partake of delicious, free ice cream.

What's Happening in Vermont?

The popular Outdoor Program allows Marlborians to take advantage of the pristine Vermont countryside. Students often suggest new activities, such as hang gliding, and as long as there are enough people (at least five) and money, the activity is organized and implemented. One student described campus athletics as "do-it-yourself sports," since no official varsity program exists. There is a soccer team, but apart from that formal competition is limited.

Marlboro's emphasis on "self-reliance" academics makes it a particularly attractive school to those who seek a rigorous curriculum balanced with a lot of attention from faculty.

The party scene is reportedly diverse. In addition to going to parties organized by the Social Activities Council, most people spend time with friends either at private parties or in the Campus Center. The Cabaret, the main social event of the year, involves an exhibition of student entertainment. Social drinking is common on campus, and some students smoke marijuana, but as one undergrad said, "Neither drugs nor alcohol are in your face. They're not a requirement for attending parties."

The small size of the college "makes it hard to have casual sex relationships," one student said, "as you invariably see your fellow classmates quite often." Another student joked that there are only "six couples" on campus. A lack of privacy is supposedly responsible for hindering random hookups.

Politically, Marlboro is predominantly liberal. Students say the gay community is quite vocal and is "very accepted" on campus. Environmental concerns are also a hot topic among students. Participation in student groups, whatever the cause, is popular, and although the student body is not ethnically diverse, its geographical diversity lends itself to many different ideas and experiences from those willing to contribute.

School spirit at Marlboro is surprisingly high for a school that lacks a formal athletics department. Most undergrads have a "fierce loyalty and love" for Marlboro, and many alumni remain active in college affairs. *The Citizen* is a bi-weekly student newspaper, and another popular group is the Live Action Role-Playing Group, a band of students who perform for the entertainment of the campus community.

Marlboro's emphasis on "self-reliance" academics makes it a particularly attractive school to those who seek a rigorous curriculum balanced with a lot of attention from faculty. The isolation of the college is great for those who want "to get away from it all," but most students warn that you really should know what you want in a school before coming to Marlboro: "Make sure you want someplace really independent," and do not forget to pack "some good sturdy shoes" for those wintertime hikes to class. —*Susannah Chu*

FYI

If you come to Marlboro you'd better bring "the ability to write because it makes the portfolio requirement less stressful, and some warm shoes for the winter."

A typical weekend schedule would be "hang out with friends at night and maybe go to a party Friday night, go hiking and study on Saturday, study on Sunday."

If there were one thing I could change about Marlboro, "I'd change how quiet it can get around here."

The three things that every student should do before graduating from Marlboro are "join an environmental rally, hang at the Campus Center, and chow some yummy Ben & Jerry's."

Middlebury College

Address: The Emma Willard House; Middlebury, VT 05753-6002
Phone: 802-443-3000
E-mail address: admissions@middlebury.edu
Web site URL: www.middlebury.edu
Founded: 1800
Private or Public: private
Religious affiliation: none
Location: small town
Undergraduate enrollment: 2,244
Total enrollment: NA
Percent Male/Female: 49%/51%
Percent Minority: 15%
Percent African-American: 2%
Percent Asian: 7%
Percent Hispanic: 5%
Percent Native-American: 1%
Percent in-state/out of state: 6%/94%
Percent Pub HS: 54%
Number of Applicants: 5,299
Percent Accepted: 27%
Percent Accepted who enroll: 41%
Entering: 586
Transfers: 12
Application Deadline: 15 Dec
Mean SAT: NA
Mean ACT: NA
Middle 50% SAT range: V 680-750, M 670-740
Middle 50% ACT range: 29-32
3 Most popular majors: English, psychology, economics
Retention: 96%
Graduation rate: 88%
On-campus housing: 96%
Fraternities: NA
Sororities: NA
Library: 950,000 volumes
Tuition and Fees: NA
Room and Board: NA
Financial aid, first-year: 37%
Varsity or Club Athletes: 42%
Early Decision or Early Action Acceptance Rate: 27%

With incomparable views of the Vermont hills, a dynamic outdoorsy student body, and Ben and Jerry's ice cream in the dining halls, Middlebury College attracts students who are smart, earthy, and unaffected by cold weather.

So Many Distributions, So Little Time

To graduate, Middlebury students must take a First-Year Seminar, classes in seven out of eight general academic distributions, and four "cultural context" classes. The eight academic categories are literature, the arts, philosophical and religious studies, historical studies, physical and life sciences, deductive reasoning and analytical processes, social analysis, and foreign languages. The four cultural classes focus on North America, Europe, Africa, Asia, Latin America, or a comparison of more than one culture. The freshman seminars are writing focused, and are the first of two writing-intensive courses that must be taken before graduation.

While the requirements seem daunting, most students appreciate the liberal arts emphasis, explaining, "The reason why I came here was because I didn't want to decide at 18 what to study." Students looking for an easy science requirement can take Physics: Human Reality and Thought, with Rich Wolf, while political science with Professor Pekkanen is described as "tough, but rewarding." Middlebury offers 44 majors, of which foreign languages, sciences, and international politics and economics are considered the most difficult. Environmental studies, on the other hand, is among the easiest: One student remarked, "All they do is frolic in the woods." About 40 percent of students double major, and approximately two-thirds of the student body go abroad at some point in their Middlebury careers. Middlebury is renowned for its language department, and offers myriad opportunities for language study during the summer, at home and abroad. Students can major in French, Spanish, Chinese, Japanese, German, Italian, or Russian, and each of these departments has links to schools or programs in their country of origin.

The school year is divided up into two semesters and a J-term, a month in the winter in which students study one topic in depth. These tend to be less traditional classes such as ballroom dancing, pinhole photography, or lego robot design, but also include many of the courses available during the year. In the liberal arts tradition, students may audit classes that they find interesting, but do not want to take for a grade. The class will not count towards distribution requirements or diploma requirements, but auditing a prerequisite to a course is sufficient for entry into that course.

Classes at Middlebury are small, generally with 20 students or less. There are no TAs, only tutors, and "all discussion sections are run by professors." Therefore, students get to know many of their professors, and find it "reasonably easy" to get into the courses they want, "especially as upperclassmen." The workload is described as intense: "I feel like we go to school more than friends of mine at other colleges," said one sophomore. Middlebury has no reading period between classes and exams, which adds to the academic crunch. However, most students have come to expect and enjoy the rigorous academic life, and still find time to explore the social activities offered on campus.

Viva Ross Vegas: A Night on the Town

Middlebury students work hard, but they also know how to have a good time. While seniors frequent the downtown bars, Mr. Ups and Two Brothers, underclassmen can often be found at the social houses, which are former fraternities and sororities transformed into coed living spaces. With names like "The Tavern," and "Zoo," the social houses throw "really fun" parties such as Sin City and the Marriage/Divorce party, where "you go get married, drink champagne, then you get divorced and drink tequila." The parties are fairly well-regulated with respect to alcohol; security officers check ID's and hand out citations for underage drinking. The Commons, which are clusters of associated dorms sharing a common courtyard, also throw parties. Ross Commons, newly built with an attached dining hall and "the nicest, biggest rooms" threw its first "Viva Ross Vegas" party last year. Students spice up their social lives with plays put on by the theater department and comedy shows by "Otter Nonsense." Particularly during the winter, hanging out in dorm rooms becomes the preferred option. "We are very possibly located in the coldest place in the world," joked one student.

Preps, Hippies, and Polar Bears

What is the typical "Midd Kid" like? In general, "a Middlebury student loves the outdoors, probably skis and hikes on the weekend, and is interested in environmental studies." However, some students would argue that the campus has two types: the wealthy, J. Crew–sporting, "private school preppy," and the "environmental type," characterized by "Birkenstocks, dreads," and clothes "from mountaineering stores." While the disparity in wealth between the two factions can sometimes be "alienating," and diversity is "less than impressive," most students are content with the student body makeup. "You find the people that you connect with," one student commented. Popular extracurricular activities include the Middlebury Mountaineering Club, intramural sports, Commons Council, and a capella singing groups. While football is not a huge spectator sport, attendance is high at varsity hockey games. For the extra-adventurous Midd Kid, there is the Polar Bear Club, whose members go skinny-dipping once a week—all year long. "They're crazy," one junior remarked.

The Lay of the Land

The Middlebury campus is centered around five residential "Commons," which are designed to serve as the backbone of student life. Each Commons has its own character and housing reputation. Ross, for example, is the newest and by some standards the nicest, although it doesn't have the charm of more classic buildings. There is a lot of new construction going on, with two new residence halls being added to Atwater Commons, and renovations proceeding in Cook Commons. The bugs are still being worked out of the Commons system, as it was newly implemented only a few years ago, but students have high hopes for the enhanced sense of community it will create. Also new on campus is the science building, Bicentennial Hall. Built in 1999, it has great "study nooks" and lounges, as well as labs and science classrooms. Rumor has it that the building has a window made from the "largest single piece of glass in the world."

"A Middlebury student loves the outdoors, probably skis and hikes on the weekend, and is interested in environmental studies."

Other notable buildings on campus include McCollough, the student center, where Midd kids hang out, study, check mail, and grab late night snacks; Proctor, one of the more popular dining halls; and Le Chateau, a gorgeous building with classrooms and a "restaurant" run by students, called Café Dolci. The food on campus is "pretty good," although it can get boring and familiar. Making an effort to support local producers, Middlebury gets its milk from area farmers, and its ice cream from both local creameries and Ben and Jerry's.

Beyond the Middlebury campus, the town of Middlebury offers "cute little shops" and restaurants for student enjoyment. Popular places to eat include Storm Café, Dog Team Tavern, American Flatbread, and Neil and Otto's, whose "pizza sticks with cheese" are perhaps "the most ordered food on campus." Students also frequent Ben Franklin's, which has great dorm apparel, although for "real" shopping, students head to Burlington, about 40 minutes away. Although most of the student body lives on campus (only seniors can live off campus, and most of them do not because of high rent and distance from classes), many of the students have cars and use them to drive around campus, to Burlington, and sometimes to Montreal or New York City.

Cool Traditions

Upon their arrival at Middlebury, freshmen attend a convocation ceremony in which a replica of the college founder's cane is passed around from student to student. Gamiliel Painter, Middlebury's founder, worked tirelessly at the college, and bequeathed to it his sturdy wooden cane. When students graduate, a replica of the cane is given to each graduating senior, and a Cane Society was created in 1989, which recognizes alumni and friends of the college who support Middlebury through gifts and donations.

Overall, Middlebury students enjoy their artistic and outdoorsy school. The lively campus is close enough to big cities for a visit, but nestled in the beautiful Vermont landscape. It is rare to hear a Middlebury student complain about their college experience; rather, most look back on their college days with fondness. —*Diana Dosik*

FYI

If you come to Middlebury, you'd better bring "a Patagonia jacket."

What's the typical weekend schedule? "Friday night; chill and watch a movie, cook with friends; Saturday, go out and hike/ski, go out to a party at the social houses at night; Sunday, study, do homework."

If I could change one thing about Middlebury, I'd "change the weather."

Three things every student at Middlebury should do before graduating are "spend a winter morning with the Polar Bear Club, check out the view from Bicentennial Hall, and hit the Bread Loaf ski slopes."

University of Vermont

Address: 194 South Prospect Street; Burlinton, VT 05401-3596
Phone: 802-656-3370
E-mail address: admissions@vuvm.edu
Web site URL: www.uvm.edu
Founded: 1791
Private or Public: public
Religious affiliation: none
Location: small town
Undergraduate enrollment: 8,792
Total enrollment: NA
Percent Male/Female: 44%/56%
Percent Minority: 5%
Percent African-American: 1%
Percent Asian: 2%
Percent Hispanic: 2%
Percent Native-American: 0%
Percent in-state/out of state: 39%/61%
Percent Pub HS: NA
Number of Applicants: 9,776
Percent Accepted: 70%
Percent Accepted who enroll: 26%
Entering: 1,841
Transfers: 405
Application Deadline: 15 Jan
Mean SAT: NA
Mean ACT: NA
Middle 50% SAT range: V 520-620, M 520-620
Middle 50% ACT range: 22-27
3 Most popular majors: business administration, English, psychology
Retention: 82%
Graduation rate: 70%
On-campus housing: 52%
Fraternities: 9%
Sororities: 6%
Library: 2,410,250 volumes
Tuition and Fees: $9,636 in; $22,688 out
Room and Board: $6,680
Financial aid, first-year: 54%
Varsity or Club Athletes: 13%
Early Decision or Early Action Acceptance Rate: 70%/80%

Life in the Vermont weather has its upsides and its downsides. The University of Vermont campus looks idyllic in the winter, with its snow-covered hills and icicle-tipped buildings. Two renowned ski resorts, Sugarbush and Stowe, are less than a half-hour drive from the university grounds, with school-organized transportation to and from the slopes. Burlington's Waterfront Park is just blocks from campus and offers outdoor ice-skating. However, with the average low in January set at an icy eight degrees, one students said the winter can "put a damper on a lot of activity. When it's 2 degrees out, no one is too motivated to go walk and find a party." During their four years' stay in the Green Mountain State, University of Vermont students learn both to love and loathe the wintry climate.

Academic Options

There is no standard set of academic requirements common to all UVM students. Mandatory classes vary depending on school, program and major. However, most students say, "requirements are fair, and easy to fulfill in four years if you know what you want to study." One freshman raved that "a lot of the classes that take care of requirements are also fun" and can be practical. Classes like Applications of Finite Math fulfill requirements while giving students vital skills for the future.

All undergraduates are required to take a Race and Culture class and two credits of physical education. PE offerings range from traditional sports, like tennis and volleyball, to more creative offerings, like figure skating and rappelling. One undergrad marveled at the fact that students receive course credit for everything from "Walking for Fitness" to "Stress Reduction."

Class size at UVM varies depending on the level of the course. According to one junior, "Intro classes are about as bad as they get . . . 500-person lecture halls, dry professors, and two exams to evaluate you." However, things improve dramatically once students get past the basics: "Upper-level classes are twenty people or less, discussion-based and much more interesting." Popular offerings include the sociology class Sex, Marriage and Family, which examines issues like how the view of sex has changed over time and how childhood experiences affect parents' behavior.

Students' primary complaint is that many students get shut out of classes. Athletes get first pick, then seniors, juniors, sophomores and finally freshman. One undergraduate complained, "Classes fill up too early and you sometimes have to wait two or three semesters to get a class you want, which screws up your class requirements for your major." The most popular programs include business administration, biology, and elementary education. UVM offers a variety of pre-professional programs, including pre-law, pre-med, and pre-vet.

All students tackle five classes a semester, leading some to groan about the "ton of work." However, others assure that the academic load is manageable. "I think it is useful to do all the work teachers give you, but for some classes it isn't really necessary," said one student. PE classes, which usually don't have homework, also lighten the load.

Home Sweet Home

UVM students call Burlington, the largest city in Vermont, their home. Downtown features a mall, nice stores and a pedestrian shopping area that is off-limits for cars. Students consider their city "quaint" and a "very spiritual place," and frequently venture into Burlington for meals, shopping and relaxation. They also take advantage of the wilderness around Burlington, enjoying the splendid scenery and wild terrain that lies just outside the city. "The best part of Vermont is often the unexplored parts," said one student. Undergraduates often spend their free time hiking, swimming and biking around Burlington.

Students also get involved in the local community, through the University's multitude of volunteer programs. UVM volunteers-in-action is the "student-run umbrella organization for twelve different volunteer programs" through which students devote their time everywhere from Burlington's soup kitchens to its battered women's homes. Every year about forty volunteers go to Burlington elementary schools to teach creative writing and produce the *Vermont Children's Magazine*. One junior described the volunteer program as "one of the most rewarding things I have done at UVM."

Hockey is *the* sport for UVM students. According to one undergrad, "the games are always filled," as everyone flocks to see the NCAA division III Catamounts face off against the ECAC. Club and intramural athletics thrive as well and "lots of people" use the campus fitness center regularly. Students also stay in shape by hitting the slopes at one of the many local ski resorts.

Room and Board

UVM underclassmen usually live on one of three mini-campuses: Main Campus, East Campus and Redstone. Most freshmen live in Harris-Millis, which is primarily doubles, with a few triples mixed in. Main Campus houses an additional group of freshman, in the infamous "shoeboxes," known for their tiny size. Freshman dorms are "fun, social places . . . but you won't get any work done there at all" and floors are single-sex. Most sophomores live on Redstone campus, which is farther from classes but "really nice and with newer furniture." One of the best parts of the UVM housing system is that it is flexible and "you have the option to move around a lot," with no deadlines for changing rooms. Juniors and seniors have the option to move off campus and many do. They often live in Burlington apartments and houses, but due to high demand, off-campus housing can be "really expensive." Students can also choose to reside in the Living and Learning Complex, in which students who share a common interest can choose to live with one another.

"At any time during the week, day or night, you can and will find people ready to party."

The on-campus food is provided by Marriott and is "pretty good" according to most students. Students pay for meals using either point or blocks. Points work like cash, paying for meals at the cafeteria, food at Alice's (think "Mobil Mart") or pizza. Blocks can only be used at the all-you-can-eat cafeteria that has nightly pasta, pizza and grill in addition to hot entrees. All students choose from a variety of meal plans, which can be entirely points, entirely blocks or some combination of the two.

Party Hardy

By all accounts, UVM lives up to its reputation as a party school. "At any time during the week, day or night, you can and will find people ready to party." Since the campus is officially dry, students party at the fraternity houses and off-campus bashes. Fraternities usually charge five dollars for admission and sometimes feature themes. One student recalls a "disease" party, where students were handed cards with the name of an illness. If partiers found the student with the matching card, they were rewarded with shots of alcohol. In addition to drinking, "all frats have music and dancing and most house parties do, too."

Most students agree that non-drinkers do not feel out of place on campus. "If you are sober, you can have a great time, too," remarked one freshman and staying in to chill with friends is pretty common. However, the party scene dominates UVM social life and despite the occasional a cappella concert or dance, alternative social gatherings are "not always an option." The administration is attempting to crack down on on-campus and underage drinking. Burlington city cops, as well as RAs, patrol the dorms and "they are not looking out for your best interests. Ever." Drug use is also widespread on campus. "The pot scene is unbelievable at UVM—practically unavoidable," said one upperclassman. Another student contends that while drugs are around, "it really depends on the people who you hang out with."

In addition to on-campus entertainment, UVM students enjoy Burlington's "hoppin' night life," letting loose at one of the city's two dance clubs or the numerous bars, which require ID. The area around UVM boasts an active concert scene. "Burlington is a young, hip city, and everything comes through: reggae, hip hop, bluegrass, you name it," as well as the jam-orientated music for which the area is particularly known. One of the most popular venues is Higher Ground, in nearby Winooski, Vermont, which features a continual stream of talented musicians.

Hippies—Too Many or Too Few?

Most undergrads say that their schoolmates have a great variety of attitudes, styles and interests. One student complained that there are "too many hippies," but another said there are not as many as she expected. One junior warned that "if you like Phish, you'll get to know a lot more about them. And if you don't, well, you better learn to tolerate them." More than half of the student body are Vermont natives and cultural and racial diversity are not the school's strongest points.

On the whole, students at the University of Vermont celebrate the fact that their peers possess "a liberal attitude and an open mind." Whether it is in the classroom, the frat houses or on Church Street in downtown Burlington, their classmates are "genuinely nice people" and receptive to different ideas, pastimes and fellow students. *—Pamela Boykoff*

FYI

If you come to UVM, you'd better bring "a winter coat."

What is the typical weekend schedule? "Skiing, snowboarding, hockey games, lake trips, coffee shops, and the outdoors—when it's pretty."

If I could change one thing about UVM, I'd "fix the parking problem."

The three things every student should do before graduating from UVM are "ski or snowboard at Stowe Mountain, learn how to balance academics and fun, and get involved in the Burlington community."

Virginia

College of William and Mary

Address: PO Box 8795, Williamsburg, VA 23187-8795
Phone: 757-221-4223
E-mail address: admiss@facstaff.wm.edu
Web site URL: www.wm.edu
Founded: 1693
Private or Public: private
Religious affiliation: none
Location: small city
Undergraduate enrollment: 5,694
Total enrollment: NA
Percent Male/Female: 44%/56%
Percent Minority: 15%
Percent African-American: 5%
Percent Asian: 7%
Percent Hispanic: 3%
Percent Native-American: 0%
Percent in-state/out of state: 66%/34%
Percent Pub HS: NA
Number of Applicants: 8,917
Percent Accepted: 32%
Percent Accepted who enroll: 43%
Entering: 1,320
Transfers: 181
Application Deadline: 5 Jan
Mean SAT: NA
Mean ACT: NA
Middle 50% SAT range: V 620-730, M 630-710
Middle 50% ACT range: 27-31
3 Most popular majors: business management, English, biology
Retention: 96%
Graduation rate: 91%
On-campus housing: 75%
Fraternities: 31%
Sororities: 33%
Library: 2,128,645 volumes
Tuition and Fees: $6,430 in; $21,130 out
Room and Board: $5,794
Financial aid, first-year: 30%
Varsity or Club Athletes: 19%
Early Decision or Early Action Acceptance Rate: 54%

Students at William and Mary quickly become accustomed to giving directions. When the weather is nice, it is not uncommon for a student to be stopped en route to class by a bewildered tourist looking for a historic landmark. After all, this is the second-oldest school in the nation, and is located in colonial Williamsburg, a popular vacation spot. While the hordes of wandering "tourons" can sometimes be irritating, students agree that the attention is flattering, and they are proud to show off their school. "Besides," explained a senior, "it's a constant reminder that we get to go to everything in colonial Williamsburg for free . . . so we might as well help out!"

A Tight-Knit Community

William and Mary's small size is relatively unusual among its public school counterparts, but students insist that is not *too* small. Says one upperclassman, "I can walk across the Sunken Gardens and run into people I know, but I could also meet someone new every day." The small size fosters a close community, which is made even tighter by a number of William and Mary traditions. Everybody looks forward to the annual Yule Log Ceremony, where representatives of different cultures explain their traditions for the holiday season and the president of the university reads to the whole student body dressed as Santa Claus. Worries are brushed away on a yule log, and the evening ends with hot cider, cookies, and a bonfire. Ghost tours of colonial Williamsburg are popular around Halloween, and spring brings the formal King and Queen's Ball. Although these "traditional" William and Mary events are beloved and well-attended, students complain that university sporting events do not enjoy the same rallied support. "This is not a spirited campus," sighed one senior. "We are an academic school, not an athletic one." Another student blamed the lack of spirit on William and Mary students' tendency to be over-committed to their own extracurriculars: "People are faithful to their own activities, but it takes a lot to make them participate in others."

The extracurriculars that command the attention of William and Mary students are many and varied. The a cappella and theater communities are "very tight," and intramural sports are extremely popular. Community service is also a big deal here, and the majority of William and Mary students participate in some form of it. Religious organizations are another strong presence; said one senior, "This is one of the most religious public schools I've seen." Although the campus is not very culturally or ethnically diverse, students here appreciate diversity and say that there is a definite emphasis on multiculturalism. Cultural events such as the "Taste of Asia" celebration are well-attended by the entire student body. "There is an interest in diversity here, but it is not exemplified," said one student. On the other hand, students also say that the size of the student body means that the campus does not self-segregate. As one student said, "groups here *have* to integrate because it is such a small community."

Students at William and Mary tend to dress relatively conservatively, but one can find styles here ranging from "hippie" to "label-conscious" and "preppy." The off-center male-female ratio can be a source of woe, prompting one female student to ask, "Where are the guys?" Students say that formal dating is not too common on campus; most relationships seem to be either "serious" or "hookups." Socializing at William and Mary is done in groups rather than couples, but those who do date will certainly have many a "relationship talk" on the benches scattered around colonial Williamsburg. According to one senior, "pretty much every relationship here starts or ends in colonial Williamsburg."

Getting Down to Business

A student from Virginia claims that the in-state reputation of William and Mary is that "all we do is study." While this is certainly an exaggeration, students at William and Mary *do* take their studies very seriously, and they say that they are continually impressed by the intellectualism of their peers. "We're not afraid to challenge ourselves," one junior asserted. Class sizes are generally small, although introductory courses are often large lectures. Students rave about their professors, describing them as "friendly," "knowledgeable," and "approachable." As one student put it, "All my professors know my name, and I can go up to them and talk about anything, whenever." Stories that illustrate professors' commitment to students abound; Professor Scholnik, for example, is known for inviting his entire American Renaissance Literature class over to his house for a winter holiday dinner.

Students who want a rewarding—if extremely challenging—academic experience often opt to take a class with Professor Hans Tiefel of the Religion Department, the best-known of which is his Death course. Tiefel's students should prepare for a heavy workload; as one senior joked, "If you get into the class, it *means* death!" Courses in economics, chemistry, and introductory philosophy are popular with students for fulfilling general requirements, although one student warns that "organic chemistry kicks everyone's butt!" Courses known for having lighter workloads include Rocks for Jocks and Physics for Non-Majors. The government and biology departments draw rave reviews from students, while the sociology department is said to offer many easy courses. A portion of the incoming freshman class is chosen to be Monroe Scholars. These students have the option of living in Monroe Hall, and they are given funds to pursue an independent study project over the summer.

While there is no specific core curriculum, students must fulfill General Education Requirements (GERs) in seven areas. They are also required to demonstrate proficiency in a foreign language, writing, and physical activity. The academic requirements are praised for being "very reasonable" and for exposing students to different subjects. As one upperclassman explained, "You fulfill a lot of [the GERs] just by moving through the school." Freshmen are required to take a writing seminar each semester. These professor-led seminars of 15 students or less are offered in a variety of focused subjects which change from year to year. "Everyone loves his or her freshman seminar," one student declared. Those with advanced academic standing—either by being upperclassmen or by matriculating with AP credits—can choose their classes (and rooms) before others, and most are eventually able to take the classes they want. However, there are so many course offerings that "even if you do not get into the class you want, you can always find something else."

Taking It All In

Despite its charm to visitors, colonial Williamsburg—or "CW," as it is referred to by the students—is not the cultural mecca many would like. The school is working with the city to provide more social options, but social life is "very campus-centered," and most students seem to like it that way. Although two-thirds of the student body hails from Virginia, the campus does not empty out on the weekends. Said one junior, "we live by the weekends here." The Greek scene is a "staple," since one-third of the campus belongs to a fraternity or sorority. However, non-Greeks can easily take advantage of the parties as well, and students are quick to point out that Greek life is only part of the social scene. Underage drinking typically occurs in private or Greek parties, as the off-campus delis and other venues require ID. William and Mary students agree that while drinking is present, it is not a huge problem and there is hardly any peer pressure. "It's a healthy environment," said one student.

> **"Pretty much every relationship here starts or ends in colonial Williamsburg."**

The university and the surrounding area offer plenty of cultural events, school-organized activities, movies, and restaurants as alternatives or additions to the party scene. There are several "delis" just off campus which function as bars for those with proper ID, and serve as hangouts for the student body in general. Undergrads also frequent Lodge One, the student center which brings in comedians and local bands for entertainment, or sip cups of java at the Daily Grind, a 24-hour on-campus coffee shop. For those who desire more nightlife, Virginia Beach, Norfolk, and Richmond are always just a short trip away.

The Campus Experience

William and Mary students describe their campus as "beautiful, colonial, and green." Everyone seems to have a favorite spot to study. "This place has so many nooks and crannies," said one freshman. There are two parts to the campus: Old Campus is distinguished by old colonial buildings, while New Campus is a mix of colonial and modern architecture. People relax in the Sunken Gardens and enjoy the beauty of the Crim Dell, a shaded pond. *Playboy* magazine listed the bridge over the Crim Dell as one of the most romantic spots on an American campus, and the legend at William and Mary is that you will marry the person you kiss on the bridge. The Crim Dell and Sunken Gardens are also part of another William and Mary tradition, the "triathlon." Before graduating, every student is supposed to streak across the Sunken Gardens, jump in the Crim Dell, and jump the wall of the Governor's Palace in colonial Williamsburg.

The food on campus is described as "pretty good," although some students complain about recent changes in the meal plans. Most eat on campus, but when they tire of college food there are plenty of off-campus options. The Trellis is famous for its desserts, and the Cheese Shop is known for its "house dressing," a recipe so secret that employees have to sign an agreement not to reveal it.

Most students live on campus at William and Mary, and rooms are chosen by a lottery system. Those who move off tend to be seniors, students who want more independence, or students with very low lottery numbers, and many of them discover that a car helps get them around. Freshmen are housed together, and most people agree that their closest friends are their hallmates from freshman year. Housing quality varies from DuPont, known as the "hotel" for freshmen, to dorms that are not renovated and lack air-conditioning. Upperclassmen with good lottery numbers can opt to live in one of the coveted lodges, which are centrally located "houses" for six or seven people. Theme and single-sex housing are also available.

Students at William and Mary love their historic and tight-knit school, and they thoroughly enjoy their experience here. The beautiful campus and dedicated professors are continually cited as big draws, but students insist that their peers are the most wonderful part of William and Mary. Said one freshman: "People here are just so friendly . . . they like you for who you are. That's why I chose this place." —*Alison Schary*

FYI

If you come to William and Mary, you'd better bring "an affinity for colonial architecture—the school is in colonial Williamsburg."

What is the typical weekend schedule? "Go to a frat party or a bar at night, then get up late the next morning and study or work on an extracurricular activity."

If I could change one thing about William and Mary, I'd "add more parking."

Three things every William and Mary student should do before graduating are "take a class in the Wren Building (the oldest building on campus), eat at the Cheese Shop, and compete in the triathlon."

George Mason University

Address: 4400 University Drive, MSN 3A4; Fairfax, VA 22030-4444
Phone: 703-993-2400
E-mail address: admissions@gmu.edu
Web site URL: www.gmu.edu
Founded: 1957
Private or Public: public
Religious affiliation: none
Location: suburban
Undergraduate enrollment: 16,687
Total enrollment: NA
Percent Male/Female: 44%/56%
Percent Minority: 33%
Percent African-American: 9%
Percent Asian: 16%
Percent Hispanic: 8%
Percent Native-American: 0%
Percent in-state/out of state: 95%/5%
Percent Pub HS: NA
Number of Applicants: 8,845
Percent Accepted: 66%
Percent Accepted who enroll: 38%
Entering: 2,552
Transfers: 2,267
Application Deadline: 15 Jan
Mean SAT: NA
Mean ACT: NA
Middle 50% SAT range: V 490-600, M 500-610
Middle 50% ACT range: 19-23
3 Most popular majors: business marketing, social sciences, communication
Retention: 78%
Graduation rate: 49%
On-campus housing: 19%
Fraternities: 3%
Sororities: 3%
Library: 1,460,524 volumes
Tuition and Fees: $5,158 in; $15,240 out
Room and Board: $5,560
Financial aid, first-year: 35%
Varsity or Club Athletes: 13%
Early Decision or Early Action Acceptance Rate: NA

Located only twenty minutes from Washington, D.C., the nation's capital, George Mason University offers students endless possibilities in both extracurricular activities and academics. Founded in 1957, the school was originally created as a two-year branch of the University of Virginia. In just fifty years, the school has made dramatic progress in the quality of academics and student life. The school has recently been dubbed Virginia's "next UVA" for its growth and progress and is attracting professors from older institutions, such as Harvard, Yale, and George Washington University.

The World of Academia

When asked about the academic requirements at George Mason, one student commented that they were "getting harder, but still manageable." The average workload for a George Mason student is fifteen credit hours per semester, which translates to about five courses. Ideally, students devote a total of forty hours to work outside of classes. Most students found the workload at George Mason to be manageable, and that they were being challenged by their studies. The University Learning Resource Center (LRC) offers students help with study skills and stress management.

To obtain a bachelor's degree, the student must fulfill a total of 120 credits within the four years. In addition, you must take at least forty-five credits of upper-level courses, which are numbered 300 and above, to count towards the bachelor's degree requirement. Up to 12 courses in which D grades have been received can be presented toward the graduation requirements. However, the requirements are subject to change, depending on the academic program or the student's area of study.

The New Century College program offers students seminar-style classes and a collaborative faculty involvement of a small college, complemented by the academic and social resources of a major research university. One aspect of this program that the students most enjoyed was that there are no tests or quizzes in these classes. "This is a major attraction," said one student. The assignments are solely based on reflections, papers and journals. Students complete the courses with a final portfolio that compiles the work they have done throughout the semester. In addition to the New Century College, George Mason offers an eclectic array of courses and special programs to its students. Gender in the Popular Culture, Beats Rhymes and Culture, and Special Events Management are only a few of the immense selection of courses from which the student can choose.

Popular majors at Mason include communications, government, nursing, economics, and English. Vernon Smith, Mason's foremost economics professor, has won the Nobel Prize for Economics. Alongside Smith, renowned figures such as Ken Starr, Chuck Robb, and Frank Sesno teach courses at the university. Because of the campus's proximity to Washington, D.C., which opens a vast number and array of opportunities to aspiring politicians, political science is considered another one of the more popular majors at Mason. Slacker majors include marketing and communications. computer science, engineering, and international politics are considered to be the harder majors.

Livin' it Up

The campus's proximity to the nation's capital opens up endless work opportunities and weekend options for the students. Washington D.C. is home to historical and world-renowned monuments and museums, great shopping, and dining options. Said one student about the opportunities provided in the capital, "D.C. is thirty minutes away, so it is easy to go clubbing or hang out at coffee shops where you have the opportunity to meet people."

Most freshmen stay on campus and go to parties hosted by frats and other organizations. "As freshmen, they are the 'coolest' thing," said one student about frat parties. "Sophomore year they are still fun, junior year it's hit or miss because there are so many freshmen . . . but they are frats, so it's free beer and good times and still fun!" Upperclassmen prefer to go to parties in nearby apartments; still another option is to frequent the bars, clubs and restaurants D.C. has to offer. Regarding the alcohol policy, there are security guards walking around campus on the weekends to make sure that no one underage is drinking and to maintain some control. Regardless, students say that underage students find ways to obtain alcohol. Greek life is a significant part of the campus community at George Mason. There are six sororities and nine fraternities on campus, and these organizations frequently host parties for the students to attend. Alpha Phi Omega, a Greek community service organization, provides service to the Fairfax community.

Extracurriculars and Athletics

The students at George Mason are mostly commuters. As a result, there is not much of a campus life at Mason, and students must make extra effort to make friends. An excellent way to get to know more people is through student-run organizations. Community service, internships, ethnic organizations, and publications are among the plethora of organizations open for all students to join and contribute. Delta Sigma Pi is the school's foremost business fraternity. Program Board is responsible for organizing various events that come to campus. *Broadside*, the school's weekly newspaper, is ranked ninth in the country and number one in Virginia. The paper produces essential information to the student body, and according to many students, is "very professional and well-respected." One student hailed, "the editors are in the office until about 3 A.M. every night before the issue is published. It takes a *great* amount of commitment to be involved there." With respect to the arts and theater scene, one student commented on the presence of "crazy-looking art" all over campus. In addition, there are frequent poetry readings with a great amount of student support and participation.

"Stepping in the grounds of the Student Union, Johnson Center, or Quad of George Mason always give the feeling as if you've stepped into a United Nations conference."

Athletics plays a significant role in campus life at Mason, in particular, the school's basketball team. Mason is a Division I school in the NCAA, and its basketball team frequently plays in the NCAA tournament. Midnight Madness provides an opportunity for the student body to demonstrate their school spirit. There is usually a large turnout of about 10,000 people, with fireworks and bands to draw out the school pride from the students. Many students who do not play team sports participate in intramurals. Soccer is "a big" IM at Mason and is "lots of fun," remarked one student.

Life on (and mostly off) Campus

Students describe the school as "quaint," "beautiful" and "modern." A lake in the middle of the campus combined with the modern architecture of the buildings makes the campus quite picturesque and attractive. Many of the facilities at Mason are either new or undergoing renovation. The Aquatics Center contains state-of-the-art equipment for the students to take advantage of. The Patriot Center is a large arena that hosts both campus events and concerts that are not affiliated with the school. In the past, the Patriot Center has hosted major sports events and big name musicians such as Marilyn Manson, 98 Degrees, and Rod Stewart. The campus is fairly small, so students can walk from one part of the campus to another in less than twenty minutes. When asked what they loved the most about campus life, one student replied, "the close proximity to everything a student could ask for and the nice people you are constantly surrounded by." Indeed, if it were not for the diverse and unique blend of people making up the student body at Mason, the school would lose much of its distinctness. George Mason boasts of its diversity, both in the student body and faculty.

Most students commute to the school, and as a result, dorm life is not influential at George Mason. Some students, however, do live on campus, and many have evaluated the quality of the dorms as being "small and dirty." The majority of the students find it extremely convenient to own a car, since the campus is located so close to the city. Students who do not have their own cars can always hitch a ride from their friends, or take the CUE bus, which goes to various stores around Fairfax.

The campus's location in the suburbs offers students an endless range of dining options. The Johnson Center, an on-campus mall food court, offers Taco Bell, La Patisserie (a café), George's Restaurant, and a handful of other eateries to choose from. The Bistro has a salad bar, and there are several other dining halls for traditional hot meals. Still another option for students is to eat in restaurants off campus. "Most of the 'really good' restaurants are slightly off campus in nearby Old Town Fairfax."

Despite the school being only 50 years old, George Mason has been and is making progress in both academics and quality of student life. The school's location near the nation's capital is ideal, for it provides students with stellar opportunities for internships, and important connections in the job market. The school is composed mostly of commuters; yet the diversity of its students and faculty go uncontested. Hundreds of different ethnicities, backgrounds, ages, and political thoughts and experiences are represented at George Mason. One student remarked, "stepping in the grounds of the Student Union, Johnson Center, or Quad of George Mason always gives the feeling as if you've stepped into a United Nations conference." —*Soo Kim*

FYI

If you come to George Mason, you'd better "bring a smile, and excitement to explore D.C."

What is the typical weekend schedule? "Friday night: bar hopping in D.C. or Old Town Fairfax. Saturday: study. Sunday: parties in D.C. or at fraternities."

If I could change one thing about George Mason, "I'd have more campus housing so more people are on campus during the weekends."

Three things every student at George Mason should do before graduating are: "get involved in Greek life, go to every Mason basketball game possible, and attend Mason Day."

Hampden-Sydney College

Address: PO Box 667; Hampden-Sydney, VA 23943
Phone: 804-223-6120
E-mail address: hsap@tiger.hsc.edu
Web site URL: www.hsc.edu
Founded: 1776
Private or Public: private
Religious affiliation: Presbyterian
Location: rural
Undergraduate enrollment: 1,038
Total enrollment: NA
Percent Male/Female: 99%/1%
Percent Minority: 7%
Percent African-American: 4%
Percent Asian: 1%
Percent Hispanic: 1%
Percent Native-American: 1%
Percent in-state/out of state: 64%/36%
Percent Pub HS: 59%
Number of Applicants: 1,028
Percent Accepted: 71%
Percent Accepted who enroll: 41%
Entering: 300
Transfers: 15
Application Deadline: 1 Mar
Mean SAT: NA
Mean ACT: NA
Middle 50% SAT range: V 510-620, M 520-620
Middle 50% ACT range: NA
3 Most popular majors: economics, history, political science
Retention: 80%
Graduation rate: 61%
On-campus housing: 94%
Fraternities: 33%
Sororities: NA
Library: 224,172 volumes
Tuition and Fees: $21,387
Room and Board: $7,020
Financial aid, first-year: 49%
Varsity or Club Athletes: NA
Early Decision or Early Action Acceptance Rate: 74%

Tradition, excellence, and honor: at all-male Hampden-Sydney, these are not just words. They are a way of life.

Academic Excellence

Excellence in academics comes in the form of the Rhetoric Program, a set of first- and second-year core requirements. Although many of their classes are predetermined by the Rhetoric Program, freshmen get a taste of the individual attention they will receive at Hampden-Sydney through faculty advisors who help plan their schedules.

The Rhetoric Program consists of challenging classes in English, writing, and speech, ten papers a semester, stringent grammar testing, and a final proficiency exam. A follow-up exam is given after the program to ensure that students have actually retained what they've learned. As one student put it, "The Rhetoric Program totally killed me my freshman year." However, students seem to appreciate the program and say that it helps later on with courses in their majors.

The economics, political science, and history departments are quite strong and popular. Languages and sciences are reportedly not as strong, yet students agree that most of the departments are quite challenging. As one sophomore put it, "If you get an A here, you really had to earn it."

The largest classes at Hampden-Sydney enroll about 35 people. Upper-level classes usually contain no more than ten students. Students know all their professors well, and some professors invite students to dinner and other social events. The accessibility of professors also comes in handy when extensions on assignments are needed. As one student reported, "Since professors know all their students so well, they're usually willing to accept a late paper or reschedule an exam if need be. It's really easy to talk to the teachers." The college also runs a Writing Center, whose staff will read and critique any written assignments. Students agree that all of these personal services help them excel.

Living Quarters

Although only freshmen are required to live on campus, almost all upperclassmen remain in campus housing. Students choose their preferred dorm before attending Hampden-Sydney. One student explained that students almost always pick the dorms they stayed in during their visits as prospective students.

Cushing, the oldest and one of the most popular dorms, houses half the freshman class. "All the freshmen want to live there," one student remarked, because of its "Animal House, party-dorm" reputation and large rooms. Other popular dorms are Carpenter, which has carpeting in all the rooms, and the Hampden House apartments, which are complete with private bathrooms. The dorms are divided into four "passages," hallways where neighboring students form strong and lasting friendships.

Typical College Food

Pannill Commons, the main dining hall on campus, serves "typical college food—not great," one student said. Most undergrads prefer the Tiger Inn restaurant, a campus hangout equivalent to a student center, with pool tables and a big-screen television. Although it's not part of the meal plan, the Tiger Inn attracts many students and even hosts bands and comedians.

Students also venture off campus to the town of Farmville for food. Some like Charlie's and Macado's for sandwiches or steak dinners. The Hitchin' Post, right off campus, draws quite a crowd for sandwiches as well. Although Farmville has about "half a dozen good restaurants," one student said, it does not have much else for the college crowd. The nearest mall is 45 minutes away, in Lynchburg, and Richmond, the largest city nearby, is an hour's drive away. Students admit that "you really need a car here, or at least have a friend with a car." Freshmen are allowed to have cars on campus, reportedly a tremendous asset for visiting the women's schools about an hour away from Hampden-Sydney.

Where the Women Are

There are four women's colleges close to Hampden-Sydney: Mary Baldwin, Sweet Briar, Randolph-Macon, and Hollins. Longwood, a co-ed state school, is also nearby. Hampden-Sydney social functions have a "definitely noticeable" female presence. The College Activities Committee occasionally hosts frequent mixers with the women's schools, and the fraternities, which include half of the student body, throw parties with the sororities from the Universities of Richmond and Virginia. As one student remarked, "It's initially really easy to meet girls. It seems like almost everyone here has a girlfriend."

Going Out

Most parties and weekend activities occur at the Circle, Hampden-Sydney's fraternity row. Despite the administration's recent enforcement of the alcohol policy by making Cushing a dry dorm, the attitude toward alcohol among students is pretty laid-back. Fraternity parties, open to all students, provide a steady supply of alcohol.

> **"It does get a little old only having 900 guys around."**

Although Greek life is a large part of the campus scene, it is not divisive. According to one non-Greek, "People consider themselves Hampden-Sydney men first, Greeks second." The Greeks are responsible for all the big parties and social events on campus. The biggest is Greek Week, an annual spring weekend of partying and dancing.

Greek Week hosts popular bands, which have included Hootie and the Blowfish, Big Head Todd and the Monsters, the Dave Matthews Band, Blues Traveler, and the Spin Doctors. Road trips to the women's colleges are also popular weekend activities.

Extracurriculars

The favorite extracurricular activity for Greeks and non-Greeks alike is intramural sports. Students organize their own teams and compete in a variety of sports, including football, basketball, and soccer. Varsity sports also receive enthusiastic student support, especially the football team, whose homecoming performance kicks off a weekend of parties with students from the competing school. The Young Republicans is one of the many popular extracurricular groups. Political sentiment on campus is conservative, and students say they are politically active. Other popular activities include the debate society, the literary organization, the Key Club, and the Outsider's Club, which sponsors white-water rafting and adventure trips.

Honorable Men

One of the most prestigious campus organizations is the student government, which is responsible for enforcing the honor code. Hampden-Sydney has a strictly enforced honor code; students can be expelled for cheating, stealing, or dishonesty. Any infraction of the honor code is addressed by the student-run honor court, which assigns the accused undergrad a student lawyer and decides his punishment. Although very few cases come in front of the court, students take their judicial process seriously. They say the honor code allows them freedom to feel safe and govern themselves.

As a result of the honor code, students report, Hampden-Sydney has almost no crime. As one student said, "I leave my books everywhere. You can walk into your friend's room and start watching TV and no one will mind. Even the dorms are always open."

With a deeply entrenched honor code and strong sense of tradition, Hampden-Sydney students enjoy a special camaraderie on campus. Although one student remarked, "It does get a little old only having 900 guys around," most students agree that the all-male environment creates a sense of true fellowship, and that the college would lose much of its special character if women were admitted. Other students point out that relationships with the faculty, strong academics, and accessibility to the many surrounding women's colleges outweigh any disadvantages. —*Susanna Chu*

FYI

The three best things about attending Hampden-Sydney are "student pride, the honor code, and the sense of security around campus."

The three worst things about attending Hampden-Sydney are "the lack of cute girls down the hall, the core requirements, and the need for a car."

Three things that every student should do before graduating from Hampden-Sydney are "walk around the dorms in boxers, spend a night at a sorority house, have a humiliating experience during Greek Week."

One thing I'd like to have known before coming here is "your really can have fun at an all-guys college."

Hollins University

Address: PO Box 9707, Roanoke, VA 24020
Phone: 540-362-6401
E-mail address: huadm@hollins.edu
Web site URL: www.hollins.edu
Founded: 1842
Private or Public: private
Religious affiliation: none
Location: suburban
Undergraduate enrollment: 847
Total enrollment: NA
Percent Male/Female: 0%/100%
Percent Minority: 11%
Percent African-American: 7%
Percent Asian: 1%
Percent Hispanic: 2%
Percent Native-American: 1%
Percent in-state/out of state: 52%/48%
Percent Pub HS: 75%
Number of Applicants: 686
Percent Accepted: 80%
Percent Accepted who enroll: 37%
Entering: 202
Transfers: 34
Application Deadline: rolling
Mean SAT: NA
Mean ACT: NA
Middle 50% SAT range: V 530-660, M 490-610
Middle 50% ACT range: 21-28
3 Most popular majors: social sciences, visual and performing arts, English
Retention: 80%
Graduation rate: 68%
On-campus housing: 90%
Fraternities: NA
Sororities: NA
Library: 163,896 volumes
Tuition and Fees: $20,675
Room and Board: $7,290
Financial aid, first-year: 65%
Varsity or Club Athletes: NA
Early Decision or Early Action Acceptance Rate: 79%

When the first frost falls on the beautiful campus of Hollins University, the entire community celebrates Tinker Day. Dorm halls are filled with the sound of seniors banging pots and pans, noise known as the Tinker Day Scares. Upon hearing the great clamor, students rise and do what classes before them have been doing for years; they go to the dining hall to eat breakfast in their pajamas. Classes are canceled for the entire day and everyone dons a crazy outfit and prepares to climb nearby Tinker Mountain, one of the many hills that surround the Hollins campus. At the top, students enjoy a huge picnic buffet and spend the rest of the day celebrating with songs and skits. Tinker Day is just one example of the many traditions observed at Hollins University. Students enjoy themselves at Hollins; they also recognize that Hollins is a place dedicated to providing a great education.

Broad-Based Academics

Hollins, a four-year women's university, divides its academic coursework into four divisions: humanities, social sciences, fine arts, and natural sciences. Each student must take eight credits from each division as part of a "broad based academic curriculum." Freshmen have to fulfill an additional writing requirement. Students praise the English department as exceptionally strong. As one undergrad said, "The department has like quadruple the number of professors of any other department." Aside from English, other popular majors include history and psychology. The political science department "is pretty good, but the professors are incomparably harder than in any other department." Although many undergraduates tend to major in the humanities, the natural sciences reportedly are "still pretty good and the facilities are up-to-date." Some students said that "easy" majors include communications and religion. Regardless of particular department credentials, most undergrads praise their professors for innovative assignments. For example, students in a sociology class were required to go into a store and write a paper on how they would steal money from that establishment. Not only do professors often "devise cool projects for class," but many live on the Hollins campus and are "always open" to student interaction, one undergrad said.

Class registration at the beginning of each term is "straightforward and fast," according to students. Few students have trouble getting into the classes they want, although some introductory classes in psychology, computer science, and art do fill up, due to caps put on course enrollment. To help students choose classes, course and faculty evaluations from previous semesters are readily accessible. Hollins students are also positive about the small class sizes. One freshman said that most of her classes "only had 15 people and the largest class I have had here has been only 45 students."

Short Term

Hollins divides the year into two semesters plus a short, four-week term that occurs in January. "Short Term is the reason I came to Hollins," said one freshman. Many upperclassmen use this time to do internships made possible through an extensive alumni network run by the career development office. Other students stay on campus for intensive seminar courses. The school also sponsors many off-campus opportunities during Short Term, such as travel to Greece, Spain, or Germany to improve language proficiency. By graduation, each student must have accumulated four Short Term credits, although as one senior noted, "Who would want to miss Short Term anyway?"

Car—a Must Have

As for social life, Hollins students often find their options limited. Many go off campus on the weekends to meet male undergrads at either Washington and Lee University or Hampden-Sydney College, both within an hour's drive. In fact, many students say having a car is a "major necessity" at Hollins. According to one senior, "There's just no bus system provided or sponsored by the administration. I have to say that it's really inconvenient not to have a car when a walk to the supermarket is half a mile." The student government does fund a taxi service on the weekends. "It's great," said one undergrad. "You can get $3 vouchers that take you to the mall or downtown." The area around Hollins is "a small district—a bit too provincial for my taste," one student said. Popular eating establishments in town include Macado's and the Mill Mountain Coffee House. One student complained, however, that "Roanoke just isn't really geared to students." Campus parties, particularly ones thrown by upperclassmen who are of age, reportedly are "uncool if you are under 21 because they won't let you near a keg."

Tradition, Tradition, Tradition

Many campus activities revolve around tradition at Hollins. Aside from Tinker Day, another popular event is Ring Night, which often "snowballs into a weeklong event." Juniors are put into groups and together do the seniors' bidding. After performing "idiotic gags and making morons of ourselves," the juniors are finally awarded their class rings. Another event is called Founder's Day, during which the seniors walk in their graduation gowns to the statue of the founder and place a wreath at its base. On certain occasions, members of a religious group called Freya don black robes and walk around campus in the middle of the night, advocating higher standards of morality.

Hollins students often criticize themselves for not "providing enough diversity." One student said that most people tend to think of Hollins students as "preppy, almost arrogant, and aloof," as many students come from higher socioeconomic backgrounds. One freshman said, "In my first few days, I did not see one person of color." One senior said that Hollins is particularly lacking in African-American students, and another said, "The diversity here tends to come from international students rather than from actual minority students from the U.S." Hollins is trying to change this image, however, in part by making substantive changes to the scholarship program for minority students.

Luxurious Housing, Crummy Food

At Hollins, all freshman live in one dorm comprised of singles and doubles. All of these rooms have built-in desks, dressers, closets, and mirrors, and air-conditioning and heating controls. One freshman living in a single said, "It's not huge, but I'm comfortable. The doubles, though, are huge." The most popular dorm on campus is Main Dorm (it "has two closets in each room as opposed to one"). Apartments across the street from the main campus house seniors and are considered "quite luxurious for on-campus housing." One of the less popular dorms is Randolph, which was built in the 1970s and reportedly "doesn't have the charm that all the other dorms do." As a result, some call it "the projects." After freshman year, housing is assigned through a lottery system, with preference given to upperclasswomen. Regardless of which dorm they live in, though, the women at Hollins are on the whole pleased with their accommodations.

The food, however, does not get such rave reviews. Though many students find campus food tolerable, others complain that it is "extremely distasteful." One student said, "I didn't expect the food to be so crummy or for there to be such a limited choice of food." Hollins only has one dining hall, with specific hours assigned for every meal. Some students find the hours inconvenient; dinner, for example, goes from 4:30 until 6:30. "I'm just not used to eating so early," one sophomore said. Despite these complaints, students praise the dining hall for its cleanliness and for "providing ice-cream sundaes every Friday at lunch as well as special theme nights every now and then." The Hollins meal plan is included in the cost of tuition. One freshman claimed, "Once you've paid, you can eat twice a week or 50 times a week." Also, as one student reported, "Probably any girl could come here and have a meal because they never check your ID." For other dining alternatives, students often go to the Rat, a place that serves as the Hollins student center and has food "like a McDonald's," or head over to the local, off-campus deli, Boomer's.

Campus Views

Hollins students are very enthusiastic about their surroundings. Many call the campus "absolutely gorgeous." The architecture is an elegant Southern/Georgian style with wide porches and grand white columns. As one student noted, "We're situated in a valley, and the surrounding mountains are just beautiful." Students praise the administration for constantly revamping and updating its buildings and facilities. In 1999, the state-of-the-art Wyndam Robertson Library was opened, which is described as "Virginia's first National Literary Landmark." One student did complain, however, that the weight room in the gym could use a little work. Another student added, "We also could use a few more male bathrooms. We do get visitors now and then."

> **"Women who are going places start at Hollins."**

Campus security issues are also important to the administration. As one student pointed out, "Hollins is isolated and it's all girls, so security concerns are pretty high." Students are encouraged to go to officials if they feel security is lacking, and "panic boxes" are posted all over campus to connect students with campus security officers.

Active Student Body

Aside from basking in the beauty of their school, Hollins students are also extremely involved in campus life. Student Government Association is a popular activity and has multiple committees that are open to any interested students. The volunteer group SHARE is also extremely well respected by Hollins women, and coordinates the large amount of community service done by students. Many students also go into the mountains to work with various ecological programs. In addition to these groups, students participate actively in sports. The riding team consistently performs well, as do the fencing and swimming teams. Hollins recruits athletes, but any student interested in a sport can find a team to join. Even students who are not active in organized sports make good use of the gym. As one student said, "Though there's a lack of treadmills, we have a climbing wall and a really great pool."

One recent area of concern on campus is that in 1998, Hollins changed from a college to a university. This change reportedly came as a result of the need for more money, but brought with it an increased selection of classes and majors, and many building upgrades. However, many upperclasswomen are not pleased about the shift in status. Although Hollins already offers co-ed graduate programs, many fear that the undergraduate program will become co-ed. As one senior commented, "They've changed our bumper sticker from reading 'Women are going places' to 'People are going places.'" One freshman reported, however, "The president says that there is absolutely no way that the school is going co-ed, and I believe her." A sophomore explained, "Hollins is still very much a small liberal arts college dedicated to personal attention and women's education."

The students of Hollins University clearly love their campus, community, academic program, and learning from each other. Though one senior said, "I wish it weren't as hard finding guy friends and developing male relationships, but I'd definitely come here again—in a flash." —*Jeff Kaplow*

FYI

The three best things about attending Hollins are "the many traditions, the women's atmosphere (it provides a big comfort level), and the fact that all the professors know you."

The three worst things about attending Hollins are "the small course selection, the lack of diversity, and the scarce resources in the library."

Three things that every student should do before graduating from Hollins are "walk on the front quad, have a rope passed down to you, and go to the Spring Cotillion."

One thing I'd like to have known before coming here is "how limited classes at a small school are."

James Madison University

Address: Sonner Hall MSC 0101, Harrisonburg, VA 22807
Phone: 540-568-6211
E-mail address: gotojmu@jmu.edu
Web site URL: www.jmu.edu
Founded: 1908
Private or Public: public
Religious affiliation: none
Location: suburban
Undergraduate enrollment: 14,828
Total enrollment: NA
Percent Male/Female: 41%/59%
Percent Minority: 11%
Percent African-American: 4%
Percent Asian: 5%
Percent Hispanic: 2%
Percent Native-American: 0%
Percent in-state/out of state: 71%/29%
Percent Pub HS: 95%
Number of Applicants: 15,639
Percent Accepted: 58%
Percent Accepted who enroll: 36%
Entering: 3,283
Transfers: 646
Application Deadline: 15 Jan
Mean SAT: NA
Mean ACT: NA
Middle 50% SAT range: V 540-620, M 540-630
Middle 50% ACT range: NA
3 Most popular majors: business and marketing, social sciences, computer sciences
Retention: 91%
Graduation rate: 79%
On-campus housing: 42%
Fraternities: 11%
Sororities: 13%
Library: 744,041 volumes
Tuition and Fees: $5,058 in; $13,280 out
Room and Board: $5,966
Financial aid, first-year: 29%
Varsity or Club Athletes: 9%
Early Decision or Early Action Acceptance Rate: 61%

Students new to James Madison University are usually struck first by the school's great academics and great people. Having grown from an obscure, state-funded teachers' college, the Madison College has become one of the foremost academic institutions in the South, impressing its students not only with its academics, but also with its relaxed and friendly atmosphere.

Abercrombie & Fitch Meets Main Street, U.S.A.

One of the "Ten Reasons You Know You're at JMU", according to a T-shirt seen on campus, is "you introduce yourself to someone new every day." Friendly, courteous, and down-to-earth, friendly people are many students' number one reason for choosing JMU. One student enthused, "I get a feeling around campus that everyone wants you to be there. You can always exchange a friendly hello with a passerby and get help when you need it." The campus atmosphere is "friendly and upbeat," conducive to meeting people and making friends. Students described the student body as "preppy" and "homogeneous." The stereotypical JMU Duke is an upper-middle-class, Abercrombie & Fitch-wearing suburban white kid from the East Coast. Minority students tend to self-segregate and sometimes have a hard time, but all are upbeat about the "nice, friendly" student body.

Party Hearty

Most Dukes follow a "work hard, play hard" philosophy, while the social scene, according to most students, revolves around "drink hard." Some students said that non-drinkers can feel out of place; one student commented that most non-drinkers tend to be more involved in extracurricular activities or have part-time jobs. Students described the dating scene as "average" and mentioned that "because of alcohol, there are more random hookups than usual." The administration provides a number of popular non-alcoholic social alternatives like Thursday and Saturday $2 movie screenings of recent releases and concerts featuring big-name bands. Recent performers include Vertical Horizon and Nine Days. Students can also choose from an incredibly wide range of extracurricular activities and club sports. Although the Greek scene is big, with about 30 percent of students involved, no students reported feeling pressure to rush.

Frat parties are a popular weekend destination, but the most popular parties—especially for non-Greeks—are those held in off-campus student apartments. One student described them as "very cool"; another said "most anybody can get in if you are dressed nice, but it helps if you have girls with you." The university has a "three strikes" alcohol policy, and campus police and RAs are described as "average" in their enforcement of rules ("so long as you aren't loud and destructive, you won't get caught"). The city police department, however, has been reported as "very ruthless" in its alcohol enforcement, and routinely breaks up off-campus parties. One of these break-ups, involving a back-to-school block party, degenerated into a riot last year. Most students felt the police department was responsible for the incident, which marked an all-time low in student-police relations. The poor relationship between students and Harrisonburg police doesn't affect campus safety, though; the campus police are "well-respected and do their jobs." The university police and student cadets patrol the campus around the clock, and blue-light security phones were recently installed. Though there was an incident involving a student rape a few years ago, students agreed that they "wouldn't think twice" if they had to walk across campus alone at night.

Major Mecca

JMU academics received rave reviews from students, who lauded the huge choice of major programs and academic flexibility the school offers. The School of Media Arts and Design (SMAD) was praised as a "hidden jewel"; other popular (and difficult) majors include business, computer science, and the prestigious College of Integrated Science and Technology (CISAT) programs.

Classes range in difficulty from the "credit-getter" introductory ROTC classes (a "guaranteed A" often taken by non-ROTC students) to "weed-out" classes like Computer Science 139 and 239, which Comp Sci majors must pass with a B. Classes are mostly quite small and almost never taught by TAs. The professors are generally very accessible and enthusiastic—especially in upper-level classes—though students report the occasional oddball who "couldn't teach a bull to charge." Most of those in the latter category teach large, mandatory (and often unpopular) Gen Ed classes. The caliber of the faculty is very high; singled out for praise by their students were writing teacher and punk singer Jennifer Holl, known to leap to windowsills during lectures; history professor Raymond Hyser; and World War II fighter ace-*cum*-English professor Geoffrey Morley-Mower. TAs are few and of widely varying quality: many students praised their TAs as "great and helpful"; a few told horror stories. One student noted that JMU's rigid academic honor code (subject, according to some students, to widespread abuse) prevents TAs from offering much assistance on assignments.

Of the 120 credits JMU students need to graduate, about 40 are general education requirements. Though they do have some latitude in choosing Gen Ed courses, most students view the requirement as an academic chore. Most majors require about 60 credits for graduation, and many students elect minors as well. Students typically take 15 to 18 credits per semester. Grading was universally described as "fair," and most said the academic programs were challenging and competitive, but not impossible for students who keep up with their work.

Food and Shelter

JMU students enjoy a choice of eleven on-campus dining options, ranging from conventional dining halls such as Gibbons Hall ("D-Hall") and Festival to commercial chains like Sbarro and Chick Fil-A. Students preferring to eat off campus can find a wide variety of restaurants nearby, including chains like Applebee's and Chili's, and ethnic restaurants like El Charro and La Italia. Most students praised the quality of the food and all were positive about the range of options.

> **"You can always exchange a friendly hello with a passerby and get help when you need it."**

There is an enormous variety of on-campus housing, and dormitories come in all forms—old and new, air-conditioned and cooled by Mother Nature, towers and conventional dorms, coed and all-women, substance-free, smoke-free, and international. Housing can be a tradeoff, though: newer dorms are generally nicer, but are located farther away from the main campus. Freshmen, who are required to live on campus, are assigned rooms based on their answers to a five-question questionnaire. Upperclassmen wishing to live on campus enter a housing lottery, but most students move off campus in their sophomore or junior years. Off-campus housing is "reasonably priced" (about $300 per month, according to one student) and readily accessible via a free bus service. RAs got high marks, and most students agreed that they "strike a good balance between enforcing the rules and being your friend."

Freight Trains and Superhighways

The JMU campus is vast, hilly, and beautiful. Interstate 81 and a railroad line run directly through the campus and divide it into "old" and "new" halves. The new half is almost completely new, built to house the College of Integrated Science and Technology. Though "prison-like" in appearance, the buildings are "high-quality and conducive to student life." The old half is home of the university's original, gorgeous bluestone buildings and the famous "Kissing Rock," a campus landmark and romantic hangout; it is also the location of the Quad, a collection of old bluestone academic buildings. Crisscrossing under the Quad are a set of tunnels which, according to campus legend, were closed off long ago, after a student died there. Her ghost is said to appear on foggy nights in the bell tower of Wilson Hall, and though the tunnels are still *verboten* to students, the adventurous will occasionally sneak in to have a look around.

Campus facilities are mostly new, popular, and of high quality, especially the five-year-old UREC recreation center, which features weight rooms, racquetball and basketball courts, a pool, a suspended track, and a climbing wall. Also popular is Taylor Down Under, a student center featuring a coffee shop, pool hall, performance space, and various information and student life offices. The only major facility that students singled out for criticism was the Carrier Library, described as "not what you'd expect at a university like ours." The city of Harrisonburg, students agree, "doesn't have anything besides JMU," and many students look forward to getting out of town.

GO, DUKES!

JMU runs a popular and successful athletic program, and students often turn out for football, soccer, basketball, and track and field events, especially against perennial rival Virginia Tech. Most teams are NCAA Division I, and the school puts a lot of money and effort into sports. Club sports are also very popular and often successful. But is the Dukes' school spirit any surprise when they attend a rising star that is rapidly becoming one of the top universities in the nation? As one freshman put it simply, "JMU is an amazing school—COME HERE!" —*Jeff Howard*

FYI

The three best things about attending JMU are "the faculty is always willing to help you out, very friendly people, beautiful campus."

The three worst things about attending JMU are "parking is not the best, registering for classes can be difficult, weather varies throughout the day."

The three things every JMU student should do before graduating are "go skiing and snow tubing at Massanutten, go to a 'dive-in' movie at the pool, and go to Melrose (an off-campus cabin that hosts parties)."

One thing I'd like to have known before coming here is "the people are very friendly, so you need to like friendly people."

Randolph-Macon Woman's College

Address: 2500 Rivermont Avenue; Lynchberg, VA 24503
Phone: 804-947-8100
E-mail address: admissions@rmwc.edu
Web site URL: www.rmwc.edu
Founded: 1891
Private or Public: private
Religious affiliation: United Methodist
Location: small city
Undergraduate enrollment: 1,154
Total enrollment: NA
Percent Male/Female: 50%/50%
Percent Minority: 8%
Percent African-American: 5%
Percent Asian: 1%
Percent Hispanic: 2%
Percent Native-American: 0%
Percent in-state/out of state: 65%/35%
Percent Pub HS: 70%
Number of Applicants: 1,689
Percent Accepted: 78%
Percent Accepted who enroll: 29%
Entering: 377
Transfers: 26
Application Deadline: 1 Mar
Mean SAT: 1167
Mean ACT: 26
Middle 50% SAT range: V 500-610, M 500-610
Middle 50% ACT range: NA
3 Most popular majors: business economics, psychology, English
Retention: 76%
Graduation rate: 73%
On-campus housing: 85%
Fraternities: 45%
Sororities: 45%
Library: 152,257 volumes
Tuition and Fees: $21,160
Room and Board: $6,030
Financial aid, first-year: 62%
Varsity or Club Athletes: 26%
Early Decision or Early Action Acceptance Rate: 73%

Lynchburg, Virginia, is the home of Randolph Macon Woman's College, a small, private, single-sex institution. The campus, which has seen few changes since its construction, consists of majestic red brick buildings surrounded by a red brick wall. Inside this wall, lives a close-knit community of women who are as serious about their commitment to their school as they are about their studies.

Noses to the Grindstone

Academics at Randolph Macon are anything but easy. Students are required to take one course each in compositional English, literature, history, European culture, women's studies, Asian or African civilization, a physical science (including a lab), math, physical education, fine arts, and a foreign language. Students say the requirements are a strong selling point of the college, as they expose students to "courses that you wouldn't think of taking." Registration is done alphabetically by last name on a rotating basis per semester. Students claim that it is very rare to get shut out of a class, even for first-years.

They also stress the benefits of their small school on student-faculty relations. Students consider the fact that there are no teaching assistants anywhere in the school to be a bonus as professors do all the grading and teaching themselves. Professors are described as "fantastic," and often become friends and mentors as well as instructors to their students. Although all departments are considered to be "academically strong," biology, math, and psychology are thought to be the most popular, primarily because these subjects encompass a wide variety of courses students find useful. Be warned, however—classes are not simple. Many science courses could be described as "death wish" classes by those who do not have a lot of time to spend on their work.

Thanks to such a demanding course load, students find themselves hitting the books more often than not. Lipscomb Library, a six-story building set in the middle of one of Macon's hills, is described as "adequate" for both studying and research. Although Lipscomb is not very large, the school offers its students a free interlibrary loan system, allowing them to obtain books from nearby schools. For those with some serious work to do, the Ethyl Center, with on-site tutors, computers, comfortable chairs, and solo study rooms, provides an ideal spot. For group work, the student center is a popular choice due to its central location.

Beautiful Rooms

Of course, students can also study in their spacious dorm rooms. While off-campus living is prohibited to those under 25, unmarried, or not living at home in Lynchburg, there are no complaints about the rooming alternatives. Room options comprise everything from singles to suites, and the rooms generally are large, carpeted, with ample windows and closet space. One student remarked, "Believe it or not, it's humungous, and bigger than my room at home!" Male visitors are allowed in the dorms until midnight Mondays through Thursdays, and allowed to stay overnight on weekends. The dorms also have TV lounges and old-fashioned "date parlors" that are used mostly for studying. The worst thing anyone reported about dorms was that they did not have elevators.

They Have Fun, Too . . .

When they are not busy studying or going to meetings for their extracurricular activities, Randolph Macon women go to coffehouses and cafés in town, rent movies, or go to school-sponsored activities such as lectures. On the weekends, students make time for low-key partying, go to local bars, or visit nearby campuses such as Hampden-Sydney. There is no need for a car at Randolph Macon, and although the town is described as "boring" by some, there are plenty of on-campus activities to choose from. Favorite events include Tacky Party, where everyone "dresses up real tacky and plays '70s music," in November, and the Senior Dinner, a formal weekend that includes a cocktail and casino night.

> **"Randolph Macon Woman's College is not for everyone: it is single-sex, small, and highly challenging."**

Students are very active in extracurricular activities, which range from sports to writing for the school newspaper the *Sundial*, or the literary magazine *Hail! Muse*, to community service projects such as BIONIC, which stands for Believe It or Not I Care. MAC, Macon Activities Counsel, arranges the school's social activities. A recently added rugby team has proved popular among students. The Black Women's Alliance both provides support for African-American students as well as sponsors dances and other social events. The organization, Bridges, provides support for gay students on campus. Randolph Macon women are also fairly politically active, and the campus chapters of the Young Democrats and Republicans enjoy a large degree of student participation. The new weight-training center, an Olympic-size pool, refurbished playing fields, and tennis and basketball courts provide ample space for the Randolph Macon Wildcats to play, and those not involved in organized sports to keep in shape.

Spoiled Rotten

As the meal plan is included in the tuition, there are no real options, but students have few complaints about the food. "The food is really good," said one student. "We get spoiled rotten." The one main dining hall has both a hot food line and "stations" where the staff cooks food to students' specifications. Vegetarians can order meals without meat. The Skellar, a student-run snack bar, provides an on-campus alternative to the dining hall. On the weekends, many students go out to eat at a variety of restaurants ranging from fast-food to Meriwhethers-Godsy, a restaurant for special occasions, run by a Macon alum.

Evens Versus Odds and Other Traditions

Tradition holds a very important place at Randolph Macon. The campus is filled with gardens and gazebos, and on beautiful days, students enjoy hanging out on front campus or in the Dell, an open-air amphitheater. There are no sororities, but some students join secret societies. There is a traditional class rivalry between "evens and odds," those whose classes end in even or odd years, which involves practical jokes and spray-painting slogans around campus. Randolph Macon women are intensely proud of their school, and report feeling "overwhelmed by school spirit." One student reported that those who do not like it transfer out, leaving a cohesive group. Another student bragged about her dorm: "It's a great community—we all get along really well. It's like having 65 sisters!" The school's small size also fosters interaction between the faculty and students. As classes are rarely bigger than 20 or 30 students, and can be as small as one, professors get to know their pupils well, even too well, for the less studious: "Many professors eat at the dining hall, so you don't want to skip class and see them there," reported one undergrad.

For some, however, the small size and relative isolation of the campus can be a drawback. There is not much to do in Lynchburg in terms of entertainment, especially for those used to big cities. While the school attracts students from all over the globe, Randolph Macon is still not as diverse as some might like it. One student complained the student body as a whole was "lacking certain aspects of American background. We are mostly white Christians from well-to-do families—Land's End, Eddie Bauer, and J. Crew kids."

A Warm Community

Randolph Macon Woman's College is not for everyone: it is single-sex, small, and highly challenging. Yet, for those who choose to attend, there is a lot to be gained from its selective atmosphere. Students have the opportunity to study abroad, as many do, during their junior year. The college also provides its students with a variety of popular internship programs. Undergrads even have the option to design their own major, for a more personalized program of study. They also cannot say enough about the pride and love they have for their school. Traditionally, RMWC has been like a second home for many students, and as with all Macon traditions, they want to keep it that way. *—Ann Zeidner*

FYI

The three best things about attending RMWC are "the personal attention, the camaraderie, and the even v. odd pranks."

The three worst things about attending RMWC are "the academic rigor, the absence of a male presence in the classroom, and the lack of diversity."

The three things that every student should do before graduating from RMWC are "go to Tacky Party, order from the J. Crew catalog, and make friends with a professor."

One thing I'd like to have known before coming here is "how much I like having men around."

Sweet Briar University

Address: PO Box B; Sweet Briar, VA 24595
Phone: 804-381-6142
E-mail address: admissions@sbc.edu
Web site URL: www.sbc.edu
Founded: 1901
Private or Public: private
Religious affiliation: none
Location: rural
Undergraduate enrollment: 688
Total enrollment: NA
Percent Male/Female: 3%/97%
Percent Minority: 10%
Percent African-American: 4%
Percent Asian: 2%
Percent Hispanic: 3%
Percent Native-American: 1%
Percent in-state/out of state: 43%/57%
Percent Pub HS: NA
Number of Applicants: 415
Percent Accepted: 86%
Percent Accepted who enroll: 42%
Entering: 151
Transfers: 13
Application Deadline: 1 Feb
Mean SAT: NA
Mean ACT: NA
Middle 50% SAT range: V 530-660, M 490-610
Middle 50% ACT range: 22-27
3 Most popular majors: English, biology, social sciences
Retention: 81%
Graduation rate: 61%
On-campus housing: 89%
Fraternities: NA
Sororities: NA
Library: 177,110 volumes
Tuition and Fees: $19,900
Room and Board: $8,040
Financial aid, first-year: 54%
Varsity or Club Athletes: 20%
Early Decision or Early Action Acceptance Rate: 88%

Sitting tranquil at the foothills of the South Ridge Mountains in Virginia, Sweet Briar College feels quaint with its old-Georgian style buildings and small town, rural setting. Rich with traditions established since its inception in 1901, Sweet Briar is also a place where "things are happening," as one student said, bringing to light the dynamic student body, the involved faculty, and the energetic environment. "You can do what you want here." Most Sweet Briar students agree that the intimate environment, the professors, and the highly motivated women make the school a tremendous learning experience and four remarkable years.

Strong Academics

As a liberal arts school, SWC emphasizes learning in a variety of disciplines with basic distribution requirements in addition to those requirements of your major. There is a core of courses in a variety of departments one must take to graduate. A student must take one course in art and literature, non-Western study, social science, history, English, physical education, an oral- and writing-intensive course, as well as quantitative reasoning. Other requirements include foreign language and community service. "I didn't find the required classes to be a problem at all," said one student. "There are not too many requirements and they are pretty flexible." For a small college (with an entering freshman class of around 160 students), Sweet Briar offers a variety of very strong departments. A student can choose from thirty-four majors or you can construct your own major, which "is really easy to do." Being the most popular major, biology has a tremendous faculty and boasts a new wing of Guion, the science building, which houses equipment capable of chromatographic and electrophoretic analyses among other things. Another popular major is government. "After taking the prerequisites I am now doing independent work on governmental urban development with a professor," said one government major. Psychology and teaching certification are also well liked.

Another aspect of Sweet Briar academics is the honors program. It offers a variety of honors seminars of all disciplines, which are team-taught by the top scholars in the field. In the spring of your junior year you have the opportunity to work closely with a faculty member and write an honors thesis over the course of three semesters, on a topic of your choice. Sweet Briar also offers cross-enrollment programs with the Seven-College Exchange program, a Dual-Degree Engineering Program with Columbia and Washington University in St. Louis, and strong junior year abroad programs.

Amazing Professors

"Professors really care about teaching you something. And after the semester is over they still remember you and are genuinely interested in what you are doing. I'm still friends with many of my professors from freshman year," said one senior. Living near or on campus, the faculty at Sweet Briar makes the academic environment what it is, since there are no teaching assistants. With introductory classes averaging around 25, close interaction with professors begins freshman year. "They learn your name and are always accessible. They really care about what they are teaching," said one English major. The administration is also well liked by students and is very involved in enhancing the Sweet Briar experience. "Our president even teaches a class." By interacting with professors in class, through research in the lab, or in a game of basketball, "you really learn to look to them as mentors and friends, not just people you see a few days a week for an hour. That really distinguishes Sweet Briar from other schools."

Room and Board

Virtually everyone lives on campus. There is a wide variety of housing available. Most fresh women live in dorms with some quads or triples, which have bedrooms and a common room attached. Residential advisors, or upperclasswomen, live among fresh women, as do professional resident coordinators. Besides having assistance with living conditions, freshwomen also have key leaders, upperclasswomen with expertise in a certain academic department or health issues, which can help with any academic or social problems students may have. "We are basically there if freshmen have problems adjusting to college life, have questions about academic stuff at Sweet Briar, or just want to hang out with some upperclasswomen," said one RA. Upperclasswomen can choose to live in corridor-style housing or there are also houses near or on campus that are very popular for seniors. The dorm rooms and houses are the most common hangout place for students. There are parlors and recreation rooms, complete with pool tables, ping-pong, TVs, and stereo systems. The new Sweet Briar Student Commons Complex was dedicated in 2002, and boasts student study, meeting, and lounge areas; large multipurpose rooms for student events; student services offices; college postal, mailing, and shipping facilities; a full-service copy center; Book Shop; a grill restaurant; and outdoor recreational areas.

> **"You can do what you want here."**

"Food here is great!" says one freshwoman. Prothro Commons, the cafeteria, offers a great variety of food that "tends to be non-greasy," SWC students have no complaints. "And when you don't like the hot meal, that's okay because there is a full salad and sandwich bar and side dishes to choose from."

Who Goes to Sweet Briar?

"We are really motivated here," said one student. "I think most of us are pretty serious about academics." At the same time, students are "genuinely friendly and good-natured." With a low minority presence and limited socioeconomic backgrounds, the term "Suzy Sweet Briar," the nickname given to the typical student, "who drives a nice car, dresses nicely, and wears pearls," holds some truth still. However, the administration is working to change that. The diversity of the activities makes up for the homogeneity of the student population. Activites range from SWEBOP (Sweet Briar Outdoor Program) to the "Learning on the Land" archeological-wildlife orientation program for freshwomen. Sweet Briar also has a unique collection of groups called tap-clubs, which vary in selectivity, themes, and seriousness. Some include "Aints-N-Asses (a loud, comic group), Taps-N-Toes (for dancers and those that help with dance concerts), Ear Phones (for loud people who can't sing), Sweet Tones (our a capella group), Chung Mungs and Tau Phi (two community service based groups)."

There are a lot of things to do on Sweet

Briar's "beautiful" campus. With "bike trails out the wazoo" and horseback riding at the on-campus Equestrian Center, "one of the best in the country," in addition to the varsity sports SBC offers, like field hockey, lacrosse, riding, soccer, swimming, tennis, and volleyball. Students often hangout at the Bistro, a restaurant in town that often hosts bands and DJs. Another popular joint is the Briar Patch, another restaurant near campus. A coffeehouse in the Meta Glass ("Glass") Dorm is a great place for students to get a little caffeine and socialize with friends. Parties on campus tend to be small, and underage drinking is prevented, so "when you turn twenty-one it's a big deal." The Administration has been trying to work with the Campus Events Organization to increase the number of events on campus. Certain events like the four dell parties, outdoor band events, and two formals through the year draw a big crowd of men and women. SWC has been able to attract many groups to campus like Richmond Ballet, Urban Bush Women, and others for SB's Babcock season. In addition, there are a variety of traditional social events throughout the year. One is the Junior Banquet, "one of the biggest nights of the year," where Juniors receive their class rings. There is also a step-singing tradition in the fall and spring. "Founders' Day and Lantern Bearing are our most beautiful traditions. For Founders' Day the seniors wear their robes and ask a sophomore to walk with them to the monument. A bagpiper leads the community on the walk to the monument where we place daisies on our founders' graves. Lantern Bearing is at the end of the year. Again, the seniors wear their robes. We ask an underclassmen to bear our lantern—a basket of flowers they get for us—as we walk around the quad at night. Then lantern bearers sing sad songs to us. This tradition definitely produces the most tears," a senior said.

But often Sweet Briar students must go off campus to find a social life, since the campus is "kind of dead" socially. A car is "definitely a must," as many students go to nearby colleges and universities. Some students go to Lynchburg, a twenty-minute drive away, "which has a little to be desired," or another option is the all-male Hampden-Sydney College. Nearby Washington and Lee and Virginia Military Institute are other popular destinations. "Guys are a big deal on the weekends," admits one student, "since we don't see many of them during the week."

Sweet Briar College offers tremendous academic experience in a tight-knit community of inspiring women. "This place does something to you," one student said. *—Staff*

FYI

The three best things about Sweet Briar College are "the food, the professors, and the academics."

The three worst things about Sweet Briar are"being far from a city, lack of diversity, no social life on campus."

Three things that every student should do before leaving campus are "get to know a professor, find a boyfriend nearby so you don't have to scramble for stuff to do on the weekends, and bear a lantern."

One thing I'd like to have known before coming here is "how homogenous this place is."

University of Richmond

Address: 28 Westhampton Way; University of Richmond, VA 23173
Phone: 804-289-8640
E-mail address: admissions@richmond.edu
Web site URL: www.richmond.edu
Founded: 1830
Private or Public: private
Religious affiliation: none
Location: suburban
Undergraduate enrollment: 2,998
Total enrollment: NA
Percent Male/Female: 47%,53%
Percent Minority: 10%
Percent African-American: 5%
Percent Asian: 3%
Percent Hispanic: 2%
Percent Native-American: 0%
Percent in-state/out of state: 16%/84%
Percent Pub HS: 65%
Number of Applicants: 5,895
Percent Accepted: 40%
Percent Accepted who enroll: 33%
Entering: 802
Transfers: 46
Application Deadline: 15 Jan
Mean SAT: NA
Mean ACT: NA
Middle 50% SAT range: V 600-690, M 620-700
Middle 50% ACT range: 27-30
3 Most popular majors: business, social sciences, English
Retention: 91%
Graduation rate: 83%
On-campus housing: 92%
Fraternities: 32%
Sororities: 49%
Library: 1,049,365 volumes
Tuition and Fees: $24,940
Room and Board: $5,160
Financial aid, first-year: 33%
Varsity or Club Athletes: 12%
Early Decision or Early Action Acceptance Rate: 54%

When you go off to college, you might wonder if you will sit next to one of the future leaders of America in the cafeteria; there's no better place for that than the University of Richmond. Richmond's leadership studies program makes the school quite unique among small liberal arts schools. The academic environment, small class sizes, a beautiful campus, and an exciting social life attract students who are ready to study hard but like to live it up in their free time.

Study Hard

Most students at Richmond feel privileged by the attention that they receive from professors. "My biggest class is 35 people," said one amazed freshman. "You know the names of people in your class, and have roundtable discussions," added a senior. The small class size contributes toward a more intimate learning environment. Professors are involved, unlike at many large universities where research or grad students have priority.

The only requirement that students complain about is CORE, a class that focuses on literature from around the world. "I hate it so much, because I could be taking classes that I am actually interested in instead," said one freshman. "Most of the reading is what I did in AP English in high school." Others don't think it's so bad: "It's annoying, but exciting at the same time. I get to be exposed to things I would never read otherwise."

Business and interdisciplinary majors offered by the School of Leadership Studies are some of the most popular at Richmond. Students agree that science majors are the hardest and political science has a reputation for being easy. One political science major defended herself saying that "the department tried to limit the number of people majoring in political science because there were so many, but we are all interested!" Most students agree, however, that "if you come to Richmond you aren't scared of hard work." The general mentality seems to be that even though "many people obsess over getting good grades," the workload is "doable" and people tend to "study hard and party harder."

Party Harder

Intense studying brings the need for a little relaxation on weekends. The general consensus is that at Richmond you can choose your own party scene, whether you drink or not, or are the frat type or not. Parties are usually at the apartments where seniors live, or at "the row," where all the frats are located. They are the center of social life for freshman, but one senior said that "social life becomes old and repetitive after a while." Drinking is "not only accessible, but prevalent," and one freshman said she felt "different" because she didn't drink. However, this does not mean that there aren't other social options. The Campus Activity Board (CAB) sponsors movies and events every weekend which are popular among those not devoted to partying all the time. Students love the hypnotist who comes every fall, describing the show as "hilarious." Most students, however, enjoy simply hanging out with friends and exploring the restaurants in the city. That Richmond has diverse dining options comes as a relief for students in need of a scene change from the main cafeteria on campus.

The Richmond Bubble

Richmond is "known for being a preppy school," said one freshman, "and it can live up to its reputation." Some students complain about the limited diversity on campus. Even though over 200 countries are represented at the school, one student described most of the population as "upper-middle class, white Northerners." However, diversity is not altogether absent. "I've met so many people that look and act differently from what I expected," said one freshman. Even though many students are "Abercrombie types," they can also be very casual at times. "Sure, people dress well, but they also go to class in their PJs" said one student. Overall, most freshmen describe the people they meet as extremely friendly, but a senior confessed that "after freshman and sophomore year you get stuck with the same group of friends."

Students describe their university as fostering the "Richmond Bubble." The campus is very self-contained," said a senior. "The administration looks after us as if they were our parents, and that doesn't prepare you for the real world." On a campus unanimously described as "gorgeous," it is easy to understand why students feel protected. "Every building is gothic, with beautiful trees all around, and the lake just enhances the beauty." Students have no fears while walking around campus, though they do watch their possessions. "I wouldn't leave my laptop in the library, but overall I feel pretty safe." There is a safety shuttle available for girls who are worried about sexual assault. Only females are allowed on the bus and on cold winter nights, jealous male friends have suffered the fate of walking home alone while the girls sit nice and cozy in the shuttle.

The Coordinate System

In years past, the campus of the University of Richmond was separated into Westhampton College for women and Richmond College for men, with one gender on each side of the lake. Although the separation still exists in the single-sex dorms, men and women now mix and mingle more on campus. The coordinate system, as it is called, inspires generally positive feelings. Each college has its own student government, which inspires leadership for both genders. "The separation is less noticeable as time passes," said one senior. A freshman commented, "I was really worried about the difference of a male and female college, but I don't even notice it." Although some students still voice discontent with single-sex dorms, it is a general consensus that "it's a lot less distracting."

"The campus is very self-contained. The administration looks after us as if they were our parents, and that doesn't prepare you for the real world."

Housing is generally considered decent. Freshmen are grouped together in one male and one female dorm, and most students are content with the size of their rooms, although a couple of dorms still don't have air-conditioning. While most students live on campus all four years, many have cars. Seniors have the option of living in the apartments, which "are great communities," and one of the centers for party life. Students have RAs throughout the four years, and while most are very friendly, "they will not hesitate to write you up if you break the rules. They are just doing their job." The most popular dorm is Grey Court, which has suites with bathrooms and big bedrooms. The only disadvantage is that "the walls are very thin . . . beware!"

Dining hall food is considered by one student to be "pretty good compared to some places," and since "everyone goes to the same place to eat, you see people more often." One student described the food as having "lots of variety, some staples." The new meal plan for seniors gives them $800 to spend anywhere on campus, which has caused much enthusiasm. For stocking up on dorm food, students venture out to U-Crops grocery store, which is a five-minute drive away. One senior blissfully exclaimed "they have a Starbucks in the library now!" For those sick of campus food, a new mall just opened in Richmond and has become "a tourist attraction," as well as a popular place for students to eat and hang out.

Not a Sporty School

While Greek life is present at Richmond, it is by no means prevalent. One student noted, "Sorority life is a way of becoming involved [on campus], but . . . people do it mainly for social purposes." However, one senior explained that the Greek scene doesn't divide the social scene. She explained, "Half my friends are in sororities and half are not. It does not limit you to not go Greek." There are no fraternity or sorority houses, so Greeks and non-Greeks reside together.

Intramurals are enormously popular at Richmond, although some students lament the lack of school spirit for varsity sports. "Students do not support athletics as much as they should. I wish sports were a bigger thing," complained one student. The basketball team is considered pretty decent, and some of the big social events of the year are the tailgates for the football games. "You can spend four years at Richmond without going to a single football game, but you cannot escape the tailgates," said one student. Most students are involved with a great number of different activities. One senior, who mentioned participating in more than three extracurricular activities, said "I do very little compared to other people."

Students at Richmond are very satisfied with their school. The small size and the contained campus help foster friendships and a positive learning environment. From the very first day students feel like they are part of the community, and they leave Richmond with a sense of accomplishment. As one freshman put it, "I am comfortable here, I feel like this is where I should be." A senior remarked, "I have received a good education and enjoyed my time here." —*Claudia Setubal*

FYI

If you come to Richmond, you'd better bring "a smile and something to share about yourself."

What is the typical weekend schedule? "Friday, party at the row; Saturday, tailgate and hang out with friends; Sunday, study, study, study."

If I could change one thing about Richmond, I would "get more people with mohawks."

Three things every student at Richmond should do before graduating are "study abroad, go mud-sliding in the IM field, and go to the pig roast."

University of Virginia

Address: PO Box 400160; Charlottesville, VA 22904-4160
Phone: 804-982-3200
E-mail address: undergrad-admission@virginia.edu
Web site URL: www.virginia.edu
Founded: 1819
Private or Public: public
Religious affiliation: none
Location: small city
Undergraduate enrollment: 12,909
Total enrollment: 19,643
Percent Male/Female: 46%/54%
Percent Minority: 4.3%
Percent African-American: 8.8%
Percent Asian: 10.9%
Percent Hispanic: 2.9%
Percent Native-American: 0.3%
Percent in-state/out of state: 69%/31%
Percent Pub HS: 74%
Number of Applicants: 14,320
Percent Accepted: 39%
Percent Accepted who enroll: 53%
Entering: 2,999
Transfers: 541
Application Deadline: 2 Jan
Mean SAT: 1320
Mean ACT: NA
Middle 50% SAT range: V 600-700, M 620-720
Middle 50% ACT range: NA
3 Most popular majors: commerce, economics, psychology
Retention: 96%
Graduation rate: 83%
On-campus housing: 47%
Fraternities: 30%
Sororities: 30%
Library: 3,300,000 volumes
Tuition and Fees: $6,148 in; $22,169 out
Room and Board: $5,591
Financial aid, first-year: 51%
Varsity or Club Athletes: NA
Early Decision or Early Action Acceptance Rate: 40%

Tradition and pride abound at the University of Virginia (UVA). Thomas Jefferson founded the school, Edgar Allen Poe went there, along with Woodrow Wilson. There are no "freshmen" and "sophomores" at UVA; instead, there are first-years and second-years and so on. Why, one may wonder? Because Mr. Jefferson believed that learning never ends; thus, a "freshman" is just in the first year of a life-long education.

The "A," The "E," The "Comm"

Undergraduates at UVA are enrolled in one of the six schools: the Engineering School, the Architecture School, the College of Arts and Sciences, the McIntire School of Commerce, the Nursing School and the Curry School of Education. Academic requirements differ based on the school and the major. The academic requirements in the College are "basic: 12 credits of math and science, eight of humanities, three of history, six of social science, and three in non-Western perspectives." In addition, there is a foreign-language requirement and a writing proficiency requirement. These requirements do not seem to bother too many students "since they are really flexible, and you can space out anything that you detest so that you aren't stuck with a ton of courses that you hate in any given semester." Another student added, "requirements give one a chance to look into unexpected and interesting academic fields." Many students think that majors in the Engineering School (E-School) and the Commerce School (Comm-School) are the hardest as well as the most competitive. In the E-School, "you don't have much choice on what classes you can take; the workload is unbearable." A lot of the TAs in the E-School reportedly "barely speak English. But usually, there is a teacher somewhere nearby (or head TA) who speaks English fluently, so there isn't any major problem with that." A second-year in the College said, "My favorite part is the review sessions which some TAs give that cover the outside reading material."

Class size "depends greatly on which classes you take." Lectures can go up to 500 whereas two people can form a small class. "Any class I felt that I wanted to be small because of its content has been small, and big lectures for the intro stuff are nice because you can find big study groups." Some classes, such as Public Speaking, are hard to get into but "a lot of times you can course action into them." UVA has its share of guts such as Physics 105 (How Things Work), Mental Health, lower-level astronomy classes, and any physical education class.

Most students are happy with their professors. Said one student, "They are interesting and they seem generally excited to be teaching, instead of being jaded." A third-year added, "the professors here want you to learn, so they try and be available as much as possible." Professor Elzinga in the Economics department, and Professor Sabato in Government and Foreign Affairs are among UVA's most famous professors. Grading is "usually tough but fair." "In some departments there is grade inflation, but generally it is not excessive and I still have to work hard to get good marks," said one student. About her overall academic experience at UVA, a third-year said, "I love it here . . . challenging but you always learn something . . ."

Sex, Drugs, and the Honor Code

UVA students are known as "Wahoos" and Charlottesville is nicknamed "Hooville" after a fish named "Wahoo," that doesn't know when to stop drinking and explodes as a result. It would be right to say that UVA students truly live up to their nicknames: "Alcohol is everywhere on campus!" However, most students say that "non-drinkers do not feel left out of it. They go to parties, too; they just don't drink." The administration is very strict on alcohol. Kegs are not allowed "on the grounds itself." Not too many people do drugs at UVA but there is a "good deal of weed use." A second-year added, "quite a lot smoke pot, but mostly casually and not too openly, and never confrontationally."

Fraternities that are lined up on Rugby Road take the center stage in the party scene. "Sometimes it's hard to get in, but not if you bring girls with you," said one male student. Being underage is a problem at bars, but not at fraternities. The fraternity parties are "okay, but get a little monotonous." There is usually no charge. Mid-Winters and the Foxfield Races are the biggest parties. Upperclassmen go to bars, house parties, other colleges, and Washington, DC in addition to fraternities. There are also apartment parties and lots of bars for upperclassmen but they are also the ones who get invites to fraternity parties.

While "some people have a lot of random hook-ups," most upperclassmen reportedly have significant others, "some of them very long-term." Dating is also said to be "very common." Most students agree that "there are enough attractive people." There is also a "good deal of sex, but most people tend to be discreet."

There are lots of occasions to get dressed up. Besides the formal events of fraternities and sororities, one tradition here is to get dressed up for the football games. According to one student, there are "tons of things to do on the weekends besides going to football games, you can go to the Downtown Mall or the Corner, both have good food and stores." Also, there are "always local bands playing all over the place." The UVA theater shows $2 movies every weekend: one old movie and one new one. Said one student, "We have great speakers that come so that is something to look forward to." The Virginia Film Festival held once a year brings big Hollywood names like Anthony Hopkins and Sigourney Weaver. The Dalai Lama and Ralph Nader were among the speakers in the last few years. Campus-wide organized activities are "wonderful, frequent, and fun." In addition, "good movies and amazing lectures" are easy to come across. One student summarized the experience: "I am very happy with the social scene at UVA—the frat people keep to themselves, and so those who are not interested in that still have plenty to do."

"Honor" at UVA is far more than a word. The Honor System provides students with substantial benefits enjoyed every day like taking un-proctored exams in your own room or in a pavilion garden. A third-year noted that "the Honor System helps develop and improve this community."

Who Are the Wahoos?

The stereotypical UVA student is: "white, preppy and well-groomed; wears khakis and polo shirts, or skirts with nice tank tops; probably upper-middle class." Opinions on the student body differ from "very diverse" to "too homogeneous (predominantly white)." Several students mentioned "the need to have more minority students" as the "admissions for minorities has decreased due to lack of applicants." An aspect of the student body that most agree on is that "there is a lot of self-segregation," which is "a big issue here." Another student added, "I don't know who the typical UVA student is, but sometimes walking to class you can sort of pick out the guy who applied early admission because his father went here and his grandfather went here and so on."

> **"The odd thing here is running . . . people are always running. It's excessive, it is just really big . . . everyone runs."**

Most people exercise and are "in good shape." "The odd thing here is running . . . people are always running, but it's excessive, if you walk around at any point in the day, you will see people running alone or in big groups, but it is just really big . . . everyone runs," said one student.

Living and Dining

First-years live on campus, either in the New Dorms or the Old Dorms. Rooms in the Old Dorms are "small" but these dorms are "more social." Those living in the New Dorms "get really big rooms with a suite area for every five rooms, and some rooms have air-conditioning." There is an RA for every 20 first-years. "Some are strict, some couldn't care less. Most are strict when they need to be," said one student. After the first year, "there are tons of people who move to live 'off Grounds,' many who relocate to fraternity and sorority houses as well as the two residential colleges on Grounds." The residential colleges, Brown and Hereford, "have personality, but other than that, the housing areas are pretty standard." There are also special houses such as the French, Spanish, and Russian Houses, where students with common interests live together. On-campus floors and bathrooms are not coed. Living off campus is "very popular," though rents and proximity to campus can vary greatly.

The dining hall food reportedly "is not terrible, but not good either, and the wait is often bad." The dining halls are "fairly clean" but some students complain about dinner ending too early. Students also have "plus points" that come with the meal plans that they can use at different stores, bakeries, or the Pav, the Castle, the Treehouse, which are food courts that house chain restaurants like Pizza Hut and Chick-Fil-A. Also, students "love delivery here, and the Castle delivers." There is also a large food selection for vegetarians, and "the restaurants in Charlottesville are great, basically one from each cost category that are about five minutes away."

The Good Ole' Song

At UVA, "almost everyone belongs to some society or another, and many belong to more than one." As one third-year said, people are "very devoted" to extracurricular activities. Some of the most well respected organizations are the Madison House (community service), the Jefferson Society (debate), *The Cavalier Daily*, and the University Guides. Community service is very popular among students. A good number of students also have real jobs and UVA offers a lot of jobs for students.

The most popular sport is football by far, but soccer and basketball are also big. Everyone, students and alumni, go to the football games. "If you walk around campus on game-days, all you see is beer everywhere and everyone dressed up," said one student. There are many traditions surrounding the football games. A student described one: "Everyone puts their arms around each other and sways while singing "The Good Ole' Song" after the team scores." There is also the "Fourth-year fifth," which is the challenge of fourth-year students drinking a fifth of bourbon at the last football game of the season." The Cavalier fans possess and express a great amount of team spirit. Besides varsity sports, the Aquatic and Fitness Center has great facilities for swimming, weight lifting, and the like. Many people do intramurals, and there are always pick-up games to be found.

History and Modernity Come Together

The campus is "beautiful . . . hilly, open, historical architecture yet with a modern vibe." "Wonderful buildings" and "lots of trees" contribute to the attractiveness of campus. The University is centered around the Lawn, which neighbors the Rotunda and hosts a statue of Homer, and Frisbee games on sunny afternoons. It is also a popular hangout on lazy Sundays.

The Scott Stadium was renovated several years ago, "making it one of the nicest stadiums in the nation," housing about 60,000 people. There are also plans to expand the basketball court, the University Hall. One student added, "they are generally just revamping the older buildings and adding to the science library."

UVA is a "really friendly place." The people are "generally enthusiastic and happy, and they don't stress out like at other schools." The "great thing about UVA is for a public university, you get an Ivy League education for about half price and the campus is great . . . plus, it's also a huge party school if you dig that sort of thing. There is something for everyone." —*Engin Yenidunya*

FYI

If you come to UVA, you'd better bring "a fan—it can get hot here."

What is the typical weekend schedule? "Partying at a frat, apartment, or bar. Oh, and some studying too."

If I could change one thing about UVA, I'd "address the parking problems."

The three things that every student should do before graduating from UVA are "go to Foxfield horse races, streak the Lawn, go to the Rocket Party at Serp."

Virginia Polytechnic Institute and State University

Address: 201 Burruss Hall; Blacksburg, VA 24061
Phone: 540-231-6267
E-mail address: vtadmiss@vt.edu
Web site URL: www.vt.edu
Founded: 1872
Private or Public: public
Religious affiliation: none
Location: rural
Undergraduate enrollment: 20,821
Total enrollment: NA
Percent Male/Female: 57%/43%
Percent Minority: 15%
Percent African-American: 6%
Percent Asian: 7%
Percent Hispanic: 2%
Percent Native-American: 0%
Percent in-state/out of state: 71%/29%
Percent Pub HS: NA
Number of Applicants: 17,895
Percent Accepted: 70%
Percent Accepted who enroll: 39%
Entering: 4,735
Transfers: NA
Application Deadline: 15 Jan
Mean SAT: 1200
Mean ACT: NA
Middle 50% SAT range: V 550-630 M 560-660
Middle 50% ACT range: NA
3 Most popular majors: business, engineering, biology
Retention: 88%
Graduation rate: 43%
On-campus housing: 40%
Fraternities: NA
Sororities: NA
Library: 2,000,000 volumes
Tuition and Fees: $5,095 in; $14,979 out
Room and Board: $5,690
Financial aid, first-year: 44%
Varsity or Club Athletes: 6%
Early Decision or Early Action Acceptance Rate: 68%

Just the school name "Virginia Polytechnic Institute gives the impression of hardcore math, science, and engineering . . . basically, we're tech, tech, tech!" Although "V-Tech" is known for its challenging science-related curriculum, whoever said Techies have more fun was right: go to classes at V-Tech for the chance to see a professor light the classroom wall on fire, a professor lay on a bed of nails and request a student to hit him with a cinder block, and yet another professor ride a fire extinguisher into the walls of the classroom. If you'd like to be taught by such a zany teacher, or your ideal coursework includes building solar-powered cars or a one-person submarine, then read on!

Not All Technical

Virginia Polytechnic University is comprised of eight colleges: Agriculture and Life Sciences; Architecture and Urban Studies; Arts and Sciences; Business; Engineering; Forestry and Wildlife Resources; Human Resources and Education; and Veterinary Medicine. Hokies—as students at Virginia Tech call themselves because of their giant, purple turkey mascot—must enroll in one of the eight colleges before they graduate. Some apply to the college of their choice early in their college career, while others begin in the University Studies program, which gives participants until the end of sophomore year to choose their college. With good grades switching colleges is not difficult, though distribution requirements and major requirements do make it tough to take many electives for academic exploration. Of the colleges, the business school seems to be the easiest for Hokies to handle due to its low number of required courses, although as one computer science major conceded, "It's still good." Of the majors, engineering, computer science, biology, and music (because each music course is only worth one credit) are known as very difficult and highly competitive.

Virginia Tech's honors program is reported to be made up mostly of preprofessionals. Right before freshman year, certain students with excellent high school grades and test scores are invited to apply for this program, which allows them to be a part of small, honors-only courses and to have priority for other classes. After matriculation, any student in any year with a 3.5 GPA is invited to apply. Once a part of the program, honors students are required to maintain a 3.5 GPA. Honors program or not, the curriculum at V-Tech is not only technical. "Although most of the student body is scientifically minded," a student noted, "non-technical majors have no problems fitting in and finding great classes." In terms of getting into classes, "The higher in level you get, the harder it is to get the schedule you want."

While Virginia Tech boasts such famous professors as Alan Turing, who decoded Nazi messages during WWII, and Dr. Kingston, who has made significant advances in cancer research, there are complaints about the lack of caring by some professors: "They don't always care about what you do and how hard you try." Another student wished that "more of the professors would care about their students, since some of them just don't take the time out of their own schedule other than for class time." Physics, chemistry and math professors are notorious for having poor English-speaking skills, and there are "simply not enough TAs when you need help." Nevertheless, as one senior put it, "I think this school is very strong in its academics and a great place to learn."

Hokies Havin' a Good Time

When not studying or doing work, students at V-Tech know how to party and have fun—with and without alcohol. Though drinking is not a must, there is a large Greek system; about 50 percent of the campus is involved with the Greek scene. As freshmen, Hokies like to hang out with their friends and find parties at apartments or at the many fraternity and sorority houses. As upperclassmen, Hokies party at friends' houses and bars, though as one student reported, "It's not usually a drinking thing with the upperclassmen; they do it all." Students report that about 50 percent of undergrads are involved in serious relationships, and that there are "quite a few random hook-ups at parties." Of these parties, some of which do charge admission, "the cool parties include the Pimp and Hoe parties, Beach parties, and the big Halloween parties." For those students who want occasions to dress-up, formals include Mid-Winters, Homecoming, and the Ring Dance.

Depends on Who You Live with

The dorms at V-Tech are co-ed by hall and floor with relatively small rooms. Of course, "the newer dorms are really nice, with air conditioning." Many rules accompany living on campus, and include visitation rights, the prohibition of alcohol, and quiet hours during exams. Freshmen must live on campus: "Freshman dorms can be small and crowded but some of them can be really nice." In their dorms, freshmen have RAs who are "not strict—they really want to be your friend." With different personalities, the dorms are defined by the students who live in each dorm. As one junior guy sheepishly admitted, "Most of the bad ones are all guys, which is sad." After their first year, most people do move off campus for nicer and more spacious townhouses and apartments; and students are not always guaranteed a room after freshman year.

Good Food to Suit All Tastes

In contrast to the opinion of students at many other universities, Hokies are very happy with their meal plan and food choices. There are quite a few options in choosing a meal plan, though many freshmen choose a plan of 19 meals per week; these meals can be eaten at a variety of the dining halls around campus. Others students are on the flex system, in which undergrads buy points to use at any of the dining halls, at franchise restaurants in the student center, on vending machines, and even at the laundromats. All in all, there is a good variety of foods to suit all tastes and a good set of hours to suit all schedules.

"This is a very high-tech university, more so than many others. Yet, this school has almost everything you could hope for in a university."

Life in Tiny Blacksburg

While students from urban or suburban areas may require some adjustment to living in tiny Blacksburg, the change is not very difficult because "everyone is friendly," and "it's easy to meet people." There are two big student centers on campus, Squires and Johnson, which are always busy. While no groups or cliques control student life, students say their groups of friends are constantly changing because of people moving off campus or graduating. Closest friends are made through dorms, classes and extracurricular activities. The congenial atmosphere at V-Tech is also reflected in students' apparel: "People wear whatever they are comfortable in—they can walk around in anything from pajamas to khakis and a nice shirt." The student body is diverse geographically and culturally, but not as much ethnically. Some students would like to have more minority students because "the population of minorities seems just too low here."

Nestled in a valley surrounded by mountains, the campus has a medieval look to it and is "just a beautiful place to be." On a lazy Sunday, you could go to Duck Pond, Drill Field, Squires, or anywhere downtown. Of course, "You do tend to want to get out of town every once in awhile." For this reason, the majority of Hokies have cars on campus, though as one student reflected, "You do not really need a car, but it certainly makes life easier." To get from place to place without a car, students may use Blacksburg's "really good bus system."

Go, Hokie Sports!

With many extracurricular options available to students at V-Tech, Hokies certainly do not neglect their sports teams. Aside from fraternity involvement, the most popular extracurricular activity on campus is athletics. The football team is definitely the most popular sports team, commanding a lot of school spirit and much support from the student body. Home football games are major occasions, particularly those against rival University of Virginia. Hokies who are not involved in varsity sports are able to actively participate in athletics through the school's popular intramural leagues. In addition, there are volleyball courts next to all the dorms and "it seems there is always someone throwing a Frisbee, baseball, football, or something." Furthermore, students report that there are almost always pick-up games somewhere on the Drill Field, a large courtyard around which all the residential and academic buildings are centered.

As one senior summarized, "This is a very high-tech university, more so than many others. Yet, this school has almost everything you could hope for in a university." Virginia Polytechnic Institute and State University is clearly a technical university, yet the number of opportunities abound for students of all academic and extracurricular interests and backgrounds. —*Victoria Yen*

FYI

If you come to Virginia Tech, you'd better bring "a good sense of humor, the ability to work hard, the ability to have some fun, and (because of the varying weather) multiple sets of clothes, including a heavy coat."

What is the typical weekend schedule? "During football season, most of the students at Virginia Tech take part in watching football on Saturdays, especially the Hokies. After that most people hang out, or party during the weekends."

If I could change one thing about Virginia Tech, I'd "make some of the classes smaller, since some have like 500 people."

Three things every student at Virginia Tech should do before graduating are: "go to a football game, make sure you do something outstanding that could be relayed as memorable, and see the mountain lake and falls."

Washington and Lee University

Address: Letcher Avenue; Lexington, VA 24450-0303
Phone: 540-463-8710
E-mail address: admissions@wlu.edu
Web site URL: www.wlu.edu
Founded: 1749
Private or Public: private
Religious affiliation: none
Location: rural
Undergraduate enrollment: 1,748
Total enrollment: 2,127
Percent Male/Female: 50%/50%
Percent Minority: 7%
Percent African-American: 4%
Percent Asian: 2%
Percent Hispanic: 1%
Percent Native-American: 0%
Percent in-state/out of state: 17%/83%
Percent Pub HS: 60%
Number of Applicants: 2,939
Percent Accepted: 31%
Percent Accepted who enroll: 49%
Entering: 458
Transfers: 3
Application Deadline: 15 Jan
Mean SAT: 1360
Mean ACT: NA
Middle 50% SAT range: V 640-720, M640-720
Middle 50% ACT range: NA
3 Most popular majors: business administration, economics, accounting
Retention: 96%
Graduation rate: 83%
On-campus housing: 64%
Fraternities: 21%
Sororities: 9%
Library: 629,723 volumes
Tuition and Fees: $23,295
Room and Board: $5,710
Financial aid, first-year: 46%
Varsity or Club Athletes: 37%
Early Decision or Early Action Acceptance Rate: 61%

Are you a Republican? Do you long for the days of chivalry and good ol' Southern hospitality? Is your wardrobe mainly comprised of khakis and polos? Are you looking for myriad social opportunities? Are you willing to work hard and play hard? If you answered "yes" to any of these questions, Washington and Lee just may be the place for you to spend the next four years.

How y'all doin'?

Nestled between the Blue Ridge and Allegheny mountains of Virginia, Washington & Lee's campus is described as "nothing less than a country club." The history that surrounds the university makes some students feel as if they have been transported back to another era in American history. Two big names have played a large role in the development of the university: George Washington, who gave the school its first major endowment, and General Robert E. Lee, a former president of the university. The school prides itself on its rich traditions. However, this tradition is much more than a requirement; some students comment that tradition fosters a sense of community and helps freshmen feel more comfortable during their first few weeks of college.

With the inspiration of General Lee, honor has been the moral cornerstone on campus. As the story goes, a student went up to Lee to ask what the rules of the college were. General Lee replied, "We have but one rule here, and it is that every student must be a gentleman." Today, that one rule is manifested in many ways. For example, the library stays open 24 hours and students leave bicycles unlocked and personal belongings unattended, confident that they will not be stolen. The honor code is knit so tightly in university tradition and history that students feel that the honor code is the single most important aspect of university life. Freshmen are not allowed to attend fall classes until they have acknowledged in writing an understanding of the honor system. The penalty for an honor violation is dismissal from Washington and Lee. One student noted, "the honor system works because the students make it work."

Hitting the Books

One sophomore confidently commented, "There are no slacker majors." The most popular programs are: accounting, economics, management, politics, and the sciences. Although the science majors are known for being extremely difficult, one junior said, "You will never find an English or history major with less than four or five hours of homework on a Tuesday night." Undergrads agree that there are no "easy A" courses at Washington and Lee. Sundays are generally spent in Leyburn Library or in the room studying. High-speed Ethernet connections are available throughout campus for student computing. Onc student said of the academic environment, "Although the students here can and do consume large quantities of alcohol, they know why they're here, and they are up to the challenge."

"The honor system works because the students make it work."

In keeping with tradition, the university sets basic general educational requirements, which ensures a broadened education. Students take courses in a foreign language, English, science, and history. The university also encourages students to engage in research and service learning. The featured program, Washington and Lee's Shepherd Program for the Interdisciplinary Study of Poverty and Human Capability, integrates academic study with community service and reflection.

It's All Greek to Me!

As much as they are studiers, W&L kids are partiers. One undergrad said, "If you're not Greek now, you will be." Social life at W&L definitely revolves around the Greek scene. One student said, "Something like 85 percent of guys are in frats and 70 percent of girls are in sororities. It may be even more. It is very rare to meet an 'independent' student." Some recent theme parties have included the Redneck Ball, Tacky Ball, Heaven & Hell, and Anything for Money. Despite the university's policy on underage drinking, one freshman said, "regardless of age, the only place you can't find alcohol is in the soft drink dispenser in the dining hall. The school is trying to tighten the alcohol policy, but it's difficult to tame 200 years of tradition."

Apart from the Greek scene, there are myriad artistic, athletic, and community service opportunities. The popular Outing Club offers students a variety of outdoor activities, ranging from backpacking, canoeing, and rock climbing to community service options. The Mock Convention, which draws students nationally, is held every four years for the political party not occupying the White House. Students do extensive political research and attempt to predict the party's nomination. According to one student, "It's definitely a lot of work, but we have so much fun doing it." Convention is also a fun week on campus—it becomes a major time for parties.

Living at W&L

All students are required to live on campus for the first two years at W&L. Freshmen live in one of four main residence halls: Baker, Davis, Gilliam, and Graham-Lees. All the frosh dorms are co-ed by floor. According to the students, approximately 50 percent of the freshmen rooms are singles; the remainder are doubles. Each fraternity and sorority has a campus house for members that offers space for chapter activities and meals, in addition to living space. Each house also has a housemother to oversee meals and event planning. Finally, students may choose to live in the Outing Club House, International House, Chavis House, or the Spanish Language House.

After their sophomore year, students may opt to live off campus or remain in on-campus housing. There are many reasonably priced apartments and houses in the community near W&L. One student said, "Robert E. Lee started the tradition of upperclassmen living off campus so that the students would mix with the Lexington citizens."

Brand Spankin' New

The university started off the 2002–2003 school year with a new president and a broad plan of improving its facilities. Recently, the university completed the science addition and renovated Reid Hall, which houses the journalism department. University Commons features Washington and Lee's bookstore, a student and faculty lounge, a snack bar, an auditorium, and a dining area. The building will also house offices and meeting rooms for student groups and the University's career services office. Also under construction is a 10,000-square-foot fitness center to meet the ever-growing campus-wide demand for physical fitness and weight training. The new art and music center, currently on the drawing board, will triple the existing space that the departments currently share.

Students looking to go to Washington and Lee can expect to partake in its timeless tradition and enjoy its commitment to keep up with the standards of modern time. —*Scott Rodney Woods*

FYI

If you come to Washington and Lee, you'd better bring "a flask."

What is the typical weekend schedule? "Friday night, go to a pre-party cookout, then hit a couple frat parties. Saturday, sleep in then go to a sporting event or just hang out until you repeat Friday night. On Sunday, wake up late, eat brunch, and head to the library to study."

If I could change one thing about Washington and Lee, "I'd make Lexington, Virginia, a bit more of a metropolis."

Three things every student at Washington & Lee should do before graduating are "hike on the Appalachian Trail, streak on the Colonnade, and rush a frat or sorority."

Washington

The Evergreen State College

Address: 2700 Evergreen Parkway NW; Olympia, WA 98505
Phone: 360-866-6000
E-mail address: admissions@evergreen.edu
Web site URL: www.evergreen.edu
Founded: 1967
Private or Public: public
Religious affiliation: none
Location: small city
Undergraduate enrollment: 4,081
Total enrollment: NA
Percent Male/Female: 49%/51%
Percent Minority: 18%
Percent African-American: 5%
Percent Asian: 4%
Percent Hispanic: 4%
Percent Native-American: 5%
Percent in-state/out of state: 77%/23%
Percent Pub HS: NA
Number of Applicants: 1,399
Percent Accepted: 93%
Percent Accepted who enroll: 37%
Entering: 492
Transfers: NA
Application Deadline: rolling
Mean SAT: NA
Mean ACT: NA
Middle 50% SAT range: V 5420-650, M 480-590
Middle 50% ACT range: NA
3 Most popular majors: social sciences, gender and cultural studies, environmental studies
Retention: 67%
Graduation rate: 51%
On-campus housing: 25%
Fraternities: NA
Sororities: NA
Library: NA
Tuition and Fees: $3,895 in; $13,255 out
Room and Board: $5,688
Financial aid, first-year: 38%
Varsity or Club Athletes: 6%
Early Decision or Early Action Acceptance Rate: NA

A state school with a lush, thousand-acre campus just outside Olympia, Washington, Evergreen was founded in the 1970s and has been popularly known ever since as that "hippie school up north." As one student put it, "the stereotype is built up that there are a lot of hippies and we all eat granola and live in the woods." However, students insist that this is nothing more than a myth and that Greeners, as they are called, offer much more. One Junior said, "[The stereotype is] that people here just smoke pot and talk about Buddhism, but I'm pretty positive I haven't had one conversation about Buddhism." Students do admit, however, that there is indeed a "liberal undertone" at the school, but one can still find a rich diversity of ideas in the classroom. As one sophomore recounted, "In my seminar, I'm reading President Bush's favorite book (next to the Bible), and half of the class agrees with it and half of the class disagrees. You don't just have a bunch of liberal kids patting each other on the back." One senior added, "One thing we do have in common is that we're all pretty open-minded on campus. A lot of people recycle and you could say, 'Oh, you're a hippie,' but we're just normal people."

Although students maintain that Evergreen's population is as diverse as any other school, the Evergreen State College has not completely abandoned the liberal ideas of the era in which it was founded. In fact, one could say that Evergreen State continues to thrive on vestiges of the 1970s, giving it a unique educational style that grants students a sense of independence and interdisciplinary integration rarely found in the modern college.

Academic Liberation

Students at the Evergreen State College eagerly talk about the remarkable degree of freedom that their school allows them in their academic pursuits. "[The freedom] can be a beautiful thing for certain people," praised one student. "For students who have a drive to learn, and who don't need someone to be constantly on their back [about] turning something in, I really think Evergreen is a great place."

Evergreen State's academic repertoire encourages students to be masters of their own scholastic destiny through four special features: academic programs, independent study contracts, internships, and study abroad. The bulk of Evergreen State's curriculum is in the form of academic programs, in which students register for a coordinated three-quarter set of classes centered on a unifying theme rather than signing up for several classes individually that, in all likelihood, would not be as integrated. One student focusing (Evergreen has no majors—only focuses) on environmental studies noted that a program called Ocean Life and Environmental Policy in his first year at Evergreen State was his main academic inspiration. "That class was basically an introduction to marine biology and ecology, but we also did environmental policy and linked it to ocean life." In order to accommodate such cross-disciplinary studies as well as to satisfy the 25:1 student-faculty ratio that every class must fulfill, programs are taught by more than one professor, with each professor specialized in the respective academic areas covered by the course.

This type of linkage across the disciplines—like biology, ecology, and politics—is the distinguishing feature of Evergreen State's programs. This integration allows the Evergreen State College to be lax when it comes to formal distribution requirements, without sacrificing learning basic skills. One student commented, "Whenever you put together a program at Evergreen, you're going to get the writing skills, the math skills, and you would have to search really hard not to get those things."

Evergreen State students also can choose contracts, in which select students can set up independent study programs in cooperation with a faculty member. "You specify the books you're going to read, where you're going to be, and how often you're going to contact your faculty member," one student said. "You could say, 'Hey, I want to do a contract about rainforest ecology.'" But students maintain that contracts are not an opportunity to avoid class, but, as the name suggests, require a substantial amount of commitment not all students are capable of. "To get a contract they choose you. [Faculty] will talk to your old professors and ask, 'How good would they be?'"

Similarly, select students are allowed to take leave from Evergreen and study abroad or do internships for credit. "You'll say what you're going to do and what you're going to be learning, and the faculty will make sure that you're doing work and not just sweeping floors," one senior said. Such internships can lead to even bigger opportunities. "My friend worked on the movie *S.W.A.T.* and was offered a job," the senior said.

"No Grading," Not "No Work"

Perhaps the most striking feature of the Evergreen State education is the lack of numerical grading. Instead, at the end of each quarter professors write what is known as a narrative evaluation, which is essentially like the recommendation letters given to students at other colleges, but with painstaking detail to a student's improvement over the course of a quarter. Students value the flexibility that the narrative evaluation system offers as opposed to numerical grading. "Everything that you do extra in class reflects [in your evaluations] because your teacher can write about it, so you're not limited to an A." Another student praised the amount of detail that can go into an evaluation; he said that with Evergreen State evaluations, employers were probably more likely to get a "better impression of me and my work ethic and to judge me as a student better as opposed to with an A, B, or a C."

Yet with such a novel approach to academics, one might wonder whether there's a temptation just to slack off at Evergreen or a necessity to be self-motivated and driven to take charge of their own work. Evergreen students insist that the case is mostly the latter. "I would say that people are very hardworking and [Evergreen's academic programs] force you to be very self-motivated," said one sophomore. Another student added, "There's not many students who just go to school. There's not really anyone who doesn't just go to class. Everyone who is here wants to be here, and everyone who is here wants to learn. And if they don't, they leave."

"[The stereotype is] that people here just smoke pot and talk about Buddhism, but I'm pretty positive I haven't had one conversation about Buddhism."

In fact, one senior noted that Evergreen State is far from a slacker's dream. "I spent 40 to 50 hours a week doing homework my first year. It's pretty common, and my friends don't look at me funny when I say, 'I have to go do work now,' because they have to, too. I wouldn't say there's too much work, but there is a lot of work." Students concurred that the work is manageable, especially because the academic program system allows professors to "coordinate so that they can assign a steady amount of homework." The senior noted that at one point during a program, "[Everyone] handed in their homework late, and the professors apologized and said that they had assigned too much work." The student concluded that this cooperation between the students and professors does help. "You can really get in the groove of a schedule that works for you," he said.

The Green and the Concrete

Evergreen State has a wide selection of rooming options. One student listed two examples, "They've got apartment-style living with four to six bedrooms with a furnished living area; they also have modular housing which is further down with their own parking lots. It's more secluded." Evergreen State offers several specialized dorms, such as "A Dorm," a freshmen-only building, and according to one sophomore, a sustainable living housing option is in the works, in which environment-conscious students can live according to the "concept of living without depleting your resources."

Yet perhaps an inevitable consequence of having so many different housing options is variation in housing quality. While one student said, "The dorms are so much bigger than anyone else's dorms I've ever seen," another said, "I lived in housing my first year and I hated it. It's cramped and pretty rowdy."

Moreover, despite the multiplicity of housing options, students living on campus are in the minority. "I wish that there were more students living on campus," complained one sophomore. "There's 4,300 students, and only 1,000 kids live on campus. Some of them commute from their hometowns [in Washington]. A lot of people live in houses or apartments off campus." She conceded, however, "It doesn't affect student life that much, but in terms of walking over to your friends' dorms to say hi, you can't really do that."

Students, however, generally agree that the food has improved leaps and bounds. Once catered by the Marriott hotel chain, Evergreen State now offers a dining option prepared by a business called Bon Appétit. "They make crepes right in front of you," one senior raved. Evergreen State also prides itself on its organic farm, much of whose produce goes to the dining halls. "Seventy percent of the food is organic, and they're working their way up to making it 100 percent," one sophomore said. Evergreen State also offers a convenience store called The Corner, which is conveniently located near the dorms of Lower Campus and offers "fruits and breads, vegetables, juice, and the basic necessities—chips and candy."

Evergreen State also offers a good range of extracurriculars to choose from, including five intercollegiate sports and many clubs. One senior spoke of his involvement with the Student CD Project, which puts out a yearly collection of songs from Evergreen student bands. Students also have good things to say about Olympia and its vibrant nightlife and rich music scene, concentrated along streets such as the famous 4th Avenue Strip. Students also enjoy a one-day festival known as Super Saturday as well as events such as a Punk Rock Prom, sponsored by an animal-rights organization.

Greeners do admit that Evergreen State does not fit the mold of other colleges, yet they insist that that necessarily isn't a bad thing. As one senior said, "It's a shame that some students may be scared off by the hippie stereotypes that abound about Evergreen State." He concluded, "I really feel sorry for people who don't how great Evergreen State is and would do well here." —*Christopher Lapinig*

FYI

If you come to The Evergreen State College, you'd better bring "an umbrella. It's basically temperate rainforest, and it rains half of the year."

What is the typical weekend schedule? "Do work, go to the gym with my friends, go to basketball or soccer or volleyball games depending on what season it is, go up to Seattle or Olympia for concerts, eat out a lot, and do homework, of course."

If I could change one thing about The Evergreen State College, I would "ask for more jobs off campus. It's really hard to find a job in Olympia, and I think most people at Evergreen work, but it's much easier to work off campus."

Three things that every student at The Evergreen State College should do before graduating are "go to the organic farm, rappel from the Clocktower, and go for a swim in the Sound on campus."

University of Puget Sound

Address: 1500 North Warner Street; Tacoma, WA 98416-0062
Phone: 253-879-3211
E-mail address: admission@ups.edu
Web site URL: www.ups.edu
Founded: 1888
Private or Public: private
Religious affiliation: none
Location: suburban
Undergraduate enrollment: 2,604
Total enrollment: NA
Percent Male/Female: 41%/59%
Percent Minority: 17%
Percent African-American: 2%
Percent Asian: 12%
Percent Hispanic: 3%
Percent Native-American: 1%
Percent in-state/out of state: 31%/69%
Percent Pub HS: 76%
Number of Applicants: 4,124
Percent Accepted: 72%
Percent Accepted who enroll: 22%
Entering: 753
Transfers: 187
Application Deadline: rolling
Mean SAT: NA
Mean ACT: NA
Middle 50% SAT range: V 580-670, M 570-670
Middle 50% ACT range: 24-29
3 Most popular majors: business management, English, biology
Retention: 85%
Graduation rate: 70%
On-campus housing: 53%
Fraternities: 25%
Sororities: 22%
Library: 463,233 volumes
Tuition and Fees: $25,360
Room and Board: $6,400
Financial aid, first-year: 70%
Varsity or Club Athletes: 6%
Early Decision or Early Action Acceptance Rate: NA

Are you interested in a college that offers a rigorous curriculum, small classes, and thoughtful professors? If so, the University of Puget Sound might be for you. Boasting 60 academic programs, more than 1,200 courses, and a tightly integrated School of Music, UPS (as students call Puget Sound) is a mid-sized college that prides itself on its strong liberal arts foundation. It is situated on a lush green campus in the heart of the Pacific Northwest and is within driving distance of Seattle, Portland, Vancouver, and Mt. Rainier.

Work Hard . . .

Every student at UPS will attest to the fact that "the workload is hard" and that "teachers expect a lot from [students]." However, most feel that the academic challenges they encounter at UPS are worthwhile and prepare them well for the real world.

Every matriculating student at UPS

must complete a core curriculum and satisfy a foreign language requirement before he or she graduates. The core curriculum consists of eight courses divided into three main subjects: Argument and Inquiry, Five Approaches to Knowing, and Interdisciplinary Experience. Within each theme, students can choose from a wide variety of courses, which makes satisfying core requirements a relatively painless, and often enjoyable, experience.

Certain majors at UPS tend to be more popular than others; among these are psychology, English, and business. In addition, a few new programs are rapidly growing in popularity, such as international political economy and theater. As if the tough workload at UPS was not enough, a few majors have earned the reputation of being especially difficult, such as politics and government, history, and biology. (Although in the case of biology, the main complaint was waking up in time for organic chemistry at 8 A.M.!) For particularly strong students, UPS offers two special programs that accepted students can apply for. One is the Honors Program, which offers students a more in-depth liberal arts curriculum. The second is the Business Leadership Program, which emphasizes problem-solving techniques and provides students with unique internship opportunities.

With an average class size of 19, UPS offers an intimate learning environment for students. Nearly every class at UPS is seminar size, allowing students to have more discussions and participation opportunities than other universities' large class sizes allow. One disadvantage stemming from small class sizes is that students do not always get into the classes of their choice. However, if students are persistent and not overly rigid about their schedule, they are usually able to take all the courses they wish to by the time they graduate.

Professors at UPS receive high praise. The consensus is that the professors are extremely approachable and interact frequently with students, both as mentors and as friends. As one senior said, "My favorite thing about UPS is probably the professors. These people truly cared about what I did, and they cared if I did well." It seems that the only negative thing students had to say about their professors was that they tended to "conspire" when setting test and due dates, which all inevitably occur at the same times. Finally, it should be noted that UPS has a "No-TA policy", meaning TAs are not allowed to teach or to grade major assignments.

Play Hard . . .

UPS students work hard when they have to, but they also know how to have fun. Although UPS is a "wet" campus in terms of allowing alcohol in students' rooms (as long as they're of age), the administration generally restricts any sort of drinking in a group setting on campus. As a result, most partying has been pushed off campus and into upperclass houses and fraternity houses. To quote one junior, "These parties usually consist of dancing and casual drinking. There is a definite presence of alcohol, but I wouldn't characterize it as a problem. Most people know not to get out of control."

The Greek life at UPS is not as strong as at other schools and has had "declining interest over the last decade" or so. However, there are still four fraternities and five sororities on campus. Rushing at UPS is delayed until second semester of freshman year, which may account for the lower interest in Greek life. However, students recommend that everyone participate in the rush process to meet new people even if they do not plan to join a frat or a sorority. Two of the fraternities, Sigma Chi and Beta Theta Pi, regularly host parties. One of the most popular parties each year is "The Beach," in which the Sigma Chi house is filled with sand and the staircases are "turned into waterfalls." As you can imagine, cleanup for this fiesta is a colossal process, but "well worth it."

Apart from parties, UPS also sponsors many alcohol-free events. These include concerts, lectures, and karaoke or movie nights. Some recent performers that UPS has attracted include Ani DiFranco and Maroon 5. The School of Music also hosts their own concerts and attracts musicians from around the world. Several endowed lecture series exist on campus, with some recent speakers including *New York Times* columnist Thomas Friedman and Nobel Peace Laureate Oscar Sanchez. There is also the "Last Lecture" series, in which UPS professors speak as if they were giving their last lectures.

In terms of extracurricular activities, UPS students are very involved. There is "Hui-o-Hawaii," which hosts the largest luau in the Northwest. There is "Praxis Imago," which is a student-run film group that puts on a student film festival, "Foolish Pleasures," each year. Singing groups are also popular with notable ones being "Underground A Cappella," "Underground Rhythm," and "Underground Jazz." Several groups perform community service around campus including "Kids Can Do" and "Circle K." In general, every student is involved with some sort of extracurricular activity, and most are involved in several. The student government at UPS is generous with funding and is usually willing to assist students with starting new clubs.

"We have a bad rep for our weather but it's really not that bad, even though it gets gray in November and stays gray until April."

In athletics, UPS is a Division III school that does not offer athletic scholarships. Although most students agree that athletics is not a strong focus for UPS, support for sports teams is still strong. The top three varsity teams at UPS are crew, soccer, and swimming, all of which have been ranked near the top of their divisions in recent years. For students not on a sports team, intramurals are quite popular. In addition, the student fitness center is a top-notch facility with a rock climbing wall, indoor tennis courts, basketball courts, and a 25-meter pool.

Life on Campus

Most students at UPS live in doubles during their freshman year, although some are housed in triples or quads. Freshman rooms are located in two main residence halls, Todd/Phibbs and Anderson/Langdon, which have in them special themed floors such as the humanities floor, the substance-free floor, and the social justice floor. Some floors are co-ed while others are single-sex; all-girls residence halls are also available. In upperclass years, suites of six with a common kitchenettes and bathrooms are available. In addition, UPS also owns approximately 60 houses on the outskirts of campus where students can live. UPS does have an RA system, but according to students, the RAs are generally not that strict.

The UPS meal plan operates on a points system in which students pay for what they eat, rather than by number of meals. Dining is centralized in the Wheelock Student Center within which there are three places to eat: a main cafeteria, a café, and a "pizza cellar." Students often praise the long operating hours of the dining service—the main cafeteria is open throughout the day until 10 P.M. Moreover, the pizza cellar, which also serves as a convenience store, is open into the wee hours of the morning. Finally, food quality was given a thumbs-up by all of the students interviewed with one student calling it "the best among colleges big and small."

When students tire of the on-campus dining options, they often walk a few blocks to the Proctor District where several shops and restaurants can be found. Some local favorites include the Metropolitan Market (gourmet grocery store) and Pomodoro's (Italian restaurant). For students with access to cars, The Waterfront is also an option.

When asked what UPS student stereotypes are, students inevitably mention Nalgenes and hiking gear. Students often dress in "earthy" or "hippie" styles with fleeces and rain jackets quite popular (and appropriate to the climate). The student body at UPS is composed largely of middle-class Caucasian and Asian students, but the administration has made attempts in recent years to increase diversity on campus. With a 55:45 male-to-female ratio in the latest incoming class, the two genders are fairly well balanced at UPS. The dating scene is relatively active, and students report that random hook-ups are quite prevalent, especially among freshmen and sophomores. Both homosexuality and interracial dating are present and accepted on campus.

Campus and Surroundings

The buildings at UPS have earned it the nickname of "Harvard of the West," thanks to their red-brick buildings with ivy running up the walls. There are grass and trees everywhere although the ground can get quite soggy during the winter months. As one student said, "We have a bad rep for our weather but it's really not that bad, even though it gets gray in November and stays gray until April."

The campus itself is situated in a residential neighbourhood and is considered very safe. Indeed, many students at UPS refer to the "bubble" that encapsulates them and separates them from the rest of Tacoma and the outside world. When the need for "big-city life" arises, most students head either to downtown Tacoma, which has an assortment of theaters, museums, malls, and restaurants, or to the bustle of Seattle. Occasionally, students also take advantage of Tacoma's proximity to Portland and Vancouver and drive to these cities for the weekend.

UPS is a challenging school that offers its students a strong liberal arts education. The university helps students realize their full potential and in the process gain a solid foundation for life after college. —*Anthony Xu*

FYI

If you come to UPS, you'd better bring "a rain jacket."

What is the typical weekend schedule? "Hang out or party on Friday night; sleep in on Saturday and lounge around or go shopping; sleep in on Sunday and do homework."

If I could change one thing about UPS, I'd "increase the diversity on campus."

Three things every student at UPS should do before graduating are "join a musical group, wade through the Thompson Fountain, and go to a fireside dinner put on by the president."

University of Washington

Address: 1410 NE Campus Parkway, 320 Schmitz Hall Box 355840; Seattle, WA 9819-5840
Phone: 206-543-9686
E-mail address: askuwadm@u.washington.edu
Web site URL: u.washington.edu
Founded: 1861
Private or Public: public
Religious affiliation: none
Location: urban
Undergraduate enrollment: 28,362
Total enrollment: NA
Percent Male/Female: 44%/56%
Percent Minority: 31%
Percent African-American: 3%
Percent Asian: 24%
Percent Hispanic: 3%
Percent Native-American: 1%
Percent in-state/out of state: 88%/12%
Percent Pub HS: NA
Number of Applicants: 13,875
Percent Accepted: 78%
Percent Accepted who enroll: 45%
Entering: 6,765
Transfers: 2,550
Application Deadline: 15 Jan
Mean SAT: NA
Mean ACT: NA
Middle 50% SAT range: V 510-640, M 540-630
Middle 50% ACT range: 22-28
3 Most popular majors: social sciences, business, English
Retention: 90%
Graduation rate: 71%
On-campus housing: 64%
Fraternities: 20%
Sororities: 29%
Library: 5,100,000 volumes
Tuition and Fees: $4,636 in; $15,337 out
Room and Board: $8,430
Financial aid, first-year: 35%
Varsity or Club Athletes: 9%
Early Decision or Early Action Acceptance Rate: 84%

At the annual Apple Cup, enthusiasm always envelops the University of Washington's football team as 'U-Dub'ers cheer their school to victory over Washington State. It is in active moments like these that this huge research university feels as small as the single cabin from whence it sprung in 1861.

A System Built on Science

UW is a "massive" university, spread out among three campuses in Seattle, Bothell, and Tacoma. Seattle is the main campus, while the latter two are much smaller and cater more towards the local populations north and south of Seattle. Because of their smaller size, Bothell and Tacoma also have smaller classes and, says one Bothell student, "professors who are more into being professors." Seattle is the hub of UW's research and student activity, however, and most students go there.

The vast majority of undergraduates at UW apply to the School of Arts and Sciences, and at the beginning of freshman year they can choose to take part in several special programs. The honors program, which enrolls 100–200 students per year, provides selected students with small classes (30 people is the norm) and a more localized educational network. Freshman may choose to join the FIG (Freshman Interest Groups) program, where small groups of students enroll together in popular fall quarter courses. These courses are quickly filled to capacity by FIG students, to such a degree that other students are often excluded from the classes. While making UW a little smaller and more intimate for FIG participators, some other students note that the program "can be very restrictive in itself."

Another program particular to UW is the early-entrance program, which selects six eighth-graders a year from the state of Washington for early entrance to the university (the eighth-graders go through one year of 'high school' and then enter college).

Once enrolled in the university, all UW students head into their university's quarter system with five requirements to fulfill. Students must take classes in the areas of social sciences, humanities, and natural sciences, as well as one year of a foreign language and one English composition course. Registering for these and other classes, however, is "one of the biggest drawbacks," as students get four specified days on which they must wake up at 6 A.M. and go online to snag spots in popular classes.

Once in classes, though, students find their coursework challenging and even inspiring. One freshman noted, "I thought it'd be easier, but that hasn't really been the case." But there are some courses which aren't considered to be rewarding. One senior commented that "lower-level classes are a joke," and classes such as Sex in Scandinavia, Children's Literature, and Dinosaurs also fall under that label. Among majors, sociology is considered to be a joke major "for the athletes."

The science departments, however, are anything but a joke. UW specializes in the sciences, and popular majors include engineering, computer science, natural sciences, and biochemistry. One popular non-science major at UW is international studies. There are a vast number of premed students at UW, many engineers, and countless resources and funding opportunities for them all. Non-science programs do not seem to be as popular or well-funded; one accounting major commented that he "didn't really know any humanities majors." Another senior made sure to point out that "there are a lot of really great people in the humanities; you just have to find them."

Students are quick to note that their university is "primarily a research school in many ways—there is great funding for certain sponsored programs, and professors focus mainly on higher-level classes." This leads to a wealth of research opportunities, as well as the fact that "half of professors end up teaching out of textbooks they wrote . . . so you know they get it."

Compared to the professors, advisors and TAs don't receive very high ratings. TAs seem to usually be fine, but there has been some strife in the past. One senior recalled how TAs went on strike for two months during his freshman year, causing him to receive only a credit instead of a letter grade. There is much academic support, however, through each major's department, as well as in the study abroad programs. The latter are widely taken advantage of, and overall students are happy with their academic life at UW and claim that "it's been fantastic."

The Key to UW

The six student dorms at UW are often categorized by what people in each dorm do: "study," "party," "live in single rooms," or "pull all-nighters." Students may pick from a multifaceted selection of dormitories—Mercer Hall is commonly referred to as "the brick prison;" the 11-story Terry-

Lander Hall is "nice, minus the elevator rides;" and "if you want to be in peace, Hansee House is where you go." Most dorm rooms are described as "nice and very spacious," and several of the dormitories have their own cafes. Among the popular on-campus dining options are the HUB (Husky Union Building) and the McMahon 8. Students describe the food as "edible . . . it fills you up."

Most UW students live on campus for their first one or two years, before moving off campus into nearby neighborhoods. As a senior in the Honors Program stated, "[the dorms] are very good for meeting people, but not good for hard studying." Dorms don't seem to be very good for hard partying either—fraternity and sorority members are usually off campus by the middle of their freshman year. One frat member commented on noticing "resentment between the dorm and frat kids."

Those who move off campus, whether into Greek houses or with smaller groups of friends, find housing in the giant rectangular U-District—"a weird little neighborhood" situated next to campus. The Ave—the popular destination for cheap food and the site of UW bookstore—sits adjacent to the district. Characterized by a vibrant mix of people, cheap eateries, and access to University Village (another popular hangout on the East Side), U-District and the Ave are pivotal points of UW culture.

"UW is primarily a research school . . . there is great funding for certain sponsored programs, and professors focus mainly on higher-level classes."

The students who enrich UW and the surrounding areas are a diverse group, and include many Asian and exchange students. One student commented on the paucity of African-Americans, but another said that "it's not too obvious to see social gaps." While there appears to be some tendency towards group segregation ("all the Asians go to the same library"), students usually stick together through shared academic interests. Honors students hang out together, and departments sponsor many events. Those involved in the Greek system also stick together and have their own culture; some students notice that "it's totally obvious they're the rich kids." As far as dating and sexuality is concerned, interracial couples are openly accepted, but the stance on homosexuality is reportedly not very liberal—"they'd rather not know."

The Husky Habitat

The UW campus stretches across a hilly part of Seattle with a "mild but continuous slope the entire way." The Quad, a central area of campus and one of the few places with open grass, is considered by many to be the loveliest spot. It leads to the Red Square, which points straight towards Drumheller Fountain. Many of the university's best-known buildings are situated in these areas, including Kane Hall, the HUB, and Suzzallo Library. Suzzallo is considered to be the best of the libraries ("really, really nice"), though recently students haven't been able to spend as much time there as some might like. Library hours have been cut down because of budget cuts, causing one student to complain, "sometimes it pisses me off when you pack up to go to the library and it's not open."

Many new buildings have sprung up on campus in recent years, often owing their sponsorship to the Gates family. Mary Gates Hall and the William H. Gates Law School are the newest additions, and a new computer science building has also just made its debut on campus.

The most popular UW building, however, is definitely the state-of-the-art IMA (Intramural Activities) center. "Everyone participates" in "IM sports" at UW; there is a wide range of skill and competition levels and many sport options, including eight different martial arts. When not doing IMs, students retreat to the lakeside area surrounding campus and the Cascade and Olympic Mountains nearby. There is plenty of physical outdoor activity at UW—one student pointed out that "Seattle on the whole is really big on hiking, fishing, skiing, swimming . . . it's beautiful and mountainous here: everywhere within a 100-mile radius of Seattle is good for outdoor sports." Another student noted, "Biking is huge in Seattle . . . I don't know anyone who doesn't have [a bike], unless it's broken or been stolen." On the whole, students report that "as a student body, people tend to focus on their physical condition."

This love for the outdoors and physical activity is further evidenced by the enthusiasm for college and Seattle sports. Football is the most watched game—the Apple Cup vs. Washington State causes major traffic problems—but the basketball and women's volleyball teams are getting more and more fans. Many students describe themselves as being "fair-weather sports fans—we're happy when we win and harshly critical when we lose." If the games aren't going well, students can always spend more time at the HUB, where movies are shown every Wednesday, or at parties and dances held by frats. It has been said that "the Greek system has an interesting relationship with campus . . . the stereotype of 'party all the time' exists." Fraternities often get a bad rep at UW, mainly because of press coverage when parties get out of hand. In October 2003 a riot on fraternity row left tipped cars and small fires. Since then, cops (some on horses) have been keeping a closer watch on the frat area.

There are many alternatives to the Greek scene, however; a large number of students keep busy with outside jobs, and others work in UW's many labs. Most find themselves hanging out with people from their academic area of interest and taking advantage of the energy in Seattle. In the end, UW students find themselves extolling their university's incredible science research atmosphere (not to mention that the city of Seattle is a hub for biotechnology and computer science) as well as the radiating energy of the outdoors. These factors encourage students as they stick out months of rain and emerge from under their umbrellas to take advantage of the winter quarter and non-stop snowboarding. With all this going for them, U-Dubers find that despite the gray climate, "by winter, everyone's happy." —*Elizabeth Dohrmann*

FYI

If you come to UW, you'd better bring "an umbrella."

What is the typical weekend schedule? "Party Thursday night; if you have a Friday class, go; snowboard or hike Friday and Saturday afternoons; party Saturday night; snowboard and work on Sunday."

If I could change one thing about UW, I'd "make it smaller and more learning-focused."

Three things every student at UW should do before graduating are "go snowboarding in the winter and boating on Lake Washington in the summer, eat at Dick's, and get to know University Village."

Washington State University

Address: French Administration Building; Pullman, WA 99164-1067	**Percent Hispanic:** 3%	**3 Most popular majors:** communication, education, management
Phone: 509-335-5586	**Percent Native-American:** 1%	**Retention:** 83%
E-mail address: admiss@wsu.edu	**Percent in-state/out of state:** 87%/13%	**Graduation rate:** 31%
Web site URL: www.wsu.edu	**Percent Pub HS:** NA	**On-campus housing:** 34%
Founded: 1890	**Number of Applicants:** 8,986	**Fraternities:** 14%
Private or Public: public	**Percent Accepted:** 77%	**Sororities:** 13%
Religious affiliation: none	**Percent Accepted who enroll:** 35%	**Library:** 2,045,438 volumes
Location: rural	**Entering:** 2,803	**Tuition and Fees:** $5,210 in; $13,312 out
Undergraduate enrollment: 18,024	**Transfers:** 2,449	**Room and Board:** $6,054
Total enrollment: NA	**Application Deadline:** 1 May	**Financial aid, first-year:** 43%
Percent Male/Female: 48%/52%	**Mean SAT:** 1060	**Varsity or Club Athletes:** 6%
Percent Minority: 14%	**Mean ACT:** NA	**Early Decision or Early Action Acceptance Rate:** NA
Percent African-American: 3%	**Middle 50% SAT range:** V 470-590, M 470-590	
Percent Asian: 5%	**Middle 50% ACT range:** NA	

If you're driving on the back roads of Eastern Washington, somewhere between Spokane and the Oregon border, eventually you're bound to drive into the small, quiet town of Pullman, home of Washington's most famous "party school." Despite such a reputation, the rolling hills of the WSU campus hold plenty to offer aside from parties and drinking.

Wake Up for Class

Students at WSU have a reputation to overcome, based on its past. Ten years ago WSU was considered little more than a party school, with rowdy, drunken students and little serious academic aspirations. At one time several years ago, students even rioted over new policies restricting alcohol on campus. These days, however, WSU has a much tamer reputation and higher academic standards.

Though WSU students know that their school is not famed for its stellar academic achievements, they never fail to mention the gratifying education they receive there. WSU is renowned for its communications program, one of its most popular and competitive majors. There is a general consensus that veterinary science is also one of the more popular and most difficult majors at WSU. Students also list business and engineering among the most difficult majors, and some feel that the psychology major is on the easier side of the spectrum. Regardless of department, most students feel that they are getting a well-rounded education and are definitely not getting a degree handed to them. As one student said about the workload, "there's not a ton, but it's not a cakewalk."

Many students note the presence of caring, helpful professors as aides to their academic success, however others feel that helpful TAs are frequently easier to get a hold of than are professors. One thing students definitely agree on is that WSU does not force you into any particular path. Students claim that the ambitious student can learn a lot by choosing challenging classes. Said one student about the academic experience, "you get out of it what you put into it. The work is there for those who want the challenge." This can be made easier or more difficult by class sizes, which range quite a bit at WSU. Upper-level classes average between 20 and 30 students. Intro classes, however, range anywhere from 100 to 500 students. Students do report that sometimes classes, particularly those in popular majors, can be difficult to get into, making it difficult to get requirements filled on time.

The Five-Day Weekend

These Cougars know how to do work when they want to, but, as in the past, they still find time to party on a regular basis. Some particularly active students claim that the weekend can start as early as Tuesday or Wednesday night and last until early Monday morning. A larger group chooses to reserve their partying for the actual weekend, going out Fridays and Saturdays and leaving Sundays for catching up on work and sleep. Either way, parties abound on this campus.

Because kegs are prohibited on campus, upperclassmen and underclassmen usually have different weekend party schedules. It's common for underclassmen to hang out together on the weekends, organizing their own parties or trying to get invites to upperclassman or Greek parties. Upperclassmen tend to take advantage of the bars on and around campus, two of the most popular being Chaser's and DaHallas. Other popular hangouts include The Coug, an old bar filled with Cougar traditional and coffeehouses like the Daily Grind. Parties on Greek row are popular among all students, though they do require an invite to get in.

For those students who are looking for other forms of entertainment, Pullman has little to offer, but WSU tries to provide an abundance of alternative activities. Movies, lectures, concerts, and other events are brought in on a regular basis. In past years Bill Cosby and Dana Carvey have been guest speakers. WSU also brings in high-quality comedians and musicians to perform in Pullman. When people really feel like staying in to have fun, the Compton Union Building, the student center, serves as a place to hang out. With eateries, including a Taco Bell, a market, a game area with a bowling alley, and a movie theater that has regular showings, the CUB is the ultimate place to relax and have fun with friends.

According to students, the WSU dating scene is almost as active as the party scene. Many people note the abundance of attractive female students as a key reason for this activity. While couples are relatively rare on campus, dating and hookups are frequent. Some students have voiced concerns about the presence of STDs on campus, but others feel that most people are responsible. Even so, the assortment of "gorgeous" people has created quite a dating scene. Said one freshman, "It is easy to find dates and lots of people go out around here. Where they go, nobody really knows." WSU is a socially active campus, and students say that most people are just trying to have fun, and WSU gives them many options. "There isn't any need to drink to find friends and you don't have to party to have fun at WSU," assured one student.

Off-Campus Living

WSU students tend to agree that living on campus isn't quite as fun as playing there. Most people claim that they were less than thrilled with their freshman dorms. The main complaint is about the small, cramped dorm rooms. In addition, some students feel that, except for the newly renovated Honors Hall, the dorms are a bit rundown. The university requires that all freshmen live in the dorms, but many students move off immediately afterwards. When relocating off campus, most people move into either the Greek houses or nearby apartments. Because Pullman is so small, virtually all off-campus housing is near campus and no one complains about the moderate prices.

"It is easy to find dates and lots of people go out around here. Where they go, nobody really knows."

Despite the dorms, most students are impressed by the appearance of the WSU campus. Along with endless rolling hills, the campus is full of trees and old-fashioned red brick buildings. Many new buildings contribute to the beauty of the campus, including the new Holland Library. The campus is large enough that buses serve as the most popular locations. Some students take the bus up the hills, but walk down. The hills are the only complaint students make about the campus. Some added that they make life especially difficult when there is snow on the ground, which in Pullman can be anywhere from two to five months of the year.

Students who want a break from Pullman, usually those with cars, can make the five-minute drive across the border to Moscow, Idaho, home to the University of Idaho. Many students feel like Moscow is also their college town. With many more restaurants than Pullman and the company of other college students, many WSU students make frequent trips to Moscow. For even more options, adventurous students can make the hour-and-a-half drive to Spokane, Washington's second-largest city.

Game Days

Among WSU's most popular attractions is their football team, the Cougars, currently the number one Pac-10 team. Far and away the most popular sport at WSU, "everyone" goes to the Saturday games. One thing WSU certainly doesn't lack is school spirit and Cougar pride. All kinds of festivities surround Cougar football games, particularly during the Apple Cup, when WSU plays their rival, the University of Washington Huskies. Other than the football team, the basketball team is also popular. While they haven't had a winning team in quite some time, students claim that a few good players make the games exciting to watch.

Though a large number of students are from Washington, particularly Seattle, and the surrounding area, the student body is described as extremely diverse. Said one student, "You name the type of student, they go to WSU." An estimated 30 percent of the student body is in a fraternity or sorority, but no one feels that there is extreme pressure to rush. While Greeks do play a prominent role in student government, they definitely are not the only ones. Everyone at WSU is involved in some type of extracurricular activity.

WSU is a large state school that prides itself on its friendly and unimposing atmosphere. Students feel that the most notable things about their school are the friendly people, the surprising academic competition, and, of course, the party atmosphere. Some students gripe about the cold weather, and everything else about Pullman, but according to them, "Wazzu is awesome." —*Lauren Rodriguez*

FYI

If you come to WSU, you'd better bring "a really warm coat!"

What is the typical weekend schedule? "Immediately after classes Friday, party, sleep, party, sleep, recover, do homework."

If I could change one thing about WSU, "I'd put in escalators."

Three things every student at WSU should do before graduating are "participate in Dad's or Mom's Weekend, eat as many products from Ferdinand's Creamery as possible, and stay awake and party for 24 hours on a Cougar Football Saturday.

Whitman College

Address: 345 Boyer Avenue; Walla Walla, WA 99362-2083
Phone: 509-527-5176
E-mail address: admission@whitman.edu
Web site URL: www.whitman.edu
Founded: 1859
Private or Public: private
Religious affiliation: none
Location: small city
Undergraduate enrollment: 1,454
Total enrollment: NA
Percent Male/Female: 43%/57%
Percent Minority: 11%
Percent African-American: 1%
Percent Asian: 6%
Percent Hispanic: 3%
Percent Native-American: 1%
Percent in-state/out of state: 45%/55%
Percent Pub HS: 76%
Number of Applicants: 2,411
Percent Accepted: 50%
Percent Accepted who enroll: 32%
Entering: 379
Transfers: 30
Application Deadline: 1 Feb
Mean SAT: 1350
Mean ACT: NA
Middle 50% SAT range: V 620-710, M 600-690
Middle 50% ACT range: 26-30
3 Most popular majors: political science, English, psychology
Retention: 93%
Graduation rate: 77%
On-campus housing: 74%
Fraternities: 30%
Sororities: 30%
Library: 282,540 volumes
Tuition and Fees: $25,626
Room and Board: $6,900
Financial aid, first-year: 43%
Varsity or Club Athletes: 35%
Early Decision or Early Action Acceptance Rate: 90%

Ever feel like exploring your natural side? If so, Whitman is the place for you. Whitties are known for their love of hiking, biking, skiing, backpacking and camping. With the tranquil Eastern Washington landscape, who could resist! However, all is not lost if you don't value your hiking boots over your life; there are plenty of on-campus organizations and, due to the laid-back nature of Whitman students, you can join or form any club you can dream up.

The Core of Academics

Besides their love of outdoors, Whitties also take their academics seriously. Academics have always been an important facet of life at Whitman. In the past, there have been seven distributional groups, including fine arts, history, language and rhetoric, physical sciences, descriptive sciences, philosophy and religion, and social sciences. However, since 2002, the requirements have been shrunk to four distributional groups. Amidst all this change there is *one* constant and that is the dreaded "Core". The "Core" is a yearlong class taken by all incoming freshmen and is officially titled Antiquity and Modernity. This is quite possibly "the worst part of Whitman." Almost all students would agree that the "Core SUCKS!" However, one student did comment that "you take it, and hopefully you're smarter for it and all freshmen take it so it's a bonding experience because you all get to complain together."

Once they get the Core out of the way and need to pick a major, students are much happier. Most of the major areas of study have similar levels of difficulty because class size is small so students are always accountable to their professor and cannot get away with doing none of the reading. However, for those desiring to push themselves to the academic limit, astrophysics is said to be the hardest major possible. Ultimately, students pick what they like so they have fun studying. And of course they leave time for other things such as lounging around Ankeny Field.

Home Sweet Home

Whitman is a small school situated around Ankeny Field. In fall and spring, many students can be seen playing intramural sports such as soccer, touch football, or rugby on the field. Ankeny is also a good place to meet friends or study in the sun. Surrounding Ankeny are all the main buildings on campus. Most of the campus architecture has an eclectic flavor to it. While some of the older administration buildings and residences have a colonial feel to them, most of the academic buildings are much more modern in style.

As for living on campus, there is a never-ending list of possibilities. All freshmen and sophomores live on campus and have required meal plans. Most freshmen live in Lyman and Jewitt Halls, which are the two biggest dorms in the center of campus next to Ankeny Field. Sophomores move into much smaller residence halls that hold fewer than eighty students and, no more than nine students in the case of language houses. There is one dorm, Prentiss Hall, which is all-female and houses the school's five sororities. All the other housing is coed. Most people live in suites, however some upperclassmen live in apartment-style housing at the edge of campus if they do not want to move off campus. Most students move off after two years. Besides dorms there are many special interest houses: anything from the Global Awareness House, to the Writing House, to the Asian Studies House and many more. According to students, the food they get is good, but repetitive. One perk about living in the language houses is that they are reputed as having the best food on campus. Also, there are four fraternities associated with Whitman—known to the students as the Tkes, Phis, Betas, and Sigs—that serve as the center of campus social life. They host most of the campus parties, both with and without alcohol.

> **"That's pretty much how Whitman is—chill."**

Chillin' Out

Partying at Whitman is what you make of it. Most students drink, but for those who do not, there is "not too much pressure because there are people at parties all the time who don't drink and there are things where drinking isn't a big part of it." There are many campus-wide school-sponsored parties that are alcohol-free but many people "pre-funk" (drink before they go to the party) with their friends. On most weekends, the place to go is the frats. According to one student, "the frats are way more chill than at state schools and there's always something going on. It's never hard to find out what parties are going on." Also, one of the most widely talked-about annual events is "The Beer Mile." The school sponsors this event and students drink lots of beer and run around the town of Walla Walla. As for getting busted by the cops, one student reports, "we can do whatever we want, they just don't look." Outside of partying, the social world is much more limited. Students report dating to be "non-existent" because "if you have a bad break-up, it makes it difficult not to see the person because the student body is so small."

Whitties

Because Whitties are small in number, with less than 1500 undergraduates, Whitman is not known for its diversity. Sometimes referred to by its students as "Whiteman," Whitman is almost entirely an "Abercrombie and Fitch wearing bunch of outdoorsy kids." However, that is changing slowly as Whitman seeks to admit a diverse class and emphasize multiculturalism through special interest housing. One such house is MECCA House (multi-ethnic house) that seeks to create a community for minority and international students at Whitman. Also, as one student points out, "there is a lot of diversity within the white." People at Whitman come from all different parts of the country and the world at large and have had many unique experiences that make them all unique, interesting people.

Athletics for All

Although Whitman is a small school, has no football team or cheerleaders and school spirit does not revolve around going out to "the Big Game," Whitman boasts a highly competitive ski team and a huge array of intramural athletic programs. The most popular intramurals are basketball and touch football. Unlike large state schools where all athletes are recruited and the jocks are set apart from the rest of the school, there is a place for everyone in Whitman athletics. According to one student, the "ulty" team (ultimate frisbee team) "is a bunch of hippies." Also, there is always the option of going hiking or backpacking in the surrounding Washington forests.

Get on Your Hiking Boots

Extracurriculars at Whitman fit all its stereotypes. There are a plethora of outdoors activities clubs that focus on hiking, skiing, biking, and camping. Also, with such a laid-back student body, Whitman students are always up for trying something weird and new that sounds even remotely enticing. There is a club for everything on campus! There is even "The SPAM Alliance." As you might have guessed, if there isn't already a club for what you want, you are encouraged to start your own. Cheese Whiz club, anyone?

Overall, even with the dreaded freshman "Core," Whitman is a place that those who attend love. As one student so eloquently put it, "if Whitman is for you, it's the best place in the world. If it's not for you, you probably wouldn't have applied in the first place!" —*Sophie Jones*

FYI

If you come to Whitman, you'd better bring "hiking boots and a warm fleece for hiking."

What is the typical weekend schedule? "pre-funk with your friends, go to a frat, sleep in, go hiking, party, sleep Sunday and do a little homework."

If I could change one thing about Whitman, I'd "increase campus diversity."

Three things that every student should do before graduating from Whitman: "streak Ankeny Field (at the center of campus), run the Beer mile (clothed or naked), and watch a sunset in the wheat fields."

West Virginia

Marshall University

Address: 400 Hall Greer Boulevard; Huntington, WV 25755
Phone: 800-642-3499
E-mail address: admissions@marshall.edu
Web site URL: www.marshall.edu
Founded: 1837
Private or Public: public
Religious affiliation: none
Location: suburban
Undergraduate enrollment: 9,823
Total enrollment: NA
Percent Male/Female: 45%/55%
Percent Minority: 7%
Percent African-American: NA
Percent Asian: NA
Percent Hispanic: NA
Percent Native-American: NA
Percent in-state/out of state: 81%/19%
Percent Pub HS: NA
Number of Applicants: 2,339
Percent Accepted: 90%
Percent Accepted who enroll: 82%
Entering: 1,889
Transfers: NA
Application Deadline: rolling
Mean SAT: NA
Mean ACT: NA
Middle 50% SAT range: NA
Middle 50% ACT range: 19-23
3 Most popular majors: education, business computer sciences
Retention: 74%
Graduation rate: 34%
On-campus housing: NA
Fraternities: NA
Sororities: NA
Library: NA
Tuition and Fees: $2,984 in; $7,986 out
Room and Board: $5,298
Financial aid, first-year: 46%
Varsity or Club Athletes: 9%
Early Decision or Early Action Acceptance Rate: 72%

Green and white or blue and gold? Almost a century and a half after West Virginia split off from its eastern neighbor to fight with the north, an affiliation with either of WV's large state universities can still pit brother against brother. For over 12,000 undergraduates, the choice is clear. Marshall University, located in the heart of downtown Huntington, West Virginia, is sometimes eclipsed by the more renowned WVU, West Virginia's other large state school. Yet, Marshall's rich traditions in service, academic excellence, and student involvement, easily allows it to stand proudly as a solid university with a wealth of offerings.

Seen and Herd

In recent years, Marshall has gained increased national exposure due to the overwhelming success of its football team, *The Thundering Herd.* This additional attention garnered by Marshall through the success of its athletic alums (including former NFL Rookie of the Year Randy Moss), has upped the influx of out of state applicants, an area in which the university is noticeably lacking. School spirit runs markedly high in Huntington, and students take pride in supporting their team, which boasts several consecutive undefeated seasons and multiple victories in the Mid-Atlantic Conference title game. However, as one undergrad jokingly notes, "the football games stop being fun after a while. We always win." Game-day is always eventful in Huntington, and fans from around the state crowd through "Tent City" on their way to the big game. Yet, despite the success of Marshall athletic teams, the university is likely better known for the tragedy that formerly surrounded its program. The away game plane crash in which all of the football players and coaches on board were killed is still associated with the school's name and reminders linger on campus in the form of the Memorial Student Center and an outdoor fountain commemorating the tragedy.

Academics

Coincidentally, many of those doing the reporting on Marshall are grads themselves. Marshall's journalism program is reportedly one of its most difficult and well respected. While majors give high praise to the faculty and curriculum, many of them complain of the higher grading scale that is used in many of the journalism classes. Communications and business programs typically enroll large numbers of students and health sciences are rapidly gaining popularity. In general, Marshall academics get high marks and while, as one student notes, "there are plenty of ways to slide by," most students agree that those who are looking for a challenging program should have no trouble finding their niche at Marshall.

The prestigious Yeager Scholars Program, requiring a separate application, awards full room and board for four years, a personal computer, a stipend for textbooks, and a travel aboard allowance for especially academically qualified students. Yeager Scholars also receive priority scheduling, special high level seminar courses, and a special mentor to guide them through their academic career and senior projects. Marshall has been recognized nationally for both this and other full and partial tuition scholarships, and is consistently ranked as one of America's "Best College Buys."

For such a large university, students point out Marshall's unusually small class sizes and the genuine enthusiasm of their professors. "It's great," one student gushes. "All my professors know my name!" "My math teacher is all about his office hours," another freshman remarked. "He comes to class angry if students didn't come and visit him the afternoon before." Students also report that its not unusual for one their fellow classmates to actually be *older* than the professor. Marshall's heavy emphasis on community education often brings in adults looking to complete a degree or earn additional credit. Marshall provides students with multiple scheduling options, allowing them to register for courses in person, over the telephone, or on the internet, although, regardless of the method, students still find registration "a giant pain in the rear."

Centralized Campus

Even if students happen to get stuck in an early morning section, however, getting to class is rarely a problem. Marshall's centralized, flat campus allows one student to "roll out of bed at 7:55 and still make it to my 8:00 class." Marshall's notorious housing shortage has made headlines in recent years when the university was forced to put up students at a local Holiday Inn while they sorted out rooming troubles. Students continue to marvel at the absurdity of a rule that requires students to live on campus for their first two years when dorms are already overcrowded. Yet, on the whole, undergrads are very satisfied with their living arrangements. Most students live in the university's massive air-conditioned Towers dorms, but its smaller rooms cause others to opt for the more spacious Buskirk and Hodges dorms. With the exception of Holderby Hall, are Marshall dorms are single sex, and each reportedly has its tradeoffs (the Hodges males notoriously complain about their group showers). All dorms are required to observe "quiet hours" beginning at 9 P.M. on weeknights and midnight on weekends and students must sign-in all guests. While students complain about rules that restrict opposite sex visitors to 11 P.M., Marshall's dorms are lauded as being very safe and are a social center for many of its students. Indeed, the campus as a whole is thought to be very secure, and many undergrads note the heavy presence of both the University Police and city officers on bike patrol.

Social Scene

When students want to get out of the dorm the surrounding area provides a lively nightlife, with Huntington's many bars pulling in the largest following, most of which line central 4th Street. Student favorites such as The Drink, The Union, and The Wild Dog attract large crowds nightly and are reportedly fairly lax about carding. However, students note that, even with the wide variety of options, most bars take on distinct personalities and students tend to frequent their one specific venue. Fraternities and sororities also play a large role in the Marshall social scene, although students feel there is a much higher pressure for males to rush than females. For non-drinkers, the Memorial Student Center holds popular evening events and their Thursday open-mike nights typically draw several undergrads. While students don't see having a car to be a necessity, many recommend some sort of transportation to get to a "real" restaurant or to the Huntington Mall and movie theaters, which are actually in nearby Barboursville. Many of Marshall's students tend to be from nearby in-state locations, causing the campus to "almost completely clear out" on the weekends, often an annoyance for many out of state undergrads.

"Everyone here is so friendly. I have my home family, and then I have my Marshall family."

Indeed, while most of Marshall's students tend to hail from West Virginia, out-of-state students typically don't report having trouble adjusting. However, several students do see the Marshall community as racially lop-sided, with Marshall having a relatively low minority population. Students note that the undergraduate population tends to self-segregate, and the university is currently attempting to implement programs which add to campus diversity and cultural awareness. Yet, students find Marshall easy to adapt to, and praise the overall friendliness of the student body. "Everyone here is so friendly," one sophomore remarks. "I have my home family, and then I have my Marshall family."

The lively undergraduate dating scene also keeps undergrads social. While students admit that "random hook-ups abound," casual and serious relationships are generally easy to come by. Whether it's an evening at a concert at the Huntington Civic Arena, only blocks from campus, or a quick lunch date at the Calamity Café, Marshall students have plenty of options for their get-togethers.

Marshall's students tend to be very involved in a wide range of extra-curriculars, with intramural sports, The Christian Center, and *The Parthenon*, the daily student newspaper, drawing several participants. Most undergrads also hold some type of part-time employment and several students participate in community outreach programs. Students remark on the usually high level of town/gown cooperation, and see the city of Huntington as taking an active interest in the life of the university and vice-versa.

Futuristic Facilities

With a top of the line science buildings and classrooms, Marshall's facilities have received lots of positive attention. One student favorite is Drinko Library, a four-floor state-of-the-art facility which provides students with several meeting rooms and quiet study clusters which can be accessed with an ID Keycard. Drinko is also home to several classrooms with "a laptop for every student," and its 1st floor is open to the Marshall community 24 hours a day.

Students can eat in one of Marshall's three large dining halls, and most rate the food as at least "average." However, those who would rather dine elsewhere can head to the student center where a Chick-Fillet, a Pizza Hut, and a student snack shop provides additional offerings to the typical student meal plan.

As Marshall continues to pick up national momentum, its role in the collegiate world will undoubtedly increase. Students, community leaders, and the administration are cooperatively working on their "Vision 2020" plan, a course of action for the university that continues to broaden its scope and includes the construction of several new state-of-the-art facilities. For now, however, Marshall manages to remain one of the nation's best kept secrets as a low cost, challenging, enthusiastic university. —*Conor Knighton*

FYI

If you come to Marshall, you better bring, "an appreciation of sports—we watch a lot of games."

What is the typical weekend schedule? "Friday—hang out in Huntington, Saturday—hang out in Huntington, Sunday—study and relax."

If I could change one thing about Marshall, I'd "try and simplify the nightmare registration process."

The three things every student at Marshall should do before graduating are: "get involved, party the whole weekend of the MAC Championship, and go to at least one football and basketball game."

West Virginia University

Address: PO Box 6009; Morgantown, WV 26506-6009
Phone: 304-293-2121
E-mail address: WVUadmissions@arc.wvu.edu
Web site URL: www.wvu.edu
Founded: 1867
Private or Public: public
Religious affiliation: none
Location: suburban
Undergraduate enrollment: 16,692
Total enrollment: NA
Percent Male/Female: 57%/43%
Percent Minority: 7%
Percent African-American: 4%
Percent Asian: 2%
Percent Hispanic: 1%
Percent Native-American: 0%
Percent in-state/out of state: 63%/37%
Percent Pub HS: NA
Number of Applicants: 8,016
Percent Accepted: 94%
Percent Accepted who enroll: 47%
Entering: 3,978
Transfers: 839
Application Deadline: rolling
Mean SAT: 1040
Mean ACT: NA
Middle 50% SAT range: V 460-560, M 470-570
Middle 50% ACT range: 20-25
3 Most popular majors: business management, engineering, social sciences
Retention: 78%
Graduation rate: 56%
On-campus housing: 21%
Fraternities: 9%
Sororities: 9%
Library: 1,500,000 volumes
Tuition and Fees: $3,548 in; $10,768 out
Room and Board: $5,822
Financial aid, first-year: 38%
Varsity or Club Athletes: 7%
Early Decision or Early Action Acceptance Rate: NA

"Almost heaven, West Virginia . . ." For over 22,000 proud Mountaineers, the words of John Denver's 1971 song still ring loudly today. Situated in the picturesque hills of Morgantown, West Virginia University boasts one of the most enthusiastic student bodies in the nation. As one student put it, "you'll never find a group of people with more school spirit than you will at WVU."

Two-Pronged Pride

Much of WVU's school spirit centers on its athletic teams. In fact, many students cite seasonal trips to Mountaineer Field as a key aspect of their college life. When not cheering on one of WVU's 20 Division I squads, students participate in a wide variety of intramural sports. As one participant explained, "you don't have to be athletic at all—everyone just comes out to have a good time. Intramurals are a great way to meet fellow Mounties."

WVU's football team draws national attention each year and often vies for one of the top slots in the Big East athletic conference. One student described the opening kick-off of the first game of the season as "the best ten seconds of the semester." The state legislature has recently mandated that the Mounties play Marshall University, WVU's state rival to the south. While football carries the largest fan base by far, sports like basketball, baseball, and gymnastics receive a smaller but equally devout following.

West Virginians take pride in their academics as well. Mountaineers are quick to point to their unusually high numbers of Rhodes scholars and to the long-term success of graduates. The much-touted University Honors Program helps high achievers get the most out of their college experience. In addition to receiving priority housing and scheduling, honors students may take exclusive "honors only" seminars taught in small groups by the university's top faculty. To be accepted into the program, students must meet specific grade and test score requirements, although those who demonstrate success once in college can also earn their way into the program.

WVU professors are described as "very clear and precise about what they want." When confusion does arise, "professors seem to go out of their way to be helpful," noted one student. However, some undergrads complain about foreign teachers being difficult to understand. "If you're going to take a math class, be sure to bring a translator," warned one undergrad. Introductory courses have been known to enroll over 500 people, but students say that the average class size is less than 30, allowing for individual interaction between student and professor.

Unfortunately, getting into classes isn't always easy. Students gripe about the university's STAR system, a telephone course registration service and the source of endless busy signals and headaches. Often, students will sacrifice precious sleeping time in order to break through before peak calling hours and schedule the classes they want. "It's much better to wake up at 6 A.M. on the first day of scheduling than to be stuck waking up at 8:30 A.M. every day of the semester," explained one student.

In 1997, WVU entered into a partnership with the F.B.I. to create the world's first biometrics program, training students in the digital verification of identity by observation of biological patterns such as fingerprint swirls or eye blood vessel webs. Students in this highly competitive major work with state-of-the-art technology and regularly hone their skills by sorting through mock crime scenes. Many others turn to the popular business, economics, and health sciences programs that are said to attract thousands of Mountaineers each year. With over 130 possible majors, students praise the wide course variety at WVU.

Campus Living

All freshmen are required to live on campus, with the majority living in one of two mammoth, air-conditioned dorms known as the Towers. Many freshmen apply to live in Boreman South, hoping to take advantage of the dorm's unique "suite-style" living areas. Honors students are assigned to Dadisman Hall, and females can elect to live in Boreman North, WVU's only single-sex dorm.

Unique among state universities is WVU's new Operation Jump Start program. The program matches an incoming freshman with one of WVU's nine residential "houses" ("a fancy way of saying 'dorm,'" explained one student), each functioning as a small community within the larger university. Students are placed near others with similar academic and extra-curricular interests, and they frequently interact with faculty member advisors who live in on-campus houses near the dorms. Operation Jump Start also helps to coordinate Fall Fest, a giant celebration at the beginning of the first semester, featuring top musical acts as Busta Ryhmes, Puff Daddy, the Verve Pipe, and the Goo Goo Dolls.

After freshman year, some students choose to live off campus in a fraternity or sorority house, or one of Morgantown's many student apartment complexes. Of those who remain, most choose to live in Stalnaker Hall, widely regarded as the best dorm on campus.

> **"[Students here are] far less likely to gain the infamous freshman fifteen . . ."**

Dining halls are generally given low marks, but Morgantown provides a wide variety of local restaurants within walking distance. Student favorites include the Boston Beanery, Pargo's, and the Mountainlair—a centrally located student union home to several fast-food chain restaurants as well as a bowling alley, a movie theater, and a game room.

One student noted that Mountaineers are "far less likely to gain the infamous freshman fifteen" than their counterparts across the nation. A general source of complaints, WVU's mountainous terrain can make for a tiring hike to class. Divided into two separate campuses—the main campus is downtown and the other is in nearby Evansdale—getting to class can often be a problem. Recently ranked as one of the best "people movers" in the nation, the PRT is an above-ground train that connects the two locations, running regular shuttles to several campus locations. Each fall during Mountaineer Week, various student organizations participate in a competition to cram as many people as possible into one of the small cars (the current record is 98). While students complain of the PRT's occasional breakdowns, one student joked that "it gives us a great excuse to miss class."

WVU's extensive campus is currently under heavy renovation, and while some complain of the rampant construction, one freshman noted that "good things come to those who wait." When all is said and done, WVU will be home to a state-of-the-art 200,000-square-foot Student Recreation Center, a brand new biology building, and an addition to the central library facility.

Social Center

With a large Greek system exerting a heavy influence over social life, weekends at WVU generally revolves around fraternity and sorority parties. Pre-game football tailgates also attract thousands of students in the fall. Unable to shake its party school reputation, Morgantown is well known for its many bars and dance clubs. Student favorites include Phantoms, Shooters, Dr. Longshot's, and the Brass Alley. For non-drinkers, one student quipped that "all three of us" still feel accepted and rarely have a problem finding alternate activities. WVU's new *Up All Night* program provides students with school-sponsored, alcohol-free activities every weekend night and generally receives high marks from the student body. Games such as Virtual Reality Soccer, Astro Bowling, and Make Your Own Music Video—coupled with "an insane amount of free food"—make *Up All Night* a popular stop on a typical weekend night.

Students are quick to point out that the best part of WVU is "its people" which are described as "incredibly friendly, outgoing, and always willing to lend a helping hand." WVU students participate in a wide range of extra-curriculars, with popular activities such as the Residence Hall Association, the drama club, and the student-written *Daily Athenian* enlisting several Mountaineers. However, many complain that the student body is too homogeneous; one student remembers being initially surprised by how few minority students there were at such a large university.

Getting Your Money's Worth

For the last several years, WVU has consistently remained a bargain in a field of increasingly expensive state schools. Many students remarked that while they could have gone to a more costly university, the money that they save now can be applied to the hefty price tag of graduate school down the line. Most importantly, Mountaineers seem happy about their choice. "I love it here," gushed one student. "I immediately felt like I was part of a family." A family that is proud to claim top-notch athletes, dedicated scholars and equally dedicated socialites among its members, WVU offers a well-rounded college experience for those who are willing to bleed blue and gold. —*Conor Knighton*

FYI

If you come to West Virginia, you'd better bring "the confidence to approach your professors because if you do this, you'll have a much more comfortable and fulfilling academic experience."

What is the typical weekend schedule? "Football, party, sleep, study."

If I could change one thing at West Virginia, I'd "flatten the hills so we don't have to trek over them all the time."

Three things that every student should do before graduating from WVU are "live in the dorm at least once; attend Fall/Spring Fest; take a "fun" course, e.g., photography, tennis, or fishing."

Wisconsin

Beloit College

Address: 700 College Avenue; Beloit, WI 53511	**Percent Asian:** 4%	**Middle 50% ACT range:** 25-29
Phone: 608-363-2500	**Percent Hispanic:** 3%	**3 Most popular majors:** creative writing, anthropology, economics
E-mail address: admiss@beloit.edu	**Percent Native-American:** 0%	**Retention:** 91%
Web site URL: www.beloit.edu	**Percent in-state/out of state:** 20%/80%	**Graduation rate:** 66%
Founded: 1846	**Percent Pub HS:** 80%	**On-campus housing:** 93%
Private or Public: private	**Number of Applicants:** 1,677	**Fraternities:** 15%
Religious affiliation: none	**Percent Accepted:** 70%	**Sororities:** 5%
Location: urban	**Percent Accepted who enroll:** 26%	**Library:** 184,000 volumes
Undergraduate enrollment: 1,281	**Entering:** 304	**Tuition and Fees:** $24,386
Total enrollment: NA	**Transfers:** 38	**Room and Board:** $5,478
Percent Male/Female: 44%/56%	**Application Deadline:** rolling	**Financial aid, first-year:** 71%
Percent Minority: 18%	**Mean SAT:** NA	**Varsity or Club Athletes:** 30%
Percent African-American: 4%	**Mean ACT:** NA	**Early Decision or Early Action Acceptance Rate:** NA
	Middle 50% SAT range: V 580-680, M 540-640	

Think of yourself as quirky and nontraditional and interested in an intimate college experience? Beloit College, located in Wisconsin, is a small liberal arts college of only 1,100 students, which means that professors are truly interested in their undergraduates and not just in doing research. A student commented that rankings do not show Beloit as it truly is—a place where love of learning is emphasized.

Cooperative Success

Another member of the Beloit community pointed out that Beloit students do not seek achievement at the expense of others but instead pursue "cooperative success." This is not a competitive place but rather "a place where you can define your interests, pursue excellence, and have the support of your peers and professors" in doing so. Just because Beloit may not have as much internal competition as other schools, particularly those on the East Coast, does not imply to students that their academics are not strong. A student commented that Beloit is exceptional because it takes average students and makes them great ones. Beloit students extolled the abilities of their professors, especially their approachability. Professors give out their home phone numbers—one is even rumored to have lent his car to a student—while others play poker with their students.

While English is the most popular major, students at Beloit are especially interested in international relations and political activism, noted one student. Sick of boring classes and of being stuck in a chair? A political science professor elaborated on why the department may be so popular: "As a department, we focus on encouraging our students to engage not only the material before them but the real-life situations to which it applies by encouraging (or requiring) students to engage in experiential learning activities such as internships with political campaigns, city hall or non-profit organizations, Model UN, and classroom role-playing exercises." Another professor in international relations recently won a national teaching award for her innovative style. However, one student commented that while political science, anthropology, chemistry, foreign languages, and theater are considered very good, there are those who look down on music and education. Beloit students are required to take two classes in the social sciences, the humanities, and the natural sciences each within the first two years, but other than this there are no formal class requirements. Just because faculty members loan out their automobiles, toss down chips, and scrawl their cell phone numbers for nervous freshmen to copy down, no one should assume that Beloit is easy academically. Students and faculty alike agree that students spend two or more hours on problem sets, readings, or studying for each one hour in class. For the four or five classes that nearly all students take every semester, this adds up to some serious work time. Programs include urban studies in Chicago, government studies in Washington, D.C., and a whole host of programs in foreign countries.

Quaint Magic

Beloit students find their campus, modeled after small New England liberal arts colleges, simply gorgeous. In describing her impressions of the campus, a Beloit student gushed, "it's absolutely beautiful here. The campus has some sort of quaint magic to it. Tall, old trees line our roads, and sidewalks and grassy lawns stretch out before our buildings. To watch the seasons change here is a truly magical experience at times. Because we have so many trees, fall is a riot of color which leads into the still, calm snow-covered winter." Needless to say, it is cold in Beloit, Wisconsin. Still, the architecture and natural beauty of the campus complement this climate and create an amazing experience.

The campus is divided into residential and academic areas, with the residential area quite large, as the vast majority of students live on campus. There is a large variety of housing available, ranging from older-style buildings to more modern architecture. There are both single-sex and co-ed dorms. There are three fraternity and two sorority houses, language dorms, and a whole host of other theme dorms. While these special-interest housings do provide a more intimate atmosphere, some complain that they take away from diversity in other housing.

The gym, the Flood Arena, is rumored to be the best in the conference, and a number of dorms have been recently renovated. The Morse Library, too, was recently renovated, but students still complain that its resources are limited. For that reason, Beloit is a member of the Wisconsin Interlibrary Loan System, which gives students access to other library facilities throughout the state.

Not a Dry Campus

Beloit students work hard, but party equally as hard. One student elaborated that this is certainly not a dry campus, but that it is a place where there is a healthy respect for what alcohol can do to the body. The policy is to follow state drinking law—you must be 21 to drink. However, in practice, at least according to students, IDs are rarely checked. Despite this, Beloit is not a party school every day of the week. Sunday through Thursday nights are spent primarily studying.

While 15 percent of Beloit students are involved in Greek life, frat parties, which are often not nearly as "Animal House" as the usual frat reputation implies, are open to all students, so whether or not a student is involved in a frat does not have a huge influence on his or her party life. Drugs are available on campus, but due to a zero-tolerance policy, their use is kept quiet. Like at any college, drinking and co-ed dorms combine to make hooking up and sex fairly common at Beloit.

Extracurriculars Galore

Beloit students have interests other than enriching their minds in the classroom and getting plastered. As a Division III school, Beloit finds that even though athletics are valued, not a tremendous emphasis is placed on varsity sports. Intramural sports, such as Frisbee Gold and Ultimate Frisbee, are very popular. Beloit students are also involved in the International Club and the Gold Key, an organization of admissions tour guides and student hosts. The Alliance, a gay support club, is also popular, evidence of the open nature of Beloit. Fine arts clubs are also very popular, including a host of dance troupes, singing groups, and theater bands.

"Beloit is exceptional because it takes average students and makes them great ones."

Food at Beloit is, as always, a matter for debate. Some students find the meals rather bad, while others praise the wide variety of options. Cereal, sandwiches, hot dishes, and soups are available at most meals. Every meal has vegan and vegetarian options, as a reported half of Beloit students are either vegan or vegetarian. Freshmen are on a meal plan that includes 20 meals per week, while older students are able to choose meal plans that include 10 or 14 meals. Most students eat in the main dining hall known as the Commons, but snack bars and off-campus restaurants are also choices.

On and Off Campus

Most people at Beloit did not go to college for the town. One student commented, "it's a tragedy that Beloit students only go into town to go to Wal-Mart." Another student described Beloit, Wisconsin, as "a run-down industrial town that is half ghetto and half white trash." Others, however, describe the town in kinder terms, citing the movie theaters, bowling alleys, and restaurants that offer a break from on-campus life. Students often take trips to Chicago, Milwaukee, and Madison, Wisconsin, so chances to get away are available. What Beloit, Wisconsin, lacks in diversity and excitement, Beloit College makes up for in its social and ethnic diversity. Although the population is largely white and significantly Midwestern (20 percent from Wisconsin and 20 percent from Illinois), Beloit has students from 49 states (missing Nevada) and a wide host of other countries.

The vast majority of Beloit students loves it there. An emphasis is placed on learning, not on grades, and Beloit students still find plenty of time to get involved and have fun. —*Christian Schaub*

FYI

If you come to Beloit, you'd better bring "an open mind and, oh yeah, a mini-fridge and other food paraphernalia for when you get sick of the food in the dining hall."

What is the typical weekend schedule? "Friday afternoon is a time for relaxing after a busy week followed by parties or one of the free on-campus movies. Everyone sleeps in on Saturday, then does work or else takes a trip off campus followed by dinner out and then the usual party circuit. Sunday is a time for community service, studying, or chilling with friends."

If I could change one thing about Beloit, "it would be the location: Beloit, Wisconsin."

Three things every Beloit student should do before graduating are "talk to someone they never would have spoken to in high school, go to a kick-ass hip-hop dance party, and have dinner at a professor's house."

Lawrence University

Address: PO Box 599; Appleton, WI 54912
Phone: 920-832-6500
E-mail address: excel@lawrence.edu
Web site URL: www.lawrence.edu
Founded: 1847
Private or Public: private
Religious affiliation: none
Location: small city
Undergraduate enrollment: 1,389
Total enrollment: NA
Percent Male/Female: 49%/51%
Percent Minority: 17%
Percent African-American: 1%
Percent Asian: 2%
Percent Hispanic: 2%
Percent Native-American: 1%
Percent in-state/out of state: 41%/59%
Percent Pub HS: 57%
Number of Applicants: 1,812
Percent Accepted: 68%
Percent Accepted who enroll: 28%
Entering: 352
Transfers: 50
Application Deadline: 15 Jan
Mean SAT: NA
Mean ACT: NA
Middle 50% SAT range: V 560-690, M 580-680
Middle 50% ACT range: 24-30
3 Most popular majors: visual/performing arts, social science, interdisciplinary studies
Retention: 88%
Graduation rate: 67%
On-campus housing: 98%
Fraternities: 30%
Sororities: 30%
Library: 370,000 volumes
Tuition and Fees: $25,089
Room and Board: $5,652
Financial aid, first-year: 62%
Varsity or Club Athletes: 25%
Early Decision or Early Action Acceptance Rate: 97%

If you're looking for a traditional private co-ed university in the Midwest, Lawrence University is about as old as they come. Founded in 1847, Lawrence University rests in the middle of the growing small metropolitan city of Appleton, Wisconsin. With a view of the Fox River, students at Lawrence share a multitude of academic resources within this close-knit community.

Small Classes . . . Lots of Love

When talking about their university, aspects that students always rave about are the class size and their animated professors. The class sizes include "one-on-one independent study, small group tutorials, and 'normal classes,'" which still stay under 40 students. As one student remarked, "I think my biggest class so far has been about 30, and I've had some of about 11. Some of the higher-level classes can be as small as four or five students." The small numbers mean that professors can really focus on individual students, a connection that most students value. One freshman thought that "the best part about Lawrence academics is that the faculty are extremely accessible and make a point to have lots of office hours." Almost all of Lawrence classes are taught by professors, not TAs—another perk of a Lawrence education.

However, don't expect the dedicated faculty at Lawrence to ease up on the workload. Students often find themselves with stacks of books to read and papers to write. Many find that there aren't too many "gut" classes, and that "even the dumb classes are still fairly intensive." So if you are looking for all party and no study, you won't be cut out for Lawrence, because "the bar is set too high for slackers."

The liberal arts education that Lawrence offers pleases most students, especially students who have no idea what their course of study will be. Freshmen are required to take two terms of Freshmen Studies, an introduction to a liberal arts education, prepping these newcomers for the critical thinking skills yet to come. Lawrence University operates on a trimester system, a schedule that doesn't seem to satisfy all students. The first trimester begins later in September and ends right before winter break. The second two are crammed into the months of

January through June. The later starting date and ending date is an inconvenience for students whose friends at other schools have different schedules. Also, students find that studies can become quite intensive with the short ten-week terms.

All undergrads are required to live on campus, which contributes to the tightly knit community feel of the campus. Ormsby Hall, with hardwood floors and a central location, and the substance-free Kohler both rank high with students. For upperclassmen, a brand new hall with "enormous suites and in-suite bathrooms," along with comfortable singles, is most desirable. In addition to the dorms, upperclassmen can choose to live in small residences owned by the university, which can house from eight to 27 people.

Where's Your Thermal Underwear?

Located in Appleton, in northeastern Wisconsin, Lawrence University sits atop a bluff overlooking the Fox River. Appleton and the surrounding cities comprise the Fox Cities, reportedly one of the fastest growing areas in Wisconsin, and "one of the best medium-sized metropolitan areas in the nation." According to one student, "Appleton is no great metropolis, but it's safe and, in it's own way, quite charming. And there are some great restaurants within five minutes of campus." The areas around campus are mostly residential and middle- to upper-class. Students feel secure walking around campus, which is "not dangerous at all." Even students without cars can enjoy the restaurants and shopping places around Appleton. Breaking out of the academic bubble seems fairly easy, for "everything that you really need is within walking distance from campus, in either direction."

The climate in Wisconsin calls for puffy down jackets and thermal underwear, if you don't want to freeze on the way to class. In the winter, students can take advantage of Appleton's park system and sled or ice skate in the parks. In addition to the multitude of bars and shops downtown, Appleton plans a downtown entertainment district that will have the new addition of $5 million mega-screen theater. When built, students will be able to *brag about* this movie theater, which will be the largest in Midwest.

The Sound of Music

Lawrence University's Conservatory of Music remains one of the leading music studies programs in the nation. The Conservatory consists of over 350 music majors and dedicated faculty that gives individual attention to each composer, performer, and scholar. Lawrence students combine the Conservatory curriculum with the liberal arts education that a Bachelor in Arts would give, as at least one-third of the courses must be taken outside of the Conservatory. Students are also given the option to pursue both a Bachelor of Arts degree and Bachelor of Music degree in a special five-year program.

Students outside of the Conservatory can also take advantage of the multitude of music courses that it has to offer. Students feel that the Conservatory students, otherwise known as "Connies," are not completely separated from the rest of the university. While some feel that there are too many "Connies," students pursuing all studies usually get along in the community feel of Lawrence.

Because of the Conservatory, there are always performances, recitals, and concerts around campus. Quite frequently, internationally renowned classical and jazz artists perform at the school. In Appleton, the recently built $45-million Fox Cities performing arts center hosts many shows and concerts, from musical performances to Broadway plays. Students find that the new center "is excellent both aesthetically and acoustically. It's wonderful from both the performing and listening perspectives."

When the Weekend Rolls Around . . .

The Greek system at Lawrence is small, with only five fraternities and three sororities. As one student commented, freshmen "are more likely to be enchanted with the novelty of a frat party." But when annual bashes such as the "Foam Party," "Beach Bash," or "Pimps and Hoes" roll around, upperclassmen flock to join in the fun. Underclassmen party in the dorms on campus, while the over-21 crowd has more options. One senior claimed, "Appleton's downtown boasts more bars than many cities twice its size." Around two dozen bars and clubs line College Avenue, a mere 20 minutes' walking distance and an even quicker ride by car. If you're feeling lazy, the "Viking Room," a campus bar, is also popular with the seniors. Students at Lawrence find that underage drinking is not a big issue. While Lawrence declares, "no underage drinking" legally, students report that the school tolerates drinking "as long as it is under control."

"The social life is perfect—something's always happening, but it's never overwhelming."

At Lawrence, you don't need to drink and party to have fun on the weekends. According to one freshman, "the social life is perfect—something's always happening, but it's never overwhelming." Many students take advantage of the fantastic music programs and attend concerts and other theatrical shows. A trip to the enormous Fox Valley Mall nearby or restaurants, like the student favorite, Taste of Thai, in downtown Appleton add variety to a weekend. The cool and trendy new late-night coffeehouse, Copper Rock, is a good place to cozy up with a date.

Positive Change and Improvement

As a small private university in central Wisconsin, Lawrence seems to lack the diversity that many other institutions embrace. Nearly half of the students are from in-state, and there are not many minority faces around. The school, however is, recruiting many international students as part of its initiative to bring a multicultural appeal to Lawrence. Lawrence International, the international students' organization, sponsors many activities, as does the Outdoor Recreation Club. Publications on campus include the biweekly *Lawrentian* and the conservative *Lawrence Review*, as well as *Tropos*, a yearly art and literary magazine. The openly GLBT population seems to be growing comfortably on campus. From the Bonsai Club to the Students of Objectivism, students find that "there are always new clubs being formed and a good amount of action within student government."

The Division III athletics at Lawrence factor into the lives of students, but definitely don't dominate their schedule. Lawrence has strong men's and women's swim teams, and volleyball and hockey teams also stand out. The fitness facilities are strategically located at the heart of campus, convenient for "ordinary students—not solely for athletes." Recently, an agreement with the local YMCA across the street from campus allows students to use those "top-notch" facilities as well. Students who like to jog or take a scenic walk away from the studious environment of the campus can stroll through the many park paths and trails along the Fox River near campus.

Lawrence has also renovated all of its science facilities, creating newer buildings and classrooms. The university also plans to renovate its student union to create a place where students can relax and socialize. Currently, hungry students can visit the Grill, a greasy campus hangout open until 12 A.M. Lawrence students feel great pride for their school, and reaffirm their decision to spend four years of their lives here. "It's hard to put down on paper: it just has a really nice feel to it," comments one senior. Lawrence is definitely not the place to look for students who crave the metropolitan experience. Instead, you can expect a friendly, supportive, and intellectually stimulating community. —*Karen Chen*

FYI

If you come to Lawrence, you'd better bring "a warm jacket . . . the wind can be especially biting."

What is the typical weekend schedule? "Party on Friday and Saturday; do homework on Sunday afternoon after the Packers game."

If I could change one thing about Lawrence, I'd "have the entire campus airlifted to a warmer climate with slightly better access to a big city."

Three things every student at Lawrence should do before graduating are "get to know several members of the faculty on a personal level, use a food tray from Downer as a sled, attend a concert, orchestral or choral, in the Chapel."

Marquette University

Address: PO Box 1881; Milwaukee, WI 53201-1881
Phone: 414-288-7302
E-mail address: admissions@marquette.edu
Web site URL: www.marquette.edu
Founded: 1881
Private or Public: private
Religious affiliation: Roman Catholic
Location: urban
Undergraduate enrollment: 7,644
Total enrollment: NA
Percent Male/Female: 46%/54%
Percent Minority: 15%
Percent African-American: 5%
Percent Asian: 4%
Percent Hispanic: 4%
Percent Native-American: 0%
Percent in-state/out of state: 47%/53%
Percent Pub HS: NA
Number of Applicants: 7,593
Percent Accepted: 83%
Percent Accepted who enroll: 30%
Entering: 1,859
Transfers: 224
Application Deadline: rolling
Mean SAT: NA
Mean ACT: NA
Middle 50% SAT range: V 520-630, M 530-640
Middle 50% ACT range: 23-28
3 Most popular majors: business marketing, communications, health professions
Retention: 89%
Graduation rate: 76%
On-campus housing: 54%
Fraternities: 6%
Sororities: 5%
Library: 720,000 volumes
Tuition and Fees: $20,724
Room and Board: $7,036
Financial aid, first-year: 65%
Varsity or Club Athletes: 3%
Early Decision or Early Action Acceptance Rate: NA

Welcome to Milwaukee, the famous Brew City of Middle America. Cold weather, cold beer, and cheese are the staples of this lovely city, dotted with parks for hiking and picnicking, and situated on the edge of the sparkling Lake Michigan. Despite the icy weather and long winter, students of Marquette University are quite happy with their location and have plenty of school spirit to prove it. College unity transcends even the sports arena at this medium-sized urban University, as its Roman Catholic affiliation pervades the student body, which takes pride in its religious traditions.

A Couple of Requirements

Marquette has much to offer in terms of diversity with its many schools, including colleges of Arts and Sciences, Communications, Journalism, Nursing, Business Administration, Engineering, the Performing Arts, Medical Technology, and Education. Students enjoy the many options and varied resources, but they sometimes feel overwhelmed with the amount of requirements: 12 philosophy credit hours, six science, three math, and six English. The university strives to maintain the Jesuit tradition of strong theological education, with nine credit hours required in that field. One student lightheartedly commented, "I am not a huge fan of all theology, but, God dammit, we go to a Jesuit university," while another said it was hard to cram everything in her schedule in addition to her major requirements.

As for majors, the ones attracting most students are political science, business, and biomedical sciences, the latter being one of the hardest, along with engineering. Many students agreed that a somewhat "lesser" course load was offered at the College of Communications. Some complained about the education program also not being so demanding, but Marquette has other strengths, such as its unique programs in dental hygiene, physical therapy, and study abroad incentives. It is also associated with the Milwaukee Institute of Art and Design, a major perk for those into art.

Class size varies from major to major, but in general, courses range from large 200-person intro lectures to 12- to 30-

student courses by junior and senior year as students further specialize. There are virtually no complaints about the courseload, as most students can afford to start partying on Thursday straight through Saturday, but spending up to 30 hours a week on school work is not uncommon at Marquette. Many seemed happy not only with the education they were receiving, but also with the personal growth afforded by close contact with professors and great study abroad opportunities. A junior political science and criminology major raved about her favorite professor: "She was very informal and had her office hours outside. She would always offer to go to the bars and things like that with us. She was great!" A couple classes that were praised were The Dynamic Media and Politics and Juvenile Delinquency, which took students to juvenile court for a field trip.

Getting Better at Diversity

Besides doing schoolwork, Marquette students fill their time up with a diverse array of extracurricular activities. There are many clubs on campus that reflect a variety of interest groups, from the medieval reenactment club to community service organizations. Basketball is definitely the biggest sport on campus and people holding tickets are referred to as "fanatics" for their enthusiastic school spirit. Games were described as "energetic, loud, lots of singing, lots of pride! Just plain fun!" by one student, who also mentioned that Notre Dame and Madison were big rival teams.

Although the extracurriculars on campus may be diverse, the same cannot be said about the student body. Many students are from the Wisconsin area, especially from Chicago, and are Caucasian and conservative. One student summed it up as "no diversity at all." Sexuality is definitely not an open issue either—when asked about what a student thought the weirdest organization on campus was, she responded, "I would say the weirdest is the Gay-Straight alliance because we are a Jesuit school and all."

Although it seems the Marquette administration is striving to diversify their homogenous population, the school still maintains its Jesuit traditions. Many students enjoy the comfort of a uniform student body, and enjoy attending the very traditional events like the Mass of the Holy Spirit at the Joan of Arc Chapel, located at the center of campus. Students take pride in this beautiful service and enjoy the Catholic affiliation of their school. Says one, "Most students are Christian so they share some sort of unity in that."

The Scoop on Brew City Living

Party all the way, dude. Yes, as you would expect at this Roman Catholic school, the weekend starts on Thursday and no one follows the "strict" alcohol policy. In the Brew City, bars and clubs are never lacking, although a timeless favorite among the student body is Haggarty's Bar. Chilling with friends often revolves around drinking at Marquette, where the drug of choice is definitely alcohol. Keggers are common and often revolve around the hype of the basketball games. Also, there is a moderately sized Greek system on campus which provides for social outlets, along with theme parties. A notable annual party is the ABC: "anything but clothing." Such partying often leads to random hook-ups, but most agree that this is an underclass trend. Because many students are from the area and get internships in the area during the summer, local summer festivals provide great entertainment. They pervade the city, and Milwaukee-ites make merry with music, parades, drinking on the streets, and dancing. Irish week is always popular among college students.

No [Insert Opposite Sex Here] Allowed!

Although students reportedly do not abide by the no-alcohol rules, they do abide by the rules in the dorms. When living with RAs and priests, there is no escaping the patrols. Although some dorms on campus are co-ed, members of the opposite sex are not allowed to visit after 1 A.M. Luckily weekends have open visiting hours, which students appreciate.

As for the dorms themselves, the frosh dorms are small and cramped, some students described them as "run-down" and "sorta ghetto," definitely "not the cleanest." The architecture of the five residence halls on campus, along with that of some other buildings, is quite remarkable. It has a modern touch that has received mixed reviews. McCormick, which holds a rep for crazy revelry at all times as it is the only co-ed freshman dorm, is a round building with pie-slice shaped rooms. Tower and East are quieter and have normally shaped, larger rooms.

"Most students are Christian so they share some sort of unity in that."

But pay no mind, because the upperclass dorms get better, not to mention that many students move off campus to nearby university-owned apartments. Part of the draw of these more spacious quarters is the lack of living restrictions and RAs, not to mention the nearby coffee shops and laudromats.

Although many Marquette students move off the main campus, no one feels isolated. Everything on campus and in the vicinity is "clumped together." This is convenient because all the main classroom buildings, the library, the Chapel of Joan of Arc, and even the main dorms are easily accessible—no trudging long distances in the icy weather! Marquette also receives much praise from its student body for its fantastic gym and athletic facilities.

Although the gym got rave reviews, the food provided by the dining halls did not. "Perhaps the worst part of the university," as one student referred to it. Not only is the food untasty, but it's unhealthy also, which means students often subsist on pizza, chicken nuggets, and burgers—if you're into Papa John's or Jimmy John's pizza, this could be the place for you. A car on campus is useful for grocery shopping if you decline to be on the meal plan and can be convenient for shopping, road trips to Chicago (only an hour and a half away), or simply to explore Milwaukee. Marquette is the sort of school that does not become a ghost town on weekends. It's fun and alive and has a lot of pride, school spirit, and a strong alumni connection. Satisfied with education and college experience they receive, most say they would do it all over again if they could. —*Carolina Galvao*

FYI

If you come to Marquette, you'd better bring "a good fake ID."

What is the typical weekend schedule? "Basketball games, bars, beer, enjoying the city of Milwaukee, and sleep."

If I could change one thing about Marquette, I would change "the food."

Three things every student at Marquette should do before graduating are "attend a game, attend at least one mass of the Holy Spirit, and study abroad."

University of Wisconsin / Madison

Address: 3rd Floor, Red Gym, 716 Langdon Street; Madison, WI 53706-1400
Phone: 608-262-3961
E-mail address: on.wisconsin@mail.admin.wisc.edu
Web site URL: www.wisc.edu
Founded: 1836
Private or Public: public
Religious affiliation: none
Location: urban
Undergraduate enrollment: 29,708
Total enrollment: NA
Percent Male/Female: 45%/55%
Percent Minority: 13%
Percent African-American: NA
Percent Asian: 5%
Percent Hispanic: 2%
Percent Native-American: 1%
Percent in-state/out of state: 70%/30%
Percent Pub HS: NA
Number of Applicants: 21,211
Percent Accepted: 60%
Percent Accepted who enroll: 43%
Entering: 5,514
Transfers: 1,294
Application Deadline: 1 Feb
Mean SAT: NA
Mean ACT: NA
Middle 50% SAT range: V 550-660, M 580-700
Middle 50% ACT range: 25-30
3 Most popular majors: communications, psychology, English
Retention: 91%
Graduation rate: 77%
On-campus housing: 26%
Fraternities: 9%
Sororities: 8%
Library: 4,800,000 volumes
Tuition and Fees: $5,140 in; $19,150 out
Room and Board: $6,130
Financial aid, first-year: 33%
Varsity or Club Athletes: 3%
Early Decision or Early Action Acceptance Rate: NA

With an undergraduate population of nearly 30,000 students, the University of Wisconsin at Madison offers its students a diversity generally not associated with the Midwest. For many students from Wisconsin and around the country, Madison is an obvious choice for its challenging academics, large sports program, and overall general appeal. As one of the highest-rated state schools in the country, Madison offers a booming college life and a solid academic program.

School Days

Academics at Madison are very stimulating, students say, although one was quick to point out that many people maintain the mantra: "Don't let school get in the way of your education." Students explain that a typical student is appreciative of the "great education at a reasonable price," but wants to be "able to enjoy life to the fullest." English, communication arts and political science are popular majors, and generally deemed to be fairly easy, while computer science and engineering are some of the harder programs. While many people from the Midwest who want to stay close to their families and friends choose Madison, students explain that the school is different because "it attracts the same type of student who could make it in notable East or West Coast schools."

Students must fulfill general education requirements in natural science, communications, humanities, and quantitative reasoning. While one student asserted that the academic requirements at Madison are "fair or too lax," most others seem to agree that they can be an obstacle. Students complained specifically about "unnecessary classes that don't have anything to do with your major." Registration can also be a problem, as many students don't get into the classes that they signed up for. There are many large lectures—as can be expected on such a large campus—although one student noted that "in small classes, I had good rapport with my professors." Most say that this is particularly the case "once you get to classes within your major." Students say that once professors get to know them well, they are "always more than willing to help with anything, even if it isn't school related." Some students also complain about foreign TAs, who are sometimes "hard to understand."

Madison has an honors program that students enter during the application process. That program, as well as the Medical Scholars program, allows students to distinguish themselves from the greater student population. In the honors program, students are required to take specific honors courses and maintain a high grade point average.

Football and Other Fun

While academics are a high priority, students admit that "football comes first at certain times of the year." Madison, already a "college town," is overrun during game days, when "you can't bike or drive through the downtown area." During football season, a large percentage of the student population spends its time at "'Camp Randall,' where hopefully the Badgers are winning." If the football game is at home, students will often get up around eight to "start pre-game parties or tailgates." The football team is a frequent Rose Bowl contender, and the basketball team is a perennial Big Ten powerhouse. Students say that you can't get enough of the team spirit at Madison—as one student explained, "Here, we are all Badgers!" Most students will say that even if the team is not number one, "We're absolutely the greatest." Another was quick to add that when there is a Badger game, "we drink before, during and after the game."

Madison is definitely known as a party school, but most students say that "things are kept under control and people stay safe." Students, many say, simply like to "maximize the social opportunities in life while attending a good school." There are a lot of parties, usually with a significant amount of drinking, but non-drinkers do not feel isolated because Madison "is such a large school that you can always be yourself and find people who share the same interests as you." Or, as another student explained, abstaining is sometimes better "because you will definitely remember everything that happens during the night." A lot of students frequent the bars on State Street, one of the main streets in Madison located near the dorms. Others, however, say that Madison "can be pretty boring" and that to find something to do "you have to go out and look for it." If there is no football game, "you don't always see a lot of students out of bed before noon on weekends." While some students "spend their weekends being productive," most do go to some parties. Freshman specifically, students say, party from Thursday night through the weekend, and others claim that "there's a fair amount of students who think [the weekend] starts on Wednesday."

While academics are a high priority, students admit that "football comes first at certain times of the year."

One student explained that Madison students tend to spend about one-fourth of their time studying. People are "pretty devoted" to extracurricular activities, which span the active fraternity scene to the Go Club, dedicated to the Asian board game. Tau Beta Pi is a well-respected fraternity at the school, and students are also very actively involved in social movements. The school is well-known for its protests of the Vietnam War, during which Sterling Hall, the physics building, was bombed. This tradition of protest continues today; as one student explained, these go on year-round. There are many religious and political organizations, and sports are also an important extracurricular for many people. Madison is a Division I school and does a fair amount of recruiting, however its top-notch athletic facilities, including "three gyms, outdoor and indoor tennis courts, volleyball and basketball courts, swimming pools, and a running track" are available to all students.

Madison, the City

Madison, the university's host city and the Wisconsin state capital, is definitely a great place to be, according to most students. As one student noted, "Madison is a city where everyone smiles when they see you." Students also say, though, that because of the college town atmosphere, "you need to go out of here just to get a taste of reality." Contrary to the situation on most college campuses, many students have off-campus jobs in the city. In general, students think Madison is a wonderful place to be. The city is surrounded by lakes and hills, giving the whole campus a very natural aura.

Madison is generally a very liberal campus with a fairly large gay community, though "there aren't any gay pride activities here." Interracial couples are also visible on campus. Students are very laid-back and can often be seen walking around in "sweat pants or pajama bottoms." While some students say that dating at Madison consists of random hookups, others do have serious relationships.

Students also praise Madison's diverse student population. Although one student identified a typical Madisonian as "reading *Badger Herald* while having lunch, wearing an Abercrombie jacket, studying and partying through the weekend," the environment of the school is changing as diversity, particularly international, increases. One international student explained that "there are so many places and activities through which you can connect with both Americans and other international students." Students also mentioned the number of ethnic festivals, and other opportunities to learn about different cultures. There are no real cliques, although people are often identified by what major they are in. The school is "full of interesting people," from MTV celebrities like Noah from Road Rules and the famous spring breakers from 1999, to alums like John Lange, the U.S. ambassador to Botswana and Jack St. Clair Kilby, a Nobel Prize winner.

Overall, Madison provides students an amazing environment for "four great years." While some are unimpressed by the gargantuan size of the school, others will assert that this provides for an amazing wealth of opportunities. From academics, to football, to the abundance of parties, students at Madison claim their school to be "one of, if not the best, universities in America!" —*Jessamyn Blau*

FYI

If you come to the University of Wisconsin/Madison, you'd better bring "a cell phone—everyone's got one."

What is the typical weekend schedule? "Drinking—parties, bars—we can drink anywhere."

If I could change one thing about the University of Wisconsin Madison, I'd "introduce a better bus system."

The three things that every student should do before graduating from University of Wisconsin Madison are "go to a Badger game, go to Memorial Union and just stare at Lake Mendota—it's beautiful—and eat Babcock's ice cream. It's the best!"

Wyoming

University of Wyoming

Address: PO Box 3434; Laramine, WY 82071
Phone: 307-766-5160
E-mail address: undergraduate. admissions@uwyo.edu
Web site URL: www.uwyo.edu
Founded: 1886
Private or Public: public
Religious affiliation: none
Location: rural
Undergraduate enrollment: 9,250
Total enrollment: NA
Percent Male/Female: 47%/53%
Percent Minority: 8%
Percent African-American: 1%
Percent Asian: 1%
Percent Hispanic: 4%
Percent Native-American: 1%
Percent in-state/out of state: 74%/26%
Percent Pub HS: NA
Number of Applicants: 2,954
Percent Accepted: 95%
Percent Accepted who enroll: 52%
Entering: 1,471
Transfers: NA
Application Deadline: 10 Aug
Mean SAT: NA
Mean ACT: NA
Middle 50% SAT range: V 460-580, M 480-600
Middle 50% ACT range: 20-26
3 Most popular majors: education, business marketing, criminal justice
Retention: 77%
Graduation rate: 25%
On-campus housing: 24%
Fraternities: 8%
Sororities: 5%
Library: 1,298,000 volumes
Tuition and Fees: $2,997 in; $8,661 out
Room and Board: $5,120
Financial aid, first-year: 43%
Varsity or Club Athletes: 6%
Early Decision or Early Action Acceptance Rate: NA

Imagine yourself amidst mountain ranges and grass plains. Look around and realize that you are engulfed in nature. Above you, nothing but big sky; below you, nothing but solid earth. Then take several high-rise dorms, classroom buildings, and 10,000 students and plop them down in the middle of the wide-open prarie. What do you see now? The University of Wyoming in Laramie, Wyoming.

Large Mountains, Large Classes

The class sizes at the University of Wyoming "really aren't bad, especially when your classes become more and more focused on your major," commented one senior. "I do have classes that go upwards of about 200 students, but 90 to 95 percent of the classes have less than 50 kids in them." Don't let the scope fool you, though; University of Wyoming has its share of caring and compassionate professors. "I have had so many professors that will really care about you as long as you show them you put in the time and effort to show concern about their subject," said one junior. The TAs receive less-than-stellar marks and "have been known to blow off the students," according to one.

The students at the University of Wyoming take pride in their academic programs. Boasting fantastic engineering and research science departments, the University of Wyoming proves that they "can roll with the big kids." Wyoming's honors program is another strong point. High school students with at least at 3.8 GPA and a 1240 SAT score are selected to participate in the program and take five required classes, two in their freshman year and one in each following year. One honors student commented on how diverse and interesting the class topics were: "The program offers several courses from chaos theory to English lit to AIDS/HIV awareness." Honors students are also given the option of living together in a special section of the dorms. The overall workload at the University of Wyoming varies. "The hardest majors by far are the engineering majors and classes in the honors program. Everything else is fairly manageable, but with frequent tests," commented one senior. Slackers usually choose to major in sports medicine or education.

Renovated Dining Halls and "Mediocre Dorms"

Because the population of Laramie, Wyoming, is so small, students often feel that it is hard to escape dorm life. Half of Laramie's 20,000 residents are Wyoming students, so when school gets out for summer break, the town "looks like an empty parking lot." Many students choose to live off campus, though the on-campus facilities are described as "very adequate." Wyoming's six dorm buildings are all located in the center of campus on a grassy field known as "Prexie's Pasture." Though each building has the same design and setup, some dorms differ in their more human aspects. "The only bad thing about one of the dorms is that all the football and basketball players live there—it really begins to smell after a while," laughed one freshman. Though Prexie's Pasture itself is pretty, it is surrounded by "lots of cement buildings and sidewalks," noted one senior. "I sure wish the school would get rid of some of the cement and replace it with grass and trees."

> **"Our wildlife and nature are really a main focus at the University of Wyoming—not many college campuses can brag about their scenic locations."**

Dining at the University of Wyoming is a college student's dream. The dining hall stays open all day until 11:30 P.M., and students can come and go as they please. The dining hall recently underwent renovations, and students are extremely happy the variety of foods now available. "The renovations removed the 'one-size-fits-all' idea and made it more like a food court in a mall where you can walk up to the Mongolian grill or pasta bar and get whatever you want," boasted one senior. There are plenty of vegetarian options, and workers are extremely friendly. Off campus, students can charge food and coffee at participating restaurants to their Campus Expre$$ ID card. "The Expre$$ ID card allows us to grab a cup of coffee or late-night snack without having cash on hand," said one sophomore. "It really gives us an excuse to get out of the dining halls sometimes."

Saddle Up, UW!

The town of Laramie doesn't have much to offer students in the way of entertainment, though there are a few bars that upperclassmen frequent. Lovejoy's and Altitudes are two local favorites. A popular hot spot for freshmen and sophomores is Cowboy, a famous nightclub that hosts 18-and-older nights. However, the town and school are *extremely* strict about alcohol consumption. "Alcohol is very accessible but the administration and town does everything to stop [underage drinking]," commented one freshman. Wyoming offers plenty of non-alcoholic alternatives for students who opt not to drink. An organization called Friday Night Fever organizes movie nights, casino nights, and comedy nights where students can "have a really fun time without paying anything." For students who would rather hit the bottle on Fridays and Saturdays, on-campus parties are often hosted by one of the university's fraternities.

However, the primary lure of Laramie, Wyoming, isn't its cowboy-themed restaurants and on-campus parties. The scenic landscape is breathtaking, and the surrounding mountains inspire many students to seek out outdoor activities. Vedawoo (pronounced vee-da-voo) has the most popular rock climbing in the area, while Snowy Range and Happy Jack are known for their camping, hiking, and skiing. "[The mountains] require having a car to get to, but since most people here have cars on campus, it never seems to be a problem," said one senior. On weekends, many students take to the outdoors to appreciate the many gorgeous mountain views. "Our wildlife and nature are really a main focus at the University of Wyoming—not many college campuses can brag about their scenic locations," boasted one freshman.

The Student's Bodies

The students of the University of Wyoming take many things seriously: their sports teams, their school activities, and their fitness. One freshman noted, "I was surprised to find so many people working out and participating in athletic activities." Several students noted that UW's Half-Acre Gym is a hot spot to hang out and one of the most noteworthy buildings on campus. "With so many athletes and nature-conscious people here, it's no wonder we have such a large population of fit people," said one sophomore. But students are definitely not image-conscious. When asked what the typical style of a UW student was, one junior responded, "A University of Wyoming sweatshirt and a pair of jeans," while another was quick to reply, "their pajamas." The relaxed atmosphere of the student body reflects their personalities. "I wouldn't want to be anywhere else—everything is just so easy-going here," commented one sophomore.

Pride Runs Along the Plains of Laramie

At Wyoming, the professors care about the students, and the students care about the school. For many students, this sense of pride in their community is the best thing about UW. "First and foremost, I go to the University of Wyoming. I think that the fact that the entire state of Wyoming is behind it and all of its programs means a lot to the students here. Also, I think that the small community brings the students here closer together . . . and the people here are amazingly friendly," bragged one freshman. When asked if she would choose to attend the University of Wyoming again, she quickly responded, "Right now, I can't picture myself anywhere else. I love it here so much, it is like no place I have ever seen. I'm proud to tell my friends back home that I go to UW." *—Nate Puksta*

FYI

If you come to the University of Wyoming, you'd better bring a "warm coat and oxygen. At 7,500 feet above sea level, UW takes a toll on the lungs."

What is the typical weekend schedule? "Hiking, camping, climbing, studying, and drinking."

If I could change one thing at the University of Wyoming, "I'd make the shower heads higher in the bathrooms and lower the dorm-room temperature at least five degrees!"

Three things every student at the University of Wyoming should do before graduating are "enjoy the great area that surrounds Laramie (it is too unique and awesome to miss), go to a UW football game, and ski in the Snowy Mountain Range."

Canada

Canada Introduction

For the American student seeking the adventure of a foreign university but reluctant to travel halfway around the world, Canada may be the ideal location. A different culture, strong programs, and low tuition are just across the border. But there's more to Canada than mountain ranges, friendly people, and cold beer; before you pack your skis and buy a plane ticket, you should know what awaits you.

Don't Say We Didn't Warn You

First, let us offer these words of warning: If generalizations about all the students in a particular university are risky, then generalizations about all the universities in a particular country are even more so. As always, there will be exceptions and differences of degree with respect to everything that follows. Research everything carefully. Individual universities, as well as different programs within the universities, can vary from the exceptional to the inadequate, and it is crucial to find out as much as possible about the school that interests you before you commit.

The greatest difference between Canadian and American universities is that in Canada there are no private colleges; all Canadian schools are government-funded. This has many implications, from overt funding problems to students' attitudes about the purpose of a university and a university education. As any administrator of a state school in the United States will tell you, legislators never seem to allocate as much funding as a school thinks it needs, and Canadian schools have suffered from budget cutbacks frequently just as American schools do. Many Canadian institutions have problems with their buildings and the quality of specialized equipment for science classes. Of course, this is not universally true, so it's important to find out which schools are strong in the subjects that interest you.

To get a general overview of all Canadian colleges, it is helpful to know if the school is situated in a French-speaking province. That can make a big difference. Ontario and British Columbia have the most colleges of the provinces, so you may want to start there in a general search.

One thing to look for in government-funded Canadian schools is a phenomenon known as "warm-body admissions." Since Canadian schools are funded based on the number of students enrolled, some schools lower their admissions standards to fill seats and raise funding. This often leads to inflated numbers of first-year students and high first-year dropout rates. This generally does not occur at the better Canadian schools, such as those included in this guide. Admissions standards tend to be based more on the students' cumulative high-school grades than on other qualities, but standards vary from school to school and from program to program. It is wise to check the standards for a particular program before you apply.

Although there are now more and more exceptions, Canadian universities often lack that elusive entity known as "school spirit" or "school unity." This can be explained in part by the size of most schools and the number of students who live at home or off campus. Unlike many Americans, most Canadians don't seem to be looking for the ideal "college experience." Instead, they are looking primarily for the right education for their future careers, and convenience is an important concern. By and large, Canadian students are unabashedly pre-professional. Students view a degree as a prerequisite for a job and attend university as a means to that end.

If you decide that a university in Canada is right for you, there are certain procedures to follow and documents to obtain. Start early! Some schools may not be prepared to handle foreign students. For information, write or call the school and ask to be put in contact with their foreign students' office. Once accepted, you will need a visa and a student authorization. These must be obtained at a Canadian embassy or consulate in the United States, not in Canada. To get the documents, you will need proof of U.S. citizenship (usually a passport or a birth certificate), a letter of acceptance to a Canadian institution, and proof of adequate funds to support yourself while in Canada. If you decide that it's for you, strap on a sense of adventure and get ready for a unique experience, but remember that it's a four-year-long trek. —*Seung Lee*

Carleton University

Address: 1125 Colonel BY Drive; 315 Robertson Hall, Ottawa, ON, K1S5B6
Phone: 613-520-3663
E-mail address: NA
Web site URL: www.carleton.ca
Founded: 1942
Private or Public: public
Religious affiliation: none
Location: urban
Undergraduate enrollment: 17,532
Total enrollment: NA
Percent Male/Female: 50%/50%
Percent Minority: NA
Percent African-American: NA
Percent Asian: NA
Percent Hispanic: NA
Percent Native-American: NA
Percent in-state/out of state: NA
Percent Pub HS: NA
Number of Applicants: NA
Percent Accepted: NA
Percent Accepted who enroll: NA
Entering: NA
Transfers: NA
Application Deadline: NA
Mean SAT: NA
Mean ACT: NA
Middle 50% SAT range: NA
Middle 50% ACT range: NA
3 Most popular majors: NA
Retention: NA
Graduation rate: NA
On-campus housing: NA
Fraternities: NA
Sororities: NA
Library: 2,000,000 volumes
Tuition and Fees: $5,416
Room and Board: $5,865 in-state
Financial aid, first-year: NA
Varsity or Club Athletes: NA
Early Decision or Early Action Acceptance Rate: NA

How often does the average university student have the best features of two provinces at their disposal? At Carleton University, students not only have the privilege of being in the capital of Canada, but also have the opportunity to venture into the primarily francophone culture of Québec. Carleton itself is located in southern Ottawa, right next to the Rideau Canal, and is in close proximity to the federal parliament buildings and offices. Ranging from aerospace engineering to architecture, Ottawa's Carleton University is known for strong programs in many different fields.

Academics: Journalism, Engineering and More!

Carleton's toughest and most well known programs are journalism, aerospace engineering, and criminology. When applying to Carleton, students must identify which particular program they are applying to and admissions are substantially based on high school GPA cutoff levels. In general, getting into classes is not too difficult. Having a good high school GPA or being on a varsity sports team will allow you to preregister for classes in your program. Large classes are the norm for popular first-year courses such as Introductory Economics, where class size is often over 100 students. However, not all classes are in the triple digits. With classes such as Russian History, you can find 20 students or less.

Carleton is a school with several excellent engineering programs. The engineering program offers multiple areas of specialty ranging from aerospace engineering to mechanical engineering with a concentration in computer-integrated manufacturing. Each specific engineering program offers a whole array of subprogram specialization veins to allow engineering students to further focus their studies. For example, all aerospace engineer majors focus on the construction of aircraft, satellites, space communication systems, or remote guidance systems. Within this program, students can choose to further explore the field by investigating areas such as accident investigation and aircraft certification. It is not rare to hear about aerospace engineering students testing cars for aerodynamic efficiency or doing other similar applications around campus. A unique aspect of this specific program is the opportunity for outstanding and driven students to participate in a co-op industrial experience throughout their academic terms at Carleton. Journalism is a popular route for English majors. The structure of the journalism degree is based on three integral components: instilling and assessing skills of journalism, exploring courses designed to probe into the nature of the news world and applying journalism skills to programs outside of the university. Not only do students appreciate this real world work exposure, but it also allows them to apply what they've learned and to meet established professionals in the field.

Manifold Social Scene

Social life at Carleton focuses mainly on the five campus pubs and residence halls. At the Unicentre, the main student hangout, one can find a cluster of bars, restaurants and Porter Hall—where bands perform. Because very few students own cars on campus, public transportation and taxis are popular forms of getting around. Approximately ten minutes from campus is "The Market." This is the main spot in Carleton and offers a wide variety of restaurants, pubs, and clubs where students can relax and dance away the week's stress. Upperclassmen and underclassmen alike find The Market a great place to relax and catch up with friends on weekend nights. The legal drinking age in Ontario is 19. Therefore, some underclassmen prefer to go to Hull, Québec, where it is 18. Hull is most accessible via taxi, which is actually less expensive than going to The Market near Carleton. There are several pubs, clubs, and bars in Hull as well, that students like to frequent. With respect to students who are non-drinkers, they are numerous on campus. Though a lot of Carleton's social life includes drinking, one student explained that, "Ottawa is a great city where there are tons of sober things to do!" Bowling, movies, and ice-skating are among the many favorites of Carleton students. The myriad museums and galleries make Ottawa a rich cultural center, displaying everything from modern art to First Nations art.

Sports: Pick-Up to Varsity

Though Carleton no longer has a football team, it has surely compensated for this with strong soccer, basketball, lacrosse, rugby and waterpolo teams. Of these teams, basketball and soccer are the campus favorites. Intramurals are relatively big on campus and you can find all sorts of different teams such as the Engineering Hockey Team. Students will often just form their own recreational teams, arrange times to practice using campus facilities and have their own sport circles. Pick-up games happen all the time: some are between certain residence floors; others are between RAs and their advisees; and some even grow to be between two different residential halls. If intramurals and varsity sports are not your thing, you can take advantage of the campus gym that is accessible by every student with their student card.

There are a multitude of campus organizations (more than a hundred) at Carleton. Similar to other Canadian universities, sororities and fraternities are forbidden at this school. In general, first-year students are not always as involved as other upperclassmen because they are not aware of all the opportunities that are available. Campus community service programs are not prevalent, but programs partnered with community efforts are quite popular. Throughout the year there are numerous foundation runs and fundraisers that link the Carleton University community with the surrounding Ottawa community.

"Ottawa is a great city where there are tons of sober things to do!"

The extensive Carleton tunnel system links all building and residences on campus. With the severely cold Ottawa winters, these tunnels are great for getting around to classes and dining halls without feeling the winter chills. One student described the campus "tunnel rats" as those students who use the underground system all winter and even show up to class in flip flops! The Rideau Canal and Rideau River are also hotspots on campus. With the winter's low temperatures, the river freezes and becomes the longest outdoor skating rink in the world. When the weather warms up, many students prefer studying by the Rideau Canal under its large shady trees and its calming quality.

Carleton is a great university for those who want to learn and take advantage of all that the university has to offer. Though it is easier to get accepted into Carleton than some other Canadian universities, specialized programs such as journalism and engineering are challenging, require more effort, and often entail more rigid requirements. The combination of Ottawa—the nation's capital—and Carleton University provide for a dynamic atmosphere where students can gain a rewarding university experience. —*Zahra Kanji*

FYI

If you come to Carleton, you'd better bring "a good supply of winter clothing."

What is the typical weekend schedule? "Attempt to do work on Saturday but instead choose going to Ottawa and having fun. Then on Sunday, you really try and get work done."

If I could change one thing about Carleton, I'd "change the cold winters."

Three things every student at Carleton should do before graduating are "skate on the Rideau Canal, visit the Parliamentary Buildings, and make use of the Tunnel System."

McGill University

Address: 845 Sherbrooke Street West; Montreal, QC, H3A 2T5
Phone: 514-398-3910
E-mail address: admissions@aro.lan.mcgill.ca
Web site URL: www.mcgill.ca
Founded: 1821
Private or Public: public
Religious affiliation: none
Location: urban
Undergraduate enrollment: 21,827
Total enrollment: 29,866
Percent Male/Female: 40%/60%
Percent Minority: NA
Percent African-American: NA
Percent Asian: NA
Percent Hispanic: NA
Percent Native-American: NA
Percent in-state/out of state: 53%/non-Quebec Canadian 29.2%/USA 7.9%/other 9.8%
Percent Pub HS: NA
Number of Applicants: 15,885
Percent Accepted: 43%
Percent Accepted who enroll: 47%
Entering: NA
Transfers: 1,930
Application Deadline: 15 Jan
Mean SAT: V 594, M 625
Mean ACT: NA
Middle 50% SAT range: NA
Middle 50% ACT range: NA
3 Most popular majors: English language and literature, mechanical engineering, psychology
Retention: NA
Graduation rate: NA
On-campus housing: 10%
Fraternities: NA
Sororities: NA
Library: 4,363,849 volumes
Tuition and Fees: $1,668 in; $3,438 out
Room and Board: $8,000
Financial aid, first-year: 7%
Varsity or Club Athletes: NA
Early Decision or Early Action Acceptance Rate: NA

Located in the heart of Montreal, McGill University offers its students the best of two worlds: a college experience in a safe urban setting. Come rain or subzero weather, McGill students can always be found gracing the streets of Montreal, taking advantage of its numerous resources. About McGill's location, one student said, "Where in the States can you find an amazing university in a safe urban setting—the key word being 'safe'?" But despite its urban location, the McGill campus is no less collegiate than a suburban or rural one. Indeed, looking at McGill's luxurious lawns and plethora of trees, a student may forget that just footsteps away from campus lies one of the world's most happening cities. All things considered, it's no wonder McGill students keep coming and never want to leave!

Learning the Canadian Way

When applying to McGill, students are asked to indicate the academic field they intend to enter. At McGill, the different academic disciplines are called "faculties." The faculties cover a wide range of interests including everything from the arts to agricultural science, with each faculty having its own department and specific requirements. Most of the faculties are housed on the main campus; only agricultural studies is on MacDonald campus.

Few students complain about the requirements. Said one student, "The requirements are extremely reasonable. They truly allow one to explore what fields one is interested in without having to be loaded down." A typical four-year B.A.-degree candidate needs about 120 credits to graduate. First-year students in the arts are required to take one class in three out of the four following disciplines—humanities, social sciences, languages, and math and science. These requirements are intended to give students a wide view of available options. After this initial year of experimentation, students declare a major and are assigned an advisor in their specific department.

But the choices given to each student do not end there. Within each department, a student can choose to complete a single or double major and an honors or joint-honors degree. Honors students typically take more specialized classes and work more closely with individual professors. In addition, an honors degree might require a senior thesis, depending on the individual department.

In terms of the classes themselves, many departments require introductory lectures that, like those at other universities, tend to be quite massive. TAs help lead discussion sections, which somewhat compensates for the immense lectures. But whereas at other universities class size shrinks as courses become more advanced, at McGill classes remain large, a cause of many student complaints. At McGill, classes are taught in English, but students can elect to take tests and write papers in French.

Canadian Cutbacks

When asked about the living environment at McGill, one student replied, "All the problems with living at McGill are due to three problems, 'Cutbacks, cutbacks, cutbacks.'" For instance, even though McGill's libraries house over 2.9 million volumes, the libraries themselves are described as pretty pitiful; few students actually study there.

> **"Where in the States can you find an amazing university in a safe urban setting—the key word being 'safe'?"**

What distinguishes McGill from many American universities is that few of its students actually live on campus. Most live off campus or commute from home. First priority in on-campus housing is given to international students, primarily first-years.

McGill dorms are formally called residences, but students refer to them as "rez." Four of the main residences are found on the hill, a location first-year students never stop complaining about. Said one student, "The rezes are not that near anything and you have to climb this huge hill."

Each "rez" has a unique reputation. Gardener is known as the place for quiet studious students, although current first-year students say that reputation is beginning to change; Molson, the typically rowdy dorm has become tamer in the past two years. McConnell remains the party dorm, as well as the rez with single-sex bathrooms. All three are co-ed. But if co-ed living is not your thing, Royal Victoria College is an all-female dorm with a more central campus location.

Students from the three dorms eat in the same cafeteria; students in Douglas, situated slightly lower down the hill, have a separate facility. Known for its aesthetic beauty, Douglas is the favorite among many. However, due to seemingly never-ending construction, Douglas has begun to lost its charm to some.

Solin Hall, the newest "rez", is also located away from the hill. Students often complain about its location, explaining it is too far from everything. With its apartment-like rooms, Solin offers more independent living for some; for others, it may be the cause of constant problems and hassles since Solin students have to cook their own meals.

But judging from the overall negative view of McGill food, cooking for yourself in Solin may not be such a bad thing after all; all other students are required to purchase a meal plan. McGill food was described as completely inedible and the meal plans as stingy because McGill limits what students can take at meals. In response to the sometimes-ludicrous dining guidelines, one student griped, "Since when is orange juice a dessert?" For vegetarians, food options are even worse or non-existent.

After the first year, students escape the meal plan as they move out of residences and, more often than not, into the "McGill ghetto." But don't be fooled by the name. In reality, the "ghetto" is a neighborhood of nice yet affordable apartment houses located just steps away from campus. Other popular places for upperclassmen include "The Plateau" or "The Main," which is situated near St. Laurent Street, a center of activity with its numerous bars and restaurants.

Extracurriculars Exist?

A McGill freshman asked to name organizations he belonged to could not list a single one. With the exception of sports, extracurricular activities do not enjoy high student participation, largely due to the high percentage of students living off campus. Greek life, too, has minimal campus presence. When asked to list a few clubs, most students would name The Stonecutters, a popular group whose sole activity is to gather and watch *The Simpsons* together every Sunday.

Students involved in sports compete at the club, intramural, and varsity levels. An interesting fact that most people don't know is that Harvard is McGill's historical rival. Indeed, the first North American football game was reportedly a McGill-versus-Harvard rugby game that took a bizarre turn, and football was "invented." Nowadays, McGill's more commonly recognized rival is Queen's University in Kingston, Ontario. And even though football is not very popular at McGill, students still get a chance to show their school spirit at the annual Homecoming game, a.k.a. the "I-didn't-know-we-had-a-football-team game." Another instance of school spirit displayed occurred when the men's soccer team won the national championship back in 1997.

For more literary minds, McGill offers numerous student publications. Published three times a week, the *McGill Daily* comes out twice a week in English and once in French. In addition, literary alternatives include the weekly *McGill Tribune* and the *Red Herring*, a humor magazine. But at McGill, out-of-class life typically revolves around off-campus venues.

Bars on Campus

For American natives, McGill's on-campus bar may be a strange sight. Unlike American schools where the majority of the students are underage, McGill social life truly capitalizes on the local drinking age, which is only eighteen. So whereas most freshman orientations at other schools center on talks and maybe pizza dinners, according to one student, the goal of freshman orientation at McGill is "to get the freshman drunk." Almost all activities revolve around drinking; even the breakfast menu features bagels and beer. Drinking is truly a central part of McGill social life.

Besides bars, other popular social spots include Peels Pub with 14-cent wings and shots for under a dollar. Angel's is known for great dancing. Gert's is the convenient and popular on-campus bar. Overall, clubbing and barhopping are the main events of a McGill student's weekend nights.

So with such a bustling social life, why would McGill students ever choose to stay in? As most McGill students would answer: the cold. Without a doubt, the freezing temperatures were one of McGill students' main complaints. But for those prospectives able to foresee themselves wearing woolen clothes for the next four years, McGill is the place to be. *—Alyssa Greenwald*

FYI

If you come to McGill, you'd better bring "a down jacket since it gets so friggin' cold!"

What is the typical weekend schedule? "Drink at a bar on campus, drink at St. Laurent, sleep. Maybe do some work here and there."

If I could change one thing about McGill, I'd "make the food edible."

Three things every student should do before graduating are "to spend a night at Peels, to go to a McGill-versus-Queens game, and to watch *The Simpsons* with The Stonecutters."

McMaster University

Address: 1280 Main Street West; L8S4L8, Hamilton, ON
Phone: 905-525-4600
E-mail address: macadmit@mcmaster.edu
Web site URL: www.mcmaster.ca
Founded: 1887
Private or Public: public
Religious affiliation: none
Location: suburban
Undergraduate enrollment: 14,130
Total enrollment: 18,806
Percent Male/Female: 43%/57%
Percent Minority: NA
Percent African-American: NA
Percent Asian: NA
Percent Hispanic: NA
Percent Native-American: NA
Percent in-state/out of state: NA
Percent Pub HS: NA
Number of Applicants: 19,652
Percent Accepted: 66%
Percent Accepted who enroll: 29%
Entering: NA
Transfers: NA
Application Deadline: 1 May
Mean SAT: NA
Mean ACT: NA
Middle 50% SAT range: NA
Middle 50% ACT range: NA
3 Most popular majors: NA
Retention: NA
Graduation rate: NA
On-campus housing: 70%
Fraternities: NA
Sororities: NA
Library: 1,700,000 volumes
Tuition and Fees: NA
Room and Board: NA
Financial aid, first-year: NA
Varsity or Club Athletes: NA
Early Decision or Early Action Acceptance Rate: NA

McMaster University, located in Hamilton, a city at the heart of the Golden Horseshoe area of Southern Ontario, is known for its dedication to innovative education and groundbreaking research. Home to about 18,000 students, many report that McMaster is second-to-none in diversity of programs offered, ethnic make-up of student body, and vibrant social scene. Named after a senator, McMaster University was founded in 1887 in Toronto but moved to its present location in 1930. The beautiful, ivy-clad buildings that intersperse the campus testify to the institution's distinguished history.

Choices Galore

If there is one thing about McMaster's academics that differentiates it from other post-secondary schools, it is the broad range of programs of study. Undergrads can choose from a whopping 141 degree programs from six faculties. Specific academic requirements vary by program, but students must take 30 percent of their courses outside of their program. Students report that the hardest programs can be found in the engineering, health sciences, and science faculties, and that the easiest ones are bunched in the social sciences, business, and humanities faculties. "I don't know how these people can say they're struggling with only 12 hours of class each week," commented a science student up to his neck with calculus problem sets and lab reports.

Students unanimously gave two thumbs up to the "elite" Arts and Science program, designed to provide students with a broad-based, liberal education. "I love the program, mainly because the classes are very small," praised one student. Said another: "The profs are as excited about teaching us as we are about learning from them. Class discussions are intelligent, and even intimidating in the first years of the program." One student reported, "after a biology teacher mentioned how asparagus makes your urine smell funny, a group of "ArtScis" cooked some up, and the professor ate them in front of the class' 300-plus students." Professors genuinely seem to care about their quality of teaching. Said one fourth-year student: "One of my profs took our class to his cottage in Algonquin for a weekend. A technology & society professor brought in a chainsaw to class to cut a pound of butter, and later in the year took a hammer to an old VCR in order to demonstrate a Neo-Luddite approach to technology."

The undergraduate M.D. program and the undergraduate nursing program are two fields of study that are often extolled. Both are well-known for their problem-based learning approach to medical education, a method that has been adopted by medical programs around the world. The interdisciplinary engineering and management program is also worth a mention, as it remains Canada's only "discipline-specific, joint engineering and business degree program."

Also highly praised is the kinesiology program, which is one of the top three programs in the country. It's a very holistic program—it takes a scientific, psychological, and sociological approach in a variety of disciplines within the realm of kinesiology.

Class size differs from program to program, but one student remarked that "compared to similar schools like the University of Toronto, Mac classes are quite small." Small classes translate into a "close-knit" academic environment, in which there is ample interaction between students and teaching staff. Students also laud the professors and TAs, describing them as "approachable," "interested in seeing you succeed," and "down-to-earth."

Not all comments concerning academics are positive, however. First-year students, in particular, are often surprised at the difficulty of the courses. "It is really hard to get good grades. You have to work hard even in intro classes," claimed one student.

Getting Rid of Stress

To relieve pent-up stress, McMaster students play hard and party hard. From huge parties to theme dances, this school has it all. Students can choose from on-campus bars such as the Rat, the Downstairs John, and the Phoenix, and off-campus bars with outlandish names like Snooty Fox, The Funky Monkey, Billy Bob's, and the Texas Border. For frosh, the school year kicks off with Welcome Week, formerly known as frosh week, during which time students get their first taste of the freedom and fun of university life by partying, gathering in bars, and attending concerts. Mac freshmen tend to travel in packs, so dating is not common during the first few months. However, according to one second-year student, by January things calm down and people begin to fall into their niches.

One of the biggest dances of the year is the McMaster Student Union's (MSU) Charity Ball, which reportedly draws as many as eight hundred students. "Besides being a great occasion to get dressed up, it also unites the school to some extent," said one student. Other big events include Frost Week—the first week back after Christmas break, homecoming, faculty formals throughout the year, public speakers, and concerts. "There's a good selection of musical groups that come to campus each year," said one undergrad.

The consensus regarding drug use is that "people definitely do them, but they aren't blatantly obvious about it." In other words, drugs are easily accessible to students looking to get high, but not perceived by the administration or the student body as being a threat to the school's reputation. After alcohol and nicotine, "marijuana is the drug of choice with mushrooms and ecstasy following," reported one insider to the drug scene. Despite the widespread drinking on and off campus, non-drinkers feel they are not left out. "You can hang out with your friends at the bars, keep your hands away from the booze, and still have a great time," reported one student.

For those who would prefer to stay away from alcohol, there are always plenty of alternative means of having a good time. "Why do you need to go out, get drunk, put a dent in your wallet, and suffer a hangover in the morning, when you could just sit back in the lounge, play pool and watch a good movie with friends?" asked one student.

Not Just for a Good-Looking Resumé

While it is true that some McMaster students join tons of extracurricular activities hoping to make themselves look good for potential employers and grad schools, most students get involved to gain new skills, for the rewarding experiences, and, of course, to have fun. One student said it well: "There's always going to be a few pre-med types who have ulterior motives behind their getting involved in volunteering, athletics, cultural organizations, special interest groups, and student government, but for the most part, people get into it just for the hell of it."

"The campus is a funny mix of beautiful, ivy-clad buildings and modern, concrete monoliths."

There are many extracurricular options open to undergraduates, from campus newspapers to intramural sports, the Conservative Party to the Queer Club. Some students say, however, that participation is lacking in many of them. Said one junior, "There are a million and one things to get into, but nobody does." Part of the reason for this is that a vast number of students live off campus, making it difficult for them to get involved. The major student-run organization is the McMaster Student Union (MSU), which basically runs all student activities, including the weekly newspaper, the *Silhouette*. The Student Union also runs two bars frequented by Mac students, a day-care center, a grocery store, and a radio station, all of which are staffed entirely by students.

On the upside, athletics at the varsity and intramural levels seem to be popular. One student on the rugby team commented, "Being a varsity athlete, most of the people I know are really into athletics at Mac. The football and basketball teams are really big here, often going to the nationals." The Pulse, the on-campus fitness center, is highly popular among students who want to stay fit but do not have the time to be on a team.

Mixed Feelings About the City

One concern often raised by prospective students is the city of Hamilton. "I spent four years at Mac and all I got was black-lung," one graduate jokingly complained. In reality, McMaster is located in suburban West Hamilton, far from the city's smog-producing steel mills. Pollution is not a problem, nor is transportation into the city. A bus pass is included in tuition fees, and the HSR, the bus network, is reportedly excellent. The city itself, however, is not so great. Apart from a strong local music scene, Hamilton offers few cultural events and loses most touring artists to nearby Toronto, located only 45 minutes away. McMaster students report that they rarely venture outside of the Westdale area around the school. The city is "rough and industrial," but there are some gems: The Hudson, "a small club that's good for beats, DJs"; The Raven, a new bar that features indie rock groups and local acts; and Hess Street, a street lined with outdoor patios packed during the summer. Most people brush off the negative aspects of the city by simply saying, "I came here for the school, not the city."

Awesome Campus, Dorms

McMaster students consistently give high ratings to the campus and residences. As one student described the campus, "It's a funny mix of beautiful, ivy-clad buildings (such as the old student building Hamilton Hall) and modern, concrete monoliths (such as the massive hospital and engineering building), mostly built around a large central green space. Come nice weather, students and Frisbees use the space well, but the campus can get eerily quiet when students go home on weekends." The most popular hangout seems to be the Togo Salmon Hall cafeteria, but students agree that this will change once the McMaster University Student Center is built. Places to study abound, but students reportedly stick to their own turf: arts students go to Mills library, engineering and science students hit the books at the Thode Science and Engineering libraries, and health science and biology students crowd the Health Science library.

Students report that they met most of their friends through their residences. Students are evenly divided in their opinion when asked whether their friends tend to be the same kind of people they hung out with in high school. "They're definitely different from the type of people I hung out with in high school," said one student, while another commented, "If you were in a clique during high school, you're most likely to join the same kind of clique at Mac." Nevertheless, the consensus is that friends are an integral part of the university experience. "They're linked to my enjoyment of life. Most of the fun comes from the things (sports, parties, classes) I do with my friends." First-years usually occupy doubles, and so have the opportunity to find out what it is like to live with a roommate. After first year, however, students may choose to live on or off campus. Theme housing is abundant at Mac—among them are La Maison Francaise, International House, and Quiet House.

On campus, there are four cafeterias that are good for school grub. Students can also eat at one of the six fast-food kiosks around campus. There is no general meal plan; instead, students can buy each meal, often in the main cafeteria, which has a fast-food court and is open 24/7, ideal for midnight snacking. The food is very expensive, however, so many undergraduates eat off campus. La Luna, a restaurant serving Lebanese food, is fairly popular due to its inexpensive menu.

An exceptional reputation and vast breadth of programs naturally leads many students towards McMaster University. And with such a vibrant community of scholastic and social stimulation, it is easy to understand why. —*Tak Nishikawa*

FYI

If you come to McMaster, you'd better bring "a readiness to study *hard.* You have to work your ass off to get good grades."

What is the typical weekend schedule? "Study, go to a local bar or hang with friends in small groups, study some more, sleep in between."

If I could change one thing about McMaster, I'd "get rid of the cliquey atmosphere."

The three things that every student should do before graduating from McMaster are "take a road trip to Toronto or beyond, make the Dean's List, and explore Hamilton for yourself."

Queen's University

Address: Kingston, Ontario, K7l3N6
Phone: 613-533-2216
E-mail address: NA
Web site URL: www.queensu.ca
Founded: 1841
Private or Public: public
Religious affiliation: none
Location: urban
Undergraduate enrollment: 13,866
Total enrollment: NA
Percent Male/Female: 41%/59%
Percent Minority: NA
Percent African-American: NA
Percent Asian: NA
Percent Hispanic: NA
Percent Native-American: NA
Percent in-state/out of state: NA
Percent Pub HS: NA
Number of Applicants: NA
Percent Accepted: 61%
Percent Accepted who enroll: NA
Entering: NA
Transfers: NA
Application Deadline: 24 Feb
Mean SAT: NA
Mean ACT: NA
Middle 50% SAT range: NA
Middle 50% ACT range: NA
3 Most popular majors: NA
Retention: NA
Graduation rate: NA
On-campus housing: NA
Fraternities: NA
Sororities: NA
Library: NA
Tuition and Fees: $3,551
Room and Board: $4,925
Financial aid, first-year: NA
Varsity or Club Athletes: NA
Early Decision or Early Action Acceptance Rate: NA

Situated on the rustic northwestern shores of Lake Ontario, Queen's University enjoys a beautiful location and a solid reputation for its undergraduate experience. One of Canada's smaller institutions at 11,000 undergrads, Queen's University has the atmosphere of an Ivy League institution without the associated Ivy League costs. Students tend to be extremely bright and motivated, and are very proud of their school. Said one undergrad, "If I could choose my university all over again, I would not even waste my time considering another institution, it would be Queen's all the way!"

Slackers Need Not Apply

"I'm happy about the academics," said one student. "I wouldn't still be here if I wasn't." Academic requirements at Queen's are quite stringent. "Queen's does not harbor any slacker students," explained one undergraduate. "Frosh 15" here does not refer to a bodyweight management issue, but to the expected grade deflation of 15 percent from one's high school GPA. However, students report that those who are not taking an honors bachelor's degree in science tend to have an easier time with their workload.

With such distinguished graduates as John Roth, the current CEO of networking giant Nortel, the commerce (business) program at Queen's is considered one of the best in Canada. The program's rigorous entry requirements also mark it as one of the most competitive. Queen's also offers competitive programs in nursing, engineering, and physical education.

Despite its relatively small overall student population, freshman classes tend to be quite large, often numbering in the hundreds. Students, however, report that the student-to-teacher ratio falls dramatically after the first year as students move beyond the necessary prerequisites. Upper-level courses and seminars tend to have no more than 20 to 30 students.

Students are generally happy with their professors, and some even go so far as to describe their professors as "cool." One student explains, "my Classics 101 prof gave me a 10 percent bonus on a midterm because I could think up five references to Greek or Roman civilization from *The Simpsons*. Finally, students report that getting into desired classes is generally not a problem provided one registers early enough.

Only Good Clean Fun

"Work hard, play harder" is definitely the student mantra at Queen's. Although Kingston, Ontario, is widely perceived as an affluent retirement community, there exists a vibrant social life on and off campus. Alcohol is a big part of the social environment, but no one feels isolated for being a non-drinker. "There is always something to do for everyone, so that no one feels alienated," said one student. Even though the drinking age is 19 in Ontario, freshmen typically take their parties off campus, as they are not permitted to bring beer bottles or kegs into the residences. Freshmen usually go clubbing on the weekends, with the most popular hangout being Cocamo. Upperclassmen tend to avoid Cocamo because of its reputation as a freshman club and head to more upscale locales such as A.J.'s Hanger, Stages, and the campus bar, Queen's Pub. Drug use among students is not conspicuous, nor is it seen by students as a major issue on campus.

The administration is strict in its alcohol policies. For example, it does not tolerate alcohol at university events unless it is in a licensed, fenced-off area. Furthermore, getting caught with a fake I.D. will get you banned from campus pubs for the rest of your academic career.

"If I could choose my university all over again, I would not even waste my time considering another institution, it would be Queen's all the way!"

Besides the bars and clubs, campus events are generally well attended. Movie nights, concerts, dances, and boat cruises are some of the most popular events. The student center or the JDUC (John Deutche University Center) is well used by many different student organizations—including the central student governing council, Alma Mater Society.

Beautiful People Abound

"There are many attractive guys and girls around," said one undergraduate. "There's always someone pleasant to adore." That said, some students complain that the student population is too homogeneous, with the majority of the student population hailing from white, upper-middle-class backgrounds. "We have a stereotype of the Gap-wearing, khaki-donning preppie school," explained one student. Geographically, the majority of the students hail from various metropolitan areas of Ontario such as Toronto and Ottawa. "The school could use some more diversity," explained another undergraduate. Nevertheless, there is a sizeable international student population from countries such as Barbados, Jamaica, Trinidad, New Guinea, Saudi Arabia, China, and India. Meeting people at Queen's is a non-issue. "It's really easy," explained an undergraduate. "People here are really friendly."

Crammed like Sardines in a Tin Can

Some students report being disappointed with the living arrangements. "I got an economy double that crammed two beds, two desks, and two metal hutches into a single-sized room my freshman year," said one sophomore. "It was more than a little cramped." Despite the disappointing quality of the living arrangements, many students find that the residence system is amenable to a great social life. "I've met my closest friends through the residence system," remarked one undergraduate.

Each residence has "floor seniors" who are typically second-year students, as well as "Floor Dons," who are fourth-year students. The Floor Seniors tend to be strict, enforcing quiet hours during the weekdays as well as guest and alcohol policies. "They just have bugs up their butts for the most part," complained one student.

Some of the dorms reportedly have different personalities. "For example, the McNeil girls are nuns, the Vic Hall kids party all the time, and the Leonard Hall boys are all rowdy and obnoxious," described one undergraduate. After first year, most students move out of the residence system into houses with four to six friends. There are many student houses in the area, as well as in an area affectionately known as the "Student Ghetto." Rent is reasonable, generally amounting to about $450 per month, and most student houses are within five minutes of campus.

The campus itself is fairly compact, only taking up three to four square blocks. The buildings tend to be a mix of modern and old, with the older buildings being based around designs from the University of Edinburgh. "The buildings are modern inside, yet historical on the outside—so it creates a nice contrast," said one student.

As a result of being located in quiet Kingston, students report feeling very safe at Queen's. Nevertheless, there exist various safety measures, such as the nighttime escort service, that bolster campus safety.

As for dining on campus, students consider the plan to be well-organized and flexible, though many consider the offerings to be repetitive and bland. "The food is alright, but it's lower than prison quality," complained one undergrad. There are vegetarian options available all the time, but nothing spectacular. "I'm getting very sick of eating pasta all the time," complained another. Luckily, dinner times tend to be social hours, and students report feeling very comfortable just sitting down with anyone and striking up a conversation. Of course, much finer dining options can be found off campus at one of Kingston's numerous upscale restaurants.

So Many Activities, So Little Time

Virtually all students tend to engage in a least one extracurricular activity during their academic career at Queen's. From debating to sports to writing for publications, Queen's has it all. "However, it depends on your personality," said one undergraduate. "If you like arguing, you hit the debate team. If you're athletic, you get in with the sports teams."

The Golden Gaels, Queen's popular football team, brings in large student crowds to all their football games. "There is tons of school spirit with lots of traditions, including many songs and chants," said one undergraduate. Homecoming is an especially festive occasion, as is the big annual game against archrival McGill University. Also, numerous on-campus athletic facilities satisfy students' desires to remain fit and active throughout college.

Scottish traditions run deep at Queen's and bring the student body together. For example, all students are given Scottish berets called Tams and are taught how to sing the school song, the "Oil Thigh." Furthermore, Queen's is also known as the Canadian university with the best orientation week. "Other places have a paltry two or three days," explained an undergraduate. "We have a full week!"

All the different faculties also have their own traditions. The engineers, for example, are known to dye themselves purple and slam their leather jackets on the ground at certain times. Every year, the engineering freshmen have to climb a 24-foot-high greased pole and grab a hat off the top of it. "We have a lot of special and fun traditions around here," said one student. "It's what makes Queen's great!"

With its proud Scottish traditions, talented student body, and ideal location, it is no wonder that Queen's students are proud to announce, "I go to Queen's!" *—Dennis Hong*

FYI

If you come to Queen's University, you'd better bring "a lot of spirit and enthusiasm."

What is the typical weekend schedule? "Attending a Golden Gael's football game wearing your Queen's Coveralls and Tams, going to a post-game party at Stages or A.J.'s Hanger, going down to the lake and reading a book under a tree, and going out to dinner at a restaurant with friends."

If I could change one thing about Queen's I would "change the sport's team name—Golden Gael's just sounds sissy!"

Three things every student should do before graduating are "go to see a homecoming football game, join the Queen's band, and jump into the lake wearing your Queen's coveralls."

University of British Columbia

Address: 1874 East Mall; Vancouver, British Colombia V6T 1Z1
Phone: 604-822-8999
E-mail address: registrar.admissions@ubc.ca
Web site URL: www.welcomeubc.ca
Founded: 1908
Private or Public: public
Religious affiliation: none
Location: urban
Undergraduate enrollment: 29,538
Total enrollment: 40,341
Percent Male/Female: 44%/56%
Percent Minority: NA
Percent African-American: NA
Percent Asian: NA
Percent Hispanic: NA
Percent Native-American: NA
Percent in-state/out of state: 94%/6%
Percent Pub HS: 98%
Number of Applicants: 19,706
Percent Accepted: 50%
Percent Accepted who enroll: 50%
Entering: 3,959
Transfers: NA
Application Deadline: 28 Feb
Mean SAT: 1300
Mean ACT: 27
Middle 50% SAT range: NA
Middle 50% ACT range: NA
3 Most popular majors: elementary education, psychology, secondary education and teaching
Retention: NA
Graduation rate: NA
On-campus housing: 20%
Fraternities: 6%
Sororities: 2%
Library: NA
Tuition and Fees: $2,295
Room and Board: $4,500
Financial aid, first-year: NA
Varsity or Club Athletes: NA
Early Decision or Early Action Acceptance Rate: NA

With its sandy beaches, majestic purple mountains, and beautiful cedar forests, the University of British Columbia is truly an outdoor paradise. Despite its calm, laid-back west coast atmosphere, the University of BC vigorously challenges its students in more ways than one to take advantage of the numerous exciting opportunities offered on its idyllic campus.

Reputed to be one of Canada's best institutions of higher learning, the University of British Columbia presents the undergraduate with an extensive range of academic offerings. From its progressive computer science and engineering programs to its competitive forestry and nursing programs, the University of BC has something for everyone. This exciting range of offerings is, however, not without its tradeoffs. With its nearly 40,000 strong student body, the University of British Columbia is huge; easily one of Canada's largest university student populations. A nervous freshman can easily feel lost amid this massive ocean of people. Nevertheless, after the initial culture shock subsides, many students discover all that the University of British Columbia provides and never want to leave.

Definitely Not a Haven for Slackers

Academic requirements at the University of British Columbia are rigorous. "There is no room for slackers here," claimed one current student. Students report that prospective engineers, who make up the majority of the student population, are among the hardest workers on campus. "Engineers take seven courses per semester; everybody else takes five," explained one undergraduate. Although students generally feel that the number of credits required to graduate is reasonable, some do complain about the distributional requirements that force science majors to take arts credits and arts majors to take science classes.

One unwelcome requirement for all freshmen is English. However, students who are lucky enough to possess good scores on the International Baccalaureate or Advanced Placement exams are able to place out of this requirement. Core courses also exist in the science and arts curriculum, although these are less dreaded. Despite the widespread distaste for the English requirement, English is still thought around campus to be an easy major.

As for classes, registration is done primarily through the Internet and priority is given to students with the best grades. The registration process can be a frustratingly time-consuming chore because of the necessity of selecting courses that fit into your schedule and are not already capped.

A Diverse Social Microcosm

Attending a very large school such as UBC has certain advantages; one of the most obvious being the extensive and diverse social atmosphere. The Student Union Building, popularly known as "The SUB," is a favorite social hotspot. "The SUB is the busiest place on campus," reported one student, "and campus-wide events are generally well attended."

Social life at UBC centers very much around the dorm and organized house system. Because of this, students find it very easy to meet people. Many students explain that the organized house system facilitates a cohesive social environment, and student spirit runs very high. "I'm friends with everybody on my floor and almost everybody in my house," one student explained. "It's a really great environment."

With the provincial drinking age at 19, alcohol plays a big part in the social scene at UBC. "The admin is very cool about drinking on campus, though underage drinking isn't sponsored, of course," explained one undergraduate. Frequent club-hopping and bar-hopping is part of the weekend nightlife. The Cheez, a local bar, is a favorite underclass hangout because "they don't card there." Upperclassmen, on the other hand, flock towards a popular club called "Koerner's" to party. Besides alcohol, drugs do not have a very big influence on campus. "Not many people do drugs, and those who do don't do them with any great frequency."

"If I had to choose again, I would definitely pick this school. I love everything about it."

For those who prefer daylight over nightlife, UBC is unique for its number of clothing-optional beaches on campus. The typical clientele of these beaches, however, consists of "fat old men and dirty peddlers."

Flexible Living Arrangements

Dorms are the typical housing for UBC students, and many report that their living arrangements are quite nice. Each dorm has RAs (Resident Advisors), who enforce quiet hours strictly, yet are known to be pretty reasonable and understanding.

Unlike at many other colleges, freshmen are not required to live in a dorm, though many still do. As one student put it, "there really isn't any worst dorm; people are put in the dorms that will most reflect their wishes." Floors in the dorms are single-sex as are the communal bathrooms. Those who choose to live on campus report that they feel safe in their surroundings. An extensive campus security phone system, a nighttime escort service, as well as on-campus bussing promote the secure feeling of the university. Furthermore, though the university is close to a large city, Vancouver has a relatively low crime rate.

So if you live in the dorms, where do you eat? While students consider the dining options on campus acceptable, many feel that the on-campus meal plan is much too limited. One common complaint is that the dining halls close much too early and that flexible operating hours in the evening would be greatly appreciated. If the dining halls aren't for you, there are many good restaurants and coffeeshops close to the university. Also, downtown Vancouver is a short bus ride away, and many students report going off campus for finer dining experiences fairly frequently.

Diversity in More Ways than One

Because the Canadian government subsidizes its universities, attending the University of British Columbia is a relatively affordable option as compared to most public colleges in the United States. Nonetheless, many prospective students are surprised to find out that much of the student body hails from upper-middle-class backgrounds in spite of the inexpensive cost of education. As one student explained, "a few people are extremely wealthy, and everybody is fairly affluent." UBC's ethnic profile is similar to that of Canada as a whole—much of the student body is Caucasian, while Chinese students form a large part of the school's minority population. However, other minorities are also represented on campus. Some students report that the Chinese students can be self-segregating, "but never to a point where it's uncomfortable." International students are definitely welcomed at UBC, and interracial and homosexual couples are also well accepted.

One student stereotyped, "UBC is a very athletic student body," and reported, "we have an enormous number of teams." Although non-athletes admit that they do not follow the university's varsity athletics very well, they report that they're proud of their fellow UBC Thunderbirds. Many students participate in intramurals and most keep active by taking advantage of the extensive athletic facilities, which include places to swim, golf, play tennis, play basketball, and rock climb. Those with more outdoorsy interests can enjoy the numerous hiking paths and various botanical gardens throughout the expansive campus.

Overall, UBC students love their school: "If I had to choose again, I would definitely pick this school. I love everything about it." With its extensive academic and social opportunities, it is not surprising that the University of British Columbia continues to maintain its reputation as one of Canada's premiere institutions. —*Dennis Hong*

FYI

If you come to the University of British Columbia, you'd better bring "an umbrella; while the administration says it's not actually as rainy as common reputation would have it, it really is."

What is the typical weekend schedule? "Getting drunk at the Cheez, going down to Wreck Beach, participating in intramurals, and hanging out in the dorm."

If I could change one thing about the University of British Columbia, I would "make it flatter—walking uphill is a pain!"

Three things every student at the University of British Columbia should do before graduating are "get a picture with a naked hippy on Wreck Beach, watch the sun set over the Rose Garden, and go to the Pit Pub nights."

University of Toronto

Address: 315 Bloor Street West, Toronto, ON, M5S1A3
Phone: 416-978-2190
E-mail address: NA
Web site URL: www.utoronto.ca
Founded: 1827
Private or Public: public
Religious affiliation: none
Location: urban
Undergraduate enrollment: 40,341
Total enrollment: NA
Percent Male/Female: 44%/56%
Percent Minority: NA
Percent African-American: NA
Percent Asian: NA
Percent Hispanic: NA
Percent Native-American: NA
Percent in-state/out of state: 96%/4%
Percent Pub HS: NA
Number of Applicants: NA
Percent Accepted: 60%
Percent Accepted who enroll: 31%
Entering: NA
Transfers: NA
Application Deadline: 1 Mar
Mean SAT: NA
Mean ACT: NA
Middle 50% SAT range: NA
Middle 50% ACT range: NA
3 Most popular majors: computer science, English language and literature, environmental studies
Retention: 95%
Graduation rate: NA
On-campus housing: 20%
Fraternities: NA
Sororities: NA
Library: NA
Tuition and Fees: $3,951 in; $8,755 out
Room and Board: $5,000
Financial aid, first-year: NA
Varsity or Club Athletes: NA
Early Decision or Early Action Acceptance Rate: NA

Known as one of the most prestigious universities in Canada, University of Toronto has much to offer to any student. With some of the top professors in every area of study, U of T has the leading edge on innovative research and the best course selection in Canada. Located in the heart of Toronto, Canada's largest city, the University of Toronto has a healthy combination of city excitement and top-notch academics.

Top in the Nation

There is a consensus that the professors at the University of Toronto are experts in their respective fields and have great accomplishments that trail after their names. There are professors who are Nobel laureates and others. It is easy for anyone to see that the University of Toronto has one of the most highly regarded academic environments. As a consequence, students have scores of courses to choose from and can tailor their schedules to personal preference. Courses are found to be challenging and professors are noted to have relatively high standards compared to most of the other Canadian universities. Some students feel lost in the large first-year classes and find the competitive nature of fellow students a little stifling. With each year, however, class sizes get much smaller and interaction with professors increases significantly. All students have access to resources such as counseling, tutorials and writing centers which are geared to help students with their rigorous course loads. Registration is done electronically by "voting" and then the computer does the first round of selections all at once based on seniority. After that, as one student commented, "Once the class fills up, you are out of luck!"

There are four main faculties at the University of Toronto: engineering, arts & science, music, and physical education & health. When applying for admission to the university, applicants apply directly to the faculty of their choice. U of T also offers a co-op program in some of its faculties. Co-op programs incorporate classroom teaching with real-world working experience; students enrolled in co-op programs switch between university work and their co-op jobs each semester. There are also many tracks offered for those interested in science. In addition, there are numerous opportunities available with professors who conduct research at nearby university-affiliated hospitals such as Sick Children's Hospital, Princess Margaret Hospital and Mount Sinai Hospital.

Break It Down

The University of Toronto has adopted a residential college system in order to create smaller communities among the relatively large student body. Seven of the nine residential colleges are located on the U of T St. George campus in downtown Toronto. The remaining two colleges, located approximately 30 minutes away from the St. George Campus, are on the Erindale and Scarborough campuses. The residence system is an effective way to meet people and get involved with student life. As one student commented, "residence events act as community builders and residence is the best way to get invited to the best parties."

> **"Being in the city provides endless opportunities that small, enclosed campuses would never be able to offer."**

Partying in the T-Dot

T-dot, a catchy short name for Toronto, is brimming with clubs, restaurants, sporting events, public festivals, theater and almost anything else someone could want in a city. Being a multicultural and cosmopolitan city, there are several ethnic pockets located close to central campus that students can explore. Ranging from Little Italy to Chinatown, there are always new corners of the city to visit and in which to hang out. Whisky Saigon and The Madison are two popular bars downtown, but these are only two from the throng of Toronto hotspots. Those who are basketball and hockey fans can catch a Toronto Raptors or Maple Leaf game at the new Air Canada Centre. With the Skydome just minutes from the St. George campus, a baseball game can easily be fit into any weekend agenda. In warmer weather, Harbourfront is a lovely place to relax. Lined with quaint lakeside restaurants and the DuMaurier Theatre, there are always plenty of attractions to be found in this area. Toronto has one of the largest, if not *the* largest, theater scenes in Canada. Roy Thompson Hall, the Ford Centre, the Hummingbird Centre, the Young Peoples' Theatre, and the Royal Alexandra Theatre are only a few examples from many Toronto theaters. Students can catch anything from entertaining Broadway shows on Theatre Row to smaller independent productions as a break from their academic routine. University of Toronto students always get discounted tickets for Toronto Symphonic Orchestra productions and there are always numerous student-run productions to enjoy as well. As one student put it, "The University of Toronto's location and opportunities make it a unique place to live and study." The TTC (or "The Rocket"), Toronto's subway, bus, and streetcar system, is quick and efficient, making it simple to get around town at any hour.

Campus Cuisine to International Cuisine

Dining options on campus have significantly widened over the past year. At most of the residential colleges, students are required to have a meal plan. Students can choose to have plans that permit a certain number of meals a week or the pay-as-you-go plan. The one exception to the meal plan rule is for students living at Innis College where the dormitories are arranged in suites and have kitchenettes where students can cook their own meals. Many places on campus now offer kosher and halal meals in addition to vegan and vegetarian options. Don't forget that U of T is located in the multicultural hub of Canada; the St. George campus is located next to Chinatown and many other ethnic communities. If you are in the mood for souvlaki or gyros, you can find a slew of Greek restaurants along Danforth Avenue or, if you're in the mood for Indian food, why not visit Gerrard Street? As one can easily tell, dining options at U of T are quite extensive and are not limited to what one can find in the residential college dining halls.

On or Off?

Much of the student body at U of T is composed of Toronto natives who are from the city itself or the Greater Toronto Area (GTA). For this reason, a significant proportion of the student body chooses not to live on campus and instead commutes each day to and from the university. There are also some who choose to rent apartments or rooms in the city and not live in the residential colleges. That being said, there are still many students who choose to live in the residential colleges. As many students agree, the residential colleges are the best way to find your social niche and feel a part of the university community. Students who live off campus repeatedly state that they miss out on the community aspect of the university. Each of the residential colleges on campus have approximately two or three residences each, with the majority being dorm style, co-ed by room or floor. Some, like Innis College, are set up in suites while others are set up like townhouses. The residences range from old and traditional dorm-style to more modern and apartment-like.

Why U of T Beats the Rest

Attending U of T offers many students the benefits of both a large and small university community experience because of the residential college system. In addition, there are incredible organizations, arts activities, and clubs that any student can join. Ranging from a local chapter of CUSO (Canadian University Students Overseas) to the running club, there are organizations to match any interest. Varsity and intramural sports are other favorites on campus. From football and field hockey to swimming and soccer, there are many teams to get involved with.

Along with superior academics, U of T boasts an array of distinguished professors, an incredibly diverse student body, countless opportunities to get involved in student organizations, and a cosmopolitan city. The University of Toronto also offers architecturally astounding buildings that range from Victorian to modern. As per countless reviews, the University of Toronto holds the torch for education in Canada. It offers only the best academics for its students and as one student effectively explained, "being in the city provides endless opportunities that small, enclosed campuses would never be able to offer." *—Zahra Kanji*

FYI

If you come to the University of Toronto, you better bring a "lot of energy in order to take advantage of all the great opportunities on campus."

What is the typical weekend schedule? "During the day, most people sleep in. Then on Friday and Saturday nights, they eat, study and go out. On Sunday, people mainly do their homework. On the weekends it can get a little less populated on campus since many students go home."

If I could change one thing about U of T, I'd "make classes smaller."

Three things every student at the University of Toronto should do before graduating are "visit every building on campus and look at the architecture, live in a residence, and join a club or team—there are countless things to do that you won't know where to begin!"

University of Waterloo

Address: 200 University Avenue West; Waterloo, ON, N2L 3G1
Phone: 519-746-2882
E-mail address: visitus@uwaterloo.ca
Web site URL: www.findoutmore.uwaterloo.ca
Founded: 1959
Private or Public: public
Religious affiliation: none
Location: urban
Undergraduate enrollment: NA
Total enrollment: 21,108
Percent Male/Female: 49%/51%
Percent Minority: NA
Percent African-American: NA
Percent Asian: NA
Percent Hispanic: NA
Percent Native-American: NA
Percent in-state/out of state: 98%/2%
Percent Pub HS: NA
Number of Applicants: NA
Percent Accepted: 61%
Percent Accepted who enroll: 33%
Entering: NA
Transfers: NA
Application Deadline: NA
Mean SAT: NA
Mean ACT: NA
Middle 50% SAT range: NA
Middle 50% ACT range: NA
3 Most popular majors: computer science, kinesiology and exercise science, mathematics
Retention: 98%
Graduation rate: NA
On-campus housing: NA
Fraternities: 1%
Sororities: 1%
Library: 2,500,000 volumes
Tuition and Fees: $3,952 in-state
Room and Board: $5,950
Financial aid, first-year: 47%
Varsity or Club Athletes: NA
Early Decision or Early Action Acceptance Rate: NA

Where else can you get great academics, great work experience, and great bratwurst, all at Canadian prices? According to students at the University of Waterloo, you can get everything you want all in one place.

A Taste of the Real World

Although it is smaller than most major Canadian universities, the University of Waterloo is well known among its peers for its rigorous and demanding academic programs. With a total of forty classes required for graduation (ten per year), there is always a lot to do particularly for students who double-major and are struggling to fit in those extra courses. Academic programs are structured around Waterloo's six faculties: applied health sciences, arts, engineering, mathematics, environmental studies, and science; each has its own requirements. In addition, there is also an Independent Studies Program for those looking for something more specialized. While math and engineering have an especially strong reputation (as Waterloo has more students enrolled in math than any other school in the world), the other departments are not slouches. There is little reported grade inflation, and professors are fairly accessible. Overall, undergrads find that the programs cater to them well. One arts student, noting the close attention students receive, commented that he could not remember taking any English classes with more than forty students per class, even freshman year.

One of Waterloo's biggest highlights is its well-developed Co-op program, where students divide the school year by alternating terms of school and employment. The Co-op program is the largest of its kind in North America with over half of the student body participating. As a result, Waterloo operates on a trimester system, with classes in session all-year long to allow students in the Co-op program to graduate within five years. Current undergrads highly recommend the program, saying, "not only can you get some much-needed cash, but you also get work experience, which is great for future employment." Being a part of the co-op system means having the opportunity to travel—not just to nearby Toronto, but to places outside of Canada as well. Students also report that coming back to school from the "real world" after working for a term provides a better perspective on classes and university life in general. One adds that "sometimes it's nice just to get away for a change of scenery and to refocus my energies."

Building Friendships

There are two main residences for students at Waterloo, called Village One and Ron Eydt Village. There are no on-campus housing requirements, but most students spend their first and second years in the dorms. Each dorm has a resident advisor, nicknamed a "don," who is an upperclassman. Many students are very enthusiastic about living within a residential church college system. The colleges include St Jerome's, St. Paul's, Conrad Grebel, and Renison. They are small colleges, religiously affiliated with the university. Offering both separate classes and housing spaces, the church colleges reportedly offer a "homier" atmosphere. Although each have their own religious background, students of any affiliation may apply for residence. Some say the church colleges have the most "spirit," and according to some, also have better food—try Conrad Grebel for Mennonite cooking, for one. On the whole, dorm rooms are small, but are the place where "we start to build lasting friendships so it isn't so bad—in a sense, we are all in it together."

Upperclassmen tend to live off campus—there is a lot of available housing conveniently near the school, and the cost of living is more affordable. By living off campus, students are able to avoid the meal plan which is reportedly "a total rip-off." Many find tastier food off campus as popular places to eat include East Side Mario's, Subway, Gino's, and the "plaza," which is open 24 hours a day. Gino's is particularly well known for allegedly holding the Guinness World Record for creating the longest pizza.

Friendly, Outdoorsy Atmosphere

Students find the town of Waterloo, Ontario, a quiet kind of university town, and are quick to differentiate it from nearby "gross, industrial, abandoned factory-like" Kitchener. For the outdoorsy types, the area around Laurel Lake provides the perfect opportunity to jog, swim, and bike. For those eager to explore the social scene, there is the Student Life Center, which organizes free movies and other recreational activities. The town of Waterloo is also famous for its great Oktoberfest celebration every year: people come from all over to sample the bratwurst, take in the dancing, and just to see what the festival is all about. Many students enthusiastically recommend the event, even if it means just taking a tour of the local breweries.

"Even the engineering students know how to relax once in a while."

As for the night life, there is Fed Hall, Canada's largest campus dance hall, where students go to party. Thursday nights are especially popular as people line up literally hours in advance to get in. Other than that, there are the usual weekend parties with plenty of alcohol available. Waterloo may have the reputation for being a studious school, but as one student commented, "even the engineering students know how to relax once in awhile." A fair number of people leave town for the weekend and head for Toronto, which is about an hour away. However, other students were quick to point out that their peers do not go to Toronto for the weekend often, preferring to hang out with friends on campus.

Intramurals and More

Extracurricular involvement at Waterloo varies as most students do not participate in many. Due to the Co-op system, many students do not have a lot of time to pursue other activities such as various employment opportunities. Extracurricular activities include an active student government and *Imprint*, the main student newspaper. Intramurals are also especially strong given a number of fine facilities available. Any student with interest can play, and the lack of pressure on the field makes the experience enjoyable. Varsity sports are very much in the background at Waterloo.

Quest for the Pink Tie

Waterloo, like all other schools, has its own unique traditions. Among them is the quest for the pink tie, which occurs during freshman week at the start of the school year. Math students, or "mathies" as they are called, go through a mild form of initiation to get the coveted pink tie. Later, a huge pink tie is hung over the side of the math building, and this often adds to the touch of rivalry between the math and engineering departments. During frosh week, engineering students try to steal the giant pink tie, while mathies try to sneak out the "tool," the engineering faculty's prized possession. As one student said, "we love to scheme and plot, but it is really just fun and games."

A Place to Grow

At Waterloo, academics are taken very seriously. "There are lots of smart people, especially in the sciences and engineering," says one undergrad. Students head to the Dana Porter Library to study, and computer clusters are readily available on campus. While the academic atmosphere may not be cutthroat, some complain that there are people who study compulsively. One student remarked that there exists a clear separation between students where "half the students study like crazy, and half have a life." Students at Waterloo can be cliquish, so school unity leaves room for improvement. However, the University of Waterloo still remains one of Canada's foremost educational institutions for the engineering, math and arts, and those who attend do take note of the good job placement rate after graduation. Above all, Waterloo students in general agree about the number of academic and social opportunities available. If there is one thing to remember about the people at Waterloo, it is that "we really know how to go after what we want." It is just that passion that keeps Waterloo growing and its students succeeding. *—Florence Han*

FYI

If you're coming to Waterloo, you'd better bring "cleats and shinguards so you can play in the intramurals."

What is the typical weekend schedule? "Eat, play sports, party, sleep."

If I could change one thing about Waterloo, I'd "knock down the ugly buildings."

Three things that every student should do before graduating from Waterloo are "go tubing in Laurel Creek, go out for a team (competitive or intramurals), and check out Oktoberfest."

University of Western Ontario

Address: 1151 Richmond Street; London, Ontario N6A 3K7
Phone: 519-679-2111
E-mail address: admissions@julian.uwo.ca
Web site URL: www.uwo.ca
Founded: 1878
Private or Public: public
Religious affiliation: none
Location: small city
Undergraduate enrollment: NA
Total enrollment: NA
Percent Male/Female: NA
Percent Minority: NA
Percent African-American: NA
Percent Asian: NA
Percent Hispanic: NA
Percent Native-American: NA
Percent in-state/out of state: NA
Percent Pub HS: NA
Number of Applicants: NA
Percent Accepted: NA
Percent Accepted who enroll: NA
Entering: NA
Transfers: NA
Application Deadline: NA
Mean SAT: NA
Mean ACT: NA
Middle 50% SAT range: NA
Middle 50% ACT range: NA
3 Most popular majors: NA
Retention: NA
Graduation rate: NA
On-campus housing: 50%
Fraternities: NA
Sororities: NA
Library: NA
Tuition and Fees: NA
Room and Board: NA
Financial aid, first-year: NA
Varsity or Club Athletes: NA
Early Decision or Early Action Acceptance Rate: NA

Located in the west end of the province in London, Ontario, the University of Western Ontario is aptly named. With about 25,000 full-time students enrolled, this university is Canada's fourth largest post-secondary institution. Established in 1878, Western has since grown to include twelve faculties collectively offering over 200 undergraduate programs, more than enough to support an extensive range of academic interests. Diversity of ethnic backgrounds as well as academic and extracurricular interests allows virtually any student to feel comfortable at Western. Even when it comes to having fun, Western offers a vibrant social scene that caters to all types of students.

Boning Up

Students report that Western has top-notch programs across the board, but that its program in business administration is in a league of its own. The prestigious and highly popular Honors Business Administration program takes the best and brightest and prepares them to become successful leaders in the business world. So outstanding is this program that it is ranked twenty-second in North America by *The Financial Times* in a 2003 survey, and many graduates of the Richard Ivey School of Business at Western go on to become CEOs, presidents and senior executives of companies in Canada and around the world.

"Major in Yourself" is UWO's celebrated catch-phrase. Here, students can immerse themselves in programs that range from the traditional to the cutting edge. For instance, in the Commercial Aviation Management program, students graduate with a commercial airline pilot's license and a university degree. Unlike most Canadian schools, where students delve into specialized study of their program right from day one of their university career, at Western, most students have their first year to explore a wide variety of disciplines. For students who want even more freedom and flexibility in their course selection, there is the Western's Scholar's Elective program, which combines a liberal education with the chance to work with a faculty mentor.

Students report large variations in class size. Said one, "First year biology has more than 1,500 students in one section, and close to 3,000 students taking the course." Another mentioned that his largest class was "SuperPsych", an introductory psychology class that typically crams 2,000 students into Alumni Hall, an enormous lecture hall. Although "almost all first year classes have more than 80 students per class," class size significantly declines for upperclassmen. Students are generally very satisfied with their professors and teaching assistants, and generously throw around words like "amazing," "approachable," and "quirky, but in a totally likeable way" when describing them. "My calculus professor had an overhead which had "Happy New Year" written in Chinese, and showed it to the class on Lunar New Year," remarked one satisfied student enrolled in Western's chemistry and economics program. Another professor "set off firecrackers and pyro" to kick off a psychology class.

Academic requirements differ depending on the faculty, and students' opinions vary. While many students find the requirements "fair" and "reasonable," others beg to differ: "There are too many. It's too complicated, especially as a first-year student." The consensus among students seems to be that the engineering program is the most demanding, while easier programs tend to be clustered in the arts and social science faculties. The workload is described as being "manageable," but students report working much more than they did in high school. One remarked that, for better or for worse, "Western seems to be immune to the grade inflation that has plagued other schools."

Play Hard, Party Hard

Students who enroll at Western will find that the school offers a vibrant and diverse array of social scenes. The majority of students enter Western as 19 year olds, owing to Ontario's five year—rather than four year—high school system. This seemingly trivial fact takes on a whole new significance when it is revealed that Canada's legal drinking age is also 19. "Too bad for college students south of the border," one student gleefully remarked. It is no surprise that Western has something of a party-school reputation. "We party like crazy," said one student succinctly. Popular pubs in London like the Rid Out Club and The Ceeps bar, as well as the on-campus nightclub The Wave, are typically jam-packed on weekends. Despite the oft-heard incidents of binge drinking on campus, not many students seem to be into hard drugs, and non-drinkers do not feel left out, as there are plenty of other opportunities for fun and entertainment ranging from formal and semi-formal dances to rock concerts. The University Community Centre features a food court, bookstore, convenience store, travel agency, pharmacy, ATM machine, gym, movie theatre, and swimming pool, and acts as a popular meeting place. It also houses the CHRW FM, Western's radio station, TV Western, and the *Gazette*, the school newspaper. "That place is like a mini-shopping mall," one student remarked. "It sort of eliminates the need to go into town."

David Letterman once named Saugeen-Maitland Hall one of the top ten "party" spots in North America.

The Greek system is popular at Western; students report that there are "at least 21 frats and six sororities." Undergrads note that, by and large, groups of friends form quickly on campus and tend to avoid change. Pulling pranks and wild tomfoolery are reportedly other means of simultaneously having fun and entertaining others: the eight-feet-tall "snow penis" recently erected by fun-loving students aroused the interest of many a passerby.

Getting Involved

At Western, students report that they are "rarely bored." There is literally something for everyone, with more than 125 clubs and associations actively making their presence felt on campus. With organizations like Western Anime Video Explosion, Women in Engineering, Young Liberals, and Medieval Society, Western's extracurricular opportunities encompass interests from ethnic heritage and politics to future careers and martial arts. Students can even join off the wall clubs like the Water Buffalo chapter, whose members congregate in large, furry blue hats with yellow horns (just like the ones Fred and Barney wore) to "drink beer and watch reruns of *The Flintstones*." In addition, there are ample community service opportunities, and the university hospital seems to be one of the hot spots for volunteerism. For the more athletically inclined student, it is good to know that Western is recognized as having an "awesome" athletic program. Many of the 36 varsity teams are among Canada's very best—in '99–'00, the men's soccer team won the national championship and twelve other Mustang teams finished in the top ten in the country. Almost one-third of Western students compete at different levels of intramural play, and "many students work out, so it's safe to say students are quite fit." If students "aren't actively participating in varsity sports or intramurals, then they are at least out supporting the Mustangs," said one student. Indeed, with their 8,000-seat TD Waterhouse Stadium, which hosted the 2001 Canada Summer Games, Western students are very enthusiastic about athletics.

The Lowdown on Campus Dorms

Students have a choice of six residences on campus, including the infamous Saugeen-Maitland Hall, which houses 1,250-odd students. (David Letterman once named Saugeen-Maitland Hall one of the top ten "party" spots in North America.) Elgin Hall, Alumni House, and Essex Hall are suite-style, meaning there are four bedrooms, a kitchen, and a bathroom in each suite. Thus, many students can enjoy "late-night instant noodles while crunching numbers, typing up a report, or just chillin'." The other three residences are traditional-style: students in a wing share bathrooms and food is served in dining halls. Although living in residence is not mandatory, students who opt to do so report enjoying fast computer network hook-ups, 24-hour front-desk staff, A/C, and parking facilities nearby. As one student explained, "Most of my friends here live on my floor. Residences are also very safe and well-maintained." Many students prefer faculty-based floors, which place students in the same area of study on the same floor. However, some have expressed a few complaints: "There's the rule that only two guests are allowed per person on weekends in your dorm room. Also, in some places, the lady bugs get annoying in late fall, but that's because people take the screens off the windows and it's breeding season for them." Moreover, students lament that the residences are great socially, but that "academically it's impossible to get any work done." A remedy for this situation lies in the numerous libraries on campus, where students can escape from the hustle and bustle of life in their dorm and hit the books. The most popular study place is the D. B. Weldon Library; the truly hard-core academics consider its facilities and study carrels first-rate.

All on-campus students, with the exception of those in Alumni House, must be on a meal plan. Cafeteria food gets a fair rating from students, who claim that "in terms of cafeteria food it's not too bad." The university food services are concerned with student feedback; the standard cafeteria fare reportedly is getting better every year because of the recent implementation of student-suggested changes. Students on the meal plan say they like being able to use their meal cards at several fast-food kiosks on campus, but warn that "if you lose your card, then you're kind of in big trouble, because the person who finds it can use it." For those who tire of dining hall food, there are several great restaurants, including T.J. Baxter's, close to campus.

To not mention the breathtaking beauty of Western's campus would be a great disservice to the school itself. In addition to the main campus, there are three affiliates: King's College, a Catholic college; Huron College, which is Anglican; and Brescia, a women's college, all located a short distance from the main campus. Well-lit footpaths, the school's own police force, and the volunteer student Foot Patrol all contribute to making Western an extremely safe campus day and night.

Students feel that London, Canada's 10th largest city, is much too homogeneous in ethnic makeup. Although the student body "reflects diverse ethnic backgrounds," this is not the case in the city, which is predominantly white. Others call the city "very rich and very white-collar." Furthermore, diversity of ethnic background and of interests on campus do not necessarily translate into demographic diversity—although there is a sizeable international student population, most students hail from within the province of Ontario.

Ontario's Country Club?

Western has been described by more than one cynical student as a "country club," and if having a good time is what you are interested in, you can find your own little party central in London, Ontario. You will also find self-described "well-rounded students" who combine the good life with a solid academic program. "This place is amazing," one student said. "It's the only school I know of where students can party as hard as they do and still succeed in athletics and academics." —*Takamitsu Nishikawa*

Index

A
Adelphi University, 571
Agnes Scott College, 260
Albion College, 471
Alfred University, 574
Allegheny College, 771
Alma College, 474
American University, 218
Amherst College, 407
Antioch College, 704
Arizona State, 83
Auburn University, 67

B
Babson College, 410
Bard College, 576
Barnard College, 579
Bates College, 377
Baylor University, 861
Beloit College, 961
Bennington College, 894
Birmingham-Southern College, 70
Boston College, 412
Boston University, 415
Bowdoin College, 381
Bowling Green State University, 707
Brandeis University, 418
Brigham Young University, 889
Brown University, 825
Bryn Mawr College, 774
Bucknell University, 777

C
California Institute of Technology, 95
California Institute of the Arts, 99
California Polytechnic State University/San Luis Obispo, 103
California State University/Chico, 105
California State University/Fresno, 108
California State University System, 102
Canada Introduction, 976
Carleton College, 491
Carleton University, 977
Carnegie Mellon University, 780
Case Western Reserve University, 710
Centre College, 365
City University of New York/City College, 583
City University of New York/Hunter College, 586
City University of New York/Queens College, 589
Claremont McKenna College, 112
Clark University, 421
Clarkson University, 591
Clemson University, 834
Colby College, 384
Colgate University, 594
College of the Atlantic, 387
College of the Holy Cross, 425
College of William and Mary, 906
College of Wooster, 713
Colorado College, 174

Colorado School of Mines, 177
Colorado State University, 180
Columbia University, 597
Connecticut College, 192
Cornell College, 347
Cornell University, 603
Creighton University, 528

D
Dartmouth College, 537
Davidson College, 682
Deep Springs College, 126
Denison University, 716
DePaul University, 286
DePauw University, 322
Dickinson College, 782
Drew University, 549
Drexel University, 786
Duke University, 685

E
Earlham College, 325
Eastman School of Music, 606
Emerson College, 428
Emory University, 264
Eugene Lang College of the New School University, 608

F
Fairfield University, 194
Florida A&M University, 235
Florida Institute of Technology, 237
Florida Southern College, 240
Florida State University, 242
Fordham University, 611
Franklin and Marshall College, 789
Furman University, 837

G
George Mason University, 909
George Washington University, 224
Georgetown University, 227
Georgia Institute of Technology, 268
Gettysburg College, 792
Goucher College, 393
Grinnell College, 349
Gustavus Adolphus College, 493

H
Hamilton College, 614
Hampden-Sydney College, 912
Hampshire College, 431
Harvard University, 435
Harvey Mudd College, 115
Haverford College, 795
Hendrix College, 89
Hobart and William Smith Colleges, 617
Hofstra University, 619
Hollins University, 915
Hope College, 477
Howard University, 229

I
Illinois State University, 289
Indiana University/Bloomington, 328
Iowa State University, 352

J
James Madison University, 918
Johns Hopkins University, 396

K
Kalamazoo College, 480
Kansas State University, 358
Kent State University, 718
Kenyon College, 721
Knox College, 292

L
Lafayette College, 798
Lake Forest College, 295
Lawrence University, 964
Lehigh University, 801
Lewis and Clark College, 756
Louisiana State University, 371
Loyola University, 298

M
Macalester College, 496
Manhattanville, 624
Marlboro College, 897
Marquette University, 967
Marshall University, 955

Massachusetts Institute of Technology, 439
McGill University, 980
McMaster University, 983
Miami University, 724
Michigan State University, 484
Middlebury College, 900
Mills College, 129
Millsaps College, 507
Mississippi State University, 509
Morehouse College, 271
Mount Holyoke College, 442
Mulhenberg College, 803

N

New College of the University of South Florida, 245
New Mexico State University, 566
New York University, 627
North Carolina School of the Arts, 689
North Carolina State University, 692
Northeastern University, 445
Northwestern University, 301

O

Oberlin College, 727
Occidental College, 133
Ohio State University, 729
Ohio University, 732
Ohio Wesleyan University, 736
Oklahoma State University, 744
Oral Roberts University, 747
Oregon State University, 760

P

Parsons School of Design, 630
Pennsylvania State University, 806
Pepperdine University, 136
Pitzer College, 118
Pomona College, 121
Princeton University, 552
Purdue University, 331

Q

Queen's University, 986
Quinnipiac University, 197

R

Randolph-Macon Woman's College, 921
Reed College, 763
Rensselaer Polytechnic Institute, 632
Rhode Island School of Design, 828
Rhodes College, 849
Rice University, 864
Rochester Institute of Technology, 635
Rollins College, 248
Rose-Hulman Institute of Technology, 333
Rutgers University, 556

S

Sarah Lawrence College, 638
Scripps College, 124
Seton Hall University, 559
Simmons College, 448
Skidmore College, 641
Smith College, 450
Southern Illinois University, 304
Southern Methodist University, 867
Spelman College, 274
St. Bonaventure University, 644
St. John's College, 398
St. John's University/College of St. Benedict, 499
St. Lawrence University, 647
St. Mary's College of California, 139
St. Mary's College, 336
St. Olaf College, 501
Stanford University, 142
State University of New York/Albany, 651
State University of New York/Binghamton, 653
State University of New York / Buffalo, 656
State University of New York/Stony Brook, 659
State University of New York System, 650
Stetson University, 251
Stevens Institute of Technology, 562
Susquehanna University, 809
Swarthmore College, 811
Sweet Briar University, 924
Syracuse University, 662

T

Temple University, 814
Texas A&M University, 870
Texas Christian University, 872
Texas Tech University, 875
The Catholic University of America, 221
The City University of New York System, 581
The Claremont Colleges, 111
The College of New Jersey, 546
The Cooper Union for the Advancement of Science and Art, 600
The Evergreen State College, 939
The Juilliard School, 621
The University of Tulsa, 753
Trinity College, 199
Trinity College, 232
Trinity University, 878
Tufts University, 453
Tulane University, 374
Tuskegee University, 72

U

Union College, 664
United States Air Force Academy, 183
United States Coast Guard Academy, 202
United States Military Academy, 667
United States Naval Academy, 401
University of Alabama, 74
University of Alaska/Fairbanks, 80
University of Arizona, 85
University of Arkansas, 91
University of British Columbia, 989
University of California/Berkeley, 146
University of California/Davis, 149
University of California/Irvine, 152
University of California/Los Angeles, 155
University of California/Riverside, 157
University of California/San Diego, 160
University of California/Santa Barbara, 163
University of California/Santa Cruz, 165
University of California System, 145
University of Chicago, 308
University of Cincinnati, 739
University of Colorado, Boulder, 186
University of Connecticut, 205
University of Dallas, 880
University of Delaware, 215
University of Denver, 189
University of Florida, 254
University of Georgia, 277
University of Hawaii, 280
University of Houston, 883
University of Idaho, 283
University of Illinois at Chicago, 311
University of Illinois at Urbana-Champaign, 315
University of Iowa, 355
University of Kansas, 362
University of Kentucky, 368
University of Maine/Orono, 390
University of Maryland/College Park, 404
University of Massachusetts/Amherst, 456
University of Miami, 256
University of Michigan, 487
University of Minnesota, 504
University of Mississippi, 512
University of Missouri/Columbia, 515
University of Missouri/Kansas City, 518
University of Montana, 524
University of Nebraska, 531
University of Nevada/Reno, 534
University of New Hampshire, 542
University of New Mexico, 568
University of North Carolina/Chapel Hill, 695
University of North Dakota, 701
University of Notre Dame, 338
University of Oklahoma, 749
University of Oregon, 766
University of Pennsylvania, 817
University of Pittsburgh, 820
University of Puget Sound, 942
University of Redlands, 168
University of Rhode Island, 831
University of Richmond, 927
University of Rochester, 670
University of South Alabama, 77
University of South Carolina, 840
University of South Dakota, 846
University of Southern California, 170
University of Tennessee, 852
University of Texas/Austin, 886
University of the South (Sewanee), 855
University of Toronto, 992
University of Utah, 891

University of Vermont, 903
University of Virginia, 930
University of Washington, 945
University of Waterloo, 995
University of Western Ontario, 997
University of Wisconsin/Madison, 970
University of Wyoming, 973

V

Valparaiso University, 341
Vanderbilt University, 858
Vassar College, 673
Villanova University, 822
Virginia Polytechnic Institute and State University, 933

W

Wabash College, 343
Wake Forest University, 698
Washington and Lee University, 936
Washington State University, 949
Washington University, 521
Wellesley College, 459
Wells College, 676
Wesleyan University, 207
West Virginia University, 958
Wheaton College, 318
Wheaton College, 461
Whitman College, 952
Willamette University, 768
Williams College, 465
Wittenberg University, 741
Wofford College, 843
Worcester Polytechnic Institute, 468

Y

Yale University, 210
Yeshiva University, 679